W9-ADK-542

The design stamped on the cover is taken from a wall painting that decorated a house in Oxford at a time when Shakespeare was a frequent visitor there, as a guest of his good friend John Davenant, a vintner. The house, which stands at No. 3, Cornmarket Street, was occupied by Davenant from about 1592 to 1614. This design was first used by the Limited Editions Club, 595 Madison Avenue, New York, who had it printed in several colors as a cover for their edition of Shakespeare's plays.

William Shakespeare

The Droeshout engraving from the title page of the First Folio.

The Play's the Thing

Seventeen of Shakespeare's Greatest Dramas

EDITED BY

Louis B. Wright and Virginia A. LaMar

HARPER & ROW, Publishers, New York, MCMLXIII

6784

Library of Congress card catalog number: 63–10980
Manufactured in the United States of America

TABLE OF CONTENTS

PREFACE

THE TEXTS of the plays in this volume are those prepared for the "Folger Library General Reader's Shakespeare" published by the Washington Square Press, which were based on a new collation of the most authoritative of the early texts. Square brackets are used to indicate that all settings and some of the stage directions and act and scene divisions do not appear in the original texts but have been added by modern editors.

As the title of this volume suggests, we have sought to place the emphasis upon a sound and legible text of seventeen of Shakespeare's most interesting plays. We have tried not to overload the text with notes, particularly antiquarian notes that might tend to distract the reader from the play as a work of literary art.

It is our observation that each teacher of Shakespeare has his own ideas as to what needs most emphasis, and it is presumptuous on the part of an editor to usurp the place of the teacher by attempting to tell the student everything that the editor thinks he ought to know about the quality of the plays, about Shakespeare's language and style, or about the Elizabethan age. The teacher will know best what should be stressed for each class, and we have accordingly kept our own annotations to the minimum consistent with an adequate explanation of essential meanings and essential facts.

We have tried to supply bibliographic suggestions that will help the student find competent discussions of various aspects of Shakespeare that may interest him. We have provided brief biographical information and a succinct statement about the state of the theatrical tradition in Shakespeare's age. A selection of commentary on Shakespeare by critics from Ben Jonson to Samuel Johnson is included to give some idea of the appreciation of Shakespeare in the century and a half after his death.

July 10, 1962

Louis B. Wright
Virginia A. LaMar

Richard and the Two Little Princes

Engraved by B. Reading after a painting by J. Northcote.

The Tragedy of RICHARD THE THIRD

INTRODUCTION

The years from September 30, 1399, to August 22, 1485, mark one of the most chaotic periods in English history. On the first date Richard II gave up his crown to Henry Bolingbroke, who became Henry IV. On the latter date Henry Tudor seized the crown from Richard III at Bosworth Field and ascended the throne as Henry VII, the first Tudor monarch. The Wars of the Roses between the houses of York and Lancaster have had many chroniclers, but the English-speaking people have learned their history from Shakespeare, for he chose to use events from Richard II to Richard III for a sequence of plays that placed on the stage the major actors in these events.

Although *Richard III* is the last in the historical chronology, it is one of the earliest plays of Shakespeare's composition, for he did not write, as most historians would, in chronological sequence. Before *Richard III,* Shakespeare had had a hand in the three parts of *Henry VI,* written between 1590 and 1592. Although scholars have accumulated a large literature on the subject, we do not know precisely how much and what scenes of the *Henry VI* plays were written by Shakespeare. It is generally agreed, however, that Shakespeare had a substantial part in the three plays as printed in the First Folio of 1623.

The historical material treated in *Henry VI* undoubtedly fascinated Shakespeare, and it was natural that he should turn his attention to the denouement of events that were left in suspense at the end of *Henry VI, Part 3.* In the next-to-last scene of that play he portrays Richard, Duke of Gloucester (later Richard III), as the murderer of Henry VI. As Richard stands astride the dead king and stabs him again, he reveals his philosophy of deliberate villainy:

> . . . Since the heavens have shap'd my body so,
> Let hell make crook'd my mind to answer it.
> I have no brother, I am like no brother;
> And this word "love," which greybeards call divine,
> Be resident in men like one another,
> And not in me! I am myself alone.

This scene has no verification in the records of history, but it was whispered that Richard of Gloucester had murdered the King. It was important to Shakespeare's plan to emphasize Richard's murder of the anointed king to justify the retribution meted to him in turn by Henry Tudor.

A cardinal principle in the doctrine of the divinity of kingship was that rebellion against a divinely appointed sovereign was impious and wicked. To justify Henry Tudor's rebellion against Richard III and the seizure of his crown, Shakespeare, following the "official" Tudor historians, had to make Richard III a monster, a triple murderer of royalty, who had not only killed with his own hands King Henry VI but had also procured the deaths of his nephews, Edward V and his brother Richard. The characterization of Richard of Gloucester in Act V, Scene vi, of *Henry VI, Part 3* is a preparation for the play that Shakespeare produced sometime between 1592 and 1593 as *The Tragedy of King Richard the Third.*

Although the play was described as a "tragedy" on the title pages of the early quartos, it was classified in the First Folio among the histories. Its technical classification of course is a matter of only academic interest; Shakespeare's audiences went to see a play about a villain whom they had all heard about, and they did not stop to ask whether it was tragedy or history.

Richard III, however, does qualify as tragedy in the Marlovian sense, for Shakespeare was still writing under the influence of Christopher Marlowe, who had popularized, in *The Jew of Malta* and other plays, the kind of tragic drama that concentrates action upon a single character and, in the case of *The Jew of Malta,* upon a consummately wicked type that Shakespeare found it easy to imitate in *Richard III.* Shakespeare's play also follows the medieval pattern of tragedy that he could have read in *The Mirror for Magistrates* (1559).

Although *Richard III* is loose and episodic in structure like the old chronicle plays, Shakespeare never lets Richard remain long off the stage, and the very perfection of his villainy gives a semblance of unity to the plot. Of all his villains, not even excepting Iago in *Othello,* Shakespeare gave to Richard the most meticulous attention, and we ourselves become so fascinated with the artistic symmetry of his villainy that we acquire a kind of morbid sympathy with the working-out of his plans.

Whether Shakespeare set out deliberately to write a play that would serve the propaganda line of the Tudors is doubtful. But there is no doubt that the authors of the sources of his plot made conscious efforts to blacken Richard's character and to glorify Henry VII as the savior of his country from a monstrous usurper. Shakespeare of course was wise enough to know that the theme and the characterization of Richard would be popular, and as a sensible playwright and producer, working for the commercial theatre, he wanted a popular play.

SOURCES, HISTORY, AND TEXT

The principal source that Shakespeare used was Raphael Holinshed's *Chronicles of England, Scotland, and Ireland* (1587), which in turn had drawn upon Edward Hall's *The Union of the Two Noble and Illustrate Families of Lancaster and York* (1548). Hall's picture of Richard as an archvillain is conventional and derives from Sir Thomas More's *The History of King Richard the Third,* written about 1513 and first printed in a garbled version by Richard Grafton in his continuation of John Hardyng's *Chronicle* (1543). William Rastell published an authentic version in 1557. More had been brought up in the household of John Morton, Bishop of Ely and later Cardinal, who had reason to hate Richard, since he had been imprisoned by him. Because of this and Morton's great service to Henry VII, it has been supposed that Morton might have written the history himself, but recent scholarship indicates that More wrote it from material supplied by Morton. It is composed in sinewy and vivid prose that paints Richard as the hunchbacked spirit of evil that he became in the Tudor legend.

Polydore Vergil, an Italian humanist who became the official historian of Henry VII and Henry VIII, made another important contribution to the Tudor legend. Vergil, like More, was a literary artist, who made the reign of Richard III the climax of long years of misrule and iniquity. Nemesis at last overtakes the wicked ruler, and Henry Tudor, the instrument of divine justice, comes to bring order to the troubled kingdom.

Modern historians have shown that Tudor writers did less than justice to Richard III, who was a brave soldier, an able general, and a competent administrator. Whether he contrived the murder of the little princes is unproved. But Shakespeare has given the world the picture of Richard that it will long retain, and not even an association established for the purpose of rehabilitating the reputation of Richard III can do much to erase the black lines that Shakespeare has drawn.

Richard III was popular in its day and has enjoyed a long stage history. It was first acted by the Lord Chamberlain's Men (Shakespeare's company), probably at the Theatre, the playhouse then used by this company. Contemporary references indicate that Richard Burbage distinguished himself in the title role. The popularity of the play is evidenced by many allusions to it in the literature of the day. The fact that six quartos of the play were printed before the First Folio printing is further evidence of its success. The theme of the wicked king was treated in numerous plays, poems, and popular ballads, and nearly every company of actors had a play on Richard III. Our knowledge of the success of Shakespeare's play is inferential, since there is little specific information on record about times and places of performances of plays in the seventeenth century, but we do have a record of its revival at court on the Queen's birthday, November 16, 1633.

After the Restoration, Shakespeare's play was eclipsed by other dramas on the subject, in particular John Caryll's *The English Princess, or, The Death of Richard III,* which bore little resemblance to Shakespeare's *Richard III.* Thomas Betterton played the role of Richard. In 1700 Colley Cibber produced his own adaptation of Shakespeare's play, which replaced the original version until the nineteenth century. Cibber shortened the play Shakespeare wrote and heightened its melodrama by inserting Richard's murder of Henry VI, as well as the murder of the princes actually on stage. Cibber's version cut out some characters and required fewer actors. This plus the fact that it was more easily staged may account for its long career. Even Garrick employed Cibber's play and played the role of Richard at intervals until 1776.

Cibber's play supplanted that of Shakespeare until late in the nineteenth century. In 1877 Henry Irving, playing the title role himself, presented a version that was very near Shakespeare's original. Later producers have generally used Shakespeare's text, but some of the stage business invented by Cibber has become traditional.

From the eighteenth century onward, *Richard III* was one of the most popular of Shakespeare's plays in America, from the eastern seaboard to the farthest frontier settlement. In 1767 it was chosen as the entertainment for a delegation of Cherokee Indian chiefs visiting New York. A New York paper reported that the Indians regarded *Richard III* "with seriousness and attention"—and perhaps with some wonder at this revelation of the white man's bloodthirsty iniquity.

The complicated textual problem of *Richard III* has never been satisfactorily resolved, but Sir Edmund Chambers' discussion of the relationship between the Quartos and the First Folio remains the most convincing. The First Quarto was published in 1597. This was followed by Quarto 2, 1598; Quarto 3, 1602; Quarto 4, 1605; Quarto 5, 1612; and Quarto 6, 1622. Each quarto seems to have reprinted the one immediately preceding it in date except Quarto 5, which was printed from Quartos 3 and 4. The Folio text seems to have been prepared by altering Quarto 6 in accordance with a manuscript, perhaps the playhouse copy. Some scholars believe that Quarto 1 is the original text and that the Folio text is a later revision. Others hold that the Folio reproduces the authentic version and that the quartos are based on an acting version first printed in Quarto 1. Sir Edmund Chambers concluded that the second theory was substantially sound.

The text printed here is based in the main on that of the 1623 Folio, with corrections from the quartos and the addition of some lines from Quarto 1 that were not in the Folio and seem to be desirable or necessary.

[Dramatis Personæ

KING EDWARD THE FOURTH.
EDWARD, PRINCE OF WALES, *afterwards* EDWARD V, } *sons to King Edward.*
RICHARD, DUKE OF YORK, }
GEORGE, DUKE OF CLARENCE, } *brothers to King Edward.*
RICHARD, DUKE OF GLOUCESTER, *afterwards* RICHARD III, }
EDWARD PLANTAGENET, *son to Clarence.*
HENRY, EARL OF RICHMOND, *afterwards* HENRY VII.
CARDINAL BOURCHIER, ARCHBISHOP OF CANTERBURY.
THOMAS ROTHERHAM, ARCHBISHOP OF YORK.
JOHN MORTON, BISHOP OF ELY.
HENRY STAFFORD, DUKE OF BUCKINGHAM.
JOHN HOWARD, DUKE OF NORFOLK.
THOMAS HOWARD, EARL OF SURREY, *son to the Duke of Norfolk.*
THOMAS GREY, MARQUESS OF DORSET, } *sons to Queen Elizabeth.*
LORD RICHARD GREY, }
ANTHONY WOODVILLE, EARL RIVERS, *brother to Queen Elizabeth.*
JOHN DE VERE, EARL OF OXFORD.
WILLIAM, LORD HASTINGS.
THOMAS, LORD STANLEY (*also called* EARL OF DERBY).
FRANCIS, LORD LOVEL.
SIR THOMAS VAUGHAN.
SIR RICHARD RATCLIFFE.
SIR WILLIAM CATESBY.
SIR JAMES TYRREL.
SIR JAMES BLUNT.
SIR WALTER HERBERT.
SIR ROBERT BRAKENBURY, *Lieutenant of the Tower.*
KEEPER *in the Tower.*
SIR WILLIAM BRANDON.
CHRISTOPHER URSWICK.
LORD MAYOR OF LONDON.
SHERIFF OF WILTSHIRE.
TRESSEL *and* BERKELEY, *gentlemen attending on Lady Anne.*

ELIZABETH, *Queen to Edward IV.*
MARGARET, *widow of Henry VI.*
DUCHESS OF YORK, *mother to Edward IV, Gloucester, and Clarence.*
LADY ANNE NEVILLE, *afterwards Queen to Richard III.*
LADY MARGARET PLANTAGENET, *daughter to Clarence.*

GHOSTS OF RICHARD'S VICTIMS.
Lords, Gentlemen, Attendants; a Pursuivant; a Page, a Scrivener; a Priest; Bishops; Citizens; Aldermen; Councilors; Murderers; Messengers; Soldiers; etc.

Scene: *England.*]

Edward IV
From John Rastell, *The Pastime of People* (1529; 1811 reprint).

The Tragedy of RICHARD THE THIRD

ACT I

Scene I. [*London. A street.*]

Enter RICHARD, DUKE OF GLOUCESTER, *solus.*

Rich. Now is the winter of our discontent
Made glorious summer by this sun of York;
And all the clouds that lowered upon our house
In the deep bosom of the ocean buried. 4
Now are our brows bound with victorious wreaths,
Our bruised arms hung up for monuments,
Our stern alarums changed to merry meetings,
Our dreadful marches to delightful measures.
Grim-visaged war hath smoothed his wrinkled front,
And now, instead of mounting barbed steeds 10
To fright the souls of fearful adversaries,
He capers nimbly in a lady's chamber
To the lascivious pleasing of a lute.
But I, that am not shaped for sportive tricks
Nor made to court an amorous looking glass; 15
I, that am rudely stamped, and want love's majesty
To strut before a wanton ambling nymph;
I, that am curtailed of this fair proportion,
Cheated of feature by dissembling Nature,
Deformed, unfinished, sent before my time 20
Into this breathing world, scarce half made up,
And that so lamely and unfashionable
That dogs bark at me as I halt by them—
Why, I, in this weak piping time of peace,
Have no delight to pass away the time, 25
Unless to see my shadow in the sun
And descant on mine own deformity.
And therefore, since I cannot prove a lover
To entertain these fair well-spoken days,
I am determined to prove a villain 30
And hate the idle pleasures of these days.
Plots have I laid, inductions dangerous,
By drunken prophecies, libels, and dreams,
To set my brother Clarence and the King
In deadly hate the one against the other; 35
And if King Edward be as true and just
As I am subtle, false, and treacherous,
This day should Clarence closely be mewed up
About a prophecy which says that G
Of Edward's heirs the murderer shall be. 40
Dive, thoughts, down to my soul: here Clarence
comes!

Enter CLARENCE, *guarded, and* BRAKENBURY,
[LIEUTENANT OF THE TOWER].

Brother, good day. What means this armed guard
That waits upon your Grace?
Clar. His Majesty,
Tend'ring my person's safety, hath appointed

2. sun . . . York: the emblem adopted by Edward IV was a blazing sun; there is a quibble on sun/son.
8. measures: dances
9. front: forehead
10. barbed: decked with the trappings of war
16. want: lack
19. feature: physical beauty; **dissembling:** Nature dissembles in fashioning men whose appearance belies their true worth.
22. unfashionable: ill-fashioned
24. piping time: i.e., time when the weak pipe is heard instead of the martial drum and fife
27. descant: ring changes on
32. inductions: preliminaries
38. mewed up: confined
44. Tend'ring: cherishing

This conduct to convey me to the Tower. 45
Rich. Upon what cause?
Clar. Because my name is George.
Rich. Alack, my lord, that fault is none of yours:
He should for that commit your godfathers.
O, belike his Majesty hath some intent 49
That you should be new-christ'ned in the Tower.
But what's the matter, Clarence, may I know?
Clar. Yea, Richard, when I know; but I protest
As yet I do not. But, as I can learn,
He hearkens after prophecies and dreams,
And from the cross-row plucks the letter G, 55
And says a wizard told him that by G
His issue disinherited should be.
And, for my name of George begins with G,
It follows in his thought that I am he.
These, as I learn, and suchlike toys as these, 60
Have moved his Highness to commit me now.
Rich. Why, this it is, when men are ruled by women:
'Tis not the King that sends you to the Tower;
My Lady Grey his wife, Clarence, 'tis she
That tempts him to this harsh extremity. 65
Was it not she, and that good man of worship,
Anthony Woodville, her brother there,
That made him send Lord Hastings to the Tower,
From whence this present day he is delivered?
We are not safe, Clarence, we are not safe. 70
Clar. By heaven, I think there is no man secure
But the Queen's kindred, and night-walking heralds
That trudge betwixt the King and Mistress Shore.
Heard you not what an humble suppliant
Lord Hastings was for his delivery? 75
Rich. Humbly complaining to her deity
Got my Lord Chamberlain his liberty.
I'll tell you what, I think it is our way,
If we will keep in favor with the King,
To be her men and wear her livery. 80
The jealous o'erworn widow and herself,
Since that our brother dubbed them gentlewomen,
Are mighty gossips in our monarchy.
Brak. I beseech your Graces both to pardon me:
His Majesty hath straitly given in charge 85
That no man shall have private conference,
Of what degree soever, with your brother.
Rich. Even so? And please your worship, Brakenbury,
You may partake of anything we say.
We speak no treason, man. We say the King 90
Is wise and virtuous, and his noble Queen
Well struck in years, fair, and not jealous.
We say that Shore's wife hath a pretty foot,
A cherry lip, a bonny eye, a passing pleasing tongue;
And that the Queen's kindred are made gentlefolks.
How say you, sir? Can you deny all this? 96
Brak. With this, my lord, myself have nought to do.
Rich. Naught to do with Mistress Shore? I tell thee, fellow,
He that doth naught with her, excepting one,
Were best to do it secretly alone. 100
Brak. What one, my lord?
Rich. Her husband, knave. Wouldst thou betray me?
Brak. I do beseech your Grace to pardon me, and withal
Forbear your conference with the noble Duke.
Clar. We know thy charge, Brakenbury, and will obey. 105
Rich. We are the Queen's abjects, and must obey.
Brother, farewell. I will unto the King;
And whatsoe'er you will employ me in,
Were it to call King Edward's widow sister,
I will perform it to enfranchise you. 110
Meantime, this deep disgrace in brotherhood
Touches me deeper than you can imagine.
Clar. I know it pleaseth neither of us well.
Rich. Well, your imprisonment shall not be long:
I will deliver you, or else lie for you. 115
Meantime, have patience.
Clar. I must perforce. Farewell.
Exit Clarence, [with Brakenbury and Guard].
Rich. Go tread the path that thou shalt ne'er return:
Simple, plain Clarence, I do love thee so
That I will shortly send thy soul to heaven,
If heaven will take the present at our hands. 120
But who comes here? The new-delivered Hastings?

Enter LORD HASTINGS.

Hast. Good time of day unto my gracious lord.
Rich. As much unto my good Lord Chamberlain.
Well are you welcome to this open air. 124
How hath your lordship brooked imprisonment?
Hast. With patience, noble lord, as prisoners must;
But I shall live, my lord, to give them thanks

45. conduct: escort
55. cross-row: alphabet, as it appeared in a hornbook
58. for: because
60. toys: fancies
64. Lady Grey: the King's wife, Elizabeth Woodville, was the widow of Sir John Grey.
66. worship: honor; dignity
80. livery: servant's uniform
83. gossips: sponsors. **Gossip** is from the Old English *godsibb* ("godparent").
85. straitly . . . charge: strictly ordered
88. And: if it
92. Well . . . years: advanced in age
94. passing: exceedingly
98. Naught: a pun on "naught" in the sense "wicked," with specific reference to sexual misconduct
106. abjects: (1) humble servants; (2) rejects
115. lie . . . you: lie in the Tower for your sake
116. perforce: "Patience perforce" was a proverbial phrase.
125. brooked: endured

That were the cause of my imprisonment.
Rich. No doubt, no doubt; and so shall Clarence too,
For they that were your enemies are his, 130
And have prevailed as much on him as you.
Hast. More pity that the eagles should be mewed,
Whiles kites and buzzards prey at liberty.
Rich. What news abroad?
Hast. No news so bad abroad as this at home: 135
The King is sickly, weak, and melancholy,
And his physicians fear him mightily.
Rich. Now, by St. John, that news is bad indeed!
O, he hath kept an evil diet long
And overmuch consumed his royal person: 140
'Tis very grievous to be thought upon.
Where is he? In his bed?
Hast. He is.
Rich. Go you before, and I will follow you.
Exit Hastings.
He cannot live, I hope, and must not die 145
Till George be packed with post horse up to heaven.
I'll in, to urge his hatred more to Clarence,
With lies well steeled with weighty arguments;
And, if I fail not in my deep intent,
Clarence hath not another day to live: 150
Which done, God take King Edward to his mercy,
And leave the world for me to bustle in!
For then I'll marry Warwick's youngest daughter.
What though I killed her husband and her father?
The readiest way to make the wench amends 155
Is to become her husband and her father:
The which will I—not all so much for love
As for another secret close intent,
By marrying her which I must reach unto.
But yet I run before my horse to market: 160
Clarence still breathes; Edward still lives and reigns;
When they are gone, then must I count my gains.
Exit.

Scene II. [*London. Another street.*]

Enter the CORSE OF HENRY THE SIXTH, *with* HALBERDS *to guard it* [*and* ATTENDANTS]; LADY ANNE *being the mourner.*

Anne. Set down, set down your honorable load—
If honor may be shrouded in a hearse—
Whilst I awhile obsequiously lament
The untimely fall of virtuous Lancaster.
[*The Bearers set down the hearse.*]
Poor key-cold figure of a holy king, 5
Pale ashes of the house of Lancaster,
Thou bloodless remnant of that royal blood,
Be it lawful that I invocate thy ghost
To hear the lamentations of poor Anne,
Wife to thy Edward, to thy slaught'red son 10
Stabbed by the selfsame hand that made these wounds!
Lo, in these windows that let forth thy life
I pour the helpless balm of my poor eyes.
O cursed be the hand that made these holes!
Cursed the heart that had the heart to do it! 15
Cursed the blood that let this blood from hence!
More direful hap betide that hated wretch
That makes us wretched by the death of thee
Than I can wish to wolves, to spiders, toads,
Or any creeping venomed thing that lives! 20
If ever he have child, abortive be it,
Prodigious, and untimely brought to light,
Whose ugly and unnatural aspect
May fright the hopeful mother at the view,
And that be heir to his unhappiness! 25
If ever he have wife, let her be made
More miserable by the death of him
Than I am made by my young lord and thee!
Come, now towards Chertsey with your holy load,
Taken from Paul's to be interred there. 30
[*The Bearers take up the hearse.*]
And still as you are weary of this weight,
Rest you, whiles I lament King Henry's corse.

Enter RICHARD, DUKE OF GLOUCESTER.

Rich. Stay, you that bear the corse, and set it down.
Anne. What black magician conjures up this fiend,
To stop devoted charitable deeds? 35
Rich. Villains, set down the corse, or, by St. Paul,
I'll make a corse of him that disobeys!
Gent. My lord, stand back, and let the coffin pass.
Rich. Unmannered dog! Stand thou, when I command!
Advance thy halberd higher than my breast, 40
Or, by St. Paul, I'll strike thee to my foot,
And spurn upon thee, beggar, for thy boldness.
[*The Bearers set down the hearse.*]
Anne. What, do you tremble? Are you all afraid?

137. fear him: fear for him
146. with . . . horse: with the utmost dispatch
153. Warwick's . . . daughter: Anne Neville
154. I . . . father: i.e., husband and father-in-law. Prince Edward, Anne's husband and son of Henry VI, died at the Battle of Tewkesbury. There is no evidence that he was murdered rather than killed in battle, but Holinshed recorded that Richard, Clarence, Hastings, and Dorset all combined to strike down the Prince.
159. By . . . unto: which I must marry her to achieve
Ent. Halberds: i.e., halberdiers

3. obsequiously: in a manner appropriate to a funeral
5. key-cold: "Cold as a key" was a proverbial expression.
17. hap: fortune; **betide:** befall
22. Prodigious: monstrous and of evil portent
25. unhappiness: wicked nature
31. still as: whenever
40. Advance: raise
42. spurn . . . thee: trample thee

Alas, I blame you not, for you are mortal,
And mortal eyes cannot endure the devil. 45
Avaunt, thou dreadful minister of hell!
Thou hadst but power over his mortal body;
His soul thou canst not have. Therefore, be gone.

Rich. Sweet saint, for charity, be not so curst.

Anne. Foul devil, for God's sake hence, and trouble us not, 50
For thou hast made the happy earth thy hell,
Filled it with cursing cries and deep exclaims.
If thou delight to view thy heinous deeds,
Behold this pattern of thy butcheries.
O gentlemen, see, see, dead Henry's wounds 55
Open their congealed mouths and bleed afresh!
Blush, blush, thou lump of foul deformity;
For 'tis thy presence that exhales this blood
From cold and empty veins where no blood dwells.
Thy deeds, inhuman and unnatural, 60
Provokes this deluge most unnatural.
O God, which this blood madest, revenge his death!
O earth, which this blood drinkst, revenge his death!
Either heav'n with lightning strike the murd'rer dead;
Or earth gape open wide and eat him quick, 65
As thou dost swallow up this good king's blood
Which his hell-governed arm hath butchered!

Rich. Lady, you know no rules of charity,
Which renders good for bad, blessings for curses.

Anne. Villain, thou knowst no law of God nor man: 70
No beast so fierce but knows some touch of pity.

Rich. But I know none, and therefore am no beast.

Anne. O wonderful, when devils tell the truth!

Rich. More wonderful, when angels are so angry.
Vouchsafe, divine perfection of a woman, 75
Of these supposed crimes, to give me leave
By circumstance but to acquit myself.

Anne. Vouchsafe, diffused infection of a man,
Of these known evils, but to give me leave
By circumstance t'accuse thy cursed self. 80

Rich. Fairer than tongue can name thee, let me have
Some patient leisure to excuse myself.

Anne. Fouler than heart can think thee, thou canst make
No excuse current but to hang thyself.

Rich. By such despair I should accuse myself. 85

Anne. And by despairing shalt thou stand excused
For doing worthy vengeance on thyself
That didst unworthy slaughter upon others.

Rich. Say that I slew them not?

Anne. Then say they were not slain.
But dead they are, and, devilish slave, by thee. 90

Rich. I did not kill your husband.

Anne. Why, then he is alive.

Rich. Nay, he is dead, and slain by Edward's hands.

Anne. In thy foul throat thou liest! Queen Margaret saw
Thy murd'rous falchion smoking in his blood;
The which thou once didst bend against her breast,
But that thy brothers beat aside the point. 96

Rich. I was provoked by her sland'rous tongue,
That laid their guilt upon my guiltless shoulders.

Anne. Thou wast provoked by thy bloody mind,
That never dreamst on aught but butcheries. 100
Didst thou not kill this king?

Rich. I grant ye.

Anne. Dost grant me, hedgehog? Then God grant me too
Thou mayst be damned for that wicked deed!
O, he was gentle, mild, and virtuous!

Rich. The better for the King of heaven that hath him. 105

Anne. He is in heaven, where thou shalt never come.

Rich. Let him thank me, that holp to send him thither;
For he was fitter for that place than earth.

Anne. And thou unfit for any place but hell.

Rich. Yes, one place else, if you will hear me name it. 110

Anne. Some dungeon.

Rich. Your bedchamber.

Anne. Ill rest betide the chamber where thou liest!

Rich. So will it, madam, till I lie with you.

Anne. I hope so.

Rich. I know so. But, gentle Lady Anne,
To leave this keen encounter of our wits 115
And fall something into a slower method;
Is not the causer of the timeless deaths
Of these Plantagenets, Henry and Edward,
As blameful as the executioner?

Anne. Thou wast the cause and most accursed effect. 120

Rich. Your beauty was the cause of that effect—
Your beauty, that did haunt me in my sleep
To undertake the death of all the world,
So I might live one hour in your sweet bosom. 124

Anne. If I thought that, I tell thee, homicide,
These nails should rent that beauty from my cheeks.

Rich. These eyes could not endure that beauty's wrack;
You should not blemish it, if I stood by:

49. curst: sharp-tongued
58. exhales: draws forth
65. quick: alive
77. circumstance: detailed explanation
78. diffused: distorted; deformed
84. current: creditable; acceptable

94. falchion: sword
107. holp: obsolete past tense of "help"
117. timeless: untimely
120. effect: effecter
127. wrack: ruin

As all the world is cheered by the sun,
So I by that. It is my day, my life. 130

Anne. Black night o'ershade thy day, and death thy life!

Rich. Curse not thyself, fair creature, thou art both.

Anne. I would I were, to be revenged on thee.

Rich. It is a quarrel most unnatural,
To be revenged on him that loveth thee. 135

Anne. It is a quarrel just and reasonable,
To be revenged on him that killed my husband.

Rich. He that bereft thee, lady, of thy husband,
Did it to help thee to a better husband. 139

Anne. His better doth not breathe upon the earth.

Rich. He lives that loves thee better than he could.

Anne. Name him.

Rich. Plantagenet.

Anne. Why, that was he.

Rich. The selfsame name, but one of better nature.

Anne. Where is he?

Rich. Here. ([*She*] *spits at him.*)
Why dost thou spit at me? 145

Anne. Would it were mortal poison, for thy sake!

Rich. Never came poison from so sweet a place.

Anne. Never hung poison on a fouler toad.
Out of my sight! Thou dost infect mine eyes. 149

Rich. Thine eyes, sweet lady, have infected mine.

Anne. Would they were basilisks, to strike thee dead!

Rich. I would they were, that I might die at once;
For now they kill me with a living death.
Those eyes of thine from mine have drawn salt tears,
Shamed their aspects with store of childish drops:
These eyes, which never shed remorseful tear, 156
No, when my father York and Edward wept
To hear the piteous moan that Rutland made
When black-faced Clifford shook his sword at him;
Nor when thy warlike father, like a child, 160
Told the sad story of my father's death,
And twenty times made pause to sob and weep,
That all the standers-by had wet their cheeks
Like trees bedashed with rain: in that sad time
My manly eyes did scorn an humble tear; 165
And what these sorrows could not thence exhale,
Thy beauty hath, and made them blind with weeping.
I never sued to friend nor enemy;
My tongue could never learn sweet smoothing word;
But, now thy beauty is proposed my fee, 170
My proud heart sues, and prompts my tongue to speak. *She looks scornfully at him.*
Teach not thy lip such scorn, for it was made
For kissing, lady, not for such contempt.
If thy revengeful heart cannot forgive,
Lo, here I lend thee this sharp-pointed sword, 175
Which if thou please to hide in this true breast,
And let the soul forth that adoreth thee,
I lay it naked to the deadly stroke;
And humbly beg the death upon my knee.
He lays his breast open. She offers at [*it*] *with his sword.*
Nay, do not pause: for I did kill King Henry—
But 'twas thy beauty that provoked me. 181
Nay, now dispatch: 'twas I that stabbed young Edward—
But 'twas thy heavenly face that set me on.
She falls the sword.
Take up the sword again, or take up me.

Anne. Arise, dissembler: though I wish thy death,
I will not be thy executioner. 186

Rich. Then bid me kill myself, and I will do it.

Anne. I have already.

Rich. That was in thy rage:
Speak it again, and even with the word,
This hand, which for thy love did kill thy love, 190
Shall for thy love kill a far truer love;
To both their deaths shalt thou be accessary.

Anne. I would I knew thy heart.

Rich. 'Tis figured in my tongue.

Anne. I fear me both are false. 195

Rich. Then never man was true.

Anne. Well, well, put up your sword.

Rich. Say, then, my peace is made.

Anne. That shalt thou know hereafter.

Rich. But shall I live in hope? 200

Anne. All men, I hope, live so.

Rich. Vouchsafe to wear this ring.

Anne. To take is not to give.
[*Richard places a ring on her finger.*]

Rich. Look how my ring encompasseth thy finger,
Even so thy breast encloseth my poor heart: 205
Wear both of them, for both of them are thine.
And if thy poor devoted servant may
But beg one favor at thy gracious hand,
Thou dost confirm his happiness forever.

Anne. What is it? 210

Rich. That it may please you leave these sad designs
To him that hath most cause to be a mourner,
And presently repair to Crosby House;
Where, after I have solemnly interred

151. basilisks: fabulous creatures with the power of death in their glances
155. aspects: appearances
158. Rutland: Richard's brother Edmund, Earl of Rutland, who was killed by Lord Clifford when his father's party was attacked near his castle at Sandal, Yorkshire
166. exhale: draw forth
169. smoothing: flattering
170. proposed . . . fee: offered as my reward
192. accessary: variant of "accessory"
202. Vouchsafe: condescend
213. presently: immediately; **Crosby House:** his town house in Bishopsgate Street, which still stands though now removed to Chelsea

At Chertsey monast'ry this noble king, 215
And wet his grave with my repentant tears,
I will with all expedient duty see you.
For divers unknown reasons, I beseech you,
Grant me this boon. 219
Anne. With all my heart; and much it joys me too,
To see you are become so penitent.
Tressel and Berkeley, go along with me.
Rich. Bid me farewell.
Anne. 'Tis more than you deserve;
But since you teach me how to flatter you,
Imagine I have said farewell already. 225
Exeunt two with Anne.
Rich. Sirs, take up the corse.
Gent. Towards Chertsey, noble lord?
Rich. No, to Whitefriars; there attend my coming.
Exit [Bearers and Guard with] Corse.
Was ever woman in this humor wooed?
Was ever woman in this humor won?
I'll have her, but I will not keep her long. 230
What! I, that killed her husband and his father,
To take her in her heart's extremest hate,
With curses in her mouth, tears in her eyes,
The bleeding witness of my hatred by,
Having God, her conscience, and these bars against me, 235
And I no friends to back my suit withal
But the plain devil and dissembling looks,
And yet to win her, all the world to nothing!
Ha!
Hath she forgot already that brave prince, 240
Edward, her lord, whom I, some three months since,
Stabbed in my angry mood at Tewkesbury?
A sweeter and a lovelier gentleman,
Framed in the prodigality of nature—
Young, valiant, wise, and, no doubt, right royal—
The spacious world cannot again afford; 246
And will she yet abase her eyes on me,
That cropped the golden prime of this sweet prince
And made her widow to a woeful bed?
On me, whose all not equals Edward's moiety? 250
On me, that halts and am misshapen thus?
My dukedom to a beggarly denier,
I do mistake my person all this while!
Upon my life, she finds, although I cannot,
Myself to be a marv'lous proper man. 255
I'll be at charges for a looking glass
And entertain a score or two of tailors
To study fashions to adorn my body:
Since I am crept in favor with myself,
I will maintain it with some little cost. 260
But first I'll turn yon fellow in his grave,
And then return lamenting to my love.
Shine out, fair sun, till I have bought a glass,
That I may see my shadow as I pass.
Exit.

Scene III. [*London. The Palace.*]

Enter the QUEEN MOTHER [ELIZABETH], LORD RIVERS, *and* LORD GREY [*with the* MARQUESS OF DORSET].

Riv. Have patience, madam; there's no doubt his Majesty
Will soon recover his accustomed health.
Grey. In that you brook it ill, it makes him worse:
Therefore, for God's sake, entertain good comfort
And cheer his Grace with quick and merry eyes. 5
Queen. If he were dead, what would betide on me?
Grey. No other harm but loss of such a lord.
Queen. The loss of such a lord includes all harms.
Grey. The heavens have blessed you with a goodly son,
To be your comforter when he is gone. 10
Queen. Ah, he is young, and his minority
Is put unto the trust of Richard Gloucester,
A man that loves not me, nor none of you.
Riv. Is it concluded he shall be Protector?
Queen. It is determined, not concluded yet: 15
But so it must be, if the King miscarry.

Enter BUCKINGHAM *and* [STANLEY, EARL OF] DERBY.

Grey. Here come the lords of Buckingham and Derby.
Buck. Good time of day unto your royal Grace!
Der. God make your Majesty joyful as you have been!
Queen. The Countess Richmond, good my Lord of Derby, 20
To your good prayer will scarcely say "Amen."
Yet, Derby, notwithstanding she's your wife
And loves not me, be you, good lord, assured
I hate not you for her proud arrogance.

217. **expedient:** speedy
237. **the . . . devil:** the devil only
238. **all . . . nothing:** with all the odds against me
244. **Framed . . . nature:** abundantly endowed by nature
247. **abase:** lower
250. **moiety:** portion
252. **denier:** a copper coin worth about a tenth of an English penny
255. **marv'lous proper:** wonderfully handsome
256. **be . . . for:** bear the cost of
257. **entertain:** hire
261. **in:** into
15. **determined . . . concluded:** i.e., the King has so determined, but it has not been made official.
16. **miscarry:** die
20. **Countess Richmond:** Margaret Beaufort, great-granddaughter of John of Gaunt and mother of Henry VII by her first husband, Edmund Tudor, Earl of Richmond. Both parents thus gave Henry VII some claim to the throne.

Der. I do beseech you, either not believe 25
The envious slanders of her false accusers;
Or, if she be accused on true report,
Bear with her weakness, which I think proceeds
From wayward sickness, and no grounded malice.
Queen. Saw you the King today, my Lord of Derby? 30
Der. But now the Duke of Buckingham and I
Are come from visiting his Majesty.
Queen. What likelihood of his amendment, lords?
Buck. Madam, good hope; his Grace speaks cheerfully.
Queen. God grant him health! Did you confer with him? 35
Buck. Ay, madam: he desires to make atonement
Between the Duke of Gloucester and your brothers,
And between them and my Lord Chamberlain,
And sent to warn them to his royal presence.
Queen. Would all were well! but that will never be: 40
I fear our happiness is at the height.

Enter RICHARD [*and* LORD HASTINGS].

Rich. They do me wrong, and I will not endure it!
Who is it that complains unto the King
That I, forsooth, am stern, and love them not?
By holy Paul, they love his Grace but lightly 45
That fill his ears with such dissentious rumors.
Because I cannot flatter and look fair,
Smile in men's faces, smooth, deceive, and cog,
Duck with French nods and apish courtesy,
I must be held a rancorous enemy. 50
Cannot a plain man live and think no harm,
But thus his simple truth must be abused
With silken, sly, insinuating Jacks?
Grey. To who in all this presence speaks your Grace? 54
Rich. To thee, that hast nor honesty nor grace.
When have I injured thee? when done thee wrong?
Or thee? or thee? or any of your faction?
A plague upon you all! His royal Grace,
Whom God preserve better than you would wish!
Cannot be quiet scarce a breathing-while 60
But you must trouble him with lewd complaints.
Queen. Brother of Gloucester, you mistake the matter:
The King, on his own royal disposition,
And not provoked by any suitor else,
Aiming, belike, at your interior hatred, 65
That in your outward action shows itself
Against my children, brothers, and myself,
Makes him to send, that he may learn the ground.
Rich. I cannot tell: the world is grown so bad 69
That wrens make prey where eagles dare not perch.
Since every Jack became a gentleman,
There's many a gentle person made a Jack.
Queen. Come, come, we know your meaning, brother Gloucester:
You envy my advancement and my friends'.
God grant we never may have need of you! 75
Rich. Meantime, God grants that I have need of you.
Our brother is imprisoned by your means,
Myself disgraced, and the nobility
Held in contempt, while great promotions
Are daily given to ennoble those 80
That scarce, some two days since, were worth a noble.
Queen. By Him that raised me to this careful height
From that contented hap which I enjoyed,
I never did incense his Majesty
Against the Duke of Clarence, but have been 85
An earnest advocate to plead for him.
My lord, you do me shameful injury
Falsely to draw me in these vile suspects.
Rich. You may deny that you were not the mean
Of my Lord Hastings' late imprisonment. 90
Riv. She may, my lord, for—
Rich. She may, Lord Rivers! Why, who knows not so?
She may do more, sir, than denying that:
She may help you to many fair preferments,
And then deny her aiding hand therein 95
And lay those honors on your high desert.
What may she not? She may, ay, marry, may she.
Riv. What, marry, may she?
Rich. What, marry, may she? Marry with a king,
A bachelor and a handsome stripling too: 100
Iwis your grandam had a worser match.
Queen. My Lord of Gloucester, I have too long borne
Your blunt upbraidings and your bitter scoffs:
By heaven, I will acquaint his Majesty
Of those gross taunts that oft I have endured. 105
I had rather be a country servant maid
Than a great queen with this condition,
To be so baited, scorned, and stormed at:

Enter OLD QUEEN MARGARET, [*unnoticed*].

26. envious: malicious
29. From . . . malice: from a distemperature that masters her, not from reasoned ill will
36. make atonement: bring about a reconciliation
39. warn: summon
48. smooth: flatter; **cog:** lie
49. French nods: bows in the French style
53. Jacks: lowborn knaves
55. grace: virtue
60. a breathing-while: the space of a breath
61. lewd: base; vicious
81. noble: coin worth six shillings eightpence
82. careful: full of care; anxious
88. draw . . . suspects: involve me in these vile suspicions
97. marry: indeed; from the oath "by the Virgin Mary"
101. Iwis: certainly; **your . . . match:** Jacquetta, Duchess of Bedford, who married Richard Woodville, a mere squire

Small joy have I in being England's queen.
Queen M. [*Aside*] And lessened be that small, God I beseech Him! 110
Thy honor, state, and seat is due to me.
Rich. What? Threat you me with telling of the King?
Tell him, and spare not. Look what I have said
I will avouch't in presence of the King:
I dare adventure to be sent to the Tower. 115
'Tis time to speak: my pains are quite forgot.
Queen M. [*Aside*] Out, devil! I do remember them too well:
Thou kill'dst my husband Henry in the Tower,
And Edward, my poor son, at Tewkesbury.
Rich. Ere you were Queen, ay, or your husband King, 120
I was a pack horse in his great affairs;
A weeder-out of his proud adversaries,
A liberal rewarder of his friends:
To royalize his blood I spent mine own.
Queen M. [*Aside*] Ay, and much better blood than his or thine. 125
Rich. In all which time you and your husband Grey
Were factious for the house of Lancaster;
And, Rivers, so were you. Was not your husband
In Margaret's battle at St. Albans slain?
Let me put in your minds, if you forget, 130
What you have been ere this, and what you are;
Withal, what I have been, and what I am.
Queen M. [*Aside*] A murd'rous villain, and so still thou art.
Rich. Poor Clarence did forsake his father, Warwick;
Ay, and forswore himself, which Jesu pardon! 135
Queen M. [*Aside*] Which God revenge!
Rich. To fight on Edward's party for the crown;
And for his meed, poor lord, he is mewed up.
I would to God my heart were flint like Edward's,
Or Edward's soft and pitiful like mine: 140
I am too childish-foolish for this world.
Queen M. [*Aside*] Hie thee to hell for shame, and leave this world,
Thou cacodemon! there thy kingdom is.
Riv. My Lord of Gloucester, in those busy days
Which here you urge to prove us enemies, 145
We followed then our lord, our sovereign king.
So should we you, if you should be our king.
Rich. If I should be? I had rather be a peddler:
Far be it from my heart, the thought thereof!
Queen. As little joy, my lord, as you suppose 150
You should enjoy, were you this country's king,
As little joy you may suppose in me
That I enjoy, being the queen thereof.
Queen M. [*Aside*] A little joy enjoys the queen thereof;
For I am she, and altogether joyless. 155
I can no longer hold me patient. [*Advancing.*]
Hear me, you wrangling pirates, that fall out
In sharing that which you have pilled from me!
Which of you trembles not that looks on me? 159
If not, that I am Queen, you bow like subjects,
Yet that, by you deposed, you quake like rebels?
Ah, gentle villain, do not turn away!
Rich. Foul wrinkled witch, what makest thou in my sight?
Queen M. But repetition of what thou hast marred:
That will I make before I let thee go. 165
Rich. Wert thou not banished on pain of death?
Queen M. I was; but I do find more pain in banishment
Than death can yield me here by my abode.
A husband and a son thou owest to me—
And thou a kingdom—all of you allegiance. 170
This sorrow that I have, by right is yours,
And all the pleasures you usurp are mine.
Rich. The curse my noble father laid on thee,
When thou didst crown his warlike brows with paper,
And with thy scorns drewst rivers from his eyes 175
And then, to dry them, gavest the Duke a clout
Steeped in the faultless blood of pretty Rutland—
His curses then, from bitterness of soul
Denounced against thee, are all fall'n upon thee;
And God, not we, hath plagued thy bloody deed.
Queen. So just is God, to right the innocent. 181
Hast. O, 'twas the foulest deed to slay that babe,
And the most merciless, that e'er was heard of!
Riv. Tyrants themselves wept when it was reported.
Dor. No man but prophesied revenge for it. 185
Buck. Northumberland, then present, wept to see it.
Queen M. What? were you snarling all before I came,
Ready to catch each other by the throat,
And turn you all your hatred now on me? 189
Did York's dread curse prevail so much with heaven
That Henry's death, my lovely Edward's death,
Their kingdom's loss, my woeful banishment,
Should all but answer for that peevish brat?
Can curses pierce the clouds and enter heaven?

111. is . . . me: i.e., is my due
113. Look what: whatever
121. pack horse: drudge
127. were . . . for: sided with
129. St. Albans: a battle between Yorkists and Lancastrians on February 17, 1461
134. father: father-in-law. Clarence was married to Warwick's daughter Isabel.
138. meed: reward
143. cacodemon: evil spirit
158. pilled: pillaged
162. gentle villain: gently-born rascal. **Villain** was used in one sense to mean simply a fellow of low birth.
176. clout: cloth
182. babe: Rutland was actually sixteen years of age at the time.

Why then, give way, dull clouds, to my quick curses!
Though not by war, by surfeit die your king, 196
As ours by murder, to make him a king!
Edward thy son, that now is Prince of Wales,
For Edward our son, that was Prince of Wales,
Die in his youth by like untimely violence! 200
Thyself a queen, for me that was a queen,
Outlive thy glory, like my wretched self!
Long mayst thou live to wail thy children's death
And see another, as I see thee now,
Decked in thy rights, as thou art stalled in mine!
Long die thy happy days before thy death, 206
And, after many lengthened hours of grief,
Die neither mother, wife, nor England's queen!
Rivers and Dorset, you were standers-by,
And so wast thou, Lord Hastings, when my son 210
Was stabbed with bloody daggers: God I pray Him
That none of you may live his natural age,
But by some unlooked accident cut off!

Rich. Have done thy charm, thou hateful withered hag!

Queen M. And leave out thee? Stay, dog, for thou shalt hear me. 215
If heaven have any grievous plague in store
Exceeding those that I can wish upon thee,
O let them keep it till thy sins be ripe,
And then hurl down their indignation 219
On thee, the troubler of the poor world's peace!
The worm of conscience still begnaw thy soul!
Thy friends suspect for traitors while thou livest,
And take deep traitors for thy dearest friends!
No sleep close up that deadly eye of thine,
Unless it be while some tormenting dream 225
Affrights thee with a hell of ugly devils!
Thou elvish-marked, abortive, rooting hog!
Thou that wast sealed in thy nativity
The slave of nature and the son of hell!
Thou slander of thy heavy mother's womb! 230
Thou loathed issue of thy father's loins!
Thou rag of honor! thou detested—

Rich. Margaret.

Queen M. Richard!

Rich. Ha!

Queen M. I call thee not.

Rich. I cry thee mercy then; for I did think 234
That thou hadst called me all these bitter names.

Queen M. Why, so I did, but looked for no reply.
O let me make the period to my curse!

Rich. 'Tis done by me, and ends in "Margaret."

Queen. Thus have you breathed your curse against yourself.

Queen M. Poor painted queen, vain flourish of my fortune! 240
Why strewst thou sugar on that bottled spider,
Whose deadly web ensnareth thee about?
Fool, fool! thou whetst a knife to kill thyself.
The day will come that thou shalt wish for me 244
To help thee curse this poisonous bunch-backed toad.

Hast. False-boding woman, end thy frantic curse,
Lest to thy harm thou move our patience.

Queen M. Foul shame upon you! you have all moved mine.

Riv. Were you well served, you would be taught your duty.

Queen M. To serve me well, you all should do me duty, 250
Teach me to be your queen, and you my subjects:
O serve me well, and teach yourselves that duty!

Dor. Dispute not with her; she is lunatic.

Queen M. Peace, Master Marquess, you are malapert:
Your fire-new stamp of honor is scarce current.
O that your young nobility could judge 256
What 'twere to lose it and be miserable!
They that stand high have many blasts to shake them,
And if they fall, they dash themselves to pieces.

Rich. Good counsel, marry! Learn it, learn it, Marquess. 260

Dor. It touches you, my lord, as much as me.

Rich. Ay, and much more; but I was born so high:
Our eyrie buildeth in the cedar's top,
And dallies with the wind and scorns the sun. 264

Queen M. And turns the sun to shade—alas! alas!
Witness my son, now in the shade of death,
Whose bright outshining beams thy cloudy wrath
Hath in eternal darkness folded up.
Your eyrie buildeth in our eyrie's nest:
O God, that seest it, do not suffer it! 270
As it is won with blood, lost be it so!

Buck. Peace, peace, for shame, if not for charity.

Queen M. Urge neither charity nor shame to me:
[*To the others*] Uncharitably with me have you dealt,
And shamefully my hopes by you are butchered.
My charity is outrage, life my shame, 276
And in that shame still live my sorrow's rage!

Buck. Have done, have done.

Queen M. O princely Buckingham, I'll kiss thy hand

195. quick: vital; vigorous
227. elvish-marked: deformed; **hog:** Richard's device was a boar.
228–29. sealed . . . nature: marked at birth as one of nature's inferior creatures
234. cry . . . mercy: beg your pardon
237. period: conclusion
240. painted queen: pictorial semblance of a queen; **flourish:** ornamental picture
241. bottled: swollen; a reference to Richard's deformed body
246. False-boding: uttering false prophecies; **frantic:** frenzied
254. malapert: impertinent
255. fire-new: freshly minted
263. eyrie: eagle's brood
270. suffer: allow

In sign of league and amity with thee: 280
Now fair befall thee and thy noble house!
Thy garments are not spotted with our blood,
Nor thou within the compass of my curse.
Buck. Nor no one here; for curses never pass
The lips of those that breathe them in the air. 285
Queen M. I will not think but they ascend the sky
And there awake God's gentle-sleeping peace.
O Buckingham, take heed of yonder dog!
Look when he fawns he bites; and when he bites,
His venom tooth will rankle to the death. 290
Have not to do with him, beware of him:
Sin, death, and hell have set their marks on him,
And all their ministers attend on him.
Rich. What doth she say, my Lord of Buckingham?
Buck. Nothing that I respect, my gracious lord.
Queen M. What, dost thou scorn me for my gentle counsel? 296
And soothe the devil that I warn thee from?
O, but remember this another day,
When he shall split thy very heart with sorrow,
And say poor Margaret was a prophetess! 300
Live each of you the subjects to his hate,
And he to yours, and all of you to God's! *Exit.*
Buck. My hair doth stand an end to hear her curses.
Riv. And so doth mine. I muse why she's at liberty.
Rich. I cannot blame her. By God's holy Mother,
She hath had too much wrong, and I repent 306
My part thereof that I have done to her.
Queen. I never did her any, to my knowledge.
Rich. Yet you have all the vantage of her wrong:
I was too hot to do somebody good 310
That is too cold in thinking of it now.
Marry, as for Clarence, he is well repaid:
He is franked up to fatting for his pains.
God pardon them that are the cause thereof!
Riv. A virtuous and a Christianlike conclusion,
To pray for them that have done scathe to us. 316
Rich. So do I ever—(*Speaks to himself*) being well advised;
For had I cursed now, I had cursed myself.

Enter CATESBY.

Cates. Madam, his Majesty doth call for you;
And for your Grace; and yours, my gracious lord.
Queen. Catesby, I come. Lords, will you go with me? 321
Riv. We wait upon your Grace.
Exeunt all but [Richard of] Gloucester.

303. an: on
304. muse: wonder
309. vantage: advantage
313. franked . . . fatting: enclosed in a sty, fattening to be killed
316. scathe: injury

Rich. I do the wrong, and first begin to brawl.
The secret mischiefs that I set abroach
I lay unto the grievous charge of others. 325
Clarence, who I, indeed, have cast in darkness,
I do beweep to many simple gulls—
Namely, to Derby, Hastings, Buckingham—
And tell them 'tis the Queen and her allies
That stir the King against the Duke my brother.
Now they believe it, and withal whet me 331
To be revenged on Rivers, Dorset, Grey.
But then I sigh, and, with a piece of Scripture,
Tell them that God bids us do good for evil:
And thus I clothe my naked villainy 335
With odd old ends stol'n forth of Holy Writ,
And seem a saint, when most I play the devil.

Enter TWO MURDERERS.

But soft! Here come my executioners.
How now, my hardy, stout, resolved mates!
Are you now going to dispatch this thing? 340
1. Mur. We are, my lord, and come to have the warrant,
That we may be admitted where he is.
Rich. Well thought upon; I have it here about me:
[*Gives the warrant.*]
When you have done, repair to Crosby Place.
But, sirs, be sudden in the execution, 345
Withal obdurate, do not hear him plead;
For Clarence is well-spoken, and perhaps
May move your hearts to pity if you mark him.
1. Mur. Tut, tut, my lord! we will not stand to prate;
Talkers are no good doers. Be assured: 350
We go to use our hands, and not our tongues.
Rich. Your eyes drop millstones, when fools' eyes fall tears.
I like you, lads: about your business straight.
Go, go, dispatch.
1. Mur. We will, my noble lord.
Exeunt.

Scene IV. [*London. The Tower.*]

Enter CLARENCE *and* KEEPER.

Keep. Why looks your Grace so heavily today?
Clar. O, I have passed a miserable night,
So full of fearful dreams, of ugly sights,

324. set abroach: let loose
327. gulls: fools
336. odd old ends: scraps
339. resolved: resolute
348. mark: heed
349. prate: chatter
1. heavily: sadly

That, as I am a Christian faithful man,
I would not spend another such a night 5
Though 'twere to buy a world of happy days,
So full of dismal terror was the time.

Keep. What was your dream, my lord? I pray you tell me.

Clar. Methoughts that I had broken from the Tower,
And was embarked to cross to Burgundy, 10
And in my company my brother Gloucester,
Who from my cabin tempted me to walk
Upon the hatches: thence we looked toward England
And cited up a thousand heavy times,
During the wars of York and Lancaster, 15
That had befall'n us. As we paced along
Upon the giddy footing of the hatches,
Methought that Gloucester stumbled, and in falling
Struck me, that thought to stay him, overboard,
Into the tumbling billows of the main. 20
O Lord! methought what pain it was to drown!
What dreadful noise of waters in mine ears!
What sights of ugly death within mine eyes!
Methoughts I saw a thousand fearful wracks;
A thousand men that fishes gnawed upon; 25
Wedges of gold, great anchors, heaps of pearl,
Inestimable stones, unvalued jewels,
All scatt'red in the bottom of the sea:
Some lay in dead men's skulls, and in the holes
Where eyes did once inhabit, there were crept, 30
As 'twere in scorn of eyes, reflecting gems,
That wooed the slimy bottom of the deep,
And mocked the dead bones that lay scatt'red by.

Keep. Had you such leisure in the time of death
To gaze upon these secrets of the deep? 35

Clar. Methought I had; and often did I strive
To yield the ghost; but still the envious flood
Stopped in my soul, and would not let it forth
To find the empty, vast, and wand'ring air,
But smothered it within my panting bulk, 40
Which almost burst to belch it in the sea.

Keep. Awaked you not in this sore agony?

Clar. No, no, my dream was lengthened after life.
O, then began the tempest to my soul!
I passed, methought, the melancholy flood, 45
With that sour ferryman which poets write of,
Unto the kingdom of perpetual night.
The first that there did greet my stranger-soul
Was my great father-in-law, renowned Warwick,
Who spake aloud, "What scourge for perjury 50
Can this dark monarchy afford false Clarence?"
And so he vanished. Then came wand'ring by
A shadow like an angel, with bright hair
Dabbled in blood, and he shrieked out aloud, 54
"Clarence is come—false, fleeting, perjured Clarence,
That stabbed me in the field by Tewkesbury:
Seize on him, Furies, take him unto torment!"
With that, methought, a legion of foul fiends
Environed me, and howled in mine ears
Such hideous cries, that with the very noise 60
I, trembling, waked, and for a season after
Could not believe but that I was in hell,
Such terrible impression made my dream.

Keep. No marvel, lord, though it affrighted you;
I am afraid, methinks, to hear you tell it. 65

Clar. Ah, Keeper, Keeper, I have done these things,
That now give evidence against my soul,
For Edward's sake, and see how he requites me!
O God! if my deep prayers cannot appease thee,
But thou wilt be avenged on my misdeeds, 70
Yet execute thy wrath in me alone:
O spare my guiltless wife and my poor children!
Keeper, I prithee sit by me awhile.
My soul is heavy, and I fain would sleep. 74

Keep. I will, my lord. God give your Grace good rest! [*Clarence sleeps*.]

Enter BRAKENBURY, THE LIEUTENANT.

Brak. Sorrow breaks seasons and reposing hours,
Makes the night morning and the noontide night:
Princes have but their titles for their glories,
An outward honor for an inward toil;
And, for unfelt imaginations, 80
They often feel a world of restless cares;
So that between their titles and low name
There's nothing differs but the outward fame.

Enter TWO MURDERERS.

1. Mur. Ho! who's here?

Brak. What wouldst thou, fellow? And how camest thou hither? 85

1. Mur. I would speak with Clarence, and I came hither on my legs.

Brak. What, so brief?

2. Mur. 'Tis better, sir, than to be tedious. Let him see our commission, and talk no more. 90

[*Brakenbury*] *reads* [*it*].

Brak. I am, in this, commanded to deliver
The noble Duke of Clarence to your hands.
I will not reason what is meant hereby,

13. hatches: decks
27. Inestimable: innumerable; **unvalued:** invaluable
37. yield: give up; **envious:** hostile
40. bulk: body
45. the . . . flood: the River Styx in Hades
46. ferryman: Charon, who ferried spirits across the Styx
50. perjury: oath-breaking
53. A . . . angel: Henry VI's son Edward
55. fleeting: fickle
64. though: if
68. requites: rewards
74. heavy: sorrowful
80. unfelt imaginations: intangible things existing only in the mind
83. fame: reputation

Because I will be guiltless from the meaning.
There lies the Duke asleep, and there the keys. 95
I'll to the King and signify to him
That thus I have resigned to you my charge.

1. Mur. You may, sir; 'tis a point of wisdom. Fare you well. *Exit [Brakenbury with Keeper]*.

2. Mur. What? Shall we stab him as he 100 sleeps?

1. Mur. No. He'll say 'twas done cowardly, when he wakes.

2. Mur. Why, he shall never wake until the great Judgment Day. 105

1. Mur. Why, then he'll say we stabbed him sleeping.

2. Mur. The urging of that word "judgment" hath bred a kind of remorse in me.

1. Mur. What? Art thou afraid? 110

2. Mur. Not to kill him, having a warrant; but to be damned for killing him, for the which no warrant can defend me.

1. Mur. I thought thou hadst been resolute.

2. Mur. So I am, to let him live. 115

1. Mur. I'll back to the Duke of Gloucester and tell him so.

2. Mur. Nay, I prithee stay a little. I hope this passionate humor of mine will change. It was wont to hold me but while one tells twenty. 120

1. Mur. How dost thou feel thyself now?

2. Mur. Some certain dregs of conscience are yet within me.

1. Mur. Remember our reward when the deed's done. 125

2. Mur. Come, he dies! I had forgot the reward.

1. Mur. Where's thy conscience now?

2. Mur. O, in the Duke of Gloucester's purse.

1. Mur. When he opens his purse to give us our reward, thy conscience flies out. 130

2. Mur. 'Tis no matter; let it go. There's few or none will entertain it.

1. Mur. What if it come to thee again?

2. Mur. I'll not meddle with it; it makes a man a coward. A man cannot steal, but it accuseth 135 him; a man cannot swear, but it checks him; a man cannot lie with his neighbor's wife, but it detects him. 'Tis a blushing shamefaced spirit that mutinies in a man's bosom. It fills a man full of obstacles. It made me once restore a purse of gold that by 140 chance I found. It beggars any man that keeps it. It is turned out of towns and cities for a dangerous thing, and every man that means to live well endeavors to trust to himself and live without it.

1. Mur. 'Tis even now at my elbow, per- 145 suading me not to kill the Duke.

2. Mur. Take the devil in thy mind, and believe him not. He would insinuate with thee but to make thee sigh.

1. Mur. I am strong-framed; he cannot 150 prevail with me.

2. Mur. Spoke like a tall man that respects thy reputation. Come, shall we fall to work?

1. Mur. Take him on the costard with the hilts of thy sword, and then throw him into the 155 malmsey butt in the next room.

2. Mur. O excellent device! and make a sop of him.

1. Mur. Soft! he wakes.

2. Mur. Strike! 160

1. Mur. No, we'll reason with him.

Clar. Where art thou, Keeper? Give me a cup of wine.

2. Mur. You shall have wine enough, my lord, anon.

Clar. In God's name, what art thou?

1. Mur. A man, as you are. 165

Clar. But not as I am, royal.

1. Mur. Nor you as we are, loyal.

Clar. Thy voice is thunder, but thy looks are humble.

1. Mur. My voice is now the King's, my looks mine own.

Clar. How darkly and how deadly dost thou speak!
Your eyes do menace me. Why look you pale? 171
Who sent you hither? Wherefore do you come?

Both. To, to, to—

Clar. To murder me?

Both. Ay, ay. 175

Clar. You scarcely have the hearts to tell me so,
And therefore cannot have the hearts to do it.
Wherein, my friends, have I offended you?

1. Mur. Offended us you have not, but the King.

Clar. I shall be reconciled to him again. 180

2. Mur. Never, my lord; therefore prepare to die.

Clar. Are you drawn forth among a world of men
To slay the innocent? What is my offense?
Where is the evidence that doth accuse me?
What lawful quest have given their verdict up 185
Unto the frowning judge? Or who pronounced
The bitter sentence of poor Clarence' death?
Before I be convict by course of law,
To threaten me with death is most unlawful:
I charge you, as you hope to have redemption 190
By Christ's dear blood shed for our grievous sins,

108. urging: mention
119. passionate humor: compassionate mood
120. tells: counts
132. entertain: retain; welcome
148. him: i.e., your conscience
152. tall: valiant
154. Take: strike; **costard:** slang for "head"
157. sop: morsel of bread or cake, used to dip in wine
161. reason: converse
168. thy . . . humble: i.e., you look like men of humble birth.
170. deadly: in a deadly manner
185. quest: inquest
188. convict: convicted

That you depart, and lay no hands on me.
The deed you undertake is damnable.
1. Mur. What we will do, we do upon command.
2. Mur. And he that hath commanded is our king.
Clar. Erroneous vassals! the great King of Kings
Hath in the table of His law commanded 197
That thou shalt do no murder. Will you then
Spurn at His edict, and fulfill a man's?
Take heed; for He holds vengeance in His hand
To hurl upon their heads that break His law. 201
2. Mur. And that same vengeance doth He hurl on thee
For false forswearing and for murder too:
Thou didst receive the sacrament to fight
In quarrel of the house of Lancaster. 205
1. Mur. And like a traitor to the name of God
Didst break that vow, and with thy treacherous blade
Unripst the bowels of thy sov'reign's son.
2. Mur. Whom thou wast sworn to cherish and defend.
1. Mur. How canst thou urge God's dreadful law to us, 210
When thou hast broke it in such dear degree?
Clar. Alas! for whose sake did I that ill deed?
For Edward, for my brother, for his sake.
He sends you not to murder me for this,
For in that sin he is as deep as I. 215
If God will be avenged for the deed,
O, know you yet, he doth it publicly!
Take not the quarrel from his pow'rful arm.
He needs no indirect or lawless course
To cut off those that have offended him. 220
1. Mur. Who made thee then a bloody minister
When gallant-springing brave Plantagenet,
That princely novice, was struck dead by thee?
Clar. My brother's love, the devil, and my rage.
1. Mur. Thy brother's love, our duty, and thy faults 225
Provoke us hither now to slaughter thee.
Clar. If you do love my brother, hate not me:
I am his brother, and I love him well.
If you are hired for meed, go back again,
And I will send you to my brother Gloucester, 230
Who shall reward you better for my life
Than Edward will for tidings of my death.
2. Mur. You are deceived. Your brother Gloucester hates you.
Clar. O, no, he loves me and he holds me dear:
Go you to him from me.
1. Mur. Ay, so we will. 235
Clar. Tell him, when that our princely father York
Blessed his three sons with his victorious arm
And charged us from his soul to love each other,
He little thought of this divided friendship:
Bid Gloucester think on this, and he will weep. 240
1. Mur. Ay, millstones, as he lessoned us to weep.
Clar. O, do not slander him, for he is kind.
1. Mur. Right, as snow in harvest. Come, you deceive yourself;
'Tis he that sends us to destroy you here. 244
Clar. It cannot be, for he bewept my fortune,
And hugged me in his arms, and swore with sobs
That he would labor my delivery.
1. Mur. Why, so he doth, when he delivers you
From this earth's thralldom to the joys of heaven.
2. Mur. Make peace with God, for you must die, my lord. 250
Clar. Have you that holy feeling in your souls
To counsel me to make my peace with God,
And are you yet to your own souls so blind
That you will war with God by murd'ring me?
O sirs, consider, they that set you on 255
To do this deed will hate you for the deed.
2. Mur. What shall we do?
Clar. Relent, and save your souls.
Which of you, if you were a prince's son,
Being pent from liberty, as I am now,
If two such murderers as yourselves came to you,
Would not entreat for life? 261
1. Mur. Relent? No, 'tis cowardly and womanish.
Clar. Not to relent is beastly, savage, devilish.
[*To 2. Murderer*] My friend, I spy some pity in thy looks.
O, if thine eye be not a flatterer, 265
Come thou on my side, and entreat for me
As you would beg, were you in my distress.
A begging prince what beggar pities not?
2. Mur. Look behind you, my lord!
1. Mur. Take that! and that! (*Stabs him.*) If all this will not do, 270
I'll drown you in the malmsey butt within.
Exit [*with the body*].
2. Mur. A bloody deed, and desperately dispatched!
How fain, like Pilate, would I wash my hands
Of this most grievous murder!

[*Re-*]*enter* FIRST MURDERER.

1. Mur. How now? What meanst thou that thou helpst me not? 275
By heaven, the Duke shall know how slack you have been.
2. Mur. I would he knew that I had saved his brother!

211. in . . . degree: so grievously
219. indirect: irregular
222. gallant-springing: springing up gallantly, i.e., giving youthful promise of nobility
241. lessoned: instructed
242. kind: naturally affectionate
259. pent: shut up

Take thou the fee and tell him what I say,
For I repent me that the Duke is slain. *Exit.*
1. Mur. So do not I. Go, coward as thou art. 280
Well, I'll go hide the body in some hole
Till that the Duke give order for his burial;
And when I have my meed, I will away,
For this will out, and then I must not stay.
Exit.

ACT II

Scene I. [*London. The Palace.*]

Flourish. Enter the KING [EDWARD,] *sick, the* QUEEN, LORD MARQUESS DORSET, [GREY,] RIVERS, HASTINGS, CATESBY, [*and*] BUCKINGHAM.

King. Why, so: now have I done a good day's work.
You peers, continue this united league.
I every day expect an embassage
From my Redeemer to redeem me hence;
And more in peace my soul shall part to heaven, 5
Since I have made my friends at peace on earth.
Hastings and Rivers, take each other's hand;
Dissemble not your hatred, swear your love.
Riv. By heaven, my soul is purged from grudging hate,
And with my hand I seal my true heart's love. 10
Hast. So thrive I as I truly swear the like!
King. Take heed you dally not before your king,
Lest He that is the supreme King of Kings
Confound your hidden falsehood, and award
Either of you to be the other's end. 15
Hast. So prosper I as I swear perfect love!
Riv. And I as I love Hastings with my heart!
King. Madam, yourself is not exempt from this;
Nor you, son Dorset; Buckingham, nor you:
You have been factious one against the other. 20
Wife, love Lord Hastings, let him kiss your hand,
And what you do, do it unfeignedly.
Queen. There, Hastings. I will never more remember
Our former hatred, so thrive I and mine!
King. Dorset, embrace him; Hastings, love Lord Marquess. 25
Dor. This interchange of love, I here protest,
Upon my part shall be inviolable.
Hast. And so swear I. [*They embrace.*]
King. Now, princely Buckingham, seal thou this league
With thy embracements to my wife's allies, 30
And make me happy in your unity.
Buck. [*To the Queen*] Whenever Buckingham doth turn his hate
Upon your Grace, but with all duteous love
Doth cherish you and yours, God punish me
With hate in those where I expect most love! 35
When I have most need to employ a friend,
And most assured that he is a friend,
Deep, hollow, treacherous, and full of guile
Be he unto me! This do I beg of heaven,
When I am cold in love to you or yours. 40
Embrace.
King. A pleasing cordial, princely Buckingham,
Is this thy vow unto my sickly heart.
There wanteth now our brother Gloucester here,
To make the blessed period of this peace.
Buck. And in good time, 45
Here comes Sir Richard Ratcliffe and the Duke.

Enter RATCLIFFE *and* [RICHARD, DUKE OF] GLOUCESTER.

Rich. Good morrow to my sovereign king and queen;
And, princely peers, a happy time of day!
King. Happy indeed, as we have spent the day:
Gloucester, we have done deeds of charity, 50
Made peace of enmity, fair love of hate,
Between these swelling wrong-incensed peers.

3. embassage: summons
5. part: depart
8. Dissemble . . . love: do not simply disguise your hatred; swear sincere love.
11. So . . . like: may I thrive as I keep the same vow.
12. dally: trifle
14. Confound: expose to shame
30. allies: kinsmen
41. cordial: restorative
44. period: conclusion; i.e., to complete it
52. swelling: haughty

Rich. A blessed labor, my most sovereign lord.
Among this princely heap, if any here
By false intelligence or wrong surmise 55
Hold me a foe;
If I unwittingly, or in my rage,
Have aught committed that is hardly borne
By any in this presence, I desire
To reconcile me to his friendly peace. 60
'Tis death to me to be at enmity:
I hate it, and desire all good men's love.
First, madam, I entreat true peace of you,
Which I will purchase with my duteous service;
Of you, my noble cousin Buckingham, 65
If ever any grudge were lodged between us;
Of you, and you, Lord Rivers, and of Dorset,
That, all without desert, have frowned on me;
Dukes, earls, lords, gentlemen—indeed, of all.
I do not know that Englishman alive 70
With whom my soul is any jot at odds
More than the infant that is born tonight.
I thank my God for my humility.

Queen. A holy day shall this be kept hereafter:
I would to God all strifes were well compounded.
My sovereign lord, I do beseech your Highness 76
To take our brother Clarence to your grace.

Rich. Why, madam, have I off'red love for this,
To be so flouted in this royal presence?
Who knows not that the gentle Duke is dead? 80
They all start.
You do him injury to scorn his corse.

King. Who knows not he is dead? Who knows he is?

Queen. All-seeing heaven, what a world is this!

Buck. Look I so pale, Lord Dorset, as the rest?

Dor. Ay, my good lord; and no man in the presence
But his red color hath forsook his cheeks. 86

King. Is Clarence dead? The order was reversed.

Rich. But he, poor man, by your first order died,
And that a winged Mercury did bear:
Some tardy cripple bare the countermand, 90
That came too lag to see him buried.
God grant that some, less noble and less loyal,
Nearer in bloody thoughts, but not in blood,
Deserve not worse than wretched Clarence did,
And yet go current from suspicion! 95

Enter [LORD STANLEY,] EARL OF DERBY.

Der. A boon, my sovereign, for my service done!
[*Kneeling.*]

King. I prithee peace. My soul is full of sorrow.

Der. I will not rise unless your Highness hear me.

King. Then say at once what is it thou requests.

Der. The forfeit, sovereign, of my servant's life,
Who slew today a riotous gentleman 101
Lately attendant on the Duke of Norfolk.

King. Have I a tongue to doom my brother's death,
And shall that tongue give pardon to a slave? 104
My brother killed no man—his fault was thought—
And yet his punishment was bitter death.
Who sued to me for him? Who, in my wrath,
Kneeled at my feet and bid me be advised?
Who spoke of brotherhood? Who spoke of love?
Who told me how the poor soul did forsake 110
The mighty Warwick and did fight for me?
Who told me, in the field at Tewkesbury,
When Oxford had me down, he rescued me
And said, "Dear brother, live, and be a king"?
Who told me, when we both lay in the field 115
Frozen almost to death, how he did lap me
Even in his garments, and did give himself,
All thin and naked, to the numb-cold night?
All this from my remembrance brutish wrath
Sinfully plucked, and not a man of you 120
Had so much grace to put it in my mind.
But when your carters or your waiting vassals
Have done a drunken slaughter and defaced
The precious image of our dear Redeemer, 124
You straight are on your knees for pardon, pardon;
And I, unjustly too, must grant it you. [*Derby rises.*]
But for my brother not a man would speak,
Nor I, ungracious, speak unto myself
For him, poor soul! The proudest of you all
Have been beholding to him in his life; 130
Yet none of you would once beg for his life.
O God! I fear thy justice will take hold
On me and you, and mine and yours, for this.
Come, Hastings, help me to my closet. Ah, poor Clarence! *Exeunt some with King and Queen.*

Rich. This is the fruits of rashness! Marked you not 135
How that the guilty kindred of the Queen
Looked pale when they did hear of Clarence' death?
O, they did urge it still unto the King!
God will revenge it. Come, lords, will you go
To comfort Edward with our company? 140

Buck. We wait upon your Grace.

Exeunt.

55. intelligence: information
58. hardly borne: deeply resented
68. all . . . desert: without my having deserved it at all
75. compounded: agreed
77. take . . . grace: i.e., forgive
79. flouted: mocked
91. lag: late
93. blood: kinship
95. go . . . suspicion: move freely and unsuspected
100. The . . . life: i.e., that his servant's life be spared
108. be advised: think it over
113. he . . . me: no such incident is recorded.
134. closet: chamber
138. still: continually
141. wait upon: attend

Scene II. [*London. The Palace.*]

Enter the Old Duchess of York, *with the* Two Children of Clarence [Edward and Margaret, Plantagenet].

Boy. Good grandam, tell us, is our father dead?
Duch. No, boy.
Girl. Why do you weep so oft, and beat your breast,
And cry "O Clarence, my unhappy son"? 4
Boy. Why do you look on us, and shake your head,
And call us orphans, wretches, castaways,
If that our noble father were alive?
Duch. My pretty cousins, you mistake me both.
I do lament the sickness of the King,
As loath to lose him, not your father's death: 10
It were lost sorrow to wail one that's lost.
Boy. Then you conclude, my grandam, he is dead.
The King mine uncle is to blame for it:
God will revenge it, whom I will importune
With earnest prayers all to that effect. 15
Girl. And so will I.
Duch. Peace, children, peace! The King doth love you well.
Incapable and shallow innocents,
You cannot guess who caused your father's death.
Boy. Grandam, we can; for my good uncle Gloucester 20
Told me the King, provoked to it by the Queen,
Devised impeachments to imprison him;
And when my uncle told me so, he wept,
And pitied me, and kindly kissed my cheek;
Bade me rely on him as on my father, 25
And he would love me dearly as a child.
Duch. Ah, that deceit should steal such gentle shape
And with a virtuous visor hide deep vice!
He is my son—ay, and therein my shame;
Yet from my dugs he drew not this deceit. 30
Boy. Think you my uncle did dissemble, grandam?
Duch. Ay, boy.
Boy. I cannot think it. Hark! What noise is this?

Enter the Queen [Elizabeth,] *with her hair about her ears,* Rivers *and* Dorset *after her.*

Queen. Ah, who shall hinder me to wail and weep,
To chide my fortune, and torment myself? 35
I'll join with black despair against my soul,
And to myself become an enemy.
Duch. What means this scene of rude impatience?
Queen. To make an act of tragic violence.
Edward, my lord, thy son, our king, is dead! 40
Why grow the branches when the root is gone?
Why wither not the leaves that want their sap?
If you will live, lament; if die, be brief,
That our swift-winged souls may catch the King's,
Or like obedient subjects follow him 45
To his new kingdom of ne'er-changing night.
Duch. Ah, so much interest have I in thy sorrow
As I had title in thy noble husband.
I have bewept a worthy husband's death,
And lived with looking on his images; 50
But now two mirrors of his princely semblance
Are cracked in pieces by malignant death,
And I for comfort have but one false glass,
That grieves me when I see my shame in him.
Thou art a widow; yet thou art a mother, 55
And hast the comfort of thy children left;
But death hath snatched my husband from mine arms
And plucked two crutches from my feeble hands,
Clarence and Edward. O, what cause have I,
Thine being but a moiety of my moan, 60
To overgo thy woes and drown thy cries!
Boy. Ah, aunt! you wept not for our father's death.
How can we aid you with our kindred tears?
Girl. Our fatherless distress was left unmoaned:
Your widow-dolor likewise be unwept! 65
Queen. Give me no help in lamentation;
I am not barren to bring forth complaints.
All springs reduce their currents to mine eyes,
That I, being governed by the watery moon,
May send forth plenteous tears to drown the world.
Ah for my husband, for my dear lord Edward! 71
Child. Ah for our father, for our dear lord Clarence!
Duch. Alas for both, both mine, Edward and Clarence!
Queen. What stay had I but Edward? and he's gone.
Child. What stay had we but Clarence? and he's gone. 75
Duch. What stays had I but they? and they are gone.
Queen. Was never widow had so dear a loss.
Child. Were never orphans had so dear a loss.
Duch. Was never mother had so dear a loss.
Alas! I am the mother of these griefs: 80
Their woes are parceled, mine is general.

8. cousins: a vague term of kinship
18. Incapable . . . shallow: ignorant and incapable of understanding
22. impeachments: accusations
28. visor: mask
42. want: lack
48. title: legal right
51. two . . . semblance: i.e., two sons that resembled him
61. overgo: exceed
65. widow-dolor: widow's sorrow
68. reduce: bring
74. stay: support; comfort
81. parceled: distributed among them; each has only one woe.

She for an Edward weeps, and so do I;
I for a Clarence weep, so doth not she:
These babes for Clarence weep, and so do I;
I for an Edward weep, so do not they. 85
Alas, you three on me, threefold distressed,
Pour all your tears! I am your sorrow's nurse,
And I will pamper it with lamentation.

Dor. Comfort, dear mother; God is much displeased
That you take with unthankfulness his doing. 90
In common worldly things 'tis called ungrateful
With dull unwillingness to repay a debt
Which with a bounteous hand was kindly lent;
Much more to be thus opposite with heaven
For it requires the royal debt it lent you. 95

Riv. Madam, bethink you like a careful mother
Of the young Prince your son. Send straight for him;
Let him be crowned; in him your comfort lives.
Drown desperate sorrow in dead Edward's grave,
And plant your joys in living Edward's throne. 100

Enter RICHARD, BUCKINGHAM, [STANLEY, EARL OF] DERBY, HASTINGS, *and* RATCLIFFE.

Rich. Sister, have comfort. All of us have cause
To wail the dimming of our shining star;
But none can help our harms by wailing them.
Madam, my mother, I do cry you mercy;
I did not see your Grace. Humbly on my knee 105
I crave your blessing.

Duch. God bless thee, and put meekness in thy breast,
Love, charity, obedience, and true duty!

Rich. Amen!—[*Aside*] and make me die a good old man!
That is the butt end of a mother's blessing; 110
I marvel that her Grace did leave it out.

Buck. You cloudy princes and heart-sorrowing peers
That bear this heavy mutual load of moan,
Now cheer each other in each other's love.
Though we have spent our harvest of this king,
We are to reap the harvest of his son. 116
The broken rancor of your high-swol'n hates,
But lately splintered, knit, and joined together,
Must gently be preserved, cherished, and kept.
Meseemeth good that, with some little train, 120
Forthwith from Ludlow the young Prince be fet
Hither to London, to be crowned our king.

Riv. Why with some little train, my Lord of Buckingham?

Buck. Marry, my lord, lest by a multitude 124
The new-healed wound of malice should break out,
Which would be so much the more dangerous
By how much the estate is green and yet ungoverned.
Where every horse bears his commanding rein
And may direct his course as please himself,
As well the fear of harm as harm apparent, 130
In my opinion, ought to be prevented.

Rich. I hope the King made peace with all of us;
And the compact is firm and true in me.

Riv. And so in me; and so, I think, in all.
Yet, since it is but green, it should be put 135
To no apparent likelihood of breach,
Which haply by much company might be urged.
Therefore I say with noble Buckingham
That it is meet so few should fetch the Prince.

Hast. And so say I. 140

Rich. Then be it so; and go we to determine
Who they shall be that straight shall post to Ludlow.
Madam, and you, my sister, will you go
To give your censures in this business?

Both. With all our hearts. 145

Exeunt. Manent Buckingham and Richard.

Buck. My lord, whoever journeys to the Prince,
For God's sake let not us two stay at home;
For by the way I'll sort occasion,
As index to the story we late talked of, 149
To part the Queen's proud kindred from the Prince.

Rich. My other self, my counsel's consistory,
My oracle, my prophet, my dear cousin,
I, as a child, will go by thy direction.
Toward Ludlow then, for we'll not stay behind.

Exeunt.

Scene III. [*London. A street.*]

Enter ONE CITIZEN *at one door and* ANOTHER *at the other.*

1. Cit. Good morrow, neighbor. Whither away so fast?

2. Cit. I promise you, I scarcely know myself.
Hear you the news abroad?

1. Cit. Yes, that the King is dead.

2. Cit. Ill news, by'r Lady—seldom comes the better:
I fear, I fear, 'twill prove a giddy world. 5

Enter ANOTHER CITIZEN.

112. cloudy: mournful
120. Meseemeth good: it seems to me good
121. fet: fetched

127. the . . . ungoverned: i.e., there has not yet been time to establish the new machinery of government.
139. meet: suitable
142. post: ride with all speed by post horse
144. censures: judgments
148. sort occasion: select opportunity
149. index: prologue
151. consistory: meeting place; the place where I seek counsel
4. seldom . . . better: proverbial pessimistic expression
5. giddy: unsettled

3. Cit. Neighbors, God speed!
1. Cit. Give you good morrow, sir.
3. Cit. Doth the news hold of good King Edward's death?
2. Cit. Ay, sir, it is too true. God help the while!
3. Cit. Then, masters, look to see a troublous world.
1. Cit. No, no! By God's good grace his son shall reign. 10
3. Cit. Woe to that land that's governed by a child!
2. Cit. In him there is a hope of government,
Which, in his nonage, council under him,
And, in his full and ripened years, himself,
No doubt shall then, and till then, govern well. 15
1. Cit. So stood the state when Henry the Sixth
Was crowned in Paris but at nine months old.
3. Cit. Stood the state so? No, no, good friends, God wot!
For then this land was famously enriched
With politic grave counsel; then the King 20
Had virtuous uncles to protect his Grace.
1. Cit. Why, so hath this, both by his father and mother.
3. Cit. Better it were they all came by his father,
Or by his father there were none at all;
For emulation who shall now be nearest 25
Will touch us all too near, if God prevent not.
O, full of danger is the Duke of Gloucester!
And the Queen's sons and brothers haught and proud;
And were they to be ruled, and not to rule,
This sickly land might solace as before. 30
1. Cit. Come, come, we fear the worst. All will be well.
3. Cit. When clouds are seen, wise men put on their cloaks;
When great leaves fall, then winter is at hand;
When the sun sets, who doth not look for night?
Untimely storms makes men expect a dearth. 35
All may be well; but if God sort it so,
'Tis more than we deserve or I expect.
2. Cit. Truly, the hearts of men are full of fear:
You cannot reason, almost, with a man
That looks not heavily and full of dread. 40
3. Cit. Before the days of change, still is it so.
By a divine instinct men's minds mistrust
Ensuing danger; as, by proof, we see
The water swell before a boist'rous storm.
But leave it all to God. Whither away? 45
2. Cit. Marry, we were sent for to the justices.
3. Cit. And so was I. I'll bear you company.
Exeunt.

8. the while: these times
11. Woe . . . child: cf. Eccles. 10:16
13. nonage: minority
18. wot: knows
20. politic: shrewd
25. emulation: envy
30. solace: be cheerful
36. sort: arrange
39. reason: talk
41. Before . . . so: it is always so when change is imminent.

Scene IV. [*London. The Palace.*]

Enter [*the*] ARCHBISHOP [OF YORK], [*the*] *young* [DUKE OF] YORK, *the* QUEEN [ELIZABETH], *and the* DUCHESS [OF YORK].

Arch. Last night, I hear, they lay at Stony Stratford;
And at Northampton they do rest tonight;
Tomorrow, or next day, they will be here.
Duch. I long with all my heart to see the Prince:
I hope he is much grown since last I saw him. 5
Queen. But I hear no. They say my son of York
Has almost overta'en him in his growth.
York. Ay, mother; but I would not have it so.
Duch. Why, my good cousin? it is good to grow.
York. Grandam, one night as we did sit at supper,
My uncle Rivers talked how I did grow 11
More than my brother. "Ay," quoth my uncle Gloucester,
"Small herbs have grace; great weeds do grow apace."
And since, methinks, I would not grow so fast, 14
Because sweet flow'rs are slow and weeds make haste.
Duch. Good faith, good faith, the saying did not hold
In him that did object the same to thee:
He was the wretched'st thing when he was young,
So long a-growing and so leisurely 19
That, if his rule were true, he should be gracious.
Arch. And so no doubt he is, my gracious madam.
Duch. I hope he is; but yet let mothers doubt.
York. Now, by my troth, if I had been remem'red,
I could have given my uncle's Grace a flout, 24
To touch his growth nearer than he touched mine.
Duch. How, my young York? I prithee let me hear it.
York. Marry, they say my uncle grew so fast
That he could gnaw a crust at two hours old:
'Twas full two years ere I could get a tooth.
Grandam, this would have been a biting jest. 30
Duch. I prithee, pretty York, who told thee this?
York. Grandam, his nurse.
Duch. His nurse? Why, she was dead ere thou wast born.

13. grace: virtue; healing power
20. gracious: virtuous
24. given . . . flout: had a laugh on his Grace, my uncle
27–28. my . . . old: the tradition that Richard was born with teeth derives originally from John Rous, *Historia regum Angliae* (*ca.* 1490).

York. If 'twere not she, I cannot tell who told me.
Queen. A parlous boy! Go to, you are too shrewd.
Duch. Good madam, be not angry with the child.
Queen. Pitchers have ears. 37

Enter a MESSENGER.

Arch. Here comes a messenger. What news?
Mess. Such news, my lord, as grieves me to report.
Queen. How doth the Prince?
Mess. Well, madam, and in health.
Duch. What is thy news? 41
Mess. Lord Rivers and Lord Grey are sent to Pomfret,
And with them Sir Thomas Vaughan, prisoners.
Duch. Who hath committed them?
Mess. The mighty Dukes, Gloucester and Buckingham.
Arch. For what offense?
Mess. The sum of all I can I have disclosed. 46
Why or for what the nobles were committed
Is all unknown to me, my gracious lord.
Queen. Ay me! I see the ruin of my house.
The tiger now hath seized the gentle hind: 50
Insulting tyranny begins to jut
Upon the innocent and aweless throne.

35. **parlous:** mischievous; **shrewd:** sharp
51. **jut:** loom threateningly
52. **aweless:** lacking the power to awe

Welcome destruction, blood, and massacre!
I see, as in a map, the end of all.
Duch. Accursed and unquiet wrangling days, 55
How many of you have mine eyes beheld!
My husband lost his life to get the crown,
And often up and down my sons were tossed
For me to joy and weep their gain and loss;
And being seated, and domestic broils 60
Clean overblown, themselves, the conquerors,
Make war upon themselves, brother to brother,
Blood to blood, self against self. O preposterous
And frantic outrage, end thy damned spleen,
Or let me die, to look on earth no more! 65
Queen. Come, come, my boy; we will to sanctuary.
Madam, farewell.
Duch. Stay, I will go with you.
Queen. You have no cause.
Arch. [*To the Queen*] My gracious lady, go,
And thither bear your treasure and your goods.
For my part, I'll resign unto your Grace 70
The seal I keep; and so betide to me
As well I tender you and all of yours!
Go, I'll conduct you to the sanctuary.

Exeunt.

54. **as . . . map:** as though a map of the future were before me
63. **preposterous:** monstrously unnatural
64. **spleen:** angry fit
71. **The seal:** the Great Seal of England

ACT III

Scene I. [*London. A street.*]

The trumpets sound. Enter young PRINCE [EDWARD OF WALES], *the* DUKE OF GLOUCESTER *and* BUCKINGHAM, LORD CARDINAL [BOURCHIER, CATESBY], *with others.*

Buck. Welcome, sweet Prince, to London, to your chamber.
Rich. Welcome, dear cousin, my thoughts' sovereign:
The weary way hath made you melancholy.
Prince. No, uncle; but our crosses on the way
Have made it tedious, wearisome, and heavy. 5
I want more uncles here to welcome me.
Rich. Sweet Prince, the untainted virtue of your years
Hath not yet dived into the world's deceit:
Nor more can you distinguish of a man
Than of his outward show, which, God he knows,
Seldom or never jumpeth with the heart. 11
Those uncles which you want were dangerous;
Your Grace attended to their sug'red words
But looked not on the poison of their hearts:
God keep you from them, and from such false friends! 15

1. **London . . . your chamber:** William Camden's *Britannia* records that London was called *camera regis* ("king's chamber") soon after the Norman Conquest.

4. **crosses:** difficulties
6. **more uncles:** i.e., his maternal uncles
11. **jumpeth:** agrees

Prince. God keep me from false friends!—but they were none.

Rich. My lord, the Mayor of London comes to greet you.

Enter LORD MAYOR [*and his* TRAIN].

May. God bless your Grace with health and happy days!

Prince. I thank you, good my lord, and thank you all. [*Exeunt Mayor and his Train.*]
I thought my mother and my brother York 20
Would long ere this have met us on the way.
Fie, what a slug is Hastings, that he comes not
To tell us whether they will come or no!

Enter LORD HASTINGS.

Buck. And, in good time, here comes the sweating lord.

Prince. Welcome, my lord. What, will our mother come? 25

Hast. On what occasion God he knows, not I,
The Queen your mother and your brother York
Have taken sanctuary. The tender Prince
Would fain have come with me to meet your Grace,
But by his mother was perforce withheld. 30

Buck. Fie, what an indirect and peevish course
Is this of hers! Lord Cardinal, will your Grace
Persuade the Queen to send the Duke of York
Unto his princely brother presently?
If she deny, Lord Hastings, go with him 35
And from her jealous arms pluck him perforce.

Card. My Lord of Buckingham, if my weak oratory
Can from his mother win the Duke of York,
Anon expect him here; but if she be obdurate
To mild entreaties, God in heaven forbid 40
We should infringe the holy privilege
Of blessed sanctuary! Not for all this land
Would I be guilty of so great a sin.

Buck. You are too senseless-obstinate, my lord,
Too ceremonious and traditional. 45
Weigh it but with the grossness of this age,
You break not sanctuary in seizing him:
The benefit thereof is always granted
To those whose dealings have deserved the place
And those who have the wit to claim the place. 50
This prince hath neither claimed it nor deserved it,
And therefore, in mine opinion, cannot have it.
Then, taking him from thence that is not there,
You break no privilege nor charter there.
Oft have I heard of sanctuary men, 55
But sanctuary children ne'er till now.

Card. My lord, you shall o'errule my mind for once.
Come on, Lord Hastings, will you go with me?

Hast. I go, my lord. 59

Prince. Good lords, make all the speedy haste you may. *Exeunt Cardinal and Hastings.*
Say, uncle Gloucester, if our brother come,
Where shall we sojourn till our coronation?

Rich. Where it seems best unto your royal self.
If I may counsel you, some day or two
Your Highness shall repose you at the Tower; 65
Then where you please, and shall be thought most fit
For your best health and recreation.

Prince. I do not like the Tower, of any place.
Did Julius Cæsar build that place, my lord? 69

Buck. He did, my gracious lord, begin that place,
Which, since, succeeding ages have re-edified.

Prince. Is it upon record, or else reported
Successively from age to age, he built it?

Buck. Upon record, my gracious lord.

Prince. But say, my lord, it were not regist'red,
Methinks the truth should live from age to age, 76
As 'twere retailed to all posterity,
Even to the general all-ending day.

Rich. [*Aside*] So wise so young, they say, do never live long.

Prince. What say you, uncle? 80

Rich. I say, without characters fame lives long.
[*Aside*] Thus, like the formal Vice, Iniquity,
I moralize two meanings in one word.

Prince. That Julius Cæsar was a famous man:
With what his valor did enrich his wit, 85
His wit set down to make his valor live.
Death makes no conquest of this conqueror,
For now he lives in fame, though not in life.
I'll tell you what, my cousin Buckingham—

Buck. What, my gracious lord? 90

Prince. An if I live until I be a man,
I'll win our ancient right in France again,
Or die a soldier as I lived a king.

Rich. [*Aside*] Short summers lightly have a forward spring.

22. slug: sluggard
26. On . . . occasion: for what reason
31. peevish: perverse
34. presently: at once
36. jealous: suspicious
44. senseless-obstinate: obstinate against reason
45. ceremonious . . . traditional: observant of traditional formality
49. whose . . . place: i.e., offenders, whose right to sanctuary was acknowledged
65. the Tower: often the residence of monarchs, including Edward IV before his coronation, but by Elizabethan times residence in the Tower was not a pleasant prospect.
68. of . . . place: of all places
69. Julius Cæsar: English chroniclers fostered a tradition that Cæsar had had the Tower erected.
71. re-edified: rebuilt
82. Vice, Iniquity: the personification of Iniquity in a morality play
94. lightly: commonly

Enter [*the*] *young* [DUKE OF] YORK, HASTINGS, *and* CARDINAL [BOURCHIER].

Buck. Now, in good time, here comes the Duke of York. 95
Prince. Richard of York, how fares our noble brother?
York. Well, my dread lord—so must I call you now.
Prince. Ay, brother, to our grief, as it is yours:
Too late he died that might have kept that title,
Which by his death hath lost much majesty. 100
Rich. How fares our cousin, noble Lord of York?
York. I thank you, gentle uncle. O my lord,
You said that idle weeds are fast in growth:
The Prince my brother hath outgrown me far.
Rich. He hath, my lord.
York. And therefore is he idle? 105
Rich. O my fair cousin, I must not say so.
York. Then he is more beholding to you than I.
Rich. He may command me as my sovereign,
But you have power in me as in a kinsman. 109
York. I pray you, uncle, give me this dagger.
Rich. My dagger, little cousin? With all my heart.
Prince. A beggar, brother?
York. Of my kind uncle, that I know will give,
And being but a toy, which is no grief to give. 114
Rich. A greater gift than that I'll give my cousin.
York. A greater gift? O, that's the sword to it.
Rich. Ay, gentle cousin, were it light enough.
York. O, then I see you will part but with light gifts!
In weightier things you'll say a beggar nay.
Rich. It is too heavy for your Grace to wear.
York. I weigh it lightly, were it heavier. 121
Rich. What, would you have my weapon, little lord?
York. I would, that I might thank you as you call me.
Rich. How?
York. Little. 125
Prince. My Lord of York will still be cross in talk.
Uncle, your Grace knows how to bear with him.
York. You mean, to bear me, not to bear with me.
Uncle, my brother mocks both you and me:
Because that I am little, like an ape, 130
He thinks that you should bear me on your shoulders.
Buck. [*Aside to Hastings*] With what a sharp-provided wit he reasons!
To mitigate the scorn he gives his uncle,
He prettily and aptly taunts himself:
So cunning, and so young, is wonderful. 135
Rich. My lord, will't please you pass along?
Myself and my good cousin Buckingham
Will to your mother, to entreat of her
To meet you at the Tower and welcome you. 139
York. What, will you go unto the Tower, my lord?
Prince. My Lord Protector needs will have it so.
York. I shall not sleep in quiet at the Tower.
Rich. Why, what should you fear?
York. Marry, my uncle Clarence' angry ghost:
My grandam told me he was murdered there. 145
Prince. I fear no uncles dead.
Rich. Nor none that live, I hope.
Prince. An if they live, I hope I need not fear.
But come, my lord; and with a heavy heart,
Thinking on them, go I unto the Tower. 150

A sennet. Exeunt Prince [*Edward*], *York, Hastings,* [*Cardinal Bourchier, and others*]. *Manent Richard, Buckingham, and Catesby.*

Buck. Think you, my lord, this little prating York
Was not incensed by his subtle mother
To taunt and scorn you thus opprobriously?
Rich. No doubt, no doubt. O, 'tis a perilous boy,
Bold, quick, ingenious, forward, capable: 155
He is all the mother's, from the top to toe.
Buck. Well, let them rest. Come hither, Catesby.
Thou art sworn as deeply to effect what we intend
As closely to conceal what we impart.
Thou knowest our reasons urged upon the way.
What thinkst thou? Is it not an easy matter 161
To make William Lord Hastings of our mind
For the installment of this noble Duke
In the seat royal of this famous isle?
Cates. He for his father's sake so loves the Prince
That he will not be won to aught against him. 166
Buck. What thinkst thou then of Stanley? Will not he?
Cates. He will do all in all as Hastings doth.
Buck. Well then, no more but this: go, gentle Catesby,
And, as it were far off, sound thou Lord Hastings
How he doth stand affected to our purpose, 171
And summon him tomorrow to the Tower
To sit about the coronation.
If thou dost find him tractable to us,
Encourage him, and tell him all our reasons: 175
If he be leaden, icy, cold, unwilling,
Be thou so too, and so break off the talk,
And give us notice of his inclination;
For we tomorrow hold divided councils,
Wherein thyself shalt highly be employed. 180

98. our: the royal plural
99. late: recently
114. toy: trifle
118. light: slight
121. weigh: value
126. cross . . . talk: inclined to punning conversation
154. perilous: dangerously clever
155. capable: intelligent
157. let . . . rest: enough talk of them
170. far off: indirectly
171. affected: inclined
179. divided councils: i.e., Richard plans a private council on the coronation as well as the official council.

Rich. Commend me to Lord William. Tell him, Catesby,
His ancient knot of dangerous adversaries
Tomorrow are let blood at Pomfret Castle,
And bid my lord, for joy of this good news,
Give Mistress Shore one gentle kiss the more. 185
Buck. Good Catesby, go effect this business soundly.
Cates. My good lords both, with all the heed I can.
Rich. Shall we hear from you, Catesby, ere we sleep?
Cates. You shall, my lord. 189
Rich. At Crosby House, there shall you find us both. *Exit Catesby.*
Buck. Now, my lord, what shall we do if we perceive
Lord Hastings will not yield to our complots?
Rich. Chop off his head! Something we will determine.
And look when I am King, claim thou of me
The earldom of Hereford and all the movables 195
Whereof the King my brother was possessed.
Buck. I'll claim that promise at your Grace's hand.
Rich. And look to have it yielded with all kindness.
Come, let us sup betimes, that afterwards
We may digest our complots in some form. 200
Exeunt.

Scene II. [*London. Before Lord Hasting's house.*]

Enter a MESSENGER *to the door of* HASTINGS.

Mess. My lord! my lord!
Hast. [*Within*] Who knocks?
Mess. One from the Lord Stanley.

Enter LORD HASTINGS.

Hast. What is't o'clock?
Mess. Upon the stroke of four. 5
Hast. Cannot my Lord Stanley sleep these tedious nights?
Mess. So it appears by that I have to say:
First, he commends him to your noble self.
Hast. What then? 9
Mess. Then certifies your lordship that this night
He dreamt the boar had rased off his helm:
Besides, he says there are two councils kept;
And that may be determined at the one
Which may make you and him to rue at the other.
Therefore he sends to know your lordship's pleasure,
If you will presently take horse with him 16
And with all speed post with him toward the North,
To shun the danger that his soul divines.
Hast. Go, fellow, go, return unto thy lord;
Bid him not fear the separated council. 20
His honor and myself are at the one,
And at the other is my good friend Catesby;
Where nothing can proceed that toucheth us
Whereof I shall not have intelligence.
Tell him his fears are shallow, without instance;
And for his dreams, I wonder he's so simple 26
To trust the mock'ry of unquiet slumbers.
To fly the boar before the boar pursues
Were to incense the boar to follow us,
And make pursuit where he did mean no chase. 30
Go, bid thy master rise and come to me,
And we will both together to the Tower,
Where he shall see the boar will use us kindly.
Mess. I'll go, my lord, and tell him what you say.
Exit.

Enter CATESBY.

Cates. Many good morrows to my noble lord!
Hast. Good morrow, Catesby; you are early stirring. 36
What news, what news, in this our tott'ring state?
Cates. It is a reeling world indeed, my lord,
And I believe will never stand upright
Till Richard wear the garland of the realm. 40
Hast. How! wear the garland! Dost thou mean the crown?
Cates. Ay, my good lord.
Hast. I'll have this crown of mine cut from my shoulders
Before I'll see the crown so foul misplaced.
But canst thou guess that he doth aim at it? 45
Cates. Ay, on my life, and hopes to find you forward
Upon his party for the gain thereof;
And thereupon he sends you this good news,
That this same very day your enemies,
The kindred of the Queen, must die at Pomfret. 50
Hast. Indeed I am no mourner for that news,
Because they have been still my adversaries;
But that I'll give my voice on Richard's side
To bar my master's heirs in true descent,
God knows I will not do it, to the death! 55

192. complots: conspiracies
193. Something . . . determine: we'll think of some pretext.
199. betimes: early
200. digest . . . form: make an orderly outline of our conspiracy
8. commends him: offers his respectful greetings
11. the boar: i.e., Richard; **rased . . . helm:** slashed off his head
25. shallow: trivial; **instance:** justification
46–47. forward . . . party: in the vanguard of his party

Cates. God keep your lordship in that gracious mind!

Hast. But I shall laugh at this a twelvemonth hence,
That they which brought me in my master's hate,
I live to look upon their tragedy.
Well, Catesby, ere a fortnight make me older, 60
I'll send some packing that yet think not on't.

Cates. 'Tis a vile thing to die, my gracious lord,
When men are unprepared and look not for it.

Hast. O, monstrous, monstrous! and so falls it out
With Rivers, Vaughan, Grey; and so 'twill do 65
With some men else, that think themselves as safe
As thou and I, who, as thou knowst, are dear
To princely Richard and to Buckingham.

Cates. The princes both make high account of you—
[*Aside*] For they account his head upon the Bridge. 70

Hast. I know they do, and I have well deserved it.

Enter Lord Stanley, [Earl of Derby].

Come on, come on! Where is your boar-spear, man?
Fear you the boar, and go so unprovided?

Der. My lord, good morrow. Good morrow, Catesby.
You may jest on, but, by the Holy Rood, 75
I do not like these several councils, I.

Hast. My lord, I hold my life as dear as yours,
And never in my days, I do protest,
Was it so precious to me as 'tis now.
Think you, but that I know our state secure, 80
I would be so triumphant as I am?

Der. The lords at Pomfret, when they rode from London,
Were jocund and supposed their states were sure,
And they indeed had no cause to mistrust;
But yet you see how soon the day o'ercast. 85
This sudden stab of rancor I misdoubt:
Pray God, I say, I prove a needless coward!
What, shall we toward the Tower? The day is spent.

Hast. Come, come, have with you. Wot you what, my lord?
Today the lords you talked of are beheaded. 90

Der. They, for their truth, might better wear their heads
Than some that have accused them wear their hats.
But come, my lord, let's away.

Enter a Pursuivant.

Hast. Go on before. I'll talk with this good fellow.
Exeunt Lord Stanley, [*Earl of Derby,*] *and Catesby.*
How now, sirrah? How goes the world with thee?

Purs. The better that your lordship please to ask. 96

Hast. I tell thee, man, 'tis better with me now
Than when thou metst me last where now we meet.
Then was I going prisoner to the Tower
By the suggestion of the Queen's allies; 100
But now I tell thee—keep it to thyself—
This day those enemies are put to death,
And I in better state than e'er I was. 103

Purs. God hold it, to your honor's good content!

Hast. Gramercy, fellow. There, drink that for me. *Throws him his purse.*

Purs. I thank your honor. *Exit Pursuivant.*

Enter a Priest.

Priest. Well met, my lord. I am glad to see your honor.

Hast. I thank thee, good Sir John, with all my heart.
I am in your debt for your last exercise;
Come the next Sabbath, and I will content you. 110
He whispers in his ear.

Priest. I'll wait upon your lordship.

Enter Buckingham.

Buck. What, talking with a priest, Lord Chamberlain?
Your friends at Pomfret, they do need the priest;
Your honor hath no shriving work in hand.

Hast. Good faith, and when I met this holy man,
The men you talk of came into my mind. 116
What, go you toward the Tower?

Buck. I do, my lord, but long I cannot stay there.
I shall return before your lordship thence.

Hast. Nay, like enough, for I stay dinner there.

Buck. [*Aside*] And supper too, although thou knowst it not.— 121
Come, will you go?

Hast. I'll wait upon your lordship.
Exeunt.

61. send . . . packing: send some to their deaths
70. the Bridge: London Bridge, where the heads of executed traitors were displayed on pikes
86. sudden . . . rancor: sudden hostile act (the executions of Rivers, Vaughan, and Grey)
89. have . . . you: let's go.

Ent. Pursuivant: a state messenger who delivered warrants
104. hold: preserve
105. Gramercy: many thanks (French *grand merci*)
108. Sir: a common title of respect for a priest
110. content: gratify; reward
114. shriving work: i.e., confession before death
120. stay: stay for

Scene III. [*Pomfret Castle.*]

Enter SIR RICHARD RATCLIFFE, *with* HALBERDS, *carrying the* NOBLES, [RIVERS, GREY, *and* VAUGHAN,] *to death at Pomfret.*

Riv. Sir Richard Ratcliffe, let me tell thee this:
Today shalt thou behold a subject die
For truth, for duty, and for loyalty.
Grey. God bless the Prince from all the pack of you!
A knot you are of damned bloodsuckers. 5
Vaugh. You live that shall cry woe for this hereafter.
Rat. Dispatch! The limit of your lives is out.
Riv. O Pomfret, Pomfret! O thou bloody prison,
Fatal and ominous to noble peers!
Within the guilty closure of thy walls 10
Richard the Second here was hacked to death;
And, for more slander to thy dismal seat,
We give to thee our guiltless blood to drink.
Grey. Now Margaret's curse is fall'n upon our heads,
When she exclaimed on Hastings, you, and I, 15
For standing by when Richard stabbed her son.
Riv. Then cursed she Richard, then cursed she Buckingham,
Then cursed she Hastings. O, remember, God,
To hear her prayer for them, as now for us!
And for my sister and her princely sons, 20
Be satisfied, dear God, with our true blood,
Which, as thou knowst, unjustly must be spilt.
Rat. Make haste. The hour of death is expiate.
Riv. Come, Grey; come, Vaughan; let us here embrace.
Farewell, until we meet again in heaven. 25
Exeunt.

Scene IV. [*London. The Tower.*]

Enter BUCKINGHAM, [LORD STANLEY, EARL OF DERBY, HASTINGS, BISHOP OF ELY, NORFOLK, RATCLIFFE, LOVEL, *with others, at a table.*

Hast. Now, noble peers, the cause why we are met
Is to determine of the coronation.
In God's name, speak. When is the royal day?
Buck. Is all things ready for the royal time?
Der. It is, and wants but nomination. 5
Ely. Tomorrow then I judge a happy day.
Buck. Who knows the Lord Protector's mind herein?
Who is most inward with the noble Duke?
Ely. Your Grace, we think, should soonest know his mind. 9
Buck. We know each other's faces; for our hearts,
He knows no more of mine than I of yours;
Or I of his, my lord, than you of mine.
Lord Hastings, you and he are near in love.
Hast. I thank his Grace, I know he loves me well;
But, for his purpose in the coronation, 15
I have not sounded him, nor he delivered
His gracious pleasure any way therein;
But you, my honorable lords, may name the time,
And in the Duke's behalf I'll give my voice,
Which, I presume, he'll take in gentle part. 20

Enter [RICHARD, DUKE OF] GLOUCESTER.

Ely. In happy time, here comes the Duke himself.
Rich. My noble lords and cousins all, good morrow.
I have been long a sleeper; but I trust
My absence doth neglect no great design 24
Which by my presence might have been concluded.
Buck. Had you not come upon your cue, my lord,
William Lord Hastings had pronounced your part—
I mean, your voice—for crowning of the King.
Rich. Than my Lord Hastings no man might be bolder.
His lordship knows me well, and loves me well. 30
My Lord of Ely, when I was last in Holborn
I saw good strawberries in your garden there.
I do beseech you send for some of them.
Ely. Marry and will, my lord, with all my heart.
Exit Bishop.
Rich. Cousin of Buckingham, a word with you.
[*Drawing him aside.*]
Catesby hath sounded Hastings in our business, 36
And finds the testy gentleman so hot
That he will lose his head ere give consent
His master's child, as worshipfully he terms it,
Shall lose the royalty of England's throne. 40
Buck. Withdraw yourself awhile. I'll go with you.
Exeunt [*Richard and Buckingham*].
Der. We have not yet set down this day of triumph:
Tomorrow, in my judgment, is too sudden;
For I myself am not so well provided
As else I would be, were the day prolonged. 45

10. closure: enclosure
12. slander: disgrace; **dismal:** ill-omened
23. The . . . expiate: your last hour has expired.

5. nomination: naming (of the day)
6. happy: opportune
34. Marry . . . will: indeed I will
39. worshipfully: respectfully
40. royalty: sovereignty
42. triumph: festivity
45. prolonged: delayed

[Re-]enter the BISHOP OF ELY.

Ely. Where is my lord the Duke of Gloucester?
I have sent for these strawberries.
Hast. His Grace looks cheerfully and smooth this morning;
There's some conceit or other likes him well 49
When that he bids good morrow with such spirit.
I think there's never a man in Christendom
Can lesser hide his love or hate than he,
For by his face straight shall you know his heart.
Der. What of his heart perceive you in his face
By any livelihood he showed today? 55
Hast. Marry, that with no man here he is offended;
For were he, he had shown it in his looks.

Enter RICHARD *and* BUCKINGHAM.

Rich. I pray you all, tell me what they deserve
That do conspire my death with devilish plots
Of damned witchcraft, and that have prevailed 60
Upon my body with their hellish charms.
Hast. The tender love I bear your Grace, my lord,
Makes me most forward in this princely presence
To doom the offenders, whosoe'er they be:
I say, my lord, they have deserved death. 65
Rich. Then be your eyes the witness of their evil.
Look how I am bewitched. Behold, mine arm
Is like a blasted sapling, withered up;
And this is Edward's wife, that monstrous witch,
Consorted with that harlot, strumpet Shore, 70
That by their witchcraft thus have marked me.
Hast. If they have done this deed, my noble lord—
Rich. If? Thou protector of this damned strumpet,
Talkst thou to me of ifs? Thou art a traitor.
Off with his head! Now, by St. Paul I swear 75
I will not dine until I see the same.
Lovel and Ratcliffe, look that it be done:
The rest that love me, rise and follow me.
Exeunt. Manent Lovel and Ratcliffe, with the Lord Hastings.
Hast. Woe, woe for England, not a whit for me!
For I, too fond, might have prevented this. 80
Stanley did dream the boar did rase our helms;
But I did scorn it and disdain to fly.
Three times today my footcloth horse did stumble,
And started when he looked upon the Tower,
As loath to bear me to the slaughterhouse. 85
O, now I need the priest that spake to me!
I now repent I told the pursuivant,
As too triumphing, how mine enemies
Today at Pomfret bloodily were butchered,
And I myself secure in grace and favor. 90
O Margaret, Margaret, now thy heavy curse
Is lighted on poor Hastings' wretched head!
Rat. Come, come, dispatch! The Duke would be at dinner.
Make a short shrift; he longs to see your head.
Hast. O momentary grace of mortal men, 95
Which we more hunt for than the grace of God!
Who builds his hope in air of your good looks
Lives like a drunken sailor on a mast,
Ready with every nod to tumble down
Into the fatal bowels of the deep. 100
Lov. Come, come, dispatch! 'Tis bootless to exclaim.
Hast. O bloody Richard! Miserable England!
I prophesy the fearful'st time to thee
That ever wretched age hath looked upon.
Come, lead me to the block; bear him my head.
They smile at me who shortly shall be dead. 106
Exeunt.

[Scene V. *London. The Tower walls.*]

Enter RICHARD, [DUKE OF GLOUCESTER,] *and* BUCKINGHAM, *in rotten armor, marvelous ill-favored.*

Rich. Come, cousin, canst thou quake, and change thy color,
Murder thy breath in middle of a word,
And then again begin, and stop again,
As if thou wert distraught and mad with terror?
Buck. Tut, I can counterfeit the deep tragedian,
Speak and look back, and pry on every side, 6
Tremble and start at wagging of a straw,
Intending deep suspicion: ghastly looks
Are at my service, like enforced smiles;
And both are ready in their offices, 10
At any time, to grace my stratagems.
But what, is Catesby gone?
Rich. He is; and see, he brings the Mayor along.

Enter the MAYOR *and* CATESBY.

Buck. Lord Mayor—
Rich. Look to the drawbridge there! 15
Buck. Hark! a drum.

49. conceit: idea; **likes:** pleases
70. Consorted: associated
74. traitor: the historical justification for Hastings' execution was his alleged complicity in the Queen's plot to set aside the Protector.
80. fond: foolish
83. footcloth horse: horse bedecked with trappings. Stumbling was considered a bad omen.

94. shrift: confession
95. grace: favor
97. builds . . . looks: builds expectations on your smile
101. bootless: useless
Ent. rotten: rusty; **ill-favored:** unsightly
8. Intending: pretending

Rich. Catesby, o'erlook the walls.
Buck. Lord Mayor, the reason we have sent—
Rich. Look back! defend thee! Here are enemies!
Buck. God and our innocency defend and guard us!

Enter LOVEL *and* RATCLIFFE, *with* HASTINGS' *head.*

Rich. Be patient, they are friends—Ratcliffe and Lovel. 21
Lov. Here is the head of that ignoble traitor,
The dangerous and unsuspected Hastings.
Rich. So dear I loved the man that I must weep:
I took him for the plainest harmless creature 25
That breathed upon the earth a Christian;
Made him my book, wherein my soul recorded
The history of all her secret thoughts.
So smooth he daubed his vice with show of virtue
That, his apparent open guilt omitted, 30
I mean, his conversation with Shore's wife,
He lived from all attainder of suspects.
Buck. Well, well, he was the covert'st shelt'red traitor
That ever lived.
Would you imagine, or almost believe, 35
Were't not that by great preservation
We live to tell it, that the subtle traitor
This day had plotted, in the council house,
To murder me and my good Lord of Gloucester?
May. Had he done so? 40
Rich. What? Think you we are Turks or infidels?
Or that we would, against the form of law,
Proceed thus rashly in the villain's death,
But that the extreme peril of the case,
The peace of England and our persons' safety, 45
Enforced us to this execution?
May. Now fair befall you! He deserved his death,
And your good Graces both have well proceeded
To warn false traitors from the like attempts.
Buck. I never looked for better at his hands 50
After he once fell in with Mistress Shore:
Yet had we not determined he should die
Until your lordship came to see his end,
Which now the loving haste of these our friends,
Something against our meanings, have prevented;
Because, my lord, I would have had you heard 56
The traitor speak, and timorously confess
The manner and the purpose of his treasons,
That you might well have signified the same
Unto the citizens, who haply may 60
Misconster us in him and wail his death.
May. But, my good lord, your Grace's words shall serve,
As well as I had seen and heard him speak;
And do not doubt, right noble princes both,
But I'll acquaint our duteous citizens 65
With all your just proceedings in this case.
Rich. And to that end we wished your Lordship here,
T'avoid the censures of the carping world.
Buck. But since you come too late of our intent,
Yet witness what you hear we did intend: 70
And so, my good Lord Mayor, we bid farewell.
Exit Mayor.
Rich. Go after, after, cousin Buckingham.
The Mayor towards Guildhall hies him in all post:
There, at your meet'st advantage of the time,
Infer the bastardy of Edward's children. 75
Tell them how Edward put to death a citizen
Only for saying he would make his son
Heir to the Crown, meaning indeed his house,
Which by the sign thereof was termed so.
Moreover, urge his hateful luxury 80
And bestial appetite in change of lust,
Which stretched unto their servants, daughters, wives,
Even where his raging eye or savage heart,
Without control, lusted to make a prey.
Nay, for a need, thus far come near my person: 85
Tell them, when that my mother went with child
Of that insatiate Edward, noble York,
My princely father, then had wars in France,
And by true computation of the time
Found that the issue was not his begot; 90
Which well appeared in his lineaments,
Being nothing like the noble Duke my father.
Yet touch this sparingly, as 'twere far off,
Because, my lord, you know my mother lives.
Buck. Doubt not, my lord, I'll play the orator
As if the golden fee for which I plead 96
Were for myself. And so, my lord, adieu.
Rich. If you thrive well, bring them to Baynard's Castle,
Where you shall find me well accompanied 99
With reverend fathers and well-learned bishops.

25. plainest harmless: most obviously harmless
27. book: diary
30. apparent open: openly displayed
31. conversation: intercourse
32. attainder . . . suspects: taint of suspicion
33. covert'st shelt'red: most closely hidden
35. almost: even
61. Misconster . . . him: misconstrue our dealing with him
74. meet'st advantage: most suitable opportunity
75. Infer: allege. **bastardy . . . children:** the Bishop of Bath and Wells reported that Edward had made a precontract with Lady Eleanor Butler. It was Richard's contention that since a precontract was considered as binding as a marriage, Edward's subsequent marriage to Elizabeth Woodville was illegal and their children illegitimate.
78. the . . . house: i.e., a tavern named the Crown
80. luxury: lust
86–87. went . . . Edward: i.e., while she was carrying Edward
96. golden fee: crown
98. Baynard's Castle: the London residence of the Duchess of York

Buck. I go; and towards three or four o'clock
Look for the news that the Guildhall affords.
Exit Buckingham.
Rich. Go, Lovel, with all speed to Doctor Shaw—
[*To Catesby*] Go thou to Friar Penker.—Bid them both
Meet me within this hour at Baynard's Castle. 105
Exeunt [*Lovel, Catesby, and Ratcliffe*].
Now will I go to take some privy order
To draw the brats of Clarence out of sight,
And to give order that no manner person
Have any time recourse unto the princes.
Exit.

[Scene VI. *London. A street.*]

Enter a SCRIVENER *with a paper in his hand.*

Scriv. Here is the indictment of the good Lord Hastings,
Which in a set hand fairly is engrossed
That it may be today read o'er in Paul's.
And mark how well the sequel hangs together:
Eleven hours I have spent to write it over, 5
For yesternight by Catesby was it sent me;
The precedent was full as long a-doing;
And yet within these five hours Hastings lived,
Untainted, unexamined, free, at liberty.
Here's a good world the while! Who is so gross 10
That cannot see this palpable device?
Yet who so bold but says he sees it not?
Bad is the world, and all will come to nought
When such ill dealing must be seen in thought.
Exit.

[Scene VII. *London. Baynard's Castle.*]

Enter RICHARD, [DUKE OF GLOUCESTER,] *and* BUCKINGHAM *at several doors.*

Rich. How now, how now, what say the citizens?
Buck. Now, by the holy Mother of our Lord,
The citizens are mum, say not a word.
Rich. Touched you the bastardy of Edward's children?
Buck. I did, with his contract with Lady Lucy 5
And his contract by deputy in France;
The unsatiate greediness of his desire
And his enforcement of the city wives;
His tyranny for trifles; his own bastardy,
As being got, your father then in France, 10
And his resemblance, being not like the Duke.
Withal I did infer your lineaments,
Being the right idea of your father
Both in your form and nobleness of mind;
Laid open all your victories in Scotland, 15
Your discipline in war, wisdom in peace,
Your bounty, virtue, fair humility;
Indeed, left nothing fitting for your purpose
Untouched or slightly handled in discourse;
And when my oratory drew toward end, 20
I bid them that did love their country's good
Cry, "God save Richard, England's royal King!"
Rich. And did they so?
Buck. No, so God help me, they spake not a word,
But, like dumb statuës or breathing stones, 25
Stared each on other, and looked deadly pale.
Which when I saw, I reprehended them
And asked the Mayor what meant this willful silence.
His answer was, the people were not used
To be spoke to but by the Recorder. 30
Then he was urged to tell my tale again:
"Thus saith the Duke, thus hath the Duke inferred,"—
But nothing spake in warrant from himself.
When he had done, some followers of mine own,
At lower end of the hall, hurled up their caps. 35
And some ten voices cried, "God save King Richard!"
And thus I took the vantage of those few:
"Thanks, gentle citizens and friends," quoth I.
"This general applause and cheerful shout
Argues your wisdoms and your love to Richard."—
And even here brake off and came away. 41
Rich. What tongueless blocks were they! Would they not speak?
Buck. No, by my troth, my lord.
Rich. Will not the Mayor then and his brethren come?
Buck. The Mayor is here at hand. Intend some fear; 45

103–4. Doctor Shaw . . . Friar Penker: popular preachers of the time. Friar Ralph Shaw made the first public reference to the alleged precontract.
2. in . . . engrossed: is written clearly in a formal hand
4. sequel: sequence of events
7. precedent: draft
9. Untainted: free of the charge of treason
10. gross: stupid
11. palpable device: obvious contrivance
14. seen . . . thought: noticed but not spoken of

5. Lady Lucy: one of Edward's mistresses, but not historically his partner in the precontract
6. contract . . . France: Warwick had negotiated for Edward a marriage with the Lady Bona of Savoy, sister-in-law of Louis IX of France, but Edward repudiated the match when he fell in love with Elizabeth Woodville.
11. resemblance: appearance
12. infer . . . lineaments: mention your features
13. right idea: true image
30. the Recorder: a man appointed by the Mayor or Aldermen, whose duty it was to record facts and recite them to the public as evidence of the truth
33. nothing . . . himself: expressed no personal guarantee of the facts
45. Intend: pretend

Be not you spoke with but by mighty suit;
And look you get a prayer book in your hand
And stand between two churchmen, good my lord,
For on that ground I'll make a holy descant.
And be not easily won to our requests; 50
Play the maid's part: still answer nay, and take it.
Rich. I go; and if you plead as well for them
As I can say nay to thee for myself,
No doubt we bring it to a happy issue.
Buck. Go, go, up to the leads! The Lord Mayor knocks. [*Exit Richard.*]

Enter the MAYOR, [ALDERMEN,] *and* CITIZENS.

Welcome, my lord. I dance attendance here; 56
I think the Duke will not be spoke withal.

Enter CATESBY.

Now, Catesby, what says your lord to my request?
Cates. He doth entreat your Grace, my noble lord,
To visit him tomorrow or next day: 60
He is within, with two right reverend fathers,
Divinely bent to meditation,
And in no worldly suits would he be moved
To draw him from his holy exercise.
Buck. Return, good Catesby, to the gracious Duke: 65
Tell him, myself, the Mayor and Aldermen,
In deep designs, in matter of great moment,
No less importing than our general good,
Are come to have some conference with his Grace.
Cates. I'll signify so much unto him straight. *Exit.*
Buck. Ah ha, my lord, this prince is not an Edward! 71
He is not lulling on a lewd love-bed,
But on his knees at meditation;
Not dallying with a brace of courtesans,
But meditating with two deep divines; 75
Not sleeping, to engross his idle body,
But praying, to enrich his watchful soul.
Happy were England, would this virtuous prince
Take on his Grace the sovereignty thereof;
But sure I fear we shall not win him to it. 80
May. Marry, God defend his Grace should say us nay!
Buck. I fear he will. Here Catesby comes again.

[*Re-*]*enter* CATESBY.

Now, Catesby, what says his Grace?
Cates. He wonders to what end you have assembled
Such troops of citizens to come to him, 85
His Grace not being warned thereof before:
He fears, my lord, you mean no good to him.
Buck. Sorry I am my noble cousin should
Suspect me that I mean no good to him:
By heaven, we come to him in perfect love; 90
And so once more return and tell his Grace.
Exit [*Catesby*].
When holy and devout religious men
Are at their beads, 'tis much to draw them thence,
So sweet is zealous contemplation.

Enter RICHARD *aloft, between* TWO BISHOPS.
[CATESBY *returns.*]

May. See where his Grace stands, 'tween two clergymen. 95
Buck. Two props of virtue for a Christian prince,
To stay him from the fall of vanity;
And see, a book of prayer in his hand—
True ornaments to know a holy man.
Famous Plantagenet, most gracious prince, 100
Lend favorable ear to our requests,
And pardon us the interruption
Of thy devotion and right Christian zeal.
Rich. My lord, there needs no such apology:
I do beseech your Grace to pardon me, 105
Who, earnest in the service of my God,
Deferred the visitation of my friends.
But, leaving this, what is your Grace's pleasure?
Buck. Even that, I hope, which pleaseth God above,
And all good men of this ungoverned isle. 110
Rich. I do suspect I have done some offense
That seems disgracious in the city's eye,
And that you come to reprehend my ignorance.
Buck. You have, my lord. Would it might please your Grace,
On our entreaties, to amend your fault! 115
Rich. Else wherefore breathe I in a Christian land?
Buck. Know then, it is your fault that you resign
The supreme seat, the throne majestical,
The scept'red office of your ancestors,
Your state of fortune and your due of birth, 120
The lineal glory of your royal house,
To the corruption of a blemished stock;
Whiles, in the mildness of your sleepy thoughts,
Which here we waken to our country's good,
The noble isle doth want her proper limbs; 125
Her face defaced with scars of infamy,

49. on . . . ground: on the basis of Richard's pious company
55. leads: lead-sheeted roof
56. dance attendance: kick my heels, waiting for an audience
72. lulling: lolling
76. engross: fatten
81. defend: forbid
97. the . . . vanity: falling to worldly temptation
112. disgracious: displeasing
125. proper: own

Her royal stock graft with ignoble plants,
And almost should'red in the swallowing gulf
Of dark forgetfulness and deep oblivion.
Which to recure, we heartily solicit 130
Your gracious self to take on you the charge
And kingly government of this your land;
Not as Protector, steward, substitute,
Or lowly factor for another's gain;
But as successively, from blood to blood, 135
Your right of birth, your empery, your own.
For this, consorted with the citizens,
Your very worshipful and loving friends,
And by their vehement instigation,
In this just cause come I to move your Grace. 140

Rich. I cannot tell if to depart in silence,
Or bitterly to speak in your reproof,
Best fitteth my degree or your condition.
If not to answer, you might haply think
Tongue-tied ambition, not replying, yielded 145
To bear the golden yoke of sovereignty
Which fondly you would here impose on me.
If to reprove you for this suit of yours,
So seasoned with your faithful love to me,
Then, on the other side, I checked my friends. 150
Therefore, to speak, and to avoid the first,
And then, in speaking, not to incur the last,
Definitively thus I answer you.
Your love deserves my thanks, but my desert
Unmeritable shuns your high request. 155
First, if all obstacles were cut away,
And that my path were even to the crown
As the ripe revenue and due of birth,
Yet so much is my poverty of spirit,
So mighty and so many my defects, 160
That I would rather hide me from my greatness,
Being a bark to brook no mighty sea,
Than in my greatness covet to be hid
And in the vapor of my glory smothered.
But, God be thanked, there is no need of me, 165
And much I need to help you, were there need:
The royal tree hath left us royal fruit,
Which, mellowed by the stealing hours of time,
Will well become the seat of majesty,
And make, no doubt, us happy by his reign. 170
On him I lay that you would lay on me,
The right and fortune of his happy stars,
Which God defend that I should wring from him!

Buck. My lord, this argues conscience in your Grace.
But the respects thereof are nice and trivial, 175
All circumstances well considered.
You say that Edward is your brother's son:
So say we too, but not by Edward's wife;
For first was he contract to Lady Lucy—
Your mother lives a witness to his vow— 180
And afterward by substitute betrothed
To Bona, sister to the King of France.
These both put off, a poor petitioner,
A care-crazed mother to a many sons,
A beauty-waning and distressed widow, 185
Even in the afternoon of her best days,
Made prize and purchase of his wanton eye,
Seduced the pitch and height of his degree
To base declension and loathed bigamy.
By her, in his unlawful bed, he got 190
This Edward, whom our manners call the Prince.
More bitterly could I expostulate,
Save that, for reverence to some alive,
I give a sparing limit to my tongue.
Then, good my lord, take to your royal self 195
This proffered benefit of dignity;
If not to bless us and the land withal,
Yet to draw forth your noble ancestry
From the corruption of abusing times
Unto a lineal true-derived course. 200

May. Do, good my lord; your citizens entreat you.

Buck. Refuse not, mighty lord, this proffered love.

Cates. O make them joyful, grant their lawful suit!

Rich. Alas, why would you heap this care on me?
I am unfit for state and majesty: 205
I do beseech you, take it not amiss,
I cannot nor I will not yield to you.

Buck. If you refuse it—as, in love and zeal,
Loath to depose the child, your brother's son;
As well we know your tenderness of heart 210
And gentle, kind, effeminate remorse,
Which we have noted in you to your kindred
And egally indeed to all estates—
Yet know, whe'er you accept our suit or no,
Your brother's son shall never reign our king, 215
But we will plant some other in the throne,
To the disgrace and downfall of your house;

127. graft: grafted. The early form of the word was "graff," **graft** being the past participle.
134. factor: agent
135. successively: by right of succession
136. empery: empire
138. worshipful: respectful
147. fondly: foolishly
150. checked: rebuked
153. Definitively: finally
157. even: smooth; unimpeded
158. the . . . birth: the inheritance now fallen to my right
159. poverty . . . spirit: humility
166. need: lack; that is, he lacks the capacity to be of help
168. stealing: slowly moving
175. respects: considerations; **nice:** overly scrupulous
181. substitute: proxy
183. petitioner: see *Henry VI, Part 3* (III.ii.), where Elizabeth Woodville appeals to Edward IV for the restoration of her dead husband's lands.
187. Made . . . of: seized upon as a prize
188. pitch . . . height: highest pitch
189. declension: decline
192. expostulate: relate in detail
211. kind: natural; **effeminate remorse:** soft-hearted pity
213. egally: equally
214. whe'er: whether

And in this resolution here we leave you.
Come, citizens. Zounds, I'll entreat no more!

Rich. O, do not swear, my lord of Buckingham.
Exeunt [all but Richard and Catesby].

Cates. Call him again, sweet prince, accept their suit: 221
If you deny them, all the land will rue it.

Rich. Will you enforce me to a world of cares?
Call them again. I am not made of stones,
But penetrable to your kind entreaties, 225
Albeit against my conscience and my soul.

[*Re-*]*enter* BUCKINGHAM *and the rest.*

Cousin of Buckingham, and sage, grave men,
Since you will buckle fortune on my back,
To bear her burden, whe'er I will or no,
I must have patience to endure the load; 230
But if black scandal or foul-faced reproach
Attend the sequel of your imposition,
Your mere enforcement shall acquittance me
From all the impure blots and stains thereof;
For God doth know, and you may partly see, 235
How far I am from the desire of this.

May. God bless your Grace! We see it and will say it.

Rich. In saying so you shall but say the truth.

Buck. Then I salute you with this royal title—
Long live King Richard, England's worthy King!

All. Amen. 241

Buck. Tomorrow may it please you to be crowned?

Rich. Even when you please, for you will have it so.

Buck. Tomorrow then we will attend your Grace,
And so most joyfully we take our leave. 245

Rich. [*To the Bishops*] Come, let us to our holy work again.—
Farewell, my cousin; farewell, gentle friends.
Exeunt.

219. **Zounds:** by God's wounds

233. **mere:** absolute; **acquittance:** furnish me with acquittal

ACT IV

Scene I. [*London. Outside the Tower.*]

Enter the QUEEN [ELIZABETH], *the* DUCHESS OF YORK, *and* MARQUESS [OF] DORSET [*at one door*]; ANNE, DUCHESS OF GLOUCESTER, [LADY MARGARET PLANTAGENET, *Clarence's daughter, at another door*].

Duch. Who meets us here? My niece Plantagenet,
Led in the hand of her kind aunt of Gloucester?
Now, for my life, she's wand'ring to the Tower
On pure heart's love, to greet the tender Prince.
Daughter, well met.

Anne. God give your Graces both 5
A happy and a joyful time of day!

Queen. As much to you, good sister. Whither away?

Anne. No farther than the Tower, and, as I guess,
Upon the like devotion as yourselves,
To gratulate the gentle princes there. 10

Queen. Kind sister, thanks. We'll enter all together.

Enter the LIEUTENANT [BRAKENBURY].

And in good time, here the Lieutenant comes.
Master Lieutenant, pray you, by your leave,
How doth the Prince, and my young son of York?

Lieut. Right well, dear madam. By your patience,
I may not suffer you to visit them; 16
The King hath strictly charged the contrary.

Queen. The King? Who's that?

Lieut. I mean the Lord Protector.

Queen. The Lord protect him from that kingly title!
Hath he set bounds between their love and me? 20
I am their mother; who shall bar me from them?

Duch. I am their father's mother; I will see them.

Anne. Their aunt I am in law, in love their mother;
Then bring me to their sights. I'll bear thy blame
And take thy office from thee on my peril. 25

1. **niece:** granddaughter. The word was used for various remote female relatives.
4. **On:** because of

10. **gratulate:** greet joyfully
16. **suffer:** permit
25. **take . . . thee:** assume your function as their guardian

Lieut. No, madam, no! I may not leave it so:
I am bound by oath, and therefore pardon me.
Exit Lieutenant.

Enter STANLEY, [EARL OF DERBY].

Der. Let me but meet you, ladies, one hour hence,
And I'll salute your Grace of York as mother
And reverend looker-on of two fair queens. 30
[*To Anne*] Come, madam, you must straight to Westminster,
There to be crowned Richard's royal queen.
Queen. Ah, cut my lace asunder,
That my pent heart may have some scope to beat,
Or else I swoon with this dead-killing news! 35
Anne. Despiteful tidings! O unpleasing news!
Dor. Be of good cheer. Mother, how fares your Grace?
Queen. O Dorset, speak not to me, get thee gone!
Death and destruction dogs thee at thy heels;
Thy mother's name is ominous to children. 40
If thou wilt outstrip death, go cross the seas,
And live with Richmond, from the reach of hell.
Go hie thee, hie thee from this slaughterhouse,
Lest thou increase the number of the dead 44
And make me die the thrall of Margaret's curse,
Nor mother, wife, nor England's counted Queen.
Der. Full of wise care is this your counsel, madam:
Take all the swift advantage of the hours.
You shall have letters from me to my son
In your behalf, to meet you on the way: 50
Be not ta'en tardy by unwise delay.
Duch. O ill-dispersing wind of misery!
O my accursed womb, the bed of death!
A cockatrice hast thou hatched to the world,
Whose unavoided eye is murderous. 55
Der. Come, madam, come! I in all haste was sent.
Anne. And I with all unwillingness will go.
O would to God that the inclusive verge
Of golden metal that must round my brow
Were red-hot steel, to sear me to the brains! 60
Anointed let me be with deadly venom
And die, ere men can say, "God save the Queen!"
Queen. Go, go, poor soul! I envy not thy glory.
To feed my humor wish thyself no harm. 64
Anne. No? Why! when he that is my husband now
Came to me as I followed Henry's corse,
When scarce the blood was well washed from his hands
Which issued from my other angel husband
And that dear saint which then I weeping followed—
O, when, I say, I looked on Richard's face, 70
This was my wish: "Be thou," quoth I, "accursed
For making me, so young, so old a widow!
And when thou wedst, let sorrow haunt thy bed;
And be thy wife, if any be so mad,
More miserable by the death of thee 75
Than thou hast made me by my dear lord's death!"
Lo, ere I can repeat this curse again,
Within so small a time, my woman's heart
Grossly grew captive to his honey words
And proved the subject of mine own soul's curse,
Which hitherto hath held mine eyes from rest; 81
For never yet one hour in his bed
Did I enjoy the golden dew of sleep,
But with his timorous dreams was still awaked.
Besides, he hates me for my father Warwick, 85
And will, no doubt, shortly be rid of me.
Queen. Poor heart, adieu! I pity thy complaining.
Anne. No more than with my soul I mourn for yours.
Dor. Farewell, thou woeful welcomer of glory.
Anne. Adieu, poor soul, that takest thy leave of it.
Duch. [*To Dorset*] Go thou to Richmond, and good fortune guide thee! 91
[*To Anne*] Go thou to Richard, and good angels tend thee!
[*To Queen*] Go thou to sanctuary, and good thoughts possess thee!
I to my grave, where peace and rest lie with me!
Eighty odd years of sorrow have I seen, 95
And each hour's joy wracked with a week of teen.
Queen. Stay, yet look back with me unto the Tower.
Pity, you ancient stones, those tender babes
Whom envy hath immured within your walls,
Rough cradle for such little pretty ones! 100
Rude ragged nurse, old sullen playfellow
For tender princes, use my babies well!
So foolish sorrow bids your stones farewell.
Exeunt.

Scene II. [*London. The Palace.*]

Sound a sennet. Enter RICHARD, *in pomp*, BUCKINGHAM, CATESBY, RATCLIFFE, LOVEL, [*a* PAGE, *and others*].

Rich. Stand all apart. Cousin of Buckingham—
Buck. My gracious sovereign?

26. it: i.e., his office
33. lace: bodice lacing
46. counted: acknowledged
54. cockatrice: another fabulous creature possessing a deadly glance like that of the basilisk
58-59. inclusive . . . metal: encircling golden crown
72. old: i.e., long
79. Grossly: stupidly
81. hitherto: ever since
96. wracked: wrecked; **teen:** misery
99. envy: malice
Ent. sennet: a trumpet call signaling the arrival of royalty or nobility

Rich. Give me thy hand.

Sound. Here he ascendeth the throne.

Thus high, by thy advice
And thy assistance, is King Richard seated:
But shall we wear these glories for a day? 5
Or shall they last, and we rejoice in them?

Buck. Still live they, and forever let them last!

Rich. Ah, Buckingham, now do I play the touch,
To try if thou be current gold indeed:
Young Edward lives. Think now what I would speak.

Buck. Say on, my loving lord. 11

Rich. Why, Buckingham, I say I would be King.

Buck. Why, so you are, my thrice-renownèd liege.

Rich. Ha! Am I King? 'Tis so. But Edward lives.

Buck. True, noble prince.

Rich. O bitter consequence,
That Edward still should live true noble Prince!
Cousin, thou wast not wont to be so dull. 17
Shall I be plain? I wish the bastards dead,
And I would have it suddenly performed.
What sayst thou now? Speak suddenly, be brief.

Buck. Your Grace may do your pleasure. 21

Rich. Tut, tut, thou art all ice; thy kindness freezes.
Say, have I thy consent that they shall die?

Buck. Give me some little breath, some pause, dear lord,
Before I positively speak in this: 25
I will resolve you herein presently.

Exit Buck[ingham].

Cates. [*Aside to a bystander*] The King is angry. See, he gnaws his lip.

Rich. I will converse with iron-witted fools
And unrespective boys. None are for me
That look into me with considerate eyes. 30
High-reaching Buckingham grows circumspect.
Boy!

Page. My lord?

Rich. Knowst thou not any whom corrupting gold
Will tempt unto a close exploit of death? 35

Page. I know a discontented gentleman
Whose humble means match not his haughty spirit:
Gold were as good as twenty orators,
And will, no doubt, tempt him to anything. 39

Rich. What is his name?

Page. His name, my lord, is Tyrrel.

Rich. I partly know the man. Go call him hither.

Exit [Page].

The deep-revolving witty Buckingham
No more shall be the neighbor to my counsels.
Hath he so long held out with me untired,
And stops he now for breath? Well, be it so. 45

Enter STANLEY, [EARL OF DERBY].

How now, Lord Stanley? What's the news?

Der. Know, my loving lord,
The Marquess Dorset, as I hear, is fled
To Richmond in the parts where he abides.

[*Stands apart.*]

Rich. Come hither, Catesby. Rumor it abroad
That Anne my wife is very grievous sick: 51
I will take order for her keeping close.
Inquire me out some mean poor gentleman,
Whom I will marry straight to Clarence' daughter.
The boy is foolish, and I fear not him. 55
Look how thou dreamst! I say again, give out
That Anne my queen is sick and like to die.
About it! for it stands me much upon
To stop all hopes whose growth may damage me.

[*Exit Catesby.*]

I must be married to my brother's daughter, 60
Or else my kingdom stands on brittle glass:
Murder her brothers, and then marry her—
Uncertain way of gain! But I am in
So far in blood that sin will pluck on sin.
Tear-falling pity dwells not in this eye. 65

Enter [PAGE, *with*] TYRREL.

Is thy name Tyrrel?

Tyr. James Tyrrel, and your most obedient subject.

Rich. Art thou indeed?

Tyr. Prove me, my gracious lord.

Rich. Darest thou resolve to kill a friend of mine?

Tyr. Please you; 70
But I had rather kill two enemies.

Rich. Why then thou hast it! Two deep enemies,
Foes to my rest and my sweet sleep's disturbers,
Are they that I would have thee deal upon:
Tyrrel, I mean those bastards in the Tower. 75

Tyr. Let me have open means to come to them,
And soon I'll rid you from the fear of them.

Rich. Thou singst sweet music. Hark, come hither, Tyrrel.
Go, by this token. Rise, and lend thine ear. (*Whispers.*)
There is no more but so: say it is done, 80

8. touch: touchstone
26. resolve: satisfy
28. iron-witted: insensitive; dull
29. unrespective: thoughtless
30. considerate: thoughtful
35. close: secret
42. deep-revolving: profoundly thoughtful; **witty:** cunning
52. for . . . close: that she be kept close
58. stands . . . upon: is extremely important for me
64. pluck on: incite
68. Prove: test
70. Please you: as you please
80. There . . . so: that's all there is to it.

And I will love thee and prefer thee for it.
Tyr. I will dispatch it straight. *Exit.*

[*Re-*]*enter* BUCKINGHAM.

Buck. My lord, I have considered in my mind
The late request that you did sound me in.
Rich. Well, let that rest. Dorset is fled to Richmond. 85
Buck. I hear the news, my lord.
Rich. Stanley, he is your wife's son. Well, look unto it.
Buck. My lord, I claim the gift, my due by promise,
For which your honor and your faith is pawned:
The earldom of Hereford and the movables 90
Which you have promised I shall possess.
Rich. Stanley, look to your wife: if she convey
Letters to Richmond, you shall answer it.
Buck. What says your Highness to my just request?
Rich. I do remember me Henry the Sixth 95
Did prophesy that Richmond should be King
When Richmond was a little peevish boy.
A king!—perhaps—perhaps—
Buck. My lord—
Rich. How chance the prophet could not at that time 100
Have told me, I being by, that I should kill him?
Buck. My lord, your promise for the earldom!
Rich. Richmond! When last I was at Exeter,
The Mayor in courtesy showed me the castle, 104
And called it Rouge-mount; at which name I started,
Because a bard of Ireland told me once
I should not live long after I saw Richmond.
Buck. My lord—
Rich. Ay, what's o'clock? 109
Buck. I am thus bold to put your Grace in mind
Of what you promised me.
Rich. Well, but what's o'clock?
Buck. Upon the stroke of ten.
Rich. Well, let it strike.
Buck. Why let it strike?
Rich. Because that, like a Jack, thou keepst the stroke
Betwixt thy begging and my meditation. 115
I am not in the giving vein today.
Buck. May it please you to resolve me in my suit.
Rich. Thou troublest me; I am not in the vein.
Exeunt [*all but Buckingham*].
Buck. And is it thus? Repays he my deep service
With such contempt? Made I him King for this?
O let me think on Hastings, and be gone 121
To Brecknock while my fearful head is on!
Exit.

81. **prefer:** advance
87. **he:** i.e., Richmond
114. **Jack:** (1) mechanical man who pantomimed the action of the clock's striking; (2) low, presumptuous fellow
122. **Brecknock:** Brecon, in South Wales

Scene [III. *London. The Palace.*]

Enter TYRREL.

Tyr. The tyrannous and bloody act is done,
The most arch deed of piteous massacre
That ever yet this land was guilty of.
Dighton and Forrest, who I did suborn
To do this piece of ruthless butchery, 5
Albeit they were fleshed villains, bloody dogs,
Melted with tenderness and mild compassion,
Wept like to children in their deaths' sad story.
"O, thus," quoth Dighton, "lay the gentle babes."
"Thus, thus," quoth Forrest, "girdling one another
Within their alablaster innocent arms. 11
Their lips were four red roses on a stalk,
And in their summer beauty kissed each other.
A book of prayers on their pillow lay,
Which once," quoth Forrest, "almost changed my mind; 15
But O! the devil"—there the villain stopped;
When Dighton thus told on—"We smothered
The most replenished sweet work of nature
That from the prime creation e'er she framed."
Hence both are gone with conscience and remorse:
They could not speak; and so I left them both, 21
To bear this tidings to the bloody King.

Enter [KING] RICHARD.

And here he comes. All health, my sovereign lord!
Rich. Kind Tyrrel, am I happy in thy news? 24
Tyr. If to have done the thing you gave in charge
Beget your happiness, be happy then,
For it is done.
Rich. But didst thou see them dead?
Tyr. I did, my lord.
Rich. And buried, gentle Tyrrel?
Tyr. The chaplain of the Tower hath buried them;
But where, to say the truth, I do not know. 30
Rich. Come to me, Tyrrel, soon at after-supper,
When thou shalt tell the process of their death.

1. **tyrannous:** violent
2. **most arch:** greatest
4. **suborn:** bribe
6. **fleshed:** experienced. Dogs and hawks were trained by giving them a taste of the blood or flesh of the quarry.
8. **in . . . story:** in telling the sad story of their deaths
11. **alablaster:** alabaster
18. **replenished:** bountifully supplied
19. **prime:** first
31. **after-supper:** reresupper, a light meal that followed the main supper
32. **process:** story

Meantime, but think how I may do thee good,
And be inheritor of thy desire. 34
Farewell till then.

Tyr. I humbly take my leave. [*Exit.*]

Rich. The son of Clarence have I pent up close,
His daughter meanly have I matched in marriage,
The sons of Edward sleep in Abraham's bosom,
And Anne my wife hath bid this world good night.
Now, for I know the Britain Richmond aims 40
At young Elizabeth, my brother's daughter,
And by that knot looks proudly on the crown,
To her go I, a jolly thriving wooer.

Enter RATCLIFFE.

Rat. My lord—

Rich. Good or bad news, that thou comest in so bluntly? 45

Rat. Bad news, my lord. Morton is fled to Richmond,
And Buckingham, backed with the hardy Welshmen,
Is in the field, and still his power increaseth.

Rich. Ely with Richmond troubles me more near
Than Buckingham and his rash-levied strength. 50
Come! I have learned that fearful commenting
Is leaden servitor to dull delay;
Delay leads impotent and snail-paced beggary.
Then fiery expedition be my wing,
Jove's Mercury, and herald for a king! 55
Go, muster men. My counsel is my shield;
We must be brief when traitors brave the field.
Exeunt.

Scene [IV. *London. Before the Palace.*]

Enter OLD QUEEN MARGARET.

Queen M. So now prosperity begins to mellow
And drop into the rotten mouth of death.
Here in these confines slily have I lurked
To watch the waning of mine enemies.
A dire induction am I witness to, 5
And will to France, hoping the consequence
Will prove as bitter, black, and tragical.
Withdraw thee, wretched Margaret! Who comes here? [*Retires.*]

Enter DUCHESS [OF YORK] *and* QUEEN [ELIZABETH].

Queen. Ah, my poor princes! ah, my tender babes!
My unblown flowers, new-appearing sweets! 10
If yet your gentle souls fly in the air
And be not fixed in doom perpetual,
Hover about me with your airy wings
And hear your mother's lamentation!

Queen M. [*Aside*] Hover about her. Say that right for right 15
Hath dimmed your infant morn to aged night.

Duch. So many miseries have crazed my voice
That my woe-wearied tongue is still and mute.
Edward Plantagenet, why art thou dead?

Queen M. [*Aside*] Plantagenet doth quit Plantagenet; 20
Edward for Edward pays a dying debt.

Queen. Wilt thou, O God, fly from such gentle lambs
And throw them in the entrails of the wolf?
When didst thou sleep when such a deed was done?

Queen M. [*Aside*] When holy Harry died, and my sweet son. 25

Duch. Dead life, blind sight, poor mortal-living ghost,
Woe's scene, world's shame, grave's due by life usurped,
Brief abstract and record of tedious days,
Rest thy unrest on England's lawful earth,
[*Sitting down.*]
Unlawfully made drunk with innocent blood! 30

Queen. Ah that thou wouldst as soon afford a grave
As thou canst yield a melancholy seat!
Then would I hide my bones, not rest them here.
Ah, who hath any cause to mourn but we?
[*Sitting down by her.*]

Queen M. [*Comes forward.*] If ancient sorrow be most reverent, 35
Give mine the benefit of seniory
And let my griefs frown on the upper hand.
If sorrow can admit society,
[*Sitting down with them.*]
Tell o'er your woes again by viewing mine.
I had an Edward, till a Richard killed him; 40

40. for: because: **Britain:** Breton. Richmond had been living in Brittany since he fled England after the Battle of Tewkesbury.
42. by . . . crown: aspires to the crown by means of that alliance
46. Morton: the Bishop of Ely, who had been in Buckingham's custody since his implication in Hastings' conspiracy
54. expedition: speed
56. My . . . shield: i.e., we must to arms without conferring on strategy.
6. consequence: conclusion
17. crazed: cracked
20. quit: pay for
21. dying debt: the debt of death
26. mortal-living: dead-alive
27. grave's . . . usurped: a being, ready for death, whom life unlawfully retains
35. reverent: entitled to respect
36. seniory: seniority
37. frown . . . hand: loom more largely; be acknowledged the greater

I had a Harry, till a Richard killed him:
Thou hadst an Edward, till a Richard killed him;
Thou hadst a Richard, till a Richard killed him.
Duch. I had a Richard too, and thou didst kill him;
I had a Rutland too, thou holpst to kill him. 45
Queen M. Thou hadst a Clarence too, and Richard killed him.
From forth the kennel of thy womb hath crept
A hellhound that doth hunt us all to death:
That dog, that had his teeth before his eyes,
To worry lambs and lap their gentle blood, 50
That foul defacer of God's handiwork,
That reigns in galled eyes of weeping souls,
That excellent grand tyrant of the earth,
Thy womb let loose to chase us to our graves.
O upright, just, and true-disposing God, 55
How do I thank thee that this carnal cur
Preys on the issue of his mother's body
And makes her pew-fellow with others' moan!
Duch. O Harry's wife, triumph not in my woes!
God witness with me, I have wept for thine. 60
Queen M. Bear with me! I am hungry for revenge,
And now I cloy me with beholding it.
Thy Edward he is dead, that killed my Edward;
Thy other Edward dead, to quit my Edward;
Young York he is but boot, because both they 65
Matched not the high perfection of my loss.
Thy Clarence he is dead that stabbed my Edward,
And the beholders of this frantic play,
The adulterate Hastings, Rivers, Vaughan, Grey,
Untimely smothered in their dusky graves. 70
Richard yet lives, hell's black intelligencer;
Only reserved their factor to buy souls
And send them thither. But at hand, at hand,
Ensues his piteous and unpitied end.
Earth gapes, hell burns, fiends roar, saints pray, 75
To have him suddenly conveyed from hence.
Cancel his bond of life, dear God, I pray,
That I may live and say, "The dog is dead."
Queen. O, thou didst prophesy the time would come
That I should wish for thee to help me curse 80
That bottled spider, that foul bunch-backed toad!
Queen M. I called thee then vain flourish of my fortune;
I called thee then poor shadow, painted queen;
The presentation of but what I was,
The flattering index of a direful pageant; 85
One heaved a-high to be hurled down below;
A mother only mocked with two fair babes;
A dream of what thou wast, a garish flag,
To be the aim of every dangerous shot;
A sign of dignity, a breath, a bubble; 90
A queen in jest, only to fill the scene.
Where is thy husband now? Where be thy brothers?
Where be thy two sons? Wherein dost thou joy?
Who sues and kneels and says, "God save the Queen"?
Where be the bending peers that flattered thee? 95
Where be the thronging troops that followed thee?
Decline all this, and see what now thou art:
For happy wife, a most distressed widow;
For joyful mother, one that wails the name;
For one being sued to, one that humbly sues; 100
For Queen, a very caitiff crowned with care;
For she that scorned at me, now scorned of me;
For she being feared of all, now fearing one;
For she commanding all, obeyed of none.
Thus hath the course of justice whirled about 105
And left thee but a very prey to time,
Having no more but thought of what thou wast,
To torture thee the more, being what thou art.
Thou didst usurp my place, and dost thou not
Usurp the just proportion of my sorrow? 110
Now thy proud neck bears half my burdened yoke,
From which even here I slip my weary head
And leave the burden of it all on thee.
Farewell, York's wife, and queen of sad mischance!
These English woes shall make me smile in France.
Queen. O thou well skilled in curses, stay awhile,
And teach me how to curse mine enemies! 117
Queen M. Forbear to sleep the nights, and fast the days;
Compare dead happiness with living woe;
Think that thy babes were sweeter than they were,
And he that slew them fouler than he is: 121
Bett'ring thy loss makes the bad causer worse;
Revolving this will teach thee how to curse.
Queen. My words are dull. O quicken them with thine! 124
Queen M. Thy woes will make them sharp and pierce like mine. *Exit* [*Queen*] *Margaret.*
Duch. Why should calamity be full of words?
Queen. Windy attorneys to their client's woes,
Airy succeeders of intestate joys.
Poor breathing orators of miseries, 129

44. Richard: her husband, the Duke of York
52. reigns . . . eyes: is supreme in causing tears of grief
53. excellent grand: surpassingly great
56. carnal: carnivorous
62. cloy me: glut myself
65. boot: an extra
68. frantic play: violent act
69. adulterate: adulterous
71. intelligencer: agent
72. Only . . . factor: retained only as their agent
85. index: prologue
88. garish flag: colored banner (symbol)
97. Decline: review in order
101. caitiff: wretch
110. proportion: degree
123. Revolving: contemplating
124. quicken: sharpen
128. succeeders . . . joys: heirs of joys that leave no trace behind

Let them have scope! Though what they will impart
Help nothing else, yet do they ease the heart.
Duch. If so, then be not tongue-tied: go with me,
And in the breath of bitter words let's smother
My damned son that thy two sweet sons smothered.
The trumpet sounds. Be copious in exclaims. 135

Enter KING RICHARD *and his* TRAIN, *marching, with Drums and Trumpets.*

Rich. Who intercepts me in my expedition?
Duch. O, she that might have intercepted thee,
By strangling thee in her accursed womb,
From all the slaughters, wretch, that thou hast done!
Queen. Hidest thou that forehead with a golden crown 140
Where't should be branded, if that right were right,
The slaughter of the prince that owed that crown
And the dire death of my poor sons and brothers?
Tell me, thou villain-slave, where are my children?
Duch. Thou toad, thou toad, where is thy brother Clarence? 145
And little Ned Plantagenet, his son?
Queen. Where is the gentle Rivers, Vaughan, Grey?
Duch. Where is kind Hastings?
Rich. A flourish, trumpets! Strike alarum, drums!
Let not the heavens hear these telltale women 150
Rail on the Lord's anointed. Strike, I say!
Flourish. Alarums.
Either be patient and entreat me fair,
Or with the clamorous report of war
Thus will I drown your exclamations.
Duch. Art thou my son? 155
Rich. Ay, I thank God, my father, and yourself.
Duch. Then patiently hear my impatience.
Rich. Madam, I have a touch of your condition,
That cannot brook the accent of reproof. 159
Duch. O let me speak!
Rich. Do then, but I'll not hear.
Duch. I will be mild and gentle in my words.
Rich. And brief, good mother, for I am in haste.
Duch. Art thou so hasty? I have stayed for thee,
God knows, in torment and in agony. 164
Rich. And came I not at last to comfort you?
Duch. No, by the Holy Rood, thou knowst it well,
Thou camest on earth to make the earth my hell.
A grievous burden was thy birth to me;
Tetchy and wayward was thy infancy;
Thy schooldays frightful, desp'rate, wild, and furious; 170
Thy prime of manhood daring, bold, and venturous;
Thy age confirmed, proud, subtle, sly, and bloody,
More mild, but yet more harmful—kind in hatred.
What comfortable hour canst thou name
That ever graced me with thy company? 175
Rich. Faith, none, but Humphrey Hour, that called your Grace
To breakfast once, forth of my company.
If I be so disgracious in your eye,
Let me march on and not offend you, madam.
Strike up the drum.
Duch. I prithee hear me speak. 180
Rich. You speak too bitterly.
Duch. Hear me a word;
For I shall never speak to thee again.
Rich. So.
Duch. Either thou wilt die, by God's just ordinance,
Ere from this war thou turn a conqueror, 185
Or I with grief and extreme age shall perish
And never more behold thy face again.
Therefore take with thee my most grievous curse,
Which in the day of battle tire thee more
Than all the complete armor that thou wearst!
My prayers on the adverse party fight, 191
And there the little souls of Edward's children
Whisper the spirits of thine enemies
And promise them success and victory!
Bloody thou art, bloody will be thy end; 195
Shame serves thy life and doth thy death attend!
Exit.
Queen. Though far more cause, yet much less spirit to curse
Abides in me. I say amen to her. 198
Rich. Stay, madam; I must talk a word with you.
Queen. I have no more sons of the royal blood
For thee to slaughter. For my daughters, Richard,
They shall be praying nuns, not weeping queens;
And therefore level not to hit their lives.
Rich. You have a daughter called Elizabeth,
Virtuous and fair, royal and gracious. 205
Queen. And must she die for this? O let her live,
And I'll corrupt her manners, stain her beauty,
Slander myself as false to Edward's bed,
Throw over her the veil of infamy:
So she may live unscarred of bleeding slaughter,
I will confess she was not Edward's daughter. 211
Rich. Wrong not her birth; she is a royal princess.
Queen. To save her life, I'll say she is not so.

142. owed: possessed
151. Rail on: exclaim against
158. condition: temperament
159. accent: language
163. stayed: waited
169. Tetchy: irritable
170. frightful: full of frights
172. age confirmed: maturity
173. kind . . . hatred: masking hatred with a semblance of kindness
176. Humphrey Hour: indigent gallants, when pressed to go to dinner, pleaded an engagement near a monument in St. Paul's Cathedral known as Duke Humphrey's. Hence to "dine with Duke Humphrey" meant to go without dinner. **Humphrey Hour** might then mean a time when she went without breakfast. The point of Richard's taunt is obscure but may refer to his mother's alleged infidelity.
203. level: aim

Rich. Her life is safest only in her birth. 214
Queen. And only in that safety died her brothers.
Rich. Lo, at their birth good stars were opposite.
Queen. No, to their lives ill friends were contrary.
Rich. All unavoided is the doom of destiny.
Queen. True, when avoided grace makes destiny:
My babes were destined to a fairer death, 220
If grace had blessed thee with a fairer life.
Rich. You speak as if that I had slain my cousins!
Queen. Cousins indeed, and by their uncle cozened
Of comfort, kingdom, kindred, freedom, life.
Whose hand soever lanched their tender hearts,
Thy head, all indirectly, gave direction. 226
No doubt the murd'rous knife was dull and blunt,
Till it was whetted on thy stone-hard heart
To revel in the entrails of my lambs. 229
But that still use of grief makes wild grief tame,
My tongue should to thy ears not name my boys
Till that my nails were anchored in thine eyes;
And I, in such a desp'rate bay of death,
Like a poor bark, of sails and tackling reft,
Rush all to pieces on thy rocky bosom. 235
Rich. Madam, so thrive I in my enterprise,
And dangerous success of bloody wars,
As I intend more good to you and yours
Than ever you or yours by me were harmed!
Queen. What good is covered with the face of heaven, 240
To be discovered, that can do me good?
Rich. The advancement of your children, gentle lady.
Queen. Up to some scaffold, there to lose their heads!
Rich. Unto the dignity and height of fortune,
The high imperial type of this earth's glory. 245
Queen. Flatter my sorrow with report of it:
Tell me, what state, what dignity, what honor
Canst thou demise to any child of mine?
Rich. Even all I have—ay, and myself and all—
Will I withal endow a child of thine, 250
So in the Lethe of thy angry soul
Thou drown the sad remembrance of those wrongs
Which thou supposest I have done to thee.
Queen. Be brief, lest that the process of thy kindness
Last longer telling than thy kindness' date. 255

215. only . . . safety: i.e., only because of their royal birth
216. opposite: hostile
218. All unavoided: completely unavoidable
219. avoided grace: wickedness
223. cozened: cheated
225. lanched: pierced
226. indirectly: underhandedly
230. But . . . grief: were it not that continual grief
234. reft: bereft
237. success: result
245. imperial type: symbol of sovereignty
248. demise: transmit
251. So: provided that; **Lethe:** the river of Hades that contained the waters of oblivion

Rich. Then know that from my soul I love thy daughter.
Queen. My daughter's mother thinks it with her soul.
Rich. What do you think?
Queen. That thou dost love my daughter from thy soul. 259
So from thy soul's love didst thou love her brothers,
And from my heart's love I do thank thee for it.
Rich. Be not so hasty to confound my meaning:
I mean that with my soul I love thy daughter
And do intend to make her Queen of England.
Queen. Well then, who dost thou mean shall be her king? 265
Rich. Even he that makes her Queen. Who else should be?
Queen. What, thou?
Rich. Even so. How think you of it?
Queen. How canst thou woo her?
Rich. That would I learn of you,
As one being best acquainted with her humor. 269
Queen. And wilt thou learn of me?
Rich. Madam, with all my heart.
Queen. Send to her by the man that slew her brothers
A pair of bleeding hearts; thereon engrave
"Edward" and "York"; then haply will she weep:
Therefore present to her—as sometime Margaret
Did to thy father, steeped in Rutland's blood—
A handkerchief, which say to her did drain 276
The purple sap from her sweet brother's body,
And bid her wipe her weeping eyes withal.
If this inducement move her not to love,
Send her a letter of thy noble deeds: 280
Tell her thou madest away her uncle Clarence,
Her uncle Rivers; ay, and for her sake,
Madest quick conveyance with her good aunt Anne.
Rich. You mock me, madam; this is not the way
To win your daughter.
Queen. There is no other way, 285
Unless thou couldst put on some other shape,
And not be Richard that hath done all this.
Rich. Say that I did all this for love of her.
Queen. Nay, then indeed she cannot choose but hate thee,
Having bought love with such a bloody spoil. 290
Rich. Look, what is done cannot be now amended:
Men shall deal unadvisedly sometimes,
Which afterhours gives leisure to repent.
If I did take the kingdom from your sons,
To make amends I'll give it to your daughter; 295

259. from . . . soul: i.e., insincerely
269. humor: disposition
274. sometime: once
283. Madest . . . with: quickly did away with
291. Look what: whatever
292. shall: will inevitably

If I have killed the issue of your womb,
To quicken your increase I will beget
Mine issue of your blood upon your daughter.
A grandam's name is little less in love
Than is the doting title of a mother; 300
They are as children but one step below,
Even of your metal, of your very blood,
Of all one pain, save for a night of groans
Endured of her for whom you bid like sorrow:
Your children were vexation to your youth, 305
But mine shall be a comfort to your age.
The loss you have is but a son being King,
And by that loss your daughter is made Queen.
I cannot make you what amends I would;
Therefore accept such kindness as I can. 310
Dorset your son, that with a fearful soul
Leads discontented steps in foreign soil,
This fair alliance quickly shall call home
To high promotions and great dignity.
The King, that calls your beauteous daughter wife,
Familiarly shall call thy Dorset brother: 316
Again shall you be mother to a king,
And all the ruins of distressful times
Repaired with double riches of content.
What! we have many goodly days to see: 320
The liquid drops of tears that you have shed
Shall come again, transformed to orient pearl,
Advantaging their love with interest
Of ten times double gain of happiness.
Go then, my mother; to thy daughter go; 325
Make bold her bashful years with your experience;
Prepare her ears to hear a wooer's tale;
Put in her tender heart the aspiring flame
Of golden sovereignty; acquaint the princess
With the sweet silent hours of marriage joys; 330
And when this arm of mine hath chastised
The petty rebel, dull-brained Buckingham,
Bound with triumphant garlands will I come
And lead thy daughter to a conqueror's bed;
To whom I will retail my conquest won, 335
And she shall be sole victress, Cæsar's Cæsar.

Queen. What were I best to say? Her father's brother
Would be her lord? Or shall I say her uncle?
Or he that slew her brothers and her uncles?
Under what title shall I woo for thee 340
That God, the law, my honor, and her love
Can make seem pleasing to her tender years?

Rich. Infer fair England's peace by this alliance.

Queen. Which she shall purchase with still-lasting war.

Rich. Tell her the King, that may command, entreats. 345

Queen. That at her hands which the King's King forbids.

Rich. Say she shall be a high and mighty queen.

Queen. To wail the title, as her mother doth.

Rich. Say I will love her everlastingly. 349

Queen. But how long shall that title "ever" last?

Rich. Sweetly in force unto her fair life's end.

Queen. But how long fairly shall her sweet life last?

Rich. As long as heaven and nature lengthens it.

Queen. As long as hell and Richard likes of it.

Rich. Say I, her sovereign, am her subject low.

Queen. But she, your subject, loathes such sovereignty. 356

Rich. Be eloquent in my behalf to her.

Queen. An honest tale speeds best being plainly told. 358

Rich. Then plainly to her tell my loving tale.

Queen. Plain and not honest is too harsh a style.

Rich. Your reasons are too shallow and too quick.

Queen. O, no, my reasons are too deep and dead—
Too deep and dead, poor infants, in their graves.

Rich. Harp not on that string, madam; that is past.

Queen. Harp on it still shall I till heartstrings break. 365

Rich. Now, by my George, my garter, and my crown—

Queen. Profaned, dishonored, and the third usurped.

Rich. I swear—

Queen. By nothing, for this is no oath:
Thy George, profaned, hath lost his lordly honor;
Thy garter, blemished, pawned his knightly virtue;
Thy crown, usurped, disgraced his kingly glory. 371
If something thou wouldst swear to be believed,
Swear then by something that thou hast not wronged.

Rich. Then by myself—

Queen. Thyself is self-misused.

Rich. Now by the world—

Queen. 'Tis full of thy foul wrongs. 375

Rich. My father's death—

Queen. Thy life hath it dishonored.

Rich. Why then, by God—

Queen. God's wrong is most of all:
If thou didst fear to break an oath with him,
The unity the King my husband made
Thou hadst not broken, nor my brothers died. 380
If thou hadst feared to break an oath by him,
The imperial metal, circling now thy head,

297. quicken . . . increase: revitalize your offspring
302. metal: substance
304. bid: endured (past tense of "abide")
322. orient: lustrous
343. Infer: suggest
356. sovereignty: i.e., a ruler
366. George: the likeness of St. George; part of the insignia of the Order of the Garter

Had graced the tender temples of my child,
And both the princes had been breathing here,
Which now, two tender bedfellows for dust, 385
Thy broken faith hath made the prey for worms.
What canst thou swear by now?
Rich. The time to come.
Queen. That thou hast wronged in the time o'erpast;
For I myself have many tears to wash
Hereafter time, for time past wronged by thee.
The children live whose fathers thou hast slaughtered, 391
Ungoverned youth, to wail it in their age;
The parents live whose children thou hast butchered,
Old barren plants, to wail it with their age.
Swear not by time to come, for that thou hast 395
Misused ere used, by times ill-used o'erpast.
Rich. As I intend to prosper and repent,
So thrive I in my dangerous affairs
Of hostile arms! Myself myself confound!
Heaven and fortune bar me happy hours! 400
Day, yield me not thy light, nor, night, thy rest!
Be opposite all planets of good luck
To my proceeding if, with dear heart's love,
Immaculate devotion, holy thoughts,
I tender not thy beauteous princely daughter! 405
In her consists my happiness and thine;
Without her, follows to myself and thee,
Herself, the land, and many a Christian soul,
Death, desolation, ruin, and decay.
It cannot be avoided but by this; 410
It will not be avoided but by this.
Therefore, dear mother—I must call you so—
Be the attorney of my love to her:
Plead what I will be, not what I have been;
Not my deserts, but what I will deserve; 415
Urge the necessity and state of times,
And be not peevish-fond in great designs.
Queen. Shall I be tempted of the devil thus?
Rich. Ay, if the devil tempt you to do good.
Queen. Shall I forget myself to be myself? 420
Rich. Ay, if yourself's remembrance wrong yourself.
Queen. Yet thou didst kill my children.
Rich. But in your daughter's womb I bury them,
Where, in that nest of spicery, they will breed
Selves of themselves, to your recomforture. 425
Queen. Shall I go win my daughter to thy will?
Rich. And be a happy mother by the deed.
Queen. I go. Write to me very shortly,
And you shall understand from me her mind. 429
Rich. Bear her my true love's kiss; and so farewell— *Exit Q[ueen Elizabeth].*
Relenting fool, and shallow, changing woman!

Enter RATCLIFFE, [CATESBY *following*].

How now? What news?
Rat. Most mighty sovereign, on the western coast
Rideth a puissant navy; to our shores
Throng many doubtful hollow-hearted friends, 435
Unarmed, and unresolved to beat them back.
'Tis thought that Richmond is their admiral;
And there they hull, expecting but the aid
Of Buckingham to welcome them ashore.
Rich. Some light-foot friend post to the Duke of Norfolk: 440
Ratcliffe, thyself—or Catesby—where is he?
Cates. Here, my good lord.
Rich. Catesby, fly to the Duke.
Cates. I will, my lord, with all convenient haste.
Rich. Ratcliffe, come hither. Post to Salisbury.
When thou comest thither—[*To Catesby*] Dull unmindful villain, 445
Why stayst thou here and goest not to the Duke?
Cates. First, mighty liege, tell me your Highness' pleasure,
What from your Grace I shall deliver to him.
Rich. O, true, good Catesby: bid him levy straight
The greatest strength and power that he can make
And meet me suddenly at Salisbury. 451
Cates. I go. *Exit.*
Rat. What, may it please you, shall I do at Salisbury?
Rich. Why, what wouldst thou do there before I go? 454
Rat. Your Highness told me I should post before.
Rich. My mind is changed.

Enter LORD STANLEY, [EARL OF DERBY].

Stanley, what news with you?
Der. None good, my liege, to please you with the hearing,
Nor none so bad but well may be reported.
Rich. Hoyday, a riddle! Neither good nor bad!
What needst thou run so many miles about, 460
When thou mayest tell thy tale the nearest way?
Once more, what news?
Der. Richmond is on the seas.
Rich. There let him sink, and be the seas on him!
White-livered runagate, what doth he there? 464
Der. I know not, mighty sovereign, but by guess.
Rich. Well, as you guess?

399. confound: destroy
405. tender: cherish
417. peevish-fond: foolishly perverse
420. forget . . . myself: forget to act like myself
425. recomforture: comfort
434. puissant: powerful
435. doubtful . . . friends: friends of dubious loyalty
464. runagate: vagabond

Der. Stirred up by Dorset, Buckingham, and Morton,
He makes for England, here to claim the crown.
Rich. Is the chair empty? is the sword unswayed?
Is the King dead? the empire unpossessed? 470
What heir of York is there alive but we?
And who is England's King but great York's heir?
Then tell me, what makes he upon the seas?
Der. Unless for that, my liege, I cannot guess.
Rich. Unless for that he comes to be your liege,
You cannot guess wherefore the Welshman comes.
Thou wilt revolt and fly to him, I fear. 477
Der. No, my good lord; therefore mistrust me not.
Rich. Where is thy power then to beat him back?
Where be thy tenants and thy followers? 480
Are they not now upon the western shore,
Safe-conducting the rebels from their ships?
Der. No, my good lord, my friends are in the North.
Rich. Cold friends to me! What do they in the North 484
When they should serve their sovereign in the West?
Der. They have not been commanded, mighty King:
Pleaseth your Majesty to give me leave,
I'll muster up my friends and meet your Grace
Where and what time your Majesty shall please.
Rich. Ay, thou wouldst be gone to join with Richmond: 490
But I'll not trust thee.
Der. Most mighty sovereign,
You have no cause to hold my friendship doubtful.
I never was nor never will be false.
Rich. Go then and muster men. But leave behind
Your son, George Stanley. Look your heart be firm,
Or else his head's assurance is but frail. 496
Der. So deal with him as I prove true to you. *Exit.*

Enter a MESSENGER.

1. *Mess.* My gracious sovereign, now in Devonshire,
As I by friends am well advertised,
Sir Edward Courtney and the haughty prelate, 500
Bishop of Exeter, his elder brother,
With many mo confederates, are in arms.

Enter ANOTHER MESSENGER.

2. *Mess.* In Kent, my liege, the Guildfords are in arms,
And every hour more competitors 504
Flock to the rebels, and their power grows strong.

Enter ANOTHER MESSENGER.

3. *Mess.* My lord, the army of great Buckingham—
Rich. Out on ye, owls! Nothing but songs of death? *He striketh him.*
There, take thou that, till thou bring better news.
3. *Mess.* The news I have to tell your Majesty
Is, that by sudden floods and fall of waters, 510
Buckingham's army is dispersed and scattered,
And he himself wand'red away alone,
No man knows whither.
Rich. I cry thee mercy:
There is my purse to cure that blow of thine.
Hath any well-advised friend proclaimed 515
Reward to him that brings the traitor in?
3. *Mess.* Such proclamation hath been made, my lord.

Enter ANOTHER MESSENGER.

4. *Mess.* Sir Thomas Lovel and Lord Marquess Dorset,
'Tis said, my liege, in Yorkshire are in arms.
But this good comfort bring I to your Highness:
The Britain navy is dispersed by tempest; 521
Richmond in Dorsetshire sent out a boat
Unto the shore, to ask those on the banks
If they were his assistants, yea or no;
Who answered him they came from Buckingham
Upon his party. He, mistrusting them, 526
Hoised sail, and made his course again for Britain.
Rich. March on, march on, since we are up in arms;
If not to fight with foreign enemies,
Yet to beat down these rebels here at home. 530

Enter CATESBY.

Cates. My liege, the Duke of Buckingham is taken.
That is the best news. That the Earl of Richmond
Is with a mighty power landed at Milford
Is colder tidings, but yet they must be told.
Rich. Away towards Salisbury! While we reason here, 535
A royal battle might be won and lost.
Someone take order Buckingham be brought
To Salisbury; the rest march on with me.
Flourish. Exeunt.

469. unswayed: unwielded
496. assurance: safety
499. advertised: informed
502. mo: more
504. competitors: associates
515. well-advised: thoughtful
526. Upon . . . party: for his cause
527. Hoised: hoisted; **Britain:** Brittany

Scene [V. *The Earl of Derby's house.*]

Enter [LORD STANLEY, EARL OF] DERBY, *and* SIR CHRISTOPHER [URSWICK].

Der. Sir Christopher, tell Richmond this from me:
That in the sty of the most deadly boar
My son George Stanley is franked up in hold;
If I revolt, off goes young George's head;
The fear of that holds off my present aid. 5
So get thee gone; commend me to thy lord.
Withal say that the Queen hath heartily consented
He should espouse Elizabeth her daughter.
But tell me, where is princely Richmond now? 9

Chris. At Pembroke, or at Ha'rford-West in Wales.
Der. What men of name resort to him?
Chris. Sir Walter Herbert, a renowned soldier,
Sir Gilbert Talbot, Sir William Stanley,
Oxford, redoubted Pembroke, Sir James Blunt,
And Rice ap Thomas, with a valiant crew, 15
And many other of great name and worth;
And towards London do they bend their power,
If by the way they be not fought withal.
Der. Well, hie thee to thy lord. I kiss his hand:
My letter will resolve him of my mind. 20
[*Gives letter.*]
Farewell.
Exeunt.

1. Sir Christopher: a priest, not a knight
6. commend me: give my respectful greetings

10. Pembroke: the seat of Richmond's uncle, Jasper Tudor; **Ha'rford-West:** Haverford West
14. redoubted: formidable; **Pembroke:** Jasper Tudor

ACT V

Scene I. [*Salisbury.*]

Enter BUCKINGHAM *with* [*the* SHERIFF *and*] HALBERDS, *led to execution.*

Buck. Will not King Richard let me speak with him?
Sher. No, my good lord; therefore be patient.
Buck. Hastings, and Edward's children, Grey and Rivers,
Holy King Henry and thy fair son Edward,
Vaughan, and all that have miscarried 5
By underhand corrupted foul injustice,
If that your moody discontented souls
Do through the clouds behold this present hour,
Even for revenge mock my destruction!
This is All Souls' Day, fellow, is it not? 10
Sher. It is.
Buck. Why, then All Souls' Day is my body's doomsday.
This is the day which, in King Edward's time,
I wished might fall on me when I was found
False to his children and his wife's allies; 15
This is the day wherein I wished to fall
By the false faith of him whom most I trusted;
This, this All Souls' Day to my fearful soul
Is the determined respite of my wrongs:
That high All-Seer which I dallied with 20
Hath turned my feigned prayer on my head
And given in earnest what I begged in jest.
Thus doth He force the swords of wicked men
To turn their own points in their masters' bosoms;
Thus Margaret's curse falls heavy on my neck: 25
"When he," quoth she, "shall split thy heart with sorrow,
Remember Margaret was a prophetess."
Come lead me, officers, to the block of shame.
Wrong hath but wrong, and blame the due of blame.
Exeunt Buckingham with Officers.

5. miscarried: died

19. determined . . . wrongs: predetermined limit of my wrongdoing
21. feigned: insincere

Scene II. [*Tamworth. The camp of Richmond.*]

Enter RICHMOND, OXFORD, [SIR JAMES] BLUNT, [SIR WALTER] HERBERT, *and others, with Drum and Colors.*

Richm. Fellows in arms, and my most loving friends,

Bruised underneath the yoke of tyranny,
Thus far into the bowels of the land
Have we marched on without impediment;
And here receive we from our father Stanley 5
Lines of fair comfort and encouragement.
The wretched, bloody, and usurping boar,
That spoiled your summer fields and fruitful vines,
Swills your warm blood like wash, and makes his trough
In your embowelled bosoms—this foul swine 10
Is now even in the center of this isle,
Near to the town of Leicester, as we learn:
From Tamworth thither is but one day's march.
In God's name cheerly on, courageous friends,
To reap the harvest of perpetual peace 15
By this one bloody trial of sharp war.
Ox. Every man's conscience is a thousand men,
To fight against this guilty homicide.
Her. I doubt not but his friends will turn to us.
Blunt. He hath no friends but what are friends for fear, 20
Which in his dearest need will fly from him.
Richm. All for our vantage. Then in God's name march!
True hope is swift and flies with swallow's wings;
Kings it makes gods, and meaner creatures kings.
Exeunt omnes.

[Scene III. *Bosworth Field.*]

Enter KING RICHARD *in arms, with* NORFOLK, RATCLIFFE, *and the* EARL OF SURREY, [*and* SOLDIERS].

Rich. Here pitch our tent, even here in Bosworth field.
My Lord of Surrey, why look you so sad?
Sur. My heart is ten times lighter than my looks.
Rich. My Lord of Norfolk—
Nor. Here, most gracious liege.
Rich. Norfolk, we must have knocks. Ha! must we not? 5
Nor. We must both give and take, my loving lord.
Rich. Up with my tent! Here will I lie tonight;
[*Soldiers begin to set up the King's tent.*]
But where tomorrow? Well, all's one for that.
Who hath descried the number of the traitors? 9
Nor. Six or seven thousand is their utmost power.
Rich. Why, our battalia trebles that account:
Besides, the King's name is a tower of strength,
Which they upon the adverse faction want.
Up with the tent! Come, noble gentlemen,
Let us survey the vantage of the ground. 15
Call for some men of sound direction:
Let's lack no discipline, make no delay,
For, lords, tomorrow is a busy day. *Exeunt.*

Enter RICHMOND, SIR WILLIAM BRANDON, OXFORD, *and* DORSET, [HERBERT, *and* BLUNT. *Some of the* SOLDIERS *pitch* RICHMOND'S *tent.*]

Richm. The weary sun hath made a golden set,
And by the bright tract of his fiery car 20
Gives token of a goodly day tomorrow.
Sir William Brandon, you shall bear my standard.
Give me some ink and paper in my tent:
I'll draw the form and model of our battle,
Limit each leader to his several charge, 25
And part in just proportion our small power.
My Lord of Oxford, you, Sir William Brandon,
And you, Sir Walter Herbert, stay with me.
The Earl of Pembroke keeps his regiment; 29
Good Captain Blunt, bear my good night to him,
And by the second hour in the morning
Desire the Earl to see me in my tent:
Yet one thing more, good Captain, do for me—
Where is Lord Stanley quartered, do you know?
Blunt. Unless I have mista'en his colors much,
Which well I am assured I have not done, 36
His regiment lies half a mile at least
South from the mighty power of the King.
Richm. If without peril it be possible,
Sweet Blunt, make some good means to speak with him 40
And give him from me this most needful note.
Blunt. Upon my life, my lord, I'll undertake it;
And so God give you quiet rest tonight!
Richm. Good night, good Captain Blunt.
[*Exit Blunt.*]
Come, gentlemen,
Let us consult upon tomorrow's business. 45
Into my tent; the dew is raw and cold.
They withdraw into the tent.

Enter, [*to his tent,* KING] RICHARD, RATCLIFFE, NORFOLK, *and* CATESBY.

Rich. What is't o'clock?
Cates. It's suppertime, my lord;
It's nine o'clock.
Rich. I will not sup tonight.
Give me some ink and paper.

5. father: stepfather
17. conscience: certainty of being in the right
5. knocks: buffets
8. all's . . . that: it doesn't matter.
11. battalia: battalions
15. the . . . ground: the strategic possibilities of the site
16. sound direction: competent leadership
20. tract: track
25. several: respective
29. keeps: stays with

What, is my beaver easier than it was? 50
And all my armor laid into my tent?

Cates. It is, my liege; and all things are in readiness.

Rich. Good Norfolk, hie thee to thy charge;
Use careful watch, choose trusty sentinels.

Nor. I go, my lord. 55

Rich. Stir with the lark tomorrow, gentle Norfolk.

Nor. I warrant you, my lord. *Exit.*

Rich. Catesby!

Cates. My lord?

Rich. Send out a pursuivant-at-arms 59
To Stanley's regiment; bid him bring his power
Before sunrising, lest his son George fall
Into the blind cave of eternal night. [*Exit Catesby.*]
Fill me a bowl of wine. Give me a watch.
Saddle white Surrey for the field tomorrow.
Look that my staves be sound and not too heavy.
Ratcliffe! 66

Rat. My lord?

Rich. Sawst thou the melancholy Lord Northumberland?

Rat. Thomas the Earl of Surrey and himself, 69
Much about cockshut time, from troop to troop
Went through the army, cheering up the soldiers.

Rich. So, I am satisfied. Give me a bowl of wine.
I have not that alacrity of spirit
Nor cheer of mind that I was wont to have.
[*Wine brought.*]
Set it down. Is ink and paper ready? 75

Rat. It is, my lord.

Rich Bid my guard watch. Leave me.
Ratcliffe, about the mid of night come to my tent
And help to arm me. Leave me, I say. *Exit Ratcliffe.*
[*King Richard withdraws into his tent.*]

Enter [LORD STANLEY, EARL OF] DERBY, *to* RICHMOND *in his tent,* [LORDS *and others attending*].

Der. Fortune and victory sit on thy helm! 79

Richm. All comfort that the dark night can afford
Be to thy person, noble father-in-law!
Tell me, how fares our loving mother?

Der. I, by attorney, bless thee from thy mother,
Who prays continually for Richmond's good:
So much for that. The silent hours steal on, 85
And flaky darkness breaks within the East.
In brief, for so the season bids us be,
Prepare thy battle early in the morning
And put thy fortune to the arbitrament
Of bloody strokes and mortal-staring war. 90
I, as I may—that which I would I cannot—
With best advantage will deceive the time
And aid thee in this doubtful shock of arms.
But on thy side I may not be too forward,
Lest, being seen, thy brother, tender George, 95
Be executed in his father's sight.
Farewell. The leisure and the fearful time
Cuts off the ceremonious vows of love
And ample interchange of sweet discourse 99
Which so-long-sund'red friends should dwell upon.
God give us leisure for these rites of love!
Once more adieu: be valiant, and speed well!

Richm. Good lords, conduct him to his regiment.
I'll strive with troubled noise to take a nap,
Lest leaden slumber peise me down tomorrow, 105
When I should mount with wings of victory:
Once more, good night, kind lords and gentlemen.
Exeunt. Manet Richmond.
O Thou, whose captain I account myself,
Look on my forces with a gracious eye;
Put in their hands thy bruising irons of wrath, 110
That they may crush down with a heavy fall
The usurping helmets of our adversaries;
Make us thy ministers of chastisement,
That we may praise thee in the victory.
To thee I do commend my watchful soul 115
Ere I let fall the windows of mine eyes:
Sleeping and waking, O defend me still! *Sleeps.*

Enter the GHOST OF PRINCE EDWARD, *son to* HENRY THE SIXTH.

Ghost. (*To Richard*) Let me sit heavy on thy soul tomorrow!
Think how thou stab'dst me in my prime of youth
At Tewkesbury: despair therefore, and die! 120
(*To Richmond*) Be cheerful, Richmond; for the wronged souls
Of butchered princes fight in thy behalf.
King Henry's issue, Richmond, comforts thee.

Enter the GHOST OF HENRY THE SIXTH.

Ghost. [*To Richard*] When I was mortal, my anointed body
By thee was punched full of deadly holes. 125
Think on the Tower and me: despair, and die!
Harry the Sixth bids thee despair, and die!

50. beaver: helmet's visor
63. watch: either a watchlight or a guard may be meant.
65. staves: lance-shafts
70. cockshut time: twilight
81. father-in-law: stepfather
83. attorney: proxy
86. flaky: streaked with remaining light
90. mortal-staring: of deadly aspect
92. With . . . time: will fool Richard as best I can
95. tender George: actually, George Stanley, Lord Strange, was a married adult.
97. leisure: time at our disposal
102. speed: prosper
105. peise: weigh
110. irons: swords
115. watchful: wakeful

(*To Richmond*) Virtuous and holy, be thou conqueror!
Harry, that prophesied thou shouldst be King, 129
Doth comfort thee in thy sleep: live, and flourish!

Enter the GHOST OF CLARENCE.

Ghost. [*To Richard*] Let me sit heavy in thy soul tomorrow—
I, that was washed to death with fulsome wine,
Poor Clarence by thy guile betrayed to death!
Tomorrow in the battle think on me, 134
And fall thy edgeless sword: despair, and die!
(*To Richmond*) Thou offspring of the house of Lancaster,
The wrongèd heirs of York do pray for thee;
Good angels guard thy battle! Live, and flourish!

Enter the GHOSTS OF RIVERS, GREY, *and* VAUGHAN.

Riv. [*To Richard*] Let me sit heavy in thy soul tomorrow, 139
Rivers, that died at Pomfret! Despair, and die!
Grey. Think upon Grey, and let thy soul despair!
Vaugh. Think upon Vaughan, and with guilty fear
Let fall thy lance: despair, and die!
All. (*To Richmond*) Awake, and think our wrongs in Richard's bosom
Will conquer him! Awake, and win the day! 145

Enter the GHOST OF LORD HASTINGS.

Ghost. [*To Richard*] Bloody and guilty, guiltily awake
And in a bloody battle end thy days!
Think on Lord Hastings: despair, and die!
(*To Richmond*) Quiet untroubled soul, awake, awake! 149
Arm, fight, and conquer, for fair England's sake!

Enter the GHOSTS OF THE TWO YOUNG PRINCES.

Ghosts. [*To Richard*] Dream on thy cousins smothered in the Tower.
Let us be lead within thy bosom, Richard,
And weigh thee down to ruin, shame and death!
Thy nephews' souls bid thee despair, and die!
(*To Richmond*) Sleep, Richmond, sleep in peace and wake in joy. 155
Good angels guard thee from the boar's annoy!
Live, and beget a happy race of kings!
Edward's unhappy sons do bid thee flourish.

Enter the GHOST OF ANNE, *his wife.*

Ghost. (*To Richard*) Richard, thy wife, that wretched Anne thy wife,
That never slept a quiet hour with thee, 160
Now fills thy sleep with perturbations:
Tomorrow in the battle think on me,
And fall thy edgeless sword: despair, and die!
(*To Richmond*) Thou quiet soul, sleep thou a quiet sleep.
Dream of success and happy victory! 165
Thy adversary's wife doth pray for thee.

Enter the GHOST OF BUCKINGHAM.

Ghost. (*To Richard*) The first was I that helped thee to the crown;
The last was I that felt thy tyranny.
O, in the battle think on Buckingham,
And die in terror of thy guiltiness! 170
Dream on, dream on, of bloody deeds and death:
Fainting, despair; despairing, yield thy breath!
(*To Richmond*) I died for hope ere I could lend thee aid;
But cheer thy heart and be thou not dismayed:
God and good angels fight on Richmond's side,
And Richard fall in height of all his pride! 176

[*The Ghosts vanish.*] *Richard starts out of his dream.*

Rich. Give me another horse! Bind up my wounds!
Have mercy, Jesu! Soft! I did but dream.
O coward conscience, how dost thou afflict me!
The lights burn blue. It is now dead midnight. 180
Cold fearful drops stand on my trembling flesh.
What do I fear? Myself? There's none else by.
Richard loves Richard: that is, I am I.
Is there a murderer here? No. Yes, I am: 184
Then fly. What, from myself? Great reason why:
Lest I revenge. What, myself upon myself?
Alack, I love myself. Wherefore? For any good
That I myself have done unto myself?
O, no! Alas, I rather hate myself
For hateful deeds committed by myself. 190
I am a villain. Yet I lie, I am not.
Fool, of thyself speak well. Fool, do not flatter.
My conscience hath a thousand several tongues,
And every tongue brings in a several tale,
And every tale condemns me for a villain. 195
Perjury, perjury, in the highest degree;
Murder, stern murder, in the direst degree;
All several sins, all used in each degree,
Throng to the bar, crying all, "Guilty! guilty!"
I shall despair. There is no creature loves me; 200
And if I die, no soul shall pity me.
Nay, wherefore should they, since that I myself

132. fulsome: satiating
135. fall: drop
156. annoy: injury
173. for hope: because of hoping to assist
198. All . . . degree: every different sin, each committed to the utmost degree

Find in myself no pity to myself?
Methought the souls of all that I had murdered
Came to my tent, and every one did threat 205
Tomorrow's vengeance on the head of Richard.

Enter RATCLIFFE.

Rat. My lord!
Rich. Who's there?
Rat. Ratcliffe, my lord, 'tis I. The early village cock
Hath twice done salutation to the morn: 210
Your friends are up and buckle on their armor.
Rich. O Ratcliffe, I have dreamed a fearful dream!
What thinkst thou? Will our friends prove all true?
Rat. No doubt, my lord.
Rich. O Ratcliffe, I fear, I fear! 214
Rat. Nay, good my lord, be not afraid of shadows.
Rich. By the apostle Paul, shadows tonight
Have struck more terror to the soul of Richard
Than can the substance of ten thousand soldiers
Armed in proof and led by shallow Richmond.
'Tis not yet near day. Come, go with me. 220
Under our tents I'll play the eavesdropper,
To hear if any mean to shrink from me.
Exeunt Richard and Ratcliffe.

Enter the LORDS *to* RICHMOND *sitting in his tent.*

Lords. Good morrow, Richmond.
Richm. Cry mercy, lords and watchful gentlemen,
That you have ta'en a tardy sluggard here. 225
Lords. How have you slept, my lord?
Richm. The sweetest sleep, and fairest-boding dreams
That ever ent'red in a drowsy head.
Have I since your departure had, my lords.
Methought their souls whose bodies Richard murdered 230
Came to my tent and cried on victory.
I promise you my heart is very jocund
In the remembrance of so fair a dream.
How far into the morning is it, lords?
Lords. Upon the stroke of four. 235
Richm. Why, then 'tis time to arm and give direction.

His Oration to his Soldiers.

More than I have said, loving countrymen,
The leisure and enforcement of the time
Forbids to dwell upon. Yet remember this:
God and our good cause fight upon our side; 240
The prayers of holy saints and wronged souls,
Like high-reared bulwarks, stand before our faces.
Richard except, those whom we fight against
Had rather have us win than him they follow.
For what is he they follow? Truly, gentlemen, 245
A bloody tyrant and a homicide;
One raised in blood and one in blood established;
One that made means to come by what he hath,
And slaughtered those that were the means to help him;
A base foul stone, made precious by the foil 250
Of England's chair, where he is falsely set;
One that hath ever been God's enemy.
Then if you fight against God's enemy,
God will in justice ward you as his soldiers;
If you do sweat to put a tyrant down, 255
You sleep in peace, the tyrant being slain;
If you do fight against your country's foes,
Your country's fat shall pay your pains the hire;
If you do fight in safeguard of your wives, 259
Your wives shall welcome home the conquerors;
If you do free your children from the sword,
Your children's children quits it in your age:
Then in the name of God and all these rights,
Advance your standards, draw your willing swords.
For me, the ransom of my bold attempt 265
Shall be this cold corpse on the earth's cold face;
But if I thrive, the gain of my attempt
The least of you shall share his part thereof.
Sound drums and trumpets boldly and cheerfully:
God and St. George! Richmond and victory! 270
[*Exeunt.*]

Enter KING RICHARD, RATCLIFFE, [*and* SOLDIERS].

Rich. What said Northumberland as touching Richmond?
Rat. That he was never trained up in arms.
Rich. He said the truth. And what said Surrey then?
Rat. He smiled and said, "The better for our purpose." 274
Rich. He was in the right, and so indeed it is.
Clock strikes.
Tell the clock there. Give me a calendar.
Who saw the sun today?
Rat. Not I, my lord.
Rich. Then he disdains to shine; for by the book
He should have braved the East an hour ago.
A black day will it be to somebody. 280
Ratcliffe!

219. proof: stout armor
224. Cry mercy: I beg your pardon
231. cried on: invoked

243. except: excepted
246. tyrant: usurper
254. ward: defend
258. fat: abundance; **pay . . . hire:** reward your pains
262. quits . . . age: repays it when you are old
264. Advance: raise
265–66. the . . . corpse: I will not compound for ransom but fight to the death
276. Tell: count its strokes

Rat. My lord?
Rich. The sun will not be seen today;
The sky doth frown and lower upon our army.
I would these dewy tears were from the ground.
Not shine today? Why, what is that to me 285
More than to Richmond? For the selfsame heaven
That frowns on me looks sadly upon him.

Enter NORFOLK.

Nor. Arm, arm, my lord; the foe vaunts in the field.
Rich. Come, bustle, bustle! Caparison my horse!
Call up Lord Stanley, bid him bring his power. 290
I will lead forth my soldiers to the plain,
And thus my battle shall be ordered:
My foreward shall be drawn out all in length,
Consisting equally of horse and foot;
Our archers shall be placed in the midst; 295
John Duke of Norfolk, Thomas Earl of Surrey,
Shall have the leading of this foot and horse.
They thus directed, we will follow
In the main battle, whose puissance on either side
Shall be well winged with our chiefest horse. 300
This, and St. George to boot! What thinkst thou, Norfolk?
Nor. A good direction, warlike sovereign.
This found I on my tent this morning.
He showeth him a paper.
Jockey of Norfolk, be not so bold,
For Dickon thy master is bought and sold. 305
Rich. A thing devised by the enemy.
Go, gentlemen, every man to his charge.
Let not our babbling dreams affright our souls;
Conscience is but a word that cowards use,
Devised at first to keep the strong in awe: 310
Our strong arms be our conscience, swords our law!
March on, join bravely, let us to't pell-mell,
If not to heaven, then hand in hand to hell.

His Oration to his Army.

What shall I say more than I have inferred?
Remember whom you are to cope withal: 315
A sort of vagabonds, rascals, and runaways,
A scum of Britains and base lackey peasants,
Whom their o'ercloyed country vomits forth
To desperate adventures and assured destruction.
You sleeping safe, they bring to you unrest; 320
You having lands, and blessed with beauteous wives,
They would restrain the one, distain the other.
And who doth lead them but a paltry fellow,
Long kept in Britain at our mother's cost,
A milksop, one that never in his life 325
Felt so much cold as over shoes in snow?
Let's whip these stragglers o'er the seas again,
Lash hence these overweening rags of France,
These famished beggars, weary of their lives,
Who, but for dreaming on this fond exploit, 330
For want of means, poor rats, had hanged themselves.
If we be conquered, let men conquer us,
And not these bastard Britains, whom our fathers
Have in their own land beaten, bobbed, and thumped, 334
And, in record, left them the heirs of shame.
Shall these enjoy our lands? lie with our wives?
Ravish our daughters? (*Drum afar off.*) Hark! I hear their drum.
Fight, gentlemen of England! Fight, bold yeomen!
Draw, archers, draw your arrows to the head! 339
Spur your proud horses hard, and ride in blood!
Amaze the welkin with your broken staves!

Enter a MESSENGER.

What says Lord Stanley? Will he bring his power?
Mess. My lord, he doth deny to come.
Rich. Off with his son George's head! 344
Nor. My lord, the enemy is past the marsh:
After the battle let George Stanley die.
Rich. A thousand hearts are great within my bosom!
Advance our standards, set upon our foes.
Our ancient word of courage, fair St. George,
Inspire us with the spleen of fiery dragons! 350
Upon them! Victory sits on our helms.
[*Exeunt.*]

[Scene IV. *Another part of the field.*]

Alarum; excursions. Enter [NORFOLK *and* FORCES; *to him*] CATESBY.

Cates. Rescue, my Lord of Norfolk, rescue, rescue!
The King enacts more wonders than a man,

287. sadly: soberly
288. vaunts . . . field: is in the field before us
289. Caparison: deck in trappings
301. to boot: in addition
304. Jockey: a nickname for John
305. Dickon: a nickname for Richard
314. inferred: mentioned
315. cope withal: encounter
316. sort: company
317. Britains: Bretons
322. distain: dishonor
324. at . . . cost: in Holinshed's *Chronicles* (1587) Richard says that Richmond was "brought vp by my moothers meanes, and mine, . . . in the court of Francis duke of Britaine"; but "mother" should probably read "brother," since Edward IV exacted a promise from the Duke that he would keep Richmond in safe custody.
334. bobbed: buffeted
341. Amaze: terrify; **welkin:** heavens
349. word: motto
350. spleen: violent rage
Ent. excursions: clashes of arms

Daring an opposite to every danger:
His horse is slain, and all on foot he fights,
Seeking for Richmond in the throat of death. 5
Rescue, fair lord, or else the day is lost!

Alarums. Enter [KING] RICHARD.

Rich. A horse! a horse! my kingdom for a horse!
Cates. Withdraw, my lord; I'll help you to a horse.
Rich. Slave, I have set my life upon a cast,
And I will stand the hazard of the die. 10
I think there be six Richmonds in the field;
Five have I slain today instead of him.
A horse! a horse! my kingdom for a horse!

[*Exeunt.*]

[Scene V. *Another part of the field.*]

Alarum. Enter [KING] RICHARD *and* RICHMOND; *they fight;* RICHARD *is slain.*

Retreat and flourish. Enter RICHMOND, [LORD STANLEY, EARL OF] DERBY, *bearing the crown with divers other* LORDS.

Richm. God and your arms be praised, victorious friends!
The day is ours; the bloody dog is dead.
Der. Courageous Richmond, well hast thou acquit thee.
Lo, here this long usurped royalty
From the dead temples of this bloody wretch 5
Have I plucked off, to grace thy brows withal.
Wear it, enjoy it, and make much of it.
Richm. Great God of heaven, say amen to all!
But tell me, is young George Stanley living? 9
Der. He is, my lord, and safe in Leicester town,
Whither, if it please you, we may now withdraw us.
Richm. What men of name are slain on either side?
Der. John Duke of Norfolk, Walter Lord Ferrers,
Sir Robert Brakenbury, and Sir William Brandon.
Richm. Inter their bodies as become their births.
Proclaim a pardon to the soldiers fled 16
That in submission will return to us;
And then, as we have ta'en the sacrament,
We will unite the White Rose and the Red.
Smile heaven upon this fair conjunction, 20
That long have frowned upon their enmity!
What traitor hears me, and says not amen?
England hath long been mad and scarred herself;
The brother blindly shed the brother's blood;
The father rashly slaughtered his own son; 25
The son, compelled, been butcher to the sire:
All this divided York and Lancaster,
Divided in their dire division,
O now let Richmond and Elizabeth,
The true succeeders of each royal house, 30
By God's fair ordinance conjoin together!
And let their heirs, God, if thy will be so,
Enrich the time to come with smooth-faced peace,
With smiling plenty, and fair prosperous days!
Abate the edge of traitors, gracious Lord, 35
That would reduce these bloody days again
And make poor England weep in streams of blood!
Let them not live to taste this land's increase
That would with treason wound this fair land's peace!
Now civil wounds are stopped, peace lives again:
That she may long live here, God say amen! 41

Exeunt.

3. Daring . . . danger: challenging every danger to combat him
9. set: wagered
10. die: one of a pair of dice

18. we . . . sacrament: I have sworn
20. conjunction: union
35. Abate: blunt
36. reduce: lead back to; restore

An Admiring Gallant

From *Stirpium, insignium nobilitatis* (1602?).

LOVE'S LABOR'S LOST

INTRODUCTION

Students of Shakespeare once considered *Love's Labor's Lost* one of the playwright's earliest plays, an example of his apprenticeship. A more careful study of the drama, however, reveals that it is far from being an immature production. On the contrary, it is a sophisticated piece satirizing current literary and social foibles and is precisely the kind of play that a young man who had fallen in with the London literary coterie in the 1590's would have tried to produce. Sir Edmund Chambers dates the first performance of the play between 1594 and 1595, which seems highly probable. This date would place the composition and performance of *Love's Labor's Lost* after the three parts of *Henry VI, Richard III, The Comedy of Errors, Titus Andronicus, The Taming of the Shrew,* and *The Two Gentlemen of Verona.* Although *Love's Labor's Lost* shows a tendency to experimentation in verse forms, its sophistication in subject matter indicates that its author had already become familiar with fashions in London, as well as with some of the characters who lent themselves to satire.

The first printed version of the play, the Quarto of 1598, described it as "A pleasant conceited comedy called *Love's Labor's Lost.* As it was presented before Her Highness this last Christmas. Newly corrected and augmented. By W. Shakespeare." This phraseology does not necessarily prove that the play had been printed earlier or that the Quarto of 1598 was vastly different from the play as first performed. Although its boast of being newly corrected and augmented may be just the publisher's advertisement, it does indicate that the play had been popular enough for performance at court during the holidays of 1597–98 and that it may have been worked over for that occasion.

Love's Labor's Lost has the characteristics of a play written for some special occasion—a celebration in some great house perhaps—but clues to the occasion have eluded scholars. Later the play was probably performed in the public playhouses. In addition to the revival in 1597 before Queen Elizabeth, it was again performed before James I and his Queen in 1605 at festivities staged at the house of the Earl of Southampton. If it enjoyed any popularity in the later seventeenth century or in the eighteenth, the records have been lost. In 1839 Charles James Mathews and Eliza Vestris revived the play at Covent Garden, and it was played at wide intervals through the nineteenth century. In the present generation it has had more frequent productions by the Old Vic Company in London and by other companies in England and the United States.

COMEDY OF GENIAL SATIRE

The comedy has a very slight plot, which revolves around the contest between the King of Navarre's academy of would-be studious courtiers and the coquettish Princess of France and her ladies; but plot is not the main interest in the play. Shakespeare makes it a pageant and spectacle with a parade of characters that are sometimes witty and gay, sometimes reminiscent of the Italian *commedia dell' arte,* sometimes merely comical with the humor of stage rustics in many an Elizabethan play. Above all the play is a vehicle for poking fun at popular fads in language and learning, at pedantry, which persists in all ages, and at the eternal conflict between men and women. This battle of the sexes is a perennial subject for dramatic treatment in every age, and Shakespeare gives it the graceful treatment of genial raillery in *Love's Labor's Lost.*

The Elizabethans particularly delighted in wordplay and in the use of fanciful language. When Shakespeare came up to London, one of the popular writers was John Lyly, a playwright and a novelist, whose most famous piece of fiction was *Euphues, the Anatomy of Wit,* first published in 1578. Before it had exhausted its popularity, it ran through seventeen editions by 1636. Its sequel, *Euphues and His England* (1580), almost as popular, had a dozen editions by 1609. These novels popularized long, balanced sentences, metaphors drawn from unnatural natural history, involved similes, fancifully turned phrases, elaborately alliterative expressions, and a plethora of fine language generally. Sir Philip Sidney had employed some of the same devices in his novel, the *Arcadia,* which had circulated widely in court circles in manuscript, and other writers indulged in similar fine language. Edmund Spenser depended for much of his poetic effect in *The Shepherd's Calendar* (1579) upon deliberate archaisms. An example of the interest in language for language's sake may be found in the work of a belated Elizabethan in Massachusetts Bay, Nathaniel Ward, who wrote *The Simple Cobbler of Aggawam* (1647). Shakespeare in *Love's Labor's Lost* not only utilized tricks of language popular at the moment but he also managed at the same time to ridicule linguistic excesses. From time immemorial, men have satirized pedantry. The pedant was a stock type in Roman and Italian comedies, and in the Elizabethan period, both in the public playhouses and on the university stages, the pedant was frequently the object of jest. Although Shakespeare's Holofernes in *Love's Labor's Lost* had an ancient lineage, some scholars have seen reflections of homegrown pedants in his characterization, perhaps a gibe at Gabriel Harvey, one of Shakespeare's contemporaries, whose learned pomposities were a matter of comment at the time. Undoubtedly there were many topical hits in this comedy, the points of which have been lost to us; but since foibles of language and character are not confined to any age, Shakespeare's comedy transcends mere allusion to local situations and personalities, and we can enjoy satire that has a universal appeal.

Shakespeare has a persistent quality of common sense and a capacity for laughing at vanity wherever he finds it. In this comedy we see him laughing at the folly of men who believe that they can resist the temptations of Eve. In the person of Berowne he mocks the affectations of the King and his scholar-courtiers, whose pretensions to learning dissolve before the smoldering eyes of the Princess and her maids. As for Berowne, he will have none of the language of fashion and he forswears pedantic affectation:

> Taffeta phrases, silken terms precise,
> Three-piled hyperboles, spruce affectation,
> Figures pedantical—these summer flies
> Have blown me full of maggot ostentation.
> I do forswear them . . . .
> Henceforth my wooing mind shall be expressed
> In russet yeas, and honest kersey noes.

Berowne serves as a sort of commentator upon the action, a kind of chorus, and perhaps as the expression of the common sense of the poet himself.

SOURCE AND TEXT

Love's Labor's Lost is one of the few plays of Shakespeare for which no definite sources can be found. If he used an older play, it has not come to light, nor has anyone identified a story or narrative which might have suggested the plot or situation. Interest in Navarre, however, was keen at the time. Though no King of Navarre was named Ferdinand, the King's followers bore the names, with slight modifications, of people "in the news," as we would say. Shakespeare could have learned the names of Berowne, Longaville, and Dumaine from newsbooks in circulation in London at the time he was writing his play. The political and religious turmoil in France resulted in the publication of numerous pamphlets and books in England, of which the following are examples: *A Caveat for France upon the Present Evils That It Now Suffereth* (1588), *Credible Reports from France and Flanders in the Month of May, 1590* (1591), *The French History* (1589), *The True History of the Civil Wars in France* (1591), *An Excellent Discourse upon the Now Present State of France* (1592), and *The History of France* (1595). These books related events which were much on the minds of Englishmen who followed the career of Henry of Navarre. Between 1589 and 1592 Queen Elizabeth gave sporadic aid to Henry in an effort to counter the influence of the Holy League. Henry's decision in 1593 that Paris was worth a Mass, and his espousal of the Catholic faith, did not diminish English interest in him or his affairs, and all of this gave timeliness to Shakespeare's use of a King of Navarre with courtiers bearing names of characters active in French politics. The Princess' visit to Navarre may be based on an actual episode when Henry's estranged wife visited him at Nérac in 1578 to discuss her dowry. It is also possible but hardly probable that Shakespeare had in mind the visit of Catherine de Medici to Henry at Saint Bris in 1586, when Catherine tried to persuade him to divorce his wife Marguerite and marry Christine of Lorraine. The idea of the ascetic academy of scholars may have been suggested by the publication of Pierre de la Primaudaye's *The French Academy* in an English translation in 1586 and several times thereafter. This encyclopedic work contains a description of the founding of an academy by four young men of Anjou.

The Quarto of 1598, the first printed version of *Love's Labor's Lost,* despite its claim of being "newly corrected," is full of printing errors, mislineations, and faulty punctuation. The copy for the First Folio of 1623 was apparently a corrected Quarto of 1598, but in printing the Folio many new errors found their way into the text. The present text is based on the Quarto of 1598, with necessary corrections and emendations. A second Quarto was published in 1631 with a title page describing it as "A witty and pleasant comedy as it was acted by His Majesty's servants at the Blackfriars and the Globe," which suggests that the play was not merely performed for a special audience but had a run in the public playhouses.

[Dramatis Personæ

FERDINAND, *King of Navarre.*

BEROWNE,
LONGAVILLE,
DUMAINE, } *lords attending the King.*

BOYET,
MARCADE, } *lords attending the Princess of France.*

DON ADRIANO DE ARMADO, *a fantastical Spaniard.*
SIR NATHANIEL, *a curate.*
HOLOFERNES, *a schoolmaster.*
ANTHONY DULL, *a constable.*
COSTARD, *a clown.*
MOTH, *page to Armado.*
A FORESTER.

THE PRINCESS OF FRANCE.

ROSALINE,
MARIA,
KATHARINE, } *ladies attending the Princess.*

JAQUENETTA, *a country wench.*

Lords, Attendants, etc.

Scene: *The King of Navarre's Park.*]

A Russian Ambassador
Cesare Vecellio, *Habiti antichi et moderni di tutto il mondo* (1598).

LOVE'S LABOR'S LOST

ACT I

[Scene I. *The King of Navarre's Park.*]

Enter FERDINAND, *King of Navarre,* BEROWNE, LONGAVILLE, *and* DUMAINE.

King. Let fame, that all hunt after in their lives,
Live regist'red upon our brazen tombs,
And then grace us in the disgrace of death;
When, spite of cormorant devouring Time,
The endeavor of this present breath may buy 5
That honor which shall bate his scythe's keen edge,
And make us heirs of all eternity.
Therefore, brave conquerors—for so you are,
That war against your own affections
And the huge army of the world's desires— 10
Our late edict shall strongly stand in force:
Navarre shall be the wonder of the world;
Our court shall be a little academe,
Still and contemplative in living art.
You three, Berowne, Dumaine, and Longaville, 15
Have sworn for three years' term to live with me
My fellow scholars, and to keep those statutes
That are recorded in this schedule here.
Your oaths are passed; and now subscribe your names,
That his own hand may strike his honor down 20
That violates the smallest branch herein:
If you are armed to do as sworn to do,
Subscribe to your deep oaths, and keep it too.
Long. I am resolved; 'tis but a three years' fast:
The mind shall banquet, though the body pine. 25
Fat paunches have lean pates; and dainty bits
Make rich the ribs, but bankrupt quite the wits.
Dum. My loving lord, Dumaine is mortified.
The grosser manner of these world's delights
He throws upon the gross world's baser slaves; 30
To love, to wealth, to pomp, I pine and die,
With all these living in philosophy.
Ber. I can but say their protestation over;
So much, dear liege, I have already sworn,
That is, to live and study here three years. 35
But there are other strict observances,
As: not to see a woman in that term,
Which I hope well is not enrolled there;
And one day in a week to touch no food,
And but one meal on every day beside, 40
The which I hope is not enrolled there;
And then to sleep but three hours in the night
And not be seen to wink of all the day—
When I was wont to think no harm all night,
And make a dark night too of half the day— 45
Which I hope well is not enrolled there.
O, these are barren tasks, too hard to keep,
Not to see ladies, study, fast, not sleep!
King. Your oath is passed to pass away from these.
Ber. Let me say no, my liege, an if you please:
I only swore to study with your Grace, 51
And stay here in your court for three years' space.

3. grace: honor; **disgrace:** misfortune
4. cormorant: voracious
6. bate: blunt
9. affections: inclinations
14. living art: the art of perfect living
21. branch: section
23. deep: strong
26. Fat . . . pates: proverbial
28. mortified: deadened in sense

Long. You swore to that, Berowne, and to the rest.
Ber. By yea and nay, sir, then I swore in jest.
What is the end of study, let me know. 55
King. Why, that to know which else we should not know.
Ber. Things hid and barred, you mean, from common sense?
King. Ay, that is study's godlike recompense.
Ber. Come on, then; I will swear to study so,
To know the thing I am forbid to know, 60
As thus: to study where I well may dine,
When I to feast expressly am forbid;
Or study where to meet some mistress fine,
When mistresses from common sense are hid;
Or, having sworn too hard-a-keeping oath, 65
Study to break it, and not break my troth.
If study's gain be thus, and this be so,
Study knows that which yet it doth not know.
Swear me to this, and I will ne'er say no. 69
King. These be the stops that hinder study quite,
And train our intellects to vain delight.
Ber. Why, all delights are vain, but that most vain
Which, with pain purchased, doth inherit pain:
As painfully to pore upon a book
To seek the light of truth; while truth the while
Doth falsely blind the eyesight of his look. 76
Light, seeking light, doth light of light beguile;
So, ere you find where light in darkness lies,
Your light grows dark by losing of your eyes.
Study me how to please the eye indeed, 80
By fixing it upon a fairer eye;
Who dazzling so, that eye shall be his heed,
And give him light that it was blinded by.
Study is like the heaven's glorious sun,
That will not be deep-searched with saucy looks;
Small have continual plodders ever won, 86
Save base authority from others' books.
These earthly godfathers of heaven's lights,
That give a name to every fixed star,
Have no more profit of their shining nights 90
Than those that walk and wot not what they are.
Too much to know is to know nought but fame;
And every godfather can give a name.
King. How well he's read, to reason against reading! 94
Dum. Proceeded well, to stop all good proceeding!
Long. He weeds the corn, and still lets grow the weeding.
Ber. The spring is near, when green geese are a-breeding.
Dum. How follows that?
Ber. Fit in his place and time.
Dum. In reason nothing.
Ber. Something then in rhyme.
Long. Berowne is like an envious sneaping frost
That bites the first-born infants of the spring. 101
Ber. Well, say I am; why should proud summer boast
Before the birds have any cause to sing?
Why should I joy in an abortive birth?
At Christmas I no more desire a rose 105
Than wish a snow in May's newfangled shows;
But like of each thing that in season grows;
So you, to study now it is too late,
Climb o'er the house to unlock the little gate. 109
King. Well, sit you out; go home, Berowne; adieu.
Ber. No, my good lord; I have sworn to stay with you;
And though I have for barbarism spoke more
Than for that angel knowledge you can say,
Yet confident I'll keep what I have swore,
And bide the penance of each three years' day.
Give me the paper; let me read the same; 116
And to the strict'st decrees I'll write my name.
King. How well this yielding rescues thee from shame!
Ber. [*Reads*]

Item. That no woman shall come within a mile of my court 120

—Hath this been proclaimed?
Long. Four days ago.
Ber. Let's see the penalty. [*Reads*]

—on pain of losing her tongue.

Who devised this penalty? 125
Long. Marry, that did I.
Ber. Sweet lord, and why?
Long. To fright them hence with that dread penalty.
Ber. A dangerous law against gentility!
[*Reads*]

Item. If any man be seen to talk with a woman 130
within the term of three years, he shall endure such public shame as the rest of the court can possibly devise.

This article, my liege, yourself must break;
For well you know here comes in embassy 134

57. common sense: everyday perception
71. train: entice
77. Light . . . beguile: i.e., the eyesight is weakened by too much seeking for the light of truth in books.
80. Study me: let me study
82. Who: i.e., the eye of the beholder; **heed:** guardian (referring to the **fairer eye**)
91. wot: know
92. Too . . . fame: reading teaches only what others have considered to be the truth
97. green geese: goslings; fools
100. envious: malicious; **sneaping:** nipping
101. first-born infants: earliest buds
102. boast: vaunt itself
115. bide: endure; **each . . . day:** each day of the three years
126. Marry: indeed
129. gentility: gentle manners

The French king's daughter, with yourself to speak—
A maid of grace and complete majesty—
About surrender up of Aquitaine
To her decrepit, sick, and bedrid father;
Therefore this article is made in vain,
Or vainly comes the admired princess hither. 140

King. What say you, lords? Why, this was quite forgot.

Ber. So study evermore is overshot.
While it doth study to have what it would,
It doth forget to do the thing it should;
And when it hath the thing it hunteth most, 145
'Tis won as towns with fire—so won, so lost.

King. We must of force dispense with this decree;
She must lie here on mere necessity.

Ber. Necessity will make us all forsworn 149
Three thousand times within this three years' space;
For every man with his affects is born,
Not by might mast'red, but by special grace.
If I break faith, this word shall speak for me:
I am forsworn on mere necessity.
So to the laws at large I write my name, 155
[*Subscribes*]
And he that breaks them in the least degree
Stands in attainder of eternal shame.
Suggestions are to other as to me;
But I believe, although I seem so loath,
I am the last that will last keep his oath. 160
But is there no quick recreation granted?

King. Ay, that there is. Our court, you know, is haunted
With a refined traveler of Spain,
A man in all the world's new fashion planted,
That hath a mint of phrases in his brain; 165
One who the music of his own vain tongue
Doth ravish like enchanting harmony;
A man of compliments, whom right and wrong
Have chose as umpire of their mutiny.
This child of fancy, that Armado hight, 170
For interim to our studies shall relate
In highborn words the worth of many a knight
From tawny Spain lost in the world's debate.
How you delight, my lords, I know not, I;
But I protest I love to hear him lie, 175
And I will use him for my minstrelsy.

Ber. Armado is a most illustrious wight,
A man of fire-new words, fashion's own knight.

Long. Costard the swain and he shall be our sport;
And so to study three years is but short. 180

Enter [DULL,] *a constable, with a letter, and* COSTARD.

Dull. Which is the Duke's own person?

Ber. This, fellow. What wouldst?

Dull. I myself reprehend his own person, for I am his Grace's tharborough; but I would see his own person in flesh and blood. 185

Ber. This is he.

Dull. Signior Arme—Arme—commends you. There's villainy abroad; this letter will tell you more.

Cost. Sir, the contempts thereof are as 190 touching me.

King. A letter from the magnificent Armado.

Ber. How low soever the matter, I hope in God for high words.

Long. A high hope for a low heaven. God 195 grant us patience!

Ber. To hear, or forbear hearing?

Long. To hear meekly, sir, and to laugh moderately; or to forbear both.

Ber. Well, sir, be it as the style shall give us 200 cause to climb in the merriness.

Cost. The matter is to me, sir, as concerning Jaquenetta. The manner of it is, I was taken with the manner.

Ber. In what manner? 205

Cost. In manner and form following, sir; all those three: I was seen with her in the manor house, sitting with her upon the form, and taken following her into the park; which, put together, is in manner and form following. Now, sir, for the manner—it is 210 the manner of a man to speak to a woman. For the form—in some form.

Ber. For the following, sir?

Cost. As it shall follow in my correction; and God defend the right! 215

King. Will you hear this letter with attention?

Ber. As we would hear an oracle.

Cost. Such is the simplicity of man to hearken after the flesh.

King. [*Reads*]

142. overshot: defeated
146. so . . . lost: conquered but destroyed in the attempt
151. affects: affections; inclinations
155. at large: in full
157. in . . . of: condemned to
158. Suggestions: temptations
161. quick: lively
162. haunted: frequented
168. compliments: courtly manners
169. mutiny: dispute
170. hight: is named
171. interim: interlude; entertainment
173. the . . . debate: battles throughout the world
176. minstrelsy: amusement

177. wight: fellow
178. fire-new: freshly coined
179. swain: rustic
183. reprehend: represent (comic error)
184. tharborough: thirdborough (petty constable)
187. commends: greets
190. contempts: contents
200. style: (1) manner; (2) stile
203–4. with . . . manner: in the act (of transgression)
208. form: bench

Great deputy, the welkin's vicegerent and sole dominator of Navarre, my soul's earth's god and body's fost'ring patron— 220

Cost. Not a word of Costard yet.
King. [*Reads*]
So it is—

Cost. It may be so; but if he say it is so, he is, in telling true, but so. 225
King. Peace!
Cost. Be to me, and every man that dares not fight!
King. No words! 230
Cost. Of other men's secrets, I beseech you.
King. [*Reads*]
So it is, besieged with sable-colored melancholy, I did commend the black oppressing humor to the most wholesome physic of thy health-giving air; and, as I am a gentleman, betook myself to walk. 235 The time When? About the sixth hour; when beasts most graze, birds best peck, and men sit down to that nourishment which is called supper. So much for the time When. Now for the ground Which? which, I mean, I walked upon; it is ycleped thy park. Then for 240 the place Where? where, I mean, I did encounter that obscene and most prepost'rous event that draweth from my snow-white pen the ebon-colored ink which here thou viewest, beholdest, surveyest, or seest. But to the place Where? It standeth north-north-east and 245 by east from the west corner of thy curious-knotted garden. There did I see that low-spirited swain, that base minnow of thy mirth,

Cost. Me?
King.
that unlettered small-knowing soul, 250

Cost. Me?
King.
that shallow vassal,

Cost. Still me?
King.
which, as I remember, hight Costard,

Cost. O, me! 255
King.
sorted and consorted, contrary to thy established proclaimed edict and continent canon; which, with, O, with—but with this I passion to say wherewith—

Cost. With a wench. 260
King.
with a child of our grandmother Eve, a female; or, for thy more sweet understanding, a woman. Him I, as my ever-esteemed duty pricks me on, have sent to thee, to receive the meed of punishment, by thy sweet Grace's officer, Anthony Dull, a man 265 of good repute, carriage, bearing, and estimation.

Dull. Me, an't shall please you; I am Anthony Dull.
King.
For Jaquenetta—so is the weaker vessel called, which I apprehended with the aforesaid swain— 270 I keep her as a vessel of thy law's fury, and shall, at the least of thy sweet notice, bring her to trial. Thine, in all compliments of devoted and heartburning heat of duty,
DON ADRIANO DE ARMADO.

Ber. This is not so well as I looked for, but 275 the best that ever I heard.
King. Ay, the best for the worst. But, sirrah, what say you to this?
Cost. Sir, I confess the wench.
King. Did you hear the proclamation? 280
Cost. I do confess much of the hearing it, but little of the marking of it.
King. It was proclaimed a year's imprisonment to be taken with a wench.
Cost. I was taken with none, sir; I was 285 taken with a damsel.
King. Well, it was proclaimed damsel.
Cost. This was no damsel neither, sir; she was a virgin.
King. It is so varied too, for it was pro- 290 claimed virgin.
Cost. If it were, I deny her virginity; I was taken with a maid.
King. This "maid" will not serve your turn, sir.
Cost. This maid will serve my turn, sir. 295
King. Sir, I will pronounce your sentence: you shall fast a week with bran and water.
Cost. I had rather pray a month with mutton and porridge.
King. And Don Armado shall be your keeper. 300
My Lord Berowne, see him delivered o'er;
And go we, lords, to put in practice that
Which each to other hath so strongly sworn.
[*Exeunt King, Longaville, and Dumaine.*]
Ber. I'll lay my head to any goodman's hat
These oaths and laws will prove an idle scorn. 305
Sirrah, come on.
Cost. I suffer for the truth, sir; for true it is I was taken with Jaquenetta, and Jaquenetta is a true girl;

220. **welkin's:** heaven's
220–21. **vicegerent:** ruler by divine appointment
221. **dominator:** lord
226. **so:** soso
233. **commend:** offer; **black . . . humor:** oppression of black bile, the humor whose excess caused melancholy
234. **physic:** medicine
240. **ycleped:** called
242. **prepost'rous:** monstrous
246. **curious-knotted garden:** flowerbeds of intricate pattern
256. **sorted:** associated
257. **continent canon:** restraining law
258. **passion:** grieve
264. **meed:** merited portion
269. **vessel:** receptacle; that which is to receive
298. **mutton:** slang for a loose woman
304. **lay:** wager; **goodman's:** yeoman's
308. **true:** honest

and therefore welcome the sour cup of prosperity! Affliction may one day smile again; and till 310 then, sit thee down, sorrow!

Exeunt.

[Scene II. *The same.*]

Enter Armado *and* Moth, *his page.*

Arm. Boy, what sign is it when a man of great spirit grows melancholy?

Moth. A great sign, sir, that he will look sad.

Arm. Why, sadness is one and the selfsame thing, dear imp. 5

Moth. No, no; O Lord, sir, no!

Arm. How canst thou part sadness and melancholy, my tender juvenal?

Moth. By a familiar demonstration of the working, my tough signior. 10

Arm. Why tough signior? Why tough signior?

Moth. Why tender juvenal? Why tender juvenal?

Arm. I spoke it, tender juvenal, as a congruent epitheton appertaining to thy young days, which we may nominate tender. 15

Moth. And I, tough signior, as an appertinent title to your old time, which we may name tough.

Arm. Pretty and apt.

Moth. How mean you, sir? I pretty, and my saying apt? or I apt, and my saying pretty? 20

Arm. Thou pretty, because little.

Moth. Little pretty, because little. Wherefore apt?

Arm. And therefore apt, because quick.

Moth. Speak you this in my praise, master?

Arm. In thy condign praise. 25

Moth. I will praise an eel with the same praise.

Arm. What, that an eel is ingenious?

Moth. That an eel is quick.

Arm. I do say thou art quick in answers; thou heatst my blood. 30

Moth. I am answered, sir.

Arm. I love not to be crossed.

Moth. [*Aside*] He speaks the mere contrary: crosses love not him.

Arm. I have promised to study three years 35 with the Duke.

Moth. You may do it in an hour, sir.

Arm. Impossible.

Moth. How many is one thrice told?

Arm. I am ill at reck'ning; it fitteth the 40 spirit of a tapster.

Moth. You are a gentleman and a gamester, sir.

Arm. I confess both: they are both the varnish of a complete man.

Moth. Then I am sure you know how much 45 the gross sum of deuce-ace amounts to.

Arm. It doth amount to one more than two.

Moth. Which the base vulgar do call three.

Arm. True.

Moth. Why, sir, is this such a piece of study? 50 Now here is three studied ere ye'll thrice wink; and how easy it is to put "years" to the word "three," and study three years in two words, the dancing horse will tell you.

Arm. A most fine figure! 55

Moth. [*Aside*] To prove you a cipher.

Arm. I will hereupon confess I am in love. And as it is base for a soldier to love, so am I in love with a base wench. If drawing my sword against the humor of affection would deliver me from the repro- 60 bate thought of it, I would take Desire prisoner, and ransom him to any French courtier for a new-devised curtsy. I think scorn to sigh; methinks I should outswear Cupid. Comfort me, boy; what great men have been in love? 65

Moth. Hercules, master.

Arm. Most sweet Hercules! More authority, dear boy, name more; and, sweet my child, let them be men of good repute and carriage.

Moth. Samson, master; he was a man of 70 good carriage, great carriage, for he carried the town gates on his back like a porter; and he was in love.

Arm. O well-knit Samson! strong-jointed Samson! I do excel thee in my rapier as much as thou didst me in carrying gates. I am in love too. Who was 75 Samson's love, my dear Moth?

Moth. A woman, master.

Arm. Of what complexion?

Moth. Of all the four, or the three, or the two, or one of the four. 80

Arm. Tell me precisely of what complexion.

Moth. Of the sea-water green, sir.

Arm. Is that one of the four complexions?

Moth. As I have read, sir; and the best of them too. 85

Arm. Green, indeed, is the color of lovers; but to have a love of that color, methinks Samson had small reason for it. He surely affected her for her wit.

8. juvenal: youth
13. congruent: suitable
14. epitheton: epithet
25. condign: deserved
34. crosses: coins stamped with crosses

43. varnish: external complement
48. vulgar: common folk
53–54. dancing horse: a performing horse, trained to indicate sums by tapping his hooves. A man named Banks and his horse Morocco flourished in the 1590's.
55. figure: piece of logic
56. cipher: zero
74. rapier: swordplay
78. complexion: temperament; specifically referring to the humor (blood, phlegm, choler, or black bile) that governed her disposition

Moth. It was so, sir; for she had a green wit.

Arm. My love is most immaculate white and red. 90

Moth. Most maculate thoughts, master, are masked under such colors.

Arm. Define, define, well-educated infant.

Moth. My father's wit and my mother's tongue assist me! 95

Arm. Sweet invocation of a child; most pretty and pathetical!

Moth. If she be made of white and red,
Her faults will ne'er be known; 100
For blushing cheeks by faults are bred,
And fears by pale white shown.
Then if she fear, or be to blame,
By this you shall not know;
For still her cheeks possess the same 105
Which native she doth owe.

A dangerous rhyme, master, against the reason of white and red.

Arm. Is there not a ballad, boy, of the King and the Beggar? 110

Moth. The world was very guilty of such a ballad some three ages since; but I think now 'tis not to be found; or if it were, it would neither serve for the writing nor the tune.

Arm. I will have that subject newly writ 115 o'er, that I may example my digression by some mighty precedent. Boy, I do love that country girl that I took in the park with the rational hind Costard; she deserves well.

Moth. [*Aside*] To be whipped; and yet a 120 better love than my master.

Arm. Sing, boy; my spirit grows heavy in love.

Moth. And that's great marvel, loving a light wench.

Arm. I say, sing. 125

Moth. Forbear till this company be past.

Enter DULL, COSTARD, *and* JAQUENETTA.

Dull. Sir, the Duke's pleasure is that you keep Costard safe; and you must suffer him to take no delight nor no penance, but 'a must fast three days a week. For this damsel, I must keep her at the 130 park; she is allowed for the daywoman. Fare you well.

Arm. I do betray myself with blushing. Maid!

Jaq. Man!

Arm. I will visit thee at the lodge. 135

Jaq. That's hereby.

Arm. I know where it is situate.

Jaq. Lord, how wise you are!

Arm. I will tell thee wonders.

Jaq. With that face? 140

Arm. I love thee.

Jaq. So I heard you say.

Arm. And so, farewell.

Jaq. Fair weather after you!

Dull. Come, Jaquenetta, away. 145

Exeunt [*Dull and Jaquenetta*].

Arm. Villain, thou shalt fast for thy offenses ere thou be pardoned.

Cost. Well, sir, I hope when I do it I shall do it on a full stomach.

Arm. Thou shalt be heavily punished. 150

Cost. I am more bound to you than your fellows, for they are but lightly rewarded.

Arm. Take away this villain; shut him up.

Moth. Come, you transgressing slave, away.

Cost. Let me not be pent up, sir; I will fast, 155 being loose.

Moth. No, sir; that were fast and loose. Thou shalt to prison.

Cost. Well, if ever I do see the merry days of desolation that I have seen, some shall see. 160

Moth. What shall some see?

Cost. Nay, nothing, Master Moth, but what they look upon. It is not for prisoners to be too silent in their words, and therefore I will say nothing. I thank God I have as little patience as another man, 165 and therefore I can be quiet.

Exeunt [*Moth and Costard*].

Arm. I do affect the very ground, which is base, where her shoe, which is baser, guided by her foot, which is basest, doth tread. I shall be forsworn, which is a great argument of falsehood, if I 170 love. And how can that be true love which is falsely attempted? Love is a familiar; Love is a devil; there is no evil angel but Love. Yet was Samson so tempted, and he had an excellent strength; yet was Solomon so seduced, and he had a very good 175 wit. Cupid's butt shaft is too hard for Hercules' club, and therefore too much odds for a Spaniard's rapier. The first and second cause will not serve my turn; the passado he respects not, the duello he regards not; his disgrace is to be called boy, but his 180

89. **green:** lively
92. **maculate:** impure
106. **native . . . owe:** she naturally possesses
109–10. **ballad . . . Beggar:** the song about King Cophetua and the beggarmaid
116. **digression:** deviation
118. **hind:** (1) rustic; (2) stag
123. **light:** wanton
128. **suffer:** allow
129. **penance:** pleasance; **'a:** he
131. **allowed:** acknowledged; **daywoman:** dairymaid
148–49. **on . . . stomach:** with courage
157. **fast . . . loose:** a conjurer's trick with a fake knot
170. **argument:** proof
172. **familiar:** evil spirit
176. **butt shaft:** blunt practice arrow
178. **The . . . cause:** insults serving as pretexts for a challenge
179. **passado:** sword thrust; **duello:** dueling code

glory is to subdue men. Adieu, valor; rust, rapier; be still, drum; for your manager is in love; yea, he loveth. Assist me, some extemporal god of rhyme, for I am sure I shall turn sonnet. Devise, wit; write, pen; for I am for whole volumes in folio. 185

Exit.

ACT II

[Scene I. *The same.*]

Enter the Princess of France, *with three attending ladies,* [(Rosaline, Maria, *and* Katharine), Boyet], *and* [Two Other] Lords.

Boy. Now, madam, summon up your dearest spirits.
Consider who the King your father sends,
To whom he sends, and what's his embassy:
Yourself, held precious in the world's esteem,
To parley with the sole inheritor 5
Of all perfections that a man may owe,
Matchless Navarre; the plea of no less weight
Than Aquitaine, a dowry for a queen.
Be now as prodigal of all dear grace
As Nature was in making graces dear, 10
When she did starve the general world beside
And prodigally gave them all to you.

Prin. Good Lord Boyet, my beauty, though but mean,
Needs not the painted flourish of your praise.
Beauty is bought by judgment of the eye, 15
Not utt'red by base sale of chapmen's tongues;
I am less proud to hear you tell my worth
Than you much willing to be counted wise
In spending your wit in the praise of mine.
But now to task the tasker: good Boyet, 20
You are not ignorant all-telling fame
Doth noise abroad Navarre hath made a vow,
Till painful study shall outwear three years,
No woman may approach his silent court.
Therefore to's seemeth it a needful course, 25
Before we enter his forbidden gates,
To know his pleasure; and in that behalf,
Bold of your worthiness, we single you
As our best-moving fair solicitor.
Tell him the daughter of the King of France, 30
On serious business, craving quick dispatch,
Importunes personal conference with his Grace.
Haste, signify so much, while we attend,
Like humble-visaged suitors, his high will.

Boy. Proud of employment, willingly I go. 35

Prin. All pride is willing pride, and yours is so.

Exit Boyet.

Who are the votaries, my loving lords,
That are vow-fellows with this virtuous duke?

1st Lord. Lord Longaville is one.

Prin. Know you the man?

Mar. I know him, madam; at a marriage feast,
Between Lord Perigort and the beauteous heir 41
Of Jaques Falconbridge, solemnized
In Normandy, saw I this Longaville.
A man of sovereign parts he is esteemed,
Well fitted in arts, glorious in arms; 45
Nothing becomes him ill that he would well.
The only soil of his fair virtue's gloss,
If virtue's gloss will stain with any soil,
Is a sharp wit matched with too blunt a will, 49
Whose edge hath power to cut, whose will still wills
It should none spare that come within his power.

Prin. Some merry mocking lord, belike; is't so?

Mar. They say so most that most his humors know.

Prin. Such short-lived wits do wither as they grow.
Who are the rest? 55

Kath. The young Dumaine, a well-accomplished youth,
Of all that virtue love for virtue loved;
Most power to do most harm, least knowing ill,
For he hath wit to make an ill shape good,

1. dearest spirits: wittiest resources
5. inheritor: possessor
6. owe: own
14. flourish: ornament
16. chapmen's: hucksters'
20. task . . . tasker: set a task for my tasker
21. fame: rumor
25. to's seemeth it: it seems to me
28. Bold: confident
29. best-moving fair: most persuasive
44. sovereign parts: peerless endowments
45. arts: skills
50. still: always

And shape to win grace though he had no wit. 60
I saw him at the Duke Alençon's once,
And much too little of that good I saw
Is my report to his great worthiness.

Ros. Another of these students at that time
Was there with him, if I have heard a truth. 65
Berowne they call him, but a merrier man,
Within the limit of becoming mirth,
I never spent an hour's talk withal.
His eye begets occasion for his wit,
For every object that the one doth catch 70
The other turns to a mirth-moving jest,
Which his fair tongue, conceit's expositor,
Delivers in such apt and gracious words
That aged ears play truant at his tales,
And younger hearings are quite ravished, 75
So sweet and voluble is his discourse.

Prin. God bless my ladies! are they all in love,
That every one her own hath garnished
With such bedecking ornaments of praise? 79

1st Lord. Here comes Boyet.

[*Re-*]*enter* BOYET.

Prin. Now, what admittance, lord?

Boy. Navarre had notice of your fair approach,
And he and his competitors in oath
Were all addressed to meet you, gentle lady,
Before I came. Marry, thus much I have learnt:
He rather means to lodge you in the field, 85
Like one that comes here to besiege his court,
Than seek a dispensation for his oath,
To let you enter his unpeopled house.

Enter KING, LONGAVILLE, DUMAINE, BEROWNE, [*and* ATTENDANTS].

Here comes Navarre.

King. Fair Princess, welcome to the court of 90
Navarre.

Prin. "Fair" I give you back again; and "welcome" I have not yet. The roof of this court is too high to be yours, and welcome to the wide fields too base to be mine. 95

King. You shall be welcome, madam, to my court.

Prin. I will be welcome then; conduct me thither.

King. Hear me, dear lady: I have sworn an oath—

Prin. Our Lady help my lord! He'll be forsworn.

King. Not for the world, fair madam, by my will.

Prin. Why, will shall break it; will, and nothing else. 101

King. Your ladyship is ignorant what it is.

Prin. Were my lord so, his ignorance were wise,
Where now his knowledge must prove ignorance.
I hear your Grace hath sworn out housekeeping.
'Tis deadly sin to keep that oath, my lord, 106
And sin to break it.
But pardon me, I am too sudden-bold;
To teach a teacher ill beseemeth me.
Vouchsafe to read the purpose of my coming, 110
And suddenly resolve me in my suit.
[*Giving a paper.*]

King. Madam, I will, if suddenly I may.

Prin. You will the sooner that I were away,
For you'll prove perjured if you make me stay.

Ber. Did not I dance with you in Brabant once?

Ros. Did not I dance with you in Brabant once?

Ber. I know you did. 117

Ros. How needless was it then to ask the question!

Ber. You must not be so quick.

Ros. 'Tis 'long of you, that spur me with such questions. 120

Ber. Your wit's too hot, it speeds too fast, 'twill tire.

Ros. Not till it leave the rider in the mire.

Ber. What time o' day?

Ros. The hour that fools should ask.

Ber. Now fair befall your mask! 125

Ros. Fair fall the face it covers!

Ber. And send you many lovers!

Ros. Amen, so you be none.

Ber. Nay, then will I be gone.

King. Madam, your father here doth intimate
The payment of a hundred thousand crowns, 131
Being but the one half of an entire sum
Disbursed by my father in his wars.
But say that he or we, as neither have,
Received that sum, yet there remains unpaid 135
A hundred thousand more, in surety of the which,
One part of Aquitaine is bound to us,
Although not valued to the money's worth.
If, then, the King your father will restore
But that one half which is unsatisfied, 140
We will give up our right in Aquitaine,
And hold fair friendship with his Majesty.
But that, it seems, he little purposeth,
For here he doth demand to have repaid
A hundred thousand crowns, and not demands,
On payment of a hundred thousand crowns, 146
To have his title live in Aquitaine;

60. grace: favor
66. Berowne . . . man: pun on "brown" (gloomy)
72. conceit's expositor: imagination's spokesman
82. competitors: partners
83. addressed: prepared
88. unpeopled: servantless

105. sworn . . . housekeeping: forsworn hospitality
109. beseemeth: becomes
111. suddenly: without delay
113. the . . . away: the sooner to get rid of me
116. Ros.: Folio; the Quarto attributes the speech to Katharine.
120. spur: a pun on the word "speer" (to ask questions)
130. intimate: make known
140. unsatisfied: unpaid

Which we much rather had depart withal,
And have the money by our father lent,
Than Aquitaine so gelded as it is. 150
Dear Princess, were not his requests so far
From reason's yielding, your fair self should make
A yielding 'gainst some reason in my breast,
And go well satisfied to France again. 154

Prin. You do the King my father too much wrong,
And wrong the reputation of your name,
In so unseeming to confess receipt
Of that which hath so faithfully been paid.

King. I do protest I never heard of it;
And, if you prove it, I'll repay it back 160
Or yield up Aquitaine.

Prin. We arrest your word.
Boyet, you can produce acquittances
For such a sum from special officers
Of Charles, his father.

King. Satisfy me so. 164

Boy. So please your Grace, the packet is not come,
Where that and other specialties are bound;
Tomorrow you shall have a sight of them.

King. It shall suffice me; at which interview
All liberal reason I will yield unto.
Meantime, receive such welcome at my hand 170
As honor, without breach of honor, may
Make tender of to thy true worthiness.
You may not come, fair Princess, within my gates;
But here without you shall be so received
As you shall deem yourself lodged in my heart,
Though so denied fair harbor in my house. 176
Your own good thoughts excuse me, and farewell.
Tomorrow shall we visit you again.

Prin. Sweet health and fair desires consort your Grace! 179

King. Thy own wish wish I thee in every place.
Exit [*with attendants*].

Ber. Lady, I will commend you to mine own heart.

Ros. Pray you, do my commendations; I would be glad to see it.

Ber. I would you heard it groan.

Ros. Is the fool sick? 185

Ber. Sick at the heart.

Ros. Alack, let it blood.

Ber. Would that do it good?

Ros. My physic says "ay."

Ber. Will you prick't with your eye? 190

Ros. No point, with my knife.

Ber. Now, God save thy life!

Ros. And yours from long living!

Ber. I cannot stay thanksgiving. [*Retiring.*]

Dum. Sir, I pray you, a word: what lady is that same? 195

Boy. The heir of Alençon, Katharine her name.

Dum. A gallant lady! Monsieur, fare you well.
Exit.

Long. I beseech you a word: what is she in the white?

Boy. A woman sometimes, an you saw her in the light.

Long. Perchance light in the light. I desire her name. 200

Boy. She hath but one for herself; to desire that were a shame.

Long. Pray you, sir, whose daughter?

Boy. Her mother's, I have heard.

Long. God's blessing on your beard!

Boy. Good sir, be not offended; 205
She is an heir of Falconbridge.

Long. Nay, my choler is ended.
She is a most sweet lady.

Boy. Not unlike, sir; that may be. *Exit Longaville.*

Ber. What's her name in the cap? 210

Boy. Rosaline, by good hap.

Ber. Is she wedded or no?

Boy. To her will, sir, or so.

Ber. You are welcome, sir; adieu! 214

Boy. Farewell to me, sir, and welcome to you.
Exit Berowne.

Mar. That last is Berowne, the merry madcap lord:
Not a word with him but a jest.

Boy. And every jest but a word.

Prin. It was well done of you to take him at his word. 218

Boy. I was as willing to grapple as he was to board.

Kath. Two hot sheeps, marry!

Boy. And wherefore not ships?
No sheep, sweet lamb, unless we feed on your lips.

Kath. You sheep and I pasture—shall that finish the jest? 222

Boy. So you grant pasture for me.
[*Offering to kiss her.*]

Kath. Not so, gentle beast.
My lips are no common, though several they be.

Boy. Belonging to whom?

Kath. To my fortunes and me.

Prin. Good wits will be jangling; but, gentles, agree: 226

150. **gelded:** mutilated (only part of Aquitaine being at stake)
157. **so . . . to:** thus seeming not to
161. **arrest:** seize upon as a guarantee
162. **acquittances:** receipts
166. **specialties:** particulars; **bound:** contained
172. **Make . . . of:** offer
179. **consort:** accompany
187. **let . . . blood:** bleed it. **It** is the old neuter genitive.
191. **No point:** not at all
194. **stay thanksgiving:** remain to thank you
200. **light . . . light:** unchaste if seen clearly
213. **or so:** or something of that sort
218. **take . . . word:** outdo him in wit
224. **common:** unenclosed land, communally farmed; **several:** private land

This civil war of wits were much better used
On Navarre and his bookmen, for here 'tis abused.
Boy. If my observation, which very seldom lies,
By the heart's still rhetoric disclosed with eyes,
Deceive me not now, Navarre is infected. 231
Prin. With what?
Boy. With that which we lovers entitle "affected."
Prin. Your reason? 234
Boy. Why, all his behaviors did make their retire
To the court of his eye, peeping thorough desire.
His heart, like an agate, with your print impressed,
Proud with his form, in his eye pride expressed;
His tongue, all impatient to speak and not see,
Did stumble with haste in his eyesight to be; 240
All senses to that sense did make their repair,
To feel only looking on fairest of fair.
Methought all his senses were locked in his eye,
As jewels in crystal for some prince to buy,
Who, tend'ring their own worth from where they were glassed, 245
Did point you to buy them, along as you passed.

228. bookmen: scholars
235–36. all . . . eye: i.e., he could do nothing but stare.
236. thorough: through
237. agate: agate stone. Agates engraved like cameos were set in rings.
246. point: direct

His face's own margent did quote such amazes
That all eyes saw his eyes enchanted with gazes.
I'll give you Aquitaine and all that is his, 249
And you give him for my sake but one loving kiss.
Prin. Come, to our pavilion: Boyet is disposed.
Boy. But to speak that in words which his eye hath disclosed;
I only have made a mouth of his eye,
By adding a tongue which I know will not lie.
Mar. Thou art an old lovemonger, and speakst skillfully. 255
Kath. He is Cupid's grandfather and learns news of him.
Ros. Then was Venus like her mother, for her father is but grim.
Boy. Do you hear, my mad wenches?
Mar. No.
Boy. What, then; do you see? 259
Mar. Ay, our way to be gone.
Boy. You are too hard for me.
Exeunt.

247. margent: margin (where explanatory notes of books were printed); forehead
251. disposed: merry

ACT III

[Scene I. *The same.*]

Enter Armado *and* Moth.

Arm. Warble, child; make passionate my sense of hearing.
Moth. Concolinel.
Arm. Sweet air! Go, tenderness of years, take this key, give enlargement to the swain, bring him 5 festinately hither; I must employ him in a letter to my love.
Moth. Master, will you win your love with a French brawl?
Arm. How meanest thou? Brawling in 10 French?
Moth. No, my complete master; but to jig off a tune at the tongue's end, canary to it with your feet, humor it with turning up your eyelids, sigh a note and sing a note, sometime through the throat, 15 as if you swallowed love with singing love, sometime through the nose, as if you snuffed up love by smelling love, with your hat penthouse-like o'er the shop of your eyes, with your arms crossed on your thin-belly doublet like a rabbit on a spit, or your 20 hands in your pocket like a man after the old painting; and keep not too long in one tune, but a snip

3. Concolinel: a trill (?); the name of a song sung at this point (?)
6. festinately: speedily
9. brawl: French *bransle,* a dance, with perhaps a pun on the civil wars in France

13. canary: dance the canaries
18. penthouse-like: i.e., slanted, like a penthouse roof
19. arms crossed: an attitude of melancholy
19–20. thin-belly doublet: i.e., meager midriff, signifying the starved appearance of the pining lover. Doublets were usually stuffed to a shape decreed by contemporary fashion.
22. snip: scrap

and away. These are compliments, these are humors; these betray nice wenches, that would be betrayed without these; and make them men of note 25 (do you note, men?) that most are affected to these.

Arm. How hast thou purchased this experience?

Moth. By my penny of observation.

Arm. But O—but O—

Moth. "The hobbyhorse is forgot." 30

Arm. Callst thou my love "hobbyhorse"?

Moth. No, master; the hobbyhorse is but a colt and your love perhaps a hackney. But have you forgot your love?

Arm. Almost I had. 35

Moth. Negligent student! learn her by heart.

Arm. By heart and in heart, boy.

Moth. And out of heart, master; all those three I will prove.

Arm. What wilt thou prove? 40

Moth. A man, if I live; and this, by, in, and without, upon the instant. By heart you love her, because your heart cannot come by her; in heart you love her, because your heart is in love with her; and out of heart you love her, being out of heart that you 45 cannot enjoy her.

Arm. I am all these three.

Moth. And three times as much more, and yet nothing at all.

Arm. Fetch hither the swain; he must carry 50 me a letter.

Moth. A message well sympathized—a horse to be ambassador for an ass.

Arm. Ha, ha!—what sayest thou?

Moth. Marry, sir, you must send the ass 55 upon the horse, for he is very slow-gaited. But I go.

Arm. The way is but short; away.

Moth. As swift as lead, sir.

Arm. The meaning, pretty ingenious?
Is not lead a metal heavy, dull, and slow? 60

Moth. Minime, honest master; or rather, master, no.

Arm. I say lead is slow.

Moth. You are too swift, sir, to say so:
Is that lead slow which is fired from a gun?

Arm. Sweet smoke of rhetoric! 65
He reputes me a cannon; and the bullet, that's he;
I shoot thee at the swain.

Moth. Thump, then, and I flee. [*Exit.*]

Arm. A most acute juvenal; voluble and free of grace!
By thy favor, sweet welkin, I must sigh in thy face;
Most rude melancholy, valor gives thee place. 71
My herald is returned.

[*Re-*]*enter* MOTH *with* COSTARD.

Moth. A wonder, master! Here's a costard broken in a shin.

Arm. Some enigma, some riddle; come, thy l'envoy; begin.

Cost. No egma, no riddle, no l'envoy; no 75 salve in the mail, sir. O, sir, plantain, a plain plantain; no l'envoy, no l'envoy; no salve, sir, but a plantain!

Arm. By virtue, thou enforcest laughter; thy silly thought, my spleen; the heaving of my lungs 80 provokes me to ridiculous smiling. O, pardon me, my stars! Doth the inconsiderate take salve for l'envoy, and the word "l'envoy" for a salve?

Moth. Do the wise think them other? Is not l'envoy a salve?

Arm. No, page, it is an epilogue or discourse to make plain 85
Some obscure precedence that hath tofore been sain.
I will example it:
The fox, the ape, and the humblebee,
Were still at odds, being but three.
There's the moral: now the l'envoy. 90

Moth. I will add the l'envoy. Say the moral again.

Arm. The fox, the ape, and the humblebee,
Were still at odds, being but three.

Moth. Until the goose came out of door,
And stayed the odds by adding four. 95
Now will I begin your moral, and do you follow with my l'envoy.
The fox, the ape, and the humblebee,
Were still at odds, being but three.

Arm. Until the goose came out of door, 100
Staying the odds by adding four.

Moth. A good l'envoy, ending in the goose; would you desire more?

Cost. The boy hath sold him a bargain, a goose, that's flat.
Sir, your pennyworth is good, an your goose be fat.
To sell a bargain well is as cunning as fast and loose;
Let me see: a fat l'envoy; ay, that's a fat goose.

30. The . . . forgot: a fragment of a song
31. hobbyhorse: loose woman
33. hackney: strumpet
52. well sympathized: appropriately disposed of
61. Minime: by no means
68. Thump: imitative of the noise of the cannon's discharge

71. gives . . . place: gives way to thee
73. costard: slang for "head," from the costard apple
74. l'envoy: concluding stanza which sums up a poem
76. salve: (1) Latin *salve* (salute), suggested by **l'envoy;** (2) ointment; **mail:** wallet; **plantain:** a leaf used to soothe bruises
80. spleen: the organ governing laughter
82. inconsiderate: thoughtless one
86. tofore . . . sain: been heretofore said
88–89. The . . . humblebee: the meaning has never been satisfactorily explained. A topical allusion, possibly to the Martin Marprelate controversy, is almost certain but has not been proved.

Arm. Come hither, come hither. How did this argument begin? 107

Moth. By saying that a costard was broken in a shin.
Then called you for the l'envoy.

Cost. True, and I for a plantain. Thus came your argument in; 110
Then the boy's fat l'envoy, the goose that you bought;
And he ended the market.

Arm. But tell me: how was there a costard broken in a shin?

Moth. I will tell you sensibly. 115

Cost. Thou hast no feeling of it, Moth; I will speak that l'envoy.
I, Costard, running out, that was safely within,
Fell over the threshold and broke my shin.

Arm. We will talk no more of this matter. 120

Cost. Till there be more matter in the shin.

Arm. Sirrah Costard, I will enfranchise thee.

Cost. O, marry me to one Frances! I smell some l'envoy, some goose, in this.

Arm. By my sweet soul, I mean setting thee 125 at liberty, enfreedoming thy person; thou wert immured, restrained, captivated, bound.

Cost. True, true; and now you will be my purgation, and let me loose.

Arm. I give thee thy liberty, set thee from 130 durance; and, in lieu thereof, impose on thee nothing but this: bear this significant [*Giving a letter*] to the country maid Jaquenetta; there is remuneration, for the best ward of mine honor is rewarding my 134 dependents. Moth, follow. [*Exit.*]

Moth. Like the sequel, I. Signior Costard, adieu.
Exit [*Moth*].

Cost. My sweet ounce of man's flesh, my incony Jew! Now will I look to his remuneration. Remuneration! O, that's the Latin word for three farthings. Three farthings—remuneration. "What's the 140 price of this inkle?"—"One penny."—"No, I'll give you a remuneration." Why, it carries it. Remuneration! Why, it is a fairer name than French crown. I will never buy and sell out of this word.

Enter BEROWNE.

Ber. My good knave Costard, exceedingly 145 well met!

Cost. Pray you, sir, how much carnation ribbon may a man buy for a remuneration?

Ber. What is a remuneration?

Cost. Marry, sir, halfpenny farthing. 150

Ber. Why, then, three-farthing worth of silk.

Cost. I thank your worship. God be wi' you!

Ber. Stay, slave, I must employ thee.
As thou wilt win my favor, good my knave,
Do one thing for me that I shall entreat. 155

Cost. When would you have it done, sir?

Ber. This afternoon.

Cost. Well, I will do it, sir; fare you well.

Ber. Thou knowest not what it is.

Cost. I shall know, sir, when I have done it. 160

Ber. Why, villain, thou must know first.

Cost. I will come to your worship tomorrow morning.

Ber. It must be done this afternoon.
Hark, slave, it is but this: 165
The Princess comes to hunt here in the park,
And in her train there is a gentle lady;
When tongues speak sweetly, then they name her name,
And Rosaline they call her. Ask for her,
And to her white hand see thou do commend 170
This sealed-up counsel. There's thy guerdon; go.

Cost. Gardon, O sweet gardon! better than remuneration; a 'leven-pence farthing better; most sweet gardon! I will do it, sir, in print. Gardon—remuneration! *Exit.*

Ber. And I, forsooth, in love! I, that have been love's whip! 176
A very beadle to a humorous sigh;
A critic, nay, a night-watch constable;
A domineering pedant o'er the boy,
Than whom no mortal so magnificent! 180
This wimpled, whining, purblind, wayward boy,
This Signior junior, giant-dwarf, Dan Cupid;
Regent of love rhymes, lord of folded arms,
The anointed sovereign of sighs and groans,
Liege of all loiterers and malcontents, 185
Dread prince of plackets, king of codpieces,
Sole imperator, and great general

112. he . . . market: cf. the proverb "Three women and a goose make a market."
124. goose: prostitute
132. significant: token
134. ward: defense
137. incony: a slang word of imprecise meaning and unknown derivation: rare, fine, remarkable, delicate, etc.
138. Jew: a complimentary epithet (perhaps also a playful shortening of "juvenal")
139. farthings: coins worth a quarter of a penny
141. inkle: tape
150. halfpenny farthing: a halfpenny and a farthing (three farthings)
171. guerdon: reward
173. a 'leven-pence farthing: eleven and a quarter pennies; Berowne's guerdon was apparently a shilling.
174. in print: to the letter
177. beadle: scourge. The **beadle** was an official who apprehended criminals and saw to their whipping. **humorous:** melancholy
180. magnificent: vainglorious
181. wimpled: scarfed (wearing a cloth over the eyes); **purblind:** totally blind
182. Signior junior: lordly youth; **Dan:** a corruption of Latin *dominus* ("master, sir")
183. folded arms: see **arms crossed,** III.i.19.
186. plackets: petticoats; women

Of trotting paritors. O my little heart!
And I to be a corporal of his field,
And wear his colors like a tumbler's hoop! 190
What! I love, I sue, I seek a wife—
A woman, that is like a German clock,
Still a-repairing, ever out of frame,
And never going aright, being a watch,
But being watched that it may still go right! 195
Nay, to be perjured, which is worst of all;
And, among three, to love the worst of all,
A whitely wanton with a velvet brow,
With two pitch balls stuck in her face for eyes;
Ay, and, by heaven, one that will do the deed, 200
Though Argus were her eunuch and her guard.
And I to sigh for her! to watch for her!
To pray for her! Go to; it is a plague
That Cupid will impose for my neglect
Of his almighty dreadful little might. 205
Well, I will love, write, sigh, pray, sue, and groan:
Some men must love my lady, and some Joan.
[*Exit.*]

188. paritors: servers of summonses for the ecclesiastical authority, often for sexual offenses
190. wear . . . hoop: flaunt tokens of my allegiance to him
198. whitely: pale
201. Argus: Juno set Argus, who had a hundred eyes, as a guard to prevent Jove's access to Io.
207. Some . . . Joan: proverbial: Joan is as good as my lady in the dark.

ACT IV

[Scene I. *The same.*]

Enter the PRINCESS, *her ladies* [(ROSALINE, MARIA, KATHARINE,) BOYET], LORDS, *and a* FORESTER.

Prin. Was that the King that spurred his horse so hard
Against the steep-up rising of the hill?
Boy. I know not; but I think it was not he.
Prin. Whoe'er 'a was, 'a showed a mounting mind.
Well, lords, today we shall have our dispatch; 5
On Saturday we will return to France.
Then, forester, my friend, where is the bush
That we must stand and play the murderer in?
For. Hereby, upon the edge of yonder coppice;
A stand where you may make the fairest shoot. 10
Prin. I thank my beauty I am fair that shoot,
And thereupon thou speakest the fairest shoot.
For. Pardon me, madam, for I meant not so.
Prin. What, what? first praise me, and again say no?
O short-lived pride! Not fair? Alack for woe! 15
For. Yes, madam, fair.
Prin. Nay, never paint me now;
Where fair is not, praise cannot mend the brow.
Here, good my glass, take this for telling true:
[*Giving him money.*]
Fair payment for foul words is more than due. 19
For. Nothing but fair is that which you inherit.
Prin. See, see, my beauty will be saved by merit.
O heresy in fair, fit for these days!
A giving hand, though foul, shall have fair praise.
But come, the bow. Now mercy goes to kill,
And shooting well is then accounted ill; 25
Thus will I save my credit in the shoot:
Not wounding, pity would not let me do't;
If wounding, then it was to show my skill,
That more for praise than purpose meant to kill.
And, out of question, so it is sometimes: 30
Glory grows guilty of detested crimes,
When, for fame's sake, for praise, an outward part
We bend to that the working of the heart;
As I for praise alone now seek to spill 34
The poor deer's blood that my heart means no ill.
Boy. Do not curst wives hold that self-sovereignty
Only for praise sake, when they strive to be
Lords o'er their lords?
Prin. Only for praise; and praise we may afford
To any lady that subdues a lord. 40

Enter COSTARD.

16. never . . . now: i.e., it's too late to flatter me.
18. good . . . glass: my faithful mirror
21. by merit: for the sake of reward, with a pun on the Catholic doctrine of salvation through good works; Protestants insisted that salvation came through divine grace.
22. heresy . . . days: an allusion to Henry of Navarre's conversion to Catholicism, July 25, 1593
23. foul: ugly
30. out . . . question: doubtless
36. curst: shrewish

Boy. Here comes a member of the commonwealth.
Cost. God dig-you-den all! Pray you, which is the head lady?
Prin. Thou shalt know her, fellow, by the rest that have no heads. 45
Cost. Which is the greatest lady, the highest?
Prin. The thickest and the tallest.
Cost. The thickest and the tallest! It is so; truth is truth.
An your waist, mistress, were as slender as my wit,
One o' these maids' girdles for your waist should be fit. 50
Are not you the chief woman? You are the thickest here.
Prin. What's your will, sir? What's your will?
Cost. I have a letter from Monsieur Berowne to one Lady Rosaline.
Prin. O, thy letter, thy letter! He's a good friend of mine.
Stand aside, good bearer. Boyet, you can carve. 55
Break up this capon.
Boy. I am bound to serve.
This letter is mistook; it importeth none here.
It is writ to Jaquenetta.
Prin. We will read it, I swear.
Break the neck of the wax, and every one give ear.
Boy. [*Reads*]

By heaven, that thou art fair is most infallible; true 60 that thou art beauteous; truth itself that thou art lovely. More fairer than fair, beautiful than beauteous, truer than truth itself, have commiseration on thy heroical vassal. The magnanimous and most illustrate King Cophetua set eye upon the pernicious and indubitate 65 beggar Zenelophon; and he it was that might rightly say, *Veni, vidi, vici;* which to annothanize in the vulgar—O base and obscure vulgar!—videlicet, He came, saw, and overcame. He came, one; saw, two; overcame, three. Who came?—the king. Why did he come?—to see. 70 Why did he see?—to overcome. To whom came he?—to the beggar. What saw he?—the beggar. Who overcame he?—the beggar. The conclusion is victory. On whose side?—the king's. The captive is enriched. On whose side?—the beggar's. The catastrophe is a nuptial. 75 On whose side?—the king's. No, on both in one, or one in both. I am the king, for so stands the comparison; thou the beggar, for so witnesseth thy lowliness. Shall I command thy love? I may. Shall I enforce thy love? I could. Shall I entreat thy love? I will. What shalt 80 thou exchange for rags?—robes; for tittles?—titles; for thyself?—me. Thus expecting thy reply, I profane my lips on thy foot, my eyes on thy picture, and my heart on thy every part.
Thine in the dearest design of industry, 85
DON ADRIANO DE ARMADO.

Thus dost thou hear the Nemean lion roar
'Gainst thee, thou lamb, that standest as his prey;
Submissive fall his princely feet before,
And he from forage will incline to play. 90
But if thou strive, poor soul, what are thou then?
Food for his rage, repasture for his den.

Prin. What plume of feathers is he that indited this letter?
What vane? What weathercock? Did you ever hear better? 94
Boy. I am much deceived but I remember the style.
Prin. Else your memory is bad, going o'er it erewhile. 96
Boy. This Armado is a Spaniard, that keeps here in court;
A phantasime, a Monarcho, and one that makes sport
To the Prince and his bookmates.
Prin. Thou fellow, a word.
Who gave thee this letter?
Cost. I told you: my lord. 100
Prin. To whom shouldst thou give it?
Cost. From my lord to my lady.
Prin. From which lord to which lady?
Cost. From my Lord Berowne, a good master of mine,
To a lady of France that he called Rosaline.
Prin. Thou hast mistaken his letter. Come, lords, away. 105
[*To Rosaline*] Here, sweet, put up this; 'twill be thine another day. *Exeunt* [*Princess and Train*].
Boy. Who is the suitor? who is the suitor?
Ros. Shall I teach you to know?
Boy. Ay, my continent of beauty.
Ros. Why, she that bears the bow.
Finely put off!
Boy. My lady goes to kill horns; but, if thou marry, 110
Hang me by the neck if horns that year miscarry.
Finely put on!
Ros. Well then, I am the shooter.
Boy. And who is your deer?
Ros. If we choose by the horns, yourself come not near.
Finely put on indeed! 115
Mar. You will wrangle with her, Boyet, and she strikes at the brow.
Boy. But she herself is hit lower. Have I hit her now?

42. God dig-you-den: God give you a good even.
55. can carve: punning meaning: "know how to please"
56. capon: love letter, from French *poulet*
64. magnanimous: noble-spirited; **illustrate:** illustrious
65. indubitate: undoubted
67. annothanize: annotate; **vulgar:** vulgar tongue; English
68. videlicet: that is to say
75. catastrophe: upshot
81. tittles: minute marks in printing; trifles
85. industry: gallantry
87. Nemean lion: a ferocious beast killed by Hercules as one of his labors
95. I . . . but: unless I am much deceived
96. going . . . it: another pun on style/stile
98. phantasime: fantastic person; **Monarcho:** a well-known eccentric who frequented Queen Elizabeth's court
107. suitor: prononounced "shooter"
108. continent: container
111. horns: proverbial signs of the cuckold (betrayed husband)
113. shooter . . . deer: suitor . . . dear
116. strikes . . . brow: has deadly aim

Ros. Shall I come upon thee with an old saying, that was a man when King Pepin of France was a little boy, as touching the hit it? 120

Boy. So I may answer thee with one as old, that was a woman when Queen Guinever of Britain was a little wench, as touching the hit it.

Ros. [*Singing*]
Thou canst not hit it, hit it, hit it,
Thou canst not hit it, my good man. 125

Boy. An I cannot, cannot, cannot,
An I cannot, another can.
[*Exeunt Rosaline and Katharine.*]

Cost. By my troth, most pleasant! How both did fit it!

Mar. A mark marvelous well shot; for they both did hit it.

Boy. A mark! O, mark but that mark! A mark, says my lady! 130
Let the mark have a prick in't, to mete at, if it may be.

Mar. Wide o' the bow hand! I' faith, your hand is out.

Cost. Indeed, 'a must shoot nearer, or he'll ne'er hit the clout.

Boy. An if my hand be out, then belike your hand is in.

Cost. Then will she get the upshoot by cleaving the pin. 135

Mar. Come, come, you talk greasily; your lips grow foul.

Cost. She's too hard for you at pricks, sir; challenge her to bowl.

Boy. I fear too much rubbing. Good night, my good owl. [*Exeunt Boyet and Maria.*]

Cost. By my soul, a swain, a most simple clown!
Lord, Lord! how the ladies and I have put him down!
O' my troth, most sweet jests, most incony vulgar wit! 141
When it comes so smoothly off, so obscenely, as it were, so fit.
Armado a the one side—O, most dainty man!
To see him walk before a lady and to bear her fan!
To see him kiss his hand, and how most sweetly 'a will swear! 145
And his page a tother side, that handful of wit!
Ah, heavens, it is a most pathetical nit!
Sola, sola! *A shout within.*
Exit Costard.

118. come upon: attack
120. the hit it: a tune sung while dancing
131. prick: central spot; **mete:** aim
132. Wide . . . hand: a wild shot
133. clout: central peg fastening the target to an upright
135. upshoot: best shot; **pin:** clout
138. too . . . rubbing: too many obstacles. A rub is something that interferes with the straight course of the bowl.
142. obscenely: an apt malapropism for "seemly"
148. Sola: a hunting call

[Scene II. *The same.*]

Enter HOLOFERNES, *the pedant,* [SIR] NATHANIEL, *and* DULL.

Nath. Very reverent sport, truly; and done in the testimony of a good conscience.

Hol. The deer was, as you know, *sanguis,* in blood; ripe as the pomewater who now hangeth like a jewel in the ear of *caelo,* the sky, the welkin, the 5 heaven, and anon falleth like a crab on the face of *terra,* the soil, the land, the earth.

Nath. Truly, Master Holofernes, the epithets are sweetly varied, like a scholar at the least; but, sir, I assure ye it was a buck of the first head. 10

Hol. Sir Nathaniel, *haud credo.*

Dull. 'Twas not a haud credo; 'twas a pricket.

Hol. Most barbarous intimation! yet a kind of insinuation, as it were, *in via,* in way, of explication; *facere,* as it were, replication, or rather, *ostentare,* to show, as it were, his inclination, after his undressed, unpolished, uneducated, unpruned, untrained, or rather unlettered, or ratherest unconfirmed fashion, to insert again my *haud credo* for a deer. 20

Dull. I said the deer was not a haud credo; 'twas a pricket.

Hol. Twice-sod simplicity, *bis coctus!*
O thou monster Ignorance, how deformed dost thou look!

Nath. Sir, he hath never fed of the dainties that are bred in a book; 25
He hath not eat paper, as it were; he hath not drunk ink; his intellect is not replenished; he is only an animal, only sensible in the duller parts;
And such barren plants are set before us that we thankful should be—
Which we of taste and feeling are—for those parts that do fructify in us more than he. 30
For as it would ill become me to be vain, indiscreet, or a fool,
So were there a patch set on learning to see him in a school.

3. in blood: in prime condition
4. pomewater: a kind of apple
6. crab: crab apple
10. of . . . head: five years old
11. Sir: a title of honor, equivalent to *dominus,* with which clergymen were addressed as holders of the degree of bachelor of arts; **haud credo:** I do not think so. Dull understands him to say "an old grey doe."
12. pricket: buck of the second year
19. insert . . . deer: repeat that my words **haud credo** mean deer
23. Twice-sod simplicity: twice-repeated stupidity; cf. the proverb "Cabbage twice sodden (stewed) is death." **bis coctus:** twice cooked
32. a . . . learning: a fool assigned the task of learning

But, *omne bene,* say I, being of an old father's mind:
Many can brook the weather that love not the wind.
Dull. You two are bookmen: can you tell me by your wit 35
What was a month old at Cain's birth that's not five weeks old as yet?
Hol. Dictynna, goodman Dull; Dictynna, goodman Dull.
Dull. What is Dictynna?
Nath. A title to Phœbe, to Luna, to the moon.
Hol. The moon was a month old when Adam was no more, 41
And raught not to five weeks when he came to five-score.
The allusion holds in the exchange.
Dull. 'Tis true, indeed; the collusion holds in the exchange. 45
Hol. God comfort thy capacity! I say the allusion holds in the exchange.
Dull. And I say the pollusion holds in the exchange; for the moon is never but a month old; and I say, beside, that 'twas a pricket that the Prin- 50 cess killed.
Hol. Sir Nathaniel, will you hear an extemporal epitaph on the death of the deer? And, to humor the ignorant, call the deer the Princess killed a pricket.
Nath. Perge, good Master Hologernes, *perge,* 55 so it shall please you to abrogate scurrility.
Hol. I will something affect the letter, for it argues facility.
The preyful Princess pierced and pricked a pretty pleasing pricket.
Some say a sore; but not a sore till now made sore with shooting.
The dogs did yell; put el to sore, then sorel jumps from thicket; 60
Or pricket sore, or else sorel; the people fall a-hooting.
If sore be sore, then L to sore makes fifty sores o' sorel.
Of one sore I an hundred make by adding but one more L.
Nath. A rare talent!
Dull. [*Aside*] If a talent be a claw, look how 65 he claws him with a talent.
Hol. This is a gift that I have, simple, simple; a foolish extravagant spirit, full of forms, figures, shapes, objects, ideas, apprehensions, motions, revolutions. These are begot in the ventricle of 70 memory, nourished in the womb of pia mater, and delivered upon the mellowing of occasion. But the gift is good in those in whom it is acute, and I am thankful for it.
Nath. Sir, I praise the Lord for you, and so 75 may my parishioners; for their sons are well tutored by you, and their daughters profit very greatly under you. You are a good member of the commonwealth.
Hol. Mehercle! if their sons be ingenious, they shall want no instruction; if their daughters be 80 capable, I will put it to them; but, *vir sapit qui pauca loquitur.* A soul feminine saluteth us.

Enter JAQUENETTA *and* COSTARD.

Jaq. God give you good morrow, Master Person.
Hol. Master Person, *quasi* pers-one. And if one should be pierced, which is the one? 85
Cost. Marry, Master Schoolmaster, he that is likest to a hogshead.
Hol. Piercing a hogshead! A good luster of conceit in a turf of earth; fire enough for a flint, pearl enough for a swine; 'tis pretty; it is well. 90
Jaq. Good Master Person, be so good as read me this letter; it was given me by Costard, and sent me from Don Armado. I beseech you, read it.
Hol. Fauste, precor gelida quando pecus omne sub umbra ruminat—and so forth. Ah, good old 95 Mantuan! I may speak of thee as the traveler doth of Venice:
Venetia, Venetia,
Chi non ti vede, non ti pretia.
Old Mantuan! old Mantuan! Who under- 100 standeth thee not, loves thee not—Ut, re, sol, la, mi, fa. Under pardon, sir, what are the contents? or, rather, as Horace says in his— What, my soul, verses?
Nath. Ay, sir, and very learned.
Hol. Let me hear a staff, a stanze, a verse; 105 *lege, domine.*

Nath. [*Reads*]
If love make me forsworn, how shall I swear to love?
Ah, never faith could hold, if not to beauty vowed!
Though to myself forsworn, to thee I'll faithful prove;

33. omne bene: all's well
42. raught: reached
43. The . . . exchange: the simile is just as apt with Cain substituted for Adam.
55. Perge: proceed
56. abrogate scurrility: omit improper language
57. something . . . letter: incline somewhat to alliteration
59. sore: four-year-old deer
60. sorel: young buck
62. L: the Roman numeral for 50
65. talent: variant of "talon"
66. claws: flatters
79. Mehercle: by Hercules
81–82. vir . . . loquitur: the wise man speaks few words.
83. Person: variant of "Parson"
84. quasi: as it were
85. pierced: pronounced "persed"
88. Piercing . . . hogshead: tapping a keg; **hogshead** was also slang for "blockhead"; **good . . . conceit:** brilliant metaphor
94–95. Fauste . . . ruminat: the first line of the first eclogue of Baptista Spagnuoli Mantuanus, known as Mantuan. His *Eclogues* were used as a school textbook.
98–99. Venetia . . . pretia: Venice, Venice, whoso seeth thee not, values thee not.
101–2. Ut . . . fa: notes of the old scale. "Do" was later substituted for **ut.**

Those thoughts to me were oaks, to thee like osiers bowed. 110
Study his bias leaves, and makes his book thine eyes,
Where all those pleasures live that art would comprehend.
If knowledge be the mark, to know thee shall suffice;
Well learned is that tongue that well can thee commend; 114
All ignorant that soul that sees thee without wonder;
Which is to me some praise that I thy parts admire.
Thy eye Jove's lightning bears, thy voice his dreadful thunder,
Which, not to anger bent, is music and sweet fire.
Celestial as thou art, O, pardon love this wrong, 119
That sings heaven's praise with such an earthly tongue.

Hol. You find not the apostrophus, and so miss the accent. Let me supervise the canzonet. Here are only numbers ratified; but, for the elegancy, facility, and golden cadence of poesy, *caret.* Ovidius Naso was the man. And why, indeed, "Naso" but 125 for smelling out the odoriferous flowers of fancy, the jerks of invention? *Imitari* is nothing: so doth the hound his master, the ape his keeper, the tired horse his rider. But, damosella virgin, was this directed to you? 130

Jaq. Ay, sir, from one Monsieur Berowne, one of the strange queen's lords.

Hol. I will overglance the superscript:

To the snow-white hand of the most beauteous Lady Rosaline. 135

I will look again on the intellect of the letter, for the nomination of the party writing to the person written unto:

Your Ladyship's in all desired employment, Berowne.

Sir Nathaniel, this Berowne is one of the votaries with the King; and here he hath framed a letter 140 to a sequent of the stranger queen's which accidentally, or by the way of progression, hath miscarried. Trip and go, my sweet; deliver this paper into the royal hand of the King; it may concern much. 145 Stay not thy compliment; I forgive thy duty. Adieu.

Jaq. Good Costard, go with me. Sir, God save your life!

Cost. Have with thee, my girl.

Exeunt [Costard and Jaquenetta].

Nath. Sir, you have done this in the fear of 150 God, very religiously; and, as a certain father saith—

Hol. Sir, tell not me of the father; I do fear colorable colors. But to return to the verses: did they please you, Sir Nathaniel?

Nath. Marvelous well for the pen. 155

Hol. I do dine today at the father's of a certain pupil of mine; where, if, before repast, it shall please you to gratify the table with a grace, I will, on my privilege I have with the parents of the foresaid child or pupil, undertake your *ben venuto;* where I 160 will prove those verses to be very unlearned, neither savoring of poetry, wit, nor invention. I beseech your society.

Nath. And thank you too; for society, saith the text, is the happiness of life. 165

Hol. And certes, the text most infallibly concludes it. [*To Dull*] Sir, I do invite you too; you shall not say me nay: *pauca verba.* Away; the gentles are at their game, and we will to our recreation.

Exeunt.

[Scene III. *The same.*]

Enter Berowne, *with a paper in his hand, alone.*

Ber. The King he is hunting the deer: I am coursing myself. They have pitched a toil: I am toiling in a pitch—pitch that defiles. Defile! a foul word! Well, "set thee down, sorrow!" for so they say the fool said, and so say I, and I am the fool. Well proved, 5 wit. By the Lord, this love is as mad as Ajax: it kills sheep; it kills me—I a sheep. Well proved again o' my side! I will not love; if I do, hang me. I' faith, I will not! O, but her eye! By this light, but for her eye, I would not love her—yes, for her two 10 eyes. Well, I do nothing in the world but lie, and lie in my throat. By heaven, I do love; and it hath taught me to rhyme, and to be melancholy; and here is part of my rhyme, and here my melancholy. Well, she hath one o' my sonnets already. The clown 15 bore it, the fool sent it, and the lady hath it: sweet clown, sweeter fool, sweetest lady! By the world, I would not care a pin if the other three were in. Here

110. osiers: willows
111. Study . . . leaves: the student leaves his normal pursuit
115. wonder: admiration
121. apostrophus: mark of elision; i.e., Nathaniel has read "vowéd" and "bowéd."
122. supervise: look over; **canzonet:** verse
123. numbers ratified: verses of regular meter
124. caret: it is wanting
127. jerks . . . invention: clever sallies; **Imitari:** to imitate
133. superscript: superscription; address
136. intellect: intelligence; contents
142. sequent: follower
146. Stay . . . duty: don't delay to make your manners; I will excuse you from curtsying.
149. Have . . . thee: let's go
152–53. colorable colors: convincing falsehoods
155. Marvelous . . . pen: i.e., the handwriting is excellent.
160. ben venuto: welcome
168. pauca verba: few words; let's say no more.
1–2. coursing: chasing
2. pitched . . . toil: laid a trap
6. Ajax: when the arms of Achilles were awarded to Ulysses, Ajax went mad and slaughtered a herd of sheep in the belief that they were his enemies.

comes one with a paper; God give him grace to groan! *He stands aside.*

Enter the KING [*with a paper*].

King. Ay me! 21

Ber. Shot, by heaven! Proceed, sweet Cupid; thou hast thumped him with thy birdbolt under the left pap. In faith, secrets!

King. [*Reads*]

So sweet a kiss the golden sun gives not 25
To those fresh morning drops upon the rose,
As thy eyebeams, when their fresh rays have smote
The night of dew that on my cheeks down flows;
Nor shines the silver moon one half so bright
Through the transparent bosom of the deep, 30
As doth thy face through tears of mine give light.
Thou shinest in every tear that I do weep;
No drop but as a coach doth carry thee;
So ridest thou triumphing in my woe.
Do but behold the tears that swell in me, 35
And they thy glory through my grief will show.
But do not love thyself; then thou wilt keep
My tears for glasses, and still make me weep.
O queen of queens! how far dost thou excel
No thought can think nor tongue of mortal tell. 40

How shall she know my griefs? I'll drop the paper—
Sweet leaves, shade folly. Who is he comes here?
Steps aside.

Enter LONGAVILLE [*with a paper*].

What, Longaville, and reading! Listen, ear.

Ber. Now, in thy likeness, one more fool appear!

Long. Ay me, I am forsworn! 45

Ber. Why, he comes in like a perjure, wearing papers.

King. In love, I hope; sweet fellowship in shame!

Ber. One drunkard loves another of the name. 49

Long. Am I the first that have been perjured so?

Ber. I could put thee in comfort: not by two that I know;
Thou makest the triumviry, the cornercap of society,
The shape of Love's Tyburn that hangs up simplicity.

Long. I fear these stubborn lines lack power to move.
O sweet Maria, empress of my love! 55
These numbers will I tear, and write in prose.

Ber. O, rhymes are guards on wanton Cupid's hose:
Disfigure not his slop.

Long. This same shall go.
He reads the sonnet.

Did not the heavenly rhetoric of thine eye,
'Gainst whom the world cannot hold argument,
Persuade my heart to this false perjury? 61
Vows for thee broke deserve not punishment.
A woman I forswore, but I will prove,
Thou being a goddess, I forswore not thee:
My vow was earthly, thou a heavenly love; 65
Thy grace being gained cures all disgrace in me.
Vows are but breath, and breath a vapor is;
Then thou, fair sun, which on my earth dost shine,
Exhalest this vapor-vow; in thee it is.
If broken then, it is no fault of mine; 70
If by me broke, what fool is not so wise
To lose an oath to win a paradise?

Ber. This is the liver-vein, which makes flesh a deity,
A green goose a goddess—pure, pure idolatry.
God amend us, God amend! we are much out o' the way! 75

Enter DUMAINE, [*with a paper*].

Long. By whom shall I send this?—Company! Stay! [*Steps aside.*]

Ber. "All hid, all hid"—an old infant play.
Like a demigod here sit I in the sky,
And wretched fools' secrets heedfully o'ereye. 79
More sacks to the mill! O heavens, I have my wish!
Dumaine transformed! Four woodcocks in a dish!

Dum. O most divine Kate!

Ber. O most profane coxcomb!

Dum. By heaven, the wonder in a mortal eye! 84

Ber. By earth, she is not, corporal: there you lie.

Dum. Her amber hair for foul hath amber quoted.

Ber. An amber-colored raven was well noted.

Dum. As upright as the cedar.

Ber. Stoop, I say;
Her shoulder is with child.

Dum. As fair as day. 89

Ber. Ay, as some days; but then no sun must shine.

Dum. O that I had my wish!

Long. And I had mine!

King. And I mine too, good Lord!

Ber. Amen, so I had mine! Is not that a good word?

Dum. I would forget her; but a fever she
Reigns in my blood, and will rememb'red be. 95

Ber. A fever in your blood? Why, then, incision
Would let her out in saucers. Sweet misprision!

Dum. Once more I'll read the ode that I have writ.

23. birdbolt: a blunt missile used to kill birds
52. cornercap: three-cornered cap of the scholar; biretta
53. Tyburn: the gallows at Tyburn was triangular in shape.
56. numbers: verses
57. guards: ornamental braid; **hose:** breeches and stockings
58. slop: full breeches

73. liver-vein: true vein of passion, which was supposed to originate in the liver
81. woodcocks: fools
85. she . . . corporal: Berowne denies that Katharine is a wonder in comparison with his Rosaline. The military title is appropriate for the champion of a lady.
86. Her . . . quoted: her hair puts to shame the color of amber.
87. was . . . noted: would be well worth noting
93. Is . . . word: is not that fair of me?
97. Sweet misprision: amiable mistake!

Ber. Once more I'll mark how love can vary wit.
Dum. *Reads his sonnet.*

On a day—alack the day!— 100
Love, whose month is ever May,
Spied a blossom passing fair
Playing in the wanton air.
Through the velvet leaves the wind,
All unseen, can passage find; 105
That the lover, sick to death,
Wished himself the heaven's breath.
"Air," quoth he, "thy cheeks may blow;
Air, would I might triumph so!
But, alack, my hand is sworn 110
Ne'er to pluck thee from thy thorn;
Vow, alack, for youth unmeet,
Youth so apt to pluck a sweet.
Do not call it sin in me
That I am forsworn for thee; 115
Thou for whom Jove would swear
Juno but an Ethiope were;
And deny himself for Jove,
Turning mortal for thy love."

This will I send; and something else more plain
That shall express my true love's fasting pain. 121
O, would the King, Berowne, and Longaville,
Were lovers too! Ill, to example ill,
Would from my forehead wipe a perjured note;
For none offend where all alike do dote. 125
Long. [*Advancing*] Dumaine, thy love is far from charity,
That in love's grief desir'st society;
You may look pale, but I should blush, I know,
To be o'erheard and taken napping so.
King. [*Advancing*] Come, sir, you blush; as his, your case is such. 130
You chide at him, offending twice as much:
You do not love Maria! Longaville
Did never sonnet for her sake compile;
Nor never lay his wreathed arms athwart
His loving bosom to keep down his heart. 135
I have been closely shrouded in this bush,
And marked you both, and for you both did blush.
I heard your guilty rhymes, observed your fashion,
Saw sighs reek from you, noted well your passion.
"Ay me!" says one. "O Jove!" the other cries. 140
One, her hairs were gold; crystal the other's eyes.
[*To Longaville*] You would for paradise break faith and troth;
[*To Dumaine*] And Jove for your love would infringe an oath.
What will Berowne say when that he shall hear
Faith infringed which such zeal did swear? 145
How will he scorn, how will he spend his wit!
How will he triumph, leap, and laugh at it!
For all the wealth that ever I did see,
I would not have him know so much by me.
Ber. [*Advancing*] Now step I forth to whip hypocrisy. 150
Ah, good my liege, I pray thee pardon me.
Good heart, what grace hast thou thus to reprove
These worms for loving, that art most in love?
Your eyes do make no coaches; in your tears
There is no certain princess that appears; 155
You'll not be perjured; 'tis a hateful thing;
Tush, none but minstrels like of sonneting.
But are you not ashamed? Nay, are you not,
All three of you, to be thus much o'ershot? 159
You found his mote; the King your mote did see;
But I a beam do find in each of three.
O, what a scene of fool'ry have I seen,
Of sighs, of groans, of sorrow, and of teen!
O me, with what strict patience have I sat.
To see a king transformed to a gnat! 165
To see great Hercules whipping a gig,
And profound Solomon to tune a jig,
And Nestor play at pushpin with the boys,
And critic Timon laugh at idle toys! 169
Where lies thy grief, O, tell me, good Dumaine?
And, gentle Longaville, where lies thy pain?
And where my liege's? All about the breast.
A caudle, ho!
King. Too bitter is thy jest.
Are we betrayed thus to thy overview?
Ber. Not you by me, but I betrayed to you. 175
I that am honest, I that hold it sin
To break the vow I am engaged in;
I am betrayed by keeping company
With moon-like men, men of inconstancy. 179
When shall you see me write a thing in rhyme?
Or groan for Joan? or spend a minute's time
In pruning me? When shall you hear that I
Will praise a hand, a foot, a face, an eye,
A gait, a state, a brow, a breast, a waist,
A leg, a limb—
King. Soft! whither away so fast? 185
A true man or a thief that gallops so?
Ber. I post from love; good lover, let me go.

Enter JAQUENETTA *and* COSTARD.

Jaq. God bless the King!
King. What present has thou there?
Cost. Some certain treason.
King. What makes treason here? 189

102. passing: exceedingly
118. deny . . . Jove: renounce his godhead
149. by: about
163. teen: grief
166. gig: top
168. Nestor: the wise Greek statesman; **pushpin:** a child's game
173. caudle: soothing drink for invalids
179. moon-like men: George Steevens' suggestion. The Quarto and Folio read "men like men."
182. pruning: preening
184. state: stately bearing
187. post: ride posthaste
188. present: presentment; notification

Cost. Nay, it makes nothing, sir.
King. If it mar nothing neither,
The treason and you go in peace away together.
Jaq. I beseech your Grace, let this letter be read;
Our person misdoubts it: 'twas treason, he said.
King. Berowne, read it over.
He [Berowne] reads the letter.
Where hadst thou it? 195
Jaq. Of Costard.
King. Where hadst thou it?
Cost. Of Dun Adramadio, Dun Adramadio.
[*Berowne tears the letter.*]
King. How now! What is in you? Why dost thou tear it?
Ber. A toy, my liege, a toy! Your Grace needs not fear it. 200
Long. It did move him to passion, and therefore let's hear it.
Dum. It is Berowne's writing, and here is his name.
[*Gathering up the pieces.*]
Ber. [*To Costard*] Ah, you whoreson loggerhead, you were born to do me shame.
Guilty, my lord, guilty! I confess, I confess.
King. What? 205
Ber. That you three fools lacked me fool to make up the mess.
He, he, and you—and you, my liege!—and I
Are pickpurses in love, and we deserve to die.
O, dismiss this audience, and I shall tell you more.
Dum. Now the number is even.
Ber. True, true, we are four.
Will these turtles be gone?
King. Hence, sirs, away. 211
Cost. Walk aside the true folk, and let the traitors stay. [*Exeunt Costard and Jaquenetta.*]
Ber. Sweet lords, sweet lovers, O, let us embrace!
As true we are as flesh and blood can be. 214
The sea will ebb and flow, heaven show his face;
Young blood doth not obey an old decree.
We cannot cross the cause why we were born,
Therefore of all hands must we be forsworn.
King. What, did these rent lines show some love of thine?
Ber. "Did they?" quoth you. Who sees the heavenly Rosaline 220
That, like a rude and savage man of Inde
At the first op'ning of the gorgeous east,
Bows not his vassal head and, strucken blind,
Kisses the base ground with obedient breast?
What peremptory eagle-sighted eye 225
Dares look upon the heaven of her brow
That is not blinded by her majesty?
King. What zeal, what fury hath inspired thee now?
My love, her mistress, is a gracious moon;
She, an attending star, scarce seen a light. 230
Ber. My eyes are then no eyes, nor I Berowne.
O, but for my love, day would turn to night!
Of all complexions the culled sovereignty
Do meet, as at a fair, in her fair cheek,
Where several worthies make one dignity, 235
Where nothing wants that want itself doth seek.
Lend me the flourish of all gentle tongues—
Fie, painted rhetoric! O, she needs it not!
To things of sale a seller's praise belongs: 239
She passes praise; then praise too short doth blot.
A withered hermit, fivescore winters worn,
Might shake off fifty, looking in her eye.
Beauty doth varnish age, as if newborn,
And gives the crutch the cradle's infancy.
O, 'tis the sun that maketh all things shine! 245
King. By heaven, thy love is black as ebony.
Ber. Is ebony like her? O, wood divine!
A wife of such wood were felicity.
O, who can give an oath? Where is a book?
That I may swear beauty doth beauty lack, 250
If that she learn not of her eye to look.
No face is fair that is not full so black.
King. O paradox! Black is the badge of hell,
The hue of dungeons, and the school of night;
And beauty's crest becomes the heavens well. 255
Ber. Devils soonest tempt, resembling spirits of light.
O, if in black my lady's brows be decked,
It mourns that painting and usurping hair
Should ravish doters with a false aspect;
And therefore is she born to make black fair. 260
Her favor turns the fashion of the days;
For native blood is counted painting now;
And therefore red that would avoid dispraise
Paints itself black, to imitate her brow. 264
Dum. To look like her are chimney sweepers black.
Long. And since her time are colliers counted bright.
King. And Ethiopes of their sweet complexion crack.
Dum. Dark needs no candles now, for dark is light.
Ber. Your mistresses dare never come in rain

193. misdoubts: suspects
200. toy: trifle
203. whoreson: good-for-nothing; **loggerhead:** blockhead
206. mess: quartet. Large banquets were broken up into "messes" of four persons each.
211. turtles: turtledoves
218. of . . . hands: on every count
219. rent: torn
233. culled sovereignty: carefully chosen queen
235. worthies: excellences; **dignity:** eminence
237. flourish: gift for florid description; **gentle:** cultivated
255. beauty's . . . well: i.e., the sign of beauty should betoken heaven, and since black is the **badge of hell,** beauty must be its opposite.
258–59. It . . . aspect: i.e., her face is dark with dismay that artificial beauty should be admired.
261. favor: face
266. colliers: coalmen
267. crack: brag

For fear their colors should be washed away. 270
King. 'Twere good yours did; for, sir, to tell you plain,
I'll find a fairer face not washed today.
Ber. I'll prove her fair, or talk till doomsday here.
King. No devil will fright thee then so much as she. 274
Dum. I never knew man hold vile stuff so dear.
Long. Look, here's thy love: my foot and her face see. [*Showing his shoe.*]
Ber. O, if the streets were paved with thine eyes,
Her feet were much too dainty for such tread!
Dun. O vile! Then, as she goes, what upward lies
The street should see as she walked overhead. 280
King. But what of this? Are we not all in love?
Ber. Nothing so sure; and thereby all forsworn.
King. Then leave this chat; and, good Berowne, now prove
Our loving lawful, and our faith not torn. 284
Dum. Ay, marry, there; some flattery for this evil.
Long. O, some authority how to proceed;
Some tricks, some quillets, how to cheat the devil!
Dum. Some salve for perjury.
Ber. 'Tis more than need.
Have at you, then, affection's men-at-arms! 290
Consider what you first did swear unto:
To fast, to study, and to see no woman—
Flat treason 'gainst the kingly state of youth.
Say, can you fast? Your stomachs are too young,
And abstinence engenders maladies. 295

And where that you have vowed to study, lords,
In that each of you have forsworn his book,
Can you still dream, and pore, and thereon look?
For when would you, my lord, or you, or you,
Have found the ground of study's excellence 300
Without the beauty of a woman's face?
From women's eyes this doctrine I derive:
They are the ground, the books, the academes,
From whence doth spring the true Promethean fire.
Why, universal plodding poisons up 305
The nimble spirits in the arteries,
As motion and long-during action tires
The sinewy vigor of the traveler.
Now, for not looking on a woman's face,
You have in that forsworn the use of eyes, 310
And study too, the causer of your vow;
For where is any author in the world
Teaches such beauty as a woman's eye?
Learning is but an adjunct to ourself,
And where we are our learning likewise is; 315
Then, when ourselves we see in ladies' eyes,
Do we not likewise see our learning there?

O, we have made a vow to study, lords,
And in that vow we have forsworn our books.
For when would you, my liege, or you, or you, 320
In leaden contemplation have found out
Such fiery numbers as the prompting eyes
Of beauty's tutors have enriched you with?
Other slow arts entirely keep the brain;
And therefore, finding barren practicers, 325
Scarce show a harvest of their heavy toil;
But love, first learned in a lady's eyes,
Lives not alone immured in the brain,
But with the motion of all elements
Courses as swift as thought in every power, 330
And gives to every power a double power,
Above their functions and their offices.
It adds a precious seeing to the eye:
A lover's eyes will gaze an eagle blind.
A lover's ear will hear the lowest sound, 335
When the suspicious head of theft is stopped.
Love's feeling is more soft and sensible
Than are the tender horns of cockled snails.
Love's tongue proves dainty Bacchus gross in taste.
For valor, is not Love a Hercules, 340
Still climbing trees in the Hesperides?
Subtle as Sphinx; as sweet and musical
As bright Apollo's lute, strung with his hair.
And when Love speaks, the voice of all the gods
Make heaven drowsy with the harmony. 345
Never durst poet touch a pen to write
Until his ink were temp'red with Love's sighs;
O, then his lines would ravish savage ears,
And plant in tyrants mild humility.
From women's eyes this doctrine I derive: 350
They sparkle still the right Promethean fire;
They are the books, the arts, the academes,
That show, contain, and nourish all the world,
Else none at all in aught proves excellent. 354
Then fools you were these women to forswear;
Or, keeping what is sworn, you will prove fools.
For wisdom's sake, a word that all men love;
Or for Love's sake, a word that loves all men;
Or for men's sake, the authors of these women;
Or women's sake, by whom we men are men— 360
Let us once lose our oaths to find ourselves,
Or else we lose ourselves to keep our oaths.
It is religion to be thus forsworn;
For charity itself fulfills the law,
And who can sever love from charity? 365
King. St. Cupid, then! and, soldiers, to the field!
Ber. Advance your standards, and upon them, lords!

287. quillets: clever dodges
296–317. And . . . there: this passage parallels a portion of lines 318–65 and was probably meant to be deleted.
304. Promethean fire: creative inspiration
322. fiery numbers: passionate verses
324. keep: stay within
336. When . . . stopped: i.e., which the ear of the wary thief cannot hear
364. charity . . . law: Rom. 13:8 and 10
367. Advance: raise; **standards:** flags

Pell-mell, down with them! But be first advised,
In conflict, that you get the sun of them. 369
Long. Now to plain dealing; lay these glozes by.
Shall we resolve to woo these girls of France?
King. And win them too; therefore let us devise
Some entertainment for them in their tents.
Ber. First, from the park let us conduct them thither;
Then homeward every man attach the hand 375
Of his fair mistress. In the afternoon
We will with some strange pastime solace them,
Such as the shortness of the time can shape;
For revels, dances, masks, and merry hours 379
Forerun fair Love, strewing her way with flowers.
King. Away, away! No time shall be omitted
That will betime, and may by us be fitted.
Ber. Allons! allons! Sowed cockle reaped no corn,
And justice always whirls in equal measure. 384
Light wenches may prove plagues to men forsworn;
If so, our copper buys no better treasure.
Exeunt.

368. **be . . . advised:** take care
369. **get . . . sun:** secure the advantage
370. **glozes:** flowery metaphors
375. **attach:** seize
381. **time:** opportunity
382. **betime:** chance
383. **cockle:** weed

ACT V

[Scene I. *The same.*]

Enter HOLOFERNES, SIR NATHANIEL, *and* DULL.

Hol. Satis quod sufficit.
Nath. I praise God for you, sir. Your reasons at dinner have been sharp and sententious; pleasant without scurrility, witty without affection, audacious without impudency, learned without opinion, 5 and strange without heresy. I did converse this quondam day with a companion of the King's who is intituled, nominated, or called, Don Adriano de Armado.
Hol. Novi hominem tanquam et. His humor is lofty, his discourse peremptory, his tongue 10 filed, his eye ambitious, his gait majestical and his general behavior vain, ridiculous, and thrasonical. He is too picked, too spruce, too affected, too odd, as it were, too peregrinate, as I may call it.
Nath. A most singular and choice epithet. 15
Draws out his table book.
Hol. He draweth out the thread of his verbosity finer than the staple of his argument. I abhor such fanatical phantasimes, such insociable and point-device companions; such rackers of orthography, as to speak "dout" fine, when he should say 20 "doubt"; "det" when he should pronounce "debt"—d, e, b, t, not d, e, t. He clepeth a calf "cauf," half "hauf"; neighbor *vocatur* "nebor"; neigh abbreviated "ne." This is abhominable—which he would call "abbominable." It insinuateth me of insanie: 25 *ne intelligis, domine?* to make frantic, lunatic.
Nath. Laus Deo, bene intelligo.
Hol. Bon, bon, fort bon! Priscian a little scratched; 'twill serve.

Enter ARMADO, MOTH, *and* COSTARD.

Nath. Videsne quis venit? 30
Hol. Video, et gaudeo.
Arm. [*To Moth*] Chirrah!

1. **Satis . . . sufficit:** enough is as good as a feast.
2. **reasons:** conversation
3. **sententious:** wise and meaningful (from Latin *sententiae*); **pleasant:** facetious
4. **scurrility:** indecency; **affection:** affectation; **audacious:** confident
5. **opinion:** self-conceit
6–7. **this . . . day:** yesterday
9. **Novi . . . te:** I know the man as well as I know you.
11. **filed:** polished
12. **thrasonical:** boastful; from the braggart Thraso in Terence's *Eunuchus*
13. **picked:** finical; **spruce:** dapper
14. **peregrinate:** foreign-fashioned; outlandish
18. **fanatical:** extravagant; **insociable:** incompatible
18–19. **point-device:** precise
22. **clepeth:** calls
23. **vocatur:** is called
24. **abhominable:** Holofernes subscribes to the contemporary error that "abominable" derives from *ab homine* instead of *ab omine*.
25. **It . . . insanie:** it seems madness to me.
26. **ne . . . domine:** do you understand, sir?
27. **Laus . . . intelligo:** praise God, I understand well.
28. **Bon . . . bon:** the Cambridge editors, Clark and Wright, suggested this for the garbled "Bome boon for boon" in the early texts. **Priscian:** Latin grammarian used in the schools
30. **Videsne . . . venit:** do you see who comes?
31. **Video . . . gaudeo:** I see and rejoice.

Hol. Quare "chirrah," not "sirrah"?

Arm. Men of peace, well encount'red.

Hol. Most military sir, salutation. 35

Moth. [*Aside to Costard*] They have been at a great feast of languages and stol'n the scraps.

Cost. O, they have lived long on the alms basket of words. I marvel thy master hath not eaten thee for a word, for thou art not so long by the head 40 as honorificabilitudinitatibus; thou art easier swallowed than a flapdragon.

Moth. Peace! the peal begins.

Arm. [*To Holofernes*] Monsieur, are you not lettered? 45

Moth. Yes, yes; he teaches boys the hornbook. What is a, b, spelt backward with the horn on his head?

Hol. Ba, *pueritia,* with a horn added.

Moth. Ba, most silly sheep with a horn. You 50 hear his learning.

Hol. Quis, quis, thou consonant?

Moth. The third of the five vowels, if you repeat them; or the fifth, if I.

Hol. I will repeat them: a, e, I— 55

Moth. The sheep; the other two concludes it: o, U.

Arm. Now, by the salt wave of the Mediterraneum, a sweet touch, a quick venue of wit!—snip, snap, quick and home. It rejoiceth my intellect. True 60 wit!

Moth. Offered by a child to an old man; which is wit-old.

Hol. What is the figure? What is the figure?

Moth. Horns! 65

Hol. Thou disputes like an infant; go whip thy gig.

Moth. Lend me your horn to make one, and I will whip about your infamy *circum circa*—a gig of a cuckold's horn.

Cost. An I had but one penny in the world, 70 thou shouldst have it to buy gingerbread. Hold, there is the very remuneration I had of thy master, thou halfpenny purse of wit, thou pigeon egg of discretion. O, an the heavens were so pleased that thou wert but my bastard, what a joyful father 75 wouldst thou make me! Go to; thou hast it *ad dunghill,* at the fingers' ends, as they say.

Hol. O, I smell false Latin: *dunghill* for *unguem.*

Arm. Artsman, preambulate; we will be singled from the barbarous. Do you not educate youth 80 at the charge house on the top of the mountain?

Hol. Or *mons,* the hill.

Arm. At your sweet pleasure, for the mountain.

Hol. I do, sans question.

Arm. Sir, it is the King's most sweet pleasure 85 and affection to congratulate the Princess at her pavilion in the posteriors of this day, which the rude multitude call the afternoon.

Hol. The posterior of the day, most generous sir, is liable, congruent, and measurable for the after- 90 noon. The word is well culled, chose; sweet, and apt, I do assure you, sir, I do assure.

Arm. Sir, the King is a noble gentleman, and my familiar, I do assure ye, very good friend. For what is inward between us, let it pass. I do beseech 95 thee, remember thy courtesy. I beseech thee, apparel thy head. And among other importunate and most serious designs, and of great import indeed, too—but let that pass; for I must tell thee it will please his Grace, by the world! sometime to lean upon 100 my poor shoulder, and with his royal finger thus dally with my excrement, with my mustachio; but, sweet heart, let that pass. By the world, I recount no fable: some certain special honors it pleaseth his greatness to impart to Armado, a soldier, a man 105 of travel, that hath seen the world; but let that pass. The very all of all is—but, sweet heart, I do implore secrecy—that the King would have me present the Princess, sweet chuck, with some delightful ostentation, or show, or pageant, or antic, or firework. 110 Now, understanding that the curate and your sweet self are good at such eruptions and sudden breaking-out of mirth, as it were, I have acquainted you withal, to the end to crave your assistance.

Hol. Sir, you shall present before her the 115 Nine Worthies. Sir Nathaniel, as concerning some entertainment of time, some show in the posterior of this day, to be rend'red by our assistance, the King's command, and this most gallant, illustrate, and

33. Quare: why?
41. honorificabilitudinitatibus (often considered to be the longest word known): honorableness, from medieval Latin *honorificabilitudo*
42. flapdragon: tidbit floated in burning brandy to be gulped as a stunt at a party game
46. hornbook: paddle-shaped board containing the alphabet, used in petty schools. A piece of horn protected the printed letters.
49. pueritia: child
52. Quis: what; **consonant:** letter that cannot be sounded without an adjacent vowel
59. venue: sally
63. wit-old: (1) half-wit; (2) cuckold
64. figure: metaphor
68. circum circa: round and about; Theobald's correction of *unum cita* in the early texts
78. unguem: i.e., *ad unguem,* "to the nail"
79. Artsman: master of arts; **preambulate:** precede us
81. the . . . mountain: possibly an allusion to a satirical passage in Erasmus' *Colloquies;* see R. David's edition of *Love's Labor's Lost* in the Arden series (London, 1951).
86. affection: inclination; **congratulate:** salute
90. liable: suitable
96. remember . . . courtesy: i.e., put on your hat (which he had removed as a courtesy).
97. importunate: pressing
102. excrement: hair; beard
110. antic: drollery
116. Nine Worthies: Hector, Alexander, Julius Cæsar, Joshua, David, Judas Maccabæus, Arthur, Charlemagne, and Guy of Warwick or Godfrey of Bouillon: three pagans, three Hebrews, and three Christian heroes

learned gentleman before the Princess—I say 120
none so fit as to present the Nine Worthies.

Nath. Where will you find men worthy enough to present them?

Hol. Joshua, yourself; myself; this gallant gentleman, Judas Maccabæus; this swain, because 125
of his great limb or joint, shall pass Pompey the Great; the page, Hercules.

Arm. Pardon, sir; error: he is not quantity enough for that Worthy's thumb; he is not so big as the end of his club. 130

Hol. Shall I have audience? He shall present Hercules in minority: his enter and exit shall be strangling a snake; and I will have an apology for that purpose.

Moth. An excellent device! So, if any of the 135
audience hiss, you may cry, "Well done, Hercules; now thou crushest the snake!" That is the way to make an offense gracious, though few have the grace to do it.

Arm. For the rest of the Worthies? 140

Hol. I will play three myself.

Moth. Thrice-worthy gentleman!

Arm. Shall I tell you a thing?

Hol. We attend.

Arm. We will have, if this fadge not, an an- 145
tic. I beseech you, follow.

Hol. Via, goodman Dull! Thou has spoken no word all this while.

Dull. Nor understood none neither, sir.

Hol. Allons! we will employ thee. 150

Dull. I'll make one in a dance, or so, or I will play
On the tabor to the Worthies, and let them dance the hay.

Hol. Most dull, honest Dull! To our sport, away!
Exeunt.

[Scene II. *The same.*]

Enter the PRINCESS, MARIA, KATHARINE, *and* ROSALINE.

Prin. Sweet hearts, we shall be rich ere we depart,
If fairings come thus plentifully in.
A lady walled about with diamonds!
Look you what I have from the loving King. 4

Ros. Madam, came nothing else along with that?

Prin. Nothing but this! Yes, as much love in rhyme
As would be crammed up in a sheet of paper
Writ o' both sides the leaf, margent and all,
That he was fain to seal on Cupid's name. 9

Ros. That was the way to make his godhead wax;
For he hath been five thousand year a boy.

Kath. Ay, and a shrewd unhappy gallows too.

Ros. You'll ne'er be friends with him: 'a killed your sister.

Kath. He made her melancholy, sad, and heavy;
And so she died. Had she been light, like you, 15
Of such a merry, nimble, stirring spirit,
She might 'a been a grandam ere she died.
And so may you; for a light heart lives long.

Ros. What's your dark meaning, mouse, of this light word?

Kath. A light condition in a beauty dark. 20

Ros. We need more light to find your meaning out.

Kath. You'll mar the light by taking it in snuff;
Therefore I'll darkly end the argument.

Ros. Look what you do, you do it still i' the dark.

Kath. So do not you; for you are a light wench.

Ros. Indeed, I weigh not you; and therefore light.

Kath. You weigh me not? O, that's you care not for me. 27

Ros. Great reason; for "past cure is still past care."

Prin. Well bandied both; a set of wit well played.
But, Rosaline, you have a favor too? 30
Who sent it? and what is it?

Ros. I would you knew.
An if my face were but as fair as yours,
My favor were as great: be witness this.
Nay, I have verses too, I thank Berowne;
The numbers true, and, were the numbering too,
I were the fairest goddess on the ground. 36
I am compared to twenty thousand fairs.
O, he hath drawn my picture in his letter!

Prin. Anything like?

Ros. Much in the letters; nothing in the praise.

Prin. Beauteous as ink—a good conclusion. 41

Kath. Fair as a text B in a copybook.

Ros. Ware pencils, ho! Let me not die your debtor,
My red dominical, my golden letter.
O that your face were not so full of oes! 45

131. **Shall . . . audience:** may I be heard?
133. **strangling . . . snake:** as the infant Hercules strangled the snakes which Juno had placed in his cradle
145. **fadge:** succeed
147. **Via:** come along
152. **tabor:** a small drum; **hay:** a country dance
2. **fairings:** gifts
10. **wax:** grow, with a pun
12. **shrewd:** malicious; **unhappy:** unlucky; **gallows:** rogue
15. **light:** (1) gay; (2) unchaste
22. **taking . . . snuff:** (1) snuffing out the light; (2) resenting her words
26. **weigh:** esteem
30. **favor:** token
33. **favor:** appearance
35. **numbering:** accounting
37. **fairs:** beauties
40. **Much . . . praise:** well penned but inaccurate
43. **Ware pencils:** beware of the painter's brush; implying that she touches up her complexion
44. **red dominical:** the initial letter "D" for Sunday (*dies dominica*), usually illuminated in gold in almanacs, etc.
45. **oes:** rounds; pockmarks

Prin. A pox of that jest! and I beshrew all shrows!
But, Katharine, what was sent to you from fair Dumaine?
Kath. Madam, this glove.
Prin. Did he not send you twain?
Kath. Yes, madam; and moreover,
Some thousand verses of a faithful lover; 50
A huge translation of hypocrisy,
Vilely compiled, profound simplicity.
Mar. This, and these pearls to me sent Longaville;
The letter is too long by half a mile. 54
Prin. I think no less. Dost thou not wish in heart
The chain were longer and the letter short?
Mar. Ay, or I would these hands might never part.
Prin. We are wise girls to mock our lovers so.
Ros. They are worse fools to purchase mocking so.
That same Berowne I'll torture ere I go. 60
O that I knew he were but in by the week!
How I would make him fawn, and beg, and seek,
And wait the season, and observe the times,
And spend his prodigal wits in bootless rhymes,
And shape his service wholly to my hests, 65
And make him proud to make me proud that jests!
So pair-taunt-like would I o'ersway his state
That he should be my fool, and I his fate.
Prin. None are so surely caught, when they are catched,
As wit turned fool; folly, in wisdom hatched, 70
Hath wisdom's warrant and the help of school,
And wit's own grace to grace a learned fool.
Ros. The blood of youth burns not with such excess
As gravity's revolt to wantonness.
Mar. Folly in fools bears not so strong a note 75
As fool'ry in the wise when wit doth dote,
Since all the power thereof it doth apply
To prove, by wit, worth in simplicity.

Enter BOYET.

Prin. Here comes Boyet, and mirth is in his face.
Boy. O, I am stabbed with laughter! Where's her Grace? 80
Prin. Thy news, Boyet?
Boy. Prepare, madam, prepare!
Arm, wenches, arm! Encounters mounted are
Against your peace. Love doth approach disguised,
Armed in arguments; you'll be surprised.
Muster your wits; stand in your own defense; 85
Or hide your heads like cowards and fly hence.
Prin. St. Denis to St. Cupid! What are they
That charge their breath against us? Say, scout, say.
Boy. Under the cool shade of a sycamore
I thought to close mine eyes some half an hour;
When, lo! to interrupt my purposed rest, 91
Toward that shade I might behold addressed
The King and his companions; warily
I stole into a neighbor thicket by,
And overheard what you shall overhear: 95
That, by-and-by, disguised they will be here.
Their herald is a pretty knavish page,
That well by heart hath conned his embassage.
Action and accent did they teach him there:
"Thus must thou speak and thus thy body bear,"
And ever and anon they made a doubt 101
Presence majestical would put him out;
"For," quoth the King, "an angel shalt thou see;
Yet fear not thou, but speak audaciously."
The boy replied, "An angel is not evil; 105
I should have feared her had she been a devil."
With that all laughed, and clapped him on the shoulder,
Making the bold wag by their praises bolder.
One rubbed his elbow, thus, and fleered, and swore
A better speech was never spoke before. 110
Another with his finger and his thumb
Cried, "Via! we will do't, come what will come."
The third he capered, and cried, "All goes well."
The fourth turned on the toe, and down he fell.
With that they all did tumble on the ground, 115
With such a zealous laughter, so profound,
That in this spleen ridiculous appears,
To check their folly, passion's solemn tears.
Prin. But what, but what, come they to visit us?
Boy. They do, they do, and are appareled thus,
Like Muscovites or Russians, as I guess. 121
Their purpose is to parley, court, and dance;
And every one his love feat will advance
Unto his several mistress; which they'll know
By favors several which they did bestow. 125
Prin. And will they so? The gallants shall be tasked,
For, ladies, we will every one be masked,
And not a man of them shall have the grace,
Despite of suit, to see a lady's face.
Hold, Rosaline, this favor thou shalt wear, 130

46. I . . . shrows: plague take all shrews!
61. in . . . week: irrevocably captured
64. bootless: unavailing
65. hests: commands
66. make him proud: dress finely
67. pair-taunt: a combination of cards that beats all other hands in the card game "Post and Pair"
70–72. folly . . . fool: the folly of an intelligent man will be superior because of his very advantages of intelligence, schooling, and wit.
74. wantonness: frivolity
75. note: stigma
84. surprised: captured
87. St. Denis: the patron saint of France
88. charge . . . breath: prepare to assault us with words
92. addressed: directed
102. put . . . out: cause him to forget his lines
109. fleered: grinned
111. with . . . thumb: snapping his fingers
118. passion's: grief's
126. tasked: hard put to it
128. grace: favor; privilege

And then the King will court thee for his dear;
Hold, take thou this, my sweet, and give me thine,
So shall Berowne take me for Rosaline.
And change you favors too; so shall your loves
Woo contrary, deceived by these removes. 135
Ros. Come on, then, wear the favors most in sight.
Kath. But, in this changing, what is your intent?
Prin. The effect of my intent is to cross theirs.
They do it but in mocking merriment,
And mock for mock is only my intent. 140
Their several counsels they unbosom shall
To loves mistook, and so be mocked withal
Upon the next occasion that we meet,
With visages displayed, to talk and greet. 144
Ros. But shall we dance, if they desire us to't?
Prin. No, to the death, we will not move a foot,
Nor to their penned speech render we no grace;
But while 'tis spoke each turn away her face.
Boy. Why, that contempt will kill the speaker's heart,
And quite divorce his memory from his part. 150
Prin. Therefore I do it; and I make no doubt
The rest will ne'er come in, if he be out.
There's no such sport as sport by sport o'erthrown,
To make theirs ours, and ours none but our own;
So shall we stay, mocking intended game, 155
And they well mocked depart away with shame.
Sound trumpet [*within*].
Boy. The trumpet sounds; be masked; the maskers come. [*The Ladies mask.*]

Enter BLACKAMOORS *with music,* MOTH *with a speech, and* THE REST OF THE LORDS, *disguised* [*as Russians*].

Moth. All hail, the richest beauties on the earth!"
Boy. Beauties no richer than rich taffeta.
Moth. "A holy parcel of the fairest dames 160
The Ladies turn their backs to him.
That ever turned their—backs—to mortal views!"
Ber. "Their eyes," villain, "their eyes."
Moth. "That ever turned their eyes to mortal views!
Out—"
Boy. True; "out" indeed. 165
Moth. "Out of your favors, heavenly spirits, vouchsafe
Not to behold—"
Ber. "Once to behold," rogue.
Moth. "Once to behold with your sun-beamed eyes
—with your sun-beamed eyes—" 170
Boy. They will not answer to that epithet;
You were best call it "daughter-beamed eyes."
Moth. They do not mark me, and that brings me out.
Ber. Is this your perfectness? Be gone, you rogue.
[*Exit Moth.*]
Ros. What would these strangers? Know their minds, Boyet. 175
If they do speak our language, 'tis our will
That some plain man recount their purposes.
Know what they would.
Boy. What would you with the Princess? 179
Ber. Nothing but peace and gentle visitation.
Ros. What would they, say they?
Boy. Nothing but peace and gentle visitation.
Ros. Why, that they have; and bid them so be gone.
Boy. She says you have it, and you may be gone.
King. Say to her we have measured many miles
To tread a measure with her on this grass. 186
Boy. They say that they have measured many a mile
To tread a measure with you on this grass.
Ros. It is not so. Ask them how many inches
Is in one mile? If they have measured many, 190
The measure, then, of one is easily told.
Boy. If to come hither you have measured miles,
And many miles, the Princess bids you tell
How many inches doth fill up one mile.
Ber. Tell her we measure them by weary steps.
Boy. She hears herself.
Ros. How many weary steps 196
Of many weary miles you have o'ergone
Are numb'red in the travail of one mile?
Ber. We number nothing that we spend for you;
Our duty is so rich, so infinite, 200
That we may do it still without account.
Vouchsafe to show the sunshine of your face,
That we, like savages, may worship it.
Ros. My face is but a moon, and clouded too.
King. Blessed are clouds, to do as such clouds do.
Vouchsafe, bright moon, and these thy stars, to shine, 206
Those clouds removed, upon our watery eyne.
Ros. O vain petitioner! beg a greater matter;
Thou now requests but moonshine in the water.
King. Then in our measure do but vouchsafe one change. 210
Thou bidst me beg; this begging is not strange.
Ros. Play music then. Nay, you must do it soon.
Not yet? No dance! Thus change I like the moon.
King. Will you not dance? How come you thus estranged?

159. rich taffeta: the material of their masks, all that is visible of their beauty

204. but . . . too: Rosaline hints that she is not the Princess but a lesser luminary; she is not "fair" but brunette; and her face is masked.
205. do . . . do: i.e., kiss her face
207. eyne: eyes
210. change: dance round

Ros. You took the moon at full, but now she's changed. 215
King. Yet still she is the moon, and I the man.
The music plays; vouchsafe some motion to it.
Ros. Our ears vouchsafe it.
King. But your legs should do it.
Ros. Since you are strangers, and come here by chance, 220
We'll not be nice; take hands. We will not dance.
King. Why take we hands then?
Ros. Only to part friends.
Curtsy, sweet hearts; and so the measure ends.
King. More measure of this measure; be not nice.
Ros. We can afford no more at such a price. 225
King. Price you yourselves. What buys your company?
Ros. Your absence only.
King. That can never be.
Ros. Then cannot we be bought; and so adieu—
Twice to your visor and half once to you! 229
King. If you deny to dance, let's hold more chat.
Ros. In private then.
King. I am best pleased with that.
[*They converse apart.*]
Ber. White-handed mistress, one sweet word with thee.
Prin. Honey, and milk, and sugar; there is three.
Ber. Nay, then, two treys, an if you grow so nice,
Metheglin, wort, and malmsey; well run dice! 235
There's half a dozen sweets.
Prin. Seventh sweet, adieu!
Since you can cog, I'll play no more with you.
Ber. One word in secret.
Prin. Let it not be sweet.
Ber. Thou grievest my gall.
Prin. Gall! bitter.
Ber. Therefore meet.
[*They converse apart.*]
Dum. Will you vouchsafe with me to change a word? 240
Mar. Name it.
Dum. Fair lady—
Mar. Say you so? Fair lord—
Take that for your fair lady.
Dum. Please it you,
As much in private, and I'll bid adieu.
[*They converse apart.*]
Kath. What, was your vizard made without a tongue? 244
Long. I know the reason, lady, why you ask.
Kath. O for your reason! Quickly, sir; I long.
Long. You have a double tongue within your mask,
And would afford my speechless vizard half.
Kath. "Veal," quoth the Dutchman. Is not "veal" a calf?
Long. A calf, fair lady!
Kath. No, a fair lord calf. 250
Long. Let's part the word.
Kath. No, I'll not be your half.
Take all and wean it; it may prove an ox.
Long. Look how you butt yourself in these sharp mocks!
Will you give horns, chaste lady? Do not so. 254
Kath. Then die a calf, before your horns do grow.
Long. One word in private with you ere I die.
Kath. Bleat softly, then; the butcher hears you cry. [*They converse apart.*]
Boy. The tongues of mocking wenches are as keen
As is the razor's edge invisible,
Cutting a smaller hair than may be seen, 260
Above the sense of sense; so sensible
Seemeth their conference; their conceits have wings,
Fleeter than arrows, bullets, wind, thought, swifter things.
Ros. Not one word more, my maids; break off, break off. 264
Ber. By heaven, all dry-beaten with pure scoff!
King. Farewell, mad wenches; you have simple wits. *Exeunt* [*King, Lords, and Blackamoors*].
Prin. Twenty adieus, my frozen muscovites.
Are these the breed of wits so wondered at?
Boy. Tapers they are, with your sweet breaths puffed out.
Ros. Well-liking wits they have; gross, gross; fat, fat. 270
Prin. O poverty in wit! kingly-poor flout!
Will they not, think you, hang themselves tonight?
Or ever but in vizards show their faces?
This pert Berowne was out of countenance quite.

221. **nice:** fussy and formal
224. **More measure:** i.e., a kiss. The formalities of a dance included a bow, a handclasp, and a kiss.
229. **visor:** mask
234. **nice:** precise
235. **Metheglin:** mead; **wort:** infusion of malt or grain for fermentation; **malmsey:** a sweet wine
237. **cog:** cheat
239. **meet:** suitable
240. **change:** exchange
244. **vizard:** variant of "visor"
247. **double tongue:** her own tongue (which utters equivocal speech) and the tongue of her mask, by which she kept it on her face
249. **Veal . . . Dutchman:** "well," as a Dutchman would pronounce it. Katharine has recognized the disguised Russian as Longaville. **Veal** is also a spelling of "veil" (mask) and a phonetic spelling of the last syllable of Longaville's name, the first syllable of which had been her last word at line 246. Longaville's name is pronounced variously in the play for the sake of rhyme, as is that of Berowne.
251. **part:** share; **half:** better half; mate
252. **ox:** fool
261. **Above . . . sense:** beyond ordinary comprehension; **sensible:** sensitive
262. **conference:** discourse; **conceits:** fancies
265. **dry-beaten:** battered
270. **Well-liking:** fat

Ros. They were all in lamentable cases! 275
The King was weeping-ripe for a good word.
Prin. Berowne did swear himself out of all suit.
Mar. Dumaine was at my service, and his sword.
"No point," quoth I; my servant straight was mute.
Kath. Lord Longaville said I came o'er his heart;
And trow you what he called me?
Prin. Qualm, perhaps. 281
Kath. Yes, in good faith.
Prin. Go, sickness as thou art!
Ros. Well, better wits have worn plain statute caps.
But will you hear? The King is my love sworn.
Prin. And quick Berowne hath plighted faith to me. 285
Kath. And Longaville was for my service born.
Mar. Dumaine is mine, as sure as bark on tree.
Boy. Madam, and pretty mistresses, give ear:
Immediately they will again be here
In their own shapes; for it can never be 290
They will digest this harsh indignity.
Prin. Will they return?
Boy. They will, they will, God knows,
And leap for joy, though they are lame with blows;
Therefore, change favors, and, when they repair,
Blow like sweet roses in this summer air. 295
Prin. How blow? how blow? Speak to be understood.
Boy. Fair ladies masked are roses in their bud:
Dismasked, their damask sweet commixture shown,
Are angels vailing clouds, or roses blown.
Prin. Avaunt, perplexity! What shall we do 300
If they return in their own shapes to woo?
Ros. Good madam, if by me you'll be advised,
Let's mock them still, as well known as disguised.
Let us complain to them what fools were here,
Disguised like Muscovites, in shapeless gear; 305
And wonder what they were, and to what end
Their shallow shows and prologue vilely penned,
And their rough carriage so ridiculous,
Should be presented at our tent to us. 309
Boy. Ladies, withdraw; the gallants are at hand.
Prin. Whip to our tents, as roes run o'er the land.
Exeunt [Princess, Rosaline, Katherine and Maria].

[*Re-*]*enter the* KING, BEROWNE, LONGAVILLE, *and* DUMAINE, [*in their proper habits*].

King. Fair sir, God save you! Where's the Princess?
Boy. Gone to her tent. Please it your Majesty
Command me any service to her thither?
King. That she vouchsafe me audience for one word. 315
Boy. I will; and so will she, I know, my lord. *Exit.*
Ber. This fellow pecks up wit as pigeons pease,
And utters it again when God doth please.
He is wit's peddler, and retails his wares 319
At wakes, and wassails, meetings, markets, fairs;
And we that sell by gross, the Lord doth know,
Have not the grace to grace it with such show.
This gallant pins the wenches on his sleeve;
Had he been Adam, he had tempted Eve.
'A can carve too, and lisp; why, this is he 325
That kissed his hand away in courtesy;
This is the ape of form, Monsieur the Nice,
That, when he plays at tables, chides the dice
In honorable terms; nay, he can sing
A mean most meanly; and in ushering, 330
Mend him who can. The ladies call him sweet;
The stairs, as he treads on them, kiss his feet.
This is the flower that smiles on every one,
To show his teeth as white as whale's bone;
And consciences that will not die in debt 335
Pay him the due of "honey-tongued Boyet."
King. A blister on his sweet tongue, with my heart,
That put Armado's page out of his part!

[*Re-*]*enter the* PRINCESS, ROSALINE, MARIA, *and* KATHARINE, [*and* BOYET].

Ber. See where it comes! Behavior, what wert thou
Till this madman showed thee? And what art thou now? 340
King. All hail, sweet madam, and fair time of day!
Prin. "Fair" in "all hail" is foul, as I conceive.
King. Construe my speeches better, if you may.
Prin. Then wish me better; I will give you leave.
King. We came to visit you, and purpose now
To lead you to our court; vouchsafe it then. 346
Prin. This field shall hold me, and so hold your vow:
Nor God, nor I, delights in perjured men.
King. Rebuke me not for that which you provoke.
The virtue of your eye must break my oath. 350
Prin. You nickname virtue: "vice" you should have spoke;
For virtue's office never breaks men's troth.
Now by my maiden honor, yet as pure
As the unsullied lily, I protest,
A world of torments though I should endure, 355

275. cases: pun on "masks"
277. swear . . . suit: carry his vows of devotion to absurd lengths
281. trow: know
283. statute caps: woolen caps of English make, which ordinary citizens were ordered by statute to wear on Sundays and holidays
298. damask: mingled white and red, like a damask rose
299. vailing: lowering; removing
307. shallow: stupid
320. wakes: church festivals
325. carve: please the ladies
328. tables: backgammon
330. mean: tenor part
350. virtue: power
351. nickname: miscall

I would not yield to be your house's guest;
So much I hate a breaking cause to be
Of heavenly oaths vowed with integrity.
King. O, you have lived in desolation here,
Unseen, unvisited, much to our shame. 360
Prin. Not so, my lord; it is not so, I swear;
We have had pastimes here, and pleasant game;
A mess of Russians left us but of late.
King. How, madam! Russians!
Prin. Ay, in truth, my lord;
Trim gallants, full of courtship and of state. 365
Ros. Madam, speak true. It is not so, my lord.
My lady, to the manner of the days,
In courtesy gives undeserving praise.
We four indeed confronted were with four
In Russian habit; here they stayed an hour 370
And talked apace; and in that hour, my lord,
They did not bless us with one happy word.
I dare not call them fools; but this I think,
When they are thirsty, fools would fain have drink.
Ber. This jest is dry to me. Gentle sweet, 375
Your wit makes wise things foolish; when we greet,
With eyes best seeing, heaven's fiery eye,
By light we lose light; your capacity
Is of that nature that to your huge store
Wise things seem foolish and rich things but poor.
Ros. This proves you wise and rich, for, in my eye— 381
Ber. I am a fool, and full of poverty.
Ros. But that you take what doth to you belong,
It were a fault to snatch words from my tongue.
Ber. O, I am yours, and all that I possess. 385
Ros. All the fool mine?
Ber. I cannot give you less.
Ros. Which of the vizards was it that you wore?
Ber. Where? when? what vizard? Why demand you this?
Ros. There, then, that vizard; that superfluous case 389
That hid the worse and showed the better face.
King. We were descried; they'll mock us now downright.
Dum. Let us confess, and turn it to a jest.
Prin. Amazed, my lord? Why looks your Highness sad?
Ros. Help, hold his brows! he'll swoon! Why look you pale?
Seasick, I think, coming from Muscovy. 395
Ber. Thus pour the stars down plagues for perjury.
Can any face of brass hold longer out?
Here stand I, lady—dart thy skill at me,
Bruise me with scorn, confound me with a flout,
Thrust thy sharp wit quite through my ignorance,
Cut me to pieces with thy keen conceit; 401
And I will wish thee never more to dance,
Nor never more in Russian habit wait.
O, never will I trust to speeches penned,
Nor to the motion of a schoolboy's tongue, 405
Nor never come in vizard to my friend,
Nor woo in rhyme, like a blind harper's song.
Taffeta phrases, silken terms precise,
Three-piled hyperboles, spruce affectation,
Figures pedantical—these summer flies 410
Have blown me full of maggot ostentation.
I do forswear them; and I here protest,
By this white glove—how white the hand, God knows!—
Henceforth my wooing mind shall be expressed
In russet yeas, and honest kersey noes. 415
And, to begin, wench—so God help me, law!—
My love to thee is sound, sans crack or flaw.
Ros. Sans "sans," I pray you.
Ber. Yet I have a trick
Of the old rage; bear with me, I am sick;
I'll leave it by degrees. Soft, let us see— 420
Write "Lord have mercy on us" on those three;
They are infected; in their hearts it lies;
They have the plague, and caught it of your eyes.
These lords are visited; you are not free,
For the Lord's tokens on you do I see. 425
Prin. No, they are free that gave these tokens to us.
Ber. Our states are forfeit; seek not to undo us.
Ros. It is not so; for how can this be true,
That you stand forfeit, being those that sue?
Ber. Peace! for I will not have to do with you.
Ros. Nor shall not, if I do as I intend. 431
Ber. Speak for yourselves; my wit is at an end.
King. Teach us, sweet madam, for our rude transgression
Some fair excuse.
Prin. The fairest is confession. 435
Were not you here but even now, disguised?
King. Madam, I was.
Prin. And were you well advised?
King. I was, fair madam.
Prin. When you then were here,
What did you whisper in your lady's ear?

367. to . . . days: in accordance with today's custom
372. happy: felicitous; fortunate

402. wish: request
403. wait: dance attendance
409. spruce: elegant
415. russet, kersey: homespun fabrics
418. Sans "sans": a word like **sans** belies his promise of plain speech.
421. Lord . . . us: a sign placed on plague-infected dwellings
424. visited: afflicted with sickness
425. the . . . tokens: a term describing the spots characteristic of the plague. Literally, the tokens are the "fairings" bestowed by the Lords.
429. you . . . sue: in a legal suit the plaintiff is not the one who pays the penalty.
430. have . . . with: that is, disagree with
437. well advised: rational

King. That more than all the world I did respect her. 440
Prin. When she shall challenge this, you will reject her.
King. Upon mine honor, no.
Prin. Peace, peace, forbear;
Your oath once broke, you force not to forswear.
King. Despise me when I break this oath of mine.
Prin. I will; and therefore keep it. Rosaline, 445
What did the Russian whisper in your ear?
Ros. Madam, he swore that he did hold me dear
As precious eyesight, and did value me
Above this world; adding thereto, moreover,
That he would wed me, or else die my lover. 450
Prin. God give thee joy of him! The noble lord
Most honorably doth uphold his word.
King. What mean you, madam? By my life, my troth,
I never swore this lady such an oath. 454
Ros. By heaven, you did; and, to confirm it plain,
You gave me this; but take it, sir, again.
King. My faith and this the Princess I did give;
I knew her by this jewel on her sleeve.
Prin. Pardon me, sir, this jewel did she wear;
And Lord Berowne, I thank him, is my dear. 460
What, will you have me, or your pearl again?
Ber. Neither of either; I remit both twain.
I see the trick on't: here was a consent,
Knowing aforehand of our merriment,
To dash it like a Christmas comedy. 465
Some carrytale, some pleaseman, some slight zany,
Some mumblenews, some trencher knight, some Dick,
That smiles his cheek in years and knows the trick
To make my lady laugh when she's disposed,
Told our intents before; which once disclosed,
The ladies did change favors; and then we, 471
Following the signs, wooed but the sign of she.
Now, to our perjury to add more terror,
We are again forsworn in will and error.
Much upon this it is; [*To Boyet*] and might not you
Forestall our sport, to make us thus untrue? 476
Do not you know my lady's foot by the squire,
And laugh upon the apple of her eye?
And stand between her back, sir, and the fire,
Holding a trencher, jesting merrily? 480
You put our page out. Go, you are allowed;
Die when you will, a smock shall be your shroud.
You leer upon me, do you? There's an eye
Wounds like a leaden sword.
Boy. Full merrily
Hath this brave manage, this career, been run. 485
Ber. Lo, he is tilting straight! Peace; I have done.

Enter COSTARD.

Welcome, pure wit! Thou partst a fair fray.
Cost. O Lord, sir, they would know
Whether the three Worthies shall come in or no?
Ber. What, are there but three?
Cost. No, sir; but it is vara fine, 490
For every one pursents three.
Ber. And three times thrice is nine.
Cost. Not so, sir; under correction, sir, I hope it is not so.
You cannot beg us, sir, I can assure you, sir; we know what we know;
I hope, sir, three times thrice, sir—
Ber. Is not nine. 495
Cost. Under correction, sir, we know whereuntil it doth amount.
Ber. By Jove, I always took three threes for nine.
Cost. O Lord, sir, it were pity you should get your living by reck'ning, sir. 500
Ber. How much is it?
Cost. O Lord, sir, the parties themselves, the actors, sir, will show whereuntil it doth amount. For mine own part, I am, as they say, but to perfect one man in one poor man, Pompion the Great, 505 sir.
Ber. Art thou one of the Worthies?
Cost. It pleased them to think me worthy of Pompey the Great; for mine own part, I know not the degree of the Worthy, but I am to stand for him. 510
Ber. Go, bid them prepare.
Cost. We will turn it finely off, sir; we will take some care. *Exit*.
King. Berowne, they will shame us; let them not approach.
Ber. We are shameproof, my lord, and 'tis some policy
To have one show worse than the King's and his company. 515
King. I say they shall not come.

443. force . . . forswear: think nothing of being forsworn
462. remit: surrender
463. consent: conspiracy
465. dash . . . comedy: as amateur holiday theatricals are traditionally made fun of
466. pleaseman: one who curries favor; **zany:** clown
467. trencher knight: formidable trencherman; **Dick:** Jack; knave
468. smile . . . years: smiles his face into premature wrinkles
475. Much . . . is: it happened much like this.
477. know . . . squire: know the exact measure of my lady's foot, i.e., know exactly how to please her
478. laugh . . . eye: jest with her familiarly
482. smock: woman's shirt; **shroud:** (1) windingsheet; (2) protection
485. brave: splendid; **manage:** exercise of horsemanship (French *manège*); **career:** headlong gallop
486. tilting: thrusting with his wit; **straight:** immediately
493. You . . . us: you cannot prove us idiots. Minors and mental incompetents owning large estates were wards of the crown, but their guardianships could be purchased or "begged" in the Court of Wards.
505. Pompion: colloquial for "pumpkin," often applied also to a big man

Prin. Nay, my good lord, let me o'errule you now.
That sport best pleases that doth least know how;
Where zeal strives to content, and the contents
Dies in the zeal of that which it presents. 520
Their form confounded makes most form in mirth,
When great things laboring perish in their birth.

Ber. A right description of our sport, my lord.

Enter ARMADO.

Arm. Anointed, I implore so much expense of thy royal sweet breath as will utter a brace of 525 words. [*Converses apart with the King, and delivers a paper.*]

Prin. Doth this man serve God?

Ber. Why ask you?

Prin. 'A speaks not like a man of God His making. 530

Arm. That is all one, my fair, sweet, honey monarch; for, I protest, the schoolmaster is exceeding fantastical; too too vain, too too vain; but we will put it, as they say, to *fortuna de la guerra.* I 534 wish you the peace of mind, most royal couplement! *Exit.*

King. Here is like to be a good presence of Worthies. He presents Hector of Troy; the swain, Pompey the Great; the parish curate, Alexander; Armado's page, Hercules; the pedant, Judas Maccabæus. 540
And if these four Worthies in their first show thrive,
These four will change habits and present the other five.

Ber. There is five in the first show.

King. You are deceived, 'tis not so.

Ber. The pedant, the braggart, the hedge 545 priest, the fool, and the boy:
Abate throw at novum, and the whole world again
Cannot pick out five such, take each one in his vein.

King. The ship is under sail, and here she comes amain. 549

Enter [COSTARD, *armed for*] POMPEY.

Cost. "I Pompey am—"

Ber. You lie, you are not he.

Cost. "I Pompey am—"

Boy. With libbard's head on knee.

Ber. Well said, old mocker; I must needs be friends with thee.

Cost. "I Pompey am, Pompey surnamed the Big—"

Dum. The "Great."

Cost. It is "Great," sir. 555
"Pompey surnamed the Great,
That oft in field, with targe and shield, did make my foe to sweat;
And traveling along this coast, I here am come by chance,
And lay my arms before the legs of this sweet lass of France."
If your ladyship would say, "Thanks, Pompey," I had done. 560

Prin. Great thanks, great Pompey.

Cost. 'Tis not so much worth; but I hope I was perfect. I made a little fault in "Great."

Ber. My hat to a halfpenny, Pompey proves the best Worthy. 564

Enter SIR NATHANIEL, *for* ALEXANDER.

Nath. "When in the world I lived, I was the world's commander;
By east, west, north, and south, I spread my conquering might.
My scutcheon plain declares that I am Alisander—"

Boy. Your nose says, no, you are not; for it stands too right.

Ber. Your nose smells "no" in this, most tender-smelling knight.

Prin. The conqueror is dismayed. Proceed, good Alexander. 570

Nath. "When in the world I lived, I was the world's commander—"

Boy. Most true, 'tis right, you were so, Alisander.

Ber. Pompey the Great!

Cost. Your servant, and Costard.

Ber. Take away the conqueror, take away 575 Alisander.

Cost. [*To Sir Nathaniel*] O, sir, you have overthrown Alisander the conqueror! You will be scraped out of the painted cloth for this. Your lion, that holds his poleax sitting on a closestool, will be 580 given to Ajax; he will be the ninth Worthy. A conqueror and afeard to speak! Run away for shame, Alisander. *Exit Nathaniel.*

524. Anointed: anointed one; your Majesty
529. God His making: an old form of the possessive
535. couplement: couple
545–46. hedge priest: an illiterate priest
547. Abate . . . novum: except for a throw at "novem quinque," a dice game played by five persons, the two principal throws of which were nine and five
551. libbard's: leopard's. Contemporary heraldry described Pompey's crest as bearing the head of a leopard.
557. targe: target; shield
567. scutcheon: shield bearing his coat of arms
568. stands . . . right: Plutarch describes Alexander as having a neck that inclined to the left.
569. your . . . no: i.e., Holofernes is not sweet-smelling, as Plutarch reported Alexander to be.
579. painted cloth: a painted hanging with a scene from romance or mythology. A favorite subject for such hangings was the Nine Worthies.
579–80. Your . . . closestool: a contemporary treatise on heraldry described Alexander's arms as consisting of a lion seated in a chair, holding a battle-ax. **closestool:** box containing a chamber pot
581. Ajax: pun on "a jakes" (privy)

There, an't shall please you, a foolish mild man; an honest man, look you, and soon dashed. He is 585
a marvelous good neighbor, faith, and a very good bowler; but for Alisander—alas! you see how 'tis—a little o'erparted. But there are Worthies a-coming will speak their mind in some other sort.

Prin. Stand aside, good Pompey. 590

Enter HOLOFERNES, *for* JUDAS; *and* MOTH, *for* HERCULES.

Hol. "Great Hercules is presented by this imp,
Whose club killed Cerberus, that three-headed *canis;*
And when he was a babe, a child, a shrimp,
Thus did he strangle serpents in his *manus.*
Quoniam he seemeth in minority, 595
Ergo I come with this apology."
Keep some state in thy exit, and vanish. *Exit Moth.*
"Judas I am—"

Dum. A Judas!

Hol. Not Iscariot, sir. 600
"Judas I am, ycliped Maccabæus."

Dum. Judas Maccabæus clipt is plain Judas.

Ber. A kissing traitor. How, art thou proved Judas?

Hol. "Judas I am—"

Dum. The more shame for you, Judas! 605

Hol. What mean you, sir?

Boy. To make Judas hang himself.

Hol. Begin, sir; you are my elder.

Ber. Well followed: Judas was hanged on an elder.

Hol. I will not be put out of countenance. 610

Ber. Because thou hast no face.

Hol. What is this?

Boy. A citternhead.

Dum. The head of a bodkin.

Ber. A death's face in a ring. 615

Long. The face of an old Roman coin, scarce seen.

Boy. The pommel of Cæsar's falchion.

Dum. The carved-bone face on a flask.

Ber. St. George's half-cheek in a brooch.

Dum. Ay, and in a brooch of lead. 620

Ber. Ay, and worn in the cap of a toothdrawer.
And now, forward; for we have put thee in countenance.

Hol. You have put me out of countenance.

Ber. False: we have given thee faces. 625

Hol. But you have outfaced them all.

Ber. An thou wert a lion we would do so.

Boy. Therefore, as he is an ass, let him go.
And so adieu, sweet Jude! Nay, why dost thou stay?

Dum. For the latter end of his name. 630

Ber. For the ass to the Jude; give it him—Jud-as, away!

Hol. This is not generous, not gentle, not humble.

Boy. A light for Monsieur Judas! It grows dark, he may stumble. [*Holofernes retires.*]

Prin. Alas, poor Maccabæus, how hath he been baited!

Enter ARMADO, [*for* HECTOR].

Ber. Hide thy head, Achilles; here comes 635
Hector in arms.

Dum. Though my mocks come home by me, I will now be merry.

King. Hector was but a Troyan in respect of this.

Boy. But is this Hector? 640

Dum. I think Hector was not so clean-timbered.

Long. His leg is too big for Hector's.

Dum. More calf, certain.

Boy. No; he is best indued in the small.

Ber. This cannot be Hector. 645

Dum. He's a god or a painter; for he makes faces.

Arm. "The armipotent Mars, of lances the almighty,
Gave Hector a gift—"

Dum. A gilt nutmeg.

Ber. A lemon. 650

Long. Stuck with cloves.

Dum. No, cloven.

Arm. Peace!
"The armipotent Mars, of lances the almighty,
Gave Hector a gift, the heir of Ilion; 655
A man so breathed that certain he would fight; yea,
From morn till night out of his pavilion.
I am that flower—"

Dum. That mint.

Long. That columbine.

Arm. Sweet Lord Longaville, rein thy tongue.

Long. I must rather give it the rein, for it 660
runs against Hector.

588. o'erparted: given a part too big for him
592. Cerberus: the three-headed dog that Hercules brought up from Hades as his eleventh labor
595. Quoniam: seeing that
596. Ergo: therefore
603. A . . . traitor: referring to the Judas kiss; **clipt** also means "kissed"; **How . . . Judas:** have I not proved you to be Judas?
608. elder: the tree on which Judas is said to have hanged himself
613. citternhead: the stringed instrument called a cittern (or cithern) often had a face carved on the head.
614. bodkin: a small dagger or lady's hairpin, both of which often had carved heads
617. falchion: sword
619. half-cheek: profile
621. worn . . . toothdrawer: toothdrawers wore brooches in their caps, apparently as a sign of their profession.
637. by: to
639. Troyan: Trojan, a slang term for a good fellow; playboy
641. clean-timbered: well-built
644. indued: endowed
647. armipotent: "mighty in arms" (Latin *armipotentem*)
649. gilt: gilded with an egg glaze
655. Ilion: Troy
656. so breathed: of such endurance

Dum. Ay, and Hector's a greyhound.

Arm. The sweet warman is dead and rotten; sweet chucks, beat not the bones of the buried; when he breathed, he was a man. But I will forward 665 with my device. [*To the Princess*] Sweet royalty, bestow on me the sense of hearing.

Berowne steps forth [*and speaks to Costard*].

Prin. Speak, brave Hector; we are much delighted.

Arm. I do adore thy sweet Grace's slipper. 669

Boy. [*Aside to Dumaine*] Loves her by the foot.

Dum. [*Aside to Boyet*] He may not by the yard.

Arm. "This Hector far surmounted Hannibal—
The party is gone—"

Cost. Fellow Hector, she is gone; she is two months on her way. 675

Arm. What meanest thou?

Cost. Faith, unless you play the honest Troyan, the poor wench is cast away. She's quick; the child brags in her belly already; 'tis yours.

Arm. Dost thou infamonize me among po- 680 tentates? Thou shalt die.

Cost. Then shall Hector be whipped for Jaquenetta that is quick by him, and hanged for Pompey that is dead by him.

Dum. Most rare Pompey! 685

Boy. Renowned Pompey!

Ber. Greater than Great! Great, great, great Pompey! Pompey the Huge!

Dum. Hector trembles.

Ber. Pompey is moved. More Ates, more 690 Ates! Stir them on! stir them on!

Dum. Hector will challenge him.

Ber. Ay, if 'a have no more man's blood in his belly than will sup a flea.

Arm. By the North Pole, I do challenge 695 thee.

Cost. I will not fight with a pole, like a northern man; I'll slash; I'll do it by the sword. I bepray you, let me borrow my arms again.

Dum. Room for the incensed Worthies! 700

Cost. I'll do it in my shirt.

Dum. Most resolute Pompey!

Moth. Master, let me take you a buttonhole lower. Do you not see Pompey is uncasing for the combat? What mean you? You will lose your reputa- 705 tion.

Arm. Gentlemen and soldiers, pardon me; I will not combat in my shirt.

Dum. You may not deny it: Pompey hath made the challenge. 710

Arm. Sweet bloods, I both may and will.

Ber. What reason have you for't?

Arm. The naked truth of it is: I have no shirt; I go woolward for penance.

Boy. True, and it was enjoined him in 715 Rome for want of linen; since when, I'll be sworn, he wore none but a dishclout of Jaquenetta's, and that 'a wears next his heart for a favor.

Enter a messenger, MONSIEUR MARCADE.

Marc. God save you, madam!

Prin. Welcome, Marcade; 720
But that thou interruptest our merriment.

Marc. I am sorry, madam; for the news I bring
Is heavy in my tongue. The King your father—

Prin. Dead, for my life!

Marc. Even so; my tale is told. 725

Ber. Worthies, away! the scene begins to cloud.

Arm. For mine own part, I breathe free breath. I have seen the day of wrong through the little hole of discretion, and I will right myself like a soldier.

Exeunt Worthies.

King. How fares your Majesty? 730

Prin. Boyet, prepare; I will away tonight.

King. Madam, not so; I do beseech you stay.

Prin. Prepare, I say. I thank you, gracious lords,
For all your fair endeavors, and entreat,
Out of a new-sad soul, that you vouchsafe 735
In your rich wisdom to excuse or hide
The liberal opposition of our spirits,
If overboldly we have borne ourselves
In the converse of breath—your gentleness
Was guilty of it. Farewell, worthy lord. 740
A heavy heart bears not a nimble tongue.
Excuse me so, coming too short of thanks
For my great suit so easily obtained.

King. The extreme parts of time extremely forms
All causes to the purpose of his speed; 745
And often at his very loose decides
That which long process could not arbitrate.
And though the mourning brow of progeny
Forbid the smiling courtesy of love
The holy suit which fain it would convince, 750
Yet, since love's argument was first on foot,
Let not the cloud of sorrow justle it
From what it purposed; since to wail friends lost
Is not by much so wholesome-profitable
As to rejoice at friends but newly found. 755

680. infamonize: defame
683. quick: (1) pregnant; (2) alive
690. Ates: Ate was the daughter of Eris (Discord).
697–98. northern man: a thief of the Border regions, whose weapon was usually a long staff
703. take . . . lower: remove your outer garment, and reduce your dignity
714. go woolward: wear wool next the skin
728–29. seen . . . discretion: proverbial
737. liberal: overfree
739. gentleness: forbearance
741. nimble: Theobald's correction of "humble" in the early texts
744–45. The . . . speed: shortness of time compels quick decision
746. at . . . loose: at the decisive moment
750. convince: establish

Prin. I understand you not; my griefs are double.
Ber. Honest plain words best pierce the ear of grief;
And by these badges understand the King:
For your fair sakes have we neglected time, 759
Played foul play with our oaths; your beauty, ladies,
Hath much deformed us, fashioning our humors
Even to the opposed end of our intents;
And what in us hath seemed ridiculous,
As love is full of unbefitting strains,
All wanton as a child, skipping and vain; 765
Formed by the eye and therefore, like the eye,
Full of straying shapes, of habits, and of forms,
Varying in subjects as the eye doth roll
To every varied object in his glance;
Which parti-coated presence of loose love 770
Put on by us, if in your heavenly eyes
Have misbecomed our oaths and gravities,
Those heavenly eyes that look into these faults
Suggested us to make. Therefore, ladies, 774
Our love being yours, the error that love makes
Is likewise yours. We to ourselves prove false,
By being once false forever to be true
To those that make us both—fair ladies, you.
And even that falsehood, in itself a sin,
Thus purifies itself and turns to grace. 780
Prin. We have received your letters, full of love;
Your favors, the ambassadors of love;
And, in our maiden council, rated them
At courtship, pleasant jest, and courtesy,
As bombast and as lining to the time; 785
But more devout than this in our respects
Have we not been; and therefore met your loves
In their own fashion, like a merriment.
Dum. Our letters, madam, showed much more than jest.
Long. So did our looks. 790
Ros. We did not quote them so.
King. Now, at the latest minute of the hour,
Grant us your loves.
Prin. A time, methinks, too short
To make a world-without-end bargain in. 795
No, no, my lord, your Grace is perjured much,
Full of dear guiltiness; and therefore this—
If for my love, as there is no such cause,
You will do aught—this shall you do for me:
Your oath I will not trust; but go with speed 800
To some forlorn and naked hermitage,
Remote from all the pleasures of the world;
There stay until the twelve celestial signs
Have brought about the annual reckoning.
If this austere insociable life 805
Change not your offer made in heat of blood,
If frosts and fasts, hard lodging and thin weeds,
Nip not the gaudy blossoms of your love,
But that it bear this trial, and last love,
Then, at the expiration of the year, 810
Come, challenge me, challenge me by these deserts;
And, by this virgin palm now kissing thine,
I will be thine; and, till that instant, shut
My woeful self up in a mourning house,
Raining the tears of lamentation 815
For the remembrance of my father's death.
If this thou do deny, let our hands part,
Neither entitled in the other's heart.
King. If this, or more than this, I would deny,
To flatter up these powers of mine with rest, 820
The sudden hand of death close up mine eye!
Hence hermit then, my heart is in thy breast.

Ber. And what to me, my love? and what to me?
Ros. You must be purged too; your sins are racked;
You are attaint with faults and perjury; 825
Therefore, if you my favor mean to get,
A twelvemonth shall you spend, and never rest,
But seek the weary beds of people sick.

Dum. But what to me, my love? but what to me?
A wife? 830
Kath. A beard, fair health, and honesty;
With threefold love I wish you all these three.
Dum. O, shall I say I thank you, gentle wife?
Kath. Not so, my lord; a twelvemonth and a day
I'll mark no words that smooth-faced wooers say.
Come when the King doth to my lady come; 836
Then, if I have much love, I'll give you some.
Dum. I'll serve thee true and faithfully till then.
Kath. Yet swear not, lest ye be forsworn again.
Long. What says Maria?
Mar. At the twelvemonth's end
I'll change my black gown for a faithful friend. 841
Long. I'll stay with patience; but the time is long.
Mar. The liker you; few taller are so young.
Ber. Studies my lady? Mistress, look on me;
Behold the window of my heart, mine eye, 845

758. **badges:** evidences
764. **strains:** impulses
765. **wanton:** playful; **skipping . . . vain:** capricious and frivolous
767. **straying:** fleeting
770. **parti-colored:** motley
774. **Suggested:** tempted
785. **bombast:** padding (used to stuff garments)
791. **quote:** interpret
797. **dear:** serious but forgivable
807. **weeds:** garments
809. **last:** remain unchanged
811. **deserts:** worthy deeds
818. **entitled in:** having a legal right to
820. **flatter . . . rest:** coddle myself
823–28. **And . . . sick:** very likely another passage meant for deletion, since it anticipates the conversation between Berowne and Rosaline that begins on line 844
825. **attaint with:** convicted of
835. **smooth-faced:** (1) clean-shaven; (2) hypocritical
841. **friend:** lover
844. **Studies:** muses

What humble suit attends thy answer there.
Impose some service on me for thy love.
Ros. Oft have I heard of you, my Lord Berowne,
Before I saw you; and the world's large tongue
Proclaims you for a man replete with mocks, 850
Full of comparisons and wounding flouts,
Which you on all estates will execute
That lie within the mercy of your wit.
To weed this wormwood from your fruitful brain,
And therewithal to win me, if you please, 855
Without the which I am not to be won,
You shall this twelvemonth term from day to day
Visit the speechless sick, and still converse
With groaning wretches; and your task shall be,
With all the fierce endeavor of your wit, 860
To enforce the pained impotent to smile.
Ber. To move wild laughter in the throat of death?
It cannot be; it is impossible;
Mirth cannot move a soul in agony. 864
Ros. Why, that's the way to choke a gibing spirit,
Whose influence is begot of that loose grace
Which shallow laughing hearers give to fools.
A jest's prosperity lies in the ear
Of him that hears it, never in the tongue
Of him that makes it; then, if sickly ears, 870
Deafed with the clamors of their own dear groans,
Will hear your idle scorns, continue then,
And I will have you and that fault withal.
But if they will not, throw away that spirit,
And I shall find you empty of that fault, 875
Right joyful of your reformation.
Ber. A twelvemonth? Well, befall what will befall,
I'll jest a twelvemonth in an hospital.
Prin. [*To the King*] Ay, sweet my lord, and so I take my leave. 879
King. No, madam; we will bring you on your way.
Ber. Our wooing doth not end like an old play:
Jack hath not Jill. These ladies' courtesy
Might well have made our sport a comedy.
King. Come, sir, it wants a twelvemonth and a day,
And then 'twill end.
Ber. That's too long for a play. 885

[*Re-*]*enter* ARMADO.

Arm. Sweet Majesty, vouchsafe me—
Prin. Was not that Hector?
Dum. The worthy knight of Troy.
Arm. I will kiss thy royal finger, and take leave. I am a votary: I have vowed to Jaquenetta to 890 hold the plow for her sweet love three year. But, most esteemed greatness, will you hear the dialogue that the two learned men have compiled in praise of the Owl and the Cuckoo? It should have followed in the end of our show. 895
King. Call them forth quickly; we will do so.
Arm. Holla! approach.

Enter ALL.

This side is Hiems, Winter; this Ver, the Spring—the one maintained by the Owl, the other by the Cuckoo. Ver, begin. 900

The Song

Spring.
When daisies pied and violets blue
And lady smocks all silver-white
And cuckoo-buds of yellow hue
Do paint the meadows with delight,
The cuckoo then on every tree 905
Mocks married men, for thus sings he:
"Cuckoo;
Cuckoo, cuckoo"—O word of fear,
Unpleasing to a married ear!

When shepherds pipe on oaten straws, 910
And merry larks are plowman's clocks;
When turtles tread, and rooks and daws,
And maidens bleach their summer smocks;
The cuckoo then on every tree
Mocks married men, for thus sings he: 915
"Cuckoo;
Cuckoo, cuckoo"—O word of fear,
Unpleasing to a married ear!

Winter.
When icicles hang by the wall,
And Dick the shepherd blows his nail, 920
And Tom bears logs into the hall,
And milk comes frozen home in pail,
When blood is nipped, and ways be foul,
Then nightly sings the staring owl:
"To-whit, Tu-who"—A merry note, 925
While greasy Joan doth keel the pot.

When all aloud the wind doth blow,
And coughing drowns the parson's saw,
And birds sit brooding in the snow,
And Marian's nose looks red and raw, 930
When roasted crabs hiss in the bowl,
Then nightly sings the staring owl:
"Tu-whit, Tu-who"—A merry note,
While greasy Joan doth keel the pot.

Arm. The words of Mercury are harsh 935 after the songs of Apollo. You that way: we this way.
Exeunt omnes.

849. large: loud
851. comparisons: satirical comments
852. estates: classes
880. bring: conduct
902. lady smocks: a wildflower, *Cardamine pratensis*
923. ways: roads; **foul:** muddy
926. keel: cool, by stirring, skimming, or adding cold liquid
928. saw: moral
931. crabs: crab apples, used in hot, spiced drinks

The Balcony Scene

Engraving by Anthony Walker (1754).

The Tragedy of ROMEO AND JULIET

INTRODUCTION

Romeo and Juliet is a romantic tragedy, written by a young man about young lovers, and it has been a favorite with young people since its first performance. The play was written shortly after *Love's Labor's Lost,* with its raillery of false sentiments and fashionable affectations, and probably dates from late 1594 or 1595. Shakespeare had just turned thirty, and though by Elizabethan standards this might have been regarded as a mature age, he retained the exuberance of youth and the lyrical vein characteristic of his early years.

Although from the beginning *Romeo and Juliet* has been one of Shakespeare's most popular plays, it is not one of the great cosmic tragedies. Unlike the Greek type of tragedy, which has for its hero an exalted person who meets disaster because of some tragic flaw, *Romeo and Juliet* is a drama of pity and pathos, which has for its protagonists a boy and a girl, two "star-crossed lovers," who are the victims of a perverse fate that they cannot escape. The spectators look on with sympathy and sadness as the lovers are cheated by a cruel destiny, but the depth of pity and fear that purged the soul in Greek tragedy—or in *King Lear*—is lacking in *Romeo and Juliet.* We regret the doleful end of the charming young lovers, but we do not feel that they typify the fate of mankind.

Nevertheless, *Romeo and Juliet* does exert a great appeal because its sentiments are perennial and universal in the Western world. Young people continue to believe in love at first sight, and they are still ready to die for love. Only crabbed age would counsel Romeo not to lose his head over Juliet because another equally charming girl will turn up tomorrow. Romantics will continue to believe that such love as Romeo and Juliet shared comes like lightning from heaven and strikes only once. This belief is one reason for the long popularity of Shakespeare's play, which for more than three and a half centuries has been read and quoted. What effect the play has had on the perpetuation of romantic concepts of love is a topic worthy of speculation.

Shakespeare reveals himself in *Romeo and Juliet* as a dramatist with a sure sense of the theatre and its potentialities. He has created a play that never flags in interest on the stage—or in the study—for he has united vivid and lyrical poetry with characterizations that strike us as genuine and true to life. Not only do we think of the protagonists as delightful and living personalities, but we are interested in a whole gallery of lesser figures who come to life: old Capulet, for example, a bustling and busy master of the house who must see to every detail; the ribald and dashing Mercutio; the old Nurse with all her worldly recollections of sensual pleasures; Friar Laurence, the very essence of the well-meaning and devoted chaplain; and even the servants, who add to the comic relief. The skill that Shakespeare lavished upon the secondary characters helps to explain why actors and actresses have always liked *Romeo and Juliet;* everybody has a part that is alive, and the stars do not run away with the show. Throughout his drama this capacity to make even minor characters into living personalities displays the quality of Shakespeare's creative imagination—and his awareness of the practical problems of the theatre.

As in *Love's Labor's Lost,* Shakespeare shows cognizance of the current fashion for fine language, and now and then he allows his characters to engage in wordplay and to employ rhetorical devices that no longer appeal to our taste. For the most part, however, the play is written with a lyrical touch that makes the lines memorable. At times, indeed, the poet simply inserts lyrical passages out of sheer poetic exuberance, as in Mercutio's speech on Queen Mab [I.iv.53 ff.], which reads like something designed for *A Midsummer Night's Dream* and has no real point in *Romeo and Juliet.* Yet many of the lyric passages rise to a pitch of great emotional tension, and some of them have taken their place among those poetic lines that young men—and old—remember through the years.

POPULARITY OF THE PLAY

Although by the time of the first performance of *Romeo and Juliet* Shakespeare was already well established as a popular playwright, this new tragedy marked a further advance in his popularity. The first printed version, the Quarto of 1597, described the play as "often (with great applause) played publicly," and there is every reason to believe that this statement is more than a mere conventional puff for the play. The play had four quarto printings before the publication of the First Folio of 1623 and a fifth quarto version in 1637. The public not only saw the play on the stage but they read it. The story has been often told of the chained copy of the First Folio in the Bodleian Library, which eager Oxford students wore out at the balcony scene.

After the Restoration *Romeo and Juliet* was one of the first of Shakespeare's plays revived. James Howard prepared an adaptation of the play with a happy ending in which Romeo and Juliet lived happily ever after. During one season, according to the Restoration prompter and stage chronicler, John Downes, the theatre played the tragedy and the tragicomedy on alternate nights.

Thomas Otway prepared an adaptation of *Romeo and Juliet* with a pseudo-Roman setting bearing the title *The History and Fall of Caius Marius* (1679), which enjoyed a certain amount of popularity for the next fifty years. Theophilus Cibber in 1744 made a new adaptation of Shakespeare's play that returned it to Renaissance Italy. In 1748 David Garrick made still another adaptation, which attempted to come somewhat closer to Shakespeare's text. During the season of 1749–50, Covent Garden and Drury Lane ran simultaneous versions of *Romeo and Juliet* in which rival actors and actresses tried to outdo each other in their interpretations of the young lovers. Various adaptations of the play held the stage in England until well into the nineteenth century. Operatic versions of *Romeo and Juliet* that reduced the play to musical spectacles attracted audiences in the mid-eighteenth century.

In America *Romeo and Juliet* has had a long history. In some form, either as an adaptation or as Shakespeare wrote it, the play appeared on the Colonial stage and remained popular throughout the nineteenth century. On the American stage from the mid-nineteenth century onward, adaptations were generally abandoned and the original play was frequently produced.

This play has enjoyed almost as much favor in non-English-speaking countries as it has had in Great Britain and America. A play by this name was acted in France before Shakespeare produced his tragedy. Dutch and German versions date from the early seventeenth century. A play based on Shakespeare's text was performed in Germany in the first half of the seventeenth century, and further adaptations were later made in German. Versions of Shakespeare's play were frequently acted on the Continent during the nineteenth century and later.

Several screen versions of the play have been attempted and have had some success.

SOURCES AND TEXT

The legend of the star-crossed lovers is an old one, elements of which may be found in classical literature. In the Renaissance the tale in some form crops up in various collections of stories. Matteo Bandello in 1554 included in his *Novelle* a story of Romeo and Juliet that Pierre Boaistuau adapted into French and included in his *Histoires tragiques* (1559). This was the version that William Painter translated into English in *The Palace of Pleasure* (1566–67). Although Shakespeare seems to have known Painter's work, his most immediate source was a long narrative poem by Arthur Brooke entitled *The Tragical History of Romeus and Juliet* (1562). Brooke was indebted to Boaistuau for his plot. Brooke himself stated that he had seen a play on the subject, and this has led some scholars to believe that Shakespeare reworked an older play. This seems doubtful. Shakespeare borrowed most of his incidents from Brooke's poem.

The textual problems of *Romeo and Juliet* are complicated by the fact that the first printed version, Quarto 1 (1597) is a so-called "Bad Quarto"—one that was pirated and apparently printed from a "reported text" prepared by one or more actors who reproduced lines from memory as best they could. Nevertheless, Quarto 1 contains some readings preferable to those in later printings and detailed stage directions not found elsewhere. Quarto 2 (1599), which the title page boasts has been "Newly corrected, augmented, and amended," appears to have been printed from a playhouse manuscript. Quarto 3 (1609) reprints Quarto 2. The First Folio of 1623 and the undated Quarto 4 reprint Quarto 3. Quarto 5 (1637) follows the text of Quarto 3.

In the preparation of the present version, the editors have used Quarto 2 as the basis of the text but have adopted readings from Quarto 1, the First Folio, and occasionally from the other early Quartos when they appear to correct obviously bad readings. Though Quarto 2 may have been based on a playhouse manuscript, perhaps Shakespeare's own script, the printed text is sometimes garbled and sometimes gives readings that are clearly wrong. The use by the printer of a playhouse text is no guarantee of legible copy, and that it was the legitimate acting version is no assurance that it represents the authentic words that Shakespeare wrote. Anyone familiar with the practices of actors and producers, Elizabethan or modern, knows that acting copy is often altered and scribbled over. The sorry state of the playhouse copy, even if originally written in Shakespeare's fairest hand, may account for the many errors in Quarto 2.

[Dramatis Personæ

CHORUS.

ESCALUS, *Prince of Verona.*
PARIS, *a young Count, kinsman to the Prince.*
MONTAGUE, } *heads of two hostile families.*
CAPULET, }
AN OLD MAN, *kin to Capulet.*
ROMEO, *son to Montague.*
MERCUTIO, *kinsman to the Prince, and friend to Romeo.*
BENVOLIO, *nephew to Montague, and friend to Romeo.*
TYBALT, *nephew to Capulet's wife.*
FRIAR LAURENCE, } *Franciscans.*
FRIAR JOHN, }
BALTHASAR, *servant to Romeo.*
ABRAM, *servant to Montague.*
SAMPSON, } *servants to Capulet.*
GREGORY, }
PETER, *servant to Juliet's nurse.*
AN APOTHECARY.
THREE MUSICIANS.
AN OFFICER.

MONTAGUE'S WIFE.
CAPULET'S WIFE.
JULIET, *daughter to Capulet.*
NURSE *to Juliet.*

Citizens of Verona; Gentlemen and Gentlewomen of both houses; Maskers, Torchbearers, Pages, Guards, Watchmen, Servants, and Attendants.

Scene: *Verona; Mantua.*]

Fencing Attacks

From Henri de Saint Didier, *Traicte contenant les secrets du premier livre sur l'espée seule* (1573; 1907 reprint).

The Tragedy of ROMEO AND JULIET

[THE PROLOGUE]

[*Enter* CHORUS.]

Chor. Two households, both alike in dignity,
In fair Verona, where we lay our scene,
From ancient grudge break to new mutiny,
Where civil blood makes civil hands unclean.
From forth the fatal loins of these two foes 5
A pair of star-crossed lovers take their life,
Whose misadventured piteous overthrows
Doth with their death bury their parents' strife.
The fearful passage of their death-marked love,
And the continuance of their parents' rage, 10
Which, but their children's end, naught could remove,
Is now the two hours' traffic of our stage,
The which if you with patient ears attend,
What here shall miss, our toil shall strive to mend.
[*Exit.*]

1. dignity: nobility
3. mutiny: dispute
4. civil: domestic, probably with a pun on the sense "gentle"
6. star-crossed: ill-destined because of unfavorable stars

ACT I

Scene I. [*A street in Verona.*]

Enter SAMPSON *and* GREGORY (*with swords and bucklers*) *of the house of Capulet.*

Samp. Gregory, on my word, we'll not carry coals.
Greg. No, for then we should be colliers.
Samp. I mean, an we be in choler, we'll draw.
Greg. Ay, while you live, draw your neck out of collar. 5
Samp. I strike quickly, being moved.
Greg. But thou art not quickly moved to strike.
Samp. A dog of the house of Montague moves me.
Greg. To move is to stir, and to be valiant is to stand. Therefore, if thou art moved, thou runnest away. 10

1. carry coals: endure humiliation. Carrying coals was considered a menial task.
3. in choler: angered
5. collar: halter; hangman's noose

Samp. A dog of that house shall move me to stand. I will take the wall of any man or maid of Montague's.

Greg. That shows thee a weak slave, for the 15 weakest goes to the wall.

Samp. 'Tis true; and therefore women, being the weaker vessels, are ever thrust to the wall. Therefore I will push Montague's men from the wall and thrust his maids to the wall. 20

Greg. The quarrel is between our masters and us their men.

Samp. 'Tis all one. I will show myself a tyrant. When I have fought with the men, I will be cruel with the maids: I will cut off their heads. 25

Greg. The heads of the maids?

Samp. Ay, the heads of the maids, or their maidenheads. Take it in what sense thou wilt.

Greg. They must take it in sense that feel it.

Samp. Me they shall feel while I am able to 30 stand; and 'tis known I am a pretty piece of flesh.

Greg. 'Tis well thou art not fish; if thou hadst, thou hadst been Poor John. Draw thy tool! Here comes two of the house of Montagues.

Enter two other Servingmen [ABRAM *and* BALTHASAR].

Samp. My naked weapon is out. Quarrel! I 35 will back thee.

Greg. How? turn thy back and run?

Samp. Fear me not.

Greg. No, marry. I fear thee!

Samp. Let us take the law of our sides; let 40 them begin.

Greg. I will frown as I pass by, and let them take it as they list.

Samp. Nay, as they dare. I will bite my thumb at them; which is disgrace to them, if they bear it. 45

Abr. Do you bite your thumb at us, sir?

Samp. I do bite my thumb, sir.

Abr. Do you bite your thumb at us, sir?

Samp. [*Aside to Gregory*] Is the law of our side if I say ay? 50

Greg. [*Aside to Sampson*] No.

Samp. No, sir, I do not bite my thumb at you, sir; but I bite my thumb, sir.

Greg. Do you quarrel, sir?

Abr. Quarrel, sir? No, sir. 55

Samp. But if you do, sir, I am for you. I serve as good a man as you.

Abr. No better.

Samp. Well, sir.

Enter BENVOLIO.

Greg. [*Aside to Sampson*] Say "better." Here 60 comes one of my master's kinsmen.

Samp. Yes, better, sir.

Abr. You lie.

Samp. Draw, if you be men. Gregory, re- 64 member thy swashing blow. *They fight.*

Ben. Part, fools! [*Beats down their swords.*] Put up your swords. You know not what you do.

Enter TYBALT.

Tyb. What, art thou drawn among these heartless hinds?
Turn thee, Benvolio! look upon thy death. 69

Ben. I do but keep the peace. Put up thy sword, Or manage it to part these men with me.

Tyb. What, drawn, and talk of peace? I hate the word
As I hate hell, all Montagues, and thee.
Have at thee, coward! [*They*] *fight.*

Enter THREE OR FOUR CITIZENS *with clubs or partisans* [*and an* OFFICER].

Officer. Clubs, bills, and partisans! Strike! 75 beat them down!

Citizens. Down with the Capulets! Down with the Montagues!

Enter OLD CAPULET *in his gown, and his* WIFE.

Cap. What noise is this? Give me my long sword, ho! 79

Wife. A crutch, a crutch! Why call you for a sword?

Cap. My sword, I say! Old Montague is come
And flourishes his blade in spite of me.

Enter OLD MONTAGUE *and his* WIFE.

Mon. Thou villain Capulet!—Hold me not, let me go.

M. Wife. Thou shalt not stir one foot to seek a foe.

Enter PRINCE ESCALUS, *with his* TRAIN.

13. take . . . of: take precedence over. The side nearest the wall in public streets was safer and more removed from the street gutters; hence it was claimed as a sign of superiority.
33. Poor John: dried, salted fish; hence, contemptible fare
39. marry: by the Virgin Mary; indeed
44. bite . . . thumb: a contemptuous gesture

68. heartless hinds: cowardly clowns, with a pun on heart/hart and on the other sense of **hind**
74. Have . . . thee: on guard
S.D. 74. partisans: short pikes with small, double-edged blades
75. bills: long-handled weapons with small blades
S.D. 78. gown: probably his dressing gown, indicating his haste to become involved in the brawl
82. spite: defiance

Prince. Rebellious subjects, enemies to peace,
Profaners of this neighbor-stained steel— 86
Will they not hear? What, ho! you men, you beasts,
That quench the fire of your pernicious rage
With purple fountains issuing from your veins!
On pain of torture, from those bloody hands 90
Throw your mistempered weapons to the ground
And hear the sentence of your moved prince.
Three civil brawls, bred of an airy word
By thee, old Capulet, and Montague,
Have thrice disturbed the quiet of our streets 95
And made Verona's ancient citizens
Cast by their grave beseeming ornaments
To wield old partisans, in hands as old,
Cankered with peace, to part your cankered hate.
If ever you disturb our streets again, 100
Your lives shall pay the forfeit of the peace.
For this time all the rest depart away.
You, Capulet, shall go along with me;
And, Montague, come you this afternoon,
To know our farther pleasure in this case, 105
To old Freetown, our common judgment place.
Once more, on pain of death, all men depart.
Exeunt [*all but Montague, his Wife, and Benvolio*].
Mon. Who set this ancient quarrel new abroach?
Speak, nephew, were you by when it began? 109
Ben. Here were the servants of your adversary
And yours, close fighting ere I did approach.
I drew to part them. In the instant came
The fiery Tybalt, with his sword prepared;
Which, as he breathed defiance to my ears,
He swung about his head and cut the winds, 115
Who, nothing hurt withal, hissed him in scorn.
While we were interchanging thrusts and blows,
Came more and more, and fought on part and part,
Till the Prince came, who parted either part.
M. Wife. O, where is Romeo? Saw you him today?
Right glad I am he was not at this fray. 121
Ben. Madam, an hour before the worshiped sun
Peered forth the golden window of the East,
A troubled mind drave me to walk abroad,
Where, underneath the grove of sycamore 125
That westward rooteth from the city's side,
So early walking did I see your son.
Towards him I made, but he was ware of me
And stole into the covert of the wood.
I—measuring his affections by my own, 130
Which then most sought where most might not be found,
Being one too many by my weary self—
Pursued my humor, not pursuing his,
And gladly shunned who gladly fled from me. 134

91. mistempered: (1) ill-natured; (2) fashioned for evil
97. grave beseeming: appropriately grave
99. Cankered . . . cankered: rusted . . . rankling
108. set . . . abroach: reopened this ancient quarrel
129. covert: concealment
130. affections: inclinations

Mon. Many a morning hath he there been seen,
With tears augmenting the fresh morning's dew,
Adding to clouds more clouds with his deep sighs;
But all so soon as the all-cheering sun
Should in the farthest East begin to draw
The shady curtains from Aurora's bed, 140
Away from light steals home my heavy son
And private in his chamber pens himself,
Shuts up his windows, locks fair daylight out,
And makes himself an artificial night.
Black and portentous must this humor prove 145
Unless good counsel may the cause remove.
Ben. My noble uncle, do you know the cause?
Mon. I neither know it nor can learn of him.
Ben. Have you importuned him by any means?
Mon. Both by myself and many other friends;
But he, his own affections' counselor, 151
Is to himself—I will not say how true—
But to himself so secret and so close,
So far from sounding and discovery,
As is the bud bit with an envious worm 155
Ere he can spread his sweet leaves to the air
Or dedicate his beauty to the sun.
Could we but learn from whence his sorrows grow,
We would as willingly give cure as know.

Enter ROMEO.

Ben. See where he comes. So please you step aside,
I'll know his grievance, or be much denied. 161
Mon. I would thou wert so happy by thy stay
To hear true shrift. Come, madam, let's away.
Exeunt [*Montague and Wife*].
Ben. Good morrow, cousin.
Rom. Is the day so young?
Ben. But new struck nine.
Rom. Ay me! sad hours seem long.
Was that my father that went hence so fast? 166
Ben. It was. What sadness lengthens Romeo's hours?
Rom. Not having that which having makes them short.
Ben. In love?
Rom. Out— 170
Ben. Of love?
Rom. Out of her favor where I am in love.
Ben. Alas that love, so gentle in his view,
Should be so tyrannous and rough in proof! 174

140. Aurora: goddess of the dawn
141. heavy: sorrowful
154. discovery: revelation
155. envious: malicious
156. he: it (the bud)
162. happy: fortunate; **stay:** waiting
163. shrift: confession
173. view: glance
174. tyrannous: violent; **proof:** trial

Rom. Alas that love, whose view is muffled still,
Should without eyes see pathways to his will!
Where shall we dine?—O me! What fray was here?—
Yet tell me not, for I have heard it all.
Here's much to do with hate, but more with love.
Why then, O brawling love! O loving hate! 180
O anything, of nothing first create!
O heavy lightness! serious vanity!
Misshapen chaos of well-seeming forms!
Feather of lead, bright smoke, cold fire, sick health!
Still-waking sleep, that is not what it is! 185
This love feel I, that feel no love in this.
Dost thou not laugh?
Ben. No, coz, I rather weep.
Rom. Good heart, at what?
Ben. At thy good heart's oppression.
Rom. Why, such is love's transgression.
Griefs of mine own lie heavy in my breast, 190
Which thou wilt propagate, to have it prest
With more of thine. This love that thou hast shown
Doth add more grief to too much of mine own.
Love is a smoke raised with the fume of sighs;
Being purged, a fire sparkling in lovers' eyes; 195
Being vexed, a sea nourished with lovers' tears.
What is it else? A madness most discreet,
A choking gall, and a preserving sweet.
Farewell, my coz.
Ben. Soft! I will go along.
An if you leave me so, you do me wrong. 200
Rom. Tut! I have lost myself; I am not here:
This is not Romeo, he's some other where.
Ben. Tell me in sadness, who is that you love?
Rom. What, shall I groan and tell thee?
Ben. Groan? Why, no;
But sadly tell me who. 205
Rom. Bid a sick man in sadness make his will.
Ah, word ill urged to one that is so ill!
In sadness, cousin, I do love a woman. 208
Ben. I aimed so near when I supposed you loved.
Rom. A right good markman! And she's fair I love.
Ben. A right fair mark, fair coz, is soonest hit.
Rom. Well, in that hit you miss. She'll not be hit
With Cupid's arrow. She hath Dian's wit,
And, in strong proof of chastity well armed, 214
From Love's weak childish bow she lives unharmed.
She will not stay the siege of loving terms,
Nor bide the encounter of assailing eyes,
Nor ope her lap to saint-seducing gold.

176. will: lust
181. create: created
182. vanity: frivolity
185. Still-waking: ever wakeful
200. An if: if
203. in sadness: seriously
205. sadly: gravely
213. Dian's wit: the wisdom of the chaste Diana
214. proof: proof (impenetrable) armor
216. stay: endure
218. ope . . . gold: i.e., like Danaë, visited by Zeus in a shower of gold

O, she is rich in beauty; only poor 219
That, when she dies, with beauty dies her store.
Ben. Then she hath sworn that she will still live chaste?
Rom. She hath, and in that sparing makes huge waste;
For beauty, starved with her severity,
Cuts beauty off from all posterity.
She is too fair, too wise, wisely too fair, 225
To merit bliss by making me despair.
She hath forsworn to love, and in that vow
Do I live dead that live to tell it now.
Ben. Be ruled by me: forget to think of her. 229
Rom. O, teach me how I should forget to think!
Ben. By giving liberty unto thine eyes:
Examine other beauties.
Rom. 'Tis the way
To call hers (exquisite) in question more.
These happy masks that kiss fair ladies' brows,
Being black, puts us in mind they hide the fair.
He that is strucken blind cannot forget 236
The precious treasure of his eyesight lost.
Show me a mistress that is passing fair,
What doth her beauty serve but as a note
Where I may read who passed that passing fair?
Farewell. Thou canst not teach me to forget. 241
Ben. I'll pay that doctrine, or else die in debt.
Exeunt.

[Scene II. *A street near the Capulet house.*]

Enter CAPULET, COUNTY PARIS, *and* [SERVANT]—*the* CLOWN.

Cap. But Montague is bound as well as I,
In penalty alike; and 'tis not hard, I think,
For men so old as we to keep the peace.
Par. Of honorable reckoning are you both,
And pity 'tis you lived at odds so long. 5
But now, my lord, what say you to my suit?
Cap. But saying o'er what I have said before:
My child is yet a stranger in the world,
She hath not seen the change of fourteen years;
Let two more summers wither in their pride 10
Ere we may think her ripe to be a bride.

220. her store: all of her, since she will leave no children
221. still: forever
225–26. wisely . . . despair: because she is so fair, and so wise as to prefer a holy chastity, she dooms me to despair because I cannot have her.
233. To . . . more: to decide that her beauty is the more exquisite
238. passing: surpassingly
239. note: reminder
240. passed: surpassed
242. pay . . . debt: make you acknowledge the virtue of forgetting or die in the attempt
Ent. County: Count

Par. Younger than she are happy mothers made.
Cap. And too soon marred are those so early made.
The earth hath swallowed all my hopes but she;
She is the hopeful lady of my earth. 15
But woo her, gentle Paris, get her heart;
My will to her consent is but a part.
An she agree, within her scope of choice
Lies my consent and fair according voice.
This night I hold an old accustomed feast, 20
Whereto I have invited many a guest,
Such as I love, and you among the store,
One more, most welcome, makes my number more.
At my poor house look to behold this night 24
Earth-treading stars that make dark heaven light.
Such comfort as do lusty young men feel
When well-appareled April on the heel
Of limping Winter treads, even such delight
Among fresh female buds shall you this night
Inherit at my house. Hear all, all see, 30
And like her most whose merit most shall be;
Which, on more view of many, mine, being one,
May stand in number, though in reck'ning none.
Come, go with me. [*To Servant, giving him a paper*]
Go, sirrah, trudge about
Through fair Verona; find those persons out 35
Whose names are written there, and to them say,
My house and welcome on their pleasure stay.
Exeunt [*Capulet and Paris*].
Serv. Find them out whose names are written here! It is written that the shoemaker should meddle with his yard and the tailor with his last, the fisher 40 with his pencil and the painter with his nets; but I am sent to find those persons whose names are here writ, and can never find what names the writing person hath here writ. I must to the learned. In good time! 45

Enter BENVOLIO *and* ROMEO.

Ben. Tut, man, one fire burns out another's burning;
One pain is lessened by another's anguish;
Turn giddy, and be holp by backward turning;
One desperate grief cures with another's languish.
Take thou some new infection to thy eye, 50
And the rank poison of the old will die.
Rom. Your plantain leaf is excellent for that.
Ben. For what, I pray thee?
Rom. For your broken shin.
Ben. Why, Romeo, art thou mad? 54
Rom. Not mad, but bound more than a madman is;
Shut up in prison, kept without my food,
Whipped and tormented and—Godden, good fellow.
Serv. God gi' godden. I pray, sir, can you read?
Rom. Ay, mine own fortune in my misery.
Serv. Perhaps you have learned it without 60 book. But I pray, can you read anything you see?
Rom. Ay, if I know the letters and the language.
Serv. Ye say honestly. Rest you merry!
Rom. Stay, fellow; I can read. *He reads.*

Signior Martino and his wife and daughters; 65
County Anselmo and his beauteous sisters;
The lady widow of Vitruvio;
Signior Placentio and his lovely nieces;
Mercutio and his brother Valentine;
Mine uncle Capulet, his wife, and daughters; 70
My fair niece Rosaline and Livia;
Signior Valentio and his cousin Tybalt;
Lucio and the lively Helena.

[*Gives back the paper.*] A fair assembly. Whither should they come?
Serv. Up. 75
Rom. Whither?
Serv. To supper, to our house.
Rom. Whose house?
Serv. My master's. 79
Rom. Indeed I should have asked you that before.
Serv. Now I'll tell you without asking. My master is the great rich Capulet; and if you be not of the house of Montagues, I pray come and crush a cup of wine. Rest you merry! *Exit.*
Ben. At this same ancient feast of Capulet's 85
Sups the fair Rosaline whom thou so lovest,
With all the admired beauties of Verona.
Go thither, and with unattainted eye
Compare her face with some that I shall show,
And I will make thee think thy swan a crow. 90
Rom. When the devout religion of mine eye
Maintains such falsehood, then turn tears to fires;
And these, who, often drowned, could never die,
Transparent heretics, be burnt for liars!
One fairer than my love? The all-seeing sun 95
Ne'er saw her match since first the world begun.
Ben. Tut! you saw her fair, none else being by,
Herself poised with herself in either eye;
But in that crystal scales let there be weighed

15. hopeful . . . earth: the lady upon whom all my earthly hopes are pinned
18. scope . . . choice: i.e., the limits of her wishes
30. Inherit: possess
32–33. mine . . . none: i.e., my daughter may be one in number but reckoned as of no account (in comparison with other beauties).
37. on . . . stay: await their pleasure
39. meddle: concern himself
44–45. In . . . time: a happy arrival (on seeing Romeo and Benvolio)
48. holp: obsolete past tense of "help"
52. plantain leaf: a remedy for wounds
53. broken shin: slang for "sexual disappointment"
57. Godden: good evening
83. crush: slang for "consume"
85. ancient: traditional
88. unattainted: unbiased
94. Transparent: obvious, as well as capable of being seen through; **heretics:** faithless ones
98. poised: balanced

Your lady's love against some other maid 100
That I will show you shining at this feast,
And she shall scant show well that now shows best.
Rom. I'll go along, no such sight to be shown,
But to rejoice in splendor of mine own.
[*Exeunt.*]

[Scene III. *Capulet's house.*]

Enter CAPULET'S WIFE, *and* NURSE.

Wife. Nurse, where's my daughter? Call her forth to me.
Nurse. Now, by my maidenhead at twelve year old,
I bade her come. What, lamb! what, ladybird!
God forbid! Where's this girl? What, Juliet!

Enter JULIET.

Jul. How now? Who calls? 5
Nurse. Your mother.
Jul. Madam, I am here. What is your will?
Wife. This is the matter—Nurse, give leave awhile,
We must talk in secret. Nurse, come back again;
I have remembered me, thou's hear our counsel.
Thou knowest my daughter's of a pretty age. 11
Nurse. Faith, I can tell her age unto an hour.
Wife. She's not fourteen.
Nurse. I'll lay fourteen of my teeth—
And yet, to my teen be it spoken, I have but four—
She's not fourteen. How long is it now 15
To Lammastide?
Wife. A fortnight and odd days.
Nurse. Even or odd, of all days in the year,
Come Lammas Eve at night shall she be fourteen.
Susan and she (God rest all Christian souls!)
Were of an age. Well, Susan is with God; 20
She was too good for me. But, as I said,
On Lammas Eve at night shall she be fourteen;
That shall she, marry; I remember it well.
'Tis since the earthquake now eleven years;
And she was weaned (I never shall forget it), 25
Of all the days of the year, upon that day;
For I had then laid wormwood to my dug,
Sitting in the sun under the dovehouse wall.
My lord and you were then at Mantua—
Nay, I do bear a brain—But, as I said, 30
When it did taste the wormwood on the nipple
Of my dug and felt it bitter, pretty fool,
To see it tetchy and fall out with the dug!
Shake, quoth the dovehouse! 'Twas no need, I trow,
To bid me trudge. 35
And since that time it is eleven years,
For then she could stand alone; nay, by the rood,
She could have run and waddled all about;
For even the day before, she broke her brow;
And then my husband (God be with his soul! 40
'A was a merry man) took up the child.
"Yea," quoth he, "dost thou fall upon thy face?
Thou wilt fall backward when thou hast more wit,
Wilt thou not, Jule?" and, by my holidam,
The pretty wretch left crying, and said "Ay." 45
To see now how a jest shall come about!
I warrant, an I should live a thousand years,
I never should forget it. "Wilt thou not, Jule?" quoth he,
And, pretty fool, it stinted, and said "Ay." 49
Wife. Enough of this. I pray thee hold thy peace.
Nurse. Yes, madam. Yet I cannot choose but laugh
To think it should leave crying and say "Ay."
And yet, I warrant, it had upon it brow
A bump as big as a young cock'rel's stone;
A perilous knock; and it cried bitterly. 55
"Yea," quoth my husband, "fallst upon thy face?
Thou wilt fall backward when thou comest to age,
Wilt thou not, Jule?" It stinted, and said "Ay."
Jul. And stint thou too, I pray thee, nurse, say I.
Nurse. Peace, I have done. God mark thee to his grace! 60
Thou wast the prettiest babe that e'er I nursed.
An I might live to see thee married once,
I have my wish.
Wife. Marry, that "marry" is the very theme
I came to talk of. Tell me, daughter Juliet, 65
How stands your disposition to be married?
Jul. It is an honor that I dream not of.
Nurse. An honor? Were not I thine only nurse,
I would say thou hadst sucked wisdom from thy teat.
Wife. Well, think of marriage now. Younger than you, 70
Here in Verona, ladies of esteem,
Are made already mothers. By my count,
I was your mother much upon these years
That you are now a maid. Thus then in brief:
The valiant Paris seeks you for his love. 75
Nurse. A man, young lady! lady, such a man
As all the world—why he's a man of wax.
Wife. Verona's summer hath not such a flower.

100. lady's love: ladylove
8. give . . . awhile: leave us for a bit
10. thou's: thou shalt
14. teen: grief
30. I . . . brain: I still have my wits
34. trow: declare
37. rood: cross
39. even: just; **broke:** cut
41. 'A: he
44. holidam: originally "halidom" (holy relic); later confused with "holy dame" and equated with the Virgin Mary
49. stinted: stopped
53. it: its
73–74. much . . . maid: at about the same age as you are now
77. a . . . wax: a model of masculine good looks

Nurse. Nay, he's a flower, in faith—a very flower.
Wife. What say you? Can you love the gentleman?
This night you shall behold him at our feast. 81
Read o'er the volume of young Paris' face,
And find delight writ there with beauty's pen;
Examine every several lineament,
And see how one another lends content; 85
And what obscured in this fair volume lies
Find written in the margent of his eyes.
This precious book of love, this unbound lover,
To beautify him only lacks a cover.
The fish lives in the sea, and 'tis much pride 90
For fair without the fair within to hide.
That book in many's eyes doth share the glory,
That in gold clasps locks in the golden story;
So shall you share all that he doth possess,
By having him making yourself no less. 95
Nurse. No less? Nay, bigger! Women grow by men.
Wife. Speak briefly, can you like of Paris' love?
Jul. I'll look to like, if looking liking move;
But no more deep will I endart mine eye 99
Than your consent gives strength to make it fly.

Enter a SERVINGMAN.

Serv. Madam, the guests are come, supper served up, you called, my young lady asked for, the nurse cursed in the pantry, and everything in extremity. I must hence to wait. I beseech you follow straight.
Wife. We follow thee. *Exit* [*Servingman*]. Juliet, the County stays. 105
Nurse. Go, girl, seek happy nights to happy days.
Exeunt.

[Scene IV. *A street near the Capulet house.*]

Enter ROMEO, MERCUTIO, BENVOLIO, *with* FIVE OR SIX OTHER MASKERS; TORCHBEARERS.

Rom. What, shall this speech be spoke for our excuse?
Or shall we on without apology?
Ben. The date is out of such prolixity.
We'll have no Cupid hoodwinked with a scarf,
Bearing a Tartar's painted bow of lath, 5
Scaring the ladies like a crowkeeper;
Nor no without-book prologue, faintly spoke
After the prompter, for our entrance;
But, let them measure us by what they will,
We'll measure them a measure, and be gone. 10
Rom. Give me a torch. I am not for this ambling;
Being but heavy, I will bear the light.
Mer. Nay, gentle Romeo, we must have you dance.
Rom. Not I, believe me. You have dancing shoes
With nimble soles; I have a soul of lead 15
So stakes me to the ground I cannot move.
Mer. You are a lover. Borrow Cupid's wings
And soar with them above a common bound.
Rom. I am too sore enpierced with his shaft
To soar with his light feathers, and so bound 20
I cannot bound a pitch above dull woe.
Under love's heavy burden do I sink.
Mer. And, to sink in it, should you burden love—
Too great oppression for a tender thing.
Rom. Is love a tender thing? It is too rough, 25
Too rude, too boist'rous, and it pricks like thorn.
Mer. If love be rough with you, be rough with love.
Prick love for pricking, and you beat love down.
Give me a case to put my visage in.
A visor for a visor! What care I 30
What curious eye doth quote deformities?
Here are the beetle brows shall blush for me.
Ben. Come, knock and enter, and no sooner in
But every man betake him to his legs.
Rom. A torch for me! Let wantons light of heart
Tickle the senseless rushes with their heels; 36
For I am proverbed with a grandsire phrase,
I'll be a candle-holder and look on;
The game was ne'er so fair, and I am done.
Mer. Tut! dun's the mouse, the constable's own word! 40
If thou art Dun, we'll draw thee from the mire
Of, save your reverence, love, wherein thou stickst
Up to the ears. Come, we burn daylight, ho!

85. **one . . . content:** each makes the other more pleasing
86–87. **what . . . eyes:** i.e., his eyes will reveal his soul. Explanatory notes were printed in the **margent** (margin) of books.
89. **a cover:** something that confines and embraces him
90. **much pride:** very fine
98. **I'll . . . move:** I'll regard him favorably if the sight of him inspires my liking
104. **straight:** at once
105. **stays:** waits
1. **shall . . . excuse:** a reference to the formal introduction usually spoken by one member of a masking party
3. **The . . . prolixity:** such wordiness is out-of-date.
4. **Cupid:** a typical conceit for the speaker of such introductions; **hoodwinked:** blindfolded
6. **crowkeeper:** a boy who protected the crops from crows
7. **without-book:** impromptu
10. **measure . . . measure:** tread a dance for them
12. **heavy:** melancholy
18. **bound:** (1) leap; (2) limit
21. **a pitch:** any distance at all
30. **visor:** mask
31. **curious:** carefully observant; **quote:** note
35. **wantons:** playful spirits
36. **rushes:** used to strew the floor
37. **a . . . phrase:** probably "He that worst may must hold the candle."
39. **done:** (1) dun (dark, gloomy); (2) finished. Another proverb is alluded to: "Leave off while the play is good."
40. **dun's . . . mouse:** a proverbial caution to be quiet
41. **Dun:** a horse's name in the proverb "Dun is in the mire."
42. **save . . . reverence:** begging your pardon; a facetious apology for comparing the state of love to a mire

Rom. Nay, that's not so.
Mer. I mean, sir, in delay
We waste our lights in vain, like lamps by day. 45
Take our good meaning, for our judgment sits
Five times in that ere once in our five wits.
Rom. And we mean well, in going to this masque;
But 'tis no wit to go.
Mer. Why, may one ask?
Rom. I dreamt a dream tonight.
Mer. And so did I. 50
Rom. Well, what was yours?
Mer. That dreamers often lie.
Rom. In bed asleep, while they do dream things true.
Mer. O, then I see Queen Mab hath been with you.
She is the fairies' midwife, and she comes
In shape no bigger than an agate stone 55
On the forefinger of an alderman,
Drawn with a team of little atomies
Athwart men's noses as they lie asleep;
Her wagon spokes made of long spinners' legs,
The cover, of the wings of grasshoppers; 60
Her traces, of the smallest spider's web;
Her collars, of the moonshine's wat'ry beams;
Her whip, of cricket's bone; the lash, of film;
Her wagoner, a small grey-coated gnat,
Not half so big as a round little worm 65
Pricked from the lazy finger of a maid;
Her chariot is an empty hazelnut,
Made by the joiner squirrel or old grub,
Time out o' mind the fairies' coachmakers.
And in this state she gallops night by night 70
Through lovers' brains, and then they dream of love;
O'er courtiers' knees, that dream on curtsies straight;
O'er lawyers' fingers, who straight dream on fees;
O'er ladies' lips, who straight on kisses dream,
Which oft the angry Mab with blisters plagues, 75
Because their breaths with sweetmeats tainted are.
Sometime she gallops o'er a courtier's nose,
And then dreams he of smelling out a suit;
And sometime comes she with a tithe-pig's tail
Tickling a parson's nose as 'a lies asleep, 80
Then dreams he of another benefice.
Sometime she driveth o'er a soldier's neck,
And then dreams he of cutting foreign throats,
Of breaches, ambuscadoes, Spanish blades,
Of healths five fathom deep; and then anon 85
Drums in his ear, at which he starts and wakes,
And being thus frighted, swears a prayer or two
And sleeps again. This is that very Mab
That plaits the manes of horses in the night
And bakes the elflocks in foul sluttish hairs, 90
Which once untangled much misfortune bodes.
This is the hag, when maids lie on their backs,
That presses them and learns them first to bear,
Making them women of good carriage.
This is she—
Rom. Peace, peace, Mercutio, peace! 95
Thou talkst of nothing.
Mer. True, I talk of dreams;
Which are the children of an idle brain,
Begot of nothing but vain fantasy;
Which is as thin of substance as the air,
And more inconstant than the wind, who woos 100
Even now the frozen bosom of the North
And, being angered, puffs away from thence,
Turning his face to the dew-dropping South.
Ben. This wind you talk of blows us from ourselves.
Supper is done, and we shall come too late. 105
Rom. I fear, too early; for my mind misgives
Some consequence, yet hanging in the stars,
Shall bitterly begin his fearful date
With this night's revels and expire the term
Of a despised life, closed in my breast, 110
By some vile forfeit of untimely death.
But he that hath the steerage of my course
Direct my sail! On, lusty gentlemen!
Ben. Strike, drum.
They march about the stage. [*Exeunt.*]

[Scene V. *Capulet's house.*]

SERVINGMEN *come forth with napkins.*

1. Serv. Where's Potpan, that he helps not to take away? He shift a trencher! he scrape a trencher!
2. Serv. When good manners shall lie all in one or two men's hands, and they unwashed too, 'tis a foul thing. 5
1. Serv. Away with the joint-stools, remove the court-cupboard, look to the plate. Good thou, save me a piece of marchpane and, as thou lovest me, let

46. good: correct
47. that: correct understanding
50. tonight: last night
65-66. worm . . . maid: idle fingers bred worms, according to an old belief.
68. joiner: cabinetmaker
90. elflocks: matted hair was believed to be due to the mischief of elves.
98. fantasy: fancy
103. dew-dropping South: rainy South wind
106. misgives: forbodes
107. consequence: sequent event
108. his: its
Exeunt: the scene break here is now traditional, but the original texts indicate continuous action, with the Servingmen entering at the end of the march.
6. joint-stools: four-legged stools made by a joiner
7. court-cupboard: sideboard; **Good thou:** thou good fellow
8. marchpane: marzipan

the porter let in Susan Grindstone and Nell. Anthony, and Potpan! 10

2. Serv. Ay, boy, ready.

1. Serv. You are looked for and called for, asked for and sought for, in the great chamber.

3. Serv. We cannot be here and there too. Cheerly, boys! Be brisk awhile, and the longer liver take 15 all. *Exeunt.*

[MASKERS *appear with* CAPULET, *his* WIFE, JULIET, *all the* GUESTS, *and* SERVANTS.]

Cap. Welcome, gentlemen! Ladies that have their toes
Unplagued with corns will have a bout with you.
Ah ha, my mistresses! which of you all 19
Will now deny to dance? She that makes dainty,
She I'll swear hath corns. Am I come near ye now?
Welcome, gentlemen! I have seen the day
That I have worn a visor and could tell
A whispering tale in a fair lady's ear, 24
Such as would please. 'Tis gone, 'tis gone, 'tis gone!
You are welcome, gentlemen! Come, musicians, play.
A hall, a hall! give room! and foot it, girls.
Music plays, and they dance.
More light, you knaves! and turn the tables up,
And quench the fire, the room is grown too hot.
Ah, sirrah, this unlooked-for sport comes well. 30
Nay, sit, nay, sit, good cousin Capulet,
For you and I are past our dancing days.
How long is't now since last yourself and I
Were in a mask?

2. Cap. By'r Lady thirty years.

Cap. What, man? 'Tis not so much, 'tis not so much! 35
'Tis since the nuptial of Lucentio,
Come Pentecost as quickly as it will,
Some five-and-twenty years, and then we masked.

2. Cap. 'Tis more, 'tis more! His son is elder, sir;
His son is thirty.

Cap. Will you tell me that? 40
His son was but a ward two years ago.

Rom. [*To a Servingman*] What lady's that, which doth enrich the hand
Of yonder knight?

Serv. I know not, sir.

Rom. O, she doth teach the torches to burn bright!
It seems she hangs upon the cheek of night 46
Like a rich jewel in an Ethiop's ear—
Beauty too rich for use, for earth too dear!
So shows a snowy dove trooping with crows
As yonder lady o'er her fellows shows. 50
The measure done, I'll watch her place of stand
And, touching hers, make blessed my rude hand.
Did my heart love till now? Forswear it, sight!
For I ne'er saw true beauty till this night.

Tyb. This, by his voice, should be a Montague.
Fetch me my rapier, boy. What, dares the slave 56
Come hither, covered with an antic face,
To fleer and scorn at our solemnity?
Now, by the stock and honor of my kin,
To strike him dead I hold it not a sin. 60

Cap. Why, how now, kinsman? Wherefore storm you so?

Tyb. Uncle, this is a Montague, our foe;
A villain, that is hither come in spite
To scorn at our solemnity this night.

Cap. Young Romeo is it?

Tyb. 'Tis he, that villain Romeo. 65

Cap. Content thee, gentle coz, let him alone.
'A bears him like a portly gentleman,
And, to say truth, Verona brags of him
To be a virtuous and well-governed youth.
I would not for the wealth of all this town 70
Here in my house do him disparagement.
Therefore be patient, take no note of him.
It is my will; the which if thou respect,
Show a fair presence and put off these frowns,
An ill-beseeming semblance for a feast. 75

Tyb. It fits when such a villain is a guest.
I'll not endure him.

Cap. He shall be endured.
What, goodman boy? I say he shall. Go to!
Am I the master here, or you? Go to!
You'll not endure him? God shall mend my soul!
You'll make a mutiny among my guests! 81
You will set cock-a-hoop! you'll be the man!

Tyb. Why, uncle, 'tis a shame.

Cap. Go to, go to!
You are a saucy boy. Is't so, indeed?
This trick may chance to scathe you. I know what.
You must contrary me! Marry, 'tis time.— 86
Well said, my hearts!—You are a princox—go!
Be quiet, or—More light, more light!—For shame!
I'll make you quiet; what!—Cheerly, my hearts!

21. Am . . . now: have I come close to the truth?
27. A hall: make space
28. turn . . . up: i.e., adjust the trestle tables to make more room. The trestles were laid on forms and could be turned out of the way when not in use.

55. should: must
57. antic: grotesque
58. fleer: mock; **solemnity:** festivity
67. portly: dignified
74. Show . . . presence: look pleasant
75. ill-beseeming semblance: unsuitable appearance
78. goodman boy: a reproach for Tybalt's presumption; **Go to:** that's enough!
80. God . . . soul: God save me!
81. mutiny: commotion
82. set cock-a-hoop: throw away all restraint. The phrase may derive from opening the tap (cock) of a keg of liquor, or possibly from cockfighting. Shakespeare in *Antony and Cleopatra* speaks of fowl fighting "inhooped," that is, in a ring.
85. scathe: harm; **what:** what I'm about
87. Well . . . hearts: well danced, my hearties; **princox:** coxcomb

Tyb. Patience perforce with willful choler meeting
Makes my flesh tremble in their different greeting.
I will withdraw; but this intrusion shall, 92
Now seeming sweet, convert to bitter gall. *Exit.*

Rom. If I profane with my unworthiest hand
This holy shrine, the gentle fine is this: 95
My lips, two blushing pilgrims, ready stand
To smooth that rough touch with a tender kiss.

Jul. Good pilgrim, you do wrong your hand too much,
Which mannerly devotion shows in this;
For saints have hands that pilgrims' hands do touch,
And palm to palm is holy palmer's kiss. 101

Rom. Have not saints lips, and holy palmers too?

Jul. Ay, pilgrim, lips that they must use in prayer.

Rom. O, then, dear saint, let lips do what hands do!
They pray; grant thou, lest faith turn to despair.

Jul. Saints do not move, though grant for prayers' sake. 106

Rom. Then move not while my prayer's effect I take.
Thus from my lips, by thine my sin is purged.
[*Kisses her.*]

Jul. Then have my lips the sin that they have took.

Rom. Sin from my lips? O trespass sweetly urged!
Give me my sin again. [*Kisses her.*]

Jul. You kiss by the book. 111

Nurse. Madam, your mother craves a word with you.

Rom. What is her mother?

Nurse. Marry, bachelor,
Her mother is the lady of the house.
And a good lady, and a wise and virtuous. 115
I nursed her daughter that you talked withal.
I tell you, he that can lay hold of her
Shall have the chinks.

Rom. Is she a Capulet?
O dear account! my life is my foe's debt.

Ben. Away, be gone, the sport is at the best. 120

Rom. Ay, so I fear; the more is my unrest.

Cap. Nay, gentlemen, prepare not to be gone;
We have a trifling foolish banquet towards.
They whisper in his ear.
Is it e'en so? Why then, I thank you all.
I thank you, honest gentlemen. Good night. 125
More torches here! [*Exeunt Maskers.*] Come on then, let's to bed.
Ah, sirrah, by my fay, it waxes late;
I'll to my rest. *Exeunt* [*all but Juliet and Nurse*].

Jul. Come hither, nurse. What is yond gentleman?

Nurse. The son and heir of old Tiberio. 130

Jul. What's he that now is going out of door?

Nurse. Marry, that, I think, be young Petruchio.

Jul. What's he that follows there, that would not dance?

Nurse. I know not.

Jul. Go ask his name.—If he be married, 135
My grave is like to be my wedding bed.

Nurse. His name is Romeo, and a Montague,
The only son of your great enemy.

Jul. My only love, sprung from my only hate!
Too early seen unknown, and known too late! 140
Prodigious birth of love it is to me
That I must love a loathed enemy.

Nurse. What's this? what's this?

Jul. A rhyme I learnt even now
Of one I danced withal.
One calls within, "Juliet."

Nurse. Anon, anon!
Come, let's away; the strangers all are gone. 145
Exeunt.

90. Patience perforce: proverbial: enforced restraint
91. different greeting: opposition
95. fine: Lewis Warburton's correction of the early reading "sin"
101. palmer: religious pilgrim
106. move: yield
118. the chinks: i.e., wealth
120. Away . . . best: the same proverb referred to at I.[iv.]39.
123. towards: in the offing
127. fay: faith
141. Prodigious: abnormal. Freakish births were considered to be omens of disaster.

[PROLOGUE]

[*Enter* CHORUS.]

Chor. Now old desire doth in his deathbed lie,
And young affection gapes to be his heir;
That fair for which love groaned for and would die,
With tender Juliet matched, is now not fair.
Now Romeo is beloved, and loves again, 5
Alike bewitched by the charm of looks;
But to his foe supposed he must complain,
And she steal love's sweet bait from fearful hooks.

3. fair: beauty
4. matched: compared

Being held a foe, he may not have access
To breathe such vows as lovers use to swear, 10
And she as much in love, her means much less
To meet her new beloved anywhere;
But passion lends them power, time means, to meet,
Temp'ring extremities with extreme sweet.

[*Exit.*]

[ACT II]

[Scene I. *A lane by the wall of Capulet's orchard.*]

Enter ROMEO *alone.*

Rom. Can I go forward when my heart is here?
Turn back, dull earth, and find thy center out.

[*Climbs the wall and leaps down within it.*]

Enter BENVOLIO *with* MERCUTIO.

Ben. Romeo! my cousin Romeo! Romeo!
Mer. He is wise,
And, on my life, hath stol'n him home to bed. 4
Ben. He ran this way, and leapt this orchard wall.
Call, good Mercutio.
Mer. Nay, I'll conjure too.
Romeo! humors! madman! passion! lover!
Appear thou in the likeness of a sigh;
Speak but one rhyme, and I am satisfied!
Cry but "Ay me!" pronounce but "love" and "dove"; 10
Speak to my gossip Venus one fair word,
One nickname for her purblind son and heir,
Young Adam Cupid, he that shot so trim
When King Cophetua loved the beggar maid!
He heareth not, he stirreth not, he moveth not; 15
The ape is dead, and I must conjure him.
I conjure thee by Rosaline's bright eyes,
By her high forehead and her scarlet lip,
By her fine foot, straight leg, and quivering thigh,
And the demesnes that there adjacent lie, 20
That in thy likeness thou appear to us!
Ben. An if he hear thee, thou wilt anger him.
Mer. This cannot anger him. 'Twould anger him
To raise a spirit in his mistress' circle
Of some strange nature, letting it there stand 25
Till she had laid it and conjured it down.
That were some spite; my invocation
Is fair and honest: in his mistress' name,
I conjure only but to raise up him.
Ben. Come, he hath hid himself among these trees
To be consorted with the humorous night. 31
Blind is his love and best befits the dark.
Mer. If love be blind, love cannot hit the mark.
Now will he sit under a medlar tree
And wish his mistress were that kind of fruit 35
As maids call medlars when they laugh alone.
O, Romeo, that she were, O that she were
An open et cetera, thou a pop'rin pear!
Romeo, good night. I'll to my truckle bed;
This field-bed is too cold for me to sleep. 40
Come, shall we go?
Ben. Go then, for 'tis in vain
To seek him here that means not to be found.

Exeunt.

2. earth: addressed to his body
11. gossip: good-natured dame
12. purblind: totally blind
13. Adam Cupid: an emendation of "Abraham Cupid" in the early texts. The hero of a popular ballad was an expert archer named "Adam Bell," which suggested the name substitution.
14. King Cophetua: the hero of another ballad, who fell in love with a beggarmaid when shot with Cupid's arrow
27. spite: injury
28. fair: decorous; **honest:** honorable
34. medlar: an apple-like fruit, also slang for a willing woman

[Scene II. *Capulet's orchard.*]

[*Enter* ROMEO.]

Rom. He jests at scars that never felt a wound.

[*Enter* JULIET *above at a window.*]

But soft! What light through yonder window breaks?
It is the East, and Juliet is the sun!
Arise, fair sun, and kill the envious moon,
Who is already sick and pale with grief 5
That thou her maid art far more fair than she.

Be not her maid, since she is envious;
Her vestal livery is but sick and green,
And none but fools do wear it; cast it off.
It is my lady; O, it is my love! 10
O that she knew she were!
She speaks, yet she says nothing. What of that?
Her eye discourses; I will answer it.
I am too bold; 'tis not to me she speaks.
Two of the fairest stars in all the heaven, 15
Having some business, do entreat her eyes
To twinkle in their spheres till they return.
What if her eyes were there, they in her head?
The brightness of her cheek would shame those stars
As daylight doth a lamp; her eyes in heaven 20
Would through the airy region stream so bright
That birds would sing and think it were not night.
See how she leans her cheek upon her hand!
O that I were a glove upon that hand,
That I might touch that cheek!

Jul. Ay me!

Rom. She speaks.
O, speak again, bright angel! for thou art 26
As glorious to this night, being o'er my head,
As is a winged messenger of heaven
Unto the white-upturned wond'ring eyes
Of mortals that fall back to gaze on him 30
When he bestrides the lazy-pacing clouds
And sails upon the bosom of the air.

Jul. O Romeo, Romeo! wherefore art thou Romeo?
Deny thy father and refuse thy name!
Or, if thou wilt not, be but sworn my love, 35
And I'll no longer be a Capulet.

Rom. [*Aside*] Shall I hear more, or shall I speak at this?

Jul. 'Tis but thy name that is my enemy.
Thou art thyself, though not a Montague.
What's Montague? It is nor hand, nor foot, 40
Nor arm, nor face, nor any other part
Belonging to a man. O, be some other name!
What's in a name? That which we call a rose
By any other name would smell as sweet.
So Romeo would, were he not Romeo called, 45
Retain that dear perfection which he owes
Without that title. Romeo, doff thy name;
And for that name, which is no part of thee,
Take all myself.

Rom. I take thee at thy word.
Call me but love, and I'll be new baptized; 50
Henceforth I never will be Romeo.

Jul. What man art thou that, thus bescreened in night,
So stumblest on my counsel?

Rom. By a name
I know not how to tell thee who I am.
My name, dear saint, is hateful to myself, 55
Because it is an enemy to thee.
Had I it written, I would tear the word.

Jul. My ears have yet not drunk a hundred words
Of that tongue's utterance, yet I know the sound.
Art thou not Romeo, and a Montague? 60

Rom. Neither, fair saint, if either thee dislike.

Jul. How camest thou hither, tell me, and wherefore?
The orchard walls are high and hard to climb,
And the place death, considering who thou art,
If any of my kinsmen find thee here. 65

Rom. With love's light wings did I o'erperch these walls;
For stony limits cannot hold love out,
And what love can do, that dares love attempt.
Therefore thy kinsmen are no let to me. 69

Jul. If they do see thee, they will murder thee.

Rom. Alack, there lies more peril in thine eye
Than twenty of their swords! Look thou but sweet,
And I am proof against their enmity.

Jul. I would not for the world they saw thee here.

Rom. I have night's cloak to hide me from their sight; 75
And but thou love me, let them find me here.
My life were better ended by their hate
Than death prorogued, wanting of thy love.

Jul. By whose direction foundst thou out this place?

Rom. By love, that first did prompt me to inquire. 80
He lent me counsel, and I lent him eyes.
I am no pilot, yet, wert thou as far
As that vast shore washed with the farthest sea,
I would adventure for such merchandise.

Jul. Thou knowst the mask of night is on my face;
Else would a maiden blush bepaint my cheek 86
For that which thou hast heard me speak tonight.
Fain would I dwell on form—fain, fain deny
What I have spoke; but farewell compliment!
Dost thou love me? I know thou wilt say "Ay"; 90
And I will take thy word. Yet, if thou swearst,
Thou mayst prove false. At lovers' perjuries,
They say Jove laughs. O gentle Romeo,
If thou dost love, pronounce it faithfully.
Or if thou thinkst I am too quickly won, 95
I'll frown, and be perverse, and say thee nay,
So thou wilt woo; but else, not for the world.
In truth, fair Montague, I am too fond,
And therefore thou mayst think my 'havior light;

8. vestal livery: virginal uniform
33. wherefore: why
46. owes: owns

69. let: hindrance
73. proof: protected by proof armor
76. but . . . me: unless you love me
78. prorogued: postponed
89. compliment: conventional formality
99. light: wanton

But trust me, gentleman, I'll prove more true 100
Than those that have more cunning to be strange.
I should have been more strange, I must confess,
But that thou overheardst, ere I was ware,
My true love's passion. Therefore pardon me,
And not impute this yielding to light love, 105
Which the dark night hath so discovered.

Rom. Lady, by yonder blessed moon I swear,
That tips with silver all these fruit-tree tops—

Jul. O, swear not by the moon, the inconstant moon,
That monthly changes in her circled orb, 110
Lest that thy love prove likewise variable.

Rom. What shall I swear by?

Jul. Do not swear at all;
Or if thou wilt, swear by thy gracious self,
Which is the god of my idolatry,
And I'll believe thee.

Rom. If my heart's dear love— 115

Jul. Well, do not swear. Although I joy in thee,
I have no joy of this contract tonight.
It is too rash, too unadvised, too sudden;
Too like the lightning, which doth cease to be 119
Ere one can say "It lightens." Sweet, good night!
This bud of love, by summer's ripening breath,
May prove a beauteous flow'r when next we meet.
Good night, good night! As sweet repose and rest
Come to thy heart as that within my breast!

Rom. O, wilt thou leave me so unsatisfied? 125

Jul. What satisfaction canst thou have tonight?

Rom. The exchange of thy love's faithful vow for mine.

Jul. I gave thee mine before thou didst request it;
And yet I would it were to give again.

Rom. Wouldst thou withdraw it? For what purpose, love? 130

Jul. But to be frank and give it thee again.
And yet I wish but for the thing I have.
My bounty is as boundless as the sea,
My love as deep; the more I give to thee,
The more I have, for both are infinite. 135
I hear some noise within. Dear love, adieu!
[*Nurse*] *calls within.*
Anon, good nurse! Sweet Montague, be true.
Stay but a little, I will come again. [*Exit.*]

Rom. O blessed, blessed night! I am afeard,
Being in night, all this is but a dream, 140
Too flattering-sweet to be substantial.

[*Re-enter* JULIET *above.*]

Jul. Three words, dear Romeo, and good night indeed.
If that thy bent of love be honorable,
Thy purpose marriage, send me word tomorrow,
By one that I'll procure to come to thee, 145
Where and what time thou wilt perform the rite;
And all my fortunes at thy foot I'll lay
And follow thee my lord throughout the world.

Nurse. (*Within*) Madam!

Jul. I come, anon.—But if thou meanst not well,
I do beseech thee— 151

Nurse. (*Within*) Madam!

Jul. By-and-by I come.—
To cease thy suit and leave me to my grief.
Tomorrow will I send.

Rom. So thrive my soul—

Jul. A thousand times good night! *Exit.* 155

Rom. A thousand times the worse, to want thy light!
Love goes toward love as schoolboys from their books;
But love from love, towards school with heavy looks.

Enter JULIET *again,* [*above*].

Jul. Hist! Romeo, hist! O for a falc'ner's voice
To lure this tassel-gentle back again! 160
Bondage is hoarse and may not speak aloud;
Else would I tear the cave where Echo lies,
And make her airy tongue more hoarse than mine
With repetition of my Romeo's name.
Romeo! 165

Rom. It is my soul that calls upon my name.
How silver-sweet sound lovers' tongues by night,
Like softest music to attending ears!

Jul. Romeo!

Rom. My sweet?

Jul. What o'clock tomorrow
Shall I send to thee?

Rom. By the hour of nine. 170

Jul. I will not fail. 'Tis twenty years till then.
I have forgot why I did call thee back.

Rom. Let me stand here till thou remember it.

Jul. I shall forget, to have thee still stand there,
Rememb'ring how I love thy company. 175

Rom. And I'll still stay, to have thee still forget,
Forgetting any other home but this.

Jul. 'Tis almost morning. I would have thee gone—
And yet no farther than a wanton's bird,
That lets it hop a little from her hand, 180
Like a poor prisoner in his twisted gyves,
And with a silk thread plucks it back again,
So loving-jealous of his liberty.

Rom. I would I were thy bird.

101. strange: distant
106. discovered: revealed
118. unadvised: heedless

143. bent: aim
160. tassel-gentle: male falcon
161. Bondage: i.e., one whose actions are controlled by another (her father)
179. wanton: playful child

Jul. Sweet, so would I.
Yet I should kill thee with much cherishing. 185
Good night, good night! Parting is such sweet sorrow,
That I shall say good night till it be morrow. [*Exit.*]
Rom. Sleep dwell upon thine eyes, peace in thy breast!
Would I were sleep and peace, so sweet to rest!
Hence will I to my ghostly father's cell, 190
His help to crave and my dear hap to tell.
Exit.

[Scene III. *Friar Laurence's cell.*]

Enter FRIAR [LAURENCE] *alone, with a basket.*

Friar. The grey-eyed morn smiles on the frowning night,
Chequ'ring the Eastern clouds with streaks of light;
And flecked darkness like a drunkard reels
From forth day's path and Titan's fiery wheels.
Now, ere the sun advance his burning eye 5
The day to cheer and night's dank dew to dry,
I must up-fill this osier cage of ours
With baleful weeds and precious-juiced flowers.
The earth that's nature's mother is her tomb,
What is her burying grave, that is her womb; 10
And from her womb children of divers kind
We sucking on her natural bosom find;
Many for many virtues excellent,
None but for some, and yet all different.
O, mickle is the powerful grace that lies 15
In plants, herbs, stones, and their true qualities;
For naught so vile that on the earth doth live
But to the earth some special good doth give;
Nor aught so good but, strained from that fair use,
Revolts from true birth, stumbling on abuse. 20
Virtue itself turns vice, being misapplied,
And vice sometime's by action dignified.
Within the infant rind of this small flower
Poison hath residence, and medicine power;
For this, being smelt, with that part cheers each part; 25
Being tasted, slays all senses with the heart.
Two such opposed kings encamp them still
In man as well as herbs—grace and rude will;
And where the worser is predominant,
Full soon the canker death eats up that plant. 30

Enter ROMEO.

Rom. Good morrow, father.
Friar. *Benedicite!*
What early tongue so sweet saluteth me?
Young son, it argues a distempered head
So soon to bid good morrow to thy bed.
Care keeps his watch in every old man's eye, 35
And where care lodges sleep will never lie;
But where unbruised youth with unstuffed brain
Doth couch his limbs, there golden sleep doth reign.
Therefore thy earliness doth me assure
Thou art uproused with some distemp'rature; 40
Or if not so, then here I hit it right—
Our Romeo hath not been in bed tonight.
Rom. That last is true, the sweeter rest was mine.
Friar. God pardon sin! Wast thou with Rosaline?
Rom. With Rosaline, my ghostly father? No. 45
I have forgot that name, and that name's woe.
Friar. That's my good son! But where hast thou been then?
Rom. I'll tell thee ere thou ask it me again.
I have been feasting with mine enemy,
Where on a sudden one hath wounded me 50
That's by me wounded. Both our remedies
Within thy help and holy physic lies.
I bear no hatred, blessed man, for, lo,
My intercession likewise steads my foe.
Friar. Be plain, good son, and homely in thy drift.
Riddling confession finds but riddling shrift. 56
Rom. Then plainly know my heart's dear love is set
On the fair daughter of rich Capulet;
As mine on hers, so hers is set on mine,
And all combined, save what thou must combine
By holy marriage. When, and where, and how 61
We met, we wooed, and made exchange of vow,
I'll tell thee as we pass; but this I pray,
That thou consent to marry us today. 64
Friar. Holy St. Francis! What a change is here!
Is Rosaline, that thou didst love so dear,
So soon forsaken? Young men's love then lies
Not truly in their hearts, but in their eyes.
Jesu Maria! What a deal of brine
Hath washed thy sallow cheeks for Rosaline! 70
How much salt water thrown away in waste,
To season love, that of it doth not taste!

190. **ghostly father:** spiritual adviser; confessor
191. **dear hap:** precious fortune
4. **Titan:** one of the sun-god's names
7. **osier:** willow
14. **None . . . some:** none but have some virtue
15. **mickle:** great; **grace:** benefit
20. **Revolts . . . birth:** rebels against the purpose for which it was created
25. **that part:** i.e., its fragrance
26. **slays . . . heart:** i.e., kills by poison
30. **canker:** cankerworm
52. **physic:** remedy
54. **My . . . foe:** my petition benefits my enemy (Juliet) as well as myself.
55. **homely:** plain
56. **shrift:** absolution
60. **all combined:** i.e., their hearts and souls are as one.
72. **season:** (1) salt; (2) preserve

The sun not yet thy sighs from heaven clears,
Thy old groans ring yet in mine ancient ears.
Lo, here upon thy cheek the stain doth sit 75
Of an old tear that is not washed off yet.
If e'er thou wast thyself, and these woes thine,
Thou and these woes were all for Rosaline.
And art thou changed? Pronounce this sentence then:
Women may fall when there's no strength in men.

Rom. Thou chidst me oft for loving Rosaline. 81

Friar. For doting, not for loving, pupil mine.

Rom. And badest me bury love.

Friar. Not in a grave
To lay one in, another out to have.

Rom. I pray thee chide not. She whom I love now
Doth grace for grace and love for love allow. 86
The other did not so.

Friar. O, she knew well
Thy love did read by rote, that could not spell.
But come, young waverer, come go with me.
In one respect I'll thy assistant be; 90
For this alliance may so happy prove
To turn your households' rancor to pure love.

Rom. O, let us hence! I stand on sudden haste.

Friar. Wisely, and slow. They stumble that run fast.

Exeunt.

[Scene IV. *A street.*]

Enter Benvolio *and* Mercutio.

Mer. Where the devil should this Romeo be?
Came he not home tonight?

Ben. Not to his father's. I spoke with his man.

Mer. Why, that same pale hard-hearted wench, that Rosaline,
Torments him so that he will sure run mad. 5

Ben. Tybalt, the kinsman to old Capulet,
Hath sent a letter to his father's house.

Mer. A challenge, on my life.

Ben. Romeo will answer it. 9

Mer. Any man that can write may answer a letter.

Ben. Nay, he will answer the letter's master, how he dares, being dared.

Mer. Alas, poor Romeo, he is already dead! stabbed with a white wench's black eye; shot through the ear with a love song; the very pin of his heart cleft 15 with the blind bow-boy's butt shaft; and is he a man to encounter Tybalt?

Ben. Why, what is Tybalt?

Mer. More than Prince of Cats, I can tell you. O, he's the courageous captain of compliments. He 20 fights as you sing pricksong—keeps time, distance, and proportion; rests me his minim rest, one, two, and the third in your bosom! the very butcher of a silk button, a duelist, a duelist! a gentleman of the very first house, of the first and second cause. 25 Ah, the immortal *passado!* the *punto reverso!* the *hay!*

Ben. The what?

Mer. The pox of such antic, lisping, affecting fantasticoes—these new tuners of accent! "By 30 Jesu, a very good blade! a very tall man! a very good whore!" Why, is not this a lamentable thing, grandsire, that we should be thus afflicted with these strange flies, these fashion-mongers, these *pardonami's,* who stand so much on the new form that 35 they cannot sit at ease on the old bench? O, their bones, their bones!

Enter Romeo.

Ben. Here comes Romeo! here comes Romeo!

Mer. Without his roe, like a dried herring. O flesh, flesh, how art thou fishified! Now is he for the 40 numbers that Petrarch flowed in. Laura, to his lady, was but a kitchen wench (marry, she had a better love to berhyme her), Dido a dowdy, Cleopatra a gypsy, Helen and Hero hildings and harlots, Thisbe a grey eye or so, but not to the purpose. Signior 45 Romeo, *bon jour!* There's a French salutation to your French slop. You gave us the counterfeit fairly last night.

Rom. Good morrow to you both. What counterfeit did I give you? 50

Mer. The slip, sir, the slip. Can you not conceive?

Rom. Pardon, good Mercutio. My business was great, and in such a case as mine a man may strain courtesy.

Mer. That's as much as to say, such a case as 55 yours constrains a man to bow in the hams.

Rom. Meaning, to curtsy.

Mer. Thou hast most kindly hit it.

73. sighs: i.e., their vapor
79. sentence: maxim (*sententia*)
93. stand: insist
16. butt shaft: practice arrow
19. Prince . . . Cats: cf. Sir Tybert, Prince of Cats, in the beast epic *Reynard the Fox.*
20. compliments: courteous formalities (of the duel)
21. pricksong: written music; i.e., notes pricked out on a sheet
22. minim rest: in musical terminology, a short pause
25. of . . . house: of the best fencing school; **cause:** motive for a duel; i.e., Tybalt is easily insulted.
26. passado: sword thrust; **punto reverso:** backhanded thrust from the left side; **hay:** Italian *hai,* a triumphant exclamation somewhat equivalent to *touché*
30. new . . . accent: affecters of the latest catchwords
31. tall: brave
35. form: (1) fashion; (2) bench
41. numbers: rhymes
44. hildings: mere baggages
47. French slop: full breeches cut in the French style
51. slip: piece of counterfeit money

Rom. A most courteous exposition.
Mer. Nay, I am the very pink of courtesy. 60
Rom. Pink for flower.
Mer. Right.
Rom. Why, then is my pump well-flowered.
Mer. Well said! Follow me this jest now till thou hast worn out thy pump, that, when the single 65 sole of it is worn, the jest may remain, after the wearing, solely singular.
Rom. O single-soled jest, solely singular for the singleness!
Mer. Come between us, good Benvolio! My 70 wits faint.
Rom. Switch and spurs, switch and spurs! or I'll cry a match.
Mer. Nay, if our wits run the wild-goose chase, I am done; for thou hast more of the wild goose 75 in one of thy wits than, I am sure, I have in my whole five. Was I with you there for the goose?
Rom. Thou wast never with me for anything when thou wast not there for the goose.
Mer. I will bite thee by the ear for that jest. 80
Rom. Nay, good goose, bite not!
Mer. Thy wit is a very bitter sweeting; it is a most sharp sauce.
Rom. And is it not, then, well served in to a sweet goose? 85
Mer. O, here's a wit of cheveril, that stretches from an inch narrow to an ell broad!
Rom. I stretch it out for that word "broad," which, added to the goose, proves thee far and wide a broad goose. 90
Mer. Why, is not this better now than groaning for love? Now art thou sociable, now art thou Romeo; now art thou what thou art, by art as well as by nature. For this driveling love is like a great natural that runs lolling up and down to hide his bauble 95 in a hole.
Ben. Stop there, stop there!
Mer. Thou desirest me to stop in my tale against the hair.
Ben. Thou wouldst else have made thy tale 100 large.
Mer. O, thou art deceived! I would have made it short; for I was come to the whole depth of my tale, and meant indeed to occupy the argument no longer.

Enter NURSE *and her Man* [PETER].

Rom. Here's goodly gear! 105
Mer. A sail, a sail!
Ben. Two, two! a shirt and a smock.
Nurse. Peter!
Peter. Anon.
Nurse. My fan, Peter. 110
Mer. Good Peter, to hide her face; for her fan's the fairer of the two.
Nurse. God ye good morrow, gentlemen.
Mer. God ye good-den, fair gentlewoman.
Nurse. Is it good-den? 115
Mer. 'Tis no less, I tell ye; for the bawdy hand of the dial is now upon the prick of noon.
Nurse. Out upon you! What a man are you!
Rom. One, gentlewoman, that God hath made for himself to mar. 120
Nurse. By my troth, it is well said. "For himself to mar," quoth 'a? Gentlemen, can any of you tell me where I may find the young Romeo?
Rom. I can tell you; but young Romeo will be older when you have found him than he was 125 when you sought him. I am the youngest of that name, for fault of a worse.
Nurse. You say well.
Mer. Yea, is the worst well? Very well took, i' faith! wisely, wisely. 130
Nurse. If you be he, sir, I desire some confidence with you.
Ben. She will endite him to some supper.
Mer. A bawd, a bawd, a bawd! So ho!
Rom. What hast thou found? 135
Mer. No hare, sir; unless a hare, sir, in a lenten pie, that is something stale and hoar ere it be spent.
He walks by them and sings.

An old hare hoar,
And an old hare hoar,
Is very good meat in Lent; 140
But a hare that is hoar
Is too much for a score
When it hoars ere it be spent.

Romeo, will you come to your father's? We'll to dinner thither. 145
Rom. I will follow you.
Mer. Farewell, ancient lady. Farewell, [*Sings*] lady, lady, lady. *Exeunt Mercutio, Benvolio.*
Nurse. Marry, farewell! I pray you, sir, what saucy merchant was this that was so full of his 150 ropery?

63. flowered: i.e., "pinked," decoratively perforated
67. solely singular: the only sole; emphatically alone
68–69. solely . . . singleness: remarkable only for its feebleness
73. cry . . . match: claim the victory
77. Was . . . goose: did my allusion to a goose score a point on you?
86. cheveril: flexible kidskin
90. broad: plainly apparent
94. natural: fool

105. goodly gear: fine stuff; handsome merchandise
127. fault: lack
133. endite: invite
137. something: somewhat
150. merchant: chap, from chapman (merchant), with a pun on "merchant ship"
151. ropery: knavery; conduct meriting the gallows

Rom. A gentleman, nurse, that loves to hear himself talk and will speak more in a minute than he will stand to in a month.

Nurse. An 'a speak anything against me, I'll 155 take him down, an 'a were lustier than he is, and twenty such Jacks; and if I cannot, I'll find those that shall. Scurvy knave! I am none of his flirt-gills; I am none of his skainsmates. And thou must stand by too, and suffer every knave to use me at his 160 pleasure!

Peter. I saw no man use you at his pleasure. If I had, my weapon should quickly have been out, I warrant you. I dare draw as soon as another man, if I see occasion in a good quarrel, and the law on my 165 side.

Nurse. Now, afore God, I am so vexed that every part about me quivers. Scurvy knave! Pray you, sir, a word; and, as I told you, my young lady bid me inquire you out. What she bid me say, I will 170 keep to myself; but first let me tell ye, if ye should lead her into a fool's paradise, as they say, it were a very gross kind of behavior, as they say; for the gentlewoman is young; and therefore, if you should deal double with her, truly it were an ill thing to be 175 offered to any gentlewoman, and very weak dealing.

Rom. Nurse, commend me to thy lady and mistress. I protest unto thee—

Nurse. Good heart, and i' faith I will tell her as much. Lord, Lord! she will be a joyful woman. 180

Rom. What wilt thou tell her, nurse? Thou dost not mark me.

Nurse. I will tell her, sir, that you do protest, which, as I take it, is a gentlemanlike offer.

Rom. Bid her devise 185
Some means to come to shrift this afternoon;
And there she shall at Friar Laurence' cell
Be shrived and married. Here is for thy pains.

Nurse. No, truly, sir; not a penny.

Rom. Go to! I say you shall. 190

Nurse. This afternoon, sir? Well, she shall be there.

Rom. And stay, good nurse, behind the abbey wall.
Within this hour my man shall be with thee
And bring thee cords made like a tackled stair,
Which to the high topgallant of my joy 195
Must be my convoy in the secret night.
Farewell. Be trusty, and I'll quit thy pains.
Farewell. Commend me to thy mistress.

Nurse. Now God in heaven bless thee! Hark you, sir.

Rom. What sayst thou, my dear nurse? 200

Nurse. Is your man secret? Did you ne'er hear say,
Two may keep counsel, putting one away?

Rom. I warrant thee my man's as true as steel.

Nurse. Well, sir, my mistress is the sweetest lady. Lord, Lord! when 'twas a little prating thing 205 —O, there is a nobleman in town, one Paris, that would fain lay knife aboard; but she, good soul, had as lief see a toad, a very toad, as see him. I anger her sometimes, and tell her that Paris is the properer man; but I'll warrant you, when I say so, she 210 looks as pale as any clout in the versal world. Doth not rosemary and Romeo begin both with a letter?

Rom. Ay, nurse, what of that? Both with an R.

Nurse. Ah, mocker! that's the dog's name. R is for the—No; I know it begins with some other 215 letter; and she hath the prettiest sententious of it, of you and rosemary, that it would do you good to hear it.

Rom. Commend me to thy lady.

Nurse. Ay, a thousand times. [*Exit Romeo.*] 220 Peter!

Peter. Anon.

Nurse. Peter, take my fan, and go before, and apace.

Exeunt.

[Scene V. *Capulet's orchard.*]

Enter JULIET.

Jul. The clock struck nine when I did send the nurse;
In half an hour she promised to return.
Perchance she cannot meet him. That's not so.
O, she is lame! Love's heralds should be thoughts,
Which ten times faster glide than the sun's beams
Driving back shadows over lowering hills. 6
Therefore do nimble-pinioned doves draw Love,
And therefore hath the wind-swift Cupid wings.
Now is the sun upon the highmost hill
Of this day's journey, and from nine till twelve 10
Is three long hours; yet she is not come.
Had she affections and warm youthful blood,
She would be as swift in motion as a ball;
My words would bandy her to my sweet love,
And his to me. 15

157. **Jacks:** rascals
158. **Scurvy:** contemptible; **flirt-gills:** light wenches
159. **skainsmates:** fellow cutthroats. A **skain** is a kind of knife used by criminals.
177. **commend . . . to:** present my respects to
194. **tackled stair:** rope ladder
195. **topgallant:** pinnacle; literally, the topmost section of a mast
197. **quit:** reward
202. **Two . . . away:** proverbial
209. **properer:** more handsome
211. **clout:** rag; **versal:** universal
216. **sententious:** i.e., *sententia*
217. **rosemary:** symbolic of remembrance
224. **apace:** speedily
7. **nimble-pinioned . . . Love:** Venus' chariot was supposed to be drawn by doves.

But old folks, many feign as they were dead—
Unwieldy, slow, heavy and pale as lead.

Enter NURSE [*and* PETER].

O God, she comes! O honey nurse, what news?
Hast thou met with him? Send thy man away.
Nurse. Peter, stay at the gate. [*Exit Peter.*] 20
Jul. Now, good sweet nurse—O Lord, why lookst thou sad?
Though news be sad, yet tell them merrily;
If good, thou shamest the music of sweet news
By playing it to me with so sour a face.
Nurse. I am aweary, give me leave awhile. 25
Fie, how my bones ache! What a jaunce have I had!
Jul. I would thou hadst my bones, and I thy news.
Nay, come, I pray thee speak. Good, good nurse, speak.
Nurse. Jesu, what haste! Can you not stay awhile?
Do you not see that I am out of breath? 30
Jul. How art thou out of breath when thou hast breath
To say to me that thou art out of breath?
The excuse that thou dost make in this delay
Is longer than the tale thou dost excuse.
Is thy news good or bad? Answer to that. 35
Say either, and I'll stay the circumstance.
Let me be satisfied, is't good or bad?
Nurse. Well, you have made a simple choice; you know not how to choose a man. Romeo? No, not he. Though his face be better than any man's, yet 40 his leg excels all men's; and for a hand and a foot, and a body, though they be not to be talked on, yet they are past compare. He is not the flower of courtesy, but, I'll warrant him, as gentle as a lamb. Go thy ways, wench; serve God. What, have you 45 dined at home?
Jul. No, no. But all this did I know before.
What says he of our marriage? What of that?
Nurse. Lord, how my head aches! What a head have I!
It beats as it would fall in twenty pieces. 50
My back o' t' other side—ah, my back, my back!
Beshrew your heart for sending me about
To catch my death with jauncing up and down!
Jul. I' faith, I am sorry that thou art not well.
Sweet, sweet, sweet nurse, tell me, what says my love? 55
Nurse. Your love says, like an honest gentleman, and a courteous, and a kind, and a handsome, and, I warrant, a virtuous—Where is your mother?
Ju. Where is my mother? Why, she is within.
Where should she be? How oddly thou repliest! 60
"Your love says, like an honest gentleman,
'Where is your mother?' "
Nurse. O God's Lady dear!
Are you so hot? Marry come up, I trow.
Is this the poultice for my aching bones?
Henceforward do your messages yourself. 65
Jul. Here's such a coil! Come, what says Romeo?
Nurse. Have you got leave to go to shrift today?
Jul. I have.
Nurse. Then hie you hence to Friar Laurence' cell;
There stays a husband to make you a wife. 70
Now comes the wanton blood up in your cheeks:
They'll be in scarlet straight at any news.
Hie you to church; I must another way,
To fetch a ladder, by the which your love
Must climb a bird's nest soon when it is dark. 75
I am the drudge, and toil in your delight;
But you shall bear the burden soon at night.
Go; I'll to dinner; hie you to the cell.
Jul. Hie to high fortune! Honest nurse, farewell.
Exeunt.

[Scene VI. *Friar Laurence's cell.*]

Enter FRIAR [LAURENCE] *and* ROMEO.

Friar. So smile the heavens upon this holy act
That after-hours with sorrow chide us not!
Rom. Amen, amen! But come what sorrow can,
It cannot countervail the exchange of joy
That one short minute gives me in her sight. 5
Do thou but close our hands with holy words,
Then love-devouring death do what he dare—
It is enough I may but call her mine.
Friar. These violent delights have violent ends
And in their triumph die, like fire and powder, 10
Which, as they kiss, consume. The sweetest honey
Is loathsome in his own deliciousness
And in the taste confounds the appetite.
Therefore love moderately: long love doth so;
Too swift arrives as tardy as too slow. 15

Enter JULIET.

Here comes the lady. O, so light a foot
Will ne'er wear out the everlasting flint.
A lover may bestride the gossamer
That idles in the wanton summer air,

16. as: as if
22. them: the news, often a plural
26. jaunce: rough journey
36. stay . . . circumstance: wait for the details.
56. honest: honorable
63. Marry . . . up: hoity-toity!
66. coil: to-do
4. countervail: outweigh
13. confounds: destroys
18. gossamer: cobweb
19. wanton: playful

And yet not fall; so light is vanity. 20
Jul. Good even to my ghostly confessor.
Friar. Romeo shall thank thee, daughter, for us both.
Jul. As much to him, else is his thanks too much.
Rom. Ah, Juliet, if the measure of thy joy
Be heaped like mine, and that thy skill be more 25
To blazon it, then sweeten with thy breath
This neighbor air, and let rich music's tongue

20. vanity: i.e., the pursuer of empty pleasure
25. that: if
26. blazon: proclaim

Unfold the imagined happiness that both
Receive in either by this dear encounter.
Jul. Conceit, more rich in matter than in words,
Brags of his substance, not of ornament. 31
They are but beggars that can count their worth;
But my true love is grown to such excess
I cannot sum up sum of half my wealth.
Friar. Come, come with me, and we will make short work; 35
For, by your leaves, you shall not stay alone
Till Holy Church incorporate two in one.
[*Exeunt.*]

30. Conceit: understanding

[ACT III]

[Scene I. *A public place.*]

Enter MERCUTIO, BENVOLIO, *and* MEN.

Ben. I pray thee, good Mercutio, let's retire.
The day is hot, the Capulets abroad,
And if we meet, we shall not scape a brawl,
For now, these hot days, is the mad blood stirring.
Mer. Thou art like one of these fellows that, 5
when he enters the confines of a tavern, claps me his sword upon the table and says "God send me no need of thee!" and by the operation of the second cup draws him on the drawer, when indeed there is no need. 10
Ben. Am I like such a fellow?
Mer. Come, come, thou art as hot a Jack in thy mood as any in Italy; and as soon moved to be moody, and as soon moody to be moved.
Ben. And what to? 15
Mer. Nay, an there were two such, we should have none shortly, for one would kill the other. Thou! why, thou wilt quarrel with a man that hath a hair more or a hair less in his beard than thou hast. Thou wilt quarrel with a man for cracking nuts, 20
having no other reason but because thou hast hazel eyes. What eye but such an eye would spy out such a quarrel? Thy head is as full of quarrels as an egg is full of meat; and yet thy head hath been beaten as addle as an egg for quarreling. Thou hast quar- 25
reled with a man for coughing in the street, because he hath wakened thy dog that hath lain asleep in the sun. Didst thou not fall out with a tailor for wearing his new doublet before Easter? with another for tying his new shoes with old ribband? And yet 30
thou wilt tutor me from quarreling!
Ben. An I were so apt to quarrel as thou art, any man should buy the fee simple of my life for an hour and a quarter.
Mer. The fee simple? O simple! 35

Enter TYBALT *and others.*

Ben. By my head, here come the Capulets.
Mer. By my heel, I care not.
Tyb. Follow me close, for I will speak to them.
Gentlemen, good-den. A word with one of you.
Mer. And but one word with one of us? 40
Couple it with something; make it a word and a blow.
Tyb. You shall find me apt enough to that, sir, an you will give me occasion.
Mer. Could you not take some occasion without giving? 45
Tyb. Mercutio, thou consortest with Romeo.
Mer. Consort? What, dost thou make us minstrels? An thou make minstrels of us, look to hear nothing

9. drawer: tapster
13–14. moved . . . moody: inclined to temper
14. moody . . . moved: angry at being crossed

33. fee simple: outright ownership
47. Consort: a term used for a company of musicians

but discords. Here's my fiddlestick; here's that shall make you dance. Zounds, consort! 50

Ben. We talk here in the public haunt of men.
Either withdraw unto some private place
And reason coldly of your grievances,
Or else depart. Here all eyes gaze on us.

Mer. Men's eyes were made to look, and let them gaze. 55
I will not budge for no man's pleasure, I.

Enter ROMEO.

Tyb. Well, peace be with you, sir. Here comes my man.

Mer. But I'll be hanged, sir, if he wear your livery.
Marry, go before to field, he'll be your follower!
Your worship in that sense may call him man. 60

Tyb. Romeo, the love I bear thee can afford
No better term than this: thou art a villain.

Rom. Tybalt, the reason that I have to love thee
Doth much excuse the appertaining rage
To such a greeting. Villain am I none. 65
Therefore farewell. I see thou knowst me not.

Tyb. Boy, this shall not excuse the injuries
That thou hast done me; therefore turn and draw.

Rom. I do protest I never injured thee,
But love thee better than thou canst devise 70
Till thou shalt know the reason of my love;
And so, good Capulet, which name I tender
As dearly as mine own, be satisfied.

Mer. O, calm, dishonorable, vile submission!
Alla stoccata carries it away. [*Draws.*] 75
Tybalt, you ratcatcher, will you walk?

Tyb. What wouldst thou have with me?

Mer. Good King of Cats, nothing but one of your nine lives. That I mean to make bold withal, and, as you shall use me hereafter, dry-beat the rest of 80 the eight. Will you pluck your sword out of his pilcher by the ears? Make haste, lest mine be about your ears ere it be out.

Tyb. I am for you. [*Draws.*]

Rom. Gentle Mercutio, put thy rapier up. 85

Mer. Come, sir, your *passado!* [*They fight.*]

Rom. Draw, Benvolio; beat down their weapons.
Gentlemen, for shame! forbear this outrage!
Tybalt, Mercutio, the Prince expressly hath
Forbid this bandying in Verona streets. 90
Hold, Tybalt! Good Mercutio!

Tybalt under Romeo's arm thrusts Mercutio in, and flies [*with his Men*].

Mer. I am hurt.
A plague o' both your houses! I am sped.
Is he gone and hath nothing?

Ben. What, art thou hurt?

Mer. Ay, ay, a scratch, a scratch. Marry, 'tis enough.
Where is my page? Go, villain, fetch a surgeon. 95
[*Exit Page.*]

Rom. Courage, man. The hurt cannot be much.

Mer. No, 'tis not so deep as a well, nor so wide as a church door; but 'tis enough, 'twill serve. Ask for me tomorrow, and you shall find me a grave man. I am peppered, I warrant, for this world. A plague 100 o' both your houses! Zounds, a dog, a rat, a mouse, a cat, to scratch a man to death! A braggart, a rogue, a villain, that fights by the book of arithmetic! Why the devil came you between us? I was hurt under your arm. 105

Rom. I thought all for the best.

Mer. Help me into some house, Benvolio,
Or I shall faint. A plague o' both your houses!
They have made worms' meat of me. I have it,
And soundly too. Your houses! 110
Exit [*supported by Benvolio*].

Rom. This gentleman, the Prince's near ally,
My very friend, hath got this mortal hurt
In my behalf—my reputation stained
With Tybalt's slander—Tybalt, that an hour
Hath been my kinsman. O sweet Juliet, 115
Thy beauty hath made me effeminate
And in my temper softened valor's steel!

Enter BENVOLIO.

Ben. O Romeo, Romeo, brave Mercutio's dead!
That gallant spirit hath aspired the clouds,
Which too untimely here did scorn the earth. 120

Rom. This day's black fate on mo days doth depend;
This but begins the woe others must end.

Enter TYBALT.

Ben. Here comes the furious Tybalt back again.

Rom. Alive in triumph, and Mercutio slain?
Away to heaven respective lenity, 125
And fire-eyed fury be my conduct now!

50. Zounds: by God's wounds
59. field: the field of honor; **follower:** quibble on another meaning: "retainer"
60. man: servant
62. villain: lowborn fellow
64. appertaining: suitable
72. tender: cherish
75. Alla stoccata: a fencing term: "at the thrust," hence, direct attack
76. ratcatcher: cat
80–81. dry-beat . . . eight: let the other eight off with a thrashing
82. pilcher: an abusive word of uncertain force. A "pilch" is a leather garment, and a "pilcher" or "pilchard" is a small fish.

90. Verona streets: a common use of a noun as an adjective
100. peppered: done for
103. the . . . arithmetic: i.e., a fencing manual with diagrams
111. ally: kinsman
112. very: true
119. aspired: attained or soared to
121. mo: more
125. respective: considerate (of consequences)

Now, Tybalt, take the "villain" back again
That late thou gavest me, for Mercutio's soul
Is but a little way above our heads,
Staying for thine to keep him company. 130
Either thou or I, or both, must go with him.

Tyb. Thou, wretched boy, that didst consort him here,
Shalt with him hence.

Rom. This shall determine that.

They fight. Tybalt falls.

Ben. Romeo, away, be gone!
The citizens are up, and Tybalt slain. 135
Stand not amazed. The Prince will doom thee death
If thou art taken. Hence, be gone, away!

Rom. O, I am fortune's fool!

Ben. Why dost thou stay?

Exit Romeo.

Enter CITIZENS.

Citizen. Which way ran he that killed Mercutio?
Tybalt, that murderer, which way ran he? 140

Ben. There lies that Tybalt.

Citizen. Up, sir, go with me.
I charge thee in the Prince's name obey.

Enter PRINCE [*with his* TRAIN], OLD MONTAGUE, CAPULET, *their* WIVES, *and* [*others*].

Prince. Where are the vile beginners of this fray?

Ben. O noble Prince, I can discover all
The unlucky manage of this fatal brawl. 145
There lies the man, slain by young Romeo,
That slew thy kinsman, brave Mercutio.

Cap. Wife. Tybalt, my cousin! O my brother's child!
O Prince! O cousin! O husband! O, the blood is spilled
Of my dear kinsman! Prince, as thou art true, 150
For blood of ours shed blood of Montague.
O cousin, cousin!

Prince. Benvolio, who began this bloody fray?

Ben. Tybalt, here slain, whom Romeo's hand did slay.
Romeo, that spoke him fair, bid him bethink 155
How nice the quarrel was, and urged withal
Your high displeasure. All this—uttered
With gentle breath, calm look, knees humbly bowed—
Could not take truce with the unruly spleen
Of Tybalt deaf to peace, but that he tilts 160
With piercing steel at bold Mercutio's breast;
Who, all as hot, turns deadly point to point,
And, with a martial scorn, with one hand beats
Cold death aside and with the other sends
It back to Tybalt, whose dexterity 165
Retorts it. Romeo he cries aloud,
"Hold, friends! friends, part!" and swifter than his tongue,
His agile arm beats down their fatal points,
And 'twixt them rushes; underneath whose arm
An envious thrust from Tybalt hit the life 170
Of stout Mercutio, and then Tybalt fled,
But by-and-by comes back to Romeo,
Who had but newly entertained revenge,
And to't they go like lightning; for ere I
Could draw to part them was stout Tybalt slain;
And as he fell did Romeo turn and fly. 176
This is the truth, or let Benvolio die.

Cap. Wife. He is a kinsman to the Montague;
Affection makes him false, he speaks not true.
Some twenty of them fought in this black strife,
And all those twenty could but kill one life. 181
I beg for justice, which thou, Prince, must give.
Romeo slew Tybalt; Romeo must not live.

Prince. Romeo slew him; he slew Mercutio. 184
Who now the price of his dear blood doth owe?

Mon. Not Romeo, Prince; he was Mercutio's friend;
His fault concludes but what the law should end,
The life of Tybalt.

Prince. And for that offense
Immediately we do exile him hence.
I have an interest in your hate's proceeding, 190
My blood for your rude brawls doth lie a-bleeding;
But I'll amerce you with so strong a fine
That you shall all repent the loss of mine.
I will be deaf to pleading and excuses; 194
Nor tears nor prayers shall purchase out abuses.
Therefore use none. Let Romeo hence in haste,
Else, when he is found, that hour is his last.
Bear hence this body, and attend our will.
Mercy but murders, pardoning those that kill.

Exeunt.

[Scene II. *Capulet's orchard.*]

Enter JULIET *alone.*

Jul. Gallop apace, you fiery-footed steeds,
Towards Phœbus' lodging! Such a wagoner

136. **amazed:** dumbstruck
138. **fool:** plaything; dupe
144. **discover:** reveal
145. **manage:** conduct
156. **nice:** trivial
166. **Retorts:** returns
170. **envious:** hostile
171. **stout:** valiant
173. **entertained:** decided on; admitted the thought of
179. **Affection:** partiality
191. **blood:** kinsman
192. **amerce:** punish
195. **purchase out:** buy immunity for

As Phaeton would whip you to the West
And bring in cloudy night immediately.
Spread thy close curtain, love-performing night, 5
That runaways' eyes may wink, and Romeo
Leap to these arms untalked of and unseen.
Lovers can see to do their amorous rites
By their own beauties; or, if love be blind,
It best agrees with night. Come, civil night, 10
Thou sober-suited matron, all in black,
And learn me how to lose a winning match,
Played for a pair of stainless maidenhoods.
Hood my unmanned blood, bating in my cheeks,
With thy black mantle; till strange love, grown bold,
Think true love acted simple modesty. 16
Come, night; come, Romeo; come, thou day in night;
For thou wilt lie upon the wings of night
Whiter than new snow upon a raven's back.
Come, gentle night; come, loving, black-browed night; 20
Give me my Romeo; and, when he shall die,
Take him and cut him out in little stars,
And he will make the face of heaven so fine
That all the world will be in love with night
And pay no worship to the garish sun. 25
O, I have bought the mansion of a love,
But not possessed it; and though I am sold,
Not yet enjoyed. So tedious is this day
As is the night before some festival
To an impatient child that hath new robes 30
And may not wear them. O, here comes my nurse,

Enter NURSE, *wringing her hands, with the ladder of cords in her lap.*

And she brings news; and every tongue that speaks
But Romeo's name speaks heavenly eloquence.
Now, nurse, what news? What hast thou there? the cords
That Romeo bid thee fetch?

Nurse. Ay, ay, the cords. 35

Jul. Ay me! what news? Why dost thou wring thy hands?

Nurse. Ah, welladay! he's dead, he's dead, he's dead!
We are undone, lady, we are undone!
Alack the day! he's gone, he's killed, he's dead!

Jul. Can heaven be so envious?

Nurse. Romeo can, 40
Though heaven cannot. O Romeo, Romeo!
Who ever would have thought it? Romeo!

Jul. What devil art thou that dost torment me thus?
This torture should be roared in dismal hell.
Hath Romeo slain himself? Say thou but "I," 45
And that bare vowel "I" shall poison more
Than the death-darting eye of cockatrice.
I am not I, if there be such an "I";
Or those eyes shut that make thee answer "I."
If he be slain, say "I"; or if not, "no." 50
Brief sounds determine of my weal or woe.

Nurse. I saw the wound, I saw it with mine eyes,
(God save the mark!) here on his manly breast.
A piteous corse, a bloody piteous corse;
Pale, pale as ashes, all bedaubed in blood, 55
All in gore blood. I swounded at the sight.

Jul. O, break, my heart! poor bankrout, break at once!
To prison, eyes; ne'er look on liberty!
Vile earth, to earth resign; end motion here,
And thou and Romeo press one heavy bier! 60

Nurse. O Tybalt, Tybalt, the best friend I had!
O courteous Tybalt! honest gentleman!
That ever I should live to see thee dead!

Jul. What storm is this that blows so contrary?
Is Romeo slaughtered, and is Tybalt dead? 65
My dear-loved cousin, and my dearer lord?
Then, dreadful trumpet, sound the general doom!
For who is living, if those two are gone?

Nurse. Tybalt is gone, and Romeo banished;
Romeo that killed him, he is banished. 70

Jul. O God! Did Romeo's hand shed Tybalt's blood?

Nurse. It did, it did! alas the day, it did!

Jul. O serpent heart, hid with a flow'ring face!
Did ever dragon keep so fair a cave?
Beautiful tyrant! fiend angelical! 75
Dove-feathered raven! wolvish-ravening lamb!
Despised substance of divinest show!
Just opposite to what thou justly seemst—
A damned saint, an honorable villain!

3. Phaeton: the rash son of Phœbus, who insisted on driving the sun's chariot and was destroyed when he could not control the horses

6. runaways' . . . wink: the eyes of unwanted observers may close. No explanation of this phrase has met with general satisfaction, and the Variorum edition of the play contains an appendix of twenty-nine pages discussing interpretation and possible emendations.

10. civil: courteous

12. learn: often used as a transitive verb in the sixteenth century

14. unmanned: untamed; **bating:** fluttering, a term from falconry. The "bating" bird was quieted by placing a hood over its head.

37. welladay: alas

40. envious: malicious

45. "I": a common spelling of the affirmative "ay"

47. cockatrice: a fabulous creature that killed with a glance; also sometimes confused with the basilisk

53. God . . . mark: God preserve us from the bad omen; a formula used on viewing or speaking of something evil or disastrous

56. swounded: swooned

57. bankrout: bankrupt

67. general doom: Last Judgment

74. keep: frequent

75. tyrant: desperado

78. Just: exact; **justly:** rightly

O nature, what hadst thou to do in hell. 80
When thou didst bower the spirit of a fiend
In mortal paradise of such sweet flesh?
Was ever book containing such vile matter
So fairly bound? O, that deceit should dwell
In such a gorgeous palace!
Nurse. There's no trust, 85
No faith, no honesty in men; all perjured,
All forsworn, all naught, all dissemblers.
Ah, where's my man? Give me some aqua vitae.
These griefs, these woes, these sorrows make me old.
Shame come to Romeo!
Jul. Blistered be thy tongue
For such a wish! He was not born to shame. 91
Upon his brow shame is ashamed to sit;
For 'tis a throne where honor may be crowned
Sole monarch of the universal earth.
O, what a beast was I to chide at him! 95
Nurse. Will you speak well of him that killed your cousin?
Jul. Shall I speak ill of him that is my husband?
Ah, poor my lord, what tongue shall smooth thy name
When I, thy three-hours' wife, have mangled it? 99
But wherefore, villain, didst thou kill my cousin?
That villain cousin would have killed my husband.
Back, foolish tears, back to your native spring!
Your tributary drops belong to woe,
Which you, mistaking, offer up to joy.
My husband lives, that Tybalt would have slain;
And Tybalt's dead, that would have slain my husband. 106
All this is comfort; wherefore weep I then?
Some word there was, worser than Tybalt's death,
That murdered me. I would forget it fain;
But O, it presses to my memory 110
Like damned guilty deeds to sinners' minds!
"Tybalt is dead, and Romeo—banished."
That "banished," that one word "banished,"
Hath slain ten thousand Tybalts. Tybalt's death
Was woe enough, if it had ended there; 115
Or, if sour woe delights in fellowship
And needly will be ranked with other griefs,
Why followed not, when she said "Tybalt's dead,"
Thy father, or thy mother, nay, or both, 119
Which modern lamentation might have moved?
But with a rearward following Tybalt's death,
"Romeo is banished"—to speak that word
Is father, mother, Tybalt, Romeo, Juliet,
All slain, all dead. "Romeo is banished"—
There is no end, no limit, measure, bound, 125
In that word's death; no words can that woe sound.
Where is my father and my mother, nurse?
Nurse. Weeping and wailing over Tybalt's corse.
Will you go to them? I will bring you thither.
Jul. Wash they his wounds with tears? Mine shall be spent, 130
When theirs are dry, for Romeo's banishment.
Take up those cords. Poor ropes, you are beguiled,
Both you and I, for Romeo is exiled.
He made you for a highway to my bed;
But I, a maid, die maiden-widowed. 135
Come, cords; come, nurse. I'll to my wedding bed;
And death, not Romeo, take my maidenhead!
Nurse. Hie to your chamber. I'll find Romeo
To comfort you. I wot well where he is.
Hark ye, your Romeo will be here at night. 140
I'll to him; he is hid at Laurence' cell.
Jul. O, find him! give this ring to my true knight
And bid him come to take his last farewell.
Exeunt.

[Scene III. *Friar Laurence's cell.*]

Enter FRIAR [LAURENCE].

Friar. Romeo, come forth; come forth, thou fearful man.
Affliction is enamored of thy parts,
And thou art wedded to calamity.

Enter ROMEO.

Rom. Father, what news? What is the Prince's doom?
What sorrow craves acquaintance at my hand 5
That I yet know not?
Friar. Too familiar
Is my dear son with such sour company.
I bring thee tidings of the Prince's doom.
Rom. What less than doomsday is the Prince's doom?
Friar. A gentler judgment vanished from his lips—
Not body's death, but body's banishment. 11
Rom. Ha, banishment? Be merciful, say "death";
For exile hath more terror in his look,
Much more than death. Do not say "banishment."
Friar. Hence from Verona art thou banished. 15
Be patient, for the world is broad and wide.
Rom. There is no world without Verona walls,
But purgatory, torture, hell itself.
Hence banished is banisht from the world,
And world's exile is death. Then "banishment" 20
Is death mistermed. Calling death "banishment,"
Thou cuttst my head off with a golden axe

87. naught: wicked
120. modern: ordinary
121. rearward: rear guard; hence, follower
139. wot: know
16. patient: calm
20. world's exile: exile from the world

And smilest upon the stroke that murders me.
Friar. O deadly sin! O rude unthankfulness!
Thy fault our law calls death; but the kind Prince,
Taking thy part, hath rushed aside the law, 26
And turned that black word death to banishment.
This is dear mercy, and thou seest it not.
Rom. 'Tis torture, and not mercy. Heaven is here,
Where Juliet lives; and every cat and dog 30
And little mouse, every unworthy thing,
Live here in heaven and may look on her;
But Romeo may not. More validity,
More honorable state, more courtship lives
In carrion flies than Romeo. They may seize 35
On the white wonder of dear Juliet's hand
And steal immortal blessing from her lips,
Who, even in pure and vestal modesty,
Still blush, as thinking their own kisses sin;
But Romeo may not—he is banished. 40
This may flies do, when I from this must fly;
They are free men, but I am banished.
And sayst thou yet that exile is not death?
Hadst thou no poison mixed, no sharp-ground knife,
No sudden mean of death, though ne'er so mean,
But "banished" to kill me—"banished"? 46
O friar, the damned use that word in hell;
Howling attends it! How hast thou the heart,
Being a divine, a ghostly confessor,
A sin-absolver, and my friend professed, 50
To mangle me with that word "banished"?
Friar. Thou fond mad man, hear me a little speak.
Rom. O, thou wilt speak again of banishment.
Friar. I'll give thee armor to keep off that word;
Adversity's sweet milk, philosophy, 55
To comfort thee, though thou art banished.
Rom. Yet "banished"? Hang up philosophy!
Unless philosophy can make a Juliet,
Displant a town, reverse a prince's doom,
It helps not, it prevails not. Talk no more. 60
Friar. O, then I see that madmen have no ears.
Rom. How should they, when that wise men have no eyes?
Friar. Let me dispute with thee of thy estate.
Rom. Thou canst not speak of that thou dost not feel.
Wert thou as young as I, Juliet thy love, 65
An hour but married, Tybalt murdered,
Doting like me, and like me banished,
Then mightst thou speak, then mightst thou tear thy hair,
And fall upon the ground, as I do now,
Taking the measure of an unmade grave. 70

Nurse knocks [within].

Friar. Arise; one knocks. Good Romeo, hide thyself.
Rom. Not I; unless the breath of heartsick groans
Mistlike infold me from the search of eyes. *Knock.*
Friar. Hark, how they knock! Who's there? Romeo, arise;
Thou wilt be taken.—Stay awhile!—stand up; 75
Knock.
Run to my study.—By-and-by!—God's will,
What simpleness is this.—I come, I come! *Knock.*
Who knocks so hard? Whence come you? What's your will?
Nurse. [*Within*] Let me come in, and you shall know my errand.
I come from Lady Juliet.
Friar. Welcome then. 80

Enter NURSE.

Nurse. O holy friar, O, tell me, holy friar,
Where is my lady's lord, where's Romeo?
Friar. There on the ground, with his own tears made drunk.
Nurse. O, he is even in my mistress' case,
Just in her case! O woeful sympathy! 85
Piteous predicament! Even so lies she,
Blubb'ring and weeping, weeping and blubbering.
Stand up, stand up! Stand, an you be a man.
For Juliet's sake, for her sake, rise and stand!
Why should you fall into so deep an O? 90
Rom. (*Rises*) Nurse—
Nurse. Ah sir! ah sir! Well, death's the end of all.
Rom. Spakest thou of Juliet? How is it with her?
Doth not she think me an old murderer,
Now I have stained the childhood of our joy 95
With blood removed but little from her own?
Where is she? and how doth she? and what says
My concealed lady to our canceled love?
Nurse. O, she says nothing, sir, but weeps and weeps;
And now falls on her bed, and then starts up, 100
And Tybalt calls; and then on Romeo cries,
And then down falls again.
Rom. As if that name,
Shot from the deadly level of a gun,
Did murder her; as that name's cursed hand
Murdered her kinsman. O, tell me, friar, tell me,
In what vile part of this anatomy 106
Doth my name lodge? Tell me, that I may sack
The hateful mansion. [*Draws his dagger.*]
Friar. Hold thy desperate hand.
Art thou a man? Thy form cries out thou art;
Thy tears are womanish, thy wild acts denote 110

26. rushed: pushed
28. dear: extraordinary
33. validity: worth
52. fond: foolish
62. when that: when
63. dispute: discuss; **estate:** condition
90. O: lamentation
94. old: an intensive
103. level: aim

The unreasonable fury of a beast.
Unseemly woman in a seeming man!
Or ill-beseeming beast in seeming both!
Thou hast amazed me. By my holy order,
I thought thy disposition better tempered. 115
Hast thou slain Tybalt? Wilt thou slay thyself?
And slay thy lady too that lives in thee,
By doing damned hate upon thyself? 118
Why railst thou on thy birth, the heaven, and earth?
Since birth and heaven and earth, all three do meet
In thee at once; which thou at once wouldst lose.
Fie, fie, thou shamest thy shape, thy love, thy wit,
Which, like a usurer, aboundst in all,
And usest none in that true use indeed 124
Which should bedeck thy shape, thy love, thy wit.
Thy noble shape is but a form of wax,
Digressing from the valor of a man;
Thy dear love sworn but hollow perjury,
Killing that love which thou hast vowed to cherish;
Thy wit, that ornament of shape and love, 130
Misshapen in the conduct of them both,
Like powder in a skill-less soldier's flask,
Is set afire by thine own ignorance,
And thou dismembered with thine own defense.
What, rouse thee, man! Thy Juliet is alive, 135
For whose dear sake thou wast but lately dead.
There art thou happy. Tybalt would kill thee,
But thou slewest Tybalt. There art thou happy.
The law, that threatened death, becomes thy friend
And turns it to exile. There art thou happy. 140
A pack of blessings light upon thy back;
Happiness courts thee in her best array;
But, like a misbehaved and sullen wench,
Thou poutst upon thy fortune and thy love.
Take heed, take heed, for such die miserable. 145
Go get thee to thy love, as was decreed,
Ascend her chamber, hence and comfort her.
But look thou stay not till the watch be set,
For then thou canst not pass to Mantua,
Where thou shalt live till we can find a time 150
To blaze your marriage, reconcile your friends,
Beg pardon of the Prince, and call thee back
With twenty hundred thousand times more joy
Than thou wentst forth in lamentation.
Go before, nurse. Commend me to thy lady, 155
And bid her hasten all the house to bed,
Which heavy sorrow makes them apt unto.
Romeo is coming.

Nurse. O Lord, I could have stayed here all the night
To hear good counsel. O, what learning is! 160
My lord, I'll tell my lady you will come.

Rom. Do so, and bid my sweet prepare to chide.

Nurse offers to go and turns again.

Nurse. Here is a ring she bid me give you, sir.
Hie you, make haste, for it grows very late. *Exit.*

Rom. How well my comfort is revived by this!

Friar. Go hence; good night; and here stands all your state: 166
Either be gone before the watch be set,
Or by the break of day disguised from hence.
Sojourn in Mantua. I'll find out your man,
And he shall signify from time to time 170
Every good hap to you that chances here.
Give me thy hand. 'Tis late. Farewell; good night.

Rom. But that a joy past joy calls out on me,
It were a grief so brief to part with thee.
Farewell.

Exeunt.

[Scene IV. *Capulet's house.*]

Enter Old Capulet, *his* Wife, *and* Paris.

Cap. Things have fall'n out, sir, so unluckily
That we have had no time to move our daughter.
Look you, she loved her kinsman Tybalt dearly,
And so did I. Well, we were born to die.
'Tis very late; she'll not come down tonight. 5
I promise you, but for your company,
I would have been abed an hour ago.

Par. These times of woe afford no time to woo.
Madam, good night. Commend me to your daughter.

Lady. I will, and know her mind early tomorrow;
Tonight she's mewed up to her heaviness. 11

Paris offers to go and Capulet calls him again.

Cap. Sir Paris, I will make a desperate tender
Of my child's love. I think she will be ruled
In all respects by me; nay more, I doubt it not.
Wife, go you to her ere you go to bed; 15
Acquaint her here of my son Paris' love
And bid her (mark you me?) on Wednesday next—
But, soft! what day is this?

Par. Monday, my lord.

Cap. Monday! ha, ha! Well, Wednesday is too soon.
A Thursday let it be—a Thursday, tell her, 20
She shall be married to this noble earl.
Will you be ready? Do you like this haste?

113. ill-beseeming beast: i.e., beast that makes a poor semblance
123. usurer: moneylender
124. use: a quibble on the sense "lend at interest"
148. the . . . set: the night watch takes its station at the gates
151. blaze: blazon; proclaim; **your friends:** your respective families

165. comfort: happiness
11. mewed . . . heaviness: a prisoner of her sorrow. Falcons were confined in "mews," from which the verb **mewed** derives.
12. desperate tender: rash offer
20. A: on

We'll keep no great ado—a friend or two;
For hark you, Tybalt being slain so late,
It may be thought we held him carelessly, 25
Being our kinsman, if we revel much.
Therefore we'll have some half a dozen friends,
And there an end. But what say you to Thursday?

Par. My lord, I would that Thursday were tomorrow.

Cap. Well, get you gone. A Thursday be it then.
Go you to Juliet ere you go to bed; 31
Prepare her, wife, against this wedding day.
Farewell, my lord.—Light to my chamber, ho!
Afore me, it is so very very late
That we may call it early by-and-by. 35
Good night.

Exeunt.

[Scene V. *Capulet's orchard.*]

Enter ROMEO *and* JULIET *aloft, at the window.*

Jul. Wilt thou be gone? It is not yet near day.
It was the nightingale, and not the lark,
That pierced the fearful hollow of thine ear.
Nightly she sings on yond pomegranate tree.
Believe me, love, it was the nightingale. 5

Rom. It was the lark, the herald of the morn;
No nightingale. Look, love, what envious streaks
Do lace the severing clouds in yonder East.
Night's candles are burnt out, and jocund day
Stands tiptoe on the misty mountain tops. 10
I must be gone and live, or stay and die.

Jul. Yond light is not daylight; I know it, I.
It is some meteor that the sun exhales
To be to thee this night a torchbearer
And light thee on thy way to Mantua. 15
Therefore stay yet; thou needst not to be gone.

Rom. Let me be ta'en, let me be put to death.
I am content, so thou wilt have it so.
I'll say yon grey is not the morning's eye,
'Tis but the pale reflex of Cynthia's brow; 20
Nor that is not the lark whose notes do beat
The vaulty heaven so high above our heads.
I have more care to stay than will to go.
Come, death, and welcome! Juliet wills it so.
How is't, my soul? Let's talk; it is not day. 25

Jul. It is, it is! Hie hence, be gone, away!
It is the lark that sings so out of tune,
Straining harsh discords and unpleasing sharps.
Some say the lark makes sweet division;
This doth not so, for she divideth us. 30
Some say the lark and loathed toad changed eyes;
O, now I would they had changed voices too,
Since arm from arm that voice doth us affray,
Hunting thee hence with hunt's-up to the day!
O, now be gone! More light and light it grows. 35

Rom. More light and light—more dark and dark our woes!

Enter NURSE, *hastily.*

Nurse. Madam!

Jul. Nurse?

Nurse. Your lady mother is coming to your chamber.
The day is broke; be wary, look about. [*Exit.*] 40

Jul. Then, window, let day in, and let life out.

Rom. Farewell, farewell! One kiss, and I'll descend. *He goeth down.*

Jul. Art thou gone so, my lord, my love, my friend?
I must hear from thee every day in the hour,
For in a minute there are many days. 45
O, by this count I shall be much in years
Ere I again behold my Romeo!

Rom. Farewell!
I will omit no opportunity
That may convey my greetings, love, to thee. 50

Jul. O, thinkst thou we shall ever meet again?

Rom. I doubt it not; and all these woes shall serve
For sweet discourses in our time to come.

Jul. O God, I have an ill-divining soul!
Methinks I see thee, now thou art below, 55
As one dead in the bottom of a tomb.
Either my eyesight fails, or thou lookst pale.

Rom. And trust me, love, in my eye so do you.
Dry sorrow drinks our blood. Adieu! adieu! *Exit.*

Jul. O Fortune, Fortune! all men call thee fickle.
If thou art fickle, what dost thou with him 61
That is renowmed for faith? Be fickle, Fortune,
For then I hope thou wilt not keep him long
But send him back.

Lady. [*Within*] Ho, daughter! are you up?

Jul. Who is't that calls? It is my lady mother. 65
Is she not down so late, or up so early?
What unaccustomed cause procures her hither?

23. **ado:** ceremony
25. **held . . . carelessly:** regarded him lightly
34. **Afore me:** my word; I declare
8. **lace:** streak; **severing:** scattering
13. **meteor:** regarded as an exhalation of gas from a star
19. **yon grey:** i.e., mingling of light with the dark
20. **reflex:** reflection; **Cynthia's brow:** the moon's face
22. **vaulty:** vaulted
23. **care:** eagerness
29. **division:** melody
31. **changed:** exchanged
33. **affray:** frighten
34. **hunt's-up:** a morning song to arouse hunters
46. **much . . . years.** many years older
54. **ill-divining:** prophesying misfortune
59. **Dry . . . blood:** it was believed that sorrow exhausted the body fluids, particularly the blood.
62. **renowmed:** renowned
67. **procures:** brings

Enter MOTHER.

Lady. Why, how now, Juliet?
Jul. Madam, I am not well.
Lady. Evermore weeping for your cousin's death?
What, wilt thou wash him from his grave with tears? 70
An if thou couldst, thou couldst not make him live.
Therefore have done. Some grief shows much of love;
But much of grief shows still some want of wit.
Jul. Yet let me weep for such a feeling loss.
Lady. So shall you feel the loss, but not the friend
Which you weep for.
Jul. Feeling so the loss, 76
I cannot choose but ever weep the friend.
Lady. Well, girl, thou weepst not so much for his death
As that the villain lives which slaughtered him.
Jul. What villain, madam?
Lady. That same villain Romeo. 80
Jul. [*Aside*] Villain and he be many miles asunder.—
God pardon him! I do, with all my heart;
And yet no man like he doth grieve my heart.
Lady. That is because the traitor murderer lives.
Jul. Ay, madam, from the reach of these my hands. 85
Would none but I might venge my cousin's death!
Lady. We will have vengeance for it, fear thou not.
Then weep no more. I'll send to one in Mantua,
Where that same banished runagate doth live,
Shall give him such an unaccustomed dram 90
That he shall soon keep Tybalt company;
And then I hope thou wilt be satisfied.
Jul. Indeed I never shall be satisfied
With Romeo till I behold him—dead—
Is my poor heart so for a kinsman vexed. 95
Madam, if you could find out but a man
To bear a poison, I would temper it;
That Romeo should, upon receipt thereof,
Soon sleep in quiet. O, how my heart abhors
To hear him named and cannot come to him, 100
To wreak the love I bore my cousin Tybalt
Upon his body that hath slaughtered him!
Lady. Find thou the means, and I'll find such a man.
But now I'll tell thee joyful tidings, girl.
Jul. And joy comes well in such a needy time.
What are they, I beseech your ladyship? 106
Lady. Well, well, thou hast a careful father, child;
One who, to put thee from thy heaviness,
Hath sorted out a sudden day of joy
That thou expects not nor I looked not for. 110
Jul. Madam, in happy time! What day is that?
Lady. Marry, my child, early next Thursday morn
The gallant, young, and noble gentleman,
The County Paris, at St. Peter's Church,
Shall happily make thee there a joyful bride. 115
Jul. Now by St. Peter's Church, and Peter too,
He shall not make me there a joyful bride!
I wonder at this haste, that I must wed
Ere he that should be husband comes to woo.
I pray you tell my lord and father, madam, 120
I will not marry yet; and when I do, I swear
It shall be Romeo, whom you know I hate,
Rather than Paris. These are news indeed!
Lady. Here comes your father. Tell him so yourself,
And see how he will take it at your hands. 125

Enter CAPULET *and* NURSE.

Cap. When the sun sets the air doth drizzle dew,
But for the sunset of my brother's son
It rains downright.
How now? a conduit, girl? What, still in tears?
Evermore show'ring? In one little body 130
Thou counterfeitst a bark, a sea, a wind:
For still thy eyes, which I may call the sea,
Do ebb and flow with tears; the bark thy body is,
Sailing in this salt flood; the winds, thy sighs,
Who, raging with thy tears and they with them,
Without a sudden calm will overset 136
Thy tempest-tossed body. How now, wife?
Have you delivered to her our decree?
Lady. Ay, sir; but she will none, she gives you thanks.
I would the fool were married to her grave! 140
Cap. Soft! take me with you, take me with you, wife.
How? Will she none? Doth she not give us thanks?
Is she not proud? Doth she not count her blest,
Unworthy as she is, that we have wrought
So worthy a gentleman to be her bridegroom? 145
Jul. Not proud you have, but thankful that you have.
Proud can I never be of what I hate,
But thankful even for hate that is meant love.
Cap. How, how, how, how, choplogic? What is this?
"Proud"—and "I thank you"—and "I thank you not"— 150
And yet "not proud"? Mistress minion you,

74. feeling: deeply felt
89. runagate: runaway
97. temper: adulterate
109. sorted out: selected

111. in . . . time: opportunely
129. conduit: fountain
141. take . . . you: let me understand you
144. wrought: arranged for
149. choplogic: quibbler
151. minion: spoiled darling

Thank me no thankings, nor proud me no prouds,
But fettle your fine joints 'gainst Thursday next
To go with Paris to St. Peter's Church,
Or I will drag thee on a hurdle thither. 155
Out, you green-sickness carrion! out, you baggage!
You tallow-face!

Lady. Fie, fie; what, are you mad?

Jul. Good father, I beseech you on my knees,

She kneels down.

Hear me with patience but to speak a word.

Cap. Hang thee, young baggage! disobedient wretch! 160
I tell thee what—get thee to church a Thursday
Or never after look me in the face.
Speak not, reply not, do not answer me!
My fingers itch. Wife, we scarce thought us blest
That God had lent us but this only child; 165
But now I see this one is one too much,
And that we have a curse in having her.
Out on her, hilding!

Nurse. God in heaven bless her!
You are to blame, my lord, to rate her so.

Cap. And why, my Lady Wisdom? Hold your tongue, 170
Good Prudence. Smatter with your gossips, go!

Nurse. I speak no treason.

Cap. O, God-i-god-en!

Nurse. May not one speak?

Cap. Peace, you mumbling fool!
Utter your gravity o'er a gossip's bowl,
For here we need it not.

Lady. You are too hot. 175

Cap. God's bread! it makes me mad. Day, night, late, early,
At home, abroad, alone, in company,
Waking or sleeping, still my care hath been
To have her matched; and having now provided
A gentleman of princely parentage, 180
Of fair demesnes, youthful, and nobly trained,
Stuffed, as they say, with honorable parts,
Proportioned as one's thought would wish a man—
And then to have a wretched puling fool,
A whining mammet, in her fortunes tender, 185
To answer "I'll not wed, I cannot love;
I am too young, I pray you pardon me"!
But, an you will not wed, I'll pardon you.
Graze where you will, you shall not house with me.
Look to't, think on't; I do not use to jest. 190
Thursday is near; lay hand on heart, advise:
An you be mine, I'll give you to my friend;
An you be not, hang, beg, starve, die in the streets,
For, by my soul, I'll ne'er acknowledge thee,
Nor what is mine shall never do thee good. 195
Trust to't. Bethink you. I'll not be forsworn. *Exit.*

Jul. Is there no pity sitting in the clouds
That sees into the bottom of my grief?
O sweet my mother, cast me not away!
Delay this marriage for a month, a week; 200
Or if you do not, make the bridal bed
In that dim monument where Tybalt lies.

Lady. Talk not to me, for I'll not speak a word.
Do as thou wilt, for I have done with thee. *Exit.*

Jul. O God!—O nurse, how shall this be prevented? 205
My husband is on earth, my faith in heaven.
How shall that faith return again to earth
Unless that husband send it me from heaven
By leaving earth? Comfort me, counsel me.
Alack, alack, that heaven should practice stratagems
Upon so soft a subject as myself! 211
What sayst thou? Hast thou not a word of joy?
Some comfort, nurse.

Nurse. Faith, here it is.
Romeo is banisht; and all the world to nothing
That he dares ne'er come back to challenge you;
Or if he do, it needs must be by stealth. 216
Then, since the case so stands as now it doth,
I think it best you married with the County.
O, he's a lovely gentleman!
Romeo's a dishclout to him. An eagle, madam, 220
Hath not so green, so quick, so fair an eye
As Paris hath. Beshrew my very heart,
I think you are happy in this second match,
For it excels your first; or if it did not,
Your first is dead—or 'twere as good he were 225
As living here and you no use of him.

Jul. Speakst thou this from thy heart?

Nurse. And from my soul too; else beshrew them both.

Jul. Amen!

Nurse. What? 230

Jul. Well, thou hast comforted me marvelous much.
Go in; and tell my lady I am gone,
Having displeased my father, to Laurence' cell,
To make confession and to be absolved. 234

Nurse. Marry, I will; and this is wisely done. *Exit.*

153. fettle: prepare
155. hurdle: a sledge on which criminals were dragged to their executions
156. green-sickness carrion: anemic piece of flesh. **Green-sickness** is an anemia of young girls.
168. hilding: good-for-nothing
169. rate: scold
171. Smatter: chatter
174. gossip's bowl: a hot punch
176. God's bread: the wafer used in Holy Communion
184. puling: whining
185. mammet: doll; **in . . . tender:** inexperienced
188. pardon you: excuse you from my company; banish you from my sight
191. advise: consider well
214. all . . . nothing: the odds are all to nothing
215. challenge: claim
220. to: compared with
221. quick: animated
226. here: i.e., on earth

Jul. Ancient damnation! O most wicked fiend!
Is it more sin to wish me thus forsworn,
Or to dispraise my lord with that same tongue
Which she hath praised him with above compare
So many thousand times? Go, counselor! 240
Thou and my bosom henceforth shall be twain.
I'll to the friar to know his remedy.
If all else fail, myself have power to die.
Exit.

236. Ancient damnation: aged devil!

241. bosom: confidence

[ACT IV]

[Scene I. *Friar Laurence's cell.*]

Enter Friar [Laurence] *and* County Paris.

Friar. On Thursday, sir? The time is very short.
Par. My father Capulet will have it so,
And I am nothing slow to slack his haste.
Friar. You say you do not know the lady's mind.
Uneven is the course; I like it not. 5
Par. Immoderately she weeps for Tybalt's death,
And therefore have I little talked of love;
For Venus smiles not in a house of tears.
Now, sir, her father counts it dangerous
That she do give her sorrow so much sway, 10
And in his wisdom hastes our marriage
To stop the inundation of her tears,
Which, too much minded by herself alone,
May be put from her by society.
Now do you know the reason of this haste. 15
Friar. [*Aside*] I would I knew not why it should be slowed.—
Look, sir, here comes the lady toward my cell.

Enter Juliet.

Par. Happily met, my lady and my wife!
Jul. That may be, sir, when I may be a wife.
Par. That may be must be, love, on Thursday next.
Jul. What must be shall be.
Friar. That's a certain text. 21
Par. Come you to make confession to this father?
Jul. To answer that, I should confess to you.
Par. Do not deny to him that you love me.
Jul. I will confess to you that I love him. 25
Par. So will ye, I am sure, that you love me.
Jul. If I do so, it will be of more price,
Being spoke behind your back, than to your face.
Par. Poor soul, thy face is much abused with tears.
Jul. The tears have got small victory by that, 30
For it was bad enough before their spite.
Par. Thou wrongst it more than tears with that report.
Jul. That is no slander, sir, which is a truth;
And what I spake, I spake it to my face.
Par. Thy face is mine, and thou hast slandered it.
Jul. It may be so, for it is not mine own. 36
Are you at leisure, holy father, now,
Or shall I come to you at evening Mass?
Friar. My leisure serves me, pensive daughter, now.
My lord, we must entreat the time alone. 40
Par. God shield I should disturb devotion!
Juliet, on Thursday early will I rouse ye.
Till then, adieu, and keep this holy kiss. *Exit.*
Jul. O, shut the door! and when thou has done so,
Come weep with me—past hope, past cure, past help! 45
Friar. Ah, Juliet, I already know thy grief;
It strains me past the compass of my wits.
I hear thou must, and nothing may prorogue it,
On Thursday next be married to this County.
Jul. Tell me not, friar, that thou hearst of this,
Unless thou tell me how I may prevent it. 51
If in thy wisdom thou canst give no help,
Do thou but call my resolution wise
And with this knife I'll help it presently.
God joined my heart and Romeo's, thou our hands;
And ere this hand, by thee to Romeo's sealed, 56
Shall be the label to another deed,

3. nothing . . . haste: too little reluctant to attempt to slow him
5. Uneven: difficult; rough

40. entreat . . . alone: request privacy
41. shield: prevent
47. strains . . . wits: taxes my wisdom; **compass:** limit
57. deed: i.e., deed of ownership

Or my true heart with treacherous revolt
Turn to another, this shall slay them both.
Therefore, out of thy long-experienced time, 60
Give me some present counsel; or, behold,
'Twixt my extremes and me this bloody knife
Shall play the umpire, arbitrating that
Which the commission of thy years and art
Could to no issue of true honor bring. 65
Be not so long to speak. I long to die
If what thou speakst speak not of remedy.

Friar. Hold, daughter. I do spy a kind of hope,
Which craves as desperate an execution
As that is desperate which we would prevent. 70
If, rather than to marry County Paris,
Thou hast the strength of will to slay thyself,
Then is it likely thou wilt undertake
A thing like death to chide away this shame,
That copest with death himself to scape from it;
And, if thou darest, I'll give thee remedy. 76

Jul. O, bid me leap, rather than marry Paris,
From off the battlements of yonder tower,
Or walk in thievish ways, or bid me lurk
Where serpents are; chain me with roaring bears,
Or shut me nightly in a charnel house, 81
O'ercovered quite with dead men's rattling bones,
With reeky shanks and yellow chapless skulls;
Or bid me go into a new-made grave
And hide me with a dead man in his shroud— 85
Things that, to hear them told, have made me tremble—
And I will do it without fear or doubt,
To live an unstained wife to my sweet love.

Friar. Hold, then. Go home, be merry, give consent
To marry Paris. Wednesday is tomorrow. 90
Tomorrow night look that thou lie alone;
Let not the nurse lie with thee in thy chamber.
Take thou this vial, being then in bed,
And this distilled liquor drink thou off;
When presently through all thy veins shall run 95
A cold and drowsy humor; for no pulse
Shall keep his native progress, but surcease;
No warmth, no breath, shall testify thou livest;
The roses in thy lips and cheeks shall fade
To paly ashes, thy eyes' windows fall 100
Like death when he shuts up the day of life;
Each part, deprived of supple government,
Shall, stiff and stark and cold, appear like death;
And in this borrowed likeness of shrunk death
Thou shalt continue two-and-forty hours, 105
And then awake as from a pleasant sleep.
Now, when the bridegroom in the morning comes
To rouse thee from thy bed, there art thou dead.
Then, as the manner of our country is,
In thy best robes, uncovered on the bier, 110
Thou shalt be borne to that same ancient vault
Where all the kindred of the Capulets lie.
In the mean time, against thou shalt awake,
Shall Romeo by my letters know our drift;
And hither shall he come; and he and I 115
Will watch thy waking, and that very night
Shall Romeo bear thee hence to Mantua.
And this shall free thee from this present shame,
If no inconstant toy nor womanish fear
Abate thy valor in the acting it. 120

Jul. Give me, give me! O, tell not me of fear!

Friar. Hold! Get you gone, be strong and prosperous
In this resolve. I'll send a friar with speed
To Mantua, with my letters to thy lord.

Jul. Love give me strength! and strength shall help afford. 125
Farewell, dear father.

Exeunt.

[Scene II. *Capulet's house.*]

Enter Father Capulet, Mother, Nurse, *and* Servingmen, two or three.

Cap. So many guests invite as here are writ.
[*Exit a Servingman.*]
Sirrah, go hire me twenty cunning cooks.

Serv. You shall have none ill, sir; for I'll try if they can lick their fingers.

Cap. How canst thou try them so? 5

Serv. Marry, sir, 'tis an ill cook that cannot lick his own fingers. Therefore he that cannot lick his fingers goes not with me.

Cap. Go, begone. *Exit Servingman.*
We shall be much unfurnished for this time. 10
What, is my daughter gone to Friar Laurence?

Nurse. Ay, forsooth.

Cap. Well, he may chance to do some good on her.
A peevish self-willed harlotry it is.

Enter Juliet.

Nurse. See where she comes from shrift with merry look. 15

64. **commission:** combination; **art:** learning
79. **in . . . ways:** in roads where thieves lurk
81. **charnel house:** a receptacle for loose bones uncovered when graves were dug
83. **reeky:** reeking; **chapless:** jawless
95. **presently:** immediately
96. **cold . . . humor:** liquid producing drowsiness
102. **supple government:** control of facility of movement
110. **uncovered:** i.e., with uncovered face
114. **drift:** intention
119. **inconstant toy:** irresolute whim
14. **peevish:** silly; **harlotry:** wench
15. **merry:** cheerful

Cap. How now, my headstrong? Where have you been gadding?
Jul. Where I have learnt me to repent the sin
Of disobedient opposition
To you and your behests, and am enjoined
By holy Laurence to fall prostrate here 20
To beg your pardon. Pardon, I beseech you!
Henceforward I am ever ruled by you.
Cap. Send for the County. Go tell him of this.
I'll have this knot knit up tomorrow morning.
Jul. I met the youthful lord at Laurence' cell 25
And gave him what becomed love I might,
Not stepping o'er the bounds of modesty.
Cap. Why, I am glad on't. This is well. Stand up.
This is as't should be. Let me see the County.
Ay, marry, go, I say, and fetch him hither. 30
Now, afore God, this reverend holy friar,
All our whole city is much bound to him.
Jul. Nurse, will you go with me into my closet
To help me sort such needful ornaments
As you think fit to furnish me tomorrow? 35
Mother. No, not till Thursday. There is time enough.
Cap. Go, nurse, go with her. We'll to church tomorrow. *Exeunt Juliet and Nurse.*
Mother. We shall be short in our provision.
'Tis now near night.
Cap. Tush, I will stir about,
And all things shall be well, I warrant thee, wife.
Go thou to Juliet, help to deck up her. 41
I'll not to bed tonight; let me alone.
I'll play the housewife for this once. What, ho!
They are all forth; well, I will walk myself
To County Paris, to prepare him up 45
Against tomorrow. My heart is wondrous light,
Since this same wayward girl is so reclaimed.
Exeunt.

[Scene III. *Juliet's chamber.*]

Enter JULIET *and* NURSE.

Jul. Ay, those attires are best; but, gentle nurse,
I pray thee leave me to myself tonight;
For I have need of many orisons
To move the heavens to smile upon my state, 4
Which, well thou knowest, is cross and full of sin.

Enter MOTHER.

19. behests: commands
26. becomed: becoming
32. bound: obligated
33. closet: boudoir
3. orisons: prayers
5. cross: irregular

Mother. What, are you busy, ho? Need you my help?
Jul. No, madam; we have culled such necessaries
As are behooveful for our state tomorrow.
So please you, let me now be left alone,
And let the nurse this night sit up with you; 10
For I am sure you have your hands full all
In this so sudden business.
Mother. Good night.
Get thee to bed and rest, for thou hast need.
Exeunt [Mother and Nurse].
Jul. Farewell! God knows when we shall meet again.
I have a faint cold fear thrills through my veins 15
That almost freezes up the heat of life.
I'll call them back again to comfort me.
Nurse!—What should she do here?
My dismal scene I needs must act alone.
Come, vial. 20
What if this mixture do not work at all?
Shall I be married then tomorrow morning?
No, no! This shall forbid it. Lie thou there.
[Lays down a dagger.]
What if it be a poison which the friar
Subtly hath ministered to have me dead, 25
Lest in this marriage he should be dishonored
Because he married me before to Romeo?
I fear it is; and yet methinks it should not,
For he hath still been tried a holy man.
How if, when I am laid into the tomb, 30
I wake before the time that Romeo
Come to redeem me? There's a fearful point!
Shall I not then be stifled in the vault,
To whose foul mouth no healthsome air breathes in,
And there die strangled ere my Romeo comes? 35
Or, if I live, is it not very like
The horrible conceit of death and night,
Together with the terror of the place—
As in a vault, an ancient receptacle
Where for this many hundred years the bones 40
Of all my buried ancestors are packed;
Where bloody Tybalt, yet but green in earth,
Lies fest'ring in his shroud; where, as they say,
At some hours in the night spirits resort—
Alack, alack, is it not like that I, 45
So early waking—what with loathsome smells,
And shrieks like mandrakes torn out of the earth,
That living mortals, hearing them, run mad—
O, if I wake, shall I not be distraught,

7. culled: chosen
8. behooveful: needful; **state:** pomp
19. dismal: dreadful
29. tried: shown by trial to be
36. like: likely
37. conceit: imagining
47. mandrakes: the roots of the *Mandragora officinarum* have a vague resemblance to a human figure. There was a popular fancy that the plant shrieked like a human when uprooted and that the sound caused madness.

Environed with all these hideous fears, 50
And madly play with my forefathers' joints,
And pluck the mangled Tybalt from his shroud,
And, in this rage, with some great kinsman's bone
As with a club dash out my desp'rate brains?
O, look! methinks I see my cousin's ghost 55
Seeking out Romeo, that did spit his body
Upon a rapier's point. Stay, Tybalt, stay!
Romeo, I come! this do I drink to thee.
She [drinks and] falls upon her bed within the curtains.

[Scene IV. *Capulet's house.*]

Enter LADY OF THE HOUSE *and* NURSE.

Lady. Hold, take these keys and fetch more spices, nurse.
Nurse. They call for dates and quinces in the pastry.

Enter OLD CAPULET.

Cap. Come, stir, stir, stir! The second cock hath crowed,
The curfew bell hath rung, 'tis three o'clock.
Look to the baked meats, good Angelica; 5
Spare not for cost.
Nurse. Go, you cot-quean, go,
Get you to bed! Faith, you'll be sick tomorrow
For this night's watching.
Cap. No, not a whit. What, I have watched ere now
All night for lesser cause, and ne'er been sick. 10
Lady. Ay, you have been a mouse-hunt in your time;
But I will watch you from such watching now.
Exeunt Lady and Nurse.
Cap. A jealous hood, a jealous hood!

Enter THREE OR FOUR [SERVANTS], *with spits and logs and baskets.*

Now, fellow,
What is there?
1. Serv. Things for the cook, sir; but I know not what. 15
Cap. Make haste, make haste. [*Exit Servant.*] Sirrah, fetch drier logs.
Call Peter; he will show thee where they are.
2. Serv. I have a head, sir, that will find out logs
And never trouble Peter for the matter.
Cap. Mass, and well said; a merry whoreson, ha!
Thou shalt be loggerhead. [*Exit Servant.*] Good faith, 'tis day. 21
The County will be here with music straight,
For so he said he would. (*Play music.*) I hear him near.
Nurse! Wife! What, ho! What, nurse, I say!

Enter NURSE.

Go waken Juliet; go and trim her up. 25
I'll go and chat with Paris. Hie, make haste,
Make haste! The bridegroom he is come already:
Make haste, I say.
[*Exeunt.*]

[Scene V. *Juliet's chamber.*]

[*Enter* NURSE.]

Nurse. Mistress! what, mistress! Juliet! Fast, I warrant her, she.
Why, lamb! why, lady! Fie, you slugabed!
Why, love, I say! madam! sweetheart! Why, bride!
What, not a word? You take your pennyworths now!
Sleep for a week; for the next night, I warrant, 5
The County Paris hath set up his rest
That you shall rest but little. God forgive me!
Marry, and amen. How sound is she asleep!
I needs must wake her. Madam, madam, madam!
Ay, let the County take you in your bed! 10
He'll fright you up, i' faith. Will it not be?
[*Opens the curtains.*]
What, dressed and in your clothes and down again?
I must needs wake you. Lady! lady! lady!
Alas, alas! Help, help! my lady's dead!
O welladay that ever I was born! 15
Some aqua vitae, ho! My lord! my lady!

Enter MOTHER.

Mother. What noise is here?
Nurse. O lamentable day!
Mother. What is the matter?
Nurse. Look, look! O heavy day!
Mother. O me, O me! My child, my only life!
Revive, look up, or I will die with thee! 20
Help, help! Call help.

57. Stay: hold your hand
2. pastry: pantry
6. cot-quean: housewife
8. For: because of; **watching:** wakefulness
11. mouse-hunt: woman-chaser; literally a term for the night-prowling weasel

20. Mass: by the Mass; **whoreson:** fellow
21. loggerhead: blockhead
6. set . . . rest: resolved

Enter FATHER.

Father. For shame, bring Juliet forth; her lord is come.

Nurse. She's dead, deceased; she's dead! Alack the day!

Mother. Alack the day, she's dead, she's dead, she's dead!

Cap. Ha! let me see her. Out alas! she's cold, 25
Her blood is settled, and her joints are stiff;
Life and these lips have long been separated.
Death lies on her like an untimely frost
Upon the sweetest flower of all the field.

Nurse. O lamentable day!

Mother. O woeful time! 30

Cap. Death, that hath ta'en her hence to make me wail,
Ties up my tongue and will not let me speak.

Enter FRIAR [LAURENCE] *and the* COUNTY [PARIS], *with* MUSICIANS.

Friar. Come, is the bride ready to go to church?

Cap. Ready to go, but never to return.
O son, the night before thy wedding day 35
Hath Death lain with thy wife. See, there she lies,
Flower as she was, deflowered by him.
Death is my son-in-law, Death is my heir;
My daughter he hath wedded. I will die
And leave him all. Life, living, all is Death's. 40

Par. Have I thought long to see this morning's face,
And doth it give me such a sight as this?

Mother. Accursed, unhappy, wretched, hateful day!
Most miserable hour that e'er time saw
In lasting labor of his pilgrimage! 45
But one, poor one, one poor and loving child,
But one thing to rejoice and solace in,
And cruel Death hath catched it from my sight!

Nurse. O woe! O woeful, woeful, woeful day!
Most lamentable day, most woeful day 50
That ever ever I did yet behold!
O day! O day! O day! O hateful day!
Never was seen so black a day as this.
O woeful day! O woeful day!

Par. Beguiled, divorced, wronged, spited, slain!
Most detestable Death, by thee beguiled, 56
By cruel cruel thee quite overthrown!
O love! O life! not life, but love in death!

Cap. Despised, distressed, hated, martyred, killed!
Uncomfortable time, why camest thou now 60
To murder, murder our solemnity?
O child! O child! my soul, and not my child!
Dead art thou, dead! alack, my child is dead,
And with my child my joys are buried!

Friar. Peace, ho, for shame! Confusion's cure lives not 65
In these confusions. Heaven and yourself
Had part in this fair maid! now heaven hath all,
And all the better is it for the maid.
Your part in her you could not keep from death,
But heaven keeps his part in eternal life. 70
The most you sought was her promotion,
For 'twas your heaven she should be advanced;
And weep ye now, seeing she is advanced
Above the clouds, as high as heaven itself?
O, in this love, you love your child so ill 75
That you run mad, seeing that she is well.
She's not well married that lives married long,
But she's best married that dies married young.
Dry up your tears and stick your rosemary
On this fair corse, and, as the custom is, 80
In all her best array bear her to church;
For though fond nature bids us all lament,
Yet nature's tears are reason's merriment.

Cap. All things that we ordained festival
Turn from their office to black funeral— 85
Our instruments to melancholy bells,
Our wedding cheer to a sad burial feast;
Our solemn hymns to sullen dirges change;
Our bridal flowers serve for a buried corse;
And all things change them to the contrary. 90

Friar. Sir, go you in; and, madam, go with him;
And go, Sir Paris. Every one prepare
To follow this fair corse unto her grave.
The heavens do lower upon you for some ill;
Move them no more by crossing their high will. 95

They all but the Nurse [and Musicians] go forth, casting rosemary on her and shutting the curtains.

1. Mus. Faith, we may put up our pipes and be gone.

Nurse. Honest good fellows, ah, put up, put up!
For well you know this is a pitiful case. [*Exit.*]

1. Mus. Ay, by my troth, the case may be amended.

Enter PETER.

Pet. Musicians, O musicians, "Heart's Ease," "Heart's Ease"! 100
O, and you will have me live, play "Heart's Ease."

1. Mus. Why "Heart's Ease"?

Pet. O, musicians, because my heart itself plays "My heart is full of woe." O, play me some merry dump to comfort me. 105

40. living: income
61. solemnity: festivity

65. Confusion's: catastrophe's
83. nature's . . . merriment: human nature is grieved at what common sense finds consoling.
87. cheer: food
88. sullen: mournful
94. ill: sin
105. dump: actually, a melancholy song or dance tune

1. Mus. Not a dump we! 'Tis no time to play now.

Pet. You will not then?

1. Mus. No.

Pet. I will then give it you soundly.

1. Mus. What will you give us? 110

Pet. No money, on my faith, but the gleek. I will give you the minstrel.

1. Mus. Then will I give you the serving-creature.

Pet. Then will I lay the serving-creature's dagger on your pate. I will carry no crotchets. I'll re 115 you, I'll fa you. Do you note me?

1. Mus. And you re us and fa us, you note us.

2. Mus. Pray you put up your dagger, and put out your wit.

Pet. Then have at you with my wit! I will 120 dry-beat you with an iron wit, and put up my iron dagger. Answer me like men.

"When griping grief the heart doth wound,
And doleful dumps the mind oppress,
Then music with her silver sound"— 125

111. gleek: taunt
112. give . . . minstrel: insult you by calling you "minstrel." Itinerant minstrels who lacked patrons were classed with rogues and beggars and were subject to statutory penalties.
115. carry: endure; **crotchets:** (1) fanciful notions; (2) quarter notes
118. put out: unsheathe
123–25. When . . . sound: a snatch from Richard Edwardes' "In Commendation of Music," the words to which appeared in *The Paradise of Dainty Devices* (1576).

Why "silver sound"? Why "music with her silver sound"? What say you, Simon Catling?

1. Mus. Marry, sir, because silver hath a sweet sound.

Pet. Pretty! What say you, Hugh Rebeck? 130

2. Mus. I say "silver sound" because musicians sound for silver.

Pet. Pretty too! What say you, James Soundpost?

3. Mus. Faith, I know not what to say.

Pet. O, I cry you mercy! you are the singer. I 135 will say for you. It is "music with her silver sound" because musicians have no gold for sounding.

"Then music with her silver sound
With speedy help doth lend redress." *Exit.*

1. Mus. What a pestilent knave is this 140 same!

2. Mus. Hang him, Jack! Come, we'll in here, tarry for the mourners, and stay dinner.

Exeunt.

127. Catling: a small lute string of catgut
130. Rebeck: an early form of violin
135. cry . . . mercy: beg your pardon
139. redress: relief
143. stay: stay for

[ACT V]

[Scene I. *A street in Mantua.*]

Enter ROMEO.

Rom. If I may trust the flattering truth of sleep,
My dreams presage some joyful news at hand.
My bosom's lord sits lightly in his throne,
And all this day an unaccustomed spirit
Lifts me above the ground with cheerful thoughts.
I dreamt my lady came and found me dead 6
(Strange dream that gives a dead man leave to think!)
And breathed such life with kisses in my lips
That I revived and was an emperor.
Ah me! how sweet is love itself possessed, 10
When but love's shadows are so rich in joy!

Enter ROMEO'S MAN BALTHASAR, *booted.*

News from Verona! How now, Balthasar?
Dost thou not bring me letters from the friar?
How doth my lady? Is my father well?
How fares my Juliet? That I ask again, 15
For nothing can be ill if she be well.

Bal. Then she is well, and nothing can be ill.
Her body sleeps in Capel's monument,
And her immortal part with angels lives.
I saw her laid low in her kindred's vault 20

3. bosom's lord: heart

And presently took post to tell it you.
O, pardon me for bringing these ill news,
Since you did leave it for my office, sir.
Rom. Is it e'en so? Then I defy you, stars!
Thou knowst my lodging. Get me ink and paper 25
And hire post horses. I will hence tonight.
Bal. I do beseech you, sir, have patience.
Your looks are pale and wild and do import
Some misadventure.
Rom. Tush, thou art deceived.
Leave me and do the thing I bid thee do. 30
Hast thou no letters to me from the friar?
Bal. No, my good lord.
Rom. No matter. Get thee gone
And hire those horses. I'll be with thee straight.
Exit [*Balthasar*].
Well, Juliet, I will lie with thee tonight.
Let's see for means. O mischief, thou art swift 35
To enter in the thoughts of desperate men!
I do remember an apothecary,
And hereabouts he dwells, which late I noted
In tattered weeds, with overwhelming brows,
Culling of simples. Meager were his looks, 40
Sharp misery had worn him to the bones;
And in his needy shop a tortoise hung,
An alligator stuffed, and other skins
Of ill-shaped fishes; and about his shelves
A beggarly account of empty boxes, 45
Green earthen pots, bladders, and musty seeds,
Remnants of packthread, and old cakes of roses
Were thinly scattered, to make up a show.
Noting this penury, to myself I said,
"An if a man did need a poison now, 50
Whose sale is present death in Mantua,
Here lives a caitiff wretch would sell it him."
O, this same thought did but forerun my need,
And this same needy man must sell it me.
As I remember, this should be the house. 55
Being holiday, the beggar's shop is shut.
What, ho! apothecary!

Enter APOTHECARY.

Apoth. Who calls so loud?
Rom. Come hither, man. I see that thou art poor.
Hold, there is forty ducats. Let me have
A dram of poison, such soon-speeding gear 60
As will disperse itself through all the veins

21. **took post:** hired a post horse
23. **office:** duty
39. **weeds:** garments; **overwhelming:** overhanging; frowning
40. **Culling:** sorting; **simples:** herbs
45. **account:** showing
47. **cakes . . . roses:** packets of rose petals for use in cosmetics and confections
52. **caitiff:** miserable
60. **gear:** stuff

That the life-weary taker may fall dead,
And that the trunk may be discharged of breath
As violently as hasty powder fired
Doth hurry from the fatal cannon's womb. 65
Apoth. Such mortal drugs I have; but Mantua's law
Is death to any he that utters them.
Rom. Art thou so bare and full of wretchedness
And fearest to die? Famine is in thy cheeks,
Need and oppression starveth in thine eyes, 70
Contempt and beggary hangs upon thy back:
The world is not thy friend, nor the world's law;
The world affords no law to make thee rich;
Then be not poor, but break it and take this.
Apoth. My poverty but not my will consents.
Rom. I pay thy poverty and not thy will. 76
Apoth. Put this in any liquid thing you will
And drink it off, and if you had the strength
Of twenty men it would dispatch you straight.
Rom. There is thy gold—worse poison to men's souls, 80
Doing more murder in this loathsome world,
Than these poor compounds that thou mayst not sell.
I sell thee poison; thou hast sold me none.
Farewell. Buy food and get thyself in flesh.
Come, cordial and not poison, go with me 85
To Juliet's grave; for there must I use thee.
Exeunt.

[Scene II. *Verona. Friar Laurence's cell.*]

Enter FRIAR JOHN *to* FRIAR LAURENCE.

John. Holy Franciscan friar, brother, ho!

Enter FRIAR LAURENCE.

Laur. This same should be the voice of Friar John.
Welcome from Mantua. What says Romeo?
Or, if his mind be writ, give me his letter.
John. Going to find a barefoot brother out, 5
One of our order to associate me,
Here in this city visiting the sick,
And finding him, the searchers of the town,
Suspecting that we both were in a house
Where the infectious pestilence did reign, 10
Sealed up the doors, and would not let us forth,
So that my speed to Mantua there was stayed.
Laur. Who bare my letter, then, to Romeo?

63. **trunk:** body
66. **mortal:** deadly
67. **utters:** distributes
85. **cordial:** stimulant; restorative
6. **associate:** accompany
8. **searchers:** officials who investigated deaths to detect cases of plague

John. I could not send it—here it is again—
Nor get a messenger to bring it thee, 15
So fearful were they of infection.
Laur. Unhappy fortune! By my brotherhood,
The letter was not nice, but full of charge,
Of dear import; and the neglecting it
May do much danger. Friar John, go hence, 20
Get me an iron crow and bring it straight
Unto my cell.
John. Brother, I'll go and bring it thee. *Exit.*
Laur. Now must I to the monument alone.
Within this three hours will fair Juliet wake.
She will beshrew me much that Romeo 25
Hath had no notice of these accidents;
But I will write again to Mantua,
And keep her at my cell till Romeo come—
Poor living corse, closed in a dead man's tomb!
Exit.

[Scene III. *A churchyard with the Capulets' tomb.*]

Enter PARIS *and his* PAGE *with flowers and* [*a torch*].

Par. Give me thy torch, boy. Hence, and stand aloof.
Yet put it out, for I would not be seen.
Under yond yew tree lay thee all along,
Holding thine ear close to the hollow ground.
So shall no foot upon the churchyard tread 5
(Being loose, unfirm, with digging up of graves)
But thou shalt hear it. Whistle then to me,
As signal that thou hearst something approach.
Give me those flowers. Do as I bid thee, go.
Page. [*Aside*] I am almost afraid to stand alone
Here in the churchyard; yet I will adventure. 11
[*Withdraws.*]
Par. Sweet flower, with flowers thy bridal bed I strew *He strews the tomb with flowers.*
(O woe! thy canopy is dust and stones)
Which with sweet water nightly I will dew;
Or, wanting that, with tears distilled by moans. 15
The obsequies that I for thee will keep
Nightly shall be to strew thy grave and weep.
Whistle Boy.
The boy gives warning something doth approach.
What cursed foot wanders this way tonight
To cross my obsequies and true love's rite? 20
What, with a torch? Muffle me, night, awhile.
[*Withdraws.*]

Enter ROMEO, *and* BALTHASAR *with a torch, a mattock, and a crow of iron.*

Rom. Give me that mattock and the wrenching iron.
Hold, take this letter. Early in the morning
See thou deliver it to my lord and father.
Give me the light. Upon thy life I charge thee, 25
Whate'er thou hearest or seest, stand all aloof
And do not interrupt me in my course.
Why I descend into this bed of death
Is partly to behold my lady's face,
But chiefly to take thence from her dead finger 30
A precious ring—a ring that I must use
In dear employment. Therefore hence, be gone.
But if thou, jealous, dost return to pry
In what I farther shall intend to do,
By heaven, I will tear thee joint by joint 35
And strew this hungry churchyard with thy limbs.
The time and my intents are savage-wild,
More fierce and more inexorable far
Than empty tigers or the roaring sea.
Bal. I will be gone, sir, and not trouble you. 40
Rom. So shalt thou show me friendship. Take thou that.
Live, and be prosperous; and farewell, good fellow.
Bal. [*Aside*] For all this same, I'll hide me hereabout.
His looks I fear, and his intents I doubt.
[*Withdraws.*]
Rom. Thou detestable maw, thou womb of death,
Gorged with the dearest morsel of the earth, 46
Thus I enforce thy rotten jaws to open,
And in despite I'll cram thee with more food.
Romeo opens the tomb.
Par. This is that banisht haughty Montague
That murdered my love's cousin—with which grief
It is supposed the fair creature died— 51
And here is come to do some villainous shame
To the dead bodies. I will apprehend him.
Stop thy unhallowed toil, vile Montague!
Can vengeance be pursued further than death? 55
Condemned villain, I do apprehend thee.
Obey, and go with me; for thou must die.
Rom. I must indeed; and therefore came I hither.
Good gentle youth, tempt not a desp'rate man.
Fly hence and leave me. Think upon these gone;
Let them affright thee. I beseech thee, youth, 61
Put not another sin upon my head
By urging me to fury. O, be gone!
By heaven, I love thee better than myself,
For I come hither armed against myself. 65

18. **nice:** trifling; **charge:** importance
25. **beshrew:** condemn
26. **accidents:** happenings
14. **sweet water:** perfume
15. **wanting:** lacking
20. **cross:** hinder
22. **mattock:** a digging tool
33. **jealous:** suspicious
45. **maw:** stomach
48. **despite:** spite

Stay not, be gone. Live, and hereafter say
A madman's mercy bid thee run away.
Par. I do defy thy conjuration
And apprehend thee for a felon here. 69
Rom. Wilt thou provoke me? Then have at thee, boy! *They fight.*
Page. O Lord, they fight! I will go call the watch. [*Exit.*]
Par. O, I am slain! [*Falls.*] If thou be merciful,
Open the tomb, lay me with Juliet. [*Dies.*]
Rom. In faith, I will. Let me peruse this face.
Mercutio's kinsman, noble County Paris! 75
What said my man when my betossed soul
Did not attend him as we rode? I think
He told me Paris should have married Juliet.
Said he not so? or did I dream it so?
Or am I mad, hearing him talk of Juliet, 80
To think it was so? O, give me thy hand,
One writ with me in sour misfortune's book!
I'll bury thee in a triumphant grave.
A grave? O, no, a lantern, slaughtered youth,
For here lies Juliet, and her beauty makes 85
This vault a feasting presence full of light.
Death, lie thou there, by a dead man interred.
[*Lays Paris in the tomb.*]
How oft when men are at the point of death
Have they been merry! which their keepers call
A lightning before death. O, how may I 90
Call this a lightning? O my love! my wife!
Death, that hath sucked the honey of thy breath,
Hath had no power yet upon thy beauty.
Thou art not conquered. Beauty's ensign yet
Is crimson in thy lips and in thy cheeks, 95
And death's pale flag is not advanced there.
Tybalt, liest thou there in thy bloody sheet?
O, what more favor can I do to thee
Than with that hand that cut thy youth in twain
To sunder his that was thine enemy? 100
Forgive me, cousin! Ah, dear Juliet,
Why art thou yet so fair? Shall I believe
That unsubstantial Death is amorous,
And that the lean abhorred monster keeps
Thee here in dark to be his paramour? 105
For fear of that I still will stay with thee
And never from this palace of dim night
Depart again. Here, here will I remain
With worms that are thy chambermaids. O, here
Will I set up my everlasting rest 110
And shake the yoke of inauspicious stars
From this world-wearied flesh. Eyes, look your last!
Arms, take your last embrace! and, lips, O you
The doors of breath, seal with a righteous kiss
A dateless bargain to engrossing death! 115
Come, bitter conduct; come, unsavory guide!
Thou desperate pilot, now at once run on
The dashing rocks thy seasick weary bark!
Here's to my love! [*Drinks.*] O true apothecary!
Thy drugs are quick. Thus with a kiss I die. 120
Falls.

Enter FRIAR [LAURENCE], *with lantern, crow, and spade.*

Friar. St. Francis be my speed! how oft tonight
Have my old feet stumbled at graves! Who's there?
Bal. Here's one, a friend, and one that knows you well.
Friar. Bliss be upon you! Tell me, good my friend,
What torch is yond that vainly lends his light 125
To grubs and eyeless skulls? As I discern,
It burneth in the Capels' monument.
Bal. It doth so, holy sir; and there's my master,
One that you love.
Friar. Who is it?
Bal. Romeo. 129
Friar. How long hath he been there?
Bal. Full half an hour.
Friar. Go with me to the vault.
Bal. I dare not, sir.
My master knows not but I am gone hence,
And fearfully did menace me with death
If I did stay to look on his intents.
Friar. Stay then; I'll go alone. Fear comes upon me. 135
O, much I fear some ill unthrifty thing.
Bal. As I did sleep under this yew tree here,
I dreamt my master and another fought,
And that my master slew him.
Friar. Romeo!
Stoops and looks on the blood and weapons.
Alack, alack, what blood is this which stains 140
The stony entrance of this sepulcher?
What mean these masterless and gory swords
To lie discolored by this place of peace?
[*Enters the tomb.*]
Romeo! O, pale! Who else? What, Paris too?
And steeped in blood? Ah, what an unkind hour
Is guilty of this lamentable chance! 146
The lady stirs. *Juliet rises.*
Jul. O comfortable friar! where is my lord?
I do remember well where I should be,
And there I am. Where is my Romeo? 150
Friar. I hear some noise. Lady, come from that nest
Of death, contagion, and unnatural sleep.

68. conjuration: bidding
83. triumphant: splendid
84. lantern: i.e., a lantern tower, as in a cathedral
86. feasting presence: festive reception room
87. Death: dead man (Paris)
115. dateless: eternal; **engrossing:** monopolizing
119. true: honest
136. unthrifty: unlucky
148. comfortable: comforting

A greater power than we can contradict
Hath thwarted our intents. Come, come away.
Thy husband in thy bosom there lies dead; 155
And Paris too. Come, I'll dispose of thee
Among a sisterhood of holy nuns.
Stay not to question, for the watch is coming.
Come, go, good Juliet. I dare no longer stay.
Jul. Go, get thee hence, for I will not away. 160
Exit [Friar].
What's here? A cup, closed in my truelove's hand?
Poison, I see, hath been his timeless end.
O churl! drunk all, and left no friendly drop
To help me after? I will kiss thy lips.
Haply some poison yet doth hang on them 165
To make me die with a restorative. [*Kisses him.*]
Thy lips are warm!
Chief Watch. [*Within*] Lead, boy. Which way?
Jul. Yea, noise? Then I'll be brief. O happy dagger! [*Snatches Romeo's dagger.*]
This is thy sheath; there rest, and let me die.
She stabs herself and falls.

Enter [PARIS'] BOY *and* WATCH.

Boy. This is the place. There, where the torch doth burn. 170
Chief Watch. The ground is bloody. Search about the churchyard.
Go, some of you; whoe'er you find attach.
[*Exeunt some of the Watch.*]
Pitiful sight! here lies the County slain;
And Juliet bleeding, warm, and newly dead,
Who here hath lain this two days buried. 175
Go, tell the Prince; run to the Capulets;
Raise up the Montagues; some others search.
[*Exeunt others of the Watch.*]
We see the ground whereon these woes do lie,
But the true ground of all these piteous woes
We cannot without circumstance descry. 180

Enter [SOME OF THE WATCH,] *with* ROMEO'S MAN [BALTHASAR].

2. Watch. Here's Romeo's man. We found him in the churchyard.
Chief Watch. Hold him in safety till the Prince come hither.

Enter FRIAR [LAURENCE] *and* ANOTHER WATCHMAN.

3. Watch. Here is a friar that trembles, sighs, and weeps.
We took this mattock and this spade from him
As he was coming from this churchyard side. 185
Chief Watch. A great suspicion! Stay the friar too.

Enter the PRINCE [*and* ATTENDANTS].

Prince. What misadventure is so early up,
That calls our person from our morning rest?

Enter CAPULET *and his* WIFE [*with others*].

Cap. What should it be, that they so shriek abroad?
Wife. The people in the street cry "Romeo," 190
Some "Juliet," and some "Paris"; and all run,
With open outcry, toward our monument.
Prince. What fear is this which startles in our ears?
Chief Watch. Sovereign, here lies the County Paris slain;
And Romeo dead; and Juliet, dead before, 195
Warm and new killed.
Prince. Search, seek, and know how this foul murder comes.
Chief Watch. Here is a friar, and slaughtered Romeo's man,
With instruments upon them fit to open
These dead men's tombs. 200
Cap. O heavens! O wife, look how our daughter bleeds!
This dagger hath mista'en, for, lo, his house
Is empty on the back of Montague,
And it missheathed in my daughter's bosom!
Wife. O me! this sight of death is as a bell 205
That warns my old age to a sepulcher.

Enter MONTAGUE [*and others*].

Prince. Come, Montague; for thou art early up
To see thy son and heir now early down.
Mon. Alas, my liege, my wife is dead tonight!
Grief of my son's exile hath stopped her breath.
What further woe conspires against mine age? 211
Prince. Look, and thou shalt see.
Mon. O thou untaught! what manners is in this,
To press before thy father to a grave?
Prince. Seal up the mouth of outrage for a while,
Till we can clear these ambiguities 216
And know their spring, their head, their true descent;
And then will I be general of your woes
And lead you even to death. Meantime forbear,

158. question: argue
162. timeless: untimely
163. churl: miser
165. Haply: perhaps
168. happy: opportune
172. attach: seize
178. woes: woeful things
180. circumstance: full explanation

186. great suspicion: very suspicious thing
202. mista'en: mistaken; missed its proper target
206. warns: summons
215. Seal . . . outrage: restrain your clamor

And let mischance be slave to patience. 220
Bring forth the parties of suspicion.
Friar. I am the greatest, able to do least,
Yet most suspected, as the time and place
Doth make against me, of this direful murder;
And here I stand, both to impeach and purge 225
Myself condemned and myself excused.
Prince. Then say at once what thou dost know in this.
Friar. I will be brief, for my short date of breath
Is not so long as is a tedious tale. 229
Romeo, there dead, was husband to that Juliet;
And she, there dead, that Romeo's faithful wife.
I married them; and their stol'n marriage day
Was Tybalt's doomsday, whose untimely death
Banisht the new-made bridegroom from this city;
For whom, and not for Tybalt, Juliet pined. 235
You, to remove that siege of grief from her,
Betrothed and would have married her perforce
To County Paris. Then comes she to me
And with wild looks bid me devise some mean
To rid her from this second marriage, 240
Or in my cell there would she kill herself.
Then gave I her (so tutored by my art)
A sleeping potion; which so took effect
As I intended, for it wrought on her 244
The form of death. Meantime I writ to Romeo
That he should hither come as this dire night
To help to take her from her borrowed grave,
Being the time the potion's force should cease.
But he which bore my letter, Friar John,
Was stayed by accident, and yesternight 250
Returned my letter back. Then all alone
At the prefixed hour of her waking
Came I to take her from her kindred's vault;
Meaning to keep her closely at my cell
Till I conveniently could send to Romeo. 255
But when I came, some minute ere the time
Of her awaking, here untimely lay
The noble Paris and true Romeo dead.
She wakes; and I entreated her come forth
And bear this work of heaven with patience; 260
But then a noise did scare me from the tomb,
And she, too desperate, would not go with me,
But, as it seems, did violence on herself.
All this I know, and to the marriage
Her nurse is privy; and if aught in this 265
Miscarried by my fault, let my old life
Be sacrificed, some hour before his time,
Unto the rigor of severest law.
Prince. We still have known thee for a holy man.
Where's Romeo's man? What can he say in this?
Bal. I brought my master news of Juliet's death;
And then in post he came from Mantua 272
To this same place, to this same monument.
This letter he early bid me give his father,
And threatened me with death, going in the vault,
If I departed not and left him there. 276
Prince. Give me the letter. I will look on it.
Where is the County's page that raised the watch?
Sirrah, what made your master in this place?
Boy. He came with flowers to strew his lady's grave; 280
And bid me stand aloof, and so I did.
Anon comes one with light to ope the tomb;
And by-and-by my master drew on him;
And then I ran away to call the watch.
Prince. This letter doth make good the friar's words, 285
Their course of love, the tidings of her death;
And here he writes that he did buy a poison
Of a poor pothecary, and therewithal
Came to this vault to die and lie with Juliet.
Where be these enemies? Capulet, Montague, 290
See what a scourge is laid upon your hate,
That heaven finds means to kill your joys with love!
And I, for winking at your discords too,
Have lost a brace of kinsmen. All are punished.
Cap. O brother Montague, give me thy hand.
This is my daughter's jointure, for no more 296
Can I demand.
Mon. But I can give thee more;
For I will raise her statue in pure gold,
That whiles Verona by that name is known,
There shall no figure at such rate be set 300
As that of true and faithful Juliet.
Cap. As rich shall Romeo's by his lady's lie—
Poor sacrifices of our enmity!
Prince. A glooming peace this morning with it brings.
The sun for sorrow will not show his head. 305
Go hence, to have more talk of these sad things;
Some shall be pardoned, and some punished;
For never was a story of more woe
Than this of Juliet and her Romeo.

Exeunt omnes.

225. **impeach:** accuse; **purge:** clear
247. **borrowed:** temporary
252. **prefixed:** previously set
254. **closely:** secretly
265. **privy:** secretly informed
269. **still:** ever
272. **in post:** posthaste
291. **scourge:** punishment
292. **your joys:** the children in whom you joyed
296. **jointure:** dowry
300. **at . . . set:** be so highly valued

Titania and Bottom

Engraving by B. Rhodes after a painting by Henry Fuseli.

A MIDSUMMER NIGHT'S DREAM

INTRODUCTION

A Midsummer Night's Dream, like *Love's Labor's Lost,* has the appearance and form of a play written for a special occasion, in this case obviously a wedding, but the precise wedding for which it was composed has been the subject of much scholarly conjecture. Its present form may represent a revision for the public playhouse. Although several weddings of noble persons have been suggested as the occasion of the play's first performance, two from their dates and circumstances seem more plausible than the others: that of William Stanley, Earl of Derby, and Elizabeth Vere, daughter of the Earl of Oxford, which took place at Greenwich on January 26, 1595; and that of Thomas Berkeley and Elizabeth Carey at Blackfriars on February 19, 1596. Obvious compliments to the Queen, such as the allusion in Act II, Scene i, to the "fair Vestal, throned by the West," may indicate that the Queen was present. Other references in the play suggest 1595–96 as the most probable date for the first performance.

This play has the quality of a masque, a type of dramatic entertainment much favored for courtly festivities. The usual masque took the form of an elaborate allegory based on some mythological anecdote or situation in which gods, goddesses, and other supernatural figures appear in a pageant-like sequence of dances, songs, and pantomimes. Frequently an antimasque consisting of satyrs, devils, savages, or plain country bumpkins is introduced for contrast with the more ethereal characters.

That Shakespeare had the structure and characteristics of the masque in mind when he put together *A Midsummer Night's Dream* is obvious, but as always he transcends the conventional in composing a poetic drama. He manages to weave together three separate elements to create a unified whole. The main plot concerns the wedding of Theseus and Hippolyta and the love story of Lysander, Demetrius, Hermia, and Helena. To provide entertainment for the wedding, the Athenian artisans plan to give the play of Pyramus and Thisbe. The quarrel of Oberon and Titania, King and Queen of the fairies, and the activities of their fairy court parallel the main plot; but by making Puck the instrument for solving the problems of the earthly lovers and increasing the confusions and comedy of the artisans the author brings all the groups together into an organic whole.

Furthermore, Shakespeare achieves something more than an evanescent entertainment for an Elizabethan wedding. We still watch or read *A Midsummer Night's Dream* with pleasure because the author provides meaning and significance deeper than the surface ripples of momentary entertainment. As in his other plays, *A Midsummer Night's Dream* is filled with commentary on life and love; and here particularly he deals with the whimsical and irresponsible aspects of love, the midsummer madness that has no explanation except in the whims of men and women or the deviltry of Robin Goodfellow. Shakespeare treats these moods and qualities in no spirit of criticism or reproof. Love can make men and women do many foolish things, but in this play we laugh gaily at such folly and accept it as the norm of life. "Lord, what fools these mortals be!" Puck exclaims; but for all of their folly mortals are rather charming beings, at least on this "wedding day at night," and neither Puck nor Shakespeare would change them. Written for a happy occasion, the comedy touches lightly on problems of love and marriage that receive more profound treatment in other plays.

Shakespeare's fairy lore has been the subject of much commentary. He gives his fairies a more benign quality than they often have in the traditional folklore. Shakespeare's age believed in witches, goblins, and ghosts, and these supernatural beings to the average superstitious Elizabethan connoted demons and hobgoblins rather than the gay "little people" portrayed in *A Midsummer Night's Dream*. The name Puck itself was a generic term for an imp and was so understood at the time. In identifying Robin Goodfellow as Puck, Shakespeare is calling him an imp; but he improved his qualities vastly over the character that he had borne before, and, ever since, Puck has been a particular personality among devilish imps. By his interpretation of the fairies as dainty beings of gauze and gossamer Shakespeare influenced most of the fairy literature that came after him.

POPULARITY OF THE PLAY

The title page of the first printed version of *A Midsummer Night's Dream*, Quarto 1 (1600), described it as a play "sundry times publicly acted by the . . . Lord Chamberlain his servants," which would indicate that it had enjoyed a run in the public playhouses as well as performance as part of some courtly entertainment. In 1604 it appears to have been one of the plays revived for the New Year's festivities before James I. Again, on Sunday, September 27, 1631, it was revived for performance before the Bishop of Lincoln and precipitated an uproar from the Puritans because a bishop had allowed a profane play to be given in his house on Sunday. During the period between 1642 and 1660, when the Puritans kept the theatres closed, a skit, or "droll," as such things were called, based on the parts of Bottom and the "rude mechanicals" apparently was given private performance. This droll was printed in 1661 and reprinted in 1672 with the title of *The Merry Conceited Humors of Bottom the Weaver*.

With the reopening of the theatres in 1660, *A Midsummer Night's Dream* returned to the stage. Samuel Pepys saw it on September 29, 1662, and confided to his *Diary* that it was "the most insipid, ridiculous play that ever I saw in my life." Henry Purcell in 1692 prepared an operatic version entitled *The Fairy Queen*. Somewhat later, in 1716, another musician, Richard Leveridge, reduced the artisans' parts to a burlesque version of an Italian opera, which enjoyed much popularity as a comic afterpiece. Charles Johnson in 1723 added the Pyramus and Thisbe episode to an adaptation of *As You Like It* which he called *Love in a Forest*. Few of Shakespeare's plays have been more often adapted than *A Midsummer Night's Dream*, and the eighteenth and nineteenth centuries saw many adapted versions. David Garrick, for example, omitted Bottom and his cohorts because, in his opinion, they violated decorum.

In 1827 Ludwig Tieck revived Shakespeare's text for a performance of the play in Berlin. For the occasion Mendelssohn composed music that has become famous. Since the mid-nineteenth century the play has had frequent performances, usually as Shakespeare wrote it, although Max Reinhardt in the 1930's staged a version at Los Angeles, California, in the Hollywood Bowl that exceeded anything yet seen in spectacle, with three hundred wedding guests winding down the Hollywood hills bearing lighted flambeaux, and Mickey Rooney playing the role of Puck. Reinhardt later staged a motion-picture version of the play that lost Shakespeare in a wilderness of stage effects. The play has been a favorite for amateur production and is frequently seen on college campuses.

SOURCES AND TEXT

A Midsummer Night's Dream is derived from no single source but instead represents the weaving-together of many elements from folklore, old tales, classical stories, and bits and pieces of legend that Shakespeare had picked up in his reading and in the oral tradition. He could have learned about the deeds of Robin Goodfellow in his native Warwickshire; he could have read about Oberon in the old romance of *Huon of Bordeaux*. Oberon had already appeared on the stage in Robert Greene's play, *James IV* (*ca.* 1591). Fairies had been discussed in Reginald Scot's *Discovery of Witchcraft* (1584). Chaucer's Knight had told a story of Theseus and Hippolyta in the *Canterbury Tales*. In *Plutarch's Lives* (North's translation, 1579) and in Ovid's *Metamorphoses* Shakespeare could have found other bits of his classical legend. The fate of Pyramus and Thisbe had long been the subject of poem and story. For the characterizations of his "rude mechanicals" and for such names of his fairies as "Cobweb" and "Peaseblossom" the author had merely to search his own fertile imagination.

The textual problems of *A Midsummer Night's Dream* are relatively simple. The play appeared in print in a quarto of 1600 as "Written by William Shakespeare. Imprinted at London, for Thomas Fisher." This Quarto 1 is fairly well printed and has fewer errors than most early texts. A Quarto 2, "Printed by James Roberts, 1600," is a pirated edition and is falsely dated, for it was actually printed in 1619. Copy for the First Folio appears to have been a corrected version of Quarto 2. The present text is based on Quarto 1, with corrections suggested by variant readings in the First Folio.

Puck

Titania and Bottom

The Fairy Sentinel

Three designs by Paul Konewka (1869).

[Dramatis Personæ

THESEUS, *Duke of Athens.*
EGEUS, *father to Hermia.*
LYSANDER, DEMETRIUS, } *in love with Hermia.*

PHILOSTRATE, *Master of the Revels to Theseus.*

PETER QUINCE, *a carpenter.*
NICK BOTTOM, *a weaver.*
FRANCIS FLUTE, *a bellows-mender.*
TOM SNOUT, *a tinker.*
SNUG, *a joiner.*
ROBIN STARVELING, *a tailor.*

HIPPOLYTA, *Queen of the Amazons, betrothed to Theseus.*
HERMIA, *daughter to Egeus, in love with Lysander.*
HELENA, *in love with Demetrius.*

OBERON, *King of the Fairies.*
TITANIA, *Queen of the Fairies.*
PUCK, *or* ROBIN GOODFELLOW.
PEASEBLOSSOM, COBWEB, MOTH, MUSTARDSEED, } *fairies.*

Other fairies attending Oberon and Titania; attendants on Theseus and Hippolyta.

Scene: *Athens, and a wood near it.*]

Titania and Oberon
A design by Paul Konewka (1869).

A MIDSUMMER NIGHT'S DREAM

ACT I

Scene I. [*Athens. The Palace of Theseus.*]

Enter THESEUS, HIPPOLYTA, [PHILOSTRATE,] *with others.*

The. Now, fair Hippolyta, our nuptial hour
Draws on apace; four happy days bring in
Another moon: but, O, methinks, how slow
This old moon wanes! she lingers my desires,
Like to a stepdame or a dowager, 5
Long withering out a young man's revenue.
Hip. Four days will quickly steep themselves in night;
Four nights will quickly dream away the time;
And then the moon, like to a silver bow
New-bent in heaven, shall behold the night 10
Of our solemnities.
The. Go, Philostrate,
Stir up the Athenian youth to merriments,
Awake the pert and nimble spirit of mirth,
Turn melancholy forth to funerals;
The pale companion is not for our pomp. 15
[*Exit Philostrate.*]
Hippolyta, I wooed thee with my sword,
And won thy love doing thee injuries;
But I will wed thee in another key,
With pomp, with triumph, and with reveling.

Enter EGEUS *and his daughter* HERMIA, LYSANDER, *and* DEMETRIUS.

Ege. Happy be Theseus, our renowned duke! 20
The. Thanks, good Egeus: what's the news with thee?
Ege. Full of vexation come I, with complaint
Against my child, my daughter Hermia.
Stand forth, Demetrius. My noble lord,
This man hath my consent to marry her. 25
Stand forth, Lysander. And, my gracious duke,
This man hath bewitched the bosom of my child.
Thou, thou, Lysander, thou hast given her rhymes
And interchanged love tokens with my child;
Thou hast by moonlight at her window sung 30
With feigning voice verses of feigning love,
And stol'n the impression of her fantasy
With bracelets of thy hair, rings, gauds, conceits,
Knacks, trifles, nosegays, sweetmeats—messengers
Of strong prevailment in unhardened youth. 35
With cunning hast thou filched my daughter's heart,
Turned her obedience, which is due to me,
To stubborn harshness. And, my gracious duke,
Be it so she will not here before your Grace
Consent to marry with Demetrius, 40
I beg the ancient privilege of Athens,
As she is mine, I may dispose of her,
Which shall be either to this gentleman

5. dowager: widow with a life interest in her husband's estate
13. pert: sprightly
15. companion: fellow (contemptuous)
16. I . . . sword: when Theseus defeated the Amazons
19. triumph: spectacle; pageantry
32. stol'n . . . fantasy: slyly made himself the object of her fancy
33. gauds: trinkets; **conceits:** fanciful gifts
34. Knacks: knickknacks
35. unhardened: impressionable
39. Be . . . so: if it be so that

Or to her death, according to our law
Immediately provided in that case. 45
The. What say you, Hermia? Be advised, fair maid,
To you your father should be as a god;
One that composed your beauties; yea, and one
To whom you are but as a form in wax
By him imprinted and within his power 50
To leave the figure or disfigure it.
Demetrius is a worthy gentleman.
Her. So is Lysander.
The. In himself he is;
But in this kind, wanting your father's voice,
The other must be held the worthier. 55
Her. I would my father looked but with my eyes.
The. Rather your eyes must with his judgment look.
Her. I do entreat your Grace to pardon me.
I know not by what power I am made bold,
Nor how it may concern my modesty 60
In such a presence here to plead my thoughts;
But I beseech your Grace that I may know
The worst that may befall me in this case
If I refuse to wed Demetrius.
The. Either to die the death, or to abjure 65
Forever the society of men.
Therefore, fair Hermia, question your desires,
Know of your youth, examine well your blood,
Whether, if you yield not to your father's choice,
You can endure the livery of a nun, 70
For aye to be in shady cloister mewed,
To live a barren sister all your life,
Chanting faint hymns to the cold fruitless moon.
Thrice blessed they that master so their blood
To undergo such maiden pilgrimage; 75
But earthlier happy is the rose distilled
Than that which, withering on the virgin thorn,
Grows, lives, and dies in single blessedness.
Her. So will I grow, so live, so die, my lord,
Ere I will yield my virgin patent up 80
Unto his lordship whose unwished yoke
My soul consents not to give sovereignty.
The. Take time to pause; and by the next new moon—
The sealing day betwixt my love and me
For everlasting bond of fellowship— 85
Upon that day either prepare to die
For disobedience to your father's will,
Or else to wed Demetrius, as he would,
Or on Diana's altar to protest
For aye austerity and single life. 90
Dem. Relent, sweet Hermia; and, Lysander, yield
Thy crazed title to my certain right.
Lys. You have her father's love, Demetrius;
Let me have Hermia's: do you marry him.
Ege. Scornful Lysander! true, he hath my love;
And what is mine my love shall render him; 96
And she is mine, and all my right of her
I do estate unto Demetrius.
Lys. I am, my lord, as well derived as he,
As well possessed; my love is more than his; 100
My fortunes every way as fairly ranked
(If not with vantage) as Demetrius';
And (which is more than all these boasts can be)
I am beloved of beauteous Hermia.
Why should not I then prosecute my right? 105
Demetrius, I'll avouch it to his head,
Made love to Nedar's daughter, Helena,
And won her soul; and she (sweet lady) dotes,
Devoutly dotes, dotes in idolatry,
Upon this spotted and inconstant man. 110
The. I must confess that I have heard so much,
And with Demetrius thought to have spoke thereof;
But, being over-full of self-affairs,
My mind did lose it. But, Demetrius, come;
And come, Egeus. You shall go with me; 115
I have some private schooling for you both.
For you, fair Hermia, look you arm yourself
To fit your fancies to your father's will;
Or else the law of Athens yields you up
(Which by no means we may extenuate) 120
To death or to a vow of single life.
Come, my Hippolyta. What cheer, my love?
Demetrius and Egeus, go along.
I must employ you in some business
Against our nuptial and confer with you 125
Of something nearly that concerns yourselves.
Ege. With duty and desire we follow you.
Exeunt. Manent Lysander and Hermia.
Lys. How now, my love? Why is your cheek so pale?
How chance the roses there do fade so fast?
Her. Belike for want of rain, which I could well
Beteem them from the tempest of my eyes. 131

45. **Immediately:** expressly
46. **Be advised:** think carefully
54. **kind:** respect; **wanting:** lacking; **voice:** approval
60. **concern:** affect
68. **blood:** emotions
70. **livery:** habit; **nun:** vestal virgin consecrated to Diana
71. **mewed:** confined; from the name of a cage where molting hawks were kept
73. **faint:** listless
75. **pilgrimage:** course of life
76. **earthlier happy:** happier by earthly standards; **distilled:** i.e., into perfume
81. **his lordship:** the mastery of any man
89. **protest:** vow
92. **crazed:** flawed
98. **estate unto:** bestow upon
99. **derived:** born
100. **possessed:** endowed
102. **vantage:** addition
110. **spotted:** morally stained
120. **extenuate:** mitigate
125. **Against:** in preparation for
126. **nearly . . . yourselves:** of immediate concern to you
127. **duty . . . desire:** eager obedience (a hendiadys)
131. **Beteem:** permit

Lys. Ay me! for aught that I could ever read,
Could ever hear by tale or history,
The course of true love never did run smooth;
But, either it was different in blood— 135
Her. O cross! too high to be enthralled to low!
Lys. Or else misgraffed in respect of years—
Her. O spite! too old to be engaged to young!
Lys. Or else it stood upon the choice of friends—
Her. O hell! to choose love by another's eyes!
Lys. Or, if there were a sympathy in choice, 141
War, death, or sickness did lay siege to it,
Making it momentany as a sound,
Swift as a shadow, short as any dream,
Brief as the lightning in the collied night, 145
That, in a spleen, unfolds both heaven and earth,
And ere a man hath power to say "Behold!"
The jaws of darkness do devour it up:
So quick bright things come to confusion.
Her. If then true lovers have been ever crossed,
It stands as an edict in destiny. 151
Then let us teach our trial patience,
Because it is a customary cross,
As due to love as thoughts and dreams and sighs,
Wishes and tears, poor Fancy's followers. 155
Lys. A good persuasion. Therefore hear me, Hermia.
I have a widow aunt, a dowager,
Of great revenue, and she hath no child:
From Athens is her house remote seven leagues;
And she respects me as her only son. 160
There, gentle Hermia, may I marry thee;
And to that place the sharp Athenian law
Cannot pursue us. If thou lovest me then,
Steal forth thy father's house tomorrow night;
And in the wood, a league without the town, 165
Where I did meet thee once with Helena
To do observance to a morn of May,
There will I stay for thee.
Her. My good Lysander!
I swear to thee by Cupid's strongest bow,
By his best arrow, with the golden head, 170
By the simplicity of Venus' doves,
By that which knitteth souls and prospers loves,
And by that fire which burned the Carthage queen
When the false Troyan under sail was seen,
By all the vows that ever men have broke 175
(In number more than ever women spoke),
In that same place thou hast appointed me
Tomorrow truly will I meet with thee.
Lys. Keep promise, love. Look, here comes Helena.

Enter HELENA.

Her. God speed fair Helena! Whither away? 180
Hel. Call you me fair? That fair again unsay.
Demetrius loves your fair. O happy fair!
Your eyes are lodestars, and your tongue's sweet air
More tuneable than lark to shepherd's ear
When wheat is green, when hawthorn buds appear.
Sickness is catching. O, were favor so, 186
Yours would I catch, fair Hermia, ere I go!
My ear should catch your voice, my eye your eye,
My tongue should catch your tongue's sweet melody.
Were the world mine, Demetrius being bated, 190
The rest I'd give to be to you translated.
O, teach me how you look, and with what art
You sway the motion of Demetrius' heart!
Her. I frown upon him, yet he loves me still.
Hel. O that your frowns would teach my smiles such skill! 195
Her. I give him curses, yet he gives me love.
Hel. O that my prayers could such affection move!
Her. The more I hate, the more he follows me.
Hel. The more I love, the more he hateth me.
Her. His folly, Helena, is no fault of mine. 200
Hel. None but your beauty: would that fault were mine!
Her. Take comfort, he no more shall see my face;
Lysander and myself will fly this place.
Before the time I did Lysander see,
Seemed Athens as a paradise to me. 205
O, then, what graces in my love do dwell
That he hath turned a heaven unto a hell!
Lys. Helen, to you our minds we will unfold:
Tomorrow night, when Phœbe doth behold
Her silver visage in the wat'ry glass, 210
Decking with liquid pearl the bladed grass
(A time that lovers' flights doth still conceal),
Through Athens gates have we devised to steal.
Her. And in the wood where often you and I

137. misgraffed: mismated
139. stood: depended
141. sympathy: harmony; suitability
143. momentany: transitory; from the Latin *momentaneus*
145. collied: coal-black
146. spleen: quick fit of temper. The spleen was considered the source of impetuous emotion.
149. confusion: destruction
150. ever: always
154. thoughts: anxieties
155. Fancy's: Love's
156. good persuasion: forceful argument
160. respects: considers
167. do . . . May: take part in May Day rites
168. stay: wait
170. his . . . head: according to Ovid, *Metamorphoses,* bk. i, the one used to inspire love
171. Venus' doves: the chariot of Venus was drawn by doves.
173. the . . . queen: Dido, who killed herself and threw her body on a funeral pyre when Æneas deserted her (Vergil, *Æneid,* bk. iv)
174. Troyan: Trojan
182. fair: beauty. Although Hermia is a brunette and Helena is blonde, Demetrius prefers Hermia.
183. lodestars: polestars; guides
186. favor: attractiveness
190. bated: excepted
191. translated: transformed
209. Phœbe: a name for the moon-goddess, Diana
213. Athens: used adjectivally

Upon faint primrose beds were wont to lie, 215
Emptying our bosoms of their counsel sweet,
There my Lysander and myself shall meet,
And thence from Athens turn away our eyes
To seek new friends and stranger companies.
Farewell, sweet playfellow. Pray thou for us; 220
And good luck grant thee thy Demetrius!
Keep word, Lysander. We must starve our sight
From lovers' food till morrow deep midnight.

Lys. I will, my Hermia. *Exit Hermia.*
Helena, adieu. 224
As you on him, Demetrius dote on you! *Exit.*

Hel. How happy some o'er other some can be!
Through Athens I am thought as fair as she.
But what of that? Demetrius thinks not so;
He will not know what all but he do know.
And as he errs, doting on Hermia's eyes, 230
So I, admiring of his qualities.
Things base and vile, holding no quantity,
Love can transpose to form and dignity.
Love looks not with the eyes, but with the mind;
Nor hath Love's mind of any judgment taste: 235
Wings, and no eyes, figure unheedy haste.
And therefore is Love said to be a child,
Because in choice he is so oft beguiled.
As waggish boys in game themselves forswear,
So the boy Love is perjured everywhere; 240
For ere Demetrius looked on Hermia's eyne,
He hailed down oaths that he was only mine;
And when this hail some heat from Hermia felt,
So he dissolved, and show'rs of oaths did melt.
I will go tell him of fair Hermia's flight. 245
Then to the wood will he tomorrow night
Pursue her; and for this intelligence
If I have thanks, it is a dear expense;
But herein mean I to enrich my pain,
To have his sight thither and back again. 250
Exit.

Scene II. [*Athens. Quince's house.*]

Enter QUINCE *the Carpenter,* SNUG *the Joiner,* BOTTOM *the Weaver,* FLUTE *the Bellows-mender,* SNOUT *the Tinker, and* STARVELING *the Tailor.*

Quince. Is all our company here?

Bot. You were best to call them generally, man by man, according to the scrip.

Quince. Here is the scroll of every man's name which is thought fit, through all Athens, to play 5 in our interlude before the duke and the duchess on his wedding day at night.

Bot. First, good Peter Quince, say what the play treats on, then read the names of the actors, and so grow to a point. 10

Quince. Marry, our play is "The most Lamentable Comedy and most Cruel Death of Pyramus and Thisbe."

Bot. A very good piece of work, I assure you, and a merry. Now, good Peter Quince, call forth 15 your actors by the scroll. Masters, spread yourselves.

Quince. Answer as I call you. Nick Bottom the weaver.

Bot. Ready. Name what part I am for, and 20 proceed.

Quince. You, Nick Bottom, are set down for Pyramus.

Bot. What is Pyramus? a lover, or a tyrant?

Quince. A lover that kills himself most gal- 25 lant for love.

Bot. That will ask some tears in the true performing of it. If I do it, let the audience look to their eyes! I will move storms; I will condole in some measure. To the rest— Yet my chief humor is 30 for a tyrant. I could play Ercles rarely, or a part to tear a cat in, to make all split.

The raging rocks
And shivering shocks
Shall break the locks 35
Of prison gates;
And Phibbus' car
Shall shine from far
And make and mar
The foolish Fates. 40

This was lofty! Now name the rest of the players. This is Ercles' vein, a tyrant's vein. A lover is more condoling.

Quince. Francis Flute the bellows-mender.

Flute. Here, Peter Quince. 45

Quince. Flute, you must take Thisbe on you.

Flute. What is Thisbe? a wand'ring knight?

Quince. It is the lady that Pyramus must love.

Flute. Nay, faith, let not me play a woman; I have a beard coming. 50

Quince. That's all one: you shall play it in a mask, and you may speak as small as you will.

215. **faint:** pale
226. **How . . . be:** how much happier some can be than others.
232. **holding . . . quantity:** having no value
235. **of . . . taste:** any touch of judgment
236. **figure:** symbolize; **unheedy:** careless
239. **waggish:** playful
248. **a . . . expense:** i.e., a return that Demetrius will be loath to give her
2. **generally:** severally
3. **scrip:** script
5. **which:** who
9. **on:** of
11. **Marry:** indeed; from "By the Virgin Mary"
29. **condole:** lament
31. **Ercles:** Hercules, whose characterization in Seneca's *Hercules Furens* was that of a ranting tyrant
37. **Phibbus' car:** the chariot of Phœbus, the sun-god
43. **condoling:** pathetic

Bot. An I may hide my face, let me play Thisbe too. I'll speak in a monstrous little voice:—"Thisne, Thisne!" "Ah, Pyramus, my lover dear! thy 55 Thisbe dear, and lady dear!"

Quince. No, no! you must play Pyramus; and, Flute, you Thisbe.

Bot. Well proceed.

Quince. Robin Starveling the tailor. 60

Starv. Here, Peter Quince.

Quince. Robin Starveling, you must play Thisbe's mother. Tom Snout the tinker.

Snout. Here, Peter Quince.

Quince. You, Pyramus' father; myself, This- 65 be's father; Snug the joiner, you the lion's part. And I hope here is a play fitted.

Snug. Have you the lion's part written? Pray you, if it be, give it me, for I am slow of study.

Quince. You may do it extempore, for it is 70 nothing but roaring.

Bot. Let me play the lion too: I will roar that I will do any man's heart good to hear me; I will roar that I will make the duke say, "Let him roar again, let him roar again." 75

Quince. An you should do it too terribly, you would fright the duchess and the ladies, that they would shriek; and that were enough to hang us all.

All. That would hang us, every mother's son.

Bot. I grant you, friends, if you should 80 fright the ladies out of their wits, they would have no more discretion but to hang us; but I will aggravate my voice so that I will roar you as gently as any sucking dove; I will roar you an 'twere any nightingale. 85

82–83. aggravate: Bottom's error for "modulate" or some similar word

Quince. You can play no part but Pyramus; for Pyramus is a sweet-faced man; a proper man as one shall see in a summer's day; a most lovely gentlemanlike man: therefore you must needs play Pyramus. 90

Bot. Well, I will undertake it. What beard were I best to play it in?

Quince. Why, what you will.

Bot. I will discharge it in either your straw-color beard, your orange-tawny beard, your purple- 95 in-grain beard, or your French-crown-color beard, your perfect yellow.

Quince. Some of your French crowns have no hair at all, and then you will play barefaced. But, masters, here are your parts; and I am to entreat you, 100 request you, and desire you, to con them by tomorrow night; and meet me in the palace wood, a mile without the town, by moonlight. There will we rehearse; for if we meet in the city, we shall be dogged with company and our devices known. In the 105 meantime I will draw a bill of properties, such as our play wants. I pray you, fail me not.

Bot. We will meet; and there we may rehearse most obscenely and courageously. Take pains; be perfect. Adieu. 110

Quince. At the duke's oak we meet.

Bot. Enough. Hold, or cut bowstrings.

Exeunt.

87. proper: handsome
95–96. purple-in-grain: permanent scarlet. The Scarlet Grain insect, *Coccus ilicis,* was the source of a permanent scarlet dye.
98. French . . . hair: i.e., bald like those who have lost their hair because of French disease (syphilis)
109. obscenely: Bottom may mean "off the scene" or perhaps "in seemly fashion"
112. Hold . . . bowstrings: keep the appointment or this company will disown you.

ACT II

[Scene I. *A wood near Athens.*]

Enter a Fairy *at one door, and* [Puck,] Robin Goodfellow *at another.*

Puck. How now, spirit! whither wander you?
Fai. Over hill, over dale,
Thorough bush, thorough brier,
Over park, over pale,
Thorough flood, thorough fire; 5
I do wander everywhere,
Swifter than the moonës sphere;
And I serve the fairy queen,
To dew her orbs upon the green.
The cowslips tall her pensioners be; 10

3. Thorough: a variant form of "through"
4. pale: enclosed ground
7. moonës: the Middle English form of the genitive
9. orbs: fairy rings
10. pensioners: a select bodyguard of tall, handsome men attended Queen Elizabeth and were known as her "Gentlemen Pensioners."

In their gold coats spots you see.
Those be rubies, fairy favors;
In those freckles live their savors.
I must go seek some dewdrops here,
And hang a pearl in every cowslip's ear. 15
Farewell, thou lob of spirits; I'll be gone.
Our queen and all her elves come here anon.

Puck. The king doth keep his revels here tonight;
Take heed the queen come not within his sight:
For Oberon is passing fell and wrath, 20
Because that she, as her attendant, hath
A lovely boy, stolen from an Indian king—
She never had so sweet a changeling—
And jealous Oberon would have the child
Knight of his train, to trace the forests wild; 25
But she perforce withholds the loved boy,
Crowns him with flowers, and makes him all her joy.
And now they never meet in grove or green,
By fountain clear or spangled starlight sheen,
But they do square, that all their elves, for fear, 30
Creep into acorn cups and hide them there.

Fai. Either I mistake your shape and making quite,
Or else you are that shrewd and knavish sprite
Called Robin Goodfellow. Are not you he
That frights the maidens of the villagery; 35
Skim milk, and sometimes labor in the quern,
And bootless make the breathless housewife churn;
And sometime make the drink to bear no barm;
Mislead night-wanderers, laughing at their harm?
Those that Hobgoblin call you, and sweet Puck, 40
You do their work, and they shall have good luck.
Are not you he?

Puck. Thou speakest aright;
I am that merry wanderer of the night.
I jest to Oberon, and make him smile
When I a fat and bean-fed horse beguile, 45
Neighing in likeness of a filly foal;
And sometime lurk I in a gossip's bowl
In very likeness of a roasted crab,
And when she drinks, against her lips I bob
And on her withered dewlap pour the ale. 50
The wisest aunt, telling the saddest tale,
Sometime for three-foot stool mistaketh me;
Then slip I from her bum, down topples she,
And "tailor" cries, and falls into a cough;
And then the whole quire hold their hips and loffe,
And waxen in their mirth, and neeze, and swear 56
A merrier hour was never wasted there.
But room, fairy! Here comes Oberon.

Fai. And here my mistress. Would that he were gone!

Enter [OBERON] *the King of Fairies, at one door, with his* TRAIN; *and the Queen,* [TITANIA], *at another, with hers.*

Ob. Ill met by moonlight, proud Titania. 60

Queen. What, jealous Oberon! Fairies, skip hence.
I have forsworn his bed and company.

Ob. Tarry, rash wanton: am not I thy lord?

Queen. Then I must be thy lady; but I know
When thou hast stolen away from fairyland, 65
And in the shape of Corin sat all day,
Playing on pipes of corn, and versing love
To amorous Phillida. Why art thou here,
Come from the farthest steppe of India,
But that, forsooth, the bouncing Amazon, 70
Your buskined mistress and your warrior love,
To Theseus must be wedded, and you come
To give their bed joy and prosperity?

Ob. How canst thou thus, for shame, Titania,
Glance at my credit with Hippolyta, 75
Knowing I know thy love to Theseus?
Didst thou not lead him through the glimmering night
From Perigouna, whom he ravished?
And make him with fair Ægles break his faith,
With Ariadne, and Antiopa? 80

Queen. These are the forgeries of jealousy;
And never, since the middle summer's spring,
Met we on hill, in dale, forest, or mead,

16. **lob:** lout
20. **passing . . . wrath:** in an exceedingly savage rage
23. **changeling:** a child exchanged for an imp. Usually the imp left by a fairy in exchange for a human child was known as a **changeling.**
25. **trace:** track
26. **perforce:** forcibly
30. **square:** quarrel
33. **shrewd:** malicious
36. **quern:** hand mill
37. **bootless:** unavailingly; by preventing the butter from turning
38. **make . . . barm:** prevent the yeast from fermenting the drink
47 **gossip's bowl:** a bowl of hot punch
48. **crab:** crab apple
51. **aunt:** old woman
52. **three-foot:** three-legged
53. **bum:** rump
54. **tailor:** an exclamation that has not been satisfactorily explained.
55. **quire:** company; **loffe:** laugh
56. **waxen:** increase; **neeze:** sneeze
58. **room:** make way
64. **thy lady:** i.e., the only woman in his life
66. **Corin:** a traditional name for a lover in pastoral romance
67. **versing love:** expressing love in poetry
71. **buskined:** probably a reference to Hippolyta's size
75. **Glance . . . Hippolyta:** seek to disgrace me by mentioning Hippolyta
78. **Perigouna:** Perigune, daughter of the brigand Sinis, fell in love with Theseus.
79. **Ægles:** another of Theseus' conquests, referred to in North's Plutarch
80. **Ariadne:** the daughter of King Minos, who helped Theseus; **Antiopa:** another Amazon, perhaps a variant name for Hippolyta
81. **forgeries:** fabrications
82. **middle . . . spring:** beginning of midsummer

By paved fountain or by rushy brook,
Or in the beached margent of the sea, 85
To dance our ringlets to the whistling wind,
But with thy brawls thou hast disturbed our sport.
Therefore the winds, piping to us in vain,
As in revenge, have sucked up from the sea
Contagious fogs; which falling in the land 90
Hath every pelting river made so proud
That they have overborne their continents.
The ox hath therefore stretched his yoke in vain,
The plowman lost his sweat, and the green corn
Hath rotted ere his youth attained a beard; 95
The fold stands empty in the drowned field,
And crows are fatted with the murrion flock;
The nine men's morris is filled up with mud,
And the quaint mazes in the wanton green
For lack of tread are undistinguishable. 100
The human mortals want their winter here.
No night is now with hymn or carol blest;
Therefore the moon, the governess of floods,
Pale in her anger, washes all the air,
That rheumatic diseases do abound. 105
And thorough this distemperature we see
The seasons alter. Hoary-headed frosts
Fall in the fresh lap of the crimson rose;
And on old Hiems' thin and icy crown
An odorous chaplet of sweet summer buds 110
Is, as in mockery, set. The spring, the summer,
The childing autumn, angry winter change
Their wonted liveries, and the mazed world,
By their increase, now knows not which is which.
And this same progeny of evils comes 115
From our debate, from our dissension;
We are their parents and original.

Ob. Do you amend it then; it lies in you.
Why should Titania cross her Oberon?
I do but beg a little changeling boy 120
To be my henchman.

Queen. Set your heart at rest.
The fairyland buys not the child of me.
His mother was a vot'ress of my order;
And in the spiced Indian air, by night,
Full often hath she gossiped by my side, 125
And sat with me on Neptune's yellow sands,
Marking the embarked traders on the flood;
When we have laughed to see the sails conceive
And grow big-bellied with the wanton wind;
Which she, with pretty and with swimming gait 130
Following (her womb then rich with my young squire)
Would imitate, and sail upon the land
To fetch me trifles, and return again,
As from a voyage, rich with merchandise.
But she, being mortal, of that boy did die, 135
And for her sake do I rear up her boy,
And for her sake I will not part with him.

Ob. How long within this wood intend you stay?

Queen. Perchance till after Theseus' wedding day.
If you will patiently dance in our round 140
And see our moonlight revels, go with us.
If not, shun me, and I will spare your haunts.

Ob. Give me that boy, and I will go with thee.

Queen. Not for thy fairy kingdom. Fairies, away!
We shall chide downright if I longer stay. 145

Exeunt [*Titania and her Train*].

Ob. Well, go thy way. Thou shalt not from this grove
Till I torment thee for this injury.
My gentle Puck, come hither. Thou remember'st
Since once I sat upon a promontory
And heard a mermaid, on a dolphin's back, 150
Uttering such dulcet and harmonious breath
That the rude sea grew civil at her song,
And certain stars shot madly from their spheres
To hear the sea-maid's music.

Puck. I remember.

Ob. That very time I saw (but thou couldst not),
Flying between the cold moon and the earth, 156
Cupid, all armed. A certain aim he took
At a fair Vestal, throned by the West,
And loosed his love-shaft smartly from his bow,
As it should pierce a hundred thousand hearts. 160
But I might see young Cupid's fiery shaft
Quenched in the chaste beams of the wat'ry moon,
And the imperial vot'ress passed on,
In maiden meditation, fancy-free.
Yet marked I where the bolt of Cupid fell. 165
It fell upon a little Western flower,
Before milk-white, now purple with love's wound,
And maidens call it love-in-idleness.
Fetch me that flow'r; the herb I showed thee once.
The juice of it, on sleeping eyelids laid, 170
Will make or man or woman madly dote
Upon the next live creature that it sees.

85. margent: margin
86. ringlets: circles
91. pelting: paltry
92. continents: containers; limits
93. stretched . . . yoke: pulled the plow
95. his: its, an old form of the genitive
97. murrion: stricken with the murrain, a cattle disease
98. nine . . . morris: pattern for a game similar to checkers, sometimes played outdoors
99. quaint: ingenious; **wanton:** luxuriant
101. want: lack
106. distemperature: abnormality; disorder
109. Hiems': winter's; a personification from the Latin *hiems*
112. childing: fruitful
113. wonted liveries: customary attire; **mazed:** bewildered
114. increase: issue; i.e., frosts or flowers
121. henchman: Middle English *hencheman,* "page"
122. The fairyland: the whole of fairyland
142. spare: avoid
149. Since: when
158. a . . . West: generally considered to be a compliment to Queen Elizabeth
161. might: could
168. love-in-idleness: a name for the pansy

Fetch me this herb, and be thou here again
Ere the Leviathan can swim a league.
Puck. I'll put a girdle round about the earth 175
In forty minutes. [*Exit.*]
Ob. Having once this juice,
I'll watch Titania when she is asleep
And drop the liquor of it in her eyes.
The next thing then she, waking, looks upon,
(Be it on lion, bear, or wolf, or bull, 180
On meddling monkey, or on busy ape)
She shall pursue it with the soul of love.
And ere I take this charm from off her sight,
(As I can take it with another herb)
I'll make her render up her page to me. 185
But who comes here? I am invisible,
And I will overhear their conference.

Enter DEMETRIUS, HELENA *following him.*

Dem. I love thee not; therefore pursue me not.
Where is Lysander and fair Hermia?
The one I'll slay, the other slayeth me. 190
Thou toldst me they were stol'n unto this wood;
And here am I, and wood within this wood
Because I cannot meet my Hermia.
Hence, get thee gone, and follow me no more!
Hel. You draw me, you hardhearted adamant!
But yet you draw not iron, for my heart 196
Is true as steel. Leave you your power to draw,
And I shall have no power to follow you.
Dem. Do I entice you? Do I speak you fair?
Or rather do I not in plainest truth 200
Tell you I do not nor I cannot love you?
Hel. And even for that do I love you the more.
I am your spaniel; and, Demetrius,
The more you beat me, I will fawn on you.
Use me but as your spaniel—spurn me, strike me,
Neglect me, lose me; only give me leave 206
(Unworthy as I am) to follow you.
What worser place can I beg in your love
And yet a place of high respect with me)
Than to be used as you use your dog? 210
Dem. Tempt not too much the hatred of my spirit,
For I am sick when I do look on thee.
Hel. And I am sick when I look not on you.
Dem. You do impeach your modesty too much
To leave the city and commit yourself 215
Into the hands of one that loves you not;
To trust the opportunity of night
And the ill counsel of a desert place
With the rich worth of your virginity.
Hel. Your virtue is my privilege: for that 220
It is not night when I do see your face,
Therefore I think I am not in the night;
Nor doth this wood lack worlds of company,
For you, in my respect, are all the world:
Then how can it be said I am alone 225
When all the world is here to look on me?
Dem. I'll run from thee and hide me in the brakes,
And leave thee to the mercy of wild beasts.
Hel. The wildest hath not such a heart as you.
Run when you will, the story shall be changed: 230
Apollo flies, and Daphne holds the chase;
The dove pursues the griffon; the mild hind
Makes speed to catch the tiger—bootless speed,
When cowardice pursues, and valor flies!
Dem. I will not stay thy questions. Let me go!
Or if thou follow me, do not believe 236
But I shall do thee mischief in the wood.
Hel. Ay, in the temple, in the town, the field,
You do me mischief. Fie, Demetrius!
Your wrongs do set a scandal on my sex. 240
We cannot fight for love, as men may do;
We should be wooed, and were not made to woo.
[*Exit Demetrius.*]
I'll follow thee, and make a heaven of hell,
To die upon the hand I love so well. *Exit.*
Ob. Fare thee well, nymph. Ere he do leave this grove, 245
Thou shalt fly him, and he shall seek thy love.

[*Re-*]*enter* PUCK.

Hast thou the flower there? Welcome, wanderer.
Puck. Ay, there it is.
Ob. I pray thee give it me.
I know a bank where the wild thyme blows,
Where oxlips and the nodding violet grows, 250
Quite over-canopied with luscious woodbine,
With sweet musk-roses, and with eglantine.
There sleeps Titania sometime of the night,
Lulled in these flowers with dances and delight;
And there the snake throws her enameled skin, 255
Weed wide enough to wrap a fairy in;
And with the juice of this I'll streak her eyes
And make her full of hateful fantasies.
Take thou some of it and seek through this grove.

174. the Leviathan: believed to be a whale by the Elizabethans
192. wood . . . wood: the first **wood** means "insane" from the Anglo-Saxon *wōd*
195. adamant: magnet
205. spurn: kick
214. impeach: discredit
218. desert: deserted
220. virtue: power of attraction
224. respect: regard
227. brakes: thickets
231. Apollo . . . Daphne: the nymph Daphne, fleeing from the amorous Apollo, was changed to a laurel tree.
232. griffon: a fabulous creature with the head and wings of an eagle and a lion's body
233. bootless: vain
235. stay . . . questions: endure further conversation with you
250. oxlips: a variety of primrose
252. eglantine: the sweetbrier, *Rosa eglanteria*
256. Weed: garment

A sweet Athenian lady is in love 260
With a disdainful youth: anoint his eyes,
But do it when the next thing he espies
May be the lady. Thou shalt know the man
By the Athenian garments he hath on.
Effect it with some care, that he may prove 265
More fond on her than she upon her love;
And look thou meet me ere the first cock crow.

Puck. Fear not, my lord; your servant shall do so.
Exeunt.

[Scene II. *Another part of the wood.*]

Enter Titania, *Queen of Fairies, with her* Train.

Queen. Come, now a roundel and a fairy song;
Then, for the third part of a minute, hence—
Some to kill cankers in the musk-rose buds,
Some war with reremice for their leathern wings, 4
To make my small elves coats, and some keep back
The clamorous owl, that nightly hoots and wonders
At our quaint spirits. Sing me now asleep.
Then to your offices, and let me rest.

Fairies sing.

1. Fai. You spotted snakes with double tongue,
Thorny hedgehogs, be not seen; 10
Newts and blindworms, do no wrong,
Come not near our Fairy Queen.

[*All.*] Philomel, with melody
Sing in our sweet lullaby;
Lulla, lulla, lullaby; lulla, lulla, lullaby;
Never harm, 16
Nor spell nor charm
Come our lovely lady nigh.
So good night, with lullaby.

1. Fai. Weaving spiders, come not here; 20
Hence, you long-legged spinners, hence!
Beetles black, approach not near;
Worm nor snail, do no offense.

[*All.*] Philomel, with melody, &c. *She sleeps.*

2. Fai. Hence, away! Now all is well. 25
One aloof stand sentinel.
[*Exeunt Fairies.*]

Enter Oberon, [*and squeezes the flower on* Titania's *eyelids*].

Ob. What thou seest when thou dost wake,
Do it for thy truelove take;
Love and languish for his sake.
Be it ounce or cat or bear, 30
Pard, or boar with bristled hair
In thy eye that shall appear
When thou wakest, it is thy dear.
Wake when some vile thing is near. [*Exit.*]

Enter Lysander *and* Hermia.

Lys. Fair love, you faint with wand'ring in the wood; 35
And to speak troth, I have forgot our way.
We'll rest us, Hermia, if you think it good,
And tarry for the comfort of the day.

Her. Be it so, Lysander. Find you out a bed;
For I upon this bank will rest my head. 40

Lys. One turf shall serve as pillow for us both;
One heart, one bed, two bosoms, and one troth.

Her. Nay, good Lysander; for my sake, my dear,
Lie further off yet, do not lie so near.

Lys. O, take the sense, sweet, of my innocence!
Love takes the meaning in love's conference. 46
I mean that my heart unto yours is knit,
So that but one heart we can make of it;
Two bosoms interchained with an oath;
So then two bosoms and a single troth. 50
Then by your side no bed-room me deny;
For lying so, Hermia, I do not lie.

Her. Lysander riddles very prettily.
Now much beshrew my manners and my pride
If Hermia meant to say Lysander lied! 55
But, gentle friend, for love and courtesy
Lie further off, in humane modesty,
Such separation as may well be said
Becomes a virtuous bachelor and a maid,
So far be distant; and good night, sweet friend, 60
Thy love ne'er alter till thy sweet life end!

Lys. Amen, amen, to that fair prayer say I,
And then end life when I end loyalty!
Here is my bed. Sleep give thee all his rest!

Her. With half that wish the wisher's eyes be pressed! *They sleep.*

Enter Puck.

1. roundel: round dance, from Old French *rondel*
4. reremice: bats
7. quaint: clever
13. Philomel: the Philomela of Greek mythology was transformed to a nightingale.

30. ounce: originally a term applied to the lynx
31. Pard: panther
42. troth: faith
45. take . . . innocence: be assured of my innocence in proposing what seems improper.
46. Love . . . conference: lovers always understand each other's meaning.
52. lie: i.e., act falsely, since my love is true. This pun on "lie" was a favorite with Elizabethans.
54. beshrew: literally, "curse"; actually a mild oath

Puck. Through the forest have I gone, 66
But Athenian found I none
On whose eyes I might approve
This flower's force in stirring love.
Night and silence! Who is here? 70
Weeds of Athens he doth wear.
This is he (my master said)
Despised the Athenian maid;
And here the maiden, sleeping sound
On the dank and dirty ground. 75
Pretty soul! she durst not lie
Near this lack-love, this kill-courtesy.
Churl, upon thy eyes I throw
All the power this charm doth owe.
When thou wakest, let love forbid 80
Sleep his seat on thy eyelid.
So awake when I am gone;
For I must now to Oberon. *Exit.*

Enter Demetrius *and* Helena, *running.*

Hel. Stay, though thou kill me, sweet Demetrius.
Dem. I charge thee, hence, and do not haunt me thus. 85
Hel. O, wilt thou darkling leave me? Do not so.
Dem. Stay, on thy peril! I alone will go. *Exit.*
Hel. O, I am out of breath in this fond chase!
The more my prayer, the lesser is my grace.
Happy is Hermia, wheresoe'er she lies; 90
For she hath blessed and attractive eyes.
How came her eyes so bright? Not with salt tears.
If so, my eyes are oft'ner washed than hers.
No, no! I am as ugly as a bear;
For beasts that meet me run away for fear. 95
Therefore no marvel though Demetrius
Do, as a monster, fly my presence thus.
What wicked and dissembling glass of mine
Made me compare with Hermia's sphery eyne?
But who is here? Lysander! on the ground? 100
Dead, or asleep? I see no blood, no wound.
Lysander, if you live, good sir, awake.
Lys. [*Waking*] And run through fire I will for thy sweet sake.
Transparent Helena! Nature shows art,
That through thy bosom makes me see thy heart.
Where is Demetrius? O, how fit a word 106
Is that vile name to perish on my sword!
Hel. Do not say so, Lysander; say not so.
What though he love your Hermia? Lord, what though?
Yet Hermia still loves you; then be content. 110
Lys. Content with Hermia? No! I do repent
The tedious minutes I with her have spent.
Not Hermia, but Helena I love.
Who will not change a raven for a dove?
The will of man is by his reason swayed; 115
And reason says you are the worthier maid.
Things growing are not ripe until their season;
So I, being young, till now ripe not to reason;
And touching now the point of human skill,
Reason becomes the marshal to my will 120
And leads me to your eyes; where I o'erlook
Love's stories, written in Love's richest book.
Hel. Wherefore was I to this keen mockery born?
When at your hands did I deserve this scorn?
Is't not enough, is't not enough, young man, 125
That I did never, no, nor never can,
Deserve a sweet look from Demetrius' eye,
But you must flout my insufficiency?
Good troth, you do me wrong! good sooth, you do!
In such disdainful manner me to woo. 130
But fare you well. Perforce I must confess
I thought you lord of more true gentleness.
O, that a lady, of one man refused,
Should of another therefore be abused! *Exit.*
Lys. She sees not Hermia. Hermia, sleep thou there, 135
And never mayst thou come Lysander near!
For, as a surfeit of the sweetest things
The deepest loathing to the stomach brings,
Or as the heresies that men do leave
Are hated most of those they did deceive, 140
So thou, my surfeit and my heresy,
Of all be hated, but the most of me!
And, all my powers, address your love and might
To honor Helen and to be her knight! *Exit.*
Her. [*Waking*] Help me, Lysander, help me! Do thy best 145
To pluck this crawling serpent from my breast!
Ay me, for pity, what a dream was here!
Lysander, look how I do quake with fear.
Methought a serpent eat my heart away,
And you sat smiling at his cruel prey. 150
Lysander! What, removed? Lysander! lord!
What, out of hearing? gone? no sound, no word?
Alack, where are you? Speak, an if you hear.
Speak, of all loves! I swoon almost with fear.
No? Then I well perceive you are not nigh: 155
Either death or you I'll find immediately.
Exit.

68. approve: demonstrate
71. Weeds: attire
79. owe: possess
86. darkling: in the dark
88. fond: foolish
89. grace: favor, with a pun
97. as: as though I were
104. Transparent: radiantly beautiful
115. will: amorous desire
119. point: highest degree
128. flout: mock
150. prey: action of preying
154. of . . . loves: in Love's name

ACT III

[Scene I. *The same. Titania lying asleep.*]

Enter the Clowns—[QUINCE, SNUG, BOTTOM, FLUTE, SNOUT *and* STARVELING].

Bot. Are we all met?

Quince. Pat, pat; and here's a marvelous convenient place for our rehearsal. This green plot shall be our stage, this hawthorn brake our tiring house, and we will do it in action as we will do it 5 before the duke.

Bot. Peter Quince!

Quince. What sayest thou, bully Bottom?

Bot. There are things in this Comedy of Pyramus and Thisbe that will never please. First, Pyra- 10 mus must draw a sword to kill himself; which the ladies cannot abide. How answer you that?

Snout. By'r lakin, a parlous fear!

Starv. I believe we must leave the killing out, when all is done. 15

Bot. Not a whit: I have a device to make all well. Write me a prologue; and let the prologue seem to say, we will do no harm with our swords, and that Pyramus is not killed indeed; and for the more better assurance, tell them that I Pyramus am 20 not Pyramus, but Bottom the weaver. This will put them out of fear.

Quince. Well, we will have such a prologue, and it shall be written in eight and six.

Bot. No, make it two more: let it be written 25 in eight and eight.

Snout. Will not the ladies be afeard of the lion?

Starv. I fear it, I promise you.

Bot. Masters, you ought to consider with yourselves, to bring in (God shield us!) a lion 30 among ladies is a most dreadful thing. For there is not a more fearful wild fowl than your lion living; and we ought to look to't.

Snout. Therefore another prologue must tell he is not a lion. 35

Bot. Nay, you must name his name, and half his face must be seen through the lion's neck, and he himself must speak through, saying thus, or to the same defect: "Ladies"—or "Fair ladies, I would wish you"—or "I would request you"—or "I 40 would entreat you—not to fear, not to tremble. My life for yours! If you think I come hither as a lion, it were pity of my life. No! I am no such thing, I am a man as other men are." And there, indeed, let him name his name and tell them plainly he 45 is Snug the joiner.

Quince. Well, it shall be so. But there is two hard things: that is, to bring the moonlight into a chamber: for, you know, Pyramus and Thisbe meet by moonlight. 50

Snout. Doth the moon shine that night we play our play?

Bot. A calendar, a calendar! Look in the almanac. Find out moonshine, find out moonshine!

Quince. Yes, it doth shine that night. 55

Bot. Why, then may you leave a casement of the great chamber window, where we play, open, and the moon may shine in at the casement.

Quince. Ay; or else one must come in with a bush of thorns and a lantern, and say he comes to 60 disfigure, or to present, the person of Moonshine. Then there is another thing: we must have a wall in the great chamber; for Pyramus and Thisbe, says the story, did talk through the chink of a wall.

Snout. You can never bring in a wall. What 65 say you, Bottom?

Bot. Some man or other must present Wall; and let him have some plaster, or some loam, or some roughcast about him, to signify wall; and let him hold his fingers thus; and through that cranny 70 shall Pyramus and Thisbe whisper.

Quince. If that may be, then all is well. Come, sit down, every mother's son, and rehearse your parts. Pyramus, you begin. When you have spoken your speech, enter into that brake; and so every one 75 according to his cue.

Enter [PUCK,] ROBIN [GOODFELLOW].

Puck. What hempen homespuns have we swagg'ring here,

2. Pat: punctually
4–5. tiring house: dressing room
13. By'r lakin: by our little lady (the Virgin); **parlous:** perilous; grave
15. when . . . done: all things considered
24. eight . . . six: jog-trot verse composed of alternate lines of eight and six syllables
43. it . . . life: it would be at peril of my life
59–60. a . . . lantern: according to an old story, the Man in the Moon was once a mortal who was transported to the moon while gathering firewood.
69. roughcast: coarse plaster

So near the cradle of the Fairy Queen?
What, a play toward? I'll be an auditor;
An actor too perhaps, if I see cause. 80

Quince. Speak, Pyramus. Thisbe, stand forth.

Bot. (*as Pyr.*) Thisbe, the flowers of odious savors sweet—

Quince. Odorous! odorous!

Bot. (*as Pyr.*)——odors savors sweet;
So hath thy breath, my dearest Thisbe dear. 85
But hark, a voice! Stay thou but here awhile,
And by-and-by I will to thee appear. *Exit.*

Puck. A stranger Pyramus than e'er played here! [*Exit.*]

Flute. Must I speak now?

Quince. Ay, marry, must you; for you must 90
understand he goes but to see a noise that he heard,
and is to come again.

Flute (*as This.*) Most radiant Pyramus, most lily-white of hue,
Of color like the red rose on triumphant brier,
Most brisky juvenal, and eke most lovely Jew, 95
As true as truest horse, that yet would never tire,
I'll meet thee, Pyramus, at Ninny's tomb.

Quince. "Ninus' tomb," man! Why, you must not
speak that yet. That you answer to Pyramus. You
speak all your part at once, cues and all. Pyra- 100
mus, enter. Your cue is past; it is "never tire."

Flute (*as This.*) O—As true as truest horse, that yet would never tire.

[*Re-enter* PUCK, *and* BOTTOM *as*] PYRAMUS *with the ass-head.*

Bot. (*as Pyr.*) If I were fair, Thisbe, I were only thine.

Quince. O monstrous! O strange! We are haunted.
Pray, masters! Fly, masters! Help! 105

The Clowns all exeunt. [*Manet Bottom*].

Puck. I'll follow you; I'll lead you about a round,
Through bog, through bush, through brake, through brier:
Sometime a horse I'll be, sometime a hound,
A hog, a headless bear, sometime a fire; 109
And neigh, and bark, and grunt, and roar, and burn,
Like horse, hound, hog, bear, fire, at every turn. *Exit.*

Bot. Why do they run away? This is a knavery of
them to make me afeard.

[*Re-*]*enter* SNOUT.

Snout. O Bottom, thou art changed! What do I see
on thee? 115

Bot. What do you see? You see an ass-head of your
own, do you? [*Exit Snout.*]

[*Re-*]*enter* QUINCE.

Quince. Bless thee, Bottom! bless thee! Thou art
translated. *Exit.*

Bot. I see their knavery: this is to make an 120
ass of me; to fright me, if they could. But I will not
stir from this place, do what they can: I will walk up
and down here, and I will sing, that they shall hear I
am not afraid. [*Sings.*]

> The woosel cock so black of hue, 125
> With orange-tawny bill,
> The throstle with his note so true,
> The wren with little quill—

Tita. [*Waking*] What angel wakes me from my flow'ry bed?

Bot. [*Sings.*]

> The finch, the sparrow, and the lark, 130
> The plain-song cuckoo gray,
> Whose note full many a man doth mark,
> And dares not answer nay.

For, indeed, who would set his wit to so foolish a
bird? Who would give a bird the lie, though he 135
cry "cuckoo" never so?

Tita. I pray thee, gentle mortal, sing again.
Mine ear is much enamored of thy note;
So is mine eye enthralled to thy shape;
And thy fair virtue's force (perforce) doth move me,
On the first view, to say, to swear, I love thee. 141

Bot. Methinks, mistress, you should have little
reason for that. And yet, to say the truth, reason and
love keep little company together nowadays. The
more the pity that some honest neighbors will 145
not make them friends. Nay, I can gleek, upon occasion.

Tita. Thou art as wise as thou art beautiful.

Bot. Not so, neither; but if I had wit enough
to get out of this wood, I have enough to 150
serve mine own turn.

Tita. Out of this wood do not desire to go:
Thou shalt remain here, whether thou wilt or no.

79. toward: in the offing
94. triumphant: magnificent
95. juvenal: youth; **eke:** moreover; **Jew:** the meaning is uncertain, but the term was one of endearment.
97. Ninny's: the tomb of Ninus, according to legend the first ruler of Assyria

119. translated: transformed
125. woosel: ousel, a variety of blackbird
127. throstle: thrush
128. quill: pipe, literally a pipe made of reed or cane
131. plain-song: i.e., singer of a plain song without variations
132–33. Whose . . . nay: the reiterated "cuckoo" aroused fear in the heart of any married man uncertain of his wife's fidelity; a "cuckold" is a man whose wife has been unfaithful.
134. set: oppose
136. never so: as never before
146. gleek: mock; jest
149. wit: wisdom

I am a spirit of no common rate,
The summer still doth tend upon my state; 155
And I do love thee. Therefore go with me.
I'll give thee fairies to attend on thee;
And they shall fetch thee jewels from the deep,
And sing while thou on pressed flowers dost sleep;
And I will purge thy mortal grossness so 160
That thou shalt like an airy spirit go.
Peaseblossom! Cobweb! Moth! and Mustardseed!

Enter [*the*] FOUR FAIRIES.

Peas. Ready.
Cob. And I.
Moth. And I. 165
Must. And I.
All. Where shall we go?
Tita. Be kind and courteous to this gentleman.
Hop in his walks and gambol in his eyes;
Feed him with apricocks and dewberries, 170
With purple grapes, green figs, and mulberries;
The honey-bags steal from the humblebees,
And for night tapers crop their waxen thighs,
And light them at the fiery glowworm's eyes,
To have my love to bed and to arise; 175
And pluck the wings from painted butterflies
To fan the moonbeams from his sleeping eyes.
Nod to him, elves, and do him courtesies.
Peas. Hail, mortal!
Cob. Hail! 180
Moth. Hail!
Must. Hail!
Bot. I cry your worships mercy, heartily. I beseech your worship's name.
Cob. Cobweb. 185
Bot. I shall desire you of more acquaintance, good Master Cobweb. If I cut my finger, I shall make bold with you. Your name, honest gentleman?
Peas. Peaseblossom.
Bot. I pray you, commend me to Mistress 190 Squash, your mother, and to Master Peasecod, your father. Good Master Peaseblossom, I shall desire you of more acquaintance too. Your name, I beseech you, sir?
Must. Mustardseed. 195
Bot. Good Master Mustardseed, I know your patience well. That same cowardly, giant-like ox-beef hath devoured many a gentleman of your house. I promise you your kindred hath made my eyes water ere now. I desire you of more acquaintance, 200 good Master Mustardseed.

Tita. Come wait upon him; lead him to my bower.
The moon, methinks, looks with a wat'ry eye;
And when she weeps, weeps every little flower,
Lamenting some enforced chastity. 205
Tie up my love's tongue, bring him silently.
Exeunt.

154. rate: rank
155. still: ever
172. humblebees: bumblebees
187–88. make . . . with: by employing him to stanch the flow of blood
191. Squash: a green peapod; **Peasecod:** a ripe peapod
197. ox-beef: usually accompanied by mustard

[Scene II. *Another part of the wood.*]

Enter [OBERON,] *King of Fairies.*

Ob. I wonder if Titania be awaked;
Then, what it was that next came in her eye,
Which she must dote on in extremity.

Enter PUCK.

Here comes my messenger. How now, mad spirit?
What night-rule now about this haunted grove? 5
Puck. My mistress with a monster is in love.
Near to her close and consecrated bower,
While she was in her dull and sleeping hour,
A crew of patches, rude mechanicals,
That work for bread upon Athenian stalls, 10
Were met together to rehearse a play,
Intended for great Theseus' nuptial day.
The shallowest thickskin of that barren sort,
Who Pyramus presented in their sport,
Forsook his scene and ent'red in a brake. 15
When I did him at this advantage take,
An ass's nole I fixed on his head.
Anon his Thisbe must be answered,
And forth my mimic comes. When they him spy,
As wild geese that the creeping fowler eye, 20
Or russet-pated choughs, many in sort,
Rising and cawing at the gun's report,
Sever themselves and madly sweep the sky;
So at his sight away his fellows fly;
And, at our stamp, here o'er and o'er one falls; 25
He murder cries and help from Athens calls.
Their sense thus weak, lost with their fears thus strong,
Made senseless things begin to do them wrong;
For briers and thorns at their apparel snatch;
Some, sleeves—some, hats; from yielders all things catch. 30

3. in extremity: excessively
5. What . . . now: what's going on tonight
7. close: concealed
9. patches: fools; **mechanicals:** artisans
13. barren sort: stupid lot
17. nole: head, from the Anglo-Saxon *hnoll*
21. russet-pated: grey-headed; russet was a homespun fabric ranging in color from grey to brown; **choughs:** jackdaws; **sort:** company
28. Made . . . wrong: (they) imagined injuries from inanimate objects
30. from . . . catch: i.e., everything attacks the runaway.

I led them on in this distracted fear
And left sweet Pyramus translated there;
When in that moment (so it came to pass)
Titania waked, and straightway loved an ass.
Ob. This falls out better than I could devise. 35
But hast thou yet latched the Athenian's eyes
With the love-juice, as I did bid thee do?
Puck. I took him sleeping (that is finished too)
And the Athenian woman by his side,
That, when he waked, of force she must be eyed.

Enter DEMETRIUS *and* HERMIA.

Ob. Stand close. This is the same Athenian. 41
Puck. This is the woman, but not this the man.
Dem. O, why rebuke you him that loves you so?
Lay breath so bitter on your bitter foe.
Her. Now I but chide; but I should use thee worse, 45
For thou, I fear, hast given me cause to curse.
If thou hast slain Lysander in his sleep,
Being o'er shoes in blood, plunge in the deep,
And kill me too.
The sun was not so true unto the day 50
As he to me. Would he have stolen away
From sleeping Hermia? I'll believe as soon
This whole earth may be bored, and that the moon
May through the center creep, and so displease
Her brother's noontide with the Antipodes. 55
It cannot be but thou hast murd'red him.
So should a murderer look, so dead, so grim.
Dem. So should the murdered look, and so should I,
Pierced through the heart with your stern cruelty.
Yet you, the murderer, look as bright, as clear, 60
As yonder Venus in her glimmering sphere.
Her. What's this to my Lysander? Where is he?
Ah, good Demetrius, wilt thou give him me?
Dem. I had rather give his carcass to my hounds.
Her. Out, dog! out, cur! Thou drivest me past the bounds 65
Of maiden's patience. Hast thou slain him then?
Henceforth be never numb'red among men!
O, once tell true! tell true, even for my sake!
Durst thou have looked upon him, being awake?
And hast thou killed him sleeping? O brave touch!
Could not a worm, an adder, do so much? 71
An adder did it; for with doubler tongue
Than thine (thou serpent!) never adder stung.
Dem. You spend your passion on a misprised mood.
I am not guilty of Lysander's blood; 75
Nor is he dead, for aught that I can tell.
Her. I pray thee, tell me then that he is well.
Dem. An if I could, what should I get therefore?
Her. A privilege never to see me more;
And from thy hated presence part I so. 80
See me no more, whether he be dead or no. *Exit*.
Dem. There is no following her in this fierce vein:
Here therefore for a while I will remain.
So sorrow's heaviness doth heavier grow
For debt that bankrout sleep doth sorrow owe; 85
Which now in some slight measure it will pay,
If for his tender here I make some stay.
Lie down [*and sleep*].
Ob. What hast thou done? Thou hast mistaken quite
And laid the love-juice on some truelove's sight.
Of thy misprision must perforce ensue 90
Some truelove turned, and not a false turned true.
Puck. Then fate o'errules, that, one man holding troth,
A million fail, confounding oath on oath.
Ob. About the wood go swifter than the wind,
And Helena of Athens look thou find. 95
All fancy-sick she is, and pale of cheer
With sighs of love, that costs the fresh blood dear.
By some illusion see thou bring her here.
I'll charm his eyes against she do appear.
Puck. I go, I go! Look how I go! 100
Swifter than an arrow from the Tartar's bow. *Exit*.

Ob. Flower of this purple dye,
Hit with Cupid's archery,
Sink in apple of his eye!
When his love he doth espy, 105
Let her shine as gloriously
As the Venus of the sky.
When thou wakest, if she be by,
Beg of her for remedy.

[*Re-*]*enter* PUCK.

Puck. Captain of our fairy band, 110
Helena is here at hand,
And the youth, mistook by me,
Pleading for a lover's fee.

36. latched: moistened
44. breath: language
55. Her brother's: referring to Phœbus, the sun; **Antipodes:** inhabitants of the other side of the earth
57. dead: deadly
60. clear: innocent
70. brave: noble
72. doubler: more deceitful
74. misprised: mistaken
84. heaviness: sadness
85. bankrout: bankrupt
87. If . . . stay: if I wait here a bit and allow sleep to offer itself
90. misprision: mistake
93. confounding: destroying
96. fancy-sick: lovesick; **cheer:** face
97. sighs . . . dear: it was thought that every sigh drew a drop of blood from the heart and thus weakened it.
99. against . . . appear: in preparation for her appearance

Shall we their fond pageant see?
Lord, what fools these mortals be! 115

Ob. Stand aside: the noise they make
Will cause Demetrius to awake.

Puck. Then will two at once woo one.
That must needs be sport alone;
And those things do best please me 120
That befall prepost'rously.

Enter LYSANDER *and* HELENA.

Lys. Why should you think that I should woo in scorn?
Scorn and derision never come in tears:
Look, when I vow, I weep; and vows so born,
In their nativity all truth appears. 125
How can these things in me seem scorn to you,
Bearing the badge of faith to prove them true?
Hel. You do advance your cunning more and more.
When truth kills truth, O devilish-holy fray! 129
These vows are Hermia's. Will you give her o'er?
Weigh oath with oath, and you will nothing weigh.
Your vows to her and me, put in two scales,
Will even weigh, and both as light as tales.
Lys. I had no judgment when to her I swore. 134
Hel. Nor none, in my mind, now you give her o'er.
Lys. Demetrius loves her, and he loves not you.
Dem. [*Waking*] O Helen, goddess, nymph, perfect, divine!
To what, my love, shall I compare thine eyne?
Crystal is muddy. O, how ripe in show 139
Thy lips, those kissing cherries, tempting grow!
That pure congealed white, high Taurus' snow,
Fanned with the eastern wind, turns to a crow
When thou holdst up thy hand: O, let me kiss
This princess of pure white, this seal of bliss!
Hel. O spite! O hell! I see you all are bent 145
To set against me for your merriment.
If you were civil and knew courtesy,
You would not do me thus much injury.
Can you not hate me, as I know you do,
But you must join in souls to mock me too? 150
If you were men, as men you are in show,
You would not use a gentle lady so;
To vow, and swear, and superpraise my parts,
When I am sure you hate me with your hearts.
You both are rivals, and love Hermia; 155
And now both rivals to mock Helena.
A trim exploit, a manly enterprise,
To conjure tears up in a poor maid's eyes
With your derision! None of noble sort
Would so offend a virgin and extort 160
A poor soul's patience, all to make you sport.
Lys. You are unkind, Demetrius. Be not so!
For you love Hermia; this you know I know;
And here, with all good will, with all my heart,
In Hermia's love I yield you up my part; 165
And yours of Helena to me bequeath,
Whom I do love, and will do to my death.
Hel. Never did mockers waste more idle breath.
Dem. Lysander, keep thy Hermia, I will none:
If e'er I loved her, all that love is gone. 170
My heart to her but as guestwise sojourned,
And now to Helen is it home returned,
There to remain.
Lys. Helen, it is not so.
Dem. Disparage not the faith thou dost not know,
Lest, to thy peril, thou aby it dear. 175
Look where thy love comes; yonder is thy dear.

Enter HERMIA.

Her. Dark night, that from the eye his function takes,
The ear more quick of apprehension makes.
Wherein it doth impair the seeing sense,
It pays the hearing double recompense. 180
Thou art not by mine eye, Lysander, found;
Mine ear, I thank it, brought me to thy sound.
But why unkindly didst thou leave me so?
Lys. Why should he stay whom love doth press to go?
Her. What love could press Lysander from my side? 185
Lys. Lysander's love, that would not let him bide,
Fair Helena; who more engilds the night
Than all yon fiery oes and eyes of light.
Why seekst thou me? Could not this make thee know,
The hate I bare thee made me leave thee so? 190
Her. You speak not as you think; it cannot be.
Hel. Lo, she is one of this confederacy!
Now I perceive they have conjoined all three
To fashion this false sport in spite of me.
Injurious Hermia! most ungrateful maid! 195
Have you conspired, have you with these contrived
To bait me with this foul derision?

114. fond: foolish; **pageant:** exhibition
119. sport alone: unparalleled sport
125. all: nothing but
127. badge . . . faith: token of faithful service, like a servant's badge
128. advance: flaunt
129. When . . . fray: if his present vow is true it destroys the truth of his previous vow to Hermia.
141. Taurus: a mountain range in Turkey
152. gentle: wellborn
157. trim: fine (ironic)
160. extort: rack; torture
168. idle: useless
169. I . . . none: I will have none of her.
175. aby . . . dear: pay dearly for it
188. oes: rounds, like spangles
195. Injurious: insulting
197. bait: torment

Is all the counsel that we two have shared,
The sisters' vows, the hours that we have spent
When we have chid the hasty-footed time 200
For parting us—O, is all forgot?
All schooldays friendship, childhood innocence?
We, Hermia, like two artificial gods,
Have with our needles created both one flower,
Both on one sampler, sitting on one cushion, 205
Both warbling of one song, both in one key;
As if our hands, our sides, voices, and minds
Had been incorporate. So we grew together,
Like to a double cherry, seeming parted,
But yet an union in partition— 210
Two lovely berries molded on one stem;
So, with two seeming bodies, but one heart;
Two of the first, like coats in heraldry,
Due but to one, and crowned with one crest.
And will you rent our ancient love asunder, 215
To join with men in scorning your poor friend?
It is not friendly, 'tis not maidenly!
Our sex, as well as I, may chide you for it,
Though I alone do feel the injury.
Her. I am amazed at your passionate words. 220
I scorn you not. It seems that you scorn me.
Hel. Have you not set Lysander, as in scorn,
To follow me and praise my eyes and face?
And made your other love, Demetrius
(Who even but now did spurn me with his foot),
To call me goddess, nymph, divine, and rare, 226
Precious, celestial? Wherefore speaks he this
To her he hates? And wherefore doth Lysander
Deny your love (so rich within his soul)
And tender me (forsooth) affection, 230
But by your setting on, by your consent?
What though I be not so in grace as you,
So hung upon with love, so fortunate;
But miserable most, to love unloved?
This you should pity rather than despise. 235
Her. I understand not what you mean by this.
Hel. Ay, do! persever, counterfeit sad looks,
Make mouths upon me when I turn my back,
Wink each at other, hold the sweet jest up:
This sport, well carried, shall be chronicled. 240
If you have any pity, grace, or manners,
You would not make me such an argument.
But fare ye well. 'Tis partly my own fault,
Which death or absence soon shall remedy.
Lys. Stay, gentle Helena; hear my excuse, 245
My love, my life, my soul, fair Helena!
Hel. O excellent!
Her. Sweet, do not scorn her so.
Dem. If she cannot entreat, I can compel.
Lys. Thou canst compel no more than she entreat.
Thy threats have no more strength than her weak prayers. 250
Helen, I love thee; by my life, I do!
I swear by that which I will lose for thee
To prove him false that says I love thee not.
Dem. I say I love thee more than he can do. 254
Lys. If thou say so, withdraw and prove it too.
Dem. Quick, come!
Her. Lysander, whereto tends all this?
Lys. Away, you Ethiope!
Her. No, no; he'll—
Dem. Seem to break loose, take on as you would follow,
But yet come not. You are a tame man, go!
Lys. Hang off, thou cat, thou burr! Vile thing, let loose, 260
Or I will shake thee from me like a serpent!
Her. Why are you grown so rude? What change is this,
Sweet love?
Lys. Thy love? Out, tawny Tartar, out!
Out, loathed med'cine! O hated potion, hence! 264
Her. Do you not jest?
Hel. Yes, sooth! and so do you.
Lys. Demetrius, I will keep my word with thee.
Dem. I would I had your bond; for I perceive
A weak bond holds you. I'll not trust your word.
Lys. What, should I hurt her, strike her, kill her dead?
Although I hate her, I'll not harm her so. 270
Her. What, can you do me greater harm than hate?
Hate me? Wherefore? O me! what news, my love?
Am not I Hermia? Are not you Lysander?
I am as fair now as I was erewhile.
Since night you loved me; yet since night you left me. 275
Why then, you left me (O, the gods forbid!)
In earnest, shall I say?
Lys. Ay, by my life!
And never did desire to see thee more.
Therefore be out of hope, of question, doubt;
Be certain, nothing truer, 'tis no jest 280
That I do hate thee, and love Helena.

198. counsel: exchange of confidence
203. artificial: skilled in art
208. incorporate: combined in one body
213–14. Two . . . one: two bodies controlled by one heart, like the arms of a man and his wife, which are combined to symbolize their union. **The first** in heraldic terms refers to the first color mentioned in describing a blazon.
215. rent: tear
220. amazed: struck dumb
230. tender: offer
232. in grace: popular
233. hung . . . love: caressed
237. persever: persevere
241. grace: goodness
242. argument: subject of sport
257. Ethiope: a scornful reference to Hermia's dark coloring
268. weak bond: i.e., woman—Hermia, who is clinging to him
275. Since . . . me: as recently as nightfall you loved me

Her. O me! you juggler! you canker blossom!
You thief of love! What, have you come by night
And stol'n my love's heart from him?
Hel. Fine, i' faith!
Have you no modesty, no maiden shame, 285
No touch of bashfulness? What, will you tear
Impatient answers from my gentle tongue?
Fie, fie! you counterfeit, you puppet you!
Her. Puppet? Why, so! Ay, that way goes the game.
Now I perceive that she hath made compare 290
Between our statures; she hath urged her height,
And with her personage, her tall personage,
Her height (forsooth), she hath prevailed with him.
And are you grown so high in his esteem
Because I am so dwarfish and so low? 295
How low am I, thou painted maypole? Speak!
How low am I? I am not yet so low
But that my nails can reach unto thine eyes.
Hel. I pray you, though you mock me, gentlemen,
Let her not hurt me. I was never curst; 300
I have no gift at all in shrewishness;
I am a right maid for my cowardice.
Let her not strike me. You perhaps may think,
Because she is something lower than myself,
That I can match her.
Her. Lower? Hark again! 305
Hel. Good Hermia, do not be so bitter with me.
I evermore did love you, Hermia,
Did ever keep your counsels, never wronged you;
Save that, in love unto Demetrius,
I told him of your stealth unto this wood. 310
He followed you; for love I followed him;
But he hath chid me hence, and threat'ned me
To strike me, spurn me; nay, to kill me too.
And now, so you will let me quiet go,
To Athens will I bear my folly back 315
And follow you no further. Let me go.
You see how simple and how fond I am.
Her. Why, get you gone! Who is't that hinders you?
Hel. A foolish heart, that I leave here behind.
Her. What, with Lysander?
Hel. With Demetrius. 320
Lys. Be not afraid, she shall not harm thee, Helena.
Dem. No, sir, she shall not, though you take her part.
Hel. O, when she is angry, she is keen and shrewd!
She was a vixen when she went to school,
And though she be but little, she is fierce. 325

Her. "Little" again? nothing but "low" and "little"?
Why will you suffer her to flout me thus?
Let me come to her.
Lys. Get you gone, you dwarf!
You minimus, of hind'ring knotgrass made!
You bead, you acorn!
Dem. You are too officious 330
In her behalf that scorns your services.
Let her alone. Speak not of Helena;
Take not her part; for if thou dost intend
Never so little show of love to her,
Thou shalt aby it.
Lys. Now she holds me not. 335
Now follow, if thou darest, to try whose right,
Of thine or mine, is most in Helena.
Dem. Follow? Nay, I'll go with thee, cheek by jowl. *Exeunt Lysander and Demetrius.*
Her. You, mistress, all this coil is 'long of you.
Nay, go not back.
Hel. I will not trust you, I, 340
Nor longer stay in your curst company.
Your hands than mine are quicker for a fray;
My legs are longer though, to run away. [*Exit.*]
Her. I am amazed, and know not what to say. *Exit.*
Ob. This is thy negligence. Still thou mistakest,
Or else committst thy knaveries willfully. 346
Puck. Believe me, king of shadows, I mistook.
Did not you tell me I should know the man
By the Athenian garments he had on?
And so far blameless proves my enterprise 350
That I have 'nointed an Athenian's eyes;
And so far am I glad it so did sort,
As this their jangling I esteem a sport.
Ob. Thou seest these lovers seek a place to fight.
Hie therefore, Robin, overcast the night. 355
The starry welkin cover thou anon
With drooping fog as black as Acheron,
And lead these testy rivals so astray
As one come not within another's way.
Like to Lysander sometime frame thy tongue, 360
Then stir Demetrius up with bitter wrong;
And sometime rail thou like Demetrius.
And from each other look thou lead them thus
Till o'er their brows death-counterfeiting sleep
With leaden legs and batty wings doth creep. 365
Then crush this herb into Lysander's eye;
Whose liquor hath this virtuous property,

282. canker blossom: stealthy corrupter, by analogy with the cankerworm that eats the heart of the blossom
288. counterfeit . . . puppet: i.e., diminutive doll
300. curst: shrewish
302. right: true
305. match her: equal her in fighting
323. keen: sharp; **shrewd:** shrewish

327. suffer: permit; **flout:** mock
329. minimus: least of beings; **of . . . made:** nourished on knotgrass, which supposedly stunted growth
333. intend: offer
335. aby: pay for
339. coil: uproar; **'long:** because
352. sort: fall out
356. welkin: sky
357. Acheron: a river in Hades, sometimes used for the whole underground region
367. virtuous property: powerful quality

To take from thence all error with his might
And make his eyeballs roll with wonted sight.
When they next wake, all this derision 370
Shall seem a dream and fruitless vision;
And back to Athens shall the lovers wend
With league whose date till death shall never end.
Whiles I in this affair do thee employ,
I'll to my queen and beg her Indian boy; 375
And then I will her charmed eye release
From monster's view, and all things shall be peace.

Puck. My fairy lord, this must be done with haste,
For night's swift dragons cut the clouds full fast,
And yonder shines Aurora's harbinger, 380
At whose approach ghosts, wand'ring here and there,
Troop home to churchyards; damned spirits all,
That in crossways and floods have burial,
Already to their wormy beds are gone,
For fear lest day should look their shames upon,
They willfully themselves exile from light, 386
And must for aye consort with black-browed night.

Ob. But we are spirits of another sort.
I with the Morning's love have oft made sport,
And, like a forester, the groves may tread 390
Even till the eastern gate, all fiery red,
Opening on Neptune, with fair blessed beams
Turns into yellow gold his salt green streams.
But notwithstanding, haste, make no delay: 394
We may effect this business yet ere day. [*Exit.*]

Puck. Up and down, up and down,
I will lead them up and down:
I am feared in field and town.
Goblin, lead them up and down.
Here comes one. 400

Enter LYSANDER.

Lys. Where art thou, proud Demetrius? Speak thou now.

Puck. Here, villain, drawn and ready. Where art thou?

Lys. I will be with thee straight.

Puck. Follow me then
To plainer ground. [*Exit Lysander.*]

Enter DEMETRIUS.

Dem. Lysander, speak again!
Thou runaway, thou coward, art thou fled? 405
Speak! In some bush? Where dost thou hide thy head?

Puck. Thou coward, art thou bragging to the stars,
Telling the bushes that thou lookst for wars,
And wilt not come? Come, recreant! come, thou child!
I'll whip thee with a rod. He is defiled 410
That draws a sword on thee.

Dem. Yea, art thou there?

Puck. Follow my voice. We'll try no manhood here.
Exeunt.

[*Enter* LYSANDER.]

Lys. He goes before me and still dares me on;
When I come where he calls, then he is gone.
The villain is much lighter-heeled than I. 415
I followed fast, but faster he did fly,
That fallen am I in dark uneven way,
And here will rest me. (*Lie down.*) Come, thou gentle day!
For if but once thou show me thy grey light, 419
I'll find Demetrius and revenge this spite. [*Sleeps.*]

Enter PUCK *and* DEMETRIUS.

Puck. Ho, ho, ho! Coward, why comest thou not?

Dem. Abide me, if thou darest; for well I wot
Thou runnest before me, shifting every place,
And darest not stand nor look me in the face.
Where art thou now?

Puck. Come hither; I am here. 425

Dem. Nay then, thou mockst me. Thou shalt buy this dear
If ever I thy face by daylight see.
Now, go thy way: faintness constraineth me
To measure out my length on this cold bed.
By day's approach look to be visited. 430
[*Lies down and sleeps.*]

Enter HELENA.

Hel. O weary night, O long and tedious night,
Abate thy hours! Shine comforts from the East,
That I may back to Athens by daylight
From these that my poor company detest; 434
And sleep, that sometimes shuts up sorrow's eye,
Steal me awhile from mine own company. *Sleep.*

Puck. Yet but three? Come one more:
Two of both kinds makes up four.
Here she comes, curst and sad.

369. wonted: accustomed
370. derision: farcical situation
371. fruitless: productive of no consequence
373. With . . . end: united by vows of love until death
380. Aurora's harbinger: the herald of the dawn, the morning star
382–83. damned . . . burial: i.e., suicides, who were buried at crossroads unless they drowned themselves so that their bodies were never found
389. the . . . love: Cephalus, beloved of Aurora, goddess of morning
403. straight: at once
409. recreant: coward; originally, one who broke his pledged faith by deserting in battle
422. Abide: wait for; **wot:** know
432. Abate: lessen
439. curst: cross

Cupid is a knavish lad 440
Thus to make poor females mad.

Enter HERMIA.

Her. Never so weary, never so in woe;
Bedabbled with the dew, and torn with briers;
I can no further crawl, no further go;
My legs can keep no pace with my desires. 445
Here will I rest me till the break of day.
Heavens shield Lysander, if they mean a fray!
[*Lies down and sleeps.*]

Puck. On the ground
Sleep sound
I'll apply 450
To your eye,
Gentle lover, remedy.
[*Squeezes the herb on Lysander's eyelids.*]
When thou wakest,
Thou takest
True delight 455
In the sight
Of thy former lady's eye;
And the country proverb known,
That every man should take his own,
In your waking shall be shown: 460
Jack shall have Jill;
Naught shall go ill;
The man shall have his mare again, and all shall be well. [*Exit.*]

ACT IV

[Scene I. *The wood. Lysander, Demetrius, Helena, and Hermia, all lying asleep.*]

Enter [TITANIA,] *Queen of Fairies, and* [BOTTOM *the*] *Clown, and* FAIRIES, [PEASEBLOSSOM, COBWEB, MOTH, MUSTARDSEED, *and others*]; *and the King,* [OBERON,] *behind them.*

Tita. Come, sit thee down upon this flow'ry bed,
While I thy amiable cheeks do coy,
And stick musk-roses in thy sleek smooth head,
And kiss thy fair large ears, my gentle joy.

Bot. Where's Peaseblossom? 5

Peas. Ready.

Bot. Scratch my head, Peaseblossom. Where's Mounsieur Cobweb?

Cob. Ready.

Bot. Mounsieur Cobweb, good mounsieur, 10 get your weapon in your hand, and kill me a red-hipped humblebee on the top of a thistle; and, good mounsieur, bring me the honey-bag. Do not fret yourself too much in the action, mounsieur; and, good mounsieur, have a care the honey-bag 15 break not. I would be loath to have you overflowen with a honey-bag, signior. Where's Mounsieur Mustardseed?

Mus. Ready.

Bot. Give me your neaf, Mounsieur Mus- 20 tardseed. Pray you, leave your curtsy, good mounsieur.

Mus. What's your will?

Bot. Nothing, good mounsieur, but to help Cavalery Peaseblossom to scratch. I must to 25 the barber's, mounsieur; for methinks I am marvelous hairy about the face; and I am such a tender ass, if my hair do but tickle me, I must scratch.

Tita. What, wilt thou hear some music, my sweet love?

Bot. I have a reasonable good ear in music. 30 Let's have the tongs and the bones.

Music, tongs, rural music.

Tita. Or say, sweet love, what thou desirest to eat.

Bot. Truly, a peck of provender. I could munch your good dry oats. Methinks I have a great desire to a bottle of hay: good hay, sweet hay, hath 35 no fellow.

Tita. I have a venturous fairy that shall seek
The squirrel's hoard, and fetch thee new nuts.

Bot. I had rather have a handful or two of dried pease. But I pray you, let none of your people 40 stir me. I have an exposition of sleep come upon me.

2. amiable: lovely; **coy:** caress
16–17. overflowen with: drowned by

20. neaf: fist
31. the . . . bones: primitive musical instruments consisting of tongs that were struck and clappers of bones
35. bottle: bundle
36. fellow: equal
41. exposition: malapropism for "disposition"

Tita. Sleep thou, and I will wind thee in my arms.
Fairies, be gone, and be all ways away.
[*Exeunt Fairies.*]
So doth the woodbine the sweet honeysuckle
Gently entwist; the female ivy so 45
Enrings the barky fingers of the elm.
O, how I love thee! how I dote on thee! [*They sleep.*]

Enter [PUCK,] ROBIN GOODFELLOW.

Ob. Welcome, good Robin. Seest thou this sweet sight?
Her dotage now I do begin to pity;
For, meeting her of late behind the wood, 50
Seeking sweet favors for this hateful fool,
I did upbraid her and fall out with her.
For she his hairy temples then had rounded
With coronet of fresh and fragrant flowers;
And that same dew which sometime on the buds 55
Was wont to swell like round and orient pearls
Stood now within the pretty flouriets' eyes,
Like tears that did their own disgrace bewail.
When I had at my pleasure taunted her,
And she in mild terms begged my patience, 60
I then did ask of her her changeling child;
Which straight she gave me, and her fairy sent
To bear him to my bower in fairyland.
And now I have the boy, I will undo
This hateful imperfection of her eyes. 65
And, gentle Puck, take this transformed scalp
From off the head of this Athenian swain;
That, he awaking when the other do,
May all to Athens back again repair,
And think no more of this night's accidents 70
But as the fierce vexation of a dream.
But first I will release the Fairy Queen.
Be as thou wast wont to be;
See as thou wast wont to see.
Dian's bud o'er Cupid's flower 75
Hath such force and blessed power.
Now, my Titania! Wake you, my sweet queen.
Tita. My Oberon, what visions have I seen!
Methought I was enamored of an ass. 79
Ob. There lies your love.
Tita. How came these things to pass?
O, how mine eyes do loathe his visage now!
Ob. Silence awhile. Robin, take off this head.
Titania, music call; and strike more dead
Than common sleep of all these five the sense. 84

43. all . . . away: off in all directions (to stand guard)
51. favors: love tokens
55. sometime: formerly
56. orient: lustrous
57. flouriets': little flowers'
65. imperfection: error
69. repair: go
70. accidents: happenings
75. Dian's bud: the antidote to the flower that inflamed love

Tita. Music, ho, music! such as charmeth sleep!
Puck. Now, when thou wakest, with thine own fool's eyes peep.
Ob. Sound, music! [*Music.*] Come, my queen, take hands with me.
And rock the ground whereon these sleepers be.
[*They dance.*]
Now thou and I are new in amity,
And will tomorrow midnight solemnly 90
Dance in Duke Theseus' house triumphantly
And bless it to all fair prosperity.
There shall the pairs of faithful lovers be
Wedded, with Theseus, all in jollity.
Puck. Fairy King, attend and mark. 95
I do hear the morning lark.
Ob. Then, my queen, in silence sad
Trip we after night's shade.
We the globe can compass soon,
Swifter than the wand'ring moon. 100
Tita. Come, my lord, and in our flight
Tell me how it came this night
That I sleeping here was found
With these mortals on the ground.
[*Exeunt.*]

Wind horn. Enter THESEUS *and all his* TRAIN; [HIPPOLYTA, EGEUS].

The. Go, one of you, find out the forester; 105
For now our observation is performed;
And since we have the vaward of the day,
My love shall hear the music of my hounds.
Uncouple in the western valley; let them go.
Dispatch, I say, and find the forester. 110
[*Exit an Attendant.*]
We will, fair queen, up to the mountain's top
And mark the musical confusion
Of hounds and echo in conjunction.
Hip. I was with Hercules and Cadmus once
When in a wood of Crete they bayed the bear 115
With hounds of Sparta. Never did I hear
Such gallant chiding; for, besides the groves,
The skies, the fountains, every region near
Seemed all one mutual cry. I never heard
So musical a discord, such sweet thunder. 120
The. My hounds are bred out of the Spartan kind;
So flewed, so sanded; and their heads are hung
With ears that sweep away the morning dew;
Crook-kneed, and dew-lapped like Thessalian bulls;
Slow in pursuit, but matched in mouth like bells,

90. solemnly: ceremoniously
91. triumphantly: magnificently; with pomp
97. sad: grave
106. observation: observation of May Day
107. vaward: vanguard; early part
114. Cadmus: brother of Europa and founder of Thebes
115. bayed: brought to bay
122. flewed: dewlapped; **sanded:** sand-colored

Each under each. A cry more tuneable 126
Was never holloaed to nor cheered with horn
In Crete, in Sparta, nor in Thessaly.
Judge when you hear. But, soft! What nymphs are these? 129

Ege. My lord, this is my daughter here asleep;
And this, Lysander; this Demetrius is;
This Helena, old Nedar's Helena.
I wonder of their being here together.

The. No doubt they rose up early to observe
The rite of May; and, hearing our intent, 135
Came here in grace of our solemnity.
But speak, Egeus. Is not this the day
That Hermia should give answer of her choice?

Ege. It is, my lord. 139

The. Go, bid the huntsmen wake them with their horns. [*Servant goes out.*]

Shout within. Wind horns. They all start up.

Good morrow, friends. Saint Valentine is past.
Begin these woodbirds but to couple now?

Lys. Pardon, my lord. [*They kneel.*]

The. I pray you all, stand up.
I know you two are rival enemies.
How comes this gentle concord in the world 145
That hatred is so far from jealousy
To sleep by hate and fear no enmity?

Lys. My lord, I shall reply amazedly,
Half sleep, half waking; but as yet, I swear,
I cannot truly say how I came here; 150
But, as I think (for truly would I speak),
And now I do bethink me, so it is—
I came with Hermia hither. Our intent
Was to be gone from Athens, where we might,
Without the peril of the Athenian law— 155

Ege. Enough, enough, my lord! you have enough.
I beg the law, the law, upon his head.
They would have stol'n away; they would, Demetrius!
Thereby to have defeated you and me—
You of your wife, and me of my consent, 160
Of my consent that she should be your wife.

Dem. My lord, fair Helen told me of their stealth,
Of this their purpose hither, to this wood;
And I in fury hither followed them,
Fair Helena in fancy following me. 165
But, my good lord, I wot not by what power
(But by some power it is) my love to Hermia,
Melted as the snow, seems to me now
As the remembrance of an idle gaud
Which in my childhood I did dote upon; 170
And all the faith, the virtue of my heart,
The object and the pleasure of mine eye,
Is only Helena. To her, my lord,
Was I betrothed ere I saw Hermia;
But, like a sickness, did I loathe this food; 175
But, as in health, come to my natural taste,
Now I do wish it, love it, long for it,
And will for evermore be true to it.

The. Fair lovers, you are fortunately met.
Of this discourse we more will hear anon. 180
Egeus, I will overbear your will;
For in the temple, by-and-by, with us,
These couples shall eternally be knit;
And, for the morning now is something worn,
Our purposed hunting shall be set aside. 185
Away with us to Athens! Three and three,
We'll hold a feast in great solemnity.
Come, Hippolyta.

[*Exeunt Duke* [*Theseus, Hippolyta,*] *Egeus,*] *and Lords.*

Dem. These things seem small and undistinguishable,
Like far-off mountains turned into clouds. 190

Her. Methinks I see these things with parted eye,
When everything seems double.

Hel. So methinks;
And I have found Demetrius like a jewel,
Mine own, and not mine own.

Dem. Are you sure
That we are awake? It seems to me 195
That yet we sleep, we dream. Do not you think
The duke was here, and bid us follow him?

Her. Yea, and my father.

Hel. And Hippolyta.

Lys. And he did bid us follow to the temple. 199

Dem. Why then, we are awake. Let's follow him,
And by the way let us recount our dreams. *Exeunt.*

Bot. (*Waking*) When my cue comes, call me, and I will answer. My next is "Most fair Pyramus." Hey-ho! Peter Quince! Flute the bellows-mender! Snout the tinker! Starveling! God's my life! 205 Stol'n hence, and left me asleep! I have had a most rare vision. I have had a dream, past the wit of man to say what dream it was. Man is but an ass if he go about to expound this dream. Methought I was— there is no man can tell what. Methought I 210 was, and methought I had—But man is but a patched fool if he will offer to say what methought I had. The eye of man hath not heard, the ear of man hath not seen, man's hand is not able to taste, his tongue to conceive, nor his heart to report what my 215

126. **Each . . . each:** graduated in tone from bass to tenor; **cry:** pack of hounds; **tuneable:** tuneful
136. **grace:** honor
146. **jealousy:** suspicion
148. **amazedly:** confusedly
165. **in fancy:** out of love
169. **gaud:** trinket
171. **virtue:** power
181. **overbear:** overrule
184. **for:** because
187. **solemnity:** pomp
194. **Mine . . . own:** not really mine and likely to be claimed by the true owner
208–9. **go about:** attempt
211. **patched:** dressed in motley
212–15. **The . . . was:** reminiscent of I Cor. 2:9

dream was. I will get Peter Quince to write a ballet of this dream. It shall be called "Bottom's Dream," because it hath no bottom; and I will sing it in the latter end of a play, before the duke. Peradventure, to make it the more gracious, I shall sing it 220 at her death.

Exit.

[Scene II. *Athens. Quince's house.*]

Enter QUINCE, FLUTE, SNOUT, *and* STARVELING.

Quince. Have you sent to Bottom's house? Is he come home yet?

Starv. He cannot be heard of. Out of doubt he is transported.

Flute. If he come not, then the play is 5 marred; it goes not forward, doth it?

Quince. It is not possible. You have not a man in all Athens able to discharge Pyramus but he.

Flute. No, he hath simply the best wit of any handicraft man in Athens. 10

Quince. Yea, and the best person too, and he is a very paramour for a sweet voice.

Flute. You must say "paragon." A paramour is (God bless us!) a thing of naught.

Enter SNUG *the Joiner.*

Snug. Masters, the duke is coming from the 15 temple, and there is two or three lords and ladies more married. If our sport had gone forward, we had all been made men.

216. ballet: ballad
3. Out . . . doubt: doubtless
4. transported: carried off by fairies
14. thing . . . naught: wicked person

Flute. O sweet bully Bottom! Thus hath he lost sixpence a day during his life. He could not 20 have scaped sixpence a day. An the duke had not given him sixpence a day for playing Pyramus, I'll be hanged! He would have deserved it. Sixpence a day in Pyramus, or nothing!

Enter BOTTOM.

Bot. Where are these lads? Where are these 25 hearts?

Quince. Bottom! O most courageous day! O most happy hour!

Bot. Masters, I am to discourse wonders; but ask me not what. For if I tell you, I am no true 30 Athenian. I will tell you everything, right as it fell out.

Quince. Let us hear, sweet Bottom.

Bot. Not a word of me. All that I will tell you is that the duke hath dined. Get your apparel 35 together, good strings to your beards, new ribbands to your pumps; meet presently at the palace; every man look o'er his part; for the short and the long is, our play is preferred. In any case, let Thisbe have clean linen; and let not him that plays the lion 40 pare his nails, for they shall hang out for the lion's claws. And, most dear actors, eat no onions nor garlic, for we are to utter sweet breath; and I do not doubt but to hear them say it is a sweet comedy. No more words. Away! go, away! 45

Exeunt.

26. hearts: hearties; good fellows
27. courageous: probably Quince means to say "fortunate."
30–31. no . . . Athenian: Acts 17:21: "For all the Athenians and strangers which were there, spent their time in nothing else but either to tell or to hear some new thing."
31. right: exactly
36. ribbands: ribbons
39. preferred: recommended

ACT V

[Scene I. *Athens. The Palace of Theseus.*]

Enter THESEUS, HIPPOLYTA, *and* PHILOSTRATE, [LORDS *and other* ATTENDANTS].

Hip. 'Tis strange, my Theseus, that these lovers speak of.

The. More strange than true. I never may believe
These antique fables nor these fairy toys.
Lovers and madmen have such seething brains,
Such shaping fantasies, that apprehend 5
More than cool reason ever comprehends.
The lunatic, the lover, and the poet,

2. may: can
3. antique: fantastic; **toys:** whimsicalities
5. fantasies: fancies

Are of imagination all compact.
One sees more devils than vast hell can hold:
That is the madman. The lover, all as frantic, 10
Sees Helen's beauty in a brow of Egypt.
The poet's eye, in a fine frenzy rolling,
Doth glance from heaven to earth, from earth to heaven;
And as imagination bodies forth
The forms of things unknown, the poet's pen 15
Turns them to shapes, and gives to airy nothing
A local habitation and a name.
Such tricks hath strong imagination
That, if it would but apprehend some joy,
It comprehends some bringer of that joy; 20
Or in the night, imagining some fear,
How easy is a bush supposed a bear!

Hip. But all the story of the night told over,
And all their minds transfigured so together,
More witnesseth than fancy's images 25
And grows to something of great constancy;
But howsoever, strange and admirable.

Enter Lovers—LYSANDER, DEMETRIUS, HERMIA, *and* HELENA.

The. Here come the lovers, full of joy and mirth.
Joy, gentle friends, joy and fresh days of love
Accompany your hearts!

Lys. More than to us 30
Wait in your royal walks, your board, your bed!

The. Come now, what masques, what dances shall we have,
To wear away this long age of three hours
Between our after-supper and bedtime?
Where is our usual manager of mirth? 35
What revels are in hand? Is there no play
To ease the anguish of a torturing hour?
Call Philostrate.

Phil. Here, mighty Theseus.

The. Say, what abridgment have you for this evening?
What masque? what music? How shall we beguile
The lazy time, if not with some delight? 41

Phil. There is a brief how many sports are ripe.
Make choice of which your Highness will see first.
[*Gives a paper.*]

The. "The battle with the Centaurs, to be sung
By an Athenian eunuch to the harp." 45
We'll none of that. That have I told my love
In glory of my kinsman Hercules.
"The riot of the tipsy Bacchanals,
Tearing the Thracian singer in their rage."
That is an old device, and it was played 50
When I from Thebes came last a conqueror.
"The thrice three Muses mourning for the death
Of Learning, late deceased in beggary."
That is some satire keen and critical,
Not sorting with a nuptial ceremony. 55
"A tedious brief scene of young Pyramus
And his love Thisbe; very tragical mirth."
Merry and tragical? tedious and brief?
That is hot ice and wondrous strange snow.
How shall we find the concord of this discord? 60

Phil. A play there is, my lord, some ten words long,
Which is as brief as I have known a play;
But by ten words, my lord, it is too long,
Which makes it tedious; for in all the play
There is not one word apt, one player fitted. 65
And tragical, my noble lord, it is;
For Pyramus therein doth kill himself.
Which when I saw rehearsed, I must confess,
Made mine eyes water; but more merry tears
The passion of loud laughter never shed. 70

The. What are they that do play it?

Phil. Hard-handed men that work in Athens here,
Which never labored in their minds till now;
And now have toiled their unbreathed memories
With this same play, against your nuptial. 75

The. And we will hear it.

Phil. No, my noble lord;
It is not for you. I have heard it over,
And it is nothing, nothing in the world;
Unless you can find sport in their intents,
Extremely stretched and conned with cruel pain, 80
To do you service.

The. I will hear that play;
For never anything can be amiss
When simpleness and duty tender it.
Go bring them in; and take your places, ladies.
[*Exit Philostrate.*]

8. Are . . . compact: are completely composed of imagination
11. brow . . . Egypt: gypsy beauty
14. bodies forth: gives birth to
20. comprehends . . . joy: includes in the conception a cause of joy
24. all . . . together: the fact that they all imagined the same thing
25. More witnesseth: attests to more
26. grows . . . constancy: achieves a certain consistency
27. howsoever: in any case; **admirable:** wondrous
34. after-supper: dessert
39. abridgment: pastime
40. beguile: while away
42. brief: list; **ripe:** ready
44. battle . . . Centaurs: the battle with the Centaurs at the wedding of Pirithous involved Theseus, but Hercules fought with Centaurs in the course of his pursuit of the Erymanthian boar; perhaps Shakespeare confused the two stories. Plutarch says that Hercules was Theseus' cousin.
49. the . . . singer: Orpheus, as told in Ovid, *Metamorphoses*, bk. xi
53. Learning . . . beggary: perhaps a topical allusion not identified
55. sorting with: befitting
74. unbreathed: unexercised
75. against: in preparation for
79–80. intents . . . stretched: i.e., they have strained their abilities in attempting the play. **conned:** learned (their lines)
83. simpleness . . . duty: innocent devotion; **tender:** offer

Hip. I love not to see wretchedness o'ercharged,
And duty in his service perishing. 86

The. Why, gentle sweet, you shall see no such thing.

Hip. He says they can do nothing in this kind.

The. The kinder we, to give them thanks for nothing.
Our sport shall be to take what they mistake; 90
And what poor duty cannot do, noble respect
Takes it in might, not merit.
Where I have come, great clerks have purposed
To greet me with premeditated welcomes;
Where I have seen them shiver and look pale, 95
Make periods in the midst of sentences,
Throttle their practiced accent in their fears,
And, in conclusion, dumbly have broke off,
Not paying me a welcome. Trust me, sweet,
Out of this silence yet I picked a welcome; 100
And in the modesty of fearful duty
I read as much as from the rattling tongue
Of saucy and audacious eloquence.
Love, therefore, and tongue-tied simplicity
In least speak most, to my capacity. 105

[*Re-enter* PHILOSTRATE.]

Phil. So please your Grace the Prologue is addressed.

The. Let him approach. *Flourish trumpets.*

Enter the PROLOGUE (QUINCE).

Pro. If we offend, it is with our good will.
That you should think, we come not to offend,
But with good will. To show our simple skill, 110
That is the true beginning of our end.
Consider then, we come but in despite.
We do not come, as minding to content you,
Our true intent is. All for your delight,
We are not here. That you should here repent you,
The actors are at hand: and, by their show, 116
You shall know all, that you are like to know.

The. This fellow doth not stand upon points.

Lys. He hath rid his prologue like a rough colt; he knows not the stop. A good moral, my 120 lord: it is not enough to speak, but to speak true.

Hip. Indeed he hath played on his prologue like a child on a recorder—a sound, but not in government.

The. His speech was like a tangled chain: nothing impaired, but all disordered. Who is next? 125

Enter PYRAMUS *and* THISBE, WALL, MOONSHINE, *and* LION.

Pro. Gentles, perchance you wonder at this show;
But wonder on, till truth make all things plain.
This man is Pyramus, if you would know;
This beauteous lady Thisbe is certain. 129
This man, with lime and roughcast, doth present
Wall, that vile Wall which did these lovers sunder;
And through Wall's chink, poor souls, they are content
To whisper. At the which let no man wonder.
This man, with lantern, dog, and bush of thorn,
Presenteth Moonshine. For, if you will know, 135
By moonshine did these lovers think no scorn
To meet at Ninus' tomb, there, there to woo.
This grisly beast, which Lion hight by name,
The trusty Thisbe, coming first by night,
Did scare away, or rather did affright; 140
And as she fled, her mantle she did fall,
Which Lion vile with bloody mouth did stain.
Anon comes Pyramus, sweet youth and tall,
And finds his trusty Thisbe's mantle slain; 144
Whereat, with blade, with bloody blameful blade,
He bravely broached his boiling bloody breast.
And Thisbe, tarrying in mulberry shade,
His dagger drew, and died. For all the rest,
Let Lion, Moonshine, Wall, and lovers twain
At large discourse while here they do remain. 150

The. I wonder if the lion be to speak.

Dem. No wonder, my lord. One lion may, when many asses do. *Exeunt* [*Prologue, Pyramus,*] *Lion, Thisbe, and Moonshine.*

Wall. In this same interlude it doth befall
That I, one Snout by name, present a wall; 155
And such a wall, as I would have you think,
That had in it a crannied hole or chink;
Through which the lovers, Pyramus and Thisbe,
Did whisper often, very secretly.
This loam, this roughcast, and this stone doth show
That I am that same wall. The truth is so. 161
And this the cranny is, right and sinister,
Through which the fearful lovers are to whisper.

85. wretchedness o'ercharged: poor wretches overburdened
86. duty . . . perishing: the failure of dutiful effort
88. in . . . kind: of this sort
91–92. noble . . . merit: a generous-minded audience will take their ability into account in assessing the merit of the performance.
93. come: traveled: **clerks:** learned men
94. premeditated welcomes: prepared speeches in Latin with which the sovereign was welcomed on formal visits to the universities
97. practiced accent: rehearsed delivery
105. capacity: understanding
106. addressed: ready
108–17. If . . . know: the speech is deliberately mispunctuated.
111. end: aim
113. minding . . . content: intending to please
118. points: punctuation
120. stop: period, with a pun on the reining of a horse
123. in government: under skillful control
126. Gentles: ladies and gentlemen
138. grisly: gruesome; **hight:** is called
143. tall: brave
146. broached: stabbed
150. At large: in full
162. right . . . sinister: right and left; horizontal, perhaps with a pun on "true and dishonest"

The. Would you desire lime and hair to speak better? 165

Dem. It is the wittiest partition that ever I heard discourse, my lord.

Enter PYRAMUS.

The. Pyramus draws near the wall. Silence!

Pyr. O grim-looked night! O night with hue so black!
O night, which ever art when day is not! 170
O night, O night! alack, alack, alack,
I fear my Thisbe's promise is forgot!
And thou, O wall, O sweet, O lovely wall,
That standst between her father's ground and mine!
Thou wall, O wall, O sweet and lovely wall, 175
Show me thy chink, to blink through with mine eyne! [*Wall holds up his fingers.*]
Thanks, courteous wall. Jove shield thee well for this!
But what see I? No Thisbe do I see.
O wicked wall, through whom I see no bliss,
Cursed be thy stones for thus deceiving me! 180

The. The wall, methinks, being sensible, should curse again.

Pyr. No, in truth, sir, he should not. "Deceiving me" is Thisbe's cue. She is to enter now, and I am to spy her through the wall. You shall see it 185 will fall pat as I told you. Yonder she comes.

Enter THISBE.

This. O wall, full often hast thou heard my moans
For parting my fair Pyramus and me!
My cherry lips have often kissed thy stones,
Thy stones with lime and hair knit up in thee. 190

Pyr. I see a voice. Now will I to the chink,
To spy an I can hear my Thisbe's face.
Thisbe!

This. My love! thou art my love, I think.

Pyr. Think what thou wilt, I am thy lover's grace;
And, like Limander, am I trusty still. 196

This. And I, like Helen, till the Fates me kill.

Pyr. Not Shafalus to Procrus was so true.

This. As Shafalus to Procrus, I to you. 199

Pyr. O kiss me through the hole of this vile wall!

This. I kiss the wall's hole, not your lips at all.

Pyr. Wilt thou at Ninny's tomb meet me straightway?

This. Tide life, tide death, I come without delay. [*Exeunt Pyramus and Thisbe.*]

Wall. Thus have I, Wall, my part discharged so;
And, being done, thus Wall away doth go. *Exit.*

The. Now is the mural down between the 206 two neighbors.

Dem. No remedy, my lord, when walls are so willful to hear without warning.

Hip. This is the silliest stuff that ever I heard. 210

The. The best in this kind are but shadows; and the worst are no worse, if imagination amend them.

Hip. It must be your imagination then, and not theirs.

The. If we imagine no worse of them than 215 they of themselves, they may pass for excellent men. Here come two noble beasts in, a man and a lion.

Enter LION *and* MOONSHINE.

Lion. You, ladies, you, whose gentle hearts do fear
The smallest monstrous mouse that creeps on floor,
May now perchance both quake and tremble here,
When lion rough in wildest rage doth roar. 221
Then know that I one Snug the joiner am,
A lion-fell, nor else no lion's dam;
For, if I should as lion come in strife
Into this place, 'twere pity on my life. 225

The. A very gentle beast, and of a good conscience.

Dem. The very best at a beast, my lord, that e'er I saw.

Lys. This lion is a very fox for his valor.

The. True; and a goose for his discretion. 230

Dem. Not so, my lord; for his valor cannot carry his discretion, and the fox carries the goose.

The. His discretion, I am sure, cannot carry his valor; for the goose carries not the fox. It is well. Leave it to his discretion, and let us listen to 235 the moon.

Moon. This lantern doth the horned moon present—

Dem. He should have worn the horns on his head.

The. He is no crescent, and his horns are 240 invisible within the circumference.

Moon. This lantern doth the horned moon present.
Myself the man i' the moon do seem to be.

The. This is the greatest error of all the rest. The man should be put into the lantern. How is it 245 else the man i' the moon?

Dem. He dares not come there for the candle; for, you see, it is already in snuff.

Hip. I am aweary of this moon; would he would change! 250

The. It appears, by his small light of discretion, that he is in the wane; but yet, in courtesy, in all reason, we must stay the time.

182. again: in return
186. fall pat: happen exactly
196. Limander: Leander, the faithful lover of Hero
197. Helen: apparently Leander and Hero and Helen and Alexander (Paris) are confused here.
198. Shafalus . . . Procrus: Cephalus and Procris, another pair of faithful lovers in Ovid's *Metamorphoses,* bk. vii
203. Tide: betide; happen
211. best . . . kind: best plays
223. lion-fell: lionskin, with a pun on "fell" meaning "fierce"
229. a . . . valor: more shrewd than valiant
231–32. his . . . discretion: his discretion exceeds his valor; cf. the proverb "Discretion is the better part of valor."
239. on . . . head: i.e., like the horns of a cuckold
248. in snuff: in a passion, with an obvious pun

Lys. Proceed, Moon.

Moon. All that I have to say is to tell you 255
that the lantern is the moon; I, the man i' the moon; this thornbush, my thornbush; and this dog, my dog.

Dem. Why, all these should be in the lantern; for all these are in the moon. But silence! Here 260
comes Thisbe.

Enter THISBE.

This. This is old Ninny's tomb. Where is my love?

Lion. O! *The Lion roars. Thisbe runs off.*

Dem. Well roared, Lion!

The. Well run, Thisbe! 265

Hip. Well shone, Moon! Truly, the moon shines with a good grace. [*The Lion tears Thisbe's mantle, and exit.*]

The. Well moused, Lion!

Dem. And then came Pyramus.

Lys. And so the Lion vanished. 270

Enter PYRAMUS.

Pyr. Sweet moon, I thank thee for thy sunny beams;
I thank thee, moon, for shining now so bright;
For, by thy gracious, golden, glittering gleams,
I trust to take of truest Thisbe sight.
But stay! O spite! 275
But mark, poor knight!
What dreadful dole is here?
Eyes, do you see?
How can it be?
O dainty duck! O dear! 280
Thy mantle good,
What, stained with blood?
Approach, ye Furies fell!
O Fates, come, come!
Cut thread and thrum; 285
Quail, crush, conclude, and quell!

The. This passion, and the death of a dear friend, would go near to make a man look sad.

Hip. Beshrew my heart but I pity the man. 289

Pyr. O, wherefore, Nature, didst thou lions frame?
Since lion vile hath here deflow'red my dear;
Which is—no, no!—which was the fairest dame
That lived, that loved, that liked, that looked with cheer.
Come, tears, confound!
Out, sword, and wound 295
The pap of Pyramus!
Ay, that left pap
Where heart doth hop. [*Stabs himself.*]
Thus die I, thus, thus, thus.
Now am I dead, 300
Now am I fled;
My soul is in the sky.
Tongue, lose thy light; 303
Moon, take thy flight. [*Exit Moonshine.*]
Now die, die, die, die, die! [*Dies.*]

Dem. No die, but an ace, for him; for he is but one.

Lys. Less than an ace, man; for he is dead, he is nothing.

The. With the help of a surgeon he might yet recover, and yet prove an ass. 310

Hip. How chance Moonshine is gone before Thisbe comes back and finds her lover?

Enter THISBE.

The. She will find him by starlight. Here she comes; and her passion ends the play.

Hip. Methinks she should not use a long 315
one for such a Pyramus. I hope she will be brief.

Dem. A mote will turn the balance, which Pyramus, which Thisbe, is the better; he for a man, God warrant us!—she for a woman, God bless us!

Lys. She has spied him already with those 320
sweet eyes.

Dem. And thus she means, videlicet:

This. Asleep, my love?
What, dead, my dove?
O Pyramus, arise! 325
Speak, speak! Quite dumb?
Dead, dead? A tomb
Must cover thy sweet eyes.
These lily lips,
This cherry nose, 330
These yellow cowslip cheeks,
Are gone, are gone.
Lovers, make moan!
His eyes were green as leeks.
O Sisters Three, 335
Come, come to me,
With hands as pale as milk;
Lay them in gore,
Since you have shore
With shears his thread of silk. 340
Tongue, not a word!
Come, trusty sword;
Come, blade, my breast imbrue!
[*Stabs herself.*]
And farewell, friends.

268. **moused:** handled as a mouse handles its prey
277. **dole:** sorrow
283. **Furies:** avenging deities of classical mythology
284. **Fates:** three goddesses who determined the length of human life. One spun the thread of life, another decided its length, and the third cut it at the appointed place.
285. **thrum:** unwoven end of thread
286. **quell:** kill
287. **passion:** sorrowful outburst
294. **confound:** destroy
306. **die:** one of a pair of dice; **ace:** the die with one spot
322. **means:** laments; **videlicet:** to wit
335. **Sisters Three:** the Fates
339. **shore:** cut
343. **imbrue:** stain with blood

Thus Thisbe ends. 345
Adieu, adieu, adieu! [*Dies.*]

The. Moonshine and Lion are left to bury the dead.

Dem. Ay, and Wall too.

Bot. [*Starts up*] No, I assure you; the wall is down that parted their fathers. Will it please 350 you to see the Epilogue, or to hear a Bergomask dance between two of our company?

The. No epilogue, I pray you; for your play needs no excuse. Never excuse; for when the players are all dead, there need none to be blamed. Marry, if 355 he that writ it had played Pyramus and hanged himself in Thisbe's garter, it would have been a fine tragedy; and so it is truly, and very notably discharged. But, come, your Bergomask! Let your Epilogue alone. 360

[*A dance.*]

The iron tongue of midnight hath told twelve.
Lovers, to bed; 'tis almost fairy time.
I fear we shall outsleep the coming morn
As much as we this night have overwatched.
This palpable gross play hath well beguiled 365
The heavy gait of night. Sweet friends, to bed.
A fortnight hold we this solemnity
In nightly revels and new jollity. *Exeunt.*

Enter Puck, [*with a broom*].

Puck. Now the hungry lion roars,
And the wolf behowls the moon; 370
Whilst the heavy plowman snores,
All with weary task fordone.
Now the wasted brands do glow,
Whilst the screech owl, screeching loud,
Puts the wretch that lies in woe 375
In remembrance of a shroud.
Now it is the time of night
That the graves, all gaping wide,
Every one lets forth his sprite,
In the churchway paths to glide; 380
And we fairies, that do run
By the triple Hecate's team
From the presence of the sun,
Following darkness like a dream,
Now are frolic. Not a mouse 385
Shall disturb this hallowed house.
I am sent, with broom, before,
To sweep the dust behind the door.

Enter King *and* Queen of Fairies, *with all their* Train.

Ob. Through the house give glimmering light,
By the dead and drowsy fire; 390
Every elf and fairy sprite
Hop as light as bird from brier;
And this ditty, after me,
Sing, and dance it trippingly.

Tita. First rehearse your song by rote, 395
To each word a warbling note.
Hand in hand, with fairy grace,
We will sing, and bless this place.

[*Song and dance.*]

Ob. Now, until the break of day,
Through this house each fairy stray. 400
To the best bride-bed will we,
Which by us shall blessed be;
And the issue there create
Ever shall be fortunate.
So shall all the couples three 405
Ever true in loving be;
And the blots of Nature's hand
Shall not in their issue stand;
Never mole, harelip, nor scar,
Nor mark prodigious, such as are 410
Despised in nativity,
Shall upon their children be.
With this field-dew consecrate,
Every fairy take his gait,
And each several chamber bless, 415
Through this palace, with sweet peace.
And the owner of it blest
Ever shall in safety rest.
Trip away; make no stay;
Meet me all by break of day. 420

Exeunt [*all but Puck*].

Puck. If we shadows have offended,
Think but this, and all is mended—
That you have but slumb'red here
While these visions did appear.
And this weak and idle theme, 425
No more yielding but a dream,
Gentles, do not reprehend.
If you pardon, we will mend.
And, as I am an honest Puck,
If we have unearned luck 430
Now to scape the serpent's tongue,
We will make amends ere long;
Else the Puck a liar call.
So, good night unto you all. 434
Give me your hands, if we be friends,
And Robin shall restore amends.

[*Exit.*]

351–52. **Bergomask dance:** a grotesque dance, named for the inhabitants of Bergamo in Italy
364. **overwatched:** remained sleepless
365. **palpable gross:** notably stupid
372. **fordone:** exhausted
382. **triple Hecate:** the goddess called Diana in her earthly aspect, Phœbe as the moon in the sky, and Hecate as a denizen of hell and mistress of nocturnal and supernatural activities
385. **frolic:** gay
403. **create:** created
407. **blots . . . hand:** physical deformities
413. **consecrate:** consecrated
425. **idle:** foolish
431. **the . . . tongue:** hisses of displeasure

Henry Irving as Shylock

From an extra-illustrated copy of Shakespeare's *Works,* edited by Henry Irving and Frank A. Marshall (New York, 1893).

THE MERCHANT OF VENICE

INTRODUCTION

The date of the first performance of *The Merchant of Venice* has been the subject of considerable debate. Some scholars have argued that it capitalizes upon interest aroused by the execution on June 7, 1594, of Roderigo Lopez, a Portuguese Jew and physician to the Queen, who was accused of attempting to poison her, and that it probably dates from sometime near the time of the Lopez incident. Sir Edmund Chambers argues for the autumn of 1596, a date which seems to the present editors reasonable. Although the title page of the first printed version, Quarto 1 (1600), states that it had been "divers times acted by the Lord Chamberlain his servants," there is no other evidence of the place of first performance or of its early reception. That it was received with favor there can be little question. It was revived at court on February 10, 1605, and so pleased King James that he commanded a repeat performance on the following Shrove Tuesday.

The identification of Shylock, the grasping moneylender and usurer, as a Jew has troubled Shakespearean students who have wondered whether Shakespeare in this characterization is expressing a spirit of anti-Semitism. Many writers have discussed the point. Sir Sidney Lee and Lucien Wolf assert that Shakespeare could have known converted Jews, chiefly from Spain and Portugal, who were then living in London, but J. L. Cardozo in *The Contemporary Jew in the Elizabethan Drama* shows that so few Jews were known to Shakespeare that he could not have been writing about any living prototype. There is little or no evidence of overt anti-Semitism in Shakespeare's day. Even the unfortunate Dr. Lopez, if he suffered from prejudice, suffered from being a Latin foreigner, not from being a Jew. Shakespeare's Shylock was simply a stock type that dated from the portrayal of Judas in the mystery plays. Judas was always shown in red wig and huge red beard, which was the traditional way of representing Shylock until the nineteenth century. A stereotype of the "wicked Jew" got into the stream of European literature in the Middle Ages and was almost entirely an artificial convention in England, where nobody thought of identifying literary or stage characters with living people. Marlowe's Barabas in *The Jew of Malta*—which may have influenced Shakespeare's concept of Shylock—was this literary stereotype. Shakespeare's characterization of Shylock does not exemplify anti-Semitism, for none existed in England in this period, but was merely the perpetuation of a literary tradition.

But Shakespeare's interest in Shylock as a human being and as a living personality—not as a Jew—gave the character such reality that Shylock almost steals the show. Indeed, many actors favor the part because of the opportunities it gives them to demonstrate their own skill in character interpretation. The older tradition, following the pattern of the Judas-types on the medieval stage, portrayed Shylock as a comic character. Beginning with Edmund Kean, however, in the nineteenth century, actors presented Shylock as a tragic figure, and Kean gave such pathos to the part that the spectators wept.

In *The Merchant of Venice* Shakespeare personifies and gives reality to the abstractions of Hate and Love and allows Love to reign supreme in the end through the instrumentality of Love's personification in Portia. Antonio is the personification of Noble Friendship, a theme much discussed in the Renaissance. Despite the revenge motif, which runs through the play as a dark undercurrent, the comedy is gay and sunny. The audience understands that Shylock will not really obtain his pound of flesh, and a happy ending is foretold from the beginning. To an Elizabethan it was all a charming and romantic tale set in that most fascinating of cities, Venice.

POPULARITY OF THE PLAY

After the revival of *The Merchant of Venice* before King James in 1605, records of performances are lacking until George Granville in 1701 brought out an adaptation with the title *The Jew of Venice,* which immediately gained a popularity that lasted forty years. Thomas Dogget, who took the part of Shylock, was famous as a comedian and of course presented Shylock as a heavy comic part. Nicholas Rowe, Shakespeare's first editor, complained of the comic interpretation and was later rewarded with Charles Macklin's representation of Shylock as a tragic villain in the 1741 revival of the play at Drury Lane.

David Garrick chose *The Merchant of Venice* as the play to inaugurate his management of Drury Lane Theatre in 1747. From that day to this *The Merchant of Venice* has been frequently performed. Few great actors and actresses of the last century failed to have some part in a revival of this comedy. The interpretation of Shylock's character varied widely, from Macklin's villain to Edmund Kean's tragic hero. The tendency in this century has been to portray Shylock sympathetically as a tragic figure. Portia has been a favorite role of actresses, some of whom gained their first fame in her portrayal. In America, from Colonial times on, *The Merchant of Venice* has been a popular play.

SOURCES AND TEXT

Shakespeare probably took the pound-of-flesh bond story from an Italian source, a collection of tales called *Il Pecorone,* first published in Italian in 1558 from a manuscript written about 1378 by Ser Giovanni of Florence. Although no English translation was available to Shakespeare, he may have had the story secondhand or may have found it in an old play that no longer survives. The choice-of-caskets theme appears in a story by Anthony Munday, *Zelauto* (1580), and in a collection of old tales, the *Gesta Romanorum* (1577). Both elements appear here and there in a number of literary analogues, and one cannot be certain where Shakespeare obtained the suggestion for combining them as he did in *The Merchant of Venice.*

The first printed version of *The Merchant of Venice* was brought out in 1600 for James Roberts. Quarto 1, a reasonably sound text, is the basis of most modern editions. A second printing in quarto appeared in 1619 but is falsely dated 1600 and merely reprints Quarto 1. The First Folio reprints Quarto 1 with corrections of confused or incorrect passages. The present edition, based on Quarto 1, includes more than fifty readings from the First Folio that correct Quarto 1.

A Venetian Lover

A Venetian Magnifico

A Venetian Merchant

A Venetian Doctor of Laws

The Doctor of Laws is from Cesare Vecellio, *Degli habiti antichi et moderni* (1590).
The others are from Jean de Glen, *Des habits, mœurs, . . . du monde* (1601).

[Dramatis Personæ

THE DUKE OF VENICE.
THE PRINCE OF MOROCCO, } *suitors to Portia.*
THE PRINCE OF ARRAGON, }

ANTONIO, *a merchant of Venice.*
BASSANIO, *his friend, suitor likewise to Portia.*
SOLANIO, }
SALERIO, } *friends to Antonio and Bassanio.*
GRATIANO, }

LORENZO, *in love with Jessica.*
SHYLOCK, *A Jew.*
TUBAL, *a Jew, his friend.*
LAUNCELOT GOBBO, *a clown, servant to Shylock.*
OLD GOBBO, *father to Launcelot.*
LEONARDO, *servant to Bassanio.*
BALTHASAR, } *servants to Portia.*
STEPHANO, }

PORTIA, *an heiress.*
NERISSA, *her waiting gentlewoman.*
JESSICA, *daughter to Shylock.*

Magnificoes, Officers, Jailer, Servants, and other Attendants.

Scene.—*Venice and Belmont.*]

The Square before St. Mark's, Venice
From Cesare Vecellio,
Degli habiti antichi et moderni (1590).

THE MERCHANT OF VENICE

ACT I

[Scene I. *A street in Venice.*]

Enter ANTONIO, SALERIO, *and* SOLANIO.

Ant. In sooth, I know not why I am so sad.
It wearies me; you say it wearies you;
But how I caught it, found it, or came by it,
What stuff 'tis made of, whereof it is born,
I am to learn; 5
And such a want-wit sadness makes of me
That I have much ado to know myself.
Saler. Your mind is tossing on the ocean;
There where your argosies with portly sail—
Like seigniors and rich burghers on the flood, 10
Or, as it were, the pageants of the sea—
Do overpeer the petty traffickers,
That curtsy to them, do them reverence,
As they fly by them with their woven wings.
Solan. Believe me, sir, had I such venture forth,
The better part of my affections would 16
Be with my hopes abroad. I should be still
Plucking the grass to know where sits the wind,
Piring in maps for ports, and piers, and roads;
And every object that might make me fear 20
Misfortune to my ventures, out of doubt
Would make me sad.
Saler. My wind, cooling my broth,
Would blow me to an ague when I thought
What harm a wind too great might do at sea.
I should not see the sandy hourglass run 25
But I should think of shallows and of flats,
And see my wealthy "Andrew" docked in sand,
Vailing her high top lower than her ribs
To kiss her burial. Should I go to church
And see the holy edifice of stone 30
And not bethink me straight of dangerous rocks,
Which, touching but my gentle vessel's side,
Would scatter all her spices on the stream,
Enrobe the roaring waters with my silks,
And, in a word, but even now worth this, 35
And now worth nothing? Shall I have the thought
To think on this, and shall I lack the thought
That such a thing bechanced would make me sad?
But tell not me! I know Antonio
Is sad to think upon his merchandise. 40
Ant. Believe me, no. I thank my fortune for it,
My ventures are not in one bottom trusted,
Nor to one place; nor is my whole estate
Upon the fortune of this present year:
Therefore my merchandise makes me not sad. 45
Solan. Why, then you are in love.
Ant. Fie, fie!
Solan. Not in love neither? Then let us say you are sad

9. argosies: merchant ships, a name deriving from the Adriatic port Ragusa, known as Arragosa in the sixteenth century; **portly:** (1) swelling; (2) majestic
11. pageants: moving spectacles, like floats, used in water festivals and ceremonial processions
17. still: ever
19. Piring: peering
21. out . . . doubt: doubtless
23. ague: chill
27. "Andrew": a ship's name, possibly a reference to the Spanish galleon the "St. Andrew," captured by the English in 1596
28. Vailing: bowing; i.e., touching her mast to the ground

Because you are not merry; and 'twere as easy
For you to laugh, and leap, and say you are merry
Because you are not sad. Now, by two-headed Janus,
Nature hath framed strange fellows in her time: 51
Some that will evermore peep through their eyes,
And laugh like parrots at a bagpiper;
And other of such vinegar aspect
That they'll not show their teeth in way of smile,
Though Nestor swear the jest be laughable. 56

Enter BASSANIO, LORENZO, *and* GRATIANO.

Here comes Bassanio, your most noble kinsman,
Gratiano, and Lorenzo. Fare ye well.
We leave you now with better company.

Saler. I would have stayed till I had made you merry, 60
If worthier friends had not prevented me.

Ant. Your worth is very dear in my regard.
I take it your own business calls on you,
And you embrace the occasion to depart.

Saler. Good morrow, my good lords. 65

Bass. Good signiors both, when shall we laugh? Say, when?
You grow exceeding strange: must it be so?

Saler. We'll make our leisures to attend on yours.
Exeunt Salerio and Solanio.

Lor. My Lord Bassanio, since you have found Antonio,
We two will leave you, but at dinnertime 70
I pray you have in mind where we must meet.

Bass. I will not fail you.

Gra. You look not well, Signior Antonio,
You have too much respect upon the world:
They lose it that do buy it with much care. 75
Believe me, you are marvelously changed.

Ant. I hold the world but as the world, Gratiano,
A stage, where every man must play a part,
And mine a sad one.

Gra. Let me play the fool,
With mirth and laughter let old wrinkles come, 80
And let my liver rather heat with wine
Than my heart cool with mortifying groans.
Why should a man whose blood is warm within
Sit like his grandsire cut in alablaster?
Sleep when he wakes? and creep into the jaundice
By being peevish? I tell thee what, Antonio— 86
I love thee, and 'tis my love that speaks—
There are a sort of men whose visages
Do cream and mantle like a standing pond,
And do a willful stillness entertain 90
With purpose to be dressed in an opinion
Of wisdom, gravity, profound conceit;
As who should say, "I am Sir Oracle,
And when I ope my lips, let no dog bark!"
O my Antonio, I do know of those 95
That therefore only are reputed wise
For saying nothing; when I am very sure,
If they should speak, would almost dam those ears
Which, hearing them, would call their brothers fools.
I'll tell thee more of this another time. 100
But fish not with this melancholy bait
For this fool gudgeon, this opinion.
Come, good Lorenzo. Fare ye well awhile.
I'll end my exhortation after dinner.

Lor. Well, we will leave you then till dinnertime.
I must be one of these same dumb wise men, 106
For Gratiano never lets me speak.

Gra. Well, keep me company but two years mo,
Thou shalt not know the sound of thine own tongue.

Ant. Fare you well. I'll grow a talker for this gear.

Gra. Thanks, i' faith, for silence is only commendable 111
In a neat's tongue dried and a maid not vendible.
Exeunt [*Gratiano and Lorenzo*].

Ant. Is that anything now?

Bass. Gratiano speaks an infinite deal of nothing, more than any man in all Venice. His reasons 115 are as two grains of wheat hid in two bushels of chaff: you shall seek all day ere you find them, and when you have them, they are not worth the search.

Ant. Well, tell me now, what lady is the same
To whom you swore a secret pilgrimage 120
That you today promised to tell me of?

Bass. 'Tis not unknown to you, Antonio,
How much I have disabled mine estate
By something showing a more swelling port
Than my faint means would grant continuance;
Nor do I now make moan to be abridged 126

50. two-headed Janus: the Roman god with two countenances facing in opposite directions
53. bagpiper: a doleful sound
56. Nestor: the wise Homeric hero, the personification of gravity
61. prevented: anticipated
67. strange: i.e., rarely seen
68. We'll . . . yours: we'll make ourselves available at your convenience.
74. respect . . . world: regard for wordly matters
80. old: abundant; **old** was commonly used for emphasis.
82. mortifying: weakening. In Elizabethan belief, every sigh drained blood from the heart.
84. alablaster: alabaster, such as was used for funeral busts
89. cream . . . mantle: become overcast with melancholy
90. stillness: silence; **entertain:** maintain
91. opinion: reputation
92. conceit: thought
98. dam: stop. Probably a remembrance of Matt. 5:22: "Whosoever shall say 'Thou fool,' shall be in danger of hellfire."
102. gudgeon: a small, easily caught fish
108. mo: more
110. for: because of; **gear:** stuff. Antonio means that Gratiano's nonsense has convinced him.
123. disabled: reduced
124. something: somewhat; **swelling port:** magnificent style of living
125. faint: slight
126. to . . . abridged: at being curtailed

From such a noble rate; but my chief care
Is to come fairly off from the great debts
Wherein my time, something too prodigal,
Hath left me gaged. To you, Antonio, 130
I owe the most in money and in love,
And from your love I have a warranty
To unburden all my plots and purposes
How to get clear of all the debts I owe.

Ant. I pray you, good Bassanio, let me know it;
And if it stand, as you yourself still do, 136
Within the eye of honor, be assured
My purse, my person, my extremest means
Lie all unlocked to your occasions.

Bass. In my schooldays, when I had lost one shaft,
I shot his fellow of the selfsame flight 141
The selfsame way with more advised watch
To find the other forth; and by adventuring both
I oft found both. I urge this childhood proof
Because what follows is pure innocence. 145
I owe you much, and, like a willful youth,
That which I owe is lost; but if you please
To shoot another arrow that self way
Which you did shoot the first, I do not doubt,
As I will watch the aim, or to find both, 150
Or bring your latter hazard back again
And thankfully rest debtor for the first.

Ant. You know me well, and herein spend but time
To wind about my love with circumstance;
And out of doubt you do me now more wrong 155
In making question of my uttermost
Than if you had made waste of all I have:
Then do but say to me what I should do,
That in your knowledge may by me be done,
And I am prest unto it: therefore speak. 160

Bass. In Belmont is a lady richly left;
And she is fair, and, fairer than that word,
Of wondrous virtues—sometimes from her eyes
I did receive fair speechless messages—
Her name is Portia, nothing undervalued 165
To Cato's daughter, Brutus' Portia.
Nor is the wide world ignorant of her worth,
For the four winds blow in from every coast
Renowned suitors, and her sunny locks
Hang on her temples like a golden fleece, 170
Which makes her seat of Belmont Colchos' strond,
And many Jasons come in quest of her.
O my Antonio, had I but the means
To hold a rival place with one of them,
I have a mind presages me such thrift 175
That I should questionless be fortunate!

Ant. Thou knowst that all my fortunes are at sea,
Neither have I money, nor commodity
To raise a present sum. Therefore go forth;
Try what my credit can in Venice do. 180
That shall be racked, even to the uttermost,
To furnish thee to Belmont to fair Portia.
Go presently inquire, and so will I,
Where money is, and I no question make
To have it of my trust, or for my sake. 185

Exeunt.

[Scene II. *Portia's house at Belmont.*]

Enter PORTIA *with her waiting woman,* NERISSA.

Por. By my troth, Nerissa, my little body is aweary of this great world.

Ner. You would be, sweet madam, if your miseries were in the same abundance as your good fortunes are; and yet, for aught I see, they are as sick 5 that surfeit with too much as they that starve with nothing. It is no mean happiness, therefore, to be seated in the mean. Superfluity comes sooner by white hairs, but competency lives longer.

Por. Good sentences, and well pronounced. 10

Ner. They would be better if well followed.

Por. If to do were as easy as to know what were good to do, chapels had been churches, and poor men's cottages princes' palaces. It is a good divine that follows his own instructions. I can easier 15 teach twenty what were good to be done than be one of the twenty to follow mine own teaching. The brain may devise laws for the blood, but a hot temper leaps o'er a cold decree: such a hare is madness the youth, to skip o'er the meshes of good counsel the 20 cripple. But this reasoning is not in the fashion to choose me a husband. O me, the word "choose"! I

127. rate: style
130. gaged: engaged; pledged
132. warranty: privilege
136–37. stand . . . honor: be recognizably honorable
139. to . . . occasions: for your necessities
141. of . . . flight: i.e., an exact duplicate that would travel the same distance
142. advised: attentive
143. forth: out
144. proof: instance
145. innocence: folly or naïveté
150. or: either
151. hazard: stake
154. wind . . . circumstance: make a roundabout request instead of appealing directly to my friendship
155. out . . . doubt: unquestionably
156. making . . . uttermost: doubting my willingness to do everything I can for you
160. prest unto: ready for
161. richly left: of rich inheritance

171. Colchos strond: the shore of Colchis, where Jason sought the Golden Fleece
175. thrift: success
178. commodity: collateral
185. of . . . sake: on the basis of my credit or in the way of friendship
7–8. to . . . mean: to be of average estate
8. Superfluity: the excessively wealthy
9. competency: one who has just enough
10. sentences: *sententiae;* maxims
18. blood: passions

may neither choose who I would nor refuse who I dislike, so is the will of a living daughter curbed by the will of a dead father. Is it not hard, Nerissa, 25 that I cannot choose one nor refuse none?

Ner. Your father was ever virtuous, and holy men at their death have good inspirations: therefore the lott'ry that he hath devised in these three chests of gold, silver, and lead, whereof who chooses 30 his meaning chooses you, will no doubt never be chosen by any rightly but one who you shall rightly love. But what warmth is there in your affection towards any of these princely suitors that are already come? 35

Por. I pray thee overname them; and as thou namest them, I will describe them; and according to my description level at my affection.

Ner. First, there is the Neapolitan prince.

Por. Ay, that's a colt indeed, for he doth 40 nothing but talk of his horse, and he makes it a great appropriation unto his own good parts that he can shoe him himself: I am much afeard my lady his mother played false with a smith.

Ner. Then is there the County Palatine. 45

Por. He doth nothing but frown, as who should say, "An you will not have me, choose!" He hears merry tales and smiles not. I fear he will prove the weeping philosopher when he grows old, being so full of unmannerly sadness in his youth. I had rather be 50 married to a death's-head with a bone in his mouth than to either of these. God defend me from these two!

Ner. How say you by the French lord, Monsieur Le Bon? 55

Por. God made him, and therefore let him pass for a man. In truth, I know it is a sin to be a mocker, but he—why, he hath a horse better than the Neapolitan's, a better bad habit of frowning than the Count Palatine. He is every man in no man. If a 60 throstle sing, he falls straight a-cap'ring; he will fence with his own shadow. If I should marry him, I should marry twenty husbands. If he would despise me, I would forgive him; for if he love me to madness, I shall never requite him. 65

Ner. What say you then to Falconbridge, the young baron of England?

Por. You know I say nothing to him, for he understands not me, nor I him. He hath neither Latin, French, nor Italian; and you will come into the 70 court and swear that I have a poor pennyworth in the English. He is a proper man's picture, but alas! who can converse with a dumb show? How oddly he is suited! I think he bought his doublet in Italy, his round hose in France, his bonnet in Germany, 75 and his behavior everywhere.

Ner. What think you of the Scottish lord, his neighbor?

Por. That he hath a neighborly charity in him, for he borrowed a box of the ear of the English- 80 man, and swore he would pay him again when he was able. I think the Frenchman became his surety and sealed under for another.

Ner. How like you the young German, the Duke of Saxony's nephew? 85

Por. Very vilely in the morning when he is sober, and most vilely in the afternoon when he is drunk. When he is best, he is a little worse than a man, and when he is worst, he is little better than a beast: an the worst fall that ever fell, I hope I shall 90 make shift to go without him.

Ner. If he should offer to choose, and choose the right casket, you should refuse to perform your father's will if you should refuse to accept him.

Por. Therefore, for fear of the worst, I pray 95 thee set a deep glass of Rhenish wine on the contrary casket, for if the devil be within and that temptation without, I know he will choose it. I will do anything, Nerissa, ere I will be married to a sponge.

Ner. You need not fear, lady, the having 100 any of these lords. They have acquainted me with their determinations, which is indeed to return to their home, and to trouble you with no more suit, unless you may be won by some other sort than your father's imposition, depending on the caskets. 105

Por. If I live to be as old as Sibylla, I will die as chaste as Diana unless I be obtained by the manner of my father's will. I am glad this parcel of wooers are so reasonable, for there is not one among them but I dote on his very absence; and I pray 110 God grant them a fair departure.

Ner. Do you not remember, lady, in your father's time, a Venetian, a scholar and a soldier, that came hither in company of the Marquis of Montferrat? 115

31. his meaning: i.e., the symbolism which Portia's father intended
33. affection: inclination
38. level: guess
45. County: count
48–49. weeping philosopher: Heraclitus of Ephesus, who wept at the sight of human folly
54. by: about
61. throstle: thrush
63. twenty husbands: i.e., because he is so capricious
72. proper: handsome
74. suited: dressed. Contemporary satirists frequently mocked the English noble's adoption of foreign dress fashions.
75. round hose: full, rounded breeches
83. sealed . . . another: i.e., the Frenchman and the Scot together were no match for the Englishman.
90. fall: befall
99. sponge: sot. Elizabethan Englishmen conventionally considered drunkenness a national characteristic of all Germans.
105. imposition: imposed condition
106. Sibylla: the Cumæan Sibyl, oracle of Apollo, who was granted as many years of life as there were grains of sand in a handful (Ovid, *Metamorphoses,* bk. xiv)

Por. Yes, yes, it was Bassanio, as I think, so was he called.

Ner. True, madam. He, of all the men that ever my foolish eyes looked upon, was the best deserving a fair lady. 120

Por. I remember him well, and I remember him worthy of thy praise.

Enter a SERVINGMAN.

How now? What news?

Serv. The four strangers seek for you, madam, to take their leave; and there is a forerunner 125 come from a fifth, the Prince of Morocco, who brings word the Prince his master will be here tonight.

Por. If I could bid the fifth welcome with so good heart as I can bid the other four farewell, I should be glad of his approach. If he have the condi- 130 tion of a saint and the complexion of a devil, I had rather he should shrive me than wive me.
Come, Nerissa. Sirrah, go before.
Whiles we shut the gate upon one wooer, another
knocks at the door. 134

Exeunt.

[Scene III. *A street in Venice.*]

Enter BASSANIO *with* SHYLOCK *the Jew.*

Shy. Three thousand ducats—well.

Bass. Ay, sir, for three months.

Shy. For three months—well.

Bass. For the which, as I told you, Antonio shall be bound. 5

Shy. Antonio shall become bound—well.

Bass. May you stead me? Will you pleasure me? Shall I know your answer?

Shy. Three thousand ducats for three months, and Antonio bound. 10

Bass. Your answer to that.

Shy. Antonio is a good man.

Bass. Have you heard any imputation to the contrary?

Shy. Ho, no, no, no, no! My meaning in say- 15 ing he is a good man is to have you understand me that he is sufficient. Yet his means are in supposition: he hath an argosy bound to Tripolis, another to the Indies. I understand, moreover, upon the Rialto, he hath a third at Mexico, a fourth for England, 20 and other ventures he hath, squand'red abroad. But ships are but boards, sailors but men; there be land rats and water rats, water thieves and land thieves—I mean pirates; and then there is the peril of waters, winds, and rocks—the man is, notwithstanding, 25 sufficient—three thousand ducats—I think I may take his bond.

Bass. Be assured you may.

Shy. I will be assured I may; and that I may be assured, I will bethink me. May I speak with 30 Antonio?

Bass. If it please you to dine with us.

Shy. Yes, to smell pork, to eat of the habitation which your prophet the Nazarite conjured the devil into! I will buy with you, sell with you, talk 35 with you, walk with you, and so following; but I will not eat with you, drink with you, nor pray with you. What news on the Rialto? Who is he comes here?

Enter ANTONIO.

Bass. This is Signior Antonio.

Shy. [*Aside*] How like a fawning publican he
looks! 40
I hate him for he is a Christian;
But more for that in low simplicity
He lends out money gratis and brings down
The rate of usance here with us in Venice.
If I can catch him once upon the hip, 45
I will feed fat the ancient grudge I bear him.
He hates our sacred nation, and he rails,
Even there where merchants most do congregate,
On me, my bargains, and my well-won thrift,
Which he calls interest. Cursed be my tribe 50
If I forgive him!

Bass. Shylock, do you hear?

Shy. I am debating of my present store,
And by the near guess of my memory
I cannot instantly raise up the gross
Of full three thousand ducats. What of that? 55
Tubal, a wealthy Hebrew of my tribe,
Will furnish me. But soft! How many months
Do you desire?—[*To Antonio*] Rest you fair, good
signior!
Your worship was the last man in our mouths.

Ant. Shylock, albeit I neither lend nor borrow
By taking nor by giving of excess, 61
Yet, to supply the ripe wants of my friend,

130–31. **condition:** character
132. **shrive me:** hear my confession
1. **ducats:** gold coins worth between $6.50 and $7.00 in modern currency
7. **May:** can; **stead:** assist
17. **sufficient:** capable of paying
19. **Rialto:** Wall Street of Venice
21. **squand'red:** dispersed
33–35. **the . . . into:** the Gadarene swine, Luke 7:32–33
40. **publican:** innkeeper
44. **usance:** interest
45. **upon . . . hip:** at a disadvantage; a wrestling term
49. **thrift:** wealth
58. **Rest . . . fair:** good luck to you
61. **By . . . excess:** i.e., with interest
62. **ripe:** urgent

I'll break a custom. [*To Bassanio*] Is he yet possessed
How much ye would?
Shy. Ay, ay, three thousand ducats.
Ant. And for three months. 65
Shy. I had forgot—three months, you told me so.
Well then, your bond. And let me see—but hear you:
Methoughts you said you neither lend nor borrow
Upon advantage.
Ant. I do never use it.
Shy. When Jacob grazed his uncle Laban's sheep—
This Jacob from our holy Abram was 71
(As his wise mother wrought in his behalf)
The third possessor; ay, he was the third—
Ant. And what of him? Did he take interest?
Shy. No, not take interest; not, as you would say,
Directly int'rest. Mark what Jacob did. 76
When Laban and himself were compromised
That all the eanlings which were streaked and pied
Should fall as Jacob's hire, the ewes, being rank,
In end of autumn turned to the rams, 80
And when the work of generation was
Between these woolly breeders in the act,
The skillful shepherd pilled me certain wands,
And, in the doing of the deed of kind,
He stuck them up before the fulsome ewes, 85
Who then conceiving, did in eaning time
Fall parti-colored lambs, and those were Jacob's.
This was a way to thrive, and he was blest;
And thrift is blessing, if men steal it not.
Ant. This was a venture, sir, that Jacob served for,
A thing not in his power to bring to pass, 91
But swayed and fashioned by the hand of heaven.
Was this inserted to make interest good?
Or is your gold and silver ewes and rams?
Shy. I cannot tell, I make it breed as fast— 95
But note me, signior.
Ant. [*Aside*] Mark you this, Bassanio,
The devil can cite Scripture for his purpose.
An evil soul, producing holy witness,
Is like a villain with a smiling cheek,
A goodly apple rotten at the heart. 100
O, what a goodly outside falsehood hath!
Shy. Three thousand ducats—'tis a good round sum.
Three months from twelve—then, let me see, the rate—
Ant. Well, Shylock, shall we be beholding to you?
Shy. Signior Antonio, many a time and oft 105
In the Rialto you have rated me
About my moneys and my usances:
Still have I borne it with a patient shrug,
For suff'rance is the badge of all our tribe.
You call me misbeliever, cutthroat dog, 110
And spet upon my Jewish gaberdine,
And all for use of that which is mine own.
Well then, it now appears you need my help:
Go to then, you come to me and you say,
"Shylock, we would have moneys." You say so—
You that did void your rheum upon my beard 116
And foot me as you spurn a stranger cur
Over your threshold. Moneys is your suit.
What should I say to you? Should I not say,
"Hath a dog money? Is it possible 120
A cur can lend three thousand ducats?" or
Shall I bend low, and in a bondman's key,
With bated breath and whisp'ring humbleness,
Say this:
"Fair sir, you spet on me on Wednesday last; 125
You spurned me such a day; another time
You called me dog; and for these courtesies
I'll lend you thus much moneys"?
Ant. I am as like to call thee so again,
To spet on thee again, to spurn thee too. 130
If thou wilt lend this money, lend it not
As to thy friends, for when did friendship take
A breed for barren metal of his friend?
But lend it rather to thine enemy,
Who if he break, thou mayst with better face 135
Exact the penalty.
Shy. Why, look you, how you storm!
I would be friends with you and have your love,
Forget the shames that you have stained me with,
Supply your present wants, and take no doit
Of usance for my moneys, 140
And you'll not hear me. This is kind I offer.
Bass. This were kindness.
Shy. This kindness will I show.
Go with me to a notary, seal me there
Your single bond; and, in a merry sport,
If you repay me not on such a day, 145

63. possessed: informed
69. Upon advantage: with interest
70. Jacob: Gen. 30:31–43
77. compromised: agreed on terms. The Quarto and Folio spell "compremyz'd."
78. eanlings: new-born lambs
79. rank: in heat
83. pilled me: peeled. This is the ethical dative, indicating the speaker's interest in the action.
84. kind: procreation
90. venture: speculation
92. swayed: controlled
106. rated: berated
107. moneys: sums of money
109. suff'rance: patience
111. spet: spat; **gaberdine:** cloak or mantle
112. use: lending at interest
114. Go to then: good enough; an interjection
117. spurn: kick
133. breed: interest; **of:** from
135. break: break his contract
139. doit: jot, from a small Dutch coin
142. were kindness: i.e., would be kindness if it should prove true
144. single: that is, without a co-signer

In such a place, such sum or sums as are
Expressed in the condition, let the forfeit
Be nominated for an equal pound
Of your fair flesh, to be cut off and taken
In what part of your body pleaseth me. 150
Ant. Content, in faith. I'll seal to such a bond,
And say there is much kindness in the Jew.
Bass. You shall not seal to such a bond for me!
I'll rather dwell in my necessity. 154
Ant. Why, fear not, man! I will not forfeit it.
Within these two months—that's a month before
This bond expires—I do expect return
Of thrice three times the value of this bond.
Shy. O father Abram, what these Christians are,
Whose own hard dealing teaches them suspect 160
The thoughts of others! Pray you tell me this:
If he should break his day, what should I gain
By the exaction of the forfeiture?
A pound of man's flesh taken from a man
Is not so estimable, profitable neither, 165
As flesh of muttons, beefs, or goats. I say,
To buy his favor I extend this friendship.
If he will take it, so; if not, adieu;
And for my love I pray you wrong me not.
Ant. Yes, Shylock, I will seal unto this bond. 170
Shy. Then meet me forthwith at the notary's;
Give him direction for this merry bond,
And I will go and purse the ducats straight,
See to my house, left in the fearful guard
Of an unthrifty knave, and presently 175
I will be with you.
Ant. Hie thee, gentle Jew.
Exit [*Shylock*].
The Hebrew will turn Christian; he grows kind.
Bass. I like not fair terms and a villain's mind.
Ant. Come on, in this there can be no dismay;
My ships come home a month before the day. 180
Exeunt.

168. so: fine
174. fearful: to be feared; untrustworthy

ACT II

[Scene I. *Portia's house at Belmont.*]

Flourish cornets. Enter [*the* PRINCE OF] MOROCCO, *a tawny Moor, all in white, and three or four* FOLLOWERS *accordingly, with* PORTIA, NERISSA, *and their* TRAIN.

Mor. Mislike me not for my complexion,
The shadowed livery of the burnished sun,
To whom I am a neighbor and near bred.
Bring me the fairest creature northward born,
Where Phœbus' fire scarce thaws the icicles, 5
And let us make incision for your love
To prove whose blood is reddest, his or mine.
I tell thee, lady, this aspect of mine
Hath feared the valiant—by my love I swear,
The best-regarded virgins of our clime 10
Have loved it too—I would not change this hue,
Except to steal your thoughts, my gentle queen.
Por. In terms of choice I am not solely led
By nice direction of a maiden's eye:
Besides, the lott'ry of my destiny 15
Bars me the right of voluntary choosing.
But, if my father had not scanted me,
And hedged me by his wit to yield myself
His wife who wins me by that means I told you,
Yourself, renowned Prince, then stood as fair 20
As any comer I have looked on yet
For my affection.
Mor. Even for that I thank you.
Therefore I pray you lead me to the caskets
To try my fortune. By this scimitar,
That slew the Sophy and a Persian prince 25
That won three fields of Sultan Solyman,
I would o'erstare the sternest eyes that look,
Outbrave the heart most daring on the earth,
Pluck the young sucking cubs from the she-bear,
Yea, mock the lion when 'a roars for prey, 30

2. shadowed livery: dark uniform which symbolizes his residence near the sun, as a servant's uniform identifies him with his master
9. feared: frightened
13. terms . . . choice: choosing
14. nice direction: dainty or fastidious command
17. scanted: limited
25. Sophy: King of Persia
26. Solyman: Solyman the Magnificent of Turkey
30. 'a: he

To win thee, lady. But alas the while!
If Hercules and Lichas play at dice
Which is the better man, the greater throw
May turn by fortune from the weaker hand:
So is Alcides beaten by his page, 35
And so may I, blind Fortune leading me,
Miss that which one unworthier may attain,
And die with grieving.

Por. You must take your chance,
And either not attempt to choose at all, 39
Or swear before you choose, if you choose wrong,
Never to speak to lady afterward
In way of marriage. Therefore be advised.

Mor. Nor will not. Come, bring me unto my chance.

Por. First, forward to the temple; after dinner
Your hazard shall be made.

Mor. Good fortune then! 45
To make me blest or cursed'st among men.

Exeunt.

[Scene II. *A street in Venice.*]

Enter [LAUNCELOT] *the Clown, alone.*

Laun. Certainly my conscience will serve me to run from this Jew my master. The fiend is at mine elbow and tempts me, saying to me, "Gobbo, Launcelot Gobbo, good Launcelot," or "good Gobbo," or "good Launcelot Gobbo, use your legs, take the start, 5 run away." My conscience says, "No. Take heed, honest Launcelot; take heed, honest Gobbo," or, as aforesaid, "honest Launcelot Gobbo, do not run; scorn running with thy heels." Well, the most courageous fiend bids me pack. "Via!" says the fiend. 10 "Away!" says the fiend. "For the heavens, rouse up a brave mind," says the fiend, "and run." Well, my conscience, hanging about the neck of my heart, says very wisely to me, "My honest friend Launcelot, being an honest man's son"—or rather an honest 15 woman's son, for indeed my father did something smack, something grow to, he had a kind of taste—Well, my conscience says, "Launcelot, budge not." "Budge," says the fiend. "Budge not," says my conscience. "Conscience," say I, "you counsel 20 well." "Fiend," say I, "you counsel well." To be ruled by my conscience, I should stay with the Jew my master, who (God bless the mark!) is a kind of devil; and, to run away from the Jew, I should be ruled by the fiend, who (saving your rever- 25 ence) is the devil himself. Certainly the Jew is the very devil incarnation, and, in my conscience, my conscience is but a kind of hard conscience to offer to counsel me to stay with the Jew. The fiend gives the more friendly counsel. I will run, fiend; 30 my heels are at your commandment; I will run.

Enter OLD GOBBO, *with a basket.*

Gob. Master young man, you, I pray you, which is the way to Master Jew's?

Laun. [*Aside*] O heavens, this is my true-begotten father! who, being more than sand-blind, 35 high-gravel-blind, knows me not. I will try confusions with him.

Gob. Master young gentleman, I pray you which is the way to Master Jew's?

Laun. Turn up on your right hand at the 40 next turning, but, at the next turning of all, on your left; marry, at the very next turning, turn of no hand, but turn down indirectly to the Jew's house.

Gob. Be God's sonties, 'twill be a hard way to hit! Can you tell me whether one Launcelot that 45 dwells with him, dwell with him or no?

Laun. Talk you of young Master Launcelot? [*Aside*] Mark me now! Now will I raise the waters. —Talk you of young Master Launcelot?

Gob. No master, sir, but a poor man's son. 50 His father, though I say't, is an honest exceeding poor man, and, God be thanked, well to live.

Laun. Well, let his father be what 'a will, we talk of young Master Launcelot.

Gob. Your worship's friend, and Launcelot, 55 sir.

Laun. But, I pray you, ergo, old man, ergo, I beseech you, talk you of young Master Launcelot?

Gob. Of Launcelot an't please your mastership.

Laun. Ergo Master Launcelot. Talk not of 60 Master Launcelot, father; for the young gentleman,

32. Lichas: an attendant of Hercules. This is not a reference to an episode in Hercules' career but a mere "for instance."
35. Alcides: one of the Greek names for Hercules, "descendant of Alcæus"; **page:** Alexander Pope's reading; the Quarto and Folio read "rage."
42. advised: cautious
43. Nor . . . not: nor will I (court another lady).
10. pack: be off; cf. the phrase "send packing"; **Via:** away; an Italian word originally used to urge a horse
13. hanging . . . heart: disheartening me
17. smack: i.e., smack of dishonesty
23. God . . . mark: God avert the evil omen: an exclamation used to offset the effect of mentioning something unpleasant or evil
25–26. saving . . . reverence: begging your pardon; similar to "God bless the mark"
27. incarnation: incarnate. Gobbo, like most clowns, is apt to misuse words for comic effect.
35. sand-blind: half-blind, from the Middle English *samblind*
36. high-gravel-blind: blind to a greater degree than "sand-blind"
42. marry: a mild oath, originally "By the Virgin Mary"
44. sonties: Holiness; probably a corruption of Old French *saintee*
48. raise . . . waters: provoke tears
52. well . . . live: well-to-do
57. ergo: therefore; a word common in formal logic, given a humorous turn by Launcelot's use

according to Fates and Destinies and such odd sayings, the Sisters Three and such branches of learning, is indeed deceased, or, as you would say in plain terms, gone to heaven. 65

Gob. Marry, God forbid! The boy was the very staff of my age, my very prop.

Laun. [*Aside*] Do I look like a cudgel or a hovel-post, a staff, or a prop?—Do you know me, father?

Gob. Alack the day, I know you not, young 70 gentleman! but I pray you tell me, is my boy (God rest his soul!) alive or dead?

Laun. Do you not know me, father?

Gob. Alack, sir, I am sand-blind! I know you not.

Laun. Nay, indeed, if you had your eyes, 75 you might fail of the knowing me. It is a wise father that knows his own child. Well, old man, I will tell you news of your son. [*Kneels.*] Give me your blessing. Truth will come to light; murder cannot be hid long—a man's son may, but in the end truth 80 will out.

Gob. Pray you, sir, stand up. I am sure you are not Launcelot, my boy.

Laun. Pray you, let's have no more fooling about it, but give me your blessing. I am Launcelot 85 —your boy that was, your son that is, your child that shall be.

Gob. I cannot think you are my son.

Laun. I know not what I shall think of that; but I am Launcelot, the Jew's man, and I am sure 90 Margery your wife is my mother.

Gob. Her name is Margery indeed. I'll be sworn, if thou be Launcelot, thou art mine own flesh and blood. Lord worshipped might he be, what a beard hast thou got! Thou hast got more hair on thy 95 chin than Dobbin my fill-horse has on his tail.

Laun. [*Rises.*] It should seem then that Dobbin's tail grows backward. I am sure he had more hair of his tail than I have of my face when I last saw him.

Gob. Lord, how art thou changed! How 100 dost thou and thy master agree? I have brought him a present. How 'gree you now?

Laun. Well, well, but, for mine own part, as I have set up my rest to run away, so I will not rest till I have run some ground. My master's a 105 very Jew. Give him a present? Give him a halter! I am famished in his service. You may tell every finger I have with my ribs. Father, I am glad you are come. Give me your present to one Master Bassanio, who indeed gives rare new liveries. If I serve 110 not him, I will run as far as God has any ground. O rare fortune! here comes the man. To him, father, for I am a Jew if I serve the Jew any longer.

Enter BASSANIO, *with* [LEONARDO *and*] *a* FOLLOWER OR TWO.

Bass. You may do so, but let it be so hasted that supper be ready at the farthest by five of the 115 clock. See these letters delivered, put the liveries to making, and desire Gratiano to come anon to my lodging. *Exit one of his men.*

Laun. To him, father.

Gob. God bless your worship! 120

Bass. Gramercy. Wouldst thou aught with me?

Gob. Here's my son, sir, a poor boy—

Laun. Not a poor boy, sir, but the rich Jew's man, that would, sir, as my father shall specify—

Gob. He hath a great infection, sir, as one 125 would say, to serve—

Laun. Indeed, the short and the long is, I serve the Jew, and have a desire, as my father shall specify—

Gob. His master and he (saving your worship's reverence) are scarce cater-cousins. 130

Laun. To be brief, the very truth is, that the Jew having done me wrong, doth cause me, as my father, being, I hope, an old man, shall frutify unto you—

Gob. I have here a dish of doves that I would bestow upon your worship; and my suit is— 135

Laun. In very brief, the suit is impertinent to myself, as your worship shall know by this honest old man; and, though I say it, though old man, yet poor man, my father.

Bass. One speak for both. What would you? 140

Laun. Serve you, sir.

Gob. That is the very defect of the matter, sir.

Bass. I know thee well; thou hast obtained thy suit.
Shylock thy master spoke with me this day
And hath preferred thee, if it be preferment 145
To leave a rich Jew's service to become
The follower of so poor a gentleman.

Laun. The old proverb is very well parted between my master Shylock and you, sir: you have the grace of God, sir, and he hath enough. 150

Bass. Thou speakst it well. Go, father, with thy son.
Take leave of thy old master and inquire
My lodging out. [*To a Servant*] Give him a livery
More guarded than his fellows'. See it done.

63. the . . . Three: another term for the Fates
94. Lord . . . be: God be praised; **beard:** presumably Launcelot kneels with his back to old Gobbo, who feels his hair.
96. fill-horse: draft-horse
104. set . . . rest: determined
106. halter: noose
107. tell: count
121. Gramercy: many thanks; a corruption of French *grand-merci*
125. infection: affection; inclination
130. cater-cousins: good friends
133. frutify: possibly, "notify" confused with "fructify"
136. impertinent: "pertinent" or "appurtenant"
142. defect: effect
145. preferred: recommended; **preferment:** advancement
148. The . . . proverb: "The grace of God is enough."
154. guarded: trimmed with braid

Laun. Father, in. I cannot get a service, no! 155
I have ne'er a tongue in my head! Well, [*Studying his palm*] if any man in Italy have a fairer table which doth offer to swear upon a book—! I shall have good fortune. Go to, here's a simple line of life! Here's a small trifle of wives! Alas, fifteen 160
wives is nothing! a 'leven widows and nine maids is a simple coming-in for one man; and then to scape drowning thrice, and to be in peril of my life with the edge of a feather bed! Here are simple scapes. Well, if Fortune be a woman, she's a good 165
wench for this gear. Father, come. I'll take my leave of the Jew in the twinkling.

Exit [*with Old Gobbo*].

Bass. I pray thee, good Leonardo, think on this:
These things being bought and orderly bestowed,
Return in haste, for I do feast tonight 170
My best-esteemed acquaintance. Hie thee, go.

Leon. My best endeavors shall be done herein.

Enter GRATIANO.

Gra. Where's your master?

Leon. Yonder, sir, he walks.

Exit.

Gra. Signior Bassanio!

Bass. Gratiano! 175

Gra. I have a suit to you.

Bass. You have obtained it.

Gra. You must not deny me, I must go with you
To Belmont.

Bass. Why, then you must. But hear thee, Gratiano. 179
Thou art too wild, too rude, and bold of voice—
Parts that become thee happily enough
And in such eyes as ours appear not faults;
But where thou art not known, why, there they show
Something too liberal. Pray thee take pain
To allay with some cold drops of modesty 185
Thy skipping spirit, lest through thy wild behavior
I be misconst'red in the place I go to
And lose my hopes.

Gra. Signior Bassanio, hear me:
If I do not put on a sober habit,
Talk with respect, and swear but now and then, 190
Wear prayer books in my pocket, look demurely,
Nay more, while grace is saying hood mine eyes
Thus with my hat, and sigh, and say amen,
Use all the observance of civility
Like one well studied in a sad ostent 195
To please his grandam, never trust me more.

Bass. Well, we shall see your bearing.

Gra. Nay, but I bar tonight; you shall not gauge me
By what we do tonight.

Bass. No, that were pity.
I would entreat you rather to put on 200
Your boldest suit of mirth, for we have friends
That purpose merriment: but fare you well,
I have some business.

Gra. And I must to Lorenzo and the rest; But we will visit you at suppertime. 205

Exeunt.

[Scene III. *Shylock's house in Venice.*]

Enter JESSICA *and* [LAUNCELOT] *the Clown.*

Jes. I am sorry thou wilt leave my father so.
Our house is hell, and thou, a merry devil,
Didst rob it of some taste of tediousness;
But fare thee well, there is a ducat for thee;
And, Launcelot, soon at supper shalt thou see 5
Lorenzo, who is thy new master's guest.
Give him this letter—do it secretly—
And so farewell: I would not have my father
See me in talk with thee.

Laun. Adieu! tears exhibit my tongue, most 10
beautiful pagan, most sweet Jew! if a Christian did not play the knave and get thee, I am much deceived. But adieu! these foolish drops do something drown my manly spirit: adieu!

Jes. Farewell, good Launcelot. *Exit* [*Launcelot*].
Alack, what heinous sin is it in me 16
To be ashamed to be my father's child!
But though I am a daughter to his blood,
I am not to his manners. O Lorenzo,
If thou keep promise, I shall end this strife, 20
Become a Christian and thy loving wife!

Exit.

157. table: i.e., that part of the palm that is read for fortunes
161. a 'leven: a common colloquial form of "eleven"
162. coming-in: income
163–64. be . . . feather bed: a colloquial phrase about the danger of marriage
165–66. she's . . . gear: i.e., this fortune proves her a good wench.
181. Parts: characteristics
183. show: appear
184. liberal: unrestrained
185. allay: temper
187. misconst'red: misjudged
189. put . . . habit: adopt a grave demeanor
190. with respect: thoughtfully

195. well . . . ostent: accustomed to appearing solemn
5. soon: i.e., tonight
10. exhibit: inhibit
11. did: the First Quarto and Folio read "doe" and some editors follow, interpreting the phrase as meaning that a Christian will marry Jessica. This is the reading of Folios 2, 3, and 4.
12. get: beget

[Scene IV. *A street in Venice.*]

Enter GRATIANO, LORENZO, SALERIO, *and* SOLANIO.

Lor. Nay, we will slink away in suppertime,
Disguise us at my lodging, and return
All in an hour.
Gra. We have not made good preparation.
Saler. We have not spoke us yet of torchbearers.
Solan. 'Tis vile, unless it may be quaintly ordered,
And better in my mind not undertook. 7
Lor. 'Tis now but four o'clock; we have two hours
To furnish us.

Enter LAUNCELOT, *with a letter.*

Friend Launcelot, what's the news?
Laun. An it shall please you to break up this, 10
it shall seem to signify.
Lor. I know the hand. In faith, 'tis a fair hand,
And whiter than the paper it writ on
Is the fair hand that writ.
Gra. Love-news, in faith!
Laun. By your leave, sir. 15
Lor. Whither goest thou?
Laun. Marry, sir, to bid my old master the Jew to
sup tonight with my new master the Christian.
Lor. Hold here, take this. Tell gentle Jessica
I will not fail her. Speak it privately. 20
[*Exit Launcelot.*]
Go, gentlemen,
Will you prepare you for this masque tonight?
I am provided of a torchbearer.
Saler. Ay, marry, I'll be gone about it straight.
Solan. And so will I.
Lor. Meet me and Gratiano 25
At Gratiano's lodging some hour hence.
Saler. 'Tis good we do so.
Exeunt [*Salerio and Solanio*].
Gra. Was not that letter from fair Jessica?
Lor. I must needs tell thee all. She hath directed
How I shall take her from her father's house; 30
What gold and jewels she is furnished with;
What page's suit she hath in readiness.
If e'er the Jew her father come to heaven,
It will be for his gentle daughter's sake;
And never dare misfortune cross her foot, 35
Unless she do it under this excuse,
That she is issue to a faithless Jew.
Come, go with me; peruse this as thou goest.
Fair Jessica shall be my torchbearer.
Exeunt.

6. quaintly: elegantly or skillfully; **ordered:** managed
10. break up: open; **seem . . . signify:** inform you. **Seem** was often used in this way in courtly Elizabethan discourse.

[Scene V. *Before Shylock's house in Venice.*]

Enter [*the*] *Jew* [SHYLOCK] *and his man* [LAUNCELOT] *that was the Clown.*

Shy. Well, thou shalt see, thy eyes shall be thy judge,
The difference of old Shylock and Bassanio.—
What, Jessica!—Thou shalt not gormandize
As thou hast done with me—What, Jessica!—
And sleep, and snore, and rend apparel out.— 5
Why, Jessica, I say!
Laun. Why, Jessica!
Shy. Who bids thee call? I do not bid thee call.
Laun. Your worship was wont to tell me I could do
nothing without bidding.

Enter JESSICA.

Jes. Call you? What is your will? 10
Shy. I am bid forth to supper, Jessica.
There are my keys: but wherefore should I go?
I am not bid for love; they flatter me.
But yet I'll go in hate, to feed upon
The prodigal Christian. Jessica, my girl, 15
Look to my house. I am right loath to go—
There is some ill a-brewing towards my rest,
For I did dream of money bags tonight.
Laun. I beseech you, sir, go. My young master
doth expect your reproach. 20
Shy. So do I his.
Laun. And they have conspired together. I will not
say you shall see a masque, but if you do, then it was
not for nothing that my nose fell a-bleeding on Black
Monday last at six o'clock i' the morning, fall- 25
ing out that year on Ash Wednesday was four year in
the afternoon.
Shy. What, are there masques? Hear you me, Jessica.
Lock up my doors; and when you hear the drum
And the vile squealing of the wry-necked fife, 30
Clamber not you up to the casements then,
Nor thrust your head into the public street
To gaze on Christian fools with varnished faces;
But stop my house's ears—I mean my casements.
Let not the sound of shallow fopp'ry enter 35
My sober house. By Jacob's staff I swear
I have no mind of feasting forth tonight;

20. reproach: approach
24. nose . . . a-bleeding: a sign of bad luck; **Black Monday:** Easter Monday
26. Ash . . . year: four years ago last Ash Wednesday. Launcelot parodies the typical jargon of a fortuneteller.
33. varnished: masked
35. fopp'ry: foolishness
36. Jacob's staff: Gen. 32:10

But I will go. Go you before me, sirrah;
Say I will come.

Laun. I will go before, sir. Mistress, look 40
out at window for all this.

There will come a Christian by
Will be worth a Jew's eye. [*Exit.*]

Shy. What says that fool of Hagar's offspring? ha?

Jes. His words were "Farewell, mistress"—nothing else. 45

Shy. The patch is kind enough, but a huge feeder,
Snail-slow in profit, and he sleeps by day
More than the wildcat. Drones hive not with me;
Therefore I part with him, and part with him
To one that I would have him help to waste 50
His borrowed purse. Well, Jessica, go in.
Perhaps I will return immediately.
Do as I bid you; shut doors after you.
Fast bind, fast find— 54
A proverb never stale in thrifty mind. *Exit.*

Jes. Farewell; and if my fortune be not crost,
I have a father, you a daughter, lost.
Exit.

[Scene VI. *A street in Venice.*]

Enter the Masquers, Gratiano *and* Salerio.

Gra. This is the penthouse under which Lorenzo
Desired us to make stand.

Saler. His hour is almost past.

Gra. And it is marvel he outdwells his hour,
For lovers ever run before the clock.

Saler. O, ten times faster Venus' pigeons fly 5
To seal love's bonds new-made than they are wont
To keep obliged faith unforfeited!

Gra. That ever holds. Who riseth from a feast
With that keen appetite that he sits down?
Where is the horse that doth untread again 10
His tedious measures with the unbated fire
That he did pace them first? All things that are
Are with more spirit chased than enjoyed.
How like a younker or a prodigal
The scarfed bark puts from her native bay, 15
Hugged and embraced by the strumpet wind!
How like the prodigal doth she return,
With over-weathered ribs and ragged sails,
Lean, rent, and beggared by the strumpet wind!

Enter Lorenzo.

Saler. Here comes Lorenzo. More of this hereafter.

Lor. Sweet friends, your patience for my long abode. 21
Not I, but my affairs, have made you wait.
When you shall please to play the thieves for wives,
I'll watch as long for you then. Approach.
Here dwells my father Jew. Ho! who's within? 25

[*Enter*] Jessica [*in boy's clothes*], *above.*

Jes. Who are you? Tell me for more certainty,
Albeit I'll swear that I do know your tongue.

Lor. Lorenzo, and thy love.

Jes. Lorenzo certain, and my love indeed,
For who love I so much? And now who knows 30
But you, Lorenzo, whether I am yours?

Lor. Heaven and thy thoughts are witness that thou art.

Jes. Here, catch this casket; it is worth the pains.
I am glad 'tis night, you do not look on me,
For I am much ashamed of my exchange. 35
But love is blind, and lovers cannot see
The pretty follies that themselves commit,
For if they could, Cupid himself would blush
To see me thus transformed to a boy. 39

Lor. Descend, for you must be my torchbearer.

Jes. What, must I hold a candle to my shames?
They in themselves, good sooth, are too too light.
Why, 'tis an office of discovery, love,
And I should be obscured.

Lor. So are you, sweet,
Even in the lovely garnish of a boy. 45
But come at once,
For the close night doth play the runaway,
And we are stayed for at Bassanio's feast.

Jes. I will make fast the doors, and gild myself
With some mo ducats, and be with you straight. 50
[*Exit above.*]

Gra. Now, by my hood, a gentle, and no Jew!

Lor. Beshrew me but I love her heartily;
For she is wise, if I can judge of her;
And fair she is, if that mine eyes be true;
And true she is, as she hath proved herself; 55

43. Jew's: spelled "Jewes" in the early texts. Pope emended to "Jewess."
46. patch: fool
1. penthouse: slanting roof
5. Venus' pigeons: the doves that drew her chariot
7. obliged: formally or legally bound
11. tedious measures: slow and stately paces
14. younker: younger son
15. scarfed: streaming pennants in the wind like scarves
35. exchange: i.e., the masculine costume she wears
42. light: improper, with a pun
43. office . . . discovery: function of revealing what is going on
45. garnish: adornment
47. close: perhaps both "compact; short of duration" and "secretive; favorable to concealment"
51. gentle: one of gentle breeding, with a pun on "Gentile." The First Quarto and First Folio read "gentle," the Second Quarto and later Folios "Gentile."
52. Beshrew me: literally, "curse me," actually a mild oath

And therefore, like herself, wise, fair, and true,
Shall she be placed in my constant soul.

[*Re-*]*enter* JESSICA, [*below*].

What, art thou come? On, gentlemen! away!
Our masquing mates by this time for us stay.
Exit [*with Jessica and Salerio*].

Enter ANTONIO.

Ant. Who's there? 60
Gra. Signior Antonio?
Ant. Fie, fie, Gratiano! Where are all the rest?
'Tis nine o'clock; our friends all stay for you.
No masque tonight. The wind is come about;
Bassanio presently will go aboard. 65
I have sent twenty out to seek for you.
Gra. I am glad on't, I desire no more delight
Than to be under sail and gone tonight.
Exeunt.

[Scene VII. *Portia's house at Belmont.*]

[*Flourish cornets.*] *Enter* PORTIA, *with* MOROCCO, *and both their* TRAINS.

Por. Go, draw aside the curtains and discover
The several caskets to this noble Prince.
Now make your choice.
Mor. The first, of gold, which this inscription bears,
"Who chooseth me shall gain what many men desire." 5
The second, silver, which this promise carries,
"Who chooseth me shall get as much as he deserves."
This third, dull lead, with warning all as blunt,
"Who chooseth me must give and hazard all he hath."
How shall I know if I do choose the right? 10
Por. The one of them contains my picture, Prince:
If you choose that, then I am yours withal.
Mor. Some god direct my judgment! Let me see.
I will survey the inscriptions back again.
What says this leaden casket? 15
"Who chooseth me must give and hazard all he hath."
Must give—for what? for lead! hazard for lead?
This casket threatens. Men that hazard all
Do it in hope of fair advantages;
A golden mind stoops not to shows of dross; 20
I'll then nor give nor hazard aught for lead.
What says the silver, with her virgin hue?
"Who chooseth me shall get as much as he deserves."
As much as he deserves? Pause there, Morocco,
And weigh thy value with an even hand. 25
If thou beest rated by thy estimation,
Thou dost deserve enough; and yet enough
May not extend so far as to the lady;
And yet to be afeard of my deserving
Were but a weak disabling of myself. 30
As much as I deserve? Why, that's the lady!
I do in birth deserve her, and in fortunes,
In graces, and in qualities of breeding;
But more than these, in love I do deserve.
What if I strayed no farther, but chose here? 35
Let's see once more this saying graved in gold:
"Who chooseth me shall gain what many men desire."
Why, that's the lady! All the world desires her.
From the four corners of the earth they come
To kiss this shrine, this mortal breathing saint. 40
The Hyrcanian deserts and the vasty wilds
Of wide Arabia are as throughfares now
For princes to come view fair Portia.
The watery kingdom, whose ambitious head
Spets in the face of heaven, is no bar 45
To stop the foreign spirits, but they come,
As o'er a brook, to see fair Portia.
One of these three contains her heavenly picture.
Is't like that lead contains her? 'Twere damnation
To think so base a thought. It were too gross 50
To rib her cerecloth in the obscure grave.
Or shall I think in silver she's immured,
Being ten times undervalued to tried gold?
O sinful thought! Never so rich a gem
Was set in worse than gold. They have in England
A coin that bears the figure of an angel 56
Stamped in gold, but that's insculped upon;
But here an angel in a golden bed
Lies all within. Deliver me the key:
Here do I choose, and thrive I as I may! 60
Por. There, take it, Prince, and if my form lie there,
Then I am yours. [*He unlocks the golden casket.*]
Mor. O hell! what have we here?
A carrion Death, within whose empty eye
There is a written scroll! I'll read the writing.

1. **discover:** reveal
14. **back again:** once more
20. **shows . . . dross:** worthless-appearing objects

22. **virgin:** silvery like the moon
25. **even:** just
30. **disabling:** depreciation
41. **Hyrcanian deserts:** a region south of the Caspian Sea
44. **watery kingdom:** ocean
46. **spirits:** persons, with a pun on "ghosts." According to popular superstition, apparitions could not cross bodies of water.
49. **like:** likely
51. **cerecloth:** wax-impregnated winding sheet. "Cere" derives from the Latin *cera* via French *cire,* "wax"; **obscure:** dark
53. **tried:** refined; pure

All that glisters is not gold— 65
Often have you heard that told;
Many a man his life hath sold
But my outside to behold;
Gilded tombs do worms infold:
Had you been as wise as bold, 70
Young in limbs, in judgment old,
Your answer had not been inscrolled.
Fare you well, your suit is cold.

Cold indeed, and labor lost.
Then farewell heat, and welcome frost. 75
Portia, adieu; I have too grieved a heart
To take a tedious leave; thus losers part.
Exit [*with his Train*].

Por. A gentle riddance. Draw the curtains, go.
Let all of his complexion choose me so.
Exeunt.

[Scene VIII. *A street in Venice.*]

Enter SALERIO *and* SOLANIO.

Saler. Why, man, I saw Bassanio under sail;
With him is Gratiano gone along;
And in their ship I am sure Lorenzo is not.
Solan. The villain Jew with outcries raised the Duke,
Who went with him to search Bassanio's ship. 5
Saler. He came too late, the ship was under sail;
But there the Duke was given to understand
That in a gondola were seen together
Lorenzo and his amorous Jessica.
Besides, Antonio certified the Duke 10
They were not with Bassanio in his ship.
Solan. I never heard a passion so confused,
So strange, outrageous, and so variable,
As the dog Jew did utter in the streets:
"My daughter! O my ducats! O my daughter! 15
Fled with a Christian! O my Christian ducats!
Justice! the law! My ducats, and my daughter!
A sealed bag, two sealed bags of ducats,
Of double ducats, stol'n from me by my daughter!
And jewels—two stones, two rich and precious stones, 20
Stol'n by my daughter! Justice! Find the girl!
She hath the stones upon her, and the ducats!"
Saler. Why, all the boys in Venice follow him,
Crying his stones, his daughter, and his ducats. 24
Solan. Let good Antonio look he keep his day,
Or he shall pay for this.
Saler. Marry, well rememb'red.
I reasoned with a Frenchman yesterday,
Who told me, in the Narrow Seas that part
The French and English there miscarried
A vessel of our country richly fraught. 30
I thought upon Antonio when he told me,
And wished in silence that it were not his.
Solan. You were best to tell Antonio what you hear.
Yet do not suddenly, for it may grieve him.
Saler. A kinder gentleman treads not the earth.
I saw Bassanio and Antonio part. 36
Bassanio told him he would make some speed
Of his return; he answered, "Do not so.
Slubber not business for my sake, Bassanio,
But stay the very riping of the time; 40
And for the Jew's bond which he hath of me,
Let it not enter in your mind of love.
Be merry, and employ your chiefest thoughts
To courtship, and such fair ostents of love
As shall conveniently become you there." 45
And even there, his eye being big with tears,
Turning his face, he put his hand behind him,
And with affection wondrous sensible
He wrung Bassanio's hand; and so they parted.
Solan. I think he only loves the world for him.
I pray thee let us go and find him out, 51
And quicken his embraced heaviness
With some delight or other.
Saler. Do we so.
Exeunt.

[Scene IX. *Portia's house at Belmont.*]

Enter NERISSA *and a* SERVITOR.

Ner. Quick, quick, I pray thee; draw the curtain straight.
The Prince of Arragon hath ta'en his oath
And comes to his election presently.

Flourish cornets. Enter ARRAGON, *his* TRAIN, *and* PORTIA [*with her* TRAIN].

65. **glisters:** glistens
69. **tombs:** Samuel Johnson's reading. The early texts read "timber."
72. **Your . . . inscrolled:** that is, instead of the scroll he would have found the portrait.
75. **heat:** passion
77. **part:** depart
19. **double ducats:** worth twice the value of ordinary ducats
27. **reasoned:** conversed
29. **miscarried:** was lost
30. **fraught:** freighted
39. **Slubber:** bungle
41. **for:** as for
42. **mind . . . love:** loving mind
44. **ostents:** shows
48. **affection . . . sensible:** that is, an extraordinary show of emotion
52. **his . . . heaviness:** the melancholy in which he is lapped
1. **straight:** at once
3. **election:** choice

Por. Behold, there stand the caskets, noble Prince.
If you choose that wherein I am contained, 5
Straight shall our nuptial rites be solemnized;
But if you fail, without more speech, my lord,
You must be gone from hence immediately.

Ar. I am enjoined by oath to observe three things:
First, never to unfold to anyone 10
Which casket 'twas I chose; next, if I fail
Of the right casket, never in my life
To woo a maid in way of marriage;
Lastly,
If I do fail in fortune of my choice, 15
Immediately to leave you and be gone.

Por. To these injunctions everyone doth swear
That comes to hazard for my worthless self.

Ar. And so have I addressed me. Fortune now
To my heart's hope! Gold, silver, and base lead. 20
"Who chooseth me must give and hazard all he hath."
You shall look fairer ere I give or hazard.
What says the golden chest? Ha, let me see!
"Who chooseth me shall gain what many men desire."
What many men desire! That "many" may be meant
By the fool multitude, that choose by show, 26
Not learning more than the fond eye doth teach,
Which pries not to the interior, but, like the martlet,
Builds in the weather on the outward wall,
Even in the force and road of casualty. 30
I will not choose what many men desire,
Because I will not jump with common spirits
And rank me with the barbarous multitude.
Why then, to thee, thou silver treasure house!
Tell me once more what title thou dost bear: 35
"Who chooseth me shall get as much as he deserves."
And well said too, for who shall go about
To cozen Fortune, and be honorable
Without the stamp of merit? Let none presume
To wear an undeserved dignity. 40
O that estates, degrees, and offices
Were not derived corruptly, and that clear honor
Were purchased by the merit of the wearer!
How many then should cover that stand bare!
How many be commanded that command! 45
How much low peasantry would then be gleaned
From the true seed of honor! and how much honor
Picked from the chaff and ruin of the times
To be new varnished! Well, but to my choice.
"Who chooseth me shall get as much as he deserves."
I will assume desert. Give me a key for this, 51
And instantly unlock my fortunes here.

[*He unlocks the silver casket.*]

Por. [*Aside*] Too long a pause for that which you find there.

Ar. What's here? The portrait of a blinking idiot,
Presenting me a schedule! I will read it. 55
How much unlike art thou to Portia!
How much unlike my hopes and my deservings!
"Who chooseth me shall have as much as he deserves."
Did I deserve no more than a fool's head?
Is that my prize? Are my deserts no better? 60

Por. To offend and judge are distinct offices
And of opposed natures.

Ar. What is here?

The fire seven times tried this.
Seven times tried that judgment is
That did never choose amiss. 65
Some there be that shadows kiss;
Such have but a shadow's bliss.
There be fools alive iwis
Silvered o'er, and so was this.
Take what wife you will to bed, 70
I will ever be your head.
So be gone; you are sped.

Still more fool I shall appear
By the time I linger here.
With one fool's head I came to woo, 75
But I go away with two.
Sweet, adieu. I'll keep my oath,
Patiently to bear my wroth.

[*Exit with his Train.*]

Por. Thus hath the candle singed the moth.
O, these deliberate fools! When they do choose, 80
They have the wisdom by their wit to lose.

Ner. The ancient saying is no heresy,
Hanging and wiving goes by destiny.

Por. Come draw the curtain, Nerissa.

Enter MESSENGER.

Mess. Where is my lady?

Por. Here. What would my lord? 85

Mess. Madam, there is alighted at your gate

19. addressed me: prepared myself
27. fond: foolish
28. martlet: the European martin
30. force . . . road: violent path (a hendiadys)
32. jump: agree
38. cozen: cheat
42. clear: unblemished
43. purchased: acquired
44. cover . . . bare: keep on their hats who now are obliged to doff them to superiors
47. true . . . honor: the truly nobly-born
55. schedule: scroll
68. iwis: certainly, from Middle English *iwis* and Old English *geweiss*
69. Silvered o'er: having an appearance of value
72. sped: done
78. wroth: vexation
80. deliberate: logical
81. wisdom: to Portia, they are wise to lose because she would not have them win.
83. Hanging . . . destiny: proverbial
85. my lord: Portia is in good spirits at her latest escape and gaily replies in kind to the messenger's salutation.

A young Venetian, one that comes before
To signify the approaching of his lord;
From whom he bringeth sensible regreets,
To wit, besides commends and courteous breath,
Gifts of rich value. Yet I have not seen 91
So likely an ambassador of love.
A day in April never came so sweet
To show how costly summer was at hand,

89. **sensible regreets:** appreciable greetings
90. **commends:** vows of devotion; **breath:** words

As this fore-spurrer comes before his lord. 95
Por. No more, I pray thee. I am half afeard
Thou wilt say anon he is some kin to thee,
Thou spendst such high-day wit in praising him.
Come, come, Nerissa, for I long to see
Quick Cupid's post that comes so mannerly. 100
Ner. Bassanio, Lord Love, if thy will it be!
Exeunt.

98. **high-day:** holiday
100. **post:** messenger

ACT III

[Scene I. *A street in Venice.*]

Enter SOLANIO *and* SALERIO.

Solan. Now what news on the Rialto?

Saler. Why, yet it lives there unchecked that Antonio hath a ship of rich lading wracked on the Narrow Seas—the Goodwins I think they call the place—a very dangerous flat, and fatal, where the car- 5 cases of many a tall ship lie buried, as they say, if my gossip Report be an honest woman of her word.

Solan. I would she were as lying a gossip in that as ever knapped ginger or made her neighbors believe she wept for the death of a third husband. But 10 it is true, without any slips of prolixity or crossing the plain highway of talk, that the good Antonio, the honest Antonio—O that I had a title good enough to keep his name company!—

Saler. Come, the full stop. 15

Solan. Ha, what sayest thou? Why, the end is, he hath lost a ship.

Saler. I would it might prove the end of his losses.

Solan. Let me say amen betimes, lest the devil cross my prayer, for here he comes in the like- 20 ness of a Jew.

Enter SHYLOCK.

How, now, Shylock? What news among the merchants?

Shy. You knew, none so well, none so well as you, of my daughter's flight. 25

Saler. That's certain. I, for my part, knew the tailor that made the wings she flew withal.

Solan. And Shylock, for his own part, knew the bird was fledged; and then it is the complexion of them all to leave the dam. 30

Shy. She is damned for it.

Saler. That's certain, if the devil may be her judge.

Shy. My own flesh and blood to rebel!

Solan. Out upon it, old carrion! Rebels it at these years? 35

Shy. I say my daughter is my flesh and my blood.

Saler. There is more difference between thy flesh and hers than between jet and ivory; more between your bloods than there is between red wine and Rhenish. But tell us, do you hear whether An- 40 tonio have had any loss at sea or no?

Shy. There I have another bad match, a bankrout, a prodigal, who dare scarce show his head on the Rialto, a beggar, that was used to come so smug upon the mart! let him look to his bond. He 45 was wont to call me usurer: let him look to his bond. He was wont to lend money for a Christian curtsy: let him look to his bond.

Saler. Why, I am sure, if he forfeit, thou wilt not take his flesh. What's that good for? 50

2. **lives . . . unchecked:** is rumored
3–4. **Narrow Seas:** the English Channel
4. **the Goodwins:** Goodwin Sands
6. **tall:** splendid
9. **knapped:** chewed. Old people were fond of nibbling on ginger.
11. **slips:** errors; **prolixity:** verbosity
19. **betimes:** promptly

29. **complexion:** disposition
34–35. **Rebels . . . years:** Solanio pretends to understand Shylock to mean that he is troubled with passion, old as he is.
42. **match:** bargain; **bankrout:** bankrupt
44. **smug:** spruce; well-dressed
48. **curtsy:** courtesy

Shy. To bait fish withal. If it will feed nothing else, it will feed my revenge. He hath disgraced me, and hind'red me half a million; laughed at my losses, mocked at my gains, scorned my nation, thwarted my bargains, cooled my friends, heated mine 55 enemies—and what's his reason? I am a Jew. Hath not a Jew eyes? Hath not a Jew hands, organs, dimensions, senses, affections, passions? fed with the same food, hurt with the same weapons, subject to the same diseases, healed by the same means, 60 warmed and cooled by the same winter and summer as a Christian is? If you prick us, do we not bleed? If you tickle us, do we not laugh? If you poison us, do we not die? And if you wrong us, shall we not revenge? If we are like you in the rest, we will 65 resemble you in that. If a Jew wrong a Christian, what is his humility? Revenge. If a Christian wrong a Jew, what should his sufferance be by Christian example? Why, revenge. The villainy you teach me I will execute, and it shall go hard but I will 70 better the instruction.

Enter a MAN FROM ANTONIO.

Man. Gentleman, my master Antonio is at his house, and desires to speak with you both.

Saler. We have been up and down to seek him.

Enter TUBAL.

Solan. Here comes another of the tribe. A 75 third cannot be matched, unless the devil himself turn Jew. *Exeunt [Solanio, Salerio, and Man].*

Shy. How now, Tubal? What news from Genoa? Hast thou found my daughter?

Tub. I often came where I did hear of her, 80 but cannot find her.

Shy. Why, there, there, there, there! A diamond gone cost me two thousand ducats in Frankford! The curse never fell upon our nation till now; I never felt it till now. Two thousand ducats in 85 that, and other precious, precious jewels. I would my daughter were dead at my foot, and the jewels in her ear: would she were hearsed at my foot, and the ducats in her coffin! No news of them? Why, so —and I know not what's spent in the search. 90 Why, thou loss upon loss! the thief gone with so much, and so much to find the thief, and no satisfaction, no revenge! nor no ill luck stirring but what lights o' my shoulders; no sighs but o' my breathing; no tears but o' my shedding. 95

Tub. Yes, other men have ill luck too. Antonio, as I heard in Genoa—

Shy. What, what, what? Ill luck, ill luck?

Tub. Hath an argosy cast away coming from Tripolis. 100

Shy. I thank God, I thank God! Is it true? is it true?

Tub. I spoke with some of the sailors that escaped the wrack.

Shy. I thank thee, good Tubal. Good news, 105 good news! ha, ha! heard in Genoa!

Tub. Your daughter spent in Genoa, as I heard, one night fourscore ducats.

Shy. Thou stickst a dagger in me—I shall never see my gold again—fourscore ducats at a sitting! 110 fourscore ducats!

Tub. There came divers of Antonio's creditors in my company to Venice that swear he cannot choose but break.

Shy. I am very glad of it. I'll plague him; 115 I'll torture him. I am glad of it.

Tub. One of them showed me a ring that he had of your daughter for a monkey.

Shy. Out upon her! Thou torturest me, Tubal. It was my turquoise; I had it of Leah when I 120 was a bachelor. I would not have given it for a wilderness of monkeys.

Tub. But Antonio is certainly undone.

Shy. Nay, that's true, that's very true. Go, Tubal, fee me an officer; bespeak him a fortnight 125 before. I will have the heart of him if he forfeit, for were he out of Venice, I can make what merchandise I will. Go, Tubal, and meet me at our synagogue; go, good Tubal; at our synagogue, Tubal.

Exeunt.

[Scene II. *Portia's house at Belmont.*]

Enter BASSANIO, PORTIA, GRATIANO, [NERISSA], *and all their* TRAINS.

Por. I pray you tarry, pause a day or two
Before you hazard, for in choosing wrong
I lose your company. Therefore forbear awhile.
There's something tells me (but it is not love)
I would not lose you, and you know yourself 5
Hate counsels not in such a quality.
But lest you should not understand me well—
And yet a maiden hath no tongue but thought—
I would detain you here some month or two
Before you venture for me. I could teach you 10
How to choose right, but then I am forsworn.

53. hind'red me: prevented my gaining
67. his: i.e., the Christian's
68. sufferance: forbearance
70. it . . . will: I shall make every effort to

113-14. cannot . . . break: must go bankrupt
125. bespeak: engage
6. quality: kind
8. a . . . thought: modesty prevents a maiden from expressing her thoughts.
11. I . . . forsworn: I would break my vow

So will I never be; so may you miss me;
But if you do, you'll make me wish a sin—
That I had been forsworn. Beshrew your eyes!
They have o'erlooked me and divided me; 15
One half of me is yours, the other half yours—
Mine own, I would say, but if mine, then yours,
And so all yours! O, these naughty times
Put bars between the owners and their rights!
And so, though yours, not yours. Prove it so, 20
Let Fortune go to hell for it, not I.
I speak too long, but 'tis to peise the time,
To eke it, and to draw it out in length,
To stay you from election.

Bass. Let me choose,
For as I am, I live upon the rack. 25

Por. Upon the rack, Bassanio? Then confess
What treason there is mingled with your love.

Bass. None but that ugly treason of mistrust,
Which makes me fear the enjoying of my love.
There may as well be amity and life 30
'Tween snow and fire as treason and my love.

Por. Ay, but I fear you speak upon the rack,
Where men enforced do speak anything.

Bass. Promise me life, and I'll confess the truth.

Por. Well then, confess and live.

Bass. "Confess and love" 35
Had been the very sum of my confession.
O happy torment, when my torturer
Doth teach me answers for deliverance!
But let me to my fortune and the caskets.

Por. Away then! I am locked in one of them;
If you do love me, you will find me out. 41
Nerissa and the rest, stand all aloof.
Let music sound while he doth make his choice;
Then, if he lose, he makes a swanlike end,
Fading in music. That the comparison 45
May stand more proper, my eye shall be the stream
And wat'ry deathbed for him. He may win;
And what is music then? Then music is
Even as the flourish when true subjects bow
To a new-crowned monarch. Such it is 50
As are those dulcet sounds in break of day
That creep into the dreaming bridegroom's ear
And summon him to marriage. Now he goes
With no less presence, but with much more love,
Than young Alcides when he did redeem 55
The virgin tribute paid by howling Troy
To the sea monster. I stand for sacrifice;
The rest aloof are the Dardanian wives,
With bleared visages come forth to view
The issue of the exploit. Go, Hercules! 60
Live thou, I live. With much much more dismay
I view the fight than thou that makest the fray.

A Song, the whilst Bassanio comments on the caskets to himself.

Tell me, where is fancy bred,
Or in the heart, or in the head?
How begot, how nourished? 65
Reply, reply.
It is engend'red in the eyes,
With gazing fed, and fancy dies
In the cradle where it lies.
Let us all ring fancy's knell. 70
I'll begin it—Ding, dong, bell.

All. Ding, dong, bell.

Bass. So may the outward shows be least themselves;
The world is still deceived with ornament.
In law, what plea so tainted and corrupt 75
But, being seasoned with a gracious voice,
Obscures the show of evil? In religion,
What damned error but some sober brow
Will bless it, and approve it with a text,
Hiding the grossness with fair ornament? 80
There is no voice so simple but assumes
Some mark of virtue on his outward parts.
How many cowards, whose hearts are all as false
As stairs of sand, wear yet upon their chins
The beards of Hercules and frowning Mars; 85
Who, inward searched, have livers white as milk!
And these assume but valor's excrement
To render them redoubted. Look on beauty,
And you shall see 'tis purchased by the weight,
Which therein works a miracle in nature, 90
Making them lightest that wear most of it.
So are those crisped snaky golden locks,
Which make such wanton gambols with the wind
Upon supposed fairness, often known
To be the dowry of a second head, 95
The skull that bred them in the sepulcher.

15. **o'erlooked:** bewitched
18. **naughty:** wicked. **Naughty** was always a much stronger word in Elizabethan English than in modern usage.
20–21. **Prove . . . it:** if I am not yours in the end, Fortune must be condemned for the fact.
22. **peise:** hang weights upon (to slow its progress)
27. **treason:** a reference to the racking of suspected traitors
29. **fear:** doubt
30. **amity . . . life:** amicable life
44. **swanlike:** swans were believed to sing when dying.
49. **flourish:** fanfare
54. **with . . . love:** Alcides undertook to rescue Hesione (the **virgin tribute**) for a reward of horses promised by her father, the King of Troy (Ovid, *Metamorphoses,* bk. xi).
57. **stand for:** represent
58. **Dardanian:** Trojan
59. **bleared:** tearstained
63. **fancy:** love
74. **still:** ever
79. **approve:** confirm
87. **excrement:** outgrowth; beard
88. **redoubted:** formidable
91. **lightest:** most wanton
92. **crisped:** curled
93–94. **Which . . . fairness:** with which the wind dallies because they appear fair
95. **the . . . head:** a wig

Thus ornament is but the guiled shore
To a most dangerous sea; the beauteous scarf
Veiling an Indian beauty; in a word, 99
The seeming truth which cunning times put on
To entrap the wisest. Therefore, thou gaudy gold,
Hard food for Midas, I will none of thee;
Nor none of thee, thou pale and common drudge
'Tween man and man: but thou, thou meager lead,
Which rather threatenst than dost promise aught,
Thy plainness moves me more than eloquence, 106
And here choose I. Joy be the consequence!

Por. [*Aside*] How all the other passions fleet to air,
As doubtful thoughts, and rash-embraced despair,
And shudd'ring fear, and green-eyed jealousy! 110
O love, be moderate; allay thy ecstasy;
In measure rein thy joy; scant this excess!
I feel too much thy blessing: make it less
For fear I surfeit!

Bass. [*Opening the leaden casket*] What find I here?
Fair Portia's counterfeit! What demigod 115
Hath come so near creation? Move these eyes?
Or whether, riding on the balls of mine,
Seem they in motion? Here are severed lips,
Parted with sugar breath—so sweet a bar 119
Should sunder such sweet friends. Here in her hairs
The painter plays the spider, and hath woven
A golden mesh t'entrap the hearts of men
Faster than gnats in cobwebs. But her eyes—
How could he see to do them? Having made one,
Methinks it should have power to steal both his
And leave itself unfurnished. Yet look, how far 126
The substance of my praise doth wrong this shadow
In underprizing it, so far this shadow
Doth limp behind the substance. Here's the scroll,
The continent and summary of my fortune. 130

You that choose not by the view
Chance as fair and choose as true.
Since this fortune falls to you,
Be content and seek no new.
If you be well pleased with this 135
And hold your fortune for your bliss,
Turn you where your lady is
And claim her with a loving kiss.

A gentle scroll. Fair lady, by your leave,
[*Kisses her.*]
I come by note, to give and to receive. 140
Like one of two contending in a prize,
That thinks he hath done well in people's eyes,
Hearing applause and universal shout,
Giddy in spirit, still gazing in a doubt
Whether those peals of praise be his or no; 145
So, thrice-fair lady, stand I, even so,
As doubtful whether what I see be true,
Until confirmed, signed, ratified by you.

Por. You see me, Lord Bassanio, where I stand,
Such as I am. Though for myself alone 150
I would not be ambitious in my wish
To wish myself much better, yet for you
I would be trebled twenty times myself,
A thousand times more fair, ten thousand times more rich,
That, only to stand high in your account, 155
I might in virtues, beauties, livings, friends,
Exceed account. But the full sum of me
Is sum of nothing, which, to term in gross,
Is an unlessoned girl, unschooled, unpracticed;
Happy in this, she is not yet so old 160
But she may learn; happier than this,
She is not bred so dull but she can learn;
Happiest of all is that her gentle spirit
Commits itself to yours to be directed,
As from her lord, her governor, her king. 165
Myself and what is mine to you and yours
Is now converted. But now I was the lord
Of this fair mansion, master of my servants,
Queen o'er myself; and even now, but now, 169
This house, these servants, and this same myself
Are yours, my lord. I give them with this ring,
Which when you part from, lose, or give away,
Let it presage the ruin of your love
And be my vantage to exclaim on you.

Bass. Madam, you have bereft me of all words,
Only my blood speaks to you in my veins, 176
And there is such confusion in my powers
As, after some oration fairly spoke
By a beloved prince, there doth appear
Among the buzzing pleased multitude, 180
Where every something, being blent together,
Turns to a wild of nothing, save of joy,
Expressed and not expressed. But when this ring
Parts from this finger, then parts life from hence!
O, then be bold to say Bassanio's dead! 185

97. guiled: guileful; treacherous
99. Indian: i.e., dark-complexioned. By contemporary standards a fair complexion was necessary for beauty.
102. Hard . . . Midas: a reference to Midas' difficulties when he had the golden touch; see Ovid, *Metamorphoses,* bk. xi.
103. pale . . . drudge: silver, which was used for currency
104. meager: poor
116. Hath . . . creation: has so nearly created a human being
126. unfurnished: incomplete (without a second eye)
130. continent: container
136. hold . . . bliss: regard your fortune as the height of happiness
140. by note: on the authority of the scroll's instruction
141. prize: contest
156. livings: revenues
157. account: accounting; calculation
158. sum . . . nothing: explained by the adjectives "unlessoned," "unschooled," "unpracticed"; **term . . . gross:** itemize
167. But now: just before this minute
169. even . . . now: at this very instant
174. vantage: opportunity; **exclaim on:** scold
181. blent: blended
182. wild: wilderness

Ner. My lord and lady, it is now our time
That have stood by and seen our wishes prosper
To cry "good joy." Good joy, my lord and lady!
Gra. My Lord Bassanio, and my gentle lady,
I wish you all the joy that you can wish; 190
For I am sure you can wish none from me;
And when your honors mean to solemnize
The bargain of your faith, I do beseech you
Even at that time I may be married too.
Bass. With all my heart, so thou canst get a wife.
Gra. I thank your lordship, you have got me one.
My eyes, my lord, can look as swift as yours. 197
You saw the mistress, I beheld the maid;
You loved, I loved; for intermission
No more pertains to me, my lord, than you. 200
Your fortune stood upon the caskets there,
And so did mine too, as the matter falls;
For wooing here until I sweat again,
And swearing till my very roof was dry
With oaths of love, at last—if promise last— 205
I got a promise of this fair one here
To have her love, provided that your fortune
Achieved her mistress.
Por. Is this true, Nerissa?
Ner. Madam, it is, so you stand pleased withal.
Bass. And do you, Gratiano, mean good faith?
Gra. Yes, faith, my lord. 211
Bass. Our feast shall be much honored in your marriage.
Gra. We'll play with them the first boy for a thousand ducats. 215
Ner. What, and stake down?
Gra. No, we shall ne'er win at that sport, and stake down.
But who comes here? Lorenzo and his infidel?
What, and my old Venetian friend Salerio?

Enter LORENZO, JESSICA, *and* SALERIO [*a Messenger from Venice*].

Bass. Lorenzo and Salerio, welcome hither, 220
If that the youth of my new int'rest here
Have power to bid you welcome. By your leave,
I bid my very friends and countrymen,
Sweet Portia, welcome.
Por. So do I, my lord.
They are entirely welcome. 225
Lor. I thank your honor. For my part, my lord,
My purpose was not to have seen you here;
But meeting with Salerio by the way,
He did entreat me, past all saying nay,
To come with him along.
Saler. I did, my lord, 230
And I have reason for it. Signior Antonio
Commends him to you. [*Gives Bassanio a letter.*]
Bass. Ere I ope his letter,
I pray you tell me how my good friend doth.
Saler. Not sick, my lord, unless it be in mind;
Nor well, unless in mind. His letter there 235
Will show you his estate.
[*Bassanio opens the letter.*]
Gra. Nerissa, cheer yond stranger; bid her welcome.
Your hand, Salerio. What's the news from Venice?
How doth that royal merchant, good Antonio?
I know he will be glad of our success. 240
We are the Jasons, we have won the Fleece.
Saler. I would you had won the fleece that he hath lost!
Por. There are some shrewd contents in yond same paper
That steals the color from Bassanio's cheek:
Some dear friend dead; else nothing in the world
Could turn so much the constitution 246
Of any constant man. What, worse and worse?
With leave, Bassanio—I am half yourself,
And I must freely have the half of anything
That this same paper brings you.
Bass. O sweet Portia,
Here are a few of the unpleasant'st words 251
That ever blotted paper! Gentle lady,
When I did first impart my love to you,
I freely told you all the wealth I had
Ran in my veins—I was a gentleman— 255
And then I told you true; and yet, dear lady,
Rating myself at nothing, you shall see
How much I was a braggart. When I told you
My state was nothing, I should then have told you
That I was worse than nothing; for indeed 260
I have engaged myself to a dear friend,
Engaged my friend to his mere enemy
To feed my means. Here is a letter, lady—
The paper as the body of my friend,
And every word in it a gaping wound 265
Issuing lifeblood. But is it true, Salerio?
Have all his ventures failed? What, not one hit?
From Tripolis, from Mexico, and England,
From Lisbon, Barbary, and India?
And not one vessel scape the dreadful touch 270
Of merchant-marring rocks?
Saler. Not one, my lord.
Besides, it should appear that, if he had
The present money to discharge the Jew,

199. intermission: time-wasting
214. play . . . boy: gamble on who has the first boy
221. int'rest: right (as one betrothed to Portia)
223. very: true
236. estate: condition
237. cheer: greet
243. shrewd: grievous; extremely distressing
247. constant: self-controlled
261. engaged: pledged
262. mere: absolute

He would not take it. Never did I know
A creature that did bear the shape of man 275
So keen and greedy to confound a man.
He plies the Duke at morning and at night,
And doth impeach the freedom of the state
If they deny him justice. Twenty merchants,
The Duke himself, and the magnificoes 280
Of greatest port have all persuaded with him;
But none can drive him from the envious plea
Of forfeiture, of justice, and his bond.
Jes. When I was with him, I have heard him swear
To Tubal and to Chus, his countrymen, 285
That he would rather have Antonio's flesh
Than twenty times the value of the sum
That he did owe him; and I know, my lord,
If law, authority, and power deny not,
It will go hard with poor Antonio. 290
Por. Is it your dear friend that is thus in trouble?
Bass. The dearest friend to me, the kindest man,
The best-conditioned and unwearied spirit
In doing courtesies, and one in whom
The ancient Roman honor more appears 295
Than any that draws breath in Italy.
Por. What sum owes he the Jew?
Bass. For me three thousand ducats.
Por. What, no more?
Pay him six thousand, and deface the bond.
Double six thousand and then treble that 300
Before a friend of this description
Shall lose a hair through Bassanio's fault.
First go with me to church and call me wife,
And then away to Venice to your friend,
For never shall you lie by Portia's side 305
With an unquiet soul. You shall have gold
To pay the petty debt twenty times over.
When it is paid, bring your true friend along.
My maid Nerissa and myself meantime
Will live as maids and widows. Come, away! 310
For you shall hence upon your wedding day.
Bid your friends welcome, show a merry cheer;
Since you are dear bought, I will love you dear.
But let me hear the letter of your friend.

Bass. Sweet Bassanio, my ships have all mis- 315
carried, my creditors grow cruel, my estate is very low,
my bond to the Jew is forfeit, and since in paying it, it
is impossible I should live, all debts are cleared between
you and I if I might but see you at my death. Notwithstanding, use your pleasure: if your love do not 320
persuade you to come, let not my letter.

Por. O love, dispatch all business and be gone!
Bass. Since I have your good leave to go away,
I will make haste; but till I come again,
No bed shall e'er be guilty of my stay, 325
Nor rest be interposer 'twixt us twain.
Exeunt.

276. **confound:** destroy
277. **plies:** solicits
278. **impeach:** impugn
280. **magnificoes:** Venetian nobility
281. **port:** importance
282. **envious:** malicious
313. **dear bought:** i.e., possibly at the cost of Antonio's life

---

[Scene III. *Before Shylock's house in Venice.*]

Enter [Shylock] *the Jew and* Solanio *and* Antonio *and the* Jailer.

Shy. Jailer, look to him—tell not me of mercy—
This is the fool that lent out money gratis.
Jailer, look to him.
Ant. Hear me yet, good Shylock.
Shy. I'll have my bond! Speak not against my bond!
I have sworn an oath that I will have my bond. 5
Thou calledst me dog before thou hadst a cause,
But, since I am a dog, beware my fangs.
The Duke shall grant me justice. I do wonder,
Thou naughty jailer, that thou art so fond
To come abroad with him at his request. 10
Ant. I pray thee hear me speak.
Shy. I'll have my bond. I will not hear thee speak.
I'll have my bond, and therefore speak no more.
I'll not be made a soft and dull-eyed fool,
To shake the head, relent, and sigh, and yield 15
To Christian intercessors. Follow not.
I'll have no speaking; I will have my bond. *Exit.*
Solan. It is the most impenetrable cur
That ever kept with men.
Ant. Let him alone.
I'll follow him no more with bootless prayers. 20
He seeks my life. His reason well I know:
I oft delivered from his forfeitures
Many that have at times made moan to me.
Therefore he hates me.
Solan. I am sure the Duke
Will never grant this forfeiture to hold. 25
Ant. The Duke cannot deny the course of law;
For the commodity that strangers have
With us in Venice, if it be denied,
Will much impeach the justice of the state,
Since that the trade and profit of the city 30
Consisteth of all nations. Therefore go.
These griefs and losses have so bated me
That I shall hardly spare a pound of flesh
Tomorrow to my bloody creditor.

19. **kept:** lived
20. **bootless:** unavailing
27. **commodity:** privilege of trade
28. **it:** the **course of law.** If Shylock, an alien, is denied his satisfaction according to the bond, the city's reputation for fair dealing will be damaged.
30. **Since that:** since
32. **bated:** abated; diminished

Well, jailer, on. Pray God Bassanio come 35
To see me pay his debt, and then I care not!

Exeunt.

[Scene IV. *Portia's house at Belmont.*]

Enter PORTIA, NERISSA, LORENZO, JESSICA, *and* [BALTHASAR,] *a* MAN OF PORTIA'S.

Lor. Madam, although I speak it in your presence,
You have a noble and a true conceit
Of godlike amity, which appears most strongly
In bearing thus the absence of your lord.
But if you knew to whom you show this honor, 5
How true a gentleman you send relief,
How dear a lover of my lord your husband,
I know you would be prouder of the work
Than customary bounty can enforce you.

Por. I never did repent for doing good, 10
Nor shall not now; for in companions
That do converse and waste the time together,
Whose souls do bear an equal yoke of love,
There must be needs a like proportion
Of lineaments, of manners, and of spirit; 15
Which makes me think that this Antonio,
Being the bosom lover of my lord,
Must needs be like my lord. If it be so,
How little is the cost I have bestowed
In purchasing the semblance of my soul 20
From out the state of hellish cruelty!
This comes too near the praising of myself,
Therefore no more of it. Hear other things:
Lorenzo, I commit into your hands
The husbandry and manage of my own house 25
Until my lord's return. For mine own part,
I have toward heaven breathed a secret vow
To live in prayer and contemplation,
Only attended by Nerissa here,
Until her husband and my lord's return. 30
There is a monastery two miles off,
And there we will abide. I do desire you
Not to deny this imposition,
The which my love and some necessity
Now lays upon you.

Lor. Madam, with all my heart. 35
I shall obey you in all fair commands.

Por. My people do already know my mind
And will acknowledge you and Jessica
In place of Lord Bassanio and myself.
So fare you well till we shall meet again. 40

Lor. Fair thoughts and happy hours attend on you!

Jes. I wish your ladyship all heart's content.

Por. I thank you for your wish, and am well pleased
To wish it back on you. Farewell, Jessica.

Exeunt [*Jessica and Lorenzo*].

Now, Balthasar, 45
As I have ever found thee honest-true,
So let me find thee still. Take this same letter,
And use thou all the endeavor of a man
In speed to Padua. See thou render this
Into my cousin's hand, Doctor Bellario; 50
And look what notes and garments he doth give thee,
Bring them, I pray thee, with imagined speed
Unto the Traject, to the common ferry
Which trades to Venice. Waste no time in words
But get thee gone. I shall be there before thee. 55

Balth. Madam, I go with all convenient speed.

Exit.

Por. Come on, Nerissa. I have work in hand
That you yet know not of; we'll see our husbands
Before they think of us.

Ner. Shall they see us?

Por. They shall, Nerissa, but in such a habit 60
That they shall think we are accomplished
With that we lack. I'll hold thee any wager,
When we are both accoutered like young men,
I'll prove the prettier fellow of the two,
And wear my dagger with the braver grace, 65
And speak between the change of man and boy
With a reed voice, and turn two mincing steps
Into a manly stride; and speak of frays
Like a fine bragging youth; and tell quaint lies,
How honorable ladies sought my love, 70
Which I denying, they fell sick and died—
I could not do withal! Then I'll repent,
And wish, for all that, that I had not killed them.
And twenty of these puny lies I'll tell,
That men shall swear I have discontinued school
Above a twelvemonth. I have within my mind 76
A thousand raw tricks of these bragging Jacks,
Which I will practice.

Ner. Why, shall we turn to men?

Por. Fie, what a question's that,
If thou wert near a lewd interpreter! 80
But come, I'll tell thee all my whole device
When I am in my coach, which stays for us

2. conceit: conception
9. customary bounty: ordinary charity
12. converse: associate; **waste:** spend
15. lineaments: distinctive characteristics
20. semblance . . . soul: one who so resembles my love
33. imposition: imposed responsibility
52. imagined speed: the speed of thought
53. Traject: ferry, from the Italian *traghetto*
61. accomplished: furnished
63. accoutered: equipped
65. braver: more gallant
69. quaint: elaborate
72. do withal: help it
77. Jacks: fellows

At the park gate; and therefore haste away,
For we must measure twenty miles today.
Exeunt.

[Scene V. *The garden at Belmont.*]

Enter [LAUNCELOT *the*] *Clown and* JESSICA.

Laun. Yes, truly; for look you, the sins of the father are to be laid upon the children. Therefore, I promise you, I fear you. I was always plain with you, and so now I speak my agitation of the matter. Therefore be o' good cheer, for truly I think you 5 are damned. There is but one hope in it that can do you any good, and that is but a kind of bastard hope neither.

Jes. And what hope is that, I pray thee?

Laun. Marry, you may partly hope that your 10 father got you not—that you are not the Jew's daughter.

Jes. That were a kind of bastard hope indeed! So the sins of my mother should be visited upon me.

Laun. Truly then I fear you are damned 15 both by father and mother. Thus when I shun Scylla, your father, I fall into Charybdis, your mother. Well, you are gone both ways.

Jes. I shall be saved by my husband. He hath made me a Christian. 20

Laun. Truly, the more to blame he! We were Christians enow before, e'en as many as could well live one by another. This making of Christians will raise the price of hogs. If we grow all to be pork-eaters, we shall not shortly have a rasher on 25 the coals for money.

Enter LORENZO.

Jes. I'll tell my husband, Launcelot, what you say. Here he comes.

Lor. I shall grow jealous of you shortly, Launcelot, if you thus get my wife into corners. 30

Jes. Nay, you need not fear us, Lorenzo, Launcelot and I are out. He tells me flatly there's no mercy for me in heaven because I am a Jew's daughter; and he says you are no good member of the commonwealth, for in converting Jews to Christians you raise 35 the price of pork.

Lor. I shall answer that better to the commonwealth than you can the getting up of the Negro's belly: the Moor is with child by you, Launcelot.

Laun. It is much that the Moor should be 40 more than reason; but if she be less than an honest woman, she is indeed more than I took her for.

Lor. How every fool can play upon the word! I think the best grace of wit will shortly turn into silence, and discourse grow commendable in 45 none only but parrots. Go in, sirrah; bid them prepare for dinner.

Laun. That is done, sir, they have all stomachs.

Lor. Goodly Lord, what a wit-snapper are you! Then bid them prepare dinner. 50

Laun. That is done too, sir. Only "cover" is the word.

Lor. Will you cover then, sir?

Laun. Not so, sir, neither! I know my duty.

Lor. Yet more quarreling with occasion? 55 Wilt thou show the whole wealth of thy wit in an instant? I pray thee understand a plain man in his plain meaning. Go to thy fellows, bid them cover the table, serve in the meat, and we will come in to dinner.

Laun. For the table, sir, it shall be served 60 in; for the meat, sir, it shall be covered; for your coming in to dinner, sir, why, let it be as humors and conceits shall govern. *Exit.*

Lor. O dear discretion, how his words are suited!
The fool hath planted in his memory 65
An army of good words; and I do know
A many fools, that stand in better place,
Garnished like him, that for a tricksy word
Defy the matter. How farest thou, Jessica?
And now, good sweet, say thy opinion— 70
How dost thou like the Lord Bassanio's wife?

Jes. Past all expressing. It is very meet
The Lord Bassanio live an upright life,
For, having such a blessing in his lady,
He finds the joys of heaven here on earth; 75
And if on earth he do not merit it,
In reason he should never come to heaven.
Why, if two gods should play some heavenly match,
And on the wager lay two earthly women,
And Portia one, there must be something else 80
Pawned with the other, for the poor rude world
Hath not her fellow.

Lor. Even such a husband
Hast thou of me as she is for a wife.

3. fear: fear for
4. agitation: possibly "cogitation"
16, 17. Scylla, Charybdis: a dangerous rock and a whirlpool in the Strait of Messina
22. enow: enough
32. out: on unfriendly terms

41. more: larger; **honest:** chaste
44–45. the . . . silence: silence (instead of brevity) will soon be considered the soul of wit.
48. stomachs: appetites
51. "cover": lay the table
54. Not . . . duty: Launcelot pretends that he has been asked to cover his head, which would be impolite in his master's presence.
55. quarreling . . . occasion: seizing opportunity for humorous misunderstanding
62, 63. humors, conceits: whims
68–69. for . . . matter: for the sake of a pun reject the meaning of what is said
76. merit: Alexander Pope's emendation of "mean" in the early texts

Jes. Nay, but ask my opinion too of that!
Lor. I will anon. First let us go to dinner. 85
Jes. Nay, let me praise you while I have a stomach.
Lor. No, pray thee, let it serve for table-talk,
Then, howsome'er thou speakst, 'mong other things
I shall digest it.
Jes. Well, I'll set you forth.
Exeunt.

89. set . . . forth: describe you at length

ACT IV

[Scene I. *A courtroom in Venice.*]

Enter the DUKE, *the* MAGNIFICOES, ANTONIO, BASSANIO, GRATIANO, [SALERIO, *and others*].

Duke. What, is Antonio here?
Ant. Ready, so please your Grace.
Duke. I am sorry for thee. Thou art come to answer
A stony adversary, an inhuman wretch,
Uncapable of pity, void and empty 5
From any dram of mercy.
Ant. I have heard
Your Grace hath ta'en great pains to qualify
His rigorous course; but since he stands obdurate,
And that no lawful means can carry me
Out of his envy's reach, I do oppose 10
My patience to his fury, and am armed
To suffer with a quietness of spirit
The very tyranny and rage of his.
Duke. Go one, and call the Jew into the court.
Saler. He is ready at the door; he comes, my lord. 15

Enter SHYLOCK.

Duke. Make room, and let him stand before our face.
Shylock, the world thinks, and I think so too,
That thou but leadest this fashion of thy malice
To the last hour of act, and then 'tis thought
Thou'lt show thy mercy and remorse more strange
Than is thy strange apparent cruelty; 21
And where thou now exacts the penalty,
Which is a pound of this poor merchant's flesh,
Thou wilt not only loose the forfeiture,
But, touched with humane gentleness and love, 25
Forgive a moiety of the principal,
Glancing an eye of pity on his losses,
That have of late so huddled on his back—
Enow to press a royal merchant down
And pluck commiseration of his state 30
From brassy bosoms and rough hearts of flint,
From stubborn Turks and Tartars, never trained
To offices of tender courtesy.
We all expect a gentle answer, Jew.
Shy. I have possessed your Grace of what I purpose, 35
And by our holy Sabbath have I sworn
To have the due and forfeit of my bond.
If you deny it, let the danger light
Upon your charter and your city's freedom!
You'll ask me why I rather choose to have 40
A weight of carrion flesh than to receive
Three thousand ducats. I'll not answer that!
But say it is my humor, is it answered?
What if my house be troubled with a rat,
And I be pleased to give ten thousand ducats 45
To have it baned? What, are you answered yet?
Some men there are love not a gaping pig,
Some that are mad if they behold a cat,
And others, when the bagpipe sings i' the nose,
Cannot contain their urine; for affection, 50
Master of passion, sways it to the mood
Of what it likes or loathes. Now for your answer:
As there is no firm reason to be rend'red
Why he cannot abide a gaping pig,
Why he a harmless necessary cat, 55
Why he a woolen bagpipe, but of force

7. qualify: weaken
13. The . . . his: his utmost violent rage (a hendiadys)
18. leadest . . . malice: continue this pretense of malice
20. remorse: compassion
24. loose: release
26. moiety: portion
46. baned: poisoned
47. gaping pig: roast pig served with open mouth
50. affection: inclination

Must yield to such inevitable shame
As to offend, himself being offended,
So can I give no reason, nor I will not,
More than a lodged hate and a certain loathing 60
I bear Antonio, that I follow thus
A losing suit against him. Are you answered?
Bass. This is no answer, thou unfeeling man,
To excuse the current of thy cruelty!
Shy. I am not bound to please thee with my answer. 65
Bass. Do all men kill the things they do not love?
Shy. Hates any man the thing he would not kill?
Bass. Every offense is not a hate at first.
Shy. What, wouldst thou have a serpent sting thee twice?
Ant. I pray you think you question with the Jew.
You may as well go stand upon the beach 71
And bid the main flood bate his usual height;
You may as well use question with the wolf,
Why he hath made the ewe bleat for the lamb;
You may as well forbid the mountain pines 75
To wag their high tops and to make no noise
When they are fretten with the gusts of heaven;
You may as well do anything most hard
As seek to soften that—than which what's harder?—
His Jewish heart. Therefore I do beseech you 80
Make no mo offers, use no farther means,
But with all brief and plain conveniency
Let me have judgment and the Jew his will.
Bass. For thy three thousand ducats here is six.
Shy. If every ducat in six thousand ducats 85
Were in six parts, and every part a ducat,
I would not draw them, I would have my bond.
Duke. How shalt thou hope for mercy, rend'ring none?
Shy. What judgment shall I dread, doing no wrong?
You have among you many a purchased slave, 90
Which, like your asses and your dogs and mules,
You use in abject and in slavish parts,
Because you bought them. Shall I say to you,
"Let them be free, marry them to your heirs!
Why sweat they under burdens? Let their beds 95
Be made as soft as yours, and let their palates
Be seasoned with such viands"? You will answer,
"The slaves are ours." So do I answer you.
The pound of flesh which I demand of him
Is dearly bought, 'tis mine, and I will have it. 100
If you deny me, fie upon your law!
There is no force in the decrees of Venice.
I stand for judgment. Answer. Shall I have it?
Duke. Upon my power I may dismiss this court
Unless Bellario, a learned doctor, 105
Whom I have sent for to determine this,
Come here today.
Solan. My lord, here stays without
A messenger with letters from the doctor,
New come from Padua. 109
Duke. Bring us the letters. Call the messenger.
Bass. Good cheer, Antonio! What, man, courage yet!
The Jew shall have my flesh, blood, bones, and all,
Ere thou shalt lose for me one drop of blood.
Ant. I am a tainted wether of the flock,
Meetest for death. The weakest kind of fruit 115
Drops earliest to the ground, and so let me.
You cannot better be employed, Bassanio,
Than to live still, and write mine epitaph.

Enter NERISSA, [*dressed like a Lawyer's Clerk*].

Duke. Came you from Padua from Bellario? 119
Ner. From both, my lord. Bellario greets your Grace. [*Presents a letter.*]
Bass. Why dost thou whet thy knife so earnestly?
Shy. To cut the forfeiture from that bankrout there.
Gra. Not on thy sole, but on thy soul, harsh Jew,
Thou makest thy knife keen; but no metal can—
No, not the hangman's axe—bear half the keenness 125
Of thy sharp envy. Can no prayers pierce thee?
Shy. No, none that thou hast wit enough to make.
Gra. O, be thou damned, inexecrable dog,
And for thy life let justice be accused!
Thou almost makest me waver in my faith, 130
To hold opinion with Pythagoras,
That souls of animals infuse themselves
Into the trunks of men. Thy currish spirit
Governed a wolf, who, hanged for human slaughter,
Even from the gallows did his fell soul fleet, 135
And, whilst thou layest in thy unhallowed dam,
Infused itself in thee; for thy desires
Are wolvish, bloody, starved, and ravenous.
Shy. Till thou canst rail the seal from off my bond,
Thou but offendst thy lungs to speak so loud. 140
Repair thy wit, good youth, or it will fall
To cureless ruin. I stand here for law.
Duke. This letter from Bellario doth commend
A young and learned doctor to our court.
Where is he?
Ner. He attendeth here hard by 145
To know your answer whether you'll admit him.

60. certain: positive; unalterable
70. think: realize; **question:** debate
77. fretten: fretted
82. with . . . conveniency: as briefly and simply as is appropriate
104. Upon: by
114. wether: castrated male sheep
135. fell: malevolent; fierce
140. offendst: harm
145. hard: near

Duke. With all my heart. Some three or four of you
Go give him courteous conduct to this place.
Meantime the court shall hear Bellario's letter.

Your Grace shall understand that at the receipt 150 of your letter I am very sick; but in the instant that your messenger came, in loving visitation was with me a young doctor of Rome—his name is Balthasar. I acquainted him with the cause in controversy between the Jew and Antonio the merchant. We turned o'er 155 many books together. He is furnished with my opinion, which, bettered with his own learning (the greatness whereof I cannot enough commend), comes with him at my importunity to fill up your Grace's request in my stead. I beseech you let his lack of years be no 160 impediment to let him lack a reverend estimation; for I never knew so young a body with so old a head. I leave him to your gracious acceptance, whose trial shall better publish his commendation.

Enter PORTIA, *for* BALTHASAR, [*dressed like a Doctor of Laws*].

Duke. You hear the learned Bellario what he writes, 165
And here, I take it, is the doctor come.
Give me your hand. Come you from old Bellario?
Por. I did, my lord.
Duke. You are welcome; take your place.
Are you acquainted with the difference
That holds this present question in the court? 170
Por. I am informed throughly of the cause.
Which is the merchant here? and which the Jew?
Duke. Antonio and old Shylock, both stand forth.
Por. Is your name Shylock?
Shy. Shylock is my name.
Por. Of a strange nature is the suit you follow;
Yet in such rule that the Venetian law 176
Cannot impugn you as you do proceed.—
You stand within his danger, do you not?
Ant. Ay, so he says.
Por. Do you confess the bond?
Ant. I do.
Por. Then must the Jew be merciful. 180
Shy. On what compulsion must I? Tell me that.
Por. The quality of mercy is not strained,
It droppeth as the gentle rain from heaven
Upon the place beneath. It is twice blest—
It blesseth him that gives, and him that takes. 185
'Tis mightiest in the mightiest. It becomes
The throned monarch better than his crown.
His scepter shows the force of temporal power,
The attribute to awe and majesty,
Wherein doth sit the dread and fear of kings; 190
But mercy is above this sceptered sway,
It is enthroned in the hearts of kings,
It is an attribute to God himself;
And earthly power doth then show likest God's
When mercy seasons justice. Therefore, Jew, 195
Though justice be thy plea, consider this,
That in the course of justice, none of us
Should see salvation. We do pray for mercy,
And that same prayer doth teach us all to render
The deeds of mercy. I have spoke thus much 200
To mitigate the justice of thy plea,
Which if thou follow, this strict court of Venice
Must needs give sentence 'gainst the merchant there.
Shy. My deeds upon my head! I crave the law,
The penalty and forfeit of my bond. 205
Por. Is he not able to discharge the money?
Bass. Yes, here I tender it for him in the court,
Yea, thrice the sum. If that will not suffice,
I will be bound to pay it ten times o'er
On forfeit of my hands, my head, my heart. 210
If this will not suffice, it must appear
That malice bears down truth. And I beseech you,
Wrest once the law to your authority.
To do a great right, do a little wrong,
And curb this cruel devil of his will. 215
Por. It must not be, there is no power in Venice
Can alter a decree established.
'Twill be recorded for a precedent,
And many an error by the same example
Will rush into the state. It cannot be. 220
Shy. A Daniel come to judgment! yea, a Daniel!
O wise young judge, how I do honor thee!
Por. I pray you let me look upon the bond.
Shy. Here 'tis, most reverend Doctor, here it is.
Por. Shylock, there's thrice thy money off'red thee.
Shy. An oath, an oath, I have an oath in heaven!
Shall I lay perjury upon my soul? 227
No, not for Venice.
Por. Why, this bond is forfeit,
And lawfully by this the Jew may claim
A pound of flesh, to be by him cut off 230
Nearest the merchant's heart. Be merciful.
Take thrice thy money; bid me tear the bond.
Shy. When it is paid, according to the tenor.
It doth appear you are a worthy judge;
You know the law, your exposition 235
Hath been most sound. I charge you by the law,
Whereof you are a well-deserving pillar,
Proceed to judgment. By my soul I swear
There is no power in the tongue of man
To alter me. I stay here on my bond. 240

161. let . . . lack: cause him to lack
163–64. whose . . . commendation: whose performance will demonstrate his worth better than I can describe it
171. throughly: thoroughly
176. in . . . rule: so much within the rules
182. strained: constrained

201. mitigate . . . plea: soften your insistence on strict justice
240. stay . . . bond: await justice according to the terms of my bond

Ant. Most heartily I do beseech the court
To give the judgment.
Por. Why then, thus it is:
You must prepare your bosom for his knife.
Shy. O noble judge! O excellent young man!
Por. For the intent and purpose of the law 245
Hath full relation to the penalty,
Which here appeareth due upon the bond.
Shy. 'Tis very true. O wise and upright judge!
How much more elder art thou than thy looks!
Por. Therefore lay bare your bosom.
Shy. Ay, his breast—
So says the bond; doth it not, noble judge? 251
Nearest his heart. Those are the very words.
Por. It is so. Are there balance here to weigh
The flesh?
Shy. I have them ready. 255
Por. Have by some surgeon, Shylock, on your charge,
To stop his wounds, lest he do bleed to death.
Shy. Is it so nominated in the bond?
Por. It is not so expressed, but what of that?
'Twere good you do so much for charity. 260
Shy. I cannot find it; 'tis not in the bond.
Por. You, merchant, have you anything to say?
Ant. But little. I am armed and well prepared.
Give me your hand, Bassanio. Fare you well!
Grieve not that I am fall'n to this for you; 265
For herein Fortune shows herself more kind
Than is her custom. It is still her use
To let the wretched man outlive his wealth
To view with hollow eye and wrinkled brow
An age of poverty; from which ling'ring penance
Of such misery doth she cut me off. 271
Commend me to your honorable wife;
Tell her the process of Antonio's end;
Say how I loved you, speak me fair in death;
And when the tale is told, bid her be judge 275
Whether Bassanio had not once a love.
Repent but you that you shall lose your friend,
And he repents not that he pays your debt;
For if the Jew do cut but deep enough,
I'll pay it instantly with all my heart. 280
Bass. Antonio, I am married to a wife
Which is as dear to me as life itself,
But life itself, my wife, and all the world
Are not with me esteemed above thy life.
I would lose all, ay, sacrifice them all 285
Here to this devil, to deliver you.
Por. Your wife would give you little thanks for that
If she were by to hear you make the offer.
Gra. I have a wife who I protest I love.
I would she were in heaven, so she could 290
Entreat some power to change this currish Jew.
Ner. 'Tis well you offer it behind her back.
The wish would make else an unquiet house.
Shy. [*Aside*] These be the Christian husbands! I have a daughter—
Would any of the stock of Barabbas 295
Had been her husband rather than a Christian!—
We trifle time. I pray thee pursue sentence.
Por. A pound of that same merchant's flesh is thine.
The court awards it, and the law doth give it.
Shy. Most rightful judge! 300
Por. And you must cut this flesh from off his breast.
The law allows it, and the court awards it.
Shy. Most learned judge! A sentence! Come, prepare!
Por. Tarry a little; there is something else.
This bond doth give thee here no jot of blood; 305
The words expressly are "a pound of flesh."
Take then thy bond, take thou thy pound of flesh;
But in the cutting it if thou dost shed
One drop of Christian blood, thy lands and goods
Are, by the laws of Venice, confiscate 310
Unto the state of Venice.
Gra. O upright judge! Mark, Jew. O learned judge!
Shy. Is that the law?
Por. Thyself shalt see the act;
For, as thou urgest justice, be assured 314
Thou shalt have justice more than thou desirest.
Gra. O learned judge! Mark, Jew. A learned judge!
Shy. I take this offer then. Pay the bond thrice,
And let the Christian go.
Bass. Here is the money.
Por. Soft!
The Jew shall have all justice. Soft! no haste. 320
He shall have nothing but the penalty.
Gra. O Jew! an upright judge! a learned judge!
Por. Therefore prepare thee to cut off the flesh.
Shed thou no blood, nor cut thou less nor more
But just a pound of flesh. If thou takest more 325
Or less than a just pound—be it but so much
As makes it light or heavy in the substance
Or the division of the twentieth part
Of one poor scruple; nay, if the scale do turn
But in the estimation of a hair— 330
Thou diest, and all thy goods are confiscate.
Gra. A second Daniel! a Daniel, Jew!
Now, infidel, I have you on the hip.

246. hath . . . penalty: applies no matter what penalty is involved
253. balance: scales
256. on . . . charge: at your expense
277. Repent: regret
280. with . . . heart: a grim joke
295. Barabbas: a thief crucified with Christ
320. all: nothing but
329. scruple: an ancient Roman unit of weight, one twenty-fourth of an ounce

Por. Why doth the Jew pause? Take thy forfeiture.
Shy. Give me my principal, and let me go. 335
Bass. I have it ready for thee; here it is.
Por. He hath refused it in the open court.
He shall have merely justice and his bond.
Gra. A Daniel still say I, a second Daniel!
I thank thee, Jew, for teaching me that word. 340
Shy. Shall I not have barely my principal?
Por. Thou shalt have nothing but the forfeiture,
To be so taken at thy peril, Jew.
Shy. Why, then the devil give him good of it!
I'll stay no longer question.
Por. Tarry, Jew, 345
The law hath yet another hold on you.
It is enacted in the laws of Venice,
If it be proved against an alien
That by direct or indirect attempts
He seeks the life of any citizen, 350
The party 'gainst the which he doth contrive
Shall seize one half his goods; the other half
Comes to the privy coffer of the state;
And the offender's life lies in the mercy
Of the Duke only, 'gainst all other voice. 355
In which predicament I say thou standst;
For it appears by manifest proceeding
That indirectly, and directly too,
Thou hast contrived against the very life
Of the defendant, and thou hast incurred 360
The danger formerly by me rehearsed.
Down, therefore, and beg mercy of the Duke.
Gra. Beg that thou mayst have leave to hang thyself!
And yet, thy wealth being forfeit to the state,
Thou hast not left the value of a cord; 365
Therefore thou must be hanged at the state's charge.
Duke. That thou shalt see the difference of our spirit,
I pardon thee thy life before thou ask it.
For half thy wealth, it is Antonio's;
The other half comes to the general state, 370
Which humbleness may drive unto a fine.
Por. Ay, for the state, not for Antonio.
Shy. Nay, take my life and all! Pardon not that!
You take my house when you do take the prop
That doth sustain my house; you take my life 375
When you do take the means whereby I live.
Por. What mercy can you render him, Antonio?
Gra. A halter gratis. Nothing else, for God's sake!
Ant. So please my lord the Duke and all the court
To quit the fine for one half of his goods, 380
I am content; so he will let me have
The other half in use, to render it
Upon his death unto the gentleman
That lately stole his daughter—
Two things provided more: that, for this favor,
He presently become a Christian; 386
The other, that he do record a gift
Here in the court of all he dies possessed
Unto his son Lorenzo and his daughter.
Duke. He shall do this, or else I do recant 390
The pardon that I late pronounced here.
Por. Art thou contented, Jew? What dost thou say?
Shy. I am content.
Por. Clerk, draw a deed of gift.
Shy. I pray you give me leave to go from hence.
I am not well. Send the deed after me, 395
And I will sign it.
Duke. Get thee gone, but do it.
Gra. In christ'ning shalt thou have two godfathers.
Had I been judge, thou shouldst have had ten more,
To bring thee to the gallows, not the font. 399
Exit [Shylock].
Duke. Sir, I entreat you home with me to dinner.
Por. I humbly do desire your Grace of pardon.
I must away this night toward Padua,
And it is meet I presently set forth.
Duke. I am sorry that your leisure serves you not.
Antonio, gratify this gentleman, 405
For in my mind you are much bound to him.
Exeunt Duke and his Train.
Bass. Most worthy gentleman, I and my friend
Have by your wisdom been this day acquitted
Of grievous penalties, in lieu whereof,
Three thousand ducats, due unto the Jew, 410
We freely cope your courteous pains withal.
Ant. And stand indebted, over and above,
In love and service to you evermore.
Por. He is well paid that is well satisfied;
And I, delivering you, am satisfied, 415
And therein do account myself well paid.
My mind was never yet more mercenary.
I pray you know me when we meet again.
I wish you well, and so I take my leave.
Bass. Dear sir, of force I must attempt you further. 420
Take some remembrance of us as a tribute,
Not as a fee. Grant me two things, I pray you—
Not to deny me, and to pardon me.

345. stay . . . question: remain for no further discussion
348. alien: as a Jew, Shylock could not become a citizen of Venice.
356. predicament: situation
361. rehearsed: enumerated
371. humbleness . . . fine: humility on your part may reduce to a mere fine
379–84. So . . . daughter: if the Duke and the court will accept a fine in lieu of half of Shylock's goods, Antonio will be satisfied with the mere use of the other half during Shylock's lifetime, to revert to Jessica's husband when Shylock dies.
405. gratify: reward
411. cope: repay

Por. You press me far, and therefore I will yield.
Give me your gloves, I'll wear them for your sake;
And for your love I'll take this ring from you. 426
Do not draw back your hand, I'll take no more,
And you in love shall not deny me this.
Bass. This ring, good sir? Alas, it is a trifle!
I will not shame myself to give you this. 430
Por. I will have nothing else but only this;
And now methinks I have a mind to it.
Bass. There's more depends on this than on the value.
The dearest ring in Venice will I give you,
And find it out by proclamation. 435
Only for this, I pray you pardon me.
Por. I see, sir, you are liberal in offers.
You taught me first to beg, and now methinks
You teach me how a beggar should be answered.
Bass. Good sir, this ring was given me by my wife,
And when she put it on, she made me vow 441
That I should neither sell nor give nor lose it.
Por. That 'scuse serves many men to save their gifts,
And if your wife be not a madwoman,
And know how well I have deserved this ring, 445
She would not hold out enemy forever
For giving it to me. Well, peace be with you!
Exeunt [*Portia and Nerissa*].
Ant. My Lord Bassanio, let him have the ring.
Let his deservings, and my love withal,
Be valued 'gainst your wive's commandment. 450
Bass. Go, Gratiano, run and overtake him.
Give him the ring and bring him, if thou canst,
Unto Antonio's house. Away! make haste.
Exit Gratiano.
Come, you and I will thither presently,
And in the morning early will we both 455
Fly toward Belmont. Come, Antonio.
Exeunt.

[Scene II. *A street in Venice.*]

Enter PORTIA *and* NERISSA.

Por. Inquire the Jew's house out, give him this deed,
And let him sign it. We'll away tonight
And be a day before our husbands home.
This deed will be well welcome to Lorenzo.

Enter GRATIANO.

Gra. Fair sir, you are well o'erta'en. 5
My Lord Bassanio, upon more advice,
Hath sent you here this ring, and doth entreat
Your company at dinner.
Por. That cannot be.
His ring I do accept most thankfully,
And so I pray you tell him. Furthermore, 10
I pray you show my youth old Shylock's house.
Gra. That will I do.
Ner. Sir, I would speak with you.
[*Aside to Portia*] I'll see if I can get my husband's ring,
Which I did make him swear to keep forever.
Por. [*Aside to Nerissa*] Thou mayst, I warrant. We shall have old swearing 15
That they did give the rings away to men;
But we'll outface them, and outswear them too.
[*Aloud*] Away! make haste. Thou knowst where I will tarry.
Ner. Come, good sir, will you show me to this house?
Exeunt.

6. upon . . . advice: after further consideration

ACT V

[Scene I. *The grounds before Portia's house at Belmont.*]

Enter LORENZO *and* JESSICA.

Lor. The moon shines bright. In such a night as this,
When the sweet wind did gently kiss the trees
And they did make no noise—in such a night
Troilus methinks mounted the Trojan walls
And sighed his soul toward the Grecian tents, 5
Where Cressid lay that night.
Jes. In such a night
Did Thisbe fearfully o'ertrip the dew,

4. Troilus: King Priam's son, whose sweetheart, Cressida, was a hostage in the Greek camp
7. Thisbe: see the rustics' entertainment in *A Midsummer Night's Dream* and Ovid, *Metamorphoses*, bk. iv.

And saw the lion's shadow ere himself,
And ran dismayed away.
Lor. In such a night
Stood Dido with a willow in her hand 10
Upon the wild sea banks, and waft her love
To come again to Carthage.
Jes. In such a night
Medea gathered the enchanted herbs
That did renew old Æson.
Lor. In such a night
Did Jessica steal from the wealthy Jew, 15
And with an unthrift love did run from Venice
As far as Belmont.
Jes. In such a night
Did young Lorenzo swear he loved her well,
Stealing her soul with many vows of faith,
And ne'er a true one.
Lor. In such a night 20
Did pretty Jessica (like a little shrew)
Slander her love, and he forgave it her.
Jes. I would out-night you, did no body come;
But, hark, I hear the footing of a man.

Enter a MESSENGER.

Lor. Who comes so fast in silence of the night? 25
Mess. A friend.
Lor. A friend? What friend? Your name, I pray you, friend?
Mess. Stephano is my name, and I bring word
My mistress will before the break of day
Be here at Belmont. She doth stray about 30
By holy crosses, where she kneels and prays
For happy wedlock hours.
Lor. Who comes with her?
Mess. None but a holy hermit and her maid.
I pray you, is my master yet returned?
Lor. He is not, nor we have not heard from him.
But go we in, I pray thee, Jessica, 36
And ceremoniously let us prepare
Some welcome for the mistress of the house.

Enter [LAUNCELOT, *the*] *Clown.*

Laun. Sola, sola! wo ha, ho! sola, sola!
Lor. Who calls? 40
Laun. Sola; Did you see Master Lorenzo and Mistress Lorenzo? Sola, sola!
Lor. Leave holloaing, man! Here.
Laun. Sola! Where? where?
Lor. Here! 45
Laun. Tell him there's a post come from my master, with his horn full of good news. My master will be here ere morning. [*Exit.*]
Lor. Sweet soul, let's in, and there expect their coming.
And yet no matter. Why should we go in? 50
My friend Stephano, signify, I pray you,
Within the house, your mistress is at hand
And bring your music forth into the air.
[*Exit Stephano.*]
How sweet the moonlight sleeps upon this bank!
Here will we sit and let the sounds of music 55
Creep in our ears. Soft stillness and the night
Become the touches of sweet harmony.
Sit, Jessica. Look how the floor of heaven
Is thick inlaid with patens of bright gold.
There's not the smallest orb which thou beholdst
But in his motion like an angel sings, 61
Still quiring to the young-eyed cherubins;
Such harmony is in immortal souls;
But whilst this muddy vesture of decay
Doth grossly close it in, we cannot hear it. 65

[*Enter* MUSICIANS.]

Come, ho, and wake Diana with a hymn!
With sweetest touches pierce your mistress' ear
And draw her home with music. *Play music.*
Jes. I am never merry when I hear sweet music.
Lor. The reason is, your spirits are attentive. 70
For do but note a wild and wanton herd,
Or race of youthful and unhandled colts,
Fetching mad bounds, bellowing and neighing loud,
Which is the hot condition of their blood:
If they but hear perchance a trumpet sound, 75
Or any air of music touch their ears,
You shall perceive them make a mutual stand,
Their savage eyes turned to a modest gaze
By the sweet power of music. Therefore the poet
Did feign that Orpheus drew trees, stones, and floods,
Since naught so stockish, hard, and full of rage 81
But music for the time doth change his nature.
The man that hath no music in himself,
Nor is not moved with concord of sweet sounds,
Is fit for treasons, stratagems, and spoils; 85
The motions of his spirit are dull as night,
And his affections dark as Erebus.
Let no such man be trusted. Mark the music.

10. Dido: Queen of Carthage, whom Æneas deserted
11. waft: waved. The willow was a symbol of forsaken love.
13. Medea: as told by Ovid, *Metamorphoses,* bk. vii
16. unthrift love: i.e., impoverished lover
59. patens: tiles
62. quiring: choiring
64. muddy . . . decay: the clothing of mortal flesh
73. Fetching: performing
79. the poet: most likely, Ovid
80. drew: attracted
81. stockish: like a stock; stolid
85. stratagems: violent deeds; **spoils:** acts of plunder
87. affections: feelings; **Erebus:** a dark underground region on the way to Hades

Enter PORTIA *and* NERISSA.

Por. That light we see is burning in my hall.
How far that little candle throws his beams! 90
So shines a good deed in a naughty world.
Ner. When the moon shone, we did not see the candle.
Por. So doth the greater glory dim the less.
A substitute shines brightly as a king
Until a king be by, and then his state 95
Empties itself, as doth an inland brook
Into the main of waters. Music! hark!
Ner. It is your music, madam, of the house.
Por. Nothing is good, I see, without respect.
Methinks it sounds much sweeter than by day. 100
Ner. Silence bestows that virtue on it, madam.
Por. The crow doth sing as sweetly as the lark
When neither is attended; and I think
The nightingale, if she should sing by day
When every goose is cackling, would be thought
No better a musician than the wren. 106
How many things by season seasoned are
To their right praise and true perfection!
Peace—how the moon sleeps with Endymion,
And would not be awaked. *Music ceases.*
Lor. That is the voice, 110
Or I am much deceived, of Portia.
Por. He knows me as the blind man knows the cuckoo,
By the bad voice.
Lor. Dear lady, welcome home.
Por. We have been praying for our husbands' welfare,
Which speed, we hope, the better for our words.
Are they returned?
Lor. Madam, they are not yet; 116
But there is come a messenger before
To signify their coming.
Por. Go in, Nerissa.
Give order to my servants that they take
No note at all of our being absent hence— 120
Nor you, Lorenzo—Jessica, nor you.
A tucket sounds.
Lor. Your husband is at hand; I hear his trumpet.
We are no telltales, madam; fear you not.
Por. This night methinks is but the daylight sick;
It looks a little paler. 'Tis a day 125
Such as the day is when the sun is hid.

Enter BASSANIO, ANTONIO, GRATIANO, *and their* FOLLOWERS.

Bass. We should hold day with the Antipodes
If you would walk in absence of the sun.
Por. Let me give light, but let me not be light,
For a light wife doth make a heavy husband, 130
And never be Bassanio so for me.
But God sort all! You are welcome home, my lord.
Bass. I thank you, madam. Give welcome to my friend.
This is the man, this is Antonio,
To whom I am so infinitely bound. 135
Por. You should in all sense be much bound to him,
For, as I hear, he was much bound for you.
Ant. No more than I am well acquitted of.
Por. Sir, you are very welcome to our house.
It must appear in other ways than words, 140
Therefore I scant this breathing courtesy.
Gra. [*To Nerissa*] By yonder moon I swear you do me wrong!
In faith, I gave it to the judge's clerk.
Would he were gelt that had it, for my part,
Since you do take it, love, so much at heart. 145
Por. A quarrel, ho, already! What's the matter?
Gra. About a hoop of gold, a paltry ring
That she did give to me, whose posy was
For all the world like cutler's poetry
Upon a knife, "Love me, and leave me not." 150
Ner. What talk you of the posy or the value?
You swore to me, when I did give it you,
That you would wear it till your hour of death,
And that it should lie with you in your grave. 154
Though not for me, yet for your vehement oaths,
You should have been respective and have kept it.
Gave it a judge's clerk! No, God's my judge,
The clerk will ne'er wear hair on's face that had it.
Gra. He will, an if he live to be a man.
Ner. Ay, if a woman live to be a man. 160
Gra. Now, by this hand, I gave it to a youth,
A kind of boy, a little scrubbed boy,
No higher than thyself, the judge's clerk,
A prating boy that begged it as a fee.
I could not for my heart deny it him. 165
Por. You were to blame—I must be plain with you—
To part so slightly with your wife's first gift,
A thing stuck on with oaths upon your finger
And so riveted with faith unto your flesh.
I gave my love a ring, and made him swear 170
Never to part with it, and here he stands:
I dare be sworn for him he would not leave it

97. main . . . waters: ocean
99. respect: respect of circumstances
107. season: seasonable occurrence
109. Endymion: the mortal lover of Selene, another name for the moon-goddess
115. speed: prosper
127. hold . . . Antipodes: have daylight at the same time as the Antipodes, on the opposite side of the world
129. be light: be unchaste
132. sort: besort; manage
141. breathing courtesy: polite verbiage
144. gelt: gelded
148. posy: rhymed inscription
156. respective: mindful
164. prating: boastful

Nor pluck it from his finger for the wealth
That the world masters. Now, in faith, Gratiano,
You give your wife too unkind a cause of grief.
An 'twere to me, I should be mad at it. 176
Bass. [*Aside*] Why, I were best to cut my left hand off
And swear I lost the ring defending it.
Gra. My Lord Bassanio gave his ring away
Unto the judge that begged it, and indeed 180
Deserved it too; and then the boy, his clerk,
That took some pains in writing, he begged mine;
And neither man nor master would take aught
But the two rings.
Por. What ring gave you, my lord?
Not that, I hope, which you received of me. 185
Bass. If I could add a lie unto a fault,
I would deny it; but you see my finger
Hath not the ring upon it—it is gone.
Por. Even so void is your false heart of truth.
By heaven, I will ne'er come in your bed 190
Until I see the ring!
Ner. Nor I in yours
Till I again see mine!
Bass. Sweet Portia,
If you did know to whom I gave the ring,
If you did know for whom I gave the ring,
And would conceive for what I gave the ring, 195
And how unwillingly I left the ring
When naught would be accepted but the ring,
You would abate the strength of your displeasure.
Por. If you had known the virtue of the ring,
Or half her worthiness that gave the ring, 200
Or your own honor to contain the ring,
You would not then have parted with the ring.
What man is there so much unreasonable,
If you had pleased to have defended it
With any terms of zeal, wanted the modesty 205
To urge the thing held as a ceremony?
Nerissa teaches me what to believe.
I'll die for't but some woman had the ring!
Bass. No, by my honor, madam, by my soul,
No woman had it, but a civil doctor, 210
Which did refuse three thousand ducats of me
And begged the ring; the which I did deny him,
And suffered him to go displeased away,
Even he that had held up the very life
Of my dear friend. What should I say, sweet lady?
I was enforced to send it after him. 216
I was beset with shame and courtesy.
My honor would not let ingratitude
So much besmear it. Pardon me, good lady,
For, by these blessed candles of the night, 220
Had you been there, I think you would have begged
The ring of me to give the worthy doctor.
Por. Let not that doctor e'er come near my house.
Since he hath got the jewel that I loved,
And that which you did swear to keep for me, 225
I will become as liberal as you;
I'll not deny him anything I have,
No, not my body, nor my husband's bed.
Know him I shall, I am well sure of it.
Lie not a night from home; watch me like Argus.
If you do not, if I be left alone, 231
Now, by mine honor, which is yet mine own,
I'll have the doctor for my bedfellow.
Ner. And I his clerk. Therefore be well advised
How you do leave me to mine own protection. 235
Gra. Well, do you so. Let not me take him then,
For if I do, I'll mar the young clerk's pen.
Ant. I am the unhappy subject of these quarrels.
Por. Sir, grieve not you. You are welcome notwithstanding.
Bass. Portia, forgive me this enforced wrong, 240
And in the hearing of these many friends
I swear to thee, even by thine own fair eyes,
Wherein I see myself—
Por. Mark you but that?
In both my eyes he doubly sees himself;
In each eye one. Swear by your double self, 245
And there's an oath of credit.
Bass. Nay, but hear me.
Pardon this fault, and by my soul I swear
I never more will break an oath with thee.
Ant. I once did lend my body for his wealth,
Which, but for him that had your husband's ring,
Had quite miscarried. I dare be bound again, 251
My soul upon the forfeit, that your lord
Will never more break faith advisedly.
Por. Then you shall be his surety. Give him this,
And bid him keep it better than the other. 255
Ant. Here, Lord Bassanio. Swear to keep this ring.
Bass. By heaven, it is the same I gave the doctor!
Por. I had it of him. Pardon me, Bassanio;
For, by this ring, the doctor lay with me.
Ner. And pardon me, my gentle Gratiano; 260
For that same scrubbed boy, the doctor's clerk,
In lieu of this, last night did lie with me.
Gra. Why, this is like the mending of highways
In summer, where the ways are fair enough.

176. mad: frantic
195. conceive: understand
201. contain: retain
206. ceremony: formal symbol
210. civil doctor: doctor of civil law
214. held up: defended

230. Argus: a hundred-eyed giant whom Juno set to watch Io
240. enforced: involuntary
245. double: deceitful
246. oath . . . credit: credible oath
251. miscarried: been destroyed
252. upon: as
263–64. this . . . summer: i.e., we didn't know when we were well off.

What, are we cuckolds ere we have deserved it? 265
Por. Speak not so grossly. You are all amazed.
Here is a letter, read it at your leisure;
It comes from Padua from Bellario.
There you shall find that Portia was the doctor,
Nerissa there her clerk. Lorenzo here 270
Shall witness I set forth as soon as you,
And even but now returned. I have not yet
Entered my house. Antonio, you are welcome,
And I have better news in store for you
Than you expect. Unseal this letter soon. 275
There you shall find three of your argosies
Are richly come to harbor suddenly.
You shall not know by what strange accident
I chanced on this letter.
Ant. I am dumb. 279
Bass. Were you the doctor, and I knew you not?
Gra. Were you the clerk that is to make me cuckold?
Ner. Ay, but the clerk that never means to do it,
Unless he live until he be a man.
Bass. Sweet Doctor, you shall be my bedfellow.
When I am absent, then lie with my wife. 285
Ant. Sweet lady, you have given me life and living;
For here I read for certain that my ships
Are safely come to road.
Por. How now, Lorenzo?
My clerk hath some good comforts too for you.
Ner. Ay, and I'll give them him without a fee.
There do I give to you and Jessica, 291
From the rich Jew, a special deed of gift,
After his death, of all he dies possessed of.
Lor. Fair ladies, you drop manna in the way
Of starved people.
Por. It is almost morning, 295
And yet I am sure you are not satisfied
Of these events at full. Let us go in,
And charge us there upon inter'gatories,
And we will answer all things faithfully.
Gra. Let it be so. The first inter'gatory 300
That my Nerissa shall be sworn on is,
Whether till the next night she had rather stay,
Or go to bed now, being two hours to day.
But were the day come, I should wish it dark
Till I were couching with the doctor's clerk. 305
Well, while I live I'll fear no other thing
So sore as keeping safe Nerissa's ring.
Exeunt.

265. cuckolds: betrayed husbands
266. amazed: dumfounded
298. charge . . . inter'gatories: compel our answers to your questions; a legal term

Falstaff Demonstrates His Courage at Gad's Hill

Etching by George Cruikshank.

The First Part of
KING HENRY THE FOURTH

INTRODUCTION

In the 1590's, plays on English history were unusually popular, and Shakespeare, who had begun his dramatic career by writing of the reign of Henry VI, looked back to earlier episodes for further dramatic material. What determined the order of his composition we do not know, for he did not follow a strict chronological sequence. By the time that he came to write of Henry IV he had already had a hand in the three parts of *Henry VI* and had staged *Richard III*, *Richard II*, and *King John*.

As a practical dramatist writing for a company that demanded fashionable plays, Shakespeare probably chose themes that he deemed of greatest appeal at the moment of composition. Gradually, however, he created sequences that provided English history in chronological order, and from his plays Englishmen ever since have taken their interpretation of the Wars of the Roses.

The first performance of *Henry IV, Part 1*, according to Professor A. R. Humphreys in the new Arden edition of the play (1960) probably dates from the winter of 1596–97. Older scholars usually dated the play about a year later. At least a year before *Henry IV*, Shakespeare had placed on the stage *Richard II*, which provides background for *Henry IV*. The popularity of *Henry IV, Part 1* was such that he was induced to write a second play to complete Henry's reign and a third play to portray the heroic deeds of Henry V. Thus, in the end, Shakespeare achieved a coherent tetralogy, beginning with *Richard II* and ending with *Henry V*. An old legend relates that Queen Elizabeth was so taken with the comedy of the Falstaff scenes in *Henry IV* that she commanded Shakespeare to write a play showing Falstaff in love and that he complied with *The Merry Wives of Windsor*. According to one theory, Shakespeare had to interrupt his historical sequence to write the comedy. The case is unproved, but there may be some basis for the legend.

In *Richard II* Shakespeare had written a lyrical drama that contrasted the poetic and dreamy Richard with the practical and efficient Henry Bolingbroke, who usurped his throne to become Henry IV. *Richard II* is a study in the qualities needed by a sovereign, and although Shakespeare portrayed Richard with a certain amount of sympathy, he emphasized the dangers to the kingdom from a weak and vacillating ruler. Although Shakespeare stressed the sin of rebellion against an anointed king, he also reflected the popular belief of the day in the necessity of having a ruler with the strength to insure order in the commonwealth. The anarchy of the Wars of the Roses remained an object lesson to Englishmen, who wanted no return of those disorders. Shakespeare's studies in the problems of kingship therefore had particular point for his contemporaries.

Though Shakespeare and his fellow countrymen could find in Henry IV's effective manipulation of public opinion and his efficient dealing with rebels who disturbed the peace much that they could approve, they, like Henry himself, were aware that he had committed a great sin in taking Richard II's crown. The curse that this sin brought upon his house and Henry's attempted expiation are themes that recur in the play. When the first scene opens, Henry reveals that he has long planned a crusade against the Saracens as one means of gaining grace but that, once more, civil strife at home has ruined his hopes. The King interprets the disasters that hover over his realm as well as the scapegrace behavior of Prince Hal as afflictions sent upon him for his sin.

Henry IV presents a series of incidents from history designed to show the King in action, but the structure is loose and episodic. Shakespeare took such liberties with facts as the requirements of the stage dictated. For example, he made Prince Hal and Hotspur about the same age and invented the combat between them. Actually Hotspur was twenty-three years older than the Prince. Shakespeare also invented Prince Hal's rescue of the King. Following an error in the source, Shakespeare confuses Edmund Mortimer, the fifth Earl of March, with his uncle, Sir Edmund Mortimer, who had been kept a prisoner by Owen Glendower. By and large, however, the play gives the generally accepted facts for events between an indefinite period in 1402 and July, 1403.

THE COMIC EFFECTS IN THE PLAY

Shakespeare created in *Henry IV* one of the immortal characters in literature in the person of John Falstaff, the fat knight who has amused generations of readers and theatregoers. In the first performance of *Henry IV* Shakespeare used the name Oldcastle, a Lollard martyr and an ancestor of William Brooke, Lord Cobham. Because of protests from the Cobham family, the dramatist changed the name to Falstaff, which also had historical connotations, for it is an adaptation of Sir John Fastolfe, an actual soldier against the French, who had already been represented incorrectly in *Henry VI* as a coward.

Traditionally upon the Elizabethan stage and earlier, comic scenes had been interspersed in serious plays, frequently without much relation to the action. Many plays preceding Shakespeare —and some that came after him—had extraneous scenes of clownery and horseplay merely to divert the audience. Shakespeare's great contribution in dramatic construction was to weld the comic subplot to the main plot in such a fashion that the play achieved something like unity. In *Henry IV* the comic scenes with Falstaff and his crew are not disjointed bits of clownery thrown in to please the groundlings but are integral parts of the play. The instrument for unifying the parts is Prince Hal, and his reaction to the comic subplot serves to further the development and revelation of his character.

Falstaff's comedy is the comedy of humor, of situation, of incongruity, as opposed to the comedy of mere wit and wordplay. It is earthy, substantial, and of universal understanding instead of being dependent upon the brittle wit that we get today in topical wisecracks of the television comics. Although the witty wisecrack may excite a flicker of gaiety, it will not bear repetition, whereas the doings of Falstaff and his fellows induce deep-seated laughter that increases with the telling. No matter how many times one has heard Falstaff's soliloquy on honor, it is always funny, and his observation, "Lord, Lord, how this world is given to lying" has become part of our comic folklore. In the presence of Falstaff's humor, pomposities and pretensions shrivel to their proper proportions.

SOURCES, HISTORY, AND TEXT

As usual in his history plays, Shakespeare went to the easiest source for his material, the second edition of Raphael Holinshed's *Chronicles of England, Scotland, and Ireland* (1587), which provided the main outline of the plot and incidental details. But he had other sources as well. An old play, *The Famous Victories of Henry the Fifth,* printed in 1598, had been performed much earlier by the Queen's Men and was known to Shakespeare. Sir John Oldcastle, the prototype of Falstaff, and other minor characters appear in the older play, and Shakespeare may have received from it the suggestion for alternating his scenes of comedy with the historical events. Shakespeare also received some suggestions from Samuel Daniel's long narrative poem *The Civil Wars* (1595), for example the combat between Prince Hal and Hotspur. Material on the riotous youth of Prince Hal may have come from John Stow's *Annals of England* (1592) or from his other chronicles.

The fact that *Henry IV, Part 1* had eight quarto printings before the closing of the theatres by the Puritans in 1642 is an indication of its popularity with the reading public. A manuscript in the Folger Library shows that sometime in the first half of the seventeenth century an adapter telescoped both parts into a single play, perhaps for a private production. The manuscript has corrections in the handwriting of Sir Edward Dering, a country gentleman of Kent, who died in 1644.

Henry IV, Part 1 has enjoyed a long popularity on the stage. It was acted at court during the reigns of James I and Charles I and was one of the earliest of Shakespeare's plays revived after the Restoration. From that time onward the play was frequently acted and was never long off the stage. In America it has been equally popular. Actors have especially liked the play because the diversity of good parts gives scope for others besides the stars. Character actors with a gift for comedy have particularly liked the role of Falstaff.

The most authoritative text for *Henry IV, Part 1* is Quarto 1, printed in 1598. Although six quarto versions appeared in succession before the First Folio in 1623, later quartos seem to have been printed successively from one another, and none has any independent authority over the first. The First Folio text of the play seems to have been taken from Quarto 5.

Falstaff and Mistress Quickly

From Francis Kirkman, *The Wits; or, Sport upon Sport* (1672).

[Dramatis Personæ

KING HENRY THE FOURTH.
HENRY, PRINCE OF WALES, } *sons to the King.*
PRINCE JOHN OF LANCASTER, } *sons to the King.*
EARL OF WESTMORLAND.
SIR WALTER BLUNT.
THOMAS PERCY, *Earl of Worcester.*
HENRY PERCY, *Earl of Northumberland.*
HENRY PERCY, *nicknamed "Hotspur," son to the Earl of Northumberland.*
EDMUND MORTIMER, *Earl of March.*
RICHARD SCROOP, *Archbishop of York.*
ARCHIBALD, *Earl of Douglas.*
OWEN GLENDOWER.
SIR RICHARD VERNON.
SIR JOHN FALSTAFF.
SIR MICHAEL, *friend to the Archbishop of York.*
POINS.
GADSHILL.
PETO.
BARDOLPH.
VINTNER *of the Boar's Head Tavern.*
FRANCIS, *a drawer.*
CHAMBERLAIN.
OSTLER.

LADY PERCY, *wife to Hotspur.*
LADY MORTIMER, *wife to Edmund Mortimer and daughter to Glendower.*
MISTRESS QUICKLY, *hostess of the Boar's Head Tavern.*

Sheriff, Carriers, Travelers, Messengers, Servants.

Scene: *England and Wales.*]

King Henry IV
From Hubert Goltzius, *Antiquissima nobilissimaque Anglorum regum* (1586).

The First Part of
KING HENRY THE FOURTH

ACT I

Scene I. [*London. The palace.*]

Enter the KING, LORD JOHN OF LANCASTER, EARL OF WESTMORLAND, [SIR WALTER BLUNT,] *with others.*

King. So shaken as we are, so wan with care,
Find we a time for frighted peace to pant
And breathe short-winded accents of new broils
To be commenced in stronds afar remote.
No more the thirsty entrance of this soil 5
Shall daub her lips with her own children's blood:
No more shall trenching war channel her fields,
Nor bruise her flow'rets with the armed hoofs
Of hostile paces. Those opposed eyes
Which, like the meteors of a troubled heaven, 10
All of one nature, of one substance bred,
Did lately meet in the intestine shock
And furious close of civil butchery,
Shall now in mutual well-beseeming ranks
March all one way and be no more opposed 15
Against acquaintance, kindred, and allies.
The edge of war, like an ill-sheathed knife,
No more shall cut his master. Therefore, friends,
As far as to the sepulcher of Christ—
Whose soldier now, under whose blessed cross 20
We are impressed and engaged to fight—
Forthwith a power of English shall we levy,
Whose arms were molded in their mother's womb
To chase these pagans in those holy fields
Over whose acres walked those blessed feet 25
Which fourteen hundred years ago were nailed
For our advantage on the bitter cross.
But this our purpose now is twelvemonth old,
And bootless 'tis to tell you we will go.
Therefor we meet not now. Then let me hear 30
Of you, my gentle cousin Westmorland,
What yesternight our council did decree
In forwarding this dear expedience.
West. My liege, this haste was hot in question
And many limits of the charge set down 35
But yesternight; when all athwart there came
A post from Wales, loaden with heavy news,
Whose worst was that the noble Mortimer,
Leading the men of Herefordshire to fight
Against the irregular and wild Glendower, 40
Was by the rude hands of that Welshman taken,
A thousand of his people butchered;
Upon whose dead corpse there was such misuse,
Such beastly shameless transformation,
By those Welshwomen done as may not be 45

4. **strronds:** strands
7. **trenching:** gashing
10. **meteors:** believed to be exhalations of gas from the heavenly bodies; hence, their offspring
12. **intestine:** internal; domestic
13. **close:** grapple
14. **mutual well-beseeming:** united and orderly
18. **his:** its
21. **engaged:** pledged
29. **bootless:** useless
30. **Therefor:** i.e., to plan the crusade
33. **dear expedience:** urgent expedition
34. **hot . . . question:** earnestly discussed
35. **limits . . . charge:** divisions of responsibility
36. **all athwart:** right in the middle (of the discussion)
37. **post:** messenger, riding posthaste; **heavy:** grave
38. **Mortimer:** Sir Edmund Mortimer
43. **corpse:** i.e., corpses

Without much shame retold or spoken of.
King. It seems then that the tidings of this broil
Brake off our business for the Holy Land.
West. This, matched with other, did, my gracious lord;
For more uneven and unwelcome news 50
Came from the North, and thus it did import:
On Holy-Rood Day the gallant Hotspur there,
Young Harry Percy, and brave Archibald,
That ever-valiant and approved Scot,
At Holmedon met, where they did spend 55
A sad and bloody hour;
As by discharge of their artillery
And shape of likelihood the news was told;
For he that brought them, in the very heat
And pride of their contention did take horse, 60
Uncertain of the issue any way.
King. Here is a dear, a true industrious friend,
Sir Walter Blunt, new lighted from his horse,
Stained with the variation of each soil
Betwixt that Holmedon and this seat of ours, 65
And he hath brought us smooth and welcome news.
The Earl of Douglas is discomfited;
Ten thousand bold Scots, two-and-twenty knights,
Balked in their own blood did Sir Walter see
On Holmedon's plains. Of prisoners, Hotspur took
Mordake, Earl of Fife, and eldest son 71
To beaten Douglas, and the Earl of Athol,
Of Murray, Angus, and Menteith.
And is not this an honorable spoil?
A gallant prize? Ha, cousin, is it not? 75
West. In faith,
It is a conquest for a prince to boast of.
King. Yea, there thou mak'st me sad, and mak'st me sin
In envy that my Lord Northumberland
Should be the father to so blest a son— 80
A son who is the theme of honor's tongue,
Amongst a grove the very straightest plant;
Who is sweet Fortune's minion and her pride;
Whilst I, by looking on the praise of him,
See riot and dishonor stain the brow 85
Of my young Harry. O that it could be proved
That some night-tripping fairy had exchanged
In cradle clothes our children where they lay,
And called mine Percy, his Plantagenet!
Then would I have his Harry, and he mine. 90
But let him from my thoughts. What think you, coz,
Of this young Percy's pride? The prisoners
Which he in this adventure hath surprised
To his own use he keeps, and sends me word
I shall have none but Mordake, Earl of Fife. 95
West. This is his uncle's teaching, this is Worcester,
Malevolent to you in all aspects,
Which makes him prune himself and bristle up
The crest of youth against your dignity.
King. But I have sent for him to answer this;
And for this cause awhile we must neglect 101
Our holy purpose to Jerusalem.
Cousin, on Wednesday next our council we
Will hold at Windsor. So inform the lords;
But come yourself with speed to us again; 105
For more is to be said and to be done
Than out of anger can be uttered.
West. I will, my liege.

Exeunt.

[Scene II. *London. An apartment of Prince Henry.*]

Enter PRINCE OF WALES *and* SIR JOHN FALSTAFF.

Fal. Now, Hal, what time of day is it, lad?

Prince. Thou art so fat-witted with drinking of old sack, and unbuttoning thee after supper, and sleeping upon benches after noon, that thou hast forgotten to demand that truly which thou wouldst truly 5 know. What a devil hast thou to do with the time of the day? Unless hours were cups of sack, and minutes capons, and clocks the tongues of bawds, and dials the signs of leaping houses, and the blessed sun himself a fair hot wench in flame-colored taf- 10 feta, I see no reason why thou shouldst be so superfluous to demand the time of the day.

Fal. Indeed you come near me now, Hal; for we that take purses go by the moon and the seven stars, and not by Phœbus, he, that wand'ring knight 15 so fair. And I prithee, sweet wag, when thou art a

50. uneven: disturbing
52. Holy-Rood Day: September 14
54. ever-valiant . . . approved: known to be habitually valiant
55. Holmedon: Humbleton, Northumberland
57–58. As . . . told: as was conjectured by the noise of their artillery
59. them: i.e., the news (often a plural)
59–60. in . . . pride: at the height of the battle
69. Balked: (1) frustrated; (2) piled up in heaps
71. Mordake, Earl of Fife: actually, Murdoch, son of the Duke of Albany, a mistake from Holinshed
73. Menteith: actually, another of Murdoch's titles
83. minion: darling
93. surprised: taken as prizes
94. To . . . use: for his own profit (from ransom)
98. prune: preen
2. old: abundant
3. sack: sherry
9. leaping houses: brothels
14. seven stars: Pleiades
15. Phœbus . . . knight: a reference to the Knight of the Sun in a romance translated from the Spanish as *The Mirror of Knighthood* (*ca.* 1578) or to *The Wandering Knight,* translated from the French of Jean Cartigny in 1581

king, as, God save thy Grace—Majesty I should say, for grace thou wilt have none—

Prince. What, none?

Fal. No, by my troth; not so much as will serve to be prologue to an egg and butter. 20

Prince. Well, how then? Come, roundly, roundly.

Fal. Marry, then, sweet wag, when thou art King, let not us that are squires of the night's body be called thieves of the day's beauty. Let us be Diana's foresters, gentlemen of the shade, minions of the moon; and let men say we be men of good government, being governed as the sea is, by our noble and chaste mistress the moon, under whose countenance we steal. 25 30

Prince. Thou sayest well, and it holds well too; for the fortune of us that are the moon's men doth ebb and flow like the sea, being governed, as the sea is, by the moon. As, for proof now: a purse of gold most resolutely snatched on Monday night and most dissolutely spent on Tuesday morning; got with swearing "Lay by," and spent with crying "Bring in"; now in as low an ebb as the foot of the ladder, and by-and-by in as high a flow as the ridge of the gallows. 35

Fal. By the Lord, thou say'st true, lad—and is not my hostess of the tavern a most sweet wench? 40

Prince. As the honey of Hybla, my old lad of the castle—and is not a buff jerkin a most sweet robe of durance?

Fal. How now, how now, mad wag? What, in thy quips and thy quiddities? What a plague have I to do with a buff jerkin? 45

Prince. Why, what a pox have I to do with my hostess of the tavern?

Fal. Well, thou hast called her to a reckoning many a time and oft. 50

Prince. Did I ever call for thee to pay thy part?

Fal. No; I'll give thee thy due, thou hast paid all there.

Prince. Yea, and elsewhere, so far as my coin would stretch; and where it would not, I have used my credit. 55

Fal. Yea, and so used it that, were it not here apparent that thou art heir apparent—But I prithee, sweet wag, shall there be gallows standing in England when thou art King? and resolution thus fubbed as it is with the rusty curb of old father antic the law? Do not thou, when thou art King, hang a thief. 60

Prince. No; thou shalt. 65

Fal. Shall I? O rare! By the Lord, I'll be a brave judge.

Prince. Thou judgest false already. I mean, thou shalt have the hanging of the thieves and so become a rare hangman. 70

Fal. Well, Hal, well; and in some sort it jumps with my humor as well as waiting in the court, I can tell you.

Prince. For obtaining of suits?

Fal. Yea, for obtaining of suits, whereof the hangman hath no lean wardrobe. 'Sblood, I am as melancholy as a gib-cat or a lugged bear. 75

Prince. Or an old lion, or a lover's lute.

Fal. Yea, or the drone of a Lincolnshire bagpipe.

Prince. What sayest thou to a hare, or the melancholy of Moor Ditch? 80

Fal. Thou hast the most unsavory similes, and art indeed the most comparative, rascalliest, sweet young prince. But, Hal, I prithee trouble me no more with vanity. I would to God thou and I knew where a commodity of good names were to be bought. An old lord of the council rated me the other day in the street about you, sir, but I marked him not; and yet he talked very wisely, but I regarded him not; and yet he talked wisely, and in the street too. 85 90

Prince. Thou didst well, for wisdom cries out in the streets, and no man regards it.

Fal. O, thou hast damnable iteration, and art indeed able to corrupt a saint. Thou hast done much harm upon me, Hal, God forgive thee for it! Before I knew thee, Hal, I knew nothing; and now am I, if a man should speak truly, little better than one of the wicked. I must give over this life, and I will give it over! By the Lord, an I do not, I am a villain! I'll be damned for never a king's son in Christendom. 95 100

Prince. Where shall we take a purse tomorrow, Jack?

Fal. Zounds, where thou wilt, lad! I'll make one. An I do not, call me villain and baffle me. 105

Prince. I see a good amendment of life in thee—from praying to purse-taking.

22. roundly: plainly
23. Marry: indeed; verily
27–28. of . . . government: well controlled
29–30. countenance: (1) face; (2) protection, approval
31. it . . . well: your metaphor is apt
37. Lay by: a bandit's demand for a traveler's goods, accompanied by curses; **Bring in:** the command to bring drink in a tavern
42. honey . . . Hybla: Mount Hybla in Sicily was famous for flavorsome honey.
43. a . . . jerkin: a leather coat such as sheriff's officers wore
44. durance: pun on the name of a durable cloth
50. reckoning: tavern account, with a double entendre
61. resolution: determination to steal
62. fubbed: baffled; **antic:** buffoon
66. brave: splendid; gallant
71. jumps: agrees
77. gib-cat: tomcat; **lugged:** baited
80. hare: proverbially melancholy in the mating season
83. comparative: satirical
85. vanity: frivolity
86. commodity: quantity
87. rated: scolded
91–92. wisdom . . . it: Prov. 1:20–24
93. damnable iteration: the devil's own ability to repeat Scripture
104. Zounds: by God's wounds
105. villain: low fellow; **baffle:** degrade; disgrace

Fal. Why, Hal, 'tis my vocation, Hal. 'Tis no sin for a man to labor in his vocation.

Enter POINS.

Poins! Now shall we know if Gadshill have set 110 a match. O, if men were to be saved by merit, what hole in hell were hot enough for him? This is the most omnipotent villain that ever cried "Stand!" to a true man.

Prince. Good morrow, Ned. 115

Poins. Good morrow, sweet Hal. What says Monsieur Remorse? What says Sir John Sack and Sugar? Jack, how agrees the devil and thee about thy soul, that thou soldest him on Good Friday last for a cup of Madeira and a cold capon's leg? 120

Prince. Sir John stands to his word, the devil shall have his bargain; for he was never yet a breaker of proverbs. He will give the devil his due.

Poins. Then art thou damned for keeping thy word with the devil. 125

Prince. Else he had been damned for cozening the devil.

Poins. But, my lads, my lads, tomorrow morning, by four o'clock early, at Gad's Hill! There are pilgrims going to Canterbury with rich offerings, 130 and traders riding to London with fat purses. I have vizards for you all; you have horses for yourselves. Gadshill lies tonight in Rochester. I have bespoke supper tomorrow night in Eastcheap. We may do it as secure as sleep. If you will go, I will stuff your 135 purses full of crowns; if you will not, tarry at home and be hanged!

Fal. Hear ye, Yedward: if I tarry at home and go not, I'll hang you for going.

Poins. You will, chops? 140

Fal. Hal, wilt thou make one?

Prince. Who, I rob? I a thief? Not I, by my faith.

Fal. There's neither honesty, manhood, nor good fellowship in thee, nor thou cam'st not of the blood royal if thou darest not stand for ten shillings. 145

Prince. Well then, once in my days I'll be a madcap.

Fal. Why, that's well said.

Prince. Well, come what will, I'll tarry at home.

Fal. By the Lord, I'll be a traitor then, when 150 thou art King.

Prince. I care not.

Poins. Sir John, I prithee, leave the Prince and me alone. I will lay him down such reasons for this adventure that he shall go. 155

Fal. Well, God give thee the spirit of persuasion and him the ears of profiting, that what thou speakest may move and what he hears may be believed, that the true Prince may (for recreation sake) prove a false thief; for the poor abuses of the time 160 want countenance. Farewell; you shall find me in Eastcheap.

Prince. Farewell, thou latter spring! farewell, All-hallown summer! [*Exit Falstaff.*]

Poins. Now, my good sweet honey lord, ride 165 with us tomorrow. I have a jest to execute that I cannot manage alone. Falstaff, Bardolph, Peto, and Gadshill shall rob those men that we have already waylaid; yourself and I will not be there; and when they have the booty, if you and I do not rob 170 them, cut this head off from my shoulders.

Prince. How shall we part with them in setting forth?

Poins. Why, we will set forth before or after them and appoint them a place of meeting, wherein 175 it is at our pleasure to fail; and then will they adventure upon the exploit themselves, which they shall have no sooner achieved, but we'll set upon them.

Prince. Yea, but 'tis like that they will know us by our horses, by our habits, and by every other 180 appointment, to be ourselves.

Poins. Tut! our horses they shall not see—I'll tie them in the wood; our vizards we will change after we leave them; and, sirrah, I have cases of buckram for the nonce, to immask our noted outward 185 garments.

Prince. Yea, but I doubt they will be too hard for us.

Poins. Well, for two of them, I know them to be as true-bred cowards as ever turned back; and 190 for the third, if he fight longer than he sees reason, I'll forswear arms. The virtue of this jest will be the incomprehensible lies that this same fat rogue will tell us when we meet at supper: how thirty, at least, he fought with; what wards, what blows, what 195 extremities he endured; and in the reproof of this lives the jest.

Prince. Well, I'll go with thee. Provide us all things necessary and meet me tonight in Eastcheap. There I'll sup. Farewell. 200

108–9. 'Tis . . . vocation: the Bible orders every man to labor in his vocation; see I Cor. 7:20.
110–11. set . . . match: arranged a robbery
111. by merit: as contrasted with salvation by grace; a point of controversy between Catholics and Protestants
114. true: honest
126. cozening: cheating
132. vizards: masks
134. Eastcheap: a section of London
140. chops: fat-jaws
145. royal: pun on the coin worth ten shillings
161. want: lack; **countenance:** permission by authority
163. latter spring: elderly youth
163–64. All-hallown summer: another way of expressing the same idea; All Hallows Day is November 1.
179. like: likely
180. habits: apparel
181. appointment: accessory
184. cases: suits; **buckram:** coarse linen cloth
185. nonce: special need; occasion; **noted:** known
195. wards: defensive postures
196. reproof: disproof

Poins. Farewell, my lord. *Exit.*

Prince. I know you all, and will awhile uphold
The unyoked humor of your idleness.
Yet herein will I imitate the sun,
Who doth permit the base contagious clouds 205
To smother up his beauty from the world,
That, when he please again to be himself,
Being wanted, he may be more wond'red at
By breaking through the foul and ugly mists
Of vapors that did seem to strangle him. 210
If all the year were playing holidays,
To sport would be as tedious as to work;
But when they seldom come, they wished-for come,
And nothing pleaseth but rare accidents.
So, when this loose behavior I throw off 215
And pay the debt I never promised,
By how much better than my word I am,
By so much shall I falsify men's hopes;
And, like bright metal on a sullen ground,
My reformation, glitt'ring o'er my fault, 220
Shall show more goodly and attract more eyes
Than that which hath no foil to set it off.
I'll so offend to make offense a skill,
Redeeming time when men think least I will.
Exit.

[Scene III. *Windsor Castle.*]

Enter the King, Northumberland, Worcester, Hotspur, Sir Walter Blunt, *with others.*

King. My blood hath been too cold and temperate,
Unapt to stir at these indignities,
And you have found me, for accordingly
You tread upon my patience; but be sure
I will from henceforth rather be myself, 5
Mighty and to be feared, than my condition,
Which hath been smooth as oil, soft as young down,
And therefore lost that title of respect
Which the proud soul ne'er pays but to the proud.

Wor. Our house, my sovereign liege, little deserves
The scourge of greatness to be used on it— 11
And that same greatness too which our own hands
Have holp to make so portly.

North. My lord—

King. Worcester, get thee gone, for I do see 15
Danger and disobedience in thine eye.
O sir, your presence is too bold and peremptory,
And majesty might never yet endure
The moody frontier of a servant brow.
You have good leave to leave us: when we need 20
Your use and counsel, we shall send for you.
Exit Worcester.
You were about to speak.

North. Yea, my good lord.
Those prisoners in your Highness' name demanded
Which Harry Percy here at Holmedon took,
Were, as he says, not with such strength denied 25
As is delivered to your Majesty.
Either envy, therefore, or misprision
Is guilty of this fault, and not my son.

Hot. My liege, I did deny no prisoners.
But I remember, when the fight was done, 30
When I was dry with rage and extreme toil,
Breathless and faint, leaning upon my sword,
Came there a certain lord, neat and trimly dressed,
Fresh as a bridegroom, and his chin new reaped
Showed like a stubble land at harvest home. 35
He was perfumed like a milliner,
And 'twixt his finger and his thumb he held
A pouncet box, which ever and anon
He gave his nose, and took't away again;
Who therewith angry, when it next came there, 40
Took it in snuff; and still he smiled and talked;
And as the soldiers bore dead bodies by,
He called them untaught knaves, unmannerly,
To bring a slovenly unhandsome corse
Betwixt the wind and his nobility. 45
With many holiday and lady terms
He questioned me, amongst the rest demanded
My prisoners in your Majesty's behalf.
I then, all smarting with my wounds being cold,
To be so pestered with a popinjay, 50
Out of my grief and my impatience
Answered neglectingly, I know not what—
He should, or he should not; for he made me mad
To see him shine so brisk, and smell so sweet,
And talk so like a waiting gentlewoman 55

203. idleness: folly
208. wanted: missed
214. accidents: happenings
218. hopes: expectations
219. sullen: dull
223. skill: clever stratagem
224. Redeeming time: making up the time I have lost
3. found me: detected this characteristic of mine
5. myself: the King
6. my condition: i.e., forbearance
13. holp: helped; **portly:** majestic

16. Danger . . . disobedience: dangerous rebellion
17. presence: behavior; **peremptory:** imperious
19. moody . . . brow: an inferior's frown; **frontier:** forehead
20. good leave: full permission
26. delivered: reported
27. envy: malice; **misprision:** misunderstanding
36. milliner: tradesman who sold delicate finery—not a maker of hats
38. pouncet box: a container with a perfumed mixture, carried by both sexes as a shield against bad odors and infection
40. Who: i.e., his nose
41. Took . . . snuff: (1) inhaled it greedily; (2) resented its removal
50. popinjay: fop
52. neglectingly: inattentively

Of guns and drums and wounds—God save the mark!—
And telling me the sovereignest thing on earth
Was parmacity for an inward bruise,
And that it was great pity, so it was,
This villainous saltpeter should be digged 60
Out of the bowels of the harmless earth,
Which many a good tall fellow had destroyed
So cowardly, and but for these vile guns,
He would himself have been a soldier.
This bald unjointed chat of his, my lord, 65
I answered indirectly, as I said,
And I beseech you, let not his report
Come current for an accusation
Betwixt my love and your high Majesty. 69

Blunt. The circumstance considered, good my lord,
Whate'er Lord Harry Percy then had said
To such a person, and in such a place,
At such a time, with all the rest retold,
May reasonably die, and never rise
To do him wrong, or any way impeach 75
What then he said, so he unsay it now.

King. Why, yet he doth deny his prisoners,
But with proviso and exception,
That we at our own charge shall ransom straight
His brother-in-law, the foolish Mortimer; 80
Who, on my soul, hath willfully betrayed
The lives of those that he did lead to fight
Against that great magician, damned Glendower,
Whose daughter, as we hear, that Earl of March
Hath lately married. Shall our coffers, then, 85
Be emptied to redeem a traitor home?
Shall we buy treason? and indent with fears
When they have lost and forfeited themselves?
No, on the barren mountains let him starve!
For I shall never hold that man my friend 90
Whose tongue shall ask me for one penny cost
To ransom home revolted Mortimer.

Hot. Revolted Mortimer?
He never did fall off, my sovereign liege,
But by the chance of war. To prove that true 95
Needs no more but one tongue for all those wounds,
Those mouthed wounds, which valiantly he took
When on the gentle Severn's sedgy bank,
In single opposition hand to hand,
He did confound the best part of an hour 100
In changing hardiment with great Glendower.
Three times they breathed, and three times did they drink,
Upon agreement, of swift Severn's flood;
Who then, affrighted with their bloody looks,
Ran fearfully among the trembling reeds 105
And hid his crisp head in the hollow bank,
Bloodstained with these valiant combatants.
Never did bare and rotten policy
Color her working with such deadly wounds;
Nor never could the noble Mortimer 110
Receive so many, and all willingly.
Then let not him be slandered with revolt.

King. Thou dost belie him, Percy, thou dost belie him!
He never did encounter with Glendower.
I tell thee 115
He durst as well have met the devil alone
As Owen Glendower for an enemy.
Art thou not ashamed? But, sirrah, henceforth
Let me not hear you speak of Mortimer.
Send me your prisoners with the speediest means,
Or you shall hear in such a kind from me 121
As will displease you. My Lord Northumberland,
We license your departure with your son.—
Send us your prisoners, or you will hear of it.

Exeunt King, [Blunt, and Train].

Hot. An if the devil come and roar for them,
I will not send them. I will after straight 126
And tell him so; for I will ease my heart,
Albeit I make a hazard of my head.

North. What, drunk with choler? Stay, and pause awhile.
Here comes your uncle.

[Re-]enter WORCESTER.

Hot. Speak of Mortimer? 130
Zounds, I will speak of him, and let my soul
Want mercy if I do not join with him!
Yea, on his part I'll empty all these veins,
And shed my dear blood drop by drop in the dust,
But I will lift the downtrod Mortimer 135

56. God . . . mark: God avert the evil omen; God forbid that he should have anything to do with such matters.
57. sovereignest: most effective
58. parmacity: spermaceti, a waxy substance from the sperm whale, used in ointments
62. tall: brave
65. bald: meaningless
66. indirectly: offhandedly
68. Come current: be credited
75. impeach: impugn; accuse
79. straight: immediately
80. brother-in-law . . . Mortimer: Sir Edmund Mortimer, Glendower's captive, is here confused with his nephew, Edmund Mortimer, Earl of March (regarded by many as the true claimant to the throne, since his dead father, Roger, 4th Earl of March, had been named as his successor by Richard II). Hotspur's wife was Sir Edmund's sister Elizabeth.
87. indent . . . fears: make a pact with one who threatens our safety; **indent** is related to the legal word "indenture"
94. fall off: desert
97. mouthed: gaping
100. confound: consume; expend
101. changing hardiment: exchanging valiant blows; fighting hand to hand
102. breathed: rested
106. his: its; **crisp:** curled; rippling
108. policy: politic cunning
109. Color: disguise
113. belie: report him falsely
128. hazard: pawn
129. choler: anger

As high in the air as this unthankful King,
As this ingrate and cankered Bolingbroke.
North. Brother, the King hath made your nephew mad.
Wor. Who struck this heat up after I was gone?
Hot. He will (forsooth) have all my prisoners;
And when I urged the ransom once again 141
Of my wive's brother, then his cheek looked pale,
And on my face he turned an eye of death,
Trembling even at the name of Mortimer. 144
Wor. I cannot blame him. Was not he proclaimed
By Richard that dead is the next of blood?
North. He was; I heard the proclamation.
And then it was when the unhappy King
(Whose wrongs in us God pardon!) did set forth
Upon his Irish expedition; 150
From whence he intercepted did return
To be deposed, and shortly murdered.
Wor. And for whose death we in the world's wide mouth
Live scandalized and foully spoken of. 154
Hot. But soft, I pray you. Did King Richard then
Proclaim my brother Edmund Mortimer
Heir to the crown?
North. He did; myself did hear it.
Hot. Nay, then I cannot blame his cousin King,
That wished him on the barren mountains starve.
But shall it be that you, that set the crown 160
Upon the head of this forgetful man,
And for his sake wear the detested blot
Of murderous subornation—shall it be
That you a world of curses undergo,
Being the agents or base second means, 165
The cords, the ladder, or the hangman rather?
O pardon me that I descend so low
To show the line and the predicament
Wherein you range under this subtle King!
Shall it for shame be spoken in these days, 170
Or fill up chronicles in time to come,
That men of your nobility and power
Did gage them both in an unjust behalf
(As both of you, God pardon it! have done)
To put down Richard, that sweet lovely rose, 175
And plant this thorn, this canker, Bolingbroke?
And shall it in more shame be further spoken
That you are fooled, discarded, and shook off
By him for whom these shames ye underwent?
No! yet time serves wherein you may redeem 180
Your banished honors and restore yourselves
Into the good thoughts of the world again;
Revenge the jeering and disdained contempt
Of this proud King, who studies day and night
To answer all the debt he owes to you 185
Even with the bloody payment of your deaths.
Therefore I say—
Wor. Peace, cousin, say no more;
And now I will unclasp a secret book,
And to your quick-conceiving discontents
I'll read you matter deep and dangerous, 190
As full of peril and adventurous spirit
As to o'erwalk a current roaring loud
On the unsteadfast footing of a spear.
Hot. If he fall in, good night, or sink or swim!
Send danger from the east unto the west, 195
So honor cross it from the north to south,
And let them grapple. O, the blood more stirs
To rouse a lion than to start a hare!
North. Imagination of some great exploit
Drives him beyond the bounds of patience. 200
Hot. By heaven, methinks it were an easy leap
To pluck bright honor from the pale-faced moon,
Or dive into the bottom of the deep,
Where fathom line could never touch the ground,
And pluck up drowned honor by the locks, 205
So he that doth redeem her thence might wear
Without corrival all her dignities;
But out upon this half-faced fellowship!
Wor. He apprehends a world of figures here,
But not the form of what he should attend. 210
Good cousin, give me audience for a while.
Hot. I cry you mercy.
Wor. Those same noble Scots
That are your prisoners—
Hot. I'll keep them all.
By God, he shall not have a Scot of them!
No, if a Scot would save his soul, he shall not. 215
I'll keep them, by this hand!
Wor. You start away
And lend no ear unto my purposes.
Those prisoners you shall keep.
Hot. Nay, I will! That's flat!
He said he would not ransom Mortimer,
Forbade my tongue to speak of Mortimer, 220
But I will find him when he lies asleep,
And in his ear I'll hollo "Mortimer."
Nay, I'll have a starling shall be taught to speak

137. cankered: spiteful; eaten by resentment and malice; **Bolingbroke:** the King, known as Henry Bolingbroke before he seized the crown
140. forsooth: truly; believe it or not!
143. eye . . . death: eye betraying mortal fear
149. in us: on our part
156. brother: brother-in-law
163. murderous subornation: incitement to murder
168. line . . . predicament: exact position
176. canker: canker or dog rose; a wild variety
183. disdained: disdainful
185. answer: repay
189. quick-conceiving discontents: discontented and therefore receptive minds
200. patience: restraint
207. corrival: partner
208. half-faced fellowship: contemptible and cowardly sharing
209. apprehends: conceives; **figures:** images
210. form: true essence; **attend:** heed
212. cry . . . mercy: beg your pardon

Nothing but "Mortimer," and give it him
To keep his anger still in motion. 225

Wor. Hear you, cousin, a word.

Hot. All studies here I solemnly defy
Save how to gall and pinch this Bolingbroke;
And that same sword-and-buckler Prince of Wales:
But that I think his father loves him not 230
And would be glad he met with some mischance,
I would have him poisoned with a pot of ale.

Wor. Farewell, kinsman. I'll talk to you
When you are better tempered to attend. 234

North. Why, what a wasp-stung and impatient fool
Art thou to break into this woman's mood,
Tying thine ear to no tongue but thine own!

Hot. Why, look you, I am whipped and scourged with rods,
Nettled, and stung with pismires when I hear
Of this vile politician, Bolingbroke. 240
In Richard's time—what do you call the place?
A plague upon it! it is in Gloucestershire;
'Twas where the madcap duke his uncle kept,
His uncle York—where I first bowed my knee
Unto this king of smiles, this Bolingbroke— 245
'Sblood!—when you and he came back from Ravenspurgh—

North. At Berkeley Castle.

Hot. You say true.
Why, what a candy deal of courtesy
This fawning greyhound then did proffer me! 250
"Look when his infant fortune came to age,"
And "gentle Harry Percy," and "kind cousin"—
O, the devil take such cozeners!—God forgive me!
Good uncle, tell your tale, for I have done.

Wor. Nay, if you have not, to it again. 255
We will stay your leisure.

Hot. I have done, i' faith.

Wor. Then once more to your Scottish prisoners.
Deliver them up without their ransom straight,
And make the Douglas' son your only mean
For powers in Scotland, which, for divers reasons
Which I shall send you written, be assured 261
Will easily be granted. [*To Northumberland*] You, my lord,
Your son in Scotland being thus employed,
Shall secretly into the bosom creep
Of that same noble prelate well-beloved, 265
The Archbishop.

Hot. Of York, is it not?

Wor. True; who bears hard
His brother's death at Bristow, the Lord Scroop.
I speak not this in estimation,
As what I think might be, but what I know 270
Is ruminated, plotted, and set down,
And only stays but to behold the face
Of that occasion that shall bring it on.

Hot. I smell it. Upon my life, it will do well.

North. Before the game is afoot thou still let'st slip. 275

Hot. Why, it cannot choose but be a noble plot.
And then the power of Scotland and of York
To join with Mortimer, ha?

Wor. And so they shall.

Hot. In faith, it is exceedingly well aimed.

Wor. And 'tis no little reason bids us speed 280
To save our heads by raising of a head;
For, bear ourselves as even as we can,
The King will always think him in our debt,
And think we think ourselves unsatisfied,
Till he hath found a time to pay us home. 285
And see already how he doth begin
To make us strangers to his looks of love.

Hot. He does, he does! We'll be revenged on him.

Wor. Cousin, farewell. No further go in this
Than I by letters shall direct your course. 290
When time is ripe, which will be suddenly,
I'll steal to Glendower and Lord Mortimer,
Where you and Douglas, and our powers at once,
As I will fashion it, shall happily meet,
To bear our fortunes in our own strong arms, 295
Which now we hold at much uncertainty.

North. Farewell, good brother. We shall thrive, I trust.

Hot. Uncle, adieu. O let the hours be short
Till fields and blows and groans applaud our sport!

Exeunt.

225. **still:** ever; continually
227. **studies:** preoccupations
229. **sword-and-buckler:** roistering. Short swords and bucklers were sometimes carried for defense by apprentices and servingmen and were therefore associated with street brawling.
239. **pismires:** ants
240. **politician:** crafty schemer
243. **kept:** resided
249. **candy . . . courtesy:** deal of saccharine politeness
251. **Look when:** whenever
253. **cozeners:** cheaters
256. **stay . . . leisure:** await your pleasure
264. **bosom:** confidence
267. **bears hard:** deeply resents
268. **Bristow:** Bristol
275. **game:** quarry; **let'st slip:** release your hunting pack
279. **aimed:** planned
281. **head:** army
282. **even:** honorably; innocently
285. **pay . . . home:** give us full payment (death)
291. **suddenly:** without delay
293. **at once:** simultaneously

ACT II

Scene I. [*Rochester. An inn yard.*]

Enter a CARRIER *with a lantern in his hand.*

1. Car. Heigh-ho! an it be not four by the day, I'll be hanged. Charles's wain is over the new chimney, and yet our horse not packed.—What, ostler!

Ostler. [*Within*] Anon, anon.

1. Car. I prithee, Tom, beat Cut's saddle, put 5 a few flocks in the point. Poor jade is wrung in the withers out of all cess.

Enter ANOTHER CARRIER.

2. Car. Peas and beans are as dank here as a dog, and that is the next way to give poor jades the bots. This house is turned upside down since Robin 10 Ostler died.

1. Car. Poor fellow never joyed since the price of oats rose. It was the death of him.

2. Car. I think this be the most villainous house in all London road for fleas. I am stung like a 15 tench.

1. Car. Like a tench? By the mass, there is ne'er a king christen could be better bit than I have been since the first cock.

2. Car. Why, they will allow us ne'er a 20 jordan, and then we leak in your chimney, and your chamber-lye breeds fleas like a loach.

1. Car. What, ostler! come away and be hanged! come away!

2. Car. I have a gammon of bacon and two 25 razes of ginger, to be delivered as far as Charing Cross.

1. Car. God's body! the turkeys in my pannier are quite starved. What, ostler! A plague on thee! hast thou never an eye in thy head? Canst not hear? 30 An 'twere not as good deed as drink to break the pate on thee, I am a very villain. Come, and be hanged! Hast no faith in thee?

Enter GADSHILL.

Gad. Good morrow, carriers. What's o'clock?

1. Car. I think it be two o'clock. 35

Gad. I prithee lend me thy lantern to see my gelding in the stable.

1. Car. Nay, by God, soft! I know a trick worth two of that, i' faith.

Gad. I pray thee lend me thine. 40

2. Car. Ay, when? canst tell? Lend me thy lantern, quoth he? Marry, I'll see thee hanged first!

Gad. Sirrah carrier, what time do you mean to come to London?

2. Car. Time enough to go to bed with a 45 candle, I warrant thee. Come, neighbor Mugs, we'll call up the gentlemen. They will along with company, for they have great charge. *Exeunt* [*Carriers*].

Gad. What, ho! chamberlain!

Enter CHAMBERLAIN.

Cham. At hand, quoth pickpurse. 50

Gad. That's even as fair as "at hand, quoth the chamberlain"; for thou variest no more from picking of purses than giving direction doth from laboring: thou layest the plot how.

Cham. Good morrow, Master Gadshill. It 55 holds current that I told you yesternight. There's a franklin in the Wild of Kent hath brought three hundred marks with him in gold. I heard him tell it to one of his company last night at supper—a kind of auditor, one that hath abundance of charge too, 60 God knows what. They are up already and call for eggs and butter. They will away presently.

1. **four . . . day:** four in the morning
2. **Charles's wain:** a popular name for the Great Bear
5. **Cut:** a horse with a docked tail
6. **flocks:** pieces of wool; **point:** front; **jade:** nag
7. **out . . . cess:** beyond measure
9. **next:** quickest; **the bots:** intestinal parasites
16. **tench:** a fish marked with red spots that resemble flea-bites
18. **king christen:** Christian king
21. **jordan:** chamberpot
22. **chamber-lye:** urine; **loach:** a fish known to be infested with fleas
25. **gammon:** flitch or side
26. **razes:** roots; **Charing Cross:** at this time a mere village between the City and Westminster
28. **pannier:** basket

31–32. **break . . . thee:** bloody your head
32. **very:** absolute
45–46. **Time . . . candle:** an evasive answer: "whenever we get there"
48. **great charge:** much money
50. **At . . . pickpurse:** proverbial
51. **fair:** exact; apt
56. **holds current:** proves true
57. **franklin:** small owner of freehold property; **Wild:** weald; forest
62. **presently:** at once

Gad. Sirrah, if they meet not with St. Nicholas' clerks, I'll give thee this neck.

Cham. No, I'll none of it. I pray thee keep 65 that for the hangman; for I know thou worshipest St. Nicholas as truly as a man of falsehood may.

Gad. What talkest thou to me of the hangman? If I hang, I'll make a fat pair of gallows; for if I hang, old Sir John hangs with me, and thou knowest 70 he is no starveling. Tut! there are other Trojans that thou dream'st not of, the which for sport sake are content to do the profession some grace; that would (if matters should be looked into) for their own credit sake make all whole. I am joined with no 75 foot land-rakers, no long-staff sixpenny strikers, none of these mad mustachio purple-hued maltworms; but with nobility and tranquillity, burgomasters and great oneyers, such as can hold in, such as will strike sooner than speak, and speak sooner than 80 drink, and drink sooner than pray; and yet, zounds, I lie; for they pray continually to their saint, the commonwealth, or rather, not pray to her, but prey on her, for they ride up and down on her and make her their boots. 85

Cham. What, the commonwealth their boots? Will she hold out water in foul way?

Gad. She will, she will! Justice hath liquored her. We steal as in a castle, cocksure. We have the receipt of fernseed, we walk invisible. 90

Cham. Nay, by my faith, I think you are more beholding to the night than to fernseed for your walking invisible.

Gad. Give me thy hand. Thou shalt have a share in our purchase, as I am a true man. 95

Cham. Nay, rather let me have it, as you are a false thief.

Gad. Go to; "homo" is a common name to all men. Bid the ostler bring my gelding out of the stable. Farewell, you muddy knave. 100

[*Exeunt.*]

63–64. St. Nicholas' clerks: highwaymen. St. Nicholas had been adopted by thieves as their patron saint.
71. Trojans: good fellows; bully boys
76. foot land-rakers: vagabond thieves; **long-staff . . . strikers:** petty thieves armed with staves
77. maltworms: topers
78. nobility . . . tranquillity: noblemen who live at their ease; **burgomasters:** officials
79. great oneyers: "great one-ers," personages; **hold in:** hold their tongues
80. speak: demand a traveler's money
85. boots: booty
87. foul: muddy
88. liquored: (1) oiled; (2) bribed
89. as . . . castle: with perfect safety; **receipt:** recipe
90. fernseed: believed to have the power to make one invisible
95. purchase: spoil; loot; **true:** honest
100. muddy: dull; stupid

Scene II. [*The highway near Gad's Hill.*]

Enter PRINCE, POINS, PETO, *and* [BARDOLPH].

Poins. Come, shelter, shelter! I have removed Falstaff's horse, and he frets like a gummed velvet.

Prince. Stand close. [*They hide.*]

Enter FALSTAFF.

Fal. Poins! Poins, and be hanged! Poins!

Prince. [*Comes forward*] Peace, ye fat- 5 kidneyed rascal! What a brawling dost thou keep!

Fal. Where's Poins, Hal?

Prince. He is walked up to the top of the hill; I'll go seek him. [*Hides.*]

Fal. I am accursed to rob in that thief's com- 10 pany. The rascal hath removed my horse and tied him I know not where. If I travel but four foot by the squire further afoot, I shall break my wind. Well, I doubt not but to die a fair death for all this, if I 'scape hanging for killing that rogue. I have 15 forsworn his company hourly any time this two-and-twenty years, and yet I am bewitched with the rogue's company. If the rascal have not given me medicines to make me love him, I'll be hanged. It could not be else: I have drunk medicines. 20 Poins! Hal! A plague upon you both! Bardolph! Peto! I'll starve ere I'll rob a foot further. An 'twere not as good a deed as drink to turn true man and to leave these rogues, I am the veriest varlet that ever chewed with a tooth. Eight yards of uneven 25 ground is threescore and ten miles afoot with me, and the stony-hearted villains know it well enough. A plague upon it when thieves cannot be true one to another! (*They whistle.*) Whew! A plague upon you all! Give me my horse, you rogues! give me my 30 horse and be hanged!

Prince. [*Steps forward*] Peace, ye fat-guts! Lie down, lay thine ear close to the ground, and list if thou canst hear the tread of travelers.

Fal. Have you any levers to lift me up again, 35 being down? 'Sblood, I'll not bear mine own flesh so far afoot again for all the coin in thy father's exchequer. What a plague mean ye to colt me thus?

Prince. Thou liest; thou art not colted, thou art uncolted. 40

2. frets . . . velvet: proverbial metaphor. Velvet was sometimes sized with gum to give it greater body, but such fabric "fretted" (wore) more quickly.
3. close: concealed
13. squire: square; foot rule
19. medicines: love potions
24. varlet: rascal
38. colt: fool

Fal. I prithee, good Prince Hal, help me to my horse, good king's son.

Prince. Out, ye rogue! Shall I be your ostler?

Fal. Go hang thyself in thine own heir-apparent garters! If I be ta'en, I'll peach for this. An I 45 have not ballads made on you all, and sung to filthy tunes, let a cup of sack be my poison. When a jest is so forward—and afoot too—I hate it.

Enter GADSHILL.

Gad. Stand!

Fal. So I do, against my will. 50

Poins. [*Steps forward*] O, 'tis our setter; I know his voice.

Bar. What news?

Gad. Case ye, case ye! On with your vizards! There's money of the King's coming down 55 the hill; 'tis going to the King's exchequer.

Fal. You lie, ye rogue! 'Tis going to the King's tavern.

Gad. There's enough to make us all.

Fal. To be hanged. 60

Prince. Sirs, you four shall front them in the narrow lane; Ned Poins and I will walk lower. If they 'scape from your encounter, then they light on us.

Peto. How many be there of them?

Gad. Some eight or ten. 65

Fal. Zounds, will they not rob us?

Prince. What, a coward, Sir John Paunch?

Fal. Indeed, I am not John of Gaunt, your grandfather, but yet no coward, Hal.

Prince. Well, we leave that to the proof. 70

Poins. Sirrah Jack, thy horse stands behind the hedge. When thou need'st him, there thou shalt find him. Farewell and stand fast.

Fal. Now cannot I strike him, if I should be hanged. 75

Prince [*Aside to Poins*] Ned, where are our disguises?

Poins. [*Aside to Prince*] Here, hard by. Stand close. [*Exeunt Prince and Poins.*]

Fal. Now, my masters, happy man be his 80 dole, say I. Every man to his business.

Enter the TRAVELERS.

Trav. Come, neighbor. The boy shall lead our horses down the hill; we'll walk afoot awhile and ease our legs.

Thieves. Stand! 85

Trav. Jesus bless us!

Fal. Strike! down with them! cut the villains' throats! Ah, whoreson caterpillars! bacon-fed knaves! they hate us youth. Down with them! fleece them! 90

Trav. O, we are undone, both we and ours forever!

Fal. Hang ye, gorbellied knaves, are ye undone? No, ye fat chuffs; I would your store were here! On, bacons, on! What, ye knaves! young men must live. You are grand jurors, are ye? We'll jure ye, 95 faith! *Here they rob them and bind them. Exeunt.*

Enter the PRINCE *and* POINS [*in buckram suits*].

Prince. The thieves have bound the true men. Now could thou and I rob the thieves and go merrily to London, it would be argument for a week, laughter for a month, and a good jest forever. 100

Poins. Stand close! I hear them coming. [*They stand aside.*]

Enter the THIEVES *again.*

Fal. Come, my masters, let us share, and then to horse before day. An the Prince and Poins be not two arrant cowards, there's no equity stirring. There's no more valor in that Poins than in a wild duck. 105

Prince. Your money!

Poins. Villains!

As they are sharing, the Prince and Poins set upon them. They all run away, and Falstaff, after a blow or two, runs away too, leaving the booty behind them.

Prince. Got with much ease. Now merrily to horse. The thieves are all scattered, and possessed with fear so strongly that they dare not meet each 110 other: each takes his fellow for an officer. Away, good Ned. Falstaff sweats to death and lards the lean earth as he walks along. Were't not for laughing, I should pity him.

Poins. How the fat rogue roared! 115

Exeunt.

Scene III. [*Warkworth Castle.*]

Enter HOTSPUR *solus, reading a letter.*

Hot. "But, for mine own part, my Lord, I could be well contented to be there, in respect of the love I

44–45. hang . . . garters: cf. the proverbial expression "hang oneself in one's own garters." As heir to the throne, the Prince was a member of the Order of the Garter.
47–48. is . . . forward: goes so far
54. Case ye: put on your masks
61. front: confront
78. hard: near
80–81. happy . . . dole: may we have good luck

88. caterpillars: parasites
92. gorbellied: great-bellied
93. chuffs: misers; **store:** entire wealth
95. grand jurors: men of wealth
99. argument: subject matter
104. arrant: downright; **there's . . . stirring:** justice is not to be had
112. lards . . . earth: i.e., with his melted fat
115. fat: found only in a fragment of the Quarto in the Folger Library
Ent. solus: alone

bear your house." He could be contented—why is he not then? In respect of the love he bears our house! He shows in this he loves his own barn better 5
than he loves our house. Let me see some more. "The purpose you undertake is dangerous"—why, that's certain! 'Tis dangerous to take a cold, to sleep, to drink; but I tell you, my lord fool, out of this nettle, danger, we pluck this flower, safety. "The pur- 10
pose you undertake is dangerous, the friends you have named uncertain, the time itself unsorted, and your whole plot too light for the counterpoise of so great an opposition." Say you so, say you so? I say unto you again, you are a shallow, cowardly 15
hind, and you lie. What a lack-brain is this! By the Lord, our plot is a good plot as ever was laid; our friends true and constant: a good plot, good friends, and full of expectation; an excellent plot, very good friends. What a frosty-spirited rogue is this! 20
Why, my Lord of York commends the plot and the general course of the action. Zounds, an I were now by this rascal, I could brain him with his lady's fan. Is there not my father, my uncle, and myself; Lord Edmund Mortimer, my Lord of York, and 25
Owen Glendower? Is there not, besides, the Douglas? Have I not all their letters to meet me in arms by the ninth of the next month, and are they not some of them set forward already? What a pagan rascal is this! an infidel! Ha! you shall see now, in very 30
sincerity of fear and cold heart will he to the King and lay open all our proceedings. O, I could divide myself and go to buffets for moving such a dish of skim milk with so honorable an action! Hang him, let him tell the King! we are prepared. I will set 35
forward tonight.

Enter his LADY.

How now, Kate? I must leave you within these two hours.

Lady. O my good lord, why are you thus alone?
For what offense have I this fortnight been
A banished woman from my Harry's bed? 40
Tell me, sweet lord, what is't that takes from thee
Thy stomach, pleasure, and thy golden sleep?
Why dost thou bend thine eyes upon the earth,
And start so often when thou sitst alone? 44
Why hast thou lost the fresh blood in thy cheeks
And given my treasures and my rights of thee
To thick-eyed musing and cursed melancholy?
In thy faint slumbers I by thee have watched,
And heard thee murmur tales of iron wars,
Speak terms of manage to thy bounding steed, 50
Cry "Courage! to the field!" And thou hast talked
Of sallies and retires, of trenches, tents,
Of palisadoes, frontiers, parapets,
Of basilisks, of cannon, culverin,
Of prisoners' ransom, and of soldiers slain, 55
And all the currents of a heady fight.
Thy spirit within thee hath been so at war,
And thus hath so bestirred thee in thy sleep,
That beads of sweat have stood upon thy brow
Like bubbles in a late-disturbed stream, 60
And in thy face strange motions have appeared,
Such as we see when men restrain their breath
On some great sudden hest. O what portents are these?
Some heavy business hath my lord in hand,
And I must know it, else he loves me not. 65

Hot. What, ho!

[*Enter a* SERVANT.]

Is Gilliams with the packet gone?

Ser. He is, my lord, an hour ago.

Hot. Hath Butler brought those horses from the sheriff?

Ser. One horse, my lord, he brought even now.

Hot. What horse? A roan, a crop-ear is it not?

Ser. It is, my lord.

Hot. That roan shall be my throne.
Well, I will back him straight. O espérance! 72
Bid Butler lead him forth into the park.

[*Exit Servant.*]

Lady. But hear you, my lord.

Hot. What say'st thou, my lady? 75

Lady. What is it carries you away?

Hot. Why, my horse, my love—my horse!

Lady. Out, you mad-headed ape!
A weasel hath not such a deal of spleen
As you are tossed with. In faith, 80
I'll know your business, Harry; that I will!
I fear my brother Mortimer doth stir
About his title and hath sent for you
To line his enterprise; but if you go—

Hot. So far afoot, I shall be weary, love. 85

Lady. Come, come, you paraquito, answer me

9–10. **out . . . safety:** cf. the proverb "Danger and delight grow both upon one stalk."
12. **unsorted:** ill-chosen
13. **for . . . of:** to offset
16. **hind:** (1) hayseed; (2) coward
19. **full . . . expectation:** very promising
33. **go . . . buffets:** let one half pummel the other
42. **stomach:** appetite
48. **faint:** light; fretful
50. **manage:** horsemanship (French *manège*)
53. **palisadoes:** barricades; **frontiers:** outer fortifications
54. **basilisks, culverin:** two types of cannon
56. **heady:** headlong
61. **motions:** signs of emotion
63. **hest:** command
64. **heavy:** grave
72. **O espérance:** the Percy motto and battle cry *Espérance en Dieu.*
79. **spleen:** nervous irritability
84. **line:** reinforce

Directly unto this question that I ask.
In faith, I'll break thy little finger, Harry,
An if thou wilt not tell me all things true.

Hot. Away, away, you trifler! Love? I love thee not; 90
I care not for thee, Kate. This is no world
To play with mammets and to tilt with lips.
We must have bloody noses and cracked crowns,
And pass them current too. Gods me, my horse!
What say'st thou, Kate? What wouldst thou have with me? 95

Lady. Do you not love me? do you not indeed?
Well, do not then; for since you love me not,
I will not love myself. Do you not love me?
Nay, tell me if you speak in jest or no.

Hot. Come, wilt thou see me ride? 100
And when I am a-horseback, I will swear
I love thee infinitely. But hark you, Kate:
I must not have you henceforth question me
Whither I go, nor reason whereabout.
Whither I must, I must, and to conclude, 105
This evening must I leave you, gentle Kate.
I know you wise, but yet no farther wise
Than Harry Percy's wife; constant you are,
But yet a woman; and for secrecy,
No lady closer, for I well believe 110
Thou wilt not utter what thou dost not know,
And so far will I trust thee, gentle Kate.

Lady. How? so far?

Hot. Not an inch further. But hark you, Kate:
Whither I go, thither shall you go too; 115
Today will I set forth, tomorrow you.
Will this content you, Kate?

Lady. It must of force.

Exeunt.

Scene IV. [*London. The Boar's Head Tavern in Eastcheap.*]

Enter PRINCE *and* POINS.

Prince. Ned, prithee come out of that fat-room and lend me thy hand to laugh a little.

Poins. Where hast been, Hal?

Prince. With three or four loggerheads amongst three or fourscore hogsheads. I have sounded the 5 very bass-string of humility. Sirrah, I am sworn brother to a leash of drawers and can call them all by their christen names, as Tom, Dick, and Francis. They take it already upon their salvation that, though I be but Prince of Wales, yet I am the king of 10 courtesy, and tell me flatly I am no proud Jack like Falstaff, but a Corinthian, a lad of mettle, a good boy (by the Lord, so they call me!), and when I am King of England I shall command all the good lads in Eastcheap. They call drinking deep, dyeing 15 scarlet; and when you breathe in your watering, they cry "hem!" and bid you play it off. To conclude, I am so good a proficient in one quarter of an hour that I can drink with any tinker in his own language during my life. I tell thee, Ned, thou hast lost 20 much honor that thou wert not with me in this action. But, sweet Ned—to sweeten which name of Ned, I give thee this pennyworth of sugar, clapped even now into my hand by an under-skinker, one that never spake other English in his life than 25 "Eight shillings and sixpence," and "You are welcome," with this shrill addition, "Anon, anon, sir! Score a pint of bastard in the Half-moon," or so—but, Ned, to drive away the time till Falstaff come, I prithee do thou stand in some by-room while I 30 question my puny drawer to what end he gave me the sugar; and do thou never leave calling "Francis!" that his tale to me may be nothing but "Anon!" Step aside, and I'll show thee a precedent.

Poins. Francis! 35

Prince. Thou art perfect.

Poins. Francis! [*Exit Poins.*]

Enter [FRANCIS, *a*] *Drawer.*

Fran. Anon, anon, sir.—Look down into the Pomgarnet, Ralph.

Prince. Come hither, Francis. 40

Fran. My lord?

Prince. How long hast thou to serve, Francis?

Fran. Forsooth, five years, and as much as to—

Poins. [*Within*] Francis!

Fran. Anon, anon, sir. 45

Prince. Five year! by'r Lady, a long lease for the clinking of pewter. But, Francis, darest thou be so

92. mammets: dolls
93. crowns: (1) heads; (2) coins
94. pass . . . current: force their acceptance. Damaged coins were not negotiable. **Gods me:** God save me
104. reason whereabout: discuss the reason for my going
1. fat-room: vat-room; taproom
4. loggerheads: blockheads
7. leash: trio. Three dogs made up a leash. **drawers:** tapsters
9. take . . . upon: swear by
11. proud Jack: presumptuous rascal
12. Corinthian: good sport; **lad . . . mettle:** fellow of spirit
15–16. dyeing scarlet: the urine of heavy drinkers was used for certain scarlet dyes.
16. watering: drinking
17. play . . . off: drink it down
24. under-skinker: tapster's apprentice
27. Anon: coming
28. Score . . . Half-Moon: charge the customers in the Half-Moon with a pint of sweet wine. The various rooms of taverns were often named.
31. puny: inferior
34. precedent: exemplary jest
38–39. Pomgarnet: Pomegranate, another room in the tavern
42. serve: i.e., to complete his apprenticeship

valiant as to play the coward with thy indenture and show it a fair pair of heels and run from it?

Fran. O Lord, sir, I'll be sworn upon all the books in England I could find in my heart— 50

Poins. [*Within*] Francis!

Fran. Anon, sir.

Prince. How old art thou, Francis?

Fran. Let me see: about Michaelmas next I shall be— 55

Poins. [*Within*] Francis!

Fran. Anon, sir. Pray stay a little, my lord.

Prince. Nay, but hark you, Francis. For the sugar thou gavest me—'twas a pennyworth, was't not? 60

Fran. O Lord! I would it had been two!

Prince. I will give thee for it a thousand pound. Ask me when thou wilt, and thou shalt have it.

Poins. [*Within*] Francis!

Fran. Anon, anon. 65

Prince. Anon, Francis? No, Francis; but tomorrow, Francis; or, Francis, a Thursday; or indeed, Francis, when thou wilt. But Francis—

Fran. My lord?

Prince. Wilt thou rob this leathern-jerkin, crystal-button, not-pated, agate-ring, puke-stocking, caddis-garter, smooth-tongue, Spanish-pouch— 70

Fran. O Lord, sir, who do you mean?

Prince. Why then, your brown bastard is your only drink; for look you, Francis, your white canvas doublet will sully. In Barbary, sir, it cannot come to so much. 75

Fran. What, sir?

Poins. [*Within*] Francis!

Prince. Away, you rogue! Dost thou not hear them call? 80 *Here they both call him. The Drawer stands amazed, not knowing which way to go.*

Enter VINTNER.

Vint. What, stand'st thou still, and hear'st such a calling? Look to the guests within. [*Exit Francis.*] My lord, old Sir John, with half a dozen more, are at the door. Shall I let them in? 85

Prince. Let them alone while, and then open the door. [*Exit Vintner.*] Poins!

Poins. [*Within*] Anon, anon, sir.

Enter POINS.

Prince. Sirrah, Falstaff and the rest of the thieves are at the door. Shall we be merry? 90

Poins. As merry as crickets, my lad. But hark ye; what cunning match have you made with this jest of the drawer? Come, what's the issue?

Prince. I am now of all humors that have showed themselves humors since the old days of goodman Adam to the pupil age of this present twelve o'clock at midnight. 95

[*Re-enter* FRANCIS.]

What's o'clock, Francis?

Fran. Anon, anon, sir. [*Exit.*]

Prince. That ever this fellow should have fewer words than a parrot, and yet the son of a woman! His industry is upstairs and downstairs, his eloquence the parcel of a reckoning. I am not yet of Percy's mind, the Hotspur of the North; he that kills me some six or seven dozen of Scots at a breakfast, washes his hands, and says to his wife, "Fie upon this quiet life! I want work." "O my sweet Harry," says she, "how many hast thou killed today?" "Give my roan horse a drench," says he, and answers "Some fourteen," an hour after, "a trifle, a trifle." I prithee call in Falstaff. I'll play Percy, and that damned brawn shall play Dame Mortimer his wife. "Rivo!" says the drunkard. Call in ribs, call in tallow. 100 105 110

Enter FALSTAFF, [GADSHILL, BARDOLPH, *and* PETO, *followed by* FRANCIS *with wine*].

Poins. Welcome, Jack. Where hast thou been?

Fal. A plague of all cowards, I say, and a vengeance too! Marry and amen! Give me a cup of sack, boy. Ere I lead this life long, I'll sew netherstocks, and mend them and foot them too. A plague of all cowards! Give me a cup of sack, rogue. Is there no virtue extant? *He drinketh.* 116 120

Prince. Didst thou never see Titan kiss a dish of butter (pitiful-hearted Titan!) that melted at the sweet tale of the sun's? If thou didst, then behold that compound. 125

Fal. You rogue, here's lime in this sack too! There is nothing but roguery to be found in villainous man. Yet a coward is worse than a cup of sack with lime in it—a villainous coward! Go thy ways, old Jack, die when thou wilt; if manhood, good man- 130

71. not-pated: short-haired; **agate-ring:** wearing a ring with an agate stone; **puke-stocking:** dark woolen-stockinged
72. caddis-garter: gartered with caddis tape; **Spanish-pouch:** wearing a purse from which he made change
74-77. Why . . . much: nonsense, intended to confuse the drawer
96. pupil age: youth
104-5. kills me: the ethical dative, meaning simply "kills"
109. drench: restorative drink
112. brawn: porker
113. Rivo: an exclamation to accompany a deep draught
118-19. netherstocks: stockings. The breeches were sometimes called "upperstocks."
121. virtue: valor
123. Titan: the sun. Helios, one name for the sun-god, was the son of a Titan.
125. compound: substance (melting butter)
126. lime: an adulterant used in sack to make it dryer and brighter

hood, be not forgot upon the face of the earth, then am I a shotten herring. There lives not three good men unhanged in England; and one of them is fat, and grows old. God help the while! A bad world, I say. I would I were a weaver; I could sing psalms or 135 anything. A plague of all cowards, I say still!

Prince. How now, woolsack? What mutter you?

Fal. A king's son! If I do not beat thee out of thy kingdom with a dagger of lath and drive all thy subjects afore thee like a flock of wild geese, I'll 140 never wear hair on my face more. You Prince of Wales?

Prince. Why, you whoreson round man, what's the matter?

Fal. Are not you a coward? Answer me to 145 that—and Poins there?

Poins. Zounds, ye fat paunch, an ye call me coward, by the Lord, I'll stab thee.

Fal. I call thee coward? I'll see thee damned ere I call thee coward, but I would give a thou- 150 sand pound I could run as fast as thou canst. You are straight enough in the shoulders; you care not who sees your back. Call you that backing of your friends? A plague upon such backing! Give me them that will face me. Give me a cup of sack. I am 155 a rogue if I drunk today.

Prince. O villain! thy lips are scarce wiped since thou drunkst last.

Fal. All is one for that. (*He drinketh.*) A plague of all cowards, still say I. 160

Prince. What's the matter?

Fal. What's the matter? There be four of us here have ta'en a thousand pound this day morning.

Prince. Where is it, Jack? where is it?

Fal. Where is it? Taken from us it is. A hun- 165 dred upon poor four of us!

Prince. What, a hundred, man?

Fal. I am a rogue if I were not at half-sword with a dozen of them two hours together. I have 'scaped by miracle. I am eight times thrust through 170 the doublet, four through the hose; my buckler cut through and through; my sword hacked like a handsaw—ecce signum! I never dealt better since I was a man. All would not do. A plague of all cowards! Let them speak. If they speak more or less 175 than truth, they are villains and the sons of darkness.

Prince. Speak, sirs. How was it?

Gad. We four set upon some dozen—

Fal. Sixteen at least, my lord.

Gad. And bound them. 180

Peto. No, no, they were not bound.

Fal. You rogue, they were bound, every man of them, or I am a Jew else—an Ebrew Jew.

Gad. As we were sharing, some six or seven fresh men set upon us— 185

Fal. And unbound the rest, and then come in the other.

Prince. What, fought you with them all?

Fal. All? I know not what you call all, but if I fought not with fifty of them, I am a bunch of 190 radish! If there were not two- or three-and-fifty upon poor old Jack, then am I no two-legged creature.

Prince. Pray God you have not murd'red some of them.

Fal. Nay, that's past praying for. I have 195 peppered two of them. Two I am sure I have paid, two rogues in buckram suits. I tell thee what, Hal—if I tell thee a lie, spit in my face, call me horse. Thou knowest my old ward. Here I lay, and thus I bore my point. Four rogues in buckram let drive at me. 200

Prince. What, four? Thou saidst but two even now.

Fal. Four, Hal. I told thee four.

Poins. Ay, ay, he said four.

Fal. These four came all afront and mainly thrust at me. I made me no more ado but took all 205 their seven points in my target, thus.

Prince. Seven? Why, there were but four even now.

Fal. In buckram?

Poins. Ay, four, in buckram suits. 210

Fal. Seven, by these hilts, or I am a villain else.

Prince. [*Aside to Poins*] Prithee let him alone. We shall have more anon.

Fal. Dost thou hear me, Hal?

Prince. Ay, and mark thee too, Jack. 215

Fal. Do so, for it is worth the list'ning to. These nine in buckram that I told thee of—

Prince. So, two more already.

Fal. Their points being broken—

Poins. Down fell their hose. 220

Fal. Began to give me ground; but I followed me close, came in, foot and hand, and with a thought seven of the eleven I paid.

Prince. O monstrous! Eleven buckram men grown out of two! 225

Fal. But, as the devil would have it, three misbe-

132. shotten: gutted; emptied of its roe
134. the while: the times
135. weaver: many weavers belonged to Puritanical sects, and their love of psalm-singing was proverbial.
159. All . . . that: that makes no difference
168. at half-sword: at swords' points
171. hose: breeches
173. dealt: fought

196. peppered: finished; **paid:** given their quietus; killed
198. horse: a contemptuous epithet
199. ward: defensive posture
204. afront: abreast; **mainly:** violently; cf. "with might and main"
206. target: shield
211. these hilts: the cross of a sword-hilt was often used to swear on.
215. mark: i.e., keep score; take note of the changing number of his assailants
219. points: a pun on another meaning of "points": laces that held breeches and hose together
222. a thought: the speed of thought

gotten knaves in Kendal green came at my back and let drive at me; for it was so dark, Hal, that thou couldst not see thy hand.

Prince. These lies are like their father that 230 begets them—gross as a mountain, open, palpable. Why, thou clay-brained guts, thou knotty-pated fool, thou whoreson obscene greasy tallow-catch—

Fal. What, art thou mad? art thou mad? Is not the truth the truth? 235

Prince. Why, how couldst thou know these men in Kendal green when it was so dark thou couldst not see thy hand? Come, tell us your reason. What sayest thou to this?

Poins. Come, your reason, Jack, your reason. 240

Fal. What, upon compulsion? Zounds, an I were at the strappado or all the racks in the world, I would not tell you on compulsion. Give you a reason on compulsion? If reasons were as plentiful as blackberries, I would give no man a reason upon 245 compulsion, I.

Prince. I'll be no longer guilty of this sin; this sanguine coward, this bed-presser, this horseback-breaker, this huge hill of flesh—

Fal. 'Sblood, you starveling, you eel-skin, 250 you dried neat's-tongue, you bull's pizzle, you stockfish—O for breath to utter what is like thee!—you tailor's yard, you sheath, you bowcase, you vile standing tuck!

Prince. Well, breathe awhile, and then to it 255 again; and when thou hast tired thyself in base comparisons, hear me speak but this.

Poins. Mark, Jack.

Prince. We two saw you four set on four, and bound them and were masters of their wealth. 260 Mark now how a plain tale shall put you down. Then did we two set on you four and with a word outfaced you from your prize, and have it; yea, and can show it you here in the house. And, Falstaff, you carried your guts away as nimbly, with as quick dex- 265 terity, and roared for mercy, and still run and roared, as ever I heard bullcalf. What a slave art thou to hack thy sword as thou hast done, and then say it was in fight! What trick, what device, what starting hole canst thou now find out to hide 270 thee from this open and apparent shame?

Poins. Come, let's hear, Jack. What trick hast thou now?

Fal. By the Lord, I knew ye as well as He that made ye. Why, hear you, my masters. Was it 275 for me to kill the heir apparent? Should I turn upon the true prince? Why, thou knowest I am as valiant as Hercules, but beware instinct. The lion will not touch the true prince. Instinct is a great matter. I was now a coward on instinct. I shall think the 280 better of myself, and thee, during my life—I for a valiant lion, and thou for a true prince. But, by the Lord, lads, I am glad you have the money. Hostess, clap to the doors. Watch tonight, pray tomorrow. Gallants, lads, boys, hearts of gold, all the titles of 285 good fellowship come to you! What, shall we be merry? Shall we have a play extempore?

Prince. Content—and the argument shall be thy running away.

Fal. Ah, no more of that, Hal, an thou 290 lovest me!

Enter HOSTESS.

Hos. O Jesu, my lord the Prince!

Prince. How now, my lady the hostess? What say'st thou to me?

Hos. Marry, my lord, there is a noble man 295 of the court at door would speak with you. He says he comes from your father.

Prince. Give him as much as will make him a royal man, and send him back again to my mother.

Fal. What manner of man is he? 300

Hos. An old man.

Fal. What doth gravity out of his bed at midnight? Shall I give him his answer?

Prince. Prithee do, Jack. 304

Fal. Faith, and I'll send him packing. *Exit.*

Prince. Now, sirs. By'r Lady, you fought fair; so did you, Peto; so did you, Bardolph. You are lions too, you ran away upon instinct, you will not touch the true prince; no—fie!

Bar. Faith, I ran when I saw others run. 310

Prince. Tell me now in earnest, how came Falstaff's sword so hacked?

Peto. Why, he hacked it with his dagger, and said he would swear truth out of England but he would make you believe it was done in fight, and per- 315 suaded us to do the like.

Bar. Yea, and to tickle our noses with speargrass to make them bleed, and then to beslubber our garments with it and swear it was the blood of true men. I did that I did not this seven year be- 320 fore—I blushed to hear his monstrous devices.

Prince. O villain! thou stolest a cup of sack eight-

227. Kendal green: cloth made in Kendal, Westmorland, traditionally the garb of Robin Hood and his men

232. knotty-pated: blockheaded

233. tallow-catch: ball of tallow

242. strappado: an instrument of torture

244. reasons: pun on "raisins"

248. sanguine coward: the sanguine man, according to the humors theory, was characterized by courage, optimism, and amorousness, but Falstaff displays only the latter two characteristics.

251–52. stockfish: dried cod

254. tuck: rapier

270. starting hole: refuge

284. Watch: stay up and make merry. Falstaff parodies Matt. 26:41.

298. royal: a coin worth ten shillings, while a **noble** was another coin, worth six shillings and eightpence

een years ago and wert taken with the manner, and ever since thou hast blushed extempore. Thou hadst fire and sword on thy side, and yet thou ran'st 325 away. What instinct hadst thou for it?

Bar. My lord, do you see these meteors? Do you behold these exhalations?

Prince. I do.

Bar. What think you they portend? 330

Prince. Hot livers and cold purses.

Bar. Choler, my lord, if rightly taken.

Prince. No, if rightly taken, halter.

[*Re-*]*enter* FALSTAFF.

Here comes lean Jack; here comes bare-bone. How now, my sweet creature of bombast? How 335 long is't ago, Jack, since thou sawest thine own knee?

Fal. My own knee? When I was about thy years, Hal, I was not an eagle's talent in the waist; I could have crept into any alderman's thumb-ring. A plague of sighing and grief! It blows a man up like a 340 bladder. There's villainous news abroad. Here was Sir John Bracy from your father. You must to the court in the morning. That same mad fellow of the North, Percy, and he of Wales that gave Amamon the bastinado, and made Lucifer cuckold, and 345 swore the devil his true liegeman upon the cross of a Welsh hook—what a plague call you him?

Poins. Owen Glendower.

Fal. Owen, Owen—the same; and his son-in-law Mortimer, and old Northumberland, and that 350 sprightly Scot of Scots, Douglas, that runs a-horseback up a hill perpendicular—

Prince. He that rides at high speed and with his pistol kills a sparrow flying.

Fal. You have hit it. 355

Prince. So did he never the sparrow.

Fal. Well, that rascal hath good metal in him; he will not run.

Prince. Why, what a rascal art thou then, to praise him so for running! 360

Fal. A-horseback, ye cuckoo! but afoot he will not budge a foot.

Prince. Yes, Jack, upon instinct.

Fal. I grant ye, upon instinct. Well, he is there too, and one Mordake, and a thousand bluecaps 365 more. Worcester is stol'n away tonight; thy father's beard is turned white with the news; you may buy land now as cheap as stinking mack'rel.

Prince. Why then, it is like, if there come a hot June, and this civil buffeting hold, we shall buy 370 maidenheads as they buy hobnails, by the hundreds.

Fal. By the mass, lad, thou sayest true; it is like we shall have good trading that way. But tell me, Hal, art not thou horrible afeard? Thou being heir apparent, could the world pick thee out three 375 such enemies again as that fiend Douglas, that spirit Percy, and that devil Glendower? Art thou not horribly afraid? Doth not thy blood thrill at it?

Prince. Not a whit, i' faith. I lack some of thy instinct. 380

Fal. Well, thou wilt be horribly chid tomorrow when thou comest to thy father. If thou love me, practice an answer.

Prince. Do thou stand for my father and examine me upon the particulars of my life. 385

Fal. Shall I? Content. This chair shall be my state, this dagger my scepter, and this cushion my crown.

Prince. Thy state is taken for a joined-stool, thy golden scepter for a leaden dagger, and thy precious rich crown for a pitiful bald crown. 390

Fal. Well, an the fire of grace be not quite out of thee, now shalt thou be moved. Give me a cup of sack to make my eyes look red, that it may be thought I have wept; for I must speak in passion, and I will do it in King Cambyses' vein. 395

Prince. Well, here is my leg.

Fal. And here is my speech. Stand aside, nobility.

Hos. O Jesu, this is excellent sport, i' faith!

Fal. Weep not, sweet queen, for trickling tears are vain. 400

Hos. O, the Father, how he holds his countenance!

Fal. For God's sake, lords, convey my tristful queen! For tears do stop the floodgates of her eyes.

Hos. O Jesu, he doth it as like one of these harlotry players as ever I see! 405

Fal. Peace, good pintpot. Peace, good ticklebrain. —Harry, I do not only marvel where thou spendest

323. with . . . manner: with stolen goods in hand
324. blushed extempore: had a permanently red face
327. meteors: red splotches on his face
328. exhalations: another name for meteors
331. Hot . . . purses: overindulgence in drink, which has heated the liver and emptied the purse
332. Choler: bile; **rightly taken:** understood correctly
333. No . . . halter: no; if apprehended, as he should be, the hangman's noose.
335. bombast: (1) cotton stuffing; (2) high-flown verbiage
338. talent: talon
344. Amamon: the name of a fiend
344–45. the bastinado: a beating
345. made . . . cuckold: gave Lucifer horns (by mating with his dam). Horns were the proverbial sign of a betrayed husband.
347. Welsh hook: pike-like weapon
357. rascal: a rascal deer was an inferior or immature specimen, not likely to provide the hounds with a good run. **metal:** (1) material; (2) spirit
365. bluecaps: Scots
370. hold: continue
386. state: chair of state
388. joined-stool: a stool so called because made by a joiner instead of a carpenter; a common article of household furniture
394. passion: grief
395. in . . . vein: in the vein of King Cambyses in Thomas Preston's drama *Cambyses, King of Persia* (1570)
396. leg: bow of homage
402. convey: remove; **tristful:** tearful
406. ticklebrain: slang for "liquor," hence a dealer in liquor

thy time, but also how thou art accompanied. For though the camomile, the more it is trodden on, the faster it grows, yet youth, the more it is 410 wasted, the sooner it wears. That thou art my son I have partly thy mother's word, partly my own opinion, but chiefly a villainous trick of thine eye and a foolish hanging of thy nether lip that doth warrant me. If then thou be son to me, here 415 lies the point: why, being son to me, art thou so pointed at? Shall the blessed sun of heaven prove a micher and eat blackberries? A question not to be asked. Shall the son of England prove a thief and take purses? A question to be asked. There is 420 a thing, Harry, which thou hast often heard of, and it is known to many in our land by the name of pitch. This pitch, as ancient writers do report, doth defile; so doth the company thou keepest. For, Harry, now I do not speak to thee in drink, but in tears; not 425 in pleasure, but in passion; not in words only, but in woes also: and yet there is a virtuous man whom I have often noted in thy company, but I know not his name.

Prince. What manner of man, an it like 430 your Majesty?

Fal. A goodly portly man, i' faith, and a corpulent; of a cheerful look, a pleasing eye, and a most noble carriage; and, as I think, his age some fifty, or, by'r Lady, inclining to threescore; and 435 now I remember me, his name is Falstaff. If that man should be lewdly given, he deceiveth me; for, Harry, I see virtue in his looks. If then the tree may be known by the fruit, as the fruit by the tree, then, peremptorily I speak it, there is virtue in that 440 Falstaff. Him keep with, the rest banish. And tell me now, thou naughty varlet, tell me where hast thou been this month?

Prince. Dost thou speak like a king? Do thou stand for me, and I'll play my father. 445

Fal. Depose me? If thou dost it half so gravely, so majestically, both in word and matter, hang me up by the heels for a rabbit-sucker, or a poulter's hare.

Prince. Well, here I am set. 450

Fal. And here I stand. Judge, my masters.

Prince. Now, Harry, whence come you?

Fal. My noble lord, from Eastcheap.

Prince. The complaints I hear of thee are grievous.

Fal. 'Sblood, my lord, they are false! 455

[*Aside*] Nay, I'll tickle ye for a young prince, i' faith.

Prince. Swearest thou, ungracious boy? Henceforth ne'er look on me. Thou art violently carried away from grace. There is a devil haunts thee 460 in the likeness of an old fat man; a tun of man is thy companion. Why dost thou converse with that trunk of humors, that bolting hutch of beastliness, that swoll'n parcel of dropsies, that huge bombard of sack, that stuffed cloakbag of guts, that 465 roasted Manningtree ox with the pudding in his belly, that reverend Vice, that grey Iniquity, that father Ruffian, that Vanity in years? Wherein is he good, but to taste sack and drink it? wherein neat and cleanly, but to carve a capon and eat it? 470 wherein cunning, but in craft? wherein crafty, but in villainy? wherein villainous, but in all things? wherein worthy, but in nothing?

Fal. I would your Grace would take me with you. Whom means your Grace? 475

Prince. That villainous abominable misleader of youth, Falstaff, that old white-bearded Satan.

Fal. My lord, the man I know.

Prince. I know thou dost.

Fal. But to say I know more harm in him 480 than in myself were to say more than I know. That he is old (the more the pity), his white hairs do witness it; but that he is (saving your reverence) a whoremaster, that I utterly deny. If sack and sugar be a fault, God help the wicked! If to be 485 old and merry be a sin, then many an old host that I know is damned. If to be fat be to be hated, then Pharaoh's lean kine are to be loved. No, my good lord: banish Peto, banish Bardolph, banish Poins; but for sweet Jack Falstaff, kind Jack Falstaff, 490 true Jack Falstaff, valiant Jack Falstaff, and therefore more valiant being, as he is, old Jack Falstaff, banish not him thy Harry's company, banish not him thy Harry's company. Banish plump Jack, and banish all the world! 495

Prince. I do, I will. [*A knocking heard.*]

[*Exeunt Hostess, Francis, and Bardolph.*]

Enter BARDOLPH, *running.*

408–11. For . . . wears: proverbial
415. warrant: assure
418. micher: truant
423. pitch . . . defile: Ecclus. 13:1
426. pleasure: sport; **passion:** sorrow
430. like: please
432. goodly: attractive; **portly:** dignified
438–39. If . . . tree: Matt. 12:33
440. peremptorily: without fear of contradiction
448. rabbit-sucker: suckling rabbit; **poulter's:** poultry dealer's
458. ungracious: wicked
462. converse: associate
463. humors: unhealthy fluids; **bolting hutch:** large bin into which grain was sifted
464. bombard: (1) leather tankard; (2) toper
466. Manningtree ox: prime beef carcass roasted whole at annual fairs at Manningtree, Essex
467–68. Vice . . . Iniquity . . . Ruffian: traditional personifications in morality plays. **Ruffian** was a slang term for the devil.
468. Vanity . . . years: elderly Vanity (another morality character), the personification of worldliness
469–70. neat . . . cleanly: precise and skillful
471. cunning: clever
474. take . . . you: let me understand you
483. saving . . . reverence: begging your pardon

Bar. O, my lord, my lord! the sheriff with a most monstrous watch is at the door.

Fal. Out, ye rogue! Play out the play. I have much to say in the behalf of that Falstaff. 500

Enter the HOSTESS.

Hos. O Jesu, my lord, my lord!

Prince. Heigh, heigh, the devil rides upon a fiddlestick! What's the matter?

Hos. The sheriff and all the watch are at the door. They are come to search the house. Shall I let 505 them in?

Fal. Dost thou hear, Hal? Never call a true piece of gold a counterfeit. Thou art essentially mad without seeming so.

Prince. And thou a natural coward without 510 instinct.

Fal. I deny your major. If you will deny the sheriff, so; if not, let him enter. If I become not a cart as well as another man, a plague on my bringing up! I hope I shall as soon be strangled with a 515 halter as another.

Prince. Go hide thee behind the arras. The rest walk up above. Now, my masters, for a true face and good conscience.

Fal. Both which I have had; but their date 520 is out, and therefore I'll hide me. *Exit.*

Prince. Call in the sheriff.

[*Exeunt all but the Prince and Peto.*]

Enter SHERIFF *and the* CARRIER.

Now, master sheriff, what is your will with me?

Sher. First, pardon me, my lord. A hue and cry
Hath followed certain men unto this house. 525

Prince. What men?

Sher. One of them is well known, my gracious lord—
A gross fat man.

Car. As fat as butter.

Prince. The man, I do assure you, is not here,
For I myself at this time have employed him. 530
And, sheriff, I will engage my word to thee
That I will by tomorrow dinnertime
Send him to answer thee, or any man,
For anything he shall be charged withal;
And so let me entreat you leave the house. 535

Sher. I will, my lord. There are two gentlemen
Have in this robbery lost three hundred marks.

Prince. It may be so. If he have robbed these men,
He shall be answerable; and so farewell.

Sher. Good night, my noble lord. 540

Prince. I think it is good morrow, is it not?

Sher. Indeed, my lord, I think it be two o'clock.

Exit [*with Carrier*].

Prince. This oily rascal is known as well as Paul's. Go call him forth.

Peto. Falstaff! Fast asleep behind the 545 arras, and snorting like a horse.

Prince. Hark how hard he fetches breath. Search his pockets.

He searcheth his pockets and findeth certain papers.

What hast thou found?

Peto. Nothing but papers, my lord. 550

Prince. Let's see what they be. Read them.

Peto. [*Reads*]			
	Item, A capon . .	ii *s.* ii *d.*	
	Item, Sauce . . .	iiii *d.*	
	Item, Sack two gallons	v *s.* viii *d.*	
	Item, Anchovies and sack after supper .	ii *s.* vi *d.*	555
	Item, Bread . . .	*ob.*	

Prince. O monstrous! but one halfpennyworth of bread to this intolerable deal of sack! What there is else, keep close; we'll read it at more ad- 560 vantage. There let him sleep till day. I'll to the court in the morning. We must all to the wars, and thy place shall be honorable. I'll procure this fat rogue a charge of foot, and I know his death will be a march of twelve score. The money shall be paid back 565 again with advantage. Be with me betimes in the morning, and so good morrow, Peto.

Peto. Good morrow, good my lord.

Exeunt.

498. watch: company of watchmen
502–3. the . . . fiddlestick: here's a to-do; proverbial
512. major: major premise
513. so: well and good
514. cart: i.e., hurdle to carry him to the gallows
517. arras: wall hanging
531. engage: pledge
543. Paul's: St. Paul's Cathedral
557. ob.: halfpenny; abbreviation for the Greek *obolus*
560. close: safe; **at . . . advantage:** at a more opportune time
564. charge . . . foot: command of a foot company
566. advantage: addition; interest; **betimes:** early

ACT III

Scene I. [*Bangor, Wales. The Archdeacon's house.*]

Enter HOTSPUR, WORCESTER, LORD MORTIMER, OWEN GLENDOWER.

Mor. These promises are fair, the parties sure,
And our induction full of prosperous hope.
Hot. Lord Mortimer, and cousin Glendower,
Will you sit down?
And uncle Worcester. A plague upon it! 5
I have forgot the map.
Glen. No, here it is. Sit, cousin Percy;
Sit, good cousin Hotspur, for by that name
As oft as Lancaster doth speak of you,
His cheek looks pale, and with a rising sigh 10
He wisheth you in heaven.
Hot. And you in hell, as oft as he hears Owen
Glendower spoke of.
Glen. I cannot blame him. At my nativity
The front of heaven was full of fiery shapes 15
Of burning cressets, and at my birth
The frame and huge foundation of the earth
Shaked like a coward.
Hot. Why, so it would have done at the same season if your mother's cat had but kittened, 20
though yourself had never been born.
Glen. I say the earth did shake when I was born.
Hot. And I say the earth was not of my mind,
If you suppose as fearing you it shook.
Glen. The heavens were all on fire, the earth did tremble. 25
Hot. O, then the earth shook to see the heavens on fire,
And not in fear of your nativity.
Diseased nature oftentimes breaks forth
In strange eruptions; oft the teeming earth
Is with a kind of colic pinched and vexed 30
By the imprisoning of unruly wind
Within her womb, which, for enlargement striving,
Shakes the old beldame earth and topples down
Steeples and mossgrown towers. At your birth
Our grandam earth, having this distemp'rature, 35
In passion shook.
Glen. Cousin, of many men
I do not bear these crossings. Give me leave
To tell you once again that at my birth
The front of heaven was full of fiery shapes, 39
The goats ran from the mountains, and the herds
Were strangely clamorous to the frighted fields.
These signs have marked me extraordinary,
And all the courses of my life do show
I am not in the roll of common men.
Where is he living, clipped in with the sea 45
That chides the banks of England, Scotland, Wales,
Which calls me pupil or hath read to me?
And bring him out that is but woman's son
Can trace me in the tedious ways of art
And hold me pace in deep experiments. 50
Hot. I think there's no man speaks better Welsh.
I'll to dinner.
Mor. Peace, cousin Percy; you will make him mad.
Glen. I can call spirits from the vasty deep.
Hot. Why, so can I, or so can any man; 55
But will they come when you do call for them?
Glen. Why, I can teach you, cousin, to command
the devil.
Hot. And I can teach thee, coz, to shame the devil— 59
By telling truth. Tell truth and shame the devil.
If thou have power to raise him, bring him hither,
And I'll be sworn I have power to shame him hence.
O, while you live, tell truth and shame the devil!
Mor. Come, come, no more of this unprofitable
chat. 65
Glen. Three times hath Harry Bolingbroke made head
Against my power; thrice from the banks of Wye
And sandy-bottomed Severn have I sent him
Bootless home and weather-beaten back. 69

2. induction: preliminary action; **prosperous hope:** expectation of success
9. Lancaster: another name for the King, whose inheritance was the Duchy of Lancaster
15. front: forehead
16. cressets: torches
32. enlargement: release
35. distemp'rature: disorder
36. passion: great distress
45. clipped . . . with: encompassed by
46. chides: beats against
47. read . . . me: given me lessons
49. trace me: keep up with me; **tedious:** painful; **art:** magic
50. hold . . . pace: keep pace with me; **deep:** occult
51. speaks . . . Welsh: i.e., is such a braggart
54. vasty deep: limitless infernal depths
66. made head: raised an army
69. Bootless: profitlessly

Hot. Home without boots, and in foul weather too?
How 'scapes he agues, in the devil's name?
Glen. Come, here is the map. Shall we divide our right
According to our threefold order ta'en?
Mor. The Archdeacon hath divided it
Into three limits very equally. 75
England, from Trent and Severn hitherto,
By south and east is to my part assigned;
All westward, Wales beyond the Severn shore,
And all the fertile land within that bound,
To Owen Glendower; and, dear coz, to you 80
The remnant northward lying off from Trent.
And our indentures tripartite are drawn,
Which being sealed interchangeably
(A business that this night may execute),
Tomorrow, cousin Percy, you and I 85
And my good Lord of Worcester will set forth
To meet your father and the Scottish power,
As is appointed us, at Shrewsbury.
My father Glendower is not ready yet,
Nor shall we need his help these fourteen days. 90
[*To Glendower*] Within that space you may have drawn together
Your tenants, friends, and neighboring gentlemen.
Glen. A shorter time shall send me to you, lords;
And in my conduct shall your ladies come,
From whom you now must steal and take no leave,
For there will be a world of water shed 96
Upon the parting of your wives and you.
Hot. Methinks my moiety, north from Burton here,
In quantity equals not one of yours.
See how this river comes me cranking in 100
And cuts me from the best of all my land
A huge half-moon, a monstrous cantle out.
I'll have the current in this place dammed up,
And here the smug and silver Trent shall run
In a new channel fair and evenly. 105
It shall not wind with such a deep indent.
To rob me of so rich a bottom here.
Glen. Not wind? It shall, it must! You see it doth.
Mor. Yea, but
Mark how he bears his course, and runs me up 110
With like advantage on the other side,
Gelding the opposed continent as much
As on the other side it takes from you.
Wor. Yea, but a little charge will trench him here
And on this north side win this cape of land; 115
And then he runs straight and even.
Hot. I'll have it so. A little charge will do it.
Glen. I will not have it alt'red.
Hot. Will not you?
Glen. No, nor you shall not.
Hot. Who shall say me nay?
Glen. Why, that will I. 120
Hot. Let me not understand you then; speak it in Welsh.
Glen. I can speak English, lord, as well as you;
For I was trained up in the English court,
Where, being but young, I framed to the harp
Many an English ditty lovely well, 125
And gave the tongue a helpful ornament—
A virtue that was never seen in you.
Hot. Marry, and I am glad of it with all my heart!
I had rather be a kitten and cry mew
Than one of these same meter ballet-mongers. 130
I had rather hear a brazen canstick turned
Or a dry wheel grate on the axletree,
And that would set my teeth nothing on edge,
Nothing so much as mincing poetry:
'Tis like the forced gait of a shuffling nag. 135
Glen. Come, you shall have Trent turned.
Hot. I do not care. I'll give thrice so much land
To any well-deserving friend;
But in the way of bargain, mark ye me,
I'll cavil on the ninth part of a hair. 140
Are the indentures drawn? Shall we be gone?
Glen. The moon shines fair; you may away by night.
I'll haste the writer, and withal
Break with your wives of your departure hence.
I am afraid my daughter will run mad, 145
So much she doteth on her Mortimer. *Exit.*
Mor. Fie, cousin Percy! how you cross my father!
Hot. I cannot choose. Sometimes he angers me
With telling me of the moldwarp and the ant,
Of the dreamer Merlin and his prophecies, 150
And of a dragon and a finless fish,
A clip-winged griffin and a molten raven,
A couching lion and a ramping cat,

72. **right:** title; legal right in territory
73. **our . . . ta'en:** the threefold division on which we have agreed
76. **hitherto:** to this point
81. **lying off:** extending
82. **indentures tripartite:** threefold agreements
83. **sealed interchangeably:** mutually confirmed
87. **father:** father-in-law
94. **conduct:** escort
98. **moiety:** portion
100. **cranking:** twisting
102. **cantle:** section
104. **smug:** trim; neat
105. **fair . . . evenly:** smoothly and straightly
107. **bottom:** bottom land
112. **continent:** boundary; shore line
114. **a . . . here:** with a little expense, a new channel can be cut
126. **gave . . . ornament:** graced the English language
127. **virtue:** excellence
130. **meter ballet-mongers:** rhymesters
131. **canstick:** candlestick
144. **Break with:** inform
149. **moldwarp:** "earth-thrower," the mole
150. **Merlin:** the Arthurian magician
153. **couching:** crouching; **ramping:** rampant

And such a deal of skimble-skamble stuff
As puts me from my faith. I tell you what—
He held me last night at least nine hours 156
In reckoning up the several devils' names
That were his lackeys. I cried "hum," and "Well, go to!"
But marked him not a word. O, he is as tedious
As a tired horse, a railing wife; 160
Worse than a smoky house. I had rather live
With cheese and garlic in a windmill far
Than feed on cates and have him talk to me
In any summerhouse in Christendom.

Mor. In faith, he is a worthy gentleman, 165
Exceedingly well read, and profited
In strange concealments, valiant as a lion,
And wondrous affable, and as bountiful
As mines of India. Shall I tell you, cousin?
He holds your temper in a high respect 170
And curbs himself even of his natural scope
When you come 'cross his humor. Faith, he does.
I warrant you that man is not alive
Might so have tempted him as you have done
Without the taste of danger and reproof. 175
But do not use it oft, let me entreat you.

Wor. In faith, my lord, you are too willful-blame,
And since your coming hither have done enough
To put him quite besides his patience. 179
You must needs learn, lord, to amend this fault.
Though sometimes it show greatness, courage, blood—
And that's the dearest grace it renders you—
Yet oftentimes it doth present harsh rage,
Defect of manners, want of government,
Pride, haughtiness, opinion, and disdain; 185
The least of which haunting a nobleman
Loseth men's hearts, and leaves behind a stain
Upon the beauty of all parts besides,
Beguiling them of commendation.

Hot. Well, I am schooled. Good manners be your speed! 190
Here come our wives, and let us take our leave.

Enter GLENDOWER *with the* LADIES.

Mor. This is the deadly spite that angers me—
My wife can speak no English, I no Welsh.

Glen. My daughter weeps; she will not part with you;
She'll be a soldier too, she'll to the wars. 195

Mor. Good father, tell her that she and my aunt Percy
Shall follow in your conduct speedily.

Glendower speaks to her in Welsh, and she answers him in the same.

Glen. She is desperate here. A peevish self-willed harlotry,
One that no persuasion can do good upon. 199

The Lady speaks in Welsh.

Mor. I understand thy looks. That pretty Welsh
Which thou pourest down from these swelling heavens
I am too perfect in; and, but for shame,
In such a parley should I answer thee.

The Lady again in Welsh.

I understand thy kisses, and thou mine,
And that's a feeling disputation. 205
But I will never be a truant, love,
Till I have learnt thy language; for thy tongue
Makes Welsh as sweet as ditties highly penned,
Sung by a fair queen in a summer's bow'r,
With ravishing division, to her lute. 210

Glen. Nay, if you melt, then will she run mad.

The Lady speaks again in Welsh.

Mor. O, I am ignorance itself in this!

Glen. She bids you on the wanton rushes lay you down
And rest your gentle head upon her lap,
And she will sing the song that pleaseth you 215
And on your eyelids crown the god of sleep,
Charming your blood with pleasing heaviness,
Making such difference 'twixt wake and sleep
As is the difference betwixt day and night
The hour before the heavenly-harnessed team 220
Begins his golden progress in the east.

Mor. With all my heart I'll sit and hear her sing.
By that time will our book, I think, be drawn.

Glen. Do so,
And those musicians that shall play to you 225
Hang in the air a thousand leagues from hence,
And straight they shall be here. Sit, and attend.

Hot. Come, Kate, thou art perfect in lying down.

154. skimble-skamble: scrambled; nonsensical
160. railing: scolding
163. cates: imported dainties
166. profited: proficient
167. concealments: mysteries
172. come . . . humor: disagree with him
175. danger . . . reproof: dangerous reproof (as example of hendiadys)
177. willful-blame: at fault for willfulness
179. besides: beyond
181. blood: fiery spirit
182. dearest grace: highest honor
184. government: self-control
185. opinion: self-conceit
188. parts: qualities
189. Beguiling: cheating
190. I . . . schooled: you have read me a lesson; **be . . . speed:** bring you prosperity

192. spite: annoyance
198. desperate: recklessly determined; **here:** on this point; **peevish:** obstinate; **harlotry:** wench
200. That . . . Welsh: i.e., tears
203. In . . . parley: in the same language
205. feeling disputation: stirring discourse
210. division: melody
213. wanton: luxuriant; **rushes:** used as a floor covering
217. blood: senses
223. our book: the tripartite indenture

Come, quick, quick, that I may lay my head in thy lap. 230

Lady P. Go, ye giddy goose. *The music plays.*

Hot. Now I perceive the devil understands Welsh;
And 'tis no marvel, he is so humorous.
By'r Lady, he is a good musician.

Lady P. Then should you be nothing but 235
musical, for you are altogether governed by humors.
Lie still, ye thief, and hear the lady sing in Welsh.

Hot. I had rather hear Lady, my brach, howl in Irish.

Lady P. Wouldst thou have thy head 240
broken?

Hot. No.

Lady P. Then be still.

Hot. Neither! 'Tis a woman's fault.

Lady P. Now God help thee! 245

Hot. To the Welsh lady's bed.

Lady P. What's that?

Hot. Peace! she sings.

Here the Lady sings a Welsh song.

Come, Kate, I'll have your song too.

Lady P. Not mine, in good sooth. 250

Hot. Not yours, in good sooth? Heart! you swear like a comfit-maker's wife. "Not you, in good sooth!" and "as true as I live!" and "as God shall mend me!" and "as sure as day!"
And givest such sarcenet surety for thy oaths 255
As if thou never walkst further than Finsbury.
Swear me, Kate, like a lady as thou art,
A good mouth-filling oath, and leave "in sooth"
And such protest of pepper gingerbread
To velvet guards and Sunday citizens. 260
Come, sing.

Lady P. I will not sing.

Hot. 'Tis the next way to turn tailor or be redbreast-teacher. An the indentures be drawn, I'll away within these two hours; and so come in when 265
ye will. *Exit.*

Glen. Come, come, Lord Mortimer. You are as slow
As hot Lord Percy is on fire to go.
By this our book is drawn; we'll but seal,
And then to horse immediately.

Mor. With all my heart. 270

Exeunt.

233. **humorous:** whimsical
238. **brach:** bitch
244. **'Tis . . . fault:** I will imitate a woman in perversity.
252. **comfit-maker's:** confectioner's
255. **sarcenet:** a fine silk; hence flimsy
256. **Finsbury:** Finsbury Fields, an area north of London where common folk went for recreation
259. **protest . . . gingerbread:** delicately spiced oaths
260. **velvet . . . citizens:** i.e., citizens whose idea of Sunday best is a garment trimmed with velvet braid
263. **tailor:** tailors, like weavers, were famed for their singing.

Scene II. [*London. The palace.*]

Enter the KING, PRINCE OF WALES, *and others.*

King. Lords, give us leave: the Prince of Wales and I
Must have some private conference; but be near at hand,
For we shall presently have need of you.

Exeunt Lords.

I know not whether God will have it so
For some displeasing service I have done, 5
That, in his secret doom, out of my blood
He'll breed revengement and a scourge for me;
But thou dost in thy passages of life
Make me believe that thou art only marked
For the hot vengeance and the rod of heaven 10
To punish my mistreadings. Tell me else,
Could such inordinate and low desires,
Such poor, such bare, such lewd, such mean attempts,
Such barren pleasures, rude society,
As thou art matched withal and grafted to, 15
Accompany the greatness of thy blood
And hold their level with thy princely heart?

Prince. So please your Majesty, I would I could
Quit all offenses with as clear excuse
As well as I am doubtless I can purge 20
Myself of many I am charged withal.
Yet such extenuation let me beg
As, in reproof of many tales devised,
Which oft the ear of greatness needs must hear
By smiling pickthanks and base newsmongers, 25
I may, for some things true wherein my youth
Hath faulty wand'red and irregular,
Find pardon on my true submission.

King. God pardon thee! Yet let me wonder, Harry,
At thy affections, which do hold a wing 30
Quite from the flight of all thy ancestors.
Thy place in council thou hast rudely lost,
Which by thy younger brother is supplied,
And art almost an alien to the hearts
Of all the court and princes of my blood. 35

8. **thy . . . life:** your general conduct
9–10. **marked/For:** intended to be
12. **inordinate:** disorderly; unbecoming one of your rank
13. **lewd:** base, not specifically lascivious; **attempts:** pursuits
15. **matched:** associated; **grafted:** unnaturally attached
17. **hold . . . level:** accord
19. **Quit:** acquit myself of
22. **extenuation:** forgiveness
23. **reproof:** disproof
25. **pickthanks:** persons who curry favor by talebearing
28. **submission:** confession
30. **affections:** inclinations; **hold . . . wing:** fly a course
32. **rudely:** violently. Holinshed reports that the Prince struck the Chief Justice because he had imprisoned a friend and was dismissed from the Council for his action.

The hope and expectation of thy time
Is ruined, and the soul of every man
Prophetically do forethink thy fall.
Had I so lavish of my presence been,
So common-hackneyed in the eyes of men, 40
So stale and cheap to vulgar company,
Opinion, that did help me to the crown,
Had still kept loyal to possession
And left me in reputeless banishment,
A fellow of no mark nor likelihood. 45
By being seldom seen, I could not stir
But, like a comet, I was wond'red at;
That men would tell their children, "This is he!"
Others would say, "Where? Which is Bolingbroke?"
And then I stole all courtesy from heaven, 50
And dressed myself in such humility
That I did pluck allegiance from men's hearts,
Loud shouts and salutations from their mouths
Even in the presence of the crowned King.
Thus did I keep my person fresh and new, 55
My presence, like a robe pontifical,
Ne'er seen but wond'red at; and so my state,
Seldom but sumptuous, showed like a feast
And won by rareness such solemnity.
The skipping King, he ambled up and down 60
With shallow jesters and rash bavin wits,
Soon kindled and soon burnt; carded his state;
Mingled his royalty with capering fools;
Had his great name profaned with their scorns
And gave his countenance, against his name, 65
To laugh at gibing boys and stand the push
Of every beardless vain comparative;
Grew a companion to the common streets,
Enfeoffed himself to popularity;
That, being daily swallowed by men's eyes, 70
They surfeited with honey and began
To loathe the taste of sweetness, whereof a little
More than a little is by much too much.
So, when he had occasion to be seen,
He was but as the cuckoo is in June, 75
Heard, not regarded—seen, but with such eyes
As, sick and blunted with community,
Afford no extraordinary gaze,
Such as is bent on sunlike majesty
When it shines seldom in admiring eyes; 80
But rather drowsed and hung their eyelids down,
Slept in his face, and rend'red such aspect
As cloudy men use to their adversaries,
Being with his presence glutted, gorged, and full.
And in that very line, Harry, standst thou; 85
For thou hast lost thy princely privilege
With vile participation. Not an eye
But is aweary of thy common sight,
Save mine, which hath desired to see thee more;
Which now doth that I would not have it do— 90
Make blind itself with foolish tenderness.

Prince. I shall hereafter, my thrice-gracious lord,
Be more myself.

King. For all the world
As thou art to this hour was Richard then
When I from France set foot at Ravenspurgh; 95
And even as I was then is Percy now.
Now, by my scepter, and my soul to boot,
He hath more worthy interest to the state
Than thou, the shadow of succession;
For of no right, nor color like to right, 100
He doth fill fields with harness in the realm,
Turns head against the lion's armed jaws,
And, being no more in debt to years than thou,
Leads ancient lords and reverend bishops on
To bloody battles and to bruising arms. 105
What never-dying honor hath he got
Against renowned Douglas! whose high deeds,
Whose hot incursions and great name in arms
Holds from all soldiers chief majority
And military title capital 110
Through all the kingdoms that acknowledge Christ.
Thrice hath this Hotspur, Mars in swathling clothes,
This infant warrior, in his enterprises
Discomfited great Douglas; ta'en him once,
Enlarged him, and made a friend of him, 115
To fill the mouth of deep defiance up
And shake the peace and safety of our throne.
And what say you to this? Percy, Northumberland,
The Archbishop's Grace of York, Douglas, Mortimer
Capitulate against us and are up. 120
But wherefore do I tell these news to thee?
Why, Harry, do I tell thee of my foes,
Which art my nearest and dearest enemy?

50. stole . . . heaven: assumed a saintly modesty
57. state: royal pomp
58. showed . . . feast: appeared festive
59. solemnity: awesome dignity
60. skipping: frivolous
61. bavin: easily kindled. A **bavin** is a bundle of brushwood.
62. carded: debased
65. countenance: (1) face; (2) favor; patronage; **against . . . name:** contrary to regal dignity
67. vain: foolish; **comparative:** satirist
69. Enfeoffed: gave himself entirely, a legal term; **popularity:** vulgar company
77. community: frequent association
82. rend'red . . . aspect: looked upon him
83. cloudy: frowning
85. line: position
87. vile participation: base association
98. interest: legal right
99. shadow . . . succession: immediate heir apparent
100. color: pretext
101. harness: armored men
102. Turns head: leads an army
103. no . . . thou: this is unhistorical; Hotspur was actually older even than the King.
109–10. Holds . . . capital: is acknowledged the most eminent warrior
112. swathling: swaddling
115. Enlarged: freed
116. To . . . up: to make a noisier show of defiance
120. Capitulate: come to agreement; **up:** in revolt

Thou that art like enough, through vassal fear,
Base inclination, and the start of spleen, 125
To fight against me under Percy's pay,
To dog his heels and curtsy at his frowns,
To show how much thou art degenerate.

Prince. Do not think so. You shall not find it so.
And God forgive them that so much have swayed
Your Majesty's good thoughts away from me. 131
I will redeem all this on Percy's head
And, in the closing of some glorious day,
Be bold to tell you that I am your son,
When I will wear a garment all of blood, 135
And stain my favors in a bloody mask,
Which, washed away, shall scour my shame with it.
And that shall be the day, whene'er it lights,
That this same child of honor and renown,
This gallant Hotspur, this all-praised knight, 140
And your unthought-of Harry chance to meet.
For every honor sitting on his helm,
Would they were multitudes, and on my head
My shames redoubled! For the time will come
That I shall make this northern youth exchange
His glorious deeds for my indignities. 146
Percy is but my factor, good my lord,
To engross up glorious deeds on my behalf;
And I will call him to so strict account
That he shall render every glory up, 150
Yea, even the slightest worship of his time,
Or I will tear the reckoning from his heart.
This in the name of God I promise here;
The which if He be pleased I shall perform,
I do beseech your Majesty may salve 155
The long-grown wounds of my intemperance.
If not, the end of life cancels all bands,
And I will die a hundred thousand deaths
Ere break the smallest parcel of this vow. 159

King. A hundred thousand rebels die in this!
Thou shalt have charge and sovereign trust herein.

Enter BLUNT.

How now, good Blunt? Thy looks are full of speed.

Blunt. So hath the business that I come to speak of.
Lord Mortimer of Scotland hath sent word
That Douglas and the English rebels met 165
The eleventh of this month at Shrewsbury.
A mighty and a fearful head they are,
If promises be kept on every hand,
As ever off'red foul play in a state.

King. The Earl of Westmorland set forth today;
With him my son, Lord John of Lancaster; 171
For this advertisement is five days old.
On Wednesday next, Harry, you shall set forward;
On Thursday we ourselves will march. Our meeting
Is Bridgenorth; and, Harry, you shall march 175
Through Gloucestershire; by which account,
Our business valued, some twelve days hence
Our general forces at Bridgenorth shall meet.
Our hands are full of business. Let's away:
Advantage feeds him fat while men delay. 180

Exeunt.

124. **vassal:** ignoble
125. **start . . . spleen:** rash impulse
136. **favors:** features
141. **unthought-of:** unvalued
146. **indignities:** shames
147. **factor:** agent
148. **engross up:** monopolize
151. **worship:** honor
156. **intemperance:** disorder
157. **bands:** bonds; obligations
159. **parcel:** portion
161. **charge:** command; **sovereign trust:** supreme responsibility
164. **Lord Mortimer:** actually, George Dunbar, the Scottish Earl of March. Shakespeare has given him the family name of the English Earls of March. The border of England and Scotland was known as the Scottish March, hence the title.
172. **advertisement:** information
177. **Our . . . value:** weighing the time necessary for our business
180. **Advantage . . . delay:** we lose the edge of opportunity by delay.

Scene III. [*London. The Boar's Head Tavern.*]

Enter FALSTAFF *and* BARDOLPH.

Fal. Bardolph, am I not fall'n away vilely since this last action? Do I not bate? Do I not dwindle? Why, my skin hangs about me like an old lady's loose gown! I am withered like an old applejohn. Well, I'll repent, and that suddenly, while I am in 5 some liking. I shall be out of heart shortly, and then I shall have no strength to repent. An I have not forgotten what the inside of a church is made of, I am a peppercorn, a brewer's horse. The inside of a church! Company, villainous company, hath 10 been the spoil of me.

Bar. Sir John, you are so fretful you cannot live long.

Fal. Why, there is it! Come, sing me a bawdy song; make me merry. I was as virtuously given as 15 a gentleman need to be, virtuous enough: swore little, diced not above seven times a week, went to a bawdy house not above once in a quarter of an hour, paid money that I borrowed three or four times, lived well, and in good compass; and now I live out 20 of all order, out of all compass.

Bar. Why, you are so fat, Sir John, that you must needs be out of all compass—out of all reasonable compass, Sir John.

Fal. Do thou amend thy face, and I'll amend 25

2. **bate:** abate; shrink
4. **applejohn:** an apple that was dried to improve its flavor
5-6. **in . . . liking:** (1) somewhat inclined (to repent); (2) fairly robust
20. **in . . . compass:** moderately

my life. Thou art our admiral, thou bearest the lantern in the poop—but 'tis in the nose of thee. Thou art the Knight of the Burning Lamp.

Bar. Why, Sir John, my face does you no harm.

Fal. No, I'll be sworn. I make as good use of 30 it as many a man doth of a death's-head or a memento mori. I never see thy face but I think upon hellfire and Dives that lived in purple; for there he is in his robes, burning, burning. If thou wert any way given to virtue, I would swear by thy face; my 35 oath should be "By this fire, that's God's angel." But thou art altogether given over, and wert indeed, but for the light in thy face, the son of utter darkness. When thou ranst up Gad's Hill in the night to catch my horse, if I did not think thou hadst been an 40 ignis fatuus or a ball of wildfire, there's no purchase in money. O, thou art a perpetual triumph, an everlasting bonfire-light! Thou hast saved me a thousand marks in links and torches, walking with thee in the night betwixt tavern and tavern; but the sack 45 that thou hast drunk me would have bought me lights as good cheap at the dearest chandler's in Europe. I have maintained that salamander of yours with fire any time this two-and-thirty years. God reward me for it! 50

Bar. 'Sblood, I would my face were in your belly!

Fal. God-a-mercy! so should I be sure to be heartburned.

Enter Hostess.

How now, Dame Partlet the hen? Have you inquired yet who picked my pocket? 55

Hos. Why, Sir John, what do you think, Sir John? Do you think I keep thieves in my house? I have searched, I have inquired, so has my husband, man by man, boy by boy, servant by servant. The tithe of a hair was never lost in my house before. 60

Fal. Ye lie, hostess. Bardolph was shaved and lost many a hair, and I'll be sworn my pocket was picked. Go to, you are a woman, go!

Hos. Who, I? No; I defy thee! God's light, I was never called so in mine own house before! 65

Fal. Go to, I know you well enough.

Hos. No, Sir John; you do not know me, Sir John. I know you, Sir John. You owe me money, Sir John, and now you pick a quarrel to beguile me of it. I bought you a dozen of shirts to your back. 70

Fal. Dowlas, filthy dowlas! I have given them away to bakers' wives; they have made bolters of them.

Hos. Now, as I am a true woman, holland of eight shillings an ell. You owe money here besides, 75 Sir John, for your diet and by-drinkings, and money lent you, four-and-twenty pound.

Fal. He had his part of it; let him pay.

Hos. He? Alas, he is poor; he hath nothing.

Fal. How? Poor? Look upon his face. What 80 call you rich? Let them coin his nose, let them coin his cheeks. I'll not pay a denier. What, will you make a younker of me? Shall I not take mine ease in mine inn but I shall have my pocket picked? I have lost a seal-ring of my grandfather's worth forty mark. 85

Hos. O Jesu, I have heard the Prince tell him, I know not how oft, that that ring was copper!

Fal. How? the Prince is a Jack, a sneak-up. 'Sblood, an he were here, I would cudgel him like a dog if he would say so. 90

Enter the Prince [*and* Peto], *marching, and* Falstaff *meets them, playing upon his truncheon like a fife.*

How now, lad? Is the wind in that door, i' faith? Must we all march?

Bar. Yea, two and two, Newgate fashion.

Hos. My lord, I pray you hear me.

Prince. What sayst thou, Mistress Quickly? 95 How doth thy husband? I love him well; he is an honest man.

Hos. Good my lord, hear me.

Fal. Prithee let her alone and list to me.

Prince. What sayst thou, Jack? 100

Fal. The other night I fell asleep here behind the arras and had my pocket picked. This house is turned bawdy house; they pick pockets.

Prince. What didst thou lose, Jack?

Fal. Wilt thou believe me, Hal, three or 105 four bonds of forty pound apiece and a seal-ring of my grandfather's.

26. admiral: flagship
31–32. memento mori: reminder of death in the form of a skull, often the device of a ring
33. Dives: Luke 16:19–31
36. By . . . angel: Psalms 104:4
37. altogether . . . over: completely abandoned to vice
42. triumph: illuminated spectacle
44. links: torches, used to light a traveler's way, since streets were not lit
48. salamander: a lizard believed to live in fire
51. 'Sblood: God's blood; **I . . . belly:** a colloquial rebuke for dwelling on the topic of his nose
52. God-a-mercy: God have mercy
54. Dame Partlet: the Hostess' agitated manner suggests Pertelote in Chaucer's "Nun's Priest's Tale."
59. tithe: tenth part
71. Dowlas: coarse linen
72. bolters: sieves
74. holland: fine linen
76. by-drinkings: odd drinks
82. denier: a French coin worth one twelfth of a sou or one tenth of an English penny
83. younker: youngster; fool
88. sneak-up: sneak
S.D. 90. truncheon: staff carried by officers as a symbol of command
91. Is . . . door: is that the way the wind blows?
93. Newgate fashion: in the manner of prisoners at Newgate

Prince. A trifle, some eightpenny matter.

Hos. So I told him, my lord, and I said I heard your Grace say so; and, my lord, he speaks 110 most vilely of you, like a foulmouthed man as he is, and said he would cudgel you.

Prince. What! he did not?

Hos. There's neither faith, truth, nor womanhood in me else. 115

Fal. There's no more faith in thee than in a stewed prune, nor no more truth in thee than in a drawn fox; and for womanhood, Maid Marian may be the deputy's wife of the ward to thee. Go, you thing, go! 120

Hos. Say, what thing? what thing?

Fal. What thing? Why, a thing to thank God on.

Hos. I am no thing to thank God on, I would thou shouldst know it! I am an honest man's wife, and, setting thy knighthood aside, thou art a knave 125 to call me so.

Fal. Setting thy womanhood aside, thou art a beast to say otherwise.

Hos. Say, what beast, thou knave, thou?

Fal. What beast? Why, an otter. 130

Prince. An otter, Sir John? Why an otter?

Fal. Why, she's neither fish nor flesh; a man knows not where to have her.

Hos. Thou art an unjust man in saying so. Thou or any man knows where to have me, thou knave, 135 thou!

Prince. Thou sayst true, hostess, and he slanders thee most grossly.

Hos. So he doth you, my lord, and said this other day you ought him a thousand pound. 140

Prince. Sirrah, do I owe you a thousand pound?

Fal. A thousand pound, Hal? A million! Thy love is worth a million; thou owest me thy love.

Hos. Nay, my lord, he called you Jack and said he would cudgel you. 145

Fal. Did I, Bardolph?

Bar. Indeed, Sir John, you said so.

Fal. Yea, if he said my ring was copper.

Prince. I say 'tis copper. Darest thou be as good as thy word now? 150

Fal. Why, Hal, thou knowest, as thou art but man, I dare; but as thou art Prince, I fear thee as I fear the roaring of the lion's whelp.

Prince. And why not as the lion?

Fal. The King himself is to be feared as the 155 lion. Dost thou think I'll fear thee as I fear thy father? Nay, an I do, I pray God my girdle break.

Prince. O, if it should, how would thy guts fall about thy knees! But, sirrah, there's no room for faith, truth, nor honesty in this bosom of 160 thine. It is all filled up with guts and midriff. Charge an honest woman with picking thy pocket? Why, thou whoreson, impudent, embossed rascal, if there were anything in thy pocket but tavern reckonings, memorandums of bawdy houses, and one poor 165 pennyworth of sugar candy to make thee long-winded—if thy pocket were enriched with any other injuries but these, I am a villain. And yet you will stand to it; you will not pocket up wrong. Art thou not ashamed? 170

Fal. Dost thou hear, Hal? Thou knowest in the state of innocency Adam fell, and what should poor Jack Falstaff do in the days of villainy? Thou seest I have more flesh than another man, and therefore more frailty. You confess then, you picked my 175 pocket?

Prince. It appears so by the story.

Fal. Hostess, I forgive thee. Go make ready breakfast. Love thy husband, look to thy servants, cherish thy guests. Thou shalt find me tractable to 180 any honest reason. Thou seest I am pacified still. Nay, prithee be gone. *Exit Hostess.* Now, Hal, to the news at court. For the robbery, lad—how is that answered?

Prince. O my sweet beef, I must still be 185 good angel to thee. The money is paid back again.

Fal. O, I do not like that paying back! 'Tis a double labor.

Prince. I am good friends with my father, and may do anything. 190

Fal. Rob me the exchequer the first thing thou doest, and do it with unwashed hands too.

Bar. Do, my lord.

Prince. I have procured thee, Jack, a charge of foot. 195

Fal. I would it had been of horse. Where shall I find one that can steal well? O for a fine thief of the age of two-and-twenty or thereabouts! I am heinously unprovided. Well, God be thanked for these rebels. They offend none but the virtuous. I 200 laud them, I praise them.

Prince. Bardolph!

Bar. My lord?

116–17. no . . . prune: stewed prunes were considered to be preventives against venereal disease and were often served in brothels.

117–18. drawn fox: a fox drawn from his lair and desperate to escape

118. Maid Marian: a character of the May Day morris games, not a model of propriety

122. on: for

133. where . . . her: i.e., whether she is forbidden on a fast day

140. ought: obsolete past tense of "owe"

157. I . . . break: referring to the proverb "Ungirt, unblessed." **Girdle** equals "sword belt."

163. embossed rascal: (1) deer exhausted and at bay; (2) swollen (extraordinary) rascal

168. injuries: valuables whose loss would be painful

169. stand . . . it: insist on your loss; **pocket . . . wrong:** endure insult

181. still: ever

192. with . . . hands: at once, without ceremony

Prince. Go bear this letter to Lord John of Lancaster,
To my brother John; this to my Lord of Westmorland. [*Exit Bardolph*.]
Go, Peto, to horse, to horse; for thou and I 206
Have thirty miles to ride yet ere dinnertime. [*Exit Peto*.]
Jack, meet me tomorrow in the Temple Hall
At two o'clock in the afternoon.
There shalt thou know thy charge, and there receive
Money and order for their furniture. 211
The land is burning; Percy stands on high;
And either they or we must lower lie. [*Exit*.]
Fal. Rare words! brave world! Hostess, my breakfast, come!
O, I could wish this tavern were my drum! 215
Exit.

211. their furniture: equipment for his company
214. brave: splendid

ACT IV

Scene I. [*The rebel camp near Shrewsbury*.]

Enter HOTSPUR, WORCESTER, *and* DOUGLAS.

Hot. Well said, my noble Scot. If speaking truth
In this fine age were not thought flattery,
Such attribution should the Douglas have
As not a soldier of this season's stamp
Should go so general current through the world. 5
By God, I cannot flatter; I do defy
The tongues of soothers; but a braver place
In my heart's love hath no man than yourself.
Nay, task me to my word; approve me, lord.
Doug. Thou art the king of honor. 10
No man so potent breathes upon the ground
But I will beard him.

Enter ONE WITH LETTERS.

Hot. Do so, and 'tis well.—
What letters hast thou there?—I can but thank you.
Mess. These letters come from your father.
Hot. Letters from him? Why comes he not himself? 15
Mess. He cannot come, my lord; he is grievous sick.
Hot. Zounds! how has he the leisure to be sick
In such a justling time? Who leads his power?
Under whose government come they along?
Mess. His letters bears his mind, not I, my lord.
Wor. I prithee tell me, doth he keep his bed? 21
Mess. He did, my lord, four days ere I set forth,
And at the time of my departure thence
He was much feared by his physicians.
Wor. I would the state of time had first been whole 25
Ere he by sickness had been visited.
His health was never better worth than now.
Hot. Sick now? droop now? This sickness doth infect
The very lifeblood of our enterprise.
'Tis catching hither, even to our camp. 30
He writes me here that inward sickness—
And that his friends by deputation could not
So soon be drawn; nor did he think it meet
To lay so dangerous and dear a trust
On any soul removed but on his own. 35
Yet doth he give us bold advertisement,
That with our small conjunction we should on,
To see how fortune is disposed to us;
For, as he writes, there is no quailing now,
Because the King is certainly possessed 40
Of all our purposes. What say you to it?

3. attribution: reputation
4. stamp: minting
5. go . . . current: be so widely credited
6. defy: disdain
7. soothers: flatterers; **braver:** finer
9. task . . . word: put my word to the test; **approve:** prove by trial
11–12. No . . . him: I will challenge any man no matter how powerful.
18. justling: belligerent
24. feared: feared for
27. better worth: more valuable
32–33. by . . . drawn: could not be assembled by deputies acting for him in so short a time
33. meet: advisable
35. any . . . removed: any other soul
36. bold advertisement: instruction to be bold
37. conjunction: combination
40. possessed: informed

Wor. Your father's sickness is a maim to us.
Hot. A perilous gash, a very limb lopped off.
And yet, in faith, it is not! His present want
Seems more than we shall find it. Were it good 45
To set the exact wealth of all our states
All at one cast? to set so rich a main
On the nice hazard of one doubtful hour?
It were not good; for therein should we read
The very bottom and the soul of hope, 50
The very list, the very utmost bound
Of all our fortunes.
Doug. Faith, and so we should;
Where now remains a sweet reversion.
We may boldly spend upon the hope
Of what is to come in. 55
A comfort of retirement lives in this.
Hot. A rendezvous, a home to fly unto,
If that the devil and mischance look big
Upon the maidenhead of our affairs. 59
Wor. But yet I would your father had been here.
The quality and hair of our attempt
Brooks no division. It will be thought
By some that know not why he is away,
That wisdom, loyalty, and mere dislike
Of our proceedings kept the Earl from hence. 65
And think how such an apprehension
May turn the tide of fearful faction
And breed a kind of question in our cause.
For well you know, we of the off'ring side
Must keep aloof from strict arbitrament, 70
And stop all sight-holes, every loop from whence
The eye of reason may pry in upon us.
This absence of your father's draws a curtain
That shows the ignorant a kind of fear
Before not dreamt of.
Hot. You strain too far. 75
I rather of his absence make this use:
It lends a luster and more great opinion,
A larger dare to our great enterprise,
Than if the Earl were here; for men must think,
If we, without his help, can make a head 80
To push against a kingdom, with his help
We shall o'erturn it topsy-turvy down.
Yet all goes well; yet all our joints are whole.
Doug. As heart can think. There is not such a word
Spoke of in Scotland as this term of fear. 85

Enter SIR RICHARD VERNON.

Hot. My cousin Vernon! welcome, by my soul.
Ver. Pray God my news be worth a welcome, lord.
The Earl of Westmorland, seven thousand strong,
Is marching hitherwards; with him Prince John.
Hot. No harm. What more?
Ver. And further, I have learned
The King himself in person is set forth, 91
Or hitherwards intended speedily,
With strong and mighty preparation.
Hot. He shall be welcome too. Where is his son,
The nimble-footed madcap Prince of Wales, 95
And his comrades, that daffed the world aside
And bid it pass?
Ver. All furnished, all in arms;
All plumed like estridges that with the wind
Bated, like eagles having lately bathed;
Glittering in golden coats like images; 100
As full of spirit as the month of May
And gorgeous as the sun at midsummer;
Wanton as youthful goats, wild as young bulls.
I saw young Harry with his beaver on,
His cushes on his thighs, gallantly armed, 105
Rise from the ground like feathered Mercury,
And vaulted with such ease into his seat
As if an angel dropped down from the clouds
To turn and wind a fiery Pegasus
And witch the world with noble horsemanship. 110
Hot. No more, no more! Worse than the sun in March,
This praise doth nourish agues. Let them come.
They come like sacrifices in their trim,
And to the fire-eyed maid of smoky war
All hot and bleeding will we offer them. 115
The mailed Mars shall on his altar sit
Up to the ears in blood. I am on fire
To hear this rich reprisal is so nigh,

44. His . . . want: our present lack of him
47. cast: dice throw; **set:** risk; **main:** stake, specifically in the game called "hazard"
48. nice: dubious
49. read: discover
51. list: limit
53. reversion: expectation; in legal terms an expectation of inheritance or succession to an office
56. comfort . . . retirement: refuge to sustain us; auxiliary strength
58–59. look . . . Upon: menace
61. hair: nature
64. mere: absolute
66. apprehension: conception
67. fearful faction: timid conspirators
68. question in: doubt of
69. off'ring: aggressive
70. keep . . . arbitrament: avoid close examination of our cause
78. dare: daring
96. daffed: thrust
97. bid . . . pass: "Let the world pass" was a popular expression.
98. estridges: ostriches
99. Bated: fluttered
103. Wanton: frisky
104. beaver: helmet
105. cushes: cuisses; thigh armor
109. turn . . . wind: put through his paces
110. witch: charm
111. the . . . March: believed to draw pestilential vapors from the marshes and cause fevers
113. trim: finest array
114. maid . . . war: Bellona, Roman goddess of war
116. mailed: armored
118. reprisal: prize

And yet not ours. Come, let me taste my horse,
Who is to bear me like a thunderbolt 120
Against the bosom of the Prince of Wales.
Harry to Harry shall, hot horse to horse,
Meet, and ne'er part till one drop down a corse.
O that Glendower were come!

Ver. There is more news.
I learned in Worcester, as I rode along, 125
He cannot draw his power this fourteen days.

Doug. That's the worst tidings that I hear of yet.

Wor. Ay, by my faith, that bears a frosty sound.

Hot. What may the King's whole battle reach unto?

Ver. To thirty thousand.

Hot. Forty let it be. 130
My father and Glendower being both away,
The powers of us may serve so great a day.
Come, let us take a muster speedily.
Doomsday is near. Die all, die merrily.

Doug. Talk not of dying. I am out of fear 135
Of death or death's hand for this one half-year.

[*Exeunt.*]

Scene II. [*A public road near Coventry.*]

Enter FALSTAFF *and* BARDOLPH.

Fal. Bardolph, get thee before to Coventry; fill me a bottle of sack. Our soldiers shall march through. We'll to Sutton Co'fil' tonight.

Bar. Will you give me money, Captain?

Fal. Lay out, lay out. 5

Bar. This bottle makes an angel.

Fal. An if it do, take it for thy labor; an if it make twenty, take them all; I'll answer the coinage. Bid my lieutenant Peto meet me at town's end. 9

Bar. I will, Captain. Farewell. *Exit.*

Fal. If I be not ashamed of my soldiers, I am a soused gurnet. I have misused the King's press damnably. I have got, in exchange of a hundred and fifty soldiers, three hundred and odd pounds. I press me none but good householders, yeomen's sons; in- 15 quire me out contracted bachelors, such as had been asked twice on the banes—such a commodity of warm slaves as had as lieve hear the devil as a drum, such as fear the report of a caliver worse than a struck fowl or a hurt wild duck. I pressed me 20 none but such toasts-and-butter, with hearts in their bellies no bigger than pins' heads, and they have bought out their services; and now my whole charge consists of ancients, corporals, lieutenants, gentlemen of companies—slaves as ragged as Lazarus in 25 the painted cloth, where the glutton's dogs licked his sores; and such as indeed were never soldiers, but discarded unjust servingmen, younger sons to younger brothers, revolted tapsters, and ostlers trade-fall'n; the cankers of a calm world and a long 30 peace; ten times more dishonorable ragged than an old feazed ancient; and such have I to fill up the rooms of them that have bought out their services that you would think that I had a hundred and fifty tattered prodigals lately come from swine- 35 keeping, from eating draff and husks. A mad fellow met me on the way, and told me I had unloaded all the gibbets and pressed the dead bodies. No eye hath seen such scarecrows. I'll not march through Coventry with them, that's flat. Nay, 40 and the villains march wide betwixt the legs, as if they had gyves on, for indeed I had the most of them out of prison. There's but a shirt and a half in all my company, and the half-shirt is two napkins tacked together and thrown over the shoulders like a 45 herald's coat without sleeves; and the shirt, to say the truth, stol'n from my host at Saint Alban's, or the red-nose innkeeper of Daventry. But that's all one; they'll find linen enough on every hedge.

Enter the PRINCE *and the* LORD OF WESTMORLAND.

Prince. How now, blown Jack? How now, 50 quilt?

Fal. What, Hal? How now, mad wag? What a devil dost thou in Warwickshire? My good Lord of Westmorland, I cry you mercy. I thought your honor had already been at Shrewsbury. 55

West. Faith, Sir John, 'tis more than time that I were there, and you too, but my powers are there al-

3. Sutton Co'fil': Sutton Coldfield, near Birmingham
5. Lay out: pay for it.
6. This . . . angel: you will owe me an angel in all if I pay for this bottle. An **angel** was a coin picturing the Archangel Michael.
8. answer . . . coinage: take responsibility for the counterfeit
12. soused gurnet: pickled gurnard (fish)
16–17. such . . . banes: three readings of the banns in church preceded the wedding.
17. commodity: lot
18. warm slaves: coddled wretches
19. caliver: musket
21. toasts-and-butter: milksops
24. ancients: ensigns; standard-bearers
24–25. gentlemen . . . companies: soldiers who ranked higher than enlisted men but whose officer status was imprecise
26. painted cloth: wall hanging, usually decorated with biblical or mythological scenes
28. unjust: dishonest
29. revolted: runaway
29–30. trade-fall'n: unemployed
30. cankers: cankerworms; destroyers
32. feazed: tattered; **ancient:** flag
36. draff: refuse
50. blown: swelled; **Jack:** pun on a soldier's quilted leather jacket
54. cry . . . mercy: beg your pardon (for failing to greet him at once)

ready. The King, I can tell you, looks for us all. We must away all night.

Fal. Tut, never fear me: I am as vigilant as a cat to steal cream. 60

Prince. I think, to steal cream indeed, for thy theft hath already made thee butter. But tell me, Jack, whose fellows are these that come after?

Fal. Mine, Hal, mine. 65

Prince. I did never see such pitiful rascals.

Fal. Tut, tut! good enough to toss; food for powder, food for powder. They'll fill a pit as well as better. Tush, man, mortal men, mortal men.

West. Ay, but, Sir John, methinks they are exceeding poor and bare—too beggarly. 70

Fal. Faith, for their poverty, I know not where they had that, and for their bareness, I am sure they never learned that of me.

Prince. No, I'll be sworn, unless you call three fingers on the ribs bare. But, sirrah, make haste. Percy is already in the field. 75 *Exit.*

Fal. What, is the King encamped?

West. He is, Sir John. I fear we shall stay too long.

Fal. Well, 80

To the latter end of a fray and the beginning of a feast

Fits a dull fighter and a keen guest.

Exeunt.

Scene III. [*The rebel camp near Shrewsbury.*]

Enter HOTSPUR, WORCESTER, DOUGLAS, VERNON.

Hot. We'll fight with him tonight.

Wor. It may not be.

Doug. You give him then advantage.

Ver. Not a whit.

Hot. Why say you so? Looks he not for supply?

Ver. So do we.

Hot. His is certain, ours is doubtful. 4

Wor. Good cousin, be advised; stir not tonight.

Ver. Do not, my lord.

Doug. You do not counsel well.

You speak it out of fear and cold heart.

Ver. Do me no slander, Douglas. By my life,

And I dare well maintain it with my life,

If well-respected honor bid me on, 10

I hold as little counsel with weak fear

As you, my lord, or any Scot that this day lives.

Let it be seen tomorrow in the battle

Which of us fears.

Doug. Yea, or tonight.

Ver. Content.

Hot. Tonight, say I. 15

Ver. Come, come, it may not be. I wonder much,

Being men of such great leading as you are,

That you foresee not what impediments

Drag back our expedition. Certain horse

Of my cousin Vernon's are not yet come up. 20

Your uncle Worcester's horse came but today;

And now their pride and mettle is asleep,

Their courage with hard labor tame and dull,

That not a horse is half the half of himself.

Hot. So are the horses of the enemy 25

In general journey-bated and brought low.

The better part of ours are full of rest.

Wor. The number of the King exceedeth ours.

For God's sake, cousin, stay till all come in. 29

The trumpet sounds a parley.

Enter SIR WALTER BLUNT.

Blunt. I come with gracious offers from the King,

If you vouchsafe me hearing and respect.

Hot. Welcome, Sir Walter Blunt, and would to God

You were of our determination.

Some of us love you well; and even those some

Envy your great deservings and good name, 35

Because you are not of our quality,

But stand against us like an enemy.

Blunt. And God defend but still I should stand so,

So long as out of limit and true rule

You stand against anointed majesty. 40

But to my charge. The King hath sent to know

The nature of your griefs, and whereupon

You conjure from the breast of civil peace

Such bold hostility, teaching his duteous land

Audacious cruelty. If that the King 45

Have any way your good deserts forgot,

Which he confesseth to be manifold,

He bids you name your griefs, and with all speed

You shall have your desires with interest,

And pardon absolute for yourself and these 50

Herein misled by your suggestion.

Hot. The King is kind, and well we know the King

Knows at what time to promise, when to pay.

67. toss: impale on pikes
81–82. To . . . guest: proverbial: "Better come at the latter end of a feast than the beginning of a fray."
3. supply: reinforcement
5. advised: cautious
10. well-respected: soundly considered
11. hold . . . with: give as little ear to
17. of . . . leading: so experienced in command
19. expedition: speed
22. pride: synonymous with **mettle**
26. journey-bated: travel-wearied
31. hearing . . . respect: respectful hearing
33. determination: conviction
36. quality: party
38. defend: forbid
43. civil: gentle
51. suggestion: incitement

My father and my uncle and myself
Did give him that same royalty he wears; 55
And when he was not six-and-twenty strong,
Sick in the world's regard, wretched and low,
A poor unminded outlaw sneaking home,
My father gave him welcome to the shore; 59
And when he heard him swear and vow to God
He came but to be Duke of Lancaster,
To sue his livery and beg his peace,
With tears of innocency and terms of zeal,
My father, in kind heart and pity moved,
Swore him assistance, and performed it too. 65
Now when the lords and barons of the realm
Perceived Northumberland did lean to him,
The more and less came in with cap and knee;
Met him in boroughs, cities, villages,
Attended him on bridges, stood in lanes, 70
Laid gifts before him, proffered him their oaths,
Gave him their heirs as pages, followed him
Even at the heels in golden multitudes.
He presently, as greatness knows itself,
Steps me a little higher than his vow 75
Made to my father while his blood was poor
Upon the naked shore at Ravenspurgh;
And now, forsooth, takes on him to reform
Some certain edicts and some strait decrees
That lie too heavy on the commonwealth; 80
Cries out upon abuses, seems to weep
Over his country's wrongs; and by this face,
This seeming brow of justice, did he win
The hearts of all that he did angle for;
Proceeded further—cut me off the heads 85
Of all the favorites that the absent King
In deputation left behind him here
When he was personal in the Irish war.
Blunt. Tut! I came not to hear this.
Hot. Then to the point. 90
In short time after, he deposed the King;
Soon after that deprived him of his life;
And in the neck of that tasked the whole state;
To make that worse, suff'red his kinsman March
(Who is, if every owner were well placed, 95
Indeed his king) to be engaged in Wales,
There without ransom to lie forfeited;
Disgraced me in my happy victories,
Sought to entrap me by intelligence;
Rated mine uncle from the council board; 100
In rage dismissed my father from the court;
Broke oath on oath, committed wrong on wrong;
And in conclusion drove us to seek out
This head of safety, and withal to pry
Into his title, the which we find 105
Too indirect for long continuance.
Blunt. Shall I return this answer to the King?
Hot. Not so, Sir Walter. We'll withdraw awhile.
Go to the King; and let there be impawned
Some surety for a safe return again, 110
And in the morning early shall mine uncle
Bring him our purposes; and so farewell.
Blunt. I would you would accept of grace and love.
Hot. And may be so we shall.
Blunt. Pray God you do.
Exeunt.

Scene IV. [*York. The Archbishop's palace.*]

Enter the ARCHBISHOP OF YORK *and* SIR MICHAEL.

Arch. Hie, good Sir Michael; bear this sealed brief
With winged haste to the Lord Marshal;
This to my cousin Scroop; and all the rest
To whom they are directed. If you knew
How much they do import, you would make haste.
Sir M. My good lord, I guess their tenor. 6
Arch. Like enough you do.
Tomorrow, good Sir Michael, is a day
Wherein the fortune of ten thousand men
Must bide the touch; for, sir, at Shrewsbury, 10
As I am truly given to understand,
The King with mighty and quick-raised power
Meets with Lord Harry; and I fear, Sir Michael,
What with the sickness of Northumberland,
Whose power was in the first proportion, 15
And what with Owen Glendower's absence thence,
Who with them was a rated sinew too
And comes not in, overruled by prophecies—
I fear the power of Percy is too weak
To wage an instant trial with the King. 20
Sir M. Why, my good lord, you need not fear;
There is Douglas and Lord Mortimer.
Arch. No, Mortimer is not there.
Sir M. But there is Mordake, Vernon, Lord Harry Percy,
And there is my Lord of Worcester, and a head 25

62. sue . . . livery: make legal claim to the inheritance due him
63. terms . . . zeal: ardent vows of devotion
74. as . . . itself: as he realizes his own power
79. strait: strict
82. face: appearance
88. personal: personally occupied
93. in . . . of: on top of; **tasked:** taxed
96. engaged: pledged as a hostage
100. Rated: scolded
104. head . . . safety: protective army
106. indirect: irregular
113. grace: mercy
1. brief: dispatch
2. Lord Marshal: Thomas Mowbray, Duke of Norfolk, son of the Mowbray with whom Bolingbroke quarreled in *Richard II*
10. bide . . . touch: endure the test
15. Whose . . . proportion: who had the greatest army
17. rated sinew: valued strength
18. overruled: mastered

Of gallant warriors, noble gentlemen.
Arch. And so there is; but yet the King hath drawn
The special head of all the land together—
The Prince of Wales, Lord John of Lancaster,
The noble Westmorland and warlike Blunt, 30
And many mo corrivals and dear men
Of estimation and command in arms.

31. mo: more; **corrivals:** associates; allies; **dear:** valuable
32. estimation . . . arms: great reputation as commanders

Sir M. Doubt not, my lord, they shall be well opposed.
Arch. I hope no less, yet needful 'tis to fear;
And, to prevent the worst, Sir Michael, speed. 35
For if Lord Percy thrive not, ere the King
Dismiss his power, he means to visit us,
For he hath heard of our confederacy,
And 'tis but wisdom to make strong against him.
Therefore make haste. I must go write again 40
To other friends; and so farewell, Sir Michael.
Exeunt.

ACT V

Scene I. [*The King's camp near Shrewsbury.*]

Enter the KING, PRINCE OF WALES, LORD JOHN OF LANCASTER, SIR WALTER BLUNT, FALSTAFF.

King. How bloodily the sun begins to peer
Above yon busky hill! The day looks pale
At his distemp'rature.
Prince. The southern wind
Doth play the trumpet to his purposes
And by his hollow whistling in the leaves 5
Foretells a tempest and a blust'ring day.
King. Then with the losers let it sympathize,
For nothing can seem foul to those that win.

The trumpet sounds. Enter WORCESTER [*and* VERNON].

How now, my Lord of Worcester? 'Tis not well
That you and I should meet upon such terms 10
As now we meet. You have deceived our trust
And made us doff our easy robes of peace
To crush our old limbs in ungentle steel.
This is not well, my lord; this is not well.
What say you to it? Will you again unknit 15
This churlish knot of all-abhorred war,
And move in that obedient orb again
Where you did give a fair and natural light,
And be no more an exhaled meteor,
A prodigy of fear, and a portent 20
Of broached mischief to the unborn times?
Wor. Hear me, my liege.
For mine own part, I could be well content
To entertain the lag-end of my life
With quiet hours, for I do protest 25
I have not sought the day of this dislike.
King. You have not sought it? How comes it then?
Fal. Rebellion lay in his way, and he found it.
Prince. Peace, chewet, peace!
Wor. It pleased your Majesty to turn your looks
Of favor from myself and all our house; 31
And yet I must remember you, my lord,
We were the first and dearest of your friends.
For you my staff of office did I break
In Richard's time, and posted day and night 35
To meet you on the way and kiss your hand
When yet you were in place and in account
Nothing so strong and fortunate as I.
It was myself, my brother, and his son
That brought you home and boldly did outdare 40
The dangers of the time. You swore to us,
And you did swear that oath at Doncaster,
That you did nothing purpose 'gainst the state,
Nor claim no further than your new-fall'n right,
The seat of Gaunt, dukedom of Lancaster. 45
To this we swore our aid. But in short space

2. busky: bosky; wooded
3. his distemp'rature: the sun's unnatural appearance
4. Doth . . . to: heralds
7. sympathize: harmonize
17. obedient orb: path of obedience

20. prodigy: omen
21. broached: released
26. dislike: dissension
29. chewet: chough (a chattering bird)
32. remember: remind
35. posted: rode post
44. new-fall'n: newly inherited

It rained down fortune show'ring on your head,
And such a flood of greatness fell on you—
What with our help, what with the absent King,
What with the injuries of a wanton time, 50
The seeming sufferances that you had borne,
And the contrarious winds that held the King
So long in his unlucky Irish wars
That all in England did repute him dead—
And from this swarm of fair advantages 55
You took occasion to be quickly wooed
To gripe the general sway into your hand;
Forgot your oath to us at Doncaster;
And, being fed by us, you used us so
As that ungentle gull, the cuckoo's bird, 60
Useth the sparrow—did oppress our nest;
Grew by our feeding to so great a bulk
That even our love durst not come near your sight
For fear of swallowing; but with nimble wing
We were enforced for safety sake to fly 65
Out of your sight and raise this present head;
Whereby we stand opposed by such means
As you yourself have forged against yourself
By unkind usage, dangerous countenance,
And violation of all faith and troth 70
Sworn to us in your younger enterprise.

King. These things, indeed, you have articulate,
Proclaimed at market crosses, read in churches,
To face the garment of rebellion
With some fine color that may please the eye 75
Of fickle changelings and poor discontents,
Which gape and rub the elbow at the news
Of hurlyburly innovation.
And never yet did insurrection want
Such water colors to impaint his cause, 80
Nor moody beggars, starving for a time
Of pell-mell havoc and confusion.

Prince. In both our armies there is many a soul
Shall pay full dearly for this encounter,
If once they join in trial. Tell your nephew 85
The Prince of Wales doth join with all the world
In praise of Henry Percy. By my hopes,
This present enterprise set off his head,
I do not think a braver gentleman,
More active-valiant or more valiant-young, 90
More daring or more bold, is now alive
To grace this latter age with noble deeds.
For my part, I may speak it to my shame,
I have a truant been to chivalry;
And so I hear he doth account me too. 95
Yet this before my father's Majesty—
I am content that he shall take the odds
Of his great name and estimation,
And will, to save the blood on either side,
Try fortune with him in a single fight. 100

King. And, Prince of Wales, so dare we venture thee,
Albeit considerations infinite
Do make against it. No, good Worcester, no!
We love our people well; even those we love
That are misled upon your cousin's part; 105
And, will they take the offer of our grace,
Both he, and they, and you, yea, every man
Shall be my friend again, and I'll be his.
So tell your cousin, and bring me word
What he will do. But if he will not yield, 110
Rebuke and dread correction wait on us,
And they shall do their office. So be gone.
We will not now be troubled with reply.
We offer fair; take it advisedly.

Exit Worcester [*with Vernon*].

Prince. It will not be accepted, on my life. 115
The Douglas and the Hotspur both together
Are confident against the world in arms.

King. Hence, therefore, every leader to his charge;
For, on their answer, will we set on them,
And God befriend us as our cause is just! 120

Exeunt. Manent Prince, Falstaff.

Fal. Hal, if thou see me down in the battle and bestride me, so! 'Tis a point of friendship.

Prince. Nothing but a colossus can do thee that friendship. Say thy prayers, and farewell.

Fal. I would 'twere bedtime, Hal, and all 125 well.

Prince. Why, thou owest God a death. [*Exit*.]

Fal. 'Tis not due yet: I would be loath to pay him before his day. What need I be so forward with him that calls not on me? Well, 'tis no matter; 130 honor pricks me on. Yea, but how if honor prick me off when I come on? How then? Can honor set to a leg? No. Or an arm? No. Or take away the grief of a wound? No. Honor hath no skill in surgery then? No. What is honor? A word. What is in that word 135 honor? What is that honor? Air—a trim reckoning! Who hath it? He that died a Wednesday. Doth he feel it? No. Doth he hear it? No. 'Tis insensible then? Yea, to the dead. But will it not live with the living? No. Why? Detraction will not suffer it. There- 140

50. injuries: wrongs; **wanton:** unruly
51. sufferances: sufferings
57. gripe: grasp
60. gull: unfledged bird
63. our love: friends such as ourselves
69. dangerous countenance: threatening behavior
72. articulate: stated article by article
74. face: decorate
75. color: disguise
78. innovation: revolution
79. want: lack
80. water colors: transparent excuses
88. set . . . head: discounted

105. misled . . . part: deceived into supporting your kinsman
111. wait . . . us: serve me
131–32. prick . . . off: select me
132. set to: heal
136. trim: fine

fore I'll none of it. Honor is a mere scutcheon—and so ends my catechism.

Exit.

Scene II. [*The rebel camp near Shrewsbury.*]

Enter WORCESTER *and* SIR RICHARD VERNON.

Wor. O, no, my nephew must not know, Sir Richard,
The liberal and kind offer of the King.
Ver. 'Twere best he did.
Wor. Then are we all undone.
It is not possible, it cannot be,
The King should keep his word in loving us. 5
He will suspect us still and find a time
To punish this offense in other faults.
Supposition all our lives shall be stuck full of eyes;
For treason is but trusted like the fox,
Who, ne'er so tame, so cherished and locked up,
Will have a wild trick of his ancestors. 11
Look how we can, or sad or merrily,
Interpretation will misquote our looks,
And we shall feed like oxen at a stall,
The better cherished still the nearer death. 15
My nephew's trespass may be well forgot;
It hath the excuse of youth and heat of blood,
And an adopted name of privilege—
A harebrained Hotspur, governed by a spleen.
All his offenses live upon my head 20
And on his father's. We did train him on;
And, his corruption being ta'en from us,
We, as the spring of all, shall pay for all.
Therefore, good cousin, let not Harry know,
In any case, the offer of the King. 25

Enter HOTSPUR [*and* DOUGLAS].

Ver. Deliver what you will, I'll say 'tis so.
Here comes your cousin.
Hot. My uncle is returned.
Deliver up my Lord of Westmorland.
Uncle, what news?
Wor. The King will bid you battle presently. 30
Doug. Defy him by the Lord of Westmorland.
Hot. Lord Douglas, go you and tell him so.
Doug. Marry, and shall, and very willingly. *Exit.*
Wor. There is no seeming mercy in the King.
Hot. Did you beg any? God forbid! 35
Wor. I told him gently of our grievances,
Of his oath-breaking, which he mended thus,
By now forswearing that he is forsworn.
He calls us rebels, traitors, and will scourge
With haughty arms this hateful name in us. 40

[*Re-*]*enter* DOUGLAS.

Doug. Arm, gentlemen! to arms! for I have thrown
A brave defiance in King Henry's teeth,
And Westmorland, that was engaged, did bear it;
Which cannot choose but bring him quickly on.
Wor. The Prince of Wales stepped forth before the King 45
And, nephew, challenged you to single fight.
Hot. O would the quarrel lay upon our heads,
And that no man might draw short breath today
But I and Harry Monmouth! Tell me, tell me,
How showed his tasking? Seemed it in contempt?
Ver. No, by my soul. I never in my life 51
Did hear a challenge urged more modestly,
Unless a brother should a brother dare
To gentle exercise and proof of arms.
He gave you all the duties of a man; 55
Trimmed up your praises with a princely tongue;
Spoke your deservings like a chronicle;
Making you ever better than his praise
By still dispraising praise valued with you;
And, which became him like a prince indeed, 60
He made a blushing cital of himself,
And chid his truant youth with such a grace
As if he mast'red there a double spirit
Of teaching and of learning instantly.
There did he pause; but let me tell the world, 65
If he outlive the envy of this day,
England did never owe so sweet a hope,
So much misconstrued in his wantonness.
Hot. Cousin, I think thou art enamored
On his follies. Never did I hear 70
Of any prince so wild a libertine.
But be he as he will, yet once ere night
I will embrace him with a soldier's arm,
That he shall shrink under my courtesy. 74
Arm, arm with speed! and, fellows, soldiers, friends,
Better consider what you have to do

141. scutcheon: funeral hatchment
18. an . . . privilege: a nickname (Hotspur) that characterizes him as rash
20–21. live . . . father's: will be charged to myself and his father
21. train: lure
23. spring: origin
33. Marry . . . shall: indeed I shall
38. forswearing: falsely denying
48. draw . . . breath: pant in battle
50. tasking: challenge
52. urged: presented
55. all . . . man: full credit for manliness
56. Trimmed up: embellished
59. dispraising . . . you: denying that any praise was worthy of you
61. cital: recital
64. instantly: at the same instant
66. envy: hostility
67. owe: own
68. misconstrued: misunderstood; **in:** because of

Than I, that have not well the gift of tongue,
Can lift your blood up with persuasion.

Enter a MESSENGER.

Mess. My lord, here are letters for you.
Hot. I cannot read them now.— 80
O gentlemen, the time of life is short!
To spend that shortness basely were too long
If life did ride upon a dial's point,
Still ending at the arrival of an hour.
An if we live, we live to tread on kings; 85
If die, brave death, when princes die with us!
Now for our consciences, the arms are fair,
When the intent of bearing them is just.

Enter ANOTHER MESSENGER.

Mess. My lord, prepare. The King comes on apace.
Hot. I thank him that he cuts me from my tale,
For I profess not talking. Only this— 91
Let each man do his best; and here draw I
A sword whose temper I intend to stain
With the best blood that I can meet withal
In the adventure of this perilous day. 95
Now, Espérance! Percy! and set on.
Sound all the lofty instruments of war,
And by that music let us all embrace;
For, heaven to earth, some of us never shall
A second time do such a courtesy. 100
Here they embrace. The trumpets sound. [*Exeunt.*]

[Scene III. *Another part of the field.*]

The KING *enters with his* POWER. *Alarum to the battle.* [*Exeunt.*] *Then enter* DOUGLAS *and* SIR WALTER BLUNT.

Blunt. What is thy name, that in battle thus
Thou crossest me? What honor dost thou seek
Upon my head?
Doug. Know then my name is Douglas,
And I do haunt thee in the battle thus
Because some tell me that thou art a king. 5
Blunt. They tell thee true.
Doug. The Lord of Stafford dear today hath bought
Thy likeness, for instead of thee, King Harry,
This sword hath ended him. So shall it thee,
Unless thou yield thee as my prisoner. 10
Blunt. I was not born a yielder, thou proud Scot;
And thou shalt find a king that will revenge
Lord Stafford's death.

They fight. Douglas kills Blunt. Then enter HOTSPUR.

Hot. O Douglas, hadst thou fought at Holmedon thus,
I never had triumphed upon a Scot. 15
Doug. All's done, all's won. Here breathless lies the King.
Hot. Where?
Doug. Here.
Hot. This, Douglas? No. I know this face full well.
A gallant knight he was, his name was Blunt; 20
Semblably furnished like the King himself.
Doug. A fool go with thy soul, whither it goes!
A borrowed title hast thou bought too dear:
Why didst thou tell me that thou wert a king? 24
Hot. The King hath many marching in his coats.
Doug. Now, by my sword, I will kill all his coats;
I'll murder all his wardrobe, piece by piece,
Until I meet the King.
Hot. Up and away!
Our soldiers stand full fairly for the day. *Exeunt.*

Alarum. Enter FALSTAFF *solus.*

Fal. Though I could 'scape shot-free at London, I fear the shot here. Here's no scoring but upon the pate. Soft! who are you? Sir Walter Blunt. There's honor for you! Here's no vanity! I am as hot as molten lead, and as heavy too. God keep lead out of me. I need no more weight than mine own bowels. I have led my rag-of-muffins where they are peppered. There's not three of my hundred and fifty left alive, and they are for the town's end, to beg during life. But who comes here? 30 35

Enter the PRINCE.

Prince. What, standst thou idle here? Lend me thy sword. 40
Many a nobleman lies stark and stiff
Under the hoofs of vaunting enemies,
Whose deaths are yet unrevenged. I prithee
Lend me thy sword.
Fal. O Hal, I prithee give me leave to breathe awhile. Turk Gregory never did such deeds in arms 45

95. adventure: hazard
99. heaven . . . earth: the odds are certain

21. Semblably . . . like: dressed to resemble
22. A fool: i.e., the title "fool"
29. stand . . . day: are in a fair way to win the day
30. shot-free: without paying my bills
31. scoring: (1) keeping accounts; (2) gashing
33. no vanity: no such vain craving for honor
37. peppered: killed
46. Turk Gregory: possibly Pope Gregory XIII, who had a reputation for ferocity in England because of his sanction of the Massacre of St. Bartholomew's Eve and his promise of an indulgence to anyone who would murder Queen Elizabeth

as I have done this day. I have paid Percy; I have made him sure.

Prince. He is indeed, and living to kill thee.
I prithee lend me thy sword. 50

Fal. Nay, before God, Hal, if Percy be alive, thou getst not my sword; but take my pistol, if thou wilt.

Prince. Give it me. What, is it in the case?

Fal. Ay, Hal. 'Tis hot, 'tis hot. There's that will sack a city. *The Prince draws it out and* 55
finds it to be a bottle of sack.

Prince. What, is it a time to jest and dally now?
He throws the bottle at him. Exit.

Fal. Well, if Percy be alive, I'll pierce him. If he do come in my way, so; if he do not, if I come in his willingly, let him make a carbonado of me. I like not such grinning honor as Sir Walter hath. Give 60 me life; which if I can save, so; if not, honor comes unlooked for, and there's an end.
Exit.

Scene [IV. *Another part of the field.*]

Alarum. Excursions. Enter the KING, *the* PRINCE, LORD JOHN OF LANCASTER, EARL OF WESTMORLAND.

King. I prithee, Harry, withdraw thyself; thou bleedest too much.
Lord John of Lancaster, go you with him.

John. Not I, my lord, unless I did bleed too.

Prince. I do beseech your Majesty make up,
Lest your retirement do amaze your friends. 5

King. I will do so.
My Lord of Westmorland, lead him to his tent.

West. Come, my lord, I'll lead you to your tent.

Prince. Lead me, my lord? I do not need your help;
And God forbid a shallow scratch should drive 10
The Prince of Wales from such a field as this,
Where stained nobility lies trodden on,
And rebels' arms triumph in massacres!

John. We breathe too long. Come, cousin Westmorland,
Our duty this way lies. For God's sake, come. 15
[*Exeunt Prince John and Westmorland.*]

Prince. By God, thou hast deceived me, Lancaster!
I did not think thee lord of such a spirit.
Before, I loved thee as a brother, John;
But now, I do respect thee as my soul.

King. I saw him hold Lord Percy at the point 20
With lustier maintenance than I did look for
Of such an ungrown warrior.

Prince. O, this boy lends mettle to us all! *Exit.*

[*Enter* DOUGLAS.]

Doug. Another King? They grow like Hydra's heads.
I am the Douglas, fatal to all those 25
That wear those colors on them. What art thou
That counterfeitst the person of a king?

King. The King himself, who, Douglas, grieves at heart
So many of his shadows thou hast met,
And not the very King. I have two boys 30
Seek Percy and thyself about the field;
But, seeing thou fallst on me so luckily,
I will assay thee. So defend thyself.

Doug. I fear thou art another counterfeit;
And yet, in faith, thou bearest thee like a king. 35
But mine I am sure thou art, whoe'er thou be,
And thus I win thee.
They fight, the King being in danger.

Enter PRINCE OF WALES.

Prince. Hold up thy head, vile Scot, or thou art like
Never to hold it up again. The spirits 39
Of valiant Shirley, Stafford, Blunt are in my arms.
It is the Prince of Wales that threatens thee,
Who never promiseth but he means to pay.
They fight. Douglas flieth.
Cheerly, my lord. How fares your Grace?
Sir Nicholas Gawsey hath for succor sent,
And so hath Clifton. I'll to Clifton straight. 45

King. Stay and breathe awhile.
Thou hast redeemed thy lost opinion,
And showed thou makest some tender of my life,
In this fair rescue thou hast brought to me.

Prince. O God, they did me too much injury 50
That ever said I heark'ned for your death.
If it were so, I might have let alone
The insulting hand of Douglas over you,
Which would have been as speedy in your end
As all the poisonous potions in the world, 55
And saved the treacherous labor of your son.

King. Make up to Clifton; I'll to Sir Nicholas Gawsey. *Exit.*

Enter HOTSPUR.

57. pierce: pronounced "perse"
59. a carbonado: a scored piece of flesh, prepared for grilling
4. make up: advance
5. amaze: terrify

24. Hydra's heads: Hydra was a mythological serpent with numerous heads, which grew two more for every one cut off.
29. shadows: likenesses
47. opinion: reputation
48. makest . . . of: have some regard for
51. heark'ned: yearned
53. insulting: proudly exultant

Hot. If I mistake not, thou art Harry Monmouth.
Prince. Thou speakst as if I would deny my name.
Hot. My name is Harry Percy.
Prince. Why, then I see 60
A very valiant rebel of the name.
I am the Prince of Wales, and think not, Percy,
To share with me in glory any more.
Two stars keep not their motion in one sphere,
Nor can one England brook a double reign 65
Of Harry Percy and the Prince of Wales.
Hot. Nor shall it, Harry, for the hour is come
To end the one of us; and would to God
Thy name in arms were now as great as mine!
Prince. I'll make it greater ere I part from thee,
And all the budding honors on thy crest 71
I'll crop to make a garland for my head.
Hot. I can no longer brook thy vanities. *They fight.*

Enter FALSTAFF.

Fal. Well said, Hal! to it, Hal! Nay, you shall find no boy's play here, I can tell you. 75

[*Re-*]*enter* DOUGLAS. *He fighteth with* FALSTAFF, *who falls down as if he were dead.* [*Exit Douglas.*] *The Prince killeth Percy.*

Hot. O Harry, thou hast robbed me of my youth!
I better brook the loss of brittle life
Than those proud titles thou hast won of me.
They wound my thoughts worse than thy sword my flesh.
But thought's the slave of life, and life time's fool,
And time, that takes survey of all the world, 81
Must have a stop. O, I could prophesy,
But that the earthy and cold hand of death
Lies on my tongue. No, Percy, thou art dust,
And food for— [*Dies.*] 85
Prince. For worms, brave Percy. Fare thee well, great heart.
Ill-weaved ambition, how much art thou shrunk!
When that this body did contain a spirit,
A kingdom for it was too small a bound;
But now two paces of the vilest earth 90
Is room enough. This earth that bears thee dead
Bears not alive so stout a gentleman.
If thou wert sensible of courtesy,
I should not make so dear a show of zeal.
But let my favors hide thy mangled face; 95
And, even in thy behalf, I'll thank myself
For doing these fair rites of tenderness.
Adieu, and take thy praise with thee to heaven.
Thy ignominy sleep with thee in the grave,
But not remembr'ed in thy epitaph. 100
He spieth Falstaff on the ground.
What, old acquaintance? Could not all this flesh
Keep in a little life? Poor Jack, farewell!
I could have better spared a better man.
O, I should have a heavy miss of thee
If I were much in love with vanity. 105
Death hath not struck so fat a deer today,
Though many dearer, in this bloody fray.
Emboweled will I see thee by-and-by;
Till then in blood by noble Percy lie. *Exit.*
Falstaff riseth up.

Fal. Emboweled? If thou embowel me to- 110 day, I'll give you leave to powder me and eat me too tomorrow. 'Sblood, 'twas time to counterfeit, or that hot termagant Scot had paid me scot and lot too. Counterfeit? I lie; I am no counterfeit. To die is to be a counterfeit, for he is but the counterfeit 115 of a man who hath not the life of a man; but to counterfeit dying when a man thereby liveth is to be no counterfeit but the true and perfect image of life indeed. The better part of valor is discretion, in the which better part I have saved my life. 120 Zounds, I am afraid of this gunpowder Percy, though he be dead. How if he should counterfeit too, and rise? By my faith, I am afraid he would prove the better counterfeit. Therefore I'll make him sure; yea, and I'll swear I killed him. Why may not 125 he rise as well as I? Nothing confutes me but eyes, and nobody sees me. Therefore, sirrah [*Stabs him*], with a new wound in your thigh, come you along with me. *He takes up Hotspur on his back.*

[*Re-*]*enter* PRINCE, *and* JOHN OF LANCASTER.

Prince. Come, brother John; full bravely hast thou fleshed 130
Thy maiden sword.
John. But, soft! whom have we here?
Did you not tell me this fat man was dead?
Prince. I did; I saw him dead,
Breathless and bleeding on the ground. Art thou alive,
Or is it fantasy that plays upon our eyesight? 135
I prithee speak. We will not trust our eyes
Without our ears. Thou art not what thou seemst.
Fal. No, that's certain, I am not a double man; but if I be not Jack Falstaff, then am I a Jack. There is Percy. If your father will do me any honor, 140 so; if not, let him kill the next Percy himself. I look to be either earl or duke, I can assure you.

71. crest: helmet
73. vanities: vain boasts
81. takes . . . of: superintends
95. favors: personal insignia
104. have . . . thee: miss thee sadly
111. powder: salt
113. termagant: savage; **scot . . . lot:** completely
121. gunpowder: hasty and violent
130. fleshed: initiated in bloodshed
138. double man: pun on a term for "ghost"
139. Jack: knave

Prince. Why, Percy I killed myself, and saw thee dead!

Fal. Didst thou? Lord, Lord, how this world is given to lying. I grant you I was down, and 145
out of breath, and so was he; but we rose both at an instant and fought a long hour by Shrewsbury clock. If I may be believed, so; if not, let them that should reward valor bear the sin upon their own heads. I'll take it upon my death, I gave him this 150
wound in the thigh. If the man were alive and would deny it, zounds! I would make him eat a piece of my sword.

John. This is the strangest tale that ever I heard.

Prince. This is the strangest fellow, brother John.
Come, bring your luggage nobly on your back. 156
For my part, if a lie may do thee grace,
I'll gild it with the happiest terms I have.

A retreat is sounded.

The trumpet sounds retreat; the day is ours.
Come, brother, let's to the highest of the field, 160
To see what friends are living, who are dead.

Exeunt [*Prince Henry and Prince John*].

Fal. I'll follow, as they say, for reward. He that rewards me, God reward him. If I do grow great, I'll grow less; for I'll purge, and leave sack, and live cleanly, as a nobleman should do. 165

Exit [*bearing off the body*].

Scene [V. *Another part of the field.*]

The trumpets sound. Enter the King, Prince of Wales, Lord John of Lancaster, Earl of Westmorland, *with* Worcester *and* Vernon *prisoners.*

King. Thus ever did rebellion find rebuke.
Ill-spirited Worcester, did not we send grace,
Pardon, and terms of love to all of you?
And wouldst thou turn our offers contrary?
Misuse the tenor of thy kinsman's trust? 5
Three knights upon our party slain today,
A noble earl, and many a creature else
Had been alive this hour,
If like a Christian thou hadst truly borne
Betwixt our armies true intelligence. 10

Wor. What I have done my safety urged me to;
And I embrace this fortune patiently,
Since not to be avoided it falls on me.

King. Bear Worcester to the death, and Vernon too;
Other offenders we will pause upon. 15

Exeunt Worcester and Vernon, [*guarded*].

How goes the field?

Prince. The noble Scot, Lord Douglas, when he saw
The fortune of the day quite turned from him,
The noble Percy slain, and all his men
Upon the foot of fear, fled with the rest; 20
And falling from a hill, he was so bruised
That the pursuers took him. At my tent
The Douglas is, and I beseech your Grace
I may dispose of him.

King. With all my heart.

Prince. Then, brother John of Lancaster, to you
This honorable bounty shall belong. 26
Go to the Douglas and deliver him
Up to his pleasure, ransomless and free.
His valors shown upon our crests today
Have taught us how to cherish such high deeds, 30
Even in the bosom of our adversaries.

John. I thank your Grace for this high courtesy,
Which I shall give away immediately.

King. Then this remains, that we divide our power.
You, son John, and my cousin Westmorland, 35
Towards York shall bend you with your dearest speed
To meet Northumberland and the prelate Scroop,
Who, as we hear, are busily in arms.
Myself and you, son Harry, will towards Wales
To fight with Glendower and the Earl of March. 40
Rebellion in this land shall lose his sway,
Meeting the check of such another day;
And since this business so fair is done,
Let us not leave till all our own be won.

Exeunt.

15. pause upon: reserve our judgment on
20. Upon . . . fear: in cowardly flight
26. honorable bounty: charitable deed that will do you honor
44. leave: leave off

King Henry V

From Hubert Goltzius, *Antiquissima nobilissimaque Anglorum regum* (1586).

The Life of KING HENRY THE FIFTH

INTRODUCTION

With the writing of the two parts of *Henry IV,* Shakespeare paved the way for the completion of his epic of the hero-king in *Henry V*. The second part of *Henry IV* shows the regeneration of Prince Hal and his acceptance of the responsibilities that must be borne by the heir to the throne. As Henry IV lies dying, he is cheered by the thought that now, perhaps in his own death, the sin of seizing the crown from Richard II will be lifted from his house. *Henry IV, Part 2* ends significantly with the entry of the new King Henry V into Westminster and his rejection of Falstaff. The scene is symbolic of Shakespeare's plan to portray the qualities of a hero-king who no longer can afford the follies and riotous companions of his youth.

Critics have sometimes worried unduly about "Falstaff's rejection" and its evidence of "priggishness" on the part of the young King. No Elizabethan in the audience would have had such a view. Shakespeare's contemporaries expected a king to act like a king, not like a clown, and for Henry V to have hobnobbed with his former friends of the Boar's Head Tavern, now that he had the awful responsibilities of kingship, would have been unthinkable. In fact, from the Elizabethan point of view, Henry V acted with royal magnanimity in promising to Falstaff and his companions some "competence for life" commensurate with the reformation that they demonstrated.

Shakespeare realized that he had created in Falstaff a character whom theatregoers would not willingly let go, and accordingly, in the Epilogue to *Henry IV, Part 2,* he promised, "If you be not too much cloyed with fat meat, our humble author will continue the story, with Sir John in it, and make you merry with fair Katherine of France. Where, for anything I know, Falstaff shall die of a sweat, unless already 'a be killed with your hard opinions. . . ." But for reasons best known to himself, Shakespeare did not continue Falstaff in *Henry V*. Perhaps he decided that in this climactic play of the series Falstaff would distract from the main purpose of illustrating the qualities of a hero-king.

The first performance of *Henry V* probably took place in the spring or early summer of 1599. The play was timely, for the country once more faced a war abroad. On March 27, 1599, the Earl of Essex, still the darling of the Queen, had marched out of London with his troops, bound for Ireland to suppress the rebellion raised by Tyrone. Essex would return in disgrace on September 28, but neither Shakespeare nor his audience could foresee that. The Chorus to Act V, describing the return of Henry

V after the victory over the French at Agincourt, tells of the citizens of London who

> Go forth and fetch their conquering Cæsar in;
> As, by a lower but by loving likelihood,
> Were now the general of our gracious Empress
> (As in good time he may) from Ireland coming,
> Bringing rebellion broached on his sword,
> How many would the peaceful city quit
> To welcome him!

Lurking in the back of every Englishman's mind in the last years of the sixteenth century was the worry over what might happen when the aging Queen, who had been revered for a generation, would pass from the scene. The kind of ruler best suited to the state was a frequent theme in the literature of the day, and every Englishman hoped that the great Queen's successor would be a sovereign who would bring glory and strength to the throne that she had graced. Consequently, a play about a hero-king from England's past could not fail to interest an audience in 1599. Any drum-and-trumpet play glorifying a royal hero would have pleased the times, but Shakespeare supplied more than that in *Henry V*. His drama breathes the spirit of the new nationalism that suffused England, and it reflects with striking immediacy the attitudes and concepts of the Elizabethan age. The representation of Henry's victory in the face of heavy odds could not fail to remind Elizabethan Englishmen of their own victory only eleven years earlier over Spain, the greatest military power in Europe. They might have remembered, too, that their own sovereign, though a frail woman, had ridden her charger to Tilbury to review the troops and had declared her readiness to lead her people against the hosts of Spain.

Shakespeare made Henry V, as the Chorus to Act II expressed it, "the mirror of all Christian kings," and he meant for his audience to see some parallels between him and the reigning queen. Henry, like Elizabeth, was a strong ruler, who won victories over foreign foes, suppressed disorder at home, and united the country under the authority of the crown. Shakespeare also portrayed Henry as God-fearing and just, qualities that the English admired, qualities that they believed their Queen possessed. *Henry V* placed on the stage the dramatist's conception of an ideal ruler, the kind that Englishmen devoutly hoped would succeed to the throne when Elizabeth was no more.

SOURCES, HISTORY, AND TEXT

As in his other history plays, Shakespeare turned to Raphael Holinshed's *Chronicles of England, Scotland, and Ireland* (1587) for the main incidents of *Henry V*. But he also appears to have used Edward Hall's *The Union of the Two Noble and Illustrate Families of Lancaster and York* (1548), which was one of Holinshed's sources. A few scholars have seen evidence that Shakespeare may have used a Latin life of Henry V, written by his chaplain, entitled *Henrici Quinti Angliae Regis Gesta* and another Latin life, *Vita et Gesta Henrici Quinti,* but it is doubtful whether the playwright went beyond Holinshed and Hall for historical material. As in *Henry IV,* he may have found some details and suggestions in *The Famous Victories of Henry the Fifth.*

The reference in the Prologue of Act I to "this wooden O" has suggested to some that the first performance took place in the newly erected Globe playhouse; but since we do not know precisely when in 1599 the Globe was opened, the reference may be to one of the other public playhouses. References to performances of *Henry V* are scanty, but it apparently was a popular play in the early seventeenth century. The interest of the reading public, at least, accounts for three quarto printings by 1619. It was revived for performance before King James in January, 1605. After the Restoration, Samuel Pepys reports seeing a play of *Henry V* at Lincoln's Inn Fields on July 6, 1668, but this probably was written by Roger Boyle.

Henry V was acted at long intervals during the eighteenth and nineteenth centuries, but it was not a favorite. David Garrick staged the play at Drury Lane in 1747 and chose for himself the role of the Chorus. When John Philip Kemble put on the play in 1789 he advertised the fact that it had not been seen on any stage for twenty years. Mid-nineteenth-century productions attempted to create interest by staging elaborate battle scenes and royal pageants. In the twentieth century the play has had fairly frequent revivals. Its most spectacular success of all time, perhaps, was the screen version in color, directed by Sir Laurence Olivier. First shown in England in November, 1944, it has had a phenomenal success on both sides of the Atlantic. It is still being shown here and there in neighborhood theatres and continues to draw crowds.

The basis of the present edition is the text found in the First Folio of 1623. *Henry V* appeared in three quarto versions before the publication of the Folio, but none provides an authoritative text. Quarto 1, printed in 1600 by Thomas Creede, is an abbreviated and corrupt text that is shorter by some two thousand lines than the Folio text. Suggestions have been made that it was put together from memory by one or more actors or that it was a truncated text cut for acting by traveling players. Quarto 2 (1602) and Quarto 3 (1619) merely reprint with some corrections the text of Quarto 1. The Folio version was apparently printed from an acceptable playhouse manuscript. Although this version is reasonably free of errors, some emendations have been necessary to arrive at what seems to be Shakespeare's meaning.

Lighting a Cannon

From Edward Webbe, *The Rare and Most Wonderful Things* (1590; 1869 reprint).

[Dramatis Personæ

CHORUS.
KING HENRY THE FIFTH.
DUKE OF GLOUCESTER, DUKE OF BEDFORD, } *brothers to the King.*
DUKE OF EXETER, *uncle to the King.*
DUKE OF YORK, *cousin to the King.*
EARL OF SALISBURY.
EARL OF WESTMORLAND.
EARL OF WARWICK.
ARCHBISHOP OF CANTERBURY.
BISHOP OF ELY.
EARL OF CAMBRIDGE.
LORD SCROOP.
SIR THOMAS GREY.
SIR THOMAS ERPINGHAM.
GOWER, *an English captain,* FLUELLEN, *a Welsh captain,* MACMORRIS, *an Irish captain,* JAMY, *a Scottish captain,* } *officers in King Henry's army.*
JOHN BATES, ALEXANDER COURT, MICHAEL WILLIAMS, } *soldiers in the same.*
PISTOL.
NYM.
BARDOLPH.
BOY.
A HERALD.
CHARLES THE SIXTH, *King of France.*
LEWIS, *the Dauphin.*
DUKE OF BURGUNDY.
DUKE OF ORLEANS.
DUKE OF BOURBON.
DUKE OF BRITAINE.
THE CONSTABLE OF FRANCE.
RAMBURES, GRANDPRÉ, BEAUMONT, } *French lords.*
GOVERNOR *of Harfleur.*
MONTJOY, *a French Herald.*
AMBASSADORS *to the King of England.*
ISABEL, *Queen of France.*
KATHERINE, *daughter to the French King and Queen.*
ALICE, *an attendant to Katherine.*
HOSTESS QUICKLY, *wife to Pistol.*

Lords, Ladies, Officers, Soldiers, Citizens, Messengers, and Attendants.

Scene: *England and France.*]

A Pikesman
From George Silver, *Paradoxes of Defense* (1599).

The Life of KING HENRY THE FIFTH

[PROLOGUE]

Enter PROLOGUE.

O for a Muse of fire, that would ascend
The brightest heaven of invention,
A kingdom for a stage, princes to act,
And monarchs to behold the swelling scene!
Then should the warlike Harry, like himself, 5
Assume the port of Mars, and at his heels
(Leashed in, like hounds) should famine, sword, and fire
Crouch for employment. But pardon, gentles all,
The flat unraised spirits that hath dared
On this unworthy scaffold to bring forth 10
So great an object. Can this cockpit hold
The vasty fields of France? Or may we cram
Within this wooden O the very casques
That did affright the air at Agincourt?
O, pardon, since a crooked figure may 15
Attest in little place a million,
And let us, ciphers to this great accompt,
On your imaginary forces work.
Suppose within the girdle of these walls
Are now confined two mighty monarchies, 20
Whose high-upreared and abutting fronts
The perilous narrow ocean parts asunder.
Piece out our imperfections with your thoughts:
Into a thousand parts divide one man
And make imaginary puissance. 25
Think, when we talk of horses, that you see them
Printing their proud hoofs i' the receiving earth.
For 'tis your thoughts that now must deck our kings,
Carry them here and there, jumping o'er times,
Turning the accomplishment of many years 30
Into an hourglass; for the which supply,
Admit me Chorus to this history,
Who, Prologue-like, your humble patience pray,
Gently to hear, kindly to judge our play.

Exit.

4. swelling: stirring
5. like himself: in his own person
6. port: bearing
8. gentles: gentlefolk
9. flat unraised: dull and uninspired
10. scaffold: platform
11. cockpit: arena
13. casques: helmets
16. Attest: stand for
17. ciphers . . . accompt: mere nothings in comparison with this great account
18. imaginary forces: forces of imagination
25. puissance: power
27. proud: high-spirited
30–31. Turning . . . hourglass: telescoping the deeds of many years
31. for . . . supply: i.e., to supply omitted information

ACT I

Scene I. [*London. An antechamber in the King's Palace.*]

Enter the two Bishops—[The Archbishop] of Canterbury *and* [The Bishop of] Ely.

Cant. My lord, I'll tell you, that self bill is urged
Which in the eleventh year of the last king's reign
Was like, and had indeed against us passed
But that the scambling and unquiet time
Did push it out of farther question. 5
Ely. But how, my lord, shall we resist it now?
Cant. It must be thought on. If it pass against us,
We lose the better half of our possession;
For all the temporal lands which men devout
By testament have given to the Church 10
Would they strip from us; being valued thus—
As much as would maintain, to the King's honor,
Full fifteen earls and fifteen hundred knights,
Six thousand and two hundred good esquires,
And, to relief of lazars and weak age, 15
Of indigent faint souls, past corporal toil,
A hundred almshouses right well supplied;
And to the coffers of the King beside,
A thousand pounds by the year. Thus runs the bill.
Ely. This would drink deep.
Cant. 'Twould drink the cup and all. 20
Ely. But what prevention?
Cant. The King is full of grace and fair regard.
Ely. And a true lover of the holy Church.
Cant. The courses of his youth promised it not.
The breath no sooner left his father's body 25
But that his wildness, mortified in him,
Seemed to die too. Yea, at that very moment
Consideration like an angel came
And whipped the offending Adam out of him,
Leaving his body as a paradise 30
T' envelop and contain celestial spirits.
Never was such a sudden scholar made;
Never came reformation in a flood
With such a heady currance scouring faults;
Nor never Hydra-headed willfulness 35
So soon did lose his seat, and all at once,
As in this king.
Ely. We are blessed in the change.
Cant. Hear him but reason in divinity,
And, all-admiring, with an inward wish
You would desire the King were made a prelate;
Hear him debate of commonwealth affairs, 41
You would say it hath been all in all his study;
List his discourse of war, and you shall hear
A fearful battle rend'red you in music;
Turn him to any cause of policy, 45
The Gordian knot of it he will unloose,
Familiar as his garter; that, when he speaks,
The air, a chartered libertine, is still,
And the mute wonder lurketh in men's ears
To steal his sweet and honeyed sentences; 50
So that the art and practic part of life
Must be the mistress to this theoric;
Which is a wonder how his Grace should glean it,
Since his addiction was to courses vain,
His companies unlettered, rude, and shallow, 55
His hours filled up with riots, banquets, sports;
And never noted in him any study,
Any retirement, any sequestration
From open haunts and popularity.
Ely. The strawberry grows underneath the nettle,
And wholesome berries thrive and ripen best 61
Neighbored by fruit of baser quality;
And so the Prince obscured his contemplation
Under the veil of wildness, which (no doubt)

1. self: same; **urged:** presented
3. Was like: i.e., like to pass
4. scambling: disorderly
9. temporal lands: i.e., lands not used for religious establishments; farmlands and the like, from which income was derived
15. lazars: lepers
22. full . . . regard: very virtuous and benevolent
26. mortified: deadened
28. Consideration: religious contemplation
33. flood: the Prince's reformation is likened to Hercules' cleansing of the Augean stables by means of the rivers Alpheus and Peneus.
34. currance: current; flux; probably from French *courrance*
35. Hydra-headed: multiheaded, like the fabulous Hydra killed by Hercules
38. divinity: theology
45. policy: statesmanship
46. Gordian knot: apparently inextricable knot, tied by Gordius, with the prediction that he who undid it would rule all Asia. Alexander fulfilled the prophecy by cutting the knot with his sword.
48. chartered: licensed; **libertine:** free spirit
49. mute . . . ears: admiration makes men silent
51–52. the . . . theoric: training and practical experience seem to govern his theory
54. vain: useless
55. shallow: stupid
58. sequestration: withdrawal
59. open . . . popularity: public places and the company of the populace

Grew like the summer grass, fastest by night, 65
Unseen, yet crescive in his faculty.
Cant. It must be so; for miracles are ceased,
And therefore we must needs admit the means
How things are perfected.
Ely. But, my good lord,
How now for mitigation of this bill 70
Urged by the commons? Doth his Majesty
Incline to it, or no?
Cant. He seems indifferent;
Or rather swaying more upon our part
Than cherishing the exhibiters against us;
For I have made an offer to his Majesty— 75
Upon our spiritual Convocation,
And in regard of causes now in hand,
Which I have opened to his Grace at large,
As touching France—to give a greater sum
Than ever at one time the clergy yet 80
Did to his predecessors part withal.
Ely. How did this offer seem received, my lord?
Cant. With good acceptance of his Majesty;
Save that there was not time enough to hear,
As I perceived his Grace would fain have done, 85
The severals and unhidden passages
Of his true titles to some certain dukedoms,
And generally to the crown and seat of France,
Derived from Edward, his great-grandfather. 89
Ely. What was the impediment that broke this off?
Cant. The French ambassador upon that instant
Craved audience; and the hour I think is come
To give him hearing. Is it four o'clock?
Ely. It is.
Cant. Then go we in to know his embassy, 95
Which I could with a ready guess declare
Before the Frenchman speak a word of it.
Ely. I'll wait upon you, and I long to hear it.
Exeunt.

[Scene II. *London. The presence chamber in the Palace.*]

Enter the KING, HUMPHREY [DUKE OF GLOUCESTER], BEDFORD, CLARENCE, WARWICK, WESTMORLAND, *and* EXETER, [*with* ATTENDANTS].

King. Where is my gracious Lord of Canterbury?
Exe. Not here in presence.

66. crescive: growing; **his:** its; **faculty:** potentiality
72. indifferent: impartial
74. exhibiters: presenters
76. Upon . . . Convocation: as a result of the meeting of the clergy
78. opened: revealed; **at large:** in full
86. severals: various points; **unhidden passages:** clear descent
98. wait upon: accompany

King. Send for him, good uncle.
West. Shall we call in the ambassador, my liege?
King. Not yet, my cousin. We would be resolved,
Before we hear him, of some things of weight, 5
That task our thoughts, concerning us and France.

Enter two BISHOPS—[THE ARCHBISHOP OF CANTERBURY *and* THE BISHOP OF ELY].

Cant. God and his angels guard your sacred throne
And make you long become it!
King. Sure we thank you.
My learned lord, we pray you to proceed
And justly and religiously unfold 10
Why the Law Salique, that they have in France,
Or should or should not bar us in our claim.
And God forbid, my dear and faithful lord,
That you should fashion, wrest, or bow your reading,
Or nicely charge your understanding soul 15
With opening titles miscreate whose right
Suits not in native colors with the truth;
For God doth know how many, now in health,
Shall drop their blood in approbation
Of what your reverence shall incite us to. 20
Therefore take heed how you impawn our person,
How you awake our sleeping sword of war.
We charge you in the name of God, take heed;
For never two such kingdoms did contend
Without much fall of blood, whose guiltless drops
Are every one a woe, a sore complaint 26
'Gainst him whose wrongs gives edge unto the swords
That makes such waste in brief mortality.
Under this conjuration speak, my lord;
For we will hear, note, and believe in heart 30
That what you speak is in your conscience washed
As pure as sin with baptism.
Cant. Then hear me, gracious sovereign, and you peers,
That owe yourselves, your lives, and services
To this imperial throne. There is no bar 35
To make against your Highness' claim to France
But this which they produce from Pharamond:
"In terram Salicam mulieres ne succedant";
"No woman shall succeed in Salique land."

4. resolved: satisfied
6. task . . . thoughts: burden my mind (the royal plural)
11. the . . . Salique: originally the code of laws of the Salian Franks; later applied to the prohibition of female succession to the French throne
12. Or: either
15. nicely: foolishly; **understanding:** fully aware
16. opening titles: revealing rights; **miscreate:** unscrupulously created
19. approbation: support
21. impawn: engage; pledge
27. wrongs gives: such disagreement of number between subject and predicate was common in Elizabethan usage.
35. imperial: including France, the domain of the English king would be an empire.
37. Pharamond: legendary king of the Salian Franks

Which Salique land the French unjustly gloze 40
To be the realm of France, and Pharamond
The founder of this law and female bar.
Yet their own authors faithfully affirm
That the land Salique is in Germany,
Between the floods of Sala and of Elbe; 45
Where Charles the Great, having subdued the Saxons,
There left behind and settled certain French;
Who, holding in disdain the German women
For some dishonest manners of their life,
Established then this law: to wit, no female 50
Should be inheritrix in Salique land;
Which Salique (as I said) 'twixt Elbe and Sala
Is at this day in Germany called Meisen.
Then doth it well appear the Salique Law
Was not devised for the realm of France; 55
Nor did the French possess the Salique land
Until four hundred one and twenty years
After defunction of King Pharamond,
Idly supposed the founder of this law,
Who died within the year of our redemption 60
Four hundred twenty-six; and Charles the Great
Subdued the Saxons, and did seat the French
Beyond the river Sala, in the year
Eight hundred five. Besides, their writers say,
King Pepin, which deposed Childeric, 65
Did, as heir general, being descended
Of Blithild, which was daughter to King Clothair,
Make claim and title to the crown of France.
Hugh Capet also—who usurped the crown
Of Charles the Duke of Lorraine, sole heir male 70
Of the true line and stock of Charles the Great—
To find his title with some shows of truth,
Though in pure truth it was corrupt and naught,
Conveyed himself as the heir to the Lady Lingare,
Daughter to Charlemain, who was the son 75
To Lewis the Emperor, and Lewis the son
Of Charles the Great. Also King Lewis the Tenth,
Who was sole heir to the usurper Capet,
Could not keep quiet in his conscience,
Wearing the crown of France, till satisfied 80
That fair Queen Isabel, his grandmother,
Was lineal of the Lady Ermengare,
Daughter to Charles the foresaid Duke of Lorraine;
By the which marriage the line of Charles the Great
Was reunited to the crown of France. 85
So that, as clear as is the summer's sun,
King Pepin's title and Hugh Capet's claim
King Lewis his satisfaction, all appear
To hold in right and title of the female.
So do the kings of France unto this day, 90
Howbeit they would hold up this Salique Law
To bar your Highness claiming from the female,
And rather choose to hide them in a net
Than amply to imbare their crooked titles
Usurped from you and your progenitors. 95

King. May I with right and conscience make this claim?

Cant. The sin upon my head, dread sovereign!
For in the Book of Numbers is it writ:
When the man dies, let the inheritance
Descend unto the daughter. Gracious lord, 100
Stand for your own, unwind your bloody flag,
Look back into your mighty ancestors;
Go, my dread lord, to your great-grandsire's tomb,
From whom you claim; invoke his warlike spirit,
And your great-uncle's, Edward the Black Prince,
Who on the French ground played a tragedy, 106
Making defeat on the full power of France,
Whiles his most mighty father on a hill
Stood smiling to behold his lion's whelp
Forage in blood of French nobility. 110
O noble English, that could entertain
With half their forces the full pride of France
And let another half stand laughing by,
All out of work and cold for action!

Ely. Awake remembrance of these valiant dead
And with your puissant arm renew their feats. 116
You are their heir; you sit upon their throne;
The blood and courage that renowned them
Runs in your veins; and my thrice-puissant liege
Is in the very May-morn of his youth 120
Ripe for exploits and mighty enterprises.

Exe. Your brother kings and monarchs of the earth
Do all expect that you should rouse yourself,
As did the former lions of your blood.

West. They know your Grace hath cause and means and might; 125
So hath your Highness. Never king of England
Had nobles richer and more loyal subjects,
Whose hearts have left their bodies here in England
And lie pavilioned in the fields of France.

Cant. O, let their bodies follow, my dear liege,
With blood and sword and fire, to win your right!
In aid whereof we of the spiritualty 132
Will raise your Highness such a mighty sum
As never did the clergy at one time
Bring in to any of your ancestors. 135

40. gloze: interpret
49. dishonest: unchaste
58. defunction: death
59. Idly: foolishly
66. heir general: heir-at-law, no matter if the claim derived from a female
72. find: render (as a jury's finding)
74. Conveyed himself: passed himself off as
75. Charlemain: historically, Charles the Bald, an error from Holinshed
77. Lewis the Tenth: i.e., Louis IX
88. his: an old form of the genitive construction
93. hide . . . net: proverbial: make use of a transparent excuse
94. imbare: expose
107. defeat: the Battle of Crécy, 1346
111. entertain: engage
114. action: i.e., lack of it
129. pavilioned: encamped in tents

King. We must not only arm t' invade the French,
But lay down our proportions to defend
Against the Scot, who will make road upon us
With all advantages.

Cant. They of those marches, gracious sovereign,
Shall be a wall sufficient to defend 141
Our inland from the pilfering borderers.

King. We do not mean the coursing snatchers only,
But fear the main intendment of the Scot,
Who hath been still a giddy neighbor to us; 145
For you shall read that my great-grandfather
Never went with his forces into France
But that the Scot on his unfurnished kingdom
Came pouring like the tide into a breach,
With ample and brim fullness of his force, 150
Galling the gleaned land with hot assays,
Girding with grievous siege castles and towns;
That England, being empty of defense,
Hath shook and trembled at the ill neighborhood.

Cant. She hath been then more feared than harmed, my liege; 155
For hear her but exampled by herself:
When all her chivalry hath been in France,
And she a mourning widow of her nobles,
She hath herself not only well defended
But taken and impounded as a stray 160
The King of Scots; whom she did send to France
To fill King Edward's fame with prisoner kings,
And make her chronicle as rich with praise
As is the ooze and bottom of the sea
With sunken wrack and sumless treasuries. 165

Ely. But there's a saying very old and true—
"If that you will France win,
Then with Scotland first begin."
For once the eagle (England) being in prey,
To her unguarded nest the weasel (Scot) 170
Comes sneaking, and so sucks her princely eggs,
Playing the mouse in absence of the cat,
To tame and havoc more than she can eat.

Exe. It follows then, the cat must stay at home.
Yet that is but a crushed necessity, 175
Since we have locks to safeguard necessaries,
And pretty traps to catch the petty thieves.
While that the armed hand doth fight abroad,
The advised head defends itself at home;
For government, though high, and low, and lower,
Put into parts, doth keep in one consent, 181
Congreeing in a full and natural close,
Like music.

Cant. Therefore doth heaven divide
The state of man in divers functions,
Setting endeavor in continual motion; 185
To which is fixed as an aim or butt
Obedience; for so work the honeybees,
Creatures that by a rule in nature teach
The act of order to a peopled kingdom.
They have a king, and officers of sorts, 190
Where some like magistrates correct at home,
Others like merchants venture trade abroad,
Others like soldiers armed in their stings
Make boot upon the summer's velvet buds,
Which pillage they with merry march bring home
To the tent-royal of their emperor, 196
Who, busied in his majesty, surveys
The singing masons building roofs of gold,
The civil citizens kneading up the honey,
The poor mechanic porters crowding in 200
Their heavy burdens at his narrow gate,
The sad-eyed justice, with his surly hum,
Delivering o'er to executors pale
The lazy yawning drone. I this infer,
That many things having full reference 205
To one consent may work contrariously,
As many arrows loosed several ways
Come to one mark, as many ways meet in one town,
As many fresh streams meet in one salt sea,
As many lines close in the dial's center; 210
So may a thousand actions, once afoot,
End in one purpose, and be all well borne
Without defeat. Therefore to France, my liege!
Divide your happy England into four,
Whereof take you one quarter into France, 215
And you withal shall make all Gallia shake.
If we, with thrice such powers left at home,
Cannot defend our own doors from the dog,
Let us be worried, and our nation lose
The name of hardiness and policy. 220

King. Call in the messengers sent from the Dauphin. [*Exeunt some Attendants.*]
Now are we well resolved, and by God's help
And yours, the noble sinews of our power,
France being ours, we'll bend it to our awe,
Or break it all to pieces. Or there we'll sit, 225
Ruling in large and ample empery
O'er France and all her (almost) kingly dukedoms,

138. road: inroad
140. marches: borders
145. giddy: unreliable
148. unfurnished: unprotected
151. Galling: harassing; **gleaned:** stripped of defense
155. feared: frightened
161. King . . . Scots: David II, captured by the English in 1346 while Edward III was in France
165. sumless: priceless
173. tame: aphetic form of "attame"; broach, pierce; **havoc:** destroy
181. keep . . . consent: stay in harmony
182. Congreeing: mutually agreeing; **close:** (1) cadence; (2) union
194. Make . . . upon: plunder
199. civil: orderly
200. mechanic: an adjective signifying unskilled labor
202. sad-eyed: grave
205–6. having . . . consent: all entirely concerned with the same end
220. name of: reputation for; **hardiness:** valor; **policy:** shrewdness
226. empery: sovereignty

Or lay these bones in an unworthy urn,
Tombless, with no remembrance over them.
Either our history shall with full mouth 230
Speak freely of our acts, or else our grave,
Like Turkish mute, shall have a tongueless mouth,
Not worshiped with a waxen epitaph.

Enter AMBASSADORS *of France,* [*attended*].

Now are we well prepared to know the pleasure
Of our fair cousin Dauphin; for we hear 235
Your greeting is from him, not from the King.

Ambassador. May't please your Majesty to give us leave
Freely to render what we have in charge;
Or shall we sparingly show you far off
The Dauphin's meaning, and our embassy? 240

King. We are no tyrant, but a Christian king,
Unto whose grace our passion is as subject
As is our wretches fett'red in our prisons.
Therefore with frank and with uncurbed plainness
Tell us the Dauphin's mind.

Ambassador. Thus then, in few: 245
Your Highness, lately sending into France,
Did claim some certain dukedoms, in the right
Of your great predecessor, King Edward the Third.
In answer of which claim, the Prince our master
Says that you savor too much of your youth, 250
And bids you be advised. There's naught in France
That can be with a nimble galliard won;
You cannot revel into dukedoms there.
He therefore sends you, meeter for your spirit,
This tun of treasure; and, in lieu of this, 255
Desires you let the dukedoms that you claim
Hear no more of you. This the Dauphin speaks.

King. What treasure, uncle?

Exe. Tennis balls, my liege.

King. We are glad the Dauphin is so pleasant with us.
His present and your pains we thank you for. 260
When we have matched our rackets to these balls,
We will in France (by God's grace) play a set
Shall strike his father's crown into the hazard.
Tell him he hath made a match with such a wrangler
That all the courts of France will be disturbed 265
With chases. And we understand him well,
How he comes o'er us with our wilder days,
Not measuring what use we made of them.
We never valued this poor seat of England,
And therefore, living hence, did give ourself 270
To barbarous license; as 'tis ever common
That men are merriest when they are from home.
But tell the Dauphin I will keep my state,
Be like a king, and show my sail of greatness,
When I do rouse me in my throne of France. 275
For that I have laid by my majesty
And plodded like a man for working days.
But I will rise there with so full a glory
That I will dazzle all the eyes of France,
Yea, strike the Dauphin blind to look on us. 280
And tell the pleasant Prince this mock of his
Hath turned his balls to gunstones, and his soul
Shall stand sore charged for the wasteful vengeance
That shall fly with them; for many a thousand widows 284
Shall this his mock mock out of their dear husbands,
Mock mothers from their sons, mock castles down;
And some are yet ungotten and unborn
That shall have cause to curse the Dauphin's scorn.
But this lies all within the will of God,
To whom I do appeal, and in whose name, 290
Tell you the Dauphin, I am coming on,
To venge me as I may and to put forth
My rightful hand in a well-hallowed cause.
So get you hence in peace. And tell the Dauphin
His jest will savor but of shallow wit 295
When thousands weep more than did laugh at it.
Convey them with safe conduct. Fare you well.

Exeunt Ambassadors.

Exe. This was a merry message.

King. We hope to make the sender blush at it.
Therefore, my lords, omit no happy hour 300
That may give furth'rance to our expedition;
For we have now no thought in us but France,
Save those to God, that run before our business.
Therefore let our proportions for these wars
Be soon collected, and all things thought upon 305
That may with reasonable swiftness add
More feathers to our wings; for, God before,
We'll chide this Dauphin at his father's door.
Therefore let every man now task his thought
That this fair action may on foot be brought. 310

Exeunt.

233. worshiped: honored; **waxen epitaph:** i.e., even a temporary obituary
245. few: few words
252. galliard: a lively dance
263. hazard: a section of a tennis court
266. chases: (1) military forays; (2) second bounces of unreturned tennis balls
275. rouse me: raise myself up
282. gunstones: cannon balls, made of stone in this period
283. sore: severely
303. those . . . business: i.e., religious observance, which must precede such an effort
307. God before: God leading us
309. task: strain to the utmost

[ACT II]

Flourish. Enter CHORUS.

Now all the youth of England are on fire,
And silken dalliance in the wardrobe lies.
Now thrive the armorers, and honor's thought
Reigns solely in the breast of every man.
They sell the pasture now to buy the horse, 5
Following the mirror of all Christian kings
With winged heels, as English Mercuries.
For now sits Expectation in the air
And hides a sword, from hilts unto the point,
With crowns imperial, crowns, and coronets 10
Promised to Harry and his followers.
The French, advised by good intelligence
Of this most dreadful preparation,
Shake in their fear and with pale policy
Seek to divert the English purposes. 15
O England! model to thy inward greatness,
Like little body with a mighty heart,
What mightst thou do that honor would thee do,
Were all thy children kind and natural!
But see, thy fault France hath in thee found out,
A nest of hollow bosoms, which he fills 21
With treacherous crowns; and three corrupted men—
One, Richard Earl of Cambridge, and the second,
Henry Lord Scroop of Masham, and the third,
Sir Thomas Grey, knight, of Northumberland—
Have, for the gilt of France (O, guilt indeed!) 26
Confirmed conspiracy with fearful France,
And by their hands this grace of kings must die,
If hell and treason hold their promises, 29
Ere he take ship for France, and in Southampton.
Linger your patience on, and we'll digest
The abuse of distance, force a play.
The sum is paid, the traitors are agreed,
The King is set from London, and the scene
Is now transported, gentles, to Southampton. 35
There is the playhouse now, there must you sit,
And thence to France shall we convey you safe
And bring you back, charming the Narrow Seas
To give you gentle pass; for, if we may,
We'll not offend one stomach with our play. 40
But, till the King come forth, and not till then,
Unto Southampton do we shift our scene.
Exit.

[Scene I. *London. A street.*]

Enter CORPORAL NYM *and* LIEUTENANT BARDOLPH.

Bard. Well met, Corporal Nym.

Nym. Good morrow, Lieutenant Bardolph.

Bard. What, are Ancient Pistol and you friends yet?

Nym. For my part, I care not. I say little; but 5 when time shall serve, there shall be smiles—but that shall be as it may. I dare not fight; but I will wink and hold out mine iron. It is a simple one; but what though? It will toast cheese, and it will endure cold as another man's sword will—and there's an 10 end.

Bard. I will bestow a breakfast to make you friends, and we'll be all three sworn brothers to France. Let't be so, good Corporal Nym.

Nym. Faith, I will live so long as I may, 15 that's the certain of it; and when I cannot live any longer, I will do as I may. That is my rest; that is the rendezvous of it.

Bard. It is certain, Corporal, that he is married to Nell Quickly, and certainly she did you wrong, 20 for you were trothplight to her.

Nym. I cannot tell. Things must be as they may. Men may sleep, and they may have their throats about them at that time, and some say knives have edges. It must be as it may. Though patience be 25 a tired mare, yet she will plod. There must be conclusions. Well, I cannot tell.

Enter PISTOL *and* HOSTESS QUICKLY.

Bard. Here comes Ancient Pistol and his wife. Good Corporal, be patient here. How now, mine host Pistol? 30

10. crowns . . . coronets: crowns for emperors, kings, and nobility
12. intelligence: information
14. pale policy: weak and fearful cunning
19. kind . . . natural: naturally loyal to their kindred
21. hollow: (1) empty; (2) heartless
28. grace . . . kings: model of a gracious king

3. Ancient: Ensign (standard-bearer)
8. iron: sword
17. rest: firm resolve
18. rendezvous: sum; all there is to it
21. trothplight: formally betrothed; in common-law usage, a contract almost as binding as marriage

Pist. Base tyke, callst thou me host?
Now by this hand I swear I scorn the term;
Nor shall my Nell keep lodgers!

Host. No, by my troth, not long; for we cannot lodge and board a dozen or fourteen gentle- 35 women that live honestly by the prick of their needles but it will be thought we keep a bawdy house straight. O welladay, Lady, if he be not here now! We shall see willful adultery and murder committed.

[*Nym and Pistol draw.*]

Bard. Good Lieutenant—good Corporal—of- 40 fer nothing here.

Nym. Pish!

Pist. Pish for thee, Iceland dog! thou prick-eared cur of Iceland!

Host. Good Corporal Nym, show thy valor, 45 and put up your sword.

Nym. Will you shog off? I would have you solus.

Pist. "Solus," egregrious dog? O viper vile!
The "solus" in thy most mervailous face!
The "solus" in thy teeth, and in thy throat, 50
And in thy hateful lungs, yea, in thy maw, perdy!
And, which is worse, within thy nasty mouth!
I do retort the "solus" in thy bowels;
For I can take, and Pistol's cock is up,
And flashing fire will follow. 55

Nym. I am not Barbason; you cannot conjure me. I have an humor to knock you indifferently well. If you grow foul with me, Pistol, I will scour you with my rapier, as I may, in fair terms. If you would walk off, I would prick your guts a little in good 60 terms, as I may, and that's the humor of it.

Pist. O braggard vile, and damned furious wight,
The grave doth gape, and doting death is near.
Therefore exhale!

Bard. Hear me, hear me what I say! He that 65 strikes the first stroke, I'll run him up to the hilts, as I am a soldier. [*Draws.*]

Pist. An oath of mickle might, and fury shall abate.

[*Pistol and Nym sheathe their swords.*]

Give me thy fist, thy forefoot to me give.
Thy spirits are most tall. 70

Nym. I will cut thy throat one time or other in fair terms. That is the humor of it.

Pist. Couple a gorge!
That is the word. I thee defy again.
O hound of Crete, thinkst thou my spouse to get?
No; to the spital go, 76
And from the powd'ring tub of infamy
Fetch forth the lazar kite of Cressid's kind,
Doll Tearsheet, she by name, and her espouse.
I have, and I will hold, the quondam Quickly 80
For the only she; and—pauca, there's enough.
Go to!

Enter the Boy.

Boy. Mine host Pistol, you must come to my master—and you, hostess. He is very sick and would to bed. Good Bardolph, put thy face between his 85 sheets and do the office of a warming pan. Faith, he's very ill.

Bard. Away, you rogue!

Host. By my troth, he'll yield the crow a pudding one of these days. The King has killed his heart. 90 Good husband, come home presently. *Exit.*

Bard. Come, shall I make you two friends? We must to France together. Why the devil should we keep knives to cut one another's throats?

Pist. Let floods o'erswell, and fiends for food 95 howl on!

Nym. You'll pay me the eight shillings I won of you at betting?

Pist. Base is the slave that pays.

Nym. That now I will have. That's the 100 humor of it.

Pist. As manhood shall compound. Push home.

They draw.

Bard. By this sword, he that makes the first thrust, I'll kill him! By this sword, I will. [*Draws.*]

Pist. "Sword" is an oath, and oaths must 105 have their course. [*Sheathes his sword.*]

Bard. Corporal Nym, an thou wilt be friends, be friends; an thou wilt not, why then be enemies with me too. Prithee put up.

Nym. I shall have my eight shillings I won 110 of you at betting?

Pist. A noble shalt thou have, and present pay;
And liquor likewise will I give to thee,
And friendship shall combine, and brotherhood.
I'll live by Nym, and Nym shall live by me. 115

31. **tyke:** mongrel
38. **here:** Charles Knight's emendation of the Folio's "hewne." The Quarto reads "O Lord heeres Corporall Nims."
47. **shog off:** come along; **solus:** alone
48. **egregious:** extraordinary
51. **maw:** stomach; **perdy:** corruption of French *par dieu*
54. **take:** take fire
56. **Barbason:** a demon
62. **wight:** fellow
68. **mickle:** great
70. **tall:** valiant
73. **Couple . . . gorge:** French *couper la gorge*
77. **pow'dring . . . infamy:** the powdering tub was used to treat venereal disease.
78. **lazar kite:** diseased whore; **of . . . kind:** in Robert Henryson's *Testament of Cresseid,* Cressida dies in leprous poverty.
80. **quondam:** erstwhile
81. **pauca:** few words
82. **Go to:** be off with you
89. **yield . . . pudding:** proverbial: be hanged and become crowbait
91. **presently:** at once
102. **compound:** determine; **Push home:** do your worst.
105. **"Sword" . . . oath:** the cross formed by the hilt of a sword was used to swear on.
112. **noble:** coin worth six shillings eightpence; **present:** immediate

Is not this just? For I shall sutler be
Unto the camp, and profits will accrue.
Give me thy hand. [*Nym sheathes his sword.*]
Nym. I shall have my noble?
Pist. In cash, most justly paid. 120
Nym. Well then, that's the humor of't.

Enter HOSTESS.

Host. As ever you come of women, come in quickly to Sir John. Ah, poor heart! he is so shaked of a burning quotidian tertian that it is most lamentable to behold. Sweet men, come to him. 125

Nym. The King hath run bad humors on the knight; that's the even of it.

Pist. Nym, thou hast spoke the right.
His heart is fracted and corroborate.

Nym. The King is a good king, but it must 130 be as it may. He passes some humors and careers.

Pist. Let us condole the knight; for, lambkins, we will live.

Exeunt.

[Scene II. *Southampton. A council chamber.*]

Enter EXETER, BEDFORD, *and* WESTMORLAND.

Bed. Fore God, his Grace is bold to trust these traitors.
Exe. They shall be apprehended by-and-by.
West. How smooth and even they do bear themselves,
As if allegiance in their bosoms sat,
Crowned with faith and constant loyalty! 5
Bed. The King hath note of all that they intend,
By interception which they dream not of.
Exe. Nay, but the man that was his bedfellow,
Whom he hath dulled and cloyed with gracious favors—
That he should, for a foreign purse, so sell 10
His sovereign's life to death and treachery!

Sound trumpets. Enter the KING, SCROOP, CAMBRIDGE, *and* GREY, [LORDS, *and* ATTENDANTS].

King. Now sits the wind fair, and we will aboard.
My Lord of Cambridge, and my kind Lord of Masham,
And you, my gentle knight, give me your thoughts.
Think you not that the pow'rs we bear with us 15
Will cut their passage through the force of France,
Doing the execution and the act
For which we have in head assembled them?
Scroop. No doubt, my liege, if each man do his best.
King. I doubt not that, since we are well persuaded
We carry not a heart with us from hence 21
That grows not in a fair consent with ours,
Nor leave not one behind that doth not wish
Success and conquest to attend on us.
Cam. Never was monarch better feared and loved
Than is your Majesty. There's not, I think, a subject
That sits in heart-grief and uneasiness 27
Under the sweet shade of your government.
Grey. True. Those that were your father's enemies
Have steeped their galls in honey and do serve you
With hearts create of duty and of zeal. 31
King. We therefore have great cause of thankfulness,
And shall forget the office of our hand
Sooner than quittance of desert and merit
According to the weight and worthiness. 35
Scroop. So service shall with steeled sinews toil,
And labor shall refresh itself with hope,
To do your Grace incessant services.
King. We judge no less. Uncle of Exeter,
Enlarge the man committed yesterday 40
That railed against our person. We consider
It was excess of wine that set him on,
And on his more advice, we pardon him.
Scroop. That's mercy, but too much security.
Let him be punished, sovereign, lest example 45
Breed (by his sufferance) more of such a kind.
King. O let us yet be merciful!
Cam. So may your Highness, and yet punish too.
Grey. Sir,
You show great mercy if you give him life 50
After the taste of much correction.
King. Alas, your too much love and care of me
Are heavy orisons 'gainst this poor wretch!
If little faults proceeding on distemper
Shall not be winked at, how shall we stretch our eye
When capital crimes, chewed, swallowed, and digested, 56
Appear before us? We'll yet enlarge that man,
Though Cambridge, Scroop, and Grey, in their dear care

116. **sutler:** provisioner
120. **justly:** exactly
124. **quotidian tertian:** a quotidian was a fever of daily occurrence; a tertian, one occurring every other day.
129. **fracted:** broken; **corroborate:** apparently considered by Pistol a synonym of "broken"
131. **passes . . . careers:** behaves capriciously
132. **condole:** condole with
3. **even:** calmly
18. **in head:** as an army
22. **consent:** agreement
33. **office:** function
34. **quittance:** full payment
40. **Enlarge:** release
43. **on . . . advice:** now that he has had time to reconsider
44. **security:** confidence in safety
46. **his sufferance:** forbearance toward him
53. **heavy orisons:** weighty appeals
54. **proceeding . . . distemper:** resulting from intoxication

And tender preservation of our person,
Would have him punished. And now to our French causes. 60
Who are the late commissioners?
Cam. I one, my lord.
Your Highness bade me ask for it today.
Scroop. So did you me, my liege.
Grey. And I, my royal sovereign. 65
King. Then, Richard Earl of Cambridge, there is yours;
There yours, Lord Scroop of Masham; and, Sir Knight,
Grey of Northumberland, this same is yours.
Read them, and know I know your worthiness.
My Lord of Westmorland, and uncle Exeter, 70
We will aboard tonight.—Why how now, gentlemen?
What see you in those papers that you lose
So much complexion?—Look ye, how they change!
Their cheeks are paper.—Why, what read you there
That hath so cowarded and chased your blood 75
Out of appearance?
Cam. I do confess my fault,
And do submit me to your Highness' mercy.
Grey, Scroop. To which we all appeal.
King. The mercy that was quick in us but late,
By your own counsel is suppressed and killed. 80
You must not dare (for shame) to talk of mercy;
For your own reasons turn into your bosoms
As dogs upon their masters, worrying you.
See you, my princes and my noble peers,
These English monsters! My Lord of Cambridge here— 85
You know how apt our love was to accord
To furnish him with all appertinents
Belonging to his honor; and this man
Hath, for a few light crowns, lightly conspired
And sworn unto the practices of France 90
To kill us here in Hampton; to the which
This knight, no less for bounty bound to us
Than Cambridge is, hath likewise sworn. But O,
What shall I say to thee, Lord Scroop, thou cruel,
Ingrateful, savage, and inhuman creature? 95
Thou that didst bear the key of all my counsels,
That knewst the very bottom of my soul,
That (almost) mightst have coined me into gold,
Wouldst thou have practiced on me for thy use—
May it be possible that foreign hire 100
Could out of thee extract one spark of evil
That might annoy my finger? 'Tis so strange
That, though the truth of it stands off as gross
As black and white, my eye will scarcely see it.
Treason and murder ever kept together, 105
As two yoke-devils sworn to either's purpose,
Working so grossly in a natural cause
That admiration did not whoop at them;
But thou ('gainst all proportion) didst bring in
Wonder to wait on treason and on murder; 110
And whatsoever cunning fiend it was
That wrought upon thee so preposterously
Hath got the voice in hell for excellence,
And other devils that suggest by treasons
Do botch and bungle up damnation 115
With patches, colors, and with forms being fetched
From glist'ring semblances of piety;
But he that tempered thee bade thee stand up,
Gave thee no instance why thou shouldst do treason,
Unless to dub thee with the name of traitor. 120
If that same demon that hath gulled thee thus
Should with his lion gait walk the whole world,
He might return to vasty Tartar back
And tell the legions, "I can never win
A soul so easy as that Englishman's." 125
O, how hast thou with jealousy infected
The sweetness of affiance! Show men dutiful?
Why, so didst thou. Seem they grave and learned?
Why, so didst thou. Come they of noble family?
Why, so didst thou. Seem they religious? 130
Why, so didst thou. Or are they spare in diet,
Free from gross passion or of mirth or anger,
Constant in spirit, not swerving with the blood,
Garnished and decked in modest complement,
Not working with the eye without the ear, 135
And but in purged judgment trusting neither?
Such and so finely bolted didst thou seem;
And thus thy fall hath left a kind of blot
To mark the full-fraught man and best indued
With some suspicion. I will weep for thee; 140
For this revolt of thine, methinks, is like

61. late: i.e., lately appointed
79. quick: alive
90. practices: plots
102. annoy: injure

107–8. Working . . . them: so obviously behaving according to their natures that they provoked no wonder
109. 'gainst . . . proportion: most unnaturally
112. preposterously: monstrously
113. voice: reputation
114. suggest: tempt to evil
115–17. botch . . . piety: clumsily fabricate a damnable deed to give it the appearance of virtuous action
118. tempered thee: molded you to his own use; **stand up:** i.e., declare yourself on the side of evil
119. instance: excuse
121. gulled: duped
122. lion gait: cf. I Pet. 5:8.
123. Tartar: Tartarus
124. legions: hosts of demons; see Mark 5:9.
126. jealousy: suspicion
127. affiance: pledged faith
132. or . . . or: either . . . or
133. blood: senses
134. modest complement: the appearance of temperance
135. Not . . . ear: acting only when appearance is confirmed by knowledge
136. but . . . judgment: only after the evidence has been well sifted
137. bolted: sifted; clear of imperfection
139. full-fraught . . . indued: man most abundantly endowed with virtues

Another fall of man. Their faults are open.
Arrest them to the answer of the law;
And God acquit them of their practices!
Exe. I arrest thee of high treason by the 145
name of Richard Earl of Cambridge.
I arrest thee of high treason by the name of Henry
Lord Scroop of Masham.
I arrest thee of high treason by the name of
Thomas Grey, knight, of Northumberland. 150
Scroop. Our purposes God justly hath discovered,
And I repent my fault more than my death,
Which I beseech your Highness to forgive,
Although my body pay the price of it.
Cam. For me, the gold of France did not seduce,
Although I did admit it as a motive 156
The sooner to effect what I intended.
But God be thanked for prevention,
Which I in sufferance heartily will rejoice,
Beseeching God, and you, to pardon me. 160
Grey. Never did faithful subject more rejoice
At the discovery of most dangerous treason
Than I do at this hour joy o'er myself,
Prevented from a damned enterprise.
My fault, but not my body, pardon, sovereign. 165
King. God quit you in his mercy! Hear your sentence.
You have conspired against our royal person,
Joined with an enemy proclaimed, and from his coffers
Received the golden earnest of our death;
Wherein you would have sold your king to slaughter,
His princes and his peers to servitude, 171
His subjects to oppression and contempt,
And his whole kingdom into desolation.
Touching our person, seek we no revenge,
But we our kingdom's safety must so tender, 175
Whose ruin you have sought, that to her laws
We do deliver you. Get you therefore hence
(Poor miserable wretches) to your death;
The taste whereof God of his mercy give
You patience to endure, and true repentance 180
Of all your dear offenses! Bear them hence.
Exeunt [Cambridge, Scroop, and Grey, guarded].
Now, lords, for France; the enterprise whereof
Shall be to you as us like glorious.
We doubt not of a fair and lucky war,
Since God so graciously hath brought to light 185
This dangerous treason, lurking in our way
To hinder our beginnings. We doubt not now
But every rub is smoothed on our way.
Then, forth, dear countrymen. Let us deliver
Our puissance into the hand of God, 190
Putting it straight in expedition.
Cheerly to sea; the signs of war advance.
No King of England, if not King of France!
Flourish. Exeunt.

[Scene III. *London. A tavern.*]

Enter PISTOL, NYM, BARDOLPH, BOY, *and* HOSTESS.

Host. Prithee, honey-sweet husband, let me bring
thee to Staines.
Pist. No; for my manly heart doth earn.
Bardolph, be blithe; Nym, rouse thy vaunting veins;
Boy, bristle thy courage up; for Falstaff he is dead,
And we must earn therefore. 6
Bard. Would I were with him, wheresome'er he is,
either in heaven or in hell!
Host. Nay sure, he's not in hell! He's in Arthur's
bosom, if ever man went to Arthur's bosom. 'A 10
made a finer end, and went away an it had been any
christom child. 'A parted ev'n just between twelve
and one, ev'n at the turning o' the tide. For after I
saw him fumble with the sheets, and play with flowers, and smile upon his finger's end, I knew 15
there was but one way; for his nose was as sharp as a
pen, and 'a babbled of green fields. "How now, Sir
John?" quoth I. "What, man? be o' good cheer." So
'a cried out "God, God, God!" three or four times.
Now I, to comfort him, bid him 'a should not 20
think of God; I hoped there was no need to trouble
himself with any such thoughts yet. So 'a bade me

142. open: evident
144. acquit: pardon
155–57. For . . . intended: Holinshed records a rumor that Cambridge's true motive was ambition for the crown, which he hoped would descend to him through his brother-in-law Edmund, Earl of March, who could not have issue. In order to save his family, he pretended a financial motive for his treason.
159. sufferance: suffering (the punishment)
169. golden . . . death: gold coins in token payment for my death
175. tender: cherish
181. dear: grievous
188. rub: obstacle
191. straight: immediately
192. advance: raise
1. bring: accompany
2. Staines: a village on the route to Southampton
3. earn: grieve
4. vaunting veins: swaggering spirits
9–10. Arthur's bosom: the Hostess' error for Abraham's bosom
10. 'A: he
12. christom: newly-christened; **parted:** departed
17. babbled: Lewis Theobald's emendation for the Folio's "table." Although it is one of the most famous emendations of Shakespeare's text, controversy about it still rages. One scholar has suggested that "table" is used in the sense "picture," and that the reference is to Richard Grenville of the "Revenge" (Grenville being pronounced "Greenfield"). The supporting arguments have not convinced many Shakespeare scholars.

lay more clothes on his feet. I put my hand into the bed and felt them, and they were as cold as any stone. Then I felt to his knees, and so upward 25 and upward, and all was as cold as any stone.

Nym. They say he cried out of sack.

Host. Ay, that 'a did.

Bard. And of women.

Host. Nay, that 'a did not. 30

Boy. Yes, that 'a did, and said they were devils incarnate.

Host. 'A could never abide carnation; 'twas a color he never liked.

Boy. 'A said once the devil would have him 35 about women.

Host. 'A did in some sort, indeed, handle women; but then he was rheumatic, and talked of the Whore of Babylon.

Boy. Do you not remember 'a saw a flea 40 stick upon Bardolph's nose, and 'a said it was a black soul burning in hell?

Bard. Well, the fuel is gone that maintained that fire. That's all the riches I got in his service.

Nym. Shall we shog? The King will be gone 45 from Southampton.

Pist. Come, let's away. My love, give me thy lips.
Look to my chattels and my movables.
Let senses rule. The word is "Pitch and pay."
Trust none; 50
For oaths are straws, men's faiths are wafer cakes,
And Holdfast is the only dog, my duck.
Therefore Caveto be thy counselor.
Go, clear thy crystals. Yoke-fellows in arms,
Let us to France, like horseleeches, my boys, 55
To suck, to suck, the very blood to suck!

Boy. And that's but unwholesome food, they say.

Pist. Touch her soft mouth, and march.

Bard. Farewell, hostess. [*Kisses her.*]

Nym. I cannot kiss, that is the humor of it; 60 but adieu!

Pist. Let housewifery appear. Keep close, I thee command.

Host. Farewell! adieu!

Exeunt.

[Scene IV. *France. The King's Palace.*]

Flourish. Enter the FRENCH KING, *the* DAUPHIN, *the* DUKES OF BERRI *and* BRITAINE, [*the* CONSTABLE, *and others*].

King. Thus comes the English with full power upon us,
And more than carefully it us concerns
To answer royally in our defenses.
Therefore the Dukes of Berri and Britaine,
Of Brabant and of Orleans, shall make forth, 5
And you, Prince Dauphin, with all swift dispatch,
To line and new repair our towns of war
With men of courage and with means defendant;
For England his approaches makes as fierce
As waters to the sucking of a gulf. 10
It fits us then to be as provident
As fear may teach us out of late examples
Left by the fatal and neglected English
Upon our fields.

Dau. My most redoubted father,
It is most meet we arm us 'gainst the foe; 15
For peace itself should not so dull a kingdom
(Though war nor no known quarrel were in question)
But that defenses, musters, preparations
Should be maintained, assembled, and collected,
As were a war in expectation. 20
Therefore I say 'tis meet we all go forth
To view the sick and feeble parts of France;
And let us do it with no show of fear—
No, with no more than if we heard that England
Were busied with a Whitsun morris dance; 25
For, my good liege, she is so idly kinged,
Her scepter so fantastically borne,
By a vain, giddy, shallow, humorous youth,
That fear attends her not.

Con. O, peace, Prince Dauphin!
You are too much mistaken in this king. 30
Question your Grace the late ambassadors,
With what great state he heard their embassy,
How well supplied with noble counselors,
How modest in exception, and withal
How terrible in constant resolution, 35

27. **of:** against; **sack:** sherry
38. **rheumatic:** feverish; probably pronounced "Rome-atic." Anti-Catholics thundered against the "Whore of Babylon."
43. **fuel:** i.e., the liquor supplied by Falstaff
45. **shog:** be off
49. **senses:** common sense; **word:** motto; **"Pitch . . . pay":** no credit
51. **wafer cakes:** fragile pastries
52. **Holdfast . . . dog:** proverbial: "Brag is a good dog, but Holdfast is better."
53. **Caveto:** caution (Latin *caveo*)
54. **clear . . . crystals:** wipe your eyes
62. **housewifery:** thrift; **Keep close:** keep all safe

Ent. Britaine: Bretagne
7. **line:** reinforce
10. **gulf:** whirlpool
12. **late examples:** i.e., Crécy and Poitiers
13. **fatal . . . neglected:** fatally neglected
14. **redoubted:** feared; formidable
15. **meet:** fitting
26. **so . . . kinged:** governed by so frivolous a ruler
27. **so . . . borne:** wielded so eccentrically
28. **vain:** worthless; **humorous:** capricious
34. **modest . . . exception:** temperate in resentment (of the Dauphin's message)

And you shall find his vanities forespent
Were but the outside of the Roman Brutus,
Covering discretion with a coat of folly;
As gardeners do with ordure hide those roots
That shall first spring and be most delicate. 40

Dau. Well, 'tis not so, my Lord High Constable!
But though we think it so, it is no matter.
In cases of defense 'tis best to weigh
The enemy more mighty than he seems.
So the proportions of defense are filled; 45
Which of a weak and niggardly projection
Doth, like a miser, spoil his coat with scanting
A little cloth.

King. Think we King Harry strong;
And, princes, look you strongly arm to meet him.
The kindred of him hath been fleshed upon us; 50
And he is bred out of that bloody strain
That haunted us in our familiar paths.
Witness our too much memorable shame
When Crécy battle fatally was struck,
And all our princes captived, by the hand 55
Of that black name, Edward, Black Prince of Wales;
Whiles that his mountain sire—on mountain standing,
Up in the air, crowned with the golden sun—
Saw his heroical seed, and smiled to see him,
Mangle the work of nature, and deface 60
The patterns that by God and by French fathers
Had twenty years been made. This is a stem
Of that victorious stock; and let us fear
The native mightiness and fate of him.

Enter a MESSENGER.

Mess. Ambassadors from Harry King of England 65
Do crave admittance to your Majesty.

King. We'll give them present audience. Go, and bring them.

[*Exeunt Messenger and certain Lords.*]

You see this chase is hotly followed, friends.

Dau. Turn head, and stop pursuit; for coward dogs
Most spend their mouths when what they seem to threaten 70
Runs far before them. Good my sovereign,
Take up the English short, and let them know
Of what a monarchy you are the head.
Self-love, my liege, is not so vile a sin 74
As self-neglecting.

Enter [LORDS, *with*] EXETER [*and* TRAIN].

King. From our brother of England?

Exe. From him, and thus he greets your Majesty:
He wills you, in the name of God Almighty,
That you devest yourself, and lay apart
The borrowed glories that by gift of heaven,
By law of nature and of nations, 'longs 80
To him and to his heirs—namely, the crown
And all wide-stretched honors that pertain
By custom, and the ordinance of times,
Unto the crown of France. That you may know
'Tis no sinister nor no awkward claim, 85
Picked from the wormholes of long-vanished days,
Nor from the dust of old oblivion raked,
He sends you this most memorable line,

[*Gives a paper.*]

In every branch truly demonstrative;
Willing you overlook this pedigree; 90
And when you find him evenly derived
From his most famed of famous ancestors,
Edward the Third, he bids you then resign
Your crown and kingdom, indirectly held
From him, the native and true challenger. 95

King. Or else what follows?

Exe. Bloody constraint; for if you hide the crown
Even in your hearts, there will he rake for it.
Therefore in fierce tempest is he coming,
In thunder and in earthquake, like a Jove; 100
That, if requiring fail, he will compel;
And bids you, in the bowels of the Lord,
Deliver up the crown, and to take mercy
On the poor souls for whom this hungry war
Opens his vasty jaws; and on your head 105
Turning the widows' tears, the orphans' cries,
The dead men's blood, the 'prived maidens' groans,
For husbands, fathers, and betrothed lovers
That shall be swallowed in this controversy.
This is his claim, his threat'ning, and my message;
Unless the Dauphin be in presence here, 111
To whom expressly I bring greeting too.

King. For us, we will consider of this further.

36. **vanities forespent:** former fooleries
37. **Brutus:** Lucius Junius Brutus, nephew of the tyrant Tarquinius Superbus, pretended idiocy while awaiting the opportunity to overthrow him.
45. **proportions . . . filled:** necessary forces are supplied
50. **hath . . . us:** have already tasted our flesh (and acquired a taste for more). Hounds and hawks were trained to pursue game by being given a taste of flesh or blood.
51. **strain:** breed
52. **haunted:** pursued
57. **mountain:** (1) great; (2) born in the mountains (?)
64. **native . . . him:** the great power for which he is destined by birth
67. **present:** immediate
83. **ordinance . . . times:** long-established law
85. **sinister:** illegitimate; **awkward:** irregular; crooked
88. **line:** table of descent
89. **truly demonstrative:** offering true proof
91. **evenly:** directly
94. **indirectly:** irregularly; **held:** withheld
95. **native . . . challenger:** true claimant by right of birth
101. **requiring:** requesting
102. **in . . . Lord:** by Christ's mercy
107. **'prived:** bereft; suggested by H. H. Walter in lieu of the Folio's "priuy" and the Quarto's "pining"

Tomorrow shall you bear our full intent 114
Back to our brother England.
Dau. For the Dauphin,
I stand here for him. What to him from England?
Exe. Scorn and defiance, slight regard, contempt,
And anything that may not misbecome
The mighty sender, doth he prize you at.
Thus says my king: An if your father's Highness
Do not, in grant of all demands at large, 121
Sweeten the bitter mock you sent his Majesty,
He'll call you to so hot an answer of it
That caves and womby vaultages of France
Shall chide your trespass, and return your mock
In second accent of his ordinance. 126
Dau. Say, if my father render fair return,
It is against my will; for I desire
Nothing but odds with England. To that end,
As matching to his youth and vanity, 130
I did present him with the Paris balls.
Exe. He'll make your Paris Louvre shake for it,
Were it the mistress court of mighty Europe;
And be assured you'll find a difference,
As we his subjects have in wonder found, 135
Between the promise of his greener days
And these he masters now. Now he weighs time
Even to the utmost grain. That you shall read
In your own losses, if he stay in France. 139
King. Tomorrow shall you know our mind at full.
Exe. Dispatch us with all speed, lest that our king
Come here himself to question our delay;
For he is footed in this land already.
King. You shall be soon dispatched with fair conditions.
A night is but small breath and little pause 145
To answer matters of this consequence.
Flourish. Exeunt.

121. at large: in full
126. second accent: echo
132–33. make . . . court: there is a pun on Louvre/lover.

ACT [III]

Enter CHORUS.

Thus with imagined wing our swift scene flies,
In motion of no less celerity
That that of thought. Suppose that you have seen
The well-appointed King at Hampton pier
Embark his royalty; and his brave fleet 5
With silken streamers the young Phœbus fanning.
Play with your fancies; and in them behold
Upon the hempen tackle shipboys climbing;
Hear the shrill whistle, which doth order give
To sounds confused; behold the threaden sails, 10
Borne with the invisible and creeping wind,
Draw the huge bottoms through the furrowed sea,
Breasting the lofty surge. O, do but think
You stand upon the rivage and behold
A city on the inconstant billows dancing; 15
For so appears this fleet majestical,
Holding due course to Harfleur. Follow, follow!
Grapple your minds to sternage of this navy,
And leave your England as dead midnight still,
Guarded with grandsires, babies, and old women,
Either past or not arrived to pith and puissance;
For who is he whose chin is but enriched 22
With one appearing hair that will not follow
These culled and choice-drawn cavaliers to France?
Work, work your thoughts, and therein see a siege.
Behold the ordinance on their carriages, 26
With fatal mouths gaping on girded Harfleur.
Suppose the ambassador from the French comes back;
Tells Harry that the King doth offer him
Katherine his daughter, and with her to dowry 30
Some petty and unprofitable dukedoms.
The offer likes not; and the nimble gunner
With linstock now the devilish cannon touches,
Alarum, and chambers go off.
And down goes all before them. Still be kind,
And eke out our performance with your mind. 35
Exit.

1. imagined wing: wings of imagination
4. Hampton: Southampton. The Folio reads "Dover," which by Elizabethan times was the usual port of embarkation for France.
5. brave: gallant; fine
6. young Phœbus: early morning sun
14. rivage: bank
21. pith: strength
24. culled . . . choice-drawn: carefully chosen
32. likes: pleases
33. linstock: a stick holding a match
S.D. 33. Alarum: trumpet signal; **chambers:** cannon

[Scene I. *France. Before Harfleur.*]

Alarum. Enter the King, Exeter, Bedford, *and* Gloucester, [*and* Soldiers *with*] *scaling ladders at Harfleur.*

King. Once more unto the breach, dear friends, once more;
Or close the wall up with our English dead!
In peace there's nothing so becomes a man
As modest stillness and humility;
But when the blast of war blows in our ears, 5
Then imitate the action of the tiger:
Stiffen the sinews, summon up the blood,
Disguise fair nature with hard-favored rage;
Then lend the eye a terrible aspect;
Let it pry through the portage of the head 10
Like the brass cannon; let the brow o'erwhelm it
As fearfully as doth a galled rock
O'erhang and jutty his confounded base,
Swilled with the wild and wasteful ocean.
Now set the teeth and stretch the nostril wide, 15
Hold hard the breath and bend up every spirit
To his full height! On, on, you noblest English,
Whose blood is fet from fathers of war proof!
Fathers that like so many Alexanders
Have in these parts from morn till even fought, 20
And sheathed their swords for lack of argument.
Dishonor not your mothers; now attest
That those whom you called fathers did beget you!
Be copy now to men of grosser blood
And teach them how to war! And you, good yeomen,
Whose limbs were made in England, show us here
The mettle of your pasture. Let us swear 27
That you are worth your breeding; which I doubt not,
For there is none of you so mean and base
That hath not noble luster in your eyes. 30
I see you stand like greyhounds in the slips,
Straining upon the start. The game's afoot!
Follow your spirit; and upon this charge
Cry "God for Harry! England and St. George!"
[*Exeunt.*] *Alarum, and chambers go off.*

7. summon: Nicholas Rowe's correction of the Folio's "commune"
9. aspect: glance
10. portage: portals; eyes
11. o'erwhelm: overhang
12. galled: chafed; fretted
13. jutty: jut over; **confounded:** destroyed
14. Swilled: swallowed
18. fet: fetched; derived; **fathers . . . war proof:** fathers of demonstrated valor
21. for . . . argument: i.e., only for lack of opposition
24. copy: model
27. mettle: quality; **pasture:** breeding
31. slips: leashes

[Scene II. *Before Harfleur.*]

Enter Nym, Bardolph, Pistol, *and* Boy.

Bard. On, on, on, on, on! to the breach, to the breach!

Nym. Pray thee, Corporal, stay. The knocks are too hot; and, for mine own part, I have not a case of lives. The humor of it is too hot; that is the 5 very plain song of it.

Pist. The plain song is most just; for humors do abound.

Knocks go and come; God's vassals drop and die;
And sword and shield 10
In bloody field
Doth win immortal fame.

Boy. Would I were in an alehouse in London! I would give all my fame for a pot of ale and safety.

Pist. And I: 15

If wishes would prevail with me,
My purpose should not fail with me,
But thither would I hie.

Boy. As duly, but not as truly,
As bird doth sing on bough. 20

Enter Fluellen.

Flu. Up to the breach, you dogs! Avaunt, you cullions! [*Drives them forward.*]

Pist. Be merciful, great duke, to men of mold!
Abate thy rage, abate thy manly rage,
Abate thy rage, great duke! 25
Good bawcock, 'bate thy rage! Use lenity, sweet chuck!

Nym. These be good humors. Your honor wins bad humors. *Exit* [*with all except Boy*].

Boy. As young as I am, I have observed these three swashers. I am boy to them all three; but all 30 they three, though they would serve me, could not be man to me; for indeed three such antics do not amount to a man. For Bardolph, he is white-livered and red-faced; by the means whereof 'a faces it out, but fights not. For Pistol, he hath a killing 35 tongue and a quiet sword; by the means whereof 'a breaks words and keeps whole weapons. For Nym, he hath heard that men of few words are the best men,

4. case: set
6. plain song: unornamented truth. A **plain song** is a simple, unvaried tune.
21. Avaunt: be off
22. cullions: base rascals
23. men . . . mold: earthy creatures; mortals
26. bawcock: fine fellow (French *beau coq*)
30. swashers: swaggerers; **boy:** page
32. antics: buffoons

and therefore he scorns to say his prayers, lest 'a should be thought a coward; but his few bad 40 words are matched with as few good deeds, for 'a never broke any man's head but his own, and that was against a post when he was drunk. They will steal anything, and call it purchase. Bardolph stole a lute-case, bore it twelve leagues, and sold it for 45 three halfpence. Nym and Bardolph are sworn brothers in filching, and in Calais they stole a fire-shovel. I knew by that piece of service the men would carry coals. They would have me as familiar with men's pockets as their gloves or their handkerchers; 50 which makes much against my manhood, if I should take from another's pocket to put into mine; for it is plain pocketing up of wrongs. I must leave them and seek some better service. Their villainy goes against my weak stomach, and therefore I 55 must cast it up. *Exit.*

Enter GOWER [*and* FLUELLEN].

Gow. Captain Fluellen, you must come presently to the mines. The Duke of Gloucester would speak with you.

Flu. To the mines? Tell you the Duke, it is 60 not so good to come to the mines; for look you, the mines is not according to the disciplines of the war. The concavities of it is not sufficient; for look you, the athversary, you may discuss unto the Duke, look you, is digt himself four yard under the coun- 65 termines. By Cheshu, I think 'a will plow up all, if there is not better directions.

Gow. The Duke of Gloucester, to whom the order of the siege is given, is altogether directed by an Irishman, a very valiant gentleman, i' faith. 70

Fly. It is Captain Macmorris, is it not?

Gow. I think it be.

Flu. By Cheshu, he is an ass, as in the world! I will verify as much in his beard. He has no more directions in the true disciplines of the wars, look 75 you, of the Roman disciplines, than is a puppy-dog.

Enter MACMORRIS *and* CAPTAIN JAMY.

Gow. Here 'a comes, and the Scots captain, Captain Jamy, with him.

Flu. Captain Jamy is a marvelous falorous gentleman, that is certain, and of great expedition 80 and knowledge in the aunchient wars, upon my particular knowledge of his directions. By Cheshu, he will maintain his argument as well as any military man in the world in the disciplines of the pristine wars of the Romans. 85

Jamy. I say gud day, Captain Fluellen.

Flu. Godden to your worship, good Captain James.

Gow. How now, Captain Macmorris? Have you quit the mines? Have the pioners given o'er?

Mac. By Chrish, law, tish ill done! The work 90 ish give over, the trompet sound the retreat. By my hand I swear, and my father's soul, the work ish ill done! It ish give over. I would have blowed up the town, so Chrish save me law! in an hour. O, tish ill done! tish ill done! By my hand, tish ill done! 95

Flu. Captain Macmorris, I beseech you now, will you voutsafe me, look you, a few disputations with you, as partly touching or concerning the disciplines of the war, the Roman wars? In the way of argument, look you, and friendly communication; 100 partly to satisfy my opinion, and partly for the satisfaction, look you, of my mind—as touching the direction of the military discipline, that is the point.

Jamy. It sall be vary gud, gud feith, gud Captens bath, and I sall quit you with gud leve, as I 105 may pick occasion. That sall I, marry.

Mac. It is no time to discourse, so Chrish save me! The day is hot, and the weather, and the wars, and the King, and the Dukes. It is no time to discourse. The town is beseeched, and the trompet call 110 us to the breach, and we talk, and, be Chrish, do nothing. 'Tis shame for us all. So God sa' me, 'tis shame to stand still, it is shame, by my hand! and there is throats to be cut, and works to be done, and there ish nothing done, so Chrish sa' me, law! 115

Jamy. By the mess, ere theise eyes of mine take themselves to slomber, I'll de gud service, or I'll lig i' the grund for it! ay, or go to death! And I'll pay't as valorously as I may, that sall I suerly do, that is the breff and the long. Marry, I wad full fain 120 heard some question 'tween you tway.

Flu. Captain Macmorris, I think, look you, under your correction, there is not many of your nation—

Mac. Of my nation? What ish my nation? Ish a villain, and a bastard, and a knave, and a ras- 125 cal. What ish my nation? Who talks of my nation?

Flu. Look you, if you take the matter otherwise than is meant, Captain Macmorris, peradventure I shall think you do not use me with that affability as in discretion you ought to use me, look 130 you, being as good a man as yourself, both in the disciplines of war, and in the derivation of my birth, and in other particularities.

Mac. I do not know you so good a man as myself. So Chrish save me, I will cut off your head! 135

48–49. carry coals: behave basely. Delivering coal was considered a menial occupation.
53. pocketing . . . wrongs: enduring insults
66. plow: blow
74. verify . . . beard: prove it to his face
74–75. directions: command; leadership

89. pioners: pioneers; miners
106. marry: indeed (by the Virgin Mary)
121. question: debate

Gow. Gentlemen both, you will mistake each other.
Jamy. Ah, that's a foul fault! *A parley* [*sounded*].
Gow. The town sounds a parley.
Flu. Captain Macmorris, when there is more better opportunity to be required, look you, I will be 140 so bold as to tell you I know the disciplines of war; and there is an end.

Exeunt.

[Scene III. *Before the gates of Harfleur.*]

Enter KING [HENRY] *and all his* TRAIN *before the gates.*

King. How yet resolves the governor of the town?
This is the latest parle we will admit.
Therefore to our best mercy give yourselves,
Or, like to men proud of destruction,
Defy us to our worst; for, as I am a soldier, 5
A name that in my thoughts becomes me best,
If I begin the batt'ry once again,
I will not leave the half-achieved Harfleur
Till in her ashes she lie buried.
The gates of mercy shall be all shut up, 10
And the fleshed soldier, rough and hard of heart,
In liberty of bloody hand shall range
With conscience wide as hell, mowing like grass
Your fresh fair virgins and your flow'ring infants.
What is it then to me if impious war, 15
Arrayed in flames like to the prince of fiends,
Do with his smirched complexion all fell feats
Enlinked to waste and desolation?
What is't to me, when you yourselves are cause,
If your pure maidens fall into the hand 20
Of hot and forcing violation?
What rein can hold licentious wickedness
When down the hill he holds his fierce career?
We may as bootless spend our vain command
Upon the enraged soldiers in their spoil 25
As send precepts to the Leviathan
To come ashore. Therefore, you men of Harfleur,
Take pity of your town and of your people
While yet my soldiers are in my command,
Whiles yet the cool and temperate wind of grace
O'erblows the filthy and contagious clouds 31
Of heady murder, spoil, and villainy.
If not—why, in a moment look to see
The blind and bloody soldier with foul hand
Defile the locks of your shrill-shrieking daughters;
Your fathers taken by the silver beards, 36
And their most reverend heads dashed to the walls;
Your naked infants spitted upon pikes,
Whiles the mad mothers with their howls confused
Do break the clouds, as did the wives of Jewry 40
At Herod's bloody-hunting slaughtermen.
What say you? Will you yield, and this avoid?
Or, guilty in defense, be thus destroyed?

Enter GOVERNOR [*on the wall*].

Gov. Our expectation hath this day an end.
The Dauphin, whom of succors we entreated, 45
Returns us that his powers are yet not ready
To raise so great a siege. Therefore, great king,
We yield our town and lives to thy soft mercy.
Enter our gates, dispose of us and ours,
For we no longer are defensible. 50
King. Open your gates. [*Exit Governor.*]
Come, uncle Exeter,
Go you and enter Harfleur, there remain
And fortify it strongly 'gainst the French.
Use mercy to them all. For us, dear uncle,
The winter coming on, and sickness growing 55
Upon our soldiers, we will retire to Calais.
Tonight in Harfleur will we be your guest;
Tomorrow for the march are we addrest.

Flourish, and enter the town.

[Scene IV. *Rouen. The King's Palace.*]

Enter KATHERINE *and* [ALICE], *an old Gentlewoman.*

Kath. Alice, tu as eté en Angleterre, et tu parles bien le langage.
Alice. Un peu, madame.
Kath. Je te prie m'enseigner; il faut que j'apprenne à parler. Comment appelez-vous la main en Anglais? 5
Alice. La main? Elle est appelée "de hand."
Kath. "De hand." Et les doigts?
Alice. Les doigts? Ma foi, j'oublie les doigts; mais je me souviendrai. Les doigts? Je pense qu'ils 10 sont appelés "de fingres"; oui, "de fingres."

140. to . . . required: available for the asking
4. proud: exultant at the thought of
11. fleshed: hardened and bloodthirsty
12. In . . . range: shall roam at large with no restraint of his bloody hand
24. bootless: vainly
26. precepts: written commands
30. grace: mercy

32. heady: headlong
34. blind: reckless, uncontrolled
43. guilty . . . defense: refusing to yield at this stage of a siege would make the city guilty of its own destruction.
50. defensible: capable of defense
58. addrest: prepared

Kath. La main, "de hand"; les doigts, "de fingres." Je pense que je suis le bon écolier; j'ai gagné deux mots d'Anglais vitement. Comment appelez-vous les ongles? 15

Alice. Les ongles? Nous les appelons "de nails."

Kath. "De nails." Ecoutez; dites-moi, si je parle bien: "de hand, de fingres," et "de nails."

Alice. C'est bien dit, madame; il est fort bon Anglais. 20

Kath. Dites-moi l'Anglais pour le bras.

Alice. "De arm," madame.

Kath. Et le coude.

Alice. "D'elbow."

Kath. "D'elbow." Je m'en fais la répétition 25 de tous les mots que vous m'avez appris dès à présent.

Alice. Il est trop difficile, madame, comme je pense.

Kath. Excusez-moi, Alice; écoutez: "d'hand, 30 de fingres, de nails, d'arma, de bilbow."

Alice. "D'elbow," madame.

Kath. O Seigneur Dieu, je m'en oublie! "D'elbow." Comment appelez-vous le col?

Alice. "De nick," madame. 35

Kath. "De nick." Et le menton?

Alice. "De chin."

Kath. "De sin." Le col, "de nick"; le menton, "de sin."

Alice. Oui. Sauf votre honneur, en vérité, 40 vous prononcez les mots aussi droit que les natifs d'Angleterre.

Kath. Je ne doute point d'apprendre, par la grâce de Dieu, et en peu de temps.

Alice. N'avez-vous pas déjà oublié ce que je 45 vous ai enseigné?

Kath. Non, je réciterai à vous promptement: "d'hand, de fingres, de mails"—

Alice. "De nails," madame.

Kath. "De nails, de arm, de ilbow." 50

Alice. Sauf votre honneur, "d'elbow."

Kath. Ainsi dis-je; "d'elbow, de nick," et "de sin." Comment appelez-vous le pied et la robe?

Alice. "De foot," madame; et "de coun."

Kath. "Le foot" et "le count"! O Seigneur 55 Dieu! ils sont mots de son mauvais, corruptible, gros et impudique, et non pour les dames d'honneur d'user: je ne voudrais prononcer ces mots devant les seigneurs de France pour tout le monde. Foh! "le foot" et "le count"! Néanmoins, je réciterai 60 une autre fois ma leçon ensemble: "d'hand, de fingre, de nails, d'arm, d'elbow, de nick, de sin, de foot, le count."

Alice. Excellent, madame!

Kath. C'est assez pour une fois: allons-nous 65 à diner.

Exeunt.

[Scene V. *Rouen. The Palace.*]

Enter the KING OF FRANCE, *the* DAUPHIN, [BRITAINE], *the* CONSTABLE OF FRANCE, *and others.*

King. 'Tis certain he hath passed the river Somme.

Con. And if he be not fought withal, my lord,
Let us not live in France; let us quit all
And give our vineyards to a barbarous people.

Dau. O Dieu vivant! Shall a few sprays of us, 5
The emptying of our fathers' luxury,
Our scions, put in wild and savage stock,
Spirt up so suddenly into the clouds
And overlook their grafters?

Brit. Normans, but bastard Normans, Norman bastards! 10
Mort de ma vie! if they march along
Unfought withal, but I will sell my dukedom
To buy a slobbery and a dirty farm
In that nook-shotten isle of Albion.

Con. Dieu de batailles! whence have they this mettle? 15
Is not their climate foggy, raw, and dull,
On whom, as in despite, the sun looks pale,
Killing their fruit with frowns? Can sodden water,
A drench for surreined jades, their barley broth,
Decoct their cold blood to such valiant heat? 20
And shall our quick blood, spirited with wine,
Seem frosty? O, for honor of our land,
Let us not hang like roping icicles
Upon our houses' thatch, whiles a more frosty people
Sweat drops of gallant youth in our rich fields—
"Poor" we may call them in their native lords! 26

Dau. By faith and honor,
Our madams mock at us and plainly say
Our mettle is bred out, and they will give
Their bodies to the lust of English youth 30
To new-store France with bastard warriors.

Brit. They bid us to the English dancing schools
And teach lavoltas high and swift corantos,
Saying our grace is only in our heels
And that we are most lofty runaways. 35

King. Where is Montjoy the herald? Speed him hence;

5. sprays . . . us: offshoots of French blood
6. luxury: lust
8. Spirt: spurt
13. slobbery: muddy
14. nook-shotten: set in a remote corner
15. mettle: spirit
18. sodden: boiled
19. drench: medicinal draught; **surreined:** overridden; **barley broth:** ale
20. Decoct: warm
33. lavoltas: dances with leaping steps; **corantos:** dances with running steps
34. grace: virtue; excellence

Let him greet England with our sharp defiance.
Up, princes! and, with spirit of honor edged,
More sharper than your swords, hie to the field.
Charles Delabreth, High Constable of France, 40
You Dukes of Orleans, Bourbon, and of Berri,
Alençon, Brabant, Bar, and Burgundy;
Jaques Chatillon, Rambures, Vaudemont,
Beaumont, Grandpré, Roussi, and Faulconbridge,
Foix, Lestrale, Bouciqualt, and Charolois, 45
High dukes, great princes, barons, lords, and knights,
For your great seats now quit you of great shames.
Bar Harry England, that sweeps through our land
With pennons painted in the blood of Harfleur.
Rush on his host as doth the melted snow 50
Upon the valleys whose low vassal seat
The Alps doth spit and void his rheum upon.
Go down upon him—you have power enough—
And in a captive chariot into Rouen
Bring him our prisoner.

Con. This becomes the great. 55
Sorry am I his numbers are so few,
His soldiers sick and famished in their march;
For I am sure, when he shall see our army,
He'll drop his heart into the sink of fear
And, for achievement, offer us his ransom. 60

King. Therefore, Lord Constable, haste on Montjoy,
And let him say to England that we send
To know what willing ransom he will give.
Prince Dauphin, you shall stay with us in Rouen.

Dau. Not so, I do beseech your Majesty. 65

King. Be patient, for you shall remain with us.
Now forth, Lord Constable and princes all,
And quickly bring us word of England's fall.

Exeunt.

[Scene VI. *The English camp in Picardy.*]

Enter CAPTAINS, *English and Welsh*—GOWER *and* FLUELLEN.

Gow. How now, Captain Fluellen? Come you from the bridge?

Flu. I assure you there is very excellent services committed at the bridge.

Gow. Is the Duke of Exeter safe? 5

Flu. The Duke of Exeter is as magnanimous as Agamemnon, and a man that I love and honor with my soul, and my heart, and my duty, and my live, and my living, and my uttermost power. He is not—God be praised and plessed!—any hurt in the 10 world, but keeps the pridge most valiantly, with excellent discipline. There is an aunchient lieutenant there at the pridge, I think in my very conscience he is as valiant a man as Mark Anthony, and he is a man of no estimation in the world, but I did see 15 him do as gallant service.

Gow. What do you call him?

Flu. He is called Aunchient Pistol.

Gow. I know him not.

Enter PISTOL.

Flu. Here is the man. 20

Pist. Captain, I thee beseech to do me favors.
The Duke of Exeter doth love thee well.

Flu. Ay, I praise God; and I have merited some love at his hands.

Pist. Bardolph, a soldier firm and sound of heart,
And of buxom valor, hath by cruel fate, 26
And giddy Fortune's furious fickle wheel—
That goddess blind,
That stands upon the rolling restless stone—

Flu. By your patience, Aunchient Pistol. 30 Fortune is painted plind, with a muffler afore her eyes, to signify to you that Fortune is plind; and she is painted also with a wheel, to signify to you, which is the moral of it, that she is turning and inconstant, and mutability, and variation; and her foot, 35 look you, is fixed upon a spherical stone, which rolls, and rolls, and rolls. In good truth, the poet makes a most excellent description of it. Fortune is an excellent moral.

Pist. Fortune is Bardolph's foe, and frowns on him; 40
For he hath stol'n a pax, and hanged must 'a be—
A damned death!
Let gallows gape for dog; let man go free,
And let not hemp his windpipe suffocate.
But Exeter hath given the doom of death 45
For pax of little price.
Therefore, go speak—the Duke will hear thy voice;
And let not Bardolph's vital thread be cut
With edge of penny cord and vile reproach.
Speak, Captain, for his life, and I will thee requite. 50

Flu. Aunchient Pistol, I do partly understand your meaning.

Pist. Why then, rejoice therefore!

Flu. Certainly, aunchient, it is not a thing to rejoice at; for if, look you, he were my brother, 55 I would desire the Duke to use his good pleasure and put him to execution; for discipline ought to be used.

47. seats: estates; positions
60. for achievement: instead of holding out for victory
6. magnanimous: noble-spirited
15. estimation: reputation
41. pax: a tablet with a depiction of the Crucifixion, kissed by communicants during Mass
50. requite: reward

Pist. Die and be damned! and figo for thy friendship!

Flu. It is well. 60

Pist. The fig of Spain! *Exit.*

Flu. Very good.

Gow. Why, this is an arrant counterfeit rascal! I remember him now—a bawd, a cutpurse.

Flu. I'll assure you, 'a utt'red as prave words 65 at the pridge as you shall see in a summer's day. But it is very well. What he has spoke to me, that is well, I warrant you, when time is serve.

Gow. Why, 'tis a gull, a fool, a rogue, that now and then goes to the wars to grace himself, at 70 his return into London, under the form of a soldier. And such fellows are perfect in the great commanders' names, and they will learn you by rote where services were done:—at such and such a sconce, at such a breach, at such a convoy; who 75 came off bravely, who was shot, who disgraced, what terms the enemy stood on; and this they con perfectly in the phrase of war, which they trick up with new-tuned oaths; and what a beard of the General's cut and a horrid suit of the camp will do among 80 foaming bottles and ale-washed wits is wonderful to be thought on. But you must learn to know such slanders of the age, or else you may be marvelously mistook.

Flu. I tell you what, Captain Gower, I do 85 perceive he is not the man that he would gladly make show to the world he is. If I find a hole in his coat, I will tell him my mind. [*Drum within.*] Hark you, the King is coming, and I must speak with him from the pridge. 90

Drum and colors. Enter the KING *and his poor* SOLDIERS, [*and* GLOUCESTER].

God pless your Majesty!

King. How now, Fluellen? Camest thou from the bridge?

Flu. Ay, so please your Majesty. The Duke of Exeter has very gallantly maintained the 95 pridge; the French is gone off, look you, and there is gallant and most prave passages. Marry, the athversary was have possession of the pridge, but he is enforced to retire, and the Duke of Exeter is master of the pridge. I can tell your Majesty, the 100 Duke is a prave man.

King. What men have you lost, Fluellen?

Flu. The perdition of the athversary hath been very great, reasonable great. Marry, for my part, I think the Duke hath lost never a man but one 105 that is like to be executed for robbing a church—one Bardolph, if your Majesty know the man. His face is all bubukles and whelks, and knobs, and flames o' fire, and his lips blows at his nose, and it is like a coal of fire, sometimes plue and sometimes red; 110 but his nose is executed, and his fire's out.

King. We would have all such offenders so cut off. And we give express charge that in our marches through the country there be nothing compelled from the villages, nothing taken but paid for; none 115 of the French upbraided or abused in disdainful language; for when lenity and cruelty play for a kingdom, the gentler gamester is the soonest winner.

Tucket. Enter MONTJOY.

Mont. You know me by my habit. 120

King. Well then, I know thee. What shall I know of thee?

Mont. My master's mind.

King. Unfold it.

Mont. Thus says my king:—Say thou to 125 Harry of England: Though we seemed dead, we did but sleep. Advantage is a better soldier than rashness. Tell him we could have rebuked him at Harfleur, but that we thought not good to bruise an injury till it were full ripe. Now we speak 130 upon our cue, and our voice is imperial. England shall repent his folly, see his weakness, and admire our sufferance. Bid him therefore consider of his ransom, which must proportion the losses we have borne, the subjects we have lost, the disgrace we 135 have digested; which in weight to re-answer, his pettiness would bow under. For our losses, his exchequer is too poor; for the effusion of our blood, the muster of his kingdom too faint a number; and for our disgrace, his own person kneeling at our 140 feet but a weak and worthless satisfaction. To this add defiance; and tell him for conclusion he hath betrayed his followers, whose condemnation is pronounced. So far my king and master; so much my office. 145

King. What is thy name? I know thy quality.

Mont. Montjoy.

King. Thou dost thy office fairly. Turn thee back,
And tell thy king I do not seek him now,
But could be willing to march on to Calais 150

58. figo: the fig of Spain; an obscenely contemptuous term accompanied by a gesture with thumb and forefinger
63. arrant: downright
75. sconce: earthwork
77. con: learn
79. new-tuned: newly current
83. slanders: disgraces
87. a . . . coat: an opportunity to shame him

103. perdition: loss
108. bubukles: probably a combination of "bubo" (abscess) and "carbuncle"; **whelks:** pimples
111. executed: i.e., slit
129. bruise: squeeze
133. sufferance: patience
139. muster: whole population

Without impeachment: for, to say the sooth,
Though 'tis no wisdom to confess so much
Unto an enemy of craft and vantage,
My people are with sickness much enfeebled,
My numbers lessened, and those few I have, 155
Almost no better than so many French;
Who when they were in health, I tell thee, herald,
I thought upon one pair of English legs
Did march three Frenchmen. Yet forgive me, God,
That I do brag thus! This your air of France 160
Hath blown that vice in me. I must repent.
Go therefore tell thy master here I am;
My ransom is this frail and worthless trunk;
My army but a weak and sickly guard;
Yet, God before, tell him we will come on, 165
Though France himself and such another neighbor
Stand in our way. There's for thy labor, Montjoy.
[*Gives a purse.*]
Go bid thy master well advise himself:
If we may pass, we will; if we be hind'red,
We shall your tawny ground with your red blood
Discolor; and so, Montjoy, fare you well. 171
The sum of all our answer is but this:
We would not seek a battle, as we are,
Nor, as we are, we say we will not shun it.
So tell your master. 175

Mont. I shall deliver so. Thanks to your Highness.
[*Exit.*]

Glouc. I hope they will not come upon us now.

King. We are in God's hand, brother, not in theirs.
March to the bridge. It now draws toward night.
Beyond the river we'll encamp ourselves, 180
And on tomorrow bid them march away.
Exeunt.

[Scene VII. *The French camp, near Agincourt.*]

Enter the CONSTABLE OF FRANCE, *the* LORD RAMBURES, ORLEANS, DAUPHIN, *with others.*

Con. Tut! I have the best armor of the world. Would it were day!

Orl. You have an excellent armor; but let my horse have his due.

Con. It is the best horse of Europe. 5

Orl. Will it never be morning?

Dau. My Lord of Orleans, and my Lord High Constable, you talk of horse and armor?

Orl. You are as well provided of both as any prince in the world. 10

Dau. What a long night is this! I would not change my horse with any that treads but on four pasterns. Ça, ha! he bounds from the earth, as if his entrails were hairs; le cheval volant, the Pegasus, avec les narines de feu! When I bestride him, I soar, I 15 am a hawk. He trots the air. The earth sings when he touches it. The basest horn of his hoof is more musical than the pipe of Hermes.

Orl. He's of the color of the nutmeg.

Dau. And of the heat of the ginger. It is a 20 beast for Perseus: he is pure air and fire; and the dull elements of earth and water never appear in him, but only in patient stillness while his rider mounts him. He is indeed a horse, and all other jades you may call beasts. 25

Con. Indeed, my lord, it is a most absolute and excellent horse.

Dau. It is the prince of palfreys. His neigh is like the bidding of a monarch, and his countenance enforces homage. 30

Orl. No more, cousin.

Dau. Nay, the man hath no wit that cannot, from the rising of the lark to the lodging of the lamb, vary deserved praise on my palfrey. It is a theme as fluent as the sea. Turn the sands into eloquent 35 tongues, and my horse is argument for them all. 'Tis a subject for a sovereign to reason on, and for a sovereign's sovereign to ride on; and for the world, familiar to us and unknown, to lay apart their particular functions and wonder at him. I once 40 writ a sonnet in his praise and began thus, "Wonder of nature!"

Orl. I have heard a sonnet begin so to one's mistress.

Dau. Then did they imitate that which I 45 composed to my courser, for my horse is my mistress.

Orl. Your mistress bears well.

Dau. Me well, which is the prescript praise and perfection of a good and particular mistress.

Con. Nay, for methought yesterday your 50 mistress shrewdly shook your back.

Dau. So perhaps did yours.

Con. Mine was not bridled.

Dau. O, then belike she was old and gentle, and

151. **impeachment:** impediment; **sooth:** truth
163. **trunk:** carcass
168. **well . . . himself:** bethink himself carefully

12. **pasterns:** used loosely for "hooves"
13–14. **as . . . hairs:** i.e., like a tennis ball, stuffed with hair
14. **Pegasus:** a winged horse that sprang from Medusa's blood when she was slain by Perseus
14–15. **avec . . . feu:** i.e., breathing fire from his nostrils
18. **pipe . . . Hermes:** Hermes (Mercury) was credited with inventing the syrinx.
24. **jades:** nags
26. **absolute:** perfect
29. **countenance:** bearing
36. **argument:** subject matter
37. **reason:** discourse
48. **prescript:** prescribed
49. **particular:** exclusively one's own
51. **shrewdly:** ill-naturedly

you rode like a kern of Ireland, your French 55
hose off, and in your strait strossers.

Con. You have good judgment in horsemanship.

Dau. Be warned by me then. They that ride so, and ride not warily, fall into foul bogs. I had rather have my horse to my mistress. 60

Con. I had as lief have my mistress a jade.

Dau. I tell thee, Constable, my mistress wears his own hair.

Con. I could make as true a boast as that, if I had a sow to my mistress. 65

Dau. "Le chien est retourné à son propre vomissement, et la truie lavée au bourbier." Thou makest use of anything.

Con. Yet do I not use my horse for my mistress, or any such proverb so little kin to the purpose. 70

Ram. My Lord Constable, the armor that I saw in your tent tonight—are those stars or suns upon it?

Con. Stars, my lord.

Dau. Some of them will fall tomorrow, I hope.

Con. And yet my sky shall not want. 75

Dau. That may be, for you bear a many superfluously, and 'twere more honor some were away.

Con. Ev'n as your horse bears your praises, who would trot as well were some of your brags dismounted. 80

Dau. Would I were able to load him with his desert! Will it never be day? I will trot tomorrow a mile, and my way shall be paved with English faces.

Con. I will not say so, for fear I should be 85
faced out of my way; but I would it were morning, for I would fain be about the ears of the English.

Ram. Who will go to hazard with me for twenty prisoners?

Con. You must first go yourself to hazard 90
ere you have them.

Dau. 'Tis midnight; I'll go arm myself. *Exit.*

Orl. The Dauphin longs for morning.

Ram. He longs to eat the English.

Con. I think he will eat all he kills. 95

Orl. By the white hand of my lady, he's a gallant prince.

Con. Swear by her foot, that she may tread out the oath.

Orl. He is simply the most active gentle- 100
man of France.

Con. Doing is activity, and he will still be doing.

Orl. He never did harm, that I heard of.

Con. Nor will do none tomorrow. He will 105
keep that good name still.

Orl. I know him to be valiant.

Con. I was told that by one that knows him better than you.

Orl. What's he? 110

Con. Marry, he told me so himself, and he said he cared not who knew it.

Orl. He needs not; it is no hidden virtue in him.

Con. By my faith, sir, but it is! Never anybody saw it but his lackey. 'Tis a hooded valor; 115
and when it appears, it will bate.

Orl. Ill will never said well.

Con. I will cap that proverb with "There is flattery in friendship."

Orl. And I will take up that with "Give the 120
devil his due."

Con. Well placed! There stands your friend for the devil. Have at the very eye of that proverb with "A pox of the devil!"

Orl. You are the better at proverbs, by 125
how much "a fool's bolt is soon shot."

Con. You have shot over.

Orl. 'Tis not the first time you were overshot.

Enter a MESSENGER.

Mess. My Lord High Constable, the English lie within fifteen hundred paces of your tents. 130

Con. Who hath measured the ground?

Mess. The Lord Grandpré.

Con. A valiant and most expert gentleman. Would it were day! Alas, poor Harry of England! He longs not for the dawning, as we do. 135

Orl. What a wretched and peevish fellow is this King of England, to mope with his fat-brained followers so far out of his knowledge!

Con. If the English had any apprehension, they would run away. 140

Orl. That they lack; for if their heads had any intellectual armor, they could never wear such heavy headpieces.

55. kern . . . Ireland: Irish foot soldier
55–56. French hose: full breeches
56. in . . . strossers: literally, in tight trousers, possibly meaning hose with which breeches would normally be worn. Irish kerns in the contemporary *Image of Ireland* by John Derricke are illustrated wearing jerkins rather than breeches and hose, and some appear to be stockingless.
61. jade: (1) nag; (2) wanton
66–67. Le . . . bourbier: cf. II Pet. 2:22.
79. brags: showy trappings
88. go . . . me: wager with me. **Hazard** was a dice game.
114–15. Never . . . lackey: i.e., he has never shown valor except in striking his servant
115–16. 'Tis . . . bate: like a hawk, his valor is kept under wraps, and when it is displayed it is soon frightened. The hawk was said to "bate" when it fluttered its wings in alarm.
127. shot over: missed the mark
128. overshot: outshot
136. peevish: silly or perverse
137–38. mope . . . knowledge: sleepwalk with his stupid company in strange country where he may lose himself. The implication is that he has unknowingly bitten off more than he can chew in this campaign.
139. apprehension: intelligent comprehension

Ram. That island of England breeds very valiant creatures. Their mastiffs are of unmatchable 145 courage.

Orl. Foolish curs, that run winking into the mouth of a Russian bear and have their heads crushed like rotten apples! You may as well say that's a valiant flea that dare eat his breakfast on the lip of 150 a lion.

Con. Just, just! and the men do sympathize with the mastiffs in robustious and rough coming on, leaving their wits with their wives; and then give them great meals of beef and iron and steel, 155 they will eat like wolves and fight like devils.

Orl. Ay, but these English are shrewdly out of beef.

Con. Then shall we find tomorrow they have only stomachs to eat and none to fight. Now is it 160 time to arm. Come, shall we about it?

Orl. It is now two o'clock; but let me see—by ten
We shall have each a hundred Englishmen.

Exeunt.

152. Just: true; **sympathize:** accord

157. shrewdly: distressingly
160. stomachs: (1) appetites; (2) courage

ACT [IV]

CHORUS.

Now entertain conjecture of a time
When creeping murmur and the poring dark
Fills the wide vessel of the universe.
From camp to camp, through the foul womb of night,
The hum of either army stilly sounds, 5
That the fixed sentinels almost receive
The secret whispers of each other's watch.
Fire answers fire, and through their paly flames
Each battle sees the other's umbered face. 9
Steed threatens steed, in high and boastful neighs
Piercing the night's dull ear; and from the tents
The armorers accomplishing the knights,
With busy hammers closing rivets up,
Give dreadful note of preparation.
The country cocks do crow, the clocks do toll 15
And the third hour of drowsy morning name.
Proud of their numbers and secure in soul,
The confident and overlusty French
Do the low-rated English play at dice;
And chide the cripple tardy-gaited night 20
Who like a foul and ugly witch doth limp
So tediously away. The poor condemned English,
Like sacrifices, by their watchful fires
Sit patiently and inly ruminate
The morning's danger; and their gesture sad, 25
Investing lank-lean cheeks and war-worn coats,
Presenteth them unto the gazing moon
So many horrid ghosts. O, now, who will behold
The royal captain of this ruined band
Walking from watch to watch, from tent to tent,
Let him cry "Praise and glory on his head!" 31
For forth he goes and visits all his host,
Bids them good morrow with a modest smile
And calls them brothers, friends, and countrymen.
Upon his royal face there is no note 35
How dread an army hath enrounded him;
Nor doth he dedicate one jot of color
Unto the weary and all-watched night,
But freshly looks, and overbears attaint
With cheerful semblance and sweet majesty; 40
That every wretch, pining and pale before,
Beholding him, plucks comfort from his looks.
A largess universal, like the sun,
His liberal eye doth give to every one,
Thawing cold fear, that mean and gentle all 45
Behold, as may unworthiness define,
A little touch of Harry in the night.

1. entertain . . . of: allow yourselves to suppose
2. poring: penetrable only by means of intent peering (poring)
5. stilly sounds: is audible in the stillness
8. paly: palelike; dividing by vertical uprights
9. battle: army; **umbered:** shadowed
12. accomplishing: completing their armor
17. Proud of: valiant because of; **secure:** overconfident
18. overlusty: unduly merry
19. play . . . dice: i.e., using them as stakes

25. gesture sad: grave demeanor
26. Investing: clothing
28. horrid: frightful; terrifying
38. all-watched: sleepless
39. overbears attaint: masters weakness
43. largess: free benefit
44. liberal: generous
45. that: so that
46. as . . . define: if the unworthy speaker may so describe it

And so our scene must to the battle fly;
Where (O for pity!) we shall much disgrace
With four or five most vile and ragged foils, 50
Right ill-disposed in brawl ridiculous,
The name of Agincourt. Yet sit and see,
Minding true things by what their mock'ries be.
Exit.

[Scene I. *France. The English camp at Agincourt.*]

Enter the KING, BEDFORD, *and* GLOUCESTER.

King. Gloucester, 'tis true that we are in great danger;
The greater therefore should our courage be.
Good morrow, brother Bedford, God Almighty!
There is some soul of goodness in things evil,
Would men observingly distill it out; 5
For our bad neighbor makes us early stirrers,
Which is both healthful, and good husbandry.
Besides, they are our outward consciences,
And preachers to us all, admonishing
That we should dress us fairly for our end. 10
Thus may we gather honey from the weed
And make a moral of the devil himself.

Enter ERPINGHAM.

Good morrow, old Sir Thomas Erpingham.
A good soft pillow for that good white head
Were better than a churlish turf of France. 15
Erp. Not so, my liege. This lodging likes me better,
Since I may say "Now lie I like a king."
King. 'Tis good for men to love their present pains
Upon example: so the spirit is eased;
And when the mind is quick'ned, out of doubt 20
The organs, though defunct and dead before,
Break up their drowsy grave and newly move
With casted slough and fresh legerity.
Lend me thy cloak, Sir Thomas. Brothers both,
Commend me to the princes in our camp; 25
Do my good morrow to them, and anon
Desire them all to my pavilion.
Glouc. We shall, my liege.
Erp. Shall I attend your Grace?
King. No, my good knight.
Go with my brothers to my lords of England. 30
I and my bosom must debate awhile,
And then I would no other company.
Erp. The Lord in heaven bless thee, noble Harry!
Exeunt [*all but the King*].
King. God-a-mercy, old heart! thou speakst cheerfully.

Enter PISTOL.

Pist. Qui va là? 35
King. A friend.
Pist. Discuss unto me, art thou officer;
Or art thou base, common, and popular?
King. I am a gentleman of a company.
Pist. Trailst thou the puissant pike? 40
King. Even so. What are you?
Pist. As good a gentleman as the Emperor.
King. Then you are a better than the King.
Pist. The King's a bawcock, and a heart of gold,
A lad of life, an imp of fame, 45
Of parents good, of fist most valiant.
I kiss his dirty shoe, and from heartstring
I love the lovely bully. What is thy name?
King. Harry le Roy.
Pist. Le Roy? A Cornish name. Art thou of Cornish crew? 50
King. No, I am a Welshman.
Pist. Knowst thou Fluellen?
King. Yes.
Pist. Tell him I'll knock his leek about his pate
Upon St. Davy's Day. 55
King. Do not you wear your dagger in your cap
that day, lest he knock that about yours.
Pist. Art thou his friend?
King. And his kinsman too.
Pist. The figo for thee then! 60
King. I thank you. God be with you!
Pist. My name is Pistol called. *Exit. Manet King.*
King. It sorts well with your fierceness.

Enter FLUELLEN *and* GOWER.

Gow. Captain Fluellen!
Flu. So! in the name of Jesu Christ, speak 65
fewer. It is the greatest admiration in the universal
world, when the true and aunchient prerogatifes and
laws of the wars is not kept. If you would take the
pains but to examine the wars of Pompey the Great,
you shall find, I warrant you, that there is no 70

50. **foils:** rapiers
53. **Minding:** picturing mentally; **mockeries:** imitations
7. **good husbandry:** thrifty management
16. **likes:** pleases
19. **Upon example:** by comparison with another's lot
23. **slough:** i.e., old skin, like that of a snake; **legerity:** nimbleness
25. **Commend me:** give my greetings
34. **God-a-mercy:** God have mercy; thanks
39. **gentleman . . . company:** an officer of disputed rank
40. **Trailst . . . pike:** are you a pikeman (in the infantry)
45. **imp . . . fame:** offspring of a famous house
55. **St. Davy's Day:** March 1, anniversary of a Welsh victory over the Saxons. The wearing of a leek was traditional to commemorate the occasion.
63. **sorts:** suits
66. **admiration:** marvel

tiddle taddle nor pibble pabble in Pompey's camp. I warrant you, you shall find the ceremonies of the wars, and the cares of it, and the forms of it, and the sobriety of it, and the modesty of it, to be otherwise. 75

Gow. Why, the enemy is loud; you hear him all night.

Flu. If the enemy is an ass and a fool and a prating coxcomb, is it meet, think you, that we should also, look you, be an ass and a fool and a prating coxcomb? In your own conscience now? 80

Gow. I will speak lower.

Flu. I pray you and beseech you that you will.

Exeunt [*Gower and Fluellen*].

King. Though it appear a little out of fashion,
There is much care and valor in this Welshman. 85

Enter THREE SOLDIERS, JOHN BATES, ALEXANDER COURT, *and* MICHAEL WILLIAMS.

Court. Brother John Bates, is not that the morning which breaks yonder?

Bates. I think it be; but we have no great cause to desire the approach of day.

Will. We see yonder the beginning of the day, but I think we shall never see the end of it. Who goes there? 90

King. A friend.

Will. Under what captain serve you?

King. Under Sir Thomas Erpingham. 95

Will. A good old commander and a most kind gentleman. I pray you, what thinks he of our estate?

King. Even as men wracked upon a sand, that look to be washed off the next tide.

Bates. He hath not told his thought to the King? 100

King. No; nor is it not meet he should. For though I speak it to you, I think the King is but a man, as I am. The violet smells to him as it doth to me; the element shows to him as it doth to me; all his senses have but human conditions. His ceremonies laid by, in his nakedness he appears but a man; and though his affections are higher mounted than ours, yet, when they stoop, they stoop with the like wing. Therefore, when he sees reason of fears, as we do, his fears, out of doubt, be of the same relish as ours are. Yet, in reason, no man should possess him with any appearance of fear, lest he, by showing it, should dishearten his army. 105 110

Bates. He may show what outward courage he will; but I believe, as cold a night as 'tis, he could wish himself in Thames up to the neck; and so I would he were, and I by him, at all adventures, so we were quit here. 115

King. By my troth, I will speak my conscience of the King: I think he would not wish himself anywhere but where he is. 120

Bates. Then I would he were here alone. So should he be sure to be ransomed, and a many poor men's lives saved. 125

King. I dare say you love him not so ill to wish him here alone, howsoever you speak this to feel other men's minds. Methinks I could not die anywhere so contented as in the King's company, his cause being just and his quarrel honorable. 130

Will. That's more than we know.

Bates. Ay, or more than we should seek after; for we know enough if we know we are the King's subjects. If his cause be wrong, our obedience to the King wipes the crime of it out of us. 135

Will. But if the cause be not good, the King himself hath a heavy reckoning to make when all those legs and arms and heads, chopped off in a battle, shall join together at the latter day and cry all "We died at such a place!" some swearing, some crying for a surgeon, some upon their wives left poor behind them, some upon the debts they owe, some upon their children rawly left. I am afeard there are few die well that die in a battle; for how can they charitably dispose of anything when blood is their argument? Now, if these men do not die well, it will be a black matter for the King that led them to it; who to disobey were against all proportion of subjection. 140 145

King. So, if a son that is by his father sent about merchandise do sinfully miscarry upon the sea, the imputation of his wickedness, by your rule, should be imposed upon his father that sent him; or if a servant, under his master's command transporting a sum of money, be assailed by robbers and die in many irreconciled iniquities, you may call the business of the master the author of the servant's damnation. But this is not so. The King is not bound to answer the particular endings of his soldiers, the father of his son, nor the master of his servant; for they purpose not their death when they purpose their services. Besides, there is no king, be his cause never so spotless, if it come to the arbitrament of swords, can try it out with all unspotted soldiers. Some (peradventure) have on them the guilt of premeditated and contrived murder; some, of be- 150 155 160 165

74. modesty: moderation; propriety
108. affections: inclinations; tastes
109. stoop: the image is that of a hawk swooping down upon its prey.
111. out . . . doubt: doubtless
112–13. possess . . . fear: show any sign of fear that he may see
118. at . . . adventures: no matter what the risk
119. quit: finished
120–21. conscience: heartfelt belief
143. rawly: prematurely
148–49. were . . . subjection: would go counter to the loyalty a subject owes his king
151. miscarry: die
156. irreconciled iniquities: unexpiated sins

guiling virgins with the broken seals of perjury; some, making the wars their bulwark, that have before gored the gentle bosom of peace with pillage and robbery. Now, if these men have defeated the 170 law and outrun native punishment, though they can outstrip men, they have no wings to fly from God. War is his beadle, war is his vengeance; so that here men are punished for before-breach of the King's laws in now the King's quarrel. Where they 175 feared the death, they have borne life away; and where they would be safe, they perish. Then if they die unprovided, no more is the King guilty of their damnation than he was before guilty of those impieties for the which they are now visited. 180 Every subject's duty is the King's, but every subject's soul is his own. Therefore should every soldier in the wars do as every sick man in his bed—wash every mote out of his conscience; and dying so, death is to him advantage; or not dying, the time 185 was blessedly lost wherein such preparation was gained; and in him that escapes, it were not sin to think that, making God so free an offer, he let him outlive that day to see his greatness and to teach others how they should prepare. 190

Will. 'Tis certain, every man that dies ill, the ill upon his own head—the King is not to answer it.

Bates. I do not desire he should answer for me, and yet I determine to fight lustily for him.

King. I myself heard the King say he would 195 not be ransomed.

Will. Ay, he said so, to make us fight cheerfully; but when our throats are cut, he may be ransomed, and we ne'er the wiser.

King. If I live to see it, I will never trust 200 his word after.

Will. You pay him then! That's a perilous shot out of an elder-gun that a poor and a private displeasure can do against a monarch! You may as well go about to turn the sun to ice with fanning 205 in his face with a peacock's feather. You'll never trust his word after! Come, 'tis a foolish saying.

King. Your reproof is something too round. I should be angry with you if the time were convenient.

Will. Let it be a quarrel between us if you 210 live.

King. I embrace it.

Will. How shall I know thee again?

King. Give me any gage of thine, and I will wear it in my bonnet. Then, if ever thou darest ac- 215 knowledge it, I will make it my quarrel.

Will. Here's my glove. Give me another of thine.

King. There.

Will. This will I also wear in my cap. If ever thou come to me and say, after tomorrow, "This 220 is my glove," by this hand, I will take thee a box on the ear.

King. If ever I live to see it, I will challenge it.

Will. Thou darest as well be hanged.

King. Well, I will do it, though I take thee 225 in the King's company.

Will. Keep thy word. Fare thee well.

Bates. Be friends, you English fools, be friends! We have French quarrels enow, if you could tell how to reckon. 230

King. Indeed the French may lay twenty French crowns to one they will beat us, for they bear them on their shoulders; but it is no English treason to cut French crowns, and tomorrow the King himself will be a clipper. *Exeunt Soldiers.*

Upon the King! Let us our lives, our souls, 236
Our debts, our careful wives,
Our children, and our sins, lay on the King!
We must bear all. O hard condition,
Twin-born with greatness, subject to the breath
Of every fool, whose sense no more can feel 241
But his own wringing! What infinite heart's-ease
Must kings neglect that private men enjoy!
And what have kings that privates have not too,
Save ceremony, save general ceremony? 245
And what art thou, thou idol Ceremony?
What kind of god art thou, that sufferst more
Of mortal griefs than do thy worshipers?
What are thy rents? What are thy comings-in?
O Ceremony, show me but thy worth! 250
What is thy soul of adoration?
Art thou aught else but place, degree, and form,
Creating awe and fear in other men?
Wherein thou art less happy being feared
Than they in fearing. 255
What drinkst thou oft, instead of homage sweet,
But poisoned flattery? O, be sick, great greatness,
And bid thy ceremony give thee cure!
Thinkst thou the fiery fever will go out
With titles blown from adulation? 260

167. broken . . . perjury: false vows of fidelity
173. beadle: an official concerned with the punishment of petty offenses
178. unprovided: unprepared; without having received the sacraments
180. visited: punished
188. making . . . offer: submitting himself so freely to God's mercy
202. pay: punish
203. elder-gun: a popgun made of elder wood
208. round: blunt
214. gage: token; pledge
232. crowns: (1) coins; (2) heads
233. English treason: clipping coin of the realm was a treasonable act.
237. careful: full of care
242. wringing: pain
249. comings-in: revenues
251. thy . . . adoration: your essential quality meriting adoration
260. titles . . . adulation: mere words administered by the breath of flattery. The secondary meaning of **blown** is "inflated."

Will it give place to flexure and low bending?
Canst thou, when thou commandst the beggar's knee,
Command the health of it? No, thou proud dream,
That playst so subtly with a king's repose.
I am a king that find thee; and I know 265
'Tis not the balm, the scepter, and the ball,
The sword, the mace, the crown imperial,
The intertissued robe of gold and pearl,
The farced title running fore the king,
The throne he sits on, nor the tide of pomp 270
That beats upon the high shore of this world—
No, not all these, thrice-gorgeous ceremony,
Not all these, laid in bed majestical,
Can sleep so soundly as the wretched slave,
Who, with a body filled, and vacant mind, 275
Gets him to rest, crammed with distressful bread;
Never sees horrid night, the child of hell;
But like a lackey, from the rise to set,
Sweats in the eye of Phœbus, and all night
Sleeps in Elysium; next day after dawn, 280
Doth rise and help Hyperion to his horse;
And follows so the ever-running year
With profitable labor to his grave;
And but for ceremony, such a wretch,
Winding up days with toil and nights with sleep,
Had the forehand and vantage of a king. 286
The slave, a member of the country's peace,
Enjoys it; but in gross brain little wots
What watch the king keeps to maintain the peace,
Whose hours the peasant best advantages. 290

Enter ERPINGHAM.

Erp. My lord, your nobles, jealous of your absence,
Seek through your camp to find you.
King. Good old knight,
Collect them all together at my tent.
I'll be before thee.
Erp. I shall do't, my lord. *Exit.* 294
King. O God of battles, steel my soldiers' hearts,
Possess them not with fear! Take from them now
The sense of reck'ning, if the opposed numbers
Pluck their hearts from then. Not today, O Lord,
O, not today, think not upon the fault
My father made in compassing the crown! 300
I Richard's body have interred new;
And on it have bestowed more contrite tears
Than from it issued forced drops of blood.
Five hundred poor I have in yearly pay,
Who twice a day their withered hands hold up 305
Toward heaven, to pardon blood; and I have built
Two chantries, where the sad and solemn priests
Sing still for Richard's soul. More will I do,
Though all that I can do is nothing worth,
Since that my penitence comes after all, 310
Imploring pardon.

Enter GLOUCESTER.

Glouc. My liege!
King. My brother Gloucester's voice. Ay.
I know thy errand; I will go with thee. 314
The day, my friends, and all things stay for me.
Exeunt.

[Scene II. *The French camp.*]

Enter the DAUPHIN, ORLEANS, RAMBURES, *and* BEAUMONT.

Orl. The sun doth gild our armor. Up, my lords!
Dau. Montez à cheval! My horse! Varlet, laquais! Ha!
Orl. O brave spirit!
Dau. Via! les eaux et la terre—
Orl. Rien puis? L'air et le feu. 5
Dau. Ciel! cousin Orleans.

Enter CONSTABLE.

Now, my Lord Constable?
Con. Hark how our steeds for present service neigh!
Dau. Mount them and make incision in their hides,
That their hot blood may spin in English eyes 10
And dout them with superfluous courage, ha!
Ram. What, will you have them weep our horses' blood?
How shall we then behold their natural tears?

Enter MESSENGER.

Mess. The English are embattailed, you French peers.
Con. To horse, you gallant princes! straight to horse! 15
Do but behold yond poor and starved band,
And your fair show shall suck away their souls,

261. flexure: bowing
265. find: judge
269. farced: stuffed; unnaturally inflated
276. distressful: painfully earned
281. Hyperion: another name for the sun-god
288. wots: knows
290. Whose hours: i.e., the King's wakeful hours; **advantages:** benefits
291. jealous of: anxious because of
300. compassing: achieving
308. still: continually
4. Via . . . terre: onward over water and earth
8. present: immediate
11. dout: extinguish; **superfluous courage:** i.e., the horse's excessive blood (valor)
14. embattailed: arrayed for battle

Leaving them but the shales and husks of men.
There is not work enough for all our hands,
Scarce blood enough in all their sickly veins 20
To give each naked curtal ax a stain
That our French gallants shall today draw out
And sheathe for lack of sport. Let us but blow on them,
The vapor of our valor will o'erturn them.
'Tis positive 'gainst all exceptions, lords, 25
That our superfluous lackeys and our peasants,
Who in unnecessary action swarm
About our squares of battle, were enow
To purge this field of such a hilding foe,
Though we upon this mountain's basis by 30
Took stand for idle speculation,
But that our honors must not. What's to say?
A very little little let us do,
And all is done. Then let the trumpets sound
The tucket sonance and the note to mount; 35
For our approach shall so much dare the field
That England shall couch down in fear and yield.

Enter GRANDPRÉ.

Grand. Why do you stay so long, my lords of France?
Yond island carrions, desperate of their bones,
Ill-favoredly become the morning field. 40
Their ragged curtains poorly are let loose,
And our air shakes them passing scornfully.
Big Mars seems bankrout in their beggared host
And faintly through a rusty beaver peeps.
The horsemen sit like fixed candlesticks 45
With torch staves in their hand; and their poor jades
Lob down their heads, dropping the hides and hips,
The gum down roping from their pale-dead eyes,
And in their pale dull mouths the gimmaled bit
Lies foul with chawed grass, still and motionless;
And their executors, the knavish crows, 51
Fly o'er them, all impatient for their hour.
Description cannot suit itself in words
To demonstrate the life of such a battle
In life so lifeless as it shows itself. 55
Con. They have said their prayers, and they stay for death.

Dau. Shall we go send them dinners and fresh suits
And give their fasting horses provender,
And after fight with them?
Con. I stay but for my guidon. To the field! 60
I will the banner from a trumpet take
And use it for my haste. Come, come away!
The sun is high, and we outwear the day.
Exeunt.

[Scene III. *The English camp.*]

Enter GLOUCESTER, BEDFORD, EXETER, ERPINGHAM *with all his host,* SALISBURY, *and* WESTMORLAND.

Glouc. Where is the King?
Bed. The King himself is rode to view their battle.
West. Of fighting men they have full threescore thousand.
Exe. There's five to one; besides, they all are fresh.
Sal. God's arm strike with us! 'Tis a fearful odds.
God be wi' you, princes all; I'll to my charge. 6
If we no more meet till we meet in heaven,
Then joyfully, my noble Lord of Bedford,
My dear Lord Gloucester, and my good Lord Exeter,
And my kind kinsman, warriors all, adieu! 10
Bed. Farewell, good Salisbury, and good luck go with thee!
Exe. Farewell, kind lord. Fight valiantly today;
And yet I do thee wrong to mind thee of it,
For thou art framed of the firm truth of valor.
[*Exit Salisbury.*]
Bed. He is as full of valor as of kindness, 15
Princely in both.

Enter the KING.

West. O that we now had here
But one ten thousand of those men in England
That do no work today!
King. What's he that wishes so?
My cousin Westmorland? No, my fair cousin.
If we are marked to die, we are enow 20
To do our country loss; and if to live,
The fewer men, the greater share of honor.
God's will! I pray thee wish not one man more.
By Jove, I am not covetous for gold,
Nor care I who doth feed upon my cost; 25
It yearns me not if men my garments wear;
Such outward things dwell not in my desires:
But if it be a sin to covet honor,

21. curtal ax: cutlass
23. for . . . sport: when the sport is finished
29. hilding: worthless
35. tucket sonance: sound of the tucket (call to the cavalry)
36. dare . . . field: daunt the enemy
39. desperate of: desperate to preserve
42. passing: exceedingly
43. bankrout: bankrupt
44. beaver: visor
47. Lob: droop
49. gimmaled bit: a double bit, hinged together
51. executors: handlers of their remains
53. suit itself: clothe itself properly
56. stay: wait

60. guidon: banner
63. outwear: consume
6. charge: duty; company under his command
20–21. enow . . . loss: enough of a loss for our country
26. yearns: distresses

I am the most offending soul alive.
No, faith, my coz, wish not a man from England.
God's peace! I would not lose so great an honor 31
As one man more methinks would share from me
For the best hope I have. O, do not wish one more!
Rather proclaim it, Westmorland, through my host,
That he which hath no stomach to this fight, 35
Let him depart; his passport shall be made,
And crowns for convoy put into his purse.
We would not die in that man's company
That fears his fellowship to die with us.
This day is called the Feast of Crispian. 40
He that outlives this day, and comes safe home,
Will stand a-tiptoe when this day is named
And rouse him at the name of Crispian.
He that shall live this day, and see old age,
Will yearly on the vigil feast his neighbors 45
And say "Tomorrow is St. Crispian."
Then will he strip his sleeve and show his scars,
And say "These wounds I had on Crispin's day."
Old men forget; yet all shall be forgot,
But he'll remember, with advantages, 50
What feats he did that day. Then shall our names,
Familiar in his mouth as household words—
Harry the King, Bedford and Exeter,
Warwick and Talbot, Salisbury and Gloucester—
Be in their flowing cups freshly rememb'red. 55
This story shall the good man teach his son;
And Crispin Crispian shall ne'er go by,
From this day to the ending of the world,
But we in it shall be remembered—
We few, we happy few, we band of brothers; 60
For he today that sheds his blood with me
Shall be my brother. Be he ne'er so vile,
This day shall gentle his condition;
And gentlemen in England now abed 64
Shall think themselves accursed they were not here,
And hold their manhoods cheap whiles any speaks
That fought with us upon St. Crispin's day.

Enter SALISBURY.

Sal. My sovereign lord, bestow yourself with speed.
The French are bravely in their battles set
And will with all expedience charge on us. 70

King. All things are ready, if our minds be so.

West. Perish the man whose mind is backward now!

King. Thou dost not wish more help from England, coz?

West. God's will, my liege! would you and I alone,
Without more help, could fight this royal battle!

King. Why, now thou hast unwished five thousand men! 76
Which likes me better than to wish us one.
You know your places. God be with you all!

Tucket. Enter MONTJOY.

Mont. Once more I come to know of thee, King Harry,
If for thy ransom thou wilt now compound, 80
Before thy most assured overthrow;
For certainly thou art so near the gulf
Thou needs must be englutted. Besides, in mercy,
The Constable desires thee thou wilt mind
Thy followers of repentance, that their souls 85
May make a peaceful and a sweet retire
From all these fields, where (wretches!) their poor bodies
Must lie and fester.

King. Who hath sent thee now?

Mont. The Constable of France.

King. I pray thee bear my former answer back:
Bid them achieve me, and then sell my bones. 91
Good God! why should they mock poor fellows thus?
The man that once did sell the lion's skin
While the beast lived, was killed with hunting him.
A many of our bodies shall no doubt 95
Find native graves; upon the which, I trust,
Shall witness live in brass of this day's work;
And those that leave their valiant bones in France,
Dying like men, though buried in your dunghills,
They shall be famed; for there the sun shall greet them 100
And draw their honors reeking up to heaven,
Leaving their earthly parts to choke your clime,
The smell whereof shall breed a plague in France.
Mark then abounding valor in our English,
That, being dead, like to the bullet's grazing, 105
Break out into a second course of mischief,
Killing in relapse of mortality.
Let me speak proudly. Tell the Constable
We are but warriors for the working day.
Our gayness and our gilt are all besmirched 110
With rainy marching in the painful field.
There's not a piece of feather in our host—
Good argument, I hope, we will not fly—
And time hath worn us into slovenry.
But, by the mass, our hearts are in the trim; 115
And my poor soldiers tell me, yet ere night
They'll be in fresher robes, or they will pluck
The gay new coats o'er the French soldiers' heads

39. fears . . . us: is afraid to be our companion in death
43. rouse him: straighten himself up with pride
50. advantages: i.e., embellishments to the truth
69. bravely . . . set: lined up in splendid battle array
70. expedience: speed

80. compound: make terms
91. achieve: vanquish
105. grazing: i.e., ricocheting
107. in . . . mortality: i.e., as though the dead had been revivified
117. or . . . pluck: if they have to pluck

And turn them out of service. If they do this 119
(As, if God please, they shall), my ransom then
Will soon be levied. Herald, save thou thy labor.
Come thou no more for ransom, gentle herald.
They shall have none, I swear, but these my joints;
Which if they have as I will leave 'em them,
Shall yield them little, tell the Constable. 125

Mont. I shall, King Harry. And so fare thee well.
Thou never shalt hear herald any more. *Exit.*

King. I fear thou wilt once more come again for ransom.

Enter YORK.

York. My lord, most humbly on my knee I beg
The leading of the vaward. 130

King. Take it, brave York. Now, soldiers, march away;
And how thou pleasest, God, dispose the day!

Exeunt.

[Scene IV. *The field of battle.*]

Alarum. Excursions. Enter PISTOL, FRENCH SOLDIER, BOY.

Pist. Yield, cur!

French. Je pense que vous êtes le gentilhomme de bonne qualité.

Pist. Quality! Callino custore me! Art thou a gentleman?
What is thy name? Discuss. 5

French. O Seigneur Dieu!

Pist. O Signieur Dew should be a gentleman.
Perpend my words, O Signieur Dew, and mark.
O Signieur Dew, thou diest on point of fox,
Except, O signieur, thou do give to me 10
Egregious ransom.

French. O, prenez miséricorde! ayez pitié de moi!

Pist. Moy shall not serve. I will have forty moys;
Or I will fetch thy rim out at thy throat
In drops of crimson blood. 15

French. Est-il impossible d'échapper la force de ton bras?

Pist. Brass, cur?
Thou damned and luxurious mountain goat,
Offerst me brass?

French. O, pardonnez-moi! 20

Pist. Sayst thou me so? Is that a ton of moys?
Come hither, boy; ask me this slave in French
What is his name.

Boy. Ecoutez. Comment êtes-vous appelé?

French. Monsieur le Fer. 25

Boy. He says his name is Master Fer.

Pist. Master Fer? I'll fer him, and firk him, and ferret him!
Discuss the same in French unto him.

Boy. I do not know the French for "fer," and "ferret," and "firk." 30

Pist. Bid him prepare, for I will cut his throat.

French. Que dit-il, monsieur?

Boy. Il me commande à vous dire que vous faites vous prêt; car ce soldat ici est disposé tout à cette heure de couper votre gorge. 35

Pist. Owy, cuppele gorge, permafoy!
Peasant, unless thou give me crowns, brave crowns;
Or mangled shalt thou be by this my sword.

French. O, je vous supplie, pour l'amour de Dieu, me pardonner! Je suis gentilhomme de bonne 40 maison. Gardez ma vie, et je vous donnerai deux cents écus.

Pist. What are his words?

Boy. He prays you to save his life. He is a gentleman of a good house, and for his ransom he will 45 give you two hundred crowns.

Pist. Tell him my fury shall abate, and I
The crowns will take.

French. Petit monsieur, que dit-il?

Boy. Encore qu'il est contre son jurement de 50 pardonner aucun prisonnier, néanmoins, pour les écus que vous l'avez promis, il est content de vous donner la liberté, le franchisement.

French. Sur mes genoux je vous donne mille remercîments; et je m'estime heureux que je suis 55 tombé entre les mains d'un chevalier, je pense, le plus brave, vaillant, et très-distingué seigneur d'Angleterre.

Pist. Expound unto me, boy.

Boy. He gives you, upon his knees, a thou- 60 sand thanks; and he esteems himself happy that he hath fall'n into the hands of one (as he thinks) the most brave, valorous, and thrice-worthy signieur of England.

Pist. As I suck blood, I will some mercy show!
Follow me, cur. [*Exit.*]

Boy. Suivez-vous le grand Capitaine. 67

[*Exit French Soldier.*]

I did never know so full a voice issue from so empty a heart; but the saying is true, "The empty vessel makes the greatest sound." Bardolph and Nym 70

130. vaward: vanguard
4. Callino . . . me: possibly an echo of a phrase from a contemporary Irish song
7. should: i.e., must. Pistol, of course, does not understand much of what the Frenchman says.
8. Perpend: consider
9. fox: sword (so called from the trade-mark stamped on a certain make)
11. Egregious: extraordinary
13. Moy: understood by Pistol to be a coin
14. rim: belly

27. firk: beat; **ferret:** harass
37. brave: splendid

had ten times more valor than this roaring devil i' the old play that every one may pare his nails with a wooden dagger; and they are both hanged; and so would this be, if he durst steal anything adventurously. I must stay with the lackeys with the 75 luggage of our camp. The French might have a good prey of us, if he knew of it; for there is none to guard it but boys.

Exit.

[Scene V. *Another part of the field of battle.*]

Enter CONSTABLE, ORLEANS, BOURBON, DAUPHIN, *and* RAMBURES.

Con. O diable!
Orl. O Seigneur! le jour est perdu, tout est perdu!
Dau. Mort de ma vie! all is confounded, all!
Reproach and everlasting shame 4
Sits mocking in our plumes. *A short alarum.*
O méchante fortune! Do not run away.
Con. Why, all our ranks are broke.
Dau. O perdurable shame! Let's stab ourselves.
Be these the wretches that we played at dice for?
Orl. Is this the king we sent to for his ransom?
Bour. Shame, and eternal shame! nothing but shame! 11
Let's die in honor. Once more back again!
And he that will not follow Bourbon now,
Let him go hence, and with his cap in hand
Like a base pander hold the chamber door 15
Whilst by a slave, no gentler than my dog,
His fairest daughter is contaminated.
Con. Disorder, that hath spoiled us, friend us now!
Let us on heaps go offer up our lives.
Orl. We are enow yet living in the field 20
To smother up the English in our throngs,
If any order might be thought upon.
Bour. The devil take order now! I'll to the throng.
Let life be short; else shame will be too long.

Exeunt.

[Scene VI. *Another part of the field.*]

Alarum. Enter the KING *and his* TRAIN, [EXETER, *and others,*] *with* PRISONERS.

King. Well have we done, thrice-valiant countrymen;
But all's not done, yet keep the French the field.
Exe. The Duke of York commends him to your Majesty.
King. Lives he, good uncle? Thrice within this hour
I saw him down; thrice up again and fighting. 5
From helmet to the spur all blood he was.
Exe. In which array, brave soldier, doth he lie,
Larding the plain; and by his bloody side,
Yoke-fellow to his honor-owing wounds,
The noble Earl of Suffolk also lies. 10
Suffolk first died; and York, all haggled over,
Comes to him, where in gore he lay insteeped,
And takes him by the beard, kisses the gashes
That bloodily did yawn upon his face,
And cries aloud, "Tarry, dear cousin Suffolk! 15
My soul shall thine keep company to heaven.
Tarry, sweet soul, for mine, then fly abreast;
As in this glorious and well-foughten field
We kept together in our chivalry!"
Upon these words I came and cheered him up. 20
He smiled me in the face, raught me his hand,
And, with a feeble gripe, says "Dear my lord,
Commend my service to my sovereign."
So did he turn, and over Suffolk's neck
He threw his wounded arm and kissed his lips; 25
And so, espoused to death, with blood he sealed
A testament of noble-ending love.
The pretty and sweet manner of it forced
Those waters from me which I would have stopped;
But I had not so much of man in me, 30
And all my mother came into mine eyes
And gave me up to tears.
King. I blame you not;
For, hearing this, I must perforce compound
With mistful eyes, or they will issue too. *Alarum.*
But hark! what new alarum is this same? 35
The French have reinforced their scattered men.
Then every soldier kill his prisoners!
Give the word through.

Exeunt.

[Scene VII. *Another part of the field.*]

Enter FLUELLEN *and* GOWER.

Flu. Kill the poys and the luggage? 'Tis expressly against the law of arms. 'Tis as arrant a piece of

71–73. **roaring . . . dagger:** the devil in morality plays was often a comic character, sometimes beaten off the stage with a wooden dagger.
3. **confounded:** routed in shame
8. **perdurable:** enduring
19. **on heaps:** in a body

8. **Larding:** enriching with his blood
9. **honor-owing:** honorable
11. **haggled:** hacked
21. **raught:** reached
22. **gripe:** grasp
23. **Commend:** tender (not praise)
33. **compound:** come to terms
34. **issue:** give forth
2. **arrant:** notorious

knavery, mark you now, as can be offert. In your conscience, now, is it not?

Gow. 'Tis certain there's not a boy left alive; 5
and the cowardly rascals that ran from the battle ha' done this slaughter. Besides, they have burned and carried away all that was in the King's tent; wherefore the King most worthily hath caused every soldier to cut his prisoner's throat. O, 'tis a gallant 10
king!

Flu. Ay, he was porn at Monmouth, Captain Gower. What call you the town's name where Alexander the Pig was born?

Gow. Alexander the Great. 15

Flu. Why, I pray you, is not "pig" great? The pig, or the great, or the mighty, or the huge, or the magnanimous are all one reckonings, save the phrase is a little variations.

Gow. I think Alexander the Great was born 20
in Macedon. His father was called Philip of Macedon, as I take it.

Flu. I think it is in Macedon where Alexander is porn. I tell you, Captain, if you look in the maps of the 'orld, I warrant you sall find, in the compar- 25
isons between Macedon and Monmouth, that the situations, look you, is both alike. There is a river in Macedon, and there is also moreover a river at Monmouth. It is called Wye at Monmouth; but it is out of my prains what is the name of the other 30
river. But 'tis all one; 'tis alike as my fingers is to my fingers, and there is salmons in both. If you mark Alexander's life well, Harry of Monmouth's life is come after it indifferent well; for there is figures in all things. Alexander, God knows and you know, 35
in his rages, and his furies, and his wraths, and his cholers, and his moods, and his displeasures, and his indignations, and also being a little intoxicates in his prains, did, in his ales and his angers, look you, kill his best friend, Cleitus. 40

Gow. Our King is not like him in that. He never killed any of his friends.

Flu. It is not well done, mark you now, to take the tales out of my mouth ere it is made and finished. I speak but in the figures and comparisons of it. 45
As Alexander killed his friend Cleitus, being in his ales and his cups, so also Harry Monmouth, being in his right wits and his good judgments, turned away the fat knight with the great belly doublet. He was full of jests, and gipes, and knaveries, and 50
mocks. I have forgot his name.

Gow. Sir John Falstaff.

Flu. That is he. I'll tell you there is good men porn at Monmouth.

Gow. Here comes his Majesty. 55

Alarum. Enter KING HARRY, [WARWICK, GLOUCESTER, EXETER, *and others,*] *with* PRISONERS. *Flourish.*

King. I was not angry since I came to France
Until this instant. Take a trumpet, herald;
Ride thou unto the horsemen on yond hill.
If they will fight with us, bid them come down,
Or void the field. They do offend our sight. 60
If they'll do neither, we will come to them
And make them skirr away as swift as stones
Enforced from the old Assyrian slings.
Besides, we'll cut the throats of those we have;
And not a man of them that we shall take 65
Shall taste our mercy. Go and tell them so.

Enter MONTJOY [*the* HERALD].

Exe. Here comes the herald of the French, my liege.

Glouc. His eyes are humbler than they used to be.

King. How now? What means this, herald? Knowst thou not
That I have fined these bones of mine for ransom?
Comest thou again for ransom?

Herald. No, great King. 71
I come to thee for charitable license
That we may wander o'er this bloody field
To book our dead, and then to bury them;
To sort our nobles from our common men; 75
For many of our princes (woe the while!)
Lie drowned and soaked in mercenary blood;
So do our vulgar drench their peasant limbs
In blood of princes; and the wounded steeds
Fret fetlock-deep in gore and with wild rage 80
Yerk out their armed heels at their dead masters,
Killing them twice. O, give us leave, great King,
To view the field in safety and dispose
Of their dead bodies!

King. I tell thee truly, herald,
I know not if the day be ours or no; 85
For yet a many of your horsemen peer
And gallop o'er the field.

Herald. The day is yours.

King. Praised be God and not our strength for it!
What is this castle called that stands hard by?

Herald. They call it Agincourt. 90

17–18. magnanimous: great-souled
34. figures: parallels
49. great . . . doublet: literally, a doublet stuffed to monstrous proportions. Doublets stuffed in a curve over the waistline were fashionable in the late sixteenth century. Falstaff, of course, needed no padding to create this fashionable line.

62. skirr: scurry
70. fined: (1) staked; (2) refined (so as to offer them in lieu of gold)
74. book: list
76. woe . . . while: alas for such a day!
77. mercenary blood: the blood of soldiers who fought for pay. Nobles fought for honor.
81. Yerk: kick
86. peer: appear
89. hard: near

King. Then call we this the field of Agincourt,
Fought on the day of Crispin Crispianus.

Flu. Your grandfather of famous memory, an't please your Majesty, and your great-uncle Edward the Plack Prince of Wales, as I have read in the 95 chronicles, fought a most prave pattle here in France.

King. They did, Fluellen.

Flu. Your Majesty says very true. If your Majesties is rememb'red of it, the Welshmen did good service in a garden where leeks did grow, wearing 100 leeks in their Monmouth caps; which your Majesty know to this hour is an honorable badge of the service; and I do believe your Majesty takes no scorn to wear the leek upon St. Tavy's day.

King. I wear it for a memorable honor; 105
For I am Welsh, you know, good countryman.

Flu. All the water in Wye cannot wash your Majesty's Welsh plood out of your pody, I can tell you that. God pless it and preserve it, as long as it pleases his grace, and his majesty too! 110

King. Thanks, good my countryman.

Flu. By Jeshu, I am your Majesty's countryman, I care not who know it! I will confess it to all the 'orld. I need not to be ashamed of your Majesty, praised be God, so long as your Majesty is an honest 115 man.

King. God keep me so!

Enter WILLIAMS.

Our heralds go with him.
Bring me just notice of the numbers dead
On both our parts. [*Exeunt Heralds with Montjoy.*]
Call yonder fellow hither.

Exe. Soldier, you must come to the King. 120

King. Soldier, why wearst thou that glove in thy cap?

Will. An't please your Majesty, 'tis the gage of one that I should fight withal, if he be alive.

King. An Englishman? 125

Will. An't please your Majesty, a rascal that swaggered with me last night; who, if 'a live and ever dare to challenge this glove, I have sworn to take him a box o' the ear; or if I can see my glove in his cap, which he swore, as he was a soldier, he would 130 wear (if alive), I will strike it out soundly.

King. What think you, Captain Fluellen? Is it fit this soldier keep his oath?

Flu. He is a craven and a villain else, an't please your Majesty, in my conscience. 135

King. It may be his enemy is a gentleman of great sort, quite from the answer of his degree.

Flu. Though he be as good a gentleman as the devil is, as Lucifer and Belzebub himself, it is necessary, look your Grace, that he keep his vow and his 140 oath. If he be perjured, see you now, his reputation is as arrant a villain and a jack sauce as ever his black shoe trod upon God's ground and his earth, in my conscience, la!

King. Then keep thy vow, sirrah, when thou 145 meetst the fellow.

Will. So I will, my liege, as I live.

King. Who servest thou under?

Will. Under Captain Gower, my liege.

Flu. Gower is a good captain and is good 150 knowledge and literatured in the wars.

King. Call him hither to me, soldier.

Will. I will, my liege. *Exit.*

King. Here, Fluellen; wear thou this favor for me and stick it in thy cap. When Alençon and my- 155 self were down together, I plucked this glove from his helm. If any man challenge this, he is a friend to Alençon and an enemy to our person. If thou encounter any such, apprehend him, an thou dost me love.

Flu. Your Grace doo's me as great honors as 160 can be desired in the hearts of his subjects. I would fain see the man, that has but two legs, that shall find himself aggriefed at this glove, that is all. But I would fain see it once, an please God of his grace that I might see. 165

King. Knowst thou Gower?

Flu. He is my dear friend, an please you.

King. Pray thee go seek him and bring him to my tent. 169

Flu. I will fetch him. *Exit.*

King. My Lord of Warwick, and my brother Gloucester,
Follow Fluellen closely at the heels.
The glove which I have given him for a favor
May haply purchase him a box o' the ear;
It is the soldier's. I by bargain should 175
Wear it myself. Follow, good cousin Warwick.
If that the soldier strike him—as I judge
By his blunt bearing, he will keep his word—
Some sudden mischief may arise of it;
For I do know Fluellen valiant, 180
And, touched with choler, hot as gunpowder,
And quickly will return an injury.
Follow, and see there be no harm between them.
Go you with me, uncle of Exeter.

Exeunt.

115. honest: honorable
118. just notice: exact reckoning
128. take: give
137. quite . . . degree: far too highborn to answer the challenge of one of his degree
138. as . . . devil: that the devil was a gentleman was a proverbial idea; cf. also *King Lear,* III.iv.145, "The prince of darkness is a gentleman."
142. jack sauce: impudent fellow
154. favor: token
174. haply: perhaps; **purchase him:** acquire for him

[Scene VIII. *Before King Henry's tent.*]

Enter GOWER *and* WILLIAMS.

Will. I warrant it is to knight you, Captain.

Enter FLUELLEN.

Flu. God's will and his pleasure, Captain, I beseech you now, come apace to the King. There is more good toward you peradventure than is in your knowledge to dream of. 5

Will. Sir, know you this glove?

Flu. Know the glove? I know the glove is a glove.

Will. I know this; and thus I challenge it.

Strikes him.

Flu. 'Sblood! an arrant traitor as any's in the universal world, or in France, or in England! 10

Gow. How now, sir? You villain!

Will. Do you think I'll be forsworn?

Flu. Stand away, Captain Gower. I will give treason his payment into plows, I warrant you.

Will. I am no traitor. 15

Flu. That's a lie in thy throat. I charge you in his Majesty's name apprehend him. He's a friend of the Duke Alençon's.

Enter WARWICK *and* GLOUCESTER.

War. How now, how now? What's the matter?

Flu. My Lord of Warwick, here is (praised 20 be God for it!) a most contagious treason come to light, look you, as you shall desire in a summer's day. Here is his Majesty.

Enter KING *and* EXETER.

King. How now? What's the matter?

Flu. My liege, here is a villain and a traitor 25 that, look your Grace, has struck the glove which your Majesty is take out of the helmet of Alençon.

Will. My liege, this was my glove, here is the fellow of it; and he that I gave it to in change promised to wear it in his cap. I promised to strike him if 30 he did. I met this man with my glove in his cap, and I have been as good as my word.

Flu. Your Majesty hear now, saving your Majesty's manhood, what an arrant, rascally, beggarly, lousy knave it is! I hope your Majesty is pear 35 me testimony and witness, and will avouchment, that this is the glove of Alençon that your Majesty is give me, in your conscience, now.

King. Give me thy glove, soldier. Look, here is the fellow of it. 40
'Twas I indeed thou promisedst to strike;
And thou hast given me most bitter terms.

Flu. An please your Majesty, let his neck answer for it, if there is any martial law in the world.

King. How canst thou make me satisfaction? 45

Will. All offenses, my lord, come from the heart. Never came any from mine that might offend your Majesty.

King. It was ourself thou didst abuse.

Will. Your Majesty came not like yourself. 50 You appeared to me but as a common man; witness the night, your garments, your lowliness. And what your Highness suffered under that shape, I beseech you take it for your own fault, and not mine; for had you been as I took you for, I made no offense. 55 Therefore I beseech your Highness pardon me.

King. Here, uncle Exeter, fill this glove with crowns
And give it to this fellow. Keep it, fellow,
And wear it for an honor in thy cap
Till I do challenge it. Give him the crowns; 60
And, Captain, you must needs be friends with him.

Flu. By this day and this light, the fellow has mettle enough in his belly. Hold, there is twelvepence for you; and I pray you to serve God, and keep you out of prawls, and prabbles, and quarrels, and 65 dissensions, and, I warrant you it is the better for you.

Will. I will none of your money.

Flu. It is with a good will. I can tell you it will serve you to mend your shoes. Come, wherefore 70 should you be so pashful? Your shoes is not so good. 'Tis a good silling, I warrant you, or I will change it.

Enter [*an English*] HERALD.

King. Now, herald, are the dead numb'red? 73

Her. Here is the number of the slaught'red French.

[*Gives a paper.*]

King. What prisoners of good sort are taken, uncle?

Exe. Charles Duke of Orleans, nephew to the King;
John Duke of Bourbon and Lord Bouciqualt:
Of other lords and barons, knights and squires,
Full fifteen hundred, besides common men.

King. This note doth tell me of ten thousand French 80
That in the field lie slain. Of princes, in this number,
And nobles bearing banners, there lie dead
One hundred twenty-six; added to these,
Of knights, esquires, and gallant gentlemen,
Eight thousand and four hundred; of the which, 85
Five hundred were but yesterday dubbed knights;
So that in these ten thousand they have lost

21. contagious: pestilent
29. change: exchange
33–34. saving . . . manhood: an apology for using the epithets that follow
36. avouchment: confirm

There are but sixteen hundred mercenaries;
The rest are princes, barons, lords, knights, squires,
And gentlemen of blood and quality. 90
The names of those their nobles that lie dead:
Charles Delabreth, High Constable of France;
Jaques of Chatillon, Admiral of France;
The master of the crossbows, Lord Rambures;
Great Master of France, the brave Sir Guichard Dau-
phin; 95
John Duke of Alençon; Anthony Duke of Brabant,
The brother to the Duke of Burgundy;
And Edward Duke of Bar; of lusty earls,
Grandpré and Roussi, Faulconbridge and Foix, 99
Beaumont and Marle, Vaudemont and Lestrale.
Here was a royal fellowship of death!
Where is the number of our English dead?
[*Herald gives another paper.*]
Edward the Duke of York, the Earl of Suffolk,
Sir Richard Ketly, Davy Gam, Esquire;
None else of name; and of all other men 105
But five-and-twenty. O God, thy arm was here!
And not to us, but to thy arm alone,
Ascribe we all! When, without stratagem,
But in plain shock and even play of battle,
Was ever known so great and little loss 110
On one part and on the other? Take it, God,
For it is none but thine!

Exe. 'Tis wonderful!

King. Come, go we in procession to the village;
And be it death proclaimed through our host
To boast of this, or take that praise from God 115
Which is his only.

Flu. Is it not lawful, an please your Majesty, to tell how many is killed?

King. Yes, Captain; but with this acknowledgment,
That God fought for us. 120

Flu. Yes, my conscience, he did us great good.

King. Do we all holy rites.
Let there be sung "Non nobis" and "Te Deum,"
The dead with charity enclosed in clay,
And then to Calais; and to England then; 125
Where ne'er from France arrived more happy men.
Exeunt.

88. **mercenaries:** common soldiers

ACT V

Enter CHORUS.

Vouchsafe to those that have not read the story
That I may prompt them; and of such as have,
I humbly pray them to admit the excuse
Of time, of numbers, and due course of things
Which cannot in their huge and proper life 5
Be here presented. Now we bear the King
Toward Calais. Grant him there. There seen,
Heave him away upon your winged thoughts
Athwart the sea. Behold, the English beach
Pales in the flood with men, wives, and boys, 10
Whose shouts and claps outvoice the deep-mouthed
sea,
Which, like a mighty whiffler fore the King,
Seems to prepare his way. So let him land,
And solemnly see him set on to London.
So swift a pace hath thought that even now 15
You may imagine him upon Blackheath;
Where that his lords desire him to have borne
His bruised helmet and his bended sword
Before him through the city. He forbids it,
Being free from vainness and self-glorious pride;
Giving full trophy, signal, and ostent 21
Quite from himself to God. But now behold,
In the quick forge and working house of thought,
How London doth pour out her citizens!
The Mayor and all his brethren in best sort— 25
Like to the senators of the antique Rome,
With the plebeians swarming at their heels—
Go forth and fetch their conqu'ring Cæsar in;
As, by a lower but by loving likelihood,
Were now the general of our gracious Empress 30
(As in good time he may) from Ireland coming,
Bringing rebellion broached on his sword,
How many would the peaceful city quit

3. **admit:** accept
10. **Pales in:** encloses
12. **whiffler:** an official who cleared the way for a procession
21. **full . . . ostent:** all symbols of victory
29. **loving likelihood:** possibility eagerly desired
30. **general:** the Earl of Essex, who commanded English troops in the effort to subdue the rebellious Irish when this play was in the writing
32. **broached:** spitted

To welcome him! Much more, and much more cause,
Did they this Harry. Now in London place him 35
(As yet the lamentation of the French
Invites the King of England's stay at home;
The Emperor's coming in behalf of France
To order peace between them) and omit
All the occurrences, whatever chanced, 40
Till Harry's back-return again to France.
There must we bring him; and myself have played
The interim, by rememb'ring you 'tis past. 43
Then brook abridgment; and your eyes advance,
After your thoughts, straight back again to France.
Exit.

[Scene I. *France. The English camp.*]

Enter Fluellen *and* Gower.

Gow. Nay, that's right. But why wear you your leek today? St. Davy's day is past.

Flu. There is occasions and causes why and wherefore in all things. I will tell you ass my friend, Captain Gower. The rascally, scauld, beggarly, lousy, 5 pragging knave, Pistol—which you and yourself and all the world know to be no petter than a fellow, look you now, of no merits—he is come to me and prings me pread and salt yesterday, look you, and bid me eat my leek. It was in a place where I could 10 not breed no contention with him; but I will be so bold as to wear it in my cap till I see him once again, and then I will tell him a little piece of my desires.

Enter Pistol.

Gow. Why, here he comes, swelling like a turkey cock. 15

Flu. 'Tis no matter for his swellings nor his turkey cocks. God pless you, Aunchient Pistol! you scurvy, lousy knave, God pless you!

Pist. Ha! art thou bedlam? Dost thou thirst, base
Trojan,
To have me fold up Parca's fatal web? 20
Hence! I am qualmish at the smell of leek.

Flu. I peseech you heartily, scurvy, lousy knave, at my desires, and my requests, and my petitions, to eat, look you, this leek. Because, look you, you do not love it, nor your affections and your appe- 25 tites and your digestions doo's not agree with it, I would desire you to eat it.

Pist. Not for Cadwallader and all his goats.

Flu. There is one goat for you. (*Strikes him.*) Will you be so good, scauld knave, as eat it? 30

Pist. Base Trojan, thou shalt die!

Flu. You say very true, scauld knave, when God's will is. I will desire you to live in the meantime, and eat your victuals. Come, there is sauce for it. [*Strikes him.*] You called me yesterday mountain- 35 squire; but I will make you today a squire of low degree. I pray you fall to. If you can mock a leek, you can eat a leek.

Gow. Enough, Captain. You have astonished him.

Flu. I say I will make him eat some part of 40 my leek, or I will peat his pate four days.—Bite, I pray you. It is good for your green wound and your ploody coxcomb.

Pist. Must I bite?

Flu. Yes, certainly, and out of doubt, and out 45 of question too, and ambiguities.

Pist. By this leek, I will most horribly revenge! I eat, and yet, I swear—

Flu. Eat, I pray you. Will you have some more sauce to your leek? There is not enough leek to 50 swear by.

Pist. Quiet thy cudgel. Thou dost see I eat.

Flu. Much good do you, scauld knave, heartily. Nay, pray you throw none away. The skin is good for your broken coxcomb. When you take occa- 55 sions to see leeks hereafter, I pray you mock at 'em; that is all.

Pist. Good.

Flu. Ay, leeks is good. Hold you, there is a groat to heal your pate. 60

Pist. Me a groat?

Flu. Yes, verily and in truth, you shall take it; or I have another leek in my pocket, which you shall eat.

Pist. I take thy groat in earnest of revenge.

Flu. If I owe you anything, I will pay you in 65 cudgels. You shall be a woodmonger and buy nothing of me but cudgels. God be wi' you, and keep you, and heal your pate. *Exit.*

Pist. All hell shall stir for this!

Gow. Go, go. You are a counterfeit cowardly 70

36–37. As . . . home: since the French are still subdued by sorrow, the King need not hurry back to consolidate his victory.
38. Emperor: Sigismund, Emperor of the Holy Roman Empire, who visited England on May 1, 1416
39. order: arrange
42–43. played . . . interim: narrated the intervening happenings in lieu of their dramatic presentation
44. brook abridgment: bear with our abridgment
5. scauld: scurvy; contemptible
19. bedlam: lunatic. Bedlam or Bethlehem Hospital housed the insane. **Trojan:** cant for a roistering fellow
20. Parca's . . . web: the Fates (*Parcae* in Latin) were three women, who respectively spun, measured, and cut the thread of human life.
21. qualmish: queasy

25. affections: inclinations; tastes
28. Cadwallader: last Welsh king. The reference to goats is merely an insult, not founded on a historical incident.
35–36. mountain-squire: i.e., owner of nothing but barren mountain lands
36–37. squire . . . degree: the title of an old ballad. Fluellen means that he will humble Pistol.
39. astonished: stunned
42. green: fresh
43. coxcomb: head

knave. Will you mock at an ancient tradition, begun upon an honorable respect and worn as a memorable trophy of predeceased valor, and dare not avouch in your deeds any of your words? I have seen you gleeking and galling at this gentleman twice or 75 thrice. You thought, because he could not speak English in the native garb, he could not therefore handle an English cudgel. You find it otherwise; and henceforth let a Welsh correction teach you a good English condition. Fare ye well. *Exit.* 80

Pist. Doth Fortune play the huswife with me now?
News have I, that my Nell is dead i' the spital
Of malady of France;
And there my rendezvous is quite cut off.
Old I do wax, and from my weary limbs 85
Honor is cudgeled. Well, bawd will I turn,
And something lean to cutpurse of quick hand.
To England will I steal, and there I'll steal;
And patches will I get unto these cudgeled scars
And swear I got them in the Gallia wars. 90
Exit.

[Scene II. *France. The King's Palace.*]

Enter, at one door, King Henry, Exeter, Bedford, [Gloucester,] Warwick, [Westmorland,] *and other* Lords; *at another,* Queen Isabel, *the* [French] King, *the* Duke of Burgundy, [*the* Princess Katherine, Alice,] *and* Other French.

King H. Peace to this meeting, wherefore we are met!
Unto our brother France and to our sister
Health and fair time of day. Joy and good wishes
To our most fair and princely cousin Katherine.
And as a branch and member of this royalty, 5
By whom this great assembly is contrived,
We do salute you, Duke of Burgundy.
And, princes French, and peers, health to you all!

France. Right joyous are we to behold your face,
Most worthy brother England. Fairly met. 10
So are you, princes English, every one.

Queen. So happy be the issue, brother England,
Of this good day and of this gracious meeting
As we are now glad to behold your eyes—
Your eyes which hitherto have borne in them, 15
Against the French that met them in their bent,
The fatal balls of murdering basilisks.
The venom of such looks, we fairly hope,
Have lost their quality, and that this day
Shall change all griefs and quarrels into love. 20

King H. To cry amen to that, thus we appear.

Queen. You English princes all, I do salute you.

Burg. My duty to you both, on equal love,
Great Kings of France and England! That I have labored
With all my wits, my pains, and strong endeavors
To bring your most imperial Majesties 26
Unto this bar and royal interview,
Your mightiness on both parts best can witness.
Since, then, my office hath so far prevailed
That, face to face and royal eye to eye, 30
You have congreeted, let it not disgrace me
If I demand, before this royal view,
What rub or what impediment there is
Why that the naked, poor, and mangled Peace,
Dear nurse of arts, plenty, and joyful births, 35
Should not, in this best garden of the world,
Our fertile France, put up her lovely visage.
Alas, she hath from France too long been chased!
And all her husbandry doth lie on heaps,
Corrupting in it own fertility. 40
Her vine, the merry cheerer of the heart,
Unpruned dies; her hedges even-pleached,
Like prisoners wildly overgrown with hair,
Put forth disordered twigs; her fallow leas
The darnel, hemlock, and rank fumitory 45
Doth root upon, while that the coulter rusts
That should deracinate such savagery.
The even mead, that erst brought sweetly forth
The freckled cowslip, burnet, and green clover,
Wanting the scythe, all uncorrected, rank, 50
Conceives by idleness and nothing teems
But hateful docks, rough thistles, kecksies, burrs,
Losing both beauty and utility.
And all our vineyards, fallows, meads, and hedges,
Defective in their natures, grow to wildness, 55
Even so our houses and ourselves and children

72. upon . . . respect: for an honorable reason
74-75. gleeking: mocking
75. galling: jeering
77. garb: manner
80. condition: character
81. huswife: hussy
84. rendezvous: refuge
86. bawd: procurer
87. something: somewhat; **cutpurse:** pickpocket
1. wherefore . . . met: for which purpose (peace) we are met

16. met . . . bent: encountered their aim
17. balls: (1) eyes; (2) cannon balls; **basilisks:** originally the basilisk was a fabulous serpent with a deadly glance; later the name was given to a type of cannon.
23. on . . . love: based on equal love for both of you
31. congreeted: greeted each other
37. put up: raise
40. it: an old form of the neuter genitive
42. even-pleached: pleated to form an even top layer of branches
45. darnel: weed growing in fields of grain; **rank:** luxuriant; **fumitory:** another weed
46. coulter: blade of the plow
47. deracinate: uproot
48. erst: formerly
51. Conceives . . . idleness: is seeded by worthless plants; **nothing teems:** produces nothing
52. kecksies: dry weed stalks

Have lost, or do not learn for want of time,
The sciences that should become our country;
But grow like savages—as soldiers will,
That nothing do but meditate on blood— 60
To swearing and stern looks, diffused attire,
And everything that seems unnatural.
Which to reduce into our former favor
You are assembled; and my speech entreats
That I may know the let why gentle Peace 65
Should not expel these inconveniences
And bless us with her former qualities.

King H. If, Duke of Burgundy, you would the peace
Whose want gives growth to the imperfections
Which you have cited, you must buy that peace 70
With full accord to all our just demands;
Whose tenures and particular effects
You have, enscheduled briefly, in your hands.

Burg. The King hath heard them; to the which as yet
There is no answer made.

King H. Well then, the peace, 75
Which you before so urged, lies in his answer.

France. I have but with a cursitory eye
O'erglanced the articles. Pleaseth your Grace
To appoint some of your Council presently
To sit with us once more, with better heed 80
To resurvey them, we will suddenly
Pass our accept and peremptory answer.

King H. Brother, we shall. Go, uncle Exeter,
And brother Clarence, and you, brother Gloucester,
Warwick, and Huntingdon—go with the King; 85
And take with you free power to ratify,
Augment, or alter, as your wisdoms best
Shall see advantageable for our dignity,
Anything in or out of our demands;
And we'll consign thereto. Will you, fair sister, 90
Go with the princes or stay here with us?

Queen. Our gracious brother, I will go with them.
Happily a woman's voice may do some good
When articles too nicely urged be stood on.

King H. Yet leave our cousin Katherine here with us. 95
She is our capital demand, comprised
Within the forerank of our articles.

Queen. She hath good leave.

Exeunt. Manent King Henry, Katherine, and the Gentlewoman [*Alice.*]

King H. Fair Katherine, and most fair!
Will you vouchsafe to teach a soldier terms
Such as will enter at a lady's ear 100
And plead his love suit to her gentle heart?

Kath. Your Majesty shall mock at me. I cannot speak your England.

King H. O fair Katherine, if you will love me soundly with your French heart, I will be glad 105 to hear you confess it brokenly with your English tongue. Do you like me, Kate?

Kath. Pardonnez-moi, I cannot tell wat is "like me."

King H. An angel is like you, Kate, and you 110 are like an angel.

Kath. Que dit-il? Que je suis semblable à les anges?

Alice. Oui, vraiment, sauf votre grâce, ainsi dit-il.

King H. I said so, dear Katherine, and I must not blush to affirm it. 115

Kath. O bon Dieu! les langues des hommes sont pleines de tromperies.

King H. What says she, fair one? that the tongues of men are full of deceits?

Alice. Oui, dat de tongues of de mans is be 120 full of deceits. Dat is de Princess.

King H. The Princess is the better Englishwoman. I' faith, Kate, my wooing is fit for thy understanding. I am glad thou canst speak no better English; for if thou couldst, thou wouldst find me such a 125 plain king that thou wouldst think I had sold my farm to buy my crown. I know no ways to mince it in love but directly to say "I love you." Then, if you urge me farther than to say, "Do you in faith?" I wear out my suit. Give me your answer; i' 130 faith, do! and so clap hands and a bargain. How say you, lady?

Kath. Sauf votre honneur, me understand well.

King H. Marry, if you would put me to verses or to dance for your sake, Kate, why, you undid 135 me. For the one I have neither words nor measure; and for the other I have no strength in measure, yet a reasonable measure in strength. If I could win a lady at leapfrog, or by vaulting into my saddle with my armor on my back, under the correction of 140 bragging be it spoken, I should quickly leap into a wife. Or if I might buffet for my love, or bound my horse for her favors, I could lay on like a butcher and sit like a jackanapes, never off. But, before God,

61. diffused: disordered
63. favor: fine appearance
65. let: hindrance
68. would: desire
69. want: lack
72. tenures: general terms
77. cursitory: cursory; hasty
79. presently: at once
82. Pass . . . answer: give our final decision as to what we will accept
90. consign: consent
93. Happily: perhaps
94. too . . . urged: mentioned only out of extreme punctiliousness; **stood:** insisted

122. the . . . Englishwoman: i.e., in preferring plain words to flattery
137. strength . . . measure: ability in dance measures
140–41. under . . . spoken: though I risk being accused of bragging in saying so
142. buffet: box
144. jackanapes: trained monkey

Kate, I cannot look greenly nor gasp out my 145
eloquence, nor I have no cunning in protestation; only downright oaths, which I never use till urged, nor never break for urging. If thou canst love a fellow of this temper, Kate, whose face is not worth sunburning, that never looks in his glass for 150
love of anything he sees there, let thine eye be thy cook. I speak to thee plain soldier. If thou canst love me for this, take me; if not, to say to thee that I shall die, is true—but for thy love, by the Lord, no; yet I love thee too. And while thou livest, dear 155
Kate, take a fellow of plain and uncoined constancy; for he perforce must do thee right, because he hath not the gift to woo in other places. For these fellows of infinite tongue that can rhyme themselves into ladies' favors, they do always reason them- 160
selves out again. What! A speaker is but a prater; a rhyme is but a ballad. A good leg will fall, a straight back will stoop, a black beard will turn white, a curled pate will grow bald, a fair face will wither, a full eye will wax hollow; but a good heart, 165
Kate, is the sun and the moon; or rather, the sun, and not the moon, for it shines bright and never changes, but keeps his course truly. If thou would have such a one, take me; and take me, take a soldier; take a soldier, take a king. And what 170
sayst thou then to my love? Speak, my fair—and fairly, I pray thee.

Kath. Is it possible dat I sould love de enemy of France?

King H. No, it is not possible you should 175
love the enemy of France, Kate; but in loving me you should love the friend of France; for I love France so well that I will not part with a village of it —I will have it all mine. And, Kate, when France is mine and I am yours, then yours is France 180
and you are mine.

Kath. I cannot tell wat is dat.

King H. No, Kate? I will tell thee in French; which I am sure will hang upon my tongue like a new-married wife about her husband's neck, 185
hardly to be shook off. Quand j'ai la possession de France, et quand vous avez la possession de moi (let me see, what then? St. Denis be my speed!), donc votre est France et vous êtes mienne. It is as easy for me, Kate, to conquer the kingdom as to speak 190
so much more French. I shall never move thee in French, unless it be to laugh at me.

Kath. Sauf votre honneur, le Français que vous parlez, il est meilleur que l'Anglais lequel je parle.

King H. No, faith, is't not, Kate. But thy 195
speaking of my tongue, and I thine, most truly-falsely, must needs be granted to be much at one. But, Kate, dost thou understand thus much English? Canst thou love me?

Kath. I cannot tell. 200

King H. Can any of your neighbors tell, Kate? I'll ask them. Come, I know thou lovest me; and at night when you come into your closet, you'll question this gentlewoman about me; and I know, Kate, you will to her dispraise those parts in me that 205
you love with your heart; but, good Kate, mock me mercifully, the rather, gentle Princess, because I love thee cruelly. If ever thou beest mine, Kate—as I have a saving faith within me tells me thou shalt—I get thee with scambling, and thou must there- 210
fore needs prove a good soldier-breeder. Shall not thou and I, between St. Denis and St. George, compound a boy, half French, half English, that shall go to Constantinople and take the Turk by the beard? Shall we not? What sayst thou, my fair 215
flower-de-luce?

Kath. I do not know dat.

King H. No; 'tis hereafter to know, but now to promise. Do but now promise, Kate, you will endeavor for your French part of such a boy; 220
and for my English moiety take the word of a king and a bachelor. How answer you, la plus belle Katherine du monde, mon très-cher et divin déesse?

Kath. Your Majestee ave fausse French enough to deceive de most sage demoiselle dat is en 225
France.

King H. Now, fie upon my false French! By mine honor in true English, I love thee, Kate; by which honor I dare not swear thou lovest me; yet my blood begins to flatter me that thou dost, notwith- 230
standing the poor and untempering effect of my visage. Now beshrew my father's ambition! He was thinking of civil wars when he got me; therefore was I created with a stubborn outside, with an aspect of iron, that, when I come to woo ladies, I 235
fright them. But in faith, Kate, the elder I wax, the better I shall appear. My comfort is, that old age, that ill layer-up of beauty, can do no more spoil upon my face. Thou hast me, if thou hast me, at the worst; and thou shalt wear me, if thou wear me, bet- 240
ter and better; and therefore tell me, most fair

145. **look greenly:** assume the expression of a languishing lover
149–50. **not . . . sunburning:** so little handsome that sunburn would not harm it
151–52. **let . . . cook:** i.e., dress my image to suit your eye, as a cook garnishes a dish to enhance its appeal
156. **uncoined:** uncounterfeited; sincere
188. **St. Denis:** patron saint of France

196–97. **truly-falsely:** sincerely if inaccurately
197. **much . . . one:** about equal
203. **closet:** private chamber
209. **saving faith:** faith in my salvation
210. **with scambling:** as the result of war
221. **moiety:** half
229. **blood:** ardor
231. **untempering:** unpersuasive
232. **beshrew:** plague take
234. **stubborn:** harsh
238. **layer-up:** preserver

Katherine, will you have me? Put off your maiden blushes; avouch the thoughts of your heart with the looks of an empress; take me by the hand, and say "Harry of England, I am thine!" which word 245 thou shalt no sooner bless mine ear withal but I will tell thee aloud "England is thine, Ireland is thine, France is thine, and Henry Plantagenet is thine"; who, though I speak it before his face, if he be not fellow with the best king, thou shalt find the 250 best king of good fellows. Come, your answer in broken music! for thy voice is music and thy English broken; therefore, queen of all Katherines, break thy mind to me in broken English. Wilt thou have me?

Kath. Dat is as it sall please de roi mon 255 père.

King H. Nay, it will please him well, Kate. It shall please him, Kate.

Kath. Den it sall also content me.

King H. Upon that I kiss your hand and I 260 call you my queen.

Kath. Laissez, mon seigneur, laissez, laissez! Ma foi, je ne veux point que vous abaissiez votre grandeur en baisant la main d'une de votre Seigneurie indigne serviteur. Excusez-moi, je vous sup- 265 plie, mon très-puissant seigneur.

King H. Then I will kiss your lips, Kate.

Kath. Les dames et demoiselles pour être baisées devant leur noces, il n'est pas la coutume de France.

King H. Madam my interpreter, what says 270 she?

Alice. Dat it is not be de fashon pour de ladies of France—I cannot tell vat is "baiser" en Anglish.

King H. To kiss.

Alice. Your Majestee entendre bettre que 275 moi.

King H. It is not a fashion for the maids in France to kiss before they are married, would she say?

Alice. Oui, vraiment.

King H. O Kate, nice customs curtsy to 280 great kings. Dear Kate, you and I cannot be confined within the weak list of a country's fashion. We are the makers of manners, Kate; and the liberty that follows our places stops the mouth of all find-faults, as I will do yours for upholding the nice fash- 285 ion of your country in denying me a kiss. Therefore patiently, and yielding. [*Kisses her*.] You have witchcraft in your lips, Kate. There is more eloquence in a sugar touch of them than in the tongues of the French Council, and they should sooner per- 290 suade Harry of England than a general petition of monarchs. Here comes your father.

Enter the FRENCH POWER *and the* ENGLISH LORDS.

Burg. God save your Majesty! My royal cousin, Teach you our princess English?

King H. I would have her learn, my fair 295 cousin, how perfectly I love her, and that is good English.

Burg. Is she not apt?

King H. Our tongue is rough, coz, and my condition is not smooth; so that, having neither 300 the voice nor the heart of flattery about me, I cannot so conjure up the spirit of love in her that he will appear in his true likeness.

Burg. Pardon the frankness of my mirth if I answer you for that. If you would conjure in her, you 305 must make a circle; if conjure up love in her in his true likeness, he must appear naked and blind. Can you blame her then, being a maid yet rosed over with the virgin crimson of modesty, if she deny the appearance of a naked blind boy in her naked seeing 310 self? It were, my lord, a hard condition for a maid to consign to.

King H. Yet they do wink and yield, as love is blind and enforces.

Burg. They are then excused, my lord, when 315 they see not what they do.

King H. Then, good my lord, teach your cousin to consent winking.

Burg. I will wink on her to consent, my lord, if you will teach her to know my meaning; for maids 320 well summered and warm kept are like flies at Bartholomewtide, blind, though they have their eyes; and then they will endure handling which before would not abide looking on.

King H. This moral ties me over to time 325 and a hot summer; and so I shall catch the fly, your cousin, in the latter end, and she must be blind too.

Burg. As love is, my lord, before it loves.

King H. It is so; and you may, some of you, thank love for my blindness, who cannot see many a 330 fair French city for one fair French maid that stands in my way.

France. Yes, my lord, you see them perspectively—the cities turned into a maid; for they are all girdled with maiden walls that war hath never 335 ent'red.

King H. Shall Kate be my wife?

France. So please you.

King H. I am content, so the maiden cities you talk of may wait on her. So the maid that 340

252. **broken music:** music played by an unmatched set of instruments
280. **nice:** fastidious
282. **list:** (1) enclosure; (2) border of fabric
284. **follows . . . places:** attends our stations in life
299–300. **condition:** characteristics; manners
314. **blind:** uncontrollable
321–22. **Bartholomewtide:** August 24
325. **ties . . . to:** constrains me to wait for
333. **perspectively:** in distorted fashion, as though through a perspective glass
340. **wait on:** attend; accompany

stood in the way for my wish shall show me the way to my will.

France. We have consented to all terms of reason.

King H. Is't so, my lords of England?

West. The King hath granted every article: 345
His daughter first; and in sequel, all,
According to their firm proposed natures.

Exe. Only he hath not yet subscribed this: Where your Majesty demands that the King of France, having any occasion to write for matter of grant, 350 shall name your Highness in this form and with this addition, in French, "Notre très-cher fils Henri, Roi d'Angleterre, héritier de France"; and thus in Latin, "Praecarissimus filius noster Henricus, Rex Angliae et haeres Franciae." 355

France. Nor this I have not, brother, so denied
But your request shall make me let it pass.

King H. I pray you then, in love and dear alliance,
Let that one article rank with the rest,
And thereupon give me your daughter. 360

France. Take her, fair son, and from her blood raise up
Issue to me, that the contending kingdoms
Of France and England, whose very shores look pale
With envy of each other's happiness,
May cease their hatred; and this dear conjunction
Plant neighborhood and Christianlike accord 366
In their sweet bosoms, that never war advance
His bleeding sword 'twixt England and fair France.

Lords. Amen!

King H. Now, welcome, Kate; and bear me witness all 370
That here I kiss her as my sovereign queen. *Flourish.*

Queen. God, the best maker of all marriages,
Combine your hearts in one, your realms in one!
As man and wife, being two, are one in love,
So be there 'twixt your kingdoms such a spousal
That never may ill office, or fell jealousy, 376
Which troubles oft the bed of blessed marriage,
Thrust in between the paction of these kingdoms
To make divorce of their incorporate league;
That English may as French, French Englishmen,
Receive each other! God speak this Amen! 381

All. Amen!

King H. Prepare we for our marriage; on which day,
My Lord of Burgundy, we'll take your oath,
And all the peers', for surety of our leagues. 385
Then shall I swear to Kate, and you to me,
And may our oaths well kept and prosp'rous be!

Sennet. Exeunt.

341. stood . . . wish: prevented me from fulfilling my wish to seize them
342. will: desire
347. According . . . natures: exactly according to the strict letter of the terms
348. subscribed: agreed to
356–57. so . . . pass: refused so firmly that your mere request could not win my acceptance
366. neighborhood: neighborliness
376. office: action; **fell:** cruel
378. paction: concord

[EPILOGUE]

Enter CHORUS.

Thus far, with rough and all-unable pen,
Our bending author hath pursued the story,
In little room confining mighty men,
Mangling by starts the full course of their glory.
Small time; but in that small, most greatly lived
This Star of England. Fortune made his sword;
By which the world's best garden he achieved, 7
And of it left his son imperial lord.
Henry the Sixth, in infant bands crowned King
Of France and England, did this king succeed;
Whose state so many had the managing 11
That they lost France and made his England bleed;
Which oft our stage hath shown; and for their sake
In your fair minds let this acceptance take.

[*Exit.*]

2. bending: humble
4. starts: disconnected bits of narrative
13. oft . . . shown: the three parts of *Henry VI* had already enjoyed great popularity. **their:** i.e., the previous plays

Julius Cæsar

From Thomas Treterus, *Romanorum imperatorum effigies* (1590).

The Tragedy of JULIUS CÆSAR

INTRODUCTION

Evidence points to the first performance of *Julius Cæsar* in the late summer of 1599. On September 21, 1599, Thomas Platter, a German traveler, records visiting a theatre on the south bank of the Thames, evidently the Globe, and seeing a play on the theme of Julius Cæsar with "at least fifteen characters." Scholars conclude that he saw Shakespeare's play. This date places the composition shortly after Shakespeare's completion of *Henry V;* and the structure of *Julius Cæsar* shows the influence of the chronicle-history, for, though it is classified as a tragedy, it has the loose construction of Shakespeare's plays dealing with English history. Perhaps the dramatist was still conscious of the public interest in history, and in *Julius Cæsar* he merely went back to an earlier period for historical episodes certain to interest playgoers of the day.

Shakespeare's contemporaries were well-versed in classical history. Every boy who had attended grammar school had read something from the Roman historians. Even those who could not read a word of Latin could read translations of Livy, Tacitus, Polybius, Appian, Cæsar, Suetonius, and others. Classical characters like Cæsar and Pompey even appeared in pageants and processions such as the Lord Mayor's Show. Many historical works in English described the deeds of the Greeks and the Romans. For example, Richard Reynolds brought out in 1571 *A Chronicle of All the Noble Emperors of the Romans from Julius Cæsar* with the expressed purpose of holding up a mirror in which princes and magistrates might see revealed the virtues and vices of the ancients. Sir Thomas North's translation of Plutarch's *Lives of the Noble Grecians and the Romans* in 1579 had at least eight editions and issues by 1613. Although this was a heavy and expensive volume, it was eminently readable, and Shakespeare and many of his contemporaries received much of their classical history from it. The Elizabethans, like American colonials in a later period, looked back to the classics, particularly to Roman history, for subject matter that was both entertaining and edifying.

Long before Shakespeare placed *Julius Cæsar* on the stage at the Globe, Cæsar plays were known both to university audiences and to the theatregoing public in London. A few years before, in 1594–95, the Lord Admiral's Men had staged two plays about Cæsar and Pompey, and they put on another Cæsar play in 1602. There is no clear evidence, however, that Shakespeare made use of these earlier plays. The lives of Cæsar, Brutus, and Antony in Plutarch provided material enough, though he may have consulted Lucan's *Pharsalia,* Appian's *Civil Wars,* Suetonius' *Lives of the Cæsars,* and other classical works, as well as an Italian play by Orlando Pescetti, *Il Cesare tragedia* (1594), as Sir Edmund Chambers points out.

Some critics have argued that Shakespeare's concern for chronicle-history prevented his concentrating interest upon a single tragic hero and that *Julius Cæsar* really has two heroes, Brutus and Cæsar. Although Brutus has an important role, Shakespeare undoubtedly intended to focus attention upon the traditional hero. Cæsar does not vanish from the play with his assassination in the first scene of Act III, but his spirit hovers over the rest of the play, and his ghost, like the conventional ghost in the revenge plays of the day, returns to pronounce vengeance on his antagonists.

Elizabethan audiences found in Cæsar some of the qualities that fascinated them in Henry IV and Henry V. They were interested in strong men who could impose order upon a chaotic world. Conquerors like Cæsar did not arouse in Elizabethan audiences the distaste that dictators arouse in a modern audience. If Cæsar sounds pompous to us, his manner was not objectionable to the spectator at the Globe; it was the manner that an Elizabethan would expect of one who had conquered most of the known world and given it stability. When the United States was a very new nation, the fathers of the country looked back to republican Rome for examples of virtue and patriotism. George Washington was often called "Cincinnatus" after one of the early Roman heroes, and the officers of Washington's army, when they created a veterans' organization, could think of nothing that better connoted their patriotic ideals than to call their group the "Society of the Cincinnati." The Elizabethans, on the contrary, looked back to imperial Rome for inspiration. They regarded Julius Cæsar as the beginning of the great line of Cæsars, the emperors who brought glory to Rome and the Pax Romana to the world. Shakespeare showed the shrewd appraisal of a successful playwright in selecting Julius Cæsar as the hero of a play that he had reason to hope would be a popular success.

HISTORY AND TEXT OF THE PLAY

Shakespeare's *Julius Cæsar* lived up to its author's expectations and proved one of his most popular and enduring plays. Allusions to it in seventeenth-century literature are frequent, and it had revivals at court before both James I and Charles I. After the Restoration it was revived as Shakespeare wrote it and did not undergo the type of alteration that was the fate of many of Shakespeare's plays. Thomas Betterton, one of the greatest actors of the Restoration, pleased audiences particularly with his interpretation of the part of Brutus. Throughout the eighteenth century the play held the stage, and it was equally popular in nineteenth- and twentieth-century theatres. In America, from the mid-eighteenth century onward, *Julius Cæsar* was often acted. Indeed, few of Shakespeare's plays have had a more enduring record than *Julius Cæsar*. It has probably been more widely read by school children than any of the other plays, and many a schoolboy has had to endure the memorizing and recitation of Mark Antony's oration over dead Cæsar.

The text of *Julius Cæsar* presents fewer problems than most of Shakespeare's plays. It was not printed in quarto, probably because Shakespeare's company carefully protected it; they did not want a popular play that was frequently revived to be published. Its first printing occurred in the Folio of 1623. The Second, Third, and Fourth Folios reprinted the text of the First Folio with few changes. The present editors have adopted a small number of corrections suggested by previous editors and now generally accepted.

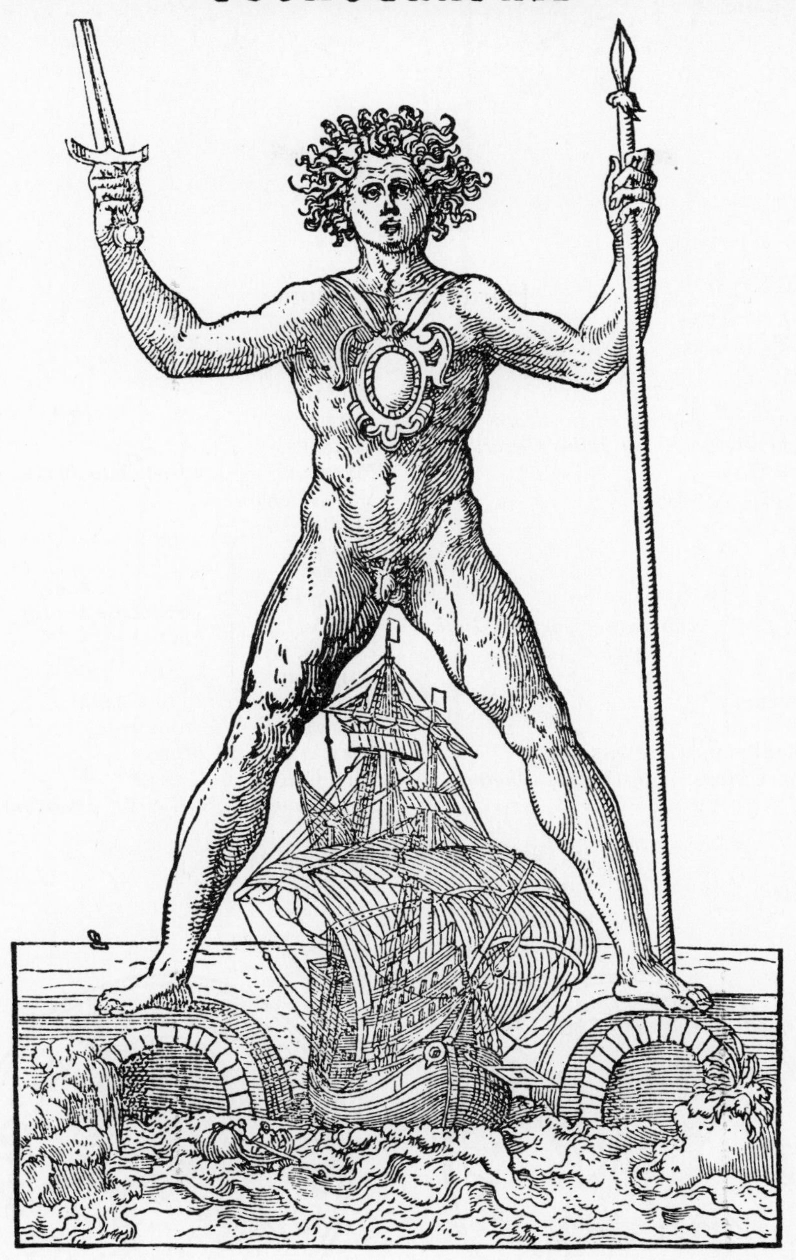

The Colossus of Rhodes
"He doth bestride the narrow world / Like a Colossus"
(*Julius Cæsar,* I.ii.135–36)
From André Thevet, *Cosmographie de Levant* (1554).

[Dramatis Personæ

JULIUS CÆSAR.
OCTAVIUS CÆSAR, MARCUS ANTONIUS, M. ÆMILIUS LEPIDUS, } *Triumvirs after the death of Julius Cæsar.*
CICERO, PUBLIUS, POPILIUS LENA, } *Senators.*
MARCUS BRUTUS, CASSIUS, CASCA, TREBONIUS, LIGARIUS, DECIUS BRUTUS, METELLUS CIMBER, CINNA, } *conspirators against Julius Cæsar.*
FLAVIUS *and* MARULLUS, *Tribunes.*
ARTEMIDORUS OF CNIDOS, *a teacher of Rhetoric.*
A SOOTHSAYER.
CINNA, *a poet.*
ANOTHER POET.
LUCILIUS, TITINIUS, MESSALA, YOUNG CATO, VOLUMNIUS, } *friends to Brutus and Cassius.*
VARRO, CLITUS, CLAUDIUS, STRATO, LUCIUS, DARDANIUS, } *servants to Brutus.*
PINDARUS, *servant to Cassius.*
CALPURNIA, *wife to Cæsar.*
PORTIA, *wife to Brutus.*
THE GHOST OF CÆSAR.
Senators, Citizens, Guards, Attendants, Servants, &c.

Scene: *Rome; near Sardis; near Philippi.*]

Brutus
From Guillaume Rouillé,
Promptuarii iconum (1553).

Calpurnia
From Guillaume Rouillé,
Promptuarii iconum (1553).

The Tragedy of JULIUS CÆSAR

ACT I

Scene I. [*Rome. A street.*]

Enter FLAVIUS, MARULLUS, *and certain* COMMONERS *over the stage.*

Flav. Hence! home, you idle creatures, get you home!
Is this a holiday? What, know you not,
Being mechanical, you ought not walk
Upon a laboring day without the sign
Of your profession? Speak, what trade art thou? 5
Car. Why, sir, a carpenter.
Mar. Where is thy leather apron and thy rule?
What dost thou with thy best apparel on?
You, sir, what trade are you?
Cob. Truly sir, in respect of a fine workman I 10
am but, as you would say, a cobbler.
Mar. But what trade art thou? Answer me directly.
Cob. A trade, sir, that I hope I may use with a safe conscience, which is indeed, sir, a mender of bad soles. 15
Mar. What trade, thou knave? Thou naughty knave, what trade?
Cob. Nay, I beseech you, sir, be not out with me.
Yet if you be out, sir, I can mend you.

3. mechanical: of the laboring class
10. in . . . of: in comparison with
11. cobbler: secondary meaning: "botcher"; one who makes clumsy repairs
12. directly: plainly
16. naughty: good-for-nothing
17. out: put out

Mar. What meanst thou by that? Mend me, thou saucy fellow?
Cob. Why, sir, cobble you. 20
Flav. Thou art a cobbler, art thou?
Cob. Truly, sir, all that I live by is with the awl. I meddle with no tradesman's matters nor women's matters, but with all. I am indeed, sir, a surgeon to old shoes. When they are in great danger, I re- 25
cover them. As proper men as ever trod upon neat's leather have gone upon my handiwork.
Flav. But wherefore art not in thy shop today?
Why dost thou lead these men about the streets?
Cob. Truly, sir, to wear out their shoes, to 30
get myself into more work. But indeed, sir, we make holiday to see Cæsar and to rejoice in his triumph.
Mar. Wherefore rejoice? What conquest brings he home?
What tributaries follow him to Rome
To grace in captive bonds his chariot wheels? 35
You blocks, you stones, you worse than senseless things!
O you hard hearts, you cruel men of Rome!
Knew you not Pompey? Many a time and oft
Have you climbed up to walls and battlements,
To tow'rs and windows, yea, to chimney tops, 40
Your infants in your arms, and there have sat
The livelong day, with patient expectation,
To see great Pompey pass the streets of Rome.
And when you saw his chariot but appear,
Have you not made an universal shout, 45
That Tiber trembled underneath her banks

26. proper: handsome

To hear the replication of your sounds
Made in her concave shores?
And do you now put on your best attire?
And do you now cull out a holiday? 50
And do you now strew flowers in his way
That comes in triumph over Pompey's blood?
Be gone!
Run to your houses, fall upon your knees,
Pray to the gods to intermit the plague 55
That needs must light on this ingratitude.

Flav. Go, go, good countrymen, and for this fault
Assemble all the poor men of your sort;
Draw them to Tiber banks, and weep your tears
Into the channel, till the lowest stream 60
Do kiss the most exalted shores of all.

Exeunt all the Commoners.

See, whe'r their basest metal be not moved.
They vanish tongue-tied in their guiltiness.
Go you down that way towards the Capitol;
This way will I. Disrobe the images 65
If you do find them decked with ceremonies.

Mar. May we do so?
You know it is the feast of Lupercal.

Flav. It is no matter. Let no images
Be hung with Cæsar's trophies. I'll about 70
And drive away the vulgar from the streets.
So do you too, where you perceive them thick.
These growing feathers plucked from Cæsar's wing
Will make him fly an ordinary pitch,
Who else would soar above the view of men 75
And keep us all in servile fearfulness.

Exeunt.

[Scene II. *The same. A public place.*]

[*Flourish.*] *Enter* CÆSAR, ANTONY (*for the course*), CALPURNIA, PORTIA, DECIUS, CICERO, BRUTUS, CASSIUS, CASCA, [*a great crowd following, among them,*] *a* SOOTHSAYER; *after them,* MARULLUS *and* FLAVIUS.

Cæs. Calpurnia.

Casca. Peace, ho! Cæsar speaks.

Cæs. Calpurnia.

Cal. Here, my lord.

Cæs. Stand you directly in Antonius' way
When he doth run his course. Antonius.

Ant. Cæsar, my lord? 5

Cæs. Forget not in your speed, Antonius,
To touch Calpurnia; for our elders say
The barren, touched in this holy chase,
Shake off their sterile curse.

Ant. I shall remember.
When Cæsar says, "Do this," it is performed. 10

Cæs. Set on, and leave no ceremony out.

Sooth. Cæsar!

Cæs. Ha! Who calls?

Casca. Bid every noise be still. Peace yet again!

Cæs. Who is it in the press that calls on me? 15
I hear a tongue shriller than all the music
Cry "Cæsar!" Speak. Cæsar is turned to hear.

Sooth. Beware the ides of March.

Cæs. What man is that?

Bru. A soothsayer bids you beware the ides of March.

Cæs. Set him before me; let me see his face. 20

Cass. Fellow, come from the throng; look upon Cæsar.

Cæs. What sayst thou to me now? Speak once again.

Sooth. Beware the ides of March.

Cæs. He is a dreamer; let us leave him. Pass.

Sennet. Exeunt. Manent Brutus and Cassius.

Cass. Will you go see the order of the course? 25

Bru. Not I.

Cass. I pray you do.

Bru. I am not gamesome. I do lack some part
Of that quick spirit that is in Antony.
Let me not hinder, Cassius, your desires. 30
I'll leave you.

Cass. Brutus, I do observe you now of late;
I have not from your eyes that gentleness
And show of love as I was wont to have.
You bear too stubborn and too strange a hand 35
Over your friend that loves you.

Bru. Cassius,
Be not deceived. If I have veiled my look,
I turn the trouble of my countenance
Merely upon myself. Vexed I am
Of late with passions of some difference, 40
Conceptions only proper to myself,
Which give some soil, perhaps, to my behaviors;
But let not therefore my good friends be grieved
(Among which number, Cassius, be you one)
Nor construe any further my neglect 45
Than that poor Brutus, with himself at war,
Forgets the shows of love to other men.

47. replication: echo
50. cull out: select (from the working days of the week)
52. blood: kin; his sons, defeated by Cæsar in Spain
55. intermit: delay
61. most . . . shores: highest banks
62. whe'r: whether; **metal:** spirit
66. ceremonies: festive decorations; the scarves mentioned at I[ii.]287.
68. the . . . Lupercal: an annual festival in honor of Lupercus, an ancient Italian god sometimes identified with Pan
74. pitch: height

25. order . . . course: running of the race
33. gentleness: courtesy
35. stubborn: harsh; **strange:** unfriendly
37–39. If . . . myself: if I have shown you a clouded face, it has been because of an entirely personal worry.
40. passions . . . difference: conflicting emotions
41. Conceptions: thoughts; **proper:** personal
42. soil: blemish

Cass. Then, Brutus, I have much mistook your passion;
By means whereof this breast of mine hath buried
Thoughts of great value, worthy cogitations. 50
Tell me, good Brutus, can you see your face?
Bru. No, Cassius, for the eye sees not itself
But by reflection, by some other things.
Cass. 'Tis just.
And it is very much lamented, Brutus, 55
That you have no such mirrors as will turn
Your hidden worthiness into your eye,
That you might see your shadow. I have heard
Where many of the best respect in Rome
(Except immortal Cæsar), speaking of Brutus 60
And groaning underneath this age's yoke,
Have wished that noble Brutus had his eyes.
Bru. Into what dangers would you lead me, Cassius,
That you would have me seek into myself
For that which is not in me? 65
Cass. Therefore, good Brutus, be prepared to hear;
And since you know you cannot see yourself
So well as by reflection, I, your glass,
Will modestly discover to yourself
That of yourself which you yet know not of. 70
And be not jealous on me, gentle Brutus.
Were I a common laugher, or did use
To stale with ordinary oaths my love
To every new protester; if you know
That I do fawn on men and hug them hard, 75
And after scandal them; or if you know
That I profess myself in banqueting
To all the rout, then hold me dangerous.
Flourish and shout.
Bru. What means this shouting? I do fear the people
Choose Cæsar for their king.
Cass. Ay, do you fear it? 80
Then must I think you would not have it so.
Bru. I would not, Cassius, yet I love him well.
But wherefore do you hold me here so long?
What is it that you would impart to me?
If it be aught toward the general good, 85
Set honor in one eye and death i' the other,
And I will look on both indifferently;
For let the gods so speed me as I love
The name of honor more than I fear death.
Cass. I know that virtue to be in you, Brutus, 90
As well as I do know your outward favor.
Well, honor is the subject of my story.
I cannot tell what you and other men
Think of this life, but for my single self,
I had as lief not be as live to be 95
In awe of such a thing as I myself.
I was born free as Cæsar, so were you;
We both have fed as well, and we can both
Endure the winter's cold as well as he.
For once, upon a raw and gusty day, 100
The troubled Tiber chafing with her shores,
Cæsar said to me, "Darest thou, Cassius, now
Leap in with me into this angry flood
And swim to yonder point?" Upon the word,
Accoutered as I was, I plunged in 105
And bade him follow. So indeed he did.
The torrent roared, and we did buffet it
With lusty sinews, throwing it aside
And stemming it with hearts of controversy.
But ere we could arrive the point proposed, 110
Cæsar cried, "Help me, Cassius, or I sink!"
I, as Æneas, our great ancestor,
Did from the flames of Troy upon his shoulder
The old Anchises bear, so from the waves of Tiber
Did I the tired Cæsar. And this man 115
Is now become a god, and Cassius is
A wretched creature and must bend his body
If Cæsar carelessly but nod on him.
He had a fever when he was in Spain,
And when the fit was on him, I did mark 120
How he did shake. 'Tis true, this god did shake.
His coward lips did from their color fly,
And that same eye whose bend doth awe the world
Did lose his luster. I did hear him groan. 124
Ay, and that tongue of his that bade the Romans
Mark him and write his speeches in their books,
Alas, it cried, "Give me some drink, Titinius,"
As a sick girl! Ye gods, it doth amaze me
A man of such a feeble temper should
So get the start of the majestic world 130
And bear the palm alone. *Shout. Flourish.*
Bru. Another general shout?
I do believe that these applauses are
For some new honors that are heaped on Cæsar.
Cass. Why, man, he doth bestride the narrow world 135
Like a Colossus, and we petty men
Walk under his huge legs and peep about

48. passion: feeling
54. just: true
58. shadow: reflection
59. respect: reputation
62. had . . . eyes: had full use of his vision
69. modestly: without exaggeration; **discover:** reveal
71. jealous on: suspicious of
72. laugher: emendation of the Folio reading "laughter"
73. stale: cheapen
76. scandal: slander
77. profess myself: make declarations of affection
78. rout: assembly
88. speed: prosper
91. favor: appearance
96. such . . . myself: a man
109. hearts . . . controversy: competitive zeal
114. Anchises: Æneas' father
123. bend: look
124. his: its. **His** is the normal Elizabethan form of the neuter genitive
130. get . . . of: outdistance
131. palm: prize
136. Colossus: a gigantic statue of Apollo at Rhodes, one of the Seven Wonders of the ancient world

To find ourselves dishonorable graves.
Men at some time are masters of their fates.
The fault, dear Brutus, is not in our stars, 140
But in ourselves, that we are underlings.
"Brutus," and "Cæsar." What should be in that "Cæsar"?
Why should that name be sounded more than yours?
Write them together: yours is as fair a name.
Sound them: it doth become the mouth as well. 145
Weigh them: it is as heavy. Conjure with 'em:
"Brutus" will start a spirit as soon as "Cæsar."
Now in the names of all the gods at once,
Upon what meat doth this our Cæsar feed
That he is grown so great? Age, thou art shamed!
Rome, thou has lost the breed of noble bloods! 151
When went there by an age since the great Flood
But it was famed with more than with one man?
When could they say (till now) that talked of Rome
That her wide walls encompassed but one man? 155
Now is it Rome indeed, and room enough,
When there is in it but one only man!
O, you and I have heard our fathers say
There was a Brutus once that would have brooked
The eternal devil to keep his state in Rome 160
As easily as a king.

Bru. That you do love me I am nothing jealous.
What you would work me to, I have some aim.
How I have thought of this, and of these times,
I shall recount hereafter. For this present, 165
I would not (so with love I might entreat you)
Be any further moved. What you have said
I will consider; what you have to say
I will with patience hear, and find a time
Both meet to hear and answer such high things. 170
Till then, my noble friend, chew upon this:
Brutus had rather be a villager
Than to repute himself a son of Rome
Under these hard conditions as this time
Is like to lay upon us.

Cass. I am glad 175
That my weak words have struck but thus much show
Of fire from Brutus.

Enter CÆSAR *and his* TRAIN.

Bru. The games are done, and Cæsar is returning.

Cass. As they pass by, pluck Casca by the sleeve,
And he will (after his sour fashion) tell you 180
What hath proceeded worthy note today.

Bru. I will do so. But look you, Cassius!
The angry spot doth glow on Cæsar's brow,
And all the rest look like a chidden train.
Calpurnia's cheek is pale, and Cicero 185
Looks with such ferret and such fiery eyes
As we have seen him in the Capitol,
Being crossed in conference by some senators.

Cass. Casca will tell us what the matter is.

Cæs. Antonius. 190

Ant. Cæsar?

Cæs. Let me have men about me that are fat,
Sleek-headed men, and such as sleep o' nights.
Yond Cassius has a lean and hungry look;
He thinks too much, such men are dangerous. 195

Ant. Fear him not, Cæsar, he's not dangerous.
He is a noble Roman, and well given.

Cæs. Would he were fatter! But I fear him not.
Yet if my name were liable to fear,
I do not know the man I should avoid 200
So soon as that spare Cassius. He reads much,
He is a great observer, and he looks
Quite through the deeds of men. He loves no plays
As thou dost, Anthony; he hears no music.
Seldom he smiles, and smiles in such a sort 205
As if he mocked himself and scorned his spirit
That could be moved to smile at anything.
Such men as he be never at heart's ease
Whiles they behold a greater than themselves,
And therefore are they very dangerous. 210
I rather tell thee what is to be feared
Than what I fear; for always I am Cæsar.
Come on my right hand, for this ear is deaf,
And tell me truly what thou thinkst of him.

Sennet. Exeunt Cæsar and his Train.
[*Manet Casca.*]

Casca. You pulled me by the cloak. Would you speak with me? 215

Bru. Ay, Casca. Tell us what hath chanced today
That Cæsar looks so sad.

Casca. Why, you were with him, were you not?

Bru. I should not then ask Casca what had chanced.

Casca. Why, there was a crown offered him; 220
and being offered him, he put it by with the back of
his hand thus; and then the people fell a-shouting.

Bru. What was the second noise for?

Casca. Why, for that too.

Cass. They shouted thrice. What was the last cry for? 225

Casca. Why, for that too.

Bru. Was the crown offered him thrice?

Casca. Ay, marry, was't! and he put it by thrice,

151. lost . . . bloods: i.e., no longer know how to breed noble men
156. Rome . . . enough: a pun on **Rome** and **room,** which were pronounced similarly. Rome (room) is an appropriate name, since the city contains only one man.
159. Brutus: Lucius Junius Brutus, from whom Marcus Brutus claimed descent, was a leader in the revolt which expelled the tyrant Tarquinius Superbus from Rome. **brooked:** allowed
162. am . . . jealous: have no doubt
163. aim: guess
170. meet: suitable
175. like: likely

186. ferret: i.e., red as a ferret's eyes
188. conference: debate
197. well given: disposed to noble behavior
217. sad: grave

every time gentler than other; and at every putting-by mine honest neighbors shouted. 230

Cass. Who offered him the crown?

Casca. Why, Antony.

Bru. Tell us the manner of it, gentle Casca.

Casca. I can as well be hanged as tell the manner of it. It was mere foolery; I did not mark it. I 235 saw Mark Antony offer him a crown—yet 'twas not a crown neither, 'twas one of these coronets—and, as I told you, he put it by once; but for all that, to my thinking, he would fain have had it. Then he offered it to him again; then he put it by again; but to 240 my thinking, he was very loath to lay his fingers off it. And then he offered it the third time. He put it the third time by; and still as he refused it, the rabblement hooted, and clapped their chapped hands, and threw up their sweaty nightcaps, and uttered 245 such a deal of stinking breath because Cæsar refused the crown that it had, almost, choked Cæsar; for he swoonded and fell down at it. And for mine own part, I durst not laugh, for fear of opening my lips and receiving the bad air. 250

Cass. But soft, I pray you. What, did Cæsar swound?

Casca. He fell down in the market place and foamed at mouth and was speechless.

Bru. 'Tis very like. He hath the falling sickness.

Cass. No, Cæsar hath it not; but you, and I, 255
And honest Casca, we have the falling sickness.

Casca. I know not what you mean by that, but I am sure Cæsar fell down. If the tag-rag people did not clap him and hiss him, according as he pleased and displeased them, as they use to do the 260 players in the theatre, I am no true man.

Bru. What said he when he came unto himself?

Casca. Marry, before he fell down, when he perceived the common herd was glad he refused the crown, he plucked me ope his doublet and 265 offered them his throat to cut. And I had been a man of any occupation, if I would not have taken him at a word I would I might go to hell among the rogues. And so he fell. When he came to himself again, he said, if he had done or said anything amiss, he 270 desired their worships to think it was his infirmity. Three or four wenches where I stood cried, "Alas, good soul!" and forgave him with all their hearts. But there's no heed to be taken of them. If Cæsar had stabbed their mothers, they would have 275 done no less.

Bru. And after that, he came thus sad away?

Casca. Ay.

Cass. Did Cicero say anything?

Casca. Ay, he spoke Greek. 280

Cass. To what effect?

Casca. Nay, an I tell you that, I'll ne'er look you i' the face again. But those that understood him smiled at one another and shook their heads; but for mine own part, it was Greek to me. I could tell you 285 more news too. Marullus and Flavius, for pulling scarfs off Cæsar's images, are put to silence. Fare you well. There was more foolery yet, if I could remember it.

Cass. Will you sup with me tonight, Casca? 290

Casca. No, I am promised forth.

Cass. Will you dine with me tomorrow?

Casca. Ay, if I be alive, and your mind hold, and your dinner worth eating.

Cass. Good. I will expect you. 295

Casca. Do so. Farewell both. *Exit.*

Bru. What a blunt fellow is this grown to be!
He was quick mettle when he went to school.

Cass. So is he now in execution
Of any bold or noble enterprise, 300
However he puts on this tardy form.
This rudeness is a sauce to his good wit,
Which gives men stomach to disgest his words
With better appetite.

Bru. And so it is. For this time I will leave you.
Tomorrow, if you please to speak with me, 306
I will come home to you; or if you will,
Come home to me, and I will wait for you.

Cass. I will do so. Till then, think of the world.
Exit Brutus.
Well, Brutus, thou art noble; yet I see 310
Thy honorable mettle may be wrought
From that it is disposed. Therefore it is meet
That noble minds keep ever with their likes;
For who so firm that cannot be seduced?
Cæsar doth bear me hard; but he loves Brutus. 315
If I were Brutus now and he were Cassius,
He should not humor me. I will this night,
In several hands, in at his windows throw,
As if they came from several citizens,
Writings, all tending to the great opinion 320
That Rome holds of his name; wherein obscurely
Cæsar's ambition shall be glanced at.
And after this let Cæsar seat him sure,
For we will shake him, or worse days endure.
Exit.

243. still: always; continually
248. swoonded: a variant of "swooned"
254. falling sickness: epilepsy
263. Marry: indeed; from "By the Virgin Mary"
265. plucked . . . ope: pulled open. The construction is the ethical dative.
266–67. a . . . occupation: a craftsman like the rest of the crowd

287. put . . . silence: deprived of further voice in state affairs. According to Plutarch, they were deprived of their tribuneships.
298. quick mettle: of lively temper
301. However: even though; **tardy form:** appearance of sluggishness
303. disgest: a variant of "digest"
312. that . . . disposed: its natural inclination
315. doth . . . hard: can scarcely stand me
322. glanced at: indirectly referred to

[Scene III. *The same. A street.*]

Thunder and lightning. Enter, [*from opposite sides,*] CASCA, [*with his sword drawn,*] *and* CICERO.

Cic. Good even, Casca. Brought you Cæsar home?
Why are you breathless? and why stare you so?
Casca. Are not you moved when all the sway of earth
Shakes like a thing unfirm? O Cicero,
I have seen tempests when the scolding winds 5
Have rived the knotty oaks, and I have seen
The ambitious ocean swell and rage and foam
To be exalted with the threat'ning clouds;
But never till tonight, never till now,
Did I go through a tempest dropping fire. 10
Either there is a civil strife in heaven,
Or else the world, too saucy with the gods,
Incenses them to send destruction.
Cic. Why, saw you anything more wonderful?
Casca. A common slave—you know him well by sight— 15
Held up his left hand, which did flame and burn
Like twenty torches joined; and yet his hand,
Not sensible of fire, remained unscorched.
Besides—I ha' not since put up my sword—
Against the Capitol I met a lion, 20
Who glared upon me, and went surly by
Without annoying me. And there were drawn
Upon a heap a hundred ghastly women,
Transformed with their fear, who swore they saw
Men, all in fire, walk up and down the streets. 25
And yesterday the bird of night did sit
Even at noonday upon the market place,
Hooting and shrieking. When these prodigies
Do so conjointly meet, let not men say,
"These are their reasons, they are natural," 30
For I believe they are portentous things
Unto the climate that they point upon.
Cic. Indeed it is a strange-disposed time.
But men may construe things after their fashion,
Clean from the purpose of the things themselves.
Comes Cæsar to the Capitol tomorrow? 36
Casca. He doth; for he did bid Antonius
Send word to you he would be there tomorrow.
Cic. Good night then, Casca. This disturbed sky
Is not to walk in.
Casca. Farewell, Cicero. *Exit Cicero.*

Enter CASSIUS.

Cass. Who's there?
Casca. A Roman.
Cass. Casca, by your voice.
Casca. Your ear is good. Cassius, what night is this! 42
Cass. A very pleasing night to honest men.
Casca. Who ever knew the heavens menace so?
Cass. Those that have known the earth so full of faults. 45
For my part, I have walked about the streets,
Submitting me unto the perilous night,
And, thus unbraced, Casca, as you see,
Have bared my bosom to the thunder-stone; 49
And when the cross blue lightning seemed to open
The breast of heaven, I did present myself
Even in the aim and very flash of it.
Casca. But wherefore did you so much tempt the heavens?
It is the part of men to fear and tremble
When the most mighty gods by tokens send 55
Such dreadful heralds to astonish us.
Cass. You are dull, Casca, and those sparks of life
That should be in a Roman you do want,
Or else you use not. You look pale, and gaze,
And put on fear, and cast yourself in wonder, 60
To see the strange impatience of the heavens;
But if you would consider the true cause
Why all these fires, why all these gliding ghosts,
Why birds and beasts, from quality and kind;
Why old men fool and children calculate; 65
Why all these things change from their ordinance,
Their natures, and performed faculties,
To monstrous quality, why, you shall find
That heaven hath infused them with these spirits
To make them instruments of fear and warning 70
Unto some monstrous state.
Now could I, Casca, name to thee a man
Most like this dreadful night
That thunders, lightens, opens graves, and roars
As doth the lion in the Capitol; 75
A man no mightier than thyself or me
In personal action, yet prodigious grown
And fearful, as these strange eruptions are.
Casca. 'Tis Cæsar that you mean. Is it not, Cassius?

3. all . . . earth: the whole of this stable globe
18. sensible: aware
21. glared: Nicholas Rowe's emendation. The Folio reads "glaz'd," which is a dialect word of the same meaning.
22. annoying: harming; **drawn . . . heap:** gathered into a huddle
26. bird . . . night: owl, a bird of ill omen
29. conjointly meet: occur simultaneously
32. climate: region
35. Clean from: quite contrary to
48. unbraced: unbuttoned. Contemporary doublet and hose is suggested by Shakespeare's allusions to dress in this play.
56. astonish: stun
58. want: lack
64. from . . . kind: i.e., act contrary to their natures
66. ordinance: order
68. monstrous quality: character greatly altered from the normal

Cass. Let it be who it is. For Romans now 80
Have thews and limbs like to their ancestors;
But woe the while! our fathers' minds are dead,
And we are governed with our mothers' spirits,
Our yoke and sufferance show us womanish.
Casca. Indeed, they say the senators tomorrow
Mean to establish Cæsar as a king, 86
And he shall wear his crown by sea and land
In every place save here in Italy.
Cass. I know where I will wear this dagger then;
Cassius from bondage will deliver Cassius. 90
Therein, ye gods, you make the weak most strong;
Therein, ye gods, you tyrants do defeat.
Nor stony tower, nor walls of beaten brass,
Nor airless dungeon, nor strong links of iron,
Can be retentive to the strength of spirit; 95
But life, being weary of these worldly bars,
Never lacks power to dismiss itself.
If I know this, know all the world besides,
That part of tyranny that I do bear
I can shake off at pleasure. *Thunder still.*
Casca. So can I. 100
So every bondman in his own hand bears
The power to cancel his captivity.
Cass. And why should Cæsar be a tyrant then?
Poor man! I know he would not be a wolf
But that he sees the Romans are but sheep; 105
He were no lion, were not Romans hinds.
Those that with haste will make a mighty fire
Begin it with weak straws. What trash is Rome,
What rubbish and what offal, when it serves
For the base matter to illuminate 110
So vile a thing as Cæsar! But, O grief,
Where hast thou led me? I, perhaps, speak this
Before a willing bondman. Then I know
My answer must be made. But I am armed,
And dangers are to me indifferent. 115
Casca. You speak to Casca, and to such a man
That is no fleering telltale. Hold, my hand.
Be factious for redress of all these griefs,
And I will set this foot of mine as far
As who goes farthest.
Cass. There's a bargain made. 120
Now know you, Casca, I have moved already
Some certain of the noblest-minded Romans
To undergo with me an enterprise
Of honorable-dangerous consequence;
And I do know, by this they stay for me 125
In Pompey's Porch; for now, this fearful night,
There is no stir or walking in the streets,
And the complexion of the element
In favor's like the work we have in hand,
Most bloody, fiery, and most terrible. 130

Enter CINNA.

Casca. Stand close awhile, for here comes one in haste.
Cass. 'Tis Cinna. I do know him by his gait.
He is a friend. Cinna, where haste you so?
Cinna. To find out you. Who's that? Metellus Cimber?
Cass. No, it is Casca, one incorporate 135
To our attempts. Am I not stayed for, Cinna?
Cinna. I am glad on't. What a fearful night is this!
There's two or three of us have seen strange sights.
Cass. Am I not stayed for? Tell me.
Cinna. Yes, you are.
O Cassius, if you could 140
But win the noble Brutus to our party—
Cass. Be you content. Good Cinna, take this paper
And look you lay it in the prætor's chair,
Where Brutus may but find it, and throw this
In at his window. Set this up with wax 145
Upon old Brutus' statue. All this done,
Repair to Pompey's Porch, where you shall find us.
Is Decius Brutus and Trebonius there?
Cinna. All but Metellus Cimber, and he's gone
To seek you at your house. Well, I will hie 150
And so bestow these papers as you bade me.
Cass. That done, repair to Pompey's Theatre.
Exit Cinna.
Come, Casca, you and I will yet ere day
See Brutus at his house. Three parts of him
Is ours already, and the man entire 155
Upon the next encounter yields him ours.
Casca. O, he sits high in all the people's hearts,
And that which would appear offense in us,
His countenance, like richest alchemy,
Will change to virtue and to worthiness. 160
Cass. Him and his worth and our great need of him
You have right well conceited. Let us go,
For it is after midnight, and ere day
We will awake him and be sure of him.
Exeunt.

81. thews: sinews
82. woe . . . while: alas for these times!
84. yoke . . . sufferance: endurance of bondage; (a hendiadys)
115. indifferent: of no consequence
117. fleering: smiling subserviently
118. Be factious: i.e., join the faction
126. Pompey's Porch: the entrance to Pompey's theatre in the Campus Martius
128. complexion: condition; **element:** sky
129. favor's: appearance's
131. close: concealed
135. incorporate: allied
136. stayed for: awaited
142. Be . . . content: don't worry about that.
148. Decius Brutus: an error for Decimus Brutus, deriving from Jacques Amyot via Thomas North's translation of Plutarch
156. him: himself
159. countenance: approval; **alchemy:** i.e., in the same way as alchemy turns base metals to gold
162. conceited: imagined

ACT II

[Scene I. *The same.*]

Enter BRUTUS *in his orchard.*

Bru. What, Lucius, ho!
I cannot by the progress of the stars
Give guess how near to day. Lucius, I say!
I would it were my fault to sleep so soundly. 4
When, Lucius, when? Awake, I say! What, Lucius!

Enter LUCIUS.

Luc. Called you, my lord?
Bru. Get me a taper in my study, Lucius.
When it is lighted, come and call me here.
Luc. I will, my lord. *Exit.*
Bru. It must be by his death; and for my part, 10
I know no personal cause to spurn at him,
But for the general. He would be crowned.
How that might change his nature, there's the question.
It is the bright day that brings forth the adder,
And that craves wary walking. Crown him that, 15
And then I grant we put a sting in him
That at his will he may do danger with.
The abuse of greatness is when it disjoins
Remorse from power. And to speak truth of Cæsar,
I have not known when his affections swayed 20
More than his reason. But 'tis a common proof
That lowliness is young ambition's ladder,
Whereto the climber-upward turns his face;
But when he once attains the upmost round,
He then unto the ladder turns his back, 25
Looks in the clouds, scorning the base degrees
By which he did ascend. So Cæsar may.
Then lest he may, prevent. And since the quarrel
Will bear no color for the thing he is,
Fashion it thus: that what he is, augmented, 30
Would run to these and these extremities;
And therefore think him as a serpent's egg,
Which, hatched, would as his kind grow mischievous,
And kill him in the shell.

Enter LUCIUS.

Luc. The taper burneth in your closet, sir. 35
Searching the window for a flint, I found
This paper, thus sealed up, and I am sure
It did not lie there when I went to bed.
Gives him the letter.
Bru. Get you to bed again; it is not day.
Is not tomorrow, boy, the ides of March? 40
Luc. I know not, sir.
Bru. Look in the calendar and bring me word.
Luc. I will, sir. *Exit.*
Bru. The exhalations, whizzing in the air,
Gives so much light that I may read by them. 45
Opens the letter and reads.

"Brutus, thou sleepst. Awake, and see thyself!
Shall Rome, &c. Speak, strike, redress!"

"Brutus, thou sleepst. Awake!"
Such instigations have been often dropped
Where I have took them up. 50
"Shall Rome, &c." Thus must I piece it out:
Shall Rome stand under one man's awe? What, Rome?
My ancestors did from the streets of Rome
The Tarquin drive when he was called a king.
"Speak, strike, redress!" Am I entreated 55
To speak and strike? O Rome, I make thee promise,
If the redress will follow, thou receiv'st
Thy full petition at the hand of Brutus!

Enter LUCIUS.

Luc. Sir, March is wasted fifteen days.
Knock within.
Bru. 'Tis good. Go to the gate, somebody knocks.
[*Exit Lucius.*]
Since Cassius first did whet me against Cæsar, 61
I have not slept.

11. **spurn:** literally, "kick"
12. **general:** general good; **would be:** would like to be
19. **Remorse:** mercy
20. **affections:** emotions in general; **swayed:** ruled
21. **common proof:** something proved by experience
28–30. **since . . . thus:** since our case against him will not be justified by his known nature, this is how our case should be made
33. **mischievous:** harmful
35. **closet:** study
40. **ides:** "first" in the Folio; corrected by Lewis Theobald
44. **exhalations:** meteors, believed to be formed of exhalations of gas from the heavenly bodies
51. **piece . . . out:** i.e., extend the meaning more fully
58. **Thy . . . petition:** what you ask to the full

Between the acting of a dreadful thing
And the first motion, all the interim is
Like a phantasma or a hideous dream. 65
The genius and the mortal instruments
Are then in council, and the state of man,
Like to a little kingdom, suffers then
The nature of an insurrection.

Enter LUCIUS.

Luc. Sir, 'tis your brother Cassius at the door,
Who doth desire to see you.

Bru. Is he alone? 71

Luc. No, sir, there are mo with him.

Bru. Do you know them?

Luc. No, sir. Their hats are plucked about their ears
And half their faces buried in their cloaks,
That by no means I may discover them 75
By any mark of favor.

Bru. Let 'em enter. [*Exit Lucius.*]
They are the faction. O conspiracy,
Sham'st thou to show thy dang'rous brow by night,
When evils are most free? O, then by day
Where wilt thou find a cavern dark enough 80
To mask thy monstrous visage? Seek none, conspiracy,
Hide it in smiles and affability!
For if thou path, thy native semblance on,
Not Erebus itself were dim enough
To hide thee from prevention. 85

Enter the CONSPIRATORS, CASSIUS, CASCA, DECIUS, CINNA, METELLUS [CIMBER], *and* TREBONIUS.

Cass. I think we are too bold upon your rest.
Good morrow, Brutus. Do we trouble you?

Bru. I have been up this hour, awake all night.
Know I these men that come along with you? 89

Cass. Yes, every man of them; and no man here
But honors you; and every one doth wish
You had but that opinion of yourself
Which every noble Roman bears of you.
This is Trebonius.

Bru. He is welcome hither.

Cass. This, Decius Brutus.

Bru. He is welcome too. 95

Cass. This, Casca; this, Cinna; and this, Metellus Cimber.

Bru. They are all welcome.
What watchful cares do interpose themselves
Betwixt your eyes and night?

Cass. Shall I entreat a word? 100

They whisper.

Dec. Here lies the east. Doth not the day break here?

Casca. No.

Cinna. O, pardon, sir, it doth; and yon grey lines
That fret the clouds are messengers of day.

Casca. You shall confess that you are both deceived. 105
Here, as I point my sword, the sun arises,
Which is a great way growing on the south,
Weighing the youthful season of the year.
Some two months hence, up higher toward the north
He first presents his fire; and the high east 110
Stands as the Capitol, directly here.

Bru. Give me your hands all over, one by one.

Cass. And let us swear our resolution.

Bru. No, not an oath. If not the face of men,
The sufferance of our souls, the time's abuse— 115
If these be motives weak, break off betimes,
And every man hence to his idle bed.
So let high-sighted tyranny range on
Till each man drop by lottery. But if these
(As I am sure they do) bear fire enough 120
To kindle cowards and to steel with valor
The melting spirits of women, then, countrymen,
What need we any spur but our own cause
To prick us to redress? what other bond
Than secret Romans that have spoke the word 125
And will not palter? and what other oath
Than honesty to honesty engaged
That this shall be, or we will fall for it?
Swear priests and cowards and men cautelous,
Old feeble carrions and such suffering souls 130
That welcome wrongs; unto bad causes swear
Such creatures as men doubt; but do not stain
The even virtue of our enterprise,
Nor the insuppressive mettle of our spirits,
To think that or our cause or our performance 135
Did need an oath, when every drop of blood
That every Roman bears, and nobly bears,
Is guilty of a several bastardy

64. **motion:** action
66. **genius:** guiding spirit; **mortal instruments:** human faculties
72. **mo:** more
75. **discover:** identify
76. **mark . . . favor:** facial characteristic
83. **path . . . on:** continue on your way undisguised
84. **Erebus:** the dark underworld of Hades

98. **watchful cares:** cares that prevent sleep
104. **fret:** lace; make a fretwork pattern
107. **a . . . south:** moving far toward the south
108. **Weighing:** considering
115. **sufferance:** suffering; **time's abuse:** current abuses
118. **high-sighted:** haughty
119. **by lottery:** in turn; according to his luck
124. **prick:** spur
126. **palter:** equivocate
127. **honesty . . . engaged:** honorable men pledged to honorable action
129. **cautelous:** crafty; therefore untrustworthy
133. **even:** exact; perfect
134. **insuppressive:** irrepressible; invincible

If he do break the smallest particle
Of any promise that hath passed from him. 140
Cass. But what of Cicero? Shall we sound him?
I think he will stand very strong with us.
Casca. Let us not leave him out.
Cinna. No, by no means.
Met. O, let us have him! for his silver hairs
Will purchase us a good opinion 145
And buy men's voices to commend our deeds.
It shall be said his judgment ruled our hands;
Our youths and wildness shall no whit appear,
But all be buried in his gravity. 149
Bru. O, name him not! Let us not break with him,
For he will never follow anything
That other men begin.
Cass. Then leave him out.
Casca. Indeed he is not fit.
Dec. Shall no man else be touched but only Cæsar? 154
Cass. Decius, well urged. I think it is not meet
Mark Antony, so well beloved of Cæsar,
Should outlive Cæsar. We shall find of him
A shrewd contriver; and you know, his means,
If he improve them, may well stretch so far
As to annoy us all; which to prevent, 160
Let Antony and Cæsar fall together.
Bru. Our course will seem too bloody, Caius Cassius,
To cut the head off and then hack the limbs,
Like wrath in death and envy afterwards;
For Antony is but a limb of Cæsar. 165
Let us be sacrificers, but not butchers, Caius.
We all stand up against the spirit of Cæsar,
And in the spirit of men there is no blood.
O that we then could come by Cæsar's spirit
And not dismember Cæsar! But, alas, 170
Cæsar must bleed for it! And, gentle friends,
Let's kill him boldly, but not wrathfully;
Let's carve him as a dish fit for the gods,
Not hew him as a carcass fit for hounds.
And let our hearts, as subtle masters do, 175
Stir up their servants to an act of rage
And after seem to chide 'em. This shall make
Our purpose necessary, and not envious;
Which so appearing to the common eyes,
We shall be called purgers, not murderers. 180
And for Mark Antony, think not of him;
For he can do no more than Cæsar's arm
When Cæsar's head is off.
Cass. Yet I fear him,
For in the ingrafted love he bears to Cæsar— 184
Bru. Alas, good Cassius, do not think of him!
If he love Cæsar, all that he can do
Is to himself—take thought, and die for Cæsar.
And that were much he should; for he is given
To sports, to wildness, and much company. 189
Treb. There is no fear in him. Let him not die,
For he will live and laugh at this hereafter.
Clock strikes.
Bru. Peace! Count the clock.
Cass. The clock hath stricken three.
Treb. 'Tis time to part.
Cass. But it is doubtful yet
Whether Cæsar will come forth today or no;
For he is superstitious grown of late, 195
Quite from the main opinion he held once
Of fantasy, of dreams, and ceremonies.
It may be these apparent prodigies,
The unaccustomed terror of this night,
And the persuasion of his augurers 200
May hold him from the Capitol today.
Dec. Never fear that. If he be so resolved,
I can o'ersway him; for he loves to hear
That unicorns may be betrayed with trees
And bears with glasses, elephants with holes, 205
Lions with toils, and men with flatterers;
But when I tell him he hates flatterers,
He says he does, being then most flattered.
Let me work,
For I can give his humor the true bent, 210
And I will bring him to the Capitol.
Cass. Nay, we will all of us be there to fetch him.
Bru. By the eighth hour. Is that the uttermost?
Cinna. Be that the uttermost, and fail not then.
Met. Caius Ligarius doth bear Cæsar hard, 215
Who rated him for speaking well of Pompey.
I wonder none of you have thought of him.
Bru. Now, good Metellus, go along by him.
He loves me well, and I have given him reasons.
Send him but hither, and I'll fashion him. 220

150. break with: reveal our plan to
158. shrewd: formidable
159. improve: make use of
160. annoy: injure
164. wrath . . . afterwards: murderous rage, followed by malice
169. come by: influence
171. gentle: noble
178. envious: malicious
184. ingrafted: deeply imbedded
187. take . . . die: grieve to death. **Thought** equals "melancholy."
188. that . . . should: that's too much to expect of him
190. no fear: nothing to fear
196. main: positive
197. fantasy: fancy; **ceremonies:** omens
198. apparent prodigies: conspicuous omens
204. with trees: i.e., by the hunter darting behind the tree pursued by the unicorn, whose horn then pierced the trunk of the tree and held him
205. glasses: mirrors; **holes:** pits
206. toils: nets
210. humor: disposition; **the . . . bent:** the very inclination we want
215. Caius . . . hard: Cæsar forgave Ligarius for his alliance with Pompey, but this generosity inspired Ligarius' resentment of Cæsar's power.
216. rated: scolded

Cass. The morning comes upon's. We'll leave you, Brutus.
And, friends, disperse yourselves; but all remember
What you have said and show yourselves true Romans.
Bru. Good gentlemen, look fresh and merrily.
Let not our looks put on our purposes, 225
But bear it as our Roman actors do,
With untired spirits and formal constancy.
And so good morrow to you every one.
Exeunt. Manet Brutus.
Boy! Lucius! Fast asleep? It is no matter.
Enjoy the honey-heavy dew of slumber. 230
Thou hast no figures nor no fantasies
Which busy care draws in the brains of men;
Therefore thou sleepst so sound.

Enter PORTIA.

Por. Brutus, my lord!
Bru. Portia! What mean you? Wherefore rise you now?
It is not for your health thus to commit 235
Your weak condition to the raw cold morning.
Por. Nor for yours neither. Y' have ungently, Brutus,
Stole from my bed. And yesternight at supper
You suddenly arose and walked about,
Musing and sighing with your arms across; 240
And when I asked you what the matter was,
You stared upon me with ungentle looks.
I urged you further, then you scratched your head
And too impatiently stamped with your foot.
Yet I insisted, yet you answered not, 245
But with an angry wafture of your hand
Gave sign for me to leave you. So I did,
Fearing to strengthen that impatience
Which seemed too much enkindled, and withal
Hoping it was but an effect of humor, 250
Which sometime hath his hour with every man.
It will not let you eat nor talk nor sleep,
And could it work so much upon your shape
As it hath much prevailed on your condition,
I should not know you Brutus. Dear my lord, 255
Make me acquainted with your cause of grief.
Bru. I am not well in health, and that is all.
Por. Brutus is wise and, were he not in health,
He would embrace the means to come by it.
Bru. Why, so I do. Good Portia, go to bed. 260
Por. Is Brutus sick, and is it physical
To walk unbraced and suck up the humors
Of the dank morning? What, is Brutus sick,
And will he steal out of his wholesome bed
To dare the vile contagion of the night, 265
And tempt the rheumy and unpurged air,
To add unto his sickness? No, my Brutus.
You have some sick offense within your mind,
Which by the right and virtue of my place
I ought to know of; and upon my knees 270
I charm you, by my once commended beauty,
By all your vows of love, and that great vow
Which did incorporate and make us one,
That you unfold to me, yourself, your half,
Why you are heavy, and what men tonight 275
Have had resort to you; for here have been
Some six or seven, who did hide their faces
Even from darkness.
Bru. Kneel not, gentle Portia.
Por. I should not need if you were gentle Brutus.
Within the bond of marriage, tell me, Brutus, 280
Is it excepted I should know no secrets
That appertain to you? Am I yourself
But, as it were, in sort or limitation?
To keep with you at meals, comfort your bed,
And talk to you sometimes? Dwell I but in the suburbs 285
Of your good pleasure? If it be no more,
Portia is Brutus' harlot, not his wife.
Bru. You are my true and honorable wife,
As dear to me as are the ruddy drops
That visit my sad heart. 290
Por. If this were true, then should I know this secret.
I grant I am a woman, but withal
A woman that Lord Brutus took to wife.
I grant I am a woman, but withal
A woman well-reputed, Cato's daughter. 295
Think you I am no stronger than my sex,
Being so fathered and so husbanded?
Tell me your counsels; I will not disclose 'em.
I have made strong proof of my constancy,
Giving myself a voluntary wound 300
Here, in the thigh. Can I bear that with patience,
And not my husband's secrets?
Bru. O ye gods,
Render me worthy of this noble wife! *Knock.*
Hark, hark! one knocks. Portia, go in awhile,
And by-and-by thy bosom shall partake 305
The secrets of my heart.

224. fresh . . . merrily: bright and cheerful
225. put on: don, like a garment; a metaphor often used by Shakespeare
227. formal constancy: ordinary composure
246. wafture: wave
250. effect . . . humor: sign of a passing mood
254. condition: disposition
255. know . . . Brutus: recognize you as Brutus
261. physical: curative; healthy
262. humors: moistures
266. rheumy: damp; **unpurged:** unpurified
268. sick offense: harmful sickness
271. charm: conjure
275. heavy: melancholy
283. in . . . limitation: in a way or with limitations
285. suburbs: the haunt of harlots
299. constancy: fortitude

All my engagements I will construe to thee,
All the charactery of my sad brows.
Leave me with haste. *Exit Portia.*
Lucius, who's that knocks? 309

Enter LUCIUS *and* [CAIUS] LIGARIUS.

Luc. Here is a sick man that would speak with you.
Bru. Caius Ligarius, that Metellus spake of.
Boy, stand aside. Caius Ligarius, how?
Caius. Vouchsafe good morrow from a feeble tongue.
Bru. O, what a time have you chose out, brave Caius,
To wear a kerchief! Would you were not sick! 315
Caius. I am not sick if Brutus have in hand
Any exploit worthy the name of honor.
Bru. Such an exploit have I in hand, Ligarius,
Had you a healthful ear to hear of it.
Caius. By all the gods that Romans bow before,
I here discard my sickness! Soul of Rome! 321
Brave son, derived from honorable loins!
Thou like an exorcist hast conjured up
My mortified spirit. Now bid me run,
And I will strive with things impossible; 325
Yea, get the better of them. What's to do?
Bru. A piece of work that will make sick men whole.
Caius. But are not some whole that we must make sick?
Bru. That must we also. What it is, my Caius,
I shall unfold to thee as we are going 330
To whom it must be done.
Caius. Set on your foot,
And with a heart new-fired I follow you,
To do I know not what; but it sufficeth
That Brutus leads me on. *Thunder.*
Bru. Follow me then.
Exeunt.

[Scene II. *The same. Cæsar's house.*]

Thunder and lightning. Enter JULIUS CÆSAR, *in his nightgown.*

Cæs. Nor heaven nor earth have been at peace tonight.
Thrice hath Calpurnia in her sleep cried out
"Help, ho! They murder Cæsar!" Who's within?

Enter a SERVANT.

Serv. My lord?
Cæs. Go bid the priests do present sacrifice, 5
And bring me their opinions of success.
Serv. I will, my lord. *Exit.*

Enter CALPURNIA.

Cal. What mean you, Cæsar? Think you to walk forth?
You shall not stir out of your house today.
Cæs. Cæsar shall forth. The things that threatened me 10
Ne'er looked but on my back. When they shall see
The face of Cæsar, they are vanished.
Cal. Cæsar, I never stood on ceremonies,
Yet now they fright me. There is one within,
Besides the things that we have heard and seen, 15
Recounts most horrid sights seen by the watch.
A lioness hath whelped in the streets,
And graves have yawned and yielded up their dead.
Fierce fiery warriors fought upon the clouds
In ranks and squadrons and right form of war, 20
Which drizzled blood upon the Capitol.
The noise of battle hurtled in the air,
Horses did neigh, and dying men did groan,
And ghosts did shriek and squeal about the streets.
O Cæsar, these things are beyond all use, 25
And I do fear them!
Cæs. What can be avoided
Whose end is purposed by the mighty gods?
Yet Cæsar shall go forth; for these predictions
Are to the world in general as to Cæsar. 29
Cal. When beggars die there are no comets seen;
The heavens themselves blaze forth the death of princes.
Cæs. Cowards die many times before their deaths;
The valiant never taste of death but once.
Of all the wonders that I yet have heard, 34
It seems to me most strange that men should fear,
Seeing that death, a necessary end,
Will come when it will come.

Enter a SERVANT.

What say the augurers?
Serv. They would not have you to stir forth today.
Plucking the entrails of an offering forth,
They could not find a heart within the beast. 40
Cæs. The gods do this in shame of cowardice.
Cæsar should be a beast without a heart
If he should stay at home today for fear.
No, Cæsar shall not. Danger knows full well
That Cæsar is more dangerous than he. 45

308. charactery: i.e., the meaning of what is written there
313. Vouchsafe: deign to accept
315. kerchief: headcloth, worn by the sick. Elizabethans believed that keeping the head warm was a prime prescription for bodily health.
324. mortified: deadened

5. present: immediate
13. stood . . . ceremonies: believed in omens
20. right form: exact manner
25. beyond . . . use: quite extraordinary

We are two lions littered in one day,
And I the elder and more terrible,
And Cæsar shall go forth.
Cal. Alas, my lord!
Your wisdom is consumed in confidence.
Do not go forth today. Call it my fear 50
That keeps you in the house and not your own.
We'll send Mark Antony to the Senate House,
And he shall say you are not well today.
Let me upon my knee prevail in this.
Cæs. Mark Antony shall say I am not well, 55
And for thy humor I will stay at home.

Enter DECIUS.

Here's Decius Brutus, he shall tell them so.
Dec. Cæsar, all hail! Good morrow, worthy Cæsar!
I come to fetch you to the Senate House.
Cæs. And you are come in very happy time 60
To bear my greeting to the senators
And tell them that I will not come today.
Cannot, is false; and that I dare not, falser:
I will not come today. Tell them so, Decius.
Cal. Say he is sick.
Cæs. Shall Cæsar send a lie? 65
Have I in conquest stretched mine arm so far
To be afeard to tell greybeards the truth?
Decius, go tell them Cæsar will not come.
Dec. Most mighty Cæsar, let me know some cause,
Lest I be laughed at when I tell them so. 70
Cæs. The cause is in my will: I will not come.
That is enough to satisfy the Senate;
But for your private satisfaction,
Because I love you, I will let you know.
Calpurnia here, my wife, stays me at home. 75
She dreamt tonight she saw my statuë,
Which, like a fountain with an hundred spouts,
Did run pure blood, and many lusty Romans
Came smiling and did bathe their hands in it.
And these does she apply for warnings and portents
And evils imminent, and on her knee 81
Hath begged that I will stay at home today.
Dec. This dream is all amiss interpreted;
It was a vision fair and fortunate.
Your statue spouting blood in many pipes, 85
In which so many smiling Romans bathed,
Signifies that from you great Rome shall suck
Reviving blood, and that great men shall press
For tinctures, stains, relics, and cognizance.
This by Calpurnia's dream is signified. 90
Cæs. And this way have you well expounded it.
Dec. I have, when you have heard what I can say:
And know it now, the Senate have concluded
To give this day a crown to mighty Cæsar.
If you shall send them word you will not come, 95
Their minds may change. Besides, it were a mock
Apt to be rendered, for some one to say
"Break up the Senate till another time,
When Cæsar's wife shall meet with better dreams."
If Cæsar hide himself, shall they not whisper 100
"Lo, Cæsar is afraid"?
Pardon me, Cæsar, for my dear dear love
To your proceeding bids me tell you this,
And reason to my love is liable.
Cæs. How foolish do your fears seem now, Calpurnia! 105
I am ashamed I did yield to them.
Give me my robe, for I will go.

Enter BRUTUS, LIGARIUS, METELLUS, CASCA, TREBONIUS, CINNA, *and* PUBLIUS.

And look where Publius is come to fetch me.
Pub. Good morrow, Cæsar.
Cæs. Welcome, Publius.
What, Brutus, are you stirred so early too? 110
Good morrow, Casca. Caius Ligarius,
Cæsar was ne'er so much your enemy
As that same ague which hath made you lean.
What is't o'clock?
Bru. Cæsar, 'tis strucken eight.
Cæs. I thank you for your pains and courtesy. 115

Enter ANTONY.

See! Antony, that revels long o' nights,
Is notwithstanding up. Good morrow, Antony.
Ant. So to most noble Cæsar.
Cæs. Bid them prepare within.
I am to blame to be thus waited for.
Now, Cinna, now, Metellus. What, Trebonius! 120
I have an hour's talk in store for you;
Remember that you call on me today;
Be near me, that I may remember you.
Treb. Cæsar, I will. [*Aside*] And so near will I be
That your best friends shall wish I had been further. 125
Cæs. Good friends, go in and taste some wine with me,
And we (like friends) will straightway go together.
Bru. [*Aside*] That every like is not the same, O Cæsar,
The heart of Brutus earns to think upon.
Exeunt.

60. in . . . time: very opportunely
75. stays: holds
89. tinctures: tints; **cognizance:** badge indicating service with a great man

97. rendered: replied
103. proceeding: advancement
104. reason . . . liable: my love for you rules my judgment.
129. earns: mourns

[Scene III. *The same. A street near the Capitol.*]

Enter ARTEMIDORUS, [*reading a paper*].

Art. Cæsar, beware of Brutus; take heed of Cassius; come not near Casca; have an eye to Cinna; trust not Trebonius; mark well Metellus Cimber; Decius Brutus loves thee not; thou hast wronged Caius Ligarius. There is but one mind in all these men, and it is bent 5 against Cæsar. If thou beest not immortal, look about you. Security gives way to conspiracy. The mighty gods defend thee!

Thy lover,
ARTEMIDORUS.

Here will I stand till Cæsar pass along 11
And as a suitor will I give him this.
My heart laments that virtue cannot live
Out of the teeth of emulation.
If thou read this, O Cæsar, thou mayst live; 15
If not, the Fates with traitors do contrive.

Exit.

[Scene IV. *Before the house of Brutus.*]

Enter PORTIA *and* LUCIUS.

Por. I prithee, boy, run to the Senate House.
Stay not to answer me, but get thee gone!
Why dost thou stay?
Luc. To know my errand, madam.
Por. I would have had thee there and here again
Ere I can tell thee what thou shouldst do there. 5
O constancy, be strong upon my side,
Set a huge mountain 'tween my heart and tongue!
I have a man's mind, but a woman's might.
How hard it is for women to keep counsel!
Art thou here yet?
Luc. Madam, what should I do? 10
Run to the Capitol and nothing else?
And so return to you and nothing else?
Por. Yes, bring me word, boy, if thy lord look well,
For he went sickly forth; and take good note
What Cæsar doth, what suitors press to him. 15
Hark, boy! What noise is that?
Luc. I hear none, madam.
Por. Prithee, listen well.
I heard a bustling rumor like a fray,
And the wind brings it from the Capitol.
Luc. Sooth, madam, I hear nothing. 20

Enter the SOOTHSAYER.

Por. Come hither, fellow. Which way hast thou been?
Sooth. At mine own house, good lady.
Por. What is't o'clock?
Sooth. About the ninth hour, lady.
Por. Is Cæsar yet gone to the Capitol?
Sooth. Madam, not yet. I go to take my stand,
To see him pass on to the Capitol. 26
Por. Thou hast some suit to Cæsar, hast thou not?
Sooth. That I have, lady. If it will please Cæsar
To be so good to Cæsar as to hear me,
I shall beseech him to befriend himself. 30
Por. Why, knowst thou any harm's intended towards him?
Sooth. None that I know will be, much that I fear may chance.
Good morrow to you. Here the street is narrow.
The throng that follows Cæsar at the heels,
Of senators, of prætors, common suitors, 35
Will crowd a feeble man almost to death.
I'll get me to a place more void and there
Speak to great Cæsar as he comes along. *Exit.*
Por. I must go in. Ay me, how weak a thing
The heart of woman is! O Brutus, 40
The heavens speed thee in thine enterprise—
Sure the boy heard me.—Brutus hath a suit
That Cæsar will not grant.—O, I grow faint.—
Run, Lucius, and commend me to my lord;
Say I am merry. Come to me again 45
And bring me word what he doth say to thee.

Exeunt [*severally*].

7. Security . . . conspiracy: false confidence admits conspiracy.
14. emulation: envy
6. constancy: self-control

18. bustling rumor: hubbub
20. Sooth: truly
45. merry: cheerful

ACT III

[Scene I. *The same. A street in front of the Capitol.*]

Flourish. Enter CÆSAR, BRUTUS, CASSIUS, CASCA, DECIUS, METELLUS, TREBONIUS, CINNA, ANTONY, LEPIDUS, ARTEMIDORUS, [POPILIUS,] PUBLIUS, *and the* SOOTHSAYER.

Cæs. The ides of March are come.
Sooth. Ay, Cæsar, but not gone.
Art. Hail, Cæsar! Read this schedule.
Dec. Trebonius doth desire you to o'erread
(At your best leisure) this his humble suit. 5
Art. O Cæsar, read mine first, for mine's a suit
That touches Cæsar nearer. Read it, great Cæsar!
Cæs. What touches us ourself shall be last served.
Art. Delay not, Cæsar! Read it instantly! 9
Cæs. What, is the fellow mad?
Pub. Sirrah, give place.
Cass. What, urge you your petitions in the street?
Come to the Capitol.

[*Cæsar goes into the Senate House, the rest following.*]

Pop. I wish your enterprise today may thrive.
Cass. What enterprise, Popilius?
Pop. Fare you well.
[*Advances to Cæsar.*]
Bru. What said Popilius Lena? 15
Cass. He wished today our enterprise might thrive.
I fear our purpose is discovered.
Bru. Look how he makes to Cæsar. Mark him.
Cass. Casca, be sudden, for we fear prevention.
Brutus, what shall be done? If this be known, 20
Cassius or Cæsar never shall turn back,
For I will slay myself.
Bru. Cassius, be constant.
Popilius Lena speaks not of our purposes,
For look, he smiles, and Cæsar doth not change.
Cass. Trebonius knows his time, for look you,
Brutus, 25
He draws Mark Antony out of the way.
[*Exeunt Antony and Trebonius.*]

Dec. Where is Metellus Cimber? Let him go
And presently prefer his suit to Cæsar.
Bru. He is addressed. Press near and second him.
Cinna. Casca, you are the first that rears your hand.
Cæs. Are we all ready? What is now amiss 31
That Cæsar and his Senate must redress?
Met. Most high, most mighty, and most puissant
Cæsar,
Metellus Cimber throws before thy seat
An humble heart. [*Kneeling.*]
Cæs. I must prevent thee, Cimber. 35
These couchings and these lowly courtesies
Might fire the blood of ordinary men
And turn preordinance and first decree
Into the law of children. Be not fond
To think that Cæsar bears such rebel blood 40
That will be thawed from the true quality
With that which melteth fools—I mean, sweet words,
Low-crooked curtsies, and base spaniel fawning.
Thy brother by decree is banished.
If thou dost bend and pray and fawn for him, 45
I spurn thee like a cur out of my way.
Know, Cæsar doth not wrong, nor without cause
Will he be satisfied.
Met. Is there no voice more worthy than my own,
To sound more sweetly in great Cæsar's ear 50
For the repealing of my banished brother?
Bru. I kiss thy hand, but not in flattery, Cæsar,
Desiring thee that Publius Cimber may
Have an immediate freedom of repeal.
Cæs. What, Brutus?
Cass. Pardon, Cæsar! Cæsar, pardon!
As low as to thy foot doth Cassius fall 56
To beg enfranchisement for Publius Cimber.
Cæs. I could be well moved, if I were as you;
If I could pray to move, prayers would move me:
But I am constant as the Northern Star, 60
Of whose true-fixed and resting quality

3. schedule: note
18. makes to: behaves toward
22. constant: calm

28. prefer: present
29. addressed: ready
33. puissant: powerful
38. preordinance . . . decree: predetermined decision
39. the . . . children: indecisiveness, children being unstable of purpose; **fond:** foolish
40. rebel blood: rebellious impulses
47–48. Cæsar . . . satisfied: Ben Jonson, quoting this line as "Cæsar did never wrong, but with just cause," considered it one of Shakespeare's absurdities. It is possible that Shakespeare altered the phraseology in the light of Jonson's criticism
51. repealing: recalling
61. resting: stable

There is no fellow in the firmament.
The skies are painted with unnumb'red sparks,
They are all fire, and every one doth shine;
But there's but one in all doth hold his place. 65
So in the world: 'tis furnished well with men,
And men are flesh and blood, and apprehensive;
Yet in the number I do know but one
That unassailable holds on his rank,
Unshaked of motion; and that I am he, 70
Let me a little show it, even in this,
That I was constant Cimber should be banished
And constant do remain to keep him so.

Cinna. O Cæsar!

Cæs. Hence! Wilt thou lift up Olympus?

Dec. Great Cæsar!

Cæs. Doth not Brutus bootless kneel?

Casca. Speak hands for me! 76

They stab Cæsar[—*Casca, the others in turn, then Brutus*].

Cæs. Et tu, Brute?—Then fall Cæsar! *Dies.*

Cinna. Liberty! Freedom! Tyranny is dead!
Run hence, proclaim, cry it about the streets!

Cass. Some to the common pulpits and cry out
"Liberty, freedom, and enfranchisement!" 81

Bru. People and Senators, be not affrighted.
Fly not; stand still. Ambition's debt is paid.

Casca. Go to the pulpit, Brutus.

Dec. And Cassius too.

Bru. Where's Publius? 85

Cinna. Here, quite confounded with this mutiny.

Met. Stand fast together, lest some friend of Cæsar's
Should chance—

Bru. Talk not of standing! Publius, good cheer.
There is no harm intended to your person 90
Nor to no Roman else. So tell them, Publius.

Cass. And leave us, Publius, lest that the people,
Rushing on us, should do your age some mischief.

Bru. Do so, and let no man abide this deed
But we the doers.

Enter TREBONIUS.

Cass. Where is Antony? 95

Treb. Fled to his house amazed.
Men, wives, and children stare, cry out, and run,
As it were doomsday.

Bru. Fates, we will know your pleasures.
That we shall die, we know, 'tis but the time,
And drawing days out, that men stand upon. 100

Cass. Why, he that cuts off twenty years of life
Cuts off so many years of fearing death.

Bru. Grant that, and then is death a benefit.
So are we Cæsar's friends, that have abridged 104
His time of fearing death. Stoop, Romans, stoop,
And let us bathe our hands in Caesar's blood
Up to the elbows and besmear our swords.
Then walk we forth, even to the market place,
And waving our red weapons o'er our heads,
Let's all cry, "Peace, freedom, and liberty!" 110

Cass. Stoop then and wash. How many ages hence
Shall this our lofty scene be acted over
In states unborn and accents yet unknown!

Bru. How many times shall Cæsar bleed in sport,
That now on Pompey's basis lies along 115
No worthier than the dust!

Cass. So oft as that shall be,
So often shall the knot of us be called
The men that gave their country liberty.

Dec. What, shall we forth?

Cass. Ay, every man away.
Brutus shall lead, and we will grace his heels 120
With the most boldest and best hearts of Rome.

Enter a SERVANT.

Bru. Soft! who comes here? A friend of Antony's.

Serv. Thus, Brutus, did my master bid me kneel;
Thus did Mark Antony bid me fall down;
And being prostrate, thus he bade me say: 125
Brutus is noble, wise, valiant, and honest;
Cæsar was mighty, bold, royal, and loving.
Say I love Brutus and I honor him;
Say I feared Cæsar, honored him, and loved him.
If Brutus will vouchsafe that Antony 130
May safely come to him and be resolved
How Cæsar hath deserved to lie in death,
Mark Antony shall not love Cæsar dead
So well as Brutus living, but will follow
The fortunes and affairs of noble Brutus 135
Thorough the hazards of this untrod state
With all true faith. So says my master Antony.

Bru. Thy master is a wise and valiant Roman.
I never thought him worse.
Tell him, so please him come unto this place, 140
He shall be satisfied and, by my honor,
Depart untouched.

Serv. I'll fetch him presently. *Exit.*

67. apprehensive: capable of reason
69. holds . . . rank: keeps a straight course
75. bootless: in vain
86. confounded: perplexed
94. abide: suffer for
100. stand upon: care about
114. sport: dramatic performance
115. basis: pedestal; the base of the statue
117. knot: closely-knit group
120. grace: dignify
127. royal: generous; munificent
131. resolved: satisfied
136. Thorough . . . state: through this hazardous period of political innovation
140. so . . . him: if he pleases to
142. presently: at once

Bru. I know that we shall have him well to friend.
Cass. I wish we may. But yet have I a mind
That fears him much; and my misgiving still 145
Falls shrewdly to the purpose.

Enter ANTONY.

Bru. But here comes Antony. Welcome, Mark Antony.
Ant. O mighty Cæsar! dost thou lie so low?
Are all thy conquests, glories, triumphs, spoils,
Shrunk to this little measure? Fare thee well. 150
I know not, gentlemen, what you intend,
Who else must be let blood, who else is rank.
If I myself, there is no hour so fit
As Cæsar's death's hour; nor no instrument
Of half that worth as those your swords, made rich
With the most noble blood of all this world. 156
I do beseech ye, if you bear me hard,
Now, whilst your purpled hands do reek and smoke,
Fulfil your pleasure. Live a thousand years,
I shall not find myself so apt to die; 160
No place will please me so, no mean of death,
As here by Cæsar, and by you cut off,
The choice and master spirits of this age.
Bru. O Antony, beg not your death of us!
Though now we must appear bloody and cruel, 165
As by our hands and this our present act
You see we do, yet see you but our hands
And this the bleeding business they have done.
Our hearts you see not. They are pitiful;
And pity to the general wrong of Rome 170
(As fire drives out fire, so pity pity)
Hath done this deed on Cæsar. For your part,
To you our swords have leaden points, Mark Antony.
Our arms in strength of malice, and our hearts
Of brothers' temper, do receive you in 175
With all kind love, good thoughts, and reverence.
Cass. Your voice shall be as strong as any man's
In the disposing of new dignities.
Bru. Only be patient till we have appeased
The multitude, beside themselves with fear, 180
And then we will deliver you the cause
Why I, that did love Cæsar when I struck him,
Have thus proceeded.
Ant. I doubt not of your wisdom.
Let each man render me his bloody hand.
First, Marcus Brutus, will I shake with you; 185
Next, Caius Cassius, do I take your hand;
Now, Decius Brutus, yours; now yours, Metellus;
Yours, Cinna; and, my valiant Casca, yours.
Though last, not least in love, yours, good Trebonius.
Gentlemen all—Alas, what shall I say? 190
My credit now stands on such slippery ground
That one of two bad ways you must conceit me,
Either a coward or a flatterer.
That I did love thee, Cæsar, O, 'tis true!
If then thy spirit look upon us now, 195
Shall it not grieve thee dearer than thy death
To see thy Antony making his peace,
Shaking the bloody fingers of thy foes,
Most noble! in the presence of thy corse?
Had I as many eyes as thou hast wounds, 200
Weeping as fast as they stream forth thy blood,
It would become me better than to close
In terms of friendship with thine enemies.
Pardon me, Julius! Here wast thou bayed, brave hart;
Here didst thou fall; and here thy hunters stand,
Signed in thy spoil, and crimsoned in thy lethe. 206
O world, thou wast the forest to this hart;
And this indeed, O world, the heart of thee!
How like a deer, strucken by many princes,
Dost thou here lie! 210
Cass. Mark Antony—
Ant. Pardon me, Caius Cassius.
The enemies of Cæsar shall say this;
Then, in a friend, it is cold modesty.
Cass. I blame you not for praising Cæsar so;
But what compact mean you to have with us? 215
Will you be pricked in number of our friends,
Or shall we on, and not depend on you?
Ant. Therefore I took your hands; but was indeed
Swayed from the point by looking down on Cæsar.
Friends am I with you all, and love you all, 220
Upon this hope, that you shall give me reasons
Why and wherein Cæsar was dangerous.
Bru. Or else were this a savage spectacle.
Our reasons are so full of good regard
That were you, Antony, the son of Cæsar, 225
You should be satisfied.
Ant. That's all I seek;
And am moreover suitor that I may
Produce his body to the market place
And in the pulpit, as becomes a friend,

143. **well . . . friend:** disposed to be a good friend
145. **still:** always
146. **Falls . . . purpose:** turns out to be distressingly accurate
152. **rank:** diseased in a way that calls for lancing or blood-letting
158. **purpled:** bloodstained
159. **Live:** if I should live
160. **apt:** ready
174. **in . . . malice:** i.e., despite their show of strength in hostility
191. **credit:** reputation
192. **conceit:** imagine
202–3. **close . . . friendship:** come to friendly terms in the end
204. **bayed:** brought to bay; hunted to death
206. **signed . . . spoil:** marked with the signs of your destruction; **lethe:** lifeblood. Lethe is the river in Hades containing the waters of oblivion, hence is associated with death.
213. **cold modesty:** cool moderation
216. **pricked:** marked down
221. **Upon:** because of
224. **good regard:** sound consideration

Speak in the order of his funeral. 230
Bru. You shall, Mark Antony.
Cass. Brutus, a word with you.
[*Aside to Brutus*] You know not what you do. Do not consent
That Antony speak in his funeral.
Know you how much the people may be moved
By that which he will utter? 235
Bru. [*Aside to Cassius*] By your pardon,
I will myself into the pulpit first
And show the reason of our Cæsar's death.
What Antony shall speak, I will protest
He speaks by leave and by permission, 240
And that we are contented Cæsar shall
Have all true rites and lawful ceremonies.
It shall advantage more than do us wrong.
Cass. [*Aside to Brutus*] I know not what may fall. I like it not.
Bru. Mark Antony, here, take you Cæsar's body.
You shall not in your funeral speech blame us, 246
But speak all good you can devise of Cæsar,
And say you do't by our permission.
Else shall you not have any hand at all
About his funeral. And you shall speak 250
In the same pulpit whereto I am going,
After my speech is ended.
Ant. Be it so.
I do desire no more.
Bru. Prepare the body then, and follow us. 254
Exeunt. Manet Antony.
Ant. O, pardon me, thou bleeding piece of earth,
That I am meek and gentle with these butchers!
Thou art the ruins of the noblest man
That ever lived in the tide of times.
Woe to the hand that shed this costly blood!
Over thy wounds now do I prophesy 260
(Which, like dumb mouths, do ope their ruby lips
To beg the voice and utterance of my tongue),
A curse shall light upon the limbs of men;
Domestic fury and fierce civil strife
Shall cumber all the parts of Italy; 265
Blood and destruction shall be so in use
And dreadful objects so familiar
That mothers shall but smile when they behold
Their infants quartered with the hands of war,
All pity choked with custom of fell deeds; 270
And Cæsar's spirit, ranging for revenge,
With Ate by his side come hot from hell,
Shall in these confines with a monarch's voice
Cry "Havoc!" and let slip the dogs of war,
That this foul deed shall smell above the earth 275
With carrion men, groaning for burial.

Enter OCTAVIUS' SERVANT.

You serve Octavius Cæsar, do you not?
Serv. I do, Mark Antony.
Ant. Cæsar did write for him to come to Rome.
Serv. He did receive his letters and is coming,
And bid me say to you by word of mouth— 281
O Cæsar!
Ant. Thy heart is big. Get thee apart and weep.
Passion, I see, is catching, for mine eyes,
Seeing those beads of sorrow stand in thine, 285
Began to water. Is thy master coming?
Serv. He lies tonight within seven leagues of Rome.
Ant. Post back with speed and tell him what hath chanced.
Here is a mourning Rome, a dangerous Rome,
No Rome of safety for Octavius yet. 290
Hie hence and tell him so. Yet stay awhile.
Thou shalt not back till I have borne this corse
Into the market place. There shall I try
In my oration how the people take
The cruel issue of these bloody men, 295
According to the which thou shalt discourse
To young Octavius of the state of things.
Lend me your hand.
Exeunt [*with Cæsar's body*].

[Scene II. *The same. The Forum.*]

Enter BRUTUS *and* CASSIUS, *with the* PLEBEIANS.

Plebeians. We will be satisfied! Let us be satisfied!
Bru. Then follow me and give me audience, friends.
Cassius, go you into the other street
And part the numbers. 4
Those that will hear me speak, let 'em stay here;
Those that will follow Cassius, go with him;
And public reasons shall be rendered
Of Cæsar's death.
1. Pleb. I will hear Brutus speak.
2. Pleb. I will hear Cassius, and compare their reasons
When severally we hear them rendered. 10
[*Exit Cassius, with some of the Plebeians.*] *Brutus goes into the pulpit.*
3. Pleb. The noble Brutus is ascended. Silence!
Bru. Be patient till the last.

230. **order:** course
244. **fall:** befall; happen
265. **cumber:** burden
270. **custom . . . deeds:** familiarity with cruelty
271. **ranging:** roaming
272. **Ate:** the personification of discord and destruction
274. **Havoc:** the military command to kill without mercy; **let slip:** unleash

295. **issue:** offspring; outcome
10. **severally:** separately

Romans, countrymen, and lovers, hear me for my cause, and be silent, that you may hear. Believe me for mine honor, and have respect to mine honor, 15 that you may believe. Censure me in your wisdom, and awake your senses, that you may the better judge. If there be any in this assembly, any dear friend of Cæsar's, to him I say that Brutus' love to Cæsar was no less than his. If then that friend demand why 20 Brutus rose against Cæsar, this is my answer: Not that I loved Cæsar less, but that I loved Rome more. Had you rather Cæsar were living, and die all slaves, than that Cæsar were dead, to live all freemen? As Cæsar loved me, I weep for him; as he was fortunate, 25 I rejoice at it; as he was valiant, I honor him, but—as he was ambitious, I slew him. There is tears for his love; joy for his fortune; honor for his valor; and death for his ambition. Who is here so base that would be a bondman? If any, speak, for him 30 have I offended. Who is here so rude that would not be a Roman? If any, speak, for him have I offended. Who is here so vile that will not love his country? If any, speak, for him have I offended. I pause for a reply. 35

All. None, Brutus, none!

Bru. Then none have I offended. I have done no more to Cæsar than you shall do to Brutus. The question of his death is enrolled in the Capitol; his glory not extenuated, wherein he was worthy, 40 nor his offenses enforced, for which he suffered death.

Enter MARK ANTONY [*and others*], *with* CÆSAR'S BODY.

Here comes his body, mourned by Mark Antony, who, though he had no hand in his death, shall receive the benefit of his dying, a place in the commonwealth, as which of you shall not? With this I depart, that, 45 as I slew my best lover for the good of Rome, I have the same dagger for myself when it shall please my country to need my death.

All. Live, Brutus! live, live!

1. Pleb. Bring him with triumph home unto his house. 50

2. Pleb. Give him a statue with his ancestors.

3. Pleb. Let him be Cæsar.

4. Pleb. Cæsar's better parts
Shall be crowned in Brutus.

1. Pleb. We'll bring him to his house with shouts and clamors.

Bru. My countrymen—

2. Pleb. Peace! silence! Brutus speaks.

1. Pleb. Peace, ho! 56

Bru. Good countrymen, let me depart alone,
And, for my sake, stay here with Antony.
Do grace to Cæsar's corpse, and grace his speech
Tending to Cæsar's glories which Mark Antony, 60
By our permission, is allowed to make.
I do entreat you, not a man depart,
Save I alone, till Antony have spoke. *Exit*.

1. Pleb. Stay, ho! and let us hear Mark Antony.

3. Pleb. Let him go up into the public chair. 65
We'll hear him. Noble Antony, go up.

Ant. For Brutus' sake I am beholding to you.
[*Goes into the pulpit*.]

4. Pleb. What does he say of Brutus?

3. Pleb. He says for Brutus' sake
He finds himself beholding to us all.

4. Pleb. 'Twere best he speak no harm of Brutus here! 70

1. Pleb. This Cæsar was a tyrant.

3. Pleb. Nay, that's certain.
We are blest that Rome is rid of him.

2. Pleb. Peace! Let us hear what Antony can say.

Ant. You gentle Romans—

All. Peace, ho! Let us hear him.

Ant. Friends, Romans, countrymen, lend me your ears; 75
I come to bury Cæsar, not to praise him.
The evil that men do lives after them;
The good is oft interred with their bones.
So let it be with Cæsar. The noble Brutus
Hath told you Cæsar was ambitious. 80
If it were so, it was a grievous fault,
And grievously hath Cæsar answered it.
Here, under leave of Brutus and the rest
(For Brutus is an honorable man;
So are they all, all honorable men), 85
Come I to speak in Cæsar's funeral.
He was my friend, faithful and just to me;
But Brutus says he was ambitious,
And Brutus is an honorable man.
He hath brought many captives home to Rome, 90
Whose ransoms did the general coffers fill.
Did this in Cæsar seem ambitious?
When that the poor have cried, Cæsar hath wept;
Ambition should be made of sterner stuff.
Yet Brutus says he was ambitious; 95
And Brutus is an honorable man.
You all did see that on the Lupercal
I thrice presented him a kingly crown,
Which he did thrice refuse. Was this ambition?
Yet Brutus says he was ambitious; 100
And sure he is an honorable man.
I speak not to disprove what Brutus spoke,
But here I am to speak what I do know.

13. lovers: dear friends
16. Censure: judge
39. question: story
40. extenuated: minimized
41. enforced: emphasized
59. grace: honor
83. under leave: by permission
97. the Lupercal: the day of the Lupercalia

You all did love him once, not without cause.
What cause withholds you then to mourn for him?
O judgment, thou art fled to brutish beasts, 106
And men have lost their reason! Bear with me,
My heart is in the coffin there with Cæsar,
And I must pause till it come back to me.

1. Pleb. Methinks there is much reason in his sayings. 110

2. Pleb. If thou consider rightly of the matter,
Cæsar has had great wrong.

3. Pleb. Has he, masters?
I fear there will a worse come in his place.

4. Pleb. Marked ye his words? He would not take the crown;
Therefore 'tis certain he was not ambitious. 115

1. Pleb. If it be found so, some will dear abide it.

2. Pleb. Poor soul! his eyes are red as fire with weeping.

3. Pleb. There's not a nobler man in Rome than Antony.

4. Pleb. Now mark him. He begins again to speak.

Ant. But yesterday the word of Cæsar might 120
Have stood against the world. Now lies he there,
And none so poor to do him reverence.
O masters! If I were disposed to stir
Your hearts and minds to mutiny and rage,
I should do Brutus wrong, and Cassius wrong, 125
Who, you all know, are honorable men.
I will not do them wrong. I rather choose
To wrong the dead, to wrong myself and you,
Than I will wrong such honorable men.
But here's a parchment with the seal of Cæsar. 130
I found it in his closet; 'tis his will.
Let but the commons hear this testament,
Which (pardon me) I do not mean to read,
And they would go and kiss dead Cæsar's wounds
And dip their napkins in his sacred blood; 135
Yea, beg a hair of him for memory,
And dying, mention it within their wills,
Bequeathing it as a rich legacy
Unto their issue. 139

4. Pleb. We'll hear the will! Read it, Mark Antony.

All. The will, the will! We will hear Cæsar's will!

Ant. Have patience, gentle friends, I must not read it.
It is not meet you know how Cæsar loved you.
You are not wood, you are not stones, but men;
And being men, hearing the will of Cæsar, 145
It will inflame you, it will make you mad.
'Tis good you know not that you are his heirs,
For if you should, O, what would come of it?

4. Pleb. Read the will! We'll hear it, Antony!
You shall read us the will, Cæsar's will! 150

Ant. Will you be patient? Will you stay awhile?
I have o'ershot myself to tell you of it.
I fear I wrong the honorable men
Whose daggers have stabbed Cæsar; I do fear it.

4. Pleb. They were traitors. Honorable men! 155

All. The will! the testament!

2. Pleb. They were villains, murderers! The will!
Read the will!

Ant. You will compel me then to read the will?
Then make a ring about the corpse of Cæsar 160
And let me show you him that made the will.
Shall I descend? and will you give me leave?

All. Come down.

2. Pleb. Descend.

3. Pleb. You shall have leave. 165

[*Antony comes down.*]

4. Pleb. A ring! Stand round.

1. Pleb. Stand from the hearse! Stand from the body!

2. Pleb. Room for Antony, most noble Antony!

Ant. Nay, press not so upon me. Stand far off.

All. Stand back! Room! Bear back! 170

Ant. If you have tears, prepare to shed them now.
You all do know this mantle. I remember
The first time ever Cæsar put it on.
'Twas on a summer's evening in his tent,
That day he overcame the Nervii. 175
Look, in this place ran Cassius' dagger through.
See what a rent the envious Casca made.
Through this the well-beloved Brutus stabbed;
And as he plucked his cursed steel away,
Mark how the blood of Cæsar followed it, 180
As rushing out of doors to be resolved
If Brutus so unkindly knocked or no;
For Brutus, as you know, was Cæsar's angel.
Judge, O you gods, how dearly Cæsar loved him!
This was the most unkindest cut of all; 185
For when the noble Cæsar saw him stab,
Ingratitude, more strong than traitors' arms,
Quite vanquished him. Then burst his mighty heart;
And in his mantle muffling up his face,
Even at the base of Pompey's statuë 190
(Which all the while ran blood) great Cæsar fell.
O, what a fall was there, my countrymen!
Then I, and you, and all of us fell down,
Whilst bloody treason flourished over us.
O, now you weep, and I perceive you feel 195
The dint of pity. These are gracious drops.
Kind souls, what, weep you when you but behold
Our Cæsar's vesture wounded? Look you here!
Here is himself, marred as you see with traitors.

1. Pleb. O piteous spectacle! 200

2. Pleb. O noble Cæsar!

113. **I . . . place:** proverbial: "Seldom comes the better."
116. **dear abide:** pay dearly for
132. **commons:** multitude
135. **napkins:** handkerchiefs
175. **Nervii:** one of the Gallic tribes
196. **dint:** dent; effect
198. **vesture:** clothing

3. Pleb. O woeful day!
4. Pleb. O traitors, villains!
1. Pleb. O most bloody sight!
2. Pleb. We will be revenged. 205
All. Revenge! About! Seek! Burn! Fire! Kill!
Slay! Let not a traitor live!
Ant. Stay, countrymen.
1. Pleb. Peace there! Hear the noble Antony.
2. Pleb. We'll hear him, we'll follow him, we'll die
with him! 211
Ant. Good friends, sweet friends, let me not stir
you up
To such a sudden flood of mutiny.
They that have done this deed are honorable.
What private griefs they have, alas, I know not, 215
That made them do it. They are wise and honorable,
And will no doubt with reasons answer you.
I come not, friends, to steal away your hearts.
I am no orator, as Brutus is,
But (as you know me all) a plain blunt man 220
That love my friend; and that they know full well
That gave me public leave to speak of him.
For I have neither wit, nor words, nor worth,
Action, nor utterance, nor the power of speech
To stir men's blood. I only speak right on. 225
I tell you that which you yourselves do know,
Show you sweet Cæsar's wounds, poor poor dumb
mouths,
And bid them speak for me. But were I Brutus,
And Brutus Antony, there were an Antony
Would ruffle up your spirits, and put a tongue 230
In every wound of Cæsar that should move
The stones of Rome to rise and mutiny.
All. We'll mutiny.
1. Pleb. We'll burn the house of Brutus.
3. Pleb. Away then! Come, seek the conspirators.
Ant. Yet hear me, countrymen. Yet hear me speak.
All. Peace, ho! Hear Antony, most noble Antony!
Ant. Why, friends, you go to do you know not
what. 237
Wherein hath Cæsar thus deserved your loves?
Alas, you know not! I must tell you then.
You have forgot the will I told you of. 240
All. Most true! The will! Let's stay and hear the
will.
Ant. Here is the will, and under Cæsar's seal.
To every Roman citizen he gives,
To every several man, seventy-five drachmas.
2. Pleb. Most noble Cæsar! We'll revenge his
death! 245
3. Pleb. O royal Cæsar!
Ant. Hear me with patience.
All. Peace, ho!

215. **griefs:** grievances
224. **Action:** eloquent gesture
230. **ruffle:** stir violently

Ant. Moreover, he hath left you all his walks,
His private arbors, and new-planted orchards, 250
On this side Tiber; he hath left them you,
And to your heirs forever—common pleasures,
To walk abroad and recreate yourselves.
Here was a Cæsar! When comes such another?
1. Pleb. Never, never! Come, away, away! 255
We'll burn his body in the holy place
And with the brands fire the traitors' houses.
Take up the body.
2. Pleb. Go fetch fire!
3. Pleb. Pluck down benches! 260
4. Pleb. Pluck down forms, windows, anything!
Exeunt Plebeians [with the body].
Ant. Now let it work. Mischief, thou art afoot,
Take thou what course thou wilt.

Enter SERVANT.

How now, fellow?
Serv. Sir, Octavius is already come to Rome.
Ant. Where is he? 265
Serv. He and Lepidus are at Cæsar's house.
Ant. And thither will I straight to visit him.
He comes upon a wish. Fortune is merry,
And in this mood will give us anything.
Serv. I heard him say Brutus and Cassius 270
Are rid like madmen through the gates of Rome.
Ant. Belike they had some notice of the people
How I had moved them. Bring me to Octavius.
Exeunt.

[Scene III. *The same. A street.*]

Enter CINNA THE POET, *and after him the* PLEBEIANS.

Cinna. I dreamt tonight that I did feast with Cæsar,
And things unluckily charge my fantasy.
I have no will to wander forth of doors,
Yet something leads me forth.
1. Pleb. What is your name? 5
2. Pleb. Whither are you going?
3. Pleb. Where do you dwell?
4. Pleb. Are you a married man or a bachelor?
2. Pleb. Answer every man directly.
1. Pleb. Ay, and briefly. 10

252. **common pleasures:** public recreation grounds
261. **forms:** benches
267. **straight:** immediately
268. **upon . . . wish:** as wished for
272. **Belike:** most likely
272–73. **of . . . them:** of the way I had moved the people
2. **things . . . fantasy:** bad omens burden my imagination
9. **directly:** straightforwardly

4. Pleb. Ay, and wisely.
3. Pleb. Ay, and truly, you were best.
Cinna. What is my name? Whither am I going? Where do I dwell? Am I a married man or a bachelor? Then, to answer every man directly and 15 briefly, wisely and truly: wisely I say, I am a bachelor.
2. Pleb. That's as much as to say they are fools that marry. You'll bear me a bang for that, I fear. Proceed—directly. 20
Cinna. Directly I am going to Cæsar's funeral.
1. Pleb. As a friend or an enemy?
Cinna. As a friend.
2. Pleb. That matter is answered directly.
4. Pleb. For your dwelling—briefly. 25

19. bear . . . bang: take a blow from me

Cinna. Briefly, I dwell by the Capitol.
3. Pleb. Your name, sir, truly.
Cinna. Truly, my name is Cinna.
1. Pleb. Tear him to pieces! He's a conspirator.
Cinna. I am Cinna the poet! I am Cinna the 30 poet!
4. Pleb. Tear him for his bad verses! Tear him for his bad verses!
Cinna. I am not Cinna the conspirator.
4. Pleb. It is no matter; his name's Cinna! 35 Pluck but his name out of his heart, and turn him going.
3. Pleb. Tear him, tear him! Come, brands, ho! firebrands! To Brutus', to Cassius'! Burn all! Some to Decius' house and some to Casca's; some to 40 Ligarius'! Away, go!

Exeunt all the Plebeians.

ACT IV

[Scene I. *The same. Antony's house.*]

Enter ANTONY, OCTAVIUS, *and* LEPIDUS.

Ant. These many, then, shall die; their names are pricked.
Oct. Your brother too must die. Consent you, Lepidus?
Lep. I do consent.
Oct. Prick him down, Antony.
Lep. Upon conditions Publius shall not live,
Who is your sister's son, Mark Antony. 5
Ant. He shall not live. Look, with a spot I damn him.
But, Lepidus, go you to Cæsar's house.
Fetch the will hither, and we shall determine
How to cut off some charge in legacies.
Lep. What? shall I find you here? 10
Oct. Or here or at the Capitol. *Exit Lepidus.*
Ant. This is a slight unmeritable man,
Meet to be sent on errands. Is it fit,
The threefold world divided, he should stand
One of the three to share it?
Oct. So you thought him, 15
And took his voice who should be pricked to die
In our black sentence and proscription.
Ant. Octavius, I have seen more days than you;
And though we lay these honors on this man
To ease ourselves of divers sland'rous loads, 20
He shall but bear them as the ass bears gold,
To groan and sweat under the business,
Either led or driven as we point the way;
And having brought our treasure where we will,
Then take we down his load, and turn him off 25
(Like to the empty ass) to shake his ears
And graze in commons.
Oct. You may do your will;
But he's a tried and valiant soldier.
Ant. So is my horse, Octavius, and for that
I do appoint him store of provender. 30
It is a creature that I teach to fight,
To wind, to stop, to run directly on,
His corporal motion governed by my spirit.
And, in some taste, is Lepidus but so.
He must be taught, and trained, and bid go forth:
A barren-spirited fellow; one that feeds 36
On objects, arts, and imitations
Which, out of use and staled by other men,
Begin his fashion. Do not talk of him,

9. cut . . . charge: reduce our expense
12. slight: of little value

32. wind: turn
34. taste: degree
36–39. feeds . . . fashion: i.e., he adopts new fads and fashions when they have become out of date.

But as a property. And now, Octavius, 40
Listen great things. Brutus and Cassius
Are levying powers. We must straight make head.
Therefore let our alliance be combined,
Our best friends made, and our best means stretched out;
And let us presently go sit in council 45
How covert matters may be best disclosed
And open perils surest answered.

Oct. Let us do so; for we are at the stake
And bayed about with many enemies;
And some that smile have in their hearts, I fear, 50
Millions of mischiefs.

Exeunt.

[Scene II. *The camp near Sardis. Before Brutus' tent.*]

Drum. Enter BRUTUS, LUCILIUS, [LUCIUS,] *and the* ARMY. TITINIUS *and* PINDARUS *meet them.*

Bru. Stand ho!

Lucil. Give the word, ho! and stand!

Bru. What now, Lucilius? Is Cassius near?

Lucil. He is at hand, and Pindarus is come
To do you salutation from his master. 5

Bru. He greets me well. Your master, Pindarus,
In his own change, or by ill officers,
Hath given me some worthy cause to wish
Things done undone; but if he be at hand,
I shall be satisfied.

Pin. I do not doubt 10
But that my noble master will appear
Such as he is, full of regard and honor.

Bru. He is not doubted. A word, Lucilius,
How he received you. Let me be resolved.

Lucil. With courtesy and with respect enough, 15
But not with such familiar instances
Nor with such free and friendly conference
As he hath used of old.

Bru. Thou hast described
A hot friend cooling. Ever note, Lucilius,
When love begins to sicken and decay 20
It useth an enforced ceremony.
There are no tricks in plain and simple faith;
But hollow men, like horses hot at hand,
Make gallant show and promise of their mettle;

Low march within.

But when they should endure the bloody spur, 25
They fall their crests, and like deceitful jades
Sink in the trial. Comes his army on?

Lucil. They mean this night in Sardis to be quartered.
The greater part, the horse in general,
Are come with Cassius.

Bru. Hark! He is arrived. 30
March gently on to meet him.

Enter CASSIUS *and his* POWERS.

Cass. Stand, ho!

Bru. Stand, ho! Speak the word along.

1. Sold. Stand!

2. Sold. Stand! 35

3. Sold. Stand!

Cass. Most noble brother, you have done me wrong.

Bru. Judge me, you gods! wrong I mine enemies?
And if not so, how should I wrong a brother? 39

Cass. Brutus, this sober form of your hides wrongs,
And when you do them—

Bru. Cassius, be content.
Speak your griefs softly. I do know you well.
Before the eyes of both our armies here
(Which should perceive nothing but love from us)
Let us not wrangle. Bid them move away. 45
Then in my tent, Cassius, enlarge your griefs,
And I will give you audience.

Cass. Pindarus,
Bid our commanders lead their charges off
A little from this ground.

Bru. Lucilius, do you the like, and let no man 50
Come to our tent till we have done our conference.
Let Lucius and Titinius guard our door.

Exeunt.

[Scene III. *The same. Brutus' tent.*]

Enter BRUTUS *and* CASSIUS.

Cass. That you have wronged me doth appear in this:
You have condemned and noted Lucius Pella

40. **property:** tool
42. **make head:** assemble an army
46. **covert matters:** hidden menaces; **disclosed:** discovered
48–49. **at . . . enemies:** that is, like a bear tied to a stake to be baited by dogs
6. **well:** opportunely
7. **In . . . officers:** because of a change of heart toward me or the defection of his subordinates
8. **worthy:** justifiable
16. **familiar instances:** signs of friendship
17. **conference:** conversation
21. **enforced:** strained
23. **hollow:** insincere; **hot . . . hand:** eager at the start
24. **mettle:** spirit
26. **jades:** nags
27. **Sink . . . trial:** fail when tested
31. **gently:** slowly
40. **sober form:** grave behavior
41. **content:** calm
46. **enlarge:** set forth in full
2. **noted:** marked with disgrace

For taking bribes here of the Sardians;
Wherein my letters, praying on his side,
Because I knew the man, were slighted off. 5

Bru. You wronged yourself to write in such a case.

Cass. In such a time as this it is not meet
That every nice offense should bear his comment.

Bru. Let me tell you, Cassius, you yourself
Are much condemned to have an itching palm, 10
To sell and mart your offices for gold
To undeservers.

Cass. I an itching palm?
You know that you are Brutus that speaks this,
Or, by the gods, this speech were else your last!

Bru. The name of Cassius honors this corruption,
And chastisement doth therefore hide his head. 16

Cass. Chastisement?

Bru. Remember March; the ides of March remember.
Did not great Julius bleed for justice' sake?
What villain touched his body that did stab 20
And not for justice? What, shall one of us,
That struck the foremost man of all this world
But for supporting robbers—shall we now
Contaminate our fingers with base bribes,
And sell the mighty space of our large honors 25
For so much trash as may be grasped thus?
I had rather be a dog and bay the moon
Than such a Roman.

Cass. Brutus, bait not me!
I'll not endure it. You forget yourself
To hedge me in. I am a soldier, I, 30
Older in practice, abler than yourself
To make conditions.

Bru. Go to! You are not, Cassius.

Cass. I am.

Bru. I say you are not.

Cass. Urge me no more! I shall forget myself. 35
Have mind upon your health, tempt me no farther.

Bru. Away, slight man!

Cass. Is't possible?

Bru. Hear me, for I will speak.
Must I give way and room to your rash choler?
Shall I be frighted when a madman stares? 40

Cass. O ye gods, ye gods! Must I endure all this?

Bru. All this? Ay, more! Fret till your proud heart break.
Go show your slaves how choleric you are
And make your bondmen tremble. Must I budge?
Must I observe you? Must I stand and crouch 45
Under your testy humor? By the gods,
You shall digest the venom of your spleen,
Though it do split you; for from this day forth
I'll use you for my mirth, yea, for my laughter,
When you are waspish.

Cass. Is it come to this? 50

Bru. You say you are a better soldier;
Let it appear so. Make your vaunting true,
And it shall please me well. For mine own part,
I shall be glad to learn of noble men.

Cass. You wrong me every way! You wrong me, Brutus! 55
I said an elder soldier, not a better.
Did I say "better"?

Bru. If you did, I care not.

Cass. When Cæsar lived he durst not thus have moved me.

Bru. Peace, peace! You durst not so have tempted him.

Cass. I durst not? 60

Bru. No.

Cass. What, durst not tempt him?

Bru. For your life you durst not.

Cass. Do not presume too much upon my love.
I may do that I shall be sorry for.

Bru. You have done that you should be sorry for.
There is no terror, Cassius, in your threats; 66
For I am armed so strong in honesty
That they pass by me as the idle wind,
Which I respect not. I did send to you
For certain sums of gold, which you denied me, 70
For I can raise no money by vile means—
By heaven, I had rather coin my heart
And drop my blood for drachmas than to wring
From the hard hands of peasants their vile trash
By any indirection. I did send 75
To you for gold to pay my legions,
Which you denied me. Was that done like Cassius?
Should I have answered Caius Cassius so?
When Marcus Brutus grows so covetous
To lock such rascal counters from his friends, 80
Be ready, gods, with all your thunderbolts,
Dash him to pieces!

Cass. I denied you not.

Bru. You did.

Cass. I did not. He was but a fool that brought
My answer back. Brutus hath rived my heart. 85
A friend should bear his friend's infirmities,
But Brutus makes mine greater than they are.

Bru. I do not, till you practice them on me.

Cass. You love me not.

Bru. I do not like your faults.

8. nice: trifling; **bear . . . comment:** be subject to criticism. **His** equals "its".
27. be . . . moon: an allusion to the proverb: "The moon does not heed the barking of dogs"—a description of utter futility
30. hedge . . . in: control my actions
35. Urge: provoke
45. observe: defer to; humor
47. digest: swallow and contain; **spleen:** the source of anger
52. vaunting: boasting
75. indirection: unjust proceeding
80. rascal counters: paltry tokens. Counters were not real coins but tokens used by shopkeepers in keeping accounts.

Cass. A friendly eye could never see such faults.
Bru. A flatterer's would not, though they do appear 91
As huge as high Olympus.
Cass. Come, Antony, and young Octavius, come!
Revenge yourselves alone on Cassius.
For Cassius is aweary of the world: 95
Hated by one he loves; braved by his brother;
Checked like a bondsman; all his faults observed,
Set in a notebook, learned and conned by rote
To cast into my teeth. O, I could weep
My spirit from mine eyes! There is my dagger,
And here my naked breast; within, a heart 101
Dearer than Pluto's mine, richer than gold:
If that thou beest a Roman, take it forth.
I, that denied thee gold, will give my heart.
Strike as thou didst at Cæsar; for I know, 105
When thou didst hate him worst, thou lovedst him better
Than ever thou lovedst Cassius.
Bru. Sheathe your dagger.
Be angry when you will; it shall have scope.
Do what you will; dishonor shall be humor.
O Cassius, you are yoked with a lamb 110
That carries anger as the flint bears fire;
Who, much enforced, shows a hasty spark,
And straight is cold again.
Cass. Hath Cassius lived
To be but mirth and laughter to his Brutus
When grief and blood ill-tempered vexeth him? 115
Bru. When I spoke that, I was ill-tempered too.
Cass. Do you confess so much? Give me your hand.
Bru. And my heart too.
Cass. O Brutus!
Bru. What's the matter?
Cass. Have you not love enough to bear with me
When that rash humor which my mother gave me
Makes me forgetful?
Bru. Yes, Cassius, and from henceforth,
When you are over-earnest with your Brutus, 122
He'll think your mother chides, and leave you so.

Enter a POET [*followed by* LUCILIUS, TITINIUS, *and* LUCIUS].

Poet. Let me go in to see the generals!
There is some grudge between 'em. 'Tis not meet
They be alone. 126
Lucil. You shall not come to them.
Poet. Nothing but death shall stay me.
Cass. How now? What's the matter?
Poet. For shame, you generals! What do you mean? 130
Love and be friends, as two such men should be,
For I have seen more years, I'm sure, than ye.
Cass. Ha, ha! How vilely doth this cynic rhyme!
Bru. Get you hence, sirrah! Saucy fellow, hence!
Cass. Bear with him, Brutus. 'Tis his fashion. 135
Bru. I'll know his humor when he knows his time.
What should the wars do with these jigging fools?
Companion, hence!
Cass. Away, away, be gone! *Exit Poet.*
Bru. Lucilius and Titinius, bid the commanders
Prepare to lodge their companies tonight. 140
Cass. And come yourselves, and bring Messala with you
Immediately to us. [*Exeunt Lucilius and Titinius.*]
Bru. Lucius, a bowl of wine.
[*Exit Lucius.*]
Cass. I did not think you could have been so angry.
Bru. O Cassius, I am sick of many griefs.
Cass. Of your philosophy you make no use 145
If you give place to accidental evils.
Bru. No man bears sorrow better. Portia is dead.
Cass. Ha! Portia?
Bru. She is dead.
Cass. How scaped I killing when I crossed you so?
O insupportable and touching loss! 151
Upon what sickness?
Bru. Impatient of my absence,
And grief that young Octavius with Mark Antony
Have made themselves so strong—for with her death
That tidings came—with this she fell distract, 155
And (her attendants absent) swallowed fire.
Cass. And died so?
Bru. Even so.
Cass. O ye immortal gods!

Enter BOY, [LUCIUS,] *with wine and tapers.*

Bru. Speak no more of her. Give me a bowl of wine.
In this I bury all unkindness, Cassius. *Drinks.*
Cass. My heart is thirsty for that noble pledge.
Fill, Lucius, till the wine o'erswell the cup. 161
I cannot drink too much of Brutus' love.
[*Drinks. Exit Lucius.*]

Enter TITINIUS *and* MESSALA.

Bru. Come in, Titinius! Welcome, good Messala.
Now sit we close about this taper here
And call in question our necessities. 165

96. braved: challenged
97. Checked: rebuked
102. Pluto's mine: the rich mines underground, Pluto's domain as god of the underworld
109. dishonor . . . humor: i.e., I shall regard your insults as mere caprice and take no offense.
112. enforced: provoked
136. know . . . humor: allow his eccentricity; **his time:** i.e., the time suitable for foolery
138. Companion: base fellow
145. your philosophy: Stoicism, which professed disregard for the blows of fate
157. Even: exactly
165. call . . . question: discuss

Cass. Portia, art thou gone?
Bru. No more, I pray you.
Messala, I have here received letters
That young Octavius and Mark Antony
Come down upon us with a mighty power,
Bending their expedition toward Philippi. 170
Mes. Myself have letters of the selfsame tenure.
Bru. With what addition?
Mes. That by proscription and bills of outlawry
Octavius, Antony, and Lepidus
Have put to death an hundred senators. 175
Bru. Therein our letters do not well agree.
Mine speak of seventy senators that died
By their proscriptions, Cicero being one.
Cass. Cicero one?
Mes. Cicero is dead,
And by that order of proscription. 180
Had you your letters from your wife, my lord?
Bru. No, Messala.
Mes. Nor nothing in your letters writ of her?
Bru. Nothing, Messala.
Mes. That methinks is strange.
Bru. Why ask you? Hear you aught of her in yours? 185
Mes. No, my lord.
Bru. Now as you are a Roman, tell me true.
Mes. Then like a Roman bear the truth I tell,
For certain she is dead, and by strange manner.
Bru. Why, farewell, Portia. We must die, Messala.
With meditating that she must die once, 191
I have the patience to endure it now.
Mes. Even so great men great losses should endure.
Cass. I have as much of this in art as you,
But yet my nature could not bear it so. 195
Bru. Well, to our work alive. What do you think
Of marching to Philippi presently?
Cass. I do not think it good.
Bru. Your reason?
Cass. This it is:
'Tis better that the enemy seek us.
So shall he waste his means, weary his soldiers, 200
Doing himself offense, whilst we, lying still,
Are full of rest, defense, and nimbleness.
Bru. Good reasons must of force give place to better.
The people 'twixt Philippi and this ground
Do stand but in a forced affection, 205
For they have grudged us contribution.
The enemy, marching along by them,
By them shall make a fuller number up,
Come on refreshed, new-added, and encouraged;
From which advantage shall we cut him off 210
If at Philippi we do face him there,
These people at our back.
Cass. Hear me, good brother.
Bru. Under your pardon. You must note beside
That we have tried the utmost of our friends,
Our legions are brimful, our cause is ripe. 215
The enemy increaseth every day;
We, at the height, are ready to decline.
There is a tide in the affairs of men
Which, taken at the flood, leads on to fortune;
Omitted, all the voyage of their life 220
Is bound in shallows and in miseries.
On such a full sea are we now afloat,
And we must take the current when it serves
Or lose our ventures.
Cass. Then, with your will, go on.
We'll along ourselves and meet them at Philippi.
Bru. The deep of night is crept upon our talk 226
And nature must obey necessity,
Which we will niggard with a little rest.
There is no more to say?
Cass. No more. Good night.
Early tomorrow will we rise and hence. 230
Bru. Lucius! (*Enter Lucius.*) My gown.
[*Exit Lucius.*]
Farewell, good Messala.
Good night, Titinius. Noble, noble Cassius,
Good night and good repose!
Cass. O my dear brother,
This was an ill beginning of the night! 235
Never come such division 'tween our souls!
Let it not, Brutus.

Enter LUCIUS, *with the gown.*

Bru. Everything is well.
Cass. Good night, my lord.
Bru. Good night, good brother.
Tit., Mes. Good night, Lord Brutus.
Bru. Farewell every one.
Exeunt [*Cassius, Titinius, and Messala*].
Give me the gown. Where is thy instrument? 240
Luc. Here in the tent.
Bru. What, thou speakst drowsily?
Poor knave, I blame thee not, thou art o'erwatched.
Call Claudius and some other of my men;
I'll have them sleep on cushions in my tent.
Luc. Varro and Claudius! 245

Enter VARRO *and* CLAUDIUS.

170. expedition: speedy course
171. tenure: tenor
194. I . . . art: I am as familiar with Stoicism
197. presently: at once
201. offense: harm
203. force: necessity
205. Do . . . affection: are friendly only upon compulsion
213. Under . . . pardon: by your leave
220. Omitted: neglected
221. bound in: confined to
224. with . . . will: as you wish
228. niggard: scant
242. o'erwatched: exhausted from sleeplessness

Var. Calls my lord?
Bru. I pray you, sirs, lie in my tent and sleep.
It may be I shall raise you by-and-by
On business to my brother Cassius.
Var. So please you, we will stand and watch your pleasure. 250
Bru. I will not have it so. Lie down, good sirs.
It may be I shall otherwise bethink me.
[*Varro and Claudius lie down.*]
Look, Lucius, here's the book I sought for so;
I put it in the pocket of my gown.
Luc. I was sure your lordship did not give it me.
Bru. Bear with me, good boy, I am much forgetful. 256
Canst thou hold up thy heavy eyes awhile,
And touch thy instrument a strain or two?
Luc. Ay, my lord, an't please you.
Bru. It does, my boy.
I trouble thee too much, but thou art willing. 260
Luc. It is my duty, sir.
Bru. I should not urge thy duty past thy might.
I know young bloods look for a time of rest.
Luc. I have slept, my lord, already.
Bru. It was well done; and thou shalt sleep again;
I will not hold thee long. If I do live, 266
I will be good to thee.
Music, and a song. [*Lucius falls asleep.*]
This is a sleepy tune. O murd'rous slumber!
Lay'st thou thy leaden mace upon my boy,
That plays thee music? Gentle knave, good night.
I will not do thee so much wrong to wake thee. 271
If thou dost nod, thou breakst thy instrument;
I'll take it from thee; and, good boy, good night.
Let me see, let me see. Is not the leaf turned down
Where I left reading? Here it is, I think. [*Sits.*]

Enter the GHOST OF CÆSAR.

How ill this taper burns! Ha! Who comes here? 276
I think it is the weakness of mine eyes
That shapes this monstrous apparition.
It comes upon me. Art thou anything?
Art thou some god, some angel, or some devil, 280
That makest my blood cold and my hair to stare?
Speak to me what thou art.
Ghost. Thy evil spirit, Brutus.
Bru. Why comest thou?
Ghost. To tell thee thou shalt see me at Philippi.
Bru. Well; then I shall see thee again? 285
Ghost. Ay, at Philippi.
Bru. Why, I will see thee at Philippi then.
[*Exit Ghost.*]
Now I have taken heart thou vanishest.
Ill spirit, I would hold more talk with thee.
Boy! Lucius! Varro! Claudius! Sirs! Awake! 290
Claudius!
Luc. The strings, my lord, are false.
Bru. He thinks he still is at his instrument.
Lucius, awake!
Luc. My lord? 295
Bru. Didst thou dream, Lucius, that thou so criedst out?
Luc. My lord, I do not know that I did cry.
Bru. Yes, that thou didst. Didst thou see anything?
Luc. Nothing, my lord.
Bru. Sleep again, Lucius. Sirrah Claudius! 300
[*To Varro*] Fellow thou, awake!
Var. My lord?
Clau. My lord?
Bru. Why did you so cry out, sirs, in your sleep?
Both. Did we, my lord?
Bru. Ay. Saw you anything?
Var. No, my lord, I saw nothing.
Clau. Nor I, my lord.
Bru. Go and commend me to my brother Cassius.
Bid him set on his pow'rs betimes before, 308
And we will follow.
Both. It shall be done, my lord.
Exeunt.

250. watch . . . pleasure: stay awake and await your command
269. mace: staff carried by a police official
308. betimes: early

ACT V

[Scene I. *The plains of Philippi.*]

Enter OCTAVIUS, ANTONY, *and their* ARMY.

Oct. Now, Antony, our hopes are answered.
You said the enemy would not come down
But keep the hills and upper regions.
It proves not so, their battles are at hand.
They mean to warn us at Philippi here, 5
Answering before we do demand of them.
Ant. Tut! I am in their bosoms and I know
Wherefore they do it. They could be content
To visit other places, and come down
With fearful bravery, thinking by this face 10
To fasten in our thoughts that they have courage.
But 'tis not so.

Enter a MESSENGER.

Mess. Prepare you, generals,
The enemy comes on in gallant show;
Their bloody sign of battle is hung out,
And something to be done immediately. 15
Ant. Octavius, lead your battle softly on
Upon the left hand of the even field
Oct. Upon the right hand I. Keep thou the left.
Ant. Why do you cross me in this exigent?
Oct. I do not cross you; but I will do so. 20
March.

Drum. Enter BRUTUS, CASSIUS, *and their* ARMY; [LUCILIUS, TITINIUS, MESSALA, *and others*].

Bru. They stand and would have parley.
Cass. Stand fast, Titinius. We must out and talk.
Oct. Mark Antony, shall we give sign of battle?
Ant. No, Cæsar, we will answer on their charge.
Make forth. The generals would have some words.
Oct. Stir not until the signal. 26
Bru. Words before blows. Is it so, countrymen?
Oct. Not that we love words better, as you do.
Bru. Good words are better than bad strokes, Octavius.
Ant. In your bad strokes, Brutus, you give good words; 30
Witness the hole you made in Cæsar's heart,
Crying "Long live! Hail, Cæsar!"
Cass. Antony,
The posture of your blows are yet unknown;
But for your words, they rob the Hybla bees,
And leave them honeyless.
Ant. Not stingless too. 35
Bru. O yes, and soundless too!
For you have stol'n their buzzing, Antony,
And very wisely threat before you sting.
Ant. Villains! you did not so when your vile daggers
Hacked one another in the sides of Cæsar. 40
You showed your teeth like apes, and fawned like hounds,
And bowed like bondmen, kissing Cæsar's feet;
Whilst damned Casca, like a cur, behind
Struck Cæsar on the neck. O you flatterers!
Cass. Flatterers? Now, Brutus, thank yourself!
This tongue had not offended so today 46
If Cassius might have ruled.
Oct. Come, come, the cause! If arguing make us sweat,
The proof of it will turn to redder drops.
Look, 50
I draw a sword against conspirators.
When think you that the sword goes up again?
Never, till Cæsar's three-and-thirty wounds
Be well avenged, or till another Cæsar
Have added slaughter to the sword of traitors. 55
Bru. Cæsar, thou canst not die by traitors' hands
Unless thou bringst them with thee.
Oct. So I hope.
I was not born to die on Brutus' sword.
Bru. O, if thou wert the noblest of thy strain,
Young man, thou couldst not die more honorable. 60
Cass. A peevish schoolboy, worthless of such honor,
Joined with a masker and a reveller!

4. **battles:** hosts
5. **warn us:** summon us to battle
7. **bosoms:** confidence
8. **could . . . content:** would be happy
10. **fearful bravery:** timorous show of defiance
14. **bloody . . . battle:** a scarlet coat was used for the signal of battle, according to North's Plutarch.
16. **softly:** slowly
19. **exigent:** crisis
34. **Hybla bees:** honey of Mount Hybla in Sicily was famous.
49. **proof:** settlement by action
61. **peevish:** childish; silly

Ant. Old Cassius still.
Oct. Come, Antony. Away!
Defiance, traitors, hurl we in your teeth.
If you dare fight today, come to the field; 65
If not, when you have stomachs.
Exeunt Octavius, Antony, and Army.
Cass. Why, now blow wind, swell billow, and swim bark!
The storm is up, and all is on the hazard.
Bru. Ho, Lucilius! Hark, a word with you.
Lucilius and Messala stand forth.
Lucil. My lord? 70
[*Brutus and Lucilius converse apart.*]
Cass. Messala.
Mes. What says my general?
Cass. Messala,
This is my birthday; as this very day
Was Cassius born. Give me thy hand, Messala.
Be thou my witness that against my will
(As Pompey was) am I compelled to set 75
Upon one battle all our liberties.
You know that I held Epicurus strong
And his opinion. Now I change my mind
And partly credit things that do presage.
Coming from Sardis, on our former ensign 80
Two mighty eagles fell, and there they perched,
Gorging and feeding from our soldiers' hands,
Who to Philippi here consorted us.
This morning are they fled away and gone,
And in their steads do ravens, crows, and kites 85
Fly o'er our heads and downward look on us
As we were sickly prey. Their shadows seem
A canopy most fatal, under which
Our army lies, ready to give up the ghost.
Mes. Believe not so.
Cass. I but believe it partly, 90
For I am fresh of spirit and resolved
To meet all perils very constantly.
Bru. Even so, Lucilius.
Cass. Now, most noble Brutus,
The gods today stand friendly, that we may,
Lovers in peace, lead on our days to age! 95
But since the affairs of men rest still incertain,
Let's reason with the worst that may befall.
If we do lose this battle, then is this
The very last time we shall speak together.
What are you then determined to do? 100
Bru. Even by the rule of that philosophy
By which I did blame Cato for the death
Which he did give himself—I know not how,
But I do find it cowardly and vile,
For fear of what might fall, so to prevent 105
The time of life—arming myself with patience
To stay the providence of some high powers
That govern us below.
Cass. Then, if we lose this battle,
You are contented to be led in triumph
Thorough the streets of Rome. 110
Bru. No, Cassius, no. Think not, thou noble Roman,
That ever Brutus will go bound to Rome.
He bears too great a mind. But this same day
Must end that work the ides of March begun,
And whether we shall meet again I know not. 115
Therefore our everlasting farewell take.
For ever and for ever farewell, Cassius!
If we do meet again, why, we shall smile;
If not, why then this parting was well made.
Cass. For ever and for ever farewell, Brutus! 120
If we do meet again, we'll smile indeed;
If not, 'tis true this parting was well made.
Bru. Why then, lead on. O that a man might know
The end of this day's business ere it come!
But it sufficeth that the day will end, 125
And then the end is known. Come, ho! Away!
Exeunt.

[Scene II. *The same. The field of battle.*]

Alarum. Enter BRUTUS *and* MESSALA.

Bru. Ride, ride, Messala, ride, and give these bills
Unto the legions on the other side. *Loud alarum.*
Let them set on at once; for I perceive
But cold demeanor in Octavius' wing,
And sudden push gives them the overthrow. 5
Ride, ride, Messala! Let them all come down.
Exeunt.

[Scene III. *Another part of the field.*]

Alarums. Enter CASSIUS *and* TITINIUS.

Cass. O, look, Titinius, look! The villains fly!
Myself have to mine own turned enemy.

63. Old Cassius still: i.e., as sharp-tongued as ever
66. stomachs: courage
68. on . . . hazard: at stake
75. set: stake
77. Epicurus: the philosopher Epicurus taught that the gods had no interest in human affairs and therefore omens had no validity.
79. presage: predict the future
80. former: foremost
83. consorted: accompanied
92. constantly: firmly
94. The . . . friendly: i.e., may the gods stand friendly today
96. rest: remain
97. reason with: consider
105–6. prevent . . . life: forestall the natural termination of life
107. stay: await
1. bills: orders
4. cold demeanor: sluggish action

This ensign here of mine was turning back;
I slew the coward and did take it from him.
Tit. O Cassius, Brutus gave the word too early, 5
Who, having some advantage on Octavius,
Took it too eagerly. His soldiers fell to spoil,
Whilst we by Antony are all enclosed.

Enter PINDARUS.

Pin. Fly further off, my lord! fly further off!
Mark Antony is in your tents, my lord. 10
Fly, therefore, noble Cassius, fly far off!
Cass. This hill is far enough. Look, look, Titinius!
Are those my tents where I perceive the fire?
Tit. They are, my lord.
Cass. Titinius, if thou lovest me;
Mount thou my horse and hide thy spurs in him 15
Till he have brought thee up to yonder troops
And here again, that I may rest assured
Whether yond troops are friend or enemy.
Tit. I will be here again even with a thought. *Exit.*
Cass. Go, Pindarus, get higher on that hill. 20
My sight was ever thick. Regard Titinius,
And tell me what thou notest about the field.
[*Pindarus ascends the hill.*]
This day I breathed first. Time is come round,
And where I did begin, there shall I end.
My life is run his compass. Sirrah, what news? 25
Pin. (*Above*) O my lord!
Cass. What news?
Pin [*Above*] Titinius is enclosed round about
With horsemen that make to him on the spur.
Yet he spurs on. Now they are almost on him. 30
Now, Titinius!
Now some light. O, he lights too! He's ta'en. (*Shout.*) And hark!
They shout for joy.
Cass. Come down; behold no more.
O coward that I am to live so long
To see my best friend ta'en before my face! 35

Enter PINDARUS [*from above*].

Come hither, sirrah.
In Parthia did I take thee prisoner,
And then I swore thee, saving of thy life,
That whatsoever I did bid thee do,
Thou shouldst attempt it. Come now, keep thine oath. 40
Now be a freeman, and with this good sword,
That ran through Cæsar's bowels, search this bosom.
Stand not to answer. Here, take thou the hilts,
And when my face is covered, as 'tis now,
Guide thou the sword. [*Pindarus stabs him.*]—Cæsar, thou art revenged 45
Even with the sword that killed thee. [*Dies.*]
Pin. So, I am free, yet would not so have been,
Durst I have done my will. O Cassius!
Far from this country Pindarus shall run, 49
Where never Roman shall take note of him. [*Exit.*]

Enter TITINIUS *and* MESSALA.

Mes. It is but change, Titinius; for Octavius
Is overthrown by noble Brutus' power,
As Cassius' legions are by Antony.
Tit. These tidings will well comfort Cassius.
Mes. Where did you leave him?
Tit. All disconsolate,
With Pindarus his bondman, on this hill. 56
Mes. Is not that he that lies upon the ground?
Tit. He lies not like the living. O my heart!
Mes. Is not that he?
Tit. No, this was he, Messala,
But Cassius is no more. O setting sun, 60
As in thy red rays thou dost sink to night,
So in his red blood Cassius' day is set!
The sun of Rome is set. Our day is gone;
Clouds, dews, and dangers come; our deeds are done!
Mistrust of my success hath done this deed. 65
Mes. Mistrust of good success hath done this deed.
O hateful Error, Melancholy's child,
Why dost thou show to the apt thoughts of men
The things that are not? O Error, soon conceived,
Thou never comest unto a happy birth, 70
But killst the mother that engend'red thee!
Tit. What, Pindarus! Where art thou, Pindarus?
Mes. Seek him, Titinius, whilst I go to meet
The noble Brutus, thrusting this report
Into his ears. I may say "thrusting" it; 75
For piercing steel and darts envenomed
Shall be as welcome to the ears of Brutus
As tidings of this sight.
Tit. Hie you, Messala,
And I will seek for Pindarus the while.
[*Exit Messala.*]
Why didst thou send me forth, brave Cassius? 80
Did I not meet thy friends, and did not they
Put on my brows this wreath of victory
And bid me give it thee? Didst thou not hear their shouts?
Alas, thou hast misconstrued everything!
But hold thee, take this garland on thy brow. 85
Thy Brutus bid me give it thee, and I
Will do his bidding. Brutus, come apace
And see how I regarded Caius Cassius.

3. ensign: standard-bearer
19. even . . . thought: as quick as thought
25. compass: full circuit
51. change: exchange
80. brave: noble

By your leave, gods. This is a Roman's part. 89
Come, Cassius' sword, and find Titinius' heart. *Dies.*

Alarum. Enter BRUTUS, MESSALA, YOUNG CATO, STRATO, VOLUMNIUS, *and* LUCILIUS.

Bru. Where, where, Messala, doth his body lie?
Mes. Lo, yonder, and Titinius mourning it.
Bru. Titinius' face is upward.
Cato. He is slain.
Bru. O Julius Cæsar, thou art mighty yet!
Thy spirit walks abroad and turns our swords 95
In our own proper entrails. *Low alarums.*
Cato. Brave Titinius!
Look whe'r he have not crowned dead Cassius.
Bru. Are yet two Romans living such as these?
The last of all the Romans, fare thee well!
It is impossible that ever Rome 100
Should breed thy fellow. Friends, I owe mo tears
To this dead man than you shall see me pay.
I shall find time, Cassius; I shall find time.
Come therefore, and to Thasos send his body.
His funerals shall not be in our camp, 105
Lest it discomfort us. Lucilius, come;
And come, young Cato. Let us to the field.
Labeo and Flavius set our battles on.
'Tis three o'clock; and, Romans, yet ere night
We shall try fortune in a second fight. 110
Exeunt.

[Scene IV. *Another part of the field.*]

Alarum. Enter BRUTUS, MESSALA, [YOUNG] CATO, LUCILIUS, *and* FLAVIUS.

Bru. Yet, countrymen, O, yet hold up your heads!
Cato. What bastard doth not? Who will go with me?
I will proclaim my name about the field.
I am the son of Marcus Cato, ho!
A foe to tyrants, and my country's friend. 5
I am the son of Marcus Cato, ho!

Enter SOLDIERS *and fight.*

Bru. And I am Brutus, Marcus Brutus I!
Brutus, my country's friend! Know me for Brutus!
[*Exit. Young Cato falls.*]
Lucil. O young and noble Cato, art thou down?
Why, now thou diest as bravely as Titinius, 10
And mayst be honored, being Cato's son.

96. proper: personal
97. whe'r: whether
101. fellow: match; **mo:** more
106. discomfort: discourage

1. Sold. Yield, or thou diest.
Lucil. Only I yield to die.
[*Offering money*] There is so much that thou wilt kill me straight.
Kill Brutus, and be honored in his death.
1. Sold. We must not. A noble prisoner! 15

Enter ANTONY.

2. Sold. Room ho! Tell Antony Brutus is ta'en.
1. Sold. I'll tell the news. Here comes the general.
Brutus is ta'en! Brutus is ta'en, my lord!
Ant. Where is he?
Lucil. Safe, Antony; Brutus is safe enough. 20
I dare assure thee that no enemy
Shall ever take alive the noble Brutus.
The gods defend him from so great a shame!
When you do find him, or alive or dead,
He will be found like Brutus, like himself. 25
Ant. This is not Brutus, friend; but, I assure you,
A prize no less in worth. Keep this man safe;
Give him all kindness. I had rather have
Such men my friends than enemies. Go on,
And see whe'r Brutus be alive or dead; 30
And bring us word unto Octavius' tent
How every thing is chanced. *Exeunt.*

[Scene V. *Another part of the field.*]

Enter BRUTUS, DARDANIUS, CLITUS, STRATO, *and* VOLUMNIUS.

Bru. Come, poor remains of friends, rest on this rock.
Cli. Statilius showed the torchlight, but, my lord,
He came not back. He is or ta'en or slain.
Bru. Sit thee down, Clitus. Slaying is the word.
It is a deed in fashion. Hark thee, Clitus. 5
[*Whispers.*]
Cli. What, I, my lord? No, not for all the world!
Bru. Peace then. No words.
Cli. I'll rather kill myself.
Bru. Hark thee, Dardanius. [*Whispers.*]
Dar. Shall I do such a deed?
Cli. O Dardanius!
Dar. O Clitus! 10
Cli. What ill request did Brutus make to thee?
Dar. To kill him, Clitus. Look, he meditates.
Cli. Now is that noble vessel full of grief,
That it runs over even at his eyes. 14
Bru. Come hither, good Volumnius. List a word.
Vol. What says my lord?

5. in fashion: both Cassius and Titinius have already killed themselves.

Bru. Why this, Volumnius.
The ghost of Cæsar hath appeared to me
Two several times by night—at Sardis once,
And this last night here in Philippi fields.
I know my hour is come.
Vol. Not so, my lord. 20
Bru. Nay, I am sure it is, Volumnius.
Thou seest the world, Volumnius, how it goes.
Our enemies have beat us to the pit. *Low alarums.*
It is more worthy to leap in ourselves
Than tarry till they push us. Good Volumnius, 25
Thou knowst that we two went to school together.
Even for that our love of old, I prithee
Hold thou my sword-hilts whilst I run on it.
Vol. That's not an office for a friend, my lord.
Alarum still.
Cli. Fly, fly, my lord! There is no tarrying here.
Bru. Farewell to you; and you; and you, Volumnius. 31
Strato, thou hast been all this while asleep.
Farewell to thee too, Strato. Countrymen,
My heart doth joy that yet in all my life
I found no man but he was true to me. 35
I shall have glory by this losing day
More than Octavius and Mark Antony
By this vile conquest shall attain unto.
So fare you well at once, for Brutus' tongue
Hath almost ended his life's history. 40
Night hangs upon mine eyes; my bones would rest,
That have but labored to attain this hour.
Alarum. Cry within: "Fly, fly, fly!"
Cli. Fly, my lord, fly!
Bru. Hence! I will follow.
[*Exeunt Clitus, Dardanius, and Volumnius.*]
I prithee, Strato, stay thou by thy lord.
Thou art a fellow of a good respect; 45
Thy life hath had some smatch of honor in it.
Hold then my sword, and turn away thy face
While I do run upon it. Wilt thou, Strato?
Stra. Give me your hand first. Fare you well, my lord.

23. **beat . . . pit:** hunted us to our graves
45. **respect:** reputation
46. **smatch:** smack; taste

Bru. Farewell, good Strato. Cæsar, now be still. 50
I killed not thee with half so good a will. *Dies.*

Alarum. Retreat. Enter OCTAVIUS, ANTONY, MESSALA, LUCILIUS, *and the* ARMY.

Oct. What man is that?
Mes. My master's man. Strato, where is thy master?
Stra. Free from the bondage you are in, Messala.
The conquerors can but make a fire of him; 55
For Brutus only overcame himself,
And no man else hath honor by his death.
Lucil. So Brutus should be found. I thank thee, Brutus,
That thou hast proved Lucilius' saying true.
Oct. All that served Brutus, I will entertain them.
Fellow, wilt thou bestow thy time with me? 61
Stra. Ay, if Messala will prefer me to you.
Oct. Do so, good Messala.
Mes. How died my master, Strato?
Stra. I held the sword, and he did run on it. 65
Mes. Octavius, then take him to follow thee,
That did the latest service to my master.
Ant. This was the noblest Roman of them all.
All the conspirators save only he
Did that they did in envy of great Cæsar; 70
He, only in a general honest thought
And common good to all, made one of them.
His life was gentle, and the elements
So mixed in him that Nature might stand up
And say to all the world, "This was a man!" 75
Oct. According to his virtue let us use him,
With all respect and rites of burial.
Within my tent his bones tonight shall lie,
Most like a soldier, ordered honorably.
So call the field to rest, and let's away 80
To part the glories of this happy day.
Exeunt omnes.

60. **entertain:** take on; employ
62. **prefer:** recommend
71–72. **in . . . all:** with honorable concern for the good of the whole commonwealth
73. **gentle:** noble
79. **ordered:** handled
81. **part:** share

The Death of Brutus

From Jean Baudoin, *Recueil d'emblèmes divers* (1638–39).

In the Forest of Arden

From an extra-illustrated copy of Shakespeare's *Works,* edited by Howard Staunton (London and New York, 1881).

AS YOU LIKE IT

INTRODUCTION

As You Like It, one of Shakespeare's most successful comedies, is written with the assurance that comes to a playwright who is conscious of his competence and has complete command of his material. Shakespeare in this play writes of a sunny world of gaiety and charm where lovers meet in a pastoral setting, experience difficulties conventional in pastoral romances, and at last live happily ever after. The play dates from shortly after *Julius Cæsar,* sometime in 1599–1600. Its first stage performance was probably at the Globe.

Shakespeare found his plot in a romance by Thomas Lodge, *Rosalynde, Euphues' Golden Legacy* (1590), written in the artificial prose that John Lyly had popularized in his own novels. Lodge in turn had taken his story from the fourteenth-century metrical romance of *Gamelyn,* which had been erroneously attributed to Chaucer as the "Cook's Tale" in some manuscript versions of the *Canterbury Tales.* Some scholars have thought that Shakespeare went back to the tale of *Gamelyn* for elements in his story, but that seems doubtful. In Lodge the story is set in the Ardennes in France. Though Shakespeare's characters masquerade as French men and women, they move about in the Forest of Arden, which is authentic Warwickshire, with the woods and flowers that Shakespeare knew and loved. Like most Englishmen of his day, Shakespeare was familiar with country scenes, country people, and country ways. The sheepcote that Rosalind set out to buy could have been a stone's throw from Shakespeare's father's farm at Snitterfield. Shakespeare usually displayed the common sense and balance that one frequently finds in men brought up in the country, and in *As You Like It* he exhibits in a marked degree qualities that reveal a man in harmony with nature.

The theme of the play is love in its various aspects, but Shakespeare never lets his treatment of the subject drift into the absurdities that were characteristic of the pastoral romances. He can laugh gaily and happily at the perplexities that love can bring, but he is neither sentimental nor cynical. Even Rosalind in love is able to display a sense of humor about love and lovers, including herself. In this play, Shakespeare is not concerned about profound overtones and cosmic truths. He is writing a play of merriment and good humor, which charmed the spectators at the Globe and has charmed audiences from that day to this.

As You Like It reveals the effects of love as it manifests itself in a variety of individuals: spirited and highborn Rosalind; brave and desperate Orlando; earthy Touchstone, content for a time with Audrey, "an ill-favored thing . . . but mine own"; selfish and thoughtless Phebe; faithful and loyal Silvius; and all the rest who are touched with an emotion universal in its influence upon men and women. Nowhere in the play does the treatment of this theme suggest anything but a healthy attitude. Shakespeare had looked upon love and had been content with what he found.

Some critics have thought that in the person of the melancholy Jaques Shakespeare reflects his own speculative and pensive quality of mind. There is little to commend this view. In few plays did the author give expression to a happier mental attitude. Jaques is a type fashionable on the stage at that moment. Although he is not quite typical of the malcontents whose cynicism was a popular theatrical convention in the last decade of the sixteenth century, he does represent a conventional attitude of affected melancholy that audiences had come to expect in a stock character. The spirit of the play, however, is that of wholesome satisfaction with a world that is essentially good. Even the usurping Duke in the end undergoes a conversion and surrenders his lands to the rightful owner. Shakespeare is too charitable to have him killed in battle, as Lodge had done in his treatment of the romance.

HISTORY AND TEXT

When *As You Like It* was first performed, the Lord Admiral's Men, who were the rivals of Shakespeare's company, were drawing crowds with a play on Robin Hood. Doubtless the Lord Chamberlain's Men felt that they had to have a merry play in a pastoral setting to compete with Robin Hood and his merry men in Sherwood Forest. So Shakespeare, their foremost playwright, supplied a comedy with a background of the Forest of Arden.

Though direct references to the early reception of the play are lacking, we can be certain that it was popular. An entry in the *Stationers' Register* for August 4, 1600, is for *As You Like It* "to be stayed," which, in effect, meant it was not to be printed. The Lord Chamberlain's Men were trying to prevent a popular play from being made available in the bookstalls.

A nineteenth-century historian, William Cory, reported a tradition in the Earl of Pembroke's family of a contemporary letter telling of a performance of *As You Like It* at Wilton House in 1603 for the entertainment of King James, with Shakespeare present. The tradition persists, but the letter cannot be found. Another tradition has assigned to Shakespeare the inconsequential role of Adam in the original cast of the play.

Although *As You Like It* was one of the plays licensed for revival at the Theatre Royal after the Restoration, its fresh country air and wholesome qualities were not the stuff that the jaded courtiers of Charles II preferred, and it had to wait until the eighteenth century for a renewal of its popularity. An adaptation by Charles Johnson was performed at Drury Lane in 1723 under the title of *Love in a Forest*. Johnson ransacked other comedies by Shakespeare for bits to make up his play, so that it is hardly recognizable as a version of *As You Like It*.

In 1740 the comedy as Shakespeare wrote it was revived at Drury Lane. Music for the songs, composed by Thomas Arne, was one of the notable innovations in this performance. From 1740 onward, *As You Like It* never again lost its appeal for theatregoers. Professor Hazelton Spencer has pointed out that the part of Rosalind was one of the favorite roles of eighteenth-century actresses, including Peg Woffington, Garrick's mistress; Perdita Robinson, the Prince Regent's mistress; and even Mrs. Sarah Siddons, the famous tragedy queen, who was something less than successful in the pastoral-comedy role. Spencer calls attention to "at least sixty notable revivals" in the nineteenth century, not including several operatic versions. This play has been particularly popular for amateur production, especially on college campuses. It has probably had more collegiate and "little theatre" productions than any other single Shakespearean play.

The first printed version of the play appeared in the First Folio of 1623, and that text is the basis of this and other modern editions. Although the Folio text is fairly free of misprints, a few emendations and corrections, suggested by earlier editors, have been adopted.

"We are still handling our ewes, and their fells you know are greasy."
(*As You Like It*, III.ii.52–53)

From T. F., *A Book of Divers Devices* (1595–1622). Folger MS V.a.311.

[Dramatis Personæ

DUKE SENIOR, *exiled.*
DUKE FREDERICK, *his brother and usurper of his dukedom.*
AMIENS, } *lords attending on Duke Senior.*
JAQUES, }
LE BEAU, *a courtier attending on Duke Frederick.*
CHARLES, *wrestler to Duke Frederick.*
OLIVER, }
JAQUES DE BOYS, } *sons of Sir Rowland de Boys.*
ORLANDO, }
ADAM, } *servants to Oliver.*
DENNIS, }
TOUCHSTONE, *a clown.*
SIR OLIVER MARTEXT, *a vicar.*
CORIN, } *shepherds.*
SILVIUS, }
WILLIAM, *a countryman, in love with Audrey.*
HYMEN, *god of marriage.*

ROSALIND, *daughter to Duke Senior.*
CELIA, *daughter to Duke Frederick.*
PHEBE, *a shepherdess.*
AUDREY, *a country wench.*

Lords, Pages, Attendants, &c.

Scene:—*Oliver's orchard; Duke Frederick's court; the Forest of Arden.*]

Diana, the Huntress
From Robert Whitcombe, *Janua divorum* (1678).

AS YOU LIKE IT

ACT I

Scene I. [*Oliver's orchard.*]

Enter ORLANDO *and* ADAM.

Orl. As I remember, Adam, it was upon this fashion bequeathed me by will but poor a thousand crowns, and, as thou sayst, charged my brother on his blessing to breed me well; and there begins my sadness. My brother Jaques he keeps at school, and report 5 speaks goldenly of his profit. For my part, he keeps me rustically at home or, to speak more properly, stays me here at home unkept; for call you that keeping for a gentleman of my birth that differs not from the stalling of an ox? His horses are bred 10 better; for, besides that they are fair with their feeding, they are taught their manage, and to that end riders dearly hired; but I, his brother, gain nothing under him but growth, for the which his animals on his dunghills are as much bound to him as I. 15 Besides this nothing that he so plentifully gives me, the something that nature gave me his countenance seems to take from me. He lets me feed with his hinds, bars me the place of a brother, and, as much as in him lies, mines my gentility with my edu- 20 cation. This is it, Adam, that grieves me; and the spirit of my father, which I think is within me, begins to mutiny against this servitude. I will no longer endure it, though yet I know no wise remedy how to avoid it. 25

Enter OLIVER.

Adam. Yonder comes my master, your brother.

Orl. Go apart, Adam, and thou shalt hear how he will shake me up. [*Adam withdraws.*]

Oli. Now, sir, what make you here?

Orl. Nothing. I am not taught to make any- 30 thing.

Oli. What mar you then, sir?

Orl. Marry, sir, I am helping you to mar that which God made, a poor unworthy brother of yours, with idleness. 35

Oli. Marry, sir, be better employed, and be naught awhile!

Orl. Shall I keep your hogs and eat husks with them? What prodigal portion have I spent that I should come to such penury? 40

Oli. Know you where you are, sir?

Orl. O, sir, very well: here in your orchard.

Oli. Know you before whom, sir?

Orl. Ay, better than him I am before knows me. I know you are my eldest brother, and in the 45 gentle condition of blood you should so know me.

2. but . . . crowns: only a paltry thousand crowns
4. breed: train
8. stays: holds
11. fair . . . feeding: well fed
12. manage: paces, from French *manège,* "horsemanship"
17. the . . . me: i.e., gentility; **countenance:** conduct
19. hinds: farmhands
20. mines: undermines

28. shake . . . up: abuse me
33. Marry: verily
36. be naught: a North-Country curse meaning "A mischief on you."
45–46. in . . . me: you should recognize that I am your brother and your equal in breeding.

The courtesy of nations allows you my better in that you are the first born; but the same tradition takes not away my blood, were there twenty brothers betwixt us. I have as much of my father in me 50 as you, albeit I confess your coming before me is nearer to his reverence.

Oli. What, boy! [*Strikes at him.*]

Orl. Come, come, elder brother, you are too young in this. 55

Oli. Wilt thou lay hands on me, villain?

Orl. I am no villain. I am the youngest son of Sir Rowland de Boys; he was my father, and he is thrice a villain that says such a father begot villains. Wert thou not my brother, I would not take this 60 hand from thy throat till this other had pulled out thy tongue for saying so. Thou hast railed on thyself.

Adam. [*Returning*] Sweet masters, be patient! For your father's remembrance, be at accord!

Oli. Let me go, I say. 65

Orl. I will not till I please. You shall hear me. My father charged you in his will to give me a good education. You have trained me like a peasant, obscuring and hiding from me all gentlemanlike qualities. The spirit of my father grows strong in me, and I 70 will no longer endure it. Therefore allow me such exercises as may become a gentleman, or give me the poor allottery my father left me by testament. With that I will go buy my fortunes.

Oli. And what wilt thou do? beg when that is 75 spent? Well, sir, get you in. I will not long be troubled with you. You shall have some part of your will. I pray you leave me.

Orl. I will no further offend you than becomes me for my good. 80

Oli. Get you with him, you old dog!

Adam. Is "old dog" my reward? Most true, I have lost my teeth in your service. God be with my old master! he would not have spoke such a word.

Exeunt Orlando, Adam.

Oli. Is it even so? Begin you to grow upon 85 me? I will physic your rankness and yet give no thousand crowns neither. Holla, Dennis!

Enter DENNIS.

Den. Calls your worship?

Oli. Was not Charles, the Duke's wrestler, here to speak with me? 90

Den. So please you, he is here at the door and importunes access to you.

Oli. Call him in. [*Exit Dennis.*] 'Twill be a good way; and tomorrow the wrestling is.

Enter CHARLES.

Cha. Good morrow to your worship. 95

Oli. Good Monsieur Charles! What's the new news at the new court?

Cha. There's no news at the court, sir, but the old news. That is, the old Duke is banished by his younger brother the new Duke, and three or 100 four loving lords have put themselves into voluntary exile with him, whose lands and revenues enrich the new Duke; therefore he gives them good leave to wander.

Oli. Can you tell if Rosalind, the Duke's 105 daughter, be banished with her father?

Cha. O, no! for the Duke's daughter her cousin so loves her, being ever from their cradles bred together, that she would have followed her exile, or have died to stay behind her. She is at the court, and no 110 less beloved of her uncle than his own daughter, and never two ladies loved as they do.

Oli. Where will the old Duke live?

Cha. They say he is already in the Forest of Arden, and a many merry men with him; and there 115 they live like the old Robin Hood of England. They say many young gentlemen flock to him every day, and fleet the time carelessly as they did in the golden world.

Oli. What, you wrestle tomorrow before the 120 new Duke?

Cha. Marry do I, sir; and I came to acquaint you with a matter. I am given, sir, secretly to understand that your younger brother, Orlando, hath a disposition to come in disguised against me to try a 125 fall. Tomorrow, sir, I wrestle for my credit, and he that escapes me without some broken limb shall acquit him well. Your brother is but young and tender, and for your love I would be loath to foil him, as I must for my own honor if he come 130 in. Therefore, out of my love to you, I came hither to acquaint you withal, that either you might stay him from his intendment, or brook such disgrace well as he shall run into, in that it is a thing of his own search and altogether against my will. 135

Oli. Charles, I thank thee for thy love to me, which thou shalt find I will most kindly requite. I had myself notice of my brother's purpose herein and have by underhand means labored to dissuade him from it; but he is resolute. I'll tell thee, 140

52. nearer . . . reverence: i.e., approaches him more nearly in the right to respect
56. villain: rascal. The term also meant a lowborn fellow.
62. railed on: abused
69. qualities: professions; accomplishments
86. physic: remedy; **rankness:** excessive growth
118. fleet: while away
118–19. golden world: the Golden Age of classical mythology
126. fall: bout
129. foil: disgrace
137. requite: reward
139. by . . . means: indirectly

Charles, it is the stubbornest young fellow of France; full of ambition, an envious emulator of every man's good parts, a secret and villainous contriver against me his natural brother. Therefore use thy discretion. I had as lief thou didst break his neck as his 145 finger. And thou wert best look to't; for if thou dost him any slight disgrace, or if he do not mightily grace himself on thee, he will practice against thee by poison, entrap thee by some treacherous device, and never leave thee till he hath ta'en thy life by 150 some indirect means or other; for I assure thee (and almost with tears I speak it) there is not one so young and so villainous this day living. I speak but brotherly of him; but should I anatomize him to thee as he is, I must blush and weep, and thou 155 must look pale and wonder.

Cha. I am heartily glad I came hither to you. If he come tomorrow, I'll give him his payment. If ever he go alone again, I'll never wrestle for prize more. And so God keep your worship! 160

Oli. Farewell, good Charles. *Exit* [*Charles*]. Now will I stir this gamester. I hope I shall see an end of him, for my soul (yet I know not why) hates nothing more than he. Yet he's gentle; never schooled and yet learned; full of noble device; of all sorts 165 enchantingly beloved, and indeed so much in the heart of the world, and especially of my own people, who best know him, that I am altogether misprized. But it shall not be so long; this wrestler shall clear all. Nothing remains but that I kindle the boy 170 thither, which now I'll go about.

Exit.

Scene II. [*A lawn before the Duke's Palace.*]

Enter ROSALIND *and* CELIA.

Cel. I pray thee, Rosalind, sweet my coz, be merry.

Ros. Dear Celia, I show more mirth than I am mistress of, and would you yet I were merrier? Unless you could teach me to forget a banished father, you must not learn me how to remember any ex- 5 traordinary pleasure.

Cel. Herein I see thou lovest me not with the full weight that I love thee. If my uncle, thy banished father, had banished thy uncle, the Duke my father, so thou hadst been still with me, I could have 10 taught my love to take thy father for mine. So wouldst thou, if the truth of thy love to me were so righteously tempered as mine is to thee.

Ros. Well, I will forget the condition of my estate to rejoice in yours. 15

Cel. You know my father hath no child but I, nor none is like to have, and truly, when he dies, thou shalt be his heir; for what he hath taken away from thy father perforce, I will render thee again in affection. By mine honor, I will! and when I break 20 that oath, let me turn monster. Therefore, my sweet Rose, my dear Rose, be merry.

Ros. From henceforth I will, coz and devise sports. Let me see. What think you of falling in love?

Cel. Marry, I prithee do, to make sport 25 withal! But love no man in good earnest, nor no further in sport neither than with safety of a pure blush thou mayst in honor come off again.

Ros. What shall be our sport then?

Cel. Let us sit and mock the good housewife 30 Fortune from her wheel, that her gifts may henceforth be bestowed equally.

Ros. I would we could do so, for her benefits are mightily misplaced, and the bountiful blind woman doth most mistake in her gifts to women. 35

Cel. 'Tis true; for those that she makes fair she scarce makes honest, and those that she makes honest she makes very ill-favoredly.

Ros. Nay, now thou goest from Fortune's office to Nature's. Fortune reigns in gifts of the world, 40 not in the lineaments of Nature.

Enter [TOUCHSTONE, *the*] CLOWN.

Cel. No? When Nature hath made a fair creature, may she not by Fortune fall into the fire? Though Nature hath given us wit to flout at Fortune, hath not Fortune sent in this fool to cut off the argu- 45 ment?

Ros. Indeed, there is Fortune too hard for Nature when Fortune makes Nature's natural the cutter-off of Nature's wit.

141. stubbornest: most unruly
142. envious: malicious
147. grace: honor
148. practice: plot
151. indirect: dishonest
153–54. but brotherly: i.e., softening his faults as a brother should; **anatomize:** dissect
159. alone: unsupported
164. gentle: well-bred
165. device: impulse
166. enchantingly beloved: adored as though he had enchanted everyone
168. misprized: scorned
5. learn: teach; common usage of the time

13. righteously tempered: compounded of the right ingredients
19. perforce: forcibly; **render:** surrender
30–31. the . . . Fortune: Fortune was conceived as controlling human destiny by means of a wheel, though here a spinning wheel seems to be meant. **Housewife** was used interchangeably with "hussy," and both senses of the word are implied, since Fortune was often called a strumpet because of her fickleness.
34. blind woman: Fortune was often pictured with blindfolded eyes.
37. honest: chaste
45–46. argument: discussion
48. natural: idiot. Some professional jesters were mentally deficient.

Cel. Peradventure this is not Fortune's work 50 neither, but Nature's, who perceiving our natural wits too dull to reason of such goddesses, hath sent this natural for our whetstone, for always the dullness of the fool is the whetstone of the wits. How now, wit? Whither wander you? 55

Touch. Mistress, you must come away to your father.

Cel. Were you made the messenger?

Touch. No, by mine honor, but I was bid to come for you. 60

Ros. Where learned you that oath, fool?

Touch. Of a certain knight that swore by his honor they were good pancakes, and swore by his honor the mustard was naught. Now I'll stand to it, the pancakes were naught, and the mustard was good, 65 and yet was not the knight forsworn.

Cel. How prove you that in the great heap of your knowledge?

Ros. Ay, marry, now unmuzzle your wisdom.

Touch. Stand you both forth now. Stroke 70 your chins, and swear by your beards that I am a knave.

Cel. By our beards (if we had them), thou art.

Touch. By my knavery (if I had it), then I were. But if you swear by that that is not, you are not 75 forsworn. No more was this knight, swearing by his honor, for he never had any; or if he had, he had sworn it away before ever he saw those pancakes or that mustard.

Cel. Prithee, who is't that thou meanst? 80

Touch. One that old Frederick, your father, loves.

Cel. My father's love is enough to honor him. Enough! Speak no more of him. You'll be whipped for taxation one of these days.

Touch. The more pity that fools may not 85 speak wisely what wise men do foolishly.

Cel. By my troth, thou sayest true; for, since the little wit that fools have was silenced, the little foolery that wise men have makes a great show. Here comes Monsieur Le Beau. 90

Enter LE BEAU.

Ros. With his mouth full of news.

Cel. Which he will put on us as pigeons feed their young.

Ros. Then shall we be news-crammed.

Cel. All the better! We shall be the more 95 marketable.—Bon jour, Monsieur Le Beau. What's the news?

Le Beau. Fair princess, you have lost much good sport.

Cel. Sport? of what color? 100

Le Beau. What color, madam? How shall I answer you?

Ros. As wit and fortune will.

Touch. Or as the Destinies decree.

Cel. Well said! That was laid on with a 105 trowel.

Touch. Nay, if I keep not my rank—

Ros. Thou losest thy old smell.

Le Beau. You amaze me, ladies. I would have told you of good wrestling, which you have lost the 110 sight of.

Ros. Yet tell us the manner of the wrestling.

Le Beau. I will tell you the beginning; and if it please your ladyships, you may see the end, for the best is yet to do; and here, where you are, 115 they are coming to perform it.

Cel. Well, the beginning, that is dead and buried.

Le Beau. There comes an old man and his three sons—

Cel. I could match this beginning with an 120 old tale.

Le Beau. Three proper young men, of excellent growth and presence.

Ros. With bills on their necks, "Be it known unto all men by these presents"— 125

Le Beau. The eldest of the three wrestled with Charles, the Duke's wrestler; which Charles in a moment threw him and broke three of his ribs, that there is little hope of life in him. So he served the second, and so the third. Yonder they lie, the 130 poor old man, their father, making such pitiful dole over them that all the beholders take his part with weeping.

Ros. Alas!

Touch. But what is the sport, monsieur, 135 that the ladies have lost?

Le Beau. Why, this that I speak of.

Touch. Thus men may grow wiser every day. It is the first time that ever I heard breaking of ribs was sport for ladies. 140

Cel. Or I, I promise thee.

Ros. But is there any else longs to see this broken music in his sides? Is there yet another dotes upon rib-breaking? Shall we see this wrestling, cousin?

Le Beau. You must, if you stay here; for 145 here is the place appointed for the wrestling, and they are ready to perform it.

Cel. Yonder sure they are coming. Let us now stay and see it.

54–55. How . . . you: a proverbial admonition to one who talked foolishly
64. naught: worthless
82. Cel.: given to Rosalind in the Folios, but editors assign to Celia.
84. taxation: i.e., criticizing his betters
100. color: kind
122. proper: handsome; well-set-up
131. dole: lamentation
142–43. broken music: music played by several different instruments rather than by a matched set of one kind

Flourish. Enter DUKE [FREDERICK], LORDS, ORLANDO, CHARLES, *and* ATTENDANTS.

Duke. Come on. Since the youth will not be entreated, his own peril on his forwardness! 150

Ros. Is yonder the man?

Le Beau. Even he, madam.

Cel. Alas, he is too young! Yet he looks successfully. 155

Duke. How now, daughter, and cousin! Are you crept hither to see the wrestling?

Ros. Ay, my liege, so please you give us leave.

Duke. You will take little delight in it, I can tell you, there is such odds in the man. In pity of 160 the challenger's youth I would fain dissuade him, but he will not be entreated. Speak to him, ladies; see if you can move him.

Cel. Call him hither, good Monsieur Le Beau.

Duke. Do so. I'll not be by. [*Moves away.*] 165

Le Beau. Monsieur the challenger, the princess calls for you.

Orl. I attend them with all respect and duty.

Ros. Young man, have you challenged Charles the wrestler? 170

Orl. No, fair princess. He is the general challenger; I come but in as others do, to try with him the strength of my youth.

Cel. Young gentleman, your spirits are too bold for your years. You have seen cruel proof of this 175 man's strength. If you saw yourself with your eyes, or knew yourself with your judgment, the fear of your adventure would counsel you to a more equal enterprise. We pray you for your own sake to embrace your own safety and give over this attempt. 180

Ros. Do, young sir. Your reputation shall not therefore be misprized. We will make it our suit to the Duke that the wrestling might not go forward.

Orl. I beseech you, punish me not with your hard thoughts, wherein I confess me much guilty to 185 deny so fair and excellent ladies anything. But let your fair eyes and gentle wishes go with me to my trial; wherein if I be foiled, there is but one shamed that was never gracious; if killed, but one dead that is willing to be so. I shall do my friends no 190 wrong, for I have none to lament me; the world no injury, for in it I have nothing. Only in the world I fill up a place, which may be better supplied when I have made it empty.

Ros. The little strength that I have, I would 195 it were with you.

Cel. And mine, to eke out hers.

Ros. Fare you well. Pray heaven I be deceived in you!

Cel. Your heart's desires be with you! 200

Cha. Come, where is this young gallant that is so desirous to lie with his mother earth?

Orl. Ready, sir; but his will hath in it a more modest working.

Duke. You shall try but one fall. 205

Cha. No, I warrant your Grace you shall not entreat him to a second that have so mightily persuaded him from a first.

Orl. You mean to mock me after. You should not have mocked me before. But come your ways! 210

Ros. Now Hercules be thy speed, young man!

Cel. I would I were invisible, to catch the strong fellow by the leg. *Wrestle.*

Ros. O excellent young man!

Cel. If I had a thunderbolt in mine eye, I 215 can tell who should down.

[*Charles is thrown.*] *Shout.*

Duke. No more, no more!

Orl. Yes, I beseech your Grace. I am not yet well breathed.

Duke. How dost thou, Charles? 220

Le Beau. He cannot speak, my lord.

Duke. Bear him away. [*Charles is borne out.*]
What is thy name, young man?

Orl. Orlando, my liege, the youngest son of Sir Rowland de Boys. 225

Duke. I would thou hadst been son to some man else!
The world esteemed thy father honorable,
But I did find him still mine enemy.
Thou shouldst have better pleased me with this deed,
Hadst thou descended from another house. 230
But fare thee well; thou art a gallant youth;
I would thou hadst told me of another father.

Exeunt Duke, [*Train, and Le Beau*].

Cel. Were I my father, coz, would I do this?

Orl. I am more proud to be Sir Rowland's son,
His youngest son, and would not change that calling
To be adopted heir to Frederick. 236

Ros. My father loved Sir Rowland as his soul,
And all the world was of my father's mind.
Had I before known this young man his son,
I should have given him tears unto entreaties 240
Ere he should thus have ventured.

Cel. Gentle cousin,
Let us go thank him and encourage him.

151. his . . . forwardness: his presumption must take the blame for his peril.
154–55. successfully: as though he would be successful
160. there . . . man: the champion is so superior to the challenger.
182. misprized: depreciated
189. gracious: honored
192–93. Only . . . place: i.e., I only fill up a space in the world.

203. will: sexual appetite
210. come . . . ways: come on
211. be . . . speed: aid you
228. still: always
240. unto: in addition to

My father's rough and envious disposition
Sticks me at heart. Sir, you have well deserved.
If you do keep your promises in love 245
But justly as you have exceeded all promise,
Your mistress shall be happy.

Ros. Gentleman,
[*Giving him a chain from her neck*]
Wear this for me, one out of suits with Fortune,
That could give more but that her hand lacks means.
Shall we go, coz?

Cel. Ay, Fare you well, fair gentleman. 250

Orl. Can I not say "I thank you"? My better parts
Are all thrown down, and that which here stands up
Is but a quintain, a mere lifeless block.

Ros. He calls us back. My pride fell with my fortunes;
I'll ask him what he would. Did you call, sir? 255
Sir, you have wrestled well, and overthrown
More than your enemies.

Cel. Will you go, coz?

Ros. Have with you. Fare you well.
Exeunt [*Rosalind and Celia*].

Orl. What passion hangs these weights upon my tongue?
I cannot speak to her, yet she urged conference.

[*Re-*]*enter* LE BEAU.

O poor Orlando, thou art overthrown! 261
Or Charles or something weaker masters thee.

Le Beau. Good sir, I do in friendship counsel you
To leave this place. Albeit you have deserved
High commendation, true applause, and love, 265
Yet such is now the Duke's condition
That he misconsters all that you have done.
The Duke is humorous. What he is, indeed,
More suits you to conceive than I to speak of. 269

Orl. I thank you, sir: and pray you tell me this—
Which of the two was daughter of the Duke,
That here was at the wrestling?

Le Beau. Neither his daughter, if we judge by manners;
But yet indeed the smaller is his daughter;
The other is daughter to the banished Duke, 275
And here detained by her usurping uncle
To keep his daughter company, whose loves
Are dearer than the natural bond of sisters.
But I can tell you that of late this Duke
Hath ta'en displeasure 'gainst his gentle niece,
Grounded upon no other argument 281
But that the people praise her for her virtues
And pity her for her good father's sake;
And, on my life, his malice 'gainst the lady
Will suddenly break forth. Sir, fare you well. 285
Hereafter, in a better world than this,
I shall desire more love and knowledge of you.

Orl. I rest much bounden to you. Fare you well.
[*Exit Le Beau.*]
Thus must I from the smoke into the smother,
From tyrant Duke unto a tyrant brother. 290
But heavenly Rosalind!
Exit.

Scene III. [*A room in the Palace.*]

Enter CELIA *and* ROSALIND.

Cel. Why, cousin! why, Rosalind! Cupid have mercy! not a word?

Ros. Not one to throw at a dog.

Cel. No, thy words are too precious to be cast away upon curs; throw some of them at me. Come, 5 lame me with reasons.

Ros. Then there were two cousins laid up, when the one should be lamed with reasons, and the other mad without any.

Cel. But is all this for your father? 10

Ros. No, some of it is for my child's father. O, how full of briers is this working-day world!

Cel. They are but burrs, cousin, thrown upon thee in holiday foolery. If we walk not in the trodden paths, our very petticoats will catch them. 15

Ros. I could shake them off my coat. These burrs are in my heart.

Cel. Hem them away.

Ros. I would try, if I could cry "hem!" and have him. 20

Cel. Come, come, wrestle with thy affections.

Ros. O, they take the part of a better wrestler than myself!

Cel. O, a good wish upon you! You will try in

243. envious: malicious
246. But justly: i.e., exactly
248. out . . . Fortune: i.e., whose suits to Fortune are not favored
249. could: would willingly
253. quintain: post used as a mark in tilting or military exercises
258. Have . . . you: I'll be with you.
259. passion: emotion
260. urged conference: offered conversation
262. Or: either
266. condition: disposition
267. misconsters: misconstrues
268. humorous: capricious
269. More . . . of: you can imagine more fittingly than I can express it
274. smaller: "taller" in the Folios; Edmond Malone's correction
285. suddenly: soon
288. rest: remain
3. Not . . . dog: proverbial; not a word though her life depended on it
9. mad: melancholy
11. child's father: i.e., future husband. Some editors emend to "father's child" after Nicholas Rowe.
19–20. cry . . . him: have him for the asking

time, in despite of a fall. But, turning these 25
jests out of service, let us talk in good earnest. Is it possible on such a sudden you should fall into so strong a liking with old Sir Rowland's youngest son?

Ros. The Duke my father loved his father dearly.

Cel. Doth it therefore ensue that you should 30
love his son dearly? By this kind of chase, I should hate him, for my father hated his father dearly; yet I hate not Orlando.

Ros. No, faith, hate him not, for my sake!

Cel. Why should I not? Doth he not deserve 35
well?

Enter DUKE [FREDERICK], *with* LORDS.

Ros. Let me love him for that; and do you love him because I do. Look, here comes the Duke.

Cel. With his eyes full of anger.

Duke. Mistress, dispatch you with your safest haste 40
And get you from our court!

Ros. Me, uncle!

Duke. You, cousin.
Within these ten days if that thou beest found
So near our public court as twenty miles,
Thou diest for it.

Ros. I do beseech your Grace
Let me the knowledge of my fault bear with me.
If with myself I hold intelligence 46
Or have acquaintance with mine own desires;
If that I do not dream or be not frantic,
As I do trust I am not—then, dear uncle,
Never so much as in a thought unborn 50
Did I offend your Highness.

Duke. Thus do all traitors.
If their purgation did consist in words,
They are as innocent as Grace itself.
Let it suffice thee that I trust thee not.

Ros. Yet your mistrust cannot make me a traitor.
Tell me whereon the likelihood depends. 56

Duke. Thou art thy father's daughter. There's enough!

Ros. So was I when your Highness took his dukedom;
So was I when your Highness banished him.
Treason is not inherited, my lord; 60
Or if we did derive it from our friends,
What's that to me? My father was no traitor.
Then, good my liege, mistake me not so much
To think my poverty is treacherous.

Cel. Dear sovereign, hear me speak. 65

Duke. Ay, Celia. We stayed her for your sake,
Else had she with her father ranged along.

Cel. I did not then entreat to have her stay;
It was your pleasure and your own remorse.
I was too young that time to value her; 70
But now I know her. If she be a traitor,
Why, so am I! We still have slept together,
Rose at an instant, learned, played, eat together;
And wheresoe'er we went, like Juno's swans,
Still we went coupled and inseparable. 75

Duke. She is too subtle for thee; and her smoothness,
Her very silence and her patience,
Speak to the people, and they pity her.
Thou art a fool. She robs thee of thy name,
And thou wilt show more bright and seem more virtuous 80
When she is gone. Then open not thy lips.
Firm and irrevocable is my doom
Which I have passed upon her. She is banished.

Cel. Pronounce that sentence then on me, my liege!
I cannot live out of her company. 85

Duke. You are a fool. You, niece, provide yourself.
If you outstay the time, upon mine honor,
And in the greatness of my word, you die.

Exeunt Duke &c.

Cel. O my poor Rosalind! whither wilt thou go?
Wilt thou change fathers? I will give thee mine.
I charge thee be not thou more grieved than I am.

Ros. I have more cause.

Cel. Thou hast not, cousin. 92
Prithee be cheerful. Knowst thou not the Duke
Hath banished me, his daughter?

Ros. That he hath not!

Cel. No? hath not? Rosalind lacks then the love
Which teacheth me that thou and I am one. 96
Shall we be sund'red? shall we part, sweet girl?
No! let my father seek another heir.
Therefore devise with me how we may fly,
Whither to go, and what to bear with us. 100
And do not seek to take your charge upon you,
To bear your griefs yourself and leave me out;
For, by this heaven, now at our sorrows pale,
Say what thou canst, I'll go along with thee!

Ros. Why, whither shall we go? 105

Cel. To seek my uncle in the Forest of Arden.

Ros. Alas, what danger will it be to us,
Maids as we are, to travel forth so far!
Beauty provoketh thieves sooner than gold.

Cel. I'll put myself in poor and mean attire 110

30. ensue: follow
31. By . . . chase: pursuing this train of logic
32. dearly: bitterly
35–36. deserve well: presumably, deserve to be hated as the son of my father's enemy
41. cousin: a vague term of near kinship
46. hold intelligence: have discourse
52. purgation: clearance
53. Grace: the Deity
69. remorse: compassion
72. still: always
74. Juno's swans: Shakespeare was probably thinking of Venus' swans; peacocks were the only fowls associated with Juno.
88. in . . . word: as surely as my word is powerful

And with a kind of umber smirch my face;
The like do you. So shall we pass along
And never stir assailants.
Ros. Were it not better,
Because that I am more than common tall,
That I did suit me all points like a man? 115
A gallant curtal ax on my thigh,
A boar-spear in my hand, and—in my heart
Lie there what hidden woman's fear there will—
We'll have a swashing and a martial outside,
As many other mannish cowards have 120
That do outface it with their semblances.

111. umber: brown earth
115. suit me: attire myself
116. curtal ax: cutlass
119. swashing: swaggering
121. outface . . . semblances: cover their cowardice with the appearance of bravery

Cel. What shall I call thee when thou art a man?
Ros. I'll have no worse a name than Jove's own page,
And therefore look you call me Ganymede.
But what will you be called? 125
Cel. Something that hath a reference to my state—
No longer Celia, but Aliena.
Ros. But, cousin, what if we assayed to steal
The clownish fool out of your father's court?
Would he not be a comfort to our travel? 130
Cel. He'll go along o'er the wide world with me.
Leave me alone to woo him. Let's away
And get our jewels and our wealth together,
Devise the fittest time and safest way
To hide us from pursuit that will be made 135
After my flight. Now go we in content
To liberty, and not to banishment.
Exeunt.

ACT II

Scene I. [*The Forest of Arden.*]

Enter Duke Senior, Amiens, *and* Two or Three Lords, *like Foresters.*

Duke S. Now, my co-mates and brothers in exile,
Hath not old custom made this life more sweet
Than that of painted pomp? Are not these woods
More free from peril than the envious court?
Here feel we but the penalty of Adam, 5
The seasons' difference; as, the icy fang
And churlish chiding of the winter's wind,
Which, when it bites and blows upon my body
Even till I shrink with cold, I smile, and say
"This is no flattery; these are counselors 10
That feelingly persuade me what I am."
Sweet are the uses of adversity,
Which, like the toad, ugly and venomous,
Wears yet a precious jewel in his head;
And this our life, exempt from public haunt, 15
Finds tongues in trees, books in the running brooks,

11. feelingly: (1) by means of my senses; (2) eagerly
14. yet: nevertheless; **precious jewel:** i.e., toadstone, used to counteract poison or as a charm. Such stones found in nature were believed to come from the heads of toads.
15. exempt . . . haunt: not frequented by the multitude

Sermons in stones, and good in everything:
I would not change it.
Ami. Happy is your Grace
That can translate the stubbornness of fortune
Into so quiet and so sweet a style. 20
Duke S. Come, shall we go and kill us venison?
And yet it irks me the poor dappled fools,
Being native burghers of this desert city,
Should, in their own confines, with forked heads
Have their round haunches gored.
1. Lord. Indeed, my lord,
The melancholy Jaques grieves at that, 26
And in that kind swears you do more usurp
Than doth your brother that hath banished you.
Today my Lord of Amiens and myself
Did steal behind him as he lay along 30
Under an oak, whose antique root peeps out
Upon the brook that brawls along this wood;
To the which place a poor sequestered stag,
That from the hunter's aim had ta'en a hurt,
Did come to languish; and indeed, my lord, 35

19. stubbornness: violent opposition
22. fools: simple creatures. The word was often used as an epithet expressing pity or affection.
24. forked heads: arrows, with a quibble on the deer's antlered heads
26. melancholy: contemplative; moody
27. kind: fashion
33. sequestered: separated (from the herd)

The wretched animal heaved forth such groans
That their discharge did stretch his leathern coat
Almost to bursting, and the big round tears
Coursed one another down his innocent nose
In piteous chase; and thus the hairy fool, 40
Much marked of the melancholy Jaques,
Stood on the extremest verge of the swift brook,
Augmenting it with tears.

Duke S. But what said Jaques?
Did he not moralize this spectacle?

1. Lord. O, yes, into a thousand similes. 45
First, for his weeping into the needless stream:
"Poor deer," quoth he, "thou mak'st a testament
As worldings do, giving thy sum of more
To that which had too much." Then, being alone,
Left and abandoned of his velvet friends: 50
" 'Tis right!" quoth he, "thus misery doth part
The flux of company." Anon a careless herd,
Full of the pasture, jumps along by him
And never stays to greet him: "Ay," quoth Jaques,
"Sweep on, you fat and greasy citizens! 55
'Tis just the fashion! Wherefore do you look
Upon that poor and broken bankrupt there?"
Thus most invectively he pierceth through
The body of the country, city, court;
Yea, and of this our life, swearing that we 60
Are mere usurpers, tyrants, and what's worse,
To fright the animals and to kill them up
In their assigned and native dwelling place.

Duke S. And did you leave him in this contemplation?

2. Lord. We did, my lord, weeping and commenting 65
Upon the sobbing deer.

Duke S. Show me the place.
I love to cope him in these sullen fits,
For then he's full of matter.

1. Lord. I'll bring you to him straight.

Exeunt.

Scene II. [*A room in the Palace.*]

Enter DUKE [FREDERICK], *with* LORDS.

Duke. Can it be possible that no man saw them?
It cannot be. Some villains of my court
Are of consent and sufferance in this.

1. Lord. I cannot hear of any that did see her.
The ladies her attendants of her chamber 5
Saw her abed, and in the morning early
They found the bed untreasured of their mistress.

2. Lord. My lord, the roynish clown at whom so oft
Your Grace was wont to laugh is also missing.
Hisperia, the princess' gentlewoman, 10
Confesses that she secretly o'erheard
Your daughter and her cousin much commend
The parts and graces of the wrestler
That did but lately foil the sinewy Charles,
And she believes, wherever they are gone, 15
That youth is surely in their company.

Duke. Send to his brother, fetch that gallant hither.
If he be absent, bring his brother to me;
I'll make him find him. Do this suddenly,
And let not search and inquisition quail 20
To bring again these foolish runaways.

Exeunt.

Scene III. [*Before Oliver's house.*]

Enter ORLANDO *and* ADAM, [*from opposite directions*].

Orl. Who's there?

Adam. What, my young master! O my gentle master!
O my sweet master! O you memory
Of old Sir Rowland! Why, what make you here?
Why are you virtuous? Why do people love you?
And wherefore are you gentle, strong, and valiant?
Why would you be so fond to overcome 7
The bonny prizer of the humorous Duke?
Your praise is come too swiftly home before you.
Know you not, master, to some kind of men 10
Their graces serve them but as enemies?
No more do yours. Your virtues, gentle master,
Are sanctified and holy traitors to you.
O, what a world is this, when what is comely
Envenoms him that bears it! 15

41. **of:** by
46. **needless:** i.e., which needed no additional water
47. **testament:** will; bequest
49. **being alone:** i.e., on the subject of the deer's lonely state
51–52. **doth . . . company:** singles one out from the common flood
56. **Wherefore:** why
61. **mere:** absolute; **tyrants:** synonymous with **usurpers; what's worse:** whatever worse thing one can be
62. **up:** i.e., off
67. **cope:** encounter; **sullen:** moody

3. **Are . . . this:** have helped to bring this about
8. **roynish:** literally, "mangy"; contemptible
13. **parts . . . graces:** physical characteristics and accomplishments
20. **inquisition:** questioning; **quail:** falter
3. **memory:** memento
4. **what . . . here:** what are you doing here; this is no place for you.
7. **fond:** foolish; **to:** as to
8. **bonny:** stalwart; **prizer:** champion
12. **No more:** no better
14. **comely:** becoming. There may be an allusion to the poisoned shirt of Nessus that destroyed Hercules; see Ovid *Metamorphoses,* bk. ix.

Orl. Why, what's the matter?
Adam. O unhappy youth,
Come not within these doors! Within this roof
The enemy of all your graces lives.
Your brother (no, no brother! yet the son—
Yet not the son—I will not call him son 20
Of him I was about to call his father)
Hath heard your praises, and this night he means
To burn the lodging where you use to lie
And you within it. If he fail of that,
He will have other means to cut you off. 25
I overheard him and his practices.
This is no place, this house is but a butchery.
Abhor it, fear it, do not enter it!
Orl. Why whither, Adam, wouldst thou have me go? 29
Adam. No matter whither, so you come not here.
Orl. What, wouldst thou have me go and beg my food,
Or with a base and boisterous sword enforce
A thievish living on the common road?
This I must do, or know not what to do.
Yet this I will not do, do how I can. 35
I rather will subject me to the malice
Of a diverted blood and bloody brother.
Adam. But do not so. I have five hundred crowns,
The thrifty hire I saved under your father,
Which I did store to be my foster nurse 40
When service should in my old limbs lie lame
And unregarded age in corners thrown.
Take that, and He that doth the ravens feed,
Yea, providently caters for the sparrow,
Be comfort to my age! Here is the gold; 45
All this I give you. Let me be your servant.
Though I look old, yet I am strong and lusty;
For in my youth I never did apply
Hot and rebellious liquors in my blood,
Nor did not with unbashful forehead woo 50
The means of weakness and debility;
Therefore my age is as a lusty winter,
Frosty, but kindly. Let me go with you;
I'll do the service of a younger man
In all your business and necessities. 55
Orl. O good old man, how well in thee appears
The constant service of the antique world,
When service sweat for duty, not for meed!
Thou art not for the fashion of these times,
Where none will sweat but for promotion, 60
And having that, do choke their service up
Even with the having. It is not so with thee.
But, poor old man, thou prunest a rotten tree
That cannot so much as a blossom yield
In lieu of all thy pains and husbandry. 65
But come thy ways! We'll go along together,
And ere we have thy youthful wages spent,
We'll light upon some settled low content.
Adam. Master, go on, and I will follow thee
To the last gasp with truth and loyalty! 70
From seventeen years till now almost fourscore
Here lived I, but now live here no more.
At seventeen years many their fortunes seek,
But at fourscore it is too late a week;
Yet fortune cannot recompense me better 75
Than to die well and not my master's debtor.
Exeunt.

Scene IV. [*Another part of the Forest of Arden.*]

Enter ROSALIND *for* GANYMEDE, CELIA *for* ALIENA, and CLOWN, *alias* TOUCHSTONE.

Ros. O Jupiter, how weary are my spirits!
Touch. I care not for my spirits if my legs were not weary.
Ros. I could find in my heart to disgrace my man's apparel and to cry like a woman; but I 5 must comfort the weaker vessel, as doublet and hose ought to show itself courageous to petticoat. Therefore, courage, good Aliena!
Cel. I pray you bear with me; I cannot go no further. 10
Touch. For my part, I had rather bear with you than bear you. Yet I should bear no cross if I did bear you, for I think you have no money in your purse.
Ros. Well, this is the Forest of Arden. 15
Touch. Ay, now am I in Arden, the more fool I! When I was at home, I was in a better place; but travelers must be content.

Enter CORIN *and* SILVIUS.

Ros. Ay, be so, good Touchstone.—Look you, who comes here,
A young man and an old in solemn talk. 20
Cor. That is the way to make her scorn you still.
Sil. O Corin, that thou knewst how I do love her!

26. practices: plots
27. butchery: slaughterhouse
28. Abhor: recoil in horror (physically rather than mentally)
32. boisterous: violent
37. diverted: alienated; **blood:** kinsman
42. unregarded . . . thrown: i.e., I shall be cast aside as an unappreciated old man.
45. Be . . . to: support; sustain
49. rebellious liquors: liquors that attack the constitution
58. meed: reward
61–62. choke . . . having: i.e., perform no more than they are paid for
63. prunest: i.e., attempt to cure
65. pains . . . husbandry: careful management
68. settled . . . content: humble place of abode where we will be content
12. cross: (1) burden; (2) coin stamped with a cross

Cor. I partly guess; for I have loved ere now.
Sil. No, Corin, being old, thou canst not guess,
Though in thy youth thou wast as true a lover 25
As ever sighed upon a midnight pillow.
But if thy love were ever like to mine
(As sure I think did never man love so),
How many actions most ridiculous
Hast thou been drawn to by thy fantasy! 30
Cor. Into a thousand that I have forgotten.
Sil. O, thou didst then never love so heartily!
If thou remem'brest not the slightest folly
That ever love did make thee run into,
Thou hast not loved. 35
Or if thou hast not sat as I do now,
Wearing thy hearer in thy mistress' praise,
Thou hast not loved.
Or if thou hast not broke from company
Abruptly, as my passion now makes me, 40
Thou hast not loved. O Phebe, Phebe, Phebe! *Exit.*
Ros. Alas, poor shepherd! Searching of thy wound,
I have by hard adventure found mine own.
Touch. And I mine. I remember, when I was in love I broke my sword upon a stone and bid 45 him take that for coming a-night to Jane Smile; and I remember the kissing of her batlet, and the cow's dugs that her pretty chopt hands had milked; and I remember the wooing of a peasecod instead of her, from whom I took two cods, and giving her 50 them again, said with weeping tears, "Wear these for my sake." We that are true lovers run into strange capers; but as all is mortal in nature, so is all nature in love mortal in folly.
Ros. Thou speakst wiser than thou art ware 55 of.
Touch. Nay, I shall ne'er be ware of mine own wit till I break my shins against it.
Ros. Jove, Jove! this shepherd's passion
Is much upon my fashion. 60
Touch. And mine, but it grows something stale with me.
Cel. I pray you, one of you question yond man
If he for gold will give us any food.
I faint almost to death.
Touch. Holla, you clown! 65
Ros. Peace, fool! he's not thy kinsman.
Cor. Who calls?
Touch. Your betters, sir.
Cor. Else are they very wretched.
Ros. Peace, I say!—Good even to you, friend.
Cor. And to you, gentle sir, and to you all.
Ros. I prithee, shepherd, if that love or gold 70
Can in this desert place buy entertainment,
Bring us where we may rest ourselves and feed.
Here's a young maid with travel much oppressed,
And faints for succor.
Cor. Fair sir, I pity her 74
And wish, for her sake more than for mine own,
My fortunes were more able to relieve her;
But I am shepherd to another man
And do not shear the fleeces that I graze.
My master is of churlish disposition
And little recks to find the way to heaven 80
By doing deeds of hospitality.
Besides, his cote, his flocks, and bounds of feed
Are now on sale, and at our sheepcote now,
By reason of his absence, there is nothing
That you will feed on; but what is, come see, 85
And in my voice most welcome shall you be.
Ros. What is he that shall buy his flock and pasture?
Cor. That young swain that you saw here but erewhile,
That little cares for buying anything.
Ros. I pray thee, if it stand with honesty, 90
Buy thou the cottage, pasture, and the flock,
And thou shalt have to pay for it of us.
Cel. And we will mend thy wages. I like this place
And willingly could waste my time in it.
Cor. Assuredly the thing is to be sold. 95
Go with me. If you like, upon report,
The soil, the profit, and this kind of life,
I will your very faithful feeder be
And buy it with your gold right suddenly.
Exeunt.

Scene V. [*Another part of the Forest.*]

Enter AMIENS, JAQUES, *and others.*

Song.

Ami. Under the greenwood tree
Who loves to lie with me,
And turn his merry note
Unto the sweet bird's throat,

30. fantasy: fancy, in the sense "amorous inclination"
43. hard adventure: ill luck
47. batlet: paddle used by laundresses
48. chopt: chapped
49. peasecod: peapod
53–54. as . . . folly: as all humans are mortal, so the folly of lovers is human.
57. wit: wisdom
65. clown: hayseed
70. if that: if
79. churlish: miserly
80. recks . . . find: counts on finding
82. cote: cottage; **bounds . . . feed:** pastures
86. in . . . voice: so far as I am concerned
88. swain: shepherd; rustic
90. stand . . . honesty: is consistent with honor
92. to . . . it: i.e., the price; **of:** from
93. mend: improve
94. waste: while away
98. feeder: dependent; servant
3–4. turn . . . throat: imitate a bird's warbling

Come hither, come hither, come hither! 5
Here shall he see
No enemy
But winter and rough weather.

Jaq. More, more, I prithee more!

Ami. It will make you melancholy, Monsieur Jaques. 10

Jaq. I thank it. More, I prithee more! I can suck melancholy out of a song as a weasel sucks eggs. More, I prithee more!

Ami. My voice is ragged. I know I cannot please you. 15

Jaq. I do not desire you to please me; I do desire you to sing. Come, more! another stanzo! Call you 'em stanzos?

Ami. What you will, Monsieur Jaques. 20

Jaq. Nay, I care not for their names; they owe me nothing. Will you sing?

Ami. More at your request than to please myself.

Jaq. Well then, if ever I thank any man, I'll thank you. But that they call compliment is like the 25 encounter of two dog-apes; and when a man thanks me heartily, methinks I have given him a penny, and he renders me the beggarly thanks. Come, sing! and you that will not, hold your tongues.

Ami. Well, I'll end the song. Sirs, cover the 30 while; the Duke will drink under this tree. He hath been all this day to look you.

Jaq. And I have been all this day to avoid him. He is too disputable for my company. I think of as many matters as he; but I give heaven thanks 35 and make no boast of them. Come, warble, come.

Song.

All together here.

Who doth ambition shun
And loves to live i' the sun,
Seeking the food he eats,
And pleased with what he gets, 40
Come hither, come hither, come hither!
Here shall he see
No enemy
But winter and rough weather.

Jaq. I'll give you a verse to this note that I 45 made yesterday in despite of my invention.

Ami. And I'll sing it.

Jaq. Thus it goes:

If it do come to pass
That any man turn ass, 50
Leaving his wealth and ease
A stubborn will to please,
Ducdame, ducdame, ducdame!
Here shall he see
Gross fools as he, 55
An if he will come to me.

Ami. What's that "ducdame"?

Jaq. 'Tis a Greek invocation to call fools into a circle. I'll go sleep, if I can; if I cannot, I'll rail against all the first-born of Egypt. 60

Ami. And I'll go seek the Duke. His banquet is prepared.

Exeunt [*severally*].

Scene VI. [*The Forest.*]

Enter ORLANDO *and* ADAM.

Adam. Dear master, I can go no further. O, I die for food! Here lie I down and measure out my grave. Farewell, kind master.

Orl. Why, how now, Adam? no greater heart in thee? Live a little, comfort a little, cheer thy- 5 self a little. If this uncouth forest yield anything savage, I will either be food for it or bring it for food to thee. Thy conceit is nearer death than thy powers. For my sake be comfortable; hold death awhile at the arm's end. I will here be with thee pres- 10 ently; and if I bring thee not something to eat, I will give thee leave to die; but if thou diest before I come, thou art a mocker of my labor. Well said! thou lookst cheerly, and I'll be with thee quickly. Yet thou liest in the bleak air. Come, I will 15 bear thee to some shelter, and thou shalt not die for lack of a dinner if there live anything in this desert. Cheerly, good Adam!

Exeunt.

5. Come hither: a simulation of some bird's call
18. stanzo: stanza; verse
21–22. I . . . nothing: an allusion to signing a moneylender's book to record a debt
25. compliment: courteous formality
26. dog-apes: dog-faced baboons
28. beggarly thanks: i.e., obsequious gratitude of a beggar
30. cover: lay the table
30–31. the while: in the meantime
32. look: seek
45. note: tune
46. in . . . invention: in spite of my poverty of imagination
52. stubborn: perverse
53. Ducdame: meaning uncertain, perhaps merely nonsense. A jest at Duke Senior's expense is certainly involved.
60. the . . . Egypt: i.e., nobles who occasion the exile of lesser men; a specific reference to Duke Senior

Scene VII. [*The Forest.*]

Enter Duke Senior, [Amiens,] *and* Lords, *like Outlaws.*

Duke S. I think he be transformed into a beast,
For I can nowhere find him like a man.
1. Lord. My lord, he is but even now gone hence.
Here was he merry, hearing of a song.
Duke S. If he, compact of jars, grow musical, 5
We shall have shortly discord in the spheres.
Go seek him; tell him I would speak with him.

Enter Jaques.

1. Lord. He saves my labor by his own approach.
Duke S. Why, how now, monsieur! what a life is this,
That your poor friends must woo your company!
What, you look merrily. 11
Jaq. A fool, a fool! I met a fool i' the forest,
A motley fool!—a miserable world!—
As I do live by food, I met a fool,
Who laid him down and basked him in the sun 15
And railed on Lady Fortune in good terms,
In good set terms—and yet a motley fool.
"Good morrow, fool," quoth I. "No, sir," quoth he,
"Call me not fool till heaven hath sent me fortune."
And then he drew a dial from his poke, 20
And looking on it with lackluster eye,
Says very wisely, "It is ten o'clock.
Thus we may see," quoth he, "how the world wags.
'Tis but an hour ago since it was nine,
And after one hour more 'twill be eleven; 25
And so, from hour to hour, we ripe and ripe,
And then, from hour to hour, we rot and rot;
And thereby hangs a tale." When I did hear
The motley fool thus moral on the time,
My lungs began to crow like chanticleer 30
That fools should be so deep contemplative;
And I did laugh sans intermission
An hour by his dial. O noble fool!
A worthy fool! Motley's the only wear!
Duke S. What fool is this? 35
Jaq. O worthy fool! One that hath been a courtier,
And says, if ladies be but young and fair,
They have the gift to know it. And in his brain,
Which is as dry as the remainder biscuit
After a voyage, he hath strange places crammed
With observation, the which he vents 41
In mangled forms. O that I were a fool!
I am ambitious for a motley coat.
Duke S. Thou shalt have one.
Jaq. It is my only suit,
Provided that you weed your better judgments 45
Of all opinion that grows rank in them
That I am wise. I must have liberty
Withal, as large a charter as the wind,
To blow on whom I please; for so fools have.
And they that are most galled with my folly, 50
They most must laugh. And why, sir, must they so?
The why is plain as way to parish church:
He that a fool doth very wisely hit
Doth very foolishly, although he smart,
Not to seem senseless of the bob. If not, 55
The wise man's folly is anatomized
Even by the squandering glances of the fool.
Invest me in my motley. Give me leave
To speak my mind, and I will through and through
Cleanse the foul body of the infected world, 60
If they will patiently receive my medicine.
Duke S. Fie on thee! I can tell what thou wouldst do.
Jaq. What, for a counter, would I do but good?
Duke S. Most mischievous foul sin, in chiding sin.
For thou thyself hast been a libertine, 65
As sensual as the brutish sting itself;
And all the embossed sores and headed evils
That thou with license of free foot hast caught,
Wouldst thou disgorge into the general world.
Jaq. Why, who cries out on pride 70
That can therein tax any private party?
Doth it not flow as hugely as the sea
Till that the wearer's very means do ebb?
What woman in the city do I name
When that I say the city woman bears 75
The cost of princes on unworthy shoulders?
Who can come in and say that I mean her,
When such a one as she, such is her neighbor?
Or what is he of basest function
That says his bravery is not on my cost, 80
Thinking that I mean him, but therein suits
His folly to the mettle of my speech?
There then! how then? what then? Let me see wherein

5. **compact . . . jars:** entirely composed of discords
13. **motley:** wearing multicolored garb characteristic of a professional fool
17. **good set:** well-phrased
20. **dial:** watch, or portable sundial: **poke:** pouch
41. **vents:** utters
45–47. **weed . . . wise:** discard your opinion of my wisdom
48. **charter:** license
50. **galled:** chafed
55. **bob:** sharp taunt
56. **anatomized:** dissected; laid bare
57. **squandering glances:** chance hits
58. **Invest:** clothe
63. **counter:** token used by merchants in keeping accounts
66. **brutish sting:** carnal impulse
67. **embossed:** swollen; **headed:** grown to a head, ready to burst
70. **pride:** rich attire
71. **tax:** blame; criticize
79. **function:** occupation
80. **bravery:** fine clothing
81–82. **suits . . . speech:** assumes the very folly that my speech has described

My tongue hath wronged him. If it do him right,
Then he hath wronged himself. If he be free, 85
Why, then my taxing like a wild goose flies,
Unclaimed of any man. But who comes here?

Enter ORLANDO.

Orl. Forbear, and eat no more!
Jaq. Why, I have eat none yet.
Orl. Nor shalt not, till necessity be served.
Jaq. Of what kind should this cock come of? 90
Duke S. Art thou thus boldened, man, by thy distress,
Or else a rude despiser of good manners,
That in civility thou seemst so empty?
Orl. You touched my vein at first. The thorny point
Of bare distress hath ta'en from me the show 95
Of smooth civility; yet am I inland bred
And know some nurture. But forbear, I say!
He dies that touches any of this fruit
Till I and my affairs are answered.
Jaq. And you will not be answered with 100
reason, I must die.
Duke S. What would you have? Your gentleness shall force
More than your force move us to gentleness.
Orl. I almost die for food, and let me have it!
Duke. S. Sit down and feed, and welcome to our table. 105
Orl. Speak you so gently? Pardon me, I pray you.
I thought that all things had been savage here,
And therefore put I on the countenance
Of stern commandment. But whate'er you are
That in this desert inaccessible, 110
Under the shade of melancholy boughs,
Lose and neglect the creeping hours of time—
If ever you have looked on better days,
If ever been where bells have knolled to church,
If ever sat at any good man's feast, 115
If ever from your eyelids wiped a tear
And know what 'tis to pity and be pitied,
Let gentleness my strong enforcement be; 118
In the which hope I blush, and hide my sword.
Duke S. True is it that we have seen better days,
And have with holy bell been knolled to church,
And sat at good men's feasts, and wiped our eyes
Of drops that sacred pity hath engendered;
And therefore sit you down in gentleness,
And take upon command what help we have 125
That to your wanting may be ministered.
Orl. Then but forbear your food a little while,
Whiles, like a doe, I go to find my fawn
And give it food. There is an old poor man
Who after me hath many a weary step 130
Limped in pure love. Till he be first sufficed,
Oppressed with two weak evils, age and hunger,
I will not touch a bit.
Duke S. Go find him out,
And we will nothing waste till you return. 134
Orl. I thank ye, and be blest for your good comfort! [*Exit.*]
Duke S. Thou seest we are not all alone unhappy.
This wide and universal theatre
Presents more woeful pageants than the scene
Wherein we play in.
Jaq. All the world's a stage,
And all the men and women merely players. 140
They have their exits and their entrances,
And one man in his time plays many parts,
His acts being seven ages. At first, the infant,
Mewling and puking in the nurse's arms.
Then the whining schoolboy, with his satchel 145
And shining morning face, creeping like snail
Unwillingly to school. And then the lover,
Sighing like furnace, with a woeful ballad
Made to his mistress' eyebrow. Then a soldier,
Full of strange oaths and bearded like the pard,
Jealous in honor, sudden and quick in quarrel, 151
Seeking the bubble reputation
Even in the cannon's mouth. And then the justice,
In fair round belly with good capon lined,
With eyes severe and beard of formal cut, 155
Full of wise saws and modern instances;
And so he plays his part. The sixth age shifts
Into the lean and slippered pantaloon,
With spectacles on nose and pouch on side;
His youthful hose, well saved, a world too wide
For his shrunk shank, and his big manly voice, 161
Turning again toward childish treble, pipes
And whistles in his sound. Last scene of all,
That ends this strange eventful history,
Is second childishness and mere oblivion, 165
Sans teeth, sans eyes, sans taste, sans everything.

Enter ORLANDO, *with* ADAM.

84. do . . . right: portray him truly
85. free: innocent
94. touched . . . vein: hit my condition
96. inland bred: bred in civilized country, instead of the backwoods
97. nurture: cultivation
100. And: if
101. reason: pronounced "raisin"
108. countenance: conduct
126. wanting: need
132. weak: weakening
134. waste: consume
144. Mewling: crying feebly
150. pard: panther
151. Jealous . . . honor: touchy about his honor
156. saws: maxims; **modern instances:** commonplaces; platitudes
158. pantaloon: Italian *pantalone,* a dotard, like the character in the *commedia dell' arte*
160. youthful hose: breeches worn in his youth
163. his: its

Duke S. Welcome. Set down your venerable burden
And let him feed.
Orl. I thank you most for him.
Adam. So had you need.
I scarce can speak to thank you for myself. 170
Duke S. Welcome, fall to. I will not trouble you
As yet to question you about your fortunes.
Give us some music; and, good cousin, sing.

Song.

Ami. Blow, blow, thou winter wind,
Thou art not so unkind 175
As man's ingratitude.
Thy tooth is not so keen,
Because thou art not seen,
Although thy breath be rude. 179
Heigh-ho, sing heigh-ho, unto the green holly!
Most friendship is feigning, most loving mere folly:
Then, heigh-ho, the holly!
This life is most jolly.

181. feigning: pretense

Freeze, freeze, thou bitter sky,
That dost not bite so nigh 185
As benefits forgot.
Though thou the waters warp,
Thy sting is not so sharp
As friend remembered not.
Heigh-ho! sing, &c. 190

Duke S. If that you were the good Sir Rowland's son—
As you have whispered faithfully you were,
And as mine eye doth his effigies witness
Most truly limned and living in your face—
Be truly welcome hither. I am the Duke 195
That loved your father. The residue of your fortune,
Go to my cave and tell me. Good old man,
Thou art right welcome, as thy master is.
Support him by the arm. Give me your hand,
And let me all your fortunes understand. 200
Exeunt.

193. effigies: likenesses
194. limned: pictured
196. residue: rest; **fortune:** story

ACT III

Scene I. [*A room in the Palace.*]

Enter Duke [Frederick], Lords, *and* Oliver.

Duke. Not see him since? Sir, sir, that cannot be!
But were I not the better part made mercy,
I should not seek an absent argument
Of my revenge, thou present. But look to it!
Find out thy brother, wheresoe'er he is; 5
Seek him with candle; bring him dead or living
Within this twelvemonth, or turn thou no more
To seek a living in our territory.
Thy lands, and all things that thou dost call thine
Worth seizure, do we seize into our hands 10
Till thou canst quit thee by thy brother's mouth
Of what we think against thee.
Oli. O that your Highness knew my heart in this!
I never loved my brother in my life.
Duke. More villain thou! Well, push him out of doors, 15
And let my officers of such a nature
Make an extent upon his house and lands.
Do this expediently and turn him going.
Exeunt.

2. the . . . mercy: composed mostly of mercy
3. argument: subject (Orlando)
6. Seek . . . candle: i.e., in every dark corner
11. quit: acquit

Scene II. [*The Forest.*]

Enter Orlando, [*hanging a paper on a tree*].

Orl. Hang there, my verse, in witness of my love;
And thou, thrice-crowned Queen of Night, survey

16. officers . . . nature: appropriate officials
17. Make . . . upon: seize by a writ of extent
18. expediently: speedily
2. thrice . . . Night: the triple moon-goddess, Diana

With thy chaste eye, from thy pale sphere above,
  Thy huntress' name that my full life doth sway.
O Rosalind! these trees shall be my books, 5
  And in their barks my thoughts I'll character,
That every eye which in this forest looks
  Shall see thy virtue witnessed everywhere.
Run, run, Orlando! carve on every tree 9
The fair, the chaste, and unexpressive she. *Exit.*

Enter CORIN *and* [TOUCHSTONE *the*] CLOWN.

Cor. And how like you this shepherd's life, Master Touchstone?

Touch. Truly, shepherd, in respect of itself, it is a good life; but in respect that it is a shepherd's life, it is naught. In respect that it is solitary, I like 15 it very well; but in respect that it is private, it is a very vile life. Now in respect it is in the fields, it pleaseth me well; but in respect it is not in the court, it is tedious. As it is a spare life, look you, it fits my humor well; but as there is no more plenty in 20 it, it goes much against my stomach. Hast any philosophy in thee, shepherd?

Cor. No more but that I know the more one sickens, the worse at ease he is; and that he that wants money, means, and content is without 25 three good friends; that the property of rain is to wet and fire to burn; that good pasture makes fat sheep, and that a great cause of the night is lack of the sun; that he that hath learned no wit by nature nor art may complain of good breeding, or 30 comes of a very dull kindred.

Touch. Such a one is a natural philosopher. Wast ever in court, shepherd?

Cor. No, truly.

Touch. Then thou art damned. 35

Cor. Nay, I hope.

Touch. Truly thou art damned, like an ill-roasted egg, all on one side.

Cor. For not being at court! Your reason.

Touch. Why, if thou never wast at court, 40 thou never sawst good manners; if thou never sawst good manners, then thy manners must be wicked; and wickedness is sin, and sin is damnation. Thou art in a parlous state, shepherd.

Cor. Not a whit, Touchstone. Those that are 45 good manners at the court are as ridiculous in the country as the behavior of the country is most mockable at the court. You told me you salute not at the court but you kiss your hands. That courtesy would be uncleanly if courtiers were shepherds. 50

Touch. Instance, briefly. Come, instance.

Cor. Why, we are still handling our ewes, and their fells you know are greasy.

Touch. Why, do not your courtier's hands sweat? and is not the grease of a mutton as wholesome 55 as the sweat of a man? Shallow, shallow! A better instance, I say. Come.

Cor. Besides, our hands are hard.

Touch. Your lips will feel them the sooner. Shallow again! A more sounder instance, come. 60

Cor. And they are often tarred over with the surgery of our sheep, and would you have us kiss tar? The courtier's hands are perfumed with civet.

Touch. Most shallow man! Thou worm's meat in respect of a good piece of flesh indeed! Learn 65 of the wise, and perpend. Civet is of a baser birth than tar—the very uncleanly flux of a cat. Mend the instance, shepherd.

Cor. You have too courtly a wit for me. I'll rest.

Touch. Wilt thou rest damned? God help 70 thee, shallow man! God make incision in thee, thou art raw!

Cor. Sir, I am a true laborer: I earn that I eat, get that I wear; owe no man hate, envy no man's happiness; glad of other men's good, content with 75 my harm; and the greatest of my pride is to see my ewes graze and my lambs suck.

Touch. That is another simple sin in you: to bring the ewes and the rams together and to offer to get your living by the copulation of cattle; to be 80 bawd to a bellwether, and to betray a she-lamb of a twelvemonth to a crooked-pated old cuckoldly ram, out of all reasonable match. If thou beest not damned for this, the devil himself will have no shepherds; I cannot see else how thou shouldst 85 scape.

Cor. Here comes young Master Ganymede, my new mistress's brother.

Enter ROSALIND, [*reading a paper*].

Ros. From the east to western Ind,
  No jewel is like Rosalind. 90
  Her worth, being mounted on the wind,
  Through all the world bears Rosalind.

4. **Thy huntress':** i.e., the particular virgin; **sway:** rule
6. **character:** write
8. **witnessed:** evidenced
10. **unexpressive:** inexpressible
16. **private:** secluded
19. **spare:** austere
29–31. **he . . . kindred:** he that has acquired no wisdom by inheritance or teaching will complain of his lack of education unless he comes from very stupid stock.
44. **parlous:** perilous
53. **fells:** pelts
65. **respect of:** comparison with
66. **perpend:** consider
67–68. **Mend . . . instance:** give a better example
71. **make . . . thee:** give thee surgical aid
72. **raw:** (1) rude; (2) sore
73. **true:** honest
75–76. **content . . . harm:** reconciled to my misfortunes
81. **bellwether:** leader of the flock
82. **cuckoldly:** horned like a cuckold (man with an unfaithful wife)
89. **western Ind:** the West Indies

All the pictures fairest lined
Are but black to Rosalind.
Let no face be kept in mind 95
But the fair of Rosalind.

Touch. I'll rhyme you so eight years together, dinners and suppers and sleeping hours excepted. It is the right butterwomen's rank to market.

Ros. Out, fool! 100

Touch. For a taste:

If a hart do lack a hind,
Let him seek out Rosalind.
If the cat will after kind,
So be sure will Rosalind. 105
Winter garments must be lined,
So must slender Rosalind.
They that reap must sheaf and bind,
Then to cart with Rosalind.
Sweetest nut hath sourest rind, 110
Such a nut is Rosalind.
He that sweetest rose will find
Must find love's prick, and Rosalind.

This is the very false gallop of verses! Why do you infect yourself with them? 115

Ros. Peace, you dull fool! I found them on a tree.

Touch. Truly the tree yields bad fruit.

Ros. I'll graff it with you and then I shall graff it with a medlar. Then it will be the earliest fruit i' the country; for you'll be rotten ere you be half 120 ripe, and that's the right virtue of the medlar.

Touch. You have said; but whether wisely or no, let the forest judge.

Enter CELIA, *with a writing.*

Ros. Peace!
Here comes my sister reading. Stand aside. 125

Cel. Why should this a desert be,
For it is unpeopled? No!
Tongues I'll hang on every tree
That shall civil sayings show:
Some, how brief the life of man 130
Runs his erring pilgrimage,
That the stretching of a span
Buckles in his sum of age;
Some, of violated vows
'Twixt the souls of friend and friend; 135
But upon the fairest boughs,
Or at every sentence end,
Will I "Rosalinda" write,
Teaching all that read to know
The quintessence of every sprite 140
Heaven would in little show.
Therefore heaven Nature charged
That one body should be filled
With all graces wide-enlarged.
Nature presently distilled 145
Helen's cheek, but not her heart,
Cleopatra's majesty,
Atalanta's better part,
Sad Lucretia's modesty.
Thus Rosalind of many parts 150
By heavenly synod was devised,
Of many faces, eyes, and hearts,
To have the touches dearest prized.
Heaven would that she these gifts should have,
And I to live and die her slave. 155

Ros. O most gentle pulpiter! what tedious homily of love have you wearied your parishioners withal, and never cried, "Have patience, good people"!

Cel. How now? Back, friends. Shepherd, go off a little. Go with him, sirrah. 160

Touch. Come, shepherd, let us make an honorable retreat; though not with bag and baggage, yet with scrip and scrippage. *Exeunt* [*Corin and Touchstone*].

Cel. Didst thou hear these verses?

Ros. O, yes, I heard them all, and more 165 too; for some of them had in them more feet than the verses would bear.

Cel. That's no matter. The feet might bear the verses.

Ros. Ay, but the feet were lame, and could 170 not bear themselves without the verse, and therefore stood lamely in the verse.

Cel. But didst thou hear without wondering how thy name should be hanged and carved upon these trees? 175

Ros. I was seven of the nine days out of the wonder before you came; for look here what I found on a palm tree. I was never so berhymed since Pythagoras' time that I was an Irish rat, which I can hardly remember. 180

Cel. Trow you who hath done this?

Ros. Is it a man?

Cel. And a chain that you once wore about his neck. Change you color?

Ros. I prithee who? 185

Cel. O Lord, Lord! it is a hard matter for friends to meet; but mountains may be removed with earthquakes, and so encounter.

93. lined: portrayed
99. right . . . market: true jog-trot rhythm
119. medlar: apple-like fruit, eaten only when nearly rotten
127. For: because
129. civil: civilized
140–41. The . . . show: that heaven intended to show in miniature the essence of every spirit
144. wide-enlarged: amply set forth
146. her heart: because it was faithless
148. Atalanta's . . . part: Atalanta was a beautiful Greek. An unsurpassed runner, she stipulated that all suitors who could not outrun her should be killed.
151. synod: assembly
153. touches: characteristics
156. pulpiter: James Spedding's emendation of the Folio's "Jupiter"
163. scrip: wallet
176. seven . . . days: proverbial: A wonder lasts but nine days.
178–79. I . . . rat: a reference to the Pythagorean theory of transmigration of souls and to rhyming spells intended to destroy rats
181. Trow: know
186–88. it . . . encounter: cf. the proverb "Friends may meet, but mountains never greet."

Ros. Nay, but who is it?

Cel. Is it possible? 190

Ros. Nay, I prithee now with most petitionary vehemence, tell me who it is.

Cel. O wonderful, wonderful, and most wonderful wonderful! and yet again wonderful, and after that, out of all hooping! 195

Ros. Good my complexion! Dost thou think, though I am caparisoned like a man, I have a doublet and hose in my disposition? One inch of delay more is a South Sea of discovery. I prithee tell me who is it quickly, and speak apace. I would thou 200 couldst stammer, that thou mightst pour this concealed man out of thy mouth as wine comes out of a narrow-mouthed bottle—either too much at once, or none at all. I prithee take the cork out of thy mouth, that I may drink thy tidings. 205

Cel. So you may put a man in your belly.

Ros. Is he of God's making? What manner of man? Is his head worth a hat? or his chin worth a beard?

Cel. Nay, he hath but a little beard. 210

Ros. Why, God will send more, if the man will be thankful! Let me stay the growth of his beard, if thou delay me not the knowledge of his chin.

Cel. It is young Orlando, that tripped up the wrestler's heels and your heart both in an in- 215 stant.

Ros. Nay, but the devil take mocking! Speak sad brow and true maid.

Cel. I' faith, coz, 'tis he.

Ros. Orlando? 220

Cel. Orlando.

Ros. Alas the day! what shall I do with my doublet and hose? What did he when thou sawst him? What said he? How looked he? Wherein went he? What makes he here? Did he ask for me? 225 Where remains he? How parted he with thee? and when shalt thou see him again? Answer me in one word.

Cel. You must borrow me Gargantua's mouth first; 'tis a word too great for any mouth of 230 this age's size. To say ay and no to these particulars is more than to answer in a catechism.

Ros. But doth he know that I am in this forest, and in man's apparel? Looks he as freshly as he did the day he wrestled? 235

Cel. It is as easy to count atomies as to resolve the propositions of a lover; but take a taste of my finding him, and relish it with good observance. I found him under a tree, like a dropped acorn.

Ros. It may well be called Jove's tree when 240 it drops forth such fruit.

Cel. Give me audience, good madam.

Ros. Proceed.

Cel. There lay he stretched along like a wounded knight. 245

Ros. Though it be pity to see such a sight, it well becomes the ground.

Cel. Cry "holla" to thy tongue, I prithee. It curvets unseasonably. He was furnished like a hunter.

Ros. O, ominous! he comes to kill my heart. 250

Cel. I would sing my song without a burden. Thou bringst me out of tune.

Ros. Do you not know I am a woman? When I think, I must speak. Sweet, say on.

Enter ORLANDO *and* JAQUES.

Cel. You bring me out. Soft! comes he not 255 here?

Ros. 'Tis he; slink by and note him.

Jaq. I thank you for your company; but, good faith, I had as lief have been myself alone.

Orl. And so had I; but yet for fashion sake 260 I thank you too for your society.

Jaq. God be wi' you! Let's meet as little as we can.

Orl. I do desire we may be better strangers.

Jaq. I pray you mar no more trees with writing love songs in their barks. 265

Orl. I pray you mar no mo of my verses with reading them ill-favoredly.

Jaq. Rosalind is your love's name?

Orl. Yes, just.

Jaq. I do not like her name. 270

Orl. There was no thought of pleasing you when she was christened.

Jaq. What stature is she of?

Orl. Just as high as my heart.

Jaq. You are full of pretty answers. Have 275 you not been acquainted with goldsmiths' wives, and conned them out of rings?

Orl. Not so; but I answer you right painted cloth, from whence you have studied your questions.

195. out . . . hooping: beyond all exclamations of wonder
196. Good . . . complexion: God help my woman's heart!
197. caparisoned: outfitted
199. a . . . discovery: as lengthy a delay as the time needed to explore the South Seas
200. apace: quickly
212. stay: wait for
217–18. sad . . . maid: seriously and honestly
224. Wherein: in what garb
234. Looks . . . freshly: is he as attractive
236. resolve: satisfy
237. propositions: questions
238. observance: attention
248. holla: whoa
248–49. curvets: frolics
249. unseasonably: inappropriately; **furnished:** dressed
250. heart: pun on hart/heart
251. burden: subordinate refrain
258–59. good faith: truly
260. fashion sake: sake of courtesy
266. mo: more
267. ill-favoredly: ungraciously
277. rings: posy rings, which had rhymes inscribed inside
278. right . . . cloth: painted hangings, cheap substitutes for tapestries, sometimes were decorated with maxims in question-and-answer form.

Jaq. You have a nimble wit; I think 'twas 280
made of Atalanta's heels. Will you sit down with
me? and we two will rail against our mistress the
world and all our misery.

Orl. I will chide no breather in the world but myself, against whom I know most faults. 285

Jaq. The worst fault you have is to be in love.

Orl. 'Tis a fault I will not change for your best
virtue. I am weary of you.

Jaq. By my troth, I was seeking for a fool when I
found you. 290

Orl. He is drowned in the brook. Look but in and
you shall see him.

Jaq. There I shall see mine own figure.

Orl. Which I take to be either a fool or a cipher.

Jaq. I'll tarry no longer with you. Farewell, 295
good Signior Love.

Orl. I am glad of your departure. Adieu, good
Monsieur Melancholy. [*Exit Jaques.*]

Ros. [*Aside to Celia*] I will speak to him like a
saucy lackey, and under that habit play the 300
knave with him.—Do you hear, forester?

Orl. Very well. What would you?

Ros. I pray you, what is't o'clock?

Orl. You should ask me, what time o' day. There's
no clock in the forest. 305

Ros. Then there is no true lover in the forest; else
sighing every minute and groaning every hour would
detect the lazy foot of Time as well as a clock.

Orl. And why not the swift foot of Time? Had not
that been as proper? 310

Ros. By no means, sir. Time travels in divers paces
with divers persons. I'll tell you who Time ambles
withal, who Time trots withal, who Time gallops
withal, and who he stands still withal.

Orl. I prithee, who doth he trot withal? 315

Ros. Marry, he trots hard with a young maid between the contract of her marriage and the day it is
solemnized. If the interim be but a se'nnight, Time's
pace is so hard that it seems the length of seven year.

Orl. Who ambles Time withal? 320

Ros. With a priest that lacks Latin and a rich man
that hath not the gout; for the one sleeps easily because he cannot study, and the other lives merrily
because he feels no pain; the one lacking the burden
of lean and wasteful learning, the other know- 325
ing no burden of heavy tedious penury. These Time
ambles withal.

Orl. Who doth he gallop withal?

Ros. With a thief to the gallows; for though he go
as softly as foot can fall, he thinks himself 330
too soon there.

Orl. Who stays it still withal?

Ros. With lawyers in the vacation; for they sleep
between term and term, and then they perceive not
how time moves. 335

Orl. Where dwell you, pretty youth?

Ros. With this shepherdess, my sister; here in the
skirts of the forest, like fringe upon a petticoat.

Orl. Are you native of this place?

Ros. As the cony that you see dwell where 340
she is kindled.

Orl. Your accent is something finer than you could
purchase in so removed a dwelling.

Ros. I have been told so of many. But indeed an
old religious uncle of mine taught me to 345
speak, who was in his youth an inland man; one
that knew courtship too well, for there he fell in love.
I have heard him read many lectures against it; and
I thank God I am not a woman, to be touched with
so many giddy offenses as he hath generally 350
taxed their whole sex withal.

Orl. Can you remember any of the principal evils
that he laid to the charge of women?

Ros. There were none principal. They were all like
one another as halfpence are, every one fault 355
seeming monstrous till his fellow-fault came to
match it.

Orl. I prithee recount some of them.

Ros. No, I will not cast away my physic but on
those that are sick. There is a man haunts the 360
forest that abuses our young plants with carving
"Rosalind" on their barks; hangs odes upon haw-
thorns, and elegies on brambles; all, forsooth, deify-
ing the name of Rosalind. If I could meet that fancy-
monger, I would give him some good counsel, 365
for he seems to have the quotidian of love upon him.

Orl. I am he that is so love-shaked. I pray you tell
me your remedy.

Ros. There is none of my uncle's marks upon you.
He taught me how to know a man in love; in 370
which cage of rushes I am sure you are not prisoner.

Orl. What were his marks?

Ros. A lean cheek, which you have not; a blue eye
and sunken, which you have not; an unquestionable
spirit, which you have not; a beard neglected, 375
which you have not. But I pardon you for that, for

294. **cipher:** nonentity
300. **lackey:** servant; **under . . . habit:** in that garb
301. **knave:** menial, as well as villain
308. **detect:** reveal
318. **se'nnight:** week
325. **wasteful:** wasting; exhausting
330. **softly:** slowly
341. **kindled:** littered
343. **purchase:** acquire
344. **of:** by
349. **touched:** marred
350. **giddy:** capricious; **offenses:** faults
364–65. **fancy-monger:** dealer in love
366. **quotidian:** fever of daily occurrence, considered a symptom of love
373. **blue:** blue-shadowed
374. **unquestionable:** not given to conversation

simply your having in beard is a younger brother's revenue. Then your hose should be ungartered, your bonnet unbanded, your sleeve unbuttoned, your shoe untied, and everything about you demon- 380 strating a careless desolation. But you are no such man: you are rather point-device in your accouterments, as loving yourself, than seeming the lover of any other.

Orl. Fair youth, I would I could make thee 385 believe I love.

Ros. Me believe it? You may as soon make her that you love believe it, which I warrant she is apter to do than to confess she does. That is one of the points in the which women still give the lie to 390 their consciences. But in good sooth, are you he that hangs the verses on the trees wherein Rosalind is so admired?

Orl. I swear to thee, youth, by the white hand of Rosalind, I am that he, that unfortunate he. 395

Ros. But are you so much in love as your rhymes speak?

Orl. Neither rhyme nor reason can express how much.

Ros. Love is merely a madness, and, I tell 400 you, deserves as well a dark house and a whip as madmen do; and the reason why they are not so punished and cured is that the lunacy is so ordinary that the whippers are in love too. Yet I profess curing it by counsel. 405

Orl. Did you ever cure any so?

Ros. Yes, one, and in this manner. He was to imagine me his love, his mistress; and I set him every day to woo me. At which time would I, being but a moonish youth, grieve, be effeminate, 410 changeable, longing, and liking, proud, fantastical, apish, shallow, inconstant, full of tears, full of smiles; for every passion something and for no passion truly anything, as boys and women are for the most part cattle of this color; would now like 415 him, now loathe him; then entertain him, then forswear him; now weep for him, then spit at him; that I drave my suitor from his mad humor of love to a living humor of madness, which was, to forswear the full stream of the world and to live in a nook 420 merely monastic. And thus I cured him; and this way will I take upon me to wash your liver as clean as a sound sheep's heart, that there shall not be one spot of love in't.

Orl. I would not be cured, youth. 425

Ros. I would cure you, if you would but call me Rosalind and come every day to my cote and woo me.

Orl. Now, by the faith of my love, I will! Tell me where it is. 430

Ros. Go with me to it, and I'll show it you; and by the way you shall tell me where in the forest you live. Will you go?

Orl. With all my heart, good youth.

Ros. Nay, you must call me Rosalind. 435 Come, sister, will you go?

Exeunt.

Scene III. [*The Forest.*]

Enter [TOUCHSTONE *the*] CLOWN, AUDREY; *and* JAQUES [*behind*].

Touch. Come apace, good Audrey. I will fetch up your goats, Audrey. And how, Audrey, am I the man yet? Doth my simple feature content you?

Aud. Your features? Lord warrant us! What features! 5

Touch. I am here with thee and thy goats, as the most capricious poet, honest Ovid, was among the Goths.

Jaq. [*Aside*] O knowledge ill inhabited, worse than Jove in a thatched house! 10

Touch. When a man's verses cannot be understood, nor a man's good wit seconded with the forward child, understanding, it strikes a man more dead than a great reckoning in a little room. Truly, I would the gods had made thee poetical. 15

Aud. I do not know what poetical is. Is it honest in deed and word? Is it a true thing?

Touch. No, truly; for the truest poetry is the most feigning, and lovers are given to poetry; and what they swear in poetry may be said, as lovers, 20 they do feign.

377–78. **your . . . revenue:** your possession of beard is slight, like the inheritance of a younger brother.

379. **unbanded:** unornamented

382–83. **point-device . . . accouterments:** perfectly turned out

400. **merely:** entirely

410. **moonish:** changeable; **effeminate:** tender

411. **liking:** responsive; **fantastical:** fanciful

412. **apish:** affected

413–14. **for . . . anything:** easily but not deeply swayed by every passing emotion

416. **entertain:** welcome

417. **that:** so that

418–19. **from . . . madness:** from his caprice of love to actual madness

421. **merely monastic:** just like a monk

422. **liver:** considered the seat of love

431–32. **by . . . way:** as we go

3. **feature:** appearance and bearing

4. **warrant:** protect

7. **capricious:** a pun on the derivation of the word from the Latin *caper* (goat); **honest:** chaste (satirical, since Ovid's poetry was characterized by flippancy about love)

8. **Goths:** a pun on Goths/goats. Ovid was exiled to live among the Getae, once identified with the Goths.

9. **ill inhabited:** ill housed

10. **Jove . . . house:** i.e., the humble home of Philemon and Baucis; cf. Ovid *Metamorphoses,* bk. viii.

14. **a . . . room:** a big bill for poor accommodations

19. **feigning:** imaginative

21. **feign:** pretend

Aud. Do you wish then that the gods had made me poetical?

Touch. I do truly. For thou swearest to me thou art honest. Now if thou wert a poet, I might 25 have some hope thou didst feign.

Aud. Would you not have me honest?

Touch. No, truly, unless thou wert hard-favored; for honesty coupled to beauty is to have honey a sauce to sugar. 30

Jaq. [*Aside*] A material fool!

Aud. Well, I am not fair; and therefore I pray the gods make me honest.

Touch. Truly, and to cast away honesty upon a foul slut were to put good meat into an un- 35 clean dish.

Aud. I am not a slut, though I thank the gods I am foul.

Touch. Well, praised be the gods for thy foulness! Sluttishness may come hereafter. But be it as 40 it may be, I will marry thee; and to that end I have been with Sir Oliver Martext, the vicar of the next village, who hath promised to meet me in this place of the forest and to couple us.

Jaq. [*Aside*] I would fain see this meeting. 45

Aud. Well, the gods give us joy!

Touch. Amen. A man may, if he were of a fearful heart, stagger in this attempt; for here we have no temple but the wood, no assembly but horn-beasts. But what though? Courage! As horns are 50 odious, they are necessary. It is said, "Many a man knows no end of his goods." Right! Many a man has good horns and knows no end of them. Well, that is the dowry of his wife; 'tis none of his own getting. Horns? Even so. Poor men alone? No, no! 55 The noblest deer hath them as huge as the rascal. Is the single man therefore blessed? No; as a walled town is more worthier than a village, so is the forehead of a married man more honorable than the bare brow of a bachelor; and by how much defense 60 is better than no skill, by so much is a horn more precious than to want.

Enter SIR OLIVER MARTEXT.

Here comes Sir Oliver. Sir Oliver Martext, you are well met. Will you dispatch us here under this tree, or shall we go with you to your chapel? 65

Sir O. Is there none here to give the woman?

Touch. I will not take her on gift of any man.

Sir O. Truly, she must be given, or the marriage is not lawful.

Jaq. [*Comes forward.*] Proceed, proceed! 70 I'll give her.

Touch. Good even, good Master What-ye-call't. How do you, sir? You are very well met. Goddild you for your last company. I am very glad to see you. Even a toy in hand here, sir. Nay, pray 75 be covered.

Jaq. Will you be married, motley?

Touch. As the ox hath his bow, sir, the horse his curb, and the falcon her bells, so man hath his desires; and as pigeons bill, so wedlock would be 80 nibbling.

Jaq. And will you, being a man of your breeding, be married under a bush like a beggar? Get you to church, and have a good priest that can tell you what marriage is. This fellow will but join you to- 85 gether as they join wainscot; then one of you will prove a shrunk panel, and like green timber warp, warp.

Touch. [*Aside*] I am not in the mind but I were better to be married of him than of another; 90 for he is not like to marry me well; and not being well married, it would be a good excuse for me hereafter to leave my wife.

Jaq. Go thou with me and let me counsel thee.

Touch. Come, sweet Audrey. 95
We must be married, or we must live in bawdry.
Farewell, good Master Oliver: not

O sweet Oliver,
O brave Oliver,
Leave me not behind thee! 100

but

Wind away,
Be gone, I say!
I will not to wedding with thee.

[*Exeunt Jaques, Touchstone, and Audrey.*]

Sir O. 'Tis no matter. Ne'er a fantastical 105 knave of them all shall flout me out of my calling. *Exit.*

25. honest: chaste, as before
28. hard-favored: ugly
31. material: full of matter
35. foul: ugly
42. Sir: here a title of respect given to priests, not a sign of knighthood
51. necessary: inevitable. The reference is to the cuckold's horns.
53. knows . . . them: is unaware of them
56. rascal: a young or inferior deer
60. defense: fencing skill
62. want: i.e., lack them
64. dispatch us: perform our marriage
73. Goddild: God yield (reward)
75. Even . . . here: just a trivial business we are engaged in
76. be covered: put on your hat (which Jaques has removed in formal courtesy)
78. bow: yoke
89. I . . . were: I am not sure but that I would be
91. like: likely
98–100. O . . . thee: a snatch of a popular song

Scene IV. [*The Forest.*]

Enter ROSALIND *and* CELIA.

Ros. Never talk to me! I will weep.

Cel. Do, I prithee; but yet have the grace to consider that tears do not become a man.

Ros. But have I not cause to weep?

Cel. As good cause as one would desire: therefore weep. 5

Ros. His very hair is of the dissembling color.

Cel. Something browner than Judas'. Marry, his kisses are Judas' own children.

Ros. I' faith, his hair is of a good color. 10

Cel. An excellent color. Your chestnut was ever the only color.

Ros. And his kissing is as full of sanctity as the touch of holy bread.

Cel. He hath bought a pair of cast lips of Diana. A nun of winter's sisterhood kisses not more religiously; the very ice of chastity is in them. 15

Ros. But why did he swear he would come this morning, and comes not?

Cel. Nay, certainly there is no truth in him. 20

Ros. Do you think so?

Cel. Yes. I think he is not a pickpurse nor a horse-stealer; but for his verity in love, I do think him as concave as a covered goblet or a worm-eaten nut.

Ros. Not true in love? 25

Cel. Yes, when he is in; but I think he is not in.

Ros. You have heard him swear downright he was.

Cel. "Was" is not "is." Besides, the oath of a lover is no stronger than the word of a tapster: they are both the confirmer of false reckonings. He attends here in the forest on the Duke your father. 30

Ros. I met the Duke yesterday and had much question with him. He asked me of what parentage I was. I told him, of as good as he. So he laughed and let me go. But what talk we of fathers when there is such a man as Orlando? 35

Cel. O, that's a brave man! He writes brave verses, speaks brave words, swears brave oaths, and breaks them bravely, quite traverse, athwart the heart of his lover; as a puisny tilter, that spurs his horse but on one side, breaks his staff like a noble goose. 40
But all's brave that youth mounts and folly guides.
Who comes here?

Enter CORIN.

Cor. Mistress and master, you have oft inquired
After the shepherd that complained of love, 45
Who you saw sitting by me on the turf,
Praising the proud disdainful shepherdess
That was his mistress.

Cel. Well, and what of him?

Cor. If you will see a pageant truly played
Between the pale complexion of true love 50
And the red glow of scorn and proud disdain,
Go hence a little, and I shall conduct you,
If you will mark it.

Ros. O, come, let us remove!
The sight of lovers feedeth those in love.
Bring us to this sight, and you shall say 55
I'll prove a busy actor in their play.

Exeunt.

7. dissembling color: red, traditionally the color of Judas' hair and a sign of a treacherous nature
15. cast: discarded
16–17. religiously: piously
22. pickpurse: pickpocket
24. concave: hollow
33. question: conversation
37. brave man: splendid man (ironic)
39. traverse: crosswise
40. puisny: unskillful
41. noble goose: magnificent simpleton

Scene V. [*Another part of the Forest.*]

Enter SILVIUS *and* PHEBE.

Sil. Sweet Phebe, do not scorn me; do not, Phebe!
Say that you love me not, but say not so
In bitterness. The common executioner,
Whose heart the accustomed sight of death makes hard,
Falls not the axe upon the humbled neck 5
But first begs pardon. Will you sterner be
Than he that dies and lives by bloody drops?

Enter ROSALIND, CELIA, *and* CORIN.

Phe. I would not be thy executioner.
I fly thee, for I would not injure thee.
Thou tellst me there is murder in mine eye: 10
'Tis pretty, sure, and very probable
That eyes, that are the frail'st and softest things,
Who shut their coward gates on atomies,
Should be called tyrants, butchers, murderers!
Now I do frown on thee with all my heart; 15
And if mine eyes can wound, now let them kill thee!
Now counterfeit to swoon; why, now fall down;
Or if thou canst not, O, for shame, for shame,
Lie not, to say mine eyes are murderers!
Now show the wound mine eye hath made in thee.
Scratch thee but with a pin, and there remains 21
Some scar of it; lean but upon a rush,

45. complained . . . love: sang a love lament
49. pageant: spectacle
5. Falls: drops

The cicatrice and capable impressure
Thy palm some moment keeps; but now mine eyes,
Which I have darted at thee, hurt thee not, 25
Nor I am sure there is no force in eyes
That can do hurt.

Sil. O dear Phebe,
If ever (as that ever may be near)
You meet in some fresh cheek the power of fancy,
Then shall you know the wounds invisible 30
That love's keen arrows make.

Phe. But till that time
Come thou not near me; and when that time comes,
Afflict me with thy mocks, pity me not,
As till that time I shall not pity thee.

Ros. And why, I pray you? Who might be your mother, 35
That you insult, exult, and all at once,
Over the wretched? What though you have no beauty—
As, by my faith, I see no more in you
Than without candle may go dark to bed!—
Must you be therefore proud and pitiless? 40
Why, what means this? Why do you look on me?
I see no more in you than in the ordinary
Of nature's salework. 'Od's my little life,
I think she means to tangle my eyes too!
No, faith, proud mistress, hope not after it. 45
'Tis not your inky brows, your black silk hair,
Your bugle eyeballs, nor your cheek of cream
That can entame my spirits to your worship.
You foolish shepherd, wherefore do you follow her,
Like foggy south, puffing with wind and rain? 50
You are a thousand times a properer man
Than she a woman. 'Tis such fools as you
That makes the world full of ill-favored children.
'Tis not her glass, but you, that flatters her,
And out of you she sees herself more proper 55
Than any of her lineaments can show her.
But, mistress, know yourself. Down on your knees,
And thank heaven, fasting, for a good man's love;
For I must tell you friendly in your ear,
Sell when you can: you are not for all markets. 60
Cry the man mercy, love him, take his offer.
Foul is most foul, being foul to be a scoffer.
So take her to thee, shepherd. Fare you well.

Phe. Sweet youth, I pray you chide a year together.
I had rather hear you chide than this man woo. 65

Ros. He's fall'n in love with your foulness, [*To Silvius*] and she'll fall in love with my anger. If it be so, as fast as she answers thee with frowning looks, I'll sauce her with bitter words.—Why look you so upon me? 70

Phe. For no ill will I bear you.

Ros. I pray you do not fall in love with me,
For I am falser than vows made in wine.
Besides, I like you not. If you will know my house,
'Tis at the tuft of olives, here hard by.— 75
Will you go, sister?—Shepherd, ply her hard.—
Come, sister.—Shepherdess, look on him better
And be not proud. Though all the world could see,
None could be so abused in sight as he.—
Come, to our flock. 80

Exeunt [Rosalind, Celia, and Corin].

Phe. Dead shepherd, now I find thy saw of might,
"Who ever loved that loved not at first sight?"

Sil. Sweet Phebe—

Phe. Ha! what sayst thou, Silvius?

Sil. Sweet Phebe, pity me.

Phe. Why, I am sorry for thee, gentle Silvius. 85

Sil. Wherever sorrow is, relief would be.
If you do sorrow at my grief in love,
By giving love your sorrow and my grief
Were both extermined. 89

Phe. Thou hast my love. Is not that neighborly?

Sil. I would have you.

Phe. Why, that were covetousness.
Silvius, the time was that I hated thee,
And yet it is not that I bear thee love;
But since that thou canst talk of love so well,
Thy company, which erst was irksome to me, 95
I will endure; and I'll employ thee too.
But do not look for further recompense
Than thine own gladness that thou art employed.

Sil. So holy and so perfect is my love,
And I in such a poverty of grace, 100
That I shall think it a most plenteous crop
To glean the broken ears after the man
That the main harvest reaps. Loose now and then
A scattered smile, and that I'll live upon.

Phe. Knowst thou the youth that spoke to me erewhile? 105

Sil. Not very well, but I have met him oft,
And he hath bought the cottage and the bounds
That the old carlot once was master of.

Phe. Think not I love him, though I ask for him.

23. **capable impressure:** visible impression
39. **Than . . . bed:** i.e., her beauty is not sufficient to provide its own light.
42–43. **the . . . salework:** the run-of-the-mill production of nature
43. **'Od's . . . life:** God save me
47. **bugle:** a black bead
55. **out . . . you:** because of you; **proper:** handsome
61. **Cry . . . mercy:** beg the man's pardon
62. **Foul . . . scoffer:** an ugly woman is even uglier when she is scornful.
64. **chide:** scold
69. **sauce:** i.e., whet her appetite
75. **hard:** near
79. **abused:** deceived
81. **Dead shepherd:** Christopher Marlowe; **saw:** maxim. The quotation is from *Hero and Leander*.
95. **erst:** formerly
100. **in . . . grace:** so little in favor
105. **erewhile:** a while ago
108. **carlot:** countryman, cognate with "carl" and "churl"

'Tis but a peevish boy; yet he talks well. 110
But what care I for words? Yet words do well
When he that speaks them pleases those that hear.
It is a pretty youth—not very pretty—
But sure he's proud; and yet his pride becomes him.
He'll make a proper man. The best thing in him
Is his complexion; and faster than his tongue 116
Did make offense, his eye did heal it up.
He is not very tall; yet for his years he's tall.
His leg is but soso; and yet 'tis well.
There was a pretty redness in his lip, 120
A little riper and more lusty red
Than that mixed in his cheek; 'twas just the difference
Betwixt the constant red and mingled damask.
There be some women, Silvius, had they marked him
In parcels as I did, would have gone near 125
To fall in love with him; but, for my part,
I love him not nor hate him not; and yet
I have more cause to hate him than to love him;
For what had he to do to chide at me?
He said mine eyes were black and my hair black;
And, now I am remembered, scorned at me. 131
I marvel why I answered not again.
But that's all one: omittance is no quittance.
I'll write to him a very taunting letter,
And thou shalt bear it. Wilt thou, Silvius? 135

Sil. Phebe, with all my heart.

Phe. I'll write it straight;
The matter's in my head and in my heart.
I will be bitter with him and passing short.
Go with me, Silvius.

Exeunt.

110. **peevish:** silly
123. **constant:** uniform
124. **marked:** noted
125. **In parcels:** item by item
131. **remembered:** reminded
133. **omittance . . . quittance:** proverbial
137. **matter's:** substance's
138. **passing short:** very curt

ACT IV

Scene I. [*The Forest.*]

Enter Rosalind *and* Celia *and* Jaques.

Jaq. I prithee, pretty youth, let me be better acquainted with thee.

Ros. They say you are a melancholy fellow.

Jaq. I am so. I do love it better than laughing.

Ros. Those that are in extremity of either are 5 abominable fellows, and betray themselves to every modern censure worse than drunkards.

Jaq. Why, 'tis good to be sad and say nothing.

Ros. Why, then, 'tis good to be a post.

Jaq. I have neither the scholar's melancholy, 10 which is emulation; nor the musician's, which is fantastical; nor the courtier's, which is proud; nor the soldier's, which is ambitious; nor the lawyer's, which is politic; nor the lady's, which is nice; nor the lover's, which is all these: but it is a melancholy of 15 mine own, compounded of many simples, extracted from many objects, and indeed the sundry contemplation of my travels, in which my often rumination wraps me in a most humorous sadness.

Ros. A traveler! By my faith, you have great 20 reason to be sad. I fear you have sold your own lands to see other men's. Then to have seen much and to have nothing is to have rich eyes and poor hands.

Jaq. Yes, I have gained my experience.

Enter Orlando.

Ros. And your experience makes you sad. I 25 had rather have a fool to make me merry than experience to make me sad—and to travel for it too!

Orl. Good day and happiness, dear Rosalind!

Jaq. Nay then, God be wi' you, an you talk in blank verse! 30

Ros. Farewell, Monsieur Traveler. Look you lisp and wear strange suits, disable all the benefits of your

7. **modern censure:** ordinary judgment
11. **emulation:** envy
14. **politic:** crafty; **nice:** finical
16. **simples:** herbs
17–18. **sundry contemplation:** varied observation
19. **humorous sadness:** moody gravity
32. **disable:** criticize

own country, be out of love with your nativity and almost chide God for making you that countenance you are; or I will scarce think you have swam 35 in a gundello. [*Exit Jaques.*] Why, how now, Orlando? Where have you been all this while? You a lover? An you serve me such another trick, never come in my sight more.

Orl. My fair Rosalind, I come within an hour 40 of my promise.

Ros. Break an hour's promise in love? He that will divide a minute into a thousand parts and break but a part of the thousandth part of a minute in the affairs of love, it may be said of him that Cupid 45 hath clapped him o' the shoulder, but I'll warrant him heart-whole.

Orl. Pardon me, dear Rosalind.

Ros. Nay, an you be so tardy, come no more in my sight. I had as lief be wooed of a snail. 50

Orl. Of a snail?

Ros. Ay, of a snail; for though he comes slowly, he carries his house on his head—a better jointure, I think, than you make a woman. Besides, he brings his destiny with him. 55

Orl. What's that?

Ros. Why, horns, which such as you are fain to be beholding to your wives for; but he comes armed in his fortune and prevents the slander of his wife.

Orl. Virtue is no horn-maker, and my Rosa- 60 lind is virtuous.

Ros. And I am your Rosalind.

Cel. It pleases him to call you so; but he hath a Rosalind of a better leer than you.

Ros. Come, woo me, woo me, for now I am 65 in a holiday humor and like enough to consent. What would you say to me now, an I were your very very Rosalind?

Orl. I would kiss before I spoke.

Ros. Nay, you were better speak first; and 70 when you were graveled for lack of matter, you might take occasion to kiss. Very good orators, when they are out, they will spit; and for lovers, lacking (God warn us!) matter, the cleanliest shift is to kiss.

Orl. How if the kiss be denied? 75

Ros. Then she puts you to entreaty, and there begins new matter.

Orl. Who could be out, being before his beloved mistress?

Ros. Marry, that should you, if I were your 80 mistress, or I should think my honesty ranker than my wit.

Orl. What, of my suit?

Ros. Not out of your apparel, and yet out of your suit. Am not I your Rosalind? 85

Orl. I take some joy to say you are, because I would be talking of her.

Ros. Well, in her person, I say I will not have you.

Orl. Then, in mine own person, I die.

Ros. No, faith, die by attorney. The poor 90 world is almost six thousand years old, and in all this time there was not any man died in his own person, videlicet, in a love cause. Troilus had his brains dashed out with a Grecian club; yet he did what he could to die before, and he is one of the pat- 95 terns of love. Leander, he would have lived many a fair year though Hero had turned nun, if it had not been for a hot midsummer night; for (good youth) he went but forth to wash him in the Hellespont, and being taken with the cramp, was drowned; 100 and the foolish chroniclers of that age found it was "Hero of Sestos." But these are all lies. Men have died from time to time, and worms have eaten them, but not for love.

Orl. I would not have my right Rosalind of 105 this mind, for I protest her frown might kill me.

Ros. By this hand, it will not kill a fly! But come, now I will be your Rosalind in a more coming-on disposition, and ask me what you will, I will grant it.

Orl. Then love me, Rosalind. 110

Ros. Yes, faith, will I, Fridays and Saturdays and all.

Orl. And wilt thou have me?

Ros. Ay, and twenty such.

Orl. What sayest thou? 115

Ros. Are you not good?

Orl. I hope so.

Ros. Why then, can one desire too much of a good thing? Come, sister, you shall be the priest and marry us. Give me your hand, Orlando. What do you 120 say, sister?

Orl. Pray thee marry us.

Cel. I cannot say the words.

Ros. You must begin, "Will you, Orlando"—

Cel. Go to. Will you, Orlando, have to wife 125 this Rosalind?

Orl. I will.

Ros. Ay, but when?

Orl. Why now, as fast as she can marry us.

Ros. Then you must say, "I take thee, Ros- 130 alind, for wife."

Orl. I take thee, Rosalind, for wife.

Ros. I might ask you for your commission; but I

33. nativity: birthplace
36. gundello: gondola
53. jointure: dower right
64. leer: countenance
71. graveled: perplexed
73. out: i.e., speechless; at a loss for words
74. shift: expedient
81. honesty: chastity; **ranker:** more lustful

90. attorney: proxy
93. videlicet: that is to say
101. chroniclers: changed by some editors, after Thomas Hanmer, to "coroners," because the word **found** is used of the decision of a coroner's jury.
133. commission: legal authority

do take thee, Orlando, for my husband. There's a girl goes before the priest, and certainly a 135 woman's thought runs before her actions.

Orl. So do all thoughts; they are winged.

Ros. Now tell me how long you would have her after you have possessed her.

Orl. For ever and a day. 140

Ros. Say "a day," without the "ever." No, no, Orlando! Men are April when they woo, December when they wed. Maids are May when they are maids, but the sky changes when they are wives. I will be more jealous of thee than a Barbary cock- 145 pigeon over his hen, more clamorous than a parrot against rain, more newfangled than an ape, more giddy in my desires than a monkey. I will weep for nothing, like Diana in the fountain, and I will do that when you are disposed to be merry; I will 150 laugh like a hyen, and that when thou art inclined to sleep.

Orl. But will my Rosalind do so?

Ros. By my life, she will do as I do.

Orl. O, but she is wise! 155

Ros. Or else she could not have the wit to do this. The wiser, the waywarder. Make the doors upon a woman's wit, and it will out at the casement; shut that, and 'twill out at the keyhole; stop that, 'twill fly with the smoke out at the chimney. 160

Orl. A man that had a wife with such a wit, he might say, "Wit, whither wilt?"

Ros. Nay, you might keep that check for it till you met your wife's wit going to your neighbor's bed.

Orl. And what wit could wit have to excuse 165 that?

Ros. Marry, to say she came to seek you there. You shall never take her without her answer unless you take her without her tongue. O, that woman that cannot make her fault her husband's occasion, 170 let her never nurse her child herself, for she will breed it like a fool!

Orl. For these two hours, Rosalind, I will leave thee.

Ros. Alas, dear love, I cannot lack thee two 175 hours!

Orl. I must attend the Duke at dinner. By two o'clock I will be with thee again.

Ros. Ay, go your ways, go your ways! I knew what you would prove. My friends told me as much, 180 and I thought no less. That flattering tongue of yours won me. 'Tis but one cast away, and so, come death! Two o'clock is your hour?

Orl. Ay, sweet Rosalind.

Ros. By my troth, and in good earnest, and 185 so God mend me, and by all pretty oaths that are not dangerous, if you break one jot of your promise or come one minute behind your hour, I will think you the most pathetical break-promise, and the most hollow lover, and the most unworthy of her you 190 call Rosalind, that may be chosen out of the gross band of the unfaithful. Therefore beware my censure and keep your promise.

Orl. With no less religion than if thou wert indeed my Rosalind. So adieu. 195

Ros. Well, Time is the old justice that examines all such offenders, and let Time try. Adieu.

Exit [*Orlando*].

Cel. You have simply misused our sex in your love-prate. We must have your doublet and hose plucked over your head, and show the world what the 200 bird hath done to her own nest.

Ros. O coz, coz, coz, my pretty little coz, that thou didst know how many fathom deep I am in love! But it cannot be sounded. My affection hath an unknown bottom, like the Bay of Portugal. 205

Cel. Or rather, bottomless, that as fast as you pour affection in, it runs out.

Ros. No, that same wicked bastard of Venus that was begot of thought, conceived of spleen, and born of madness, that blind rascally boy that 210 abuses every one's eyes because his own are out—let him be judge how deep I am in love. I'll tell thee, Aliena, I cannot be out of the sight of Orlando. I'll go find a shadow, and sigh till he come.

Cel. And I'll sleep. 215

Exeunt.

Scene II. [*The Forest.*]

Enter JAQUES, *and* LORDS [*like*] *Foresters*) [*with a dead deer*].

Jaq. Which is he that killed the deer?

Lord. Sir, it was I.

Jaq. Let's present him to the Duke like a Roman conqueror; and it would do well to set the deer's horns upon his head for a branch of victory. 5 Have you no song, forester, for this purpose?

Lord. Yes, sir.

Jaq. Sing it. 'Tis no matter how it be in tune, so it make noise enough. *Music.*

135. goes before: anticipates
147. against: before
149. Diana . . . fountain: a popular subject for garden statuary was Diana bathing.
170. her . . . occasion: i.e., her husband's fault
191. gross: great
194. religion: faith
209. thought: melancholy; **spleen:** rashness
211. abuses: deceives
3-4. like . . . conqueror: i.e., triumphantly
5. branch . . . victory: laurel wreath

Song.

What shall he have that killed the deer? 10
His leather skin and horns to wear.
Then sing him home.
(*The rest shall bear this burden.*)
Take thou no scorn to wear the horn;
It was a crest ere thou wast born:
Thy father's father wore it, 15
And thy father bore it.
The horn, the horn, the lusty horn,
Is not a thing to laugh to scorn.
Exeunt.

Scene III. [*The Forest.*]

Enter Rosalind *and* Celia.

Ros. How say you now? Is it not past two o'clock? and here much Orlando!

Cel. I warrant you, with pure love and troubled brain, he hath ta'en his bow and arrows, and is gone forth to sleep. 5

Enter Silvius.

Look who comes here.
Sil. My errand is to you, fair youth.
My gentle Phebe bid me give you this.
[*Gives a letter.*]
I know not the contents; but, as I guess
By the stern brow and waspish action 10
Which she did use as she was writing of it,
It bears an angry tenure. Pardon me;
I am but as a guiltless messenger.
Ros. Patience herself would startle at this letter
And play the swaggerer. Bear this, bear all! 15
She says I am not fair, that I lack manners;
She calls me proud, and that she could not love me,
Were man as rare as phoenix. 'Od's my will!
Her love is not the hare that I do hunt.
Why writes she so to me? Well, shepherd, well, 20
This is a letter of your own device.
Sil. No, I protest, I know not the contents.
Phebe did write it.
Ros. Come, come, you are a fool,
And turned into the extremity of love.
I saw her hand. She has a leathern hand, 25
A freestone-colored hand. I verily did think
That her old gloves were on, but 'twas her hands.
She has a housewife's hand; but that's no matter.
I say she never did invent this letter;
This is a man's invention and his hand. 30
Sil. Sure it is hers.
Ros. Why, 'tis a boisterous and a cruel style,
A style for challengers. Why, she defies me
Like Turk to Christian! Women's gentle brain
Could not drop forth such giant-rude invention, 35
Such Ethiop words, blacker in their effect
Than in their countenance. Will you hear the letter?
Sil. So please you, for I never heard it yet—
Yet heard too much of Phebe's cruelty. 39
Ros. She Phebes me. Mark how the tyrant writes.
Read.

Art thou god to shepherd turned,
That a maiden's heart hath burned?

Can a woman rail thus?
Sil. Call you this railing?
Ros. *Read.*

Why, thy godhead laid apart, 45
Warrest thou with a woman's heart?

Did you ever hear such railing?

Whiles the eye of man did woo me,
That could do no vengeance to me.

Meaning me a beast. 50

If the scorn of your bright eyne
Have power to raise such love in mine,
Alack, in me what strange effect
Would they work in mild aspect!
Whiles you chid me, I did love; 55
How then might your prayers move!
He that brings this love to thee
Little knows this love in me;
And by him seal up thy mind,
Whether that thy youth and kind 60
Will the faithful offer take
Of me and all that I can make,
Or else by him my love deny,
And then I'll study how to die.

Sil. Call you this chiding? 65
Cel. Alas, poor shepherd!
Ros. Do you pity him? No, he deserves no pity. Wilt thou love such a woman? What, to make thee an instrument, and play false strains upon thee? Not to be endured! Well, go your way to her (for I 70 see love hath made thee a tame snake) and say this to her: that if she love me, I charge her to love thee;

S.D. 12. bear . . . burden: sing this refrain
13. Take . . . scorn: be not ashamed
2. here . . . Orlando: here's a fine lot of Orlando!
12. tenure: tenor
18. rare . . . phoenix: the mythical phoenix existed in only one exemplar, which, on attaining a great age, destroyed itself on a funeral pyre, after which a new bird arose from the ashes. **'Od's . . . will:** God save me.
24. turned . . . love: changed into the very essence of love

51. eyne: eyes
59. seal up: certify

if she will not, I will never have her unless thou entreat for her. If you be a true lover, hence, and not a word; for here comes more company. 75

Exit Silvius.

Enter OLIVER.

Oli. Good morrow, fair ones. Pray you, if you know,
Where in the purlieus of this forest stands
A sheepcote, fenced about with olive trees?
Cel. West of this place, down in the neighbor bottom.
The rank of osiers by the murmuring stream 80
Left on your right hand brings you to the place.
But at this hour the house doth keep itself;
There's none within.
Oli. If that an eye may profit by a tongue,
Then should I know you by description— 85
Such garments and such years: "The boy is fair,
Of female favor, and bestows himself
Like a ripe sister; the woman low,
And browner than her brother." Are not you
The owner of the house I did inquire for? 90
Cel. It is no boast, being asked, to say we are.
Oli. Orlando doth commend him to you both,
And to that youth he calls his Rosalind
He sends this bloody napkin. Are you he? 94
Ros. I am. What must we understand by this?
Oli. Some of my shame, if you will know of me
What man I am, and how, and why, and where
This handkercher was stained.
Cel. I pray you tell it.
Oli. When last the young Orlando parted from you,
He left a promise to return again 100
Within an hour; and pacing through the forest,
Chewing the food of sweet and bitter fancy,
Lo, what befell! He threw his eye aside,
And mark what object did present itself: 104
Under an oak, whose boughs were mossed with age
And high top bald with dry antiquity,
A wretched ragged man, o'ergrown with hair,
Lay sleeping on his back. About his neck
A green and gilded snake had wreathed itself, 109
Who with her head, nimble in threats, approached
The opening of his mouth; but suddenly,
Seeing Orlando, it unlinked itself
And with indented glides did slip away
Into a bush, under which bush's shade
A lioness, with udders all drawn dry, 115
Lay couching, head on ground, with catlike watch
When that the sleeping man should stir; for 'tis
The royal disposition of that beast
To prey on nothing that doth seem as dead.
This seen, Orlando did approach the man 120
And found it was his brother, his elder brother.
Cel. O, I have heard him speak of that same brother,
And he did render him the most unnatural
That lived amongst men.
Oli. And well he might so do,
For well I know he was unnatural. 125
Ros. But, to Orlando! Did he leave him there,
Food to the sucked and hungry lioness?
Oli. Twice did he turn his back and purposed so;
But kindness, nobler ever than revenge,
And nature, stronger than his just occasion, 130
Made him give battle to the lioness,
Who quickly fell before him; in which hurtling
From miserable slumber I awaked.
Cel. Are you his brother?
Ros. Was it you he rescued?
Cel. Was't you that did so oft contrive to kill him?
Oli. 'Twas I. But 'tis not I! I do not shame 136
To tell you what I was, since my conversion
So sweetly tastes, being the thing I am.
Ros. But, for the bloody napkin?
Oli. By-and-by.
When from the first to last, betwixt us two, 140
Tears our recountments had most kindly bathed,
As how I came into that desert place—
In brief, he led me to the gentle Duke,
Who gave me fresh array and entertainment,
Committing me unto my brother's love, 145
Who led me instantly unto his cave,
There stripped himself, and here upon his arm
The lioness had torn some flesh away,
Which all this while had bled; and now he fainted,
And cried, in fainting, upon Rosalind. 150
Brief, I recovered him, bound up his wound;
And after some small space, being strong at heart,
He sent me hither, stranger as I am,
To tell this story, that you might excuse
His broken promise, and to give this napkin, 155
Dyed in his blood, unto the shepherd youth
That he in sport doth call his Rosalind.

[*Rosalind swoons.*]

Cel. Why, how now, Ganymede? sweet Ganymede!
Oli. Many will swoon when they do look on blood.
Cel. There is more in it. Cousin Ganymede! 160
Oli. Look, he recovers.
Ros. I would I were at home.

77. purlieus: borders
79. neighbor bottom: nearby meadow
80. rank: line; **osiers:** willows
87. favor: appearance
87–88. bestows . . . sister: behaves like a mature woman
92. commend him: send his greetings
94. napkin: handkerchief
113. indented glides: serpentine turnings

130. occasion: reason
132. hurtling: commotion
141. recountments: narratives
151. Brief: in brief

Cel. We'll lead you thither. I pray you, will you take him by the arm?

Oli. Be of good cheer, youth. You a man? 165 You lack a man's heart.

Ros. I do so, I confess it. Ah, sirrah, a body would think this was well counterfeited! I pray you tell your brother how well I counterfeited. Heigh-ho!

Oli. This was not counterfeit. There is too 170 great testimony in your complexion that it was a passion of earnest.

169. counterfeited: pretended
172. passion . . . earnest: genuine fainting fit

Ros. Counterfeit, I assure you.

Oli. Well then, take a good heart and counterfeit to be a man. 175

Ros. So I do; but, i' faith, I should have been a woman by right.

Cel. Come, you look paler and paler. Pray you draw homewards. Good sir, go with us.

Oli. That will I; for I must bear answer back 180
How you excuse my brother, Rosalind.

Ros. I shall devise something. But I pray you commend my counterfeiting to him. Will you go?

Exeunt.

ACT V

Scene I. [*The Forest.*]

Enter [Touchstone *the*] Clown *and* Audrey.

Touch. We shall find a time, Audrey. Patience, gentle Audrey.

Aud. Faith, the priest was good enough, for all the old gentleman's saying.

Touch. A most wicked Sir Oliver, Audrey, a 5 most vile Martext! But, Audrey, there is a youth here in the forest lays claim to you.

Aud. Ay, I know who 'tis. He hath no interest in me in the world. Here comes the man you mean.

Enter William.

Touch. It is meat and drink to me to see a 10 clown. By my troth, we that have good wits have much to answer for. We shall be flouting; we cannot hold.

Will. Good even, Audrey.

Aud. God ye good even, William. 15

Will. And good even to you, sir.

Touch. Good even, gentle friend. Cover thy head, cover thy head. Nay, prithee be covered. How old are you, friend?

Will. Five-and-twenty, sir. 20

Touch. A ripe age. Is thy name William?

11. clown: rustic
12–13. We . . . hold: we cannot help mocking

Will. William, sir.

Touch. A fair name. Wast born i' the forest here?

Will. Ay, sir, I thank God.

Touch. "Thank God." A good answer. Art 25 rich?

Will. Faith, sir, soso.

Touch. "Soso" is good, very good, very excellent good; and yet it is not, it is but soso. Art thou wise?

Will. Ay, sir, I have a pretty wit. 30

Touch. Why, thou sayst well. I do now remember a saying, "The fool doth think he is wise, but the wise man knows himself to be a fool." The heathen philosopher, when he had a desire to eat a grape, would open his lips when he put it into his mouth, 35 meaning thereby that grapes were made to eat and lips to open. You do love this maid?

Will. I do, sir.

Touch. Give me your hand. Art thou learned?

Will. No, sir. 40

Touch. Then learn this of me: to have is to have; for it is a figure in rhetoric that drink, being poured out of a cup into a glass, by filling the one doth empty the other; for all your writers do consent that *ipse* is he. Now, you are not *ipse,* for I am he. 45

Will. Which he, sir?

Touch. He, sir, that must marry this woman. Therefore, you clown, abandon (which is in the vulgar, leave) the society (which in the boorish is, company) of this female (which in the common is, 50 woman); which together is, abandon the society of this female, or, clown, thou perishest; or, to thy better understanding, diest; or, to wit, I kill thee, make thee away, translate thy life into death, thy

liberty into bondage. I will deal in poison with 55
thee, or in bastinado, or in steel. I will bandy with
thee in faction; I will o'errun thee with policy; I will
kill thee a hundred and fifty ways. Therefore tremble
and depart.

Aud. Do, good William. 60

Will. God rest you merry, sir. *Exit.*

Enter CORIN.

Cor. Our master and mistress seeks you. Come
away, away!

Touch. Trip, Audrey! trip, Audrey! I attend, I attend. 65

Exeunt.

Scene II. [*The Forest.*]

Enter ORLANDO *and* OLIVER.

Orl. Is't possible that on so little acquaintance you
should like her? that but seeing, you should love her?
and loving, woo? and wooing, she should grant? And
will you persever to enjoy her?

Oli. Neither call the giddiness of it in question, 5
the poverty of her, the small acquaintance, my sudden wooing, nor her sudden consenting; but say with
me, I love Aliena; say with her that she loves me;
consent with both that we may enjoy each other. It
shall be to your good; for my father's house, 10
and all the revenue that was old Sir Rowland's, will I
estate upon you, and here live and die a shepherd.

Enter ROSALIND.

Orl. You have my consent. Let your wedding be
tomorrow. Thither will I invite the Duke and all's
contented followers. Go you and prepare 15
Aliena; for look you, here comes my Rosalind.

Ros. God save you, brother.

Oli. And you, fair sister. [*Exit.*]

Ros. O my dear Orlando, how it grieves me to see
thee wear thy heart in a scarf! 20

Orl. It is my arm.

Ros. I thought thy heart had been wounded with
the claws of a lion.

Orl. Wounded it is, but with the eyes of a lady.

Ros. Did your brother tell you how I coun- 25
terfeited to swoon when he showed me your handkercher?

Orl. Ay, and greater wonders than that.

Ros. O, I know where you are! Nay, 'tis true. There
was never anything so sudden but the fight of 30
two rams and Cæsar's thrasonical brag of "I came,
saw, and overcame." For your brother and my sister
no sooner met but they looked; no sooner looked but
they loved; no sooner loved but they sighed; no
sooner sighed but they asked one another the 35
reason; no sooner knew the reason but they sought
the remedy: and in these degrees have they made a
pair of stairs to marriage, which they will climb incontinent, or else be incontinent before marriage.
They are in the very wrath of love, and they 40
will together. Clubs cannot part them.

Orl. They shall be married tomorrow, and I will
bid the Duke to the nuptial. But, O, how bitter a
thing it is to look into happiness through another
man's eyes! By so much the more shall I to- 45
morrow be at the height of heart-heaviness, by how
much I shall think my brother happy in having what
he wishes for.

Ros. Why then, tomorrow I cannot serve your turn
for Rosalind? 50

Orl. I can live no longer by thinking.

Ros. I will weary you then no longer with idle talking. Know of me then (for now I speak to some purpose) that I know you are a gentleman of good conceit. I speak not this that you should bear a 55
good opinion of my knowledge, insomuch I say I
know you are; neither do I labor for a greater esteem
than may in some little measure draw a belief from
you, to do yourself good, and not to grace me. Believe then, if you please, that I can do strange 60
things. I have, since I was three year old, conversed
with a magician, most profound in his art and yet not
damnable. If you do love Rosalind so near the heart
as your gesture cries it out, when your brother mar-
ries Aliena shall you marry her. I know into 65
what straits of fortune she is driven; and it is not impossible to me, if it appear not inconvenient to you,
to set her before your eyes tomorrow human as she is,
and without any danger.

Orl. Speakst thou in sober meanings? 70

Ros. By my life, I do! which I tender dearly,

56. bastinado: beating
56–57. bandy . . . faction: dispute with you
57. oer'run . . . policy: best you by a stratagem
4. persever: accent on the second syllable

29. where . . . are: your meaning
31. thrasonical: boastful (from the braggart Thraso in Terence's *Eunuchus*)
38–39. incontinent . . . incontinent: without delay . . . unchaste
41. Clubs . . . them: i.e., they cannot be beaten apart.
53–54. to . . . purpose: earnestly
54–55. conceit: intelligence
56. insomuch: because
59. grace: honor
61. conversed: associated
62–63. not damnable: i.e., white magic only
64. gesture: behavior
67. inconvenient: improper
68. human . . . is: in her own person, not as a spirit
71. tender: cherish

though I say I am a magician. Therefore put you in your best array, bid your friends; for if you will be married tomorrow, you shall; and to Rosalind, if you will. 75

Enter SILVIUS *and* PHEBE.

Look, here comes a lover of mine and a lover of hers.
Phe. Youth, you have done me much ungentleness
To show the letter that I writ to you.
Ros. I care not if I have. It is my study
To seem despiteful and ungentle to you. 80
You are there followed by a faithful shepherd.
Look upon him, love him; he worships you.
Phe. Good shepherd, tell this youth what 'tis to love.
Sil. It is to be all made of sighs and tears;
And so am I for Phebe. 85
Phe. And I for Ganymede.
Orl. And I for Rosalind.
Ros. And I for no woman.
Sil. It is to be all made of faith and service;
And so am I for Phebe. 90
Phe. And I for Ganymede.
Orl. And I for Rosalind.
Ros. And I for no woman.
Sil. It is to be all made of fantasy,
All made of passion, and all made of wishes, 95
All adoration, duty, and observance,
All humbleness, all patience, and impatience,
All purity, all trial, all obedience;
And so am I for Phebe.
Phe. And so am I for Ganymede. 100
Orl. And so am I for Rosalind.
Ros. And so am I for no woman.
Phe. [*To Rosalind*] If this be so, why blame you me to love you?
Sil. [*To Phebe*] If this be so, why blame you me to love you?
Orl. If this be so, why blame you me to love you? 105
Ros. Why do you speak too, "Why blame you me to love you?"
Orl. To her that is not here, nor doth not hear.
Ros. Pray you, no more of this; 'tis like the howling of Irish wolves against the moon. [*To Silvius*] I will help you if I can.—[*To Phebe*] I would 110 love you if I could.—Tomorrow meet me all together.—[*To Phebe*] I will marry you if ever I marry woman, and I'll be married tomorrow.—[*To Orlando*] I will satisfy you if ever I satisfied man, and you shall be married tomorrow.—[*To Silvius*] 115 I will content you if what pleases you contents you, and you shall be married tomorrow.—[*To Orlando*] As you love Rosalind, meet.—[*To Silvius*] As you love Phebe, meet.—And as I love no woman, I'll meet. So fare you well. I have left you commands. 120
Sil. I'll not fail if I live.
Phe. Nor I.
Orl. Nor I.

Exeunt.

Scene III. [*The Forest.*]

Enter [TOUCHSTONE *the*] CLOWN *and* AUDREY.

Touch. Tomorrow is the joyful day, Audrey; tomorrow will we be married.
Aud. I do desire it with all my heart; and I hope it is no dishonest desire to desire to be a woman of the world. Here come two of the banished Duke's 5 pages.

Enter TWO PAGES.

1. Page. Well met, honest gentleman.
Touch. By my troth, well met. Come, sit, sit, and a song!
2. Page. We are for you. Sit i' the middle. 10
1. Page. Shall we clap into't roundly, without hawking or spitting or saying we are hoarse, which are the only prologues to a bad voice?
2. Page. I' faith, i' faith! and both in a tune, like two gypsies on a horse. 15

Song.

It was a lover and his lass—
With a hey, and a ho, and a hey nonino—
That o'er the green cornfield did pass
In springtime, the only pretty ring-time,
When birds do sing, hey ding a ding, ding. 20
Sweet lovers love the spring.

Between the acres of the rye—
With a hey, and a ho, and a hey nonino—
These pretty country folks would lie
In springtime, &c. 25

72. though . . . magician: despite my confession of magic art
77. done . . . ungentleness: treated me most uncivilly
79. study: deliberate intent
80. despiteful: spiteful
96. observance: devoted attention

4. dishonest: improper
4–5. woman . . . world: i.e., a married woman
11. clap . . . roundly: plunge into it at once
14. in . . . tune: in the same tune
18. cornfield: wheat field
19. only . . . ring-time: best time for wedding

This carol they began that hour—
With a hey, and a ho, and a hey nonino—
How that a life was but a flower
In springtime, &c.

And therefore take the present time— 30
With a hey, and a ho, and a hey nonino—
For love is crowned with the prime
In springtime, &c.

Touch. Truly, young gentlemen, though there was no great matter in the ditty, yet the note was 35 very untunable.

1. Page. You are deceived, sir. We kept time, we lost not our time.

Touch. By my troth, yes! I count it but time lost to hear such a foolish song. God be wi' you, 40 and God mend your voices! Come, Audrey.

Exeunt.

Scene IV. [*The Forest.*]

Enter DUKE SENIOR, AMIENS, JAQUES, ORLANDO, OLIVER, CELIA.

Duke S. Dost thou believe, Orlando, that the boy
Can do all this that he hath promised?

Orl. I sometimes do believe, and sometimes do not,
As those that fear they hope, and know they fear.

Enter ROSALIND, SILVIUS, *and* PHEBE.

Ros. Patience once more, whiles our compact is urged. 5
You say, if I bring in your Rosalind,
You will bestow her on Orlando here?

Duke S. That would I, had I kingdoms to give with her.

Ros. And you say you will have her when I bring her?

Orl. That would I, were I of all kingdoms king.

Ros. You say you'll marry me, if I be willing? 11

Phe. That will I, should I die the hour after.

Ros. But if you do refuse to marry me,
You'll give yourself to this most faithful shepherd?

Phe. So is the bargain. 15

Ros. You say that you'll have Phebe, if she will?

Sil. Though to have her and death were both one thing.

Ros. I have promised to make all this matter even.
Keep you your word, O Duke, to give your daughter;
You yours, Orlando, to receive his daughter; 20
Keep you your word, Phebe, that you'll marry me,
Or else, refusing me, to wed this shepherd;
Keep your word, Silvius, that you'll marry her
If she refuse me; and from hence I go,
To make these doubts all even. 25

Exeunt Rosalind and Celia.

Duke S. I do remember in this shepherd boy
Some lively touches of my daughter's favor.

Orl. My lord, the first time that I ever saw him
Methought he was a brother to your daughter.
But, my good lord, this boy is forest-born, 30
And hath been tutored in the rudiments
Of many desperate studies by his uncle,
Whom he reports to be a great magician,
Obscured in the circle of this forest.

Enter [TOUCHSTONE *the*] CLOWN *and* AUDREY.

Jaq. There is, sure, another flood toward, and 35 these couples are coming to the ark. Here comes a pair of very strange beasts, which in all tongues are called fools.

Touch. Salutation and greeting to you all!

Jaq. Good my lord, bid him welcome. This is 40 the motley-minded gentleman that I have so often met in the forest. He hath been a courtier, he swears.

Touch. If any man doubt that, let him put me to my purgation. I have trod a measure; I have flattered a lady; I have been politic with my 45 friend, smooth with mine enemy; I have undone three tailors; I have had four quarrels, and like to have fought one.

Jaq. And how was that ta'en up?

Touch. Faith, we met, and found the quarrel 50 was upon the seventh cause.

Jaq. How seventh cause? Good my lord, like this fellow.

Duke S. I like him very well.

Touch. Goddild you, sir; I desire you of the 55 like. I press in here, sir, amongst the rest of the country copulatives, to swear and to forswear, according as marriage binds and blood breaks. A poor virgin, sir, an ill-favored thing, sir, but mine own. A poor humor of mine, sir, to take that that no man 60

32. **prime:** spring
35. **ditty:** verses; **note:** tune
36. **untunable:** untuneful
4. **fear . . . hope:** are afraid to hope for fear of disappointment
5. **urged:** presented
18. **make . . . even:** smooth out all these matters
27. **lively touches:** vivid traits; **favor:** physiognomy
32. **desperate:** dangerous
34. **Obscured:** hidden
35. **toward:** in the offing
41. **motley-minded:** foolish
44. **purgation:** trial; **measure:** dance
46. **undone:** ruined (by not paying them)
47–48. **like . . . one:** nearly had to fight one
49. **ta'en up:** settled
57. **copulatives:** couples
58. **blood breaks:** passion breaks the marriage vows

else will. Rich honesty dwells like a miser, sir, in a poor house, as your pearl in your foul oyster.

Duke S. By my faith, he is very swift and sententious.

Touch. According to the fool's bolt, sir, and 65 such dulcet diseases.

Jaq. But, for the seventh cause. How did you find the quarrel on the seventh cause?

Touch. Upon a lie seven times removed (bear your body more seeming, Audrey): as thus, sir. I did 70 dislike the cut of a certain courtier's beard. He sent me word, if I said his beard was not cut well, he was in the mind it was. This is called the Retort Courteous. If I sent him word again it was not well cut, he would send me word he cut it to please himself. 75 This is called the Quip Modest. If again, it was not well cut, he disabled my judgment. This is called the Reply Churlish. If again, it was not well cut, he would answer I spake not true. This is called the Reproof Valiant. If again, it was not well cut, he 80 would say I lie. This is called the Countercheck Quarrelsome and so to the Lie Circumstantial and the Lie Direct.

Jaq. And how oft did you say his beard was not well cut? 85

Touch. I durst go no further than the Lie Circumstantial, nor he durst not give me the Lie Direct; and so we measured swords and parted.

Jaq. Can you nominate in order now the degrees of the lie? 90

Touch. O sir, we quarrel in print, by the book, as you have books for good manners. I will name you the degrees. The first, the Retort Courteous; the second, the Quip Modest; the third, the Reply Churlish; the fourth, the Reproof Valiant; the fifth, the 95 Countercheck Quarrelsome; the sixth, the Lie with Circumstance; the seventh, the Lie Direct. All these you may avoid but the Lie Direct, and you may avoid that too, with an If. I knew when seven justices could not take up a quarrel, but when the 100 parties were met themselves, one of them thought but of an If: as, "If you said so, then I said so"; and they shook hands and swore brothers. Your If is the only peacemaker. Much virtue in If.

Jaq. Is not this a rare fellow, my lord? He's 105 as good at anything, and yet a fool.

Duke S. He uses his folly like a stalking horse, and under the presentation of that he shoots his wit.

Enter HYMEN, ROSALIND, *and* CELIA. *Still music.*

Hym. Then is there mirth in heaven
When earthly things made even 110
Atone together.
Good Duke, receive thy daughter;
Hymen from heaven brought her,
Yea, brought her hither, 114
That thou mightst join her hand with his
Whose heart within his bosom is.

Ros. To you I give myself, for I am yours. [*To Duke*]
To you I give myself, for I am yours. [*To Orlando*]

Duke S. If there be truth in sight, you are my daughter.

Orl. If there be truth in sight, you are my Rosalind.

Phe. If sight and shape be true, 121
Why then, my love adieu!

Ros. I'll have no father, if you be not he. [*To Duke*]
I'll have no husband, if you be not he. [*To Orlando*]
Nor ne'er wed woman, if you be not she. [*To Phebe*]

Hym. Peace ho! I bar confusion. 126
'Tis I must make conclusion
Of these most strange events.
Here's eight that must take hands
To join in Hymen's bands, 130
If truth holds true contents.
[*To Orlando and Rosalind*]
You and you no cross shall part.
[*To Oliver and Celia*]
You and you are heart in heart.
[*To Phebe*]
You to his love must accord,
Or have a woman to your lord. 135
[*To Touchstone and Audrey*]
You and you are sure together
As the winter to foul weather.
Whiles a wedlock hymn we sing,
Feed yourselves with questioning,
That reason wonder may diminish 140
How thus we met, and these things finish.

Song.

Wedding is great Juno's crown—
O blessed bond of board and bed!

63–64. swift . . . sententious: quick with maxims (*sententiae*)
65. According . . . bolt: cf. the proverb "The fool's bolt is soon shot."
66. dulcet diseases: pleasant failings
70. seeming: decorously
76. Modest: moderate
77. disabled: disqualified
82. Circumstantial: indirect
88. measured swords: touching sword to sword was preliminary to a fencing bout.

107. stalking horse: a hunter's blind in the shape of a horse
108. presentation: semblance
S.D. 108. Hymen: Greek god of marriage
110. made even: reconciled
111. Atone together: are made one
131. If . . . contents: if faithfulness can bring true happiness
136. sure together: securely united

'Tis Hymen peoples every town;
High wedlock then be honored. 145
Honor, high honor, and renown
To Hymen, god of every town!

Duke S. O my dear niece, welcome thou art to me,
Even daughter, welcome, in no less degree!
Phe. [*To Silvius*] I will not eat my word, now thou art mine; 150
Thy faith my fancy to thee doth combine.

Enter SECOND BROTHER, [JAQUES DE BOYS].

2. Bro. Let me have audience for a word or two.
I am the second son of old Sir Rowland
That bring these tidings to this fair assembly.
Duke Frederick, hearing how that every day 155
Men of great worth resorted to this forest,
Addressed a mighty power, which were on foot
In his own conduct, purposely to take
His brother here and put him to the sword;
And to the skirts of this wild wood he came, 160
Where, meeting with an old religious man,
After some question with him, was converted
Both from his enterprise and from the world,
His crown bequeathing to his banished brother,
And all their lands restored to them again 165
That were with him exiled. This to be true
I do engage my life.
Duke S. Welcome, young man.
Thou offerst fairly to thy brothers' wedding:
To one, his lands withheld; and to the other,
A land itself at large, a potent dukedom. 170
First, in this forest let us do those ends
That here were well begun and well begot;
And after, every of this happy number
That have endured shrewd days and nights with us
Shall share the good of our returned fortune, 175
According to the measure of their states.
Meantime forget this new-fallen dignity
And fall into our rustic revelry.
Play, music, and you brides and bridegrooms all,
With measure heaped in joy, to the measures fall.
Jaq. Sir, by your patience. If I heard you rightly,
The Duke hath put on a religious life 182
And thrown into neglect the pompous court.
2. Bro. He hath.
Jaq. To him will I. Out of these convertites 185
There is much matter to be heard and learned.
[*To Duke*] You to your former honor I bequeath;
Your patience and your virtue well deserves it.
[*To Orlando*] You to a love that your true faith doth merit;
[*To Oliver*] You to your land and love and great allies; 190
[*To Silvius*] You to a long and well-deserved bed;
[*To Touchstone*] And you to wrangling, for thy loving voyage
Is but for two months victualed.—So, to your pleasures!
I am for other than for dancing measures.
Duke S. Stay, Jaques, stay. 195
Jaq. To see no pastime I! What you would have
I'll stay to know at your abandoned cave. *Exit.*
Duke S. Proceed, proceed. We will begin these rites,
As we do trust they'll end, in true delights.
[*The dance begins.*]

149. Even daughter: my true daughter
157. Addressed: prepared
158. In . . . conduct: under his personal command
162. question: conversation
167. engage: pledge
171. do . . . ends: fulfill those plans
174. shrewd: wretched
176. measure . . . states: i.e., proportionate status
180. to . . . fall: begin dancing
185. convertites: converts
193. Is . . . victualed: is equipped to last only two months

[EPILOGUE]

Ros. It is not the fashion to see the lady the epilogue; but it is no more unhandsome than to see the lord the prologue. If it be true that good wine needs no bush, 'tis true that a good play needs no epilogue. Yet to good wine they do use good bushes, and 5 good plays prove the better by the help of good epilogues. What a case am I in then, that am neither a good epilogue, nor cannot insinuate with you in the behalf of a good play! I am not furnished like a beggar; therefore to beg will not become me. My 10 way is to conjure you, and I'll begin with the women. I charge you, O women, for the love you bear to men, to like as much of this play as please you; and I charge you, O men, for the love you bear to women (as I perceive by your simp'ring none of you 15 hates them), that between you and the women the play may please. If I were a woman, I would kiss as many of you as had beards that pleased me, complexions that liked me, and breaths that I defied not; and I am sure, as many as have good beards, 20 or good faces, or sweet breaths, will, for my kind offer, when I make curtsy, bid me farewell.

Exeunt.

2. unhandsome: inappropriate
3–4. good . . . bush: the old sign of an alehouse was a bunch of ivy hanging over the door, possibly a custom connected with the god Bacchus.
11. conjure: exhort solemnly

19. liked: pleased; **defied:** resented

Hamlet and the Gravedigger

Engraved by G[eorg?] Goldberg after a painting by Friedrich Pecht.

The Tragedy of HAMLET

INTRODUCTION

Elizabethan audiences took special delight in sensational plays of murder and revenge. One of Shakespeare's earliest plays, *Titus Andronicus,* had catered to this taste, and Thomas Kyd had supplied in *The Spanish Tragedy* enough bloodshed and brutality to satisfy the most eager appetite for this type of drama. Shakespeare's *Hamlet* is an extraordinary example of a play that conforms to the current fashion for tragedies of revenge and yet succeeds in transcending sensationalism to achieve greatness as a profound study of human nature. As a practical playwright, writing for a company in which he had a financial interest, Shakespeare was concerned to produce plays that would attract the largest number of paying customers. Hence he was ready to supply a fashionable play when his company needed a revenge tragedy in the Senecan manner to meet competition from Philip Henslowe's rival players. The theme, and the name Hamlet, were already familiar on the English stage when Shakespeare sat down to write his play. Thomas Lodge, in *Wit's Misery* (1596), describes an old play of Hamlet in which the ghost "cried so miserably at the Theatre like an oyster-wife, 'Hamlet, revenge!' "

The most likely date for the first production of Shakespeare's play is 1600. James Roberts had the play entered in the *Stationers' Register* on July 26, 1602, and in 1603 a corrupt version known as Quarto 1 appeared—a pirated text probably put together by an actor or actors with less than perfect memories for the parts. Its title page described the play as "divers times acted by His Highness' servants in the City of London, as also in the two universities of Cambridge and Oxford and elsewhere." Clearly, by 1603 Shakespeare's play was already well known. To correct a version which misrepresented the true text of the play there appeared in 1604 Quarto 2: *The Tragical History of Hamlet, Prince of Denmark. By William Shakespeare. Newly imprinted and enlarged to almost as much again as it was, according to the true and perfect copy.* Sir Edmund Chambers comments that Quarto 2 "may very possibly be from the author's manuscript, but if so, numerous misprints suggest that this was not very legible." He thinks, however, that Quarto 1 and subsequent texts all derive from Quarto 2.

THE HAMLET "PROBLEM"

The interpretation of Hamlet's character has fascinated critics of Shakespeare since the nineteenth century. A vast literature has resulted from attempts to explain Hamlet's inability to take decisive action, his treatment of Ophelia, his madness, real or feigned, and a variety of other questions called forth by his actions. Shakespeare's own audience was not aware of a "Hamlet problem," and it was many generations before Hamlet became the subject of minute character analysis. When someone raised the question of Hamlet's delay in seeking his revenge, Thomas Hanmer, an eighteenth-century critic, observed that if the Prince had gone "naturally to work" in the first act the play would have ended there. When Shakespeare's audience went to the Globe in 1600 they expected to see a rousing melodrama, and that is what Shakespeare supplied—a sensational play with all the trappings of Senecan tragedy, including a great deal of suspense and a violent denouement filled with swordplay in the last act. Although *Hamlet* has in it much more than this, it is well to remember how the play appeared to an audience in 1600.

Since Coleridge's day, the reader's interest has focused upon the character of Hamlet himself. The play, after all, is about his problems, and the care that Shakespeare took in writing his lines shows his own concern with the interpretation of that part. We may be sure, however, that Shakespeare never intended to portray Hamlet as a delicate flower, a Bunthorne who would have "walked down Piccadilly with a lily in his hand." On the contrary, Hamlet reflected qualities that an Englishman in 1600 would have understood as those to be expected in a prince who had been educated to rule his country. The ideal of education for a leader was a proper balance between the contemplative and the active life, as exemplified, for instance, in Sir Philip Sidney. By implication, and by the words of other characters in the play, Shakespeare gives to Hamlet qualities familiar in the best of Renaissance Englishmen. Although Hamlet did not neglect the active life, he found his greatest pleasure in the cultivation of his mind. Such a man, brought back to the sordid realities of the Danish court, might well complain against the cursed spite of fate that forced him to set right the evils round him. Complain though he might, he would not neglect his duty. Instead, he would study the problems before him and attempt their solution when he had satisfied his reason. If Hamlet's methods of working out his problems are indirect and time-consuming, he is merely following the pattern of behavior of the thoughtful and speculative type of individual. Contrasted with Hamlet is Laertes, who reacts spontaneously and predictably.

Hamlet's qualities may be seen in many intellectual figures who enter public life and are brought face to face with the realities of practical politics. The happy politician is one who, unhampered by a philosophic mind, can respond automatically in accordance with the required conventions of behavior. The speculative thinker finds it difficult to react instantly and decisively in political crises. Perhaps one reason for the enduring popularity of *Hamlet* is the sympathy which all thoughtful and studious persons must feel for the Prince, and their self-identification with his type.

SOURCES, HISTORY, AND TEXT

Shakespeare perhaps based his own play upon the older *Hamlet,* but since this earlier play, if printed, has not survived, we can only conjecture what use he made of it. The plot derives ultimately from a late-twelfth-century history, Saxo Grammaticus' *Historia Danica,* first printed in 1514, but there is no evidence that Shakespeare knew the original source. The Hamlet story appears in François de Belleforest's *Histoires tragiques* (1582), and it was translated from Belleforest into English and printed in 1608 as *The History of Hamblet*. Shakespeare's play derives either directly or through the older *Hamlet* from Belleforest. Variations of the Hamlet legend are found in many analogues in European folk literature.

Hamlet has been the most popular of all of Shakespeare's plays. It has been translated into most of the important languages of the world and has been frequently acted ever since 1600. It was in the repertory of a company of English actors in Germany in 1626, and it has become almost as familiar on foreign stages as it is in the English theatre.

Frequent contemporary references indicate that *Hamlet* was one of Shakespeare's greatest stage successes. The first actor to play the role of

Hamlet was Richard Burbage, and since that time nearly every tragedian, including some women and children, have attempted the role, with varying degrees of success. *Hamlet* was the first of Shakespeare's plays revived by Sir William Davenant after the Restoration, with the great actor Thomas Betterton in the title role. Davenant, who remembered Burbage, passed on to Betterton his recollection of Burbage's interpretation, and Betterton transmitted to later actors the tradition of the melancholy Dane. *Hamlet* has been almost continuously on the stage since the seventeenth century. David Garrick was the most famous Hamlet of the eighteenth century, but many other actors challenged his pre-eminence. Garrick played the part in the court dress of the period. *Hamlet* in modern dress has a long tradition. John Philip Kemble, who began playing Hamlet in 1783, went back to the traditional black robes of the gloomy Dane. *Hamlet* was one of the early plays performed in Colonial America and has been almost continuously on the American stage ever since. The English stage in the nineteenth century saw many versions of *Hamlet,* including an incredible performance in 1803 by Master William Henry West Betty, a juvenile of twelve, and various interpretations of the Prince of Denmark by women, the most famous—if not the best—being the rendition at the end of the century by Sarah Bernhardt.

Hamlet is an unusually long play, and it clearly was cut for the Elizabethan stage. The performance in 1938 in New York of a full-length *Hamlet,* staged by Margaret Webster and Maurice Evans, proved a surprising success, but its length required an intermission for dinner.

The present text of *Hamlet* follows the usual practice of modern editors of collating Quarto 2 and the First Folio version. Quarto 2 provides the fullest text, having more than two hundred lines not found in the Folio, but it leaves out about eighty-five lines of the Folio. Sir Edmund Chambers thinks that Quarto 2 and the Folio "show a common origin," but he suggests that the copy from which the printers set the Folio text had been altered for use as a prompt copy. A third Quarto appeared in 1611, but it is merely a reprint of Quarto 2.

[Dramatis Personæ

CLAUDIUS, *King of Denmark.*
HAMLET, *nephew to the King.*
POLONIUS, *counselor to the King.*
HORATIO, *friend to Hamlet.*
LAERTES, *son to Polonius.*
VOLTEMAND,
CORNELIUS,
ROSENCRANTZ,
GUILDENSTERN, } *courtiers.*
OSRIC,
A GENTLEMAN,
MARCELLUS,
BERNARDO, } *soldiers.*
FRANCISCO,
REYNALDO, *servant to Polonius.*
FORTINBRAS, *Prince of Norway.*
PLAYERS.
TWO CLOWNS, *gravediggers.*
A NORWEGIAN CAPTAIN.
ENGLISH AMBASSADORS.
GERTRUDE, *Queen of Denmark, mother to Hamlet.*
OPHELIA, *daughter to Polonius.*
GHOST OF HAMLET'S FATHER.

Lords, Ladies, Priests, Officers, Soldiers, Sailors, Messengers, Attendants.

Scene: *Elsinore.*]

Defense with Rapier and Dagger
George Silver, *Paradoxes of Defense* (1599).

The Tragedy of HAMLET

ACT I

Scene I. [*Elsinore Castle. The platform of the watch.*]

Enter BERNARDO *and* FRANCISCO, *two sentinels* [*from opposite directions*].

Ber. Who's there?
Fran. Nay, answer me. Stand and unfold yourself.
Ber. Long live the King!
Fran. Bernardo?
Ber. He. 5
Fran. You come most carefully upon your hour.
Ber. 'Tis now struck twelve. Get thee to bed, Francisco.
Fran. For this relief much thanks. 'Tis bitter cold,
And I am sick at heart.
Ber. Have you had quiet guard?
Fran. Not a mouse stirring. 10
Ber. Well, good night.
If you do meet Horatio and Marcellus,
The rivals of my watch, bid them make haste.

Enter HORATIO *and* MARCELLUS.

Fran. I think I hear them. Stand! Who's there?
Hor. Friends to this ground.
Mar. And liegemen to the Dane. 15
Fran. Give you good night.
Mar. O, farewell, honest soldier.
Who hath relieved you?
Fran. Bernardo hath my place.
Give you good night. *Exit.*
Mar. Holla, Bernardo!
Ber. Say—
What, is Horatio there?
Hor. A piece of him. 19
Ber. Welcome, Horatio. Welcome, good Marcellus.
Mar. What, has this thing appeared again tonight?
Ber. I have seen nothing.
Mar. Horatio says 'tis but our fantasy,
And will not let belief take hold of him
Touching this dreaded sight, twice seen of us. 25
Therefore I have entreated him along,
With us to watch the minutes of this night,
That, if again this apparition come,
He may approve our eyes and speak to it.
Hor. Tush, tush, 'twill not appear.
Ber. Sit down awhile, 30
And let us once again assail your ears,
That are so fortified against our story,
What we two nights have seen.
Hor. Well, sit we down,
And let us hear Bernardo speak of this.
Ber. Last night of all, 35
When yond same star that's westward from the pole
Had made his course t' illume that part of heaven
Where now it burns, Marcellus and myself,
The bell then beating one—

Enter GHOST.

13. rivals: partners
15. Dane: King of Denmark
23. fantasy: fancy
29. approve: confirm
37. his: its; a common form of the neuter genitive

Mar. Peace! break thee off! Look where it comes again! 40
Ber. In the same figure, like the King that's dead.
Mar. Thou art a scholar; speak to it, Horatio.
Ber. Looks it not like the King? Mark it, Horatio.
Hor. Most like. It harrows me with fear and wonder.
Ber. It would be spoke to.
Mar. Question it, Horatio. 45
Hor. What art thou that usurpst this time of night
Together with that fair and warlike form
In which the majesty of buried Denmark
Did sometimes march? By heaven I charge thee speak!
Mar. It is offended.
Ber. See, it stalks away! 50
Hor. Stay! Speak, speak! I charge thee speak! *Exit Ghost.*
Mar. 'Tis gone and will not answer.
Ber. How now, Horatio? You tremble and look pale.
Is not this something more than fantasy?
What think you on't? 55
Hor. Before my God, I might not this believe
Without the sensible and true avouch
Of mine own eyes.
Mar. Is it not like the King?
Hor. As thou art to thyself.
Such was the very armor he had on 60
When he the ambitious Norway combated;
So frowned he once when, in an angry parle,
He smote the sledded Polacks on the ice.
'Tis strange.
Mar. Thus twice before, and jump at this dead hour, 65
With martial stalk hath he gone by our watch.
Hor. In what particular thought to work I know not;
But, in the gross and scope of my opinion,
This bodes some strange eruption to our state.
Mar. Good now, sit down, and tell me he that knows, 70
Why this same strict and most observant watch
So nightly toils the subject of the land,
And why such daily cast of brazen cannon
And foreign mart for implements of war;
Why such impress of shipwrights, whose sore task
Does not divide the Sunday from the week; 76
What might be toward, that this sweaty haste
Doth make the night joint-laborer with the day?
Who is't that can inform me?
Hor. That can I.
At least, the whisper goes so. Our last King, 80
Whose image even but now appeared to us,
Was, as you know, by Fortinbras of Norway,
Thereto pricked on by a most emulate pride,
Dared to the combat; in which our valiant Hamlet
(For so this side of our known world esteemed him)
Did slay this Fortinbras; who, by a sealed compact,
Well ratified by law and heraldry, 87
Did forfeit, with his life, all those his lands
Which he stood seized of, to the conqueror;
Against the which a moiety competent 90
Was gaged by our King; which had returned
To the inheritance of Fortinbras,
Had he been vanquisher, as, by the same comart
And carriage of the article designed,
His fell to Hamlet. Now, sir, young Fortinbras, 95
Of unimproved mettle hot and full,
Hath in the skirts of Norway, here and there,
Sharked up a list of lawless resolutes,
For food and diet to some enterprise
That hath a stomach in't; which is no other, 100
As it doth well appear unto our state,
But to recover of us, by strong hand
And terms compulsatory, those foresaid lands
So by his father lost; and this, I take it,
Is the main motive of our preparations, 105
The source of this our watch, and the chief head
Of this post-haste and romage in the land.
Ber. I think it be no other but e'en so.
Well may it sort that this portentous figure 109
Comes armed through our watch, so like the King
That was and is the question of these wars.
Hor. A mote it is to trouble the mind's eye.
In the most high and palmy state of Rome,
A little ere the mightiest Julius fell,
The graves stood tenantless, and the sheeted dead
Did squeak and gibber in the Roman streets; 116

48. buried Denmark: the dead King of Denmark
49. sometimes: formerly
57–58. the . . . eyes: confirmation by my sense of sight, the evidence of which must be true
61. Norway: King of Norway
63. Polacks: Edmond Malone's suggestion for "pollax" (spelled variously in the early texts)
65. jump: exactly
68. gross . . . scope: general range
70. Good now: if you will be so good
72. toils: wearies; **subject:** subjects
83. emulate: envious
86. by . . . compact: in accordance with agreed terms
87. law . . . heraldry: heraldic law; the rules agreed between the two nations (a hendiadys)
89. stood . . . of: possessed
90. moiety competent: adequate portion
91. gaged: pledged
93. comart: compact; the reading of the Second Quarto. The Folio reads "cou'nant."
94. carriage: tenor
96. unimproved: unemployed; i.e., never tested or not presently in use
98. Sharked . . . list: hastily enlisted; **resolutes:** adventurers
99. For . . . diet: as cannon fodder
100. hath . . . in't: requires courage
101. state: government
107. post-haste . . . romage: hasty preparation
109. Well . . . sort: it may well be appropriate
113. palmy: flourishing

As stars with trains of fire, and dews of blood,
Disasters in the sun; and the moist star
Upon whose influence Neptune's empire stands
Was sick almost to doomsday with eclipse. 120
And even the like precurse of fierce events,
As harbingers preceding still the fates
And prologue to the omen coming on,
Have heaven and earth together demonstrated
Unto our climatures and countrymen. 125

Enter GHOST *again.*

But soft! behold! Lo, where it comes again!
I'll cross it, though it blast me.—Stay, illusion!
If thou hast any sound, or use of voice,
Speak to me.
If there be any good thing to be done, 130
That may to thee do ease, and grace to me,
Speak to me.
If thou art privy to thy country's fate,
Which happily foreknowing may avoid,
O, speak! 135
Or if thou hast uphoarded in thy life
Extorted treasure in the womb of earth
(For which, they say, you spirits oft walk in death),
The cock crows.
Speak of it! Stay, and speak!—Stop it, Marcellus!
Mar. Shall I strike at it with my partisan? 140
Hor. Do, if it will not stand.
Ber. 'Tis here!
Hor. 'Tis here!
Mar. 'Tis gone! *Exit Ghost.*
We do it wrong, being so majestical,
To offer it the show of violence;
For it is as the air, invulnerable, 145
And our vain blows malicious mockery.
Ber. It was about to speak, when the cock crew.
Hor. And then it started, like a guilty thing
Upon a fearful summons. I have heard
The cock, that is the trumpet to the morn, 150
Doth with his lofty and shrill-sounding throat
Awake the god of day; and at his warning,
Whether in sea or fire, in earth or air,
The extravagant and erring spirit hies
To his confine; and of the truth herein 155
This present object made probation.
Mar. It faded on the crowing of the cock.
Some say that ever 'gainst that season comes
Wherein our Saviour's birth is celebrated,
The bird of dawning singeth all night long; 160
And then, they say, no spirit dare stir abroad,
The nights are wholesome, then no planets strike,
No fairy takes, nor witch hath power to charm,
So hallowed and so gracious is the time.
Hor. So have I heard and do in part believe it.
But look, the morn, in russet mantle clad, 166
Walks o'er the dew of yon high eastern hill.
Break we our watch up; and by my advice
Let us impart what we have seen tonight
Unto young Hamlet; for, upon my life, 170
This spirit, dumb to us, will speak to him.
Do you consent we shall acquaint him with it,
As needful in our loves, fitting our duty?
Mar. Let's do't, I pray; and I this morning know
Where we shall find him most conveniently. 175
Exeunt.

117. As stars, etc.: a line may be missing here. **Stars with trains of fire** are meteors.
118. Disasters: omens of disaster; **moist star:** moon
119. Upon . . . stands: i.e., which controls the ocean
120. sick . . . eclipse: almost eclipsed, as the Bible foretells it will be on the Day of Judgment (Matt. 24:29)
121. precurse: precursor
122. harbingers: literally, officials who preceded important people to arrange for their reception; **still:** ever
123. omen: calamity
134. happily: perhaps
140. partisan: a long-handled spear with a lateral blade
146. malicious mockery: ineffectual malice, because it cannot hurt a ghost
154. extravagant . . . erring: straying from its proper haunts
156. made probation: proved
158. 'gainst: just before
162. strike: exert malign influence
163. fairy: fiend; **takes:** bewitches

Scene II. [*Elsinore Castle. An audience chamber.*]

Flourish. Enter CLAUDIUS, *King of Denmark,* GERTRUDE *the Queen,* HAMLET, POLONIUS, LAERTES, *and his sister* OPHELIA, LORDS ATTENDANT.

King. Though yet of Hamlet our dear brother's death
The memory be green, and that it us befitted
To bear our hearts in grief, and our whole kingdom
To be contracted in one brow of woe,
Yet so far hath discretion fought with nature 5
That we with wisest sorrow think on him
Together with remembrance of ourselves.
Therefore our sometime sister, now our queen,
The imperial jointress to this warlike state,
Have we, as 'twere with a defeated joy, 10
With an auspicious, and a dropping eye,
With mirth in funeral, and with dirge in marriage,
In equal scale weighing delight and dole,
Taken to wife; nor have we herein barred
Your better wisdoms, which have freely gone 15
With this affair along. For all, our thanks.
Now follows, that you know, young Fortinbras,

9. jointress: widow with rights in her husband's estate
10. defeated: overcome
13. dole: grief

Holding a weak supposal of our worth,
Or thinking by our late dear brother's death
Our state to be disjoint and out of frame, 20
Colleagued with this dream of his advantage,
He hath not failed to pester us with message
Importing the surrender of those lands
Lost by his father, with all bands of law,
To our most valiant brother. So much for him. 25

Enter VOLTEMAND *and* CORNELIUS.

Now for ourself and for this time of meeting.
Thus much the business is: we have here writ
To Norway, uncle of young Fortinbras,
Who, impotent and bedrid, scarcely hears
Of this his nephew's purpose, to suppress 30
His further gait herein, in that the levies,
The lists, and full proportions are all made
Out of his subject; and we here dispatch
You, good Cornelius, and you, Voltemand,
For bearers of this greeting to old Norway, 35
Giving to you no further personal power
To business with the King more than the scope
Of these dilated articles allow. [*Gives a paper.*]
Farewell, and let your haste commend your duty.

Cor., Volt. In that, and all things, will we show our duty. 40

King. We doubt it nothing. Heartily farewell.

Exeunt Voltemand and Cornelius.

And now, Laertes, what's the news with you?
You told us of some suit. What is't, Laertes?
You cannot speak of reason to the Dane 44
And lose your voice. What wouldst thou beg, Laertes,
That shall not be my offer, not thy asking?
The head is not more native to the heart,
The hand more instrumental to the mouth,
Than is the throne of Denmark to thy father.
What wouldst thou have, Laertes?

Laer. My dear lord,
Your leave and favor to return to France, 51
From whence though willingly I came to Denmark
To show my duty in your coronation,
Yet now I must confess, that duty done, 54
My thoughts and wishes bend again toward France
And bow them to your gracious leave and pardon.

King. Have you your father's leave? What says Polonius?

Pol. He hath, my lord, wrung from me my slow leave
By laborsome petition, and at last
Upon his will I sealed my hard consent. 60
I do beseech you give him leave to go.

King. Take thy fair hour, Laertes. Time be thine,
And thy best graces spend it at thy will!
But now, my cousin Hamlet, and my son—

Ham. [*Aside*] A little more than kin, and less than kind! 65

King. How is it that the clouds still hang on you?

Ham. Not so, my lord. I am too much i' the sun.

Queen. Good Hamlet, cast thy nighted color off,
And let thine eye look like a friend on Denmark.
Do not forever with thy vailed lids 70
Seek for thy noble father in the dust.
Thou knowst 'tis common, all that lives must die,
Passing through nature to eternity.

Ham. Ay, madam, it is common.

Queen. If it be,
Why seems it so particular with thee? 75

Ham. Seems, madam? Nay, it is. I know not "seems."
'Tis not alone my inky cloak, good mother,
Nor customary suits of solemn black,
Nor windy suspiration of forced breath,
No, nor the fruitful river in the eye, 80
Nor the dejected havior of the visage,
Together with all forms, moods, shapes of grief,
That can denote me truly. These indeed seem,
For they are actions that a man might play;
But I have that within which passeth show— 85
These but the trappings and the suits of woe.

King. 'Tis sweet and commendable in your nature, Hamlet,
To give these mourning duties to your father;
But you must know, your father lost a father;
That father lost, lost his, and the survivor bound
In filial obligation for some term 91
To do obsequious sorrow. But to persever
In obstinate condolement is a course
Of impious stubbornness. 'Tis unmanly grief;
It shows a will most incorrect to heaven, 95
A heart unfortified, a mind impatient,
An understanding simple and unschooled;
For what we know must be, and is as common

18. weak supposal: poor estimation; **our:** my
21. Colleagued: allied; **advantage:** superiority
22. pester . . . message: bother me with frequent messages
24. all . . . law: complete legality
31. gait: proceeding
38. dilated: set forth in detail
39. let . . . duty: show your duty in a speedy departure rather than courteous farewells.
47. native: naturally akin
51. leave . . . favor: favorable leave
63. thy . . . will: may your best qualities govern the way you spend it.
65. more . . . kind: i.e., Claudius is Hamlet's stepfather as well as his uncle, but Hamlet does not feel kindly toward him. The word **cousin** was a vague term of kinship.
67. sun: a pun on sun/son
68. nighted: dark
70. vailed: downcast
80. fruitful: copious
81. havior: behavior
92. obsequious sorrow: sorrow suitable for a funeral; **persever:** persevere
93. obstinate condolement: inconsolable sorrow

As any the most vulgar thing to sense,
Why should we in our peevish opposition 100
Take it to heart? Fie! 'tis a fault to heaven,
A fault against the dead, a fault to nature,
To reason most absurd, whose common theme
Is death of fathers, and who still hath cried,
From the first corse till he that died today, 105
"This must be so." We pray you throw to earth
This unprevailing woe, and think of us
As of a father; for let the world take note
You are the most immediate to our throne,
And with no less nobility of love 110
Than that which dearest father bears his son
Do I impart toward you. For your intent
In going back to school in Wittenberg,
It is most retrograde to our desire;
And we beseech you, bend you to remain 115
Here in the cheer and comfort of our eye,
Our chiefest courtier, cousin, and our son.

Queen. Let not thy mother lose her prayers, Hamlet:
I pray thee stay with us, go not to Wittenberg. 119

Ham. I shall in all my best obey you, madam.

King. Why, 'tis a loving and a fair reply.
Be as ourself in Denmark. Madam, come.
This gentle and unforced accord of Hamlet
Sits smiling to my heart; in grace whereof,
No jocund health that Denmark drinks today 125
But the great cannon to the clouds shall tell,
And the King's rouse the heaven shall bruit again,
Respeaking earthly thunder. Come away.

Flourish. Exeunt all but Hamlet.

Ham. O that this too too solid flesh would melt,
Thaw, and resolve itself into a dew! 130
Or that the Everlasting had not fixed
His canon 'gainst self-slaughter! O God! God!
How weary, stale, flat, and unprofitable
Seem to me all the uses of this world!
Fie on't! ah, fie! 'Tis an unweeded garden 135
That grows to seed; things rank and gross in nature
Possess it merely. That it should come to this!
But two months dead—nay, not so much, not two!
So excellent a king, that was to this
Hyperion to a satyr; so loving to my mother 140
That he might not beteem the winds of heaven
Visit her face too roughly. Heaven and earth!
Must I remember? Why, she would hang on him
As if increase of appetite had grown
By what it fed on; and yet, within a month— 145
Let me not think on't! Frailty, thy name is woman!—
A little month, or ere those shoes were old
With which she followed my poor father's body
Like Niobe, all tears—why she, even she 149
(O God! a beast that wants discourse of reason
Would have mourned longer) married with my uncle;
My father's brother, but no more like my father
Than I to Hercules. Within a month,
Ere yet the salt of most unrighteous tears
Had left the flushing in her galled eyes, 155
She married. O, most wicked speed, to post
With such dexterity to incestuous sheets!
It is not, nor it cannot come to good.
But break my heart, for I must hold my tongue!

Enter HORATIO, MARCELLUS, *and* BERNARDO.

Hor. Hail to your lordship!

Ham. I am glad to see you well. 160
Horatio—or I do forget myself!

Hor. The same, my lord, and your poor servant ever.

Ham. Sir, my good friend—I'll change that name with you.
And what make you from Wittenberg, Horatio?
Marcellus? 165

Mar. My good lord!

Ham. I am very glad to see you.—[*To Bernardo*] Good even, sir.—
But what, in faith, make you from Wittenberg?

Hor. A truant disposition, good my lord.

Ham. I would not hear your enemy say so, 170
Nor shall you do my ear that violence
To make it truster of your own report
Against yourself. I know you are no truant.
But what is your affair in Elsinore?
We'll teach you to drink deep ere you depart. 175

Hor. My lord, I came to see your father's funeral.

Ham. I prithee do not mock me, fellow student,
I think it was to see my mother's wedding.

Hor. Indeed, my lord, it followed hard upon.

Ham. Thrift, thrift, Horatio! The funeral baked meats 180

99. most . . . sense: most common object of perception
100. peevish: childish
107. unprevailing: vain
112. impart: express my mind
114. retrograde: contrary
115. bend you: submit yourself
124. grace: honor
127. rouse: carousal; **bruit:** report
129. solid: the First Folio reading. The Second Quarto reading "sallied" is preferred by some editors and the passage has become a bibliographical crux. But **solid** is a forceful and reasonable word in the context. A recent article by Sidney Warhaft in *ELH*, XXVIII (1961), 21–30, offers additional support for **solid** in the light of Elizabethan physiological theory.

141. beteem: permit
149. Niobe: a woman whose boasting of her children offended the goddess Leto, with the result that all were killed and Niobe herself was transformed to a stone from which tears flowed perpetually
150. wants: lacks; **discourse . . . reason:** rationality
154. unrighteous: i.e., hypocritical
155. flushing: inflammation; **galled:** irritated
163. change: exchange
179. hard upon: soon after

Did coldly furnish forth the marriage tables.
Would I had met my dearest foe in heaven
Or ever I had seen that day, Horatio!
My father—methinks I see my father.
Hor. O, where, my lord?
Ham. In my mind's eye, Horatio. 185
Hor. I saw him once. He was a goodly king.
Ham. He was a man, take him for all in all.
I shall not look upon his like again.
Hor. My lord, I think I saw him yesternight.
Ham. Saw? who? 190
Hor. My lord, the King your father.
Ham. The King my father?
Hor. Season your admiration for a while
With an attent ear, till I may deliver,
Upon the witness of these gentlemen,
This marvel to you.
Ham. For God's love let me hear! 195
Hor. Two nights together had these gentlemen
(Marcellus and Bernardo) on their watch
In the dead waste and middle of the night
Been thus encount'red. A figure like your father,
Armed at point exactly, cap-a-pe, 200
Appears before them and with solemn march
Goes slow and stately by them. Thrice he walked
By their oppressed and fear-surprised eyes,
Within his truncheon's length; whilst they, distilled
Almost to jelly with the act of fear, 205
Stand dumb and speak not to him. This to me
In dreadful secrecy impart they did,
And I with them the third night kept the watch;
Where, as they had delivered, both in time, 209
Form of the thing, each word made true and good,
The apparition comes. I knew your father:
These hands are not more like.
Ham. But where was this?
Mar. My lord, upon the platform where we watched.
Ham. Did you not speak to it?
Hor. My lord, I did;
But answer made it none. Yet once methought 215
It lifted up it head and did address
Itself to motion, like as it would speak;
But even then the morning cock crew loud,
And at the sound it shrunk in haste away
And vanished from our sight.
Ham. 'Tis very strange. 220
Hor. As I do live, my honored lord, 'tis true;
And we did think it writ down in our duty
To let you know of it.
Ham. Indeed, indeed, sirs, but this troubles me.
Hold you the watch tonight?
Both [*Mar. and Ber.*] We do, my lord. 225
Ham. Armed, say you?
Both. Armed, my lord.
Ham. From top to toe?
Both. My lord, from head to foot.
Ham. Then saw you not his face?
Hor. O, yes, my lord! He wore his beaver up.
Ham. What, looked he frowningly? 231
Hor. A countenance more in sorrow than in anger.
Ham. Pale or red?
Hor. Nay, very pale.
Ham. And fixed his eyes upon you?
Hor. Most constantly.
Ham. I would I had been there. 235
Hor. It would have much amazed you.
Ham. Very like, very like. Stayed it long?
Hor. While one with moderate haste might tell a hundred.
Both. Longer, longer.
Hor. Not when I saw't.
Ham. His beard was grizzled—no? 240
Hor. It was, as I have seen it in his life,
A sable silvered.
Ham. I will watch tonight.
Perchance 'twill walk again.
Hor. I warr'nt it will.
Ham. If it assume my noble father's person,
I'll speak to it, though hell itself should gape 245
And bid me hold my peace. I pray you all,
If you have hitherto concealed this sight,
Let it be tenable in your silence still;
And whatsoever else shall hap tonight,
Give it an understanding but no tongue. 250
I will requite your loves. So, fare you well.
Upon the platform, 'twixt eleven and twelve,
I'll visit you.
All. Our duty to your honor.
Ham. Your loves, as mine to you. Farewell.
Exeunt [*all but Hamlet*].
My father's spirit—in arms? All is not well. 255
I doubt some foul play. Would the night were come!
Till then sit still, my soul. Foul deeds will rise,
Though all the earth o'erwhelm them, to men's eyes.
Exit.

182. dearest: bitterest. The word derives from Old English *deor* (dire).
192. admiration: wonder
193. deliver: report
198. dead waste: empty expanse
200. at point: fully; **cap-a-pe:** from head to foot
203. oppressed . . . fear-surprised: overcome by surprise
204. truncheon: a baton carried by a military officer
216. it: its
218. even: just
230. beaver: visor
237. Very like: most likely
240. grizzled: mingled with gray
245. hell . . . gape: if the spirit was an evil one it would be dangerous to speak to it, and it might indeed carry the speaker off to hell.
248. tenable: held
254. Your . . . you: Hamlet insists on friendship rather than deference.
256. doubt: fear

Scene III. [*Elsinore. Polonius' house.*]

Enter LAERTES *and* OPHELIA.

Laer. My necessaries are embarked. Farewell.
And, sister, as the winds give benefit
And convoy is assistant, do not sleep,
But let me hear from you.
Oph. Do you doubt that?
Laer. For Hamlet, and the trifling of his favor,
Hold it a fashion, and a toy in blood; 6
A violet in the youth of primy nature,
Forward, not permanent—sweet, not lasting;
The perfume and suppliance of a minute;
No more.
Oph. No more but so?
Laer. Think it no more. 10
For nature crescent does not grow alone
In thews and bulk, but as this temple waxes,
The inward service of the mind and soul
Grows wide withal. Perhaps he loves you now,
And now no soil nor cautel doth besmirch 15
The virtue of his will; but you must fear,
His greatness weighed, his will is not his own,
For he himself is subject to his birth.
He may not, as unvalued persons do,
Carve for himself, for on his choice depends 20
The safety and health of this whole state,
And therefore must his choice be circumscribed
Unto the voice and yielding of that body
Whereof he is the head. Then if he says he loves you,
It fits your wisdom so far to believe it 25
As he in his particular act and place
May give his saying deed, which is no further
Than the main voice of Denmark goes withal.
Then weigh what loss your honor may sustain
If with too credent ear you list his songs, 30
Or lose your heart, or your chaste treasure open
To his unmast'red importunity.
Fear it, Ophelia, fear it, my dear sister,
And keep you in the rear of your affection,
Out of the shot and danger of desire. 35
The chariest maid is prodigal enough
If she unmask her beauty to the moon.
Virtue itself scapes not calumnious strokes.
The canker galls the infants of the spring
Too oft before their buttons be disclosed, 40
And in the morn and liquid dew of youth
Contagious blastments are most imminent.
Be wary then; best safety lies in fear.
Youth to itself rebels, though none else near.
Oph. I shall the effect of this good lesson keep 45
As watchman to my heart. But, good my brother,
Do not, as some ungracious pastors do,
Show me the steep and thorny way to heaven,
Whiles, like a puffed and reckless libertine,
Himself the primrose path of dalliance treads 50
And recks not his own rede.
Laer. O, fear me not!

Enter POLONIUS.

I stay too long. But here my father comes.
A double blessing is a double grace;
Occasion smiles upon a second leave. 54
Pol. Yet here, Laertes? Aboard, aboard, for shame!
The wind sits in the shoulder of your sail,
And you are stayed for. There—my blessing with thee!
And these few precepts in thy memory
Look thou character. Give thy thoughts no tongue,
Nor any unproportioned thought his act. 60
Be thou familiar, but by no means vulgar:
Those friends thou hast, and their adoption tried,
Grapple them to thy soul with hoops of steel;
But do not dull thy palm with entertainment 64
Of each new-hatched, unfledged comrade. Beware
Of entrance to a quarrel; but being in,
Bear't that the opposed may beware of thee.
Give every man thine ear, but few thy voice;
Take each man's censure, but reserve thy judgment.
Costly thy habit as thy purse can buy, 70
But not expressed in fancy; rich, not gaudy;
For the apparel oft proclaims the man,
And they in France of the best rank and station

2–4. **as . . . you:** do not neglect opportunities offered by favorable winds and convenient convoys to write me regularly.
5. **For:** as for
6. **fashion:** fad; **toy . . . blood:** whim inspired by the amorous instinct of youth
7. **youth . . . nature:** early spring of life
8. **Forward:** precocious
9. **suppliance:** supply; pastime
11. **nature:** a living creature; **crescent:** growing
12. **thews:** strength; **temple:** body
14. **withal:** at the same time
15. **cautel:** deceit
17. **His . . . weighed:** considering his greatness
20. **Carve for:** gratify
23. **voice . . . yielding:** assenting voice; approval
30. **credent:** credulous
34. **affection:** feelings
35. **shot . . . danger:** dangerous range
36. **chariest:** most careful
39. **canker:** cankerworm; **infants . . . spring:** early spring blossoms
40. **buttons:** buds
44. **Youth . . . near:** the unstable temper of the young responds to the slightest temptation.
47. **ungracious:** ungodly
51. **recks:** heeds; **rede:** counsel
54. **Occasion:** opportunity
57. **stayed:** waited
59. **Look . . . character:** see that you inscribe
60. **unproportioned:** immoderate
61. **familiar:** friendly; **vulgar:** commonly accessible
64. **entertainment:** welcome (by handshaking)
69. **censure:** synonymous with **judgment**
71. **in fancy:** i.e., fantastically

Are most select and generous, chief in that.
Neither a borrower nor a lender be; 75
For loan oft loses both itself and friend,
And borrowing dulls the edge of husbandry.
This above all: to thine own self be true,
And it must follow, as the night the day,
Thou canst not then be false to any man. 80
Farewell. My blessing season this in thee!

Laer. Most humbly do I take my leave, my lord.

Pol. The time invites you. Go, your servants tend.

Laer. Farewell, Ophelia, and remember well
What I have said to you.

Oph. 'Tis in my memory locked, 85
And you yourself shall keep the key of it.

Laer. Farewell. *Exit.*

Pol. What is't, Ophelia, he hath said to you?

Oph. So please you, something touching the Lord Hamlet.

Pol. Marry, well bethought! 90
'Tis told me he hath very oft of late
Given private time to you, and you yourself
Have of your audience been most free and bounteous.
If it be so—as so 'tis put on me,
And that in way of caution—I must tell you 95
You do not understand yourself so clearly
As it behooves my daughter and your honor.
What is between you? Give me up the truth.

Oph. He hath, my lord, of late made many tenders
Of his affection to me. 100

Pol. Affection? Pooh! You speak like a green girl,
Unsifted in such perilous circumstance.
Do you believe his tenders, as you call them?

Oph. I do not know, my lord, what I should think.

Pol. Marry, I will teach you! Think yourself a baby 105
That you have ta'en these tenders for true pay,
Which are not sterling. Tender yourself more dearly,
Or (not to crack the wind of the poor phrase,
Running it thus) you'll tender me a fool. 109

Oph. My lord, he hath importuned me with love
In honorable fashion.

Pol. Ay, fashion you may call it. Go to, go to!

Oph. And hath given countenance to his speech, my lord,
With almost all the holy vows of heaven. 114

Pol. Ay, springes to catch woodcocks! I do know,
When the blood burns, how prodigal the soul
Lends the tongue vows. These blazes, daughter,
Giving more light than heat, extinct in both
Even in their promise, as it is a-making,
You must not take for fire. From this time 120
Be somewhat scanter of your maiden presence.
Set your entreatments at a higher rate
Than a command to parley. For Lord Hamlet,
Believe so much in him, that he is young,
And with a larger tether may he walk 125
Than may be given you. In few, Ophelia,
Do not believe his vows; for they are brokers,
Not of that dye which their investments show,
But mere implorators of unholy suits,
Breathing like sanctified and pious bawds, 130
The better to beguile. This is for all:
I would not, in plain terms, from this time forth
Have you so slander any moment leisure
As to give words or talk with the Lord Hamlet.
Look to't, I charge you. Come your ways. 135

Oph. I shall obey, my lord.

Exeunt.

[Scene IV. *Elsinore Castle. The platform of the watch.*]

Enter HAMLET, HORATIO, *and* MARCELLUS.

Ham. The air bites shrewdly; it is very cold.

Hor. It is a nipping and an eager air.

Ham. What hour now?

Hor. I think it lacks of twelve.

Mar. No, it is struck.

Hor. Indeed? I heard it not. It then draws near the season 5
Wherein the spirit held his wont to walk.

A flourish of trumpets, and two pieces go off.

What does this mean, my lord?

Ham. The King doth wake tonight and takes his rouse,

77. **husbandry:** thrift
83. **tend:** await thee
90. **Marry:** a mild oath, derived from "By the Virgin Mary"
99. **tenders:** offers
102. **Unsifted:** untried
106. **tenders:** pun on the sense "legal tender"
107. **Tender . . . dearly:** set a higher value on yourself
108–9. **not . . . thus:** not to force the metaphor until it is exhausted. **Running** is J. P. Collier's conjecture; the Folio reads "Roaming" and the Second Quarto "Wrong."
109. **tender . . . fool:** offer me a fool for a daughter
113. **countenance:** support
115. **springes:** snares; **woodcocks:** gullible fools
122. **entreatments:** dealings
123. **command . . . parley:** it was a commonplace to refer to the courting of women in terms of a military siege.
125. **larger tether:** more latitude
127. **brokers:** panders
128. **Not . . . show:** not holy, as their clothing would signify. **Investments** is used in the sense "clothing," with a quibble carrying out the metaphor begun with the word **brokers.**
129. **implorators:** urgers
130. **Breathing . . . bawds:** speaking piously to disguise their bawdy nature. **Bawds** was suggested by Lewis Theobald; the Second Quarto and First Folio read "bonds."
131. **This . . . all:** this is my final word.
133. **slander:** misuse disgracefully; **moment leisure:** leisure of a moment
1. **shrewdly:** keenly
2. **eager:** sharp, from the French *aigre*
6. **held . . . wont:** was accustomed

Keeps wassail, and the swagg'ring upspring reels,
And, as he drains his draughts of Rhenish down, 10
The kettledrum and trumpet thus bray out
The triumph of his pledge.
Hor. Is it a custom?
Ham. Ay, marry, is't;
But to my mind, though I am native here
And to the manner born, it is a custom 15
More honored in the breach than the observance.
This heavy-headed revel east and west
Makes us traduced and taxed of other nations;
They clepe us drunkards and with swinish phrase
Soil our addition; and indeed it takes 20
From our achievements, though performed at height,
The pith and marrow of our attribute.
So oft it chances in particular men
That for some vicious mole of nature in them,
As in their birth,—wherein they are not guilty, 25
Since nature cannot choose his origin,—
By their o'ergrowth of some complexion,
Oft breaking down the pales and forts of reason,
Or by some habit that too much o'erleavens
The form of plausive manners, that these men 30
Carrying, I say, the stamp of one defect,
Being nature's livery, or fortune's star,
Their virtues else—be they as pure as grace,
As infinite as man may undergo—
Shall in the general censure take corruption 35
From that particular fault. The dram of e'il
Doth all the noble substance often dout
To his own scandal.

Enter GHOST.

Hor. Look, my lord, it comes!
Ham. Angels and ministers of grace defend us!
Be thou a spirit of health or goblin damned, 40
Bring with thee airs from heaven or blasts from hell,
Be thy intents wicked or charitable,
Thou comest in such a questionable shape
That I will speak to thee. I'll call thee Hamlet,
King, father, royal Dane. O, answer me! 45
Let me not burst in ignorance, but tell
Why thy canonized bones, hearsed in death,
Have burst their cerements; why the sepulcher
Wherein we saw thee quietly inurned
Hath oped his ponderous and marble jaws 50
To cast thee up again. What may this mean
That thou, dead corse, again in complete steel,
Revisits thus the glimpses of the moon,
Making night hideous, and we fools of nature
So horridly to shake our disposition 55
With thoughts beyond the reaches of our souls?
Say, why is this? wherefore? What should we do?
Ghost beckons Hamlet.
Hor. It beckons you to go away with it,
As if it some impartment did desire
To you alone.
Mar. Look with what courteous action 60
It waves you to a more removed ground.
But do not go with it!
Hor. No, by no means!
Ham. It will not speak. Then will I follow it.
Hor. Do not, my lord!
Ham. Why, what should be the fear?
I do not set my life at a pin's fee; 65
And for my soul, what can it do to that,
Being a thing immortal as itself?
It waves me forth again. I'll follow it.
Hor. What if it tempt you toward the flood, my lord,
Or to the dreadful summit of the cliff 70
That beetles o'er his base into the sea,
And there assume some other, horrible form
Which might deprive your sovereignty of reason
And draw you into madness? Think of it.
The very place puts toys of desperation, 75
Without more motive, into every brain
That looks so many fathoms to the sea
And hears it roar beneath.
Ham. It waves me still.
Go on, I'll follow thee.
Mar. You shall not go, my lord.
Ham. Hold off your hands! 80
Hor. Be ruled, you shall not go.
Ham. My fate cries out
And makes each petty artery in this body
As hardy as the Nemean lion's nerve.
[*Ghost beckons.*]

9. upspring: a German dance
10. Rhenish: Rhine wine
12. triumph . . . pledge: the triumphant feat of proposing a toast and draining his cup
16. breach: neglect
18. taxed: censured
19. clepe: call
20. addition: title
22. pith . . . marrow: very essence; **attribute:** reputation
23. particular: individual
24. mole . . . nature: natural fault
27. o'ergrowth . . . complexion: overdevelopment of some trait of their temperament. The human **complexion** was the compound of humors that determined personality.
28. pales . . . forts: synonymous: "limits"
30. plausive: pleasing
32. nature's livery: inherent distinguishing characteristic; **fortune's star:** acquired trait determined by fortune
35. censure: judgment
36. e'il: evil
37. dout: efface
38. scandal: disgrace
47. canonized: buried with religious rites
48. cerements: graveclothes
54. fools . . . nature: humans whose comprehension is limited to natural phenomena
73. sovereignty . . . reason: rational control
75. toys . . . desperation: desperate fancies
83. Nemean lion: an invulnerable beast finally slain by Hercules

Still am I called. Unhand me, gentlemen— 84
By heaven, I'll make a ghost of him that lets me!
I say, away!—Go on, I'll follow thee.
Exeunt Ghost and Hamlet.

Hor. He waxes desperate with imagination.
Mar. Let's follow; 'tis not fit thus to obey him.
Hor. Have after. To what issue will this come?
Mar. Something is rotten in the state of Denmark. 90
Hor. Heaven will direct it.
Mar. Nay, let's follow him.
Exeunt.

[Scene V. *Same. Another part of the ramparts.*]

Enter GHOST *and* HAMLET.

Ham. Whither wilt thou lead me? Speak, I'll go no further.
Ghost. Mark me.
Ham. I will.
Ghost. My hour is almost come,
When I to sulph'rous and tormenting flames
Must render up myself.
Ham. Alas, poor ghost! 4
Ghost. Pity me not, but lend thy serious hearing
To what I shall unfold.
Ham. Speak, I am bound to hear.
Ghost. So art thou to revenge, when thou shalt hear.
Ham. What?
Ghost. I am thy father's spirit,
Doomed for a certain term to walk the night, 10
And for the day confined to fast in fires,
Till the foul crimes done in my days of nature
Are burnt and purged away. But that I am forbid
To tell the secrets of my prison house,
I could a tale unfold whose lightest word 15
Would harrow up thy soul, freeze thy young blood,
Make thy two eyes, like stars, start from their spheres,
Thy knotted and combined locks to part,
And each particular hair to stand on end
Like quills upon the fretful porpentine. 20
But this eternal blazon must not be
To ears of flesh and blood. List, list, O, list!
If thou didst ever thy dear father love—
Ham. O God!
Ghost. Revenge his foul and most unnatural murder. 25
Ham. Murder?
Ghost. Murder most foul, as in the best it is;
But this most foul, strange, and unnatural.
Ham. Haste me to know't, that I, with wings as swift
As meditation or the thoughts of love, 30
May sweep to my revenge.
Ghost. I find thee apt;
And duller shouldst thou be than the fat weed
That rots itself in ease on Lethe wharf,
Wouldst thou not stir in this. Now, Hamlet, hear:
'Tis given out that, sleeping in my orchard, 35
A serpent stung me; so the whole ear of Denmark
Is by a forged process of my death
Rankly abused; but know, thou noble youth,
The serpent that did sting thy father's life
Now wears his crown.
Ham. O my prophetic soul! 40
My uncle?
Ghost. Ay, that incestuous, that adulterate beast,
With witchcraft of his wit, with traitorous gifts—
O wicked wit and gifts, that have the power
So to seduce!—won to his shameful lust 45
The will of my most seeming-virtuous queen.
O Hamlet, what a falling-off was there,
From me, whose love was of that dignity
That it went hand in hand even with the vow
I made to her in marriage, and to decline 50
Upon a wretch whose natural gifts were poor
To those of mine!
But virtue, as it never will be moved,
Though lewdness court it in a shape of heaven,
So lust, though to a radiant angel linked, 55
Will sate itself in a celestial bed
And prey on garbage.
But soft! methinks I scent the morning air.
Brief let me be. Sleeping within my orchard,
My custom always of the afternoon, 60
Upon my secure hour thy uncle stole,
With juice of cursed hebenon in a vial,
And in the porches of my ears did pour
The leperous distilment, whose effect
Holds such an enmity with blood of man 65
That swift as quicksilver it courses through
The natural gates and alleys of the body,
And with a sudden vigor it doth posset
And curd, like eager droppings into milk,
The thin and wholesome blood; so did it mine, 70

85. lets: hinders
20. porpentine: porcupine
21. eternal blazon: revelation of eternity
32. fat: thick and sluggish
33. Lethe wharf: the shores of Lethe, the river in Hades that contained the waters of oblivion
37. process: relation
38. Rankly abused: utterly deceived
42. adulterate: adulterous
61. secure: carefree; unconscious of danger
62. hebenon: probably henbane, *Hyoscyamus niger*
64. leperous: producing a leprous eruption
68. posset: curdle
69. eager: sharp; acid

And a most instant tetter barked about,
Most lazar-like, with vile and loathsome crust
All my smooth body.
Thus was I, sleeping, by a brother's hand
Of life, of crown, of queen, at once dispatched; 75
Cut off even in the blossoms of my sin,
Unhous'led, disappointed, unaneled,
No reck'ning made, but sent to my account
With all my imperfections on my head.

Ham. O, horrible! O, horrible! most horrible! 80

Ghost. If thou hast nature in thee, bear it not.
Let not the royal bed of Denmark be
A couch for luxury and damned incest.
But, howsoever thou pursuest this act,
Taint not thy mind, nor let thy soul contrive 85
Against thy mother aught. Leave her to heaven,
And to those thorns that in her bosom lodge
To prick and sting her. Fare thee well at once,
The glowworm shows the matin to be near
And gins to pale his uneffectual fire. 90
Adieu, adieu, adieu! Remember me. *Exit.*

Ham. O all you host of heaven! O earth! What else?
And shall I couple hell? O fie! Hold, hold, my heart!
And you, my sinews, grow not instant old,
But bear me stiffly up. Remember thee? 95
Ay, thou poor ghost, while memory holds a seat
In this distracted globe. Remember thee?
Yea, from the table of my memory
I'll wipe away all trivial fond records,
All saws of books, all forms, all pressures past 100
That youth and observation copied there,
And thy commandment all alone shall live
Within the book and volume of my brain,
Unmixed with baser matter. Yes, by heaven!
O most pernicious woman! 105
O villain, villain, smiling, damned villain!
My tables, my tables! Meet it is I set it down
That one may smile, and smile, and be a villain;
At least I'm sure it may be so in Denmark. [*Writes.*]
So, uncle, there you are. Now to my word: 110
It is "Adieu, adieu! Remember me."
I have sworn't.

Hor. (*Within*) My lord, my lord!

Enter HORATIO *and* MARCELLUS.

Mar. Lord Hamlet!

Hor. Heaven secure him!

Ham. So be it!

Mar. Illo, ho, ho, my lord! 115

Ham. Hillo, ho, ho, boy! Come, bird, come.

Mar. How is't, my noble lord?

Hor. What news, my lord?

Ham. O, wonderful!

Hor. Good my lord, tell it.

Ham. No, you'll reveal it.

Hor. Not I, my lord, by heaven!

Mar. Nor I, my lord. 120

Ham. How say you then? Would heart of man once think it?
But you'll be secret?

Both. Ay, by heaven, my lord.

Ham. There's ne'er a villain dwelling in all Denmark
But he's an arrant knave.

Hor. There needs no ghost, my lord, come from the grave 125
To tell us this.

Ham. Why, right! You are in the right!
And so, without more circumstance at all,
I hold it fit that we shake hands and part;
You, as your business and desires shall point you,
For every man hath business and desire, 130
Such as it is; and for my own poor part,
Look you, I'll go pray.

Hor. These are but wild and whirling words, my lord.

Ham. I am sorry they offend you, heartily;
Yes, faith, heartily.

Hor. There's no offense, my lord. 135

Ham. Yes, by Saint Patrick, but there is, Horatio,
And much offense too. Touching this vision here,
It is an honest ghost, that let me tell you.
For your desire to know what is between us,
O'ermaster't as you may. And now, good friends,
As you are friends, scholars, and soldiers, 141
Give me one poor request.

Hor. What is't, my lord? We will.

Ham. Never make known what you have seen tonight.

Both. My lord, we will not.

Ham. Nay, but swear't.

Hor. In faith, 145
My lord, not I.

Mar. Nor I, my lord—in faith.

Ham. Upon my sword.

71. tetter: skin eruption; **barked about:** covered like a bark
72. lazar-like: leper-like
75. dispatched: deprived
77. Unhous'led: without benefit of the last sacrament; **disappointed:** unprepared for eternity; **unaneled:** unanointed in the rite of extreme unction
83. luxury: lust
97. this . . . globe: i.e., Hamlet's mind
98. table: table book; tablet
99. fond: foolish
100. saws: maxims; **forms:** images; **pressures:** impressions
101. youth . . . observation: youthful observation
110. word: motto
113. secure: safeguard
116. Hillo . . . boy: a call used by a falconer to summon his bird
124. arrant: absolute
127. circumstance: ceremony
138. honest ghost: i.e., not an evil spirit
147. sword: the sword-hilt formed a cross.

Mar. We have sworn, my lord, already.
Ham. Indeed, upon my sword, indeed.

GHOST *cries under the stage.*

Ghost. Swear.
Ham. Aha boy, sayst thou so? Art thou there, truepenny? 150
Come on! You hear this fellow in the cellarage.
Consent to swear.
Hor. Propose the oath, my lord.
Ham. Never to speak of this that you have seen.
Swear by my sword.
Ghost. [*Beneath*] Swear. 155
Ham. Hic et ubique? Then we'll shift our ground.
Come hither, gentlemen,
And lay your hands again upon my sword.
Never to speak of this that you have heard:
Swear by my sword. 160
Ghost. [*Beneath*] Swear by his sword.
Ham. Well said, old mole! Canst work i' the earth so fast?
A worthy pioner! Once more remove, good friends.
Hor. O day and night, but this is wondrous strange!
Ham. And therefore, as a stranger give it welcome.
There are more things in heaven and earth, Horatio,

150. truepenny: "good fellow"
156. Hic . . . ubique: here and everywhere
163. pioner: pioneer; miner
165. as . . . stranger: i.e., courteously

Than are dreamt of in your philosophy. 167
But come!
Here, as before, never, so help you mercy,
How strange or odd soe'er I bear myself 170
(As I perchance hereafter shall think meet
To put an antic disposition on),
That you, at such times seeing me, never shall,
With arms encumb'red thus, or this headshake,
Or by pronouncing of some doubtful phrase, 175
As "Well, well, we know," or "We could, an if we would,"
Or "If we list to speak," or "There be, an if they might,"
Or such ambiguous giving out, to note
That you know aught of me—this not to do,
So grace and mercy at your most need help you, 180
Swear.
Ghost. [*Beneath*] Swear. [*They swear.*]
Ham. Rest, rest, perturbed spirit! So, gentlemen,
With all my love I do commend me to you;
And what so poor a man as Hamlet is 185
May do t' express his love and friending to you,
God willing, shall not lack. Let us go in together;
And still your fingers on your lips, I pray.
The time is out of joint. O cursed spite
That ever I was born to set it right! 190
Nay, come, let's go together.

Exeunt.

167. your philosophy: philosophy in general
178. giving out: hint

ACT II

[Scene I. *Elsinore. Polonius' house.*]

Enter POLONIUS *and* REYNALDO.

Pol. Give him this money and these notes, Reynaldo.
Rey. I will, my lord.
Pol. You shall do marvel's wisely, good Reynaldo,
Before you visit him, to make inquire
Of his behavior.
Rey. My lord, I did intend it. 5

3. marvel's: marvelous

Pol. Marry, well said, very well said. Look you, sir,
Inquire me first what Danskers are in Paris;
And how, and who, what means, and where they keep,
What company, at what expense; and finding
By this encompassment and drift of question 10
That they do know my son, come you more nearer
Than your particular demands will touch it.
Take you, as 'twere, some distant knowledge of him;
As thus, "I know his father and his friends,
And in part him." Do you mark this, Reynaldo? 15

7. Danskers: Danes
10. encompassment . . . question: roundabout inquiry
11. come you: i.e., you may come
12. particular demands: specific questions

Rey. Ay, very well, my lord.
Pol. "And in part him, but," you may say, "not well.
But if't be he I mean, he's very wild,
Addicted so and so"; and there put on him
What forgeries you please; marry, none so rank 20
As may dishonor him—take heed of that;
But, sir, such wanton, wild, and usual slips
As are companions noted and most known
To youth and liberty.
Rey. As gaming, my lord.
Pol. Ay, or drinking, fencing, swearing, quarreling,
Drabbing. You may go so far. 26
Rey. My lord, that would dishonor him.
Pol. Faith, no, as you may season it in the charge.
You must not put another scandal on him,
That he is open to incontinency. 30
That's not my meaning. But breathe his faults so quaintly
That they may seem the taints of liberty,
The flash and outbreak of a fiery mind,
A savageness in unreclaimed blood,
Of general assault.
Rey. But, my good lord— 35
Pol. Wherefore should you do this?
Rey. Ay, my lord,
I would know that.
Pol. Marry, sir, here's my drift,
And I believe it is a fetch of warrant.
You laying these slight sullies on my son
As 'twere a thing a little soiled i' the working, 40
Mark you,
Your party in converse, him you would sound,
Having ever seen in the prenominate crimes
The youth you breathe of guilty, be assured
He closes with you in this consequence: 45
"Good sir," or so, or "friend," or "gentleman"—
According to the phrase or the addition
Of man and country—
Rey. Very good, my lord.
Pol. And then, sir, does he this—he does—What was I about to say? By the mass, I was about 50
to say something! Where did I leave?
Rey. At "closes in the consequence," at "friend or so," and "gentleman."
Pol. At "closes in the consequence"—Ay, marry!
He closes thus: "I know the gentleman. 55
I saw him yesterday, or t'other day,
Or then, or then, with such or such; and, as you say,
There was he gaming; there o'ertook in 's rouse;
There falling out at tennis"; or perchance,
"I saw him enter such a house of sale," 60
Videlicet, a brothel, or so forth.
See you now—
Your bait of falsehood takes this carp of truth;
And thus do we of wisdom and of reach,
With windlasses and with assays of bias, 65
By indirections find directions out.
So, by my former lecture and advice,
Shall you my son. You have me, have you not?
Rey. My lord, I have.
Pol. God be wi' you, fare you well!
Rey. Good my lord! 70
Pol. Observe his inclination in yourself.
Rey. I shall, my lord.
Pol. And let him ply his music.
Rey. Well, my lord.
Pol. Farewell! *Exit Reynaldo.*

Enter OPHELIA.

How now, Ophelia? What's the matter?
Oph. O my lord, my lord, I have been so affrighted! 75
Pol. With what, i' the name of God?
Oph. My lord, as I was sewing in my closet,
Lord Hamlet, with his doublet all unbraced,
No hat upon his head, his stockings fouled,
Ungart'red, and down-gyved to his ankle; 80
Pale as his shirt, his knees knocking each other,
And with a look so piteous in purport
As if he had been loosed out of hell
To speak of horrors—he comes before me.
Pol. Mad for thy love?
Oph. My lord, I do not know, 85
But truly I do fear it.
Pol. What said he?
Oph. He took me by the wrist and held me hard;
Then goes he to the length of all his arm,
And, with his other hand thus o'er his brow,
He falls to such perusal of my face 90
As he would draw it. Long stayed he so.
At last, a little shaking of mine arm,
And thrice his head thus waving up and down,
He raised a sigh so piteous and profound

19. **put . . . him:** charge him with
20. **forgeries:** fabrications; **rank:** gross
26. **Drabbing:** whoring
28. **season:** temper; soften
30. **incontinency:** overindulgence in any vice
31. **quaintly:** ingeniously
32. **taints . . . liberty:** faults due to lack of control
34. **unreclaimed:** untamed
35. **Of . . . assault:** common to all
38. **fetch . . . warrant:** guaranteed device
40. **a . . . working:** slightly soiled, like cloth that has been handled
58. **o'ertook . . . rouse:** overcome by drink
61. **Videlicet:** namely
64. **reach:** comprehension
65. **windlasses . . . bias:** winding turns and oblique approaches. **Assays of bias** is a bowling term.
71. **in yourself:** with your own eyes
73. **ply . . . music:** do as he pleases
77. **closet:** boudoir
78. **doublet:** a man's jacket, which decorum required to be fastened in public
80. **down-gyved:** fallen in coils

As it did seem to shatter all his bulk 95
And end his being. That done, he lets me go,
And with his head over his shoulder turned
He seemed to find his way without his eyes,
For out o' doors he went without their help
And to the last bended their light on me. 100

Pol. Come, go with me. I will go seek the King.
This is the very ecstasy of love,
Whose violent property fordoes itself
And leads the will to desperate undertakings
As oft as any passion under heaven 105
That does afflict our natures. I am sorry.
What, have you given him any hard words of late?

Oph. No, my good lord; but, as you did command,
I did repel his letters and denied
His access to me.

Pol. That hath made him mad. 110
I am sorry that with better heed and judgment
I had not quoted him. I feared he did but trifle
And meant to wrack thee; but beshrew my jealousy!
By heaven, it is as proper to our age
To cast beyond ourselves in our opinions 115
As it is common for the younger sort
To lack discretion. Come, go we to the King.
This must be known; which, being kept close, might move
More grief to hide than hate to utter love.
Come. 120

Exeunt.

Scene II. [*Elsinore. A room in the Castle.*]

Flourish. Enter KING *and* QUEEN, ROSENCRANTZ *and* GUILDENSTERN, *cum aliis.*

King. Welcome, dear Rosencrantz and Guildenstern.
Moreover that we much did long to see you,
The need we have to use you did provoke
Our hasty sending. Something have you heard
Of Hamlet's transformation. So I call it, 5
Sith nor the exterior nor the inward man
Resembles that it was. What it should be,
More than his father's death, that thus hath put him
So much from the understanding of himself,
I cannot dream of. I entreat you both 10
That, being of so young days brought up with him,
And since so neighbored to his youth and havior,
That you vouchsafe your rest here in our court
Some little time; so by your companies
To draw him on to pleasures, and to gather 15
So much as from occasion you may glean,
Whether aught to us unknown afflicts him thus
That, opened, lies within our remedy.

Queen. Good gentlemen, he hath much talked of you,
And sure I am two men there are not living 20
To whom he more adheres. If it will please you
To show us so much gentry and good will
As to expend your time with us awhile
For the supply and profit of our hope,
Your visitation shall receive such thanks 25
As fits a king's remembrance.

Ros. Both your Majesties
Might, by the sovereign power you have of us,
Put your dread pleasures more into command
Than to entreaty.

Guil. But we both obey,
And here give up ourselves, in the full bent, 30
To lay our service freely at your feet,
To be commanded.

King. Thanks, Rosencrantz and gentle Guildenstern.

Queen. Thanks, Guildenstern and gentle Rosencrantz.
And I beseech you instantly to visit 35
My too much changed son.—Go, some of you,
And bring these gentlemen where Hamlet is.

Guil. Heavens make our presence and our practices
Pleasant and helpful to him!

Queen. Ay, amen!

Exeunt Rosencrantz and Guildenstern, [*with some Attendants*].

Enter POLONIUS.

Pol. The ambassadors from Norway, my good lord,
Are joyfully returned. 41

King. Thou still hast been the father of good news.

Pol. Have I, my lord? Assure you, my good liege,
I hold my duty as I hold my soul,
Both to my God and to my gracious king; 45
And I do think—or else this brain of mine
Hunts not the trail of policy so sure
As it hath used to do—that I have found
The very cause of Hamlet's lunacy. 49

King. O, speak of that! That do I long to hear.

95. **bulk:** body. This does not imply that Hamlet was of heavy build.
102. **ecstasy:** madness
103. **property:** characteristic; **fordoes:** destroys
112. **quoted:** noted; interpreted
113. **beshrew:** curse; **jealousy:** suspicion
115. **cast . . . ourselves:** overestimate our wisdom
118–19. **being . . . love:** might cause more grief by its concealment than displeasure at its revelation. Polonius thinks of the reaction of the King and Queen.
6. **Sith:** since
13. **vouchsafe . . . rest:** deign to stay
18. **opened:** revealed
22. **gentry:** courtesy
30. **in . . . bent:** to the utmost
47. **policy:** cunning

Pol. Give first admittance to the ambassadors,
My news shall be the fruit to that great feast.
King. Thyself do grace to them, and bring them in.
[*Exit Polonius.*]
He tells me, my dear Gertrude, he hath found
The head and source of all your son's distemper. 55
Queen. I doubt it is no other but the main,
His father's death and our o'erhasty marriage.
King. Well, we shall sift him.

Enter POLONIUS, VOLTEMAND, *and* CORNELIUS.

Welcome, my good friends.
Say, Voltemand, what from our brother Norway?
Volt. Most fair return of greetings and desires. 60
Upon our first, he sent out to suppress
His nephew's levies, which to him appeared
To be a preparation 'gainst the Polack,
But better looked into, he truly found
It was against your Highness; whereat grieved, 65
That so his sickness, age, and impotence
Was falsely borne in hand, sends out arrests
On Fortinbras; which he, in brief, obeys,
Receives rebuke from Norway, and, in fine,
Makes vow before his uncle never more 70
To give the assay of arms against your Majesty.
Whereon old Norway, overcome with joy,
Gives him three thousand crowns in annual fee
And his commission to employ those soldiers,
So levied as before, against the Polack; 75
With an entreaty, herein further shown,
[*Gives a paper.*]
That it might please you to give quiet pass
Through your dominions for this enterprise,
On such regards of safety and allowance
As therein are set down.
King. It likes us well; 80
And at our more considered time we'll read,
Answer, and think upon this business.
Meantime we thank you for your well-took labor.
Go to your rest; at night we'll feast together.
Most welcome home! *Exeunt Ambassadors.*
Pol. This business is well ended.
My liege, and madam, to expostulate 86
What majesty should be, what duty is,
Why day is day, night night, and time is time,
Were nothing but to waste night, day, and time.
Therefore, since brevity is the soul of wit, 90
And tediousness the limbs and outward flourishes,
I will be brief. Your noble son is mad.
Mad call I it; for, to define true madness,
What is't but to be nothing else but mad?
But let that go.
Queen. More matter, with less art. 95
Pol. Madam, I swear I use no art at all.
That he is mad, 'tis true: 'tis true 'tis pity;
And pity 'tis 'tis true. A foolish figure!
But farewell it, for I will use no art.
Mad let us grant him then. And now remains 100
That we find out the cause of this effect—
Or rather say, the cause of this defect,
For this effect defective comes by cause.
Thus it remains, and the remainder thus.
Perpend: 105
I have a daughter (have while she is mine),
Who in her duty and obedience, mark,
Hath given me this. Now gather, and surmise.
[*Reads*] *the letter.*

To the celestial, and my soul's idol, the most beautified Ophelia,—

That's an ill phrase, a vile phrase; "beautified" 110
is a vile phrase. But you shall hear. Thus: [*Reads*]

In her excellent white bosom, these, &c.

Queen. Came this from Hamlet to her?
Pol. Good madam, stay awhile. I will be faithful.
[*Reads*]

Doubt thou the stars are fire; 115
Doubt that the sun doth move;
Doubt truth to be a liar;
But never doubt I love.

O dear Ophelia, I am ill at these numbers; I have not art to reckon my groans; but that I love thee best, O, most best, believe it. Adieu. 121
Thine evermore, most dear lady, whilst this machine is to him, HAMLET.

This, in obedience, hath my daughter shown me;
And more above, hath his solicitings, 125
As they fell out by time, by means, and place,
All given to mine ear.
King. But how hath she
Received his love?
Pol. What do you think of me?
King. As of a man faithful and honorable.
Pol. I would fain prove so. But what might you think, 130
When I had seen this hot love on the wing
(As I perceived it, I must tell you that,
Before my daughter told me), what might you,
Or my dear Majesty your queen here, think,

53. **grace:** honor
67. **borne . . . hand:** deceived
79. **On . . . allowance:** according to such terms as you think safe and permissible
80. **likes:** pleases
81. **at . . . time:** when we have time for due consideration
90. **wit:** wisdom
98. **figure:** figure of speech
105. **Perpend:** consider
119. **ill . . . numbers:** unskilled in writing poetry
122. **machine:** body

If I had played the desk or table book, 135
Or given my heart a winking, mute and dumb,
Or looked upon this love with idle sight?
What might you think? No, I went round to work
And my young mistress thus I did bespeak:
"Lord Hamlet is a prince, out of thy star. 140
This must not be." And then I precepts gave her,
That she should lock herself from his resort,
Admit no messengers, receive no tokens.
Which done, she took the fruits of my advice,
And he, repulsed, a short tale to make, 145
Fell into a sadness, then into a fast,
Thence to a watch, thence into a weakness,
Thence to a lightness, and, by this declension,
Into the madness wherein now he raves,
And all we mourn for.

King. Do you think 'tis this? 150

Queen. It may be, very like.

Pol. Hath there been such a time—I would fain know that—
That I have positively said " 'Tis so,"
When it proved otherwise?

King. Not that I know.

Pol. [*Points to his head and shoulder.*] Take this from this, if this be otherwise. 155
If circumstances lead me, I will find
Where truth is hid, though it were hid indeed
Within the center.

King. How may we try it further?

Pol. You know sometimes he walks four hours together
Here in the lobby.

Queen. So he does indeed. 160

Pol. At such a time I'll loose my daughter to him.
Be you and I behind an arras then.
Mark the encounter. If he love her not,
And be not from his reason fall'n thereon,
Let me be no assistant for a state, 165
But keep a farm and carters.

King. We will try it.

Enter HAMLET, *reading on a book.*

Queen. But look where sadly the poor wretch comes reading.

Pol. Away, I do beseech you, both away!
I'll board him presently. O, give me leave.

Exeunt King and Queen, [*with Attendants*].

How does my good Lord Hamlet? 170

Ham. Well, God-a-mercy.

Pol. Do you know me, my lord?

Ham. Excellent well. You are a fishmonger.

Pol. Not I, my lord. 174

Ham. Then I would you were so honest a man.

Pol. Honest, my lord?

Ham. Ay, sir. To be honest, as this world goes, is to be one man picked out of ten thousand.

Pol. That's very true, my lord. 179

Ham. For if the sun breed maggots in a dead dog, being a god kissing carrion—Have you a daughter?

Pol. I have, my lord.

Ham. Let her not walk i' the sun. Conception is a blessing, but not as your daughter may conceive. Friend, look to't. 185

Pol. [*Aside*] How say you by that? Still harping on my daughter. Yet he knew me not at first. He said I was a fishmonger. He is far gone, far gone! And truly in my youth I suff'red much extremity for love —very near this. I'll speak to him again.— 190
What do you read, my lord?

Ham. Words, words, words.

Pol. What is the matter, my lord?

Ham. Between who?

Pol. I mean, the matter that you read, my 195 lord.

Ham. Slanders, sir; for the satirical rogue says here that old men have grey beards; that their faces are wrinkled; their eyes purging thick amber and plum-tree gum; and that they have a plenti- 200 ful lack of wit, together with most weak hams. All which, sir, though I most powerfully and potently believe, yet I hold it not honesty to have it thus set down; for you yourself, sir, should be old as I am if, like a crab, you could go backward. 205

Pol. [*Aside*] Though this be madness, yet there is method in't.—Will you walk out of the air, my lord?

Ham. Into my grave?

Pol. Indeed, that is out o' the air. [*Aside*] How pregnant sometimes his replies are! a happi- 210 ness that often madness hits on, which reason and sanity could not so prosperously be delivered of. I will leave him and suddenly contrive the means of meeting between him and my daughter.—My honorable lord, I will most humbly take my leave 215 of you.

Ham. You cannot, sir, take from me anything that I will more willingly part withal—except my life, except my life, except my life.

Enter ROSENCRANTZ *and* GUILDENSTERN.

135. played . . . book: acted as a silent container of the information
136. given . . . winking: stifled my concern
137. idle: fruitless; without being moved to action
138. round: directly
147. watch: sleepless state
148. declension: deterioration
158. center: heart of the earth
162. arras: wall hanging
169. board: accost

181. god: i.e., the sun-god. William Warburton suggested **god** for "good" in the Folio and Quarto.
186. by: about
203. honesty: honorable conduct
210–11. happiness: aptness

Pol. Fare you well, my lord. 220

Ham. These tedious old fools!

Pol. You go to seek the Lord Hamlet. There he is.

Ros. [*To Polonius*] God save you, sir!

Exit [*Polonius*].

Guil. My honored lord!

Ros. My most dear lord! 225

Ham. My excellent good friends! How dost thou, Guildenstern? Ah, Rosencrantz! Good lads, how do ye both?

Ros. As the indifferent children of the earth.

Guil. Happy in that we are not over-happy. 230
On Fortune's cap we are not the very button.

Ham. Nor the soles of her shoe?

Ros. Neither, my lord.

Ham. Then you live about her waist, or in the middle of her favors? 235

Guil. Faith, her privates we.

Ham. In the secret parts of Fortune? O, most true! she is a strumpet. What news?

Ros. None, my lord, but that the world's grown honest. 240

Ham. Then is doomsday near! But your news is not true. Let me question more in particular. What have you, my good friends, deserved at the hands of Fortune that she sends you to prison hither?

Guil. Prison, my lord? 245

Ham. Denmark's a prison.

Ros. Then is the world one.

Ham. A goodly one; in which there are many confines, wards, and dungeons, Denmark being one o' the worst. 250

Ros. We think not so, my lord.

Ham. Why, then 'tis none to you, for there is nothing either good or bad but thinking makes it so. To me it is a prison.

Ros. Why, then your ambition makes it 255
one. 'Tis too narrow for your mind.

Ham. O God, I could be bounded in a nutshell and count myself a king of infinite space, were it not that I have bad dreams.

Guil. Which dreams indeed are ambition; 260
for the very substance of the ambitious is merely the shadow of a dream.

Ham. A dream itself is but a shadow.

Ros. Truly, and I hold ambition of so airy and light a quality that it is but a shadow's 265
shadow.

Ham. Then are our beggars bodies, and our monarchs and outstretched heroes the beggars' shadows. Shall we to the court? for, by my fay, I cannot reason. 270

Both. We'll wait upon you.

Ham. No such matter! I will not sort you with the rest of my servants; for, to speak to you like an honest man, I am most dreadfully attended. But in the beaten way of friendship, what make you at 275
Elsinore?

Ros. To visit you, my lord; no other occasion.

Ham. Beggar that I am, I am even poor in thanks; but I thank you; and sure, dear friends, my thanks are too dear a halfpenny. Were you not sent 280
for? Is it your own inclining? Is it a free visitation? Come, deal justly with me. Come, come! Nay, speak.

Guil. What should we say, my lord?

Ham. Why, anything, but to the purpose. 285
You were sent for, and there is a kind of confession in your looks, which your modesties have not craft enough to color. I know the good King and Queen have sent for you.

Ros. To what end, my lord? 290

Ham. That you must teach me. But let me conjure you by the rights of our fellowship, by the consonancy of our youth, by the obligation of our ever-preserved love, and by what more dear a better proposer could charge you withal, be even and 295
direct with me, whether you were sent for or no.

Ros. [*Aside to Guildenstern*] What say you?

Ham. [*Aside*] Nay then, I have an eye of you. If you love me, hold not off.

Guil. My lord, we were sent for. 300

Ham. I will tell you why, so shall my anticipation prevent your discovery, and your secrecy to the King and Queen moult no feather. I have of late—but wherefore I know not—lost all my mirth, forgone all custom of exercises; and indeed, it goes so 305
heavily with my disposition that this goodly frame, the earth, seems to me a sterile promontory; this most excellent canopy, the air, look you, this brave o'erhanging firmament, this majestical roof fretted with golden fire—why, it appeareth no other 310
thing to me than a foul and pestilent congregation of vapors. What a piece of work is a man! how noble in reason! how infinite in faculties! in form and moving

229. **indifferent:** unremarkable; average
238. **a strumpet:** fickle of favor
248. **goodly:** roomy
267–68. **Then . . . shadows:** if ambition is but a "shadow's shadow," then unambitious beggars are substantial, while the ambitious great ones are only shadows.

269. **fay:** faith
271. **wait upon:** accompany
272. **matter:** thing; **sort:** classify
274. **dreadfully attended:** probably both "poorly served" and "accompanied by horrors"
274–75. **in . . . friendship:** i.e., speaking as old friends
280. **too dear:** not worth
288. **color:** disguise
292–93. **consonancy . . . youth:** our youthful congeniality
302. **prevent:** forestall; **discovery:** revelation; **secrecy:** promise of secrecy
307. **sterile promontory:** barren headland in space
309. **fretted:** decorated
310. **golden fire:** stars

how express and admirable! in action how like an angel! in apprehension how like a god! the 315 beauty of the world, the paragon of animals! And yet to me what is this quintessence of dust? Man delights not me—no, nor woman neither, though by your smiling you seem to say so.

Ros. My lord, there was no such stuff in my 320 thoughts.

Ham. Why did you laugh then, when I said, "Man delights not me"?

Ros. To think, my lord, if you delight not in man, what lenten entertainment the players shall 325 receive from you. We coted them on the way, and hither are they coming to offer you service.

Ham. He that plays the king shall be welcome—his Majesty shall have tribute of me; the adventurous knight shall use his foil and target; the 330 lover shall not sigh gratis; the humorous man shall end his part in peace; the clown shall make those laugh whose lungs are tickle o' the sere; and the lady shall say her mind freely, or the blank verse shall halt for't. What players are they? 335

Ros. Even those you were wont to take such delight in, the tragedians of the city.

Ham. How chances it they travel? Their residence, both in reputation and profit, was better both ways.

Ros. I think their inhibition comes by the 340 means of the late innovation.

Ham. Do they hold the same estimation they did when I was in the city? Are they so followed?

Ros. No indeed are they not.

Ham. How comes it? Do they grow rusty? 345

Ros. Nay, their endeavor keeps in the wonted pace; but there is, sir, an eyrie of children, little eyases, that cry out on the top of question and are most tyrannically clapped for't. These are now the fashion, and so berattle the common stages 350 (so they call them) that many wearing rapiers are afraid of goosequills and dare scarce come thither.

Ham. What, are they children? Who maintains 'em? How are they escoted? Will they pursue the quality no longer than they can sing? Will they 355 not say afterwards, if they should grow themselves to common players (as it is most like, if their means are no better), their writers do them wrong to make them exclaim against their own succession?

Ros. Faith, there has been much to do on 360 both sides; and the nation holds it no sin to tarre them to controversy. There was, for a while, no money bid for argument unless the poet and the player went to cuffs in the question.

Ham. Is't possible? 365

Guil. O, there has been much throwing about of brains.

Ham. Do the boys carry it away?

Ros. Ay, that they do, my lord—Hercules and his load too. 370

Ham. It is not very strange; for my uncle is King of Denmark, and those that would make mows at him while my father lived give twenty, forty, fifty, a hundred ducats apiece for his picture in little. 'Sblood, there is something in this more than 375 natural, if philosophy could find it out.

Flourish for the Players.

Guil. There are the players.

Ham. Gentlemen, you are welcome to Elsinore. Your hands, come! The appurtenance of welcome is fashion and ceremony. Let me comply with 380 you in this garb, lest my extent to the players (which I tell you must show fairly outwards) should more appear like entertainment than yours. You are welcome. But my uncle-father and aunt-mother are deceived. 385

Guil. In what, my dear lord?

Ham. I am but mad north-north-west. When the wind is southerly I know a hawk from a handsaw.

Enter POLONIUS.

Pol. Well be with you, gentlemen! 390

Ham. Hark you, Guildenstern—and you too—at

314. express: precise
317. quintessence: concentrated essence
325. lenten entertainment: meager reception
326. coted: passed by
330. foil . . . target: sword and shield
331. humorous man: actor who plays a role characterizing a particular humor
333. tickle . . . sere: quick on the trigger. A **sere** is the catch in a gunlock
333–35. the . . . for't: the lady will be allowed to talk without interruption, lest the meter of the speeches be marred.
340. inhibition: prohibition (from the city)
341. the . . . innovation: the new competition of boy acting companies
347. eyrie: brood
348. eyases: literally, unfledged hawks; **cry . . . question:** outclamor all competition
349. tyrannically: violently
350. berattle . . . stages: deride the public playhouses. The boy companies played in private theatres to more exclusive audiences.
354. escoted: supported
355. quality: profession; **no . . . sing:** until their voices change
359. succession: subsequent course of action
361. tarre: incite
362–64. There . . . question: for a time no money would be paid for a play which did not contain satire on the players.
369–70. Hercules . . . load: the sign of the Globe theatre showed Hercules supporting the world on his shoulders.
372. mows: mouths
374. picture . . . little: a miniature
379. appurtenance: accessory
380. comply with: compliment
381. extent: extension of courtesy
387. north-north-west: according to Timothy Bright's *Treatise of Melancholy* (1586), melancholy was affected in degree by the condition of the wind and would be most severe under the influence of the north wind.
388–89. handsaw: possibly a quibble on "heronshaw" (heron), but the phrase is proverbial

each ear a hearer! That great baby you see there is not yet out of his swaddling clouts.

Ros. Happily he's the second time come to them; for they say an old man is twice a child. 395

Ham. I will prophesy he comes to tell me of the players. Mark it.—You say right, sir; a Monday morning; 'twas so indeed.

Pol. My lord, I have news to tell you.

Ham. My lord, I have news to tell you: 400 when Roscius was an actor in Rome—

Pol. The actors are come hither, my lord.

Ham. Buzz, buzz!

Pol. Upon my honor—

Ham. Then came each actor on his ass— 405

Pol. The best actors in the world, either for tragedy, comedy, history, pastoral, pastoral-comical, historical-pastoral, tragical-historical, tragical-comical-historical-pastoral; scene individable, or poem unlimited. Seneca cannot be too heavy, 410 nor Plautus too light. For the law of writ and the liberty, these are the only men.

Ham. O Jephthah, judge of Israel, what a treasure hadst thou!

Pol. What a treasure had he, my lord? 415

Ham. Why,

> One fair daughter, and no more,
> The which he loved passing well.

Pol. [*Aside*] Still on my daughter.

Ham. Am I not i' the right, old Jephthah? 420

Pol. If you call me Jephthah, my lord, I have a daughter that I love passing well.

Ham. Nay, that follows not.

Pol. What follows then, my lord?

Ham. Why, 425

> As by lot, God wot,

and then, you know,

> It came to pass, as most like it was.

The first row of the pious chanson will show you more; for look where my abridgment comes. 430

Enter four or five PLAYERS.

You are welcome, masters; welcome, all.—I am glad to see thee well.—Welcome, good friends.—O, my old friend? Why, thy face is valanced since I saw thee last. Comest thou to beard me in Denmark?—What, my young lady and mistress? By'r Lady, 435 your ladyship is nearer to heaven than when I saw you last by the altitude of a chopine. Pray God your voice, like a piece of uncurrent gold, be not cracked within the ring.—Masters, you are all welcome. We'll e'en to't like French falconers, fly at 440 anything we see. We'll have a speech straight. Come, give us a taste of your quality. Come, a passionate speech.

1. Play. What speech, my good lord?

Ham. I heard thee speak me a speech once, 445 but it was never acted; or if it was, not above once; for the play, I remember, pleased not the million, 'twas caviary to the general; but it was (as I received it, and others, whose judgments in such matters cried in the top of mine) an excellent 450 play, well digested in the scenes, set down with as much modesty as cunning. I remember one said there were no sallets in the line to make the matter savory, nor no matter in the phrase that might indict the author of affectation; but called it an honest 455 method, as wholesome as sweet, and by very much more handsome than fine. One speech in it I chiefly loved. 'Twas Æneas' tale to Dido, and thereabout of it especially where he speaks of Priam's slaughter. If it live in your memory, begin at this line—let 460 me see, let me see:

> The rugged Pyrrhus, like the Hyrcanian beast—

'Tis not so; it begins with Pyrrhus:

> The rugged Pyrrhus, he whose sable arms,
> Black as his purpose, did the night resemble 465
> When he lay couched in the ominous horse,
> Hath now this dread and black complexion smeared
> With heraldry more dismal. Head to foot
> Now is he total gules, horridly tricked 469
> With blood of fathers, mothers, daughters, sons,
> Baked and impasted with the parching streets,
> That lend a tyrannous and a damned light

393. clouts: clothes
394. Happily: perhaps
401. Roscius: a famous actor of Cicero's time
409–10. scene . . . unlimited: plays that observe unity in time and place and plays that do not
410. Seneca: Roman dramatist whose bloody tragedies had much influence on Elizabethan playwrights
411. Plautus: Roman writer of comedies
411–12. law . . . liberty: writings observing the rules of composition and writings overlooking such rules
413. Jephthah: see Judges 11:34–39.
418. passing: exceedingly
429. row: stanza
433. valanced: fringed, with a beard
435. young lady: a lad who played feminine roles
437. chopine: a shoe elevated by a thick sole
438–39. uncurrent . . . ring: a coin with a crack was not negotiable. Hamlet refers to the boy's change of voice.
448. caviary . . . general: too choice for general popularity
450. cried . . . of: spoke with more authority than
453. sallets: spicy bits
455. honest: chaste
457. handsome: seemly; **fine:** ornate
458. Æneas: hero of Vergil's *Æneid.* The style of this speech may have been inspired by Marlowe and Nashe, *Dido, Queen of Carthage.*
462. Pyrrhus: son of the Greek hero Achilles; **Hyrcanian beast:** tiger of Hyrcania, a region on the Caspian Sea
464. sable arms: arms marked with a black device
469. gules: the heraldic word for "red"; **tricked:** decorated; another heraldic term
472. tyrannous: fierce

To their lord's murder. Roasted in wrath and fire,
And thus o'ersized with coagulate gore,
With eyes like carbuncles, the hellish Pyrrhus 475
Old grandsire Priam seeks.

So, proceed you.

Pol. Fore God, my lord, well spoken, with good accent and good discretion.

1. Play. Anon he finds him, 480
Striking too short at Greeks. His antique sword,
Rebellious to his arm, lies where it falls,
Repugnant to command. Unequal matched,
Pyrrhus at Priam drives, in rage strikes wide;
But with the whiff and wind of his fell sword 485
The unnerved father falls. Then senseless Ilium,
Seeming to feel this blow, with flaming top
Stoops to his base, and with a hideous crash
Takes prisoner Pyrrhus' ear. For lo! his sword,
Which was declining on the milky head 490
Of reverend Priam, seemed i' the air to stick.
So, as a painted tyrant, Pyrrhus stood,
And, like a neutral to his will and matter,
Did nothing.
But, as we often see, against some storm, 495
A silence in the heavens, the rack stand still,
The bold winds speechless, and the orb below
As hush as death—anon the dreadful thunder
Doth rend the region; so, after Pyrrhus' pause,
Aroused vengeance sets him new awork; 500
And never did the Cyclops' hammers fall
On Mars' armor, forged for proof eterne,
With less remorse than Pyrrhus' bleeding sword
Now falls on Priam. 504
Out, out, thou strumpet Fortune! All you gods,
In general synod take away her power;
Break out the spokes and fellies from her wheel,
And bowl the round nave down the hill of heaven,
As low as to the fiends!

Pol. This is too long. 510

Ham. It shall to the barber's, with your beard.—Prithee say on. He's for a jig or a tale of bawdry, or he sleeps. Say on; come to Hecuba.

1. Play. But who, O who, had seen the mobled queen—

Ham. "The mobled queen"? 515

Pol. That's good! "Mobled queen" is good.

1. Play. Run barefoot up and down, threat'ning the flames
With bisson rheum; a clout upon that head
Where late the diadem stood, and for a robe,
About her lank and all o'erteemed loins, 520
A blanket, in the alarm of fear caught up—
Who this had seen, with tongue in venom steeped
'Gainst Fortune's state would treason have pronounced.
But if the gods themselves did see her then,
When she saw Pyrrhus make malicious sport 525
In mincing with his sword her husband's limbs,
The instant burst of clamor that she made
(Unless things mortal move them not at all)
Would have made milch the burning eyes of heaven
And passion in the gods. 530

Pol. Look, whe'r he has not turned his color, and has tears in's eyes. Prithee no more!

Ham. 'Tis well. I'll have thee speak out the rest of this soon.—Good my lord, will you see the players well bestowed? Do you hear? Let them be 535 well used; for they are the abstract and brief chronicles of the time. After your death you were better have a bad epitaph than their ill report while you live.

Pol. My lord, I will use them according to 540 their desert.

Ham. God's bodykins, man, much better! Use every man after his desert, and who should scape whipping? Use them after your own honor and dignity. The less they deserve, the more merit is 545 in your bounty. Take them in.

Pol. Come, sirs.

Ham. Follow him, friends. We'll hear a play tomorrow.

Exeunt Polonius and Players [*except the First*].

Dost thou hear me, old friend? Can you play 550 "The Murder of Gonzago"?

1. Play. Ay, my lord.

Ham. We'll ha't tomorrow night. You could, for a need, study a speech of some dozen or sixteen lines which I would set down and insert in't, could 555 you not?

1. Play. Ay, my lord.

Ham. Very well. Follow that lord—and look you mock him not. [*Exit First Player.*] My good friends, I'll leave you till night. You are welcome to 560 Elsinore.

Ros. Good my lord!

Ham. Ay, so, God be wi' ye!

Exeunt [*Rosencrantz and Guildenstern*].

Now I am alone.
O, what a rogue and peasant slave am I!
Is it not monstrous that this player here, 565

474. **o'ersized:** overglazed
475. **like carbuncles:** glowing red
483. **Repugnant:** disobedient
485. **fell:** deadly
486. **Ilium:** i.e., the walls of Troy
488. **his:** its
496. **rack:** cloud formation
497. **orb:** earth
499. **region:** upper air
502. **proof eterne:** eternal impenetrability
503. **remorse:** compassion
507. **fellies:** sections of a wheel's rim; **wheel:** the wheel of Fortune, by which she was supposed to regulate human destinies
508. **nave:** hub
512. **jig:** a brief farce or comic turn
514. **mobled:** muffled
518. **bisson rheum:** blinding tears
520. **o'erteemed:** exhausted from excessive childbearing
529. **milch:** wet with tears
531. **wh'er:** whether
535. **bestowed:** accommodated
542. **bodykins:** little body

But in a fiction, in a dream of passion,
Could force his soul so to his own conceit
That, from her working, all his visage wanned,
Tears in his eyes, distraction in's aspect,
A broken voice, and his whole function suiting 570
With forms to his conceit? And all for nothing!
For Hecuba!
What's Hecuba to him, or he to Hecuba,
That he should weep for her? What would he do,
Had he the motive and the cue for passion 575
That I have? He would drown the stage with tears
And cleave the general ear with horrid speech;
Make mad the guilty and appal the free,
Confound the ignorant, and amaze indeed
The very faculties of eyes and ears. 580
Yet I,
A dull and muddy-mettled rascal, peak
Like John-a-dreams, unpregnant of my cause,
And can say nothing! No, not for a king,
Upon whose property and most dear life 585
A damned defeat was made. Am I a coward?
Who calls me villain? breaks my pate across?
Plucks off my beard and blows it in my face?
Tweaks me by the nose? gives me the lie i' the throat
As deep as to the lungs? Who does me this, ha? 590
'Swounds, I should take it! for it cannot be
But I am pigeon-livered and lack gall
To make oppression bitter, or ere this
I should have fatted all the region kites
With this slave's offal. Bloody, bawdy villain! 595
Remorseless, treacherous, lecherous, kindless villain!
O, vengeance!
Why, what an ass am I! This is most brave,
That I, the son of a dear father murdered,
Prompted to my revenge by heaven and hell, 600
Must (like a whore) unpack my heart with words
And fall a-cursing like a very drab,
A scullion!
Fie upon't! foh! About, my brain! I have heard
That guilty creatures, sitting at a play, 605
Have by the very cunning of the scene
Been struck so to the soul that presently
They have proclaimed their malefactions;
For murder, though it have no tongue, will speak
With most miraculous organ. I'll have these players
Play something like the murder of my father 611
Before mine uncle. I'll observe his looks,
I'll tent him to the quick; if he but blench,
I know my course. The spirit that I have seen
May be a devil; and the devil hath power 615
T' assume a pleasing shape; yea, and perhaps
Out of my weakness and my melancholy,
As he is very potent with such spirits,
Abuses me to damn me. I'll have grounds
More relative than this. The play's the thing 620
Wherein I'll catch the conscience of the King.

Exit.

567. conceit: imagination
568. her: i.e., conceit's
578. free: innocent
579. amaze: dumfound
582. dull . . . muddy-mettled: abject and cowardly; **peak:** mope
583. John-a-dreams: a habitual dreamer; **unpregnant of:** unmoved by
586. defeat: destruction
591. 'Swounds: God's wounds
594. region kites: kites (birds of prey) of the air
596. kindless: unnatural, having gone against nature in killing his brother and marrying his brother's wife
601. unpack: relieve
603. scullion: kitchen servant
607. presently: at once
613. tent: probe
618. spirits: moods
620. relative: closely related; relevant

[ACT III]

[Scene I. *Elsinore. A room in the Castle.*]

Enter KING, QUEEN, POLONIUS, OPHELIA, ROSENCRANTZ, GUILDENSTERN, *and* LORDS.

King. And can you by no drift of circumstance
Get from him why he puts on this confusion,
Grating so harshly all his days of quiet
With turbulent and dangerous lunacy? 4
Ros. He does confess he feels himself distracted,
But from what cause he will by no means speak.
Guil. Nor do we find him forward to be sounded,
But with a crafty madness keeps aloof
When we would bring him on to some confession
Of his true state.
Queen. Did he receive you well? 10
Ros. Most like a gentleman.
Guil. But with much forcing of his disposition.

1. drift . . . circumstance: turn of talk

Ros. Niggard of question, but of our demands
Most free in his reply.
Queen. Did you assay him
To any pastime? 15
Ros. Madam, it so fell out that certain players
We o'erraught on the way. Of these we told him,
And there did seem in him a kind of joy
To hear of it. They are here about the court,
And, as I think, they have already order 20
This night to play before him.
Pol. 'Tis most true;
And he beseeched me to entreat your Majesties
To hear and see the matter.
King. With all my heart, and it doth much content me
To hear him so inclined. 25
Good gentlemen, give him a further edge
And drive his purpose on to these delights.
Ros. We shall, my lord.
Exeunt Rosencrantz and Guildenstern.
King. Sweet Gertrude, leave us too;
For we have closely sent for Hamlet hither,
That he, as t'were by accident, may here 30
Affront Ophelia.
Her father and myself (lawful espials)
Will so bestow ourselves that, seeing unseen,
We may of their encounter frankly judge
And gather by him, as he is behaved, 35
If't be the affliction of his love, or no,
That thus he suffers for.
Queen. I shall obey you;
And for your part, Ophelia, I do wish
That your good beauties be the happy cause
Of Hamlet's wildness. So shall I hope your virtues
Will bring him to his wonted way again, 41
To both your honors.
Oph. Madam, I wish it may.
[*Exit Queen.*]
Pol. Ophelia, walk you here.—Gracious, so please you,
We will bestow ourselves.—[*To Ophelia*] Read on this book,
That show of such an exercise may color 45
Your loneliness.—We are oft to blame in this,
'Tis too much proved, that with devotion's visage
And pious action we do sugar o'er
The devil himself.
King. [*Aside*] O, 'tis too true!
How smart a lash that speech doth give my conscience! 50
The harlot's cheek, beautied with plast'ring art,
Is not more ugly to the thing that helps it
Than is my deed to my most painted word.
O heavy burden! 54
Pol. I hear him coming. Let's withdraw, my lord.
Exeunt [*King and Polonius*].

Enter HAMLET.

Ham. To be, or not to be, that is the question:
Whether 'tis nobler in the mind to suffer
The slings and arrows of outrageous fortune
Or to take arms against a sea of troubles,
And by opposing end them. To die—to sleep— 60
No more; and by a sleep to say we end
The heartache, and the thousand natural shocks
That flesh is heir to. 'Tis a consummation
Devoutly to be wished. To die—to sleep. 64
To sleep—perchance to dream: ay, there's the rub!
For in that sleep of death what dreams may come
When we have shuffled off this mortal coil,
Must give us pause. There's the respect
That makes calamity of so long life. 69
For who would bear the whips and scorns of time,
The oppressor's wrong, the proud man's contumely,
The pangs of despised love, the law's delay,
The insolence of office, and the spurns
That patient merit of the unworthy takes,
When he himself might his quietus make 75
With a bare bodkin? Who would these fardels bear,
To grunt and sweat under a weary life,
But that the dread of something after death—
The undiscovered country, from whose bourn
No traveler returns—puzzles the will, 80
And makes us rather bear those ills we have
Than fly to others that we know not of?
Thus conscience does make cowards of us all,
And thus the native hue of resolution
Is sicklied o'er with the pale cast of thought, 85
And enterprises of great pith and moment
With this regard their currents turn awry
And lose the name of action.—Soft you now!
The fair Ophelia!—Nymph, in thy orisons
Be all my sins rememb'red.
Oph. Good my lord, 90
How does your honor for this many a day?

13. **Niggard . . . question:** sparing in talk
14. **assay:** try to tempt
17. **o'erraught:** reached and passed
29. **closely:** secretly
31. **Affront:** confront
32. **espials:** spies
45–46. **color . . . loneliness:** give a pretext for your solitude
52. **to:** compared with
65. **rub:** obstacle (specifically, in bowling)
67. **mortal coil:** either "human trouble" or "fleshly encumbrance"
69. **makes . . . life:** makes us endure calamity through a long life
71. **contumely:** humiliation
73. **office:** officialdom
75. **quietus:** release; from the legal phrase *Quietus est* ("He is quit")
76. **bodkin:** dagger; **fardels:** burdens
79. **undiscovered:** unexplored; **bourn:** boundary
85. **thought:** melancholy
87. **With . . . regard:** because of this meditation

Ham. I humbly thank you; well, well, well.

Oph. My lord, I have remembrances of yours
That I have longed long to redeliver.
I pray you, now receive them.

Ham. No, not I! 95
I never gave you aught.

Oph. My honored lord, you know right well you did,
And with them words of so sweet breath composed
As made the things more rich. Their perfume lost,
Take these again; for to the noble mind 100
Rich gifts wax poor when givers prove unkind.
There, my lord.

Ham. Ha, ha! Are you honest?

Oph. My lord?

Ham. Are you fair? 105

Oph. What means your lordship?

Ham. That if you be honest and fair, your honesty should admit no discourse to your beauty.

Oph. Could beauty, my lord, have better commerce than with honesty? 110

Ham. Ay, truly; for the power of beauty will sooner transform honesty from what it is to a bawd than the force of honesty can translate beauty into his likeness. This was sometime a paradox, but now the time gives it proof. I did love you once. 115

Oph. Indeed, my lord, you made me believe so.

Ham. You should not have believed me; for virtue cannot so inoculate our old stock but we shall relish of it. I loved you not.

Oph. I was the more deceived. 120

Ham. Get thee to a nunnery! Why wouldst thou be a breeder of sinners? I am myself indifferent honest, but yet I could accuse me of such things that it were better my mother had not borne me. I am very proud, revengeful, ambitious; with more offenses at my beck than I have thoughts to put them in, imagination to give them shape, or time to act them in. What should such fellows as I do, crawling between earth and heaven? We are arrant knaves all; believe none of us. Go thy ways to a nunnery. 130 Where's your father?

Oph. At home, my lord.

Ham. Let the doors be shut upon him, that he may play the fool nowhere but in's own house. Farewell.

Oph. O, help him, you sweet heavens! 135

Ham. If thou dost marry, I'll give thee this plague for thy dowry: be thou as chaste as ice, as pure as snow, thou shalt not escape calumny. Get thee to a nunnery. Go, farewell. Or if thou wilt needs marry, marry a fool; for wise men know well 140 enough what monsters you make of them. To a nunnery, go; and quickly too. Farewell.

Oph. O heavenly powers, restore him!

Ham. I have heard of your paintings too, well enough. God hath given you one face, and you 145 make yourselves another. You jig, you amble, and you lisp; you nickname God's creatures and make your wantonness your ignorance. Go to, I'll no more on't! it hath made me mad. I say, we will have no mo marriages. Those that are married already— 150 all but one—shall live; the rest shall keep as they are. To a nunnery, go. *Exit.*

Oph. O, what a noble mind is here o'erthrown!
The courtier's, soldier's, scholar's, eye, tongue, sword,
The expectancy and rose of the fair state, 155
The glass of fashion and the mold of form,
The observed of all observers—quite, quite down!
And I, of ladies most deject and wretched,
That sucked the honey of his music vows,
Now see that noble and most sovereign reason, 160
Like sweet bells jangled, out of tune and harsh;
That unmatched form and feature of blown youth
Blasted with ecstasy. O, woe is me
T' have seen what I have seen, see what I see! 164

Enter KING *and* POLONIUS.

King. Love? his affections do not that way tend;
Nor what he spake, though it lacked form a little,
Was not like madness. There's something in his soul
O'er which his melancholy sits on brood;
And I do doubt the hatch and the disclose
Will be some danger; which for to prevent, 170
I have in quick determination
Thus set it down: he shall with speed to England
For the demand of our neglected tribute.
Haply the seas, and countries different,
With variable objects, shall expel 175
This something-settled matter in his heart
Whereon his brains still beating puts him thus
From fashion of himself. What think you on't?

Pol. It shall do well. But yet do I believe
The origin and commencement of his grief 180
Sprung from neglected love.—How now, Ophelia?
You need not tell us what Lord Hamlet said,
We heard it all.—My lord, do as you please;
But if you hold it fit, after the play
Let his queen mother all alone entreat him 185
To show his grief. Let her be round with him;
And I'll be placed, so please you, in the ear
Of all their conference. If she find him not,

118. inoculate: change by grafting; **old stock:** i.e., as descendants of Adam
122–23. indifferent honest: reasonably virtuous
141. monsters: horned cuckolds (betrayed husbands)

147–48. make . . . ignorance: blame your caprices on ignorance
155. expectancy . . . state: the one who is expected to be the country's chief ornament
156. mold . . . form: model of behavior
157. observed: honored
165. affections: feelings
176. something-settled: somewhat fixed
186. round: blunt
188. find . . . not: does not find out his secret

To England send him; or confine him where
Your wisdom best shall think.

King. It shall be so. 190
Madness in great ones must not unwatched go.

Exeunt.

[Scene II. *Elsinore. A hall in the Castle.*]

Enter HAMLET *and* THREE OF THE PLAYERS.

Ham. Speak the speech, I pray you, as I pronounced it to you, trippingly on the tongue. But if you mouth it, as many of our players do, I had as lief the town crier spoke my lines. Nor do not saw the air too much with your hand, thus, but use all 5 gently; for in the very torrent, tempest, and (as I may say) whirlwind of your passion, you must acquire and beget a temperance that may give it smoothness. O, it offends me to the soul to hear a robustious periwig-pated fellow tear a passion to 10 tatters, to very rags, to split the ears of the groundlings, who (for the most part) are capable of nothing but inexplicable dumb shows and noise. I would have such a fellow whipped for o'erdoing Termagant. It out-herods Herod. Pray you avoid it. 15

Player. I warrant your Honor.

Ham. Be not too tame neither; but let your own discretion be your tutor. Suit the action to the word, the word to the action; with this special observance, that you o'erstep not the modesty of nature: 20 for anything so overdone is from the purpose of playing, whose end, both at the first and now, was and is, to hold, as 'twere, the mirror up to nature; to show virtue her own feature, scorn her own image, and the very age and body of the time his form and 25 pressure. Now this overdone, or come tardy off, though it make the unskillful laugh, cannot but make the judicious grieve; the censure of the which one must in your allowance o'erweigh a whole theatre of others. O, there be players that I have seen 30 play, and heard others praise, and that highly (not to speak it profanely), that, neither having the accent of Christians, nor the gait of Christian, pagan, nor man, have so strutted and bellowed that I have thought some of Nature's journeymen had 35 made men, and not made them well, they imitated humanity so abominably.

Player. I hope we have reformed that indifferently with us, sir.

Ham. O, reform it altogether! And let those 40 that play your clowns speak no more than is set down for them. For there be of them that will themselves laugh, to set on some quantity of barren spectators to laugh too, though in the mean time some necessary question of the play be then to be considered. 45 That's villainous and shows a most pitiful ambition in the fool that uses it. Go make you ready.

Exeunt Players.

Enter POLONIUS, ROSENCRANTZ, *and* GUILDENSTERN.

How now, my lord? Will the King hear this piece of work?

Pol. And the Queen too, and that presently. 50

Ham. Bid the players make haste. (*Exit Polonius.*)
Will you two help to hasten them?

Both. We will, my lord. *Exeunt they two.*

Ham. What, ho, Horatio!

Enter HORATIO.

Hor. Here, sweet lord, at your service. 55

Ham. Horatio, thou art e'en as just a man
As e'er my conversation coped withal.

Hor. O, my dear lord!

Ham. Nay, do not think I flatter;
For what advancement may I hope from thee,
That no revenue hast but thy good spirits 60
To feed and clothe thee? Why should the poor be flattered?
No, let the candied tongue lick absurd pomp,
And crook the pregnant hinges of the knee
Where thrift may follow fawning. Dost thou hear?
Since my dear soul was mistress of her choice 65
And could of men distinguish, her election
Hath sealed thee for herself. For thou hast been
As one, in suff'ring all, that suffers nothing;
A man that Fortune's buffets and rewards 69
Hast ta'en with equal thanks; and blest are those
Whose blood and judgment are so well commingled
That they are not a pipe for Fortune's finger
To sound what stop she please. Give me that man
That is not passion's slave, and I will wear him

11–12. **groundlings:** the lowest class of spectators, who stood in the yard of the playhouse
12. **capable:** capable of appreciating
14. **Termagant:** the name of a supposed Saracen god who appeared in many morality plays
15. **Herod:** traditionally portrayed as a ranting tyrant
20. **modesty:** temperance
21. **from:** contrary to
24–25. **the . . . body:** the true image as to both age and physical shape
26. **pressure:** impression; **come . . . off:** inadequately performed
27. **unskillful:** ignorant
29. **allowance:** acknowledgment; i.e., you must regard the censure of one judicious spectator as more weighty than the applause of a whole theatre of others.

43. **barren:** stupid
56. **just:** well-balanced
57. **conversation:** human intercourse; **coped withal:** met; encountered
63. **pregnant:** ready
64. **thrift:** profit
66. **election:** choice

In my heart's core, ay, in my heart of heart, 75
As I do thee. Something too much of this!
There is a play tonight before the King.
One scene of it comes near the circumstance,
Which I have told thee, of my father's death.
I prithee, when thou seest that act afoot, 80
Even with the very comment of thy soul
Observe my uncle. If his occulted guilt
Do not itself unkennel in one speech,
It is a damned ghost that we have seen,
And my imaginations are as foul 85
As Vulcan's stithy. Give him heedful note;
For I mine eyes will rivet to his face,
And after we will both our judgments join
In censure of his seeming.

Hor. Well, my lord.
If he steal aught the whilst this play is playing, 90
And scape detecting, I will pay the theft.

Sound a flourish. Enter Trumpets and Kettledrums. Danish march. Enter KING, QUEEN, POLONIUS, OPHELIA, ROSENCRANTZ, GUILDENSTERN, *and other* LORDS *attendant, with his [the* KING'S*]* GUARD *carrying torches.*

Ham. They are coming to the play: I must be idle. Get you a place.

King. How fares our cousin Hamlet?

Ham. Excellent, i' faith, of the chameleon's 95 dish: I eat the air, promise-crammed. You cannot feed capons so.

King. I have nothing with this answer, Hamlet. These words are not mine.

Ham. No, nor mine now. [*To Polonius*] 100 My lord, you played once i' the university, you say?

Pol. That did I, my lord, and was accounted a good actor.

Ham. What did you enact?

Pol. I did enact Julius Cæsar; I was killed i' 105 the Capitol; Brutus killed me.

Ham. It was a brute part of him to kill so capital a calf there. Be the players ready?

Ros. Ay, my lord. They stay upon your patience.

Queen. Come hither, my dear Hamlet, sit 110 by me.

Ham. No, good mother, here's metal more attractive.

Pol. [*Aside to the King*] O, ho! do you mark that?

Ham. Lady, shall I lie in your lap? 115

Oph. No, my lord.

Ham. I mean, my head upon your lap?

Oph. Ay, my lord.

Ham. Do you think I meant country matters?

Oph. I think nothing, my lord. 120

Ham. That's a fair thought to lie between maids' legs.

Oph. What is, my lord?

Ham. Nothing.

Oph. You are merry, my lord. 125

Ham. Who, I?

Oph. Ay, my lord.

Ham. O God, your only jig-maker! What should a man do but be merry? For look you how cheerfully my mother looks, and my father died within 's 130 two hours.

Oph. Nay, 'tis twice two months, my lord.

Ham. So long? Nay then, let the devil wear black, for I'll have a suit of sables. O heavens! die two months ago, and not forgotten yet? Then 135 there's hope a great man's memory may outlive his life half a year. But, by'r Lady, he must build churches then; or else shall he suffer not thinking on, with the hobbyhorse, whose epitaph is "For O, for O, the hobbyhorse is forgot!" 140

Hautboys play. The dumb show enters.

Enter a KING *and a* QUEEN *very lovingly; the* QUEEN *embracing him. She kneels, and makes show of protestation unto him. He takes her up and declines his head upon her neck. He lays him down upon a bank of flowers. She, seeing him asleep, leaves him. Anon comes in a fellow, takes off his crown, kisses it, pours poison in the* KING'S *ears, and exits. The* QUEEN *returns, finds the* KING *dead, and makes passionate action. The* POISONER, *with some two or three* MUTES, *comes in again, seeming to lament with her. The dead body is carried away. The* POISONER *woos the* QUEEN *with gifts; she seems loath and unwilling awhile, but in the end accepts his love.*

Exeunt.

Oph. What means this, my lord?

Ham. Marry, this is miching malicho; it means mischief.

Oph. Belike this show imports the argument of the play. 145

81. **comment:** observation
82. **occulted:** concealed
86. **stithy:** forge
95–96. **the . . . dish:** i.e., air. The chameleon was believed to live on air, possibly because its tongue flicks up small insects that the observer's eye cannot see.
96. **promise-crammed:** stuffed with promises of my future succession to the throne
99. **These . . . mine:** i.e., they do not bear on my question.
109. **stay . . . patience:** await your willingness to hear them
119. **country:** indelicate; obscene
128. **your . . . jig-maker:** the best comic of them all
134. **sables:** sable furs; i.e., rich clothing
138. **suffer . . . on:** endure being forgotten
139. **hobbyhorse:** a mock horse used in the morris dances, which were suppressed by the Puritans
139–40. **For . . . forgot:** a line from a lost ballad
S.D. 140. **Hautboys:** oboes
142. **miching malicho:** skulking crime. *Malhecho* is Spanish for "misdeed."
144. **Belike:** probably

Enter PROLOGUE.

Ham. We shall know by this fellow. The players cannot keep counsel; they'll tell all.

Oph. Will he tell us what this show meant?

Ham. Ay, or any show that you'll show him. Be not you ashamed to show, he'll not shame to tell 150 you what it means.

Oph. You are naught, you are naught! I'll mark the play.

Pro. For us, and for our tragedy,
Here stooping to your clemency, 155
We beg your hearing patiently. [*Exit.*]

Ham. Is this a prologue, or the posy of a ring?

Oph. 'Tis brief, my lord.

Ham. As woman's love.

Enter [TWO PLAYERS,] KING *and* QUEEN.

King. Full thirty times hath Phœbus' cart gone round
Neptune's salt wash and Tellus' orbed ground, 161
And thirty dozen moons with borrowed sheen
About the world have times twelve thirties been,
Since love our hearts, and Hymen did our hands,
Unite comutual in most sacred bands. 165

Queen. So many journeys may the sun and moon
Make us again count o'er ere love be done!
But woe is me! you are so sick of late,
So far from cheer and from your former state,
That I distrust you. Yet, though I distrust, 170
Discomfort you, my lord, it nothing must;
For women's fear and love holds quantity,
In neither aught, or in extremity.
Now what my love is, proof hath made you know;
And as my love is sized, my fear is so. 175
Where love is great, the littlest doubts are fear;
Where little fears grow great, great love grows there.

King. Faith, I must leave thee, love, and shortly too;
My operant powers their functions leave to do.
And thou shalt live in this fair world behind, 180
Honored, beloved, and haply one as kind
For husband shalt thou—

Queen. O, confound the rest!
Such love must needs be treason in my breast.
In second husband let me be accurst!
None wed the second but who killed the first. 185

Ham. [*Aside*] Wormwood, wormwood!

Queen. The instances that second marriage move
Are base respects of thrift, but none of love.
A second time I kill my husband dead
When second husband kisses me in bed. 190

King. I do believe you think what now you speak;
But what we do determine oft we break.
Purpose is but the slave to memory,
Of violent birth, but poor validity;
Which now, like fruit unripe, sticks on the tree, 195
But fall unshaken when they mellow be.
Most necessary 'tis that we forget
To pay ourselves what to ourselves is debt.
What to ourselves in passion we propose,
The passion ending, doth the purpose lose. 200
The violence of either grief or joy
Their own enactures with themselves destroy.
Where joy most revels, grief doth most lament;
Grief joys, joy grieves, on slender accident.
This world is not for aye, nor 'tis not strange 205
That even our loves should with our fortunes change;
For 'tis a question left us yet to prove,
Whether love lead fortune, or else fortune love.
The great man down, you mark his favorite flies,
The poor advanced makes friends of enemies; 210
And hitherto doth love on fortune tend,
For who not needs shall never lack a friend,
And who in want a hollow friend doth try,
Directly seasons him his enemy.
But, orderly to end where I begun, 215
Our wills and fates do so contrary run
That our devices still are overthrown;
Our thoughts are ours, their ends none of our own.
So think thou wilt no second husband wed;
But die thy thoughts when thy first lord is dead. 220

Queen. Nor earth to me give food, nor heaven light,
Sport and repose lock from me day and night,
To desperation turn my trust and hope,
An anchor's cheer in prison be my scope,
Each opposite that blanks the face of joy 225
Meet what I would have well, and it destroy,
Both here and hence pursue me lasting strife,
If, once a widow, ever I be wife!

Ham. If she should break it now!

King. 'Tis deeply sworn. Sweet, leave me here awhile.
My spirits grow dull, and fain I would beguile 231
The tedious day with sleep.

Queen. Sleep rock thy brain,
[*He*] *sleeps.*
And never come mischance between us twain! *Exit.*

Ham. Madam, how like you this play?

Queen. The lady doth protest too much, methinks.

Ham. O, but she'll keep her word. 236

King. Have you heard the argument? Is there no offense in't?

Ham. No, no! They do but jest, poison in jest; no offense i' the world. 240

King. What do you call the play?

152. naught: wicked
157. posy: inscribed motto in verse
161. Tellus' . . . ground: the earth. **Tellus** was an ancient Italian earth goddess.
164. Hymen: the Greek god of marriage
170. distrust: fear for
172. holds quantity: are equal
173. In . . . extremity: i.e., nonexistent or extreme
179. My . . . do: my faculties cease functioning.
187. instances: inducements
194. validity: strength
197–98. Most . . . debt: since a resolution is only a promise to oneself, it is inevitable that one will forget it.
201–2. The . . . destroy: violent emotion wears itself out and destroys at the same time the impulses to action born with it.
204. on . . . accident: because of trivial happenings
214. seasons: matures
224. anchor's: hermit's: **cheer:** fare
225. opposite . . . joy: misfortune that obliterates joy
237. argument: summary of the plot

Ham. "The Mousetrap." Marry, how? Tropically. This play is the image of a murder done in Vienna. Gonzago is the duke's name: his wife, Baptista. You shall see anon. 'Tis a knavish piece of work; 245 but what o' that? Your Majesty, and we that have free souls, it touches us not. Let the galled jade wince; our withers are unwrung.

Enter LUCIANUS.

This is one Lucianus, nephew to the King.

Oph. You are as good as a chorus, my lord. 250

Ham. I could interpret between you and your love, if I could see the puppets dallying.

Oph. You are keen, my lord, you are keen.

Ham. It would cost you a groaning to take off my edge. 255

Oph. Still better, and worse.

Ham. So you must take your husbands.—Begin, murderer. Pox, leave thy damnable faces, and begin! Come, the croaking raven doth bellow for revenge.

Luc. Thoughts black, hands apt, drugs fit, and time
agreeing; 260
Confederate season, else no creature seeing;
Thou mixture rank, of midnight weeds collected,
With Hecate's ban thrice blasted, thrice infected,
Thy natural magic and dire property
On wholesome life usurp immediately. 265

Pours the poison in his ears.

Ham. He poisons him i' the garden for's estate; his name's Gonzago. The story is extant, and writ in choice Italian. You shall see anon how the murderer gets the love of Gonzago's wife.

Oph. The King rises. 270

Ham. What, frighted with false fire?

Queen. How fares my lord?

Pol. Give o'er the play.

King. Give me some light! Away!

All. Lights, lights, lights! 275

Exeunt all but Hamlet and Horatio.

Ham. Why, let the strucken deer go weep,
The hart ungalled play;
For some must watch, while some must
sleep:
Thus runs the world away.
Would not this, sir, and a forest of feathers— 280
if the rest of my fortunes turn Turk with me—with two Provincial roses on my razed shoes, get me a fellowship in a cry of players, sir?

Hor. Half a share.

Ham. A whole one I! 285
For thou dost know, O Damon dear,
This realm dismantled was
Of Jove himself; and now reigns here
A very, very—pajock.

Hor. You might have rhymed. 290

Ham. O good Horatio, I'll take the ghost's word for a thousand pound! Didst perceive?

Hor. Very well, my lord.

Ham. Upon the talk of the poisoning?

Hor. I did very well note him. 295

Ham. Aha! Come, some music! Come, the recorders!
For if the King like not the comedy,
Why then, belike he likes it not, perdy.
Come, some music!

Enter ROSENCRANTZ *and* GUILDENSTERN.

Guil. Good my lord, vouchsafe me a word 300 with you.

Ham. Sir, a whole history.

Guil. The King, sir—

Ham. Ay, sir, what of him?

Guil. Is in his retirement, marvelous dis- 305 tempered.

Ham. With drink, sir?

Guil. No, my lord; rather with choler.

Ham. Your wisdom should show itself more richer to signify this to his doctor; for, for me to put 310 him to his purgation would perhaps plunge him into far more choler.

Guil. Good my lord, put your discourse into some frame, and start not so wildly from my affair.

Ham. I am tame, sir; pronounce. 315

242. **Tropically:** by a trope (figure of speech), with a pun on "trap"
247. **galled jade:** horse with a gall (sore spot)
248. **withers:** area between the shoulderblades
250. **chorus:** actor who interpreted the action and supplied background information
256. **better . . . worse:** wittier and more obscene
259. **the . . . revenge:** a parody of the line "The screeking raven sits croaking for revenge," from *The True Tragedy of Richard III* (1594)
261. **Confederate season:** the time acting as a confederate
262. **midnight weeds:** special potency was attributed to ingredients for magic gathered at midnight.
263. **Hecate:** one aspect of Diana as controller of magic and witchcraft; **ban:** curse
271. **false fire:** a blank discharge of arms or fireworks
280. **feathers:** trimmings such as an actor might wear
281. **turn Turk:** prove faithless
282: **Provincial roses:** rosettes of ribbons. The damask rose was also known as *Rosa provincialis;* **razed:** slashed decoratively
283. **cry:** pack, usually applied to hunting dogs
286. **Damon:** the loyal friend of Pythias. Hamlet trusts Horatio to be equally loyal. The verse may be a fragment of a song.
289. **pajock:** peacock, a creature of repulsive habits according to contemporary natural history
298. **perdy:** from French *par dieu*
305–6. **distempered:** disordered
308. **choler:** (1) anger; (2) bile. Hamlet puns on both meanings.
311. **purgation:** physical and spiritual cleansing

Guil. The Queen, your mother, in most great affliction of spirit hath sent me to you.

Ham. You are welcome.

Guil. Nay, good my lord, this courtesy is not of the right breed. If it shall please you to make 320 me a wholesome answer, I will do your mother's commandment; if not, your pardon and my return shall be the end of my business.

Ham. Sir, I cannot.

Guil. What, my lord? 325

Ham. Make you a wholesome answer; my wit's diseased. But, sir, such answer as I can make, you shall command; or rather, as you say, my mother. Therefore no more, but to the matter! My mother, you say— 330

Ros. Then thus she says: your behavior hath struck her into amazement and admiration.

Ham. O wonderful son, that can so astonish a mother! But is there no sequel at the heels of this mother's admiration? Impart. 335

Ros. She desires to speak with you in her closet ere you go to bed.

Ham. We shall obey, were she ten times our mother. Have you any further trade with us?

Ros. My lord, you once did love me. 340

Ham. And do still, by these pickers and stealers!

Ros. Good my lord, what is your cause of distemper? You do surely bar the door upon your own liberty, if you deny your griefs to your friend.

Ham. Sir, I lack advancement. 345

Ros. How can that be, when you have the voice of the King himself for your succession in Denmark?

Ham. Ay, sir, but "while the grass grows"—the proverb is something musty.

Enter the PLAYERS *with recorders.*

O, the recorders! Let me see one. To with- 350 draw with you—why do you go about to recover the wind of me, as if you would drive me into a toil?

Guil. O my lord, if my duty be too bold, my love is too unmannerly.

Ham. I do not well understand that. Will 355 you play upon this pipe?

Guil. My lord, I cannot.

Ham. I pray you.

Guil. Believe me, I cannot.

Ham. I do beseech you. 360

Guil. I know no touch of it, my lord.

Ham. It is as easy as lying. Govern these ventages with your finger and thumb, give it breath with your mouth, and it will discourse most eloquent music. Look you, these are the stops. 365

Guil. But these cannot I command to any utt'rance of harmony. I have not the skill.

Ham. Why, look you now, how unworthy a thing you make of me! You would play upon me; you would seem to know my stops; you would 370 pluck out the heart of my mystery; you would sound me from my lowest note to the top of my compass; and there is much music, excellent voice, in this little organ, yet cannot you make it speak. 'Sblood, do you think I am easier to be played on than a pipe? 375 Call me what instrument you will, though you can fret me, you cannot play upon me.

Enter POLONIUS.

God bless you, sir!

Pol. My lord, the Queen would speak with you, and presently. 380

Ham. Do you see yonder cloud that's almost in shape of a camel?

Pol. By the mass, and 'tis like a camel indeed.

Ham. Methinks it is like a weasel.

Pol. It is backed like a weasel. 385

Ham. Or like a whale.

Pol. Very like a whale.

Ham. Then will I come to my mother by-and-by. They fool me to the top of my bent.—I will come by-and-by. 390

Pol. I will say so. *Exit.*

Ham. "By-and-by" is easily said.—Leave me, friends. [*Exeunt all but Hamlet.*]

'Tis now the very witching time of night, 394
When churchyards yawn, and hell itself breathes out
Contagion to this world. Now could I drink hot blood
And do such bitter business as the day
Would quake to look on. Soft! now to my mother!
O heart, lose not thy nature; let not ever
The soul of Nero enter this firm bosom. 400
Let me be cruel, not unnatural;
I will speak daggers to her, but use none.
My tongue and soul in this be hypocrites—
How in my words somever she be shent,
To give them seals never, my soul, consent! 405
Exit.

321. **wholesome:** sane
332. **amazement, admiration:** consternation
341. **pickers . . . stealers:** hands. The Anglican Catechism forbids "picking and stealing."
348. **while . . . grows:** "While the grass grows, the horse starves." The proverb dates back as far as 1243.
351–52. **go . . . toil:** attempt to get on my windward side, where I cannot smell you out, in order to force me into a trap
353–54. **if . . . unmannerly:** my love matches my duty and both must be blamed for any offense.
356. **pipe:** recorder
362. **ventages:** openings; stops
374. **organ:** instrument
377. **fret:** (1) annoy; (2) furnish with "frets" for tuning, as on a stringed instrument
388. **by-and-by:** immediately
389. **to . . . bent:** to the utmost. The metaphor is from the bending of a bow.
400. **Nero:** who murdered his mother, Agrippina
404. **shent:** shamed
405. **give . . . seals:** confirm them with action

[Scene III. *The same. A room in the Castle.*]

Enter KING, ROSENCRANTZ, *and* GUILDENSTERN.

King. I like him not, nor stands it safe with us
To let his madness range. Therefore prepare you;
I your commission will forthwith dispatch,
And he to England shall along with you.
The terms of our estate may not endure 5
Hazard so near us as doth hourly grow
Out of his lunacies.

Guil. We will ourselves provide.
Most holy and religious fear it is
To keep those many many bodies safe
That live and feed upon your Majesty. 10

Ros. The single and peculiar life is bound
With all the strength and armor of the mind
To keep itself from noyance; but much more
That spirit upon whose weal depends and rests
The lives of many. The cease of majesty 15
Dies not alone, but like a gulf doth draw
What's near it with it. It is a massy wheel,
Fixed on the summit of the highest mount,
To whose huge spokes ten thousand lesser things
Are mortised and adjoined; which when it falls, 20
Each small annexment, petty consequence,
Attends the boist'rous ruin. Never alone
Did the king sigh, but with a general groan.

King. Arm you, I pray you, to this speedy voyage;
For we will fetters put upon this fear, 25
Which now goes too free-footed.

Both. We will haste us.

Exeunt Gentlemen [*Rosencrantz and Guildenstern*].

Enter POLONIUS.

Pol. My lord, he's going to his mother's closet.
Behind the arras I'll convey myself
To hear the process. I'll warrant she'll tax him home;
And, as you said, and wisely was it said, 30
'Tis meet that some more audience than a mother,
Since nature makes them partial, should o'erhear
The speech, of vantage. Fare you well, my liege.
I'll call upon you ere you go to bed
And tell you what I know.

King. Thanks, dear my lord. 35

Exit [*Polonius*].

O, my offense is rank, it smells to heaven;
It hath the primal eldest curse upon't,
A brother's murder! Pray can I not,
Though inclination be as sharp as will.
My stronger guilt defeats my strong intent, 40
And, like a man to double business bound,
I stand in pause where I shall first begin,
And both neglect. What if this cursed hand
Were thicker than itself with brother's blood,
Is there not rain enough in the sweet heavens 45
To wash it white as snow? Whereto serves mercy
But to confront the visage of offense?
And what's in prayer but this twofold force,
To be forestalled ere we come to fall,
Or pardoned being down? Then I'll look up; 50
My fault is past. But, O, what form of prayer
Can serve my turn? "Forgive me my foul murder"?
That cannot be; since I am still possessed
Of those effects for which I did the murder—
My crown, mine own ambition, and my queen. 55
May one be pardoned and retain the offense?
In the corrupted currents of this world
Offense's gilded hand may shove by justice,
And oft 'tis seen the wicked prize itself
Buys out the law; but 'tis not so above. 60
There is no shuffling; there the action lies
In his true nature, and we ourselves compelled,
Even to the teeth and forehead of our faults,
To give in evidence. What then? What rests?
Try what repentance can. What can it not? 65
Yet what can it when one cannot repent?
O wretched state! O bosom black as death!
O limed soul, that, struggling to be free,
Art more engaged! Help, angels! Make assay.
Bow, stubborn knees; and heart with strings of steel,
Be soft as sinews of the new-born babe! 71
All may be well. [*He kneels.*]

Enter HAMLET.

Ham. Now might I do it pat, now he is praying;
And now I'll do't. And so he goes to heaven,
And so am I revenged. That would be scanned. 75
A villain kills my father; and for that,
I, his sole son, do this same villain send
To heaven.
Why, this is hire and salary, not revenge!
He took my father grossly, full of bread, 80
With all his crimes broad blown, as flush as May;
And how his audit stands, who knows save heaven?
But in our circumstance and course of thought,

5. terms . . . estate: my position as king
11. peculiar: private
13. noyance: harm
14. weal: well-being
16. gulf: whirlpool
24. Arm: prepare
29. tax . . . home: scold him thoroughly
33. of vantage: from a favorable spot
56. offense: profits of offense
58. gilded: filled with bribing gold
61–62. the . . . nature: legally, the action is admissible only on the basis of truth.
68. limed: entrapped, like a bird in birdlime
80. grossly . . . bread: with all the gross sins of the flesh upon him
83. in . . . thought: as we humans regard such circumstances

'Tis heavy with him; and am I then revenged,
To take him in the purging of his soul, 85
When he is fit and seasoned for his passage?
No.
Up, sword, and know thou a more horrid hent.
When he is drunk asleep; or in his rage;
Or in the incestuous pleasure of his bed; 90
At gaming, swearing, or about some act
That has no relish of salvation in't—
Then trip him, that his heels may kick at heaven,
And that his soul may be as damned and black
As hell, whereto it goes. My mother stays. 95
This physic but prolongs thy sickly days. *Exit.*

King. [*Rises*] My words fly up, my thoughts remain below;
Words without thoughts never to heaven go. *Exit.*

[Scene IV. *The same. The Queen's closet.*]

Enter QUEEN *and* POLONIUS.

Pol. He will come straight. Look you lay home to him.
Tell him his pranks have been too broad to bear with,
And that your Grace hath screened and stood between
Much heat and him. I'll silence me even here.
Pray you be round with him. 5

Ham.[*Within*] Mother, mother, mother!

Queen. I'll warrant you; fear me not. Withdraw; I hear him coming. [*Polonius hides behind the arras.*]

Enter HAMLET.

Ham. Now, mother, what's the matter?

Queen. Hamlet, thou hast thy father much offended. 10

Ham. Mother, you have my father much offended.

Queen. Come, come, you answer with an idle tongue.

Ham. Go, go, you question with a wicked tongue.

Queen. Why, how now, Hamlet?

Ham. What's the matter now?

Queen. Have you forgot me?

Ham. No, by the rood, not so! 15
You are the Queen, your husband's brother's wife,
And—would it were not so—you are my mother.

Queen. Nay, then I'll set those to you that can speak.

Ham. Come, come, and sit you down, you shall not budge!
You go not till I set you up a glass 20
Where you may see the inmost part of you.

Queen. What wilt thou do? Thou wilt not murder me?
Help, help, ho!

Pol. [*Behind*] What, ho! help, help, help!

Ham. [*Draws*] How now? a rat? Dead for a ducat, dead! 25
[*Stabs through the arras and*] *kills Polonius.*

Pol. [*Behind*] O, I am slain!

Queen. O me, what hast thou done?

Ham. Nay, I know not. Is it the King?

Queen. O, what a rash and bloody deed is this!

Ham. A bloody deed—almost as bad, good mother,
As kill a king, and marry with his brother. 30

Queen. As kill a king?

Ham. Ay, lady, 'twas my word.
[*Pulls aside arras and sees Polonius.*]
Thou wretched, rash, intruding fool, farewell!
I took thee for thy better. Take thy fortune.
Thou findst to be too busy is some danger.—
Leave wringing of your hands. Peace! sit you down
And let me wring your heart; for so I shall 36
If it be made of penetrable stuff;
If damned custom have not brazed it so
That it is proof and bulwark against sense.

Queen. What have I done that thou darest wag thy tongue 40
In noise so rude against me?

Ham. Such an act
That blurs the grace and blush of modesty;
Calls virtue hypocrite; takes off the rose
From the fair forehead of an innocent love,
And sets a blister there; makes marriage vows 45
As false as dicers' oaths. O, such a deed
As from the body of contraction plucks
The very soul, and sweet religion makes
A rhapsody of words! Heaven's face doth glow;
Yea, this solidity and compound mass, 50
With tristful visage, as against the doom,
Is thought-sick at the act.

Queen. Ay me, what act,
That roars so loud and thunders in the index?

Ham. Look here upon this picture, and on this,

88. hent: opportunity
95. stays: waits
96. physic: spiritual purgation; **thy:** i.e., Claudius'
2. broad: flagrant
4. silence . . . here: remain silent in this hiding place
12. idle: foolish
15. rood: cross
38. brazed: hardened
39. proof . . . bulwark: an armored bulwark; **sense:** feeling
45. blister: the brand of a harlot
47. contraction: the marriage contract
48. sweet religion: holy marriage vows
50. solidity . . . mass: globe of earth
51. tristful: sad; **against . . . doom:** when Judgment Day looms
52. thought-sick: overcome with sorrow
53. index: preface

The counterfeit presentment of two brothers. 55
See what a grace was seated on this brow;
Hyperion's curls; the front of Jove himself;
An eye like Mars, to threaten and command;
A station like the herald Mercury
New lighted on a heaven-kissing hill: 60
A combination and a form indeed
Where every god did seem to set his seal
To give the world assurance of a man.
This was your husband. Look you now what follows.
Here is your husband, like a mildewed ear 65
Blasting his wholesome brother. Have you eyes?
Could you on this fair mountain leave to feed,
And batten on this moor? Ha! have you eyes?
You cannot call it love; for at your age
The heyday in the blood is tame, it's humble, 70
And waits upon the judgment; and what judgment
Would step from this to this? Sense sure you have,
Else could you not have motion; but sure that sense
Is apoplexed; for madness would not err,
Nor sense to ecstasy was ne'er so thralled 75
But it reserved some quantity of choice
To serve in such a difference. What devil was't
That thus hath cozened you at hoodman-blind?
Eyes without feeling, feeling without sight,
Ears without hands or eyes, smelling sans all, 80
Or but a sickly part of one true sense
Could not so mope.
O shame! where is thy blush? Rebellious hell,
If thou canst mutiny in a matron's bones,
To flaming youth let virtue be as wax 85
And melt in her own fire. Proclaim no shame
When the compulsive ardor gives the charge,
Since frost itself as actively doth burn,
And reason panders will.

Queen. O Hamlet, speak no more!
Thou turnst mine eyes into my very soul, 90
And there I see such black and grained spots
As will not leave their tinct.

Ham. Nay, but to live
In the rank sweat of an enseamed bed,
Stewed in corruption, honeying and making love
Over the nasty sty!

Queen. O, speak to me no more! 95
These words like daggers enter in mine ears.
No more, sweet Hamlet!

Ham. A murderer and a villain!
A slave that is not twentieth part the tithe
Of your precedent lord; a vice of kings;
A cutpurse of the empire and the rule, 100
That from a shelf the precious diadem stole
And put it in his pocket!

Queen. No more!

Enter GHOST.

Ham. A king of shreds and patches!—
Save me and hover o'er me with your wings,
You heavenly guards! What would your gracious figure? 105

Queen. Alas, he's mad!

Ham. Do you not come your tardy son to chide,
That, lapsed in time and passion, lets go by
The important acting of your dread command?
O, say! 110

Ghost. Do not forget. This visitation
Is but to whet thy almost blunted purpose.
But look, amazement on thy mother sits.
O, step between her and her fighting soul!
Conceit in weakest bodies strongest works. 115
Speak to her, Hamlet.

Ham. How is it with you, lady?

Queen. Alas, how is't with you,
That you do bend your eye on vacancy,
And with the incorporal air do hold discourse?
Forth at your eyes your spirits wildly peep; 120
And, as the sleeping soldiers in the alarm,
Your bedded hairs, like life in excrements,
Start up and stand on end. O gentle son,
Upon the heat and flame of thy distemper
Sprinkle cool patience! Whereon do you look? 125

Ham. On him, on him! Look you how pale he glares!
His form and cause conjoined, preaching to stones,
Would make them capable.—Do not look upon me,
Lest with this piteous action you convert
My stern effects. Then what I have to do 130
Will want true color—tears perchance for blood.

Queen. To whom do you speak this?

Ham. Do you see nothing there?

Queen. Nothing at all; yet all that is I see.

Ham. Nor did you nothing hear?

Queen. No, nothing but ourselves.

Ham. Why, look you there! Look how it steals away! 135

57. **Hyperion:** the sun-god, who personified male beauty; **front:** forehead; countenance
59. **station:** upright posture
65–66. **mildewed . . . brother:** Gen. 41:5–7
67. **leave . . . feed:** stop feeding
68. **batten:** gorge; **moor:** barren land
78. **cozened:** cheated; **hoodman-blind:** blindman's buff
80. **sans:** without
91. **grained:** dyed "in grain," i.e., permanently
93. **enseamed:** grease-laden
99. **vice . . . kings:** clown among kings, referring to the Vice in morality plays
100. **cutpurse:** pickpocket; thief
108. **lapsed . . . passion:** neglectful of opportunity and passionate motive
115. **Conceit:** imagination
119. **incorporal:** bodiless; empty
122. **excrements:** outgrowths of the body, including hair and nails
128. **capable:** susceptible to feeling
130. **effects:** deeds

My father, in his habit as he lived!
Look where he goes even now out at the portal!
Exit Ghost.

Queen. This is the very coinage of your brain.
This bodiless creation ecstasy
Is very cunning in.

Ham. Ecstasy? 140
My pulse as yours doth temperately keep time
And makes as healthful music. It is not madness
That I have utt'red. Bring me to the test,
And I the matter will reword; which madness
Would gambol from. Mother, for love of grace,
Lay not that flattering unction to your soul, 146
That not your trespass but my madness speaks.
It will but skin and film the ulcerous place,
Whilst rank corruption, mining all within,
Infects unseen. Confess yourself to heaven; 150
Repent what's past; avoid what is to come;
And do not spread the compost on the weeds
To make them ranker. Forgive me this my virtue;
For in the fatness of these pursy times
Virtue itself of vice must pardon beg— 155
Yea, curb and woo for leave to do him good.

Queen. O Hamlet, thou hast cleft my heart in twain.

Ham. O, throw away the worser part of it,
And live the purer with the other half.
Good night—but go not to my uncle's bed. 160
Assume a virtue, if you have it not.
That monster, custom, who all sense doth eat
Of habits evil, is angel yet in this,
That to the use of actions fair and good
He likewise gives a frock or livery, 165
That aptly is put on. Refrain tonight,
And that shall lend a kind of easiness
To the next abstinence; the next more easy;
For use almost can change the stamp of nature,
And either [. . .] the devil, or throw him out 170
With wondrous potency. Once more, good night;
And when you are desirous to be blest,
I'll blessing beg of you.—For this same lord,
I do repent; but heaven hath pleased it so,
To punish me with this, and this with me, 175
That I must be their scourge and minister.
I will bestow him, and will answer well
The death I gave him. So again, good night.
I must be cruel, only to be kind;
Thus bad begins, and worse remains behind. 180
One word more, good lady.

Queen. What shall I do?

Ham. Not this, by no means, that I bid you do:
Let the bloat King tempt you again to bed;
Pinch wanton on your cheek; call you his mouse;
And let him, for a pair of reechy kisses, 185
Or paddling in your neck with his damned fingers,
Make you to ravel all this matter out,
That I essentially am not in madness,
But mad in craft. 'Twere good you let him know;
For who that's but a queen, fair, sober, wise, 190
Would from a paddock, from a bat, a gib,
Such dear concernings hide? Who would do so?
No, in despite of sense and secrecy,
Unpeg the basket on the house's top,
Let the birds fly, and like the famous ape, 195
To try conclusions, in the basket creep
And break your own neck down.

Queen. Be thou assured, if words be made of breath,
And breath of life, I have no life to breathe
What thou hast said to me. 200

Ham. I must to England; you know that?

Queen. Alack,
I had forgot! 'Tis so concluded on.

Ham. There's letters sealed; and my two school-fellows,
Whom I will trust as I will adders fanged,
They bear the mandate; they must sweep my way
And marshal me to knavery. Let it work; 206
For 'tis the sport to have the enginer
Hoist with his own petar; and 't shall go hard
But I will delve one yard below their mines
And blow them at the moon. O, 'tis most sweet 210
When in one line two crafts directly meet.
This man shall set me packing.
I'll lug the guts into the neighbor room.—
Mother, good night.—Indeed, this counselor
Is now most still, most secret, and most grave, 215
Who was in life a foolish prating knave.
Come, sir, to draw toward an end with you.
Good night, mother.
Exeunt (Hamlet tugging in Polonius).

136. habit: costume
145. gambol: leap erratically
146. flattering unction: soothing salve
151. what . . . come: i.e., future sin
154. pursy: fat and ill-conditioned
156. curb: bow
162–63. monster . . . evil: custom is a monster in destroying our awareness of the evil of our habits. Theobald suggested **evil** for the reading "devil" in the Second Quarto; the Folio omits.
166. aptly: readily
170. either . . . the devil: the word "master" is added by some editors from the Fourth Quarto, which reads "And master the devil."
176. scourge . . . minister: agent of punishment
180. remains behind: is yet to come
185. reechy: greasy; foul
191. paddock: toad; **gib:** tomcat
192. dear concernings: important matters
195. famous ape: a lost story, apparently concerning an ape that frees birds from a basket and, seeing them fly, enters the basket himself and attempts to fly from it, only to fall and break his neck.
196. try conclusions: experiment
207. enginer: engineer; contriver
208. Hoist: hoisted; **petar:** petard (bomb); booby-trap
211. two crafts: i.e., the tactics of two enemies
212. packing: (1) carrying off (Polonius); (2) departing hastily

[ACT IV]

[Scene I. *Elsinore. A room in the Castle.*]

Enter King *and* Queen, *with* Rosencrantz *and* Guildenstern.

King. There's matter in these sighs. These profound heaves
You must translate; 'tis fit we understand them.
Where is your son?
Queen. Bestow this place on us a little while.
[*Exeunt Rosencrantz and Guildenstern.*]
Ah, mine own lord, what have I seen tonight! 5
King. What, Gertrude? How does Hamlet?
Queen. Mad as the sea and wind when both contend
Which is the mightier. In his lawless fit,
Behind the arras hearing something stir,
Whips out his rapier, cries "A rat, a rat!" 10
And in this brainish apprehension kills
The unseen good old man.
King. O heavy deed!
It had been so with us, had we been there.
His liberty is full of threats to all—
To you yourself, to us, to everyone. 15
Alas, how shall this bloody deed be answered?
It will be laid to us, whose providence
Should have kept short, restrained, and out of haunt
This mad young man. But so much was our love
We would not understand what was most fit, 20
But, like the owner of a foul disease,
To keep it from divulging, let it feed
Even on the pith of life. Where is he gone?
Queen. To draw apart the body he hath killed,
O'er whom his very madness, like some ore 25
Among a mineral of metals base,
Shows itself pure. He weeps for what is done.
King. O Gertrude, come away!
The sun no sooner shall the mountains touch
But we will ship him hence; and this vile deed 30
We must with all our majesty and skill
Both countenance and excuse. Ho, Guildenstern!

Enter Rosencrantz *and* Guildenstern.

Friends both, go join you with some further aid.
Hamlet in madness hath Polonius slain, 34
And from his mother's closet hath he dragged him.
Go seek him out; speak fair, and bring the body
Into the chapel. I pray you haste in this.
Exeunt [*Rosencrantz and Guildenstern*].
Come, Gertrude, we'll call up our wisest friends
And let them know both what we mean to do
And what's untimely done, 40
Whose whisper o'er the world's diameter—
As level as the cannon to his blank
Transports his pois'ned shot—may miss our name
And hit the woundless air.—O, come away!
My soul is full of discord and dismay. 45
Exeunt.

11. brainish apprehension: brainsick fancy
17. providence: prudent management
18. short: closely reined; **out . . . haunt:** in confinement
32. countenance: sanction

40. done: it has been thought that a phrase is omitted here. But **Whose** may mean "of which," that is, the whisper of what's untimely done. Edward Capell inserted the words "So haply slander."
42. level: well-aimed; **his blank:** its target
44. woundless: invulnerable

[Scene II. *The same. A passage in the Castle.*]

Enter Hamlet.

Ham. Safely stowed.
Gentlemen. (*Within*) Hamlet! Lord Hamlet!
Ham. But soft! What noise? Who calls on Hamlet? O, here they come.

Enter Rosencrantz *and* Guildenstern.

Ros. What have you done, my lord, with the dead body? 5
Ham. Compounded it with dust, whereto 'tis kin.
Ros. Tell us where 'tis, that we may take it thence
And bear it to the chapel.
Ham. Do not believe it.
Ros. Believe what? 10
Ham. That I can keep your counsel, and not mine own. Besides, to be demanded of a sponge, what replication should be made by the son of a king?
Ros. Take you me for a sponge, my lord?
Ham. Ay, sir, that soaks up the King's 15 countenance, his rewards, his authorities. But such

12. to . . . of: being questioned by
13. replication: reply
16. countenance: favor

officers do the King best service in the end. He keeps them, like an ape, in the corner of his jaw; first mouthed, to be last swallowed. When he needs what you have gleaned, it is but squeezing you and, 20
sponge, you shall be dry again.

Ros. I understand you not, my lord.

Ham. I am glad of it: a knavish speech sleeps in a foolish ear.

Ros. My lord, you must tell us where the 25
body is and go with us to the King.

Ham. The body is with the King, but the King is not with the body. The King is a thing—

Guil. A thing, my lord?

Ham. Of nothing. Bring me to him. Hide 30
fox, and all after.

Exeunt.

[Scene III. *The same. A room as before.*]

Enter KING.

King. I have sent to seek him and to find the body.
How dangerous is it that this man goes loose!
Yet must not we put the strong law on him.
He's loved of the distracted multitude,
Who like not in their judgment but their eyes; 5
And where 'tis so, the offender's scourge is weighed,
But never the offense. To bear all smooth and even,
This sudden sending him away must seem
Deliberate pause. Diseases desperate grown
By desperate appliance are relieved, 10
Or not at all.

Enter ROSENCRANTZ.

How now? What hath befall'n?

Ros. Where the dead body is bestowed, my lord,
We cannot get from him.

King. But where is he?

Ros. Without, my lord; guarded, to know your pleasure.

King. Bring him before us. 15

Ros. Ho, Guildenstern! Bring in my lord.

Enter HAMLET *and* GUILDENSTERN [*with* ATTENDANTS].

King. Now, Hamlet, where's Polonius?

Ham. At supper.

King. At supper? Where?

Ham. Not where he eats, but where he is 20
eaten. A certain convocation of politic worms are e'en at him. Your worm is your only emperor for diet. We fat all creatures else to fat us, and we fat ourselves for maggots. Your fat king and your lean beggar is but variable service—two dishes, but 25
to one table. That's the end.

King. Alas, alas!

Ham. A man may fish with the worm that hath eat of a king, and eat of the fish that hath fed of that worm. 30

King. What dost thou mean by this?

Ham. Nothing but to show you how a king may go a progress through the guts of a beggar.

King. Where is Polonius?

Ham. In heaven. Send thither to see. If your 35
messenger find him not there, seek him i' the other place yourself. But indeed, if you find him not within this month, you shall nose him as you go up the stairs into the lobby.

King. Go seek him there. [*To Attendants.*] 40

Ham. He will stay till you come.

[*Exeunt Attendants.*]

King. Hamlet, this deed, for thine especial safety,—
Which we do tender as we dearly grieve
For that which thou hast done,—must send thee hence
With fiery quickness. Therefore prepare thyself.
The bark is ready and the wind at help, 46
The associates tend, and everything is bent
For England.

Ham. For England?

King. Ay, Hamlet.

Ham. Good.

King. So is it, if thou knewst our purposes.

Ham. I see a cherub that sees them. But 50
come, for England! Farewell, dear mother.

King. Thy loving father, Hamlet.

Ham. My mother! Father and mother is man and wife; man and wife is one flesh; and so, my mother. Come, for England! *Exit.*

King. Follow him at foot; tempt him with speed aboard; 56
Delay it not, I'll have him hence tonight.
Away! for everything is sealed and done
That else leans on the affair. Pray you make haste.

[*Exeunt Rosencrantz and Guildenstern.*]

23–24. **a . . . ear:** probably refers to the proverb "Better be a fool than a knave."
28, 30. **a thing . . . nothing:** a mere mortal. Hamlet is contemptuous and threatening.
30–31. **Hide . . . after:** a cry for hide-and-seek. Traditional stage business has Hamlet make a sudden dash off the stage.
4. **distracted:** of unstable judgment; confused
9. **Deliberate pause:** the result of careful thought

21. **convocation . . . worms:** a punning reference to the Diet of Worms, summoned by the Emperor of the Holy Roman Empire in 1521 to hear the case of Martin Luther. Polonius prided himself on being **politic.**
25. **variable:** varied
33. **progress:** the state journey of a monarch through his realm
43. **tender:** care for
50. **I . . . them:** heaven's cherubim see everything, and Hamlet himself can guess.

And, England, if my love thou holdst at aught,—
As my great power thereof may give thee sense, 61
Since yet thy cicatrice looks raw and red
After the Danish sword, and thy free awe
Pays homage to us,—thou mayst not coldly set
Our sovereign process, which imports at full, 65
By letters congruing to that effect,
The present death of Hamlet. Do it, England;
For like the hectic in my blood he rages,
And thou must cure me. Till I know 'tis done,
Howe'er my haps, my joys were ne'er begun. 70
Exit.

[Scene IV. *Near Elsinore Castle.*]

Enter FORTINBRAS *with his* ARMY *over the stage.*

For. Go, Captain, from me greet the Danish king.
Tell him that by his license Fortinbras
Craves the conveyance of a promised march
Over his kingdom. You know the rendezvous.
If that his Majesty would aught with us, 5
We shall express our duty in his eye;
And let him know so.
Capt. I will do't, my lord.
For. Go softly on. *Exeunt* [*all but the Captain*].

Enter HAMLET, ROSENCRANTZ, [GUILDENSTERN,] *and others.*

Ham. Good sir, whose powers are these?
Capt. They are of Norway, sir. 10
Ham. How purposed, sir, I pray you?
Capt. Against some part of Poland.
Ham. Who commands them, sir?
Capt. The nephew to old Norway, Fortinbras.
Ham. Goes it against the main of Poland, sir, 15
Or for some frontier?
Capt. Truly to speak, and with no addition,
We go to gain a little patch of ground
That hath in it no profit but the name.
To pay five ducats, five, I would not farm it; 20
Nor will it yield to Norway or the Pole
A ranker rate, should it be sold in fee.
Ham. Why, then the Polack never will defend it.
Capt. Yes, it is already garrisoned.
Ham. Two thousand souls and twenty thousand ducats 25
Will not debate the question of this straw.
This is the imposthume of much wealth and peace,
That inward breaks, and shows no cause without
Why the man dies.—I humbly thank you, sir. 29
Capt. God be wi' you, sir. [*Exit.*]
Ros. Will't please you go, my lord?
Ham. I'll be with you straight. Go a little before.
[*Exeunt all but Hamlet.*]
How all occasions do inform against me
And spur my dull revenge! What is a man,
If his chief good and market of his time
Be but to sleep and feed? A beast, no more. 35
Sure he that made us with such large discourse,
Looking before and after, gave us not
That capability and godlike reason
To fust in us unused. Now, whether it be
Bestial oblivion, or some craven scruple 40
Of thinking too precisely on the event,—
A thought which, quartered, hath but one part wisdom
And ever three parts coward,—I do not know
Why yet I live to say "This thing's to do,"
Sith I have cause, and will, and strength, and means
To do't. Examples gross as earth exhort me. 46
Witness this army of such mass and charge,
Led by a delicate and tender prince,
Whose spirit, with divine ambition puffed,
Makes mouths at the invisible event, 50
Exposing what is mortal and unsure
To all that fortune, death, and danger dare,
Even for an eggshell. Rightly to be great
Is not to stir without great argument,
But greatly to find quarrel in a straw 55
When honor's at the stake. How stand I then,
That have a father killed, a mother stained,
Excitements of my reason and my blood,
And let all sleep, while to my shame I see
The imminent death of twenty thousand men, 60
That for a fantasy and trick of fame
Go to their graves like beds, fight for a plot
Whereon the numbers cannot try the cause,

60. **holdst . . . aught:** value at all
61. **As . . . sense:** as you should, in view of my great power
62. **cicatrice:** wound
63. **free:** freely given
64. **set:** regard
65. **process:** command
67. **present:** immediate
68. **the hectic:** severe fever
70. **Howe'er . . . haps:** however my fortunes turn
3. **conveyance:** escort
6. **in . . . eye:** before his person
8. **softly:** slowly
17. **addition:** exaggeration
20. **farm:** rent
22. **ranker:** greater; **in fee:** outright
26. **debate . . . straw:** settle a trivial matter like this
27. **imposthume:** festering growth
33. **dull:** sluggish
34. **market:** profit
36. **discourse:** reasoning ability
37. **Looking . . . after:** reasoning from cause to effect
39. **fust:** mildew
46. **gross . . . earth:** as evident as the very earth
50. **event:** outcome
53–56. **Rightly . . . stake:** the truly great will not stir without good reason, but when honor is at stake a trifling thing should be sufficient motive.
61. **trick . . . fame:** trifle affecting reputation
63. **Whereon . . . cause:** smaller than will contain the combatants

Which is not tomb enough and continent
To hide the slain? O, from this time forth, 65
My thoughts be bloody, or be nothing worth!

Exit.

[Scene V. *Elsinore. A room in the Castle.*]

Enter QUEEN, HORATIO, *and a* GENTLEMAN.

Queen. I will not speak with her.
Gent. She is importunate, indeed distract;
Her mood will needs be pitied.
Queen. What would she have?
Gent. She speaks much of her father; says she hears
There's tricks i' the world, and hems, and beats her heart; 5
Spurns enviously at straws; speaks things in doubt,
That carry but half sense. Her speech is nothing,
Yet the unshaped use of it doth move
The hearers to collection; they aim at it, 9
And botch the words up fit to their own thoughts;
Which, as her winks and nods and gestures yield them,
Indeed would make one think there might be thought,
Though nothing sure, yet much unhappily.
Hor. 'Twere good she were spoken with; for she may strew
Dangerous conjectures in ill-breeding minds. 15
Queen. Let her come in. [*Exit Gentleman.*]
[*Aside*] To my sick soul (as sin's true nature is)
Each toy seems prologue to some great amiss.
So full of artless jealousy is guilt
It spills itself in fearing to be spilt. 20

Enter OPHELIA *distracted.*

Oph. Where is the beauteous Majesty of Denmark?
Queen. How now, Ophelia?
Oph. (*Sings*)
How should I your truelove know
From another one?
By his cockle hat and staff 25
And his sandal shoon.

Queen. Alas, sweet lady, what imports this song?
Oph. Say you? Nay, pray you mark.

(*Sings*) He is dead and gone, lady,
He is dead and gone; 30
At his head a grass-green turf,
At his heels a stone.

O, ho!
Queen. Nay, but Ophelia—
Oph. Pray you mark. 35

(*Sings*) White his shroud as the mountain snow—

Enter KING.

Queen. Alas, look here, my lord!

Oph. (*Sings*)
Larded all with sweet flowers;
Which bewept to the grave did not go
With truelove showers. 40

King. How do you, pretty lady?
Oph. Well. Goddild you! They say the owl was a baker's daughter. Lord, we know what we are, but know not what we may be. God be at your table!
King. Conceit upon her father. 45
Oph. Pray let's have no words of this; but when they ask you what it means, say you this:

(*Sings*) Tomorrow is Saint Valentine's day,
All in the morning betime,
And I a maid at your window, 50
To be your Valentine.

Then up he rose and donned his clo'es
And dupped the chamber door,
Let in the maid, that out a maid
Never departed more. 55

King. Pretty Ophelia!
Oph. Indeed, la, without an oath, I'll make an end on't!

[*Sings*] By Gis and by Saint Charity,
Alack, and fie for shame! 60
Young men will do't if they come to't.
By Cock, they are to blame.

Quoth she, "Before you tumbled me,
You promised me to wed."

He answers: 65

"So would I 'a' done, by yonder sun,
An thou hadst not come to my bed."

64. continent: receptacle
6. Spurns: shies; **enviously:** suspiciously
8–9. the . . . collection: i.e., formless as it is, its nature is such that hearers are moved to draw inferences from it.
9. aim: guess
10. botch: patch
11. yield them: present them (her words)
18. toy: trifle; **amiss:** misfortune
19. artless jealousy: awkward suspicion
25. cockle hat: hat with a cockleshell in the band, the symbol of a completed pilgrimage to the shrine of St. James of Compostela in Spain
26. shoon: shoes
38. Larded: garnished
42. Goddild: God yield (reward); **the owl:** in an old tale a baker's daughter was changed to an owl by Jesus because of her lack of generosity.
45. Conceit . . . father: i.e., imaginings about her father are the cause of this.
53. dupped: opened
59. Gis: Jesus
62. Cock: a corruption of "God"

King. How long hath she been thus?

Oph. I hope all will be well. We must be patient; but I cannot choose but weep to think they 70 would lay him i' the cold ground. My brother shall know of it; and so I thank you for your good counsel. Come, my coach! Good night, ladies. Good night, sweet ladies. Good night, good night. *Exit*.

King. Follow her close; give her good watch, I pray you. [*Exit Horatio*.]
O, this is the poison of deep grief; it springs 76
All from her father's death. O Gertrude, Gertrude,
When sorrows come, they come not single spies,
But in battalions! First, her father slain;
Next, your son gone, and he most violent author 80
Of his own just remove; the people muddied,
Thick and unwholesome in their thoughts and whispers
For good Polonius' death, and we have done but greenly
In hugger-mugger to inter him; poor Ophelia
Divided from herself and her fair judgment, 85
Without the which we are pictures or mere beasts;
Last, and as much containing as all these,
Her brother is in secret come from France;
Feeds on his wonder, keeps himself in clouds,
And wants not buzzers to infect his ear 90
With pestilent speeches of his father's death,
Wherein necessity, of matter beggared,
Will nothing stick our person to arraign
In ear and ear. O my dear Gertrude, this,
Like to a murd'ring piece, in many places 95
Gives me superfluous death. *A noise within*.

Queen. Alack, what noise is this?

King. Where are my Switzers? Let them guard the door.

Enter a MESSENGER.

What is the matter?

Mess. Save yourself, my lord:
The ocean, overpeering of his list,
Eats not the flats with more impetuous haste 100
Than young Laertes, in a riotous head,
O'erbears your officers. The rabble call him lord;
And, as the world were now but to begin,
Antiquity forgot, custom not known,
The ratifiers and props of every word, 105
They cry "Choose we, Laertes shall be king!"
Caps, hands, and tongues applaud it to the clouds,
"Laertes shall be king! Laertes king!" *A noise within*.

Queen. How cheerfully on the false trail they cry!
O, this is counter, you false Danish dogs! 110

King. The doors are broke.

Enter LAERTES *with others*.

Laer. Where is this king?—Sirs, stand you all without.

All. No, let's come in!

Laer. I pray you give me leave.

All. We will, we will!

Laer. I thank you. Keep the door.
[*Exeunt his Followers*.]
O thou vile king,
Give me my father!

Queen. Calmly, good Laertes. 116

Laer. That drop of blood that's calm proclaims me bastard;
Cries cuckold to my father; brands the harlot
Even here between the chaste unsmirched brows
Of my true mother.

King. What is the cause, Laertes,
That thy rebellion looks so giantlike? 121
Let him go, Gertrude. Do not fear our person.
There's such divinity doth hedge a king
That treason can but peep to what it would,
Acts little of his will. Tell me, Laertes, 125
Why thou art thus incensed. Let him go, Gertrude.
Speak, man.

Laer. Where is my father?

King. Dead.

Queen. But not by him!

King. Let him demand his fill. 129

Laer. How came he dead? I'll not be juggled with:
To hell, allegiance! vows, to the blackest devil!
Conscience and grace, to the profoundest pit!
I dare damnation. To this point I stand,
That both the worlds I give to negligence,
Let come what comes; only I'll be revenged 135
Most throughly for my father.

King. Who shall stay you?

Laer. My will, not all the world!
And for my means, I'll husband them so well
They shall go far with little.

King. Good Laertes,
If you desire to know the certainty 140
Of your dear father's death, is't writ in your revenge

83. greenly: foolishly
84. hugger-mugger: secrecy
89. wonder: speculation; **clouds:** confusion
90. buzzers: gossips
93. nothing: not at all; **stick:** scruple
94. ear . . . ear: every ear
95. murd'ring piece: cannon that discharged scattered missiles
97. Switzers: Swiss guards
99. overpeering: towering over; overflowing; **list:** bound
101. in . . . head: leading a riotous force
105. word: motto
110. counter: in the wrong direction, a hunting term
118. cuckold: betrayed husband
122. fear: fear for
124. peep to: look furtively at
136. throughly: thoroughly; **stay:** stop
137. My . . . world: not all the world shall stop me from having my will.

That swoopstake you will draw both friend and foe,
Winner and loser?

Laer. None but his enemies.

King. Will you know them then?

Laer. To his good friends thus wide I'll ope my arms 145
And, like the kind life-rend'ring pelican,
Repast them with my blood.

King. Why, now you speak
Like a good child and a true gentleman.
That I am guiltless of your father's death,
And am most sensibly in grief for it, 150
It shall as level to your judgment pierce
As day does to your eye.

A noise within: "Let her come in."

Laer. How now? What noise is that?

Enter OPHELIA.

O heat, dry up my brains! Tears seven times salt
Burn out the sense and virtue of mine eye! 155
By heaven, thy madness shall be paid by weight
Till our scale turn the beam. O rose of May!
Dear maid, kind sister, sweet Ophelia!
O heavens! is't possible a young maid's wits
Should be as mortal as an old man's life? 160
Nature is fine in love, and where 'tis fine,
It sends some precious instance of itself
After the thing it loves.

Oph. (*Sings*)

They bore him barefaced on the bier
(Hey non nony, nony, hey nony) 165
And in his grave rained many a tear.

Fare you well, my dove!

Laer. Hadst thou thy wits, and didst persuade revenge,
It could not move thus.

Oph. You must sing "A-down, a-down," and 170 you, "Call him a-down-a." O, how the wheel becomes it! It is the false steward, that stole his master's daughter.

Laer. This nothing's more than matter.

Oph. There's rosemary, that's for remem- 175 brance. Pray you, love, remember. And there is pansies, that's for thoughts.

Laer. A document in madness! Thoughts and remembrance fitted.

Oph. There's fennel for you, and colum- 180 bines. There's rue for you, and here's some for me. We may call it herb of grace o' Sundays. O, you must wear your rue with a difference! There's a daisy. I would give you some violets, but they withered all when my father died. They say he 185 made a good end.

[*Sings*] For bonny sweet Robin is all my joy.

Laer. Thought and affliction, passion, hell itself,
She turns to favor and to prettiness.

Oph. (*Sings*)

And will he not come again? 190
And will he not come again?
No, no, he is dead;
Go to thy deathbed;
He never will come again.

His beard was as white as snow, 195
All flaxen was his poll.
He is gone, he is gone,
And we cast away moan.
God 'a' mercy on his soul!

And of all Christian souls, I pray God. God 200 be wi' you. *Exit.*

Laer. Do you see this, O God?

King. Laertes, I must commune with your grief,
Or you deny me right. Go but apart, 204
Make choice of whom your wisest friends you will,
And they shall hear and judge 'twixt you and me.
If by direct or by collateral hand
They find us touched, we will our kingdom give,
Our crown, our life, and all that we call ours,
To you in satisfaction; but if not, 210
Be you content to lend your patience to us,
And we shall jointly labor with your soul
To give it due content.

Laer. Let this be so.
His means of death, his obscure funeral—
No trophy, sword, nor hatchment o'er his bones,
No noble rite nor formal ostentation,— 216
Cry to be heard, as 'twere from heaven to earth,
That I must call't in question.

King. So you shall;
And where the offense is let the great axe fall.
I pray you go with me. 220

Exeunt.

142. swoopstake: indiscriminately, as one might gather up all stakes in a game

146. life-rend'ring: the pelican was believed to feed its young with its own flesh and blood.

150. sensibly: feelingly

155. virtue: power

171. wheel: probably, spinning wheel. Ophelia sings excerpts of spinning songs.

172. false steward: a reference to some lost story

178. document: lesson

180–84. The plants symbolize the following: **fennel,** flattery; **columbines,** disloyalty or ingratitude; **rue,** sorrow and repentance; **daisies,** infidelity; **violet,** faithfulness; **herb of grace** was another name for **rue.**

183. difference: heraldic term for a variation in a coat of arms to distinguish between different branches of a family. The rue was probably given to the Queen, for whom it would symbolize repentance; for Ophelia herself it would mean sorrow.

188. passion: grief

189. favor: attractiveness

196. poll: head

207. collateral: indirect

215. hatchment: memorial tablet bearing a coat of arms

[Scene VI. *The same. Another room in the Castle.*]

Enter HORATIO *with an* ATTENDANT.

Hor. What are they that would speak with me?
Servant. Sailors, sir. They say they have letters for you.
Hor. Let them come in. [*Exit Attendant.*]
I do not know from what part of the world
I should be greeted, if not from Lord Hamlet. 5

Enter SAILORS.

Sailor. God bless you, sir.
Hor. Let him bless thee too.
Sailor. He shall, sir, an't please him. There's a letter for you, sir,—it comes from the ambassador that was bound for England—if your name be 10 Horatio, as I am let to know it is.

Hor. (*Reads the letter.*) Horatio, when thou shalt have overlooked this, give these fellows some means to the King. They have letters for him. Ere we were two days old at sea, a pirate of very warlike appointment 15 gave us chase. Finding ourselves too slow of sail, we put on a compelled valor, and in the grapple I boarded them. On the instant they got clear of our ship; so I alone became their prisoner. They have dealt with me like thieves of mercy; but they knew what they 20 did: I am to do a good turn for them. Let the King have the letters I have sent, and repair thou to me with as much speed as thou wouldst fly death. I have words to speak in thine ear will make thee dumb; yet are they much too light for the bore of the matter. These 25 good fellows will bring thee where I am. Rosencrantz and Guildenstern hold their course for England. Of them I have much to tell thee. Farewell.
He that thou knowest thine, HAMLET.

Come, I will give you way for these your letters,
And do't the speedier that you may direct me 31
To him from whom you brought them.
Exeunt.

[Scene VII. *The same. Another room in the Castle.*]

Enter KING *and* LAERTES.

King. Now must your conscience my acquittance seal,
And you must put me in your heart for friend,

20. **thieves . . . mercy:** merciful thieves
25. **bore:** caliber; import
30. **way:** admittance

Sith you have heard, and with a knowing ear,
That he which hath your noble father slain
Pursued my life.
Laer. It well appears. But tell me 5
Why you proceeded not against these feats
So crimeful and so capital in nature,
As by your safety, wisdom, all things else,
You mainly were stirred up.
King. O, for two special reasons,
Which may to you, perhaps, seem much unsinewed,
But yet to me they are strong. The Queen his mother
Lives almost by his looks; and for myself,— 12
My virtue or my plague, be it either which,—
She's so conjunctive to my life and soul
That, as the star moves not but in his sphere, 15
I could not but by her. The other motive
Why to a public count I might not go
Is the great love the general gender bear him,
Who, dipping all his faults in their affection, 19
Would, like the spring that turneth wood to stone,
Convert his gyves to graces; so that my arrows,
Too slightly timbered for so loud a wind,
Would have reverted to my bow again,
And not where I had aimed them.
Laer. And so have I a noble father lost; 25
A sister driven into desp'rate terms,
Whose worth, if praises may go back again,
Stood challenger on mount of all the age
For her perfections. But my revenge will come.
King. Break not your sleeps for that. You must not think 30
That we are made of stuff so flat and dull
That we can let our beard be shook with danger,
And think it pastime. You shortly shall hear more.
I loved your father, and we love ourself,
And that, I hope, will teach you to imagine— 35

Enter a MESSENGER *with letters.*

How now? What news?
Mess. Letters, my lord, from Hamlet:
This to your Majesty; this to the Queen.
King. From Hamlet? Who brought them? 38
Mess. Sailors, my lord, they say; I saw them not.
They were given me by Claudio; he received them
Of him that brought them.
King. Laertes, you shall hear them.
Leave us. *Exit Messenger.*

9. **mainly:** mightily
14. **conjunctive:** united
17. **count:** reckoning
18. **general gender:** common people
20. **spring . . . stone:** several such springs were known in England.
21. **gyves:** shackles; **graces:** honors
26. **terms:** conditions
27. **back again:** i.e., to her former state

[*Reads*] High and Mighty,—You shall know I am set naked on your kingdom. Tomorrow shall I beg leave to see your kingly eyes; when I shall (first asking 45 your pardon thereunto) recount the occasion of my sudden and more strange return. HAMLET.

What should this mean? Are all the rest come back?
Or is it some abuse, and no such thing?
Laer. Know you the hand?
King. 'Tis Hamlet's character.
"Naked!" 51
And in a postscript here, he says "alone."
Can you advise me?
Laer. I am lost in it, my lord. But let him come!
It warms the very sickness in my heart 55
That I shall live and tell him to his teeth,
"Thus didest thou."
King. If it be so, Laertes
(As how should it be so? how otherwise?),
Will you be ruled by me?
Laer. Ay, my lord,
So you will not o'errule me to a peace. 60
King. To thine own peace. If he be now returned,
As checking at his voyage, and that he means
No more to undertake it, I will work him
To an exploit now ripe in my device,
Under the which he shall not choose but fall; 65
And for his death no wind of blame shall breathe,
But even his mother shall uncharge the practice
And call it accident.
Laer. My lord, I will be ruled;
The rather if you could devise it so
That I might be the organ.
King. It falls right. 70
You have been talked of since your travel much,
And that in Hamlet's hearing, for a quality
Wherein they say you shine. Your sum of parts
Did not together pluck such envy from him
As did that one; and that, in my regard, 75
Of the unworthiest siege.
Laer. What part is that, my lord?
King. A very ribband in the cap of youth—
Yet needful too; for youth no less becomes
The light and careless livery that it wears
Than settled age his sables and his weeds, 80
Importing health and graveness. Two months since
Here was a gentleman of Normandy.
I have seen myself, and served against, the French,
And they can well on horseback; but this gallant
Had witchcraft in't. He grew unto his seat, 85
And to such wondrous doing brought his horse
As had he been incorpsed and demi-natured
With the brave beast. So far he topped my thought
That I, in forgery of shapes and tricks,
Come short of what he did.
Laer. A Norman was't? 90
King. A Norman.
Laer. Upon my life, Lamound.
King. The very same.
Laer. I know him well. He is the brooch indeed
And gem of all the nation.
King. He made confession of you; 95
And gave you such a masterly report
For art and exercise in your defense,
And for your rapier most especially,
That he cried out 'twould be a sight indeed
If one could match you. The scrimers of their nation
He swore had neither motion, guard, nor eye, 101
If you opposed them. Sir, this report of his
Did Hamlet so envenom with his envy
That he could nothing do but wish and beg
Your sudden coming o'er to play with him. 105
Now, out of this—
Laer. What out of this, my lord?
King. Laertes, was your father dear to you?
Or are you like the painting of a sorrow,
A face without a heart?
Laer. Why ask you this?
King. Not that I think you did not love your father; 110
But that I know love is begun by time,
And that I see, in passages of proof,
Time qualifies the spark and fire of it.
There lives within the very flame of love
A kind of wick or snuff that will abate it; 115
And nothing is at a like goodness still;
For goodness, growing to a plurisy,
Dies in his own too-much. That we would do,
We should do when we would; for this "would" changes,
And hath abatements and delays as many 120
As there are tongues, are hands, are accidents;
And then this "should" is like a spendthrift sigh,
That hurts by easing. But to the quick o' the ulcer!
Hamlet comes back. What would you undertake

44. **naked:** unequipped
49. **abuse:** trick
50. **character:** handwriting
62. **checking at:** rebelling against; in falconry the **action** of the hawk in deserting the quarry to pursue another bird
67. **uncharge . . . practice:** acquit the method of treachery
73. **parts:** abilities; accomplishments
76. **siege:** rank
77. **ribband:** ribbon
79. **livery:** characteristic dress
80. **weeds:** garments
81. **health:** lack of concern about health, referring to the **careless livery of youth; since:** ago
87. **incorpsed . . . demi-natured:** grown into the same body with (his horse), like a centaur
88. **brave:** noble; **thought:** imagination
89. **forgery:** invention; **shapes . . . tricks:** intricate paces of horsemanship
95. **made . . . of:** acknowledged your acquaintance
100. **scrimers:** fencers
112. **passages . . . proof:** confirmatory happenings
117. **plurisy:** excess
123. **hurts:** i.e., by drawing blood from the heart, thus weakening its action according to contemporary physiology

To show yourself your father's son in deed 125
More than in words?
Laer. To cut his throat i' the church!
King. No place indeed should murder sanctuarize;
Revenge should have no bounds. But, good Laertes,
Will you do this? Keep close within your chamber.
Hamlet returned shall know you are come home.
We'll put on those shall praise your excellence 131
And set a double varnish on the fame
The Frenchman gave you; bring you in fine together
And wager on your heads. He, being remiss,
Most generous, and free from all contriving, 135
Will not peruse the foils; so that with ease,
Or with a little shuffling, you may choose
A sword unbated, and, in a pass of practice,
Requite him for your father.
Laer. I will do't!
And for that purpose I'll anoint my sword. 140
I bought an unction of a mountebank
So mortal that, but dip a knife in it,
Where it draws blood no cataplasm so rare,
Collected from all simples that have virtue 144
Under the moon, can save the thing from death
That is but scratched withal. I'll touch my point
With this contagion, that, if I gall him slightly,
It may be death.
King. Let's further think of this,
Weigh what convenience both of time and means
May fit us to our shape. If this should fail, 150
And that our drift look through our bad performance,
'Twere better not assayed. Therefore this project
Should have a back or second, that might hold
If this did blast in proof. Soft! let me see.
We'll make a solemn wager on your cunnings—
I ha't! 156
When in your motion you are hot and dry—
As make your bouts more violent to that end—
And that he calls for drink, I'll have prepared him
A chalice for the nonce; whereon but sipping, 160
If he by chance escape your venomed stuck,
Our purpose may hold there.—But stay, what noise?

Enter QUEEN.

How now, sweet queen?
Queen. One woe doth tread upon another's heel,
So fast they follow. Your sister's drowned, Laertes.
Laer. Drowned! O, where? 166
Queen. There is a willow grows aslant a brook,
That shows his hoar leaves in the glassy stream.
There with fantastic garlands did she come
Of crowflowers, nettles, daisies, and long purples,
That liberal shepherds give a grosser name, 171
But our cold maids do dead men's fingers call them.
There on the pendent boughs her coronet weeds
Clamb'ring to hang, an envious sliver broke,
When down her weedy trophies and herself 175
Fell in the weeping brook. Her clothes spread wide
And, mermaid-like, awhile they bore her up;
Which time she chanted snatches of old tunes,
As one incapable of her own distress,
Or like a creature native and indued 180
Unto that element; but long it could not be
Till that her garments, heavy with their drink,
Pulled the poor wretch from her melodious lay
To muddy death.
Laer. Alas, then she is drowned?
Queen. Drowned, drowned. 185
Laer. Too much of water hast thou, poor Ophelia,
And therefore I forbid my tears; but yet
It is our trick; nature her custom holds,
Let shame say what it will. When these are gone,
The woman will be out. Adieu, my lord. 190
I have a speech of fire, that fain would blaze
But that this folly douts it. *Exit.*
King. Let's follow, Gertrude.
How much I had to do to calm his rage!
Now fear I this will give it start again;
Therefore let's follow. 195
Exeunt.

131. **put on:** incite
133. **in fine:** finally
138. **unbated:** unblunted; **pass . . . practice:** treacherous thrust
141. **mountebank:** quack
143. **cataplasm:** poultice
144. **simples:** herbs
150. **fit . . . shape:** suit our design
151. **drift:** intention
154. **blast . . . proof:** burst in trial
155. **cunnings:** respective skills
160. **nonce:** specific occasion
161. **stuck:** thrust
162. **hold:** prevail
170. **long purples:** a species of orchid
171. **liberal:** plain-spoken
174. **sliver:** branch
179. **incapable of:** uncomprehending
180. **indued:** adapted
188. **our trick:** the way of humans
190. **The . . . out:** my feminine weakness will be exhausted.

[ACT V]

[Scene I. *The same. A churchyard.*]

Enter two CLOWNS, [*with spades and pickaxes*].

Clown. Is she to be buried in Christian burial that willfully seeks her own salvation?

Other. I tell thee she is; therefore make her grave straight. The crowner hath sat on her, and finds it Christian burial. 5

Clown. How can that be, unless she drowned herself in her own defense?

Other. Why, 'tis found so.

Clown. It must be *se offendendo;* it cannot be else. For here lies the point: if I drown myself 10 wittingly, it argues an act; and an act hath three branches—it is to act, to do, and to perform; argal, she drowned herself wittingly.

Other. Nay, but hear you, Goodman Delver!

Clown. Give me leave. Here lies the water; 15 good. Here stands the man; good. If the man go to this water and drown himself, it is, will he nill he, he goes—mark you that. But if the water come to him and drown him, he drowns not himself. Argal, he that is not guilty of his own death shortens not his 20 own life.

Other. But is this law?

Clown. Ay, marry, is't—crowner's quest law.

Other. Will you ha' the truth on't? If this had not been a gentlewoman, she should have been 25 buried out o' Christian burial.

Clown. Why, there thou sayst! And the more pity that great folk should have count'nance in this world to drown or hang themselves more than their even-Christian. Come, my spade! There is no an- 30 cient gentlemen but gard'ners, ditchers, and grave-makers. They hold up Adam's profession.

Other. Was he a gentleman?

Clown. He was the first that ever bore arms.

Other. Why, he had none. 35

Clown. What, art a heathen? How dost thou understand the Scripture? The Scripture says Adam digged. Could he dig without arms? I'll put another question to thee. If thou answerest me not to the purpose, confess thyself— 40

Other. Go to!

Clown. What is he that builds stronger than either the mason, the shipwright, or the carpenter?

Other. The gallows-maker; for that frame outlives a thousand tenants. 45

Clown. I like thy wit well, in good faith. The gallows does well. But how does it well? It does well to those that do ill. Now, thou dost ill to say the gallows is built stronger than the church. Argal, the gallows may do well to thee. To't again, come! 50

Other. Who builds stronger than a mason, a shipwright, or a carpenter?

Clown. Ay, tell me that, and unyoke.

Other. Marry, now I can tell!

Clown. To't. 55

Other. Mass, I cannot tell.

Enter HAMLET *and* HORATIO *afar off.*

Clown. Cudgel thy brains no more about it, for your dull ass will not mend his pace with beating; and when you are asked this question next, say "a grave-maker." The houses he makes lasts till 60 doomsday. Go, get thee to Yaughan; fetch me a stoup of liquor. [*Exit Second Clown.*]

[*Clown digs and*] *sings.*

In youth when I did love, did love,
Methought it was very sweet;
To contract—O—the time for—a—my behove,
O, methought there—a—was nothing—a—meet.

4. straight: at once; **crowner:** coroner
9. se offendendo: in self-offense; the clown's mistake for *se defendendo,* a common legal phrase
12. argal: a mistake for *ergo*
15. Give . . . leave: let me continue.
23. quest: inquest
27. there . . . sayst: you said it.
28. count'nance: allowance
29–30. even-Christian: fellow Christian
32. hold up: maintain
34. arms: only gentlemen had the right to bear coats of arms. Some heraldry books display Adam's spade as the oldest escutcheon, explaining the traditional shape of the heraldic shield.
40. confess thyself: "and be hanged," a common proverb
53. unyoke: unharness yourself, your work will be finished.
56. Mass: by the Mass
61. Yaughan: probably a London tavern-keeper
62. stoup: two-quart container
63–66, 73–76. In . . . such: the clown's version of a poem printed in Richard Tottel's *Miscellany* (1557) and attributed to Lord Vaux.
65. contract: shorten; **behove:** benefit

Ham. Has this fellow no feeling of his business, that he sings at grave-making? 67

Hor. Custom hath made it in him a property of easiness. 70

Ham. 'Tis e'en so. The hand of little employment hath the daintier sense.

Clown. (*Sings*)

But age with his stealing steps
Hath clawed me in his clutch,
And hath shipped me intil the land, 75
As if I had never been such.
[*Throws up a skull.*]

Ham. That skull had a tongue in it and could sing once. How the knave jowls it to the ground, as if 'twere Cain's jawbone, that did the first murder! This might be the pate of a politician, which 80 this ass now o'erreaches; one that would circumvent God, might it not?

Hor. It might, my lord.

Ham. Or of a courtier, which could say "Good morrow, sweet lord! How dost thou, good 85 lord?" This might be my Lord Such-a-one, that praised my Lord Such-a-one's horse when he meant to beg it—might it not?

Hor. Ay, my lord.

Ham. Why, e'en so! and now my Lady 90 Worm's, chapless, and knocked about the mazzard with a sexton's spade. Here's fine revolution, if we had the trick to see't. Did these bones cost no more the breeding but to play at loggets with 'em? Mine ache to think on't. 95

Clown. (*Sings*)

A pickaxe and a spade, a spade,
For and a shrouding sheet;
O, a pit of clay for to be made
For such a guest is meet.
[*Throws up another skull.*]

Ham. There's another. Why may not that be 100 the skull of a lawyer? Where be his quiddities now, his quillets, his cases, his tenures, and his tricks? Why does he suffer this rude knave now to knock him about the sconce with a dirty shovel, and will not tell him of his action of battery? Hum! 105 This fellow might be in's time a great buyer of land, with his statutes, his recognizances, his fines, his double vouchers, his recoveries. Is this the fine of his fines, and the recovery of his recoveries, to have his fine pate full of fine dirt? Will his vouchers 110 vouch him no more of his purchases, and double ones too, than the length and breadth of a pair of indentures? The very conveyances of his lands will scarcely lie in this box; and must the inheritor himself have no more, ha? 115

Hor. Not a jot more, my lord.

Ham. Is not parchment made of sheepskins?

Hor. Ay, my lord, and of calveskins too.

Ham. They are sheep and calves which seek out assurance in that. I will speak to this fellow. 120 Whose grave's this, sirrah?

Clown. Mine, sir.

[*Sings*] O, a pit of clay for to be made
For such a guest is meet.

Ham. I think it be thine indeed, for thou 125 liest in't.

Clown. You lie out on't, sir, and therefore 'tis not yours. For my part, I do not lie in't, yet it is mine.

Ham. Thou dost lie in't, to be in't and say it is thine. 'Tis for the dead, not for the quick; 130 therefore thou liest.

Clown. 'Tis a quick lie, sir; 'twill away again from me to you.

Ham. What man dost thou dig it for?

Clown. For no man, sir. 135

Ham. What woman then?

Clown. For none neither.

Ham. Who is to be buried in't?

Clown. One that was a woman, sir; but, rest her soul, she's dead. 140

Ham. How absolute the knave is! We must speak by the card, or equivocation will undo us. By the Lord, Horatio, this three years I have taken note of it, the age is grown so picked that the toe of the peasant comes so near the heel of the courtier he 145 galls his kibe.—How long hast thou been a grave-maker?

Clown. Of all the days i' the year, I came to't that day that our last king Hamlet overcame Fortinbras. 150

Ham. How long is that since?

Clown. Cannot you tell that? Every fool can tell that. It was the very day that young Hamlet was born—he that is mad, and sent into England.

69–70. **Custom . . . easiness:** custom has made him easy in it.
72. **daintier sense:** greater sensitivity
75. **shipped . . . land:** returned me to the dust
78. **jowls:** knocks
81. **o'erreaches:** gets the better of
91. **chapless:** jawless: **mazzard:** a slang term for "head"
94. **loggets:** a game played with pieces of wood
101. **quiddities:** logical subtleties
102. **quillets:** quibbles
104. **sconce:** head
107. **statutes . . . recognizances, etc.:** terms dealing with property laws
112–13. **indentures:** conveyances or contracts, which were prepared in duplicate
130. **quick:** living
141. **absolute:** precise
142. **by . . . card:** to the point, as by a compass; **equivocation:** a term in logic meaning a fallacy resulting from ambiguity
144. **picked:** refined
146. **kibe:** chilblain; i.e., peasants now come close to courtiers in elegance.

Ham. Ay, marry, why was he sent into England? 155

Clown. Why, because he was mad. He shall recover his wits there; or, if he do not, 'tis no great matter there.

Ham. Why? 160

Clown. 'Twill not be seen in him there. There the men are as mad as he.

Ham. How came he mad?

Clown. Very strangely, they say.

Ham. How strangely? 165

Clown. Faith, e'en with losing his wits.

Ham. Upon what ground?

Clown. Why, here in Denmark. I have been sexton here, man and boy, thirty years.

Ham. How long will a man lie i' the earth ere he rot? 170

Clown. Faith, if he be not rotten before he die (as we have many pocky corses nowadays that will scarce hold the laying in), he will last you some eight year or nine year. A tanner will last you nine year. 175

Ham. Why he more than another?

Clown. Why, sir, his hide is so tanned with his trade that he will keep out water a great while; and your water is a sore decayer of your whoreson dead body. Here's a skull now: this skull hath lien i' the earth three-and-twenty years. 180

Ham. Whose was it?

Clown. A whoreson mad fellow's it was. Whose do you think it was? 185

Ham. Nay, I know not.

Clown. A pestilence on him for a mad rogue! He poured a flagon of Rhenish on my head once. This same skull, sir, was Yorick's skull, the King's jester.

Ham. This? 190

Clown. E'en that.

Ham. Let me see. [*Takes the skull.*] Alas, poor Yorick! I knew him, Horatio. A fellow of infinite jest, of most excellent fancy. He hath borne me on his back a thousand times. And now how abhorred in my imagination it is! My gorge rises at it. Here hung those lips that I have kissed I know not how oft. Where be your gibes now? your gambols? your songs? your flashes of merriment that were wont to set the table on a roar? Not one now, to mock your own grinning? Quite chapfall'n? Now get you to my lady's chamber, and tell her, let her paint an inch thick, to this favor she must come. Make her laugh at that. Prithee, Horatio, tell me one thing. 195 200 205

Hor. What's that, my lord?

Ham. Dost thou think Alexander looked o' this fashion i' the earth?

Hor. E'en so. 209

Ham. And smelt so? Pah! [*Puts down the skull.*]

Hor. E'en so, my lord.

Ham. To what base uses we may return, Horatio! Why may not imagination trace the noble dust of Alexander till he find it stopping a bunghole?

Hor. 'Twere to consider too curiously, to consider so. 215

Ham. No, faith, not a jot; but to follow him thither with modesty enough, and likelihood to lead it; as thus: Alexander died, Alexander was buried, Alexander returneth into dust; the dust is earth; of earth we make loam; and why of that loam (whereto he was converted) might they not stop a beer barrel? 220

Imperious Cæsar, dead and turned to clay,
Might stop a hole to keep the wind away. 225
O, that that earth which kept the world in awe
Should patch a wall t' expel the winter's flaw!

But soft! but soft! aside! Here comes the King—

Enter KING, QUEEN, LAERTES, *and a coffin, with* [PRIESTS *and*] LORDS *attendant.*

The Queen, the courtiers. Who is this they follow?
And with such maimed rites? This doth betoken
The corse they follow did with desp'rate hand 231
Fordo it own life. 'Twas of some estate.
Couch we awhile, and mark. [*Retires with Horatio.*]

Laer. What ceremony else?

Ham. That is Laertes,
A very noble youth. Mark. 235

Laer. What ceremony else?

Priest. Her obsequies have been as far enlarged
As we have warranty. Her death was doubtful;
And, but that great command o'ersways the order,
She should in ground unsanctified have lodged 240
Till the last trumpet. For charitable prayers,
Shards, flints, and pebbles should be thrown on her.
Yet here she is allowed her virgin crants,
Her maiden strewments, and the bringing home
Of bell and burial. 245

Laer. Must there no more be done?

Priest. No more be done.
We should profane the service of the dead
To sing a requiem and such rest to her
As to peace-parted souls.

Laer. Lay her i' the earth,
And from her fair and unpolluted flesh 250
May violets spring! I tell thee, churlish priest,

173. pocky: diseased
180. whoreson: a jocular word of no precise meaning
203. favor: cast of countenance

215. curiously: ingeniously
227. flaw: gust of wind
232. Fordo: destroy
233. Couch: hide
242. Shards: pieces of pottery
243. crants: garlands, from the German *kranz*
249. peace-parted souls: souls who departed in peace

A minist'ring angel shall my sister be
When thou liest howling.
Ham. What, the fair Ophelia?
Queen. Sweets to the sweet! Farewell. 254
[*Scatters flowers.*]
I hoped thou shouldst have been my Hamlet's wife;
I thought thy bride-bed to have decked, sweet maid,
And not have strewed thy grave.
Laer. O, treble woe
Fall ten times treble on that cursed head
Whose wicked deed thy most ingenious sense
Deprived thee of! Hold off the earth awhile, 260
Till I have caught her once more in mine arms.
Leaps in the grave.
Now pile your dust upon the quick and dead
Till of this flat a mountain you have made
T' o'ertop old Pelion or the skyish head
Of blue Olympus. 265
Ham. [*Advancing*] What is he whose grief
Bears such an emphasis? whose phrase of sorrow
Conjures the wand'ring stars, and makes them stand
Like wonder-wounded hearers? This is I,
Hamlet the Dane. [*Leaps in after Laertes.*]
Laer. The devil take thy soul! 270
[*Grappling with him.*]
Ham. Thou prayst not well.
I prithee take thy fingers from my throat;
For, though I am not splenitive and rash,
Yet have I in me something dangerous,
Which let thy wisdom fear. Hold off thy hand! 275
King. Pluck them asunder.
Queen. Hamlet, Hamlet!
All. Gentlemen!
Hor. Good my lord, be quiet.
[*Attendants part them, and they leave the grave.*]
Ham. Why, I will fight with him upon this theme
Until my eyelids will no longer wag.
Queen. O my son, what theme? 280
Ham. I loved Ophelia. Forty thousand brothers
Could not (with all their quantity of love)
Make up my sum. What wilt thou do for her?
King. O, he is mad, Laertes.
Queen. For love of God, forbear him! 285
Ham. 'Swounds, show me what thou't do.
Woo't weep? woo't fight? woo't fast? woo't tear thyself?
Woo't drink up eisell? eat a crocodile?
I'll do't. Dost thou come here to whine?
To outface me with leaping in her grave? 290
Be buried quick with her, and so will I.
And if thou prate of mountains, let them throw
Millions of acres on us, till our ground,
Singeing his pate against the burning zone,
Make Ossa like a wart! Nay, an thou'lt mouth, 295
I'll rant as well as thou.
Queen. This is mere madness;
And thus a while the fit will work on him.
Anon, as patient as the female dove
When that her golden couplets are disclosed,
His silence will sit drooping.
Ham. Hear you, sir! 300
What is the reason that you use me thus?
I loved you ever. But it is no matter.
Let Hercules himself do what he may,
The cat will mew, and dog will have his day. *Exit.*
King. I pray thee, good Horatio, wait upon him.
Exit Horatio.
[*To Laertes*] Strengthen your patience in our last night's speech. 306
We'll put the matter to the present push.—
Good Gertrude, set some watch over your son.—
This grave shall have a living monument.
An hour of quiet shortly shall we see; 310
Till then in patience our proceeding be.
Exeunt.

[Scene II. *The same. A hall in the Castle.*]

Enter HAMLET *and* HORATIO.

Ham. So much for this, sir; now shall you see the other.
You do remember all the circumstance?
Hor. Remember it, my lord!
Ham. Sir, in my heart there was a kind of fighting
That would not let me sleep. Methought I lay 5
Worse than the mutines in the bilboes. Rashly—
And praised be rashness for it; let us know,
Our indiscretion sometime serves us well
When our deep plots do pall; and that should learn us
There's a divinity that shapes our ends, 10
Rough-hew them how we will—
Hor. That is most certain.
Ham. Up from my cabin,
My sea-gown scarfed about me, in the dark
Groped I to find out them; had my desire,
Fingered their packet, and in fine withdrew 15
To mine own room again; making so bold
(My fears forgetting manners) to unseal

264. Pelion: the mountain that the giants of Greek mythology piled on Mount Ossa in an attempt to reach Olympus
273. splenitive: synonymous with **rash**
285. forbear him: leave him alone
286. thou't: thou wilt
287. Woo't: wilt thou
288. eisell: vinegar, supposed to heighten grief
294. burning zone: belt between the tropics of Cancer and Capricorn
299. golden couplets: two young ones covered with yellow down
307. the . . . push: immediate execution
6. mutines: mutineers; **bilboes:** ship's stocks
9. pall: fail

Their grand commission; where I found, Horatio
(O royal knavery!), an exact command,
Larded with many several sorts of reasons, 20
Importing Denmark's health, and England's too,
With, ho! such bugs and goblins in my life—
That, on the supervise, no leisure bated,
No, not to stay the grinding of the axe,
My head should be struck off.

Hor. Is't possible? 25

Ham. Here's the commission; read it at more leisure.
But wilt thou hear me how I did proceed?

Hor. I beseech you.

Ham. Being thus benetted round with villainies,
Ere I could make a prologue to my brains, 30
They had begun the play. I sat me down;
Devised a new commission; wrote it fair.
I once did hold it, as our statists do,
A baseness to write fair, and labored much
How to forget that learning; but, sir, now 35
It did me yeoman's service. Wilt thou know
The effect of what I wrote?

Hor. Ay, good my lord.

Ham. An earnest conjuration from the King,
As England was his faithful tributary,
As love between them like the palm might flourish,
As peace should still her wheaten garland wear 41
And stand a comma 'tween their amities,
And many suchlike as's of great charge,
That, on the view and knowing of these contents,
Without debatement further, more or less, 45
He should the bearers put to sudden death,
Not shriving time allowed.

Hor. How was this sealed?

Ham. Why, even in that was heaven ordinant.
I had my father's signet in my purse,
Which was the model of that Danish seal; 50
Folded the writ up in the form of the other,
Subscribed it, gave't the impression, placed it safely,
The changeling never known. Now, the next day
Was our sea-fight; and what to this was sequent
Thou knowst already. 55

Hor. So Guildenstern and Rosencrantz go to't.

Ham. Why, man, they did make love to this employment!
They are not near my conscience; their defeat
Does by their own insinuation grow.
'Tis dangerous when the baser nature comes 60
Between the pass and fell incensed points
Of mighty opposites.

Hor. Why, what a king is this!

Ham. Does it not, thinkst thee, stand me now upon—
He that hath killed my king, and whored my mother;
Popped in between the election and my hopes; 65
Thrown out his angle for my proper life,
And with such coz'nage—is't not perfect conscience
To quit him with this arm? And is't not to be damned
To let this canker of our nature come
In further evil? 70

Hor. It must be shortly known to him from England
What is the issue of the business there.

Ham. It will be short; the interim is mine,
And a man's life's no more than to say "one."
But I am very sorry, good Horatio, 75
That to Laertes I forgot myself;
For by the image of my cause I see
The portraiture of his. I'll court his favors.
But sure the bravery of his grief did put me
Into a tow'ring passion.

Hor. Peace! Who comes here? 80

Enter young Osric, *a courtier.*

Osr. Your lordship is right welcome back to Denmark.

Ham. I humbly thank you, sir. [*Aside to Horatio*] Dost know this waterfly?

Hor. [*Aside to Hamlet*] No, my good lord. 85

Ham. [*Aside to Horatio*] Thy state is the more gracious; for 'tis a vice to know him. He hath much land, and fertile. Let a beast be lord of beasts, and his crib shall stand at the king's mess. 'Tis a chough; but, as I say, spacious in the possession of 90 dirt.

Osr. Sweet lord, if your lordship were at lei-

20. **Larded:** filled out
22. **bugs . . . goblins:** illusory dangers
23. **on . . . bated:** on reading the instruction, wasting no time
30–31. **Ere . . . play:** without preliminary my mind instinctively began to work.
33. **statists:** statesmen
37. **effect:** tenor
42. **stand . . . amities:** i.e., prevent their amities from clashing; unite their friendships
47. **shriving:** confession and absolution
48. **ordinant:** the agency that determined the outcome
53. **changeling:** exchange
56. **to't:** to death
58. **defeat:** destruction
59. **insinuation:** i.e., action designed to insinuate themselves with the King
61. **pass:** thrust; **fell:** deadly
63. **Does . . . upon:** am I not now bound
65. **election:** election to the throne by the people
66. **proper:** own
67. **coz'nage:** trickery
68. **quit:** pay
70. **In:** into
79. **bravery:** ostentation
84. **waterfly:** showy trifler
87. **gracious:** virtuous
89. **at . . . mess:** among the King's dinner companions. Banquets were usually made up of "messes" of four. **chough:** magpie

sure, I should impart a thing to you from his Majesty.

Ham. I will receive it, sir, with all diligence 95 of spirit. Put your bonnet to his right use, 'tis for the head.

Osr. I thank your lordship, it is very hot.

Ham. No, believe me, 'tis very cold; the wind is northerly. 100

Osr. It is indifferent cold, my lord, indeed.

Ham. But yet methinks it is very sultry and hot for my complexion.

Osr. Exceedingly, my lord; it is very sultry, as 'twere—I cannot tell how. But, my lord, his 105 Majesty bade me signify to you that he has laid a great wager on your head. Sir, this is the matter—

Ham. I beseech you remember.

[*Hamlet moves him to put on his hat.*]

Osr. Nay, good my lord; for mine ease, in good faith. Sir, here is newly come to court Laertes; 110 believe me, an absolute gentleman, full of most excellent differences, of very soft society and great showing. Indeed, to speak feelingly of him, he is the card or calendar of gentry; for you shall find in him the continent of what part a gentleman would 115 see.

Ham. Sir, his definement suffers no perdition in you; though, I know, to divide him inventorially would dozy the arithmetic of memory, and yet but yaw neither in respect of his quick sail. But, in 120 the verity of extolment, I take him to be a soul of great article, and his infusion of such dearth and rareness as, to make true diction of him, his semblable is his mirror, and who else would trace him, his umbrage, nothing more. 125

Osr. Your lordship speaks most infallibly of him.

Ham. The concernancy, sir? Why do we wrap the gentleman in our more rawer breath?

Osr. Sir?

Hor. [*Aside to Hamlet*] Is't not possible to 130 understand in another tongue? You will do't, sir, really.

Ham. What imports the nomination of this gentleman?

Osr. Of Laertes? 135

Hor. [*Aside*] His purse is empty already; all's golden words are spent.

Ham. Of him, sir.

Osr. I know you are not ignorant—

Ham. I would you did, sir; yet, in faith, if 140 you did, it would not much approve me. Well, sir?

Osr. You are not ignorant of what excellence Laertes is—

Ham. I dare not confess that, lest I should compare with him in excellence; but to know a 145 man well were to know himself.

Osr. I mean, sir, for his weapon; but in the imputation laid on him by them, in his meed he's unfellowed.

Ham. What's his weapon? 150

Osr. Rapier and dagger.

Ham. That's two of his weapons—but well.

Osr. The King, sir, hath wagered with him six Barbary horses; against the which he has imponed, as I take it, six French rapiers and poniards, 155 with their assigns, as girdle, hangers, and so. Three of the carriages, in faith, are very dear to fancy, very responsive to the hilts, most delicate carriages, and of very liberal conceit.

Ham. What call you the carriages? 160

Hor. [*Aside to Hamlet*] I knew you must be edified by the margent ere you had done.

Osr. The carriages, sir, are the hangers.

Ham. The phrase would be more germane to the matter if we could carry cannon by our sides. 165 I would it might be hangers till then. But on! Six Barbary horses against six French swords, their assigns, and three liberal-conceited carriages: that's the French bet against the Danish. Why is this all imponed, as you call it? 170

Osr. The King, sir, hath laid that, in a dozen passes between yourself and him, he shall not exceed you three hits; he hath laid on twelve for nine, and

96. **Put . . . use:** put on your hat. Osric insists on politely doffing his hat and protests in the elegant terms decreed by courtesy books.
103. **complexion:** compound of humors; temperament
111. **absolute:** perfect
112. **differences:** accomplishments that distinguish him; **soft society:** gentle manners
112–13. **great showing:** noble appearance
113. **feelingly:** with accurate perception
113–14. **the . . . gentry:** a veritable handbook of courtesy
115. **continent:** container; **what part:** all the qualities
117. **perdition:** loss
118. **divide . . . inventorially:** inventory his qualities
119. **dozy:** dizzy
120. **yaw:** off course (a nautical term meaning to veer back and forth off the course); **neither:** at that
122. **great article:** many excellencies; **infusion:** character with which he is infused
123–24. **his . . . mirror:** he can only be matched by his own reflection; **trace:** pursue competitively
125. **umbrage:** shadow
127. **concernancy:** relevance
128. **our . . . breath:** our words, which are too crude to describe him
131. **do't:** outdo Osric in fancy expression
133. **nomination:** naming
140–41. **I . . . me:** in other words, Osric's opinion is of little worth one way or the other.
147–48. **imputation:** reputation
148. **them:** his weapons; **meed:** merits
148–49. **unfellowed:** unmatched
154. **imponed:** staked
156. **assigns:** accessories; **girdle:** belt; **hangers:** straps attaching the weapons to the girdle
157. **dear . . . fancy:** tastefully designed
158. **responsive:** harmoniously patterned
159. **liberal conceit:** imaginative pattern
161–62. **must . . . margent:** i.e., would need some explanation. The **margent** (margin) of books contained any necessary explanatory notes.
171. **laid:** bet

it would come to immediate trial if your lordship would vouchsafe the answer. 175

Ham. How if I answer no?

Osr. I mean, my lord, the opposition of your person in trial.

Ham. Sir, I will walk here in the hall. If it please his Majesty, it is the breathing time of day 180 with me. Let the foils be brought, the gentleman willing, and the King hold his purpose, I will win for him if I can; if not, I will gain nothing but my shame and the odd hits.

Osr. Shall I redeliver you e'en so? 185

Ham. To this effect, sir, after what flourish your nature will.

Osr. I commend my duty to your lordship.

Ham. Yours, yours. [*Exit Osric.*] He does well to commend it himself; there are no tongues else 190 for's turn.

Hor. This lapwing runs away with the shell on his head.

Ham. He did comply with his dug before he sucked it. Thus has he, and many more of the same 195 bevy that I know the drossy age dotes on, only got the tune of the time and outward habit of encounter —a kind of yeasty collection, which carries them through and through the most fanned and winnowed opinions; and do but blow them to their trial 200 —the bubbles are out.

Enter a LORD.

Lord. My lord, his Majesty commended him to you by young Osric, who brings back to him, that you attend him in the hall. He sends to know if your pleasure hold to play with Laertes, or that 205 you will take longer time.

Ham. I am constant to my purposes; they follow the King's pleasure. If his fitness speaks, mine is ready; now or whensoever, provided I be so able as now. 210

Lord. The King and Queen and all are coming down.

Ham. In happy time.

Lord. The Queen desires you to use some gentle entertainment to Laertes before you fall to play. 215

Ham. She well instructs me. [*Exit Lord.*]

Hor. You will lose this wager, my lord.

Ham. I do not think so. Since he went into France I have been in continual practice; I shall win at the odds. But thou wouldst not think how ill all's 220 here about my heart. But it is no matter.

Hor. Nay, good my lord—

Ham. It is but foolery; but it is such a kind of gaingiving as would perhaps trouble a woman.

Hor. If your mind dislike anything, obey it. 225 I will forestall their repair hither and say you are not fit.

Ham. Not a whit, we defy augury; there's a special providence in the fall of a sparrow. If it be now, 'tis not to come; if it be not to come, it will 230 be now; if it be not now, yet it will come: the readiness is all. Since no man has aught of what he leaves, what is't to leave betimes? Let be.

Enter KING, QUEEN, LAERTES, [OSRIC], *and* LORDS, *with other* ATTENDANTS *with foils and gauntlets. A table and flagons of wine on it.*

King. Come, Hamlet, come, and take this hand from me. [*He puts Laertes' hand into Hamlet's.*]

Ham. Give me your pardon, sir. I have done you wrong; 235
But pardon't, as you are a gentleman.
This presence knows,
And you must needs have heard, how I am punished
With sore distraction. What I have done
That might your nature, honor, and exception 240
Roughly awake, I here proclaim was madness.
Was't Hamlet wronged Laertes? Never Hamlet.
If Hamlet from himself be ta'en away,
And when he's not himself does wrong Laertes,
Then Hamlet does it not, Hamlet denies it. 245
Who does it, then? His madness. If't be so,
Hamlet is of the faction that is wronged;
His madness is poor Hamlet's enemy.
Sir, in this audience,
Let my disclaiming from a purposed evil 250
Free me so far in your most generous thoughts
That I have shot my arrow o'er the house
And hurt my brother.

Laer. I am satisfied in nature,
Whose motive in this case should stir me most
To my revenge. But in my terms of honor 255
I stand aloof, and will no reconcilement
Till by some elder masters of known honor
I have a voice and precedent of peace

175. the answer: to answer the challenge
191. for's turn: to serve his purpose
192–93. This . . . head: this upstart is as precocious as the lapwing, which runs away when it is barely hatched. Osric has put on his hat.
194. comply with: compliment
196. bevy: a term for a covey of quails; **drossy:** worthless
197. outward . . . encounter: superficial clothing of social grace
198. yeasty: insubstantial
199. fanned . . . winnowed: refined; discriminating. The First Folio reads "fond" for **fanned** (suggested by William Warburton), while the Second Quarto reads "prophane and trennowed."
213. In . . . time: "I am glad to hear it" or the like
214–15. use . . . entertainment: show a civil welcome
219–20. at . . . odds: with the advantage I possess
232–33. Since . . . betimes: since all we possess are our personal endowments, what does it matter when we leave the world?
253. in nature: personally
258. voice: authority

To keep my name ungored. But till that time
I do receive your offered love like love, 260
And will not wrong it.

Ham. I embrace it freely,
And will this brother's wager frankly play.
Give us the foils. Come on.

Laer. Come, one for me.

Ham. I'll be your foil, Laertes. In mine ignorance
Your skill shall, like a star i' the darkest night 265
Stick fiery off indeed.

Laer. You mock me, sir.

Ham. No, by this hand.

King. Give them the foils, young Osric. Cousin Hamlet,
You know the wager?

Ham. Very well, my lord.
Your Grace has laid the odds o' the weaker side. 270

King. I do not fear it, I have seen you both;
But since he is bettered, we have therefore odds.

Laer. This is too heavy; let me see another.

Ham. This likes me well. These foils have all a length? *Prepare to play.*

Osr. Ay, my good lord. 275

King. Set me the stoups of wine upon that table.
If Hamlet give the first or second hit,
Or quit in answer of the third exchange,
Let all the battlements their ordnance fire;
The King shall drink to Hamlet's better breath, 280
And in the cup an union shall he throw
Richer than that which four successive kings
In Denmark's crown have worn. Give me the cups;
And let the kettle to the trumpet speak,
The trumpet to the cannoneer without, 285
The cannons to the heavens, the heaven to earth,
"Now the King drinks to Hamlet." Come, begin.
And you the judges, bear a wary eye.

Ham. Come on, sir.

Laer. Come, my lord. *They play.*

Ham. One.

Laer. No.

Ham. Judgment!

Osr. A hit, a very palpable hit.

Laer. Well, again! 290

King. Stay, give me drink. Hamlet, this pearl is thine;
Here's to thy health.

Drum; trumpets sound; a piece goes off [*within*].

Give him the cup.

Ham. I'll play this bout first; set it by awhile.
Come. (*They play.*) Another hit. What say you?

Laer. A touch, a touch; I do confess. 295

King. Our son shall win.

Queen. He's fat, and scant of breath.
Here, Hamlet, take my napkin, rub thy brows.
The Queen carouses to thy fortune, Hamlet.

Ham. Good madam!

King. Gertrude, do not drink. 299

Queen. I will, my lord; I pray you pardon me. [*Drinks.*]

King. [*Aside*] It is the poisoned cup; it is too late.

Ham. I dare not drink yet, madam; by-and-by.

Queen. Come, let me wipe thy face.

Laer. My lord, I'll hit him now.

King. I do not think't.

Laer. [*Aside*] And yet it is almost against my conscience. 305

Ham. Come for the third, Laertes! You but dally;
I pray you pass with your best violence;
I am afeard you make a wanton of me.

Laer. Say you so? Come on. *Play.*

Osr. Nothing neither way. 310

Laer. Have at you now!

[*Laertes wounds Hamlet; then,*] *in scuffling, they change rapiers,* [*and Hamlet wounds Laertes*].

King. Part them! They are incensed.

Ham. Nay come! again! [*The Queen falls.*]

Osr. Look to the Queen there, ho!

Hor. They bleed on both sides. How is it, my lord?

Osr. How is't, Laertes?

Laer. Why, as a woodcock to mine own springe, Osric. 315
I am justly killed with mine own treachery.

Ham. How does the Queen?

King. She swoons to see them bleed.

Queen. No, no! the drink, the drink! O my dear Hamlet!
The drink, the drink! I am poisoned. [*Dies.*]

Ham. O villainy! Ho! let the door be locked. 320
Treachery! Seek it out. [*Laertes falls.*]

Laer. It is here, Hamlet. Hamlet, thou art slain;
No med'cine in the world can do thee good.
In thee there is not half an hour of life.
The treacherous instrument is in thy hand, 325
Unbated and envenomed. The foul practice
Hath turned itself on me. Lo, here I lie,
Never to rise again. Thy mother's poisoned.
I can no more. The King, the King's to blame.

Ham. The point envenomed too? 330
Then, venom, to thy work. *Hurts the King.*

All. Treason! treason!

King. O, yet defend me, friends! I am but hurt.

Ham. Here, thou incestuous, murd'rous, damned Dane,
Drink off this potion! Is thy union here? 335
Follow my mother. *King dies.*

Laer. He is justly served.
It is a poison tempered by himself.

259. ungored: unmarred
264. foil: i.e., contrast
281. union: large pearl
296. fat: probably "out of condition"

297. napkin: handkerchief
308. make . . . me: toy with me

Exchange forgiveness with me, noble Hamlet. 338
Mine and my father's death come not upon thee,
Nor thine on me! *Dies.*

Ham. Heaven make thee free of it! I follow thee.
I am dead, Horatio. Wretched queen, adieu!
You that look pale and tremble at this chance,
That are but mutes or audience to this act,
Had I but time (as this fell sergeant, Death, 345
Is strict in his arrest) O, I could tell you—
But let it be. Horatio, I am dead;
Thou livest; report me and my cause aright
To the unsatisfied.

Hor. Never believe it.
I am more an antique Roman than a Dane. 350
Here's yet some liquor left.

Ham. As th'art a man,
Give me the cup. Let go! By heaven, I'll have't.
O good Horatio, what a wounded name
(Things standing thus unknown) shall live behind me!
If thou didst ever hold me in thy heart, 355
Absent thee from felicity awhile,
And in this harsh world draw thy breath in pain,
To tell my story. *March afar off, and shot within.*
What warlike noise is this?

Osr. Young Fortinbras, with conquest come from Poland,
To the ambassadors of England gives 360
This warlike volley.

Ham. O, I die, Horatio!
The potent poison quite o'ercrows my spirit.
I cannot live to hear the news from England,
But I do prophesy the election lights
On Fortinbras. He has my dying voice. 365
So tell him, with the occurrents, more and less,
Which have solicited—the rest is silence. *Dies.*

Hor. Now cracks a noble heart. Good night, sweet prince,
And flights of angels sing thee to thy rest!
[*March within.*]
Why does the drum come hither? 370

Enter FORTINBRAS *and* ENGLISH AMBASSADORS, *with Drum, Colors, and* ATTENDANTS.

Fort. Where is this sight?

Hor. What is it you would see?
If aught of woe or wonder, cease your search.

Fort. This quarry cries on havoc. O proud Death,
What feast is toward in thine eternal cell
That thou so many princes at a shot 375
So bloodily hast struck?

Ambassador. The sight is dismal;
And our affairs from England come too late.
The ears are senseless that should give us hearing
To tell him his commandment is fulfilled,
That Rosencrantz and Guildenstern are dead. 380
Where should we have our thanks?

Hor. Not from his mouth,
Had it the ability of life to thank you.
He never gave commandment for their death.
But since, so jump upon this bloody question,
You from the Polack wars, and you from England,
Are here arrived, give order that these bodies 386
High on a stage be placed to the view;
And let me speak to the yet unknowing world
How these things came about. So shall you hear
Of carnal, bloody, and unnatural acts; 390
Of accidental judgments, casual slaughters;
Of deaths put on by cunning and forced cause;
And, in this upshot, purposes mistook
Fall'n on the inventors' heads. All this can I
Truly deliver.

Fort. Let us haste to hear it, 395
And call the noblest to the audience.
For me, with sorrow I embrace my fortune.
I have some rights of memory in this kingdom,
Which now to claim my vantage doth invite me.

Hor. Of that I shall have also cause to speak, 400
And from his mouth whose voice will draw on more.
But let this same be presently performed,
Even while men's minds are wild, lest more mischance
On plots and errors happen.

Fort. Let four captains
Bear Hamlet like a soldier to the stage; 405
For he was likely, had he been put on,
To have proved most royally; and for his passage
The soldiers' music and the rites of war
Speak loudly for him.
Take up the bodies. Such a sight as this 410
Becomes the field, but here shows much amiss.
Go, bid the soldiers shoot.
Exeunt marching; after the which a peal of ordnance are shot off.

341. free: innocent
367. solicited: evoked (the happenings)
373. This . . . havoc: this heap of dead proclaims indiscriminate slaughter.
384. jump upon: exactly coincident with; **question:** matter
387. stage: platform
399. vantage: opportunity
401. whose . . . more: whose authority will attract the approval of others
404. On: because of
406. put on: put to the test

From Angelo Vizani, *Trattato dello schermo* (1588).

The Reluctant Duelists

From an extra-illustrated copy of Shakespeare's *Works,* edited by Howard Staunton (London and New York, 1881).

TWELFTH NIGHT

INTRODUCTION

In the opinion of many critics *Twelfth Night* is Shakespeare's finest achievement in sheer comedy of merriment. Although Victorian commentators occasionally professed to see a tragic element in the discomfiture of Malvolio, Shakespeare intended the episode to be nothing more than a practical joke played on a pompous steward who deserved the resulting embarrassment. Throughout the play there prevails a madcap gaiety untinged with any overtones of melancholy. *Twelfth Night,* written in the sunny spirit of *As You Like It,* followed hard upon that play. Its first performance probably dates from sometime in 1600 or 1601.

This comedy was performed at a night of revels at the Middle Temple on February 2, 1602, and we have the record of the impression that it made on one member of the Temple, John Manningham, who wrote in his diary:

> At our feast we had a play called *Twelfth Night, or, What You Will,* much like the *Comedy of Errors,* or *Menaechmi* in Plautus, but most like and near to that in Italian called *Inganni.* A good practice in it to make the steward believe his lady widow was in love with him, by counterfeiting a letter as from his lady in general terms, telling him what she liked best in him, and prescribing his gesture in smiling, his apparel, etc., and then when he came to practice, making him believe they took him to be mad.

The possibility that *Twelfth Night* was written for some special occasion has been often discussed. Professor Leslie Hotson wrote an ingenious book, *The First Night of Twelfth Night* (New York, 1954), to prove that Shakespeare prepared the play in eleven days after his company was called upon to get something ready for the festivities at Whitehall on January 6, 1601, when the Queen entertained Virginio Orsino, Duke of Bracciano, who had come to England on an official mission. Although it is interesting to speculate that Shakespeare might have received a suggestion for the name of his Duke of Illyria from that of the visiting Italian ambassador, the portrayal of the lovesick Orsino in *Twelfth Night* would hardly have flattered a dignitary whom Queen Elizabeth wished to please. It is more plausible to believe that Shakespeare wrote the comedy with some later occasion in mind, when there would be no risk of offending the Queen's visitor. The memory of Orsino's recent mission to London would have given a small element of topicality to the use of the name in the play.

Sir Edmund Chambers has suggested that, although Shakespeare was not likely to have meddled in affairs of state, the characterization of Malvolio may reflect a bit of backstairs gossip of the court. About this time there was talk of the pomposity and folly of Sir William Knollys, Comptroller of the Royal Household, an unpopular official, whose quarters adjoined those of the Queen's maids of honor. Pretending to great virtue, he reproved the young women for their gaiety and frivolity, while at the same time he attempted to pursue one of them, Mary Fitton, who led him on for sport, though she was carrying on a serious love affair with the Earl of Pembroke. Knollys' character and behavior so paralleled Malvolio's that it is easy to believe that some courtier supplied Shakespeare with information for a caricature that would have pleased everyone except Sir William.

SOURCES, HISTORY, AND TEXT

The elements in the main plot of *Twelfth Night* are found in various sources that Shakespeare may have known. Manningham, in the diary entry already cited, called attention to the similarity of the play to an Italian comedy which he called *Inganni.* This may have been a comedy by Curzio Gonzaga, which had a character called Cesare; or more likely it may refer to a play of 1537, performed by the Academy of Intronati, which has closer parallels to Shakespeare's play. The plot is common to a number of stories. The most convenient source for Shakespeare was probably the tale "Of Apolonius and Silla" in Barnabe Rich's *Rich His Farewell to Military Profession* (1581). Matteo Bandello told the story in No. 36, Part 2, of his *Novelle,* and it was translated into French by François de Belleforest and included in his *Histoires tragiques.* A Latin play entitled *Laelia,* translated from the *Ingannati,* was performed in 1595 at Queen's College, Cambridge.

Although Shakespeare may have picked up suggestions for names of characters from various sources, the working-out of the subplot is essentially Shakespeare's invention. As in his other plays, he shows an advance over most of his contemporaries in the way that he weaves the subplot into the structure of the play.

We can be certain that the members of the Middle Temple who chose *Twelfth Night* for their revels in 1602 were not the only ones who took delight in the play. It was revived at court before James I in 1618 and before Charles I in 1623. Leonard Digges, in commendatory verses to Shakespeare's *Poems* (1640), described the play's popularity with audiences who flocked "To hear Malvolio, that cross-gartered gull." After the Restoration, *Twelfth Night* was the second of Shakespeare's plays revived by Sir William Davenant, *Hamlet* being the first. Samuel Pepys in 1661 wrote in his diary that while walking one night past the playhouse in Lincoln's Inn Fields he observed that the King was attending "a new play, *Twelfth Night,*" and despite a resolution to stay away he "could not forbear to go in, which did make the play seem a burden to me and I took no pleasure at all in it; and so after it was done went home with my mind troubled for my going thither after my swearing to my wife that I would never go to a play without her." Although Pepys' bad conscience prevented his enjoyment of the play on this occasion, he saw it twice more, in 1663 and in 1669, an indication that it remained for a long time on the boards. Repetition, however, did not make Pepys like *Twelfth Night,* which he described as no more than "a silly play" and "one of the weakest plays that ever I saw on the stage." But his was a minority opinion.

An adaptation, made by William Burnaby with the title *Love Betrayed, or, The Agreeable Disappointment,* had a brief run at Lincoln's Inn Fields in 1703 and again in 1705. Shakespeare's original play was not acted again, so far as the records show, until a performance at Drury Lane in 1741. The play regained its earlier popularity and has continued to attract audiences from that day to this. George Frederic Reynolds was responsible for an operatic version in 1820.

Throughout the nineteenth century *Twelfth Night* was frequently revived. Most of the great actresses were happy to appear in the role of Viola. It has been equally popular in the twentieth century. *Twelfth Night* has long been a favorite of the Old Vic Company, and their productions of the play in 1958 and 1959 were particularly noteworthy. Few English plays have enjoyed such consistent popularity over the years as *Twelfth Night.*

The textual problems of *Twelfth Night* are uncomplicated. No printing occurred before the First Folio, and that text has fewer errors than occur in most of the plays. It contains stage directions and indications for music that suggest that the Folio text may have been printed from a good prompt copy. All later versions of course are based on the First Folio.

The Duke Hears a Love Song
From the Staunton edition (1881).

[Dramatis Personæ

ORSINO, *Duke of Illyria.*
SEBASTIAN, *brother to Viola.*
ANTONIO, *a sea captain, friend to Sebastian.*
A SEA CAPTAIN, *friend to Viola.*
VALENTINE,
CURIO, } *gentlemen attending the Duke.*
SIR TOBY BELCH, *uncle to Olivia.*
SIR ANDREW AGUECHEEK.
MALVOLIO, *steward to Olivia.*
FABIAN,
FESTE, *a Clown,* } *servants to Olivia.*
OLIVIA, *a countess.*
VIOLA, *sister to Sebastian.*
MARIA, *attendant to Olivia.*

Lords, a Priest, Sailors, Officers, Musicians, and Attendants.

Scene: *A city in Illyria, and the nearby seacoast.*]

Malvolio
From the Staunton edition (1881).

TWELFTH NIGHT

ACT I

Scene I. [*The Duke's Palace.*]

Enter ORSINO (DUKE OF ILLYRIA), CURIO *and other* LORDS; [*and* MUSICIANS.]

Duke. If music be the food of love, play on;
Give me excess of it, that, surfeiting,
The appetite may sicken, and so die.
That strain again! It had a dying fall;
O, it came o'er my ear like the sweet sound 5
That breathes upon a bank of violets,
Stealing and giving odor! Enough, no more!
'Tis not so sweet now as it was before.
O spirit of love, how quick and fresh art thou,
That, notwithstanding thy capacity 10
Receiveth as the sea, nought enters there,
Of what validity and pitch soe'er,
But falls into abatement and low price
Even in a minute! So full of shapes is fancy
That it alone is high fantastical. 15
Cur. Will you go hunt, my lord?
Duke. What, Curio?
Cur. The hart.
Duke. Why, so I do, the noblest that I have.
O, when mine eyes did see Olivia first,
Methought she purged the air of pestilence! 20
That instant was I turned into a hart,
And my desires, like fell and cruel hounds,
E'er since pursue me.

Enter VALENTINE.

How now? What news from her?
Val. So please my lord, I might not be admitted.
But from her handmaid do return this answer: 25
The element itself, till seven years' heat,
Shall not behold her face at ample view;
But like a cloistress she will veiled walk,
And water once a day her chamber round
With eye-offending brine: all this to season 30
A brother's dead love, which she would keep fresh
And lasting in her sad remembrance.
Duke. O, she that hath a heart of that fine frame
To pay this debt of love but to a brother,
How will she love when the rich golden shaft 35
Hath killed the flock of all affections else

4. **fall:** cadence
5–7. **it . . . odor:** it was as captivating to my ear as a zephyr that has blown over a bank of violets and borne their scent along with it.
9. **quick . . . fresh:** speedily responsive
11. **Receiveth as:** i.e., equals
12. **validity . . . pitch:** value
13. **falls . . . price:** decreases in value
14. **Even:** exactly; **shapes:** images; **fancy:** a lover's imagination
15. **high fantastical:** capable of the greatest flights of imagination
18. **Why . . . do:** i.e., he hunts Olivia's heart.
21–23. **turned . . . me:** an image from the story of Actæon, who was turned to a stag by Diana and hunted by his own hounds (Ovid, *Metamorphoses,* bk. iii)
22. **fell:** savage; fierce
26. **element:** sky; **till . . . heat:** till seven years have elapsed
30. **season:** preserve
31. **A . . . love:** her love for a dead brother
35. **golden shaft:** Cupid's arrow for inducing love. Another arrow with leaden tip was employed to inspire dislike (Ovid, *Metamorphoses,* bk. i).

That live in her; when liver, brain, and heart,
These sovereign thrones, are all supplied and filled,
Her sweet perfections, with one self king!
Away before me to sweet beds of flowers! 40
Love-thoughts lie rich when canopied with bowers.

Exeunt.

Scene II. [*The seacoast.*]

Enter VIOLA, *a* CAPTAIN, *and* SAILORS.

Vio. What country, friends, is this?
Capt. This is Illyria, lady.
Vio. And what should I do in Illyria?
My brother he is in Elysium. 4
Perchance he is not drowned: what think you, sailors?
Capt. It is perchance that you yourself were saved.
Vio. O my poor brother! and so perchance may he be.
Capt. True, madam; and, to comfort you with chance,
Assure yourself, after our ship did split, 9
When you, and those poor number saved with you,
Hung on our driving boat, I saw your brother,
Most provident in peril, bind himself
(Courage and hope both teaching him the practice)
To a strong mast that lived upon the sea;
Where, like Arion on the dolphin's back, 15
I saw him hold acquaintance with the waves
So long as I could see.
Vio. For saying so, there's gold.
Mine own escape unfoldeth to my hope,
Whereto thy speech serves for authority, 20
The like of him. Knowst thou this country?
Capt. Ay, madam, well, for I was bred and born
Not three hours' travel from this very place.
Vio. Who governs here?
Capt. A noble duke, in nature as in name. 25
Vio. What is his name?
Capt. Orsino.
Vio. Orsino! I have heard my father name him.
He was a bachelor then.
Capt. And so is now, or was so very late; 30
For but a month ago I went from hence,
And then 'twas fresh in murmur (as you know
What great ones do, the less will prattle of)
That he did seek the love of fair Olivia.

37. liver: the organ governing love; **heart:** source of all emotion
39. one . . . king: one single master
11. driving: drifting
13. practice: trick
15. Arion: a lengendary poet and musician. Herodotus reports that Arion jumped overboard to escape murderous sailors and rode to safety on a dolphin's back. Shakespeare's source is probably Ovid, *Fasti,* ii.93–118.
30. late: recently

Vio. What's she? 35
Capt. A virtuous maid, the daughter of a count
That died some twelvemonth since; then leaving her
In the protection of his son, her brother,
Who shortly also died; for whose dear love,
They say, she hath abjured the sight 40
And company of men.
Vio. O that I served that lady,
And might not be delivered to the world,
Till I had made mine own occasion mellow,
What my estate is!
Capt. That were hard to compass,
Because she will admit no kind of suit; 45
No, not the Duke's.
Vio. There is a fair behavior in thee, Captain;
And though that nature with a beauteous wall
Doth oft close in pollution, yet of thee
I will believe thou hast a mind that suits 50
With this thy fair and outward character.
I prithee (and I'll pay thee bounteously)
Conceal me what I am, and be my aid
For such disguise as haply shall become
The form of my intent. I'll serve this duke. 55
Thou shalt present me as an eunuch to him;
It may be worth thy pains. For I can sing,
And speak to him in many sorts of music
That will allow me very worth his service.
What else may hap, to time I will commit; 60
Only shape thou thy silence to my wit.
Capt. Be you his eunuch, and your mute I'll be.
When my tongue blabs, then let mine eyes not see.
Vio. I thank thee. Lead me on.

Exeunt.

Scene III. [*Olivia's house.*]

Enter SIR TOBY *and* MARIA.

To. What a plague means my niece to take the death of her brother thus? I am sure care's an enemy to life.

Mar. By my troth, Sir Toby, you must come in earlier o' nights. Your cousin, my lady, takes 5 great exceptions to your ill hours.

43–44. might . . . is: could conceal my true identity until the moment seemed ripe to me
44. were: would be; **compass:** achieve
48. though that: though
51. fair . . . character: what is fairly written on your exterior; your virtuous appearance
54. haply: perchance
54–55. become . . . intent: suit my intention
56. eunuch: singer with an immature tenor voice. Young men whose high tenors had been preserved by castration (*castrati*) were popular in Italy.
59. allow me: cause me to be acknowledged
61. shape . . . wit: do not reveal whatever stratagem I may devise.
5. cousin: term for a near relation

To. Why, let her except before excepted!

Mar. Ay, but you must confine yourself within the modest limits of order.

To. Confine? I'll confine myself no finer than 10 I am. These clothes are good enough to drink in, and so be these boots too. An they be not, let them hang themselves in their own straps.

Mar. That quaffing and drinking will undo you. I heard my lady talk of it yesterday; and of a 15 foolish knight that you brought in one night here to be her wooer.

To. Who? Sir Andrew Aguecheek?

Mar. Ay, he.

To. He's as tall a man as any's in Illyria. 20

Mar. What's that to the purpose?

To. Why, he has three thousand ducats a year.

Mar. Ay, but he'll have but a year in all these ducats. He's a very fool and a prodigal.

To. Fie that you'll say so! He plays o' the 25 viol de gamboys, and speaks three or four languages word for word without book, and hath all the good gifts of nature.

Mar. He hath, indeed, almost natural! for, besides that he's a fool, he's a great quarreler; and but 30 that he hath the gift of a coward to allay the gust he hath in quarreling, 'tis thought among the prudent he would quickly have the gift of a grave.

To. By this hand, they are scoundrels and substractors that say so of him. Who are they? 35

Mar. They that add, moreover, he's drunk nightly in your company.

To. With drinking healths to my niece. I'll drink to her as long as there is a passage in my throat and drink in Illyria. He's a coward and a coistrel 40 that will not drink to my niece till his brains turn o' the toe like a parish top. What, wench! Castiliano vulgo! for here comes Sir Andrew Agueface.

Enter SIR ANDREW.

And. Sir Toby Belch! How now, Sir Toby Belch?

To. Sweet Sir Andrew! 45

And. Bless you, fair shrew.

Mar. And you too, sir.

To. Accost, Sir Andrew, accost.

And. What's that?

To. My niece's chambermaid. 50

And. Good Mistress Accost, I desire better acquaintance.

Mar. My name is Mary, sir.

And. Good Mistress Mary Accost—

To. You mistake, knight. "Accost" is front 55 her, board her, woo her, assail her.

And. By my troth, I would not undertake her in this company. Is that the meaning of "accost"?

Mar. Fare you well, gentlemen.

To. An thou let part so, Sir Andrew, would 60 thou mightst never draw sword again!

And. An you part so, mistress, I would I might never draw sword again! Fair lady, do you think you have fools in hand?

Mar. Sir, I have not you by the hand. 65

And. Marry, but you shall have! and here's my hand.

Mar. Now, sir, thought is free. I pray you, bring your hand to the buttery bar and let it drink.

And. Wherefore, sweetheart? What's your 70 metaphor?

Mar. It's dry, sir.

And. Why, I think so. I am not such an ass but I can keep my hand dry. But what's your jest?

Mar. A dry jest, sir. 75

And. Are you full of them?

Mar. Ay, sir, I have them at my fingers' ends. Marry, now I let go your hand, I am barren. *Exit*.

To. O knight, thou lackst a cup of canary! When did I see thee so put down? 80

And. Never in your life, I think, unless you see canary put me down. Methinks sometimes I have no more wit than a Christian or an ordinary man has. But I am a great eater of beef, and I believe that does harm to my wit. 85

To. No question.

And. An I thought that, I'd forswear it. I'll ride home tomorrow, Sir Toby.

To. *Pourquoi*, my dear knight?

And. What is *"pourquoi"?* Do, or not do? I 90 would I had bestowed that time in the tongues that I have in fencing, dancing, and bear-baiting. O, had I but followed the arts!

To. Then hadst thou had an excellent head of hair.

And. Why, would that have mended my hair? 95

7. except . . . excepted: except previous exceptions (a legal term); past offenses should be forgiven.
10. confine myself: i.e., clothe myself
20. tall: fine
24. very: downright
26. viol . . . gamboys: viol da gamba; bass viol
29. natural: like a natural (idiot)
31. gust: gusto
34–35. substractors: slanderers
40. coistrel: base wretch
42. parish top: a large top kept at the village market place for the recreation of villagers; **Castiliano vulgo:** the meaning of Sir Toby's admonition has never been satisfactorily determined.
43. Agueface: a play on Sir Andrew's name, "Aguecheek," which describes his pale and thin face.
60. let part: let her depart
64. have . . . hand: are dealing with fools
66. Marry: by the Virgin Mary; verily
69. buttery bar: drinking bar
70. Wherefore: why
78. barren: drained of jests
79. lackst: need; **canary:** sweet wine
83. Christian . . . man: any ordinary man, Christians being equal in God's sight
93. arts: liberal arts

To. Past question, for thou seest it will not curl by nature.

And. But it becomes me well enough, does't not?

To. Excellent. It hangs like flax on a distaff; and I hope to see a housewife take thee between her 100 legs and spin it off.

And. Faith, I'll home tomorrow, Sir Toby. Your niece will not be seen; or if she be, it's four to one she'll none of me. The Count himself here hard by woos her. 105

To. She'll none o' the Count. She'll not match above her degree, neither in estate, years, nor wit; I have heard her swear't. Tut, there's life in't, man.

And. I'll stay a month longer. I am a fellow o' the strangest mind i' the world. I delight in 110 masques and revels sometimes altogether.

To. Art thou good at these kickshawses, knight?

And. As any man in Illyria, whatsoever he be, under the degree of my betters; and yet I will not compare with an old man. 115

To. What is thy excellence in a galliard, knight?

And. Faith, I can cut a caper.

To. And I can cut the mutton to't.

And. And I think I have the back-trick simply as strong as any man in Illyria. 120

To. Wherefore are these things hid? Wherefore have these gifts a curtain before 'em? Are they like to take dust, like Mistress Mall's picture? Why dost thou not go to church in a galliard and come home in a coranto? My very walk should be a jig. I 125 would not so much as make water but in a sinkapace. What dost thou mean? Is it a world to hide virtues in? I did think, by the excellent constitution of thy leg, it was formed under the star of a galliard.

And. Ay, 'tis strong, and it does indifferent 130 well in a flame-colored stock. Shall we set about some revels?

To. What shall we do else? Were we not born under Taurus?

And. Taurus? That's sides and heart. 135

To. No, sir; it is legs and thighs. Let me see thee caper. [*Sir Andrew dances.*] Ha, higher! Ha, ha, excellent!

Exeunt.

96. curl by: Lewis Theobald's emendation. The Folio reads "coole my."
104. hard: near
108. there's . . . in't: you have a good chance
111. altogether: more than anything
112. kickshawses: French *quelque chose* (kickshaws)
113–14. under . . . betters: no better than myself in rank and skill
115. old: experienced
116. galliard: lively contemporary dance
119. back-trick: backward step
122. like: likely
123. Mall: a common feminine nickname. **Mistress Mall** is a hypothetical rather than a specific person.
125. coranto: a running dance
126. sinkapace: *cinquepace* ("five steps"), a dance similar to the galliard
131. stock: stocking
136. legs . . . thighs: some contemporary astrologers held that Taurus governed the legs and thighs.

Scene IV. [*The Duke's Palace.*]

Enter VALENTINE, *and* VIOLA *in man's attire.*

Val. If the Duke continue these favors towards you, Cesario, you are like to be much advanced. He hath known you but three days, and already you are no stranger.

Vio. You either fear his humor or my negli- 5 gence, that you call in question the continuance of his love. Is he inconstant, sir, in his favors?

Val. No, believe me.

Enter DUKE, CURIO, *and* ATTENDANTS.

Vio. I thank you. Here comes the Count.

Duke. Who saw Cesario, ho? 10

Vio. On your attendance, my lord, here.

Duke. Stand you awhile aloof.—Cesario,
Thou knowst no less but all. I have unclasped
To thee the book even of my secret soul.
Therefore, good youth, address thy gait unto her;
Be not denied access, stand at her doors, 16
And tell them there thy fixed foot shall grow
Till thou have audience.

Vio. Sure, my noble lord,
If she be so abandoned to her sorrow
As it is spoke, she never will admit me. 20

Duke. Be clamorous and leap all civil bounds
Rather than make unprofited return.

Vio. Say I do speak with her, my lord, what then?

Duke. O, then unfold the passion of my love;
Surprise her with discourse of my dear faith! 25
It shall become thee well to act my woes.
She will attend it better in thy youth
Than in a nuncio's of more grave aspect.

Vio. I think not so, my lord.

Duke. Dear lad, believe it;
For they shall yet belie thy happy years 30
That say thou art a man. Diana's lip
Is not more smooth and rubious; thy small pipe
Is as the maiden's organ, shrill and sound,
And all is semblative a woman's part.
I know thy constellation is right apt 35

21. civil: courteous
25. Surprise: capture; captivate
28. nuncio's: i.e., that of an older messenger
32. rubious: ruby-colored
33. sound: flawless
34. is . . . part: resembles a woman's characteristics
35. constellation: i.e., qualities determined by stellar influence

For this affair. Some four or five attend him—
All, if you will; for I myself am best
When least in company. Prosper well in this,
And thou shalt live as freely as thy lord
To call his fortunes thine.

Vio. I'll do my best 40
To woo your lady. [*Aside*] Yet a barful strife!
Whoe'er I woo, myself would be his wife.

Exeunt.

Scene V. [*Olivia's house.*]

Enter MARIA *and* CLOWN.

Mar. Nay, either tell me where thou hast been, or I will not open my lips so wide as a bristle may enter in way of thy excuse. My lady will hang thee for thy absence.

Clown. Let her hang me! He that is well 5 hanged in this world needs to fear no colors.

Mar. Make that good.

Clown. He shall see none to fear.

Mar. A good lenten answer. I can tell thee where that saying was born, of "I fear no colors." 10

Clown. Where, good Mistress Mary?

Mar. In the wars; and that may you be bold to say in your foolery.

Clown. Well, God give them wisdom that have it; and those that are fools, let them use their tal- 15 ents.

Mar. Yet you will be hanged for being so long absent, or to be turned away—is not that as good as a hanging to you?

Clown. Many a good hanging prevents a bad 20 marriage; and for turning away, let summer bear it out.

Mar. You are resolute then?

Clown. Not so, neither; but I am resolved on two points. 25

Mar. That if one break, the other will hold; or if both break, your gaskins fall.

Clown. Apt, in good faith; very apt. Well, go thy way! If Sir Toby would leave drinking, thou wert as witty a piece of Eve's flesh as any in Illyria. 30

Mar. Peace, you rogue; no more o' that. Here comes my lady. Make your excuse wisely, you were best. [*Exit.*]

Enter LADY OLIVIA *with* MALVOLIO.

Clown. Wit, an't be thy will, put me into good fooling! Those wits that think they have thee 35 do very oft prove fools; and I that am sure I lack thee may pass for a wise man. For what says Quinapalus? "Better a witty fool than a foolish wit."—God bless thee, lady!

Oli. Take the fool away. 40

Clown. Do you not hear, fellows? Take away the lady.

Oli. Go to, y'are a dry fool! I'll no more of you. Besides, you grow dishonest.

Clown. Two faults, madonna, that drink and 45 good counsel will amend. For give the dry fool drink, then is the fool not dry. Bid the dishonest man mend himself: if he mend, he is no longer dishonest; if he cannot, let the botcher mend him. Anything that's mended is but patched; virtue that transgresses 50 is but patched with sin, and sin that amends is but patched with virtue. If that this simple syllogism will serve, so; if it will not, what remedy? As there is no true cuckold but calamity, so beauty's a flower. The lady bade take away the fool; therefore, I say 55 again, take her away.

Oli. Sir, I bade them take away you.

Clown. Misprision in the highest degree! Lady, *cucullus non facit monachum.* That's as much to say as, I wear not motley in my brain. Good ma- 60 donna, give me leave to prove you a fool.

Oli. Can you do it?

Clown. Dexteriously, good madonna.

Oli. Make your proof.

Clown. I must catechize you for it, madonna. 65 Good my mouse of virtue, answer me.

Oli. Well, sir, for want of other idleness, I'll bide your proof.

Clown. Good madonna, why mournest thou?

Oli. Good fool, for my brother's death. 70

Clown. I think his soul is in hell, madonna.

41. barful strife: effort beset with difficulties
6. fear . . . colors: proverbial: "Truth fears no colors [enemy flags]." The Clown puns on colors/collars (nooses).
7. Make . . . good: prove that.
9. good . . . answer: i.e., poor answer
14–16 God . . . talents: God help the wise to make the best use of their wits; we fools must do our best with the wit at our command.
21–22. bear . . . out: make it bearable
25. points: secondary meaning: laces used to connect doublet, breeches, and hose
27. gaskins: hose
29–30. as . . . flesh: i.e., as clever a wife

34. an't: if it
37–38. Quinapalus: a mythical sage invented by the Clown
43. Go to: be off; no more; **dry:** barren of invention
44. dishonest: dishonorable
49. botcher: tailor who specialized in repairs
53. so: well and good
53–54. no . . . calamity: i.e., no true betrayal but that of Fortune, to whom everyone is bound as though married. A **cuckold** is a man whose wife has been unfaithful. **Calamity** is the person who has suffered calamity.
58. Misprision: error
59. cucullus . . . monachum: proverbial: "A cowl does not make a monk."
60. motley: the parti-colored clothing of a fool
63. Dexteriously: variant of "dexterously"
66. Good . . . virtue: my good little virtuous mouse
67. idleness: pastime

Oli. I know his soul is in heaven, fool.

Clown. The more fool, madonna, to mourn for your brother's soul being in heaven. Take away the fool, gentlemen. 75

Oli. What think you of this fool, Malvolio? Doth he not mend?

Mal. Yes, and shall do till the pangs of death shake him. Infirmity, that decays the wise, doth ever make the better fool. 80

Clown. God send you, sir, a speedy infirmity, for the better increasing your folly! Sir Toby will be sworn that I am no fox; but he will not pass his word for twopence that you are no fool.

Oli. How say you to that, Malvolio? 85

Mal. I marvel your ladyship takes delight in such a barren rascal. I saw him put down the other day with an ordinary fool that has no more brain than a stone. Look you now, he's out of his guard already. Unless you laugh and minister occasion to him, 90 he is gagged. I protest I take these wise men that crow so at these set kind of fools no better than the fools' zanies.

Oli. O, you are sick of self-love, Malvolio, and taste with a distempered appetite. To be generous, 95 guiltless, and of free disposition, is to take those things for bird bolts that you deem cannon bullets. There is no slander in an allowed fool, though he do nothing but rail; nor no railing in a known discreet man, though he do nothing but reprove. 100

Clown. Now Mercury indue thee with leasing, for thou speakest well of fools!

Enter MARIA.

Mar. Madam, there is at the gate a young gentleman much desires to speak with you.

Oli. From the Count Orsino, is it? 105

Mar. I know not, madam. 'Tis a fair young man, and well attended.

Oli. Who of my people hold him in delay?

Mar. Sir Toby, madam, your kinsman.

Oli. Fetch him off, I pray you. He speaks 110 nothing but madman. Fie on him! [*Exit Maria.*] Go you, Malvolio. If it be a suit from the Count, I am sick, or not at home. What you will, to dismiss it. (*Exit Malvolio.*) Now you see, sir, how your fooling grows old, and people dislike it. 115

Clown. Thou hast spoke for us, madonna, as if thy eldest son should be a fool; whose skull Jove cram with brains!

Enter SIR TOBY.

for—here he comes—one of thy kin has a most weak *pia mater.* 120

Oli. By mine honor, half drunk! What is he at the gate, cousin?

To. A gentleman.

Oli. A gentleman? What gentleman?

To. 'Tis a gentleman here. A plague o' these 125 pickle-herring! How now, sot?

Clown. Good Sir Toby!

Oli. Cousin, cousin, how have you come so early by this lethargy?

To. Lechery? I defy lechery. There's one at 130 the gate.

Oli. Ay, marry, what is he?

To. Let him be the devil an he will, I care not! Give me faith, say I. Well, it's all one. *Exit.*

Oli. What's a drunken man like, fool? 135

Clown. Like a drowned man, a fool, and a madman. One draught above heat makes him a fool, the second mads him, and a third drowns him.

Oli. Go thou and seek the crowner, and let him sit o' my coz; for he's in the third degree of drink 140 —he's drowned. Go look after him.

Clown. He is but mad yet, madonna, and the fool shall look to the madman. [*Exit.*]

Enter MALVOLIO.

Mal. Madam, yond young fellow swears he will speak with you. I told him you were sick: he 145 takes on him to understand so much, and therefore comes to speak with you. I told him you were asleep: he seems to have a foreknowledge of that too, and therefore comes to speak with you. What is to be said to him, lady? He's fortified against any denial. 150

Oli. Tell him he shall not speak with me.

Mal. Has been told so; and he says he'll stand at your door like a sheriff's post, and be the supporter to a bench, but he'll speak with you.

77. mend: improve
79–80. Infirmity . . . fool: when old age weakens the intellect, it makes a man more foolish.
87. barren: witless
88. ordinary fool: i.e., an idiot
89. out . . . guard: unable to defend himself
90. minister occasion: supply opportunity
93. zanies: stooges
95. distempered: disordered
97. bird bolts: blunt arrows used to hunt birds
98–100. There . . . reprove: an acknowledged fool is allowed any amount of slanderous talk, and a noted wise man may criticize at will without offense.
101. Mercury: noted for his trickiness; **indue:** endow; **leasing:** the gift of lying
101–2. for . . . fools: you will need an ability to lie if you are going to praise fools.
115. old: stale
120. pia mater: brain
125–26. A . . . pickle-herring: an excuse for a drunken hiccup
126. sot: blockhead; fool
137. heat: enough to heat him
139. crowner: coroner
139–40. sit o': hold an inquest on
146. takes . . . him: pretends
152. Has: he has

Oli. What kind o' man is he? 155

Mal. Why, of mankind.

Oli. What manner of man?

Mal. Of very ill manner. He'll speak with you, will you or no.

Oli. Of what personage and years is he? 160

Mal. Not yet old enough for a man nor young enough for a boy; as a squash is before 'tis a peasecod, or a codling when 'tis almost an apple. 'Tis with him in standing water, between boy and man. He is very well-favored and he speaks very shrew- 165 ishly. One would think his mother's milk were scarce out of him.

Oli. Let him approach. Call in my gentlewoman.

Mal. Gentlewoman, my lady calls. *Exit.*

Enter MARIA.

Oli. Give me my veil; come, throw it o'er 170 my face. We'll once more hear Orsino's embassy.

Enter VIOLA.

Vio. The honorable lady of the house, which is she?

Oli. Speak to me; I shall answer for her. Your will?

Vio. Most radiant, exquisite, and unmatch- 175 able beauty—I pray you tell me if this be the lady of the house, for I never saw her. I would be loath to cast away my speech; for, besides that it is excellently well penned, I have taken great pains to con it. Good beauties, let me sustain no scorn. I 180 am very comptible, even to the least sinister usage.

Oli. Whence came you, sir?

Vio. I can say little more than I have studied, and that question's out of my part. Good gentle one, give me modest assurance if you be the lady of the 185 house, that I may proceed in my speech.

Oli. Are you a comedian?

Vio. No, my profound heart; and yet (by the very fangs of malice I swear) I am not that I play. Are you the lady of the house? 190

Oli. If I do not usurp myself, I am.

Vio. Most certain, if you are she, you do usurp yourself; for what is yours to bestow is not yours to reserve. But this is from my commission. I will on with my speech in your praise and then show 195 you the heart of my message.

Oli. Come to what is important in't. I forgive you the praise.

Vio. Alas, I took great pains to study it, and 'tis poetical. 200

Oli. It is the more like to be feigned; I pray you keep it in. I heard you were saucy at my gates; and allowed your approach rather to wonder at you than to hear you. If you be not mad, be gone; if you have reason, be brief. 'Tis not that time of moon 205 with me to make one in so skipping a dialogue.

Mar. Will you hoist sail, sir? Here lies your way.

Vio. No, good swabber; I am to hull here a little longer. Some mollification for your giant, sweet lady!

Oli. Tell me your mind. 210

Vio. I am a messenger.

Oli. Sure you have some hideous matter to deliver, when the courtesy of it is so fearful. Speak your office.

Vio. It alone concerns your ear. I bring no 215 overture of war, no taxation of homage. I hold the olive in my hand. My words are as full of peace as matter.

Oli. Yet you began rudely. What are you? What would you? 220

Vio. The rudeness that hath appeared in me have I learned from my entertainment. What I am, and what I would, are as secret as maidenhead: to your ears, divinity; to any other's, profanation.

Oli. Give us the place alone; we will hear 225 this divinity. [*Exit Maria.*] Now, sir, what is your text?

Vio. Most sweet lady—

Oli. A comfortable doctrine, and much may be said of it. Where lies your text? 230

Vio. In Orsino's bosom.

Oli. In his bosom? In what chapter of his bosom?

Vio. To answer by the method, in the first of his heart.

Oli. O, I have read it! it is heresy. Have you 235 no more to say?

Vio. Good madam, let me see your face.

Oli. Have you any commission from your lord to negotiate with my face? You are now out of your text. But we will draw the curtain and show 240

162. squash: unripe peasecod (pea pod)
163. codling: green apple
164. in . . . water: halfway, like water just before the tide turns
165. well-favored: handsome
165–66. shrewishly: shrilly
179. con: learn
181. comptible . . . usage: sensitive to the slightest discourtesy
185. modest: reasonable
187. comedian: actor
188. profound heart: i.e., intelligent lady
194. from . . . commission: not a part of my message
197. forgive: excuse the omission of
201. feigned: insincere
205–6. 'Tis . . . dialogue: the moon is in the wrong phase to put me in the mood for lunatic nonsense.
208. swabber: clearer of the decks; **hull:** lie becalmed
209. giant: facetious. Maria is obviously tiny, from other references.
216. taxation: demand
222. entertainment: reception
224. divinity: sacred conversation
229. comfortable: comforting
233. by . . . method: in accordance with your pretense that I am a preacher

you the picture. [*Unveils.*] Look you, sir, such a one I was this present. Is't not well done?

Vio. Excellently done, if God did all.

Oli. 'Tis in grain, sir; 'twill endure wind and weather. 245

Vio. 'Tis beauty truly blent, whose red and white
Nature's own sweet and cunning hand laid on.
Lady, you are the cruel'st she alive
If you will lead these graces to the grave,
And leave the world no copy. 250

Oli. O, sir, I will not be so hard-hearted. I will give out divers schedules of my beauty. It shall be inventoried, and every particle and utensil labeled to my will:—as, item, two lips, indifferent red; item, two grey eyes, with lids to them; item, one 255 neck, one chin, and so forth. Were you sent hither to praise me?

Vio. I see you what you are—you are too proud;
But if you were the devil, you are fair.
My lord and master loves you. O, such love 260
Could be but recompensed though you were crowned
The nonpareil of beauty!

Oli. How does he love me?

Vio. With adorations, fertile tears,
With groans that thunder love, with sighs of fire.

Oli. Your lord does know my mind; I cannot love him. 265
Yet I suppose him virtuous, know him noble,
Of great estate, of fresh and stainless youth;
In voices well divulged, free, learned, and valiant,
And in dimension and the shape of nature
A gracious person. But yet I cannot love him. 270
He might have took his answer long ago.

Vio. If I did love you in my master's flame,
With such a suff'ring, such a deadly life,
In your denial I would find no sense; 274
I would not understand it.

Oli. Why, what would you?

Vio. Make me a willow cabin at your gate
And call upon my soul within the house;
Write loyal cantons of contemned love
And sing them loud even in the dead of night;
Halloa your name to the reverberate hills 280
And make the babbling gossip of the air
Cry out "Olivia!" O, you should not rest
Between the elements of air and earth
But you should pity me! 284

Oli. You might do much. What is your parentage?

Vio. Above my fortunes, yet my state is well.
I am a gentleman.

Oli. Get you to your lord.
I cannot love him. Let him send no more,
Unless, perchance, you come to me again
To tell me how he takes it. Fare you well. 290
I thank you for your pains. Spend this for me.

Vio. I am no fee'd post, lady; keep your purse;
My master, not myself, lacks recompense.
Love make his heart of flint that you shall love;
And let your fervor, like my master's, be 295
Placed in contempt! Farewell, fair cruelty. *Exit.*

Oli. "What is your parentage?"
"Above my fortunes, yet my state is well.
I am a gentleman." I'll be sworn thou art. 299
Thy tongue, thy face, thy limbs, actions, and spirit
Do give thee fivefold blazon. Not too fast! soft, soft!
Unless the master were the man. How now?
Even so quickly may one catch the plague?
Methinks I feel this youth's perfections
With an invisible and subtle stealth 305
To creep in at mine eyes. Well, let it be.
What ho, Malvolio!

Enter MALVOLIO.

Mal. Here, madam, at your service.

Oli. Run after that same peevish messenger,
The County's man. He left this ring behind him,
Would I or not. Tell him I'll none of it. 310
Desire him not to flatter with his lord
Nor hold him up with hopes. I am not for him.
If that the youth will come this way tomorrow,
I'll give him reasons for't. Hie thee, Malvolio. 314

Mal. Madam, I will. *Exit.*

Oli. I do I know not what, and fear to find
Mine eye too great a flatterer for my mind.
Fate, show thy force! Ourselves we do not owe.
What is decreed must be—and be this so!

[*Exit.*]

244. **in grain:** dyed in grain. Permanent dye was obtained from cochineal (Kermes or Scarlet Grain).
253–54. **labeled . . . will:** inventoried along with my will
257. **praise:** appraise
263. **fertile:** plentiful
268. **In . . . divulged:** according to general report; **free:** liberal; generous
269. **in . . . nature:** natural form and dimension
270. **gracious:** graced with beauty
272. **in . . . flame:** with my master's ardor
273. **With . . . life:** suffering so intensely that life seems a lingering death
277. **soul:** beloved
278. **cantons . . . love:** songs lamenting my unsuccessful love
280. **reverberate:** echoing
281. **the . . . air:** Echo
284. **But . . . me:** unless you took pity upon me
292. **fee'd post:** hired messenger
294. **make . . . love:** i.e., make the object of your love hard-hearted
301. **give . . . blazon:** proclaim you five times over. A **blazon** is a description of a heraldic device.
309. **County's:** Count's (Duke Orsino's)
317. **Mine . . . mind:** that my eye has approved one whom my judgment would reject
318. **Ourselves . . . owe:** i.e., we do not control our own fates. **Owe** means "possess."

ACT II

Scene I. [*The seacoast.*]

Enter Antonio *and* Sebastian.

Ant. Will you stay no longer? nor will you not that I go with you?

Seb. By your patience, no. My stars shine darkly over me; the malignancy of my fate might perhaps distemper yours. Therefore I shall crave of you 5 your leave, that I may bear my evils alone. It were a bad recompense for your love to lay any of them on you.

Ant. Let me yet know of you whither you are bound. 10

Seb. No, sooth, sir. My determinate voyage is mere extravagancy. But I perceive in you so excellent a touch of modesty that you will not extort from me what I am willing to keep in; therefore it charges me in manners the rather to express myself. You 15 must know of me then, Antonio, my name is Sebastian, which I called Roderigo. My father was that Sebastian of Messaline whom I know you have heard of. He left behind him myself and a sister, both born in an hour. If the heavens had been pleased, 20 would we had so ended! But you, sir, altered that, for some hour before you took me from the breach of the sea was my sister drowned.

Ant. Alas the day!

Seb. A lady, sir, though it was said she much 25 resembled me, was yet of many accounted beautiful. But though I could not with such estimable wonder overfar believe that, yet thus far I will boldly publish her: she bore a mind that envy could not but call fair. She is drowned already, sir, with salt wa- 30 ter, though I seem to drown her remembrance again with more.

Ant. Pardon me, sir, your bad entertainment.

Seb. O good Antonio, forgive me your trouble!

Ant. If you will not murder me for my love, 35 let me be your servant.

Seb. If you will not undo what you have done, that is, kill him whom you have recovered, desire it not. Fare ye well at once. My bosom is full of kindness; and I am yet so near the manners of my mother 40 that, upon the least occasion more, mine eyes will tell tales of me. I am bound to the Count Orsino's court. Farewell. *Exit.*

Ant. The gentleness of all the gods go with thee!
I have many enemies in Orsino's court, 45
Else would I very shortly see thee there.
But come what may, I do adore thee so
That danger shall seem sport, and I will go.
Exit.

3. **By . . . patience:** if you will forgive me
11. **sooth:** truly
11–12. **My . . . extravagancy:** I have no set course except to wander. **Extravagancy** means "wandering."
15. **in manners:** as a matter of courtesy
22. **breach:** breaking waves
27. **with . . . wonder:** despite my esteem and admiration
29. **envy:** malice personified
33. **bad entertainment:** evil welcome (to his country)
35. **If . . . love:** if you do not want my affection for you to kill me
40. **the . . . mother:** i.e., womanly tears

Scene II. [*A street.*]

Enter Viola *and* Malvolio *at several doors.*

Mal. Were not you even now with the Countess Olivia?

Vio. Even now, sir. On a moderate pace I have since arrived but hither.

Mal. She returns this ring to you, sir. You 5 might have saved me my pains, to have taken it away yourself. She adds, moreover, that you should put your lord into a desperate assurance she will none of him. And one thing more, that you be never so hardy to come again in his affairs, unless it be to re- 10 port your lord's taking of this. Receive it so.

Vio. She took the ring of me. I'll none of it.

Mal. Come, sir, you peevishly threw it to her; and her will is, it should be so returned. If it be worth stooping for, there it lies, in your eye; if not, be 15 it his that finds it. *Exit.*

Vio. I left no ring with her. What means this lady?
Fortune forbid my outside have not charmed her!
She made good view of me; indeed, so much
That methought her eyes had lost her tongue, 20
For she did speak in starts distractedly.
She loves me sure; the cunning of her passion

8. **desperate:** hopeless

Invites me in this churlish messenger.
None of my lord's ring? Why, he sent her none!
I am the man. If it be so—as 'tis— 25
Poor lady, she were better love a dream!
Disguise, I see thou art a wickedness
Wherein the pregnant enemy does much.
How easy is it for the proper false
In women's waxen hearts to set their forms! 30
Alas, our frailty is the cause, not we!
For such as we are made of, such we be.
How will this fadge? My master loves her dearly;
And I (poor monster) fond as much on him;
And she (mistaken) seems to dote on me. 35
What will become of this? As I am man,
My state is desperate for my master's love.
As I am woman (now alas the day!),
What thriftless sighs shall poor Olivia breathe!
O Time, thou must untangle this, not I; 40
It is too hard a knot for me t'untie!

[*Exit.*]

Scene III. [*Olivia's house.*]

Enter SIR TOBY *and* SIR ANDREW.

To. Approach, Sir Andrew. Not to be abed after midnight is to be up betimes; and *diluculo surgere,* thou knowst—

And. Nay, by my troth, I know not; but I know to be up late is to be up late. 5

To. A false conclusion! I hate it as an unfilled can. To be up after midnight, and to go to bed then, is early; so that to go to bed after midnight is to go to bed betimes. Does not our life consist of the four elements? 10

And. Faith, so they say; but I think it rather consists of eating and drinking.

To. Th'art a scholar! Let us therefore eat and drink. Marian I say! a stoup of wine!

Enter CLOWN.

And. Here comes the fool, i' faith. 15

Clown. How now, my hearts? Did you never see the picture of We Three?

To. Welcome, ass. Now let's have a catch.

And. By my troth, the fool has an excellent breast. I had rather than forty shillings I had such a 20 leg, and so sweet a breath to sing, as the fool has. In sooth, thou wast in very gracious fooling last night, when thou spokest of Pigrogromitus, of the Vapians passing the equinoctial of Queubus. 'Twas very good, i' faith. I sent thee sixpence for thy leman. 25 Hadst it?

Clown. I did impeticos thy gratillity; for Malvolio's nose is no whipstock. My lady has a white hand, and the Myrmidons are no bottle-alehouses.

And. Excellent! Why, this is the best fooling, when all is done. Now a song! 30

To. Come on! there is sixpence for you. Let's have a song.

And. There's a testril of me too. If one knight give a— 35

Clown. Would you have a love song, or a song of good life?

To. A love song, a love song.

And. Ay, ay! I care not for good life.

Clown sings.

O mistress mine, where are you roaming? 40
O, stay and hear! your truelove's coming,
That can sing both high and low.
Trip no further, pretty sweeting;
Journeys end in lovers meeting,
Every wise man's son doth know. 45

And. Excellent good, i' faith!

To. Good, good!

Clown [*sings*].

What is love? 'Tis not hereafter;
Present mirth hath present laughter;
What's to come is still unsure: 50
In delay there lies no plenty;
Then come kiss me, sweet and twenty!
Youth's a stuff will not endure.

28. pregnant enemy: i.e., the devil, ever ready to seize an opportunity
29. proper false: handsome deceiver
32. such . . . be: i.e., our actions accord with our frailty.
33. How . . . fadge: what will be the result of this?
34. monster: i.e., a creature neither masculine nor feminine; **fond:** dote
39. thriftless: unprofitable
2. betimes: early; **diluculo surgere:** the full quotation is a wise saying from Lily's Latin Grammar: *Diluculo surgere saluberrimum est* ("To rise early is most healthful").
9–10. our . . . elements: the constituents of life were believed to be fire, air, earth, and water.
14. stoup: tankard
16. hearts: hearties
17. the . . . Three: a satirical picture, sometimes appearing on inn signs, of two fools, with the legend "We Three," or, more explicitly, "We three loggerheads [blockheads] be," the observer being the third.
18. catch: i.e., sing a round
19. breast: voice
23–24. Pigrogromitus . . . Queubus: nonsense, but apparently considered witty by Sir Andrew
25. leman: sweetheart
27. impeticos . . . gratillity: impetticoat thy gratuity; give your tip to my mistress
29. Myrmidons: Achilles' soldiers. The rest of the passage is nonsense.
34. testril: a diminutive of the French *tester* (sixpence)
36–37. of . . . life: i.e., imparting a moral
52. sweet . . . twenty: sweet maiden of twenty years

And. A mellifluous voice, as I am true knight.

To. A contagious breath. 55

And. Very sweet and contagious, i' faith.

To. To hear by the nose, it is dulcet in contagion. But shall we make the welkin dance indeed? Shall we rouse the night owl in a catch that will draw three souls out of one weaver? Shall we do that? 60

And. An you love me, let's do't! I am dog at a catch.

Clown. By'r Lady, sir, and some dogs will catch well.

And. Most certain. Let our catch be "Thou 65 knave."

Clown. "Hold thy peace, thou knave," knight? I shall be constrained in't to call thee knave, knight.

And. 'Tis not the first time I have constrained one to call me knave. Begin, fool. It begins, "Hold 70 thy peace."

Clown. I shall never begin if I hold my peace.

And. Good, i' faith! Come, begin.

Catch sung. Enter MARIA.

Mar. What a caterwauling do you keep here! If my lady have not called up her steward Mal- 75 volio and bid him turn you out of doors, never trust me.

To. My lady's a Cataian, we are politicians, Malvolio's a Peg-a-Ramsey, and [*Sings*] "Three merry men be we." Am not I consanguineous? Am I 80 not of her blood? Tilly-vally, lady! [*Sings*] "There dwelt a man in Babylon, lady, lady!"

Clown. Beshrew me, the knight's in admirable fooling.

And. Ay, he does well enough if he be dis- 85 posed, and so do I too. He does it with a better grace, but I do it more natural.

To. [*Sings*] "O' the twelfth day of December"—

Mar. For the love o' God, peace!

Enter MALVOLIO.

Mal. My masters, are you mad? or what are 90 you? Have you no wit, manners, nor honesty, but to gabble like tinkers at this time of night? Do ye make an alehouse of my lady's house, that ye squeak out your coziers' catches without any mitigation or remorse of voice? Is there no respect of place, 95 persons, nor time in you?

To. We did keep time, sir, in our catches. Sneck up!

Mal. Sir Toby, I must be round with you. My lady bade me tell you that, though she harbors you 100 as her kinsman, she's nothing allied to your disorders. If you can separate yourself and your misdemeanors, you are welcome to the house. If not, and it would please you to take leave of her, she is very willing to bid you farewell. 105

To. [*Sings*] "Farewell, dear heart, since I must needs be gone."

Mar. Nay, good Sir Toby!

Clown. [*Sings*] "His eyes do show his days are almost done."

Mal. Is't even so?

To. "But I will never die." 110

Clown. Sir Toby, there you lie.

Mal. This is much credit to you!

To. "Shall I bid him go?"

Clown. "What an if you do?"

To. "Shall I bid him go, and spare not?" 115

Clown. "O, no, no, no, no, you dare not!"

To. Out o' tune, sir? Ye lie. Art any more than a steward? Dost thou think, because thou art virtuous, there shall be no more cakes and ale?

Clown. Yes, by St. Anne! and ginger shall 120 be hot i' the mouth too.

To. Th'art i' the right.—Go, sir, rub your chain with crumbs. A stoup of wine, Maria!

Mal. Mistress Mary, if you prized my lady's favor at anything more than contempt, you would 125 not give means for this uncivil rule. She shall know of it, by this hand. *Exit.*

Mar. Go shake your ears!

And. 'Twere as good a deed as to drink when a man's ahungry, to challenge him the field, and 130 then to break promise with him and make a fool of him.

To. Do't, knight. I'll write thee a challenge; or I'll deliver thy indignation to him by word of mouth.

Mar. Sweet Sir Toby, be patient for to- 135

55. contagious breath: catchy voice
57. To . . . contagion: i.e., his breath sounds sweet but smells offensive.
58. welkin: sky
60. weaver: many weavers, said to be fond of singing, belonged to Puritanical sects.
61. dog: expert
65–66. "Thou knave": in this catch each of the singers in turn is addressed "Thou knave."
78. Cataian: native of Cathay, usually applied to a cheat. Toby merely means to express his lack of concern for what Olivia may say.
79. Peg-a-Ramsey: the name of a merry song
81. Tilly-vally: "pish-tush" or the like, a contemptuous dismissal
83. Beshrew: plague take
85–86. disposed: in good spirits
91. honesty: decorum
94. coziers': cobblers'
94–95. remorse: literally, pity
97–98. Sneck up: be hanged. **Sneck,** of uncertain derivation, originally meant "latch."
99. round: blunt
101. allied: related; associated
106. "Farewell . . . gone": This line and the other snatches sung through line 116 are from "Corydon's Farewell to Phyllis."
120. ginger: often used to spice ale
122–23. rub . . . crumbs: i.e., polish your chain (the badge of his office as steward).
126. uncivil rule: disorderly behavior

night. Since the youth of the Count's was today with my lady, she is much out of quiet. For Monsieur Malvolio, let me alone with him. If I do not gull him into a nayword, and make him a common recreation, do not think I have wit enough to lie straight 140 in my bed. I know I can do it.

To. Possess us, possess us! Tell us something of him.

Mar. Marry, sir, sometimes he is a kind of Puritan.

And. O, if I thought that, I'd beat him like 145 a dog!

To. What, for being a Puritan? Thy exquisite reason, dear knight?

And. I have no exquisite reason for't, but I have reason good enough. 150

Mar. The devil a Puritan that he is, or anything constantly but a time-pleaser; an affectioned ass, that cons state without book and utters it by great swarths; the best persuaded of himself; so crammed, as he thinks, with excellencies that it is his 155 grounds of faith that all that look on him love him; and on that vice in him will my revenge find notable cause to work.

To. What wilt thou do?

Mar. I will drop in his way some obscure 160 epistles of love, wherein by the color of his beard, the shape of his leg, the manner of his gait, the expressure of his eye, forehead, and complexion, he shall find himself most feelingly personated. I can write very like my lady your niece; on a for- 165 gotten matter we can hardly make distinction of our hands.

To. Excellent! I smell a device.

And. I have't in my nose too.

To. He shall think by the letters that thou 170 wilt drop that they come from my niece, and that she's in love with him.

Mar. My purpose is indeed a horse of that color.

And. And your horse now would make him an ass.

Mar. Ass, I doubt not. 175

And. O, 'twill be admirable!

Mar. Sport royal, I warrant you. I know my physic will work with him. I will plant you two, and let the fool make a third, where he shall find the letter. Observe his construction of it. For this night, to 180 bed, and dream on the event. Farewell. *Exit.*

To. Good night, Penthesilea.

And. Before me, she's a good wench.

To. She's a beagle true-bred, and one that adores me. What o' that? 185

And. I was adored once too.

To. Let's to bed, knight. Thou hadst need send for more money.

And. If I cannot recover your niece, I am a foul way out. 190

To. Send for money, knight. If thou hast her not i' the end, call me Cut.

And. If I do not, never trust me, take it how you will.

To. Come, come; I'll go burn some sack. 195 'Tis too late to go to bed now. Come, knight; come, knight.

Exeunt.

Scene IV. [*The Duke's Palace.*]

Enter Duke, Viola, Curio, *and others.*

Duke. Give me some music. Now good morrow, friends.
Now, good Cesario, but that piece of song,
That old and antique song we heard last night.
Methought it did relieve my passion much,
More than light airs and recollected terms 5
Of these most brisk and giddy-paced times.
Come, but one verse.

Cur. He is not here, so please your lordship, that should sing it.

Duke. Who was it? 10

Cur. Feste the jester, my lord, a fool that the Lady Olivia's father took much delight in. He is about the house.

Duke. Seek him out. [*Exit Curio.*] And play the tune the while. *Music plays.*
Come hither, boy. If ever thou shalt love, 15
In the sweet pangs of it remember me;
For such as I am all true lovers are,
Unstaid and skittish in all motions else
Save in the constant image of the creature
That is beloved. How dost thou like this tune? 20

138. let . . . him: leave him to me; **gull:** fool
142. Possess: inform
152. constantly: faithfully; **time-pleaser:** toady; **affectioned:** affected
153. cons . . . book: learns stately deportment by heart
153–54. utters . . . swarths: distributes it largely. **Swarth** is a variant of "swath."
154. the . . . himself: holding the best opinion of himself
164. feelingly personated: convincingly characterized
165–66. on . . . matter: i.e., when a piece of writing concerns a matter now forgotten
181. on: of; **event:** outcome
182. Penthesilea: queen of the Amazons
183. Before me: on my word
189. recover: acquire legal possession of
190. out: out of pocket (for money spent on courtship and in making loans to Sir Toby)
192. Cut: a dock-tailed or gelded horse. Horses were held in contempt as stupid animals.
195. burn: heat; **sack:** sherry
3. antique: old-fashioned; quaint
4. passion: grief
5. recollected terms: i.e., phrases requiring study, unlike the old songs, which seem spontaneous utterances
18. motions: movers of emotion

Vio. It gives a very echo to the seat
Where Love is throned.
Duke. Thou dost speak masterly.
My life upon't, young though thou art, thine eye
Hath stayed upon some favor that it loves.
Hath it not, boy?
Vio. A little, by your favor. 25
Duke. What kind of woman is't?
Vio. Of your complexion.
Duke. She is not worth thee then. What years, i' faith?
Vio. About your years, my lord.
Duke. Too old, by heaven! Let still the woman take
An elder than herself: so wears she to him, 30
So sways she level in her husband's heart;
For, boy, however we do praise ourselves,
Our fancies are more giddy and unfirm,
More longing, wavering, sooner lost and won,
Than women's are.
Vio. I think it well, my lord. 35
Duke. Then let thy love be younger than thyself,
Or thy affection cannot hold the bent;
For women are as roses, whose fair flower,
Being once displayed, doth fall that very hour.
Vio. And so they are; alas, that they are so! 40
To die, even when they to perfection grow!

Enter CURIO *and* CLOWN.

Duke. O, fellow, come, the song we had last night.
Mark it, Cesario; it is old and plain.
The spinsters and the knitters in the sun,
And the free maids that weave their thread with bones, 45
Do use to chant it. It is silly sooth,
And dallies with the innocence of love,
Like the old age.
Clown. Are you ready, sir? 49
Duke. Ay; prithee sing. *Music.*

The Song.

Come away, come away, death,
And in sad cypress let me be laid.
Fly away, fly away, breath;
I am slain by a fair cruel maid.
My shroud of white, stuck all with yew, 55
O, prepare it!
My part of death, no one so true
Did share it.

Not a flower, not a flower sweet,
On my black coffin let there be strown; 60
Not a friend, not a friend greet
My poor corpse, where my bones shall be thrown.
A thousand thousand sighs to save,
Lay me, O, where
Sad true lover never find my grave, 65
To weep there!

Duke. There's for thy pains.
Clown. No pains, sir. I take pleasure in singing, sir.
Duke. I'll pay thy pleasure then.
Clown. Truly, sir, and pleasure will be paid 70
one time or another.
Duke. Give me now leave to leave thee.
Clown. Now the melancholy god protect thee, and the tailor make thy doublet of changeable taffeta, for thy mind is a very opal! I would have men of 75
such constancy put to sea, that their business might be everything, and their intent everywhere; for that's it that always makes a good voyage of nothing. Farewell. *Exit.*
Duke. Let all the rest give place.
[*Exeunt Curio and Attendants.*]
Once more, Cesario,
Get thee to yond same sovereign cruelty. 81
Tell her, my love, more noble than the world,
Prizes not quantity of dirty lands.
The parts that Fortune hath bestowed upon her,
Tell her I hold as giddily as Fortune; 85
But 'tis that miracle and queen of gems
That nature pranks her in, attracts my soul.
Vio. But if she cannot love you, sir—
Duke. I cannot be so answered.
Vio. Sooth, but you must.
Say that some lady, as perhaps there is, 90
Hath for your love as great a pang of heart
As you have for Olivia: You cannot love her;
You tell her so. Must she not then be answered?
Duke. There is no woman's sides
Can bide the beating of so strong a passion 95

21–22. It . . . throned: it exactly echoes the heart of a lover.
24. stayed: rested; **favor:** face
25. by . . . favor: if you will have it so (with a double meaning)
26. complexion: disposition
29. still: ever
30. wears . . . him: she molds herself to his liking
31. sways . . . heart: she retains a constant command of her husband's heart
33. fancies: amorous inclinations
37. hold . . . bent: maintain the same pitch of ardor
45. free: carefree; **bones:** bone bobbins (used in making bone lace)
46. Do use: are accustomed; **silly sooth:** unadorned truth
48. Like . . . age: in an old-fashioned way
52. sad: somber; dark; **cypress:** coffin of cypress wood
57–58. My . . . it: no one ever so faithfully performed a dying role as I do.
61. greet: lament
70. paid: paid for
77. intent: destination
77–78. that's . . . nothing: i.e., such purposelessness never accomplishes anything.
80. give place: clear away
81. sovereign cruelty: cruel mistress
84. parts: worldly possessions
85. hold: regard; **giddily:** casually; **as Fortune:** as does Fortune (who bestows her favors carelessly)
87. pranks: dresses
95. bide: endure

As love doth give my heart; no woman's heart
So big to hold so much; they lack retention.
Alas, their love may be called appetite—
No motion of the liver, but the palate—
That suffers surfeit, cloyment, and revolt; 100
But mine is all as hungry as the sea
And can digest as much. Make no compare
Between that love a woman can bear me
And that I owe Olivia.

Vio. Ay, but I know—

Duke. What dost thou know? 105

Vio. Too well what love women to men may owe.
In faith, they are as true of heart as we.
My father had a daughter loved a man
As it might be perhaps, were I a woman, 109
I should your lordship.

Duke. And what's her history?

Vio. A blank, my lord. She never told her love,
But let concealment, like a worm i' the bud,
Feed on her damask cheek. She pined in thought;
And, with a green and yellow melancholy,
She sat like Patience on a monument, 115
Smiling at grief. Was not this love indeed?
We men may say more, swear more; but indeed
Our shows are more than will; for still we prove
Much in our vows but little in our love. 119

Duke. But died thy sister of her love, my boy?

Vio. I am all the daughters of my father's house,
And all the brothers too—and yet I know not.
Sir, shall I to this lady?

Duke. Ay, that's the theme.
To her in haste! Give her this jewel. Say
My love can give no place, bide no denay. 125

Exeunt.

Scene V. [*Olivia's garden.*]

Enter Sir Toby, Sir Andrew, *and* Fabian.

To. Come thy ways, Signior Fabian.

Fab. Nay, I'll come. If I lose a scruple of this sport, let me be boiled to death with melancholy.

To. Wouldst thou not be glad to have the niggardly rascally sheepbiter come by some notable shame? 5

Fab. I would exult, man. You know he brought me out o' favor with my lady about a bear-baiting here.

To. To anger him we'll have the bear again; and we will fool him black and blue. Shall we not, Sir Andrew? 10

And. An we do not, it is pity of our lives.

Enter Maria.

To. Here comes the little villain. How now, my metal of India?

Mar. Get ye all three into the box tree. Malvolio's coming down this walk. He has been yonder i' the sun practicing behavior to his own shadow this half hour. Observe him, for the love of mockery; for I know this letter will make a contemplative idiot of him. Close, in the name of jesting! Lie thou there [*Throws down a letter*]; for here comes the trout that must be caught with tickling. *Exit.* 15 20

Enter Malvolio.

Mal. 'Tis but fortune; all is fortune. Maria once told me she did affect me; and I have heard herself come thus near, that, should she fancy, it should be one of my complexion. Besides, she uses me with a more exalted respect than anyone else that follows her. What should I think on't? 25

To. Here's an overweening rogue!

Fab. O, peace! Contemplation makes a rare turkey cock of him. How he jets under his advanced plumes! 30

And. 'Slight, I could so beat the rogue!

Fab. Peace, I say.

Mal. To be Count Malvolio! 35

To. Ah, rogue!

And. Pistol him, pistol him!

Fab. Peace, peace!

Mal. There is example for't. The Lady of the Strachy married the yeoman of the wardrobe. 40

And. Fie on him, Jezebel!

Fab. O, peace! Now he's deeply in. Look how imagination blows him.

Mal. Having been three months married to her, sitting in my state— 45

To. O for a stonebow, to hit him in the eye!

Mal. Calling my officers about me, in my branched

99. **motion:** movement
100. **cloyment:** satiation; **revolt:** revulsion (from excess)
113. **thought:** melancholy
118. **Our . . . will:** our pretense of love is greater than our actual desire.
125. **denay:** denial
2. **scruple:** little bit
5. **sheepbiter:** sneak

14. **metal . . . India:** a term for "gold," i.e., treasure
20. **Close:** hide yourselves
24. **affect:** favor
26. **complexion:** temperament
28. **follows:** serves; **on't:** of it
31. **jets:** swaggers
33. **'Slight:** by God's light
39–40. **The . . . wardrobe:** the exact meaning of the allusion has escaped detection. A **yeoman of the wardrobe** was a retainer who had responsibility for the clothing of a noble household.
41. **Jezebel:** i.e., proud one
43. **blows:** swells
45. **state:** chair of state
46. **stonebow:** a bow or catapult used to shoot fowl
47. **branched:** patterned with branches and foliage

velvet gown; having come from a day bed, where I have left Olivia sleeping—

To. Fire and brimstone! 50

Fab. O, peace, peace!

Mal. And then to have the humor of state; and after a demure travel of regard—telling them I know my place, as I would they should do theirs—to ask for my kinsman Toby— 55

To. Bolts and shackles!

Fab. O, peace, peace, peace! Now, now.

Mal. Seven of my people, with an obedient start, make out for him. I frown the while, and perchance wind up my watch, or play with my—some 60 rich jewel. Toby approaches; curtsies there to me—

To. Shall this fellow live?

Fab. Though our silence be drawn from us with cars, yet peace!

Mal. I extend my hand to him thus, quench- 65 ing my familiar smile with an austere regard of control—

To. And does not Toby take you a blow o' the lips then?

Mal. Saying, "Cousin Toby, my fortunes 70 having cast me on your niece, give me this prerogative of speech."

To. What, what?

Mal. "You must amend your drunkenness."

To. Out, scab! 75

Fab. Nay, patience, or we break the sinews of our plot.

Mal. "Besides, you waste the treasure of your time with a foolish knight"—

And. That's me, I warrant you. 80

Mal. "One Sir Andrew"—

And. I knew 'twas I, for many do call me fool.

Mal. What employment have we here?

[*Picks up the letter.*]

Fab. Now is the woodcock near the gin.

To. O, peace! and the spirit of humors inti- 85 mate reading aloud to him!

Mal. By my life, this is my lady's hand! These be her very C's, her U's, and her T's; and thus makes she her great P's. It is, in contempt of question, her hand. 90

And. Her C's, her U's, and her T's? Why that?

Mal. [*Reads*] "To the unknown beloved, this, and my good wishes." Her very phrases! By your leave, wax. Soft! and the impressure her Lucrece, with which she uses to seal! 'Tis my lady. To whom 95 should this be?

Fab. This wins him, liver and all.

Mal. [*Reads*]

Jove knows I love—
But who?
Lips, do not move; 100
No man must know.

"No man must know." What follows? The numbers altered! "No man must know." If this should be thee, Malvolio?

To. Marry, hang thee, brock! 105

Mal. [*Reads*]

I may command where I adore;
But silence, like a Lucrece knife,
With bloodless stroke my heart doth gore.
M. O. A. I. doth sway my life.

Fab. A fustian riddle! 110

To. Excellent wench, say I.

Mal. "M. O. A. I. doth sway my life." Nay, but first, let me see, let me see, let me see.

Fab. What dish o' poison has she dressed him!

To. And with what wing the staniel checks 115 at it!

Mal. "I may command where I adore." Why, she may command me: I serve her; she is my lady. Why, this is evident to any formal capacity. There is no obstruction in this. And the end—what should 120 that alphabetical position portend? If I could make that resemble something in me! Softly! M. O. A. I.

To. O, ay, make up that! He is now at a cold scent.

Fab. Sowter will cry upon't for all this, though it be as rank as a fox. 125

Mal. M.—Malvolio. M.—Why, that begins my name!

Fab. Did not I say he would work it out? The cur is excellent at faults.

Mal. M.—But then there is no consonancy 130 in the sequel. That suffers under probation. A should follow, but O does.

Fab. And O shall end, I hope.

52. **have . . . state:** feel like giving audience
53. **a . . . regard:** an aloof survey of the company
59. **make . . . him:** set out to fetch him
66–67. **austere . . . control:** stern look of mastery
68. **take:** give
75. **scab:** scurvy fellow
84. **gin:** snare
85. **spirit . . . humors:** controller of impulse
89. **in . . . question:** without any doubt
93–94. **By . . . wax:** an apology to the seal as he breaks it
97. **wins . . . all:** i.e., it will even inspire a reciprocal ardor.
102–3. **numbers altered:** verses in different meter
105. **brock:** badger (despised as a dirty and stinking creature)
110. **fustian riddle:** i.e., gibberish
114. **dressed:** prepared
115. **staniel:** kestrel (a variety of hawk). This is Hanmer's correction of the Folio reading "stallion."
115–16. **checks . . . it:** is diverted from the scent or pursues a false quarry
119. **formal capacity:** average intelligence
123. **make up:** interpret
124. **Sowter:** term for a bungler, used as the name of a hound
124–25. **though . . . fox:** though the trick should be obvious
129. **excellent . . . faults:** clever at making sense of a set of unintelligible clues. In hunting, a **fault** is an interruption of the scent or a complete loss of the quarry.
130. **consonancy:** consistency
131. **suffers . . . probation:** will not bear examination
133. **O:** lamentation (i.e., Malvolio's discomfiture)

To. Ay, or I'll cudgel him, and make him cry O!

Mal. And then I comes behind. 135

Fab. Ay, an you had any eye behind you, you might see more detraction at your heels than fortunes before you.

Mal. M, O, A, I. This simulation is not as the former; and yet, to crush this a little, it would 140 bow to me, for every one of these letters are in my name. Soft! here follows prose.

[*Reads*] If this fall into thy hand, revolve. In my stars I am above thee; but be not afraid of greatness. Some are born great, some achieve greatness, and some 145 have greatness thrust upon 'em. Thy Fates open their hands; let thy blood and spirit embrace them; and to inure thyself to what thou art like to be, cast thy humble slough and appear fresh. Be opposite with a kinsman, surly with servants. Let thy tongue tang ar- 150 guments of state; put thyself into the trick of singularity. She thus advises thee that sighs for thee. Remember who commended thy yellow stockings and wished to see thee ever cross-gartered. I say, remember. Go to, thou art made, if thou desirest to be so. If not, 155 let me see thee a steward still, the fellow of servants, and not worthy to touch Fortune's fingers. Farewell. She that would alter services with thee,

THE FORTUNATE UNHAPPY.

Daylight and champian discovers not more. 160 This is open. I will be proud, I will read politic authors, I will baffle Sir Toby, I will wash off gross acquaintance, I will be point-device the very man. I do not now fool myself, to let imagination jade me; for every reason excites to this, that my lady 165 loves me. She did commend my yellow stockings of late, she did praise my leg being cross-gartered; and in this she manifests herself to my love, and with a kind of injunction drives me to these habits of her liking. I thank my stars, I am happy. I will 170 be strange, stout, in yellow stockings, and cross-gartered, even with the swiftness of putting on. Jove and my stars be praised! Here is yet a postscript.

Thou canst not choose but know who I am. If thou entertainst my love, let it appear in thy smiling. 175 Thy smiles become thee well. Therefore in my presence still smile, dear my sweet, I prithee.

Jove, I thank thee. I will smile; I will do everything that thou wilt have me. *Exit.*

Fab. I will not give my part of this sport 180 for a pension of thousands to be paid from the Sophy.

To. I could marry this wench for this device—

And. So could I too.

To. And ask no other dowry with her but 185 such another jest.

Enter MARIA.

And. Nor I neither.

Fab. Here comes my noble gull-catcher.

To. Wilt thou set thy foot o' my neck?

And. Or o' mine either? 190

To. Shall I play my freedom at tray-trip and become thy bondslave?

And. I' faith, or I either?

To. Why, thou hast put him in such a dream that, when the image of it leaves him, he must run 195 mad.

Mar. Nay, but say true, does it work upon him?

To. Like aqua vitae with a midwife.

Mar. If you will, then, see the fruits of the sport, mark his first approach before my lady. He 200 will come to her in yellow stockings, and 'tis a color she abhors, and cross-gartered, a fashion she detests; and he will smile upon her, which will now be so unsuitable to her disposition, being addicted to a melancholy as she is, that it cannot but turn him 205 into a notable contempt. If you will see it, follow me.

To. To the gates of Tartar, thou most excellent devil of wit!

And. I'll make one too.

Exeunt.

139–41. This . . . me: this disguised message is not as clear as the previous phrase, but with a little force I can master it.
143. revolve: consider; **stars:** birth
148. inure: accustom; **like:** likely
149. humble slough: lowly semblance. **Slough** is literally an outer casing or skin.
150–51. tang . . . state: discuss questions of policy
151–52. put . . . singularity: adopt an air of superiority
154. cross-gartered: gartered with ribbons that crossed back of the knee and tied in a bow above the knee in front
158. alter services: exchange roles
160. champian: flat, open country; **discovers:** reveals
162. baffle: disgrace publicly
163. point-device: in every point
164. jade: trick
168. manifests . . . love: reveals her love for me
169–70. habits . . . liking: garments that please her
170. happy: fortunate
171. strange: distant; **stout:** arrogant
175. entertainst: welcomest
177. still: always
182. Sophy: Shah of Persia
188. gull-catcher: catcher of fools
191. tray-trip: a dice game
207. Tartar: Tartarus; hell
209. make one: go along

ACT III

Scene I. [*Olivia's garden.*]

Enter VIOLA, *and* CLOWN [*with a tabor and pipe*].

Vio. Save thee, friend, and thy music! Dost thou live by thy tabor?

Clown. No, sir, I live by the church.

Vio. Art thou a churchman?

Clown. No such matter, sir. I do live by the 5 church; for I do live at my house, and my house doth stand by the church.

Vio. So thou mayst say, the king lies by a beggar, if a beggar dwell near him; or, the church stands by thy tabor, if thy tabor stand by the church. 10

Clown. You have said, sir. To see this age! A sentence is but a chev'ril glove to a good wit. How quickly the wrong side may be turned outward!

Vio. Nay, that's certain. They that dally nicely with words may quickly make them wanton. 15

Clown. I would therefore my sister had had no name, sir.

Vio. Why, man?

Clown. Why, sir, her name's a word, and to dally with that word might make my sister wanton. 20 But indeed words are very rascals since bonds disgraced them.

Vio. Thy reason, man?

Clown. Troth, sir, I can yield you none without words, and words are grown so false I am loath 25 to prove reason with them.

Vio. I warrant thou art a merry fellow and carest for nothing.

Clown. Not so, sir; I do care for something; but in my conscience, sir, I do not care for you. If 30 that be to care for nothing, sir, I would it would make you invisible.

Vio. Art not thou the Lady Olivia's fool?

Clown. No, indeed, sir. The Lady Olivia has no folly. She will keep no fool, sir, till she be mar- 35 ried; and fools are as like husbands as pilchards are to herrings—the husband's the bigger. I am indeed not her fool, but her corrupter of words.

Vio. I saw thee late at the Count Orsino's.

Clown. Foolery, sir, does walk about the orb 40 like the sun; it shines everywhere. I would be sorry, sir, but the fool should be as oft with your master as with my mistress. I think I saw your wisdom there.

Vio. Nay, an thou pass upon me, I'll no more with thee. Hold, there's expenses for thee. 45

[*Gives a piece of money.*]

Clown. Now Jove, in his next commodity of hair, send thee a beard!

Vio. By my troth, I'll tell thee, I am almost sick for one, though I would not have it grow on my chin. Is thy lady within? 50

Clown. Would not a pair of these have bred, sir?

Vio. Yes, being kept together and put to use.

Clown. I would play Lord Pandarus of Phrygia, sir, to bring a Cressida to this Troilus.

Vio. I understand you, sir. 'Tis well begged. 55

Clown. The matter, I hope, is not great, sir, begging but a beggar: Cressida was a beggar. [*Viola tosses him another coin.*] My lady is within, sir. I will conster to them whence you come. Who you are and what you would are out of my welkin—I 60 might say "element," but the word is over-worn. *Exit.*

Vio. This fellow is wise enough to play the fool,
And to do that well craves a kind of wit.
He must observe their mood on whom he jests,
The quality of persons, and the time; 65
Not, like the haggard, check at every feather
That comes before his eye. This is a practice
As full of labor as a wise man's art;
For folly that he wisely shows, is fit;
But wise men, folly-fall'n, quite taint their wit. 70

Ent. tabor: a small drum
12. chev'ril: flexible kidskin
14. dally nicely: play lasciviously
21–22. since . . . them: i.e., since men began to require bonds instead of trusting another's word in making bargains
29–30. in . . . conscience: as conscience is my judge
36. pilchards: small fish of the herring family
40. orb: earth
41–43. I . . . mistress: i.e., I would regret to think my mistress more foolish than your master.
44. pass . . . me: offer a duel
46. commodity: consignment
49. one: i.e., a man with a beard
51. these: coins
52. use: lending at interest
56–57. begging . . . beggar: a reference to the practice of "begging" the wardship of wealthy minors through the Court of Wards
59. conster: construe; explain
60. welkin: sky (element)
63. craves: requires; **wit:** intelligence
66. haggard: an untrained hawk
67. practice: craft
69. wisely: deliberately (to earn a living); **fit:** suitable

Enter SIR TOBY *and* [SIR] ANDREW.

To. Save you, gentleman!

Vio. And you, sir.

And. Dieu vous garde, monsieur.

Vio. Et vous aussi; votre serviteur.

And. I hope, sir, you are, and I am yours. 75

To. Will you encounter the house? My niece is desirous you should enter, if your trade be to her.

Vio. I am bound to your niece, sir. I mean, she is the list of my voyage.

To. Taste your legs, sir; put them to motion. 80

Vio. My legs do better understand me, sir, than I understand what you mean by bidding me taste my legs.

To. I mean, to go, sir, to enter.

Vio. I will answer you with gait and entrance. But we are prevented. 85

Enter OLIVIA *and* GENTLEWOMAN [MARIA].

Most excellent accomplished lady, the heavens rain odors on you!

And. [*Aside*] That youth's a rare courtier. "Rain odors"—well! 90

Vio. My matter hath no voice, lady, but to your own most pregnant and vouchsafed ear.

And. [*Aside*] "Odors," "pregnant," and "vouchsafed"—I'll get 'em all three all ready.

Oli. Let the garden door be shut, and leave me to my hearing. [*Exeunt Sir Toby, Sir Andrew, and Maria.*] Give me your hand, sir. 95

Vio. My duty, madam, and most humble service.

Oli. What is your name? 99

Vio. Cesario is your servant's name, fair princess.

Oli. My servant, sir? 'Twas never merry world
Since lowly feigning was called compliment.
Y'are servant to the Count Orsino, youth. 103

Vio. And he is yours, and his must needs be yours.
Your servant's servant is your servant, madam.

Oli. For him, I think not on him; for his thoughts,
Would they were blanks, rather than filled with me!

Vio. Madam, I come to whet your gentle thoughts
On his behalf.

Oli. O, by your leave, I pray you!
I bade you never speak again of him; 110
But, would you undertake another suit,
I had rather hear you to solicit that
Than music from the spheres.

Vio. Dear lady—

Oli. Give me leave, beseech you. I did send,
After the last enchantment you did here, 115
A ring in chase of you. So did I abuse
Myself, my servant, and, I fear me, you.
Under your hard construction must I sit,
To force that on you in a shameful cunning
Which you knew none of yours. What might you think? 120
Have you not set mine honor at the stake
And baited it with all the unmuzzled thoughts
That tyrannous heart can think? To one of your receiving
Enough is shown; a cypress, not a bosom,
Hides my heart. So, let me hear you speak. 125

Vio. I pity you.

Oli. That's a degree to love.

Vio. No, not a grise; for 'tis a vulgar proof
That very oft we pity enemies.

Oli. Why then, methinks 'tis time to smile again.
O world, how apt the poor are to be proud! 130
If one should be a prey, how much the better
To fall before the lion than the wolf! *Clock strikes.*
The clock upbraids me with the waste of time.
Be not afraid, good youth, I will not have you;
And yet, when wit and youth is come to harvest,
Your wife is like to reap a proper man. 136
There lies your way, due west.

Vio. Then westward ho!
Grace and good disposition attend your ladyship!
You'll nothing, madam, to my lord by me?

Oli. Stay. 140
I prithee tell me what thou thinkst of me.

Vio. That you do think you are not what you are.

Oli. If I think so, I think the same of you.

Vio. Then think you right. I am not what I am.

Oli. I would you were as I would have you be!

Vio. Would it be better, madam, than I am? 146
I wish it might; for now I am your fool.

Oli. O, what a deal of scorn looks beautiful
In the contempt and anger of his lip!

76. **encounter:** enter
77. **trade:** business
79. **list:** end; limit
86. **prevented:** forestalled
92. **pregnant:** ready; **vouchsafed:** proffered
102. **lowly feigning:** pretense of humility; **compliment:** courtesy
106. **For:** as for
116. **abuse:** deceive
118. **Under . . . sit:** you must have a poor opinion of me
123. **tyrannous:** fierce; uncontrollable; **receiving:** understanding
124. **cypress:** transparent fabric (so called from its origin in Cyprus)
126. **degree:** step
127. **grise:** another name for "step"; **a . . . proof:** something proved by common experience
129. **'tis . . . again:** i.e., if the youth is hostile, Olivia might as well cease pining for him and assume a cheerful disposition.
132. **fall . . . wolf:** succumb to the king of beasts rather than to a heartless inferior
135. **is . . . harvest:** have matured
137. **westward ho:** a call used to summon a boatman for a westward passage on the Thames
142. **you . . . are:** i.e., you are deceived.
143. **I . . . you:** Olivia thinks Cesario has implied that she is out of her wits and answers that he also must be mad to reject her.
147. **fool:** plaything

A murd'rous guilt shows not itself more soon 150
Than love that would seem hid: love's night is noon.
Cesario, by the roses of the spring,
By maidhood, honor, truth, and everything,
I love thee so that, mauger all thy pride,
Nor wit nor reason can my passion hide. 155
Do not extort thy reasons from this clause,
For that I woo, thou therefore hast no cause;
But rather reason thus with reason fetter:
Love sought is good, but given unsought is better.

Vio. By innocence I swear, and by my youth,
I have one heart, one bosom, and one truth, 161
And that no woman has; nor never none
Shall mistress be of it, save I alone.
And so adieu, good madam. Never more
Will I my master's tears to you deplore. 165

Oli. Yet come again; for thou perhaps mayst move
That heart which now abhors to like his love.
Exeunt.

Scene II. [*Olivia's house.*]

Enter Sir Toby, Sir Andrew, *and* Fabian.

And. No, faith, I'll not stay a jot longer.

To. Thy reason, dear venom; give thy reason.

Fab. You must needs yield your reason, Sir Andrew.

And. Marry, I saw your niece do more favors 5
to the Count's servingman than ever she bestowed upon me. I saw't i' the orchard.

To. Did she see thee the while, old boy? Tell me that.

And. As plain as I see you now. 10

Fab. This was a great argument of love in her toward you.

And. 'Slight! will you make an ass o' me?

Fab. I will prove it legitimate, sir, upon the oaths of judgment and reason. 15

To. And they have been grand-jurymen since before Noah was a sailor.

Fab. She did show favor to the youth in your sight only to exasperate you, to awake your dormouse valor, to put fire in your heart and brimstone in 20
your liver. You should then have accosted her; and with some excellent jests, fire-new from the mint, you should have banged the youth into dumbness. This was looked for at your hand, and this was balked. The double gilt of this opportunity you 25
let time wash off, and you are now sailed into the North of my lady's opinion, where you will hang like an icicle on a Dutchman's beard unless you do redeem it by some laudable attempt either of valor or policy. 30

And. An't be any way, it must be with valor; for policy I hate. I had as lief be a Brownist as a politician.

To. Why then, build me thy fortunes upon the basis of valor. Challenge me the Count's youth 35
to fight with him; hurt him in eleven places. My niece shall take note of it; and assure thyself there is no love-broker in the world can more prevail in man's commendation with woman than report of valor.

Fab. There is no way but this, Sir Andrew. 40

And. Will either of you bear me a challenge to him?

To. Go, write it in a martial hand. Be curst and brief; it is no matter how witty, so it be eloquent and full of invention. Taunt him with the license of 45
ink. If thou thou'st him some thrice, it shall not be amiss; and as many lies as will lie in thy sheet of paper, although the sheet were big enough for the bed of Ware in England, set 'em down. Go, about it! Let there be gall enough in thy ink, though thou 50
write with a goose-pen, no matter. About it!

And. Where shall I find you?

To. We'll call thee at the cubiculo. Go.
Exit Sir Andrew.

Fab. This is a dear manikin to you, Sir Toby.

To. I have been dear to him, lad—some two 55
thousand strong, or so.

Fab. We shall have a rare letter from him—but you'll not deliver't?

To. Never trust me then; and by all means stir on the youth to an answer. I think oxen and wain- 60
ropes cannot hale them together. For Andrew, if he were opened, and you find so much blood in his liver as will clog the foot of a flea, I'll eat the rest of the anatomy.

Fab. And his opposite, the youth, bears in his 65
visage no great presage of cruelty.

Enter Maria.

151. love's . . . noon: love is as visible at night as by daylight.
154. mauger: despite
156–59. Do . . . better: do not reason that I am not worth having because I do the wooing; love freely offered is better than love solicited.
25. balked: passed up

30. policy: craft
32. Brownist: member of the Puritanical sect founded by Robert Browne
43. curst: ill-tempered
45–46. with . . . ink: as freely as pen can write
46. thou'st: address him with the familiar "thou," appropriate only to intimates and inferiors
48–49. the . . . Ware: a four-poster bed famous for its size (now in the Victoria and Albert Museum in London)
49–51. Let . . . goose-pen: do not express yourself foolishly and timidly just because you write with a goose-quill.
53. cubiculo: cubicle; i.e., Sir Andrew's chamber (?)
55. dear: expensive
60–61. wainropes: wagon ropes
65. opposite: opponent
66. presage: threat

To. Look where the youngest wren of mine comes.
Mar. If you desire the spleen, and will laugh yourselves into stitches, follow me. Yond gull Malvolio is turned heathen, a very renegado; for there is 70 no Christian that means to be saved by believing rightly can ever believe such impossible passages of grossness. He's in yellow stockings!
To. And cross-gartered?
Mar. Most villainously; like a pedant that 75 keeps a school i' the church. I have dogged him like his murderer. He does obey every point of the letter that I dropped to betray him. He does smile his face into more lines than is in the new map with the augmentation of the Indies. You have not seen 80 such a thing as 'tis. I can hardly forbear hurling things at him. I know my lady will strike him. If she do, he'll smile, and take't for a great favor.
To. Come bring us, bring us where he is!
Exeunt omnes.

Scene III. [*A street.*]

Enter SEBASTIAN *and* ANTONIO.

Seb. I would not by my will have troubled you;
But since you make your pleasure of your pains,
I will no further chide you.
Ant. I could not stay behind you. My desire,
More sharp than filed steel, did spur me forth; 5
And not all love to see you (though so much
As might have drawn one to a longer voyage)
But jealousy what might befall your travel,
Being skill-less in these parts; which to a stranger,
Unguided and unfriended, often prove 10
Rough and unhospitable. My willing love,
The rather by these arguments of fear,
Set forth in your pursuit.
Seb. My kind Antonio,
I can no other answer make but thanks,
And thanks, and ever thanks; and oft good turns
Are shuffled off with such uncurrent pay. 16
But, were my worth as is my conscience firm,
You should find better dealing. What's to do?
Shall we go see the relics of this town?
Ant. Tomorrow, sir; best first go see your lodging.
Seb. I am not weary, and 'tis long to night. 21
I pray you let us satisfy our eyes
With the memorials and the things of fame
That do renown this city.
Ant. Would you'ld pardon me.
I do not without danger walk these streets. 25
Once in a sea-fight 'gainst the Count his galleys
I did some service; of such note indeed
That, were I ta'en here, it would scarce be answered.
Seb. Belike you slew great number of his people?
Ant. The offense is not of such a bloody nature,
Albeit the quality of the time and quarrel 31
Might well have given us bloody argument.
It might have since been answered in repaying
What we took from them, which for traffic's sake
Most of our city did. Only myself stood out; 35
For which, if I be lapsed in this place,
I shall pay dear.
Seb. Do not then walk too open.
Ant. It doth not fit me. Hold, sir, here's my purse.
In the south suburbs at the Elephant
Is best to lodge. I will bespeak our diet, 40
Whiles you beguile the time and feed your knowledge
With viewing of the town. There shall you have me.
Seb. Why I your purse?
Ant. Haply your eye shall light upon some toy
You have desire to purchase; and your store 45
I think is not for idle markets, sir.
Seb. I'll be your purse-bearer, and leave you for
An hour.
Ant. To the Elephant.
Seb. I do remember.
Exeunt.

Scene IV. [*Olivia's garden.*]

Enter OLIVIA *and* MARIA.

Oli. I have sent after him; he says he'll come.
How shall I feast him? what bestow of him?
For youth is bought more oft than begged or borrowed.
I speak too loud.
Where is Malvolio? He is sad and civil, 5
And suits well for a servant with my fortunes.
Where is Malvolio?

67. the . . . mine: i.e., my diminutive pet
68. the spleen: a fit of laughter
70. renegado: renegade; traitor to the faith
72–73. impossible . . . grossness: obviously impossible things
79–80. new . . . Indies: probably Edward Wright's map, printed in Richard Hakluyt's *Principal Navigations* (1598–1600)
8. jealousy: anxiety
9. skill-less: inexperienced
16. uncurrent: unnegotiable
17. worth: i.e., wealth
28. it . . . answered: i.e., the punishment he could expect would be severe.
34. for . . . sake: for the sake of continued trade
36. lapsed: caught unawares
40. bespeak: order
44. toy: trifle
45–46. your . . . markets: you have too little money for frivolous spending.
2. of: on
5. sad: grave; **civil:** decorous

Mar. He's coming, madam; but in very strange manner. He is sure possessed, madam.

Oli. Why, what's the matter? Does he rave? 10

Mar. No, madam, he does nothing but smile. Your ladyship were best to have some guard about you if he come, for sure the man is tainted in's wits.

Oli. Go call him hither. [*Exit Maria.*] I am as mad as he,
If sad and merry madness equal be. 15

Enter [MARIA, *with*] MALVOLIO.

How now, Malvolio?

Mal. Sweet lady, ho, ho!

Oli. Smilest thou?
I sent for thee upon a sad occasion.

Mal. Sad, lady? I could be sad. This does 20 make some obstruction in the blood, this cross-gartering; but what of that? If it please the eye of one, it is with me as the very true sonnet is, "Please one, and please all."

Oli. Why, how dost thou, man? What is the 25 matter with thee?

Mal. Not black in my mind, though yellow in my legs. It did come to his hands, and commands shall be executed. I think we do know the sweet Roman hand. 30

Oli. Wilt thou go to bed, Malvolio?

Mal. To bed? Ay, sweetheart; and I'll come to thee.

Oli. God comfort thee! Why dost thou smile so, and kiss thy hand so oft? 35

Mar. How do you, Malvolio?

Mal. At your request? Yes, nightingales answer daws!

Mar. Why appear you with this ridiculous boldness before my lady? 40

Mal. "Be not afraid of greatness." 'Twas well writ.

Oli. What meanst thou by that, Malvolio?

Mal. "Some are born great"—

Oli. Ha?

Mal. "Some achieve greatness"— 45

Oli. What sayst thou?

Mal. "And some have greatness thrust upon them."

Oli. Heaven restore thee!

Mal. "Remember who commended thy yellow stockings"— 50

Oli. Thy yellow stockings?

Mal. "And wished to see thee cross-gartered."

Oli. Cross-gartered?

Mal. "Go to, thou art made, if thou desirest to be so"— 55

Oli. Am I made?

Mal. "If not, let me see thee a servant still."

Oli. Why, this is very midsummer madness.

Enter SERVANT.

Ser. Madam, the young gentleman of the Count Orsino's is returned. I could hardly entreat him 60 back. He attends your ladyship's pleasure.

Oli. I'll come to him. [*Exit Servant.*] Good Maria, let this fellow be looked to. Where's my cousin Toby? Let some of my people have a special care of him. I would not have him miscarry for the half 65 of my dowry. *Exit* [*Olivia; then Maria*].

Mal. O ho! do you come near me now? No worse man than Sir Toby to look to me! This concurs directly with the letter. She sends him on purpose, that I may appear stubborn to him; for she 70 incites me to that in the letter. "Cast thy humble slough," says she; "be opposite with a kinsman, surly with servants; let thy tongue tang with arguments of state; put thyself into the trick of singularity";—and consequently sets down the manner how: 75 as, a sad face, a reverend carriage, a slow tongue, in the habit of some sir of note, and so forth. I have limed her; but it is Jove's doing, and Jove make me thankful! And when she went away now, "Let this fellow be looked to." "Fellow!" not "Malvo- 80 lio," nor after my degree, but "fellow." Why, everything adheres together, that no dram of a scruple, no scruple of a scruple, no obstacle, no incredulous or unsafe circumstance—What can be said? Nothing that can be can come between me and the full 85 prospect of my hopes. Well, Jove, not I, is the doer of this, and he is to be thanked.

Enter [SIR] TOBY, FABIAN, *and* MARIA.

To. Which way is he, in the name of sanctity? If all the devils of hell be drawn in little, and Legion himself possessed him, yet I'll speak to him. 90

Fab. Here he is, here he is! How is't with you, sir? How is't with you, man?

Mal. Go off; I discard you. Let me enjoy my private. Go off.

Mar. Lo, how hollow the fiend speaks within 95 him! Did not I tell you? Sir Toby, my lady prays you to have a care of him.

19. upon . . . occasion: in a grave moment
29–30. Roman hand: Italian cursive script, the forerunner of most modern hands
37–38. At . . . daws: Malvolio disdains to answer familiar questions from an inferior, as a nightingale would ignore a jackdaw.

58. midsummer madness: madness was believed to be particularly common around Midsummer Eve.
65. miscarry: come to harm
67. come . . . now: begin to perceive my situation
70. appear . . . him: treat him harshly
77. habit: garb
78. limed: caught in birdlime
83. incredulous: incredible
89. Legion: cf. Mark 5:9.
93. discard: reject
93–94. private: privacy

Mal. Aha! does she so?

To. Go to, go to; peace, peace! We must deal gently with him. Let me alone. How do you, 100 Malvolio? How is't with you? What, man! defy the devil! Consider, he's an enemy to mankind.

Mal. Do you know what you say?

Mar. La you, an you speak ill of the devil, how he takes it at heart! Pray God he be not be- 105 witched!

Fab. Carry his water to the wise woman.

Mar. Marry, and it shall be done tomorrow morning if I live. My lady would not lose him for more than I'll say. 110

Mal. How now, mistress?

Mar. O Lord!

To. Prithee hold thy peace. This is not the way. Do you not see you move him? Let me alone with him. 115

Fab. No way but gentleness; gently, gently. The fiend is rough and will not be roughly used.

To. Why, how now, my bawcock? How dost thou, chuck?

Mal. Sir! 120

To. Ay, biddy, come with me. What, man! 'tis not for gravity to play at cherry-pit with Satan. Hang him, foul collier!

Mar. Get him to say his prayers. Good Sir Toby, get him to pray. 125

Mal. My prayers, minx?

Mar. No, I warrant you, he will not hear of godliness.

Mal. Go hang yourselves all! You are idle shallow things; I am not of your element. You shall 130 know more hereafter. *Exit.*

To. Is't possible?

Fab. If this were played upon a stage now, I could condemn it as an improbable fiction.

To. His very genius hath taken the infec- 135 tion of the device, man.

Mar. Nay, pursue him now, lest the device take air and taint.

Fab. Why, we shall make him mad indeed.

Mar. The house will be the quieter. 140

To. Come, we'll have him in a dark room and bound. My niece is already in the belief that he's mad. We may carry it thus, for our pleasure and his penance, till our very pastime, tired out of breath, prompt us to have mercy on him; at which 145 time we will bring the device to the bar and crown thee for a finder of madmen. But see, but see!

Enter SIR ANDREW.

Fab. More matter for a May morning.

And. Here's the challenge; read it. I warrant there's vinegar and pepper in't. 150

Fab. Is't so saucy?

And. Ay, is't, I warrant him. Do but read.

To. Give me. [*Reads*]

Youth, whatsoever thou art, thou art but a scurvy fellow. 155

Fab. Good, and valiant.

To. [*Reads*]

Wonder not nor admire not in thy mind why I do call thee so, for I will show thee no reason for't.

Fab. A good note! That keeps you from the blow of the law. 160

To. [*Reads*]

Thou comest to the Lady Olivia, and in my sight she uses thee kindly. But thou liest in thy throat; that is not the matter I challenge thee for.

Fab. Very brief, and to exceeding good sense—less. 165

To. [*Reads*]

I will waylay thee going home; where if it be thy chance to kill me—

Fab. Good.

To. [*Reads*]

Thou killst me like a rogue and a villain.

Fab. Still you keep o' the windy side of the 170 law. Good.

To. [*Reads*]

Fare thee well, and God have mercy upon one of our souls! He may have mercy upon mine, but my hope is better; and so look to thyself. Thy friend, as thou usest him, and thy sworn enemy, 175

ANDREW AGUECHEEK.

If this letter move him not, his legs cannot. I'll give't him.

Mar. You may have a very fit occasion for't. He is now in some commerce with my lady and 180 will by-and-by depart.

To. Go, Sir Andrew! Scout me for him at the corner of the orchard like a bum-baily. So soon as ever thou seest him, draw; and as thou drawst, swear horrible; for it comes to pass oft that a terrible 185 oath, with a swaggering accent sharply twanged off, gives manhood more approbation than ever proof itself would have earned him. Away!

And. Nay, let me alone for swearing. *Exit.*

104. La: behold
114. move: excite
118. bawcock: fine fellow (French *beau coq*)
119. chuck: another endearment
122. gravity: a sober person; **cherry-pit:** a child's game
123. collier: dealer in coal; therefore, "black one"
135. genius: ruling spirit
137–38. take . . . taint: become known and thus be spoiled
148. May morning: antic season
157. admire: marvel
180. commerce: communication
183. bum-baily: bailiff (who made arrests for a sheriff)
187. approbation: confirmation
189. let . . . swearing: no one can equal me in swearing.

To. Now will not I deliver his letter; for 190
the behavior of the young gentleman gives him out
to be of good capacity and breeding; his employment between his lord and my niece confirms no less.
Therefore this letter, being so excellently ignorant,
will breed no terror in the youth. He will find 195
it comes from a clodpoll. But, sir, I will deliver
his challenge by word of mouth, set upon Aguecheek
a notable report of valor, and drive the gentleman
(as I know his youth will aptly receive it) into a
most hideous opinion of his rage, skill, fury, 200
and impetuosity. This will so fright them both that
they will kill one another by the look, like cockatrices.

Enter OLIVIA *and* VIOLA.

Fab. Here he comes with your niece. Give them
way till he take leave, and presently after him.

To. I will meditate the while upon some 205
horrid message for a challenge.

[*Exeunt Sir Toby, Fabian, and Maria.*]

Oli. I have said too much unto a heart of stone
And laid mine honor too unchary out.
There's something in me that reproves my fault;
But such a headstrong potent fault it is 210
That it but mocks reproof.

Vio. With the same 'havior that your passion bears
Goes on my master's grief.

Oli. Here, wear this jewel for me; 'tis my picture.
Refuse it not; it hath no tongue to vex you. 215
And I beseech you come again tomorrow.
What shall you ask of me that I'll deny,
That honor, saved, may upon asking give?

Vio. Nothing but this—your true love for my master. 219

Oli. How with mine honor may I give him that
Which I have given to you?

Vio. I will acquit you.

Oli. Well, come again tomorrow. Fare thee well.
A fiend like thee might bear my soul to hell. [*Exit.*]

Enter [SIR] TOBY *and* FABIAN.

To. Gentleman, God save thee!

Vio. And you, sir. 225

To. That defense thou hast, betake thee to't. Of
what nature the wrongs are thou hast done him, I
know not; but thy intercepter, full of despite, bloody
as the hunter, attends thee at the orchard end. Dismount thy tuck, be yare in thy preparation; 230
for thy assailant is quick, skillful, and deadly.

Vio. You mistake, sir. I am sure no man hath any
quarrel to me. My remembrance is very free and clear
from any image of offense done to any man.

To. You'll find it otherwise, I assure you. 235
Therefore, if you hold your life at any price, betake
you to your guard; for your opposite hath in him
what youth, strength, skill, and wrath can furnish
man withal.

Vio. I pray you, sir, what is he? 240

To. He is knight, dubbed with unhatched rapier
and on carpet consideration; but he is a devil in
private brawl. Souls and bodies hath he divorced
three; and his incensement at this moment is so implacable that satisfaction can be none but by 245
pangs of death and sepulcher. "Hob, nob" is his
word; "give't or take't."

Vio. I will return again into the house and desire
some conduct of the lady. I am no fighter. I have
heard of some kind of men that put quarrels 250
purposely on others to taste their valor. Belike this
is a man of that quirk.

To. Sir, no. His indignation derives itself out of a
very competent injury; therefore get you on and give
him his desire. Back you shall not to the house, 255
unless you undertake that with me which with as
much safety you might answer him. Therefore on!
or strip your sword stark naked; for meddle you
must, that's certain, or forswear to wear iron about
you. 260

Vio. This is as uncivil as strange. I beseech you do
me this courteous office, as to know of the knight
what my offense to him is. It is something of my
negligence, nothing of my purpose.

To. I will do so. Signior Fabian, stay you 265
by this gentleman till my return. *Exit.*

Vio. Pray you, sir, do you know of this matter?

Fab. I know the knight is incensed against you,
even to a mortal arbitrament; but nothing of the
circumstance more. 270

Vio. I beseech you, what manner of man is he?

Fab. Nothing of that wonderful promise, to read
him by his form, as you are like to find him in the
proof of his valor. He is indeed, sir, the most skillful,
bloody, and fatal opposite that you could 275
possibly have found in any part of Illyria. Will you
walk towards him? I will make your peace with him
if I can.

Vio. I shall be much bound to you for't. I am one
that had rather go with sir priest than sir 280
knight. I care not who knows so much of my mettle.
Exeunt.

196. **clodpoll:** blockhead
202. **cockatrices:** fabulous creatures with deadly glances
203–4. **Give . . . way:** leave them alone
208. **unchary:** generously
221. **acquit:** release
228. **despite:** defiance; **bloody:** bloodthirsty
230. **tuck:** sword; **yare:** quick
237. **guard:** defense
241–42. **knight . . . consideration:** a knight dubbed with an ornamental sword at court, for reasons unconnected with his valor (possibly, for a fee)
246. **"Hob, nob":** have or have not
254. **competent:** sufficient
258. **meddle:** fight
269. **mortal arbitrament:** fatal conclusion

Enter [Sir] Toby *and* [Sir] Andrew.

To. Why, man, he's a very devil; I have not seen such a virago. I had a pass with him, rapier, scabbard, and all, and he gives me the stuck-in with such a mortal motion that it is inevitable; and 285
on the answer he pays you as surely as your feet hit the ground they step on. They say he has been fencer to the Sophy.

And. Pox on't. I'll not meddle with him.

To. Ay, but he will not now be pacified. 290
Fabian can scarce hold him yonder.

And. Plague on't, an I thought he had been valiant, and so cunning in fence, I'd have seen him damned ere I'd have challenged him. Let him let the matter slip, and I'll give him my horse, grey Capilet. 295

To. I'll make the motion. Stand here; make a good show on't. This shall end without the perdition of souls. [*Aside*] Marry, I'll ride your horse as well as I ride you.

Enter Fabian *and* Viola.

I have his horse to take up the quarrel. I have 300
persuaded him the youth's a devil.

Fab. He is as horribly conceited of him; and pants and looks pale, as if a bear were at his heels.

To. There's no remedy, sir; he will fight with you for's oath sake. Marry, he hath better be- 305
thought him of his quarrel, and he finds that now scarce to be worth talking of. Therefore draw for the supportance of his vow. He protests he will not hurt you.

Vio. [*Aside*] Pray God defend me! A little 310
thing would make me tell them how much I lack of a man.

Fab. Give ground if you see him furious.

To. Come, Sir Andrew, there's no remedy. The gentleman will for his honor's sake have one 315
bout with you; he cannot by the duello avoid it; but he has promised me, as he is a gentleman and a soldier, he will not hurt you. Come on, to't!

And. Pray God he keep his oath! [*Draws.*]

Enter Antonio.

Vio. I do assure you 'tis against my will. 320
[*Draws.*]

Ant. Put up your sword. If this young gentleman
Have done offense, I take the fault on me;
If you offend him, I for him defy you.

To. You, sir? Why, what are you?

Ant. [*Draws*] One, sir, that for his love dares yet do more 325
Than you have heard him brag to you he will.

To. Nay, if you be an undertaker, I am for you. [*Draws.*]

Enter Officers.

Fab. O good Sir Toby, hold! Here come the officers.

To. I'll be with you anon. 330

Vio. Pray, sir, put your sword up, if you please.

And. Marry, will I, sir; and for that I promised you, I'll be as good as my word. He will bear you easily, and reins well.

1. Off. This is the man; do thy office. 335

2. Off. Antonio, I arrest thee at the suit
Of Count Orsino.

Ant. You do mistake me, sir.

1. Off. No, sir, no jot. I know your favor well,
Though now you have no sea-cap on your head.
Take him away. He knows I know him well. 340

Ant. I must obey. [*To Viola*] This comes with seeking you.
But there's no remedy; I shall answer it.
What will you do, now my necessity
Makes me to ask you for my purse? It grieves me
Much more for what I cannot do for you 345
Than what befalls myself. You stand amazed,
But be of comfort.

2. Off. Come, sir, away.

Ant. I must entreat of you some of that money.

Vio. What money, sir? 350
For the fair kindness you have showed me here,
And part being prompted by your present trouble,
Out of my lean and low ability
I'll lend you something. My having is not much.
I'll make division of my present with you. 355
Hold, there's half my coffer.

Ant. Will you deny me now?
Is't possible that my deserts to you
Can lack persuasion? Do not tempt my misery,
Lest that it make me so unsound a man
As to upbraid you with those kindnesses 360
That I have done for you.

Vio. I know of none,
Nor know I you by voice or any feature.
I hate ingratitude more in a man

283. **virago:** fire-eater
284. **stuck-in:** thrust (Italian *stoccata*)
285. **mortal motion:** deadly movement; **inevitable:** impossible to avoid
286. **on . . . you:** in reply he jabs you
296. **motion:** offer
297. **perdition:** loss
300. **take up:** resolve
302. **He . . . him:** Cesario has as terrifying a picture of Sir Andrew.
316. **duello:** dueling code
327. **undertaker:** helper
330. **anon:** at once
338. **favor:** features
355. **my present:** the funds in my possession
359. **unsound:** weak

Than lying, vainness, babbling drunkenness,
Or any taint of vice whose strong corruption 365
Inhabits our frail blood.

Ant. O heavens themselves!

2. Off. Come, sir, I pray you go.

Ant. Let me speak a little. This youth that you see here
I snatched one half out of the jaws of death;
Relieved him with such sanctity of love, 370
And to his image, which methought did promise
Most venerable worth, did I devotion.

1. Off. What's that to us? The time goes by. Away!

Ant. But, O, how vile an idol proves this god!
Thou hast, Sebastian, done good feature shame.
In nature there's no blemish but the mind; 376
None can be called deformed but the unkind.
Virtue is beauty; but the beauteous evil
Are empty trunks, o'erflourished by the devil.

1. Off. The man grows mad. Away with him! Come, come, sir. 380

Ant. Lead me on. *Exit [with Officers].*

Vio. Methinks his words do from such passion fly
That he believes himself; so do not I.
Prove true, imagination, O, prove true,
That I, dear brother, be now ta'en for you! 385

To. Come hither, knight; come hither, Fabian.
We'll whisper o'er a couplet or two of most sage saws.

Vio. He named Sebastian. I my brother know
Yet living in my glass. Even such and so
In favor was my brother, and he went 390
Still in this fashion, color, ornament,
For him I imitate. O, if it prove,
Tempests are kind, and salt waves fresh in love! [*Exit.*]

To. A very dishonest paltry boy, and more a coward than a hare. His dishonesty appears in leav- 395 ing his friend here in necessity and denying him; and for his cowardship, ask Fabian.

Fab. A coward, a most devout coward; religious in it. 399

And. 'Slid, I'll after him again and beat him!

To. Do; cuff him soundly, but never draw thy sword.

And. An I do not— [*Exit.*]

Fab. Come, let's see the event. 404

To. I dare lay any money 'twill be nothing yet. *Exeunt.*

372. Most . . . worth: worthiness of the highest respect; **devotion:** homage
375. feature: appearance
377. unkind: unnatural
379. trunks: chests; bodies; **o'erflourished:** embellished
387. saws: maxims
388–89. I . . . glass: i.e., when I look into a mirror, I see my brother.
394. paltry: contemptible
400. 'Slid: by God's eyelid
404. event: outcome

ACT IV

Scene I. [*Before Olivia's house.*]

Enter SEBASTIAN *and* CLOWN.

Clown. Will you make me believe that I am not sent for you?

Seb. Go to, go to, thou art a foolish fellow. Let me be clear of thee.

Clown. Well held out, i' faith! No, I do not 5 know you; nor I am not sent to you by my lady, to bid you come speak with her; nor your name is not Master Cesario; nor this is not my nose neither. Nothing that is so is so.

Seb. I prithee vent thy folly somewhere else. 10 Thou knowst not me.

Clown. Vent my folly! He has heard that word of some great man, and now applies it to a fool. Vent my folly! I am afraid this great lubber, the world, will prove a cockney. I prithee now, ungird 15 thy strangeness, and tell me what I shall vent to my lady. Shall I vent to her that thou art coming?

Seb. I prithee, foolish Greek, depart from me.

10. vent: utter
14. lubber: lout
15. cockney: milksop; fop
15–16. ungird . . . strangeness: cast off thy pretense of being a stranger

There's money for thee. If you tarry longer,
I shall give worse payment. 20

Clown. By my troth, thou hast an open hand. These wise men that give fools money get themselves a good report—after fourteen years' purchase.

Enter [SIR] ANDREW, [SIR] TOBY, *and* FABIAN.

And. Now, sir, have I met you again? There's for you! [*Striking Sebastian.*] 25

Seb. Why, there's for thee, and there, and there! [*Returning the blow.*]
Are all the people mad?

To. Hold, sir, or I'll throw your dagger o'er the house.

Clown. This will I tell my lady straight. I 30 would not be in some of your coats for twopence. [*Exit.*]

To. Come on, sir; hold!

And. Nay, let him alone. I'll go another way to work with him. I'll have an action of battery against him, if there be any law in Illyria. Though I 35 stroke him first, yet it's no matter for that.

Seb. Let go thy hand.

To. Come, sir, I will not let you go. Come, my young soldier, put up your iron. You are well fleshed. Come on. 40

Seb. I will be free from thee. What wouldst thou now?
If thou darest tempt me further, draw thy sword.

To. What, what? Nay then, I must have an ounce or two of this malapert blood from you. [*Draws.*]

Enter OLIVIA.

Oli. Hold, Toby! On thy life I charge thee hold!

To. Madam! 46

Oli. Will it be ever thus? Ungracious wretch,
Fit for the mountains and the barbarous caves,
Where manners ne'er were preached! Out of my sight!
Be not offended, dear Cesario. 50
Rudesby, be gone!
[*Exeunt Sir Toby, Sir Andrew, and Fabian.*]
I prithee, gentle friend,
Let thy fair wisdom, not thy passion, sway
In this uncivil and unjust extent
Against thy peace. Go with me to my house,
And hear thou there how many fruitless pranks 55
This ruffian hath botched up, that thou thereby
Mayst smile at this. Thou shalt not choose but go;
Do not deny. Beshrew his soul for me!
He started one poor heart of mine, in thee. 59

Seb. What relish is in this? How runs the stream?
Or I am mad, or else this is a dream.
Let fancy still my sense in Lethe steep;
If it be thus to dream, still let me sleep!

Oli. Nay, come, I prithee. Would thou'dst be ruled by me!

Seb. Madam, I will.

Oli. O, say so, and be so! 65
Exeunt.

Scene II. [*Olivia's house.*]

Enter MARIA *and* CLOWN.

Mar. Nay, I prithee put on this gown and this beard; make him believe thou art Sir Topas the curate; do it quickly. I'll call Sir Toby the whilst. [*Exit.*]

Clown. Well, I'll put it on, and I will dissemble myself in't, and I would I were the first that 5 ever dissembled in such a gown. I am not tall enough to become the function well, nor lean enough to be thought a good student; but to be said an honest man and a good housekeeper goes as fairly as to say a careful man and a great scholar. The competi- 10 tors enter.

Enter [SIR] TOBY [*and* MARIA].

To. Jove bless thee, Master Parson.

Clown. Bonos dies, Sir Toby; for, as the old hermit of Prague, that never saw pen and ink, very wittily said to a niece of King Gorboduc, "That 15 that is is"; so I, being Master Parson, am Master Parson; for what is "that" but "that," and "is" but "is"?

To. To him, Sir Topas.

Clown. What ho, I say. Peace in this prison! 20

To. The knave counterfeits well; a good knave.

MALVOLIO *within.*

Mal. Who calls there?

Clown. Sir Topas the curate, who comes to visit Malvolio the lunatic.

23. fourteen . . . purchase: paying for it for a term of fourteen years
36. stroke: struck
39. are . . . fleshed: have had an ample taste of blood
44. malapert: impudent
47. Ungracious: boorish
51. Rudesby: barbarian
53. extent: demonstration
59. started: (1) stirred; (2) flushed from covert; **heart:** pun on "hart"
60. What . . . this: what does this mean?
61. Or: either
62. Lethe: the waters of oblivion
4. dissemble: disguise
9. housekeeper: i.e., hospitable neighbor
10–11. competitors: colleagues
13–18. as . . . "is": pseudo-learned nonsense
21. knave: boy

Mal. Sir Topas, Sir Topas, good Sir Topas, 25
go to my lady.

Clown. Out, hyperbolical fiend! How vexest thou this man! Talkest thou nothing but of ladies?

To. Well said, Master Parson.

Mal. Sir Topas, never was man thus wronged. 30
Good Sir Topas, do not think I am mad. They have laid me here in hideous darkness.

Clown. Fie, thou dishonest Satan! I call thee by the most modest terms; for I am one of those gentle ones that will use the devil himself with cour- 35
tesy. Sayst thou that house is dark?

Mal. As hell, Sir Topas.

Clown. Why, it hath bay windows transparent as barricadoes, and the clerestories toward the south north are as lustrous as ebony; and yet com- 40
plainest thou of obstruction?

Mal. I am not mad, Sir Topas. I say to you this house is dark.

Clown. Madman, thou errest. I say there is no darkness but ignorance, in which thou art more 45
puzzled than the Egyptians in their fog.

Mal. I say this house is as dark as ignorance, though ignorance were as dark as hell; and I say there was never man thus abused. I am no more mad than you are. Make the trial of it in any constant ques- 50
tion.

Clown. What is the opinion of Pythagoras concerning wild fowl?

Mal. That the soul of our grandam might happily inhabit a bird. 55

Clown. What thinkst thou of his opinion?

Mal. I think nobly of the soul and no way approve his opinion.

Clown. Fare thee well. Remain thou still in darkness. Thou shalt hold the opinion of Pythagoras 60
ere I will allow of thy wits, and fear to kill a woodcock, lest thou dispossess the soul of thy grandam. Fare thee well.

Mal. Sir Topas, Sir Topas!

To. My most exquisite Sir Topas! 65

Clown. Nay, I am for all waters.

Mar. Thou mightest have done this without thy beard and gown. He sees thee not.

To. To him in thine own voice, and bring me word how thou findst him. I would we were well 70
rid of this knavery. If he may be conveniently delivered, I would he were; for I am now so far in offense with my niece that I cannot pursue with any safety this sport to the upshot. Come by-and-by to my chamber. *Exit [with Maria].*

Clown. [*Singing*] "Hey, Robin, jolly Robin, 76
Tell me how thy lady does."

Mal. Fool!

Clown. "My lady is unkind, perdie!"

Mal. Fool! 80

Clown. "Alas, why is she so?"

Mal. Fool, I say!

Clown. "She loves another"—Who calls, ha?

Mal. Good fool, as ever thou wilt deserve well at my hand, help me to a candle, and pen, ink, 85
and paper. As I am a gentleman, I will live to be thankful to thee for't.

Clown. Master Malvolio?

Mal. Ay, good fool.

Clown. Alas, sir, how fell you besides your 90
five wits?

Mal. Fool, there was never man so notoriously abused. I am as well in my wits, fool, as thou art.

Clown. But as well? Then you are mad indeed, if you be no better in your wits than a fool. 95

Mal. They have here propertied me; keep me in darkness, send ministers to me, asses, and do all they can to face me out of my wits.

Clown. Advise you what you say. The minister is here.—Malvolio, Malvolio, thy wits the heav- 100
ens restore! Endeavor thyself to sleep and leave thy vain bibble babble.

Mal. Sir Topas!

Clown. Maintain no words with him, good fellow.—Who, I, sir? Not I, sir. God be wi' you, 105
good Sir Topas!—Marry, amen.—I will, sir, I will.

Mal. Fool, fool, fool, I say!

Clown. Alas, sir, be patient. What say you, sir? I am shent for speaking to you.

Mal. Good fool, help me to some light and 110
some paper. I tell thee, I am as well in my wits as any man in Illyria.

Clown. Welladay that you were, sir!

Mal. By this hand, I am. Good fool, some ink, paper, and light; and convey what I will set 115
down to my lady. It shall advantage thee more than ever the bearing of letter did.

Clown. I will help you to't. But tell me true, are you not mad indeed? or do you but counterfeit?

Mal. Believe me, I am not. I tell thee true. 120

Clown. Nay, I'll ne'er believe a madman till I see his brains. I will fetch you light and paper and ink.

Mal. Fool, I'll requite it in the highest degree. I prithee be gone.

Clown. [*Singing*]
I am gone, sir; 125
And anon, sir,

27. hyperbolical: extravagant in speech
39. barricadoes: barricades; **clerestories:** upper windows
50–51. constant question: rational discussion
54. happily: haply; perchance
61. allow . . . wits: acknowledge your sanity
66. Nay . . . waters: indeed, I can do anything.
71–72. delivered: released

79. perdie: *par dieu,* indeed
96. propertied me: treated me like a thing
99. Advise you: consider carefully
109. shent: scolded

I'll be with you again,
In a trice,
Like to the old Vice,
Your need to sustain; 130
Who, with dagger of lath,
In his rage and his wrath,
Cries "aha!" to the devil.
Like a mad lad,
"Pare thy nails, dad." 135
Adieu, goodman devil.

Exit.

Scene III. [*Olivia's garden.*]

Enter SEBASTIAN.

Seb. This is the air; that is the glorious sun;
This pearl she gave me, I do feel't and see't;
And though 'tis wonder that enwraps me thus,
Yet 'tis not madness. Where's Antonio then?
I could not find him at the Elephant; 5
Yet there he was; and there I found this credit,
That he did range the town to seek me out.
His counsel now might do me golden service;
For though my soul disputes well with my sense
That this may be some error, but no madness, 10
Yet doth this accident and flood of fortune
So far exceed all instance, all discourse,
That I am ready to distrust mine eyes
And wrangle with my reason, that persuades me
To any other trust but that I am mad, 15
Or else the lady's mad. Yet, if 'twere so,
She could not sway her house, command her followers,
Take and give back affairs and their dispatch
With such a smooth, discreet, and stable bearing
As I perceive she does. There's something in't 20
That is deceivable. But here the lady comes.

Enter OLIVIA *and* PRIEST.

Oli. Blame not this haste of mine. If you mean well,
Now go with me and with this holy man
Into the chantry by. There, before him,
And underneath that consecrated roof, 25
Plight me the full assurance of your faith,
That my most jealous and too doubtful soul
May live at peace. He shall conceal it
Whiles you are willing it shall come to note,
What time we will our celebration keep 30
According to my birth. What do you say?

Seb. I'll follow this good man and go with you,
And, having sworn truth, ever will be true.

Oli. Then lead the way, good father; and heavens so shine
That they may fairly note this act of mine! 35

Exeunt.

129. **Vice:** personification of vice in a morality play
6. **credit:** belief
11. **accident:** happening
12. **instance:** precedent; **discourse:** rationality

17. **sway:** rule
18. **Take . . . dispatch:** listen to reports, make decisions, and order business to be taken care of
21. **deceivable:** deceptive
24. **chantry by:** nearby chapel
27. **jealous:** skeptical
29. **Whiles:** until
30. **What time:** at which time
31. **birth:** rank
35. **That . . . note:** to indicate approval of

ACT V

Scene I. [*Before Olivia's house.*]

Enter CLOWN *and* FABIAN.

Fab. Now as thou lovest me, let me see his letter.

Clown. Good Master Fabian, grant me another request.

Fab. Anything.

Clown. Do not desire to see this letter. 5

Fab. This is to give a dog, and in recompense desire my dog again.

Enter DUKE, VIOLA, CURIO, *and* LORDS.

Duke. Belong you to the Lady Olivia, friends?

Clown. Ay, sir, we are some of her trappings.

Duke. I know thee well. How dost thou, my good fellow? 10

Clown. Truly, sir, the better for my foes, and the worse for my friends.

Duke. Just the contrary: the better for thy friends.

Clown. No, sir, the worse. 15

Duke. How can that be?

Clown. Marry, sir, they praise me and make an ass of me. Now my foes tell me plainly I am an ass; so that by my foes, sir, I profit in the knowledge of myself, and by my friends I am abused; so that, 20 conclusions to be as kisses, if your four negatives make your two affirmatives, why then, the worse for my friends and the better for my foes.

Duke. Why, this is excellent.

Clown. By my troth, sir, no; though it please 25 you to be one of my friends.

Duke. Thou shalt not be the worse for me. There's gold.

Clown. But that it would be double-dealing, sir, I would you could make it another. 30

Duke. O, you give me ill counsel.

Clown. Put your grace in your pocket, sir, for this once, and let your flesh and blood obey it.

Duke. Well, I will be so much a sinner to be a double-dealer. There's another. 35

Clown. Primo, secundo, tertio is a good play; and the old saying is "The third pays for all." The triplex, sir, is a good tripping measure; or the bells of St. Bennet, sir, may put you in mind—one, two, three.

Duke. You can fool no more money out of 40 me at this throw. If you will let your lady know I am here to speak with her, and bring her along with you, it may awake my bounty further.

Clown. Marry, sir, lullaby to your bounty till I come again! I go, sir; but I would not have you 45 to think that my desire of having is the sin of covetousness. But, as you say, sir, let your bounty take a nap; I will awake it anon. *Exit.*

Enter ANTONIO *and* OFFICERS.

Vio. Here comes the man, sir, that did rescue me.

Duke. That face of his I do remember well; 50
Yet when I saw it last, it was besmeared
As black as Vulcan in the smoke of war.
A baubling vessel was he captain of,
For shallow draught and bulk unprizable,
With which such scathful grapple did he make 55
With the most noble bottom of our fleet
That very envy and the tongue of loss
Cried fame and honor on him. What's the matter?

1. Off. Orsino, this is that Antonio
That took the "Phœnix" and her fraught from
Candy; 60
And this is he that did the "Tiger" board
When your young nephew Titus lost his leg.
Here in the streets, desperate of shame and state,
In private brabble did we apprehend him. 64

Vio. He did me kindness, sir; drew on my side;
But in conclusion put strange speech upon me.
I know not what 'twas but distraction.

Duke. Notable pirate, thou salt-water thief!
What foolish boldness brought thee to their mercies
Whom thou in terms so bloody and so dear 70
Hast made thine enemies?

Ant. Orsino, noble sir,
Be pleased that I shake off these names you give me.
Antonio never yet was thief or pirate,
Though I confess, on base and ground enough,
Orsino's enemy. A witchcraft drew me hither. 75
That most ingrateful boy there by your side
From the rude sea's enraged and foamy mouth
Did I redeem. A wrack past hope he was.
His life I gave him, and did thereto add
My love without retention or restraint, 80
All his in dedication. For his sake
Did I expose myself (pure for his love)
Into the danger of this adverse town;
Drew to defend him when he was beset;
Where being apprehended, his false cunning 85
(Not meaning to partake with me in danger)
Taught him to face me out of his acquaintance,
And grew a twenty years removed thing
While one would wink; denied me mine own purse,
Which I had recommended to his use 90
Not half an hour before.

Vio. How can this be?

Duke. When came he to this town?

Ant. Today, my lord; and for three months before,
No int'rim, not a minute's vacancy,
Both day and night did we keep company. 95

Enter OLIVIA *and* ATTENDANTS.

Duke. Here comes the Countess; now heaven walks on earth.

20. abused: deceived
32. grace: virtue (with a pun on the title "your Grace")
33. it: the ill counsel
37. triplex: triple time
41. throw: turn of the dice game
53. baubling: trifling
54. unprizable: worthless
55. scathful: injurious
56. bottom: vessel
57. very . . . loss: those who had lost by his hostile action
60. fraught: freight; **Candy:** Candia (ancient name for Crete)
63. desperate: reckless
64. brabble: brawl
66. put . . . me: spoke to me strangely
74. on . . . enough: for sufficient reason
78. wrack: ruin
82. pure: purely
83. adverse: hostile
87. face . . . acquaintance: pretend that he did not know me
90. recommended: offered
94. No int'rim: without interruption

But for thee, fellow—fellow, thy words are madness.
Three months this youth hath tended upon me;
But more of that anon. Take him aside.
Oli. What would my lord, but that he may not have, 100
Wherein Olivia may seem serviceable?
Cesario, you do not keep promise with me.
Vio. Madam!
Duke. Gracious Olivia— 104
Oli. What do you say, Cesario?—Good my lord—
Vio. My lord would speak; my duty hushes me.
Oli. If it be aught to the old tune, my lord,
It is as fat and fulsome to mine ear
As howling after music.
Duke. Still so cruel?
Oli. Still so constant, lord. 110
Duke. What, to perverseness? You uncivil lady,
To whose ingrate and unauspicious altars
My soul the faithful'st off'rings hath breathed out
That e'er devotion tendered! What shall I do?
Oli. Even what it please my lord, that shall become him. 115
Duke. Why should I not, had I the heart to do it,
Like to the Egyptian thief at point of death,
Kill what I love?—a savage jealousy
That sometimes savors nobly. But hear me this:
Since you to non-regardance cast my faith, 120
And that I partly know the instrument
That screws me from my true place in your favor,
Live you the marble-breasted tyrant still.
But this your minion, whom I know you love,
And whom, by heaven I swear, I tender dearly,
Him will I tear out of that cruel eye 126
Where he sits crowned in his master's spite.
Come, boy, with me. My thoughts are ripe in mischief.
I'll sacrifice the lamb that I do love
To spite a raven's heart within a dove. 130
Vio. And I, most jocund, apt, and willingly,
To do you rest a thousand deaths would die.
Oli. Where goes Cesario?
Vio. After him I love
More than I love these eyes, more than my life,
More, by all mores, than e'er I shall love wife. 135
If I do feign, you witnesses above
Punish my life for tainting of my love!
Oli. Ay me detested! how am I beguiled!
Vio. Who does beguile you? Who does do you wrong?
Oli. Hast thou forgot thyself? Is it so long? 140
Call forth the holy father. [*Exit an Attendant.*]
Duke. [*To Viola*] Come, away!
Oli. Whither, my lord? Cesario, husband, stay.
Duke. Husband?
Oli. Ay, husband. Can he that deny?
Duke. Her husband, sirrah?
Vio. No, my lord, not I.
Oli. Alas, it is the baseness of thy fear 145
That makes thee strangle thy propriety.
Fear not, Cesario; take thy fortunes up;
Be that thou knowest thou art, and then thou art
As great as that thou fearest.

Enter PRIEST.

O, welcome, father!
Father, I charge thee by thy reverence 150
Here to unfold—though lately we intended
To keep in darkness what occasion now
Reveals before 'tis ripe—what thou dost know
Hath newly passed between this youth and me.
Priest. A contract of eternal bond of love, 155
Confirmed by mutual joinder of your hands,
Attested by the holy close of lips,
Strengthened by interchangement of your rings;
And all the ceremony of this compact
Sealed in my function, by my testimony; 160
Since when, my watch hath told me, toward my grave
I have traveled but two hours.
Duke. O thou dissembling cub! What wilt thou be
When time hath sowed a grizzle on thy case?
Or will not else thy craft so quickly grow 165
That thine own trip shall be thine overthrow?
Farewell, and take her; but direct thy feet
Where thou and I, henceforth, may never meet.
Vio. My lord, I do protest—
Oli. O, do not swear! 169
Hold little faith, though thou hast too much fear.

Enter SIR ANDREW.

And. For the love of God, a surgeon! Send one presently to Sir Toby.
Oli. What's the matter?

108. fat . . . fulsome: sickening
112. ingrate: ungrateful; **unauspicious:** unfavorable
114. tendered: offered
117. Egyptian thief: a character in Heliodorus' story of Theagenes and Chariclea, who offered to kill his mistress rather than lose her
119. savors nobly: smacks of nobility
120. to . . . faith: discard my devotion
124. minion: pet
125. tender: cherish
127. in . . . spite: despite his master
128. ripe in: ready for
131. jocund: cheerfully; **apt:** eagerly
132. do . . . rest: give you ease
136. feign: pretend
146. strangle: smother (conceal); **propriety:** identity
147. take . . . up: accept thy good fortune
148. that . . . art: i.e., Olivia's husband
150. thy reverence: the respect you command
160. Sealed . . . function: confirmed by the performance of my priestly office
164. Sowed . . . case: scattered gray in your hair
166. trip: tripping of another
170. Hold . . . faith: retain some remnant of fidelity

And. Has broke my head across, and has given Sir Toby a bloody coxcomb too. For the love of 175 God, your help! I had rather than forty pound I were at home.

Oli. Who has done this, Sir Andrew?

And. The Count's gentleman, one Cesario. We took him for a coward, but he's the very devil 180 incardinate.

Duke. My gentleman Cesario?

And. Od's lifelings, here he is! You broke my head for nothing; and that that I did, I was set on to do't by Sir Toby. 185

Vio. Why do you speak to me? I never hurt you.
You drew your sword upon me without cause,
But I bespake you fair and hurt you not.

Enter [SIR] TOBY *and* CLOWN.

And. If a bloody coxcomb be a hurt, you have hurt me. I think you set nothing by a bloody cox- 190 comb. Here comes Sir Toby halting—you shall hear more. But if he had not been in drink, he would have tickled you othergates than he did.

Duke. How now, gentleman? How is't with you?

To. That's all one! Has hurt me, and there's 195 the end on't.—Sot, didst see Dick Surgeon, sot?

Clown. O, he's drunk, Sir Toby, an hour agone. His eyes were set at eight i' the morning.

To. Then he's a rogue and a passy measures pavin. I hate a drunken rogue. 200

Oli. Away with him! Who hath made this havoc with them?

And. I'll help you, Sir Toby, because we'll be dressed together.

To. Will you help—an ass-head and a cox- 205 comb and a knave—a thin-faced knave, a gull?

Oli. Get him to bed, and let his hurt be looked to.
[*Exeunt Sir Toby, Sir Andrew, Clown, and Fabian.*]

Enter SEBASTIAN.

Seb. I am sorry, madam, I have hurt your kinsman;
But had it been the brother of my blood,
I must have done no less with wit and safety. 210
You throw a strange regard upon me, and by that
I do perceive it hath offended you.
Pardon me, sweet one, even for the vows
We made each other but so late ago.

Duke. One face, one voice, one habit, and two persons! 215
A natural perspective, that is and is not!

Seb. Antonio! O my dear Antonio!
How have the hours racked and tortured me
Since I have lost thee! 219

Ant. Sebastian are you?

Seb. Fearst thou that, Antonio?

Ant. How have you made division of yourself?
An apple cleft in two is not more twin
Than these two creatures. Which is Sebastian?

Oli. Most wonderful! 224

Seb. Do I stand there? I never had a brother;
Nor can there be that deity in my nature
Of here and everywhere. I had a sister,
Whom the blind waves and surges have devoured.
Of charity, what kin are you to me? 229
What countryman? what name? what parentage?

Vio. Of Messaline; Sebastian was my father—
Such a Sebastian was my brother too;
So went he suited to his watery tomb.
If spirits can assume both form and suit,
You come to fright us.

Seb. A spirit I am indeed, 235
But am in that dimension grossly clad
Which from the woman I did participate.
Were you a woman, as the rest goes even,
I should my tears let fall upon your cheek
And say, "Thrice welcome, drowned Viola!" 240

Vio. My father had a mole upon his brow—

Seb. And so had mine.

Vio. And died that day when Viola from her birth
Had numbered thirteen years.

Seb. O, that record is lively in my soul! 245
He finished indeed his mortal act
That day that made my sister thirteen years.

Vio. If nothing lets to make us happy both
But this my masculine usurped attire,
Do not embrace me till each circumstance 250
Of place, time, fortune do cohere and jump
That I am Viola; which to confirm,
I'll bring you to a captain in this town,
Where lie my maiden weeds; by whose gentle help
I was preserved to serve this noble Count. 255

175. **coxcomb:** head
181. **incardinate:** incarnate
183. **Od's lifelings:** God's little life
190. **set . . . by:** think nothing of
191. **halting:** limping
193. **othergates:** otherwise
196. **Sot:** fool
199. **passy . . . pavin:** literally, a slow and stately dance
204. **dressed:** treated
210. **wit:** wisdom
211. **regard:** glance
215. **habit:** costume
216. **natural perspective:** illusion created by nature
220. **Fearst thou:** do you doubt
226. **deity:** divine power
227. **Of . . . everywhere:** of being several places at once
229. **Of charity:** kindly tell me
233. **suited:** dressed
236. **dimension:** shape; **grossly:** fleshily
237. **participate:** possess
238. **as . . . even:** i.e., as you should be, since other facts indicate that you are my sister.
248. **lets:** hinders
251. **jump:** agree
254. **weeds:** garments

All the occurrence of my fortune since
Hath been between this lady and this lord.
Seb. [*To Olivia*] So comes it, lady, you have been mistook.
But nature to her bias drew in that.
You would have been contracted to a maid; 260
Nor are you therein, by my life, deceived:
You are betrothed both to a maid and man.
Duke. Be not amazed; right noble is his blood.
If this be so, as yet the glass seems true,
I shall have share in this most happy wrack. 265
[*To Viola*] Boy, thou hast said to me a thousand times
Thou never shouldst love woman like to me.
Vio. And all those sayings will I overswear,
And all those swearings keep as true in soul
As doth that orbed continent the fire 270
That severs day from night.
Duke. Give me thy hand,
And let me see thee in thy woman's weeds.
Vio. The captain that did bring me first on shore
Hath my maid's garments. He upon some action
Is now in durance, at Malvolio's suit, 275
A gentleman, and follower of my lady's.
Oli. He shall enlarge him. Fetch Malvolio hither.
And yet alas! now I remember me,
They say, poor gentleman, he's much distract.

Enter CLOWN *with a letter, and* FABIAN.

A most extracting frenzy of mine own 280
From my remembrance clearly banished his.
How does he, sirrah?
Clown. Truly, madam, he holds Belzebub at the stave's end as well as a man in his case may do. Has here writ a letter to you; I should have given't 285 you today morning. [*Offers the letter.*] But as a madman's epistles are no gospels, so it skills not much when they are delivered.
Oli. Open't and read it.
Clown. Look then to be well edified, when 290 the fool delivers the madman. [*Reads loudly*] "By the Lord, madam"—
Oli. How now? Art thou mad?
Clown. No, madam, I do but read madness. An your ladyship will have it as it ought to be, 295 you must allow vox.
Oli. Prithee read i' thy right wits.
Clown. So I do, madonna; but to read his right wits is to read thus. Therefore perpend, my princess, and give ear. 300
Oli. [*To Fabian*] Read it you, sirrah.
Fab. (*Reads*)

By the Lord, madam, you wrong me, and the world shall know it. Though you have put me into darkness, and given your drunken cousin rule over me, yet have I the benefit of my senses as well as your ladyship. 305 I have your own letter that induced me to the semblance I put on; with the which I doubt not but to do myself much right, or you much shame. Think of me as you please. I leave my duty a little unthought of, and speak out of my injury. 310
THE MADLY USED MALVOLIO.

Oli. Did he write this?
Clown. Ay, madam.
Duke. This savors not much of distraction.
Oli. See him delivered, Fabian; bring him hither.
[*Exit Fabian.*]
My lord, so please you, these things further thought on, 316
To think me as well a sister as a wife,
One day shall crown the alliance on't, so please you,
Here at my house and at my proper cost.
Duke. Madam, I am most apt t' embrace your offer. 320
[*To Viola*] Your master quits you; and for your service done him,
So much against the mettle of your sex,
So far beneath your soft and tender breeding,
And since you called me master, for so long,
Here is my hand: you shall from this time be 325
Your master's mistress.
Oli. A sister! you are she.

Enter [FABIAN, *with*] MALVOLIO.

Duke. Is this the madman?
Oli. Ay, my lord, this same.
How now, Malvolio?
Mal. Madam, you have done me wrong,
Notorious wrong.
Oli. Have I, Malvolio? No.
Mal. Lady, you have. Pray you peruse that letter.
You must not now deny it is your hand. 331
Write from it if you can, in hand or phrase,
Or say 'tis not your seal, not your invention.
You can say none of this. Well, grant it then,

259. nature . . . that: you followed a natural inclination thereby. **Bias** is a bowling term.
263. amazed: dumfounded
264. as . . . true: as it must be, since the (perspective) glass seems to be accurate
270. that . . . continent: the sun
274. upon: because of
275. durance: confinement
276. follower: retainer
277. enlarge: release
280. extracting: distracting
283–84. holds . . . end: resists the devil
287–88. skills . . . much: matters little
291. delivers: reports
296. vox: audible voice
299. perpend: consider
319. proper: personal
320. apt: eager
321. quits: releases
322. mettle: spirit; nature

And tell me, in the modesty of honor, 335
Why you have given me such clear lights of favor,
Bade me come smiling and cross-gartered to you,
To put on yellow stockings, and to frown
Upon Sir Toby and the lighter people;
And, acting this in an obedient hope, 340
Why have you suffered me to be imprisoned,
Kept in a dark house, visited by the priest,
And made the most notorious geck and gull
That e'er invention played on? Tell me why.

Oli. Alas, Malvolio, this is not my writing, 345
Though I confess much like the character;
But, out of question, 'tis Maria's hand.
And now I do bethink me, it was she
First told me thou wast mad. Thou camest in smiling,
And in such forms which here were presupposed
Upon thee in the letter. Prithee be content. 351
This practice hath most shrewdly passed upon thee;
But when we know the grounds and authors of it,
Thou shalt be both the plaintiff and the judge
Of thine own cause.

Fab. Good madam, hear me speak,
And let no quarrel, nor no brawl to come, 356
Taint the condition of this present hour,
Which I have wond'red at. In hope it shall not,
Most freely I confess myself and Toby
Set this device against Malvolio here, 360
Upon some stubborn and uncourteous parts
We had conceived against him. Maria writ
The letter, at Sir Toby's great importance,
In recompense whereof he hath married her.
How with a sportful malice it was followed 365
May rather pluck on laughter than revenge,
If that the injuries be justly weighed
That have on both sides passed.

Oli. Alas poor fool, how have they baffled thee!

Clown. Why, "some are born great, some 370 achieve greatness, and some have greatness thrown upon them." I was one, sir, in this interlude—one Sir Topas, sir; but that's all one. "By the Lord, fool, I am not mad!" But do you remember—"Madam, why laugh you at such a barren rascal? An you 375 smile not, he's gagged"? And thus the whirligig of time brings in his revenges.

Mal. I'll be revenged on the whole pack of you!
[*Exit.*]

Oli. He hath been most notoriously abused.

Duke. Pursue him and entreat him to a peace.
He hath not told us of the captain yet, 381
When that is known, and golden time convents,
A solemn combination shall be made
Of our dear souls. Meantime, sweet sister,
We will not part from hence. Cesario, come— 385
For so you shall be while you are a man;
But when in other habits you are seen,
Orsino's mistress and his fancy's queen.
Exeunt [*all but the Clown*].

Clown sings.

When that I was and a little tiny boy,
With hey, ho, the wind and the rain, 390
A foolish thing was but a toy,
For the rain it raineth every day.

But when I came to man's estate,
With hey, ho, the wind and the rain,
'Gainst knaves and thieves men shut their gate, 395
For the rain it raineth every day.

But when I came, alas! to wive,
With hey, ho, the wind and the rain,
By swaggering could I never thrive,
For the rain it raineth every day. 400

But when I came unto my beds,
With hey, ho, the wind and the rain,
With tosspots still had drunken heads,
For the rain it raineth every day.

A great while ago the world begun, 405
With hey, ho, the wind and the rain;
But that's all one, our play is done,
And we'll strive to please you every day.
[*Exit.*]

335. **in . . . honor:** with appropriate honesty
336. **lights:** signs
339. **lighter:** lesser
343. **geck:** simpleton; **gull:** fool
352. **practice:** plot; **shrewdly:** maliciously; **passed . . . thee:** taken you in
361. **Upon:** because of; **stubborn:** harsh; **parts:** occasions
363. **importance:** importunity
372. **interlude:** farce
382. **convents:** suits
388. **fancy's queen:** ladylove
393. **estate:** condition

Othello Contemplates the Sleeping Desdemona

From an extra-illustrated edition of Shakespeare's *Works* edited by Henry Irving and Frank A. Marshall (New York, 1893).

The Tragedy of OTHELLO
the Moor of Venice

INTRODUCTION

Evidence points to sometime in 1604 as the date of the first performance of *Othello*. It was played before King James I at Whitehall on November 1, 1604, and probably had appeared on the public stage earlier in the year. After writing the dark comedies, *All's Well That Ends Well* and *Measure for Measure,* Shakespeare in *Othello* returned to tragedy and achieved a great success. In the opinion of many critics, *Othello* is Shakespeare's best-constructed play. It was a tradition of the Elizabethan stage for plays, both tragedies and comedies, to have comic subplots that frequently bore little relation to the main action. We have seen how in *Henry IV* Shakespeare conformed to this traditional practice yet wove the subplot into the structure of the play to give it coherence. But in *Othello* he abandoned the subplot altogether and concentrated all of the action upon the main theme, the struggle between good and evil and the gradual corrosion of the soul of a noble character under the malevolent influence of a supreme villain.

Othello is not a Greek type of tragedy, describing the catastrophe overtaking a king or great personage because of Fate or some tragic flaw. On the contrary, its principal characters move on a plane of ordinary life within the experience, or at least the vicarious experience, of the audience for whom the play was written. The protagonists are human rather than superhuman, and their reactions are such that spectators and readers have no difficulty in identifying them as fellow creatures. The play is a tragedy of pity and pathos concerned with elemental human emotions universally understood and described dramatically in moving and poetic language.

The action moves swiftly from the first scene to the denouement. We never get lost in a multiplicity of incidents and a multitude of characters. Our attention never falters as we focus upon the archvillainy of Iago and his plot to plant in Othello's mind a corroding belief in his wife's faithlessness. In the working-out of this plot the author maintains suspense until the very end. No obscurity of language, characterization, or presentation puzzles spectator or reader.

The initial setting of the play in Venice made certain the attention of the Elizabethan playgoer, for Venice held a morbid fascination for Shakespeare's age, which regarded all Italy as a land of both romance and wickedness. Venice especially was noted for the beauty and complaisance of its women, the jealousy and quick tempers of its men, and the bloody deeds of its bravoes. The hypnotic interest of Englishmen in Italy, particularly in Venice, made it easy for

Shakespeare to create an atmosphere in which a character like Iago might be expected.

Iago is the type of villain that Elizabethans had learned about in Italian short stories and from the reports of travelers. Garbled interpretations of Machiavelli were also quoted to reveal the deep-dyed villainy that could be expected in Italy. Consummate villains had been popular on the stage since the morality plays, in which personifications of good and evil struggled for the soul of man. Richard III, who consciously preferred evil to good as a means of attaining his ends, should be compared with Iago, who made evil an end in itself.

Yet to give plausibility to Iago's wickedness, Shakespeare makes him hint at his hatred of Othello for promoting Cassio ahead of him and for being intimate with his own wife, Emilia. But this last is hardly more than an afterthought to rationalize a hate and an envy that are part of Iago's nature. To make the irony deeper, Shakespeare gives Iago an outward appearance of honest virtue and has Othello refer to him as "honest Iago." Othello himself is by nature courageous, open, generous, unsuspecting, and naïve. Desdemona is warmhearted, tender, faithful, and much in love with her husband, which increases the poignancy of the tragedy. No thought is further from Desdemona's mind than that of infidelity. The tension of the play heightens as we watch Iago subtly poison Othello's mind and witness Desdemona's bewilderment, despair, and ultimate death; and this tension is sustained until the last lines of the final scene, when the spectator is left contemplating the tortures awaiting Iago as he is dragged off the stage to execution.

The question of the color and race that Shakespeare intended to portray in Othello the Moor has resulted in a great deal of discussion, much of it beside the point. Shakespeare and his age were not much concerned about racial matters; there is little to indicate that Elizabethans would have interpreted the union of Othello and Desdemona as a problem in mixed marriage or that they would have regarded racial differences as of much concern. To the Elizabethans, Othello was a foreigner and an exotic, and such interest as always attached to exotics attached to the Moor. On the Elizabethan stage, a Russian or a Pole would probably have been an even stranger character than a Moor.

The interest in Moors was persistent because of the stories of the Moors in Spain and, more recently, because of forays of Moslem pirates from North Africa into the English Channel. Moorish soldiers had taken part in the siege of Malta in 1565, a struggle which Beaumont and Fletcher dramatized in 1618 in *The Knight of Malta*. The King of Portugal lost his life in the Battle of Alcazar in 1578, and Englishmen were familiar enough with the story of this Moroccan episode to make George Peele's play *The Battle of Alcazar* (acted about 1578) a popular piece. Other plays were concerned with Moors or Moorish themes.

SOURCE, HISTORY, AND TEXT

Shakespeare's plot derives from a collection of Italian short stories, the *Hecatommithi* of Giraldi Cinthio, first published in 1565. It was not translated into English in Shakespeare's time, but a French version was published in Paris in 1584. Whether Shakespeare read the Italian or the French version, or whether he got the story at second hand from somebody else, nobody knows. A comparison of the original story with the dramatic interpretation made by Shakespeare is useful in showing the way that the playwright could transform an uninspired and pedestrian story into a work of vivid characterization and poetic power.

From the first, *Othello* was a popular play. Evidence exists of several revivals before the closing of the theatres in 1642: in 1610, 1629, and 1635; it had court performances in 1604, 1612–13, and 1636. After the Restoration, when women replaced the boys who had played women's roles on the earlier stage, the part of Desdemona was perhaps the first role played by a woman on an English public stage. *Othello* was frequently performed throughout the later seventeenth century and continued to be a stage favorite during the eighteenth, nineteenth, and twentieth centuries. Between 1826 and 1852 the American Negro actor Ira Aldridge made a reputation playing Othello in England and Germany. Nearly a century later Paul Robeson played Othello successfully in England and later in the United States. Actors and actresses have found in this play, particularly in the roles of Othello, Desdemona, and Iago, scope for their talents, and they have long regarded it as a favorite vehicle of their histrionic art.

Othello was first printed in a quarto version in 1622 with the statement on the title page that "it hath been divers times acted at the Globe and at the Blackfriars by His Majesty's servants." A second quarto version appeared in 1630, and a third quarto was printed in 1655, but these have no authority. Quarto 1 and the First Folio text of 1623, in the opinion of many scholars, are based on manuscripts that are independent but ultimately derive from a common original, perhaps a playhouse copy. In preparing the present text the editors have in general followed the Folio but have made corrections based on Quarto 1 when its readings seemed preferable.

A Sea Battle
From Olaus Magnus, *Historia de gentibus septentrionalibus* (1555).

The Names of the Actors

DUKE OF VENICE.
BRABANTIO, [*a Senator*], *father to Desdemona.*
SENATORS.
GRATIANO, [*brother to Brabantio*], } *two noble*
LODOVICO, [*kinsman to Brabantio*], } *Venetians.*
OTHELLO, *the Moor.*
CASSIO, [*his*] *honorable Lieutenant.*
IAGO, [*Othello's Ancient*], *a villain.*
RODERIGO, *a gulled gentleman.*
MONTANO, [*retiring*] *Governor of Cyprus.*
CLOWN, [*servant to Othello*].

DESDEMONA, [*daughter to Brabantio and*] *wife to Othello.*
EMILIA, *wife to Iago.*
BIANCA, *a courtesan.*

Sailor, [*Messenger, Herald, Officers, Gentlemen, Musicians, Attendants*].

[Scene: *Venice; Cyprus.*]

A Venetian Gentleman of Substance [Brabantio]
From Giacomo Franco,
Habiti d'huomeni et donne Venetiane (1609?).

The Tragedy of OTHELLO *the Moor of Venice*

ACT I

Scene I. [*Venice. A street.*]

Enter RODERIGO *and* IAGO.

Rod. Tush, never tell me! I take it much unkindly
That thou, Iago, who hast had my purse
As if the strings were thine, shouldst know of this.

Iago. 'Sblood, but you'll not hear me!
If ever I did dream of such a matter, 5
Abhor me.

Rod. Thou toldst me thou didst hold him in thy hate.

Iago. Despise me if I do not. Three great ones of the city,
In personal suit to make me his lieutenant,
Off-capped to him; and, by the faith of man, 10
I know my price, I am worth no worse a place.
But he, as loving his own pride and purposes,
Evades them with a bombast circumstance,
Horribly stuffed with epithets of war;
And, in conclusion, 15
Nonsuits my mediators; for, "Certes," says he,
"I have already chose my officer."
And what was he?
Forsooth, a great arithmetician,
One Michael Cassio, a Florentine 20
(A fellow almost damned in a fair wife),
That never set a squadron in the field,
Nor the division of a battle knows
More than a spinster; unless the bookish theoric,
Wherein the toged consuls can propose 25
As masterly as he. Mere prattle, without practice,
Is all his soldiership. But he, sir, had the election;
And I (of whom his eyes had seen the proof
At Rhodes, at Cyprus, and on other grounds
Christian and heathen) must be be-leed and calmed
By debitor and creditor, this counter-caster. 31
He (in good time!) must his lieutenant be,
And I (God bless the mark!) his Moorship's ancient.

Rod. By heaven, I rather would have been his hangman.

Iago. Why, there's no remedy; 'tis the curse of service. 35
Preferment goes by letter and affection,
And not by old gradation, where each second

4. 'Sblood: by God's blood
10. Off-capped . . . him: pleaded Iago's case humbly, with hats in hand
13. a . . . circumstance: lofty but irrelevant rhetoric. **Bombast** means also "cotton stuffing."
16. Nonsuits: denies the suit of
19. arithmetician: one whose knowledge of military tactics is merely theoretical
21. almost . . . wife: the idea that a man was "damned in a fair wife" was proverbial. Since Cassio is not married, this may be a slip on Shakespeare's part, or it may refer to Bianca's pursuit of him, although she does not appear until Act IV.
25. toged consuls: robed statesmen. The toga symbolizes peace.
28. proof: trial in combat
30. be-leed . . . calmed: stopped in my course
31. debitor . . . counter-caster: i.e., a man whose only skill is in keeping accounts; another reference to Cassio's bookish knowledge of warfare
32. in . . . time: ironic: a fine piece of luck for me!
33. God . . . mark: heaven forbid; **ancient:** ensign
36. Preferment: promotion; **letter . . . affection:** influence and personal liking
37. old gradation: seniority

Stood heir to the first. Now, sir, be judge yourself
Whether I in any just term am affined
To love the Moor.

Rod. I would not follow him then. 40

Iago. O, sir, content you.
I follow him to serve my turn upon him.
We cannot all be masters, nor all masters
Cannot be truly followed. You shall mark
Many a duteous and knee-crooking knave 45
That, doting on his own obsequious bondage,
Wears out his time, much like his master's ass,
For naught but provender; and when he's old, cashiered.
Whip me such honest knaves! Others there are
Who, trimmed in forms and visages of duty, 50
Keep yet their hearts attending on themselves;
And, throwing but shows of service on their lords,
Do well thrive by them, and when they have lined their coats,
Do themselves homage. These fellows have some soul;
And such a one do I profess myself. For, sir, 55
It is as sure as you are Roderigo,
Were I the Moor, I would not be Iago.
In following him, I follow but myself.
Heaven is my judge, not I for love and duty,
But seeming so, for my peculiar end; 60
For when my outward action doth demonstrate
The native act and figure of my heart
In compliment extern, 'tis not long after
But I will wear my heart upon my sleeve
For daws to peck at. I am not what I am. 65

Rod. What a full fortune does the thick-lips owe
If he can carry't thus!

Iago. Call up her father:
Rouse him, make after him, poison his delight,
Proclaim him in the streets, incense her kinsmen,
And though he in a fertile climate dwell, 70
Plague him with flies; though that his joy be joy,
Yet throw such changes of vexation on't
As it may lose some color.

Rod. Here is her father's house. I'll call aloud.

Iago. Do, with like timorous accent and dire yell
As when, by night and negligence, the fire 76
Is spied in populous cities.

Rod. What, ho, Brabantio! Signior Brabantio, ho!

Iago. Awake! What, ho, Brabantio! Thieves! thieves! thieves!
Look to your house, your daughter, and your bags!
Thieves! thieves! 81

[*Enter*] BRABANTIO *above, at a window.*

Bra. What is the reason of this terrible summons?
What is the matter there?

Rod. Signior, is all your family within?

Iago. Are your doors locked?

Bra. Why, wherefore ask you this?

Iago. Zounds, sir, y'are robbed! For shame, put on your gown! 86
Your heart is burst; you have lost half your soul.
Even now, now, very now, an old black ram
Is tupping your white ewe. Arise, arise!
Awake the snorting citizens with the bell, 90
Or else the devil will make a grandsire of you.
Arise, I say!

Bra. What, have you lost your wits?

Rod. Most reverend signior, do you know my voice?

Bra. Not I. What are you? 94

Rod. My name is Roderigo.

Bra. The worser welcome!
I have charged thee not to haunt about my doors.
In honest plainness thou hast heard me say
My daughter is not for thee; and now, in madness,
Being full of supper and distemp'ring draughts,
Upon malicious knavery dost thou come 100
To start my quiet.

Rod. Sir, sir, sir—

Bra. But thou must needs be sure
My spirit and my place have in their power
To make this bitter to thee.

Rod. Patience, good sir.

Bra. What tellst thou me of robbing? This is Venice; 105
My house is not a grange.

Rod. Most grave Brabantio,
In simple and pure soul I come to you.

Iago. Zounds, sir, you are one of those that will not serve God if the devil bid you. Because we have to do you service, and you think we are ruffians, 110 you'll have your daughter covered with a Barbary

39. affined: bound
44. shall mark: must notice
50. trimmed . . . duty: decked out in a semblance of devotion
54. Do . . . homage: serve themselves
57. Were . . . Iago: i.e., I am Iago and not the Moor, and my first duty is to myself; and I would certainly prefer to be the master instead of the subordinate.
60. peculiar: personal
62. act . . . figure: function and motivation
63. compliment extern: external appearance
64. But: that
66. owe: own
70–71. though . . . flies: though he is enjoying good luck, plague him with petty irritations
75. timorous: terrifying
76. night . . . negligence: nocturnal negligence
86. Zounds: God's wounds
89. tupping: covering
90. snorting: snoring
99. distemp'ring: intoxicating
100. Upon: intent upon
101. start: disturb
106. grange: isolated farmhouse

horse; you'll have your nephews neigh to you; you'll have coursers for cousins, and gennets for germans.

Bra. What profane wretch art thou?

Iago. I am one, sir, that comes to tell you 115 your daughter and the Moor are now making the beast with two backs.

Bra. Thou art a villain.

Iago. You are a senator.

Bra. This thou shalt answer. I know thee, Roderigo.

Rod. Sir, I will answer anything. But I beseech you, 120
If't be your pleasure and most wise consent
(As partly I find it is) that your fair daughter,
At this odd-even and dull watch o' the night,
Transported, with no worse nor better guard
But with a knave of common hire, a gondolier, 125
To the gross clasps of a lascivious Moor—
If this be known to you, and your allowance,
We then have done you bold and saucy wrongs;
But if you know not this, my manners tell me
We have your wrong rebuke. Do not believe 130
That, from the sense of all civility,
I thus would play and trifle with your reverence.
Your daughter, if you have not given her leave,
I say again, hath made a gross revolt,
Tying her duty, beauty, wit, and fortunes 135
In an extravagant and wheeling stranger
Of here and everywhere. Straight satisfy yourself.
If she be in her chamber, or your house,
Let loose on me the justice of the state
For thus deluding you.

Bra. Strike on the tinder, ho! 140
Give me a taper! Call up all my people!
This accident is not unlike my dream:
Belief of it oppresses me already.
Light, I say! light! *Exit [above].*

Iago. Farewell, for I must leave you.
It seems not meet, nor wholesome to my place, 145
To be produced (as, if I stay, I shall)
Against the Moor. For I do know, the state,
However this may gall him with some check,
Cannot with safety cast him; for he's embarked
With such loud reason to the Cyprus wars, 150
Which even now stand in act, that for their souls
Another of his fathom they have none
To lead their business; in which regard,
Though I do hate him as I do hell pains,
Yet, for necessity of present life, 155
I must show out a flag and sign of love,
Which is indeed but sign. That you shall surely find him,
Lead to the Sagittary the raised search;
And there will I be with him. So farewell. *Exit.*

Enter, [below,] BRABANTIO, *in his nightgown, and* SERVANTS *with torches.*

Bra. It is too true an evil. Gone she is; 160
And what's to come of my despised time
Is naught but bitterness. Now, Roderigo,
Where didst thou see her?—O unhappy girl!—
With the Moor, sayst thou?—Who would be a father?—
How didst thou know 'twas she?—O, she deceives me
Past thought!—What said she to you?—Get mo tapers! 166
Raise all my kindred!—Are they married, think you?

Rod. Truly I think they are.

Bra. O heaven! How got she out? O treason of the blood!
Fathers, from hence trust not your daughters' minds
By what you see them act. Is there not charms 171
By which the property of youth and maidhood
May be abused? Have you not read, Roderigo,
Of some such thing?

Rod. Yes, sir, I have indeed.

Bra. Call up my brother.—O, would you had had her!— 175
Some one way, some another.—Do you know
Where we may apprehend her and the Moor?

Rod. I think I can discover him, if you please
To get good guard and go along with me.

Bra. Pray you lead on. At every house I'll call;
I may command at most.—Get weapons, ho! 181
And raise some special officers of night.—
On, good Roderigo. I'll deserve your pains.
Exeunt.

Scene II. [*Venice. Before the Sagittary.*]

Enter OTHELLO, IAGO, ATTENDANTS, *with torches.*

Iago. Though in the trade of war I have slain men,
Yet do I hold it very stuff o' the conscience
To do no contrived murder. I lack iniquity

113. gennets: horses of Spanish breed; **germans:** relations
123. odd-even . . . night: midnight
127. your allowance: with your sanction
131. from: contrary to
134. gross: great
136. extravagant: "wandering beyond bounds," vagrant
148. gall . . . check: cause him annoyance by a rebuke
149. cast: dismiss
150. loud: important
152. fathom: capacity
158. Sagittary: probably an inn of that name
161. despised time: old age
166. mo: more
172. property: nature
173. abused: deceived
182. special . . . night: members of the watch
183. deserve . . . pains: reward your efforts
2. very . . . o': the essence of

Sometimes to do me service. Nine or ten times
I had thought t' have yerked him here under the ribs.
Oth. 'Tis better as it is.
Iago. Nay, but he prated, 6
And spoke such scurvy and provoking terms
Against your honor,
That with the little godliness I have
I did full hard forbear him. But I pray you, sir, 10
Are you fast married? Be assured of this,
That the magnifico is much beloved,
And hath in his effect a voice potential
As double as the Duke's. He will divorce you,
Or put upon you what restraint and grievance 15
The law, with all his might to enforce it on,
Will give him cable.
Oth. Let him do his spite.
My services which I have done the signiory
Shall out-tongue his complaints. 'Tis yet to know—
Which, when I know that boasting is an honor, 20
I shall promulgate—I fetch my life and being
From men of royal siege; and my demerits
May speak (unbonneted) to as proud a fortune
As this that I have reached. For know, Iago,
But that I love the gentle Desdemona, 25
I would not my unhoused free condition
Put into circumscription and confine
For the sea's worth.

Enter CASSIO, *and* OFFICERS *with torches.*

But look what lights come yond.
Iago. Those are the raised father and his friends.
You were best go in.
Oth. Not I. I must be found. 30
My parts, my title, and my perfect soul
Shall manifest me rightly. Is it they?
Iago. By Janus, I think no.
Oth. The servants of the Duke? and my lieutenant?
The goodness of the night upon you, friends! 35
What is the news?
Cas. The Duke does greet you, General;
And he requires your haste-post-haste appearance
Even on the instant.

Oth. What's the matter, think you?
Cas. Something from Cyprus, as I may divine.
It is a business of some heat. The galleys 40
Have sent a dozen sequent messengers
This very night at one another's heels;
And many of the consuls, raised and met,
Are at the Duke's already. You have been hotly called for;
When, being not at your lodging to be found, 45
The Senate hath sent about three several quests
To search you out.
Oth. 'Tis well I am found by you.
I will but spend a word here in the house,
And go with you. [*Exit.*]
Cas. Ancient, what makes he here?
Iago. Faith, he tonight hath boarded a land carrack. 50
If it prove lawful prize, he's made forever.
Cas. I do not understand.
Iago. He's married.
Cas. To who?

[*Enter* OTHELLO.]

Iago. Marry, to—Come, Captain, will you go?
Oth. Have with you.
Cas. Here comes another troop to seek for you.

Enter BRABANTIO, RODERIGO, *and* OFFICERS *with torches and weapons.*

Iago. It is Brabantio. General, be advised; 55
He comes to bad intent.
Oth. Holla! stand there!
Rod. Signior, it is the Moor.
Bra. Down with him, thief!
[*Both parties draw swords.*]
Iago. You, Roderigo! Come, sir, I am for you.
Oth. Keep up your bright swords, for the dew will rust them.
Good signior, you shall more command with years
Than with your weapons. 61
Bra. O thou foul thief, where hast thou stowed my daughter?
Damned as thou art, thou hast enchanted her!
For I'll refer me to all things of sense,
If she in chains of magic were not bound, 65
Whether a maid so tender, fair, and happy,
So opposite to marriage that she shunned
The wealthy curled darlings of our nation,
Would ever have (t' incur a general mock)
Run from her guardage to the sooty bosom 70

5. yerked: jabbed
6. prated: chattered
7. scurvy: contemptible
10. full . . . him: hardly restrain myself from attacking him
11. fast: securely
12. the magnifico: Brabantio
13–14. a . . . Duke's: an influence as great as the Duke's
16. enforce . . . on: force it to the limit
17. cable: rope; latitude
18. signiory: governing body of Venice
19. yet . . . know: not yet known
22. siege: station; **demerits:** merits
23. unbonneted: on equal terms, but courteously
28. the . . . worth: all the treasure buried in the sea
37. haste-post-haste: speedy. The phrase was a direction for the quick delivery of letters.

41. sequent: consecutive
46. several: separate
50. carrack: cargo ship
53. Have . . . you: come along
55. advised: careful
64. refer: appeal

Of such a thing as thou—to fear, not to delight.
Judge me the world if 'tis not gross in sense
That thou hast practiced on her with foul charms,
Abused her delicate youth with drugs or minerals
That weaken motion. I'll have't disputed on. 75
'Tis probable, and palpable to thinking.
I therefore apprehend and do attach thee
For an abuser of the world, a practicer
Of arts inhibited and out of warrant.
Lay hold upon him. If he do resist, 80
Subdue him at his peril.

Oth. Hold your hands,
Both you of my inclining and the rest.
Were it my cue to fight, I should have known it
Without a prompter. Where will you that I go
To answer this your charge?

Bra. To prison, till fit time
Of law and course of direct session 86
Call thee to answer.

Oth. What if I do obey?
How may the Duke be therewith satisfied,
Whose messengers are here about my side
Upon some present business of the state 90
To bring me to him?

Officer. 'Tis true, most worthy signior.
The Duke's in council, and your noble self,
I am sure, is sent for.

Bra. How? The Duke in council?
In this time of the night? Bring him away!
Mine's not an idle cause. The Duke himself, 95
Or any of my brothers of the state,
Cannot but feel this wrong as 'twere their own;
For if such actions may have passage free,
Bondslaves and pagans shall our statesmen be.

Exeunt.

Scene III. [*Venice. A chamber in the Senate House.*]

Enter DUKE *and* SENATORS, *set at a table, with lights and* ATTENDANTS.

Duke. There is no composition in these news
That gives them credit.

1. Sen. Indeed they are disproportioned.
My letters say a hundred and seven galleys.

Duke. And mine a hundred forty.

2. Sen. And mine two hundred.
But though they jump not on a just account 5
(As in these cases where the aim reports
'Tis oft with difference), yet do they all confirm
A Turkish fleet, and bearing up to Cyprus.

Duke. Nay, it is possible enough to judgment.
I do not so secure me in the error 10
But the main article I do approve
In fearful sense.

Sailor. (*Within*) What, ho! what, ho! what, ho!

Enter SAILOR.

Officer. A messenger from the galleys.

Duke. Now, what's the business?

Sailor. The Turkish preparation makes for Rhodes. 15
So was I bid report here to the state
By Signior Angelo.

Duke. How say you by this change?

1. Sen. This cannot be
By no assay of reason. 'Tis a pageant
To keep us in false gaze. When we consider 20
The importancy of Cyprus to the Turk,
And let ourselves again but understand
That, as it more concerns the Turk than Rhodes,
So may he with more facile question bear it,
For that it stands not in such warlike brace, 25
But altogether lacks the abilities
That Rhodes is dressed in—if we make thought of this,
We must not think the Turk is so unskillful
To leave that latest which concerns him first,
Neglecting an attempt of ease and gain 30
To wake and wage a danger profitless.

Duke. Nay, in all confidence he's not for Rhodes.

Officer. Here is more news.

Enter a MESSENGER.

Mess. The Ottomites, reverend and gracious,
Steering with due course toward the isle of Rhodes,
Have there injointed them with an after fleet. 36

1. Sen. Ay, so I thought. How many, as you guess?

71. fear: frighten
72. Judge . . . world: let the world judge; **gross in sense:** notably apparent
74. Abused: deceived
75. motion: understanding; good judgment
77. attach: arrest
79. arts inhibited: forbidden arts; magic; **out . . . warrant:** disallowed
86. course . . . session: regular session of court
1. composition: agreement; **these news:** commonly a plural (Latin *res novae*)
5. jump . . . account: do not agree on the exact number
6. the aim: conjecture
10–12. I . . . sense: the error does not so reassure me that I fail to find the general tenor alarming.
18. How . . . by: what do you say about
18–19. This . . . reason: this is completely contrary to logic.
19. pageant: pretense. A **pageant** was an elaborate float used in ceremonial street processions and water festivals.
24. with . . . it: more easily take it
25. For that: because
36. injointed: joined

Mess. Of thirty sail; and now they do re-stem
Their backward course, bearing with frank appearance
Their purposes toward Cyprus. Signior Montano,
Your trusty and most valiant servitor, 41
With his free duty recommends you thus,
And prays you to believe him.
Duke. 'Tis certain then for Cyprus.
Marcus Luccicos, is not he in town? 45
1. Sen. He's now in Florence.
Duke. Write from us to him; post-post-haste dispatch.

Enter BRABANTIO, OTHELLO, CASSIO, IAGO, RODERIGO, *and* OFFICERS.

1. Sen. Here comes Brabantio and the valiant Moor.
Duke. Valiant Othello, we must straight employ you
Against the general enemy Ottoman. 50
[*To Brabantio*] I did not see you. Welcome, gentle signior.
We lacked your counsel and your help tonight.
Bra. So did I yours. Good your Grace, pardon me.
Neither my place, nor aught I heard of business,
Hath raised me from my bed; nor doth the general care 55
Take hold on me; for my particular grief
Is of so floodgate and o'erbearing nature
That it engluts and swallows other sorrows,
And it is still itself.
Duke. Why, what's the matter?
Bra. My daughter! O, my daughter!
All. Dead?
Bra. Ay, to me!
She is abused, stol'n from me, and corrupted 61
By spells and medicines bought of mountebanks;
For nature so prepost'rously to err,
Being not deficient, blind, or lame of sense,
Sans witchcraft could not. 65
Duke. Whoe'er he be that in this foul proceeding
Hath thus beguiled your daughter of herself,
And you of her, the bloody book of law
You shall yourself read in the bitter letter 69
After your own sense; yea, though our proper son
Stood in your action.
Bra. Humbly I thank your Grace.
Here is the man—this Moor, whom now, it seems,
Your special mandate, for the state affairs,
Hath hither brought.
All. We are very sorry for't.
Duke. [*To Othello*] What, in your own part, can you say to this? 75
Bra. Nothing, but this is so.
Oth. Most potent, grave, and reverend signiors,
My very noble, and approved good masters:
That I have ta'en away this old man's daughter,
It is most true; true I have married her. 80
The very head and front of my offending
Hath this extent, no more. Rude am I in my speech,
And little blessed with the soft phrase of peace;
For since these arms of mine had seven years' pith,
Till now some nine moons wasted, they have used
Their dearest action in the tented field; 86
And little of this great world can I speak
More than pertains to feats of broil and battle;
And therefore little shall I grace my cause
In speaking for myself. Yet, by your gracious patience, 90
I will a round unvarnished tale deliver
Of my whole course of love—what drugs, what charms,
What conjuration, and what mighty magic
(For such proceeding am I charged withal)
I won his daughter.
Bra. A maiden never bold; 95
Of spirit so still and quiet that her motion
Blushed at herself; and she—in spite of nature,
Of years, of country, credit, everything—
To fall in love with what she feared to look on!
It is a judgment maimed and most imperfect 100
That will confess perfection so could err
Against all rules of nature, and must be driven
To find out practices of cunning hell
Why this should be. I therefore vouch again
That with some mixtures pow'rful o'er the blood,
Or with some dram, conjured to this effect, 106
He wrought upon her.
Duke. To vouch this is no proof,
Without more certain and more overt test
Than these thin habits and poor likelihoods
Of modern seeming do prefer against him. 110
1. Sen. But, Othello, speak.
Did you by indirect and forced courses

42. **With . . . thus:** offers his wholehearted duty in reporting thus
56. **particular:** personal
62. **mountebanks:** charlatans, called **mountebanks** because they stood on benches to cry their wares
65. **Sans:** without
67. **beguiled . . . herself:** robbed your daughter of her judgment
70. **After . . . sense:** as you choose to interpret it; **proper:** own
71. **Stood . . . action:** was answerable in the action
78. **approved good:** demonstrated to be good
84. **pith:** power
85. **Till . . . wasted:** until nine months ago
86. **dearest:** most important; chief
91. **round:** plain
96. **motion:** thought
103. **practices:** tricks
109. **thin habits:** flimsy appearances
110. **modern:** ordinary; mere
112. **indirect:** devious; **forced:** unnatural

Subdue and poison this young maid's affections?
Or came it by request, and such fair question
As soul to soul affordeth?

Oth. I do beseech you, 115
Send for the lady to the Sagittary
And let her speak of me before her father.
If you do find me foul in her report,
The trust, the office I do hold of you
Not only take away, but let your sentence 120
Even fall upon my life.

Duke. Fetch Desdemona hither.

Oth. Ancient, conduct them; you best know the place.

Exeunt [Iago and] two or three [Attendants].

And till she come, as truly as to heaven
I do confess the vices of my blood,
So justly to your grave ears I'll present 125
How I did thrive in this fair lady's love,
And she in mine.

Duke. Say it, Othello.

Oth. Her father loved me, oft invited me;
Still questioned me the story of my life 130
From year to year—the battles, sieges, fortunes
That I have passed.
I ran it through, even from my boyish days
To the very moment that he bade me tell it.
Wherein I spake of most disastrous chances, 135
Of moving accidents by flood and field;
Of hairbreadth scapes i' the imminent deadly breach;
Of being taken by the insolent foe
And sold to slavery; of my redemption thence
And portance in my travel's history; 140
Wherein of antres vast and deserts idle,
Rough quarries, rocks, and hills whose heads touch heaven,
It was my hint to speak—such was the process;
And of the Cannibals that each other eat,
The Anthropophagi, and men whose heads 145
Do grow beneath their shoulders. This to hear
Would Desdemona seriously incline;
But still the house affairs would draw her thence;
Which ever as she could with haste dispatch,
She'd come again, and with a greedy ear 150
Devour up my discourse. Which I observing,
Took once a pliant hour, and found good means
To draw from her a prayer of earnest heart
That I would all my pilgrimage dilate,
Whereof by parcels she had something heard, 155
But not intentively. I did consent,
And often did beguile her of her tears
When I did speak of some distressful stroke
That my youth suffered. My story being done,
She gave me for my pains a world of sighs. 160
She swore, in faith, 'twas strange, 'twas passing strange;
'Twas pitiful, 'twas wondrous pitiful.
She wished she had not heard it; yet she wished
That heaven had made her such a man. She thanked me;
And bade me, if I had a friend that loved her, 165
I should but teach him how to tell my story,
And that would woo her. Upon this hint I spake.
She loved me for the dangers I had passed,
And I loved her that she did pity them.
This only is the witchcraft I have used. 170
Here comes the lady: let her witness it.

Enter DESDEMONA, IAGO, ATTENDANTS

Duke. I think this tale would win my daughter too.
Good Brabantio,
Take up this mangled matter at the best.
Men do their broken weapons rather use 175
Than their bare hands.

Bra. I pray you hear her speak.
If she confess that she was half the wooer,
Destruction on my head if my bad blame
Light on the man! Come hither, gentle mistress.
Do you perceive in all this noble company 180
Where most you owe obedience?

Des. My noble father,
I do perceive here a divided duty.
To you I am bound for life and education;
My life and education both do learn me
How to respect you: you are the lord of duty; 185
I am hitherto your daughter. But here's my husband;
And so much duty as my mother showed
To you, preferring you before her father,
So much I challenge that I may profess
Due to the Moor my lord.

Bra. God be with you! I have done.
Please it your Grace, on to the state affairs. 191
I had rather to adopt a child than get it.
Come hither, Moor.
I here do give thee that with all my heart

114. **question:** conversation
130. **Still:** continually
137. **imminent deadly:** threatening death
140. **portance:** comportment
141. **antres:** caves
143. **hint:** opportunity; **process:** relation
145. **Anthropophagi:** Scythians, reportedly eaters of human flesh
152. **pliant:** convenient
154. **dilate:** relate in full
155. **by parcels:** bit by bit
156. **intentively:** without distraction
161. **passing:** exceedingly
167. **hint:** opportunity, as at line 143
174. **Take . . . best:** make the best of this sorry business
175–76: **Men . . . hands:** another way of saying "you must make the best of things." Possibly derives from the proverb "A wise man never wants (lacks) a weapon."
178. **bad:** unjust
186. **I . . . daughter:** i.e., until now I have been exclusively yours.
189. **challenge:** claim

Which, but thou hast already, with all my heart
I would keep from thee. For your sake, jewel, 196
I am glad at soul I have no other child;
For thy escape would teach me tyranny,
To hang clogs on them. I have done, my lord.
Duke. Let me speak like yourself and lay a sentence 200
Which, as a grise or step, may help these lovers
Into your favor.
When remedies are past, the griefs are ended
By seeing the worst, which late on hopes depended.
To mourn a mischief that is past and gone 205
Is the next way to draw new mischief on.
What cannot be preserved when Fortune takes,
Patience her injury a mock'ry makes.
The robbed that smiles steals something from the thief;
He robs himself that spends a bootless grief. 210
Bra. So let the Turk of Cyprus us beguile:
We lose it not, so long as we can smile.
He bears the sentence well that nothing bears
But the free comfort which from thence he hears;
But he bears both the sentence and the sorrow 215
That to pay grief must of poor patience borrow.
These sentences, to sugar, or to gall,
Being strong on both sides, are equivocal.
But words are words: I never yet did hear 219
That the bruised heart was pierced through the ear.
I humbly beseech you, proceed to the affairs of state.
Duke. The Turk with a most mighty preparation makes for Cyprus. Othello, the fortitude of the place is best known to you; and though we have there a substitute of most allowed sufficiency, yet 225 opinion, a sovereign mistress of effects, throws a more safer voice on you. You must therefore be content to slubber the gloss of your new fortunes with this more stubborn and boist'rous expedition.
Oth. The tyrant custom, most grave senators,
Hath made the flinty and steel couch of war 231
My thrice-driven bed of down. I do agnize
A natural and prompt alacrity
I find in hardness; and do undertake
These present wars against the Ottomites. 235
Most humbly, therefore, bending to your state,
I crave fit disposition for my wife;
Due reference of place and exhibition,
With such accommodation and besort
As levels with her breeding.
Duke. If you please, 240
Be't at her father's.
Bra. I'll not have it so.
Oth. Nor I.
Des. Nor would I there reside,
To put my father in impatient thoughts
By being in his eye. Most gracious Duke,
To my unfolding lend your prosperous ear, 245
And let me find a charter in your voice,
T' assist my simpleness.
Duke. What would you, Desdemona?
Des. That I did love the Moor to live with him,
My downright violence, and storm of fortunes, 250
May trumpet to the world. My heart's subdued
Even to the very quality of my lord.
I saw Othello's visage in his mind,
And to his honors and his valiant parts
Did I my soul and fortunes consecrate. 255
So that, dear lords, if I be left behind,
A moth of peace, and he go to the war,
The rights for which I love him are bereft me,
And I a heavy interim shall support
By his dear absence. Let me go with him. 260
Oth. Let her have your voice.
Vouch with me heaven, I therefore beg it not
To please the palate of my appetite,
Nor to comply with heat, the young affects
In my defunct and proper satisfaction; 265
But to be free and bounteous to her mind.
And heaven defend your good souls that you think
I will your serious and great business scant
For she is with me. No, when light-winged toys
Of feathered Cupid seel with wanton dullness 270
My speculative and officed instruments,
That my disports corrupt and taint my business,

199. **clogs:** restraints
200. **like yourself:** as you should
201. **grise:** synonymous with **step**
210. **bootless:** unavailing
218. **equivocal:** equal
225. **allowed sufficiency:** acknowledged capability
226. **sovereign:** dominant
226–27. **throws . . . you:** cries out that in your command lies greater safety
228. **slubber:** dull
229. **stubborn:** dangerous; **boist'rous:** violent
232. **thrice-driven:** i.e., unusually choice; **agnize:** confess
237. **fit disposition:** suitable accommodation
238. **Due . . . exhibition:** assignment of an appropriate living-place and allowance
239. **accommodation . . . besort:** appropriate comfort
245. **prosperous:** favorable
246–47. **let . . . simpleness:** support my unskilled pleading with your authority.
250. **violence . . . fortunes:** violent taking of my fortune by storm, instead of fulfilling my father's expectations
251. **subdued:** conquered
252. **quality:** profession
254. **honors . . . parts:** reputation and military prowess
257. **moth:** idle thing
259. **heavy:** sorrowful
261. **voice:** approval
264. **heat:** passion
264–65. **the . . . satisfaction:** my newly conceived affection, which has not yet been satisfied. **Defunct** means "postponed."
266. **mind:** wishes
269. **For:** because
270. **seel:** blind, from French *ciller.* The term means to sew up the eyelid of a falcon. This was done to accustom it to darkness so that it would tolerate wearing a hood.
271. **speculative . . . instruments:** faculties of perception assigned to duty

Let housewives make a skillet of my helm,
And all indign and base adversities
Make head against my estimation! 275

Duke. Be it as you shall privately determine,
Either for her stay or going. The affair cries haste,
And speed must answer it. You must away tonight.

Oth. With all my heart.

Duke. At nine i' the morning here we'll meet again.
Othello, leave some officer behind, 281
And he shall our commission bring to you;
With such things else of quality and respect
As doth import you.

Oth. So please your Grace, my ancient.
A man he is of honesty and trust. 285
To his conveyance I assign my wife,
With what else needful your good Grace shall think
To be sent after me.

Duke. Let it be so.
Good night to every one. [*To Brabantio*] And, noble signior,
If virtue no delighted beauty lack, 290
Your son-in-law is far more fair than black.

1. Sen. Adieu, brave Moor. Use Desdemona well.

Bra. Look to her, Moor, if thou hast eyes to see.
She has deceived her father, and may thee.

Exit [*with Duke, Senators, Officers, etc.*].

Oth. My life upon her faith!—Honest Iago, 295
My Desdemona must I leave to thee.
I prithee let thy wife attend on her,
And bring them after in the best advantage.
Come, Desdemona. I have but an hour
Of love, of worldly matters and direction, 300
To spend with thee. We must obey the time.

Exeunt Moor and Desdemona.

Rod. Iago.

Iago. What sayst thou, noble heart?

Rod. What will I do, thinkst thou?

Iago. Why, go to bed and sleep. 305

Rod. I will incontinently drown myself.

Iago. If thou dost, I shall never love thee after. Why, thou silly gentleman!

Rod. It is silliness to live when to live is torment; and then have we a prescription to die when 310 death is our physician.

Iago. O villainous! I have looked upon the world for four times seven years; and since I could distinguish betwixt a benefit and an injury, I never found man that knew how to love himself. Ere 315 I would say I would drown myself for the love of a guinea hen, I would change my humanity with a baboon.

Rod. What should I do? I confess it is my shame to be so fond, but it is not in my virtue to 320 amend it.

Iago. Virtue? a fig! 'Tis in ourselves that we are thus or thus. Our bodies are our gardens, to the which our wills are gardeners; so that if we will plant nettles or sow lettuce, set hyssop and 325 weed up thyme, supply it with one gender of herbs or distract it with many—either to have it sterile with idleness or manured with industry—why, the power and corrigible authority of this lies in our wills. If the balance of our lives had not one scale of rea- 330 son to poise another of sensuality, the blood and baseness of our natures would conduct us to most prepost'rous conclusions. But we have reason to cool our raging motions, our carnal stings, our unbitted lusts; whereof I take this that you call love to 335 be a sect or scion.

Rod. It cannot be.

Iago. It is merely a lust of the blood and a permission of the will. Come, be a man! Drown thyself? Drown cats and blind puppies! I have 340 professed me thy friend, and I confess me knit to thy deserving with cables of perdurable toughness. I could never better stead thee than now. Put money in thy purse. Follow thou the wars; defeat thy favor with an usurped beard. I say, put money 345 in thy purse. It cannot be that Desdemona should long continue her love to the Moor—put money in thy purse—nor he his to her. It was a violent commencement, and thou shalt see an answerable sequestration. Put but money in thy purse. 350 These Moors are changeable in their wills. Fill thy purse with money. The food that to him now is as luscious as locusts shall be to him shortly as bitter as coloquintida. She must change for youth. When she is sated with his body, she will find the error 355 of her choice. She must have change, she must. Therefore put money in thy purse. If thou wilt needs damn thyself, do it a more delicate way than drowning. Make all the money thou canst. If sanctimony and a frail vow betwixt an erring barbarian 360 and a supersubtle Venetian be not too hard for my wits and all the tribe of hell, thou shalt enjoy her.

274. indign: shameful
275. Make . . . estimation: assault my reputation
290. delighted: delightful
298. in . . . advantage: when the best opportunity offers
306. incontinently: without delay
317. guinea hen: woman (contemptuous)

325. hyssop: an aromatic herb
331. poise: balance
333. prepost'rous: monstrous
334. unbitted: uncurbed
336. sect, scion: graft or cutting; offshoot
342. perdurable: imperishable
343. stead: assist
344–45. defeat . . . favor: destroy your facial appearance; **usurped:** assumed
350. sequestration: separation
351. wills: carnal appetites
353. locusts: possibly the locust fruit known as "St. John's bread"
354. coloquintida: a bitter fruit from which a purgative is made
360. erring: wandering

Therefore make money. A pox of drowning thyself! It is clean out of the way. Seek thou rather to be hanged in compassing thy joy than to be 365 drowned and go without her.

Rod. Wilt thou be fast to my hopes, if I depend on the issue?

Iago. Thou art sure of me. Go, make money. I have told thee often, and I re-tell thee again 370 and again, I hate the Moor. My cause is hearted; thine hath no less reason. Let us be conjunctive in our revenge against him. If thou canst cuckold him, thou dost thyself a pleasure, me a sport. There are many events in the womb of time, which 375 will be delivered. Traverse! go! provide thy money! We will have more of this tomorrow. Adieu.

Rod. Where shall we meet i' the morning?

Iago. At my lodging.

Rod. I'll be with thee betimes. 380

Iago. Go to, farewell.—Do you hear, Roderigo?

Rod. What say you?

Iago. No more of drowning, do you hear?

Rod. I am changed. I'll go sell all my land. *Exit.*

364. out . . . way: the wrong thing to do
365. compassing: achieving
367. fast: faithful
371. hearted: heartfelt
373. cuckold him: i.e., seduce his wife
376. Traverse: a military term: "about face and march"
380. betimes: early
381. Go to: get on with you

Iago. Thus do I ever make my fool my purse;
For I mine own gained knowledge should profane
If I would time expend with such a snipe 387
But for my sport and profit. I hate the Moor;
And it is thought abroad that 'twixt my sheets
'Has done my office. I know not if't be true; 390
Yet I, for mere suspicion in that kind,
Will do as if for surety. He holds me well;
The better shall my purpose work on him.
Cassio's a proper man. Let me see now:
To get his place, and to plume up my will 395
In double knavery—How, how? Let's see.
After some time, to abuse Othello's ear
That he is too familiar with his wife.
He hath a person and a smooth dispose
To be suspected—framed to make women false. 400
The Moor is of a free and open nature
That thinks men honest that but seem to be so,
And will as tenderly be led by the nose
As asses are.
I have't! It is engend'red! Hell and night 405
Must bring this monstrous birth to the world's light.
Exit.

387. snipe: fool; dupe
394. proper: handsome
395. plume up: glorify
398. he: Cassio
399–400. He . . . suspected: his looks and gallant manner will make such a suspicion plausible.
403. tenderly: gently

ACT II

Scene I. [*A seaport in Cyprus. An open place near the harbor.*]

Enter MONTANO *and* TWO GENTLEMEN.

Mon. What from the cape can you discern at sea?

1. Gent. Nothing at all, it is a high-wrought flood;
I cannot 'twixt the heaven and the main
Descry a sail.

Mon. Methinks the wind hath spoke aloud at land;
A fuller blast ne'er shook our battlements. 6
If it hath ruffianed so upon the sea,
What ribs of oak, when mountains melt on them,
Can hold the mortise? What shall we hear of this?

9. hold . . . mortise: hold at the joints

2. Gent. A segregation of the Turkish fleet. 10
For do but stand upon the foaming shore,
The chidden billow seems to pelt the clouds;
The wind-shaked surge, with high and monstrous mane,
Seems to cast water on the burning Bear
And quench the Guards of the ever-fixed pole. 15
I never did like molestation view
On the enchafed flood.

Mon. If that the Turkish fleet
Be not ensheltered and embayed, they are drowned.
It is impossible they bear it out.

10. segregation: scattering
14. the . . . Bear: Ursa Minor
15. the . . . pole: two bright stars in Ursa Minor on a line with the polestar
16. like: similar
17. enchafed: raging; **If that:** if

Enter a THIRD GENTLEMAN.

3. Gent. News, lads! Our wars are done. 20
The desperate tempest hath so banged the Turks
That their designment halts. A noble ship of Venice
Hath seen a grievous wrack and sufferance
On most part of their fleet.
Mon. How? Is this true?
3. Gent. The ship is here put in,
A Veronesa; Michael Cassio, 26
Lieutenant to the warlike Moor Othello,
Is come on shore; the Moor himself at sea,
And is in full commission here for Cyprus.
Mon. I am glad on't. 'Tis a worthy governor. 30
3. Gent. But this same Cassio, though he speak of comfort
Touching the Turkish loss, yet he looks sadly
And prays the Moor be safe, for they were parted
With foul and violent tempest.
Mon. Pray heaven he be;
For I have served him, and the man commands 35
Like a full soldier. Let's to the seaside, ho!
As well to see the vessel that's come in
As to throw out our eyes for brave Othello,
Even till we make the main and the aerial blue
An indistinct regard.
3. Gent. Come, let's do so; 40
For every minute is expectancy
Of more arrivance.

Enter CASSIO.

Cas. Thanks you, the valiant of this warlike isle,
That so approve the Moor! O, let the heavens
Give him defense against the elements, 45
For I have lost him on a dangerous sea!
Mon. Is he well shipped?
Cas. His bark is stoutly timbered, and his pilot
Of very expert and approved allowance.
Therefore my hopes (not surfeited to death) 50
Stand in bold cure.
(*Within*) "A sail, a sail, a sail!"

Enter a MESSENGER.

Cas. What noise?
Mess. The town is empty; on the brow o' the sea
Stand ranks of people, and they cry "A sail!" 54
Cas. My hopes do shape him for the Governor.
A shot.
2. Gent. They do discharge their shot of courtesy.
Our friends at least.
Cas. I pray you, sir, go forth
And give us truth who 'tis that is arrived. 58
2. Gent. I shall. *Exit.*
Mon. But, good Lieutenant, is your general wived?
Cas. Most fortunately. He hath achieved a maid
That paragons description and wild fame; 62
One that excels the quirks of blazoning pens,
And in the essential vesture of creation
Does tire the ingener.

Enter SECOND GENTLEMAN.

How now? Who has put in?
2. Gent. 'Tis one Iago, ancient to the General. 66
Cas. Has had most favorable and happy speed.
Tempests themselves, high seas, and howling winds,
The guttered rocks and congregated sands,
Traitors ensteeped to clog the guiltless keel, 70
As having sense of beauty, do omit
Their mortal natures, letting go safely by
The divine Desdemona.
Mon. What is she?
Cas. She that I spake of, our great captain's captain,
Left in the conduct of the bold Iago, 75
Whose footing here anticipates our thoughts
A se'nnight's speed. Great Jove, Othello guard,
And swell his sail with thine own pow'rful breath,
That he may bless this bay with his tall ship,
Make love's quick pants in Desdemona's arms, 80
Give renewed fire to our extincted spirits,
And bring all Cyprus comfort!

Enter DESDEMONA, IAGO, RODERIGO, *and* EMILIA [*with* ATTENDANTS].

O, behold!
The riches of the ship is come on shore!
You men of Cyprus, let her have your knees.
Hail to thee, lady! and the grace of heaven, 85
Before, behind thee, and on every hand,
Enwheel thee round!
Des. I thank you, valiant Cassio.
What tidings can you tell me of my lord?
Cas. He is not yet arrived; nor know I aught
But that he's well and will be shortly here. 90
Des. O, but I fear! How lost you company?

23. sufferance: disaster
26. Veronesa: Veronese ship, in Venetian service
42. arrivance: arrivals
49. approved allowance: demonstrated ability
50–51. my . . . cure: Prov. 13:12: "Hope deferred maketh the heart sick."
61. achieved: won
62. paragons: surpasses; **wild fame:** exaggerated reputation
63. quirks: fanciful expressions; **blazoning:** praising
64–65. in . . . ingener: her natural endowments exhaust the ingenuity of anyone who would praise her. **Ingener** means "engineer," "contriver."
70. ensteeped: sunken
71. omit: neglect
72. mortal: deadly
79. tall: fine, splendid
81. extincted: extinguished

Cas. The great contention of the sea and skies
Parted our fellowship.
(*Within*) "A sail, a sail!" [*A shot.*]
But hark. A sail!

2. Gent. They give their greeting to the citadel.
This likewise is a friend.

Cas. See for the news. 95
[*Exit Gentleman.*]
Good ancient, you are welcome. [*To Emilia*] Welcome, mistress.
Let it not gall your patience, good Iago,
That I extend my manners. 'Tis my breeding
That gives me this bold show of courtesy.
[*Kisses her.*]

Iago. Sir, would she give you so much of her lips
As of her tongue she oft bestows on me, 101
You would have enough.

Des. Alas, she has no speech!

Iago. In faith, too much.
I find it still when I have list to sleep.
Marry, before your ladyship, I grant, 105
She puts her tongue a little in her heart
And chides with thinking.

Emil. You have little cause to say so.

Iago. Come on, come on! You are pictures out of doors,
Bells in your parlors, wildcats in your kitchens,
Saints in your injuries, devils being offended, 111
Players in your housewifery, and housewives in your beds.

Des. O, fie upon thee, slanderer!

Iago. Nay, it is true, or else I am a Turk.
You rise to play, and go to bed to work. 115

Emil. You shall not write my praise.

Iago. No, let me not.

Des. What wouldst thou write of me, if thou shouldst praise me?

Iago. O gentle lady, do not put me to't,
For I am nothing if not critical.

Des. Come on, assay.—There's one gone to the harbor? 120

Iago. Ay, madam.

Des. I am not merry; but I do beguile
The thing I am by seeming otherwise.
Come, how wouldst thou praise me? 124

Iago. I am about it; but indeed my invention
Comes from my pate as birdlime does from frieze—
It plucks out brains and all. But my Muse labors,
And thus she is delivered:

If she be fair and wise, fairness and wit—
The one's for use, the other useth it. 130

Des. Well praised! How if she be black and witty?

Iago. If she be black, and thereto have a wit,
She'll find a white that shall her blackness fit.

Des. Worse and worse!

Emil. How if fair and foolish? 135

Iago. She never yet was foolish that was fair,
For even her folly helped her to an heir.

Des. These are old fond paradoxes to make fools laugh i' the alehouse. What miserable praise hast thou for her that's foul and foolish? 140

Iago. There's none so foul, and foolish thereunto,
But does foul pranks which fair and wise ones do.

Des. O heavy ignorance! Thou praisest the worst best. But what praise couldst thou bestow on a deserving woman indeed—one that, in the authority of her merit, did justly put on the vouch of very malice itself? 145

Iago. She that was ever fair, and never proud;
Had tongue at will, and yet was never loud;
Never lacked gold, and yet went never gay; 150
Fled from her wish, and yet said "Now I may";
She that, being angered, her revenge being nigh,
Bade her wrong stay, and her displeasure fly;
She that in wisdom never was so frail
To change the cod's head for the salmon's tail; 155
She that could think and ne'er disclose her mind;
See suitors following and not look behind:
She was a wight (if ever such wight were)—

Des. To do what?

Iago. To suckle fools and chronicle small beer. 160

Des. O most lame and impotent conclusion! Do not learn of him, Emilia, though he be thy husband.

104. still: ever; **list:** desire
109. pictures . . . doors: pretty as pictures when on public display
110. Bells . . . parlors: sweet and musical of voice when acting the hostess
112. Players: triflers; **housewives:** hussies
120. assay: make a try
126. pate: noggin; **birdlime:** a sticky preparation used to catch birds; **frieze:** cloth with a heavy nap
130. The . . . it: her wit uses her beauty as a commodity.
131. black: dark-complexioned
133. white: punningly used for "wight," fellow
138. fond: foolish
140. foul: ugly
145–46. in . . . of: by virtue of
146–47. justly . . . itself: rightly claim the approval of even the most malicious
155. change . . . tail: make a bad bargain
160. chronicle . . . beer: keep household accounts

How say you, Cassio? Is he not a most profane and liberal counselor?

Cas. He speaks home, madam. You may 165
relish him more in the soldier than in the scholar.

Iago. [*Aside*] He takes her by the palm. Ay, well said, whisper! With as little a web as this will I ensnare as great a fly as Cassio. Ay, smile upon her, do! I will gyve thee in thine own courtship. You 170
say true; 'tis so, indeed! If such tricks as these strip you out of your lieutenantry, it had been better you had not kissed your three fingers so oft—which now again you are most apt to play the sir in. Very good! well kissed! an excellent curtsy! 'Tis so, in- 175
deed. Yet again your fingers to your lips? Would they were clyster pipes for your sake! (*Trumpet within.*) The Moor! I know his trumpet.

Cas. 'Tis truly so.

Des. Let's meet him and receive him. 180

Cas. Lo, where he comes!

Enter OTHELLO *and* ATTENDANTS.

Oth. O my fair warrior!

Des. My dear Othello!

Oth. It gives me wonder great as my content
To see you here before me. O my soul's joy!
If after every tempest come such calms, 185
May the winds blow till they have wakened death!
And let the laboring bark climb hills of seas
Olympus-high, and duck again as low
As hell's from heaven! If it were now to die,
'Twere now to be most happy; for I fear 190
My soul hath her content so absolute
That not another comfort like to this
Succeeds in unknown fate.

Des. The heavens forbid
But that our loves and comforts should increase
Even as our days do grow!

Oth. Amen to that, sweet powers! 195
I cannot speak enough of this content;
It stops me here; it is too much of joy.
And this, and this, the greatest discords be
They kiss.
That e'er our hearts shall make!

Iago. [*Aside*] O, you are well tuned now!
But I'll set down the pegs that make this music,
As honest as I am.

Oth. Come, let us to the castle. 201
News, friends! Our wars are done; the Turks are drowned.
How does my old acquaintance of this isle?—
Honey, you shall be well desired in Cyprus;
I have found great love amongst them. O my sweet,
I prattle out of fashion, and I dote 206
In mine own comforts. I prithee, good Iago,
Go to the bay and disembark my coffers.
Bring thou the master to the citadel.
He is a good one, and his worthiness 210
Does challenge much respect.—Come, Desdemona,
Once more well met at Cyprus.

Exeunt [*all but Iago and Roderigo*].

Iago. Do thou meet me presently at the harbor. Come hither. If thou beest valiant (as they say base men being in love have then a nobility in their 215
natures more than is native to them), list me. The Lieutenant tonight watches on the court of guard. First, I must tell thee this: Desdemona is directly in love with him.

Rod. With him? Why, 'tis not possible. 220

Iago. Lay thy finger thus, and let thy soul be instructed. Mark me with what violence she first loved the Moor, but for bragging and telling her fantastical lies; and will she love him still for prating? Let not thy discreet heart think it. Her eye must be 225
fed; and what delight shall she have to look on the devil? When the blood is made dull with the act of sport, there should be, again to inflame it and to give satiety a fresh appetite, loveliness in favor, sympathy in years, manners, and beauties; all which the 230
Moor is defective in. Now for want of these required conveniences, her delicate tenderness will find itself abused, begin to heave the gorge, disrelish and abhor the Moor. Very nature will instruct her in it and compel her to some second choice. Now, sir, 235
this granted (as it is a most pregnant and unforced position), who stands so eminent in the degree of this fortune as Cassio does? A knave very voluble; no further conscionable than in putting on the mere form of civil and humane seeming for the bet- 240
ter compass of his salt and most hidden loose affection? Why, none! why, none! A slipper and subtle knave; a finder of occasion; that has an eye can stamp and counterfeit advantages, though true advantage never present itself; a devilish knave! 245
Besides, the knave is handsome, young, and hath all those requisites in him that folly and green minds

164. liberal: licentious
165. home: bluntly
175. curtsy: courtesy
177. clyster pipes: syringe for an enema
192. comfort: delight
200. set . . . music: destroy your harmony. The reference is to the tuning of a stringed instrument.

204. desired: loved
206. out . . . fashion: unsuitably
206–7. dote . . . comforts: become a fool over my pleasures
211. challenge: demand
221. thus: on your lips
229. favor: physical appearance
234. Very: mere
236. pregnant . . . unforced: readily apparent and natural
239. conscionable: conscientious
241. salt, loose: lecherous
242. slipper: slippery
243. finder . . . occasion: opportunist
244. stamp . . . counterfeit: i.e., make his own

look after. A pestilent complete knave! and the woman hath found him already.

Rod. I cannot believe that in her. She's full of most blessed condition. 250

Iago. Blessed fig's-end! The wine she drinks is made of grapes. If she had been blessed, she would never have loved the Moor. Blessed pudding! Didst thou not see her paddle with the palm of his hand? Didst not mark that? 255

Rod. Yes, that I did; but that was but courtesy.

Iago. Lechery, by this hand! an index and obscure prologue to the history of lust and foul thoughts. They met so near with their lips that their breaths embraced together. Villainous thoughts, Roderigo! When these mutualities so marshal the way, hard at hand comes the master and main exercise, the incorporate conclusion. Pish! But, sir, be you ruled by me. I have brought you from Venice. Watch you tonight; for the command, I'll lay't upon you. Cassio knows you not. I'll not be far from you. Do you find some occasion to anger Cassio; either by speaking too loud, or tainting his discipline, or from what other course you please which the time shall more favorably minister. 260 265 270

Rod. Well.

Iago. Sir, he is rash and very sudden in choler, and haply with his truncheon may strike at you. Provoke him that he may; for even out of that will I cause these of Cyprus to mutiny; whose qualification shall come into no true taste again but by the displanting of Cassio. So shall you have a shorter journey to your desires by the means I shall then have to prefer them; and the impediment most profitably removed without the which there were no expectation of our prosperity. 275 280

Rod. I will do this if I can bring it to any opportunity.

Iago. I warrant thee. Meet me by-and-by at the citadel.
I must fetch his necessaries ashore. Farewell. 285

Rod. Adieu. *Exit.*

Iago. That Cassio loves her, I do well believe it;
That she loves him, 'tis apt and of great credit.
The Moor (howbeit that I endure him not)
Is of a constant, loving, noble nature, 290
And I dare think he'll prove to Desdemona
A most dear husband. Now I do love her too;
Not out of absolute lust (though peradventure
I stand accountant for as great a sin)
But partly led to diet my revenge, 295
For that I do suspect the lusty Moor
Hath leaped into my seat; the thought whereof
Doth, like a poisonous mineral, gnaw my inwards;
And nothing can or shall content my soul
Till I am evened with him, wife for wife; 300
Or failing so, yet that I put the Moor
At least into a jealousy so strong
That judgment cannot cure. Which thing to do
If this poor trash of Venice, whom I trace
For his quick hunting, stand the putting on, 305
I'll have our Michael Cassio on the hip,
Abuse him to the Moor in the right garb
(For I fear Cassio with my nightcap too),
Make the Moor thank me, love me, and reward me
For making him egregiously an ass 310
And practicing upon his peace and quiet
Even to madness. 'Tis here, but yet confused.
Knavery's plain face is never seen till used.

Exit.

252–53. The . . . grapes: i.e., she's only human.
269. tainting: discrediting
274. truncheon: baton
276–77. whose . . . taste: who will not be satisfied
288. of . . . credit: easily believable
295. diet: feed
301. yet that: until
304–5. whom . . . hunting: whose footsteps I dog to stir him on
306. on . . . hip: a wrestling term: "at a disadvantage"
307. garb: manner
310. egregiously: grossly
311. practicing upon: plotting against
312. 'Tis . . . confused: i.e., I have all the makings of a successful plot; I have only to work out the details.

Scene II. [*Cyprus. Before Othello's Castle.*]

Enter OTHELLO'S HERALD, *with a proclamation;* [*people following*].

Her. It is Othello's pleasure, our noble and valiant general, that, upon certain tidings now arrived, importing the mere perdition of the Turkish fleet, every man put himself into triumph; some to dance, some to make bonfires, each man to what sport and revels his addiction leads him. For, besides these beneficial news, it is the celebration of his nuptial. So much was his pleasure should be proclaimed. All offices are open, and there is full liberty of feasting from this present hour of five till the bell have told eleven. Heaven bless the isle of Cyprus and our noble general Othello! 5 10

Exeunt.

3. mere perdition: absolute destruction
8–9. offices: the rooms from which food and drink are dispensed

[Scene III. *Cyprus. Within the Castle.*]

Enter OTHELLO, DESDEMONA, CASSIO, *and* ATTENDANTS.

Oth. Good Michael, look you to the guard tonight.
Let's teach ourselves that honorable stop
Not to outsport discretion.

Cas. Iago hath direction what to do;
But notwithstanding, with my personal eye 5
Will I look to't.

Oth. Iago is most honest.
Michael, good night. Tomorrow with your earliest
Let me have speech with you.—Come, my dear love.
The purchase made, the fruits are to ensue;
That profit's yet to come 'tween me and you.— 10
Good night. *Exeunt Othello and Desdemona* [*with Attendants*].

Enter Iago.

Cas. Welcome, Iago. We must to the watch.

Iago. Not this hour, Lieutenant; 'tis not yet ten o' the clock. Our general cast us thus early for the love of his Desdemona; who let us not therefore 15 blame. He hath not yet made wanton the night with her, and she is sport for Jove.

Cas. She's a most exquisite lady.

Iago. And I'll warrant her, full of game.

Cas. Indeed, she's a most fresh and delicate 20 creature.

Iago. What an eye she has! Methinks it sounds a parley to provocation.

Cas. An inviting eye; and yet methinks right modest. 25

Iago. And when she speaks, is it not an alarum to love?

Cas. She is indeed perfection.

Iago. Well, happiness to their sheets! Come, Lieutenant, I have a stoup of wine, and here with- 30 out are a brace of Cyprus gallants that would fain have a measure to the health of black Othello.

Cas. Not tonight, good Iago. I have very poor and unhappy brains for drinking. I could well wish courtesy would invent some other custom of enter- 35 tainment.

Iago. O, they are our friends. But one cup! I'll drink for you.

Cas. I have drunk but one cup tonight, and that was craftily qualified too; and behold what in- 40 novation it makes here. I am unfortunate in the infirmity and dare not task my weakness with any more.

Iago. What, man! 'Tis a night of revels. The gallants desire it. 45

Cas. Where are they?

Iago. Here at the door. I pray you call them in.

Cas. I'll do't, but it dislikes me. *Exit.*

Iago. If I can fasten but one cup upon him
With that which he hath drunk tonight already, 50
He'll be as full of quarrel and offense
As my young mistress' dog. Now my sick fool Rod-
erigo,
Whom love hath turned almost the wrong side out,
To Desdemona hath tonight caroused
Potations pottle-deep; and he's to watch. 55
Three lads of Cyprus—noble swelling spirits,
That hold their honors in a wary distance,
The very elements of this warlike isle—
Have I tonight flustered with flowing cups,
And they watch too. Now, 'mongst this flock of
drunkards 60
Am I to put our Cassio in some action
That may offend the isle.

Enter Cassio, Montano, *and* Gentlemen; [Servant *with wine*].

But here they come.
If consequence do but approve my dream,
My boat sails freely, both with wind and stream.

Cas. Fore God, they have given me a rouse 65 already.

Mon. Good faith, a little one; not past a pint, as I am a soldier.

Iago. Some wine, ho!
[*Sings*]

And let me the canakin clink, clink; 70
And let me the canakin clink.
A soldier's a man;
A life's but a span,
Why then, let a soldier drink.

Some wine, boys! 75

Cas. Fore God, an excellent song!

Iago. I learned it in England, where indeed they are most potent in potting. Your Dane, your German, and your swag-bellied Hollander—Drink, ho! —are nothing to your English. 80

Cas. Is your Englishman so expert in his drinking?

Iago. Why, he drinks you with facility your Dane dead drunk; he sweats not to overthrow your Almain; he gives your Hollander a vomit ere the next pottle can be filled. 85

Cas. To the health of our General!

Mon. I am for it, Lieutenant, and I'll do you justice.

30. **stoup:** a two-quart container
32. **measure:** draught
37–38. **I'll . . . you:** I'll answer for you when a toast is proposed.
40. **qualified:** diluted
40–41. **innovation:** disturbance
48. **dislikes:** displeases
54. **caroused:** swilled
55. **pottle-deep:** by the tankard
56. **swelling:** stately
57. **hold . . . distance:** are touchy about their honor
58. **elements:** essences; that is, their warlike natures personify the warlike isle
63. **If . . . dream:** if the outcome confirms my expectation
65. **rouse:** deep draught
83–84. **sweats . . . Almain:** has no difficulty outdrinking a German
87–88. **do . . . justice:** match your toast

Iago. O sweet England!

[*Sings*]

King Stephen was and a worthy peer; 90
His breeches cost him but a crown;
He held 'em sixpence all too dear,
With that he called the tailor lown.
He was a wight of high renown,
And thou art but of low degree. 95
'Tis pride that pulls the country down;
Then take thine auld cloak about thee.

Some wine, ho!

Cas. Fore God, this is a more exquisite song than the other. 100

Iago. Will you hear't again?

Cas. No, for I hold him unworthy of his place that does those things. Well, God's above all; and there be souls must be saved, and there be souls must not be saved. 105

Iago. It's true, good Lieutenant.

Cas. For mine own part—no offense to the General, nor any man of quality—I hope to be saved.

Iago. And so do I too, Lieutenant.

Cas. Ay, but, by your leave, not before me. 110
The lieutenant is to be saved before the ancient. Let's have no more of this; let's to our affairs. God forgive us our sins! Gentlemen, let's look to our business. Do not think, gentlemen, I am drunk. This is my ancient. This is my right hand, and this is 115
my left. I am not drunk now. I can stand well enough, and speak well enough.

All. Excellent well!

Cas. Why, very well then. You must not think then that I am drunk. *Exit.*

Mon. To the platform, masters. Come, let's set the watch. 121

Iago. You see this fellow that is gone before.
He is a soldier fit to stand by Cæsar
And give direction; and do but see his vice.
'Tis to his virtue a just equinox, 125
The one as long as the other. 'Tis pity of him.
I fear the trust Othello puts him in,
On some odd time of his infirmity,
Will shake this island.

Mon. But is he often thus?

Iago. 'Tis evermore the prologue to his sleep.
He'll watch the horologe a double set 131
If drink rock not his cradle.

Mon. It were well
The General were put in mind of it.
Perhaps he sees it not, or his good nature
Prizes the virtue that appears in Cassio 135
And looks not on his evils. Is not this true?

Enter RODERIGO.

Iago. [*Aside to him*] How now, Roderigo?
I pray you after the Lieutenant, go! *Exit Roderigo.*

Mon. And 'tis great pity that the noble Moor
Should hazard such a place as his own second 140
With one of an engraffed infirmity.
It were an honest action to say
So to the Moor.

Iago. Not I, for this fair island!
I do love Cassio well and would do much
To cure him of this evil.

(*Within*) "Help! Help!"
But hark! What noise?

Enter CASSIO, *driving in* RODERIGO.

Cas. Zounds, you rogue! you rascal! 146

Mon. What's the matter, Lieutenant?

Cas. A knave teach me my duty?
I'll beat the knave into a twiggen bottle.

Rod. Beat me?

Cas. Dost thou prate, rogue? [*Strikes him.*]

Mon. Nay, good Lieutenant! 150
[*Takes his arm.*]
I pray you, sir, hold your hand.

Cas. Let me go, sir,
Or I'll knock you o'er the mazzard.

Mon. Come, come, you're drunk!

Cas. Drunk? *They fight.*

Iago. [*Aside to Roderigo*] Away, I say! Go out and cry a mutiny! *Exit Roderigo.*
Nay, good Lieutenant. God's will, gentlemen! 155
Help, ho!—Lieutenant—sir—Montano—sir—
Help, masters!—Here's a goodly watch indeed!
A bell rung.
Who's that which rings the bell? Diablo, ho!
The town will rise. God's will, Lieutenant, hold!
You will be shamed forever.

Enter OTHELLO *and* ATTENDANTS.

Oth. What is the matter here? 160

Mon. I bleed still. I am hurt to the death. He dies!

Oth. Hold for your lives!

Iago. Hold, hold! Lieutenant—sir—Montano—gentlemen!
Have you forgot all sense of place and duty?
Hold! The General speaks to you. Hold, hold, for shame! 165

90–97. **King Stephen, etc.:** a well-known song
93. **lown:** lout
125. **equinox:** equivalent
126. **'Tis . . . him:** it's a pity about him.
131. **watch:** remain wakeful; **horologe:** clock; **double set:** twenty-four hours
141. **engraffed:** deeply engrained
149. **twiggen:** wicker-covered
152. **mazzard:** slang term for "head"

Oth. Why, how now, ho? From whence ariseth this?
Are we turned Turks, and to ourselves do that
Which heaven hath forbid the Ottomites?
For Christian shame put by this barbarous brawl!
He that stirs next to carve for his own rage 170
Holds his soul light; he dies upon his motion.
Silence that dreadful bell! It frights the isle
From her propriety. What's the matter, masters?
Honest Iago, that looks dead with grieving,
Speak. Who began this? On thy love, I charge thee.

Iago. I do not know. Friends all but now, even now, 176
In quarter, and in terms like bride and groom
Devesting them for bed; and then, but now
(As if some planet had unwitted men)
Swords out, and tilting one at other's breast 180
In opposition bloody. I cannot speak
Any beginning to this peevish odds,
And would in action glorious I had lost
Those legs that brought me to a part of it!

Oth. How comes it, Michael, you are thus forgot?

Cas. I pray you pardon me; I cannot speak. 186

Oth. Worthy Montano, you were wont be civil;
The gravity and stillness of your youth
The world hath noted, and your name is great
In mouths of wisest censure. What's the matter
That you unlace your reputation thus 191
And spend your rich opinion for the name
Of a night-brawler? Give me answer to't.

Mon. Worthy Othello, I am hurt to danger.
Your officer, Iago, can inform you, 195
While I spare speech, which something now offends me,
Of all that I do know; nor know I aught
By me that's said or done amiss this night,
Unless self-charity be sometimes a vice,
And to defend ourselves it be a sin 200
When violence assails us.

Oth. Now, by heaven,
My blood begins my safer guides to rule,
And passion, having my best judgment collied,
Assays to lead the way. If I once stir
Or do but lift this arm, the best of you 205
Shall sink in my rebuke. Give me to know
How this foul rout began, who set it on;
And he that is approved in this offense,
Though he had twinned with me, both at a birth,
Shall lose me. What! in a town of war, 210
Yet wild, the people's hearts brimful of fear,
To manage private and domestic quarrel?
In night, and on the court and guard of safety?
'Tis monstrous. Iago, who began 't?

Mon. If partially affined, or leagued in office,
Thou dost deliver more or less than truth, 216
Thou art no soldier.

Iago. Touch me not so near.
I had rather have this tongue cut from my mouth
Than it should do offense to Michael Cassio.
Yet I persuade myself, to speak the truth 220
Shall nothing wrong him. Thus it is, General.
Montano and myself being in speech,
There comes a fellow crying out for help,
And Cassio following him with determined sword
To execute upon him. Sir, this gentleman 225
Steps in to Cassio and entreats his pause.
Myself the crying fellow did pursue,
Lest by his clamor (as it so fell out)
The town might fall in fright. He, swift of foot,
Outran my purpose; and I returned the rather 230
For that I heard the clink and fall of swords,
And Cassio high in oath; which till tonight
I ne'er might say before. When I came back
(For this was brief) I found them close together
At blow and thrust, even as again they were 235
When you yourself did part them.
More of this matter cannot I report;
But men are men; the best sometimes forget.
Though Cassio did some little wrong to him,
As men in rage strike those that wish them best,
Yet surely Cassio I believe received 241
From him that fled some strange indignity,
Which patience could not pass.

Oth. I know, Iago,
Thy honesty and love doth mince this matter,
Making it light to Cassio. Cassio, I love thee; 245
But never more be officer of mine.

Enter DESDEMONA, *attended.*

Look if my gentle love be not raised up!
I'll make thee an example.

Des. What's the matter, dear?

Oth. All's well now, sweeting; come away to bed.
[*To Montano*] Sir, for your hurts, myself will be your surgeon. 250
Lead him off. [*Exit Montano, attended.*]

167–68. **that . . . Ottomites:** i.e., murder each other, which heaven prevented the Turks from doing by destroying their fleet
170. **carve for:** please
177. **In quarter:** orderly
182. **peevish odds:** silly quarrel
190. **censure:** judgment
191. **unlace:** disarray; expose
192. **rich:** valuable; **opinion:** reputation
196. **something:** somewhat; **offends:** hurts
202. **blood:** anger
203. **collied:** obscured; literally, "darkened with coal"
208. **approved . . . offense:** proved to be the author of the fight
212. **domestic:** personal
213. **on . . . safety:** in the very headquarters of the watch
215. **partially affined:** bound by affection; **leagued . . . office:** allied with a comrade
225. **execute:** i.e., express his anger
244. **mince:** belittle

Iago, look with care about the town
And silence those whom this vile brawl distracted.
Come, Desdemona. 'Tis the soldiers' life 254
To have their balmy slumbers waked with strife.
Exeunt [*all but Iago and Cassio*].

Iago. What, are you hurt, Lieutenant?

Cas. Ay, past all surgery.

Iago. Marry, God forbid!

Cas. Reputation, reputation, reputation! O, I have lost my reputation! I have lost the immortal 260 part of myself, and what remains is bestial. My reputation, Iago, my reputation!

Iago. As I am an honest man, I thought you had received some bodily wound; there is more sense in that than in reputation. Reputation is an idle 265 and most false imposition; oft got without merit and lost without deserving. You have lost no reputation at all unless you repute yourself such a loser. What, man! there are ways to recover the General again. You are but now cast in his mood—a punish- 270 ment more in policy than in malice, even so as one would beat his offenseless dog to affright an imperious lion. Sue to him again, and he's yours.

Cas. I will rather sue to be despised than to deceive so good a commander with so slight, so 275 drunken, and so indiscreet an officer. Drunk? and speak parrot? and squabble? swagger? swear? and discourse fustian with one's own shadow? O thou invisible spirit of wine, if thou hast no name to be known by, let us call thee devil! 280

Iago. What was he that you followed with your sword? What had he done to you?

Cas. I know not.

Iago. Is't possible?

Cas. I remember a mass of things, but noth- 285 ing distinctly; a quarrel, but nothing wherefore. O God, that men should put an enemy in their mouths to steal away their brains! that we should with joy, pleasance, revel, and applause transform ourselves into beasts! 290

Iago. Why, but you are now well enough. How came you thus recovered?

Cas. It hath pleased the devil drunkenness to give place to the devil wrath. One unperfectness shows me another, to make me frankly despise 295 myself.

Iago. Come, you are too severe a moraler. As the time, the place, and the condition of this country stands, I could heartily wish this had not so befall'n; but since it is as it is, mend it for your own 300 good.

Cas. I will ask him for my place again: he shall tell me I am a drunkard! Had I as many mouths as Hydra, such an answer would stop them all. To be now a sensible man, by-and-by a fool, and 305 presently a beast! O strange! Every inordinate cup is unblest, and the ingredient is a devil.

Iago. Come, come, good wine is a good familiar creature if it be well used. Exclaim no more against it. And, good Lieutenant, I think you think I 310 love you.

Cas. I have well approved it, sir. I drunk?

Iago. You or any man living may be drunk at a time, man. I'll tell you what you should do. Our General's wife is now the General. I may say 315 so in this respect, for that he hath devoted and given up himself to the contemplation, mark, and denotement of her parts and graces. Confess yourself freely to her. Importune her help to put you in your place again. She is of so free, so kind, so apt, so 320 blessed a disposition she holds it a vice in her goodness not to do more than she is requested. This broken joint between you and her husband entreat her to splinter; and my fortunes against any lay worth naming, this crack of your love shall 325 grow stronger than 'twas before.

Cas. You advise me well.

Iago. I protest, in the sincerity of love and honest kindness.

Cas. I think it freely; and betimes in the 330 morning will I beseech the virtuous Desdemona to undertake for me. I am desperate of my fortunes if they check me here.

Iago. You are in the right. Good night, Lieutenant; I must to the watch. 335

Cas. Good night, honest Iago. *Exit.*

Iago. And what's he then that says I play the villain,
When this advice is free I give and honest,
Probal to thinking, and indeed the course
To win the Moor again? For 'tis most easy 340
The inclining Desdemona to subdue
In any honest suit. She's framed as fruitful
As the free elements. And then for her
To win the Moor—were't to renounce his baptism,
All seals and symbols of redeemed sin— 345
His soul is so enfettered to her love
That she may make, unmake, do what she list,
Even as her appetite shall play the god
With his weak function. How am I then a villain
To counsel Cassio to this parallel course 350

277. parrot: nonsense
278. fustian: another word for "nonsense"
289. pleasance: merriment

306. inordinate: excessive
308. familiar: Iago puns on the word. A **familiar** was an evil spirit supplied by the devil to attend a witch or magician.
312. approved: proved
320. free: generous; **apt:** responsive
324. splinter: splint together; **lay:** stake
330. freely: without qualification
339. Probal: probable
341. inclining: compliant
349. function: faculties

Directly to his good? Divinity of hell!
When devils will the blackest sins put on,
They do suggest at first with heavenly shows,
As I do now. For whiles this honest fool
Plies Desdemona to repair his fortune, 355
And she for him pleads strongly to the Moor,
I'll pour this pestilence into his ear—
That she repeals him for her body's lust;
And by how much she strives to do him good,
She shall undo her credit with the Moor. 360
So will I turn her virtue into pitch,
And out of her own goodness make the net
That shall enmesh them all.

Enter RODERIGO.

How now, Roderigo?

Rod. I do follow here in the chase, not like a hound that hunts, but one that fills up the cry. 365 My money is almost spent; I have been tonight exceedingly well cudgelled; and I think the issue will be, I shall have so much experience for my pains; and so, with no money at all, and a little more wit, return again to Venice. 370

Iago. How poor are they that have not patience!
What wound did ever heal but by degrees?
Thou knowst we work by wit, and not by witchcraft;
And wit depends on dilatory time.
Does't not go well? Cassio hath beaten thee, 375
And thou by that small hurt hast cashiered Cassio.
Though other things grow fair against the sun,
Yet fruits that blossom first will first be ripe.
Content thyself awhile. By the mass, 'tis morning!
Pleasure and action make the hours seem short.
Retire thee; go where thou art billeted. 381
Away, I say! Thou shalt know more hereafter.
Nay, get thee gone! *Exit Roderigo.*
Two things are to be done:
My wife must move for Cassio to her mistress;
I'll set her on; 385
Myself a while to draw the Moor apart
And bring him jump when he may Cassio find
Soliciting his wife. Ay, that's the way!
Dull not device by coldness and delay.

Exit.

351. **Divinity of hell:** hell's own theology
352. **put on:** urge
353. **suggest:** tempt
355. **Plies:** beseeches
358. **repeals:** seeks his restoration
365. **fills . . . cry:** rounds out the pack

ACT III

Scene I. [*Cyprus. Before the Castle.*]

Enter CASSIO, *with* MUSICIANS.

Cas. Masters, play here, I will content your pains:
Something that's brief; and bid "Good morrow, General." *They play.*

Enter the CLOWN.

Clown. Why, masters, have your instruments been at Naples, that they speak i' the nose thus?

Mus. How, sir, how? 5

Clown. Are these, I pray, called wind instruments?

Mus. Ay, marry, are they, sir.

Clown. O, thereby hangs a tail.

Mus. Whereby hangs a tale, sir?

Clown. Marry, sir, by many a wind instrument that I know. But, masters, here's money for you; and the General so likes your music that he desires you, of all loves, to make no more noise with it. 10

Mus. Well, sir, we will not. 15

Clown. If you have any music that may not be heard, to't again. But, as they say, to hear music the General does not greatly care.

Mus. We have none such, sir.

Clown. Then put up your pipes in your bag, for I'll away. Go, vanish into air, away! 20

Exeunt Musicians.

Cas. Dost thou hear, my honest friend?

Clown. No, I hear not your honest friend. I hear you.

1. **content:** reward
2. **bid . . . General:** i.e., play a morning serenade, as was customary for a newly married couple
4. **Naples:** a reference to the "Neapolitan" disease (syphilis), which sometimes eats away the nose

13. **of . . . loves:** for the love you bear him

Cas. Prithee keep up thy quillets. There's a poor piece of gold for thee. If the gentlewoman that attends the General's wife be stirring, tell her there's one Cassio entreats her a little favor of speech. Wilt thou do this? 25

Clown. She is stirring, sir. If she will stir hither, I shall seem to notify unto her. 30

Cas. Do, good my friend. *Exit Clown.*

Enter IAGO.

In happy time, Iago.

Iago. You have not been abed then?

Cas. Why, no. The day had broke
Before we parted. I have made bold, Iago, 35
To send in to your wife. My suit to her
Is that she will to virtuous Desdemona
Procure me some access.

Iago. I'll send her to you presently;
And I'll devise a mean to draw the Moor
Out of the way, that your converse and business
May be more free. 41

Cas. I humbly thank you for't. *Exit* [*Iago*].
I never knew
A Florentine more kind and honest.

Enter EMILIA.

Emil. Good morrow, good Lieutenant. I am sorry
For your displeasure; but all will sure be well. 45
The General and his wife are talking of it,
And she speaks for you stoutly. The Moor replies
That he you hurt is of great fame in Cyprus
And great affinity, and that in wholesome wisdom
He might not but refuse you. But he protests he loves
you, 50
And needs no other suitor but his likings
To take the safest occasion by the front
To bring you in again.

Cas. Yet I beseech you,
If you think fit, or that it may be done,
Give me advantage of some brief discourse 55
With Desdemon alone.

Emil. Pray you come in.
I will bestow you where you shall have time
To speak your bosom freely.

Cas. I am much bound to you.
Exeunt.

25. keep up: put away; **quillets:** puns
32. In . . . time: fortunately met
42–43. I . . . honest: i.e., he matches my own townsmen in honesty.
45. displeasure: loss of favor
48–49. of . . . affinity: related to influential people
49. wholesome wisdom: discretion
52. occasion: opportunity; proverbial: "Take Time [Occasion] by the forelock, for he is bald behind."

Scene II. [*Cyprus, Within the Castle.*]

Enter OTHELLO, IAGO, *and* GENTLEMEN.

Oth. These letters give, Iago, to the pilot
And by him do my duties to the senate.
That done, I will be walking on the works.
Repair there to me.

Iago. Well, my good lord, I'll do't.

Oth. This fortification, gentlemen, shall we see't?

Gent. We'll wait upon your lordship. 6
Exeunt.

Scene III. [*Cyprus. The garden of the Castle.*]

Enter DESDEMONA, CASSIO, *and* EMILIA.

Des. Be thou assured, good Cassio, I will do
All my abilities in thy behalf.

Emil. Good madam, do. I warrant it grieves my
husband
As if the cause were his.

Des. O, that's an honest fellow. Do not doubt,
Cassio, 5
But I will have my lord and you again
As friendly as you were.

Cas. Bounteous madam,
Whatever shall become of Michael Cassio,
He's never anything but your true servant. 9

Des. I know't; I thank you. You do love my lord;
You have known him long; and be you well assured
He shall in strangeness stand no farther off
Than in a politic distance.

Cas. Ay, but, lady,
That policy may either last so long,
Or feed upon such nice and waterish diet, 15
Or breed itself so out of circumstance,
That, I being absent, and my place supplied,
My general will forget my love and service.

Des. Do not doubt that. Before Emilia here
I give thee warrant of thy place. Assure thee, 20
If I do vow a friendship, I'll perform it
To the last article. My lord shall never rest;
I'll watch him tame and talk him out of patience;
His bed shall seem a school, his board a shrift;

3. works: fortified walls
12–13. stand . . . distance: be no more unfriendly than policy requires
15. feed . . . diet: grow by such minute and trivial additions
16. breed . . . circumstance: be so perpetuated by new happenings
23. watch . . . tame: subdue him by keeping him awake, a trick used in training hawks
24. shrift: confessional, where he admits his errors

I'll intermingle everything he does 25
With Cassio's suit. Therefore be merry, Cassio,
For thy solicitor shall rather die
Than give thy cause away.

Enter OTHELLO *and* IAGO.

Emil. Madam, here comes my lord.
Cas. Madam, I'll take my leave. 30
Des. Why, stay, and hear me speak.
Cas. Madam, not now. I am very ill at ease,
Unfit for mine own purposes.
Des. Well, do your discretion. *Exit Cassio.*
Iago. Ha! I like not that.
Oth. What dost thou say? 35
Iago. Nothing, my lord; or if—I know not what.
Oth. Was not that Cassio parted from my wife?
Iago. Cassio, my lord? No, sure, I cannot think it,
That he would steal away so guilty-like,
Seeing you coming.
Oth. I do believe 'twas he. 40
Des. How now, my lord?
I have been talking with a suitor here,
A man that languishes in your displeasure.
Oth. Who is't you mean?
Des. Why, your lieutenant, Cassio. Good my lord,
If I have any grace or power to move you, 46
His present reconciliation take;
For if he be not one that truly loves you,
That errs in ignorance, and not in cunning,
I have no judgment in an honest face. 50
I prithee call him back.
Oth. Went he hence now?
Des. Yes, faith; so humbled
That he hath left part of his grief with me
To suffer with him. Good love, call him back. 54
Oth. Not now, sweet Desdemon; some other time.
Des. But shall't be shortly?
Oth. The sooner, sweet, for you.
Des. Shall't be tonight at supper?
Oth. No, not tonight.
Des. Tomorrow dinner then?
Oth. I shall not dine at home.
I meet the captains at the citadel.
Des. Why then, tomorrow night, or Tuesday morn,
Or Tuesday noon or night, or Wednesday morn. 61
I prithee name the time, but let it not
Exceed three days. I' faith, he's penitent;
And yet his trespass, in our common reason
(Save that, they say, the wars must make examples
Out of their best) is not almost a fault 66
T' incur a private check. When shall he come?
Tell me, Othello. I wonder in my soul
What you could ask me that I should deny
Or stand so mamm'ring on. What? Michael Cassio, 70
That came a-wooing with you, and so many a time,
When I have spoke of you dispraisingly,
Hath ta'en your part—to have so much to do
To bring him in? Trust me, I could do much—
Oth. Prithee no more. Let him come when he will!
I will deny thee nothing.
Des. Why, this is not a boon; 76
'Tis as I should entreat you wear your gloves,
Or feed on nourishing dishes, or keep you warm,
Or sue to you to do a peculiar profit
To your own person. Nay, when I have a suit 80
Wherein I mean to touch your love indeed,
It shall be full of poise and difficult weight,
And fearful to be granted.
Oth. I will deny thee nothing!
Whereon I do beseech thee grant me this,
To leave me but a little to myself. 85
Des. Shall I deny you? No. Farewell, my lord.
Oth. Farewell, my Desdemon. I'll come to thee straight.
Des. Emilia, come.—Be as your fancies teach you.
Whate'er you be, I am obedient.
Exeunt Desdemona and Emilia.
Oth. Excellent wretch! Perdition catch my soul
But I do love thee! and when I love thee not, 91
Chaos is come again.
Iago. My noble lord—
Oath. What dost thou say, Iago?
Iago. Did Michael Cassio, when you wooed my lady,
Know of your love? 95
Oth. He did, from first to last. Why dost thou ask?
Iago. But for a satisfaction of my thought;
No further harm.
Oth. Why of thy thought, Iago?
Iago. I did not think he had been acquainted with her.
Oth. O, yes, and went between us very oft. 100
Iago. Indeed?
Oth. Indeed? Ay, indeed! Discernst thou aught in that?
Is he not honest?
Iago. Honest, my lord?
Oth. Honest? Ay, honest.
Iago. My lord, for aught I know.
Oth. What dost thou think?
Iago. Think, my lord?
Oth. Think, my lord? 106
By heaven, he echoes me,

47. reconciliation: submission
64. in . . . reason: by ordinary lights
66–67. not . . . check: hardly merits a private rebuke

70. stand . . . on: so hesitate about
82. poise: weight
83. fearful: provoking anxiety
90. wretch: a term of affection
103. honest: honorable

As if there were some monster in his thought
Too hideous to be shown. Thou dost mean something.
I heard thee say even now, thou likest not that,
When Cassio left my wife. What didst not like?
And when I told thee he was of my counsel 111
In my whole course of wooing, thou criedst "Indeed?"
And didst contract and purse thy brow together,
As if thou then hadst shut up in thy brain
Some horrible conceit. If thou dost love me, 115
Show me thy thought.

Iago. My lord, you know I love you.

Oth. I think thou dost;
And, for I know thou'rt full of love and honesty
And weighst thy words before thou givest them breath,
Therefore these stops of thine fright me the more;
For such things in a false disloyal knave 121
Are tricks of custom; but in a man that's just
They are close dilations, working from the heart
That passion cannot rule.

Iago. For Michael Cassio,
I dare be sworn I think that he is honest. 125

Oth. I think so too.

Iago. Men should be what they seem;
Or those that be not, would they might seem none!

Oth. Certain, men should be what they seem.

Iago. Why then, I think Cassio's an honest man.

Oth. Nay, yet there's more in this. 130
I prithee speak to me, as to thy thinkings,
As thou dost ruminate, and give thy worst of thoughts
The worst of words.

Iago. Good my lord, pardon me.
Though I am bound to every act of duty,
I am not bound to that all slaves are free to. 135
Utter my thoughts? Why, say they are vile and false,
As where's that palace whereinto foul things
Sometimes intrude not? Who has a breast so pure
But some uncleanly apprehensions
Keep leets and law days, and in session sit 140
With meditations lawful?

Oth. Thou dost conspire against thy friend, Iago,
If thou but thinkst him wronged, and makest his ear
A stranger to thy thoughts.

Iago. I do beseech you—
Though I perchance am vicious in my guess 145
(As I confess it is my nature's plague
To spy into abuses, and oft my jealousy
Shapes faults that are not)—that your wisdom
From one that so imperfectly conceits
Would take no notice, nor build yourself a trouble
Out of his scattering and unsure observance. 151
It were not for your quiet nor your good,
Nor for my manhood, honesty, or wisdom,
To let you know my thoughts.

Oth. What dost thou mean?

Iago. Good name in man and woman, dear my lord,
Is the immediate jewel of their souls. 156
Who steals my purse steals trash; 'tis something, nothing;
'Twas mine, 'tis his, and has been slave to thousands;
But he that filches from me my good name
Robs me of that which not enriches him 160
And makes me poor indeed.

Oth. By heaven, I'll know thy thoughts!

Iago. You cannot, if my heart were in your hand;
Nor shall not whilst 'tis in my custody.

Oth. Ha!

Iago. O, beware, my lord, of jealousy! 165
It is the green-eyed monster, which doth mock
The meat it feeds on. That cuckold lives in bliss
Who, certain of his fate, loves not his wronger;
But O, what damned minutes tells he o'er
Who dotes, yet doubts; suspects, yet strongly loves!

Oth. O misery! 171

Iago. Poor and content is rich, and rich enough;
But riches fineless is as poor as winter
To him that ever fears he shall be poor.
Good heaven, the souls of all my tribe defend 175
From jealousy!

Oth. Why, why is this?
Thinkst thou I'd make a life of jealousy,
To follow still the changes of the moon
With fresh suspicions? No! To be once in doubt
Is once to be resolved. Exchange me for a goat 180
When I shall turn the business of my soul
To such exsufflicate and blown surmises,
Matching thy inference. 'Tis not to make me jealous
To say my wife is fair, feeds well, loves company,
Is free of speech, sings, plays, and dances well. 185
Where virtue is, these are more virtuous.
Nor from mine own weak merits will I draw
The smallest fear or doubt of her revolt,
For she had eyes, and chose me. No, Iago;
I'll see before I doubt; when I doubt, prove; 190
And on the proof there is no more but this—
Away at once with love or jealousy!

Iago. I am glad of it; for now I shall have reason

115. conceit: imagining
120. stops: hesitations
122. tricks . . . custom: customary characteristics
123. close dilations: accurate signs of sincere emotion
135. that . . . to: i.e., revelation of his every thought
140. leets: regular court sessions
145. Though: since; **vicious:** erring; wicked
147. jealousy: suspicion
149. conceits: imagines
151. scattering: random
156. immediate: nearest; most valuable
166. mock: toy with
173. fineless: limitless
180. resolved: satisfied
182. exsufflicate: contemptible; probably from the Latin *exsufflare;* **blown:** flyblown
188. revolt: infidelity

To show the love and duty that I bear you
With franker spirit. Therefore, as I am bound, 195
Receive it from me. I speak not yet of proof.
Look to your wife; observe her well with Cassio;
Wear your eye thus, not jealous nor secure.
I would not have your free and noble nature,
Out of self-bounty, be abused. Look to't. 200
I know our country disposition well:
In Venice they do let heaven see the pranks
They dare not show their husbands; their best conscience
Is not to leave't undone, but keep't unknown.

Oth. Dost thou say so? 205

Iago. She did deceive her father, marrying you;
And when she seemed to shake and fear your looks,
She loved them most.

Oth. And so she did.

Iago. Why, go to then!
She that, so young, could give out such a seeming
To seel her father's eyes up close as oak— 210
He thought 'twas witchcraft—but I am much to blame.
I humbly do beseech you of your pardon
For too much loving you.

Oth. I am bound to thee forever.

Iago. I see this hath a little dashed your spirits.

Oth. Not a jot, not a jot.

Iago. I' faith, I fear it has.
I hope you will consider what is spoke 216
Comes from my love. But I do see y'are moved.
I am to pray you not to strain my speech
To grosser issues nor to larger reach
Than to suspicion. 220

Oth. I will not.

Iago. Should you do so, my lord,
My speech should fall into such vile success
As my thoughts aim not at. Cassio's my worthy friend—
My lord, I see y' are moved.

Oth. No, not much moved.
I do not think but Desdemona's honest. 225

Iago. Long live she so! and long live you to think so!

Oth. And yet, how nature erring from itself—

Iago. Ay, there's the point! as (to be bold with you)
Not to affect many proposed matches
Of her own clime, complexion, and degree, 230
Whereto we see in all things nature tends—
Foh! one may smell in such a will most rank,
Foul disproportion, thoughts unnatural—
But pardon me—I do not in position
Distinctly speak of her; though I may fear 235
Her will, recoiling to her better judgment,
May fall to match you with her country forms,
And happily repent.

Oth. Farewell, farewell!
If more thou dost perceive, let me know more.
Set on thy wife to observe. Leave me, Iago. 240

Iago. My lord, I take my leave. [*Walks away.*]

Oth. Why did I marry? This honest creature doubtless
Sees and knows more, much more, than he unfolds.

Iago. [*Returns*] My lord, I would I might entreat your Honor
To scan this thing no further. Leave it to time. 245
Although 'tis fit that Cassio have his place,
For sure he fills it up with great ability,
Yet, if you please to hold him off awhile,
You shall by that perceive him and his means.
Note if your lady strain his entertainment 250
With any strong or vehement importunity.
Much will be seen in that. In the mean time
Let me be thought too busy in my fears
(As worthy cause I have to fear I am)
And hold her free, I do beseech your Honor. 255

Oth. Fear not my government.

Iago. I once more take my leave. *Exit.*

Oth. This fellow's of exceeding honesty,
And knows all qualities, with a learned spirit
Of human dealings. If I do prove her haggard, 260
Though that her jesses were my dear heartstrings,
I'd whistle her off and let her down the wind
To prey at fortune. Haply, for I am black
And have not those soft parts of conversation
That chamberers have, or for I am declined 265
Into the vale of years (yet that's not much),
She's gone. I am abused, and my relief
Must be to loathe her. O curse of marriage,
That we can call these delicate creatures ours,
And not their appetites! I had rather be a toad 270
And live upon the vapor of a dungeon
Than keep a corner in the thing I love
For others' uses. Yet 'tis the plague of great ones;
Prerogatived are they less than the base.

200. **self-bounty:** natural charity
219. **grosser:** greater
222. **success:** consequence
225. **honest:** chaste
229. **affect:** prefer
230. **complexion:** temperament
232. **will:** sexual appetite
233. **disproportion:** abnormality
234. **in position:** in formalizing this theory
236–37. **Her . . . forms:** her appetite, conquered by her better judgment, may begin to compare you with her countrymen.
238. **happily:** perhaps
250. **strain . . . entertainment:** press for his reinstatement
255. **free:** innocent
256. **government:** self-control
260. **haggard:** faithless, like a falcon whose training is incomplete
261. **jesses:** straps which tethered the falcon
262. **down the wind:** i.e., to fend for herself
264. **parts:** accomplishments; **conversation:** manners; social presence
265. **chamberers:** gallants
274. **Prerogatived:** privileged

'Tis destiny unshunnable, like death: 275
Even then this forked plague is fated to us
When we do quicken. Desdemona comes.

Enter DESDEMONA *and* EMILIA.

If she be false, O, then heaven mocks itself!
I'll not believe't.

Des. How now, my dear Othello?
Your dinner, and the generous islanders 280
By you invited, do attend your presence.

Oth. I am to blame.

Des. Why do you speak so faintly?
Are you not well?

Oth. I have a pain upon my forehead, here.

Des. Faith, that's with watching; 'twill away again.
Let me but bind it hard, within this hour 286
It will be well.

Oth. Your napkin is too little.

[*He pushes it away and it drops.*]

Let it alone. Come, I'll go in with you.

Des. I am very sorry that you are not well.

Exeunt Othello and Desdemona.

Emil. I am glad I have found this napkin. 290
This was her first remembrance from the Moor.
My wayward husband hath a hundred times
Wooed me to steal it; but she so loves the token
(For he conjured her she should ever keep it)
That she reserves it evermore about her 295
To kiss and talk to. I'll have the work ta'en out
And give't Iago.
What he will do with it heaven knows, not I;
I nothing but to please his fantasy.

Enter IAGO.

Iago. How now? What do you here alone? 300

Emil. Do not you chide; I have a thing for you.

Iago. A thing for me? It is a common thing—

Emil. Ha?

Iago. To have a foolish wife. 304

Emil. O, is that all? What will you give me now
For that same handkerchief?

Iago. What handkerchief?

Emil. What handkerchief?
Why, that the Moor first gave to Desdemona;
That which so often you did bid me steal.

Iago. Hast stol'n it from her? 310

Emil. No, faith; she let it drop by negligence,
And to the advantage, I, being here, took't up.
Look, here it is.

Iago. A good wench! Give it me.

Emil. What will you do with't, that you have been so earnest
To have me filch it?

Iago. Why, what's that to you? 315

[*Snatches it.*]

Emil. If it be not for some purpose of import,
Give't me again. Poor lady, she'll run mad
When she shall lack it.

Iago. Be not you acknown on't; I have use for it.
Go, leave me. *Exit Emilia.*
I will in Cassio's lodging lose this napkin 321
And let him find it. Trifles light as air
Are to the jealous confirmations strong
As proofs of holy writ. This may do something.
The Moor already changes with my poison. 325
Dangerous conceits are in their natures poisons
Which at the first are scarce found to distaste,
But with a little act upon the blood
Burn like the mines of sulphur.

Enter OTHELLO.

I did say so.
Look where he comes! Not poppy nor mandragora,
Nor all the drowsy syrups of the world, 331
Shall ever medicine thee to that sweet sleep
Which thou ow'dst yesterday.

Oth. Ha! ha! false to me?

Iago. Why, how now, General? No more of that!

Oth. Avaunt! be gone! Thou hast set me on the rack. 335
I swear 'tis better to be much abused
Than but to know't a little.

Iago. How now, my lord?

Oth. What sense had I of her stol'n hours of lust?
I saw't not, thought it not, it harmed not me.
I slept the next night well, was free and merry; 340
I found not Cassio's kisses on her lips.
He that is robbed, not wanting what is stol'n,
Let him not know't, and he's not robbed at all.

Iago. I am sorry to hear this.

Oth. I had been happy if the general camp, 345
Pioners and all, had tasted her sweet body,
So I had nothing known. O, now forever
Farewell the tranquil mind! farewell content!
Farewell the plumed troop, and the big wars
That make ambition virtue! O, farewell! 350
Farewell the neighing steed and the shrill trump,
The spirit-stirring drum, the ear-piercing fife,

276. forked plague: the horns of the cuckold
277. quicken: come alive
280. generous: illustrious; i.e., the gentry
285. watching: sleeplessness
287. napkin: handkerchief
296. work: embroidery
299. fantasy: fancy; whim
312. to . . . advantage: fortunately
319. Be . . . on't: pretend you know nothing of it
328. with . . . act: after brief action
330. mandragora: *Mandragora officinarum,* used for sleeping potions
333. ow'dst: possessed
340. free: carefree
342. wanting: missing
346. Pioners: pioneers; miners

The royal banner, and all quality,
Pride, pomp, and circumstance of glorious war!
And O ye mortal engines whose rude throats 355
The immortal Jove's dread clamors counterfeit,
Farewell! Othello's occupation's gone!
Iago. Is't possible, my lord?
Oth. Villain, be sure thou prove my love a whore!
Be sure of it; give me the ocular proof; 360
Or, by the worth of man's eternal soul,
Thou hadst been better have been born a dog
Than answer my waked wrath!
Iago. Is't come to this?
Oth. Make me to see't; or at the least so prove it
That the probation bear no hinge nor loop 365
To hang a doubt on—or woe upon thy life!
Iago. My noble lord—
Oth. If thou dost slander her and torture me,
Never pray more; abandon all remorse;
On horror's head horrors accumulate; 370
Do deeds to make heaven weep, all earth amazed;
For nothing canst thou to damnation add
Greater than that.
Iago. O grace! O heaven forgive me!
Are you a man? Have you a soul or sense?—
God b' wi' you! take mine office. O wretched fool,
That livest to make thine honesty a vice! 376
O monstrous world! Take note, take note, O world,
To be direct and honest is not safe.
I thank you for this profit; and from hence
I'll love no friend, sith love breeds such offense.
Oth. Nay, stay. Thou shouldst be honest. 381
Iago. I should be wise; for honesty's a fool
And loses that it works for.
Oth. By the world,
I think my wife be honest, and think she is not;
I think that thou art just, and think thou art not.
I'll have some proof. Her name, that was as fresh
As Dian's visage, is now begrimed and black 387
As mine own face. If there be cords, or knives,
Poison, or fire, or suffocating streams,
I'll not endure it. Would I were satisfied! 390
Iago. I see, sir, you are eaten up with passion.
I do repent me that I put it to you.
You would be satisfied?
Oth. Would? Nay, I will.
Iago. And may. But how? how satisfied, my lord?
Would you, the supervisor, grossly gape on? 395
Behold her topped?
Oth. Death and damnation! O!
Iago. It were a tedious difficulty, I think,
To bring them to that prospect. Damn them then,
If ever mortal eyes do see them bolster
More than their own! What then? How then? 400
What shall I say? Where's satisfaction?
It is impossible you should see this,
Were they as prime as goats, as hot as monkeys,
As salt as wolves in pride, and fools as gross
As ignorance made drunk. But yet, I say, 405
If imputation and strong circumstances
Which lead directly to the door of truth
Will give you satisfaction, you may have't.
Oth. Give me a living reason she's disloyal.
Iago. I do not like the office. 410
But sith I am entered in this cause so far,
Pricked to't by foolish honesty and love,
I will go on. I lay with Cassio lately,
And being troubled with a raging tooth,
I could not sleep. 415
There are a kind of men so loose of soul
That in their sleeps will mutter their affairs.
One of this kind is Cassio.
In sleep I heard him say, "Sweet Desdemona,
Let us be wary, let us hide our loves!" 420
And then, sir, would he gripe and wring my hand,
Cry "O sweet creature!" and then kiss me hard,
As if he plucked up kisses by the roots
That grew upon my lips; then laid his leg 424
Over my thigh, and sighed, and kissed, and then
Cried "Cursed fate that gave thee to the Moor!"
Oth. O monstrous! monstrous!
Iago. Nay, this was but his dream.
Oth. But this denoted a foregone conclusion.
'Tis a shrewd doubt, though it be but a dream. 429
Iago. And this may help to thicken other proofs
That do demonstrate thinly.
Oth. I'll tear her all to pieces!
Iago. Nay, but be wise. Yet we see nothing done;
She may be honest yet. Tell me but this—
Have you not sometimes seen a handkerchief 434
Spotted with strawberries in your wive's hand?
Oth. I gave her such a one; 'twas my first gift.
Iago. I know not that; but such a handkerchief
(I am sure it was your wive's) did I today
See Cassio wipe his beard with.
Oth. If't be that—
Iago. If it be that, or any that was hers, 440
It speaks against her, with the other proofs.
Oth. O, that the slave had forty thousand lives!
One is too poor, too weak for my revenge.
Now do I see 'tis true. Look here, Iago:
All my fond love thus do I blow to heaven. 445
'Tis gone.
Arise, black vengeance, from the hollow hell!
Yield up, O love, thy crown and hearted throne

354. circumstance: pageantry
355. mortal: deadly; **engines:** cannon
365. probation: proof
371. amazed: horrorstruck
380. sith: since
404. pride: heat
406. strong circumstances: weighty circumstantial evidence
409. living reason: actual proof
428. forgone conclusion: previous happening
429. shrewd doubt: extremely suspicious thing

To tyrannous hate! Swell, bosom, with thy fraught,
For 'tis of aspics' tongues!

Iago. Yet be content. 450

Oth. O, blood, blood, blood!

Iago. Patience, I say. Your mind perhaps may change.

Oth. Never, Iago. Like to the Pontic sea,
Whose icy current and compulsive course
Ne'er feels retiring ebb, but keeps due on 455
To the Propontic and the Hellespont;
Even so my bloody thoughts, with violent pace,
Shall ne'er look back, ne'er ebb to humble love,
Till that a capable and wide revenge
Swallow them up. (*He kneels.*) Now, by yond marble heaven, 460
In the due reverence of a sacred vow
I here engage my words.

Iago. Do not rise yet. *Iago kneels.*
Witness, you ever-burning lights above,
You elements that clip us round about,
Witness that here Iago doth give up 465
The execution of his wit, hands, heart
To wronged Othello's service! Let him command,
And to obey shall be in me remorse,
What bloody business ever. [*They rise.*]

Oth. I greet thy love,
Not with vain thanks but with acceptance bounteous, 470
And will upon the instant put thee to't.
Within these three days let me hear thee say
That Cassio's not alive.

Iago. My friend is dead; 'tis done at your request.
But let her live.

Oth. Damn her, lewd minx! O, damn her!
Come, go with me apart. I will withdraw 476
To furnish me with some swift means of death
For the fair devil. Now art thou my lieutenant.

Iago. I am your own forever.

Exeunt.

Scene IV. [*Cyprus. Before the Castle.*]

Enter DESDEMONA, EMILIA, *and* CLOWN.

Des. Do you know, sirrah, where Lieutenant Cassio lies?

449. fraught: burden
450. aspics: asps; **be content:** control yourself
453. Pontic: Black
456. Propontic: Sea of Marmora; **Hellespont:** Bosporus
459. capable: sufficient
460. marble: marbled with clouds
462. engage: pledge
464. clip: enfold
466. execution: performance
468. to . . . remorse: pity shall make me obey
469. greet: match

Clown. I dare not say he lies anywhere.

Des. Why man?

Clown. He's a soldier; and for one to say a soldier lies is stabbing. 5

Des. Go to. Where lodges he?

Clown. To tell you where he lodges is to tell you where I lie.

Des. Can anything be made of this? 10

Clown. I know not where he lodges; and for me to devise a lodging, and say he lies here or he lies there, were to lie in mine own throat.

Des. Can you inquire him out, and be edified by report? 15

Clown. I will catechize the world for him; that is, make questions, and by them answer.

Des. Seek him, bid him come hither. Tell him I have moved my lord on his behalf and hope all will be well. 20

Clown. To do this is within the compass of man's wit, and therefore I'll attempt the doing it. *Exit.*

Des. Where should I lose that handkerchief, Emilia?

Emil. I know not, madam. 25

Des. Believe me, I had rather have lost my purse
Full of crusadoes; and but my noble Moor
Is true of mind, and made of no such baseness
As jealous creatures are, it were enough
To put him to ill thinking.

Emil. Is he not jealous? 30

Des. Who? he? I think the sun where he was born
Drew all such humors from him.

Enter OTHELLO.

Emil. Look where he comes.

Des. I will not leave him now till Cassio
Be called to him.—How is't with you, my lord?

Oth. Well, my good lady. [*Aside*] O, hardness to dissemble!— 35
How do you, Desdemona?

Des. Well, my good lord.

Oth. Give me your hand. This hand is moist, my lady.

Des. It yet hath felt no age nor known no sorrow.

Oth. This argues fruitfulness and liberal heart.
Hot, hot, and moist. This hand of yours requires 40
A sequester from liberty, fasting and prayer,
Much castigation, exercise devout;
For here's a young and sweating devil here
That commonly rebels. 'Tis a good hand,
A frank one.

Des. You may, indeed, say so; 45
For 'twas that hand that gave away my heart.

14. edified: instructed
27. crusadoes: Portuguese gold coins stamped with a cross
40. Hot . . . moist: indicative of a sensual nature
42. castigation: discipline

Oth. A liberal hand! The hearts of old gave hands;
But our new heraldry is hands, not hearts.
Des. I cannot speak of this. Come now, your promise!
Oth. What promise, chuck? 50
Des. I have sent to bid Cassio come speak with you.
Oth. I have a salt and sorry rheum offends me.
Lend me thy handkerchief.
Des. Here, my lord.
Oth. That which I gave you.
Des. I have it not about me.
Oth. Not?
Des. No indeed, my lord.
Oth. That is a fault. 55
That handkerchief
Did an Egyptian to my mother give.
She was a charmer, and could almost read
The thoughts of people. She told her, while she kept it,
'Twould make her amiable and subdue my father 60
Entirely to her love; but if she lost it
Or made a gift of it, my father's eye
Should hold her loathed, and his spirits should hunt
After new fancies. She, dying, gave it me,
And bid me, when my fate would have me wive, 65
To give it her. I did so; and take heed on't;
Make it a darling like your precious eye.
To lose't or give't away were such perdition
As nothing else could match.
Des. Is't possible?
Oth. 'Tis true. There's magic in the web of it. 70
A sibyl that had numb'red in the world
The sun to course two hundred compasses,
In her prophetic fury sewed the work;
The worms were hallowed that did breed the silk;
And it was dyed in mummy which the skillful 75
Conserved of maidens' hearts.
Des. I' faith? Is't true?
Oth. Most veritable. Therefore look to't well.
Des. Then would to God that I had never seen't!
Oth. Ha! Wherefore? 79
Des. Why do you speak so startingly and rash?
Oth. Is't lost? Is't gone? Speak, is it out o' the way?
Des. Heaven bless us!
Oth. Say you?

48. heraldry: symbolism; **hands . . . hearts:** modern marriage involves the exchange of hands but the heart does not necessarily accompany the hand.
52. salt . . . rheum: miserable cold
60. amiable: lovable
68. perdition: loss
71–72. that . . . compasses: that had lived two hundred years
75. mummy: a magical compound made from an embalmed corpse
76. Conserved: preserved
80. startingly: abruptly

Des. It is not lost. But what an if it were?
Oth. How? 85
Des. I say it is not lost.
Oth. Fetch't, let me see't!
Des. Why, so I can, sir; but I will not now.
This is a trick to put me from my suit.
Pray you let Cassio be received again.
Oth. Fetch me the handkerchief! My mind misgives. 90
Des. Come, come!
You'll never meet a more sufficient man.
Oth. The handkerchief!
Des. I pray talk me of Cassio.
Oth. The handkerchief!
Des. A man that all his time
Hath founded his good fortunes on your love, 95
Shared dangers with you—
Oth. The handkerchief!
Des. In sooth, you are to blame.
Oth. Away! *Exit.*
Emil. Is not this man jealous? 100
Des. I ne'er saw this before.
Sure there's some wonder in this handkerchief.
I am most unhappy in the loss of it.
Emil. 'Tis not a year or two shows us a man.
They are all but stomachs, and we all but food; 105
They eat us hungerly, and when they are full,
They belch us.

Enter IAGO *and* CASSIO.

Look you—Cassio and my husband!
Iago. There is no other way; 'tis she must do't.
And lo the happiness! Go and importune her.
Des. How now, good Cassio? What's the news with you? 110
Cas. Madam, my former suit. I do beseech you
That by your virtuous means I may again
Exist, and be a member of his love
Whom I with all the office of my heart
Entirely honor. I would not be delayed. 115
If my offense be of such mortal kind
That neither service past, nor present sorrows,
Nor purposed merit in futurity,
Can ransom me into his love again,
But to know so must be my benefit. 120
So shall I clothe me in a forced content,
And shut myself up in some other course,
To Fortune's alms.
Des. Alas, thrice-gentle Cassio!
My advocation is not now in tune.
My lord is not my lord; nor should I know him, 125

92. sufficient: capable
106. hungerly: hungrily
122. shut . . . in: confine myself to
123. To . . . alms: at the mercy of Fortune
124. in tune: opportune

Were he in favor as in humor altered.
So help me every spirit sanctified
As I have spoken for you all my best
And stood within the blank of his displeasure
For my free speech! You must awhile be patient.
What I can do I will; and more I will 131
Than for myself I dare. Let that suffice you.

Iago. Is my lord angry?

Emil. He went hence but now,
And certainly in strange unquietness.

Iago. Can he be angry? I have seen the cannon
When it hath blown his ranks into the air 136
And, like the devil, from his very arm
Puffed his own brother—and can he be angry?
Something of moment then. I will go meet him.
There's matter in't indeed if he be angry. 140

Des. I prithee do so. *Exit* [*Iago*].
Something sure of state,
Either from Venice or some unhatched practice
Made demonstrable here in Cyprus to him,
Hath puddled his clear spirit; and in such cases
Men's natures wrangle with inferior things, 145
Though great ones are their object. 'Tis even so.
For let our finger ache, and it endues
Our other healthful members even to that sense
Of pain. Nay, we must think men are not gods,
Nor of them look for such observancy 150
As fits the bridal. Beshrew me much, Emilia,
I was (unhandsome warrior as I am!)
Arraigning his unkindness with my soul;
But now I find I had suborned the witness,
And he's indicted falsely. 155

Emil. Pray heaven it be state matters, as you think,
And no conception nor no jealous toy
Concerning you.

Des. Alas the day! I never gave him cause.

Emil. But jealous souls will not be answered so.
They are not ever jealous for the cause, 161
But jealous for they are jealous. 'Tis a monster
Begot upon itself, born on itself.

Des. Heaven keep that monster from Othello's mind!

Emil. Lady, amen. 165

Des. I will go seek him. Cassio, walk here about.
If I do find him fit, I'll move your suit
And seek to effect it to my uttermost.

Cas. I humbly thank your ladyship.
Exeunt Desdemona and Emilia.

Enter BIANCA.

Bian. Save you, friend Cassio!

Cas. What make you from home?
How is it with you, my most fair Bianca? 171
I' faith, sweet love, I was coming to your house.

Bian. And I was going to your lodging, Cassio.
What, keep a week away? seven days and nights?
Eightscore eight hours? and lovers' absent hours,
More tedious than the dial eightscore times? 176
O weary reck'ning!

Cas. Pardon me, Bianca.
I have this while with leaden thoughts been pressed;
But I shall in a more convenient time
Strike off this score of absence. Sweet Bianca, 180
[*Gives her Desdemona's handkerchief*.]
Take me this work out.

Bian. O Cassio, whence came this?
This is some token from a newer friend.
To the felt absence now I feel a cause.
Is't come to this? Well, well.

Cas. Go to, woman!
Throw your vile guesses in the devil's teeth, 185
From whence you have them. You are jealous now
That this is from some mistress, some remembrance.
No, by my faith, Bianca.

Bian. Why, whose is it?

Cas. I know not, sweet. I found it in my chamber.
I like the work well. Ere it be demanded, 190
As like enough it will, I would have it copied.
Take it and do't, and leave me for this time.

Bian. Leave you? Wherefore?

Cas. I do attend here on the General
And think it no addition, nor my wish, 195
To have him see me womaned.

Bian. Why, I pray you?

Cas. Not that I love you not.

Bian. But that you do not love me!
I pray you bring me on the way a little,
And say if I shall see you soon at night.

Cas. 'Tis but a little way that I can bring you,
For I attend here; but I'll see you soon. 201

Bian. 'Tis very good. I must be circumstanced.
Exeunt.

129. **blank:** center of a target
141. **Something . . . state:** some state business certainly
142. **unhatched practice:** unexecuted stratagem
147. **endues:** subdues
150. **observancy:** consideration
151. **Beshrew:** curse; a mild oath
152. **unhandsome:** unfair
154. **suborned:** falsified; **witness:** evidence
157. **toy:** whim
176. **dial:** circuit of the clock's hands
180. **Strike . . . absence:** make up for the absence you have been marking down against me
195. **addition:** credit
198. **bring:** escort
199. **soon . . . night:** tonight
202. **be circumstanced:** take what comes

ACT IV

Scene I. [*Cyprus. Before the Castle.*]

Enter OTHELLO *and* IAGO.

Iago. Will you think so?
Oth. Think so, Iago?
Iago. What,
To kiss in private?
Oth. An unauthorized kiss.
Iago. Or to be naked with her friend in bed
An hour, or more, not meaning any harm?
Oth. Naked in bed, Iago, and not mean harm? 5
It is hypocrisy against the devil.
They that mean virtuously, and yet do so,
The devil their virtue tempts, and they tempt heaven.
Iago. So they do nothing, 'tis a venial slip.
But if I give my wife a handkerchief— 10
Oth. What then?
Iago. Why, then 'tis hers, my lord; and being hers,
She may, I think, bestow't on any man.
Oth. She is protectress of her honor too.
May she give that? 15
Iago. Her honor is an essence that's not seen;
They have it very oft that have it not.
But for the handkerchief—
Oth. By heaven, I would most gladly have forgot it!
Thou saidst (O, it comes o'er my memory 20
As doth the raven o'er the infected house,
Boding to all!) he had my handkerchief.
Iago. Ay, what of that?
Oth. That's not so good now.
Iago. What
If I had said I had seen him do you wrong?
Or heard him say—as knaves be such abroad 25
Who having, by their own importunate suit,
Or voluntary dotage of some mistress,
Convinced or supplied them, cannot choose
But they must blab—
Oth. Hath he said anything?
Iago. He hath, my lord; but be you well assured,
No more than he'll unswear.
Oth. What hath he said? 31
Iago. Faith, that he did—I know not what he did.
Oth. What? what?
Iago. Lie—
Oth. With her?
Iago. With her, on her; what you will.
Oth. Lie with her? lie on her—We say lie on 35
her when they belie her.—Lie with her! Zounds, that's fulsome.—Handkerchief—confessions—handkerchief!—To confess, and be hanged for his labor—first to be hanged, and then to confess! I tremble at it. Nature would not invest herself in such 40
shadowing passion without some instruction. It is not words that shakes me thus.—Pish! Noses, ears, and lips? Is't possible?—Confess?—handkerchief?—O devil! *Falls in a trance.*
Iago. Work on, 45
My medicine, work! Thus credulous fools are caught,
And many worthy and chaste dames even thus,
All guiltless, meet reproach.—What, ho! my lord!
My lord, I say! Othello!

Enter CASSIO.

How now, Cassio?
Cas. What's the matter? 50
Iago. My lord is fall'n into an epilepsy.
This is his second fit; he had one yesterday.
Cas. Rub him about the temples.
Iago. No, forbear.
The lethargy must have his quiet course.
If not, he foams at mouth, and by-and-by 55
Breaks out to savage madness. Look, he stirs.
Do you withdraw yourself a little while.
He will recover straight. When he is gone,
I would on great occasion speak with you.
[*Exit Cassio.*]
How is it, General? Have you not hurt your head?
Oth. Dost thou mock me?
Iago. I mock you? No, by heaven. 61
Would you would bear your fortune like a man!
Oth. A horned man's a monster and a beast.
Iago. There's many a beast then in a populous city,
And many a civil monster. 65
Oth. Did he confess it?

6. hypocrisy . . . devil: i.e., innocence pretending evil
17. it: the reputation for honor
22. Boding: ominous
25. as: since
28. Convinced: seduced; **supplied:** satisfied

40. Nature: i.e., Othello's natural calm
41. instruction: intuition
61. mock me: Othello thinks of the cuckold's horns.
65. civil: civilized

Iago. Good sir, be a man.
Think every bearded fellow that's but yoked
May draw with you. There's millions now alive
That nightly lie in those unproper beds 69
Which they dare swear peculiar. Your case is better.
O, 'tis the spite of hell, the fiend's arch-mock,
To lip a wanton in a secure couch,
And to suppose her chaste! No, let me know;
And knowing what I am. I know what she shall be.

Oth. O, thou art wise! 'Tis certain.

Iago. Stand you awhile apart; 75
Confine yourself but in a patient list.
Whilst you were here, o'erwhelmed with your grief
(A passion most unfitting such a man),
Cassio came hither. I shifted him away
And laid good 'scuse upon your ecstasy; 80
Bade him anon return, and here speak with me;
The which he promised. Do but encave yourself
And mark the fleers, the gibes, and notable scorns
That dwell in every region of his face;
For I will make him tell the tale anew— 85
Where, how, how oft, how long ago, and when
He hath, and is again to cope your wife.
I say, but mark his gesture. Marry, patience!
Or I shall say you are all in all in spleen,
And nothing of a man.

Oth. Dost thou hear, Iago? 90
I will be found most cunning in my patience;
But (dost thou hear?) most bloody.

Iago. That's not amiss;
But yet keep time in all. Will you withdraw?
[*Othello retires.*]
Now will I question Cassio of Bianca,
A huswife that by selling her desires 95
Buys herself bread and clothes. It is a creature
That dotes on Cassio, as 'tis the strumpet's plague
To beguile many and be beguiled by one.
He, when he hears of her, cannot refrain
From the excess of laughter. Here he comes. 100

Enter CASSIO.

As he shall smile, Othello shall go mad;
And his unbookish jealousy must conster
Poor Cassio's smiles, gestures, and light behavior
Quite in the wrong. How do you now, Lieutenant?

Cas. The worser that you give me the addition
Whose want even kills me. 106

Iago. Ply Desdemona well, and you are sure on't.
Now, if this suit lay in Bianca's power,
How quickly should you speed!

Cas. Alas, poor caitiff!

Oth. Look how he laughs already! 110

Iago. I never knew woman love man so.

Cas. Alas, poor rogue! I think, i' faith, she loves me.

Oth. Now he denies it faintly, and laughs it out.

Iago. Do you hear, Cassio?

Oth. Now he importunes him
To tell it o'er. Go to! Well said, well said! 115

Iago. She gives it out that you shall marry her.
Do you intend it?

Cas. Ha, ha, ha!

Oth. Do you triumph, Roman? Do you triumph?

Cas. I marry her? What, a customer? 120
Prithee bear some charity to my wit; do not think it so unwholesome. Ha, ha, ha!

Oth. So, so, so, so! Laugh that wins!

Iago. Faith, the cry goes that you shall marry her.

Cas. Prithee say true. 125

Iago. I am a very villain else.

Oth. Have you scored me? Well.

Cas. This is the monkey's own giving out. She is persuaded I will marry her out of her own love and flattery, not out of my promise. 130

Oth. Iago beckons me. Now he begins the story.

Cas. She was here even now; she haunts me in every place. I was t'other day talking on the sea bank with certain Venetians, and thither comes the bauble, and, by this hand, she falls me thus 135
about my neck—

Oth. Crying "O dear Cassio!" as it were. His gesture imports it.

Cas. So hangs, and lolls, and weeps upon me; so hales and pulls me! Ha, ha, ha! 140

Oth. Now he tells how she plucked him to my chamber. O, I see that nose of yours, but not that dog I shall throw't to.

Cas. Well, I must leave her company.

Enter BIANCA.

Iago. Before me! Look where she comes. 145

Cas. 'Tis such another fitchew! marry, a perfumed one. What do you mean by this haunting of me?

67–68. every . . . you: every married man may bear the same burden
69–70. unproper . . . peculiar: beds not exclusively their own, though they would swear otherwise
76. in . . . list: within the limits of patience
78. passion: fit
80. ecstasy: swoon
82. encave: hide
87. cope: encounter amorously
88. gesture: behavior
89. all . . . spleen: all made up of anger. The spleen was believed to be the source of anger.
93. time: measure
95. huswife: hussy
102. unbookish: ignorant; **conster:** construe
105. addition: title
109. caitiff: wretch
119. Roman: probably used with thought of a Roman triumph
120. customer: prostitute
123. Laugh . . . wins: proverbial: "They laugh that win."
135. bauble: trifle
146. such another: such a (emphatic); **fitchew:** polecat, slang for "whore"

Bian. Let the devil and his dam haunt you! What did you mean by that same handkerchief you gave me even now? I was a fine fool to take it. I 150 must take out the work? A likely piece of work that you should find it in your chamber and know not who left it there! This is some minx's token, and I must take out the work? There! give it your hobby-horse. Wheresoever you had it, I'll take out 155 no work on't.

Cas. How now, my sweet Bianca? How now? how now?

Oth. By heaven, that should be my handkerchief!

Bian. An you'll come to supper tonight, you 160 may; an you will not, come when you are next prepared for. *Exit.*

Iago. After her, after her!

Cas. Faith, I must; she'll rail i' the street else.

Iago. Will you sup there? 165

Cas. Yes, I intend so.

Iago. Well, I may chance to see you; for I would very fain speak with you.

Cas. Prithee come. Will you? 169

Iago. Go to! say no more. *Exit Cassio.*

Oth. [*Comes forward*] How shall I murder him, Iago?

Iago. Did you perceive how he laughed at his vice?

Oth. O Iago!

Iago. And did you see the handkerchief? 175

Oth. Was that mine?

Iago. Yours, by this hand! And to see how he prizes the foolish woman your wife! She gave it him, and he hath giv'n it his whore.

Oth. I would have him nine years a-killing! 180 —A fine woman! a fair woman! a sweet woman!

Iago. Nay, you must forget that.

Oth. Ay, let her rot, and perish, and be damned tonight, for she shall not live. No, my heart is turned to stone: I strike it, and it hurts my hand. O, the 185 world hath not a sweeter creature! She might lie by an emperor's side and command him tasks.

Iago. Nay, that's not your way.

Oth. Hang her! I do but say what she is. So delicate with her needle! an admirable musician! 190 O, she will sing the savageness out of a bear! of so high and plenteous wit and invention!

Iago. She's the worse for all this.

Oth. O, a thousand thousand times! And then, of so gentle a condition! 195

Iago. Ay, too gentle.

Oth. Nay, that's certain. But yet the pity of it, Iago! O Iago, the pity of it, Iago!

Iago. If you are so fond over her iniquity, give her patent to offend; for if it touch not you, it 200 comes near nobody.

Oth. I will chop her into messes! Cuckold me!

Iago. O, 'tis foul in her.

Oth. With mine officer!

Iago. That's fouler. 205

Oth. Get me some poison, Iago, this night. I'll not expostulate with her, lest her body and beauty unprovide my mind again. This night, Iago!

Iago. Do it not with poison. Strangle her in her bed, even the bed she hath contaminated. 210

Oth. Good, good! The justice of it pleases. Very good!

Iago. And for Cassio, let me be his undertaker. You shall hear more by midnight.

Oth. Excellent good! *A trumpet.*
What trumpet is that same? 215

Iago. Something from Venice, sure.

Enter LODOVICO, DESDEMONA, *and* ATTENDANTS.

'Tis Lodovico,
Come from the Duke; and see, your wife is with him.

Lod. God save you, worthy General!

Oth. With all my heart, sir.

Lod. The Duke and Senators of Venice greet you.
[*Gives him a letter.*]

Oth. I kiss the instrument of their pleasures. 220
[*Opens the letter and reads.*]

Des. And what's the news, good cousin Lodovico?

Iago. I am very glad to see you, signior.
Welcome to Cyprus.

Lod. I thank you. How does Lieutenant Cassio?

Iago. Lives, sir.

Des. Cousin, there's fall'n between him and my lord 225
An unkind breach; but you shall make all well.

Oth. Are you sure of that?

Des. My lord?

Oth. [*Reads*] "This fail you not to do, as you will—"

Lod. He did not call; he's busy in the paper. 230
Is there division 'twixt thy lord and Cassio?

Des. A most unhappy one. I would do much
T' atone them, for the love I bear to Cassio.

Oth. Fire and brimstone!

Des. My lord?

Oth. Are you wise?

Des. What, is he angry?

Lod. May be the letter moved him; 235
For, as I think, they do command him home,
Deputing Cassio in his government.

Des. By my troth, I am glad on't.

154–55. hobbyhorse: sweetheart
159. should: must
195. condition: temperament
199. fond: foolish
200. patent: license
213. undertaker: i.e., the one who takes care of him
218. With . . . heart: amen
233. atone: reconcile

Oth. Indeed?
Des. My lord?
Oth. I am glad to see you mad.
Des. Why, sweet Othello!
Oth. Devil! [*Strikes her.*]
Des. I have not deserved this. 241
Lod. My lord, this would not be believed in Venice,
Though I should swear I saw't. 'Tis very much.
Make her amends; she weeps.
Oth. O devil, devil!
If that the earth could teem with woman's tears,
Each drop she falls would prove a crocodile. 246
Out of my sight!
Des. I will not stay to offend you. [*Going.*]
Lod. Truly, an obedient lady.
I do beseech your lordship call her back.
Oth. Mistress!
Des. My lord?
Oth. What would you with her, sir?
Lod. Who? I, my lord? 251
Oth. Ay! You did wish that I would make her turn.
Sir, she can turn, and turn, and yet go on,
And turn again; and she can weep, sir, weep;
And she's obedient; as you say, obedient, 255
Very obedient.—Proceed you in your tears.—
Concerning this, sir (O well-painted passion!),
I am commanded home.—Get you away;
I'll send for you anon.—Sir, I obey the mandate
And will return to Venice.—Hence, avaunt! 260
[*Exit Desdemona.*]
Cassio shall have my place. And, sir, tonight
I do entreat that we may sup together.
You are welcome, sir, to Cyprus.—Goats and monkeys! *Exit.*
Lod. Is this the noble Moor whom our full senate
Call all in all sufficient? Is this the nature 265
Whom passion could not shake? whose solid virtue
The shot of accident nor dart of chance
Could neither graze nor pierce?
Iago. He is much changed.
Lod. Are his wits safe? Is he not light of brain?
Iago. He's that he is. I may not breathe my censure. 270
What he might be—if what he might he is not—
I would to heaven he were!
Lod. What, strike his wife?
Iago. Faith, that was not so well; yet would I knew
That stroke would prove the worst!
Lod. Is it his use?
Or did the letters work upon his blood 275
And new-create this fault?
Iago. Alas, alas!
It is not honesty in me to speak
What I have seen and known. You shall observe him,
And his own courses will denote him so
That I may save my speech. Do but go after 280
And mark how he continues.
Lod. I am sorry that I am deceived in him.
Exeunt.

Scene II. [*Cyprus. Within the Castle.*]

Enter Othello *and* Emilia.

Oth. You have seen nothing then?
Emil. Nor ever heard, nor ever did suspect.
Oth. Yes, you have seen Cassio and she together.
Emil. But then I saw no harm, and then I heard
Each syllable that breath made up between them. 5
Oth. What, did they never whisper?
Emil. Never, my lord.
Oth. Nor send you out o' the way?
Emil. Never.
Oth. To fetch her fan, her gloves, her mask, nor nothing?
Emil. Never, my lord. 10
Oth. That's strange.
Emil. I durst, my lord, to wager she is honest,
Lay down my soul at stake. If you think other,
Remove your thought; it doth abuse your bosom.
If any wretch have put this in your head, 15
Let heaven requite it with the serpent's curse!
For if she be not honest, chaste, and true,
There's no man happy; the purest of their wives
Is foul as slander.
Oth. Bid her come hither. Go. *Exit Emilia.*
She says enough; yet she's a simple bawd 20
That cannot say as much. This is a subtle whore,
A closet lock and key of villainous secrets;
And yet she'll kneel and pray; I have seen her do't.

Enter Desdemona *and* Emilia.

Des. My lord, what is your will?
Oth. Pray, chuck, come hither.
Des. What is your pleasure?
Oth. Let me see your eyes. 25
Look in my face.
Des. What horrible fancy's this?
Oth. [*To Emilia*] Some of your function, mistress.
Leave procreants alone and shut the door;
Cough or cry hem if anybody come.
Your mystery, your mystery! Nay, dispatch! 30
Exit Emilia.

245. teem: conceive
257. passion: emotion
277. honesty: honorable action

18. happy: lucky
27–30. Some . . . mystery: Othello speaks as though Emilia is a bawd and Desdemona a whore.

Des. Upon my knees, what doth your speech import?
I understand a fury in your words,
But not the words.
Oth. Why, what art thou?
Des. Your wife, my lord; your true
And loyal wife.
Oth. Come, swear it, damn thyself; 35
Lest, being like one of heaven, the devils themselves
Should fear to seize thee. Therefore be double-damned—
Swear thou art honest.
Des. Heaven doth truly know it.
Oth. Heaven truly knows that thou art false as hell.
Des. To whom, my lord? With whom? How am I false? 40
Oth. Ah, Desdemon! away! away! away!
Des. Alas the heavy day! Why do you weep?
Am I the motive of these tears, my lord?
If haply you my father do suspect
An instrument of this your calling back, 45
Lay not your blame on me. If you have lost him,
Why, I have lost him too.
Oth. Had it pleased heaven
To try me with affliction, had they rained
All kinds of sores and shames on my bare head,
Steeped me in poverty to the very lips, 50
Given to captivity me and my utmost hopes,
I should have found in some place of my soul
A drop of patience. But, alas, to make me
A fixed figure for the time of scorn
To point his slow and moving finger at! 55
Yet could I bear that too; well, very well.
But there where I have garnered up my heart,
Where either I must live or bear no life,
The fountain from the which my current runs
Or else dries up—to be discarded thence, 60
Or keep it as a cistern for foul toads
To knot and gender in—turn thy complexion there,
Patience, thou young and rose-lipped cherubin!
I here look grim as hell! 64
Des. I hope my noble lord esteems me honest.
Oth. O, ay! as summer flies are in the shambles,
That quicken even with blowing. O thou weed,
Who art so lovely fair, and smellst so sweet,
That the sense aches at thee, would thou hadst ne'er been born! 69
Des. Alas, what ignorant sin have I committed?
Oth. Was this fair paper, this most goodly book,
Made to write "whore" upon? What committed?
Committed? O thou public commoner!
I should make very forges of my cheeks
That would to cinders burn up modesty, 75
Did I but speak thy deeds. What committed?
Heaven stops the nose at it, and the moon winks;
The bawdy wind, that kisses all it meets,
Is hushed within the hollow mine of earth
And will not hear it. What committed? 80
Impudent strumpet!
Des. By heaven, you do me wrong!
Oth. Are not you a strumpet?
Des. No, as I am a Christian!
If to preserve this vessel for my lord
From any other foul unlawful touch
Be not to be a strumpet, I am none. 85
Oth. What, not a whore?
Des. No, as I shall be saved!
Oth. Is't possible?
Des. O, heaven forgive us!
Oth. I cry you mercy then.
I took you for that cunning whore of Venice
That married with Othello.—You, mistress, 90
That have the office opposite to Saint Peter
And keep the gate of hell!

Enter EMILIA.

You, you, ay, you!
We have done our course. There's money for your pains.
I pray you turn the key, and keep our counsel. *Exit.*
Emil. Alas, what does this gentleman conceive?
How do you, madam? How do you, my good lady?
Des. Faith, half asleep. 97
Emil. Good madam, what's the matter with my lord?
Des. With who?
Emil. Why, with my lord, madam. 100
Des. Who is thy lord?
Emil. He that is yours, sweet lady.
Des. I have none. Do not talk to me, Emilia.
I cannot weep; nor answer have I none
But what should go by water. Prithee tonight
Lay on my bed my wedding sheets, remember; 105
And call thy husband hither.
Emil. Here's a change indeed! *Exit.*
Des. 'Tis meet I should be used so, very meet.
How have I been behaved, that he might stick
The small'st opinion on my least misuse?

Enter IAGO *and* EMILIA.

Iago. What is your pleasure, madam? How is't with you? 110
Des. I cannot tell. Those that do teach young babes

43. motive: mover
54. time . . . scorn: scornful time
66. shambles: slaughterhouse
73. commoner: prostitute
88. cry . . . mercy: beg your pardon
108–9. stick . . . misuse: note the slightest action worthy of censure

Do it with gentle means and easy tasks.
He might have chid me so; for, in good faith,
I am a child to chiding.
Iago. What is the matter, lady?
Emil. Alas, Iago, my lord hath so bewhored her,
Thrown such despite and heavy terms upon her 116
As true hearts cannot bear.
Des. Am I that name, Iago?
Iago. What name, fair lady?
Des. Such as she says my lord did say I was.
Emil. He called her whore. A beggar in his drink
Could not have laid such terms upon his callet. 121
Iago. Why did he so?
Des. I do not know. I am sure I am none such.
Iago. Do not weep, do not weep. Alas the day!
Emil. Hath she forsook so many noble matches,
Her father and her country, all her friends, 126
To be called whore? Would it not make one weep?
Des. It is my wretched fortune.
Iago. Beshrew him for't!
How comes this trick upon him?
Des. Nay, heaven doth know.
Emil. I will be hanged if some eternal villain, 130
Some busy and insinuating rogue,
Some cogging, cozening slave, to get some office,
Have not devised this slander. I'll be hanged else.
Iago. Fie, there is no such man! It is impossible.
Des. If any such there be, heaven pardon him!
Emil. A halter pardon him! and hell gnaw his bones! 136
Why should he call her whore? Who keeps her company?
What place? what time? what form? what likelihood?
The Moor's abused by some most villainous knave,
Some base notorious knave, some scurvy fellow. 140
O heaven, that such companions thou'dst unfold,
And put in every honest hand a whip
To lash the rascals naked through the world
Even from the East to the West!
Iago. Speak within door.
Emil. O, fie upon them! Some such squire he was
That turned your wit the seamy side without 146
And made you to suspect me with the Moor.
Iago. You are a fool. Go to.
Des. O good Iago,
What shall I do to win my lord again?
Good friend, go to him; for, by this light of heaven,
I know not how I lost him. Here I kneel. 151
If e'er my will did trespass 'gainst his love
Either in discourse of thought or actual deed,
Or that mine eyes, mine ears, or any sense
Delighted them in any other form, 155
Or that I do not yet, and ever did,
And ever will (though he do shake me off
To beggarly divorcement) love him dearly,
Comfort forswear me! Unkindness may do much;
And his unkindness may defeat my life, 160
But never taint my love. I cannot say "whore."
It doth abhor me now I speak the word;
To do the act that might the addition earn
Not the world's mass of vanity could make me.
Iago. I pray you be content. 'Tis but his humor.
The business of the state does him offense, 166
And he does chide with you.
Des. If 'twere no other—
Iago. 'Tis but so, I warrant.
[*Trumpets within.*]
Hark how these instruments summon you to supper.
The messengers of Venice stay the meat. 170
Go in, and weep not. All things shall be well.
Exeunt Desdemona and Emilia.

Enter RODERIGO.

How now, Roderigo?
Rod. I do not find that thou dealst justly with me.
Iago. What in the contrary?
Rod. Every day thou daffst me with some 175 device, Iago, and rather, as it seems to me now, keepst from me all conveniency than suppliest me with the least advantage of hope. I will indeed no longer endure it; nor am I yet persuaded to put up in peace what already I have foolishly suffered. 180
Iago. Will you hear me, Roderigo?
Rod. Faith, I have heard too much; for your words and performances are no kin together.
Iago. You charge me most unjustly.
Rod. With naught but truth. I have wasted 185 myself out of means. The jewels you have had from me to deliver to Desdemona would half have corrupted a votarist. You have told me she hath received them, and returned me expectations and comforts of sudden respect and acquaintance; 190 but I find none.
Iago. Well, go to; very well.
Rod. Very well! go to! I cannot go to, man; nor 'tis not very well. Nay, I think it is scurvy, and begin to find myself fopped in it. 195
Iago. Very well.
Rod. I tell you 'tis not very well. I will make my-

121. **callet:** trull
129. **trick:** whim
132. **cogging, cozening:** lying, cheating
136. **halter:** noose
141. **companions:** base fellows
154. **that:** if
160. **defeat:** destroy
170. **the meat:** dinner
175. **daffst me:** put me off
177. **conveniency:** opportunity
179–80. **put . . . peace:** accept peaceably
188. **votarist:** nun
195. **fopped:** made a fool of

self known to Desdemona. If she will return me my jewels, I will give over my suit and repent my unlawful solicitation. If not, assure yourself I will 200
seek satisfaction of you.

Iago. You have said now.

Rod. Ay, and said nothing but what I protest intendment of doing.

Iago. Why, now I see there's mettle in 205
thee; and even from this instant do build on thee a better opinion than ever before. Give me thy hand, Roderigo. Thou hast taken against me a most just exception; but yet I protest I have dealt most directly in thy affair. 210

Rod. It hath not appeared.

Iago. I grant indeed it hath not appeared; and your suspicion is not without wit and judgment. But, Roderigo, if thou hast that in thee indeed which I have greater reason to believe now than ever 215
(I mean purpose, courage, and valor), this night show it. If thou the next night following enjoy not Desdemona, take me from this world with treachery and devise engines for my life.

Rod. Well, what is it? Is it within reason 220
and compass?

Iago. Sir, there is especial commission come from Venice to depute Cassio in Othello's place.

Rod. Is that true? Why, then Othello and Desdemona return again to Venice. 225

Iago. O, no. He goes into Mauretania and takes away with him the fair Desdemona, unless his abode be lingered here by some accident; wherein none can be so determinate as the removing of Cassio.

Rod. How do you mean removing of him? 230

Iago. Why, by making him uncapable of Othello's place—knocking out his brains.

Rod. And that you would have me to do?

Iago. Ay, if you dare do yourself a profit and a right. He sups tonight with a harlotry, and 235
thither will I go to him. He knows not yet of his honorable fortune. If you will watch his going thence, which I will fashion to fall out between twelve and one, you may take him at your pleasure. I will be near to second your attempt, and he 240
shall fall between us. Come, stand not amazed at it, but go along with me. I will show you such a necessity in his death that you shall think yourself bound to put it on him. It is now high suppertime, and the night grows to waste. About it! 245

Rod. I will hear further reason for this.

Iago. And you shall be satisfied.

Exeunt.

202. **You . . . now:** that's the way to talk.
219. **engines for:** ingenious contrivances against
228. **accident:** happening
235. **harlotry:** harlot
241. **amazed:** dumfounded
245. **grows . . . waste:** wastes away

Scene III. [*Cyprus. Another room in the Castle.*]

Enter OTHELLO, LODOVICO, DESDEMONA, EMILIA, *and* ATTENDANTS.

Lod. I do beseech you, sir, trouble yourself no further.

Oth. O, pardon me; 'twill do me good to walk.

Lod. Madam, good night. I humbly thank your ladyship.

Des. Your Honor is most welcome.

Oth. Will you walk, sir?
O, Desdemona— 5

Des. My lord?

Oth. Get you to bed on the instant. I will be returned forthwith. Dismiss your attendant there. Look't be done.

Des. I will, my lord. 10

Exeunt [*Othello, Lodovico, and Attendants*].

Emil. How goes it now? He looks gentler than he did.

Des. He says he will return incontinent.
He hath commanded me to go to bed,
And bid me to dismiss you.

Emil. Dismiss me? 14

Des. It was his bidding. Therefore, good Emilia,
Give me my nightly wearing, and adieu.
We must not now displease him.

Emil. I would you had never see him! 18

Des. So would not I. My love doth so approve him
That even his stubbornness, his checks, his frowns
(Prithee unpin me) have grace and favor in them.

Emil. I have laid those sheets you bade me on the bed.

Des. All's one. Good faith, how foolish are our minds!
If I do die before thee, prithee shroud me 24
In one of those same sheets.

Emil. Come, come! You talk.

Des. My mother had a maid called Barbary.
She was in love; and he she loved proved mad
And did forsake her. She had a song of "Willow."
An old thing 'twas; but it expressed her fortune,
And she died singing it. That song tonight 30
Will not go from my mind. I have much to do
But to go hang my head all at one side
And sing it like poor Barbary. Prithee dispatch.

Emil. Shall I go fetch your nightgown?

Des. No, unpin me here.
This Lodovico is a proper man. 35

12. **incontinent:** immediately
20. **stubbornness:** harshness
23. **All's one:** no matter.
32. **But to:** not to

Emil. A very handsome man.

Des. He speaks well.

Emil. I know a lady in Venice would have walked barefoot to Palestine for a touch of his nether lip. 40

Des. (*Sings*)

> The poor soul sat sighing by a sycamore tree,
> Sing all a green willow:
> Her hand on her bosom, her head on her knee,
> Sing willow, willow, willow.
> The fresh streams ran by her and murmured her moans; 45
> Sing willow, willow, willow;
> Her salt tears fell from her, and soft'ned the stones.
> Sing willow—

Lay by these.

> willow, willow; 50

Prithee hie thee; he'll come anon.

> Sing all a green willow must be my garland.
> Let nobody blame him; his scorn I approve—

Nay, that's not next. Hark! who is't that knocks?

Emil. It is the wind. 55

Des.

> I called my love false love; but what said he then?
> Sing willow, willow, willow:
> If I court mo women, you'll couch with mo men.

So, get thee gone; good night. Mine eyes do itch. 59
Doth that bode weeping?

Emil. 'Tis neither here nor there.

Des. I have heard it said so. O, these men, these men!
Dost thou in conscience think—tell me, Emilia—
That there be women do abuse their husbands
In such gross kind?

Emil. There be some such, no question.

Des. Wouldst thou do such a deed for all the world? 65

Emil. Why, would not you?

Des. No, by this heavenly light!

Emil. Nor I neither by this heavenly light.
I might do't as well i' the dark.

Des. Wouldst thou do such a deed for all the world?

Emil. The world's a huge thing. It is a great 70 price for a small vice.

Des. In troth, I think thou wouldst not.

Emil. In troth, I think I should; and undo't when I had done it. Marry, I would not do such a thing for a joint-ring, nor for measures of lawn, nor 75 for gowns, petticoats, nor caps, nor any petty exhibition; but, for all the whole world—'Ud's pity! who would not make her husband a cuckold to make him a monarch? I should venture purgatory for't.

Des. Beshrew me if I would do such a wrong 80
For the whole world.

Emil. Why, the wrong is but a wrong i' the world; and having the world for your labor, 'tis a wrong in your own world, and you might quickly make it right. 85

Des. I do not think there is any such woman.

Emil. Yes, a dozen; and as many to the vantage as would store the world they played for.
But I do think it is their husbands' faults
If wives do fall. Say that they slack their duties 90
And pour our treasures into foreign laps;
Or else break out in peevish jealousies,
Throwing restraint upon us; or say they strike us,
Or scant our former having in despite— 94
Why, we have galls; and though we have some grace,
Yet have we some revenge. Let husbands know
Their wives have sense like them. They see, and smell,
And have their palates both for sweet and sour,
As husbands have. What is it that they do
When they change us for others? Is it sport? 100
I think it is. And doth affection breed it?
I think it doth. Is't frailty that thus errs?
It is so too. And have not we affections,
Desires for sport, and frailty, as men have?
Then let them use us well; else let them know, 105
The ills we do, their ills instruct us so.

Des. Good night, good night. Heaven me such uses send,
Not to pick bad from bad, but by bad mend!

Exeunt.

60. 'Tis . . . there: it means nothing.

75. joint-ring: a traditional love token
76–77. exhibition: gift
77. 'Ud's pity: God's pity!
87. to . . . vantage: in addition
92. peevish: foolish
94. scant: lessen
95. galls: capacities for resentment; **grace:** virtue
96. revenge: vengefulness
101. affection: amorous fancy
108. pick . . . mend: return evil for evil but learn from my misfortune

ACT V

Scene I. [*Cyprus. A street.*]

Enter IAGO *and* RODERIGO.

Iago. Here, stand behind this bulk; straight will he come.
Wear thy good rapier bare, and put it home.
Quick, quick! Fear nothing; I'll be at thy elbow.
It makes us, or it mars us—think on that,
And fix most firm thy resolution. 5

Rod. Be near at hand. I may miscarry in't.

Iago. Here, at thy hand. Be bold, and take thy stand. [*Stands aside.*]

Rod. I have no great devotion to the deed,
And yet he hath given me satisfying reasons.
'Tis but a man gone. Forth my sword! He dies! 10

Iago. I have rubbed this young quat almost to the sense,
And he grows angry. Now whether he kill Cassio,
Or Cassio him, or each do kill the other,
Every way makes my gain. Live Roderigo,
He calls me to a restitution large 15
Of gold and jewels that I bobbed from him
As gifts to Desdemona.
It must not be. If Cassio do remain,
He hath a daily beauty in his life
That makes me ugly; and besides, the Moor 20
May unfold me to him; there stand I in much peril.
No, he must die. But so! I hear him coming.

Enter CASSIO.

Rod. I know his gait. 'Tis he. Villain, thou diest! [*Makes a pass at Cassio.*]

Cas. That thrust had been mine enemy indeed
But that my coat is better than thou knowst. 25
I will make proof of thine. [*Draws, and wounds Roderigo.*]

Rod. O, I am slain!

[*Iago comes forward, wounds Cassio from behind, and exits.*]

Cas. I am maimed forever. Help, ho! Murder! murder! [*Falls.*]

Enter OTHELLO.

Oth. The voice of Cassio. Iago keeps his word.

Rod. O, villain that I am!

Oth. It is even so.

Cas. O, help, ho! light! a surgeon! 30

Oth. 'Tis he. O brave Iago, honest and just,
That hast such noble sense of thy friend's wrong!
Thou teachest me. Minion, your dear lies dead,
And your unblest fate hies. Strumpet, I come.
Forth of my heart those charms, thine eyes, are blotted. 35
Thy bed, lust-stained, shall with lust's blood be spotted. *Exit.*

Enter LODOVICO *and* GRATIANO.

Cas. What, ho? No watch? No passage? Murder! murder!

Gra. 'Tis some mischance. The cry is very direful.

Cas. O, help!

Lod. Hark! 40

Rod. O wretched villain!

Lod. Two or three groan. It is a heavy night.
These may be counterfeits. Let's think't unsafe
To come in to the cry without more help.

Rod. Nobody come? Then shall I bleed to death.

Lod. Hark! 46

Enter IAGO.

Gra. Here's one comes in his shirt, with light and weapons.

Iago. Who's there? Whose noise is this that cries on murder?

Lod. We do not know.

Iago. Did not you hear a cry?

Cas. Here, here! For heaven's sake, help me!

Iago. What's the matter?

Gra. This is Othello's ancient, as I take it. 51

Lod. The same indeed, a very valiant fellow.

1. bulk: buttress
2. home: i.e., into a vital spot
11. quat: literally, "pimple"; **sense:** quick
16. bobbed: tricked
21. unfold: reveal
26. proof: trial
31. brave: noble
33. Minion: darling (meaning Desdemona)
37. passage: passers-by
42. heavy: overcast; dark

Iago. What are you here that cry so grievously?
Cas. Iago? O, I am spoiled, undone by villains!
Give me some help. 55
Iago. O me, Lieutenant! What villains have done this?
Cas. I think that one of them is hereabout
And cannot make away.
Iago. O treacherous villains!
What are you there? Come in, and give some help.
[*To Lodovico and Gratiano.*]
Rod. O, help me here! 60
Cas. That's one of them.
Iago. O murd'rous slave! O villain!
[*Stabs Roderigo.*]
Rod. O damned Iago! O inhuman dog!
Iago. Kill men i' the dark? Where be these bloody thieves?
How silent is this town! Ho! murder! murder!
What may you be? Are you of good or evil? 65
Lod. As you shall prove us, praise us.
Iago. Signior Lodovico?
Lod. He, sir.
Iago. I cry you mercy. Here's Cassio hurt by villains.
Gra. Cassio? 70
Iago. How is it, brother?
Cas. My leg is cut in two.
Iago. Marry, heaven forbid!
Light, gentlemen. I'll bind it with my shirt.

Enter BIANCA.

Bian. What is the matter, ho? Who is't that cried?
Iago. Who is't that cried? 75
Bian. O my dear Cassio! my sweet Cassio!
O Cassio, Cassio, Cassio!
Iago. O notable strumpet!—Cassio, may you suspect
Who they should be that thus have mangled you?
Cas. No. 80
Gra. I am sorry to find you thus. I have been to seek you.
Iago. Lend me a garter. So. O for a chair
To bear him easily hence!
Bian. Alas, he faints! O Cassio, Cassio, Cassio!
Iago. Gentlemen all, I do suspect this trash 85
To be a party in this injury.—
Patience awhile, good Cassio.—Come, come!
Lend me a light. Know we this face or no?
Alas, my friend and my dear countryman
Roderigo? No. Yes, sure. O heaven! Roderigo. 90
Gra. What, of Venice?
Iago. Even he, sir. Did you know him?
Gra. Know him? Ay.
Iago. Signior Gratiano? I cry you gentle pardon.
These bloody accidents must excuse my manners
That so neglected you.
Gra. I am glad to see you. 95
Iago. How do you, Cassio?—O, a chair, a chair!
Gra. Roderigo?
Iago. He, he, 'tis he! [*A chair brought in*] O, that's well said! the chair.
Some good man bear him carefully from hence.
I'll fetch the General's surgeon. [*To Bianca*] For you, mistress, 100
Save you your labor.—He that lies slain here, Cassio,
Was my dear friend. What malice was between you?
Cas. None in the world; nor do I know the man.
Iago. [*To Bianca*] What, look you pale?—O, bear him out o' the air.
[*Cassio and Roderigo are borne off.*]
Stay you, good gentlemen.—Look you pale, mistress?— 105
Do you perceive the gastness of her eye?—
Nay, an you stare, we shall hear more anon.
Behold her well; I pray you look upon her.
Do you see, gentlemen? Nay, guiltiness will speak,
Though tongues were out of use. 110

Enter EMILIA.

Emil. 'Las, what's the matter? What's the matter, husband?
Iago. Cassio hath here been set on in the dark
By Roderigo, and fellows that are scaped.
He's almost slain, and Roderigo dead. 114
Emil. Alas, good gentleman! alas, good Cassio!
Iago. This is the fruit of whoring. Prithee, Emilia,
Go know of Cassio where he supped tonight.
[*To Bianca*] What, do you shake at that?
Bian. He supped at my house; but I therefore shake not.
Iago. O, did he so? I charge you go with me. 120
Emil. Fie, fie upon thee, strumpet!
Bian. I am no strumpet, but of life as honest
As you that thus abuse me.
Emil. As I? Foh! fie upon thee!
Iago. Kind gentlemen, let's go see poor Cassio dressed.
[*To Bianca*] Come, mistress, you must tell's another tale.— 125
Emilia, run you to the citadel
And tell my lord and lady what hath happed.—
Will you go on afore? [*Aside*] This is the night
That either makes me or fordoes me quite.
Exeunt.

54. spoiled: mutilated
82. chair: litter
106. gastness: terror
129. fordoes: destroys

Scene II. [*Cyprus. A bedchamber in the Castle.*]

DESDEMONA *in her bed. Enter* OTHELLO *with a light.*

Oth. It is the cause, it is the cause, my soul.
Let me not name it to you, you chaste stars!
It is the cause. Yet I'll not shed her blood,
Nor scar that whiter skin of hers than snow,
And smooth as monumental alablaster. 5
Yet she must die, else she'll betray more men.
Put out the light, and then put out the light.
If I quench thee, thou flaming minister,
I can again thy former light restore,
Should I repent me; but once put out thy light, 10
Thou cunning'st pattern of excelling nature,
I know not where is that Promethean heat
That can thy light relume. When I have plucked the rose,
I cannot give it vital growth again;
It needs must wither. I'll smell it on the tree. 15
He kisses her.
O balmy breath, that dost almost persuade
Justice to break her sword! One more, one more!
Be thus when thou art dead, and I will kill thee,
And love thee after. One more, and this the last!
So sweet was ne'er so fatal. I must weep, 20
But they are cruel tears. This sorrow's heavenly,
It strikes where it doth love. She wakes.
Des. Who's there? Othello?
Oth. Ay, Desdemona.
Des. Will you come to bed, my lord?
Oth. Have you prayed tonight, Desdemon?
Des. Ay, my lord.
Oth. If you bethink yourself of any crime 26
Unreconciled as yet to heaven and grace,
Solicit for it straight.
Des. Alack, my lord, what may you mean by that?
Oth. Well, do it, and be brief; I will walk by. 30
I would not kill thy unprepared spirit.
No, heaven forfend! I would not kill thy soul.
Des. Talk you of killing?
Oth. Ay, I do.
Des. Then heaven
Have mercy on me!
Oth. Amen, with all my heart!
Des. If you say so, I hope you will not kill me.
Oth. Humh! 36
Des. And yet I fear you; for you are fatal then
When your eyes roll so. Why I should fear I know not,
Since guiltiness I know not; but yet I feel I fear.
Oth. Think on thy sins.
Des. They are loves I bear to you. 40
Oth. Ay, and for that thou diest.
Des. That death's unnatural that kills for loving.
Alas, why gnaw you so your nether lip?
Some bloody passion shakes your very frame.
These are portents; but yet I hope, I hope, 45
They do not point on me.
Oth. Peace and be still!
Des. I will so. What's the matter?
Oth. That handkerchief which I so loved and gave thee
Thou gavest to Cassio.
Des. No, by my life and soul!
Send for the man and ask him.
Oth. Sweet soul, take heed,
Take heed of perjury; thou art on thy deathbed.
Des. Ay, but not yet to die.
Oth. Yes, presently. 52
Therefore confess thee freely of thy sin;
For to deny each article with oath
Cannot remove nor choke the strong conception 55
That I do groan withal. Thou art to die.
Des. Then Lord have mercy on me!
Oth. I say amen.
Des. And have you mercy too! I never did
Offend you in my life; never loved Cassio
But with such general warranty of heaven 60
As I might love. I never gave him token.
Oth. By heaven, I saw my handkerchief in's hand!
O perjured woman! thou dost stone my heart,
And makest me call what I intend to do
A murder, which I thought a sacrifice. 65
I saw the handkerchief.
Des. He found it then.
I never gave it him. Send for him hither.
Let him confess a truth.
Oth. He hath confessed.
Des. What, my lord? 69
Oth. That he hath used thee.
Des. How? unlawfully?
Oth. Ay.
Des. He will not say so.
Oth. No, his mouth is stopped.
Honest Iago hath ta'en order for't.
Des. O, my fear interprets. What, is he dead?
Oth. Had all his hairs been lives, my great revenge
Had stomach for them all. 75
Des. Alas, he is betrayed, and I undone!
Oth. Out, strumpet! Weepst thou for him to my face?
Des. O, banish me, my lord, but kill me not!
Oth. Down, strumpet!
Des. Kill me tomorrow; let me live tonight! 80

5. alablaster: alabaster
8. minister: servant
13. relume: relight
32. forfend: forbid
63. stone: turn to stone
75. stomach: appetite or resentment

Oth. Nay, an you strive—
Des. But half an hour!
Oth. Being done, there is no pause.
Des. But while I say one prayer!
Oth. It is too late. *He smothers her.*
Emilia calls within, at the door.
Emil. My lord, my lord! What, ho, my lord, my lord!
Oth. What noise is this? Not dead? not yet quite dead? 85
I that am cruel am yet merciful;
I would not have thee linger in thy pain.
So, so.
Emil. [*Within*] What, ho! my lord, my lord!
Oth. Who's there?
Emil. [*Within*] O, good my lord, I would speak a word with you! 90
Oth. Yes.—'Tis Emilia.—By-and-by.—She's dead.—
'Tis like she comes to speak of Cassio's death:
The noise was high. Ha! no more moving?
Still as the grave.—Shall she come in? Were't good?—
I think she stirs again. No.—What's best to do? 95
If she come in, she'll sure speak to my wife.
My wife! my wife! what wife? I have no wife.
O, insupportable! O heavy hour!
Methinks it should be now a huge eclipse
Of sun and moon, and that the affrighted globe 100
Should yawn at alteration.
Emil. [*Within*] I do beseech you
That I may speak with you, O good my lord!
Oth. I had forgot thee. O, come in, Emilia.
Soft, by-and-by.—Let me the curtains draw.—
Where art thou? [*Opens the door.*]

Enter EMILIA.

What's the matter with thee now?
Emil. O my good lord, yonder's foul murder done!
Oth. What? Now? 107
Emil. But now, my lord.
Oth. It is the very error of the moon.
She comes more near the earth than she was wont
And makes men mad. 111
Emil. Cassio, my lord, hath killed a young Venetian
Called Roderigo.
Oth. Roderigo killed?
And Cassio killed?
Emil. No, Cassio is not killed.
Oth. Not Cassio killed? Then murder's out of tune,
And sweet revenge grows harsh. 116
Des. O, falsely, falsely murdered!
Emil. O Lord! what cry is that?
Oth. That? What?
Emil. Out and alas! that was my lady's voice.
Help! help, ho! help! O lady, speak again! 120
Sweet Desdemona! O sweet mistress, speak!
Des. A guiltless death I die.
Emil. O, who hath done this deed?
Des. Nobody—I myself. Farewell. 124
Commend me to my kind lord. O, farewell! *She dies.*
Oth. Why, how should she be murd'red?
Emil. Alas, who knows?
Oth. You heard her say herself, it was not I.
Emil. She said so. I must needs report a truth.
Oth. She's like a liar gone to burning hell!
'Twas I that killed her.
Emil. O, the more angel she, 130
And you the blacker devil!
Oth. She turned to folly, and she was a whore.
Emil. Thou dost belie her, and thou art a devil.
Oth. She was false as water.
Emil. Thou art rash as fire to say
That she was false. O, she was heavenly true! 135
Oth. Cassio did top her. Ask thy husband else.
O, I were damned beneath all depth in hell
But that I did proceed upon just grounds
To this extremity. Thy husband knew it all.
Emil. My husband? 140
Oth. Thy husband.
Emil. That she was false to wedlock?
Oth. Ay, with Cassio. Nay, had she been true,
If heaven would make me such another world
Of one entire and perfect chrysolite, 145
I'd not have sold her for it.
Emil. My husband?
Oth. Ay, 'twas he that told me first.
An honest man he is, and hates the slime
That sticks on filthy deeds.
Emil. My husband?
Oth. What needs this iterance, woman? I say, thy husband. 150
Emil. O mistress, villainy hath made mocks with love!
My husband say that she was false?
Oth. He, woman.
I say, thy husband. Dost understand the word?
My friend, thy husband; honest, honest Iago.
Emil. If he say so, may his pernicious soul 155
Rot half a grain a day! he lies to the heart.
She was too fond of her most filthy bargain.
Oth. Ha!
Emil. Do thy worst.
This deed of thine is no more worthy heaven 160

82. Being . . . pause: it's too late to stop now.
101. yawn . . . alteration: gape as the result of an earthquake caused by the cosmic upheaval
109. error: aberration (in wandering from her course)
132. folly: unchastity
134. false . . . water: proverbial, presumably because water assumes the shape of the container into which it is put
151. mocks: sport

Than thou wast worthy her.
Oth. Peace, you were best.
Emil. Thou hast not half the power to do me harm
As I have to be hurt. O gull! O dolt!
As ignorant as dirt! thou hast done a deed— 164
I care not for thy sword; I'll make thee known,
Though I lost twenty lives. Help! help, ho! help!
The Moor hath killed my mistress! Murder! murder!

Enter MONTANO, GRATIANO, IAGO, *and others.*

Mon. What is the matter? How now, General?
Emil. O, are you come, Iago? You have done well,
That men must lay their murders on your neck.
Gra. What is the matter? 171
Emil. Disprove this villain, if thou beest a man:
He says thou toldst him that his wife was false.
I know thou didst not; thou'rt not such a villain.
Speak, for my heart is full. 175
Iago. I told him what I thought, and told no more
Than what he found himself was apt and true.
Emil. But did you ever tell him she was false?
Iago. I did.
Emil. You told a lie, an odious damned lie! 180
Upon my soul, a lie! a wicked lie!
She false with Cassio? Did you say with Cassio?
Iago. With Cassio, mistress. Go to, charm your tongue.
Emil. I will not charm my tongue; I am bound to speak:
My mistress here lies murdered in her bed— 185
All. O heavens forfend!
Emil. And your reports have set the murder on.
Oth. Nay, stare not, masters. It is true indeed.
Gra. 'Tis a strange truth. 189
Mon. O monstrous act!
Emil. Villainy, villainy, villainy!
I think upon't, I think! I smell't! O villainy!
I thought so then. I'll kill myself for grief.
O villainy, villainy!
Iago. What, are you mad? I charge you get you home. 194
Emil. Good gentlemen, let me have leave to speak.
'Tis proper I obey him, but not now.
Perchance, Iago, I will ne'er go home.
Oth. O! O! O! *Falls on the bed.*
Emil. Nay, lay thee down and roar!
For thou hast killed the sweetest innocent 199
That e'er did lift up eye.
Oth. O, she was foul! [*Rises.*]
I scarce did know you, uncle. There lies your niece,
Whose breath, indeed, these hands have newly stopped.
I know this act shows horrible and grim.

Gra. Poor Desdemon! I am glad thy father's dead.
Thy match was mortal to him, and pure grief 205
Shore his old thread in twain. Did he live now,
This sight would make him do a desperate turn;
Yea, curse his better angel from his side,
And fall to reprobance.
Oth. 'Tis pitiful; but yet Iago knows 210
That she with Cassio hath the act of shame
A thousand times committed. Cassio confessed it;
And she did gratify his amorous works
With that recognizance and pledge of love
Which I first gave her; I saw it in his hand: 215
It was a handkerchief, an antique token
My father gave my mother.
Emil. O God! O heavenly pow'rs!
Iago. Zounds, hold your peace!
Emil. 'Twill out, 'twill out! I peace?
No, I will speak as liberal as the North. 220
Let heaven and men and devils, let them all,
All, all, cry shame against me, yet I'll speak.
Iago. Be wise, and get you home.
Emil. I will not.
[*Iago draws and threatens Emilia.*]
Gra. Fie!
Your sword upon a woman?
Emil. O thou dull Moor, that handkerchief thou speakst of 225
I found by fortune, and did give my husband;
For often with a solemn earnestness
(More than indeed belonged to such a trifle)
He begged of me to steal't.
Iago. Villainous whore!
Emil. She gave it Cassio? No, alas, I found it, 230
And I did give't my husband.
Iago. Filth, thou liest!
Emil. By heaven, I do not, I do not, gentlemen.
O murd'rous coxcomb! what should such a fool
Do with so good a wife?
Oth. Are there no stones in heaven 234
But what serves for the thunder? Precious villain!
The Moor runs at Iago, [*but is disarmed by Montano*]. *Iago kills his wife.*
Gra. The woman falls. Sure he hath killed his wife.
Emil. Ay, ay. O, lay me by my mistress' side.
Exit Iago.
Gra. He's gone, but his wife's killed.
Mon. 'Tis a notorious villain. Take you this weapon,
Which I have here recovered from the Moor. 240
Come, guard the door without. Let him not pass,

162–63. Thou . . . hurt: i.e., he can harm her body but not her soul.

206. Shore: cut
207. turn: act
209. reprobance: unregenerate damnation
214. recognizance: symbol
220. liberal: freely; **North:** north wind
239. notorious: notable

But kill him rather. I'll after that same villain,
For 'tis a damned slave.

Exeunt Montano and Gratiano [*with others. Manent Othello and Emilia*].

Oth. I am not valiant neither;
But every puny whipster gets my sword.
But why should honor outlive honesty? 245
Let it go all.

Emil. What did thy song bode, lady?
Hark, canst thou hear me? I will play the swan,
And die in music. [*Sings*] "Willow, willow, willow."
Moor, she was chaste; she loved thee, cruel Moor.
So come my soul to bliss as I speak true. 250
So speaking as I think, I die, I die. *She dies.*

Oth. I have another weapon in this chamber;
It is a sword of Spain, the ice-brook's temper.
O, here it is.—Uncle, I must come forth.

Gra. (*Within*) If thou attempt it, it will cost thee dear. 255
Thou hast no weapon, and perforce must suffer.

Oth. Look in upon me then and speak with me,
Or, naked as I am, I will assault thee.

[*Enter* GRATIANO.]

Gra. What is the matter?

Oth. Behold, I have a weapon.
A better never did itself sustain 260
Upon a soldier's thigh. I have seen the day
That with this little arm and this good sword
I have made my way through more impediments
Than twenty times your stop. But, O vain boast!
Who can control his fate? 'Tis not so now. 265
Be not afraid, though you do see me weaponed.
Here is my journey's end, here is my butt,
And very seamark of my utmost sail.
Do you go back dismayed? 'Tis a lost fear.
Man but a rush against Othello's breast, 270
And he retires. Where should Othello go?—
Now, how dost thou look now? O ill-starred wench!
Pale as thy smock! When we shall meet at compt,
This look of thine will hurl my soul from heaven,
And fiends will snatch at it. Cold, cold, my girl? 275
Even like thy chastity.—O cursed slave!
Whip me, ye devils,
From the possession of this heavenly sight!
Blow me about in winds! roast me in sulphur!

244. whipster: contemptible fellow
245. why . . . honesty: why should the reputation of honor outlive the reality?
253. ice-brook's temper: tempered in ice-cold water, as were some Spanish blades
258. naked: unarmed
267. butt: archery target; goal
268. seamark: mark of the ship's destination
269. lost: vain
270. rush: reed
273. compt: judgment
274. look: innocent expression

Wash me in steep-down gulfs of liquid fire! 280
O Desdemona, Desdemona! dead!
O! O! O!

Enter LODOVICO, CASSIO, MONTANO, *and* IAGO, *with* OFFICERS.

Lod. Where is this rash and most unfortunate man?

Oth. That's he that was Othello. Here I am. 284

Lod. Where is that viper? Bring the villain forth.

Oth. I look down towards his feet—but that's a fable.
If that thou beest a devil, I cannot kill thee.
[*Wounds Iago.*]

Lod. Wrench his sword from him.
[*Othello is disarmed.*]

Iago. I bleed, sir, but not killed.

Oth. I am not sorry neither. I'd have thee live;
For in my sense, 'tis happiness to die. 290

Lod. O thou Othello that wert once so good,
Fall'n in the practice of a damned slave,
What shall be said to thee?

Oth. Why, anything:
An honorable murderer, if you will;
For naught did I in hate, but all in honor. 295

Lod. This wretch hath part confessed his villainy.
Did you and he consent in Cassio's death?

Oth. Ay.

Cas. Dear General, I never gave you cause.

Oth. I do believe it, and I ask your pardon. 300
Will you, I pray, demand that demidevil
Why he hath thus ensnared my soul and body?

Iago. Demand me nothing. What you know, you know.
From this time forth I never will speak word. 304

Lod. What, not to pray?

Gra. Torments will ope your lips.

Oth. Well, thou dost best.

Lod. Sir, you shall understand what hath befall'n,
Which, as I think, you know not. Here is a letter
Found in the pocket of the slain Roderigo;
And here another. The one of them imports 310
The death of Cassio to be undertook
By Roderigo.

Oth. O villain!

Cas. Most heathenish and most gross!

Lod. Now here's another discontented paper
Found in his pocket too; and this, it seems, 315
Roderigo meant t' have sent this damned villain;
But that, belike, Iago in the interim
Came in and satisfied him.

Oth. O thou pernicious caitiff!—
How came you, Cassio, by that handkerchief
That was my wife's?

286. feet: to see whether he has cloven hooves
313. gross: flagrant

Cas. I found it in my chamber; 320
And he himself confessed but even now
That there he dropped it for a special purpose
Which wrought to his desire.
Oth. O fool! fool! fool!
Cas. There is besides in Roderigo's letter,
How he upbraids Iago that he made him 325
Brave me upon the watch; whereon it came
That I was cast; and even but now he spake,
After long seeming dead—Iago hurt him,
Iago set him on. 329
Lod. You must forsake this room and go with us.
Your power and your command is taken off,
And Cassio rules in Cyprus. For this slave,
If there be any cunning cruelty
That can torment him much and hold him long,
It shall be his. You shall close prisoner rest 335
Till that the nature of your fault be known
To the Venetian state. Come, bring away.
Oth. Soft you! a word or two before you go.
I have done the state some service, and they know't—
No more of that. I pray you, in your letters, 340
When you shall these unlucky deeds relate,
Speak of me as I am. Nothing extenuate,
Nor set down aught in malice. Then must you speak
Of one that loved not wisely, but too well;
Of one not easily jealous, but, being wrought, 345
Perplexed in the extreme; of one whose hand
(Like the base Indian) threw a pearl away
Richer than all his tribe; of one whose subdued eyes,
Albeit unused to the melting mood,
Drop tears as fast as the Arabian trees 350
Their med'cinable gum. Set you down this;
And say besides that in Aleppo once,
Where a malignant and a turbaned Turk
Beat a Venetian and traduced the state,
I took by the throat the circumcised dog 355
And smote him—thus. *He stabs himself.*
Lod. O bloody period!
Gra. All that's spoke is marred.
Oth. I kissed thee ere I killed thee. No way but this—
Killing myself, to die upon a kiss.
He [falls across Desdemona and] dies.
Cas. This did I fear, but thought he had no weapon; 360
For he was great of heart.
Lod. O Spartan dog,
More fell than anguish, hunger, or the sea!
Look on the tragic loading of this bed.
This is thy work. The object poisons sight;
Let it be hid. Gratiano, keep the house, 365
And seize upon the fortunes of the Moor,
For they succeed on you. To you, Lord Governor,
Remains the censure of this hellish villain.
The time, the place, the torture—O, enforce it!
Myself will straight aboard, and to the state 370
This heavy act with heavy heart relate.
Exeunt omnes.

326. **Brave:** challenge
345. **wrought:** worked upon
346. **Perplexed:** completely distracted
347. **the . . . Indian:** if this refers to some tale, it has not been identified. Possibly it means only an ignorant savage.
351. **med'cinable:** medicinal
357. **period:** ending
362. **fell:** fierce
365. **keep:** guard

Lear Crowned with Flowers

Engraved by one of the Brothers Dalziel.

The Tragedy of KING LEAR

INTRODUCTION

The first performance of *King Lear* probably occurred late in 1605, and the play apparently was presented at court during the following Christmas holidays. The first printing of the play, Quarto 1 of 1608, has an unusually descriptive title page: *M. William Shakespeare, His True Chronicle History of the Life and Death of King Lear and His Three Daughters. With the Unfortunate Life of Edgar, Son and Heir to the Earl of Gloucester, and His Sullen and Assumed Humor of Tom of Bedlam. As It Was Played before the King's Majesty at Whitehall upon St. Stephen's Night in Christmas Holidays. By His Majesty's Servants Playing Usually at the Globe on the Bankside.* This version, printed for Nathaniel Butter, whose shop was at the sign of the Pied Bull in St. Paul's churchyard, is known as the "Pied Bull Quarto." John Munro, in the introduction to his edition of *King Lear* (the London Shakespeare) suggests that the title page was made deliberately explicit to distinguish Shakespeare's play from an older play, *The True Chronicle History of King Leir,* which had been printed in 1605 as "lately acted." Shakespeare had found in the old *King Leir* plot elements that he reworked, but his play is a complete transformation of the original and has only superficial resemblances to it.

Shakespeare's tragedy, one of the most moving that he ever wrote, reaches such heights of emotional tension that some critics have maintained that it is impossible to represent it properly on the stage; the play, they believe, is more suitable to the library, where the imagination can supply the inadequacies of actors. This was Charles Lamb's opinion, and many later critics have agreed with him. To Lamb and those who share his views, the emotions are too intense for theatrical representation, the characters are conceived in terms that transcend normal human qualities, and the language exceeds that which is characteristic of the stage. In short, the play is a tragic poem, dark and intense, rather than a stage piece.

That the play is a grand and tragic poetic drama, one can concede, but that does not eliminate the possibility of its representation on the stage by human actors who can approximate the concepts that Shakespeare wrote into his lines. Both Granville-Barker and Tucker Brooke have pointed out that Shakespeare's play was designed for the stage and successfully performed there. It was a success on first production, and King James thought it a suitable play for court performance. Whatever his faults, Granville-Barker adds, James was a shrewd judge of good drama.

Tucker Brooke goes further, in an essay on "*King Lear* on the Stage," and contends that though the tragedy is conceived on a vast scale, it is not "a play apart, a voicing of lyric or philosophic rather than dramatic ideas." On the contrary, it is a drama that grafts aristocratic themes and emotions upon characters essentially bourgeois:

> Not only has he chosen to present under the tattered veil of mythical royalty a bourgeois family group; he has even dethroned all the conventional tragic passions and elevated to the highest place in the whole hierarchy of sin his detested petty vice of selfishness.

Even if one accepts this concept of *King Lear,* it does not follow that the play is any less cosmic in its sweeping power or less universal in its appeal. Lear in his person represents the eternal tragedy of age that has not acquired wisdom, and the play in essence is a study of Lear's re-education and purification. But Lear is not just a particular individual; the dramatist subsumes in his person the whole of the human race with those faults of vanity, rage, and selfishness that must be purged away before true wisdom can be attained. In the early scenes of the play the spectator or the reader forgets that Lear is a king of Britain. He is a rash, stubborn, impetuous, and spoiled old man who, by his folly, brings upon his head punishments that chasten him until, in the end, he is transfigured.

In its philosophic implications *King Lear* is pagan and pessimistic. No comfortable belief in the best of all possible worlds lightens this play. Man is in the hands of Fate, an implacable Fate that turns the wheel of Fortune mechanically. "As flies to wanton boys are we to the gods; / They kill us for their sport" is the comment of Gloucester, who voices the pagan doctrine of the play. Some biographers of Shakespeare have seen in *King Lear* a reflection of personal tragedy in the author's life, but we have no evidence for such a belief. *King Lear* may simply reflect the fatalistic and stoical attitudes that characterized much of the writing of the Jacobean period. "Men must endure / Their going hence, even as their coming hither; / Ripeness is all," Edgar observes in one of the passages that indicate the stoical acceptance of the decisions of Fate. It was a belief forced upon many men in this age of shifting fortunes and the rise and fall of reputations.

SOURCES, HISTORY, AND TEXT

The immediate source for Shakespeare's play was *The True Chronicle History of King Leir,* which was entered in the *Stationers' Register* as early as May 14, 1594, and finally printed in 1605, but the story was already familiar to English readers. Geoffrey of Monmouth told the tale of the old king and his three daughters in his *Historia Regum Britanniae,* which dates from about 1135; Raphael Holinshed includes the story as veritable history in his *Chronicles of England, Scotland, and Ireland* (1st ed., 1577; 2nd ed., 1587) and dates the reign of Lear as "the year of the world 3105"; Edmund Spenser in Book II of *The Faerie Queene* (1590) gives an account of Lear; and John Higgins in his additions to *The Mirror for Magistrates* (ed. of 1574) includes the Lear story as one of the tragedies. The subplot, dealing with the troubles of Gloucester, Shakespeare took from a story told in Sir Philip Sidney's *Arcadia* (1590).

One has only to compare the source material with Shakespeare's finished play to realize the skill that the dramatist displays in the composition of *King Lear*. For example, the subplot concerning the sufferings of old Gloucester at the hands of his grasping bastard son Edmund is something more than the conventional addition of bustle and action characteristic of Elizabethan plays, for it parallels the main plot and helps to intensify the emotional impact of Lear's plight without distracting from the theme of the drama. The employment of the Fool as a sort of chorus commenting on Lear's condition is another instance of Shakespeare's use of a conventional device of Elizabethan drama to reflect at times the vague thoughts flitting through the old king's mind and to add subtle emphasis to his tragedy.

King Lear was one of the earliest of Shakespeare's plays staged after the Restoration by Sir William Davenant, who revived it again in 1675. The tragedy was too overpowering for Restoration tastes, however, and Nahum Tate undertook to revise the plot to give it a happy ending, producing, in Hazelton Spencer's words, "the most notorious of all the Restoration perversions of Shakespeare." Tate, in his wisdom, decided that a love affair between Cordelia and Edgar was required to improve the play, and he took pride in an ending with "a success to the innocent distressed persons." Whatever later critics may think of Tate's atrocities, his version held the stage for a century and a half, though Garrick did modify Tate's play by replacing some portions with Shakespeare's original. Nevertheless, Tate's version remained the normal stage text until Charles W. Macready in 1838 returned Shakespeare's tragedy to the theatre. Although the play offers many problems in staging and interpretation, it has been constantly acted since Macready's day. Occasionally it has lent itself to eccentric staging. For example, a Canadian company in 1961 gave the play a prehistoric northern setting and dressed the cast like Eskimos to convey an idea of its dark, mysterious quality.

In the present edition we have followed the practice of most modern editors in using the version in the First Folio as the basic text, but we have adopted readings from Quarto 1 in passages requiring correction. The First Folio omitted approximately 300 lines found in Quarto 1 and added approximately 100 lines not appearing there. As is the practice of modern editors, we have restored these omitted lines.

The question of the source of the copy for Quarto 1 and the First Folio version has been the subject of much scholarly discussion, which is admirably summarized in the introduction to Munro's edition. After surveying the evidence, Munro concludes that Quarto 1 was produced by actors' reconstruction of the text from memory and that the Folio text was based on a copy of Quarto 1 corrected by a current playhouse promptbook. Two later quartos, printed in 1619 and 1655, have no independent authority.

Lear and the Fool in the Storm
Engraved by one of the Brothers Dalziel.

[Dramatis Personæ

LEAR, *King of Britain.*
KING OF FRANCE.
DUKE OF BURGUNDY.
DUKE OF CORNWALL, *Regan's husband.*
DUKE OF ALBANY, *Goneril's husband.*
EARL OF KENT.
EARL OF GLOUCESTER.
EDGAR, *Gloucester's son.*
EDMUND, *Gloucester's bastard son.*
CURAN, *a courtier.*
OLD MAN, *Gloucester's tenant.*
DOCTOR.
THE FOOL.
OSWALD, *Goneril's steward.*
A CAPTAIN *in Edmund's employ.*
GENTLEMEN.
A HERALD.
SERVANTS *of Cornwall.*

GONERIL, REGAN, CORDELIA, } *Lear's daughters.*

Knights in Lear's service, Officers, Messengers, Soldiers, Attendants.

Scene.—*Britain.*]

Tom o' Bedlam
From a broadside ballad.

The Tragedy of KING LEAR

ACT I

Scene I. [*Inside Lear's Palace.*]

Enter KENT, GLOUCESTER, *and* EDMUND [*in rear*].

Kent. I thought the King had more affected the Duke of Albany than Cornwall.

Glou. It did always seem so to us; but now, in the division of the kingdom, it appears not which of the Dukes he values most, for qualities are so weighed that curiosity in neither can make choice of either's moiety. 5

Kent. Is not this your son, my lord?

Glou. His breeding, sir, hath been at my charge. I have so often blushed to acknowledge him that now I am brazed to it. 10

Kent. I cannot conceive you.

Glou. Sir, this young fellow's mother could, whereupon she grew round-wombed, and had indeed, sir, a son for her cradle ere she had a husband for her bed. Do you smell a fault? 15

Kent. I cannot wish the fault undone, the issue of it being so proper.

Glou. But I have a son, sir, by order of law, some year elder than this, who yet is no dearer in my account. Though this knave came something saucily to the world before he was sent for, yet was his mother fair, there was good sport at his making, and the whoreson must be acknowledged.—Do you know this noble gentleman, Edmund? 20 25

Edm. [*Advancing*] No, my lord.

Glou. My Lord of Kent: remember him hereafter as my honorable friend.

Edm. My services to your lordship.

Kent. I must love you, and sue to know you better.

Edm. Sir, I shall study deserving. 31

Glou. He hath been out nine years, and away he shall again. (*Sound a sennet.*) The King is coming.

Enter one bearing a coronet, KING LEAR, CORNWALL, ALBANY, GONERIL, REGAN, CORDELIA, *and* ATTENDANTS.

Lear. Attend the lords of France and Burgundy, Gloucester. 35

Glou. I shall, my lord.

[*Exeunt Gloucester and Edmund.*]

Lear. Meantime we shall express our darker purpose.
Give me the map there. Know that we have divided
In three our kingdom, and 'tis our fast intent
To shake all cares and business from our age, 40
Conferring them on younger strengths while we
Unburdened crawl toward death. Our son of Cornwall,

1. more affected: favored
6. curiosity: consideration in minute detail
7. moiety: portion
11. brazed: brazened
12. conceive: understand
18. proper: handsome
21. knave: fellow (jocular)
24. whoreson: bastard (also jocular)
30. sue: endeavor
S.D. 32. sennet: a distinctive trumpet call announcing an important arrival
34. Attend: escort them in
37. darker: less obvious
39. fast intent: firm intention

And you, our no less loving son of Albany,
We have this hour a constant will to publish
Our daughters' several dowers, that future strife 45
May be prevented now. The princes, France and Burgundy,
Great rivals in our youngest daughter's love,
Long in our court have made their amorous sojourn,
And here are to be answered. Tell me, my daughters
(Since now we will divest us both of rule, 50
Interest of territory, cares of state),
Which of you shall we say doth love us most?
That we our largest bounty may extend
Where nature doth with merit challenge. Goneril,
Our eldest-born, speak first. 55

Gon. Sir, I love you more than word can wield the matter;
Dearer than eyesight, space, and liberty;
Beyond what can be valued, rich or rare;
No less than life, with grace, health, beauty, honor;
As much as child e'er loved, or father found; 60
A love that makes breath poor, and speech unable.
Beyond all manner of so much I love you.

Cor. [*Aside*] What shall Cordelia speak? Love, and be silent.

Lear. Of all these bounds, even from this line to this,
With shadowy forests and with champaigns riched,
With plenteous rivers and wide-skirted meads, 66
We make thee lady. To thine and Albany's issues
Be this perpetual.—What says our second daughter,
Our dearest Regan, wife of Cornwall? Speak.

Reg. I am made 70
Of that self metal as my sister,
And prize me at her worth. In my true heart
I find she names my very deed of love,
Only she comes too short, that I profess
Myself an enemy to all other joys 75
Which the most precious square of sense possesses,
And find I am alone felicitate
In your dear Highness' love.

Cor. [*Aside*] Then poor Cordelia!
And yet not so, since I am sure my love's
More ponderous than my tongue. 80

Lear. To thee and thine hereditary ever
Remain this ample third of our fair kingdom,
No less in space, validity, and pleasure
Than that conferred on Goneril.—Now, our joy,
Although our last and least; to whose young love 85
The vines of France and milk of Burgundy
Strive to be interessed; what can you say to draw
A third more opulent than your sisters? Speak.

Cor. Nothing, my lord.

Lear. Nothing? 90

Cor. Nothing.

Lear. Nothing will come of nothing. Speak again.

Cor. Unhappy that I am, I cannot heave
My heart into my mouth. I love your Majesty
According to my bond, no more nor less. 95

Lear. How, how, Cordelia? Mend your speech a little,
Lest you may mar your fortunes.

Cor. Good my lord,
You have begot me, bred me, loved me; I
Return those duties back as are right fit,
Obey you, love you, and most honor you. 100
Why have my sisters husbands, if they say
They love you all? Happily, when I shall wed,
That lord whose hand must take my plight shall carry
Half my love with him, half my care and duty.
Sure I shall never marry like my sisters, 105
To love my father all.

Lear. But goes thy heart with this?

Cor. Ay, good my lord.

Lear. So young, and so untender?

Cor. So young, my lord, and true.

Lear. Let it be so! thy truth then be thy dower!
For, by the sacred radiance of the sun, 111
The mysteries of Hecate and the night;
By all the operation of the orbs
From whom we do exist and cease to be;
Here I disclaim all my paternal care, 115
Propinquity and property of blood,
And as a stranger to my heart and me
Hold thee from this forever. The barbarous Scythian,
Or he that makes his generation messes
To gorge his appetite, shall to my bosom 120
Be as well neighbored, pitied, and relieved,
As thou my sometime daughter.

Kent. Good my liege—

Lear. Peace, Kent!

44. constant will: synonymous with **fast intent**
45. several: respective
51. Interest: rightful claim
54. nature . . . challenge: natural affection makes a claim as strong as that of merit.
65. champaigns: fertile plains
71. self: same
73. very deed: exact description
76. square: measure (foot rule); **sense:** sensibility
77. felicitate: made happy
81. hereditary: descendants
83. validity: worth
85. least: youngest and smallest. The Quarto reads "last not least."
87. be interessed: have a legal right in
92. Nothing . . . nothing: proverbial: *Ex nihilo nihil fit.*
95. bond: obligation
102. Happily: perhaps
103. plight: plighted troth
112. Hecate: one of the aspects of the goddess Diana as the nocturnal moon and ruler of witches
113. orbs: stars
116. Propinquity . . . blood: close kinship and possession of the same blood
119. makes . . . messes: eats his young
121. neighbored: treated kindly
122. sometime: erstwhile, now disowned

Come not between the dragon and his wrath.
I loved her most, and thought to set my rest 125
On her kind nursery.—Hence and avoid my sight!—
So be my grave my peace as here I give
Her father's heart from her! Call France! Who stirs?
Call Burgundy! Cornwall and Albany,
With my two daughters' dowers digest the third;
Let pride, which she calls plainness, marry her. 131
I do invest you jointly with my power,
Preëminence, and all the large effects
That troop with majesty. Ourself, by monthly course,
With reservation of an hundred knights 135
By you to be sustained, shall our abode
Make with you by due turn. Only we shall retain
The name, and all the additions to a king. The sway,
Revenue, execution of the rest,
Beloved sons, be yours; which to confirm, 140
This coronet part between you.

Kent. Royal Lear,
Whom I have ever honored as my king,
Loved as my father, as my master followed,
As my great patron thought on in my prayers—

Lear. The bow is bent and drawn, make from the shaft. 145

Kent. Let it fall rather, though the fork invade
The region of my heart! Be Kent unmannerly
When Lear is mad. What wouldst thou do, old man?
Thinkest thou that duty shall have dread to speak
When power to flattery bows? To plainness honor's bound 150
When majesty falls to folly. Reserve thy state
And in thy best consideration check
This hideous rashness. Answer my life my judgment,
Thy youngest daughter does not love thee least,
Nor are those empty-hearted whose low sounds 155
Reverb no hollowness.

Lear. Kent, on thy life, no more!

Kent. My life I never held but as a pawn
To wage against thine enemies, nor fear to lose it,
Thy safety being motive.

Lear. Out of my sight!

Kent. See better, Lear, and let me still remain 160
The true blank of thine eye.

Lear. Now by Apollo—

Kent. Now by Apollo, King,
Thou swearest thy gods in vain.

Lear. O vassal! miscreant!
[*Reaches for his sword.*]

Alb., Corn. Dear sir, forbear!

Kent. Kill thy physician and thy fee bestow 165
Upon the foul disease. Revoke thy gift,
Or, whilst I can vent clamor from my throat,
I'll tell thee thou dost evil.

Lear. Hear me, recreant!
On thine allegiance, hear me! 169
That thou hast sought to make us break our vows,
Which we durst never yet, and with strained pride
To come betwixt our sentence and our power,
Which nor our nature nor our place can bear,
Our potency made good, take thy reward.
Five days we do allot thee for provision 175
To shield thee from disasters of the world,
And on the sixth to turn thy hated back
Upon our kingdom. If, on the tenth day following,
Thy banished trunk be found in our dominions,
The moment is thy death. Away! By Jupiter, 180
This shall not be revoked.

Kent. Fare thee well, King. Since thus thou wilt appear,
Freedom lives hence, and banishment is here.
[*To Cordelia*] The gods to their dear shelter take thee, maid,
That justly thinkest and hast most rightly said! 185
[*To Regan and Goneril*] And your large speeches may your deeds approve,
That good effects may spring from words of love.
Thus Kent, O princes, bids you all adieu;
He'll shape his old course in a country new. *Exit.*

Flourish. Enter GLOUCESTER, *with* FRANCE *and* BURGUNDY; ATTENDANTS.

Glou. Here's France and Burgundy, my noble lord. 190

Lear. My Lord of Burgundy,
We first address toward you, who with this king
Hath rivalled for our daughter. What in the least
Will you require in present dower with her,
Or cease your quest of love?

Bur. Most royal Majesty, 195
I crave no more than hath your Highness offered,
Nor will you tender less.

Lear. Right noble Burgundy,
When she was dear to us, we did hold her so,
But now her price is fallen. Sir, there she stands.
If aught within that little seeming substance, 200

125–26. thought . . . nursery: counted on her affection as my refuge
131. Let . . . her: let her pride be her sole dowry.
138. additions: titles
145. make . . . shaft: avoid the arrow; don't make yourself the target of my wrath.
156. Reverb: reverberate
161. true blank: dead center of a target; that is, "the main focus of your attention when you need sound advice"
163. miscreant: faithless wretch
168. recreant: traitor
170. That: since
174. Our . . . good: in proof of my authority
179. trunk: body
186. approve: demonstrate
S.D. 189. flourish: fanfare
197. tender: offer
198. hold: regard
200. little . . . substance: quantity that does not look like much

Or all of it, with our displeasure pieced,
And nothing more, may fitly like your Grace,
She's there, and she is yours.

Bur. I know no answer.

Lear. Will you, with those infirmities she owes,
Unfriended, new adopted to our hate, 205
Dowered with our curse, and strangered with our oath,
Take her, or leave her?

Bur. Pardon me, royal sir.
Election makes not up in such conditions.

Lear. Then leave her, sir; for by the power that made me,
I tell you all her wealth. [*To France*] For you, great King, 210
I would not from your love make such a stray
To match you where I hate; therefore beseech you
To avert your liking a more worthier way
Than on a wretch whom nature is ashamed
Almost to acknowledge hers.

France. This is most strange, 215
That she whom even but now was your best object,
The argument of your praise, balm of your age,
The best, the dearest, should in this trice of time
Commit a thing so monstrous to dismantle
So many folds of favor. Sure her offense 220
Must be of such unnatural degree
That monsters it, or your fore-vouched affection
Fall into taint; which to believe of her
Must be a faith that reason without miracle
Should never plant in me.

Cor. I yet beseech your Majesty
(If for I want that glib and oily art 226
To speak and purpose not, since what I well intend,
I'll do it before I speak), that you make known
It is no vicious blot, murder, or foulness,
No unchaste action or dishonored step, 230
That hath deprived me of your grace and favor;
But even for want of that for which I am richer,
A still-soliciting eye, and such a tongue
As I am glad I have not, though not to have it
Hath lost me in your liking.

Lear. Better thou 235
Hadst not been born than not to have pleased me better.

France. Is it but this—a tardiness in nature
Which often leaves the history unspoke
That it intends to do? My Lord of Burgundy,
What say you to the lady? Love's not love 240
When it is mingled with regards that stand
Aloof from the entire point. Will you have her?
She is herself a dowry.

Bur. Royal King,
Give but that portion which yourself proposed,
And here I take Cordelia by the hand, 245
Duchess of Burgundy.

Lear. Nothing! I have sworn; I am firm.

Bur. I am sorry then you have so lost a father
That you must lose a husband.

Cor. Peace be with Burgundy!
Since that respect and fortunes are his love, 250
I shall not be his wife.

France. Fairest Cordelia, that art most rich, being poor;
Most choice, forsaken; and most loved, despised!
Thee and thy virtues here I seize upon.
Be it lawful I take up what's cast away. 255
Gods, gods! 'tis strange that from their coldest neglect
My love should kindle to inflamed respect.
Thy dowerless daughter, King, thrown to my chance,
Is queen of us, of ours, and our fair France.
Not all the dukes of waterish Burgundy 260
Can buy this unprized precious maid of me.
Bid them farewell, Cordelia, though unkind.
Thou losest here, a better where to find.

Lear. Thou hast her, France; let her be thine; for we
Have no such daughter, nor shall ever see 265
That face of hers again. Therefore be gone
Without our grace, our love, our benison.
Come, noble Burgundy.

Flourish. Exeunt Lear, Burgundy, [*Cornwall, Albany, Gloucester, and Attendants*].

France. Bid farewell to your sisters. 269

Cor. The jewels of our father, with washed eyes
Cordelia leaves you. I know you what you are;
And, like a sister, am most loath to call
Your faults as they are named. Love well our father.
To your professed bosoms I commit him;
But yet, alas, stood I within his grace, 275
I would prefer him to a better place!
So farewell to you both.

Gon. Prescribe not us our duty.

Reg. Let your study
Be to content your lord, who hath received you 279
At Fortune's alms. You have obedience scanted,

201. **pieced:** supplemented
202. **like:** please
204. **owes:** possesses
208. **Election:** choice; **makes . . . up:** cannot be made
217. **argument:** subject
218. **trice:** moment; literally, in the time needed to make one tug, from Middle English *tricen*
222. **monsters it:** is worthy only of a monster; **fore-vouched:** previously affirmed
223. **Fall . . . taint:** come to be doubted
226. **for:** because
233. **still-soliciting:** ever begging
235. **lost . . . liking:** lost my place in your affection
237. **tardiness . . . nature:** natural reluctance
242. **entire:** perfect and complete in itself; i.e., the only point really relevant
267. **grace:** favor
270. **washed:** tearful
276. **prefer:** recommend
280. **At . . . alms:** as a trifling gift from Fortune

And well are worth the want that you have wanted.

Cor. Time shall unfold what plighted cunning hides,
Who covers faults, at last with shame derides.
Well may you prosper!

France. Come, my fair Cordelia.

Exeunt France and Cordelia.

Gon. Sister, it is not little I have to say of 285
what most nearly appertains to us both. I think our father will hence tonight.

Reg. That's most certain, and with you; next month with us.

Gon. You see how full of changes his age is. 290
The observation we have made of it hath not been little. He always loved our sister most, and with what poor judgment he hath now cast her off appears too grossly.

Reg. 'Tis the infirmity of his age; yet he 295
hath ever but slenderly known himself.

Gon. The best and soundest of his time hath been but rash; then must we look from his age to receive, not alone the imperfections of long-engraffed condition, but therewithal the unruly waywardness 300
that infirm and choleric years bring with them.

Reg. Such unconstant starts are we like to have from him as this of Kent's banishment.

Gon. There is further compliment of leave-taking between France and him. Pray you let's hit 305
together. If our father carry authority with such disposition as he bears, this last surrender of his will but offend us.

Reg. We shall further think of it.

Gon. We must do something, and i' the heat. 310

Exeunt.

Scene II. [*Inside Gloucester's Castle.*]

Enter [Edmund *the*] Bastard, [*a letter in his hand*].

Edm. Thou, Nature, art my goddess; to thy law
My services are bound. Wherefore should I
Stand in the plague of custom and permit
The curiosity of nations to deprive me, 4
For that I am some twelve or fourteen moonshines
Lag of a brother? Why bastard? wherefore base?
When my dimensions are as well compact,
My mind as generous, and my shape as true,
As honest madam's issue? Why brand they us 9
With base? with baseness? bastardy? base, base?
Who, in the lusty stealth of nature, take
More composition and fierce quality
Than doth, within a dull, stale, tired bed,
Go to the creating a whole tribe of fops
Got 'tween asleep and wake? Well then, 15
Legitimate Edgar, I must have your land.
Our father's love is to the bastard Edmund
As to the legitimate. Fine word, "legitimate"!
Well, my legitimate, if this letter speed
And my invention thrive, Edmund the base 20
Shall top the legitimate; I grow; I prosper.
Now, gods, stand up for bastards!

Enter Gloucester.

Glou. Kent banished thus? and France in choler parted?
And the King gone tonight? prescribed his power?
Confined to exhibition? All this done 25
Upon the gad? Edmund, how now? What news?

Edm. So please your lordship, none.

[*Puts away the letter.*]

Glou. Why so earnestly seek you to put up that letter?

Edm. I know no news, my lord.

Glou. What paper were you reading? 30

Edm. Nothing, my lord.

Glou. No? What needed then that terrible dispatch of it into your pocket? The quality of nothing hath not such need to hide itself. Let's see. Come, if it be nothing, I shall not need spectacles. 35

Edm. I beseech you, sir, pardon me. It is a letter from my brother that I have not all o'erread; and for so much as I have perused, I find it not fit for your o'erlooking.

Glou. Give me the letter, sir. 40

Edm. I shall offend, either to detain or give it. The contents, as in part I understand them, are to blame.

Glou. Let's see, let's see!

281. **well . . . wanted:** deserve the like unnatural treatment from your husband
282. **plighted:** pleated; concealed by intricate pleats
299. **long-engraffed:** firmly attached for a long time
302. **unconstant starts:** capricious motions
304. **compliment:** ceremony
305–6. **hit together:** agree on how to handle him
307–8. **this . . . us:** i.e., the division of the kingdom between them will only cause them trouble, since along with Cordelia's share they will have to assume her burden of filial duty.
310. **i' . . . heat:** while the iron's hot
3. **Stand . . . custom:** endure conventional decree; accept the imposition of traditional custom
4. **curiosity . . . nations:** the fine discriminations of human law
6. **Lag of:** behind
7. **well compact:** well put together
8. **generous:** gentlemanly
9. **honest:** respectable
12. **composition:** strength; **fierce quality:** energy
23. **parted:** departed
24. **prescribed:** limited
25. **exhibition:** mere subsistence
26. **Upon . . . gad:** on the spur of the moment

Edm. I hope, for my brother's justification, he wrote this but as an essay or taste of my virtue. 45

Glou. (*Reads*) This policy and reverence of age makes the world bitter to the best of our times; keeps our fortunes from us till our oldness cannot relish them. I begin to find an idle and fond bondage in the oppression of aged tyranny, who sways, not as it hath power, 50 but as it is suffered. Come to me, that of this I may speak more. If our father would sleep till I waked him, you should enjoy half his revenue forever, and live the beloved of your brother. EDGAR.

Hum! Conspiracy? "Sleep till I waked him, 55 you should enjoy half his revenue." My son Edgar! Had he a hand to write this? a heart and brain to breed it in? When came you to this? Who brought it?

Edm. It was not brought me, my lord; there's 60 the cunning of it. I found it thrown in at the casement of my closet.

Glou. You know the character to be your brother's?

Edm. If the matter were good, my lord, I 65 durst swear it were his; but in respect of that, I would fain think it were not.

Glou. It is his.

Edm. It is his hand, my lord, but I hope his heart is not in the contents. 70

Glou. Hath he never before sounded you in this business?

Edm. Never, my lord. But I have heard him oft maintain it to be fit that, sons at perfect age, and fathers declined, the father should be as ward 75 to the son, and the son manage his revenue.

Glou. O villain, villain! His very opinion in the letter! Abhorred villain! Unnatural, detested, brutish villain! worse than brutish! Go, sirrah, seek him. I'll apprehend him. Abominable villain! Where is 80 he?

Edm. I do not well know, my lord. If it shall please you to suspend your indignation against my brother till you can derive from him better testimony of his intent, you should run a certain course; 85 where, if you violently proceed against him, mistaking his purpose, it would make a great gap in your own honor and shake in pieces the heart of his obedience. I dare pawn down my life for him that he hath writ this to feel my affection to your 90 honor, and to no other pretense of danger.

Glou. Think you so?

Edm. If your honor judge it meet, I will place you where you shall hear us confer of this and by an auricular assurance have your satisfaction, and 95 that without any further delay than this very evening.

Glou. He cannot be such a monster.

Edm. Nor is not, sure.

Glou. To his father, that so tenderly and 100 entirely loves him. Heaven and earth! Edmund, seek him out; wind me into him, I pray you; frame the business after your own wisdom. I would unstate myself to be in a due resolution.

Edm. I will seek him, sir, presently, convey 105 the business as I shall find means, and acquaint you withal.

Glou. These late eclipses in the sun and moon portend no good to us. Though the wisdom of nature can reason it thus and thus, yet nature 110 finds itself scourged by the sequent effects. Love cools, friendship falls off, brothers divide. In cities, mutinies; in countries, discord; in palaces, treason; and the bond cracked 'twixt son and father. This villain of mine comes under the prediction; 115 there's son against father: the King falls from bias of nature; there's father against child. We have seen the best of our time. Machinations, hollowness, treachery, and all ruinous disorders follow us disquietly to our graves. Find out this villain, Edmund; 120 it shall lose thee nothing; do it carefully. And the noble and true-hearted Kent banished! his offense, honesty! 'Tis strange. *Exit.*

Edm. This is the excellent foppery of the world, that, when we are sick in fortune, often the 125 surfeits of our own behavior, we make guilty of our disasters the sun, the moon, and stars; as if we were villains on necessity; fools by heavenly compulsion; knaves, thieves, and treachers by spherical predominance; drunkards, liars, and adulterers 130 by an enforced obedience of planetary influence; and all that we are evil in, by a divine thrusting on. An admirable evasion of whoremaster man, to lay his goatish disposition to the charge of a star! My fa-

45. essay: trial
46–47. This . . . times: the habit of deferring to age embitters the lives of young men like us.
49. idle . . . fond: synonymous: "foolish"
50. sways: rules
51. suffered: permitted
62. closet: private chamber
63. character: handwriting
71. sounded you: tested your attitude
78. Unnatural: unfilial
85. run . . . course: be certain of following the right course
91. pretense . . . danger: dangerous intent
93. meet: suitable
95. auricular: aural; through the ear
102. wind . . . him: find out what is in his mind
103–4. unstate myself: give up all I have
104. in . . . resolution: satisfied of the truth
105. presently: immediately
109–11. Though . . . effects: though science offers explanations for these phenomena which deny their effect on human fate, human conduct still shows their influence.
116–17. bias . . . nature: natural inclination
124. foppery: foolishness
129. treachers: traitors
132. divine . . . on: supernatural incitement
134. goatish: lustful

ther compounded with my mother under the 135
Dragon's Tail, and my nativity was under Ursa Major, so that it follows I am rough and lecherous. Fut! I should have been that I am had the maidenliest star in the firmament twinkled on my bastardizing.

Enter EDGAR.

Pat! he comes, like the catastrophe of the old 140
comedy. My cue is villainous melancholy, with a sigh like Tom o' Bedlam. O, these eclipses do portend these divisions! Fa, sol, la, mi.

Edg. How now, brother Edmund? What serious contemplation are you in? 145

Edm. I am thinking, brother, of a prediction I read this other day, what should follow these eclipses.

Edg. Do you busy yourself with that?

Edm. I promise you, the effects he writes of succeed unhappily: as of unnaturalness between 150
the child and the parent; death, dearth, dissolutions of ancient amities; divisions in state, menaces and maledictions against king and nobles; needless diffidences, banishment of friends, dissipation of cohorts, nuptial breaches, and I know not what. 155

Edg. How long have you been a sectary astronomical?

Edm. When saw you my father last?

Edg. The night gone by.

Edm. Spake you with him? 160

Edg. Ay, two hours together.

Edm. Parted you in good terms? Found you no displeasure in him by word nor countenance?

Edg. None at all.

Edm. Bethink yourself wherein you may 165
have offended him; and at my entreaty forbear his presence until some little time hath qualified the heat of his displeasure, which at this instant so rageth in him that with the mischief of your person it would scarcely allay. 170

Edg. Some villain hath done me wrong.

Edm. That's my fear. I pray you have a continent forbearance till the speed of his rage goes slower; and, as I say, retire with me to my lodging, from whence I will fitly bring you to hear my lord 175
speak. Pray ye, go! There's my key. If you do stir abroad, go armed.

Edg. Armed, brother?

Edm. Brother, I advise you to the best. I am no honest man if there be any good meaning to- 180
ward you. I have told you what I have seen and heard; but faintly, nothing like the image and horror of it. Pray you, away!

Edg. Shall I hear from you anon? 184

Edm. I do serve you in this business. *Exit Edgar.*

A credulous father! and a brother noble,
Whose nature is so far from doing harms
That he suspects none; on whose foolish honesty
My practices ride easy! I see the business.
Let me, if not by birth, have lands by wit; 190
All with me's meet that I can fashion fit.

Exit.

Scene III. [*Inside the Duke of Albany's Palace.*]

Enter GONERIL *and* [OSWALD, *her*] STEWARD.

Gon. Did my father strike my gentleman for chiding of his fool?

Osw. Ay, madam.

Gon. By day and night, he wrongs me! Every hour
He flashes into one gross crime or other
That sets us all at odds. I'll not endure it. 5
His knights grow riotous, and himself upbraids us
On every trifle. When he returns from hunting,
I will not speak with him. Say I am sick.
If you come slack of former services,
You shall do well; the fault of it I'll answer. 10

[*Horns within.*]

Osw. He's coming, madam; I hear him.

Gon. Put on what weary negligence you please,
You and your fellows. I'd have it come to question.
If he distaste it, let him to my sister,
Whose mind and mine I know in that are one, 15
Not to be overruled. Idle old man,
That still would manage those authorities
That he hath given away! Now, by my life,
Old fools are babes again, and must be used
With checks as flatteries, when they are seen abused.
Remember what I have said.

Osw. Very well, madam. 21

Gon. And let his knights have colder looks among you.

136. **Dragon's Tail:** the descending node of the moon or a planet
140. **catastrophe:** final tragedy which ends the play
142. **Tom o' Bedlam:** a madman released from Bethlehem Hospital (Bedlam) with a license to beg for his living
149–50. **succeed:** follow
153–54. **diffidences:** distrustings
154–55. **dissipation . . . cohorts:** disbandment of troops
156–57. **sectary astronomical:** believer in astrology
163. **countenance:** behavior
169. **the . . . person:** your bodily harm
172. **continent:** self-contained
175. **fitly:** at a suitable time
182. **image . . . horror:** horrible actuality (a hendiadys)
189. **practices:** stratagems
191. **All's . . . fit:** anything suits me that I can turn to good use.
4. **gross:** great; **crime:** offense
9. **come . . . services:** offer less service than formerly
13. **question:** open discussion
14. **distaste:** dislike
20. **With . . . abused:** with rebukes instead of flatteries when flattery has been excessive

What grows of it, no matter. Advise your fellows so.
I would breed from hence occasions, and I shall,
That I may speak. I'll write straight to my sister 25
To hold my very course. Prepare for dinner.
Exeunt.

Scene IV. [*Inside the Duke of Albany's Palace.*]

Enter KENT, [*disguised*].

Kent. If but as well I other accents borrow,
That can my speech diffuse, my good intent
May carry through itself to that full issue
For which I razed my likeness. Now, banished Kent,
If thou canst serve where thou dost stand condemned, 5
So may it come, thy master, whom thou lovest,
Shall find thee full of labors.

Horns within. Enter LEAR, [KNIGHTS,] *and* ATTENDANTS.

Lear. Let me not stay a jot for dinner; go get it ready. [*Exit an Attendant.*] How now? What art thou? 10

Kent. A man, sir.

Lear. What dost thou profess? What wouldst thou with us?

Kent. I do profess to be no less than I seem, to serve him truly that will put me in trust, to 15 love him that is honest, to converse with him that is wise and says little, to fear judgment, to fight when I cannot choose, and to eat no fish.

Lear. What art thou?

Kent. A very honest-hearted fellow, and as 20 poor as the King.

Lear. If thou beest as poor for a subject as he is for a king, thou art poor enough. What wouldst thou?

Kent. Service.

Lear. Who wouldst thou serve? 25

Kent. You.

Lear. Dost thou know me, fellow?

Kent. No, sir, but you have that in your countenance which I would fain call master.

Lear. What's that? 30

Kent. Authority.

Lear. What services canst thou do?

Kent. I can keep honest counsel, ride, run, mar a curious tale in telling it, and deliver a plain message bluntly. That which ordinary men are fit for, I 35 am qualified in, and the best of me is diligence.

Lear. How old art thou?

Kent. Not so young, sir, to love a woman for singing, nor so old to dote on her for anything. I have years on my back forty-eight. 40

Lear. Follow me; thou shalt serve me. If I like thee no worse after dinner, I will not part from thee yet. Dinner, ho, dinner! Where's my knave? my fool? Go you and call my fool hither.
[*Exit an Attendant.*]

Enter [OSWALD *the*] STEWARD.

You, you, sirrah, where's my daughter? 45

Osw. So please you— *Exit.*

Lear. What says the fellow there? Call the clotpoll back. [*Exit a Knight.*] Where's my fool, ho? I think the world's asleep.

[*Enter* KNIGHT.]

How now? Where's that mongrel? 50

Knight. He says, my lord, your daughter is not well.

Lear. Why came not the slave back to me when I called him?

Knight. Sir, he answered me in the roundest 55 manner, he would not.

Lear. He would not?

Knight. My lord, I know not what the matter is, but to my judgment your Highness is not entertained with that ceremonious affection as you 60 were wont. There's a great abatement of kindness appears as well in the general dependants as in the Duke himself also and your daughter.

Lear. Ha! sayest thou so?

Knight. I beseech you pardon me, my lord, 65 if I be mistaken, for my duty cannot be silent when I think your Highness wronged.

Lear. Thou but rememberest me of mine own conception. I have perceived a most faint neglect of late, which I have rather blamed as mine own jeal- 70 ous curiosity than as a very pretense and purpose of unkindness. I will look further into it. But where's my fool? I have not seen him this two days.

Knight. Since my young lady's going into France, sir, the fool hath much pined away. 75

24. **occasions:** excuses (to correct her father)
25. **straight:** immediately
2. **diffuse:** disorder
4. **razed . . . likeness:** destroyed my true appearance (with a disguise)
12. **profess:** follow as a profession
18. **eat . . . fish:** observe prescribed fast days
34. **curious:** complicated
47. **clotpoll:** blockhead
55. **roundest:** bluntest
59–60. **entertained:** treated
60. **ceremonious affection:** demonstration of due respect
68. **rememberest:** remindest
70–71. **jealous curiosity:** suspicious vigilance
71. **very:** actual

Lear. No more of that; I have noted it well. Go you and tell my daughter I would speak with her. [*Exit Knight*.] Go you, call hither my fool.
[*Exit an Attendant*.]

[*Re-*]*enter* STEWARD.

O, you, sir, you! Come you hither, sir. Who am I, sir?
Osw. My lady's father. 80
Lear. "My lady's father"? My lord's knave! You whoreson dog! you slave! you cur!
Osw. I am none of these, my lord! I beseech your pardon.
Lear. Do you bandy looks with me, you 85 rascal? [*Strikes him*.]
Osw. I'll not be strucken, my lord.
Kent. Nor tripped neither, you base football player? [*Trips him*.]
Lear. I thank thee, fellow. Thou servest me, 90 and I'll love thee.
Kent. Come, sir, arise, away! I'll teach you differences. Away, away! If you will measure your lubber's length again, tarry; but away! Go to! Have you wisdom? So. [*Exit Oswald*.]
Lear. Now, my friendly knave, I thank thee. 96

Enter FOOL.

There's earnest of thy service. [*Gives Kent money*.]
Fool. Let me hire him too. Here's my coxcomb.
[*Offers Kent his cap*.]
Lear. How now, my pretty knave? How dost thou?
Fool. Sirrah, you were best take my cox- 100 comb.
Kent. Why, fool?
Fool. Why? For taking one's part that's out of favor. Nay, an thou canst not smile as the wind sits, thou'lt catch cold shortly. There, take my 105 coxcomb! Why, this fellow has banished two on's daughters, and did the third a blessing against his will. If thou follow him, thou must needs wear my coxcomb.—How now, nuncle? Would I had two coxcombs and two daughters! 110
Lear. Why, my boy?
Fool. If I gave them all my living, I'd keep my coxcombs myself. There's mine! beg another of thy daughters.
Lear. Take heed, sirrah—the whip. 115
Fool. Truth's a dog must to kennel; he must be whipped out, when the Lady Brach may stand by the fire and stink.
Lear. A pestilent gall to me!
Fool. Sirrah, I'll teach thee a speech. 120
Lear. Do.
Fool. Mark it, nuncle.

Have more than thou showest,
Speak less than thou knowest,
Lend less than thou owest, 125
Ride more than thou goest,
Learn more than thou trowest,
Set less than thou throwest;
Leave thy drink and thy whore,
And keep in-a-door, 130
And thou shalt have more
Than two tens to a score.

Kent. This is nothing, fool.
Fool. Then 'tis like the breath of an unfee'd lawyer —you gave me nothing for it. Can you make 135 no use of nothing, nuncle?
Lear. Why, no, boy. Nothing can be made out of nothing.
Fool. [*To Kent*] Prithee tell him, so much the rent of his land comes to. He will not believe 140 a fool.
Lear. A bitter fool!
Fool. Dost thou know the difference, my boy, between a bitter fool and a sweet one?
Lear. No, lad; teach me. 145
Fool. That lord that counselled thee
To give away thy land,
Come place him here by me—
Do thou for him stand.
The sweet and bitter fool 150
Will presently appear;
The one in motley here,
The other found out there.
Lear. Dost thou call me fool, boy?
Fool. All thy other titles thou hast given 155 away; that thou wast born with.
Kent. This is not altogether fool, my lord.

85. bandy looks: trade look for look; regard me as an equal
88–89. base . . . player: football was despised as a game played by boys and the lower classes rather than by gentlemen.
92–93. differences: social distinctions
93. lubber: lout
94. Go to: be off!
97. earnest: advance payment in part to seal an agreement
98. coxcomb: the conventional headgear of a clown, shaped like a cock's comb
104–5. an . . . shortly: if you can't curry favor with the great, you'll soon suffer for it.
109. nuncle: a contraction of "mine uncle"
116–18. Truth's . . . stink: Truth is ordered out of the house, while fawning flattery, personified as a hound, may enjoy the fire no matter how she smells. This is the Folio reading, emended by many editors to "Lady the brach" because "Lady" was a common name for a bitch.
125. owest: ownest
126. goest: walkest
127. Learn . . . trowest: don't believe everything you hear
128. Set . . . throwest: don't risk all your money on one throw
134. breath: words; advice
152. motley: multicolored clothing
157. altogether fool: completely foolish. The Fool pretends he has been accused of monopolizing foolishness, and denies it.

Fool. No, faith; lords and great men will not let me. If I had a monopoly out, they would have part on't. And ladies too, they will not let me have 160 all the fool to myself; they'll be snatching. Nuncle, give me an egg, and I'll give thee two crowns.

Lear. What two crowns shall they be?

Fool. Why, after I have cut the egg i' the middle and eat up the meat, the two crowns of the 165 egg. When thou clovest thy crown i' the middle and gavest away both parts, thou borest thine ass on thy back o'er the dirt. Thou hadst little wit in thy bald crown when thou gavest thy golden one away. If I speak like myself in this, let him be whipped 170 that first finds it so.

[*Sings*] Fools had ne'er less grace in a year,
For wise men are grown foppish;
And know not how their wits to wear,
Their manners are so apish. 175

Lear. When were you wont to be so full of songs, sirrah?

Fool. I have used it, nuncle, ever since thou madest thy daughters thy mother; for when thou gavest them the rod, and puttest down thine 180 own breeches,

[*Sings*] Then they for sudden joy did weep,
And I for sorrow sung,
That such a king should play bopeep
And go the fools among. 185

Prithee, nuncle, keep a schoolmaster that can teach thy fool to lie. I would fain learn to lie.

Lear. An you lie, sirrah, we'll have you whipped.

Fool. I marvel what kin thou and thy daughters are. They'll have me whipped for speaking 190 true; thou'lt have me whipped for lying; and sometimes I am whipped for holding my peace. I had rather be any kind o' thing than a fool! And yet I would not be thee, nuncle. Thou hast pared thy wit o' both sides and left nothing i' the middle. 195 Here comes one o' the parings.

Enter GONERIL.

Lear. How now, daughter? What makes that frontlet on? You are too much o' late i' the frown.

Fool. Thou wast a pretty fellow when thou hadst no need to care for her frowning. Now thou 200 art an O without a figure. I am better than thou art now: I am a fool, thou art nothing. [*To Goneril*] Yes, forsooth, I will hold my tongue. So your face bids me, though you say nothing. Mum, mum!

He that keeps nor crust nor crum, 205
Weary of all, shall want some.—

[*Pointing at Lear*] That's a shealed peasecod.

Gon. Not only, sir, this your all-licensed fool,
But other of your insolent retinue
Do hourly carp and quarrel, breaking forth 210
In rank and not-to-be-endured riots. Sir,
I had thought, by making this well known unto you,
To have found a safe redress; but now grow fearful,
By what yourself too late have spoke and done,
That you protect this course, and put it on 215
By your allowance; which if you should, the fault
Would not scape censure, nor the redresses sleep,
Which, in the tender of a wholesome weal,
Might in their working do you that offense
Which else were shame, that then necessity 220
Must call discreet proceeding.

Fool. For you know, nuncle,
The hedge-sparrow fed the cuckoo so long
That it's had it head bit off by it young.
So out went the candle, and we were left darkling.

Lear. Are you our daughter? 226

Gon. I would you would make use of your good wisdom,
Whereof I know you are fraught, and put away
These dispositions which of late transport you
From what you rightly are. 230

Fool. May not an ass know when the cart draws the horse? Whoop, Jug, I love thee!

Lear. Does any here know me? This is not Lear.
Does Lear walk thus? speak thus? Where are his eyes?
Either his notion weakens, or his discernings 235
Are lethargied—Sleeping or waking? Ha! Sure 'tis not so!
Who is it that can tell me who I am?

Fool. Lear's shadow.

Lear. I would learn that; for, by the marks of sovereignty,
Knowledge, and reason, I should be false persuaded
I had daughters. 241

Fool. Which they will make an obedient father.

Lear. Your name, fair gentlewoman?

Gon. This admiration, sir, is much o' the savor

167–68. **borest . . . dirt:** like the man in Æsop's fable
169–71. **If . . . so:** if my plain speech is foolish, yet whip the fool who first recognizes the truth of what I say (i.e., Lear himself).
172–73. **Fools . . . foppish:** fools have little favor nowadays because wise men behave just as foolishly.
175. **apish:** foolishly affected
184. **play bopeep:** conceal himself (his royalty) like the player of a child's game
197–98. **frontlet:** forehead band; frown
201. **O:** nothing
207. **shealed:** shelled
215. **put it on:** encourage it
216. **allowance:** indulgence
216–21. **the . . . proceeding:** the error would not go uncriticized nor unpunished for the safety of the commonwealth, perhaps in a manner that would be a shameful abuse of you were it not that discretion made it necessary.
224. **it:** its, a common form of the genitive
228. **fraught:** freighted
229. **dispositions:** capricious moods
232. **Jug:** a diminutive form of "Joan"—a common feminine name
235. **notion:** understanding
244. **admiration:** pretense of wonder

Of other your new pranks. I do beseech you 245
To understand my purposes aright.
As you are old and reverend, you should be wise.
Here do you keep a hundred knights and squires;
Men so disordered, so debauched, and bold 249
That this our court, infected with their manners,
Shows like a riotous inn. Epicurism and lust
Make it more like a tavern or a brothel
Than a graced palace. The shame itself doth speak
For instant remedy. Be then desired
By her that else will take the thing she begs 255
A little to disquantity your train,
And the remainders that shall still depend
To be such men as may besort your age,
Which know themselves and you.

Lear. Darkness and devils!
Saddle my horses! Call my train together! 260
Degenerate bastard, I'll not trouble thee;
Yet have I left a daughter.

Gon. You strike my people, and your disordered rabble
Make servants of their betters.

Enter ALBANY.

Lear. Woe that too late repents!—O, sir, are you come? 265
Is it your will? Speak, sir!—Prepare my horses.
Ingratitude, thou marble-hearted fiend,
More hideous when thou showest thee in a child
Than the sea-monster!

Alb. Pray, sir, be patient.

Lear. [*To Goneril*] Detested kite, thou liest!
My train are men of choice and rarest parts, 271
That all particulars of duty know
And in the most exact regard support
The worships of their name.—O most small fault,
How ugly didst thou in Cordelia show! 275
Which, like an engine, wrenched my frame of nature
From the fixed place; drew from my heart all love
And added to the gall. O Lear, Lear, Lear!
Beat at this gate that let thy folly in 279
[*Beats his forehead with his fist.*]
And thy dear judgment out! Go, go, my people.

Alb. My lord, I am guiltless, as I am ignorant
Of what hath moved you.

Lear. It may be so, my lord.
Hear, Nature, hear! dear goddess, hear!
Suspend thy purpose, if thou didst intend
To make this creature fruitful. 285
Into her womb convey sterility;
Dry up in her the organs of increase;
And from her derogate body never spring
A babe to honor her! If she must teem,
Create her child of spleen, that it may live 290
And be a thwart disnatured torment to her.
Let it stamp wrinkles in her brow of youth,
With cadent tears fret channels in her cheeks,
Turn all her mother's pains and benefits
To laughter and contempt, that she may feel 295
How sharper than a serpent's tooth it is
To have a thankless child! Away, away! *Exit.*

Alb. Now, gods that we adore, whereof comes this?

Gon. Never afflict yourself to know more of it,
But let his disposition have that scope 300
As dotage gives it.

[*Re-*]*enter* LEAR.

Lear. What, fifty of my followers at a clap?
Within a fortnight?

Alb. What's the matter, sir?

Lear. I'll tell thee. [*To Goneril*] Life and death! I am ashamed 304
That thou hast power to shake my manhood thus;
That these hot tears, which break from me perforce,
Should make thee worth them. Blasts and fogs upon thee!
The untented woundings of a father's curse
Pierce every sense about thee!—Old fond eyes,
Beweep this cause again, I'll pluck ye out, 310
And cast you, with the waters that you loose,
To temper clay. Yea, is it come to this?
Ha! Let it be so. I have another daughter,
Who I am sure is kind and comfortable.
When she shall hear this of thee, with her nails 315
She'll flay thy wolvish visage. Thou shalt find
That I'll resume the shape which thou dost think
I have cast off for ever.
Exeunt [*Lear, Kent, and Attendants*].

Gon. Do you mark that, my lord?

Alb. I cannot be so partial, Goneril, 320
To the great love I bear you—

Gon. Pray you, content.—What, Oswald, ho!
[*To the Fool*] You, sir, more knave than fool, after your master!

Fool. Nuncle Lear, nuncle Lear, tarry!
Take the fool with thee. 325

A fox, when one has caught her,
And such a daughter,
Should sure to the slaughter,
If my cap would buy a halter.
So the fool follows after. *Exit.*

257. **depend:** remain as dependents
258. **besort:** become
274. **worships:** dignities; honors
276. **engine:** machine; probably an instrument of torture like the rack
288. **derogate:** debased
293. **cadent:** falling
308. **untented:** unprobable; too deep to be reached with a "tent" (a probe used to cleanse wounds)
329. **halter:** noose

Gon. This man hath had good counsel! A hundred knights? 331
'Tis politic and safe to let him keep
At point a hundred knights; yes, that on every dream,
Each buzz, each fancy, each complaint, dislike,
He may enguard his dotage with their powers 335
And hold our lives in mercy.—Oswald, I say!
Alb. Well, you may fear too far.
Gon. Safer than trust too far.
Let me still take away the harms I fear,
Not fear still to be taken. I know his heart.
What he hath uttered I have writ my sister. 340
If she sustain him and his hundred knights,
When I have showed the unfitness—

Enter STEWARD.

How now, Oswald?
What, have you writ that letter to my sister?
Osw. Yes, madam. 344
Gon. Take you some company, and away to horse!
Inform her full of my particular fear,
And thereto add such reasons of your own
As may compact it more. Get you gone,
And hasten your return. [*Exit Oswald.*] No, no, my lord!
This milky gentleness and course of yours, 350
Though I condemn not, yet, under pardon,
You are much more at task for want of wisdom
Than praised for harmful mildness.
Alb. How far your eyes may pierce I cannot tell.
Striving to better, oft we mar what's well. 355
Gon. Nay then—
Alb. Well, well; the event.
Exeunt.

Scene V. [*A courtyard of the Duke of Albany's Palace.*]

Enter LEAR, KENT, *and* FOOL.

Lear. Go you before to Gloucester with these letters. Acquaint my daughter no further with anything you know than comes from her demand out of the letter. If your diligence be not speedy, I shall be there afore you. 5
Kent. I will not sleep, my lord, till I have delivered your letter. *Exit.*

Fool. If a man's brains were in's heels, were it not in danger of kibes?
Lear. Ay, boy. 10
Fool. Then I prithee be merry. Thy wit shall not go slipshod.
Lear. Ha, ha, ha!
Fool. Shalt see thy other daughter will use thee kindly; for though she's as like this as a crab's 15 like an apple, yet I can tell what I can tell.
Lear. What canst tell, boy?
Fool. She'll taste as like this as a crab does to a crab. Thou canst tell why one's nose stands i' the middle on's face? 20
Lear. No.
Fool. Why, to keep one's eyes of either side's nose, that what a man cannot smell out, he may spy into.
Lear. I did her wrong.
Fool. Canst tell how an oyster makes his 25 shell?
Lear. No.
Fool. Nor I neither; but I can tell why a snail has a house.
Lear. Why? 30
Fool. Why, to put's head in; not to give it away to his daughters, and leave his horns without a case.
Lear. I will forget my nature. So kind a father!—Be my horses ready?
Fool. Thy asses are gone about 'em. The rea- 35 son why the seven stars are no mo than seven is a pretty reason.
Lear. Because they are not eight?
Fool. Yes indeed. Thou wouldst make a good fool.
Lear. To take it again perforce! Monster in- 40 gratitude!
Fool. If thou wert my fool, nuncle, I'd have thee beaten for being old before thy time.
Lear. How's that?
Fool. Thou shouldst not have been old till 45 thou hadst been wise.
Lear. O, let me not be mad, not mad, sweet heaven!
Keep me in temper; I would not be mad!

[*Enter a* GENTLEMAN.]

How now? Are the horses ready?
Gent. Ready, my lord. 50
Lear. Come, boy.
Fool. She that's a maid now, and laughs at my departure,
Shall not be a maid long, unless things be cut shorter.
Exeunt.

333. At point: fully armed
336. in mercy: at his mercy
338. still: always
346. particular: personal
348. compact . . . more: add to its substance
351. under pardon: pardon me for saying so
352. at task: blameful
357. the event: let's see what will happen.

9. kibes: chilblains
11–12. Thy . . . slipshod: since you lack brains, you will never need to wear slippers to protect them from chilblains.
18. crab: crab apple
36. seven stars: the Pleiades; **mo:** more
40. To . . . perforce: Lear contemplates regaining his kingdom by force.

ACT II

Scene I. [*A courtyard inside Gloucester's Castle.*]

Enter [EDMUND *the*] BASTARD *and* CURAN, *severally.*

Edm. Save thee, Curan.

Cur. And you, sir. I have been with your father, and given him notice that the Duke of Cornwall and Regan his Duchess will be here with him this night.

Edm. How comes that? 5

Cur. Nay, I know not. You have heard of the news abroad—I mean the whispered ones, for they are yet but ear-bussing arguments?

Edm. Not I. Pray you, what are they?

Cur. Have you heard of no likely wars toward 'twixt the Dukes of Cornwall and Albany? 10

Edm. Not a word.

Cur. You may do, then, in time. Fare you well, sir. *Exit.*

Edm. The Duke be here tonight? The better! best!
This weaves itself perforce into my business. 15
My father hath set guard to take my brother;
And I have one thing, of a queasy question,
Which I must act. Briefness and fortune, work!
Brother, a word! Descend! Brother, I say!

Enter EDGAR.

My father watches. O sir, fly this place! 20
Intelligence is given where you are hid.
You have now the good advantage of the night.
Have you not spoken 'gainst the Duke of Cornwall?
He's coming hither; now, i' the night, i' the haste,
And Regan with him. Have you nothing said 25
Upon his party 'gainst the Duke of Albany?
Advise yourself.

Edg. I am sure on't, not a word.

Edm. I hear my father coming. Pardon me!
In cunning I must draw my sword upon you. 29
Draw, seem to defend yourself; now quit you well.—
Yield! Come before my father. Light, ho, here!
Fly, brother.—Torches, torches!—So farewell.
Exit Edgar.

Some blood drawn on me would beget opinion
Of my more fierce endeavor. [*Stabs his arm.*] I have seen drunkards
Do more than this in sport.—Father, father!— 35
Stop, stop! No help?

Enter GLOUCESTER, *and* SERVANTS *with torches.*

Glou. Now, Edmund, where's the villain?

Edm. Here stood he in the dark, his sharp sword out,
Mumbling of wicked charms, conjuring the moon
To stand auspicious mistress.

Glou. But where is he? 39

Edm. Look, sir, I bleed.

Glou. Where is the villain, Edmund?

Edm. Fled this way, sir. When by no means he could—

Glou. Pursue him, ho! Go after. [*Exeunt some Servants.*] By no means what?

Edm. Persuade me to the murder of your lordship;
But that I told him the revenging gods
'Gainst parricides did all the thunder bend; 45
Spoke with how manifold and strong a bond
The child was bound to the father—sir, in fine,
Seeing how loathly opposite I stood
To his unnatural purpose, in fell motion
With his prepared sword he charges home 50
My unprovided body, lanched mine arm;
And when he saw my best alarumed spirits,
Bold in the quarrel's right, roused to the encounter,
Or whether gasted by the noise I made,
Full suddenly he fled.

Glou. Let him fly far. 55
Not in this land shall he remain uncaught;
And found—dispatch. The noble Duke my master,
My worthy arch and patron, comes tonight.
By his authority I will proclaim it,
That he which finds him shall deserve our thanks,
Bringing the murderous coward to the stake; 61
He that conceals him, death.

Edm. When I dissuaded him from his intent

1. Save: God bless
8. ear-bussing: ear-kissing; whispered
10–11. toward: in prospect
17. queasy question: ticklish nature
27. Advise yourself: consider carefully
30. quit you well: defend yourself

33–34. beget . . . endeavor: convince that I have fought fiercely
39. stand . . . mistress: favor his fortune
49. fell: deadly
51. unprovided: undefended; **lanched:** wounded
54. gasted: terrified
57. found—dispatch: kill on sight
58. arch . . . patron: chief patron

And found him pight to do it, with curst speech
I threatened to discover him. He replied, 65
"Thou unpossessing bastard, dost thou think,
If I would stand against thee, would the reposal
Of any trust, virtue, or worth in thee
Make thy words faithed? No. What I should deny
(As this I would; ay, though thou didst produce 70
My very character), I'd turn it all
To thy suggestion, plot, and damned practice;
And thou must make a dullard of the world,
If they not thought the profits of my death
Were very pregnant and potential spirits 75
To make thee seek it."

Glou. O strange and fastened villain!
Would he deny his letter, said he? I never got him.

Tucket within.

Hark, the Duke's trumpets! I know not why he comes.
All ports I'll bar; the villain shall not scape;
The Duke must grant me that. Besides, his picture
I will send far and near, that all the kingdom 81
May have due note of him, and of my land,
Loyal and natural boy, I'll work the means
To make thee capable.

Enter CORNWALL, REGAN *and* ATTENDANTS.

Corn. How now, my noble friend? Since I came hither 85
(Which I can call but now) I have heard strange news.

Reg. If it be true, all vengeance comes too short
Which can pursue the offender. How dost, my lord?

Glou. O madam, my old heart is cracked, it's cracked!

Reg. What, did my father's godson seek your life?
He whom my father named? Your Edgar? 91

Glou. O lady, lady, shame would have it hid!

Reg. Was he not companion with the riotous knights
That tended upon my father?

Glou. I know not, madam. 'Tis too bad, too bad!

Edm. Yes, madam, he was of that consort. 96

Reg. No marvel then though he were ill affected.
'Tis they have put him on the old man's death,
To have the expense and waste of his revenues.
I have this present evening from my sister 100
Been well informed of them, and with such cautions
That, if they come to sojourn at my house,
I'll not be there.

Corn. Nor I, assure thee, Regan.
Edmund, I hear that you have shown your father
A childlike office.

Edm. 'Twas my duty, sir. 105

Glou. He did bewray his practice, and received
This hurt you see, striving to apprehend him.

Corn. Is he pursued?

Glou. Ay, my good lord.

Corn. If he be taken, he shall never more 109
Be feared of doing harm. Make your own purpose,
How in my strength you please. For you, Edmund,
Whose virtue and obedience doth this instant
So much commend itself, you shall be ours.
Natures of such deep trust we shall much need;
You we first seize on.

Edm. I shall serve you, sir, 115
Truly, however else.

Glou. For him I thank your Grace.

Corn. You know not why we came to visit you—

Reg. Thus out of season, threading dark-eyed night.
Occasions, noble Gloucester, of some prize,
Wherein we must have use of your advice. 120
Our father he hath writ, so hath our sister,
Of differences, which I best thought it fit
To answer from our home. The several messengers
From hence attend dispatch. Our good old friend,
Lay comforts to your bosom, and bestow 125
Your needful counsel to our businesses,
Which craves the instant use.

Glou. I serve you, madam.
Your Graces are right welcome.

Exeunt. Flourish.

64. **pight:** determined; **curst:** angry
65. **discover:** denounce
69. **faithed:** credited
72. **suggestion:** temptation; **practice:** stratagem
75. **pregnant . . . spirits:** pressing and powerful incitements
76. **strange:** unnatural; **fastened:** confirmed
77. **got:** fathered
S.D. 77. **Tucket:** trumpet signal for troops to move
83. **natural:** (1) illegitimate; (2) natural in filial devotion
84. **capable:** sufficient; wealthy, as Gloucester's heir
97. **though:** if; **ill affected:** evilly inclined
106. **bewray:** expose
110–11. **Make . . . please:** my power is at your pleasure.
116. **Truly . . . else:** faithfully at least (if not usefully)
119. **prize:** importance
123. **from:** away from

Scene II. [*Without the gates of Gloucester's Castle.*]

Enter KENT *and* [OSWALD *the*] STEWARD, *severally.*

Osw. Good dawning to thee, friend. Art of this house?

Kent. Ay.

Osw. Where may we set our horses?

Kent. I' the mire. 5

Osw. Prithee, if thou lovest me, tell me.

Kent. I love thee not.

Osw. Why then, I care not for thee.

Kent. If I had thee in Lipsbury Pinfold, I would make thee care for me. 10

Osw. Why dost thou use me thus? I know thee not.

Kent. Fellow, I know thee.

Osw. What dost thou know me for?

Kent. A knave, a rascal, an eater of broken meats; a base, proud, shallow, beggarly, three-suited, 15 hundred-pound, filthy, worsted-stocking knave; a lily-livered, action-taking, whoreson, glass-gazing, superserviceable, finical rogue; one-trunk-inheriting slave; one that wouldst be a bawd in way of good service, and art nothing but the composition of 20 a knave, beggar, coward, pander, and the son and heir of a mongrel bitch; one whom I will beat into clamorous whining if thou denyst the least syllable of thy addition.

Osw. Why, what a monstrous fellow art thou, 25 thus to rail on one that's neither known of thee nor knows thee!

Kent. What a brazen-faced varlet art thou, to deny thou knowest me! Is it two days ago since I tripped up thy heels and beat thee before the King? 30 [*Draws his sword.*] Draw, you rogue! for, though it be night, yet the moon shines. I'll make a sop o' the moonshine of you. You whoreson cullionly barbermonger, draw!

Osw. Away! I have nothing to do with thee. 35

Kent. Draw, you rascal! You come with letters against the King, and take Vanity the puppet's part against the royalty of her father. Draw, you rogue, or I'll so carbonado your shanks! Draw, you rascal! Come your ways! 40

Osw. Help, ho! murder! help!

Kent. Strike, you slave! Stand, rogue! Stand, you neat slave! Strike! [*Beats him.*]

Osw. Help, ho! murder! murder!

Enter EDMUND, *with his rapier drawn.*

Edm. How now? What's the matter? 45
Parts [*them*].

Kent. With you, goodman boy, if you please! Come, I'll flesh ye! Come on, young master!

Enter GLOUCESTER, CORNWALL, REGAN, SERVANTS.

Glou. Weapons? arms? What's the matter here?

Corn. Keep peace, upon your lives!
He dies that strikes again. What is the matter? 50

Reg. The messengers from our sister and the King.

Corn. What is your difference? Speak.

Osw. I am scarce in breath, my lord.

Kent. No marvel, you have so bestirred your valor. You cowardly rascal, nature disclaims in 55 thee; a tailor made thee.

Corn. Thou art a strange fellow. A tailor make a man?

Kent. A tailor, sir: a stonecutter or a painter could not have made him so ill, though they had been 60 but two hours at the trade.

Corn. Speak yet, how grew your quarrel?

Osw. This ancient ruffian, sir, whose life I have spared
At suit of his grey beard—

Kent. Thou whoreson zed! thou unnecessary 65 letter! My lord, if you'll give me leave, I will tread this unbolted villain into mortar and daub the wall of a jakes with him. "Spare my grey beard," you wagtail?

Corn. Peace, sirrah! 70
You beastly knave, know you no reverence?

Kent. Yes, sir, but anger hath a privilege.

Corn. Why art thou angry?

Kent. That such a slave as this should wear a sword,
Who wears no honesty. Such smiling rogues as these,
Like rats, oft bite the holy cords atwain 76
Which are too intrinse to unloose; smooth every passion
That in the natures of their lords rebel,
Being oil to fire, snow to the colder moods;
Renege, affirm, and turn their halcyon beaks 80
With every gale and vary of their masters,
Knowing naught (like dogs) but following.
A plague upon your epileptic visage!
Smile you my speeches, as I were a fool?
Goose, if I had you upon Sarum Plain, 85
I'd drive ye cackling home to Camelot.

9. **Lipsbury Pinfold:** probably, "in my jaws," "in my power." A **pinfold** is a cattle pen; **Lipsbury** may mean "Liptown."
17. **action-taking:** cowardly, relying on legal instead of manly defense
18. **superserviceable:** officious; **finical:** foppish; **one-trunk-inheriting:** owning but one pair of trunk hose
24. **thy addition:** the designations I have indicated
26. **rail on:** scold
32–33. **make . . . you:** puncture you so that your body sops up the moonlight
33. **cullionly:** base
33–34. **barbermonger:** dandy
37. **Vanity . . . puppet:** Lady Vanity, a morality character; i.e., Goneril
39. **carbonado:** slash like a **carbonado** for broiling
40. **Come . . . ways:** come on
43. **neat:** dandified
47. **flesh ye:** give you your first taste of blood (from the practice of "fleshing" dogs and hawks for hunting)
55–56. **disclaims . . . thee:** denies having created thee
64. **At . . . of:** on account of
65. **zed:** the letter "z"
67. **unbolted:** unadulterated; complete
68. **jakes:** privy
77. **intrinse:** intricate
80. **halcyon:** a seabird which it was believed would turn with the wind if hung up by the beak
84. **Smile you:** do you laugh at
85. **Sarum Plain:** Salisbury Plain, near the site of the legendary Camelot, which was inhabited by flocks of geese

Corn. What, art thou mad, old fellow?
Glou. How fell you out? Say that.
Kent. No contraries hold more antipathy
Than I and such a knave. 90
Corn. Why dost thou call him knave? What is his fault?
Kent. His countenance likes me not.
Corn. No more perchance does mine, nor his, nor hers.
Kent. Sir, 'tis my occupation to be plain:
I have seen better faces in my time 95
Than stands on any shoulder that I see
Before me at this instant.
Corn. This is some fellow
Who, having been praised for bluntness, doth affect
A saucy roughness, and constrains the garb
Quite from his nature. He cannot flatter, he, 100
An honest mind and plain, he must speak truth:
An they will take it, so; if not, he's plain.
These kind of knaves I know which in this plainness
Harbor more craft and more corrupter ends
Than twenty silly-ducking observants 105
That stretch their duties nicely.
Kent. Sir, in good faith, in sincere verity,
Under the allowance of your great aspect,
Whose influence, like the wreath of radiant fire 109
On flickering Phœbus' front—
Corn. What meanest by this?
Kent. To go out of my dialect, which you discommend so much. I know, sir, I am no flatterer. He that beguiled you in a plain accent was a plain knave, which, for my part, I will not be, though I should win your displeasure to entreat me to it. 115
Corn. What was the offense you gave him?
Osw. I never gave him any.
It pleased the King his master very late
To strike at me, upon his misconstruction; 119
When he, compact, and flattering his displeasure,
Tripped me behind; being down, insulted, railed
And put upon him such a deal of man
That worthied him, got praises of the King
For him attempting who was self-subdued;
And, in the fleshment of this dread exploit, 125
Drew on me here again.

Kent. None of these rogues and cowards
But Ajax is their fool.
Corn. Fetch forth the stocks!
You stubborn ancient knave, you reverend braggart,
We'll teach you—
Kent. Sir, I am too old to learn.
Call not your stocks for me. I serve the King, 130
On whose employment I was sent to you.
You shall do small respect, show too bold malice
Against the grace and person of my master,
Stocking his messenger.
Corn. Fetch forth the stocks! As I have life and honor, 135
There shall he sit till noon.
Reg. Till noon? Till night, my lord, and all night too!
Kent. Why, madam, if I were your father's dog,
You should not use me so.
Reg. Sir, being his knave, I will.
Corn. This is a fellow of the selfsame color 140
Our sister speaks of. Come, bring away the stocks!
Stocks are brought out.
Glou. Let me beseech your Grace not to do so.
His fault is much, and the good King his master
Will check him for it. Your purposed low correction
Is such as basest and contemnedest wretches 145
For pilferings and most common trespasses
Are punished with. The King must take it ill
That he, so slightly valued in his messenger,
Should have him thus restrained.
Corn. I'll answer that.
Reg. My sister may receive it much more worse,
To have her gentleman abused, assaulted, 151
For following her affairs. Put in his legs.
[*Kent is put in the stocks.*]
Come, my good lord, away.
Exeunt [*all but Gloucester and Kent*].
Glou. I am sorry for thee, friend. 'Tis the Duke's pleasure,
Whose disposition, all the world well knows, 155
Will not be rubbed nor stopped. I'll entreat for thee.
Kent. Pray do not, sir. I have watched and traveled hard.
Some time I shall sleep out, the rest I'll whistle.
A good man's fortune may grow out at heels.
Give you good morrow! 160
Glou. The Duke's to blame in this; 'twill be ill taken. *Exit.*
Kent. Good King, that must approve the common saw,

92. likes: pleases
99–100. constrains . . . nature: falsifies his nature by overacting the part
102. so: so much the better
105. silly-ducking observants: low-bowing flunkies
106. nicely: meticulously
115. win . . . it: overcome your displeasure so that you sued for my service
119. upon . . . misconstruction: because he misunderstood an action of mine
120. compact: acting in accord with the King
122. put . . . man: pretended so much heroism
123. worthied him: made him seem worthy
125. in . . . of: excited by

127. Ajax . . . fool: i.e., they boast themselves as superior to the hero Ajax
133. grace . . . person: honorable person
140. color: kind
149. answer: take responsibility for
156. rubbed: hindered
157. watched: remained sleepless
162. approve: demonstrate; **saw:** maxim

Thou out of heaven's benediction comest
To the warm sun!
Approach, thou beacon to this under globe, 165
That by thy comfortable beams I may
Peruse this letter. Nothing almost sees miracles
But misery. I know 'tis from Cordelia,
Who hath most fortunately been informed
Of my obscured course—and [*Reads*] "shall find time 170
From this enormous state, seeking to give
Losses their remedies"—All weary and o'erwatched,
Take vantage, heavy eyes, not to behold
This shameful lodging.
Fortune, good night; smile once more, turn thy wheel. 175

Sleeps.

[Scene III. *Open country in the neighborhood of Gloucester's Castle.*]

Enter EDGAR.

Edg. I heard myself proclaimed,
And by the happy hollow of a tree
Escaped the hunt. No port is free, no place
That guard and most unusual vigilance
Does not attend my taking. Whiles I may scape, 5
I will preserve myself; and am bethought
To take the basest and most poorest shape
That ever penury, in contempt of man,
Brought near to beast. My face I'll grime with filth,
Blanket my loins, elf all my hair in knots, 10
And with presented nakedness outface
The winds and persecutions of the sky.
The country gives me proof and precedent
Of Bedlam beggars, who, with roaring voices,
Strike in their numbed and mortified bare arms 15
Pins, wooden pricks, nails, sprigs of rosemary;
And with this horrible object, from low farms,
Poor pelting villages, sheepcotes, and mills, 18
Sometime with lunatic bans, sometime with prayers,
Enforce their charity. "Poor Turlygod! poor Tom!"
That's something yet! Edgar I nothing am.

Exit.

[Scene IV. *Without the gates of Gloucester's Castle; Kent in the stocks.*]

Enter LEAR, FOOL *and* GENTLEMAN.

Lear. 'Tis strange that they should so depart from home,
And not send back my messenger.
Gent. As I learned,
The night before there was no purpose in them
Of this remove.
Kent. Hail to thee, noble master!
Lear. Ha! 5
Makest thou this shame thy pastime?
Kent. No, my lord.
Fool. Ha, ha! he wears cruel garters. Horses are tied by the head, dogs and bears by the neck, monkeys by the loins, and men by the legs. When a man's over-lusty at legs, then he wears wooden 10 netherstocks.
Lear. What's he that hath so much thy place mistook
To set thee here?
Kent. It is both he and she—
Your son and daughter.
Lear. No. 15
Kent. Yes.
Lear. No, I say.
Kent. I say yea.
Lear. No, no, they would not!
Kent. Yes, they have. 20
Lear. By Jupiter, I swear no!
Kent. By Juno, I swear ay!
Lear. They durst not do it;
They could not, would not do it. 'Tis worse than murder
To do upon respect such violent outrage.
Resolve me with all modest haste which way 25
Thou mightst deserve or they impose this usage,
Coming from us.
Kent. My lord, when at their home
I did commend your Highness' letters to them,

163–64. out . . . sun: i.e., from the blessed shade to the sun's full heat
167–68. Nothing . . . misery: none come closer to believing in miracles than the miserable, who would otherwise be without hope.
170. obscured course: what I am doing in disguise
171. From: away from; **enormous state:** disordered kingdom
172. o'erwatched: exhausted from lack of sleep
173. vantage: advantage; opportunity
175. Fortune . . . wheel: proverbially Fortune, personified as a woman, regulated human destiny by the turn of a wheel.
2. happy: opportune
10. elf: i.e., mat into elflocks
15. mortified: synonymous with **numbed**
17. object: spectacle
18. pelting: miserable
19. bans: curses

20. Poor . . . Tom: a rehearsal of Tom o' Bedlam's plaint. **Turlygod,** though of uncertain origin, may have been a familiar bedlam character of the time.
21. Edgar . . . am: as Edgar I am completely lost.
7. cruel: a pun on crewel (worsted yarn)
10. over-lusty . . . legs: of vagrant habit
11. netherstocks: stockings
12. so . . . mistook: misunderstood your status thus
24. upon respect: deliberately
25. Resolve: inform; **modest haste:** deliberate speed
28. commend: offer

Ere I was risen from the place that showed
My duty kneeling, came there a reeking post, 30
Stewed in his haste, half breathless, panting forth
From Goneril his mistress salutations;
Delivered letters, spite of intermission,
Which presently they read; on whose contents,
They summoned up their meinie, straight took horse,
Commanded me to follow and attend 36
The leisure of their answer, gave me cold looks,
And meeting here the other messenger,
Whose welcome I perceived had poisoned mine—
Being the very fellow which of late 40
Displayed so saucily against your Highness—
Having more man than wit about me, drew.
He raised the house with loud and coward cries.
Your son and daughter found this trespass worth
The shame which here it suffers. 45

Fool. Winter's not gone yet, if the wild geese fly that way.

Fathers that wear rags
Do make their children blind;
But fathers that bear bags 50
Shall see their children kind.
Fortune, that arrant whore,
Ne'er turns the key to the poor.

But for all this, thou shalt have as many dolors for thy daughters as thou canst tell in a year. 55

Lear. O, how this mother swells up toward my heart!
Hysterica passio! Down, thou climbing sorrow,
Thy element's below! Where is this daughter?

Kent. With the Earl, sir, here within.

Lear. Follow me not; 59
Stay here. *Exit.*

Gent. Made you no more offense but what you speak of?

Kent. None.
How chance the King comes with so small a number?

Fool. An thou hadst been set i' the stocks for 65 that question, thou'dst well deserved it.

Kent. Why, fool?

Fool. We'll set thee to school to an ant, to teach thee there's no laboring i' the winter. All that follow their noses are led by their eyes but blind men, 70 and there's not a nose among twenty but can smell him that's stinking. Let go thy hold when a great wheel runs down a hill, lest it break thy neck with following it; but the great one that goes upward, let him draw thee after. When a wise man gives 75 thee better counsel, give me mine again: I would have none but knaves follow it, since a fool gives it.

That sir which serves and seeks for gain,
And follows but for form,
Will pack when it begins to rain 80
And leave thee in the storm.
But I will tarry; the fool will stay,
And let the wise man fly.
The knave turns fool that runs away;
The fool no knave, perdy. 85

Kent. Where learned you this, fool?

Fool. Not i' the stocks, fool.

Enter LEAR *and* GLOUCESTER.

Lear. Deny to speak with me? They are sick! they are weary!
They have traveled all the night! Mere fetches—
The images of revolt and flying off! 90
Fetch me a better answer.

Glou. My dear lord,
You know the fiery quality of the Duke,
How unremovable and fixed he is
In his own course.

Lear. Vengeance! plague! death! confusion! 95
Fiery? What quality? Why, Gloucester, Gloucester,
I'd speak with the Duke of Cornwall and his wife.

Glou. Well, my good lord, I have informed them so.

Lear. Informed them? Dost thou understand me, man?

Glou. Ay, my good lord. 100

Lear. The King would speak with Cornwall; the dear father
Would with his daughter speak, commands, tends service.
Are they informed of this? My breath and blood!
Fiery? the fiery Duke? Tell the hot Duke that—
No, but not yet! May be he is not well. 105
Infirmity doth still neglect all office
Whereto our health is bound. We are not ourselves
When nature, being oppressed, commands the mind
To suffer with the body. I'll forbear;
And am fallen out with my more headier will, 110
To take the indisposed and sickly fit
For the sound man. [*Looks at Kent.*] Death on my state! Wherefore
Should he sit here? This act persuades me
That this remotion of the Duke and her
Is practice only. Give me my servant forth. 115
Go tell the Duke and's wife I'd speak with them—

30. post: messenger
33. spite . . . intermission: although it interrupted me
34. presently: at once
35. meinie: household
52. arrant whore: notorious strumpet (because her favor is capricious)
54. dolors: sorrows, with a pun on "dollars"
55. tell: count
56. mother: hysteria, derived from the stomach and producing a choked feeling in the throat. **Hysterica passio** is synonymous.

85. perdy: *par dieu,* verily
89. fetches: pretexts
106. still: ever; **office:** function
110. am . . . will: deplore my hastier inclination
114. remotion: removal

Now, presently. Bid them come forth and hear me,
Or at their chamber door I'll beat the drum
Till it cry sleep to death. 119

Glou. I would have all well betwixt you. *Exit.*

Lear. O me, my heart, my rising heart! But down!

Fool. Cry to it, nuncle, as the cockney did to the eels when she put 'em i' the paste alive. She knapped 'em o' the coxcombs with a stick and cried "Down, wantons, down!" 'Twas her brother that, in 125 pure kindness to his horse, buttered his hay.

Enter CORNWALL, REGAN, GLOUCESTER, SERVANTS.

Lear. Good morrow to you both.

Corn. Hail to your Grace!
Kent here set at liberty.

Reg. I am glad to see your Highness.

Lear. Regan, I think you are; I know what reason
I have to think so. If thou shouldst not be glad,
I would divorce me from thy mother's tomb, 131
Sepulchring an adultress. [*To Kent*] O, are you free?
Some other time for that.—Beloved Regan,
Thy sister's naught. O Regan, she hath tied 134
Sharp-toothed unkindness, like a vulture, here!
[*Points to his heart.*]
I can scarce speak to thee. Thou'lt not believe
With how depraved a quality—O Regan!

Reg. I pray you, sir, take patience. I have hope
You less know how to value her desert
Than she to scant her duty.

Lear. Say, how is that? 140

Reg. I cannot think my sister in the least
Would fail her obligation. If, sir, perchance
She have restrained the riots of your followers,
'Tis on such ground, and to such wholesome end,
As clears her from all blame. 145

Lear. My curses on her!

Reg. O, sir, you are old!
Nature in you stands on the very verge
Of her confine. You should be ruled, and led
By some discretion that discerns your state
Better than you yourself. Therefore I pray you
That to our sister you do make return; 151
Say you have wronged her.

Lear. Ask her forgiveness?
Do you but mark how this becomes the house:
[*Kneeling*] "Dear daughter, I confess that I am old.
Age is unnecessary. On my knees I beg 155
That you'll vouchsafe me raiment, bed, and food."

Reg. Good sir, no more! These are unsightly tricks.
Return you to my sister.

Lear. [*Stands up.*] Never, Regan!
She hath abated me of half my train;
Looked black upon me; struck me with her tongue,
Most serpent-like, upon the very heart. 161
All the stored vengeances of heaven fall
On her ingrateful top! Strike her young bones,
You taking airs, with lameness!

Corn. Fie, sir, fie!

Lear. You nimble lightnings, dart your blinding flames 165
Into her scornful eyes! Infect her beauty,
You fen-sucked fogs, drawn by the powerful sun,
To fall and blister!

Reg. O the blest gods! so will you wish on me
When the rash mood is on. 170

Lear. No, Regan, thou shalt never have my curse.
Thy tender-hefted nature shall not give
Thee o'er to harshness. Her eyes are fierce, but thine
Do comfort and not burn. 'Tis not in thee
To grudge my pleasures, to cut off my train, 175
To bandy hasty words, to scant my sizes,
And, in conclusion, to oppose the bolt
Against my coming in. Thou better knowest
The offices of nature, bond of childhood,
Effects of courtesy, dues of gratitude. 180
Thy half of the kingdom hast thou not forgot,
Wherein I thee endowed.

Reg. Good sir, to the purpose.

Lear. Who put my man in the stocks?
Tucket within.

Corn. What trumpet's that?

Reg. I know it—my sister's. This approves her letter
That she would soon be here.

Enter [OSWALD *the*] STEWARD.

Is your lady come? 185

Lear. This is a slave, whose easy, borrowed pride
Dwells in the fickle grace of her he follows.
Out, varlet, from my sight!

Corn. What means your Grace?

Lear. Who stocked my servant? Regan, I have good hope 189
Thou didst not know on't.

Enter GONERIL.

Who comes here? O heavens,
If you do love old men, if your sweet sway
Allow obedience, if you yourselves are old,

122. **cockney:** various meanings: "milksop," "townsman," "Londoner," but here apparently "simpleton," or "cook"
123. **knapped:** rapped
131–32. **I . . . adultress:** i.e., I would disown your mother because I could no longer believe you were my child.
134. **naught:** wicked
139–40. **You . . . duty:** if analyzed, this sentence says the opposite of what is meant.
147. **Nature:** i.e., your natural term of life
149. **some discretion:** some other discreet person
164. **taking:** infectious
172. **tender-hefted:** tender, or susceptible to tenderness
176. **scant . . . sizes:** give me scanty allowance
184. **approves:** confirms

Make it your cause! Send down, and take my part!
[*To Goneril*] Art not ashamed to look upon this beard?—
O Regan, will you take her by the hand? 195
Gon. Why not by the hand, sir? How have I offended?
All's not offense that indiscretion finds
And dotage terms so.
Lear. O sides, you are too tough!
Will you yet hold? How came my man i' the stocks?
Corn. I set him there, sir, but his own disorders 200
Deserved much less advancement.
Lear. You? Did you?
Reg. I pray you, father, being weak, seem so.
If, till the expiration of your month,
You will return and sojourn with my sister,
Dismissing half your train, come then to me. 205
I am now from home, and out of that provision
Which shall be needful for your entertainment.
Lear. Return to her, and fifty men dismissed?
No, rather I abjure all roofs, and choose
To wage against the enmity o' the air, 210
To be a comrade with the wolf and owl—
Necessity's sharp pinch! Return with her?
Why, the hot-blooded France, that dowerless took
Our youngest born, I could as well be brought
To knee his throne, and, squire-like, pension beg
To keep base life afoot. Return with her? 216
Persuade me rather to be slave and sumpter
To this detested groom. [*Pointing at Oswald.*]
Gon. At your choice, sir.
Lear. I prithee, daughter, do not make me mad.
I will not trouble thee, my child; farewell. 220
We'll no more meet, no more see one another.
But yet thou art my flesh, my blood, my daughter;
Or rather a disease that's in my flesh,
Which I must needs call mine. Thou art a boil,
A plague sore or embossed carbuncle, 225
In my corrupted blood. But I'll not chide thee.
Let shame come when it will, I do not call it.
I do not bid the Thunder-bearer shoot,
Nor tell tales of thee to high-judging Jove.
Mend when thou canst; be better at thy leisure;
I can be patient; I can stay with Regan, 231
I and my hundred knights.
Reg. Not altogether so.
I looked not for you yet, nor am provided
For your fit welcome. Give ear, sir, to my sister;
For those that mingle reason with your passion
Must be content to think you old, and so— 236
But she knows what she does.
Lear. Is this well spoken?
Reg. I dare avouch it, sir. What, fifty followers?
Is it not well? What should you need of more? 239
Yea, or so many, sith that both charge and danger
Speak 'gainst so great a number? How in one house
Should many people, under two commands,
Hold amity? 'Tis hard; almost impossible.
Gon. Why might not you, my lord, receive attendance
From those that she calls servants, or from mine?
Reg. Why not, my lord? If then they chanced to slack ye, 246
We could control them. If you will come to me
(For now I spy a danger), I entreat you
To bring but five-and-twenty. To no more
Will I give place or notice. 250
Lear. I gave you all—
Reg. And in good time you gave it!
Lear. Made you my guardians, my depositaries;
But kept a reservation to be followed
With such a number. What, must I come to you
With five-and-twenty, Regan? Said you so? 255
Reg. And speak it again, my lord. No more with me.
Lear. Those wicked creatures yet do look well-favored
When others are more wicked; not being the worst
Stands in some rank of praise. [*To Goneril*] I'll go with thee.
Thy fifty yet doth double five-and-twenty, 260
And thou art twice her love.
Gon. Hear me, my lord.
What need you five-and-twenty, ten, or five,
To follow in a house where twice so many
Have a command to tend you?
Reg. What need one?
Lear. O, reason not the need! Our basest beggars
Are in the poorest thing superfluous. 266
Allow not nature more than nature needs,
Man's life is cheap as beast's. Thou art a lady:
If only to go warm were gorgeous, 269
Why, nature needs not what thou gorgeous wearest,
Which scarcely keeps thee warm. But, for true need—
You heavens, give me that patience, patience I need!
You see me here, you gods, a poor old man,
As full of grief as age; wretched in both.
If it be you that stirs these daughters' hearts 275
Against their father, fool me not so much
To bear it tamely; touch me with noble anger,
And let not women's weapons, water drops,
Stain my man's cheeks! No, you unnatural hags!

200. disorders: misbehavior
217. sumpter: pack animal
240. sith that: since
246. slack: neglect
257–59. Those . . . praise: i.e., Goneril now looks virtuous in comparison with Regan.
265–66. basest . . . superfluous: even beggars, whose possessions are but poor, have a little more than they need for mere survival.
276–77. fool . . . tamely: let me not be such a fool as to endure it mildly

I will have such revenges on you both 280
That all the world shall—I will do such things—
What they are yet, I know not; but they shall be
The terrors of the earth! You think I'll weep.
No, I'll not weep. [*Sounds of an approaching storm.*]
I have full cause of weeping, but this heart 285
Shall break into a hundred thousand flaws
Or ere I'll weep. O fool, I shall go mad!
[*Exeunt Lear, Gloucester, Kent, and Fool.*]

Corn. Let us withdraw, 'twill be a storm.

Reg. This house is little; the old man and's people
Cannot be well bestowed. 290

Gon. 'Tis his own blame; hath put himself from rest
And must needs taste his folly.

Reg. For his particular, I'll receive him gladly,
But not one follower.

Gon. So am I purposed.
Where is my Lord of Gloucester? 295

Corn. Followed the old man forth.

286. **flaws:** fragments
290. **bestowed:** accommodated
293. **his particular:** himself

Enter GLOUCESTER.

He is returned.

Glou. The King is in high rage.

Corn. Whither is he going?

Glou. He calls to horse, but will I know not whither.

Corn. 'Tis best to give him way, he leads himself.

Gon. My lord, entreat him by no means to stay.

Glou. Alack, the night comes on, and the bleak winds 301
Do sorely ruffle. For many miles about
There's scarce a bush.

Reg. O, sir, to willful men
The injuries that they themselves procure
Must be their schoolmasters. Shut up your doors.
He is attended with a desperate train, 306
And what they may incense him to, being apt
To have his ear abused, wisdom bids fear.

Corn. Shut up your doors, my lord; 'tis a wild night. 309
My Regan counsels well. Come out o' the storm.
[*Exeunt.*]

302. **sorely ruffle:** grievously rage
308. **abused:** deceived

ACT III

[Scene I. *A heath.*]

Storm still. Enter KENT *and a* GENTLEMAN, *severally.*

Kent. Who's there, besides foul weather?

Gent. One minded like the weather, most unquietly.

Kent. I know you. Where's the King?

Gent. Contending with the fretful elements;
Bids the wind blow the earth into the sea, 5
Or swell the curled waters 'bove the main,
That things might change or cease; tears his white hair,
Which the impetuous blasts, with eyeless rage,
Catch in their fury and make nothing of;
Strives in his little world of man to outscorn 10
The to-and-fro-conflicting wind and rain.
This night, wherein the cub-drawn bear would couch,
The lion and the belly-pinched wolf
Keep their fur dry, unbonneted he runs, 14
And bids what will take all.

Kent. But who is with him?

Gent. None but the fool, who labors to outjest
His heart-struck injuries.

Kent. Sir, I do know you,
And dare upon the warrant of my note
Commend a dear thing to you. There is division
(Although as yet the face of it is covered 20
With mutual cunning) 'twixt Albany and Cornwall;
Who have (as who have not, that their great stars
Throned and set high?) servants, who seem no less,
Which are to France the spies and speculations
Intelligent of our state. What hath been seen, 25

9. **make . . . of:** treat with no respect

12. **cub-drawn:** drained from suckling young
18. **upon . . . note:** on the basis of my knowledge
19. **dear:** important
24. **speculations:** spies

Either in snuffs and packings of the Dukes,
Or the hard rein which both of them have borne
Against the old kind King, or something deeper,
Whereof, perchance, these are but furnishings—
But, true it is, from France there comes a power
Into this scattered kingdom, who already, 31
Wise in our negligence, have secret feet
In some of our best ports and are at point
To show their open banner. Now to you:
If on my credit you dare build so far 35
To make your speed to Dover, you shall find
Some that will thank you, making just report
Of how unnatural and bemadding sorrow
The King hath cause to plain.
I am a gentleman of blood and breeding, 40
And from some knowledge and assurance offer
This office to you.

Gent. I will talk further with you.

Kent. No, do not.
For confirmation that I am much more
Than my out-wall, open this purse and take 45
What it contains. If you shall see Cordelia
(As fear not but you shall), show her this ring,
And she will tell you who that fellow is
That yet you do not know. Fie on this storm!
I will go seek the King. 50

Gent. Give me your hand. Have you no more to say?

Kent. Few words, but, to effect, more than all yet:
That, when we have found the King (in which your pain
That way, I'll this), he that first lights on him
Holla the other. 55

Exeunt [severally].

Scene II. [*Another part of the heath.*]

Storm still. Enter Lear *and* Fool.

Lear. Blow, winds, and crack your cheeks! rage! blow!
You cataracts and hurricanoes, spout
Till you have drenched our steeples, drowned the cocks!
You sulph'rous and thought-executing fires,
Vaunt-couriers of oak-cleaving thunderbolts, 5
Singe my white head! And thou, all-shaking thunder,
Strike flat the thick rotundity o' the world,
Crack Nature's molds, all germens spill at once,
That make ingrateful man!

Fool. O nuncle, court holy water in a dry 10
house is better than this rain water out o' door. Good
nuncle, in; ask thy daughters' blessing! Here's a
night pities neither wise men nor fools.

Lear. Rumble thy bellyfull! Spit, fire! Spout, rain!
Nor rain, wind, thunder, fire are my daughters.
I tax not you, you elements, with unkindness. 16
I never gave you kingdom, called you children,
You owe me no subscription. Then let fall
Your horrible pleasure. Here I stand your slave,
A poor, infirm, weak, and despised old man. 20
But yet I call you servile ministers,
That will with two pernicious daughters join
Your high-engendered battles 'gainst a head
So old and white as this! O, ho! 'tis foul!

Fool. He that has a house to put's head in 25
has a good headpiece.

The codpiece that will house
Before the head has any,
The head and he shall louse:
So beggars marry many. 30
The man that makes his toe
What he his heart should make
Shall of a corn cry woe,
And turn his sleep to wake.

For there was never yet fair woman but she 35
made mouths in a glass.

Enter Kent.

Lear. No, I will be the pattern of all patience; I
will say nothing.

Kent. Who's there?

Fool. Marry, here's grace and a codpiece; 40
that's a wise man and a fool.

Kent. Alas, sir, are you here? Things that love night
Love not such nights as these. The wrathful skies
Gallow the very wanderers of the dark 44
And make them keep their caves. Since I was man,
Such sheets of fire, such bursts of horrid thunder,
Such groans of roaring wind and rain, I never
Remember to have heard. Man's nature cannot carry
The affliction nor the fear.

Lear. Let the great gods,
That keep this dreadful pudder o'er our heads, 50

26. snuffs: hasty quarrels; **packings:** plottings
29. furnishings: outward manifestations
39. plain: complain
45. out-wall: outward appearance
2. cataracts, hurricanoes: waterspouts
3. cocks: weathercocks
4. thought-executing: acting with the speed of thought
5. Vaunt-couriers: heralds
8. germens: sperm
10. court . . . water: flattery
18. subscription: allegiance
27–30. The . . . many: the man who hastily begets children when he has no roof over his head will become a lousy vagrant.
31–34. The . . . wake: the man who cherishes a meaner member as much as his heart will suffer from trivial woes. The Fool has in mind Lear's poor judgment in evaluating his daughters.
44. Gallow: terrify
50. pudder: disturbance

Find out their enemies now. Tremble, thou wretch,
That hast within thee undivulged crimes
Unwhipped of justice. Hide thee, thou bloody hand;
Thou perjured, and thou simular of virtue
That art incestuous. Caitiff, to pieces shake 55
That under covert and convenient seeming
Hast practiced on man's life. Close pent-up guilts,
Rive your concealing continents, and cry
These dreadful summoners grace. I am a man
More sinned against than sinning.

Kent. Alack, bareheaded? 60
Gracious my lord, hard by here is a hovel;
Some friendship will it lend you 'gainst the tempest.
Repose you there, while I to this hard house
(More harder than the stones whereof 'tis raised,
Which even but now, demanding after you, 65
Denied me to come in) return, and force
Their scanted courtesy.

Lear. My wits begin to turn.
Come on, my boy. How dost, my boy? Art cold?
I am cold myself. Where is this straw, my fellow?
The art of our necessities is strange, 70
And can make vile things precious. Come, your hovel.
Poor fool and knave, I have one part in my heart
That's sorry yet for thee.

Fool. [*Sings*]
He that has and a little tiny wit,
With hey, ho, the wind and the rain, 75
Must make content with his fortunes fit,
Though the rain it raineth every day.

Lear. True, boy. Come, bring us to this hovel.
Exeunt [*Lear and Kent*].

Fool. This is a brave night to cool a courtesan. I'll speak a prophecy ere I go: 80
When priests are more in word than matter;
When brewers mar their malt with water;
When nobles are their tailors' tutors,
No heretics burned, but wenches' suitors;
When every case in law is right; 85
No squire in debt nor no poor knight;
When slanders do not live in tongues;
Nor cutpurses come not to throngs;
When usurers tell their gold i' the field;
And bawds and whores do churches build: 90
Then shall the realm of Albion
Come to great confusion.
Then comes the time, who lives to see't,
That going shall be used with feet.
This prophecy Merlin shall make, for I live before his time. 95
Exit.

54. simular: simulator
56. under . . . seeming: under a cloak of hypocrisy
58. Rive: split; **continents:** containers
58–59. cry . . . grace: beg mercy of
61. hard: near
79. brave: splendid
80–94. When . . . feet: a parody of verses known as "Merlin's prophecy," at one time mistakenly attributed to Chaucer. The Quarto edition omits, as do some editors.
88. cutpurses: pickpockets
89. usurers: moneylenders
91. Albion: an ancient name, chiefly poetic, for Britain

Scene III. [*Inside Gloucester's Castle.*]

Enter GLOUCESTER *and* EDMUND.

Glou. Alack, alack, Edmund, I like not this unnatural dealing! When I desired their leave that I might pity him, they took from me the use of mine own house; charged me on pain of perpetual displeasure neither to speak of him, entreat for 5 him, nor any way sustain him.

Edm. Most savage and unnatural!

Glou. Go to; say you nothing. There is division between the Dukes, and a worse matter than that. I have received a letter this night—'tis danger- 10 ous to be spoken—I have locked the letter in my closet. These injuries the King now bears will be revenged home; there is part of a power already footed; we must incline to the King. I will look him and privily relieve him. Go you and maintain talk 15 with the Duke, that my charity be not of him perceived. If he ask for me, I am ill and gone to bed. If I die for it, as no less is threatened me, the King my old master must be relieved. There are strange 19 things toward, Edmund. Pray you be careful. *Exit.*

Edm. This courtesy, forbid thee, shall the Duke
Instantly know, and of that letter too.
This seems a fair deserving, and must draw me
That which my father loses—no less than all.
The younger rises when the old doth fall. 25
Exit.

Scene IV. [*Before a hovel on the heath.*]

Storm still. Enter LEAR, KENT, *and* FOOL.

Kent. Here is the place, my lord. Good my lord, enter.
The tyranny of the open night's too rough
For nature to endure.

Lear. Let me alone.

Kent. Good my lord, enter here.

Lear. Wilt break my heart?

13. home: completely; **footed:** abroad in the land
14. look: seek out
15. privily: secretly
23. fair deserving: action meriting reward
2. tyranny: violence

Kent. I had rather break mine own. Good my lord, enter. 5

Lear. Thou thinkest 'tis much that this contentious storm
Invades us to the skin. So 'tis to thee;
But where the greater malady is fixed,
The lesser is scarce felt. Thou'dst shun a bear;
But if thy flight lay toward the roaring sea, 10
Thou'dst meet the bear i' the mouth. When the mind's free,
The body's delicate. The tempest in my mind
Doth from my senses take all feeling else
Save what beats there. Filial ingratitude!
Is it not as this mouth should tear this hand 15
For lifting food to it? But I will punish home!
No, I will weep no more. In such a night
To shut me out! Pour on; I will endure.
In such a night as this! O Regan, Goneril!
Your old kind father, whose frank heart gave all!
O, that way madness lies; let me shun that! 21
No more of that.

Kent. Good my lord, enter here.

Lear. Prithee go in thyself; seek thine own ease.
This tempest will not give me leave to ponder
On things would hurt me more. But I'll go in. 25
[*To the Fool*] In, boy; go first.—You houseless poverty—
Nay, get thee in. I'll pray, and then I'll sleep.

[*The Fool enters the hovel.*]

Poor naked wretches, wheresoe'er you are,
That bide the pelting of this pitiless storm, 29
How shall your houseless heads and unfed sides,
Your looped and windowed raggedness, defend you
From seasons such as these? O, I have ta'en
Too little care of this! Take physic, pomp;
Expose thyself to feel what wretches feel,
That thou mayst shake the superflux to them 35
And show the heavens more just.

Edg. [*Within*] Fathom and half, fathom and half! Poor Tom!

[*Re-*]*enter* FOOL.

Fool. Come not in here, nuncle, here's a spirit. Help me, help me! 40

Kent. Give me thy hand. Who's there?

Fool. A spirit, a spirit! He says his name's poor Tom.

Kent. What art thou that dost grumble there i' the straw? Come forth. 45

Enter EDGAR.

Edg. Away! the foul fiend follows me! Through the sharp hawthorn blow the winds Humh! go to thy bed, and warm thee.

Lear. Didst thou give all to thy two daughters. And art thou come to this? 50

Edg. Who gives anything to poor Tom? whom the foul fiend hath led through fire and through flame, through ford and whirlpool, o'er bog and quagmire; that hath laid knives under his pillow and halters in his pew, set ratsbane by his porridge, made him 55 proud of heart, to ride on a bay trotting horse over four-inched bridges, to course his own shadow for a traitor. Bless thy five wits! Tom's acold. O, do de, do de, do de. Bless thee from whirlwinds, star-blasting, and taking! Do poor Tom some charity, 60 whom the foul fiend vexes. There could I have him now, and there, and there again, and there!

Storm still.

Lear. Have his daughters brought him to this pass? Couldst thou save nothing? Wouldst thou give 'em all? 65

Fool. Nay, he reserved a blanket, else we had been all shamed.

Lear. Now all the plagues that in the pendulous air
Hang fated o'er men's faults light on thy daughters!

Kent. He hath no daughters, sir. 70

Lear. Death, traitor! Nothing could have subdued nature
To such a lowness but his unkind daughters.
Is it the fashion that discarded fathers
Should have thus little mercy on their flesh?
Judicious punishment! 'Twas this flesh begot 75
Those pelican daughters.

Edg. Pillicock sat on Pillicock Hill. Alow, alow, loo, loo!

Fool. This cold night will turn us all to fools and madmen. 80

Edg. Take heed o' the foul fiend; obey thy parents; keep thy word's justice; swear not; commit not with man's sworn spouse; set not thy sweet heart on proud array. Tom's acold.

Lear. What hast thou been? 85

Edg. A servingman, proud in heart and mind; that curled my hair, wore gloves in my cap; served the lust of my mistress' heart and did the act of darkness with her; swore as many oaths as I spake words, and

9. shun: flee, not merely avoid
31. looped . . . windowed: tattered
32–33. ta'en . . . this: given too little thought to the unfortunate
35. superflux: superfluity; your own excess

54–55. that . . . porridge: fiends were supposed to tempt men to suicide.
57. course: pursue
58. five wits: common wit, imagination, fantasy, estimation, and memory, as listed by Stephen Hawes, *The Pastime of Pleasure* (1509); **do de:** imitating the chattering of teeth
59. star-blasting: evil astronomical influence
60. taking: seizure by illness or enchantment
76. pelican daughters: it was popularly believed that pelicans fed their offspring with their own flesh and blood.
77. Pillicock: a term equivalent to "darling"; also a euphemism for phallus
77–78. Alow . . . loo: a hunter's shout

broke them in the sweet face of heaven; one 90
that slept in the contriving of lust, and waked to do it. Wine loved I deeply, dice dearly; and in woman out-paramoured the Turk. False of heart, light of ear, bloody of hand; hog in sloth, fox in stealth, wolf in greediness, dog in madness, lion in prey. Let 95
not the creaking of shoes nor the rustling of silks betray thy poor heart to woman. Keep thy foot out of brothels, thy hand out of plackets, thy pen from lender's books, and defy the foul fiend. Still through the hawthorn blows the cold wind; says suum, 100
mun, hey, no, nonny. Dolphin my boy, my boy, sessa! let him trot by. *Storm still.*

Lear. Thou wert better in thy grave than to answer with thy uncovered body this extremity of the skies. Is man no more than this? Consider him well. 105
Thou owest the worm no silk, the beast no hide, the sheep no wool, the cat no perfume. Ha! Here's three on's are sophisticated! Thou art the thing itself; unaccommodated man is no more but such a poor, bare, forked animal as thou art. Off, off, you lend- 110
ings! Come, unbutton here. [*Tearing his garments.*]

Fool. Prithee, nuncle, be contented! 'Tis a naughty night to swim in. Now a little fire in a wild field were like an old lecher's heart—a small spark, all the rest on's body cold. Look, here comes a walking 115
fire.

Enter GLOUCESTER *with a torch.*

Edg. This is the foul Flibbertigibbet. He begins at curfew, and walks till the first cock. He gives the web and the pin, squints the eye, and makes the harelip; mildews the white wheat, and hurts the poor 120
creature of earth.

Swithold footed thrice the 'old;
He met the nightmare, and her nine fold;
Bid her alight
And her troth plight, 125
And aroint thee, witch, aroint thee!

Kent. How fares your Grace?

Lear. What's he?

Kent. Who's there? What is't you seek?

Glou. What are you there? Your names? 130

Edg. Poor Tom, that eats the swimming frog, the toad, the tadpole, the wall-newt and the water; that in the fury of his heart, when the foul fiend rages, eats cow-dung for sallets, swallows the old rat and the ditch-dog, drinks the green mantle of the 135
standing pool; who is whipped from tithing to tithing, and stock-punished and imprisoned; who hath had three suits to his back, six shirts to his body, horse to ride, and weapon to wear;

But mice and rats, and such small deer, 140
Have been Tom's food for seven long year.

Beware my follower. Peace, Smulkin! peace, thou fiend!

Glou. What, hath your Grace no better company?

Edg. The prince of darkness is a gentleman! 145
Modo he's called, and Mahu.

Glou. Our flesh and blood, my lord, is grown so vile,
That it doth hate what gets it.

Edg. Poor Tom's acold.

Glou. Go in with me. My duty cannot suffer
T' obey in all your daughters' hard commands. 151
Though their injunction be to bar my doors
And let this tyrannous night take hold upon you,
Yet have I ventured to come seek you out
And bring you where both fire and food is ready.

Lear. First let me talk with this philosopher. 156
What is the cause of thunder?

Kent. Good my lord, take his offer; go into the house.

Lear. I'll talk a word with this same learned Theban.
What is your study? 160

Edg. How to prevent the fiend and to kill vermin.

Lear. Let me ask you one word in private.

Kent. Importune him once more to go, my lord.
His wits begin to unsettle.

Glou. Canst thou blame him?
Storm still.
His daughters seek his death. Ah, that good Kent!
He said it would be thus—poor banished man! 166
Thou sayest the King grows mad: I'll tell thee, friend,
I am almost mad myself. I had a son,
Now outlawed from my blood. He sought my life
But lately, very late. I loved him, friend— 170
No father his son dearer. True to tell thee,

96. creaking . . . shoes: a fashionable affectation
98. plackets: petticoats; hence women
100–102. suum . . . by: Edgar first imitates the wind's sound, then trails into snatches of songs which have not been identified. **Sessa,** spelled "sesey" in the Folio, may be the French *cessez* ("cease"), suggested by **Dolphin,** the contemporary spelling of "Dauphin."
107. cat: civet cat, the source of musk
107–8. Here's . . . sophisticated: i.e., the three present who are fully clothed
108–9. unaccommodated: unclothed
112. naughty: wicked
117. Flibbertigibbet: a fiend, probably found by Shakespeare in Samuel Harsnett, *A Declaration of Egregious Popish Impostures* (1603), which satirized beliefs about demonic possession
118–19. the . . . pin: a kind of cataract
122–26. Swithold . . . thee: a charm to avert nightmare (an incubus supposed literally to ride men at night). **Swithold** is St. Withold or Vitalis, but the same story is sometimes attached to St. George. **'old:** wold; meadow; **aroint thee:** be off with thee

132. water: water newt
134. sallets: salad greens
135. mantle: scum
136. tithing: a division of rural areas, originally ten households or one tenth of a hundred
148. gets: begets
161. prevent: forestall

The grief hath crazed my wits. What a night's this!
I do beseech your Grace—

Lear. O, cry you mercy, sir.
Noble philosopher, your company.

Edg. Tom's acold. 175

Glou. In, fellow, there, into the hovel; keep thee warm.

Lear. Come, let's in all.

Kent. This way, my lord.

Lear. With him!
I will keep still with my philosopher.

Kent. Good my lord, soothe him; let him take the fellow.

Glou. Take him you on. 180

Kent. Sirrah, come on; go along with us.

Lear. Come, good Athenian.

Glou. No words, no words! hush.

Edg. Child Rowland to the dark tower came;
His word was still 185
Fie, foh, and fum!
I smell the blood of a British man.

Exeunt.

Scene V. [*Inside Gloucester's Castle.*]

Enter CORNWALL *and* EDMUND.

Corn. I will have my revenge ere I depart his house.

Edm. How, my lord, I may be censured, that nature thus gives way to loyalty, something fears me to think of. 5

Corn. I now perceive it was not altogether your brother's evil disposition made him seek his death; but a provoking merit, set a-work by a reprovable badness in himself.

Edm. How malicious is my fortune that I 10 must repent to be just! This is the letter he spoke of, which approves him an intelligent party to the advantages of France. O heavens! that this reason were not, or not I the detector!

Corn. Go with me to the Duchess. 15

Edm. If the matter of this paper be certain, you have mighty business in hand.

Corn. True or false, it hath made thee Earl of Gloucester. Seek out where thy father is, that he may be ready for our apprehension. 20

Edm. [*Aside*] If I find him comforting the King, it will stuff his suspicion more fully. [*Aloud*] I will persevere in my course of loyalty, though the conflict be sore between that and my blood.

Corn. I will lay trust upon thee, and thou 25 shalt find a dearer father in my love.

Exeunt.

Scene VI. [*An outbuilding near Gloucester's Castle.*]

Enter GLOUCESTER *and* KENT.

Glou. Here is better than the open air; take it thankfully. I will piece out the comfort with what addition I can. I will not be long from you.

Kent. All the power of his wits have given way to his impatience. The gods reward your kindness! 5

Exit [*Gloucester*].

[*Enter* LEAR, EDGAR, *and* FOOL.]

Edg. Frateretto calls me, and tells me Nero is an angler in the lake of darkness. Pray, innocent, and beware the foul fiend.

Fool. Prithee, nuncle, tell me whether a madman be a gentleman or a yeoman. 10

Lear. A king, a king!

Fool. No, he's a yeoman that has a gentleman to his son; for he's a mad yeoman that sees his son a gentleman before him.

Lear. To have a thousand with red burning spits
Come hizzing in upon 'em— 16

Edg. The foul fiend bites my back.

Fool. He's mad that trusts in the tameness of a wolf, a horse's health, a boy's love, or a whore's oath.

Lear. It shall be done; I will arraign them straight. 20
[*To Edgar*] Come, sit thou here, most learned justicer.
[*To the Fool*] Thou, sapient sir, sit here. Now, you she-foxes!

Edg. Look, where he stands and glares! Wantest thou eyes at trial, madam?
Come o'er the bourn, Bessy, to me. 25

Fool. Her boat hath a leak,
And she must not speak
Why she dares not come over to thee.

Edg. The foul fiend haunts poor Tom in the voice of a nightingale. Hoppedance cries in Tom's 30

184. Child Rowland: a fragment from a ballad about Charlemagne's nephew, the hero Roland. **Child** was the term for a candidate for knighthood.
4. something fears: frightens somewhat
8. provoking merit: a provocation in the fact that he deserved death
11. to be: being
12. intelligent party: informer
21. comforting: abetting

6. Frateretto: another fiend
7. lake . . . darkness: i.e., in hell
21. justicer: judge
25. Come . . . me: the refrain of a song; **bourn:** brook
30. Hoppedance: Hoberdidance, one of Harsnett's devils. Harsnett relates that the rumble of a stomach was sometimes interpreted as the croaking of a devil in the form of a frog.

belly for two white herring. Croak not, black angel;
I have no food for thee.

Kent. How do you, sir? Stand you not so amazed.
Will you lie down and rest upon the cushions?

Lear. I'll see their trial first. Bring in their evidence. 35
[*To Edgar*] Thou, robed man of justice, take thy place.
[*To the Fool*] And thou, his yokefellow of equity,
Bench by his side. [*To Kent*] You are o' the commission,
Sit you too.

Edg. Let us deal justly. 40
Sleepest or wakest thou, jolly shepherd?
Thy sheep be in the corn;
And for one blast of thy minikin mouth
Thy sheep shall take no harm.
Purr! the cat is grey. 45

Lear. Arraign her first. 'Tis Goneril. I here take my oath before this honorable assembly, she kicked the poor King her father.

Fool. Come hither, mistress. Is your name Goneril?

Lear. She cannot deny it. 50

Fool. Cry you mercy, I took you for a joint-stool.

Lear. And here's another, whose warped looks proclaim
What store her heart is made on. Stop her there!
Arms, arms! sword! fire! Corruption in the place!
False justicer, why hast thou let her scape? 55

Edg. Bless thy five wits!

Kent. O pity! Sir, where is the patience now
That you so oft have boasted to retain?

Edg. [*Aside*] My tears begin to take his part so much
They mar my counterfeiting. 60

Lear. The little dogs and all,
Tray, Blanch, and Sweetheart, see, they bark at me.

Edg. Tom will throw his head at them. Avaunt, you curs!
Be thy mouth or black or white, 65
Tooth that poisons if it bite;
Mastiff, greyhound, mongrel grim,
Hound or spaniel, brach or lym,
Bobtail tyke or trundle-tail—
Tom will make him weep and wail; 70
For, with throwing thus my head,
Dogs leap the hatch, and all are fled.
Do de, de, de. Sessa! Come, march to wakes and fairs and market towns. Poor Tom, thy horn is dry.

Lear. Then let them anatomize Regan. See 75 what breeds about her heart. Is there any cause in nature that makes these hard hearts? [*To Edgar*] You, sir, I entertain for one of my hundred; only I do not like the fashion of your garments. You'll say they are Persian; but let them be changed. 80

Kent. Now, good my lord, lie here and rest awhile.

Lear. Make no noise, make no noise; draw the curtains.
So, so. We'll go to supper i' the morning.

Fool. And I'll go to bed at noon.

Enter GLOUCESTER.

Glou. Come hither, friend. Where is the King my master? 85

Kent. Here, sir; but trouble him not; his wits are gone.

Glou. Good friend, I prithee take him in thy arms.
I have o'erheard a plot of death upon him.
There is a litter ready; lay him in it
And drive toward Dover, friend, where thou shalt meet 90
Both welcome and protection. Take up thy master.
If thou shouldst dally half an hour, his life,
With thine, and all that offer to defend him,
Stand in assured loss. Take up, take up!
And follow me, that will to some provision 95
Give thee quick conduct.

Kent. Oppressed nature sleeps.
This rest might yet have balmed thy broken sinews,
Which, if convenience will not allow,
Stand in hard cure. [*To the Fool*] Come, help to bear thy master. 99
Thou must not stay behind.

Glou. Come, come, away!

Exeunt [*all but Edgar*].

Edg. When we our betters see bearing our woes,
We scarcely think our miseries our foes.
Who alone suffers suffers most i' the mind,
Leaving free things and happy shows behind; 104
But then the mind much sufferance doth o'erskip
When grief hath mates, and bearing fellowship.

33. amazed: dumfounded
43. for: during; **minikin:** diminutive and shrill-voiced
45. Purr: another demon's name
51. Cry . . . joint-stool: a facetious apology for overlooking a person's presence. In this case, the person is really a **joint-stool** (a sturdy four-legged stool which was a common piece of household furniture).
53. store: material
68. lym: lyam or lymmer, a kind of bloodhound
69. tyke: mongrel; **trundle-tail:** a dog with a long curled tail
73. wakes: church festivals
74. thy . . . dry: the typical Bedlam beggar wore a drinking horn, which he would attempt to fill by repeating this phrase at inns and homes. Edgar also means that his inspiration to play mad is beginning to falter.
75. anatomize: dissect
78. entertain: hire
80. Persian: understood to be rich and gorgeous. Lear is ironical.
94. Stand . . . loss: are threatened with certain loss
99. Stand . . . cure: will be difficult to cure
103. Who . . . mind: solitary suffering brings the greatest mental anguish
105. sufferance: suffering
106. bearing: endurance

How light and portable my pain seems now,
When that which makes me bend makes the King bow,
He childed as I fathered! Tom, away!
Mark the high noises, and thyself bewray 110
When false opinion, whose wrong thoughts defile thee,
In thy just proof repeals and reconciles thee.
What will hap more tonight, safe scape the King!
Lurk, lurk.

[*Exit.*]

Scene VII. [*Inside Gloucester's Castle.*]

Enter CORNWALL, REGAN, GONERIL, [EDMUND *the*] BASTARD, *and* SERVANTS.

Corn. [*To Goneril*] Post speedily to my lord your husband, show him this letter. The army of France is landed.—Seek out the traitor Gloucester.

[*Exeunt some of the Servants.*]

Reg. Hang him instantly.
Gon. Pluck out his eyes. 5
Corn. Leave him to my displeasure. Edmund, keep you our sister company. The revenges we are bound to take upon your traitorous father are not fit for your beholding. Advise the Duke where you are going, to a most festinate preparation. We are 10 bound to the like. Our posts shall be swift and intelligent betwixt us. Farewell, dear sister; farewell, my Lord of Gloucester.

Enter [OSWALD *the*] STEWARD.

How now? Where's the King?
Osw. My Lord of Gloucester hath conveyed him hence. 15
Some five- or six-and-thirty of his knights,
Hot questrists after him, met him at gate;
Who, with some other of the lord's dependants,
Are gone with him toward Dover, where they boast
To have well-armed friends.
Corn. Get horses for your mistress.
Gon. Farewell, sweet lord, and sister. 21
Corn. Edmund, farewell.

Exeunt Goneril, [*Edmund, and Oswald*].

Go seek the traitor Gloucester,
Pinion him like a thief, bring him before us.

[*Exeunt other Servants.*]

Though well we may not pass upon his life
Without the form of justice, yet our power 25
Shall do a court'sy to our wrath, which men
May blame, but not control.

Enter GLOUCESTER, *brought in by two or three.*

Who's there? the traitor?
Reg. Ingrateful fox! 'tis he.
Corn. Bind fast his corky arms.
Glou. What mean your Graces? Good my friends, consider 30
You are my guests. Do me no foul play, friends.
Corn. Bind him, I say. [*Servants bind him.*]
Reg. Hard, hard. O filthy traitor!
Glou. Unmerciful lady as you are, I am none.
Corn. To this chair bind him. Villain, thou shalt find— [*Regan pulls his beard.*]
Glou. By the kind gods, 'tis most ignobly done
To pluck me by the beard. 36
Reg. So white, and such a traitor!
Glou. Naughty lady,
These hairs which thou dost ravish from my chin
Will quicken, and accuse thee. I am your host.
With robber's hands my hospitable favors 40
You should not ruffle thus. What will you do?
Corn. Come sir, what letters had you late from France?
Reg. Be simple-answered, for we know the truth.
Corn. And what confederacy have you with the traitors
Late footed in the kingdom? 45
Reg. To whose hands you have sent the lunatic King?
Speak.
Glou. I have a letter guessingly set down,
Which came from one that's of a neutral heart,
And not from one opposed.
Corn. Cunning.
Reg. And false. 50
Corn. Where hast thou sent the King?
Glou. To Dover.
Reg. Wherefore to Dover? Wast thou not charged at peril—
Corn. Wherefore to Dover? Let him answer that.
Glou. I am tied to the stake, and I must stand the course.
Reg. Wherefore to Dover? 55
Glou. Because I would not see thy cruel nails
Pluck out his poor old eyes; nor thy fierce sister
In his anointed flesh rash boarish fangs.

110. Mark . . . noises: note the discords in high places; **bewray:** expose
112. repeals: recalls you to your rightful place
10. to . . . preparation: to make speedy preparation
10–11. are . . . like: intend the same preparation
11–12. be . . . intelligent: bear speedy intelligence
17. questrists: pursuers
25–26. our . . . wrath: our legal power shall bow to our anger
29. corky: withered and sapless
39. quicken: come alive
40. hospitable favors: i.e., the features of myself, your host
41. ruffle: handle roughly
45. Late footed: recently landed
58. rash: slash as a boar might with his tusks

The sea, with such a storm as his bare head
In hell-black night endured, would have buoyed up
And quenched the stelled fires. 61
Yet, poor old heart, he holp the heavens to rain.
If wolves had at thy gate howled that dern time,
Thou shouldst have said, "Good porter, turn the key."
All cruels else subscribe: but I shall see 65
The winged vengeance overtake such children.

Corn. See it shalt thou never. Fellows, hold the chair.
Upon these eyes of thine I'll set my foot.

Glou. He that will think to live till he be old,
Give me some help!—O cruel! O you gods! 70

Reg. One side will mock another. The other too!

Corn. If you see vengeance—

1. Serv. Hold your hand, my lord!
I have served you ever since I was a child,
But better service have I never done you
Than now to bid you hold.

Reg. How now, you dog? 75

1. Serv. If you did wear a beard upon your chin,
I'd shake it on this quarrel.

Reg. What do you mean?

Corn. My villain! *[They] draw and fight.*

1. Serv. Nay, then, come on, and take the chance of anger. 79

Reg. Give me thy sword. A peasant stand up thus? *She takes a sword and runs at him behind.*

1. Serv. O, I am slain! My lord, you have one eye left
To see some mischief on him. O! *He dies.*

Corn. Lest it see more, prevent it. Out, vile jelly!
Where is thy luster now?

Glou. All dark and comfortless! Where's my son Edmund? 85
Edmund, enkindle all the sparks of nature
To quit this horrid act.

Reg. Out, treacherous villain!
Thou callest on him that hates thee. It was he
That made the overture of thy treasons to us,
Who is too good to pity thee. 90

Glou. O my follies! Then Edgar was abused.
Kind gods, forgive me that, and prosper him!

Reg. Go thrust him out at gates, and let him smell
His way to Dover. *Exit [a Servant] with Gloucester.*
How is't, my lord? How look you?

Corn. I have received a hurt. Follow me, lady. 95
Turn out that eyeless villain. Throw this slave
Upon the dunghill. Regan, I bleed apace.
Untimely comes this hurt. Give me your arm.
Exit [Cornwall, led by Regan].

2. Serv. I'll never care what wickedness I do,
If this man come to good.

3. Serv. If she live long, 100
And in the end meet the old course of death,
Women will all turn monsters.

2. Serv. Let's follow the old Earl, and get the bedlam
To lead him where he would. His roguish madness
Allows itself to anything. 105

3. Serv. Go thou. I'll fetch some flax and whites of eggs
To apply to his bleeding face. Now heaven help him!
Exeunt.

60. buoyed: swelled
61. stelled fires: stars
62. holp: helped
63. dern: dark; dreadful
65. All . . . subscribe: all other cruel things yield up their cruelty
66. winged: i.e., divine
69. will . . . to: hopes to
86. sparks . . . nature: filial affection
87. quit: requite
89. overture: disclosure
94. How . . . you: how are things with you?
101. old: usual
104–5. His . . . anything: being a mad wanderer, he will lend himself to anything.
106. flax: a contemporary remedy for an eye injury

ACT IV

Scene I. [*The heath.*]

Enter EDGAR.

Edg. Yet better thus, and known to be contemned,
Than still contemned and flattered. To be worst,
The lowest and most dejected thing of Fortune,
Stands still in esperance, lives not in fear.
The lamentable change is from the best; 5
The worst returns to laughter. Welcome then,
Thou unsubstantial air that I embrace!
The wretch that thou hast blown unto the worst
Owes nothing to thy blasts.

Enter GLOUCESTER, *led by an* OLD MAN.

But who comes here?
My father, poorly led? World, world, O world! 10
But that thy strange mutations make us hate thee,
Life would not yield to age.
Old Man. O my good lord,
I have been your tenant, and your father's tenant,
These fourscore years.
Glou. Away, get thee away! Good friend, be gone.
Thy comforts can do me no good at all; 16
Thee they may hurt.
Old Man. You cannot see your way.
Glou. I have no way, and therefore want no eyes;
I stumbled when I saw. Full oft 'tis seen
Our means secure us, and our mere defects 20
Prove our commodities. O dear son Edgar,
The food of thy abused father's wrath;
Might I but live to see thee in my touch,
I'd say I had eyes again!
Old Man. How now? Who's there?
Edg. [*Aside*] O gods! Who is't can say "I am at the worst"? 25
I am worse than e'er I was.
Old Man. 'Tis poor mad Tom.
Edg. [*Aside*] And worse I may be yet. The worst is not
So long as we can say "This is the worst."
Old Man. Fellow, where goest?
Glou. Is it a beggarman?
Old Man. Madman and beggar too. 30
Glou. He has some reason, else he could not beg.
I' the last night's storm I such a fellow saw,
Which made me think a man a worm. My son
Came then into my mind, and yet my mind
Was then scarce friends with him. I have heard more since. 35
As flies to wanton boys are we to the gods.
They kill us for their sport.
Edg. [*Aside*] How should this be?
Bad is the trade that must play fool to sorrow,
Angering itself and others.—Bless thee, master!
Glou. Is that the naked fellow?
Old Man. Ay, my lord. 40
Glou. Get thee away. If for my sake
Thou wilt o'ertake us hence a mile or twain
I' the way toward Dover, do it for ancient love;
And bring some covering for this naked soul,
Which I'll entreat to lead me.
Old Man. Alack, sir, he is mad!
Glou. 'Tis the time's plague when madmen lead the blind. 46
Do as I bid thee, or rather do thy pleasure.
Above the rest, be gone.
Old Man. I'll bring him the best 'parel that I have,
Come on't what will. *Exit.*
Glou. Sirrah naked fellow— 50
Edg. Poor Tom's acold. [*Aside*] I cannot daub it further.
Glou. Come hither, fellow.
Edg. [*Aside*] And yet I must.—Bless thy sweet eyes, they bleed.
Glou. Knowest thou the way to Dover?
Edg. Both stile and gate, horseway and foot- 55
path. Poor Tom hath been scared out of his good
wits. Bless thee, good man's son, from the foul fiend!
Five fiends have been in poor Tom at once: of lust,
as Obidicut; Hobbididence, prince of dumbness;
Mahu, of stealing; Modo, of murder; Flib- 60

1–2. Yet . . . flattered: better to be in my present position, an object of open scorn, than in a position of power, flattered but secretly despised.
6. The . . . laughter: when at the worst, any change of fortune must be for the better.
11–12. But . . . age: only hatred of your capriciousness causes men to age and die.
20–21. Our . . . commodities: our advantages provide only false security, and our misfortunes turn out to be benefits; cf. the proverb "Every commodity hath its discommodity."
22. abused: deceived
27–28. The . . . worst: we have not reached the worst if we have hope enough to believe that nothing worse can come.
51. daub . . . further: maintain the disguise of madness
59. Obidicut: Hoberdicut in Harsnett

bertigibbet, of mopping and mowing, who since possesses chambermaids and waiting women. So, bless thee, master!

Glou. Here, take this purse, thou whom the heavens' plagues 64
Have humbled to all strokes. That I am wretched
Makes thee the happier. Heavens, deal so still!
Let the superfluous and lust-dieted man,
That slaves your ordinance, that will not see
Because he does not feel, feel your power quickly;
So distribution should undo excess, 70
And each man have enough. Dost thou know Dover?

Edg. Ay, master.

Glou. There is a cliff, whose high and bending head
Looks fearfully in the confined deep.
Bring me but to the very brim of it, 75
And I'll repair the misery thou dost bear
With something rich about me. From that place
I shall no leading need.

Edg. Give me thy arm.
Poor Tom shall lead thee.

Exeunt.

Scene II. [*Outside the Duke of Albany's Palace.*]

Enter GONERIL *and* [EDMUND *the*] BASTARD.

Gon. Welcome, my lord. I marvel our mild husband
Not met us on the way.

Enter [OSWALD *the*] STEWARD.

Now where's your master?

Osw. Madam, within, but never man so changed.
I told him of the army that was landed:
He smiled at it. I told him you were coming: 5
His answer was, "The worse." Of Gloucester's treachery
And of the loyal service of his son
When I informed him, then he called me sot
And told me I had turned the wrong side out.
What most he should dislike seems pleasant to him;
What like, offensive. 11

Gon. [*To Edmund*] Then shall you go no further.
It is the cowish terror of his spirit,
That dares not undertake. He'll not feel wrongs 14
Which tie him to an answer. Our wishes on the way
May prove effects. Back, Edmund, to my brother.
Hasten his musters and conduct his powers.
I must change arms at home and give the distaff
Into my husband's hands. This trusty servant
Shall pass between us. Ere long you are like to hear
(If you dare venture in your own behalf) 21
A mistress's command. Wear this; [*Gives a favor*]
Spare speech;
Decline your head: this kiss, if it durst speak,
Would stretch thy spirits up into the air.
Conceive, and fare thee well. 25

Edm. Yours in the ranks of death! *Exit.*

Gon. My most dear Gloucester!
O, the difference of man and man!
To thee a woman's services are due;
My fool usurps my body.

Osw. Madam, here comes my lord. *Exit.*

Enter ALBANY.

Gon. I have been worth the whistle.

Alb. O Goneril, 30
You are not worth the dust which the rude wind
Blows in your face! I fear your disposition.
That nature which contemns it origin
Cannot be bordered certain in itself.
She that herself will sliver and disbranch 35
From her material sap, perforce must wither
And come to deadly use.

Gon. No more! The text is foolish.

Alb. Wisdom and goodness to the vile seem vile;
Filths savor but themselves. What have you done?
Tigers, not daughters, what have you performed?
A father, and a gracious aged man, 42
Whose reverence even the head-lugged bear would lick,
Most barbarous, most degenerate, have you madded.
Could my good brother suffer you to do it? 45
A man, a prince, by him so benefited!
If that the heavens do not their visible spirits
Send quickly down to tame these vile offenses,
It will come,
Humanity must perforce prey on itself, 50
Like monsters of the deep.

Gon. Milk-livered man!

61. mopping . . . mowing: grimacing. Harsnett comments on the demonic possession of three chambermaids. Edgar's statement satirizes the affectations of court attendants trying to be fashionable.
67. superfluous: possessed of a surplus; **lust-dieted:** pleasure-sated
68. slaves . . . ordinance: behaves as though superior to your laws
8. sot: blockhead
13. cowish: cowardly
14–15. He'll . . . answer: he overlooks injuries which call for revenge.
18. arms, distaff: the symbols of man and woman
25. Conceive: understand me
29. fool: husband
30. I . . . whistle: ironic: once, you would have met me.
33. it origin: its parentage
34. Cannot . . . itself: i.e., can be expected to lack self-control
35. sliver . . . disbranch: sever
36. material sap: vital fluid; i.e., the parent who has given her life
43. head-lugged: led by a neck chain

That bearest a cheek for blows, a head for wrongs;
Who hast not in thy brows an eye discerning
Thine honor from thy suffering; that not knowest
Fools do those villains pity who are punished 55
Ere they have done their mischief. Where's thy drum?
France spreads his banners in our noiseless land,
With plumed helm thy state begins to threat,
Whiles thou, a moral fool, sittest still, and cries
"Alack, why does he so?"

Alb. See thyself, devil! 60
Proper deformity shows not in the fiend
So horrid as in woman.

Gon. O vain fool!

Alb. Thou changed and self-covered thing, for shame!
Bemonster not thy feature! Were't my fitness
To let these hands obey my blood, 65
They are apt enough to dislocate and tear
Thy flesh and bones. Howe'er thou art a fiend,
A woman's shape doth shield thee.

Gon. Marry, your manhood—mew!

Enter a GENTLEMAN.

Alb. What news? 70

Gent. O, my good lord, the Duke of Cornwall's dead,
Slain by his servant, going to put out
The other eye of Gloucester.

Alb. Gloucester's eyes?

Gent. A servant that he bred, thrilled with remorse,
Opposed against the act, bending his sword 75
To his great master; who, thereat enraged,
Flew on him, and amongst them felled him dead;
But not without that harmful stroke which since
Hath plucked him after.

Alb. This shows you are above,
You justicers, that these our nether crimes 80
So speedily can venge! But O poor Gloucester!
Lost he his other eye?

Gent. Both, both, my lord.
This letter, madam, craves a speedy answer.
'Tis from your sister.

Gon. [*Aside*] One way I like this well;
But being widow, and my Gloucester with her, 85
May all the building in my fancy pluck
Upon my hateful life. Another way
The news is not so tart.—I'll read, and answer. *Exit.*

Alb. Where was his son when they did take his eyes? 89

Gent. Come with my lady hither.

Alb. He is not here.

Gent. No, my good lord; I met him back again.

Alb. Knows he the wickedness?

Gent. Ay, my good lord: 'twas he informed against him,
And quit the house on purpose, that their punishment
Might have the freer course.

Alb. Gloucester, I live 95
To thank thee for the love thou showedst the King,
And to revenge thine eyes. Come hither, friend.
Tell me what more thou knowest.

Exeunt.

[Scene III. *The French camp near Dover.*]

Enter KENT *and a* GENTLEMAN.

Kent. Why the King of France is so suddenly gone back, know you no reason?

Gent. Something he left imperfect in the state, which since his coming forth is thought of, which imports to the kingdom so much fear and 5 danger that his personal return was most required and necessary.

Kent. Who hath he left behind him general?

Gent. The Marshal of France, Monsieur La Far.

Kent. Did your letters pierce the Queen to 10 any demonstration of grief?

Gent. Ay, sir. She took them, read them in my presence,
And now and then an ample tear trilled down
Her delicate cheek. It seemed she was a queen
Over her passion, who, most rebel-like, 15
Sought to be king o'er her.

Kent. O, then it moved her?

Gent. Not to a rage. Patience and sorrow strove
Who should express her goodliest. You have seen
Sunshine and rain at once: her smiles and tears
Were like. A better way: those happy smilets 20
That played on her ripe lip seemed not to know
What guests were in her eyes, which parted thence
As pearls from diamonds dropped. In brief,
Sorrow would be a rarity most beloved,
If all could so become it.

Kent. Made she no verbal question?

53–54. discerning . . . suffering: discriminating between forbearance and neglect of honor
61–62. Proper . . . woman: deformity, being appropriate to a fiend, is not so repulsive as in a woman.
62. vain: useless
63. changed . . . thing: Goneril's evil distorts her face so that she looks fiendish, but Albany knows that her expression reflects her true nature.
64. Were't . . . fitness: if it were fitting for a man to so treat a woman
69. mew: an exclamation of contempt
74. remorse: compassion
86–87. May . . . life: may pull down my castle in the air and destroy me

91. back again: on his way back
5. imports: portends
18. express . . . goodliest: become her best
25. so . . . it: express it so becomingly

Gent. Faith, once or twice she heaved the name of father 26
Pantingly forth, as if it pressed her heart;
Cried "Sisters, sisters! Shame of ladies! Sisters!
Kent! father! sisters! What, i' the storm? i' the night?
Let pity not be believed!" There she shook 30
The holy water from her heavenly eyes,
And clamor moistened. Then away she started
To deal with grief alone.

Kent. It is the stars,
The stars above us, govern our conditions;
Else one self mate and make could not beget 35
Such different issues. You spoke not with her since?

Gent. No.

Kent. Was this before the King returned?

Gent. No, since.

Kent. Well, sir, the poor distressed Lear's i' the town;
Who sometime, in his better tune, remembers 40
What we are come about, and by no means
Will yield to see his daughter.

Gent. Why, good sir?

Kent. A sovereign shame so elbows him; his own unkindness,
That stripped her from his benediction, turned her
To foreign casualties, gave her dear rights 45
To his dog-hearted daughters—these things sting
His mind so venomously that burning shame
Detains him from Cordelia.

Gent. Alack, poor gentleman!

Kent. Of Albany's and Cornwall's powers you heard not?

Gent. 'Tis so; they are afoot. 50

Kent. Well, sir, I'll bring you to our master Lear
And leave you to attend him. Some dear cause
Will in concealment wrap me up awhile.
When I am known aright, you shall not grieve
Lending me this acquaintance. I pray you go 55
Along with me.

Exeunt.

Scene [IV. *Same.*]

Enter, with Drum and Colors, CORDELIA, DOCTOR, *and* SOLDIERS.

Cor. Alack, 'tis he! Why, he was met even now
As mad as the vexed sea, singing aloud,

32. clamor moistened: her outcry was moistened by tears.
35. make: mate
40. in . . . tune: in saner moments
43. sovereign: overpowering
45. casualties: chances
52. dear: important
54. grieve: regret

Crowned with rank fumiter and furrow-weeds,
With hardocks, hemlock, nettles, cuckoo-flowers,
Darnel, and all the idle weeds that grow 5
In our sustaining corn. A century send forth.
Search every acre in the high-grown field
And bring him to our eye. [*Exit an Officer.*] What can man's wisdom
In the restoring his bereaved sense?
He that helps him take all my outward worth. 10

Doct. There is means, madam.
Our foster nurse of nature is repose,
The which he lacks. That to provoke in him
Are many simples operative, whose power
Will close the eye of anguish.

Cor. All blest secrets, 15
All you unpublished virtues of the earth,
Spring with my tears! be aidant and remediate
In the good man's distress! Seek, seek for him!
Lest his ungoverned rage dissolve the life
That wants the means to lead it.

Enter MESSENGER.

Mess. News, madam. 20
The British powers are marching hitherward.

Cor. 'Tis known before. Our preparation stands
In expectation of them. O dear father,
It is thy business that I go about.
Therefore great France 25
My mourning and importuned tears hath pitied.
No blown ambition doth our arms incite,
But love, dear love, and our aged father's right.
Soon may I hear and see him!

Exeunt.

Scene [V. *Inside Gloucester's Castle.*]

Enter REGAN *and* [OSWALD *the*] STEWARD.

Reg. But are my brother's powers set forth?

Osw. Ay, madam.

3. fumiter: fumitory, a plant of the genus *Fumaria*, especially *F. officinalis*
4. hardocks: a coarse weed, not certainly identified
5. Darnel: another weed
6. century: body of a hundred soldiers
8. What . . . wisdom: what can science do
14. simples: herbal remedies
16. unpublished . . . earth: little-known medicinal plants
17. aidant: helpful; **remediate:** curative
19. rage: delirious frenzy
26. importuned: importunate
27. blown: inflated

Reg. Himself in person there?
Osw. Madam, with much ado:
Your sister is the better soldier.
Reg. Lord Edmund spake not with your lord at home?
Osw. No madam. 5
Reg. What might import my sister's letter to him?
Osw. I know not, lady.
Reg. Faith, he is posted hence on serious matter.
It was great ignorance, Gloucester's eyes being out,
To let him live. Where he arrives he moves 10
All hearts against us. Edmund, I think, is gone,
In pity of his misery, to dispatch
His nighted life; moreover, to descry
The strength o' the enemy.
Osw. I must needs after him, madam, with my letter. 15
Reg. Our troops set forth tomorrow. Stay with us.
The ways are dangerous.
Osw. I may not, madam.
My lady charged my duty in this business.
Reg. Why should she write to Edmund? Might not you
Transport her purposes by word? Belike, 20
Some things—I know not what—I'll love thee much—
Let me unseal the letter.
Osw. Madam, I had rather—
Reg. I know your lady does not love her husband;
I am sure of that; and at her late being here
She gave strange eliads and most speaking looks 25
To noble Edmund. I know you are of her bosom.
Osw. I, madam?
Reg. I speak in understanding. Y'are! I know't.
Therefore I do advise you take this note.
My lord is dead; Edmund and I have talked, 30
And more convenient is he for my hand
Than for your lady's. You may gather more.
If you do find him, pray you give him this;
And when your mistress hears thus much from you,
I pray desire her call her wisdom to her. 35
So fare you well.
If you do chance to hear of that blind traitor,
Preferment falls on him that cuts him off.
Osw. Would I could meet him, madam! I should show
What party I do follow.
Reg. Fare thee well. 40
Exeunt.

Scene [VI. *Open country near Dover.*]

Enter GLOUCESTER, *and* EDGAR [*clothed as a countryman*].

Glou. When shall I come to the top of that same hill?
Edg. You do climb up it now. Look how we labor.
Glou. Methinks the ground is even.
Edg. Horrible steep.
Hark, do you hear the sea?
Glou. No, truly.
Edg. Why, then, your other senses grow imperfect
By your eyes' anguish.
Glou. So may it be indeed. 6
Methinks thy voice is altered, and thou speakest
In better phrase and matter than thou didst.
Edg. Y'are much deceived. In nothing am I changed
But in my garments.
Glou. Methinks y'are better spoken.
Edg. Come on, sir; here's the place. Stand still. How fearful 11
And dizzy 'tis to cast one's eyes so low!
The crows and choughs that wing the midway air
Show scarce so gross as beetles. Halfway down
Hangs one that gathers sampire—dreadful trade!
Methinks he seems no bigger than his head. 16
The fishermen that walk upon the beach
Appear like mice; and yond tall anchoring bark,
Diminished to her cock; her cock, a buoy
Almost too small for sight. The murmuring surge
That on the unnumbered idle pebble chafes 21
Cannot be heard so high. I'll look no more,
Lest my brain turn, and the deficient sight
Topple down headlong.
Glou. Set me where you stand.
Edg. Give me your hand; you are now within a foot 25
Of the extreme verge; for all beneath the moon
Would I not leap upright.
Glou. Let go my hand.
Here, friend, 's another purse; in it a jewel
Well worth a poor man's taking. Fairies and gods
Prosper it with thee! Go thou further off; 30
Bid me farewell, and let me hear thee going.
Edg. Now fare ye well, good sir.
Glou. With all my heart.

2. **with . . . ado:** reluctantly
13. **nighted:** darkened
25. **eliads:** œillades, amorous glances
26. **of . . . bosom:** in her confidence
29. **take . . . note:** note what I say
31. **convenient:** appropriate
38. **Preferment:** advancement; favor

13. **choughs:** birds of the crow family
14. **gross:** large
15. **sampire:** a succulent herb which grew on cliffs. The name is a corruption of *herbe de Saint Pierre*. It was valued for use in relish.
19. **cock:** cockboat, a small ship's boat
21. **unnumbered:** innumerable

Edg. [*Aside*] Why I do trifle thus with his despair
Is done to cure it.
Glou. O you mighty gods! *He kneels.*
This world I do renounce, and, in your sights, 35
Shake patiently my great affliction off.
If I could bear it longer and not fall
To quarrel with your great opposeless wills,
My snuff and loathed part of nature should
Burn itself out. If Edgar live, O, bless him! 40
Now, fellow, fare thee well.
He falls [*forward and faints*].
Edg. Gone, sir, farewell.—
And yet I know not how conceit may rob
The treasury of life when life itself
Yields to the theft. Had he been where he thought,
By this had thought been past.—Alive or dead? 45
Ho you, sir! friend! Hear you, sir? Speak!—
Thus might he pass indeed. Yet he revives.
What are you, sir?
Glou. Away, and let me die.
Edg. Hadst thou been aught but gossamer, feathers, air,
So many fathom down precipitating, 50
Thou'dst shivered like an egg; but thou dost breathe;
Hast heavy substance; bleedest not; speakest; art sound.
Ten masts at each make not the altitude
Which thou hast perpendicularly fell.
Thy life's a miracle. Speak yet again. 55
Glou. But have I fallen, or no?
Edg. From the dread summit of this chalky bourn.
Look up a-height. The shrill-gorged lark so far
Cannot be seen or heard. Do but look up.
Glou. Alack, I have no eyes! 60
Is wretchedness deprived that benefit
To end itself by death? 'Twas yet some comfort
When misery could beguile the tyrant's rage
And frustrate his proud will.
Edg. Give me your arm. 64
Up—so. How is't? Feel you your legs? You stand.
Glou. Too well, too well.
Edg. This is above all strangeness.
Upon the crown o' the cliff what thing was that
Which parted from you?
Glou. A poor unfortunate beggar.
Edg. As I stood here below, methought his eyes
Were two full moons; he had a thousand noses, 70
Horns whelked and waved like the enridged sea:
It was some fiend; therefore, thou happy father,
Think that the clearest gods, who make them honors
Of men's impossibilities, have preserved thee.
Glou. I do remember now. Henceforth I'll bear
Affliction till it do cry out itself 76
"Enough, enough," and die. That thing you speak of,
I took it for a man. Often 'twould say
"The fiend, the fiend"—he led me to that place.
Edg. Bear free and patient thoughts.

Enter LEAR, *mad,* [*garlanded with wild flowers*].

But who comes here? 80
The safer sense will ne'er accommodate
His master thus.
Lear. No, they cannot touch me for coining;
I am the King himself.
Edg. O thou side-piercing sight! 85
Lear. Nature's above art in that respect. There's your press money. That fellow handles his bow like a crow-keeper. Draw me a clothier's yard. Look, look, a mouse! Peace, peace; this piece of toasted cheese will do it. There's my gauntlet; I'll prove it on 90 a giant. Bring up the brown bills. O, well flown, bird! i' the clout, i' the clout! Hewgh! Give the word.
Edg. Sweet marjoram.
Lear. Pass.
Glou. I know that voice. 95
Lear. Ha! Goneril with a white beard? They flattered me like a dog, and told me I had white hairs in my beard ere the black ones were there. To say "ay" and "no" to everything that I said! "Ay" and "no" too was no good divinity. When the rain came 100 to wet me once, and the wind to make me chatter; when the thunder would not peace at my bidding; there I found 'em, there I smelt 'em out. Go to, they are not men o' their words! They told me I was everything. 'Tis a lie—I am not ague-proof. 105

38. opposeless: irresistible
39. My . . . nature: the useless remainder of my life
42. conceit: imagination. Edgar fears that Gloucester may have expected death so firmly that his heart will actually stop.
53. at each: placed end to end
57. bourn: boundary (of the sea)
58. shrill-gorged: shrill-voiced
71. whelked: twisted; **enridged:** furrowed
72. happy: fortunate; **father:** old man
73. clearest: purest
73–74. who . . . impossibilities: who win men's honor by performing tasks impossible to them
80. free: cheerful
81–82. The . . . thus: a sane man would not dress thus.
83. coining: counterfeiting, a treasonable offense
86. Nature's . . . respect: Nature has created the King, and human agencies cannot change his authority.
87. press money: enlistment pay. Lear imagines that he is recruiting men.
88. crow-keeper: awkward archer, like a boy employed to scare crows away; **clothier's yard:** the measure for a standard English arrow
90. prove it: i.e., defend my cause (symbolized by the gauntlet); **on:** against
91. brown bills: foot soldiers armed with **brown bills,** halberds painted to prevent rust; **well flown:** the flight of an imaginary arrow is compared to the flight of a bird.
92. clout: center of the target; **word:** password
97–98. I . . . there: I was as wise as a bearded old man before I had any beard.
99–100. "Ay" . . . divinity: a reference to the biblical injunction to "let your yea be yea, and your nay, nay, lest ye fall into damnation" (Jas. 5:12)
100. divinity: theology

Glou. The trick of that voice I do well remember.
Is't not the King?
Lear. Ay, every inch a king!
When I do stare, see how the subject quakes.
I pardon that man's life. What was thy cause?
Adultery? 110
Thou shalt not die. Die for adultery? No.
The wren goes to it, and the small gilded fly
Does lecher in my sight.
Let copulation thrive; for Gloucester's bastard son
Was kinder to his father than my daughters 115
Got 'tween the lawful sheets.
To it, luxury, pell-mell! for I lack soldiers.
Behold yond simpering dame,
Whose face between her forks presages snow,
That minces virtue, and does shake the head 120
To hear of pleasure's name.
The fitchew nor the soiled horse goes to it
With a more riotous appetite.
Down from the waist they are Centaurs,
Though women all above. 125
But to the girdle do the gods inherit,
Beneath is all the fiend's.
There's hell, there's darkness, there is the sulphurous pit; burning, scalding, stench, consumption. Fie, fie, fie! pah, pah! Give me an ounce of civet; 130 good apothecary, sweeten my imagination. There's money for thee.
Glou. O, let me kiss that hand!
Lear. Let me wipe it first; it smells of mortality.
Glou. O ruined piece of nature! This great world 135
Shall so wear out to naught. Dost thou know me?
Lear. I remember thine eyes well enough. Dost thou squint at me? No, do thy worst, blind Cupid! I'll not love. Read thou this challenge; mark but the penning of it. 140
Glou. Were all thy letters suns, I could not see.
Edg. [*Aside*] I would not take this from report. It is,
And my heart breaks at it.
Lear. Read.
Glou. What, with the case of eyes? 145
Lear. O, ho, are you there with me? No eyes in your head, nor no money in your purse? Your eyes are in a heavy case, your purse in a light. Yet you see how this world goes.
Glou. I see it feelingly. 150
Lear. What, art mad? A man may see how this world goes with no eyes. Look with thine ears. See how yond justice rails upon yond simple thief. Hark in thine ear. Change places and, handy-dandy, which is the justice, which is the thief? Thou hast 155 seen a farmer's dog bark at a beggar?
Glou. Ay, sir.
Lear. And the creature run from the cur? There thou mightst behold the great image of authority: a dog's obeyed in office. 160
Thou rascal beadle, hold thy bloody hand!
Why dost thou lash that whore? Strip thine own back.
Thou hotly lusts to use her in that kind
For which thou whippest her. The usurer hangs the cozener. 164
Through tattered clothes small vices do appear;
Robes and furred gowns hide all. Plate sin with gold,
And the strong lance of justice hurtless breaks;
Arm it in rags, a pygmy's straw does pierce it.
None does offend, none, I say, none; I'll able 'em:
Take that of me, my friend, who have the power
To seal the accuser's lips. Get thee glass eyes 171
And, like a scurvy politician, seem
To see the things thou dost not. Now, now, now, now!
Pull off my boots. Harder, harder! So.
Edg. O, matter and impertinency mixed! 175
Reason in madness!
Lear. If thou wilt weep my fortunes, take my eyes.
I know thee well enough; thy name is Gloucester.
Thou must be patient. We came crying hither; 179
Thou knowest, the first time that we smell the air
We wawl and cry. I will preach to thee: mark.
Glou. Alack, alack the day!
Lear. When we are born, we cry that we are come
To this great stage of fools. This' a good block.
It were a delicate stratagem to shoe 185
A troop of horse with felt. I'll put't in proof,
And when I have stolen upon these sons-in-law,
Then kill, kill, kill, kill, kill, kill!

Enter a GENTLEMAN [*with* ATTENDANTS].

Gent. O, here he is! Lay hand upon him.—Sir,
Your most dear daughter— 190

117. luxury: lust
119. forks: probably, the peaked dressing of her hair; **presages snow:** resembles snow in its white purity
120. minces virtue: affects chastity
122. fitchew: polecat; also a cant term for "prostitute"
126. inherit: possess
135. piece: masterpiece
145. case: rim; sockets
146. Are . . . me: is that what you mean?
150. see . . . feelingly: perceive it by feeling and feel it keenly
154. handy-dandy: a child's game of choosing which hand has a hidden object
158. creature: human being
159. image: personification
161. beadle: official who punished criminals
164. cozener: petty swindler
169. able: vouch for
172. scurvy: scabby; contemptible
175. matter . . . impertinency: sense and nonsense
184. This': this is; **block:** perhaps Lear handles a hat, which makes him think of the felt he refers to in the next line.
185. delicate: subtle

Lear. No rescue? What, a prisoner? I am even
The natural fool of fortune. Use me well;
You shall have ransom. Let me have surgeons;
I am cut to the brains.
Gent. You shall have anything.
Lear. No seconds? All myself? 195
Why, this would make a man a man of salt,
To use his eyes for garden waterpots,
Ay, and laying autumn's dust. I will die bravely,
Like a smug bridegroom. What! I will be jovial.
Come, come, I am a king; masters, know you that?
Gent. You are a royal one, and we obey you. 201
Lear. Then there's life in't. Come, an you get it, you shall get it by running. Sa, sa, sa, sa!
Exit running [followed by Attendants].
Gent. A sight most pitiful in the meanest wretch,
Past speaking of in a king! Thou hast one daughter
Who redeems nature from the general curse 206
Which twain have brought her to.
Edg. Hail, gentle sir.
Gent. Sir, speed you. What's your will?
Edg. Do you hear aught, sir, of a battle toward?
Gent. Most sure and vulgar. Every one hears that
Which can distinguish sound.
Edg. But, by your favor, 211
How near's the other army?
Gent. Near and on speedy foot. The main descry
Stands on the hourly thought.
Edg. I thank you, sir. That's all.
Gent. Though that the Queen on special cause is here. 215
Her army is moved on.
Edg. I thank you, sir.
Exit [Gentleman].
Glou. You ever-gentle gods, take my breath from me;
Let not my worser spirit tempt me again
To die before you please!
Edg. Well pray you, father.
Glou. Now, good sir, what are you? 220
Edg. A most poor man, made tame to fortune's blows,
Who, by the art of known and feeling sorrows,
Am pregnant to good pity. Give me your hand;
I'll lead you to some biding.
Glou. Hearty thanks.
The bounty and the benison of heaven 225
To boot, and boot!

Enter [OSWALD *the*] STEWARD.

Osw. A proclaimed prize! Most happy!
That eyeless head of thine was first framed flesh
To raise my fortunes. Thou old unhappy traitor,
Briefly thyself remember: the sword is out 229
That must destroy thee.
Glou. Now let thy friendly hand
Put strength enough to't. [*Edgar interposes.*]
Osw. Wherefore, bold peasant,
Darest thou support a published traitor? Hence!
Lest that the infection of his fortune take
Like hold on thee. Let go his arm. 234
Edg. Chill not let go, zir, without vurther 'casion.
Osw. Let go, slave, or thou diest!
Edg. Good gentleman, go your gait, and let poor volk pass. An chud ha' bin zwagger'd out of my life, 'twould not ha' bin zo long as 'tis by a vortnight. Nay, come not near the old man. Keep out, 240 che vor' ye, or Ise try whither your costard or my ballow be the harder. Chill be plain with you.
Osw. Out, dunghill!
Edg. Chill pick your teeth, zir. Come! No matter vor your foins. [*They fight and Oswald falls.*]
Osw. Slave, thou hast slain me. Villain, take my purse. 246
If ever thou wilt thrive, bury my body,
And give the letters which thou findst about me
To Edmund Earl of Gloucester. Seek him out
Upon the English party. O, untimely death! Death!
He dies.
Edg. I know thee well. A serviceable villain, 251
As duteous to the vices of thy mistress
As badness would desire.
Glou. What, is he dead?
Edg. Sit you down, father; rest you.
Let's see these pockets; the letters that he speaks of
May be my friends. He's dead; I am only sorry 256
He had no other deathsman. Let us see.
Leave, gentle wax; and manners, blame us not:
To know our enemies' minds, we rip their hearts;
Their papers is more lawful. *Reads the letter.*

Let our reciprocal vows be remembered. You 261 have many opportunities to cut him off. If your will want not, time and place will be fruitfully offered. There is nothing done if he return the conqueror. Then am I

192. fool: plaything
198. bravely: courageously and splendidly (referring to his weed-bedecked clothing)
199. smug: spruce
202. there's . . . it: all is not lost.
203. Sa, sa: French *çà, çà,* "here, here"; a cry to urge hounds to the chase
210. vulgar: commonly known
213–14. The . . . thought: the main force should be sighted any hour
223. pregnant: susceptible
224. biding: abode
226. To . . . boot: as compensation into the bargain
229. thyself remember: review thy sins
235. Chill: I will. Edgar assumes a rustic dialect.
238. chud: I could
241. che . . . ye: I warn you; **Ise:** I shall; **costard:** an apple, also a humorous term for "head"
242. ballow: presumably a cudgel. Corrected copies of the First Quarto read "bat."
245. foins: sword thrusts

the prisoner, and his bed my jail; from the loathed 265
warmth whereof deliver me, and supply the place for
your labor.
Your (wife, so I would say) affectionate servant,
GONERIL.

O indistinguished space of woman's will!
A plot upon her virtuous husband's life, 270
And the exchange my brother! Here in the sands
Thee I'll rake up, the post unsanctified
Of murderous lechers; and in the mature time
With this ungracious paper strike the sight
Of the death-practiced Duke. For him 'tis well 275
That of thy death and business I can tell.

Glou. The King is mad. How stiff is my vile sense,
That I stand up, and have ingenious feeling
Of my huge sorrows! Better I were distract.
So should my thoughts be severed from my griefs,
And woes by wrong imaginations lose 281
The knowledge of themselves. *A drum afar off.*

Edg. Give me your hand.
Far off methinks I hear the beaten drum.
Come, father, I'll bestow you with a friend.
Exeunt.

Scene VII. [*A tent in the French camp.*]

Enter CORDELIA, KENT, DOCTOR, *and* GENTLEMAN.

Cor. O thou good Kent, how shall I live and work
To match thy goodness? My life will be too short
And every measure fail me.

Kent. To be acknowledged, madam, is o'erpaid.
All my reports go with the modest truth; 5
Nor more nor clipped, but so.

Cor. Be better suited:
These weeds are memories of those worser hours:
I prithee put them off.

Kent. Pardon, dear madam.
Yet to be known shortens my made intent.
My boon I make it that you know me not 10
Till time and I think meet.

Cor. Then be it so, my good lord. [*To the Doctor*]
How does the King?

Doct. Madam, sleeps still.

Cor. O you kind gods,
Cure this great breach in his abused nature! 15
The untuned and jarring senses, O, wind up
Of this child-changed father!

Doct. So please your Majesty
That we may wake the King? He hath slept long.

Cor. Be governed by your knowledge, and proceed
I' the sway of your own will. Is he arrayed? 20

Enter LEAR *in a chair carried by* SERVANTS.

Gent. Ay, madam. In the heaviness of sleep
We put fresh garments on him.

Doct. Be by, good madam, when we do awake him.
I doubt not of his temperance.

Cor. Very well. [*Music.*]

Doct. Please you draw near. Louder the music
there! 25

Cor. O my dear father, restoration hang
Thy medicine on my lips, and let this kiss
Repair those violent harms that my two sisters
Have in thy reverence made!

Kent. Kind and dear princess!

Cor. Had you not been their father, these white
flakes 30
Had challenged pity of them. Was this a face
To be opposed against the warring winds?
To stand against the deep dread-bolted thunder?
In the most terrible and nimble stroke
Of quick, cross lightning? to watch—poor perdu!—
With this thin helm? Mine enemy's dog, 36
Though he had bit me, should have stood that night
Against my fire; and wast thou fain, poor father,
To hovel thee with swine and rogues forlorn,
In short and musty straw? Alack, alack! 40
'Tis wonder that thy life and wits at once
Had not concluded all.—He wakes; speak to him.

Doct. Madam, do you; 'tis fittest.

Cor. How does my royal lord? How fares your
Majesty?

Lear. You do me wrong to take me out o' the
grave. 45
Thou art a soul in bliss; but I am bound
Upon a wheel of fire, that mine own tears
Do scald like molten lead.

Cor. Sir, do you know me?

Lear. You are a spirit, I know. Where did you die?

Cor. Still, still, far wide! 50

Doct. He's scarce awake. Let him alone awhile.

Lear. Where have I been? Where am I? Fair daylight?
I am mightily abused. I should e'en die with pity,

269. indistinguished . . . will: limitless scope of woman's lust
272. rake up: bury
273. in . . . time: when the time is ripe
274. ungracious: wicked
275. death-practiced: whose death has been plotted
278–79. have . . . of: acutely perceive
6. Nor . . . clipped: neither enlarged nor abbreviated
7. weeds: garments
9. Yet . . . intent: to reveal myself now would prevent the completion of my purpose.

24. temperance: sanity
30. flakes: locks of hair
31. challenged: demanded
35. perdu: *sentinelle perdue,* one stationed in so dangerous a position that his death seems certain
38. fain: forced
42. concluded all: both ended
50. wide: wide of the mark; wandering in his wits

To see another thus. I know not what to say.
I will not swear these are my hands. Let's see: 55
I feel this pin prick. Would I were assured
Of my condition!
Cor. O, look upon me, sir,
And hold your hands in benediction o'er me.
No, sir, you must not kneel.
Lear. Pray, do not mock me.
I am a very foolish fond old man, 60
Fourscore and upward, not an hour more nor less;
And, to deal plainly,
I fear I am not in my perfect mind.
Methinks I should know you, and know this man;
Yet I am doubtful; for I am mainly ignorant 65
What place this is; and all the skill I have
Remembers not these garments; nor I know not
Where I did lodge last night. Do not laugh at me;
For (as I am a man) I think this lady
To be my child Cordelia.
Cor. And so I am. I am. 70
Lear. Be your tears wet? Yes, faith. I pray weep not.
If you have poison for me, I will drink it.
I know you do not love me, for your sisters
Have, as I do remember, done me wrong:
You have some cause, they have not.
Cor. No cause, no cause.
Lear. Am I in France?
Kent. In your own kingdom, sir.

65. **mainly:** completely

Lear. Do not abuse me. 77
Doct. Be comforted, good madam. The great rage
You see is killed in him; and yet it is danger
To make him even o'er the time he has lost. 80
Desire him to go in. Trouble him no more
Till further settling.
Cor. Will't please your Highness walk?
Lear. You must bear with me.
Pray you now, forget and forgive. I am old and foolish.
Exeunt [*Lear, Cordelia, Doctor, and Attendants*].
Gent. Holds it true, sir, that the Duke of 85
Cornwall was so slain?
Kent. Most certain, sir.
Gent. Who is conductor of his people?
Kent. As 'tis said, the bastard son of Gloucester.
Gent. They say Edgar, his banished son, is 90
with the Earl of Kent in Germany.
Kent. Report is changeable. 'Tis time to look
about; the powers of the kingdom approach apace.
Gent. The arbitrament is like to be bloody. 94
Fare you well, sir. [*Exit.*]
Kent. My point and period will be throughly wrought,
Or well or ill, as this day's battle's fought.
Exit.

80. **even o'er:** fill in; recall to mind
82. **settling:** calming
94. **arbitrament:** settlement
96. **point . . . period:** final end; **throughly:** thoroughly

ACT V

Scene I. [*The British camp near Dover.*]

Enter, with Drum and Colors, Edmund, Regan, Gentlemen *and* Soldiers.

Edm. Know of the Duke if his last purpose hold,
Or whether since he is advised by aught
To change the course. He's full of alteration
And self-reproving. Bring his constant pleasure.
[*Exit an Officer.*]

4. **constant pleasure:** firm decision

Reg. Our sister's man is certainly miscarried. 5
Edm. 'Tis to be doubted, madam.
Reg. Now, sweet lord,
You know the goodness I intend upon you.
Tell me, but truly, but then speak the truth,
Do you not love my sister?
Edm. In honored love. 9
Reg. But have you never found my brother's way
To the forfended place?
Edm. That thought abuses you.

5. **miscarried:** dead
6. **doubted:** feared
11. **forfended:** prohibited

Reg. I am doubtful that you have been conjunct
And bosomed with her, as far as we call hers.
Edm. No, by mine honor, madam.
Reg. I never shall endure her. Dear my lord, 15
Be not familiar with her.
Edm. Fear me not.
She and the Duke her husband!

Enter, with Drum and Colors, ALBANY, GONERIL, SOLDIERS.

Gon. [*Aside*] I had rather lose the battle than that sister
Should loosen him and me.
Alb. Our very loving sister, well bemet. 20
Sir, this I hear: the King is come to his daughter,
With others whom the rigor of our state
Forced to cry out. Where I could not be honest,
I never yet was valiant. For this business,
It touches us as France invades our land, 25
Not bolds the King, with others, whom, I fear,
Most just and heavy causes make oppose.
Edm. Sir, you speak nobly.
Reg. Why is this reasoned?
Gon. Combine together 'gainst the enemy;
For these domestic and particular broils 30
Are not the question here.
Alb. Let's then determine
With the ancient of war on our proceeding.
Edm. I shall attend you presently at your tent.
Reg. Sister, you'll go with us?
Gon. No. 35
Reg. 'Tis most convenient; pray go with us.
Gon. [*Aside*] O, ho, I know the riddle.—I will go.

[*As they are going out,*] *enter* EDGAR [*disguised*].

Edg. If e'er your Grace had speech with man so poor,
Hear me one word.
Alb. I'll overtake you.
Exeunt [*all but Albany and Edgar*].
Speak.
Edg. Before you fight the battle, ope this letter.
If you have victory, let the trumpet sound 41
For him that brought it. Wretched though I seem,
I can produce a champion that will prove
What is avouched there. If you miscarry,
Your business of the world hath so an end, 45
And machination ceases. Fortune love you!
Alb. Stay till I have read the letter.
Edg. I was forbid it.
When time shall serve, let but the herald cry,
And I'll appear again. 49
Alb. Why, fare thee well. I will o'erlook thy paper.
Exit [*Edgar*].

Enter EDMUND.

Edm. The enemy's in view; draw up your powers.
Here is the guess of their true strength and forces
By diligent discovery; but your haste
Is now urged on you.
Alb. We will greet the time. *Exit.*
Edm. To both these sisters have I sworn my love;
Each jealous of the other, as the stung 56
Are of the adder. Which of them shall I take?
Both? one? or neither? Neither can be enjoyed
If both remain alive. To take the widow
Exasperates, makes mad her sister Goneril; 60
And hardly shall I carry out my side,
Her husband being alive. Now then, we'll use
His countenance for the battle, which being done,
Let her who would be rid of him devise
His speedy taking off. As for the mercy 65
Which he intends to Lear and to Cordelia,
The battle done, and they within our power,
Shall never see his pardon; for my state
Stands on me to defend, not to debate.
Exit.

Scene II. [*A field between the two camps.*]

Alarum within. Enter, with Drum and Colors, LEAR, CORDELIA, *and the* POWERS OF FRANCE *over the stage, and exeunt.*

Enter EDGAR *and* GLOUCESTER.

Edg. Here, father, take the shadow of this tree
For your good host. Pray that the right may thrive.
If ever I return to you again,
I'll bring you comfort.
Glou. Grace go with you, sir!
Exit [*Edgar*].

Alarum and retreat within. Enter EDGAR.

12. doubtful: fearful; **conjunct . . . hers:** as intimate with her as it is possible to be
25–26. It . . . King: i.e., our concern is with the French invasion of our land, not with any assistance France may lend the King. The difficult syntax suggests corruption in the text.
28. Why . . . reasoned: why is this conversation necessary?
30. particular: personal; **broils:** quarrels
32. ancient . . . war: seasoned officers
36. convenient: suitable

46. machination: plotting
53. discovery: scouting
54. greet . . . time: be prepared when the time comes
56. jealous: suspiciously watchful
63. countenance: authority
68–69. my . . . debate: the security of my position requires active defense; I cannot afford to consider moral issues.

Edg. Away, old man! give me thy hand! away! 5
King Lear hath lost, he and his daughter ta'en.
Give me thy hand! come on!
Glou. No further, sir. A man may rot even here.
Edg. What, in ill thoughts again? Men must endure
Their going hence, even as their coming hither; 10
Ripeness is all. Come on.
Glou. And that's true too.
Exeunt.

Scene III. [*The British camp, near Dover.*]

Enter, in conquest, with Drum and Colors, EDMUND; LEAR *and* CORDELIA *as prisoners;* SOLDIERS, CAPTAIN.

Edm. Some officers take them away. Good guard
Until their greater pleasures first be known
That are to censure them.
Cor. We are not the first
Who with best meaning have incurred the worst.
For thee, oppressed king, I am cast down; 5
Myself could else outfrown false Fortune's frown.
Shall we not see these daughters and these sisters?
Lear. No, no, no, no! Come, let's away to prison.
We two alone will sing like birds i' the cage.
When thou dost ask me blessing, I'll kneel down 10
And ask of thee forgiveness. So we'll live,
And pray, and sing, and tell old tales, and laugh
At gilded butterflies, and hear poor rogues
Talk of court news; and we'll talk with them too,
Who loses and who wins; who's in, who's out; 15
And take upon's the mystery of things,
As if we were God's spies; and we'll wear out,
In a walled prison, packs and sects of great ones
That ebb and flow by the moon.
Edm. Take them away.
Lear. Upon such sacrifices, my Cordelia, 20
The gods themselves throw incense. Have I caught thee?
He that parts us shall bring a brand from heaven
And fire us hence like foxes. Wipe thine eyes.
The goodyears shall devour 'em, flesh and fell,
Ere they shall make us weep! We'll see 'em starved first. 25
Come. *Exeunt* [*Lear and Cordelia, guarded*].
Edm. Come hither, Captain; hark.
Take thou this note [*Gives a paper*]. Go follow them to prison.
One step I have advanced thee; if thou dost
As this instructs thee, thou dost make thy way 30
To noble fortunes. Know thou this, that men
Are as the time is; to be tender-minded
Does not become a sword. Thy great employment
Will not bear question; either say thou'lt do't,
Or thrive by other means.
Capt. I'll do't, my lord. 35
Edm. About it! and write happy when th' hast done.
Mark—I say, instantly; and carry it so
As I have set it down. 38
Capt. I cannot draw a cart, nor eat dried oats;
If it be man's work, I'll do't. *Exit.*

Flourish. Enter ALBANY, GONERIL, REGAN, SOLDIERS.

Alb. Sir, you have showed today your valiant strain,
And fortune led you well. You have the captives
Who were the opposites of this day's strife;
I do require them of you, so to use them
As we shall find their merits and our safety 45
May equally determine.
Edm. Sir, I thought it fit
To send the old and miserable King
To some retention and appointed guard;
Whose age had charms in it, whose title more,
To pluck the common bosom on his side 50
And turn our impressed lances in our eyes
Which do command them. With him I sent the Queen,
My reason all the same; and they are ready
Tomorrow, or at further space, t' appear
Where you shall hold your session. At this time 55
We sweat and bleed: the friend hath lost his friend,
And the best quarrels, in the heat, are cursed
By those that feel their sharpness.
The question of Cordelia and her father
Requires a fitter place.
Alb. Sir, by your patience, 60
I hold you but a subject of this war,
Not as a brother.
Reg. That's as we list to grace him.
Methinks our pleasure might have been demanded
Ere you had spoke so far. He led our powers,
Bore the commission of my place and person, 65
The which immediacy may well stand up
And call itself your brother.
Gon. Not so hot!
In his own grace he doth exalt himself
More than in your addition.

2. their . . . pleasures: the wishes of those with higher authority
3. censure: judge
4. meaning: intentions
16. take . . . things: undertake to decide the meaning of things
24. goodyears: a term of obscure origin meaning a malevolent agency; **fell:** skin

37. carry . . . so: so perform it
41. strain: blood; birth
51. impressed lances: the weapons of our conscripted men
61. hold: regard
62. list: please
66. immediacy: immediate representation of myself

Reg. In my rights
By me invested, he compeers the best. 70
Gon. That were the most if he should husband you.
Reg. Jesters do oft prove prophets.
Gon. Holla, holla!
That eye that told you so looked but asquint.
Reg. Lady, I am not well; else I should answer
From a full-flowing stomach. General, 75
Take thou my soldiers, prisoners, patrimony;
Dispose of them, of me; the walls are thine.
Witness the world that I create thee here
My lord and master.
Gon. Mean you to enjoy him?
Alb. The let-alone lies not in your good will. 80
Edm. Nor in thine, lord.
Alb. Half-blooded fellow, yes.
Reg. [*To Edmund*] Let the drum strike, and prove my title thine.
Alb. Stay yet; hear reason. Edmund, I arrest thee
On capital treason; and, in thine attaint,
This gilded serpent [*Points to Goneril*]. For your claim, fair sister, 85
I bar it in the interest of my wife.
'Tis she is sub-contracted to this lord,
And I, her husband, contradict your banes.
If you will marry, make your loves to me;
My lady is bespoke.
Gon. An interlude! 90
Alb. Thou art armed, Gloucester. Let the trumpet sound.
If none appear to prove upon thy person
Thy heinous, manifest, and many treasons,
There is my pledge [*Throws down a glove*]! I'll make it on thy heart,
Ere I taste bread, thou art in nothing less 95
Than I have here proclaimed thee.
Reg. Sick, O, sick!
Gon. [*Aside*] If not, I'll ne'er trust medicine.
Edm. There's my exchange [*Throws down a glove*]. What in the world he is
That names me traitor, villain-like he lies.
Call by thy trumpet. He that dares approach, 100
On him, on you, who not? I will maintain
My truth and honor firmly.
Alb. A herald, ho!
Edm. A herald, ho, a herald!

70. **compeers:** equals
73. **That . . . asquint:** cf. the proverb "Love, being jealous, makes a good eye look asquint."
77. **the . . . thine:** i.e., I surrender to you the fortress of my person.
78. **Witness . . . world:** let the world note
81. **Half-blooded:** illegitimate
84. **in . . . attaint:** as a partner to your treason
88. **contradict:** forbid; **banes:** banns
90. **An interlude:** ironic: "A pretty farce!"
94. **make it:** make it good
101. **maintain:** defend

Alb. Trust to thy single virtue; for thy soldiers,
All levied in my name, have in my name 105
Took their discharge.
Reg. My sickness grows upon me.
Alb. She is not well. Convey her to my tent.
[*Exit Regan, led.*]

Enter a HERALD.

Come hither, herald. Let the trumpet sound,
And read out this. 109
Capt. Sound, trumpet! *A trumpet sounds.*

Her. (*Reads*) If any man of quality or degree within the lists of the army will maintain upon Edmund, supposed Earl of Gloucester, that he is a manifold traitor, let him appear by the third sound of the trumpet. He is bold in his defense. 115
First trumpet.
Her. Again! *Second trumpet.*
Her. Again! *Third trumpet.*
Trumpet answers within.

Enter EDGAR, *armed, a Trumpet before him.*

Alb. Ask him his purposes, why he appears
Upon this call o' the trumpet.
Her. What are you?
Your name, your quality? and why you answer 120
This present summons?
Edg. Know my name is lost;
By treason's tooth bare-gnawn and canker-bit.
Yet am I noble as the adversary
I come to cope.
Alb. Which is that adversary?
Edg. What's he that speaks for Edmund Earl of Gloucester? 125
Edm. Himself. What sayest thou to him?
Edg. Draw thy sword,
That, if my speech offend a noble heart,
Thy arm may do thee justice. Here is mine.
Behold, it is the privilege of mine honors,
My oath, and my profession. I protest, 130
Mauger thy strength, place, youth, and eminence,
Despite thy victor sword and fire-new fortune,
Thy valor and thy heart, thou art a traitor,
False to thy gods, thy brother, and thy father;
Conspirant 'gainst this high illustrious prince; 135
And from the extremest upward of thy head
To the descent and dust beneath thy foot,
A most toad-spotted traitor. Say thou "no,"
This sword, this arm, and my best spirits are bent
To prove upon thy heart, whereto I speak, 140
Thou liest.

104. **virtue:** valor
122. **canker-bit:** maliciously undermined
124. **cope:** fight
131. **Mauger:** despite
132. **fire-new:** brand-new

Edm. In wisdom I should ask thy name;
But since thy outside looks so fair and warlike,
And that thy tongue some say of breeding breathes,
What safe and nicely I might well delay
By rule of knighthood I disdain and spurn; 145
Back do I toss those treasons to thy head,
With the hell-hated lie o'erwhelm thy heart,
Which, for they yet glance by and scarcely bruise,
This sword of mine shall give them instant way
Where they shall rest forever. Trumpets, speak!
Alarums. Fight. [*Edmund falls.*]
Alb. Save him, save him!
Gon. This is mere practice, Gloucester. 151
By the law of arms thou wast not bound to answer
An unknown opposite. Thou art not vanquished,
But cozened and beguiled.
Alb. Shut your mouth, dame,
Or with this paper shall I stop it. [*Shows her her letter to Edmund.*]—[*To Edmund*] Hold, sir.
[*To Goneril*] Thou worse than any name, read thine own evil. 156
No tearing, lady! I perceive you know it.
Gon. Say if I do—the laws are mine, not thine.
Who can arraign me for't?
Alb. Most monstrous! O! 159
Knowest thou this paper?
Gon. Ask me not what I know.
Exit.
Alb. Go after her. She's desperate; govern her.
[*Exit an Officer.*]
Edm. What you have charged me with, that have I done,
And more, much more. The time will bring it out.
'Tis past, and so am I. But what art thou
That hast this fortune on me? If thou'rt noble, 165
I do forgive thee.
Edg. Let's exchange charity.
I am no less in blood than thou art, Edmund;
If more, the more th' hast wronged me.
My name is Edgar and thy father's son.
The gods are just, and of our pleasant vices 170
Make instruments to plague us.
The dark and vicious place where thee he got
Cost him his eyes.
Edm. Th' hast spoken right; 'tis true.
The wheel is come full circle; I am here.
Alb. Methought thy very gait did prophesy 175
A royal nobleness. I must embrace thee.
Let sorrow split my heart if ever I
Did hate thee, or thy father!
Edg. Worthy prince, I know't.

143. say: smack; taste
144. safe . . . nicely: cautiously and fastidiously
151. practice: trickery
153. opposite: opponent
166. charity: forgiveness
167. no . . . art: my blood is as good as yours
174. The wheel: Fortune's wheel

Alb. Where have you hid yourself? 179
How have you known the miseries of your father?
Edg. By nursing them, my lord. List a brief tale;
And when 'tis told, O that my heart would burst!
The bloody proclamation to escape
That followed me so near (O, our lives' sweetness!
That we the pain of death would hourly die 185
Rather than die at once!) taught me to shift
Into a madman's rags, t' assume a semblance
That very dogs disdained; and in this habit
Met I my father with his bleeding rings,
Their precious stones new lost; became his guide,
Led him, begged for him, saved him from despair;
Never (O fault!) revealed myself unto him 192
Until some half hour past, when I was armed;
Not sure, though hoping of this good success,
I asked his blessing, and from first to last 195
Told him my pilgrimage. But his flawed heart
(Alack, too weak the conflict to support!)
'Twixt two extremes of passion, joy and grief,
Burst smilingly.
Edm. This speech of yours hath moved me,
And shall perchance do good; but speak you on;
You look as you had something more to say. 201
Alb. If there be more, more woeful, hold it in;
For I am almost ready to dissolve,
Hearing of this.
Edg. This would have seemed a period
To such as love not sorrow; but another, 205
To amplify too much, would make much more,
And top extremity.
Whilst I was big in clamor, came there a man,
Who, having seen me in my worst estate, 209
Shunned my abhorred society; but then, finding
Who 'twas that so endured, with his strong arms
He fastened on my neck, and bellowed out
As he'd burst heaven; threw him on my father;
Told the most piteous tale of Lear and him
That ever ear received; which in recounting 215
His grief grew puissant, and the strings of life
Began to crack. Twice then the trumpets sounded,
And there I left him tranced.
Alb. But who was this?
Edg. Kent, sir, the banished Kent; who in disguise
Followed his enemy king and did him service 220
Improper for a slave.

Enter a GENTLEMAN *with a bloody knife.*

Gent. Help, help! O, help!
Edg. What kind of help?
Alb. Speak, man.
Edg. What means this bloody knife?

196. flawed: cracked
208. big: loud
216. puissant: potent

Gent. 'Tis hot, it smokes.
It came even from the heart of—O, she's dead!
Alb. Who dead? Speak, man. 225
Gent. Your lady, sir, your lady! and her sister
By her is poisoned; she hath confessed it.
Edm. I was contracted to them both. All three
Now marry in an instant.
Edg. Here comes Kent.

Enter KENT.

Alb. Produce the bodies, be they alive or dead.
[*Exit Gentleman.*]
This judgment of the heavens, that makes us tremble, 231
Touches us not with pity. [*To Kent*] O, is this he?
The time will not allow the compliment
Which very manners urges.
Kent. I am come
To bid my king and master aye good night. 235
Is he not here?
Alb. Great thing of us forgot!
Speak, Edmund, where's the King? and where's Cordelia?
The bodies of Goneril and Regan are brought in.
Seest thou this object, Kent?
Kent. Alack, why thus?
Edm. Yet Edmund was beloved.
The one the other poisoned for my sake, 240
And after slew herself.
Alb. Even so. Cover their faces.
Edm. I pant for life. Some good I mean to do,
Despite of mine own nature. Quickly send
(Be brief in't) to the castle; for my writ 245
Is on the life of Lear and on Cordelia.
Nay, send in time.
Alb. Run, run, O, run!
Edg. To who, my lord? Who has the office? Send
Thy token of reprieve.
Edm. Well thought on. Take my sword; 250
Give it the Captain.
Edg. Haste thee for thy life. [*Exit an Officer.*]
Edm. He hath commission from thy wife and me
To hang Cordelia in the prison and
To lay the blame upon her own despair
That she fordid herself. 255
Alb. The gods defend her! Bear him hence awhile.
[*Edmund is borne off.*]

Enter LEAR, *with* CORDELIA *in his arms,* [CAPTAIN *and others following*].

Lear. Howl, howl, howl! O, you are men of stones.
Had I your tongues and eyes, I'd use them so
That heaven's vault should crack. She's gone forever!
I know when one is dead, and when one lives. 260
She's dead as earth. Lend me a looking glass.
If that her breath will mist or stain the stone,
Why, then she lives.
Kent. Is this the promised end?
Edg. Or image of that horror?
Alb. Fall and cease!
Lear. This feather stirs; she lives! If it be so,
It is a chance which does redeem all sorrows 266
That ever I have felt.
Kent. O my good master!
Lear. Prithee away!
Edg. 'Tis noble Kent, your friend.
Lear. A plague upon you, murderers, traitors all!
I might have saved her; now she's gone forever!
Cordelia, Cordelia! stay a little. Ha! 271
What is't thou sayest? Her voice was ever soft,
Gentle, and low—an excellent thing in woman.
I killed the slave that was a-hanging thee.
Capt. 'Tis true, my lords, he did.
Lear. Did I not, fellow?
I have seen the day, with my good biting falchion
I would have made 'em skip. I am old now, 277
And these same crosses spoil me. Who are you?
Mine eyes are not o' the best, I'll tell you straight.
Kent. If fortune brag of two she loved and hated,
One of them we behold. 281
Lear. This is a dull sight. Are you not Kent?
Kent. The same;
Your servant Kent. Where is your servant Caius?
Lear. He's a good fellow, I can tell you that.
He'll strike, and quickly too. He's dead and rotten.
Kent. No, my good lord; I am the very man—
Lear. I'll see that straight. 287
Kent. That from your first of difference and decay
Have followed your sad steps.
Lear. You are welcome hither.
Kent. Nor no man else! All's cheerless, dark, and deadly. 290
Your eldest daughters have fordone themselves,
And desperately are dead.
Lear. Ay, so I think.
Alb. He knows not what he says; and vain is it
That we present us to him.
Edg. Very bootless.

Enter a CAPTAIN.

234. **very:** mere
255. **fordid:** killed

262. **stone:** crystal surface of a mirror
264. **Fall and cease:** Albany addresses the heavens.
276. **falchion:** sword
278. **crosses:** troubles
282. **dull:** depressing
288. **first . . . decay:** beginning of your decline of fortune
290. **Nor . . . else:** "how can anyone be welcome at a time like this!"
294. **bootless:** unprofitable

Capt. Edmund is dead, my lord.
Alb. That's but a trifle here. 295
You lords and noble friends, know our intent.
What comfort to this great decay may come
Shall be applied. For us, we will resign,
During the life of this old Majesty,
To him our absolute power; [*To Edgar and Kent*] you to your rights; 300
With boot, and such addition as your honors
Have more than merited. All friends shall taste
The wages of their virtue, and all foes
The cup of their deservings.—O, see, see!
Lear. And my poor fool is hanged! No, no, no life!
Why should a dog, a horse, a rat, have life, 306
And thou no breath at all? Thou'lt come no more,
Never, never, never, never, never!
Pray you undo this button. Thank you, sir.
Do you see this? Look on her! look! her lips! 310
Look there, look there! *He dies.*

297. this . . . decay: this ruined man
301. addition: title
305. fool: endearment referring to Cordelia

Edg. He faints! My lord, my lord!
Kent. Break, heart; I prithee break!
Edg. Look up, my lord.
Kent. Vex not his ghost. O, let him pass! He hates him
That would upon the rack of this tough world
Stretch him out longer.
Edg. He is gone indeed. 315
Kent. The wonder is, he hath endured so long.
He but usurped his life.
Alb. Bear them from hence. Our present business
Is general woe. [*To Kent and Edgar*] Friends of my soul, you twain
Rule in this realm, and the gored state sustain. 320
Kent. I have a journey, sir, shortly to go.
My master calls me; I must not say no.
Edg. The weight of this sad time we must obey,
Speak what we feel, not what we ought to say.
The oldest hath borne most; we that are young
Shall never see so much, nor live so long. 326
Exeunt with a dead march.

317. usurped . . . life: i.e., he had borne more than was natural for a human to bear.

Fortune's Wheel
From Sebastian Brant, *The Ship of Fools* (1497).

Macbeth's Vision of the Line of Stuart Kings Stretching out "to the Crack of Doom" (IV.i)

Etching by J. Moyr Smith; from an extra-illustrated copy of Shakespeare's *Works,* edited by Henry Irving and Frank A. Marshall.

The Tragedy of MACBETH

INTRODUCTION

Soon after producing *King Lear,* Shakespeare turned his attention again to legendary history —this time to the history of Scotland—and brought out *Macbeth,* which the evidence indicates was first performed in 1606. Taking his main plot elements from Holinshed's *Chronicles,* Shakespeare created a Macbeth to suit his own fancy; the historical Scottish king, who was a contemporary of Edward the Confessor, King of England from 1042 to 1066, was in many respects quite different from the character in the play. Shakespeare is concerned with a study in evil, and he makes Macbeth conform to the requirements of a quasi-morality play portraying the struggle of good and evil for the soul of the king.

Critics have seen in *Macbeth* a concentration upon the theme of ambition or upon the manifestations of fear and its devastating results. It is more accurate to say that Shakespeare is attempting to show the corroding effects produced by his protagonist's choice of Evil as his good. In the morality plays, the contest between good and evil angels for the soul of man was made explicit, and even in such a sophisticated play as Marlowe's *Doctor Faustus* one sees the continuation of this tradition. In other plays the conflict is symbolized in certain less stereotyped characters. In *Macbeth* the contest for the soul of the protagonist is not prolonged, because he falls an easy victim to the promptings of ambition, stimulated by the witches' prophecies; but weak as the struggle is, the audience is aware of a conflict in Macbeth's own conscience, and it is Lady Macbeth, playing the role of an evil angel, who finally pushes her husband to a point beyond which there is no return.

Having succumbed to the temptation to gain the crown by the murder of Duncan, Macbeth finds himself inexorably committed to a career of evil that leads to inevitable ruin. He can never turn back and seek redemption. Once set upon his course, he moves from one violent act to another in an effort to ward off disaster. In the vain effort to insure the security of the throne that he has obtained by violence, he adds evil to evil until his name is a byword in Scotland for tyranny and cruelty. Yet Shakespeare does not make a monster of Macbeth, for that would have changed the nature of the play and made its chief protagonist less tragic. When the play opens we see a hero returning from the victorious defense of his country. He is ambitious, it is true, but he is willing to be patient and leave the future to Fate. As one near of kin to Duncan, he may be chosen his successor. Only when Duncan names his son Malcolm to succeed him is Macbeth ripe for violence.

Lady Macbeth is of sterner stuff, but she is not the virago that some actresses have made her. Ambitious for her husband, eager for him to possess the crown, she suppresses her good impulses, deliberately chooses Evil, and invokes the Powers of Darkness. Henceforth she is Macbeth's own Evil Genius. As in the case of Macbeth, Shakespeare does not make Lady Macbeth a monster either. She is capable of remorse, and that remorse drives her to the self-revelation of the great sleepwalking scene and eventually to her hinted suicide.

Shakespeare's interest in human beings rather than personified abstractions gives *Macbeth* a reality that is lacking in the strict morality plays. In this play Shakespeare reveals the tragedy that befalls two people who elect to follow a course of evil for the sake of their own ambitions. They are people whom the audience can recognize as veritable personalities, comprehensible to any sensate human being. Though their positions are exalted and their actions beyond those of normal human experience, their feelings and motivations are within the realm of ordinary human understanding, and the spectator can experience the catharsis of pity and fear that comes from identification with the protagonist of a great tragedy.

Macbeth is one of Shakespeare's shortest plays, and its action is concentrated. Some critics maintain that its brevity is the result of haste and that the play was written at the command of King James to be used as part of the entertainment of his brother-in-law, Christian IV of Denmark, who visited London in the summer of 1606. Others think that the play, written for the Globe, was abbreviated for court performance. Still others think that Shakespeare deliberately chose to write a compact and swiftly moving drama to suit the theme that he had chosen. Whatever the motivation of its writing, the play does contain an elaborate compliment to King James in the characterization of his ancestor, Banquo, and in the dumb show of the Eight Kings, with still other Stuarts to follow, until Macbeth exclaims, "Will the line stretch out to the crack of doom?"

SOURCES, HISTORY, AND TEXT

As in other plays dealing with British legend, Shakespeare took the essential material for *Macbeth* from Holinshed, who himself drew on ancient Scottish chronicles. Some material comes from folklore. The witches may derive from King James's *Demonology* (1597); Shakespeare was undoubtedly aware that the royal pedant would be flattered to see his own work recognized as an authority. Reginald Scot's *Discovery of Witchcraft* (1584) also may have furnished suggestions for the witch scenes. Scholars have written learnedly about the nature of the witches and have found likenesses to the Norns and the Valkyries of Norse folklore and to the Fates of Greek mythology.

Macbeth was one of Shakespeare's most popular plays. It apparently remained in the repertory of the King's Men for many years after its first production and was frequently acted. The astrologer Dr. Simon Forman saw a performance at the Globe on April 20, 1611, and wrote a long summary of the action in a manuscript preserved in the Bodleian Library at Oxford. On the reopening of the theatres after the Restoration, *Macbeth* was one of the plays first chosen for presentation. Sir William Davenant, however, chose to rewrite the play into a sort of opera with music, dancing, and witches flying across the stage on trapezes. On April 19, 1667, Samuel Pepys noted in his diary his enjoyment of a performance of *Macbeth,* "which, though I have seen it often, yet is one of the best plays for the stage, for variety of dancing and music, that ever I saw." Thomas Betterton found in the role of Macbeth one of his most popular parts. His wife, who played Lady Macbeth, was succeeded in the role by Elizabeth Barry, one of the reigning favorites of the Restoration stage.

Davenant's operatic play remained the favorite version until near the middle of the eighteenth century, when, in 1744, David Garrick revised the play and restored most of Shakespeare's scenes, though he "improved" Shakespeare by writing a dying speech for Macbeth in which the villain-hero, breathing his last, bewails his imminent damnation. Garrick himself played the part of Macbeth.

Charles Macklin in 1773 introduced an innovation by dressing the actors in Scottish costumes. When John Philip Kemble took over the management of Drury Lane in 1788, he went back to Davenant's version for operatic effects. His sister, Mrs. Siddons, made Lady Macbeth one of her most effective roles. Her rendition of the sleepwalking scene was so effective that one spectator declared, "I smelt blood! I swear that I smelt blood!"

In some form *Macbeth* has remained on the stage almost continuously since the seventeenth century. It has been one of Shakespeare's most popular plays, both on the stage and in the study. *Macbeth* and *Julius Cæsar* have been the two plays most often read by school children.

Perhaps because of its great contemporary popularity, the King's Men took care not to let *Macbeth* get into print until the Folio of 1623. The Folio version, therefore, is the basis of all modern texts. The copy used by the printers of the Folio was, in Sir Edmund Chambers' opinion, a theatrical prompt copy, but he notes that it is not a very satisfactory text because of abridgments and alterations. The only play shorter than Macbeth is *The Comedy of Errors*. Chambers and others agree that there is some evidence of interpolation of non-Shakespearean matter in the Folio version, but there is no general agreement about the extent of this. Chambers would confine the interpolations to three passages in the witch scenes. Two songs in Act III, Scene v, and Act IV, Scene i, were added from Thomas Middleton's *The Witch,* which was performed at the Blackfriars sometime before 1623; the inclusion of these songs has led scholars to believe that other matter written by Middleton or someone else may have been interpolated. The scenes generally accepted as non-Shakespearean are those in which Hecate appears (III.v and IV.i).

Macbeth's Coronation
From Holinshed, *The History of Scotland* (1577).

[Dramatis Personæ

DUNCAN, *King of Scotland.*
MALCOLM, } *his sons.*
DONALBAIN, }
MACBETH, } *Generals of the Scottish Army.*
BANQUO, }
MACDUFF, }
LENNOX, }
ROSS, } *Noblemen of Scotland.*
MENTEITH, }
ANGUS, }
CAITHNESS, }
FLEANCE, *son to Banquo.*
SIWARD, *Earl of Northumberland, General of the English forces.*
YOUNG SIWARD, *his son.*
SEYTON, *an Officer attending on Macbeth.*

BOY, *son to Macduff.*
A CAPTAIN.
AN ENGLISH DOCTOR.
A SCOTTISH DOCTOR.
A PORTER.
AN OLD MAN.
LADY MACBETH.
LADY MACDUFF.
A GENTLEWOMAN *attending on Lady Macbeth.*
HECATE.
THREE WITCHES.
THE GHOST OF BANQUO.
APPARITIONS.

Lords, Gentlemen, Officers, Soldiers, Murderers, Messengers, Attendants.

Scene: *Scotland and England.*]

The Murder of Banquo
From Holinshed, *The History of Scotland* (1577).

The Tragedy of MACBETH

ACT I

Scene I. [*Scotland. An open place.*]

Thunder and lightning. Enter THREE WITCHES.

1. Witch. When shall we three meet again?
In thunder, lightning, or in rain?
2. Witch. When the hurlyburly's done,
When the battle's lost and won.
3. Witch. That will be ere the set of sun. 5
1. Witch. Where the place?
2. Witch. Upon the heath.
3. Witch. There to meet with Macbeth.
1. Witch. I come, Graymalkin!
2. Witch. Paddock calls.
3. Witch. Anon!
All. Fair is foul, and foul is fair. 10
Hover through the fog and filthy air.
Exeunt.

Scene II. [*A camp near Forres.*]

Alarum within. Enter KING [DUNCAN], MALCOLM, DONALBAIN, LENNOX, *with* ATTENDANTS, *meeting a bleeding* CAPTAIN.

King. What bloody man is that? He can report,
As seemeth by his plight, of the revolt
The newest state.

8. Graymalkin: a familiar spirit in the shape of a cat
9. Paddock: a toad, the familiar of the Second Witch

Mal. This is the sergeant
Who like a good and hardy soldier fought
'Gainst my captivity. Hail, brave friend! 5
Say to the King the knowledge of the broil
As thou didst leave it.
Capt. Doubtful it stood,
As two spent swimmers that do cling together
And choke their art. The merciless Macdonwald
(Worthy to be a rebel, for to that 10
The multiplying villainies of nature
Do swarm upon him) from the Western Isles
Of kerns and gallowglasses is supplied;
And Fortune, on his damned quarrel smiling,
Showed like a rebel's whore. But all's too weak; 15
For brave Macbeth (well he deserves that name),
Disdaining Fortune, with his brandished steel,
Which smoked with bloody execution
(Like valor's minion), carved out his passage
Till he faced the slave; 20
Which ne'er shook hands nor bade farewell to him
Till he unseamed him from the nave to the chops
And fixed his head upon our battlements.
King. O valiant cousin! worthy gentleman!
Capt. As whence the sun 'gins his reflection 25
Shipwracking storms and direful thunders break,

10. that: that end
13. kerns: lightly armed foot soldiers, a term usually applied to Irish freebooters, but sometimes to Scottish Highlanders as well; **gallowglasses:** mounted soldiers of a more professional caliber
14. damned: accursed; **quarrel:** Thomas Hanmer's emendation of the Folio's "quarry"
15. Showed: appeared
19. minion: favorite
22. unseamed . . . chops: laid him open from navel to jaws
26. break: suggested by Alexander Pope. The Folio has no verb; Folios 2-4 read "breaking."

So from that spring whence comfort seemed to come
Discomfort swells. Mark, King of Scotland, mark.
No sooner justice had, with valor armed, 29
Compelled these skipping kerns to trust their heels
But the Norweyan lord, surveying vantage,
With furbished arms and new supplies of men,
Began a fresh assault.
King. Dismayed not this
Our captains, Macbeth and Banquo?
Capt. Yes,
As sparrows eagles, or the hare the lion. 35
If I say sooth, I must report they were
As cannons overcharged with double cracks; so they
Doubly redoubled strokes upon the foe.
Except they meant to bathe in reeking wounds,
Or memorize another Golgotha, 40
I cannot tell—
But I am faint; my gashes cry for help.
King. So well thy words become thee as thy wounds;
They smack of honor both. Go get him surgeons.
[*Exit Captain, attended.*]

Enter Ross *and* Angus.

Who comes here?
Mal. The worthy Thane of Ross. 45
Len. What a haste looks through his eyes! So should he look
That seems to speak things strange.
Ross. God save the King!
King. Whence camest thou, worthy thane?
Ross. From Fife, great King,
Where the Norweyan banners flout the sky
And fan our people cold. Norway himself, 50
With terrible numbers,
Assisted by that most disloyal traitor
The Thane of Cawdor, began a dismal conflict,
Till that Bellona's bridegroom, lapped in proof,
Confronted him with self-comparisons, 55
Point against point, rebellious arm 'gainst arm,
Curbing his lavish spirit; and to conclude,
The victory fell on us.
King. Great happiness!
Ross. That now
Sweno, the Norways' king, craves composition;
Nor would we deign him burial of his men 60
Till he disbursed, at Saint Colme's Inch,
Ten thousand dollars to our general use.
King. No more that Thane of Cawdor shall deceive
Our bosom interest. Go pronounce his present death
And with his former title greet Macbeth. 65
Ross. I'll see it done.
Dun. What he hath lost noble Macbeth hath won.
Exeunt.

Scene III. [*A heath near Forres.*]

Thunder. Enter the Three Witches.

1. Witch. Where hast thou been, sister?
2. Witch. Killing swine.
3. Witch. Sister, where thou?
1. Witch. A sailor's wife had chestnuts in her lap
And mounched and mounched and mounched. "Give me," quoth I. 5
"Aroint thee, witch!" the rump-fed ronyon cries.
Her husband's to Aleppo gone, master o' the "Tiger";
But in a sieve I'll thither sail,
And like a rat without a tail
I'll do, I'll do, and I'll do. 10
2. Witch. I'll give thee a wind.
1. Witch. Th' art kind.
3. Witch. And I another.
1. Witch. I myself have all the other,
And the very ports they blow, 15
All the quarters that they know
I' the shipman's card.
I'll drain him dry as hay.
Sleep shall neither night nor day
Hang upon his penthouse lid. 20
He shall live a man forbid.
Weary sev'nights, nine times nine,
Shall he dwindle, peak, and pine.
Though his bark cannot be lost,
Yet it shall be tempest-tost. 25
Look what I have.
2. Witch. Show me! show me!

31. Norweyan lord: King of Norway; **vantage:** opportunity
37. cracks: cannon balls
40. memorize . . . Golgotha: make the place as memorable for slaughter as Golgotha, where Christ was crucified
45. Thane: the chief of a clan, equal in rank to an earl's son
47. seems . . . strange: whose appearance is as strange as his news
49. flout: defy
53. dismal: seemingly ill-omened
54. Bellona's bridegroom: Macbeth, partner of the Roman goddess of war; **proof:** proof armor, made to be proof against penetration
55. Confronted . . . self-comparisons: defied him and matched his prowess
57. lavish: undisciplined
59. composition: agreement on peace terms
61. Saint Colme's Inch: Inchcolm in the Firth of Forth
64. Our . . . interest: my most vital concerns; **present:** immediate
6. Aroint thee: begone; **rump-fed:** fat-rumped; **ronyon:** good-for-nothing
9. like . . . tail: in the shape of a tailless rat. Witches supposedly could take the form of animals, but such likenesses, it was believed, could not be perfect.
17. card: chart or compass card
20. penthouse lid: eyelid, which slants like a penthouse roof
21. forbid: accursed

1. Witch. Here I have a pilot's thumb,
Wracked as homeward he did come. *Drum within.*
3. Witch. A drum, a drum! 30
Macbeth doth come.
All. The Weird Sisters, hand in hand,
Posters of the sea and land,
Thus do go about, about:
Thrice to thine, and thrice to mine, 35
And thrice again, to make up nine.
Peace! The charm's wound up.

Enter MACBETH *and* BANQUO.

Macb. So foul and fair a day I have not seen.
Ban. How far is't called to Forres? What are these,
So withered, and so wild in their attire, 40
That look not like the inhabitants o' the earth,
And yet are on't? Live you? or are you aught
That man may question? You seem to understand me,
By each at once her choppy finger laying
Upon her skinny lips. You should be women, 45
And yet your beards forbid me to interpret
That you are so.
Macb. Speak, if you can. What are you?
1. Witch. All hail, Macbeth! Hail to thee, Thane of Glamis!
2. Witch. All hail, Macbeth! Hail to thee, Thane of Cawdor!
3. Witch. All hail, Macbeth, that shalt be King hereafter! 50
Ban. Good sir, why do you start and seem to fear
Things that do sound so fair? I' the name of truth,
Are ye fantastical, or that indeed
Which outwardly ye show? My noble partner
You greet with present grace and great prediction
Of noble having and of royal hope, 56
That he seems rapt withal. To me you speak not.
If you can look into the seeds of time
And say which grain will grow and which will not,
Speak then to me, who neither beg nor fear 60
Your favors nor your hate.
1. Witch. Hail!
2. Witch. Hail!
3. Witch. Hail!
1. Witch. Lesser than Macbeth, and greater. 65
2. Witch. Not so happy, yet much happier.
3. Witch. Thou shalt get kings, though thou be none.
So all hail, Macbeth and Banquo!
1. Witch. Banquo and Macbeth, all hail! 69
Macb. Stay, you imperfect speakers, tell me more!
By Sinel's death I know I am Thane of Glamis,
But how of Cawdor? The Thane of Cawdor lives,
A prosperous gentleman; and to be King
Stands not within the prospect of belief,
No more than to be Cawdor. Say from whence 75
You owe this strange intelligence, or why
Upon this blasted heath you stop our way
With such prophetic greeting. Speak, I charge you.
Witches vanish.
Ban. The earth hath bubbles, as the water has,
And these are of them. Whither are they vanished?
Macb. Into the air, and what seemed corporal melted 81
As breath into the wind. Would they had stayed!
Ban. Were such things here as we do speak about?
Or have we eaten on the insane root
That takes the reason prisoner? 85
Macb. Your children shall be kings.
Ban. You shall be King.
Macb. And Thane of Cawdor too. Went it not so?
Ban. To the selfsame tune and words. Who's here?

Enter ROSS *and* ANGUS.

Ross. The King hath happily received, Macbeth,
The news of thy success; and when he reads 90
Thy personal venture in the rebels' fight,
His wonders and his praises do contend
Which should be thine or his. Silenced with that,
In viewing o'er the rest o' the selfsame day,
He finds thee in the stout Norweyan ranks, 95
Nothing afeard of what thyself didst make,
Strange images of death. As thick as hail
Came post with post, and every one did bear
Thy praises in his kingdom's great defense
And poured them down before him.
Ang. We are sent 100
To give thee from our royal master thanks;
Only to herald thee into his sight,
Not pay thee.
Ross. And for an earnest of a greater honor,
He bade me, from him, call thee Thane of Cawdor;
In which addition, hail, most worthy Thane! 106
For it is thine.
Ban. What, can the devil speak true?
Macb. The Thane of Cawdor lives. Why do you dress me
In borrowed robes?

32. Weird: fateful. The Folio spells "weyward" here, "weyard" elsewhere. The word derives from Old English *wyrd.* The witches are analogous to the Fates of classical and the Norns of Norse mythology.
33. Posters: speedy travelers
44. choppy: chapped
53. fantastical: illusory; figments of fancy
55. grace: honor
67. get: beget
71. Sinel: Macbeth's father
76. owe: possess
84. insane: productive of madness. Hemlock and henbane were both supposed to have such an effect.
92–93. His . . . his: he is almost speechless with admiration when he tries to praise you.
98. post . . . post: messenger after messenger
104. earnest: token payment
106. addition: title

Ang. Who was the Thane lives yet,
But under heavy judgment bears that life 110
Which he deserves to lose. Whether he was combined
With those of Norway, or did line the rebel
With hidden help and vantage, or that with both
He labored in his country's wrack, I know not;
But treasons capital, confessed and proved, 115
Have overthrown him.

Macb. [*Aside*] Glamis, and Thane of Cawdor!
The greatest is behind.—[*To Ross and Angus*]
Thanks for your pains.
[*Aside to Banquo*] Do you not hope your children shall be kings,
When those that gave the Thane of Cawdor to me
Promised no less to them?

Ban. [*Aside to Macbeth*] That, trusted home,
Might yet enkindle you unto the crown, 121
Besides the Thane of Cawdor. But 'tis strange!
And oftentimes, to win us to our harm,
The instruments of darkness tell us truths,
Win us with honest trifles, to betray's 125
In deepest consequence.—
Cousins, a word, I pray you.

Macb. [*Aside*] Two truths are told,
As happy prologues to the swelling act
Of the imperial theme.—I thank you, gentlemen.—
[*Aside*] This supernatural soliciting 130
Cannot be ill; cannot be good. If ill,
Why hath it given me earnest of success,
Commencing in a truth? I am Thane of Cawdor.
If good, why do I yield to that suggestion
Whose horrid image doth unfix my hair 135
And make my seated heart knock at my ribs
Against the use of nature? Present fears
Are less than horrible imaginings.
My thought, whose murder yet is but fantastical,
Shakes so my single state of man that function 140
Is smothered in surmise, and nothing is
But what is not.

Ban. Look how our partner's rapt.

Macb. [*Aside*] If chance will have me King, why, chance may crown me,
Without my stir.

Ban. New honors come upon him,
Like our strange garments, cleave not to their mold
But with the aid of use.

Macb. [*Aside*] Come what come may, 146
Time and the hour runs through the roughest day.

Ban. Worthy Macbeth, we stay upon your leisure.

Macb. Give me your favor. My dull brain was wrought
With things forgotten. Kind gentlemen, your pains
Are registered where every day I turn 151
The leaf to read them. Let us toward the King.
[*Aside to Banquo*] Think upon what hath chanced, and, at more time,
The interim having weighed it, let us speak
Our free hearts each to other.

Ban. [*Aside to Macbeth*] Very gladly. 155

Macb. [*Aside to Banquo*] Till then, enough.—
Come, friends.

Exeunt.

Scene IV. [*Forres. The Palace.*]

Flourish. Enter KING [DUNCAN], LENNOX, MALCOLM, DONALBAIN, *and* ATTENDANTS.

King. Is execution done on Cawdor? Are not
Those in commission yet returned?

Mal. My liege,
They are not yet come back. But I have spoke
With one that saw him die; who did report
That very frankly he confessed his treasons, 5
Implored your Highness' pardon, and set forth
A deep repentance. Nothing in his life
Became him like the leaving it. He died
As one that had been studied in his death
To throw away the dearest thing he owed 10
As 'twere a careless trifle.

King. There's no art
To find the mind's construction in the face.
He was a gentleman on whom I built
An absolute trust.

Enter MACBETH, BANQUO, ROSS, *and* ANGUS.

O worthiest cousin,
The sin of my ingratitude even now 15
Was heavy on me! Thou art so far before
That swiftest wing of recompense is slow
To overtake thee. Would thou hadst less deserved,
That the proportion both of thanks and payment
Might have been mine! Only I have left to say, 20

112. **line:** reinforce
113. **vantage:** synonymous with **help**
117. **behind:** to follow
120. **home:** to the limit
126. **In . . . consequence:** i.e., at the hour of death
128. **swelling:** majestic
136. **seated:** fixed
137. **Against . . . nature:** unnaturally; **fears:** real dangers
139. **fantastical:** imaginary
140. **single:** self-contained
141–42. **nothing . . . not:** nothing exists for me but imagined future events.
147. **Time . . . day:** proverbial: "The longest day must have an end."
149. **favor:** indulgence
154. **The . . . it:** the interim having allowed further consideration of it
155. **free:** frank
2. **in commission:** entrusted to carry out the execution
9. **studied:** rehearsed
10. **owed:** owned
15. **even:** just
16. **before:** ahead
19. **proportion:** greater measure

More is thy due than more than all can pay.
Macb. The service and the loyalty I owe,
In doing it pays itself. Your Highness' part
Is to receive our duties; and our duties 24
Are to your throne and state children and servants,
Which do but what they should by doing everything
Safe toward your love and honor.
King. Welcome hither.
I have begun to plant thee and will labor
To make thee full of growing. Noble Banquo,
That hast no less deserved, nor must be known 30
No less to have done so, let me infold thee
And hold thee to my heart.
Ban. There if I grow,
The harvest is your own.
King. My plenteous joys,
Wanton in fullness, seek to hide themselves
In drops of sorrow. Sons, kinsmen, thanes, 35
And you whose places are the nearest, know
We will establish our estate upon
Our eldest, Malcolm, whom we name hereafter
The Prince of Cumberland; which honor must
Not unaccompanied invest him only, 40
But signs of nobleness, like stars, shall shine
On all deservers. From hence to Inverness,
And bind us further to you.
Macb. The rest is labor which is not used for you.
I'll be myself the harbinger, and make joyful 45
The hearing of my wife with your approach;
So, humbly take my leave.
King. My worthy Cawdor!
Macb. [*Aside*] The Prince of Cumberland! That is a step
On which I must fall down, or else o'erleap,
For in my way it lies. Stars, hide your fires! 50
Let not light see my black and deep desires.
The eye wink at the hand; yet let that be,
Which the eye fears, when it is done, to see. *Exit.*
King. True, worthy Banquo: he is full so valiant,
And in his commendations I am fed; 55
It is a banquet to me. Let's after him,
Whose care is gone before to bid us welcome.
It is a peerless kinsman.
Flourish. Exeunt.

Scene V. [*Inverness. Macbeth's Castle.*]

Enter MACBETH'S WIFE, *alone, with a letter.*

Lady [*Reads*] They met me in the day of success; and I have learned by the perfect'st report they have more in them than mortal knowledge. When I burned in desire to question them further, they made themselves air, into which they vanished. Whiles I stood rapt in the 5 wonder of it, came missives from the King, who all-hailed me Thane of Cawdor, by which title, before, these Weird Sisters saluted me, and referred me to the coming on of time with "Hail, King that shalt be!" This have I thought good to deliver thee, my dearest partner 10 of greatness, that thou mightst not lose the dues of rejoicing by being ignorant of what greatness is promised thee. Lay it to thy heart, and farewell.

Glamis thou art, and Cawdor, and shalt be
What thou art promised. Yet do I fear thy nature.
It is too full o' the milk of human kindness 16
To catch the nearest way. Thou wouldst be great;
Art not without ambition, but without
The illness should attend it. What thou wouldst highly,
That wouldst thou holily; wouldst not play false,
And yet wouldst wrongly win. Thou'ldst have, great Glamis, 21
That which cries "Thus thou must do," if thou have it;
And that which rather thou dost fear to do
Than wishest should be undone. Hie thee hither,
That I may pour my spirits in thine ear 25
And chastise with the valor of my tongue
All that impedes thee from the golden round
Which fate and metaphysical aid doth seem
To have thee crowned withal.

Enter MESSENGER.

What is your tidings?
Mess. The King comes here tonight.
Lady. Thou'rt mad to say it! 30
Is not thy master with him? who, were't so,
Would have informed for preparation.
Mess. So please you, it is true. Our Thane is coming.
One of my fellows had the speed of him,
Who, almost dead for breath, had scarcely more 35
Than would make up his message.
Lady. Give him tending;
He brings great news. *Exit Messenger.*
The raven himself is hoarse
That croaks the fatal entrance of Duncan
Under my battlements. Come, you spirits
That tend on mortal thoughts, unsex me here, 40
And fill me, from the crown to the toe, top-full

34. **Wanton:** unrestrained
44. **rest:** leisure
45. **harbinger:** forerunner; literally, an underling who prepared the way for a noble person
52. **wink at:** refuse to see
54. **full so:** every bit as

6. **missives:** messengers
10. **deliver:** report to
19. **illness:** evil
27. **round:** crown
28. **metaphysical:** supernatural
34. **had . . . of:** i.e., outrode
40. **mortal:** deadly

Of direst cruelty! Make thick my blood;
Stop up the access and passage to remorse,
That no compunctious visitings of nature
Shake my fell purpose nor keep peace between 45
The effect and it! Come to my woman's breasts
And take my milk for gall, you murd'ring ministers,
Wherever in your sightless substances
You wait on nature's mischief! Come, thick night,
And pall thee in the dunnest smoke of hell, 50
That my keen knife see not the wound it makes,
Nor heaven peep through the blanket of the dark
To cry "Hold, hold!"

Enter MACBETH.

Great Glamis! worthy Cawdor!
Greater than both, by the all-hail hereafter!
Thy letters have transported me beyond 55
This ignorant present, and I feel now
The future in the instant.

Macb. My dearest love,
Duncan comes here tonight.

Lady. And when goes hence?

Macb. Tomorrow, as he purposes.

Lady. O, never
Shall sun that morrow see! 60
Your face, my Thane, is as a book where men
May read strange matters. To beguile the time,
Look like the time; bear welcome in your eye,
Your hand, your tongue; look like the innocent flower,
But be the serpent under't. He that's coming 65
Must be provided for; and you shall put
This night's great business into my dispatch,
Which shall to all our nights and days to come
Give solely sovereign sway and masterdom.

Macb. We will speak further.

Lady. Only look up clear.
To alter favor ever is to fear. 71
Leave all the rest to me.

Exeunt.

Scene VI. [*The same. Before Macbeth's Castle.*]

Hautboys and torches. Enter KING [DUNCAN], MALCOLM, DONALBAIN, BANQUO, LENNOX, MACDUFF, ROSS, ANGUS, *and* ATTENDANTS.

King. This castle hath a pleasant seat. The air
Nimbly and sweetly recommends itself
Unto our gentle senses.

Ban. This guest of summer,
The temple-haunting martlet, does approve
By his loved mansionry that the heaven's breath 5
Smells wooingly here. No jutty, frieze,
Buttress, nor coign of vantage, but this bird
Hath made his pendent bed and procreant cradle.
Where they most breed and haunt, I have observed,
The air is delicate.

Enter LADY [MACBETH].

King. See, see, our honored hostess! 10
The love that follows us sometime is our trouble,
Which still we thank as love. Herein I teach you
How you shall bid God 'ield us for your pains
And thank us for your trouble.

Lady. All our service
In every point twice done, and then done double,
Were poor and single business to contend 16
Against those honors deep and broad wherewith
Your Majesty loads our house. For those of old,
And the late dignities heaped up to them,
We rest your hermits.

King. Where's the Thane of Cawdor?
We coursed him at the heels and had a purpose 21
To be his purveyor; but he rides well,
And his great love, sharp as his spur, hath holp him
To his home before us. Fair and noble hostess,
We are your guest tonight.

Lady. Your servants ever 25
Have theirs, themselves, and what is theirs, in compt,

43. **remorse:** compassion
44. **compunctious . . . nature:** natural pangs of conscience
45. **fell:** savage
45–46. **keep . . . it:** maintain a quiet interval between my purpose and its accomplishment; delay the carrying out of my intent
47. **ministers:** agents
48. **sightless:** invisible
50. **pall:** shroud; **dunnest:** darkest
56. **ignorant:** uninformed (of the future)
57. **the instant:** this moment
62–63. **beguile . . . time:** deceive the world, behave as occasion requires
67. **dispatch:** management
69. **solely . . . masterdom:** absolute rule of the kingdom
70. **clear:** innocently
71. **favor:** countenance; **fear:** betray a troubled mind

Ent. **Hautboys:** oboes
3. **gentle:** gentled; soothed
4. **martlet:** house martin; **approve:** confirm
5. **loved mansionry:** favorite nesting-place
6. **jutty:** projection
7. **coign . . . vantage:** suitable corner
11–14. **The . . . trouble:** love is sometimes troublesome to its object but nevertheless inspires gratitude; this fact should teach you to ask God to reward me for the trouble that my visit, inspired by love, is causing you.
16. **single:** inadequate
20. **rest:** remain; **hermits:** beadsmen, who pray for you out of gratitude
21. **coursed:** pursued
22. **purveyor:** synonymous with **harbinger** (I.iv.45)
23. **holp:** helped
26. **compt:** trust

To make their audit at your Highness' pleasure,
Still to return your own.
King. Give me your hand;
Conduct me to mine host. We love him highly
And shall continue our graces towards him. 30
By your leave, hostess.
Exeunt.

Scene VII. [*The same. Macbeth's Castle.*]

Hautboys, Torches. Enter a SEWER, *and divers* SERVANTS *with dishes and service over the stage. Then enter* MACBETH.

Macb. If it were done when 'tis done, then 'twere well
It were done quickly. If the assassination
Could trammel up the consequence, and catch,
With his surcease, success, that but this blow
Might be the be-all and the end-all here, 5
But here, upon this bank and shoal of time,
We'ld jump the life to come. But in these cases
We still have judgment here, that we but teach
Bloody instructions, which, being taught, return 9
To plague the inventor. This even-handed justice
Commends the ingredience of our poisoned chalice
To our own lips. He's here in double trust:
First, as I am his kinsman and his subject,
Strong both against the deed; then, as his host,
Who should against his murderer shut the door, 15
Not bear the knife myself. Besides, this Duncan
Hath borne his faculties so meek, hath been
So clear in his great office, that his virtues
Will plead like angels, trumpet-tongued, against
The deep damnation of his taking-off; 20
And pity, like a naked new-born babe,
Striding the blast, or heaven's cherubin, horsed
Upon the sightless couriers of the air,
Shall blow the horrid deed in every eye,
That tears shall drown the wind. I have no spur 25
To prick the sides of my intent, but only
Vaulting ambition, which o'erleaps itself
And falls on the other—

Enter LADY [MACBETH].

How now? What news?
Lady. He has almost supped. Why have you left the chamber?
Macb. Hath he asked for me?
Lady. Know you not he has? 30
Macb. We will proceed no further in this business.
He hath honored me of late, and I have bought
Golden opinions from all sorts of people,
Which would be worn now in their newest gloss,
Not cast aside so soon.
Lady. Was the hope drunk 35
Wherein you dressed yourself? Hath it slept since?
And wakes it now to look so green and pale
At what it did so freely? From this time
Such I account thy love. Art thou afeard
To be the same in thine own act and valor 40
As thou art in desire? Wouldst thou have that
Which thou esteemst the ornament of life,
And live a coward in thine own esteem,
Letting "I dare not" wait upon "I would,"
Like the poor cat i' the adage?
Macb. Prithee peace! 45
I dare do all that may become a man.
Who dares do more is none.
Lady. What beast was't then
That made you break this enterprise to me?
When you durst do it, then you were a man;
And to be more than what you were, you would 50
Be so much more the man. Nor time nor place
Did then adhere, and yet you would make both.
They have made themselves, and that their fitness now
Does unmake you. I have given suck, and know
How tender 'tis to love the babe that milks me. 55
I would, while it was smiling in my face,
Have plucked my nipple from his boneless gums
And dashed the brains out, had I so sworn as you
Have done to this.
Macb. If we should fail?
Lady. We fail?
But screw your courage to the sticking place, 60
And we'll not fail. When Duncan is asleep
(Whereto the rather shall his day's hard journey
Soundly invite him), his two chamberlains
Will I with wine and wassail so convince
That memory, the warder of the brain, 65
Shall be a fume, and the receipt of reason

28. Still: always
Ent. Sewer: steward
1. were: would be
3. trammel up: catch in a net
4. his surcease: Duncan's death; **success:** termination; the end of the matter
6. But: only; i.e., on earth; **shoal:** Lewis Theobald's emendation of the Folio's "schoole"
7. jump: hazard
11. Commends: offers; **ingredience:** composition
17. faculties: powers
18. clear: pure
22. Striding . . . blast: riding the wind
23. sightless: invisible, as at I.v.48
45. cat . . . adage: "The cat would eat fish, and would not wet her feet," John Heywood's *Proverbs* (1546)
53. that . . . fitness: their very fitness
60. sticking place: height of resolution, an image from the cranks used to tighten the cords of crossbows
64. convince: overcome
65. warder: guardian
66. receipt: container

A limbeck only. When in swinish sleep
Their drenched natures lie as in a death,
What cannot you and I perform upon
The unguarded Duncan? what not put upon 70
His spongy officers, who shall bear the guilt
Of our great quell?
Macb. Bring forth men-children only,
For thy undaunted mettle should compose
Nothing but males. Will it not be received, 74

67. limbeck: alembic, the cap of a still
68. drenched: drowned
71. spongy: sodden with drink
72. quell: murder

When we have marked with blood those sleepy two
Of his own chamber and used their very daggers,
That they have done't?
Lady. Who dares receive it other,
As we shall make our griefs and clamor roar
Upon his death?
Macb. I am settled and bend up
Each corporal agent to this terrible feat. 80
Away, and mock the time with fairest show;
False face must hide what the false heart doth know.
Exeunt.

81. mock . . . time: deceive all observers

ACT II

Scene I. [*The same. Court of Macbeth's Castle.*]

Enter BANQUO, *and* FLEANCE *with a torch before him.*

Ban. How goes the night, boy?
Fle. The moon is down; I have not heard the clock.
Ban. And she goes down at twelve.
Fle. I take't, 'tis later, sir.
Ban. Hold, take my sword. There's husbandry in heaven;
Their candles are all out. Take thee that too. 5
A heavy summons lies like lead upon me,
And yet I would not sleep. Merciful powers,
Restrain in me the cursed thoughts that nature
Gives way to in repose!

Enter MACBETH, *and a* SERVANT *with a torch.*

Give me my sword.
Who's there? 10
Macb. A friend.
Ban. What, sir, not yet at rest? The King's abed.
He hath been in unusual pleasure and
Sent forth great largess to your offices.
This diamond he greets your wife withal 15
By the name of most kind hostess, and shut up
In measureless content.

4. husbandry: thrifty management
14. offices: i.e., servants
16. shut up: concluded

Macb. Being unprepared,
Our will became the servant to defect,
Which else should free have wrought.
Ban. All's well.
I dreamt last night of the three Weird Sisters. 20
To you they have showed some truth.
Macb. I think not of them.
Yet when we can entreat an hour to serve,
We would spend it in some words upon that business,
If you would grant the time.
Ban. At your kind'st leisure. 24
Macb. If you shall cleave to my consent, when 'tis,
It shall make honor for you.
Ban. So I lose none
In seeking to augment it but still keep
My bosom franchised and allegiance clear,
I shall be counseled.
Macb. Good repose the while!
Ban. Thanks, sir. The like to you! 30
Exeunt Banquo [and Fleance].
Macb. Go bid thy mistress, when my drink is ready,
She strike upon the bell. Get thee to bed.
Exit [Servant].
Is this a dagger which I see before me,
The handle toward my hand? Come, let me clutch thee!
I have thee not, and yet I see thee still. 35

18. Our . . . defect: our desire to entertain him lavishly had to submit to our deficiency
25. cleave . . . consent: stick by me
28. franchised: free (of guilt); **clear:** unblemished
29. counseled: receptive to your words

Art thou not, fatal vision, sensible
To feeling as to sight? or art thou but
A dagger of the mind, a false creation,
Proceeding from the heat-oppressed brain?
I see thee yet, in form as palpable 40
As this which now I draw.
Thou marshalst me the way that I was going,
And such an instrument I was to use.
Mine eyes are made the fools o' the other senses,
Or else worth all the rest. I see thee still; 45
And on thy blade and dudgeon gouts of blood,
Which was not so before. There's no such thing.
It is the bloody business which informs
Thus to mine eyes. Now o'er the one half-world
Nature seems dead, and wicked dreams abuse 50
The curtained sleep. Witchcraft celebrates
Pale Hecate's offerings; and withered murder,
Alarumed by his sentinel, the wolf,
Whose howl's his watch, thus with his stealthy pace,
With Tarquin's ravishing strides, towards his design
Moves like a ghost. Thou sure and firm-set earth, 56
Hear not my steps which way they walk, for fear
Thy very stones prate of my whereabout
And take the present horror from the time, 59
Which now suits with it. Whiles I threat, he lives;
Words to the heat of deeds too cold breath gives.
A bell rings.
I go, and it is done. The bell invites me.
Hear it not, Duncan, for it is a knell
That summons thee to heaven, or to hell.
Exit.

Scene II. [*The same.*]

Enter LADY [MACBETH].

Lady. That which hath made them drunk hath made me bold;
What hath quenched them hath given me fire. Hark! Peace!
It was the owl that shrieked, the fatal bellman
Which gives the stern'st good-night. He is about it.
The doors are open, and the surfeited grooms 5
Do mock their charge with snores. I have drugged their possets,
That death and nature do contend about them
Whether they live or die.
Macb. [*Within*] Who's there? What, ho?
Lady. Alack, I am afraid they have awaked, 9
And 'tis not done! The attempt, and not the deed,
Confounds us. Hark! I laid their daggers ready;
He could not miss 'em. Had he not resembled
My father as he slept, I had done't.

Enter MACBETH.

My husband!
Macb. I have done the deed. Didst thou not hear a noise? 14
Lady. I heard the owl scream and the crickets cry.
Did not you speak?
Macb. When?
Lady. Now.
Macb. As I descended?
Lady. Ay.
Macb. Hark!
Who lies i' the second chamber?
Lady. Donalbain.
Macb. This is a sorry sight. 20
Lady. A foolish thought, to say a sorry sight.
Macb. There's one did laugh in's sleep, and one cried "Murder!"
That they did wake each other. I stood and heard them.
But they did say their prayers and addressed them
Again to sleep.
Lady. There are two lodged together. 25
Macb. One cried "God bless us!" and "Amen!" the other,
As they had seen me with these hangman's hands,
List'ning their fear. I could not say "Amen!"
When they did say "God bless us!"
Lady. Consider it not so deeply. 30
Macb. But wherefore could not I pronounce "Amen"?
I had most need of blessing, and "Amen"
Stuck in my throat.
Lady. These deeds must not be thought
After these ways. So, it will make us mad.
Macb. Methought I heard a voice cry "Sleep no more! 35
Macbeth does murder sleep"—the innocent sleep,
Sleep that knits up the raveled sleave of care,
The death of each day's life, sore labor's bath,

36–37. sensible . . . feeling: tangible
42. marshalst: leadest
46. dudgeon: handle made of wood
48. informs: takes shape
50. abuse: deceive
52. Hecate: ruler of witches, another manifestation of the moon-goddess
55. Tarquin's . . . stride: Tarquin's rape of Lucrece is the theme of Shakespeare's narrative poem.
3. bellman: the town crier, who also tolled the bell for condemned criminals
6. charge: responsibility; **possets:** hot, spiced drinks containing milk and liquor
11. Confounds: destroys
27. hangman's hands: bloody hands. The hangman quartered and disemboweled condemned traitors.
37. raveled sleave: tangled skein

Balm of hurt minds, great nature's second course,
Chief nourisher in life's feast.

Lady. What do you mean? 40

Macb. Still it cried "Sleep no more!" to all the house;
"Glamis hath murdered sleep, and therefore Cawdor
Shall sleep no more! Macbeth shall sleep no more!"

Lady. Who was it that thus cried? Why, worthy Thane,
You do unbend your noble strength to think 45
So brainsickly of things. Go get some water
And wash this filthy witness from your hand.
Why did you bring these daggers from the place?
They must lie there. Go carry them and smear
The sleepy grooms with blood.

Macb. I'll go no more. 50
I am afraid to think what I have done;
Look on't again I dare not.

Lady. Infirm of purpose!
Give me the daggers. The sleeping and the dead
Are but as pictures. 'Tis the eye of childhood
That fears a painted devil. If he do bleed, 55
I'll gild the faces of the grooms withal,
For it must seem their guilt. *Exit. Knocking within.*

Macb. Whence is that knocking?
How is't with me when every noise appals me? 58
What hands are here? Ha! they pluck out mine eyes!
Will all great Neptune's ocean wash this blood
Clean from my hand? No. This my hand will rather
The multitudinous seas incarnadine,
Making the green one red.

Enter LADY [MACBETH].

Lady. My hands are of your color, but I shame
To wear a heart so white. (*Knock.*) I hear a knocking 65
At the south entry. Retire we to our chamber.
A little water clears us of this deed.
How easy is it then! Your constancy
Hath left you unattended. (*Knock.*) Hark! more knocking.
Get on your nightgown, lest occasion call us 70
And show us to be watchers. Be not lost
So poorly in your thoughts.

Macb. To know my deed, 'twere best not know myself. *Knock.*
Wake Duncan with thy knocking! I would thou couldst!

Exeunt.

39. second course: i.e., after food
47. witness: evidence
68. constancy: composure
71. watchers: wakers
73. To . . . myself: rather than face what I have done, it would be better to lose my reason.

Scene III. [*The same.*]

Enter a PORTER. *Knocking within.*

Port. Here's a knocking indeed! If a man were porter of hell gate, he should have old turning the key. (*Knock.*) Knock, knock, knock! Who's there, i' the name of Belzebub? Here's a farmer that hanged himself on the expectation of plenty. Come in 5 time! Have napkins enow about you; here you'll sweat for't. (*Knock.*) Knock, knock! Who's there, in the other devil's name? Faith, here's an equivocator, that could swear in both the scales against either scale; who committed treason enough 10 for God's sake, yet could not equivocate to heaven. O, come in, equivocator! (*Knock.*) Knock, knock, knock! Who's there? Faith, here's an English tailor come hither for stealing out of a French hose. Come in, tailor. Here you may roast your goose. 15 (*Knock.*) Knock, knock! Never at quiet! What are you? But this place is too cold for hell. I'll devil-porter it no further. I had thought to have let in some of all professions that go the primrose way to the everlasting bonfire. (*Knock.*) Anon, 20 anon! [*Opens the gate.*] I pray you remember the porter.

Enter MACDUFF *and* LENNOX.

Macd. Was it so late, friend, ere you went to bed,
That you do lie so late?

Port. Faith, sir, we were carousing till the 25 second cock; and drink, sir, is a great provoker of three things.

Macd. What three things does drink especially provoke?

Port. Marry, sir, nose-painting, sleep, and urine. Lechery, sir, it provokes, and unprovokes: it 30 provokes the desire, but it takes away the performance. Therefore much drink may be said to be an equivocator with lechery: it makes him, and it mars him; it sets him on, and it takes him off; it persuades him, and disheartens him; makes him 35

2. old: plenty of
4–5. hanged . . . plenty: i.e., because he had hoarded grain to make a profit
5–6. Come . . . time: you are welcome; **napkins:** handkerchiefs
8–9. equivocator: one who answers evasively, a habit ascribed to the Jesuits when questioned about treasonable activities. This is considered a reference to Father Garnet, a Jesuit who was executed in 1606 for implication in the Gunpowder Plot.
14. stealing . . . hose: skimping on the garment in order to steal cloth. If attempted in the making of the tightfitting breeches known as "French hose," the theft would be easily noted.
15. goose: pressing iron

stand to, and not stand to; in conclusion, equivocates him in a sleep, and, giving him the lie, leaves him.

Macd. I believe drink gave thee the lie last night.

Port. That it did, sir, i' the very throat on me; but I requited him for his lie; and, I think, being 40 too strong for him, though he took up my legs sometime, yet I made a shift to cast him.

Macd. Is thy master stirring?

Enter MACBETH.

Our knocking has awaked him; here he comes.

Len. Good morrow, noble sir.

Macb. Good morrow, both. 45

Macd. Is the King stirring, worthy Thane?

Macb. Not yet.

Macd. He did command me to call timely on him;
I have almost slipped the hour.

Macb. I'll bring you to him.

Macd. I know this is a joyful trouble to you;
But yet 'tis one. 50

Macb. The labor we delight in physics pain.
This is the door.

Macd. I'll make so bold to call,
For 'tis my limited service. *Exit.*

Len. Goes the King hence today?

Macb. He does; he did appoint so. 54

Len. The night has been unruly. Where we lay,
Our chimneys were blown down; and, as they say,
Lamentings heard i' the air, strange screams of death,
And prophesying, with accents terrible,
Of dire combustion and confused events 59
New hatched to the woeful time. The obscure bird
Clamored the livelong night. Some say the earth
Was feverous and did shake.

Macb. 'Twas a rough night.

Len. My young remembrance cannot parallel
A fellow to it. 64

Enter MACDUFF.

Macd. O horror, horror, horror! Tongue nor heart
Cannot conceive nor name thee!

Macb. and Len. What's the matter?

Macd. Confusion now hath made his masterpiece!
Most sacrilegious murder hath broke ope
The Lord's anointed temple and stole thence
The life o' the building!

Macb. What is't you say? the life? 70

Len. Mean you his Majesty?

Macd. Approach the chamber, and destroy your sight
With a new Gorgon. Do not bid me speak.
See, and then speak yourselves.

Exeunt Macbeth and Lennox.

Awake, awake!
Ring the alarum bell. Murder and treason! 75
Banquo and Donalbain! Malcolm! awake!
Shake off this downy sleep, death's counterfeit,
And look on death itself! Up, up, and see
The great doom's image! Malcolm! Banquo!
As from your graves rise up and walk like sprites
To countenance this horror! Ring the bell! 81

Bell rings.

Enter LADY [MACBETH].

Lady. What's the business,
That such a hideous trumpet calls to parley
The sleepers of the house? Speak, speak!

Macd. O gentle lady,
'Tis not for you to hear what I can speak! 85
The repetition in a woman's ear
Would murder as it fell.

Enter BANQUO.

O Banquo, Banquo,
Our royal master's murdered!

Lady. Woe, alas!
What, in our house?

Ban. Too cruel anywhere.
Dear Duff, I prithee contradict thyself 90
And say it is not so.

Enter MACBETH, LENNOX, *and* ROSS.

Macb. Had I but died an hour before this chance,
I had lived a blessed time; for from this instant
There's nothing serious in mortality;
All is but toys; renown and grace is dead; 95
The wine of life is drawn, and the mere lees
Is left this vault to brag of.

Enter MALCOLM *and* DONALBAIN.

Don. What is amiss?

Macb. You are, and do not know't.
The spring, the head, the fountain of your blood
Is stopped, the very source of it is stopped. 100

41. took . . . legs: overturned me, like a wrestler
42. made . . . shift: managed; **cast:** (1) throw; (2) vomit
51. physics: remedies
53. limited: appointed
59. combustion: uproar
60. obscure bird: dark bird; owl, which is active at night
67. Confusion: destruction
69. The . . . temple: the body of the King

73. Gorgon: the mythological creature whose glance turned the beholder to stone
79. The . . . image: a likeness of Judgment Day
80. sprites: spirits
81. countenance: conform with
94. mortality: human life
95. toys: trifles
96. drawn: drawn off

Macd. Your royal father's murdered.
Mal. O, by whom?
Len. Those of his chamber, as it seemed, had done't.
Their hands and faces were all badged with blood;
So were their daggers, which unwiped we found
Upon their pillows. 105
They stared and were distracted. No man's life
Was to be trusted with them.
Macb. O, yet I do repent me of my fury
That I did kill them.
Macd. Wherefore did you so?
Macb. Who can be wise, amazed, temp'rate and furious, 110
Loyal and neutral, in a moment? No man.
The expedition of my violent love
Outrun the pauser, reason. Here lay Duncan,
His silver skin laced with his golden blood, 114
And his gashed stabs looked like a breach in nature
For ruin's wasteful entrance; there, the murderers,
Steeped in the colors of their trade, their daggers
Unmannerly breeched with gore. Who could refrain
That had a heart to love and in that heart
Courage to make's love known?
Lady. Help me hence, ho! 120
Macd. Look to the lady.
Mal. [*Aside to Donalbain*] Why do we hold our tongues,
That most may claim this argument for ours?
Don. [*Aside to Malcolm*] What should be spoken here,
Where our fate, hid in an auger hole, 125
May rush and seize us? Let's away,
Our tears are not yet brewed.
Mal. [*Aside to Donalbain*] Nor our strong sorrow
Upon the foot of motion.
Ban. Look to the lady.
[*Lady Macbeth is carried out.*]
And when we have our naked frailties hid, 130
That suffer in exposure, let us meet
And question this most bloody piece of work,
To know it further. Fears and scruples shake us.
In the great hand of God I stand, and thence
Against the undivulged pretense I fight 135
Of treasonous malice.
Macd. And so do I.
All. So all.
Macb. Let's briefly put on manly readiness
And meet i' the hall together.
All. Well contented.
Exeunt [*all but Malcolm and Donalbain*].

103. **badged:** marked, as with a badge
110. **amazed:** dumfounded
112. **expedition:** speed
118. **breeched:** sheathed
123. **argument:** subject
125. **an . . . hole:** i.e., where we cannot detect it
132. **question:** discuss
135. **pretense:** intention

Mal. What will you do? Let's not consort with them.
To show an unfelt sorrow is an office 140
Which the false man does easy. I'll to England.
Don. To Ireland I. Our separated fortune
Shall keep us both the safer. Where we are,
There's daggers in men's smiles; the near in blood,
The nearer bloody.
Mal. This murderous shaft that's shot
Hath not yet lighted, and our safest way 146
Is to avoid the aim. Therefore to horse!
And let us not be dainty of leave-taking
But shift away. There's warrant in that theft
Which steals itself when there's no mercy left. 150
Exeunt.

Scene IV. [*The same. Without Macbeth's Castle.*]

Enter Ross *with an* Old Man.

Old Man. Threescore and ten I can remember well;
Within the volume of which time I have seen
Hours dreadful and things strange; but this sore night
Hath trifled former knowings.
Ross. Ah, good father,
Thou seest the heavens, as troubled with man's act,
Threaten his bloody stage. By the clock 'tis day, 6
And yet dark night strangles the traveling lamp.
Is't night's predominance, or the day's shame,
That darkness does the face of earth entomb
When living light should kiss it?
Old Man. 'Tis unnatural, 10
Even like the deed that's done. On Tuesday last
A falcon, tow'ring in her pride of place,
Was by a mousing owl hawked at and killed.
Ross. And Duncan's horses (a thing most strange and certain),
Beauteous and swift, the minions of their race, 15
Turned wild in nature, broke their stalls, flung out,
Contending 'gainst obedience, as they would make
War with mankind.
Old Man. 'Tis said they eat each other.

144–45. **the . . . bloody:** i.e., our nearest of kin offers our greatest danger.
148. **dainty of:** particular about (in observing ceremony)
149. **warrant:** justification
149–50. **that . . . itself:** i.e., their stealthy departure
3. **sore:** terrible
4. **trifled:** made trifles of; **former knowings:** previous experience
12. **tow'ring . . . place:** proudly soaring to her greatest height
15. **minions:** darlings; choicest examples

Ross. They did so, to the amazement of mine eyes
That looked upon't.

Enter Macduff.

Here comes the good Macduff. 20
How goes the world, sir, now?
Macd. Why, see you not?
Ross. Is't known who did this more than bloody deed?
Macd. Those that Macbeth hath slain.
Ross. Alas, the day!
What good could they pretend?
Macd. They were suborned.
Malcolm and Donalbain, the King's two sons, 25
Are stol'n away and fled, which puts upon them
Suspicion of the deed.
Ross. 'Gainst nature still!
Thriftless ambition, that will raven up
Thine own live's means! Then 'tis most like
The sovereignty will fall upon Macbeth. 30
Macd. He is already named, and gone to Scone
To be invested.
Ross. Where is Duncan's body?
Macd. Carried to Colmekill,
The sacred storehouse of his predecessors
And guardian of their bones.
Ross. Will you to Scone? 35
Macd. No, cousin, I'll to Fife.
Ross. Well, I will thither.
Macd. Well, may you see things well done there. Adieu,
Lest our old robes sit easier than our new!
Ross. Farewell, father.
Old Man. God's benison go with you, and with those 40
That would make good of bad, and friends of foes!
Exeunt omnes.

24. pretend: intend; **suborned:** bribed
28. raven up: devour rapaciously
33. Colmekill: the island of Iona

ACT III

Scene I. [*Forres. The Palace.*]

Enter Banquo.

Ban. Thou hast it now—King, Cawdor, Glamis, all,
As the Weird Women promised; and I fear
Thou playedst most foully for't. Yet it was said
It should not stand in thy posterity,
But that myself should be the root and father 5
Of many kings. If there come truth from them
(As upon thee, Macbeth, their speeches shine),
Why, by the verities on thee made good,
May they not be my oracles as well
And set me up in hope? But, hush, no more! 10

Sennet sounded. Enter Macbeth, *as King;* Lady [Macbeth, *as Queen*]; Lennox, Ross, Lords, *and* Attendants.

Macb. Here's our chief guest.
Lady. If he had been forgotten,
It had been as a gap in our great feast,
And all-thing unbecoming.
Macb. Tonight we hold a solemn supper, sir,
And I'll request your presence.
Ban. Let your Highness 15
Command upon me, to the which my duties
Are with a most indissoluble tie
Forever knit.
Macb. Ride you this afternoon?
Ban. Ay, my good lord.
Macb. We should have else desired your good advice 20
(Which still hath been both grave and prosperous)
In this day's council; but we'll take tomorrow.
Is't far you ride?
Ban. As far, my lord, as will fill up the time
'Twixt this and supper. Go not my horse the better,
I must become a borrower of the night 26
For a dark hour or twain.
Macb. Fail not our feast.
Ban. My lord, I will not.

4. stand: continue
8. on . . . good: proved in your case
13. all-thing: altogether
14. solemn: festive
21. prosperous: profitable

Macb. We hear our bloody cousins are bestowed
In England and in Ireland, not confessing 30
Their cruel parricide, filling their hearers
With strange invention. But of that tomorrow,
When therewithal we shall have cause of state
Craving us jointly. Hie you to horse. Adieu,
Till you return at night. Goes Fleance with you? 35
Ban. Ay, my good lord. Our time does call upon's.
Macb. I wish your horses swift and sure of foot,
And so I do commend you to their backs.
Farewell. *Exit Banquo.*
Let every man be master of his time 40
Till seven at night. To make society
The sweeter welcome, we will keep ourself
Till suppertime alone. While then, God be with you!
Exeunt Lords [*and others. Manent Macbeth and a Servant*].
Sirrah, a word with you. Attend those men
Our pleasure? 45
Serv. They are, my lord, without the palace gate.
Macb. Bring them before us. *Exit Servant.*
To be thus is nothing,
But to be safely thus. Our fears in Banquo
Stick deep, and in his royalty of nature
Reigns that which would be feared. 'Tis much he dares, 50
And to that dauntless temper of his mind
He hath a wisdom that doth guide his valor
To act in safety. There is none but he
Whose being I do fear; and under him
My genius is rebuked, as it is said 55
Mark Antony's was by Cæsar. He chid the Sisters
When first they put the name of King upon me,
And bade them speak to him. Then, prophet-like,
They hailed him father to a line of kings.
Upon my head they placed a fruitless crown 60
And put a barren scepter in my gripe,
Thence to be wrenched with an unlineal hand,
No son of mine succeeding. If't be so,
For Banquo's issue have I filed my mind;
For them the gracious Duncan have I murdered;
Put rancors in the vessel of my peace 66
Only for them, and mine eternal jewel
Given to the common enemy of man
To make them kings, the seed of Banquo kings!
Rather than so, come, Fate, into the list, 70
And champion me to the utterance! Who's there?

Enter SERVANT *and* TWO MURDERERS.

Now go to the door and stay there till we call.
Exit Servant.
Was it not yesterday we spoke together?
Murderers. It was, so please your Highness.
Macb. Well then, now
Have you considered of my speeches? Know 75
That it was he, in the times past, which held you
So under fortune, which you thought had been
Our innocent self. This I made good to you
In our last conference, passed in probation with you
How you were borne in hand, how crossed; the instruments; 80
Who wrought with them; and all things else that might
To half a soul and to a notion crazed
Say "Thus did Banquo."
1. Mur. You made it known to us.
Macb. I did so; and went further, which is now
Our point of second meeting. Do you find 85
Your patience so predominant in your nature
That you can let this go? Are you so gospeled
To pray for this good man and for his issue,
Whose heavy hand hath bowed you to the grave
And beggared yours forever?
1. Mur. We are men, my liege. 90
Macb. Ay, in the catalogue ye go for men,
As hounds and greyhounds, mongrels, spaniels, curs,
Shoughs, water-rugs, and demi-wolves are clept
All by the name of dogs. The valued file
Distinguishes the swift, the slow, the subtle, 95
The housekeeper, the hunter, every one
According to the gift which bounteous nature
Hath in him closed; whereby he does receive
Particular addition, from the bill
That writes them all alike; and so of men. 100
Now, if you have a station in the file,
Not i' the worst rank of manhood, say't;
And I will put that business in your bosoms
Whose execution takes your enemy off,
Grapples you to the heart and love of us, 105
Who wear our health but sickly in his life,
Which in his death were perfect.
2. Mur. I am one, my liege,
Whom the vile blows and buffets of the world
Have so incensed that I am reckless what
I do to spite the world.
1. Mur. And I another, 110
So weary with disasters, tugged with fortune,

42. **ourself:** the royal plural
43. **While then:** in the meantime
49. **royalty:** nobility
55. **genius:** ruling spirit; **rebuked:** checked; inhibited
64. **filed:** defiled
70. **list:** field of combat
71. **champion:** challenge; **utterance:** French *outrance,* "utmost"
79. **passed . . . you:** discussed with you the proof
80. **borne . . . hand:** deceived
82. **notion:** understanding
87. **gospeled:** ruled by gospel teachings to forgive your enemies
94. **valued file:** list containing evaluations
99. **Particular addition:** a distinguishing adjective or title; **from:** unlike

That I would set my life on any chance,
To mend it or be rid on't.

Macb. Both of you
Know Banquo was your enemy.

Murderers. True, my lord.

Macb. So is he mine, and in such bloody distance
That every minute of his being thrusts 116
Against my near'st of life; and though I could
With barefaced power sweep him from my sight
And bid my will avouch it, yet I must not,
For certain friends that are both his and mine, 120
Whose loves I may not drop, but wail his fall
Who I myself struck down. And thence it is
That I to your assistance do make love,
Masking the business from the common eye
For sundry weighty reasons.

2. Mur. We shall, my lord, 125
Perform what you command us.

1. Mur. Though our lives—

Macb. Your spirits shine through you. Within this hour at most
I will advise you where to plant yourselves,
Acquaint you with the perfect spy o' the time,
The moment on't; for't must be done tonight, 130
And something from the palace (always thought
That I require a clearness), and with him,
To leave no rubs nor botches in the work,
Fleance his son, that keeps him company,
Whose absence is no less material to me 135
Than is his father's, must embrace the fate
Of that dark hour. Resolve yourselves apart;
I'll come to you anon.

Murderers. We are resolved, my lord.

Macb. I'll call upon you straight. Abide within.
[*Exeunt Murderers.*]
It is concluded. Banquo, thy soul's flight, 140
If it find heaven, must find it out tonight.
Exit.

Scene II. [*The same.*]

Enter MACBETH'S LADY *and a* SERVANT.

Lady. Is Banquo gone from court?

Serv. Ay, madam, but returns again tonight.

Lady. Say to the King I would attend his leisure
For a few words.

Serv. Madam, I will. *Exit.*

Lady. Naught's had, all's spent,
Where our desire is got without content. 5
'Tis safer to be that which we destroy
Than by destruction dwell in doubtful joy.

Enter MACBETH.

How now, my lord? Why do you keep alone,
Of sorriest fancies your companions making, 9
Using those thoughts which should indeed have died
With them they think on? Things without all remedy
Should be without regard. What's done is done.

Macb. We have scotched the snake, not killed it.
She'll close and be herself, whilst our poor malice
Remains in danger of her former tooth. 15
But let the frame of things disjoint, both the worlds suffer,
Ere we will eat our meal in fear and sleep
In the affliction of these terrible dreams
That shake us nightly. Better be with the dead,
Whom we, to gain our peace, have sent to peace, 20
Than on the torture of the mind to lie
In restless ecstasy. Duncan is in his grave;
After life's fitful fever he sleeps well.
Treason has done his worst: nor steel nor poison,
Malice domestic, foreign levy, nothing, 25
Can touch him further.

Lady. Come on.
Gentle my lord, sleek o'er your rugged looks;
Be bright and jovial among your guests tonight.

Macb. So shall I, love; and so, I pray, be you.
Let your remembrance apply to Banquo; 30
Present him eminence both with eye and tongue:
Unsafe the while, that we
Must lave our honors in these flattering streams
And make our faces vizards to our hearts,
Disguising what they are.

Lady. You must leave this. 35

Macb. O, full of scorpions is my mind, dear wife!
Thou knowst that Banquo, and his Fleance, lives.

Lady. But in them Nature's copy's not eterne.

Macb. There's comfort yet; they are assailable.
Then be thou jocund. Ere the bat hath flown 40
His cloistered flight, ere to black Hecate's summons

115. **in . . . distance:** to such a degree of bloody hostility
117. **near'st . . . life:** heart; very life
119. **bid . . . it:** justify it solely on the basis that I willed it
129. **the . . . time:** the most precise intelligence of Banquo's movements
131. **something:** somewhat; **thought:** remembering
133. **rubs:** imperfections
137. **Resolve . . . apart:** withdraw and decide

9. **sorriest:** most wretched
11–12. **Things . . . regard:** proverbial: "Past cure, past care."
13. **scotched:** wounded
14. **close:** heal
16. **frame . . . things:** universe
22. **restless ecstasy:** anxious frenzy
30. **Let . . . to:** be particularly attentive to
32. **the while:** for the time; **that:** so that
33. **lave:** cleanse
34. **vizards:** masks
38. **Nature's . . . eterne:** i.e., they are mortal. **Copy** may be used in the sense of "copyhold tenure."
41. **cloistered:** i.e., through cloisters or similar enclosures

The shard-borne beetle with his drowsy hums
Hath rung night's yawning peal, there shall be done
A deed of dreadful note.

Lady. What's to be done?

Macb. Be innocent of the knowledge, dearest chuck, 45
Till thou applaud the deed. Come, seeling night,
Scarf up the tender eye of pitiful day,
And with thy bloody and invisible hand
Cancel and tear to pieces that great bond
Which keeps me pale! Light thickens, and the crow
Makes wing to the rooky wood. 51
Good things of day begin to droop and drowse,
Whiles night's black agents to their preys do rouse.
Thou marvelst at my words; but hold thee still:
Things bad begun make strong themselves by ill.
So prithee go with me. 56

Exeunt.

Scene III. [*The same. A park near the Palace.*]

Enter THREE MURDERERS.

1. Mur. But who did bid thee join with us?

3. Mur. Macbeth.

2. Mur. He needs not our mistrust, since he delivers
Our offices, and what we have to do,
To the direction just.

1. Mur. Then stand with us.
The west yet glimmers with some streaks of day.
Now spurs the lated traveler apace 6
To gain the timely inn, and near approaches
The subject of our watch.

3. Mur. Hark! I hear horses.

Ban. (*Within*) Give us a light there, ho!

2. Mur. Then 'tis he! The rest
That are within the note of expectation 10
Already are i' the court.

1. Mur. His horses go about.

3. Mur. Almost a mile; but he does usually,
So all men do, from hence to the palace gate
Make it their walk.

Enter BANQUO, *and* FLEANCE *with a torch.*

2. Mur. A light, a light!

3. Mur. 'Tis he.

1. Mur. Stand to't. 15

Ban. It will be rain tonight.

1. Mur. Let it come down!

[*They set upon Banquo.*]

Ban. O, treachery! Fly, good Fleance, fly, fly, fly!
Thou mayst revenge. O slave!

[*Dies. Fleance escapes.*]

3. Mur. Who did strike out the light?

1. Mur. Was't not the way?

3. Mur. There's but one down; the son is fled.

2. Mur. We have lost 20
Best half of our affair.

1. Mur. Well, let's away, and say how much is done.

Exeunt.

Scene IV. [*The same. Hall in the Palace.*]

Banquet prepared. Enter MACBETH, LADY [MACBETH], ROSS, LENNOX, LORDS, *and* ATTENDANTS.

Macb. You know your own degrees, sit down. At first
And last the hearty welcome.

Lords. Thanks to your Majesty.

Macb. Ourself will mingle with society
And play the humble host.
Our hostess keeps her state, but in best time 5
We will require her welcome.

Lady. Pronounce it for me, sir, to all our friends,
For my heart speaks they are welcome.

Enter FIRST MURDERER [*to the door*].

Macb. See, they encounter thee with their hearts' thanks.
Both sides are even: here I'll sit i' the midst. 10
Be large in mirth; anon we'll drink a measure
The table round. [*Moves toward Murderer at door.*]
There's blood upon thy face.

Mur. 'Tis Banquo's then.

Macb. 'Tis better thee without than he within.
Is he dispatched? 15

Mur. My lord, his throat is cut. That I did for him.

Macb. Thou art the best o' the cutthroats! Yet he's good

42. shard-borne: borne on scaly wings. Shard also means "dung," and there may be a deliberate quibble referring to the beetle that is born in dung.
46. seeling: blinding; in falconry, the process of sewing the eyelids of a bird during the taming process
47. Scarf up: blindfold
49. that . . . bond: Banquo's lease on life
2. delivers: reports
3. offices: duties
4. To . . . just: exactly as Macbeth has already directed
6. lated: belated
10. within . . . expectation: on the list of expected guests

1. degrees: ranks; hence, their appropriate places at table
5. keeps . . . state: remains in her chair of state; **in . . . time:** at the proper moment
6. require: request
9. encounter: respond to
11. large: unrestrained

That did the like for Fleance. If thou didst it,
Thou art the nonpareil.
Mur. Most royal sir,
Fleance is scaped. 20
Macb. [*Aside*] Then comes my fit again. I had else been perfect;
Whole as the marble, founded as the rock,
As broad and general as the casing air.
But now I am cabined, cribbed, confined, bound in
To saucy doubts and fears.—But Banquo's safe? 25
Mur. Ay, my good lord. Safe in a ditch he bides,
With twenty trenched gashes on his head,
The least a death to nature.
Macb. Thanks for that!
There the grown serpent lies; the worm that's fled
Hath nature that in time will venom breed, 30
No teeth for the present. Get thee gone. Tomorrow
We'll hear ourselves again. *Exit Murderer.*
Lady. My royal lord,
You do not give the cheer. The feast is sold
That is not often vouched, while 'tis a-making, 34
'Tis given with welcome. To feed were best at home.
From thence, the sauce to meat is ceremony;
Meeting were bare without it.

Enter the GHOST OF BANQUO, *and sits in Macbeth's place.*

Macb. Sweet remembrancer!
Now good digestion wait on appetite,
And health on both!
Len. May't please your Highness sit.
Macb. Here had we now our country's honor, roofed, 40
Were the graced person of our Banquo present;
Who may I rather challenge for unkindness
Than pity for mischance!
Ross. His absence, sir,
Lays blame upon his promise. Please't your Highness
To grace us with your royal company? 45
Macb. The table's full.
Len. Here is a place reserved, sir.
Macb. Where?
Len. Here, my good lord. What is't that moves your Highness?
Macb. Which of you have done this?
Lords. What, my good lord?
Macb. Thou canst not say I did it. Never shake
Thy gory locks at me. 51
Ross. Gentlemen, rise. His Highness is not well.

22. **founded:** firmly based
23. **broad . . . general:** free and unlimited; **casing:** enveloping everything
25. **safe:** harmless
33. **give:** offer spontaneously
33–35. **The . . . welcome:** private hospitality is no better than that of an inn if the guests are not assured of welcome.
35. **To feed:** mere eating

Lady. Sit, worthy friends. My lord is often thus,
And hath been from his youth. Pray you keep seat.
The fit is momentary; upon a thought 55
He will again be well. If much you note him,
You shall offend him and extend his passion.
Feed, and regard him not.—Are you a man?
Macb. Ay, and a bold one, that dare look on that
Which might appal the devil.
Lady. O proper stuff! 60
This is the very painting of your fear.
This is the air-drawn dagger which you said
Led you to Duncan. O, these flaws and starts
(Impostors to true fear) would well become
A woman's story at a winter's fire, 65
Authorized by her grandam. Shame itself!
Why do you make such faces? When all's done,
You look but on a stool.
Macb. Prithee see there! behold! look! lo! How say you?
Why, what care I? If thou canst nod, speak too. 70
If charnel houses and our graves must send
Those that we bury back, our monuments
Shall be the maws of kites. [*Exit Ghost.*]
Lady. What, quite unmanned in folly?
Macb. If I stand here, I saw him.
Lady. Fie, for shame!
Macb. Blood hath been shed ere now, i' the olden time, 75
Ere humane statute purged the gentle weal;
Ay, and since too, murders have been performed
Too terrible for the ear. The time has been
That, when the brains were out, the man would die,
And there an end! But now they rise again, 80
With twenty mortal murders on their crowns,
And push us from our stools. This is more strange
Than such a murder is.
Lady. My worthy lord,
Your noble friends do lack you.
Macb. I do forget.
Do not muse at me, my most worthy friends. 85
I have a strange infirmity, which is nothing
To those that know me. Come, love and health to all!
Then I'll sit down. Give me some wine, fill full.

Enter GHOST.

I drink to the general joy o' the whole table,
And to our dear friend Banquo, whom we miss. 90

55. **upon . . . thought:** in an instant
57. **passion:** fit
63. **flaws:** outbursts of emotion
64. **Impostors . . . fear:** i.e., they result from imaginary rather than actual dangers.
66. **Authorized:** attested to
71. **charnel houses:** repositories of the bones of the dead
72–73. **our . . . kites:** our bodies will be thrown to vultures instead of being buried; **maws:** stomachs
76. **purged . . . weal:** purged the state of violence and thus gentled it
81. **mortal murders:** fatal wounds

Would he were here! To all, and him, we thirst,
And all to all.

Lords. Our duties, and the pledge.

Macb. Avaunt, and quit my sight! Let the earth hide thee!
Thy bones are marrowless, thy blood is cold;
Thou hast no speculation in those eyes 95
Which thou dost glare with!

Lady. Think of this, good peers,
But as a thing of custom. 'Tis no other.
Only it spoils the pleasure of the time.

Macb. What man dare, I dare.
Approach thou like the rugged Russian bear, 100
The armed rhinoceros, or the Hyrcan tiger;
Take any shape but that, and my firm nerves
Shall never tremble. Or be alive again
And dare me to the desert with thy sword.
If trembling I inhabit then, protest me 105
The baby of a girl. Hence, horrible shadow!
Unreal mock'ry, hence! [*Exit Ghost.*]
Why, so! Being gone,
I am a man again. Pray you sit still.

Lady. You have displaced the mirth, broke the good meeting
With most admired disorder.

Macb. Can such things be, 110
And overcome us like a summer's cloud
Without our special wonder? You make me strange
Even to the disposition that I owe,
When now I think you can behold such sights
And keep the natural ruby of your cheeks 115
When mine is blanched with fear.

Ross. What sights, my lord?

Lady. I pray you speak not. He grows worse and worse;
Question enrages him. At once, good night.
Stand not upon the order of your going,
But go at once.

Len. Good night, and better health 120
Attend his Majesty!

Lady. A kind good night to all!
Exeunt Lords [and Attendants].

Macb. It will have blood, they say: blood will have blood.
Stones have been known to move and trees to speak;
Augures and understood relations have 124
By maggot-pies and choughs and rooks brought forth
The secret'st man of blood. What is the night?

Lady. Almost at odds with morning, which is which.

Macb. How sayst thou that Macduff denies his person
At our great bidding?

Lady. Did you send to him, sir?

Macb. I hear it by the way; but I will send. 130
There's not a one of them but in his house
I keep a servant fee'd. I will tomorrow
(And betimes I will) to the Weird Sisters.
More shall they speak; for now I am bent to know
By the worst means the worst. For mine own good
All causes shall give way. I am in blood 136
Stepped in so far that, should I wade no more,
Returning were as tedious as go o'er.
Strange things I have in head, that will to hand,
Which must be acted ere they may be scanned. 140

Lady. You lack the season of all natures, sleep.

Macb. Come, we'll to sleep. My strange and self-abuse
Is the initiate fear that wants hard use.
We are yet but young in deed.
Exeunt.

Scene V. [*A heath.*]

Thunder. Enter the Three Witches, *meeting* Hecate.

1. Witch. Why, how now, Hecate? You look angerly.

Hec. Have I not reason, beldams as you are,
Saucy and overbold? How did you dare
To trade and traffic with Macbeth
In riddles and affairs of death; 5
And I, the mistress of your charms,
The close contriver of all harms,
Was never called to bear my part

91–92. To . . . all: here's a toast to you all, including Banquo; everyone drink to the health of all.
92. Our . . . pledge: our allegiance to your Majesty and health to everyone
95. speculation: discernment; rational sight
101. Hyrcan tiger: tiger of the Hyrcanian desert, near the Caspian Sea
104. to . . . desert: to fight you in a solitary place
105. inhabit: abide (at home), refusing your challenge
106. baby . . . girl: girl's doll
110. admired: amazing
112–13. You . . . owe: i.e., you deny the bravery that is natural to me.
119. Stand . . . going: forget protocol in departing
124. Augures: auguries; predictions; **understood relations:** prophetic interpretations
125. maggot-pies: magpies; **choughs:** birds of the crow family; **brought forth:** revealed
126. man . . . blood: murderer
128. How . . . thou: what do you say to the fact
130. by . . . way: i.e., from spies
133. betimes: early
139. to hand: be executed
141. season: preservative
142. self-abuse: delusion
143. initiate . . . use: timidity proper to a beginner who is not hardened by custom
Scene V is generally believed to be an interpolation by a hand other than Shakespeare's. The song indicated at line 34 is from Thomas Middleton's *The Witch* (written *ca.* 1609).
2. beldams: hags
7. close: secret

Or show the glory of our art?
And, which is worse, all you have done 10
Hath been but for a wayward son,
Spiteful and wrathful, who, as others do,
Loves for his own ends, not for you.
But make amends now. Get you gone
And at the pit of Acheron 15
Meet me i' the morning. Thither he
Will come to know his destiny.
Your vessels and your spells provide,
Your charms and everything beside.
I am for the air. This night I'll spend 20
Unto a dismal and a fatal end.
Great business must be wrought ere noon.
Upon the corner of the moon
There hangs a vap'rous drop profound.
I'll catch it ere it come to ground; 25
And that, distilled by magic sleights,
Shall raise such artificial sprites
As by the strength of their illusion
Shall draw him on to his confusion.
He shall spurn fate, scorn death, and bear 30
His hopes 'bove wisdom, grace, and fear;
And you all know security
Is mortals' chiefest enemy.

Music and a song within. "Come away, come away," &c.

Hark! I am called. My little spirit, see, 35
Sits in a foggy cloud and stays for me. [*Exit.*]

1. Witch. Come, let's make haste. She'll soon be back again.

Exeunt.

15. **Acheron:** a river in Hades
21. **dismal:** disastrous
24. **vap'rous . . . profound:** a heavy drop of moisture
32. **security:** overconfidence

Scene VI. [*Forres. The Palace.*]

Enter LENNOX *and* ANOTHER LORD.

Len. My former speeches have but hit your thoughts,
Which can interpret farther. Only I say
Things have been strangely borne. The gracious Duncan
Was pitied of Macbeth. Marry, he was dead!
And the right valiant Banquo walked too late; 5
Whom, you may say (if't please you) Fleance killed,
For Fleance fled. Men must not walk too late.
Who cannot want the thought how monstrous
It was for Malcolm and for Donalbain
To kill their gracious father? Damned fact! 10
How it did grieve Macbeth! Did he not straight,
In pious rage, the two delinquents tear,
That were the slaves of drink and thralls of sleep?
Was not that nobly done? Ay, and wisely too!
For 'twould have angered any heart alive 15
To hear the men deny't. So that I say
He has borne all things well; and I do think
That, had he Duncan's sons under his key
(As, an't please heaven, he shall not), they should find
What 'twere to kill a father. So should Fleance. 20
But peace! for from broad words, and 'cause he failed
His presence at the tyrant's feast, I hear
Macduff lives in disgrace. Sir, can you tell
Where he bestows himself?

Lord. The son of Duncan,
From whom this tyrant holds the due of birth, 25
Lives in the English court, and is received
Of the most pious Edward with such grace
That the malevolence of fortune nothing
Takes from his high respect. Thither Macduff
Is gone to pray the holy King upon his aid 30
To wake Northumberland and warlike Siward;
That by the help of these (with Him above
To ratify the work) we may again
Give to our tables meat, sleep to our nights, 34
Free from our feasts and banquets bloody knives,
Do faithful homage and receive free honors—
All which we pine for now. And this report
Hath so exasperate the King that he
Prepares for some attempt of war.

Len. Sent he to Macduff?

Lord. He did; and with an absolute "Sir, not I!"
The cloudy messenger turns me his back 41
And hums, as who should say, "You'll rue the time
That clogs me with this answer."

Len. And that well might
Advise him to a caution t' hold what distance
His wisdom can provide. Some holy angel 45
Fly to the court of England and unfold
His message ere he come, that a swift blessing
May soon return to this our suffering country
Under a hand accursed!

Lord. I'll send my prayers with him.

Exeunt.

4. **Marry:** indeed; literally, "By the Virgin Mary"
8. **want . . . thought:** fail to think
10. **fact:** crime
25. **holds . . . birth:** withholds the birthright
27. **Edward:** Edward the Confessor: **grace:** honor
30. **upon . . . aid:** in Malcolm's behalf
35. **Free . . . knives:** free feasts and banquets from bloody knives
36. **free:** liberal and untainted
38. **exasperate:** exasperated
41. **cloudy:** frowning; **turns me:** turns; the ethical dative
43. **clogs:** burdens

ACT IV

Scene I. [*A cavern. In the middle, a boiling cauldron.*]

Thunder. Enter the THREE WITCHES.

1. Witch. Thrice the brinded cat hath mewed.
2. Witch. Thrice, and once the hedge-pig whined.
3. Witch. Harpier cries; 'tis time.
1. Witch. Round about the cauldron go;
In the poisoned entrails throw. 5
Toad, that under cold stone
Days and nights has thirty-one
Swelt'red venom sleeping got,
Boil thou first i' the charmed pot.
All. Double, double, toil and trouble; 10
Fire burn, and cauldron bubble.
2. Witch. Fillet of a fenny snake,
In the cauldron boil and bake;
Eye of newt, and toe of frog,
Wool of bat, and tongue of dog, 15
Adder's fork, and blindworm's sting,
Lizard's leg, and howlet's wing;
For a charm of pow'rful trouble
Like a hell-broth boil and bubble.
All. Double, double, toil and trouble; 20
Fire burn, and cauldron bubble.
3. Witch. Scale of dragon, tooth of wolf,
Witch's mummy, maw and gulf
Of the ravined salt-sea shark,
Root of hemlock, digged i' the dark; 25
Liver of blaspheming Jew,
Gall of goat, and slips of yew
Slivered in the moon's eclipse;
Nose of Turk and Tartar's lips;
Finger of birth-strangled babe 30
Ditch-delivered by a drab:
Make the gruel thick and slab.

1. brinded: brindled; streaked
3. Harpier: the Third Witch's familiar
8. Swelt'red: sweated; **got:** created
12. fenny: fen-inhabiting
16. blindworm: a small, harmless lizard
17. howlet: owlet
23. mummy: preserved corpse, believed to have potent magical properties; **maw . . . gulf:** stomach and gullet
24. ravined: voracious
25. i' . . . dark: i.e., at midnight, when its potency would be greatest
31. drab: whore
32. slab: sticky

Add thereto a tiger's chaudron
For the ingredience of our cauldron.
All. Double, double, toil and trouble; 35
Fire burn, and cauldron bubble.
2. Witch. Cool it with a baboon's blood,
Then the charm is firm and good.

Enter HECATE *and the* OTHER THREE WITCHES.

Hec. O, well done! I commend your pains,
And every one shall share i' the gains. 40
And now about the cauldron sing
Like elves and fairies in a ring,
Enchanting all that you put in.
Music and a song, "Black spirits," &c.
2. Witch. By the pricking of my thumbs,
Something wicked this way comes. 45
Open locks,
Whoever knocks!

Enter MACBETH.

Macb. How now, you secret, black, and midnight hags?
What is't you do?
All. A deed without a name. 49
Macb. I conjure you by that which you profess
(Howe'er you come to know it), answer me.
Though you untie the winds and let them fight
Against the churches; though the yesty waves
Confound and swallow navigation up;
Though bladed corn be lodged and trees blown down; 55
Though castles topple on their warders' heads;
Though palaces and pyramids do slope
Their heads to their foundations; though the treasure
Of nature's germens tumble all together,
Even till destruction sicken—answer me 60
To what I ask you.
1. Witch. Speak.
2. Witch. Demand.
3. Witch. We'll answer.

33. chaudron: entrails
50. that . . . profess: i.e., your magic arts
53. yesty: foaming
55. bladed corn: ripe wheat; **lodged:** beaten flat
59. nature's germens: all the seeds of creation

1. Witch. Say, if th' hadst rather hear it from our mouths
Or from our masters.
Macb. Call 'em! Let me see 'em.
1. Witch. Pour in sow's blood, that hath eaten
Her nine farrow; grease that's sweaten 65
From the murderer's gibbet throw
Into the flame.
All. Come, high or low;
Thyself and office deftly show!

Thunder. FIRST APPARITION, *an Armed Head.*

Macb. Tell me, thou unknown power—
1. Witch. He knows thy thought.
Hear his speech, but say thou naught. 70
1. Appar. Macbeth! Macbeth! Macbeth! Beware Macduff;
Beware the Thane of Fife. Dismiss me. Enough.
He descends.
Macb. Whate'er thou art, for thy good caution thanks!
Thou hast harped my fear aright. But one word more—
1. Witch. He will not be commanded. Here's another, 75
More potent than the first.

Thunder. SECOND APPARITION, *a Bloody Child.*

2. Appar. Macbeth! Macbeth! Macbeth!
Macb. Had I three ears, I'ld hear thee.
2. Appar. Be bloody, bold, and resolute; laugh to scorn
The pow'r of man, for none of woman born 80
Shall harm Macbeth. *Descends.*
Macb. Then live, Macduff. What need I fear of thee?
But yet I'll make assurance double sure
And take a bond of fate. Thou shalt not live!
That I may tell pale-hearted fear it lies 85
And sleep in spite of thunder.

Thunder. THIRD APPARITION, *a Child Crowned, with a tree in his hand.*

What is this
That rises like the issue of a king
And wears upon his baby-brow the round
And top of sovereignty?
All. Listen, but speak not to't.
3. Appar. Be lion-mettled, proud, and take no care 90
Who chafes, who frets, or where conspirers are.
Macbeth shall never vanquished be until
Great Birnam Wood to high Dunsinane Hill
Shall come against him. *Descends.*
Macb. That will never be.
Who can impress the forest, bid the tree 95
Unfix his earth-bound root? Sweet bodements, good!
Rebellious dead rise never till the wood
Of Birnam rise, and our high-placed Macbeth
Shall live the lease of nature, pay his breath
To time and mortal custom. Yet my heart 100
Throbs to know one thing. Tell me, if your art
Can tell so much—shall Banquo's issue ever
Reign in this kingdom?
All. Seek to know no more.
Macb. I will be satisfied. Deny me this, 104
And an eternal curse fall on you! Let me know.
Why sinks that cauldron? and what noise is this?
Hautboys.

1. Witch. Show!
2. Witch. Show!
3. Witch. Show!
All. Show his eyes, and grieve his heart! 110
Come like shadows, so depart!

A show of EIGHT KINGS, [*the eighth*] *with a glass in his hand, and* BANQUO *last.*

Macb. Thou art too like the spirit of Banquo. Down!
Thy crown does sear mine eyeballs. And thy hair,
Thou other gold-bound brow, is like the first.
A third is like the former. Filthy hags! 115
Why do you show me this? A fourth? Start, eyes!
What, will the line stretch out to the crack of doom?
Another yet? A seventh? I'll see no more.
And yet the eighth appears, who bears a glass
Which shows me many more; and some I see 120
That twofold balls and treble scepters carry.
Horrible sight! Now I see 'tis true;
For the blood-boltered Banquo smiles upon me
And points at them for his. [*Apparitions descend.*]
What? Is this so?
1. Witch. Ay, sir, all this is so. But why 125
Stands Macbeth thus amazedly?
Come, sisters, cheer we up his sprites
And show the best of our delights.

S.D. 68. Armed Head: symbolic of Macbeth's coming combat with Macduff
74. harped: sounded
S.D. 76. a Bloody Child: symbolizing Macduff, who was prematurely born
84. take . . . fate: bind fate by a contract
S.D. 86. a Child Crowned: the image of Duncan's son Malcolm, bearing a symbol of the trees with which his men disguise themselves in their advance on Dunsinane
95. impress: conscript
96. bodements: omens
106. noise: music
S.D. 111. glass: mirror
121. twofold . . . scepters: prophesying the union of England and Scotland under one monarch (James I)
123. blood-boltered: having hair matted with blood
127. sprites: spirits

I'll charm the air to give a sound
While you perform your antic round, 130
That this great king may kindly say
Our duties did his welcome pay.

Music. The Witches dance, and vanish.

Macb. Where are they? Gone? Let this pernicious hour
Stand aye accursed in the calendar! 134
Come in, without there!

Enter LENNOX.

Len. What's your Grace's will?

Macb. Saw you the Weird Sisters?

Len. No, my lord.

Macb. Came they not by you?

Len. No indeed, my lord.

Macb. Infected be the air whereon they ride,
And damned all those that trust them! I did hear
The galloping of horse. Who was't came by? 140

Len. 'Tis two or three, my lord, that bring you word
Macduff is fled to England.

Macb. Fled to England?

Len. Ay, my good lord.

Macb. [*Aside*] Time, thou anticipatest my dread exploits.
The flighty purpose never is o'ertook 145
Unless the deed go with it. From this moment
The very firstlings of my heart shall be
The firstlings of my hand. And even now,
To crown my thoughts with acts, be it thought and done!
The castle of Macduff I will surprise, 150
Seize upon Fife, give to the edge o' the sword
His wife, his babes, and all unfortunate souls
That trace him in his line. No boasting like a fool!
This deed I'll do before this purpose cool.
But no more sights!—Where are these gentlemen?
Come, bring me where they are. 156

Exeunt.

Scene II. [*Fife. Macduff's Castle.*]

Enter MACDUFF'S WIFE, *her* SON, *and* ROSS.

Wife. What had he done to make him fly the land?

Ross. You must have patience, madam.

Wife. He had none.
His flight was madness. When our actions do not,
Our fears do make us traitors.

Ross. You know not
Whether it was his wisdom or his fear. 5

Wife. Wisdom? To leave his wife, to leave his babes,
His mansion, and his titles, in a place
From whence himself does fly? He loves us not,
He wants the natural touch. For the poor wren,
(The most diminutive of birds) will fight, 10
Her young ones in her nest, against the owl.
All is the fear, and nothing is the love,
As little is the wisdom, where the flight
So runs against all reason.

Ross. My dearest coz,
I pray you school yourself. But for your husband,
He is noble, wise, judicious, and best knows 16
The fits o' the season. I dare not speak much further;
But cruel are the times, when we are traitors
And do not know ourselves; when we hold rumor
From what we fear, yet know not what we fear, 20
But float upon a wild and violent sea
Each way and move—I take my leave of you.
Shall not be long but I'll be here again.
Things at the worst will cease, or else climb upward
To what they were before.—My pretty cousin, 25
Blessing upon you!

Wife. Fathered he is, and yet he's fatherless.

Ross. I am so much a fool, should I stay longer,
It would be my disgrace and your discomfort.
I take my leave at once. *Exit.*

Wife. Sirrah, your father's dead;
And what will you do now? How will you live? 31

Son. As birds do, mother.

Wife. What, with worms and flies?

Son. With what I get, I mean; and so do they.

Wife. Poor bird! thou'dst never fear the net nor lime,
The pitfall nor the gin. 35

Son. Why should I, mother? Poor birds they are not set for.
My father is not dead, for all your saying.

Wife. Yes, he is dead. How wilt thou do for a father?

Son. Nay, how will you do for a husband?

Wife. Why, I can buy me twenty at any market.

Son. Then you'll buy 'em to sell again. 41

Wife. Thou speakst with all thy wit; and yet, i' faith,
With wit enough for thee.

130. antic round: grotesque round dance
145. flighty: fleet
153. trace: succeed; descend from
4. Our . . . traitors: i.e., fear makes us betray the treachery in our hearts.

9. wants . . . touch: lacks natural feeling
14. coz: cousin; kinswoman
15. school: control
17. fits: disorders; **season:** the present
19. do . . . ourselves: i.e., unwittingly
19–20. hold . . . fear: believe what our fears dictate
29. It . . . disgrace: i.e., I would be moved to tears.
34. lime: birdlime, in which birds were caught
35. pitfall . . . gin: two traps for birds
36. Poor: worthless

Son. Was my father a traitor, mother?
Wife. Ay, that he was! 45
Son. What is a traitor?
Wife. Why, one that swears, and lies.
Son. And be all traitors that do so?
Wife. Every one that does so is a traitor and must be hanged.
Son. And must they all be hanged that swear and lie? 50
Wife. Every one.
Son. Who must hang them?
Wife. Why, the honest men.
Son. Then the liars and swearers are fools; for there are liars and swearers enow to beat the 55 honest men and hang up them.
Wife. Now God help thee, poor monkey!
But how wilt thou do for a father?
Son. If he were dead, you'ld weep for him. If you would not, it were a good sign that I should 60 quickly have a new father.
Wife. Poor prattler, how thou talkst!

Enter a MESSENGER.

Mess. Bless you, fair dame! I am not to you known,
Though in your state of honor I am perfect.
I doubt some danger does approach you nearly. 65
If you will take a homely man's advice,
Be not found here. Hence with your little ones!
To fright you thus methinks I am too savage;
To do worse to you were fell cruelty,
Which is too nigh your person. Heaven preserve you! 70
I dare abide no longer. *Exit.*
Wife. Whither should I fly?
I have done no harm. But I remember now
I am in this earthly world, where to do harm
Is often laudable, to do good sometime
Accounted dangerous folly. Why then, alas, 75
Do I put up that womanly defense
To say I have done no harm?—What are these faces?

Enter MURDERERS.

Mur. Where is your husband?
Wife. I hope, in no place so unsanctified 79
Where such as thou mayst find him.
Mur. He's a traitor.
Son. Thou liest, thou shag-eared villain!
Mur. What, you egg!
[*Stabbing him.*]
Young fry of treachery!

64. **in . . . perfect:** I know you well for a noble lady.
65. **doubt:** fear
69. **fell:** savage
81. **shag-eared:** shaggy-haired

Son. He has killed me, mother.
Run away, I pray you! [*Dies.*]
Exit [*Lady Macduff*], *crying* "Murder!" [*followed by Murderers.*]

Scene III. [*England. Before the King's Palace.*]

Enter MALCOLM *and* MACDUFF.

Mal. Let us seek out some desolate shade, and there
Weep our sad bosoms empty.
Macd. Let us rather
Hold fast the mortal sword and, like good men,
Bestride our downfall'n birthdom. Each new morn
New widows howl, new orphans cry, new sorrows
Strike heaven on the face, that it resounds 6
As if it felt with Scotland and yelled out
Like syllable of dolor.
Mal. What I believe, I'll wail;
What know, believe; and what I can redress,
As I shall find the time to friend, I will. 10
What you have spoke, it may be so perchance.
This tyrant, whose sole name blisters our tongues,
Was once thought honest; you have loved him well;
He hath not touched you yet. I am young; but something
You may discern of him through me, and wisdom
To offer up a weak, poor, innocent lamb 16
T' appease an angry god.
Macd. I am not treacherous.
Mal. But Macbeth is.
A good and virtuous nature may recoil
In an imperial charge. But I shall crave your pardon. 20
That which you are, my thoughts cannot transpose.
Angels are bright still, though the brightest fell.
Though all things foul would wear the brows of grace,
Yet grace must still look so.
Macd. I have lost my hopes.
Mal. Perchance even there where I did find my doubts. 25

3. **mortal:** deadly
4. **Bestride . . . birthdom:** stand over our downtrodden country and fight to preserve it.
8. **Like . . . dolor:** similar sorrowful words
10. **the . . . friend:** favorable opportunity
12. **sole:** mere
13. **honest:** honorable
15. **through me:** by betraying me to him; **and wisdom:** and discern wisdom
19–20. **recoil . . . charge:** shrink from the anger of a king
21. **transpose:** transform
22. **the brightest:** Lucifer
23–24. **Though . . . so:** i.e., the fact that vice can simulate virtue should not cause us to doubt the existence of virtue.

Why in that rawness left you wife and child,
Those precious motives, those strong knots of love,
Without leave-taking? I pray you,
Let not my jealousies be your dishonors,
But mine own safeties. You may be rightly just, 30
Whatever I shall think.

Macd. Bleed, bleed, poor country!
Great tyranny, lay thou thy basis sure,
For goodness dare not check thee! Wear thou thy wrongs;
The title is affeered! Fare thee well, lord.
I would not be the villain that thou thinkst 35
For the whole space that's in the tyrant's grasp
And the rich East to boot.

Mal. Be not offended.
I speak not as in absolute fear of you.
I think our country sinks beneath the yoke;
It weeps, it bleeds, and each new day a gash 40
Is added to her wounds. I think withal
There would be hands uplifted in my right;
And here from gracious England have I offer
Of goodly thousands. But, for all this,
When I shall tread upon the tyrant's head 45
Or wear it on my sword, yet my poor country
Shall have more vices than it had before,
More suffer and more sundry ways than ever,
By him that shall succeed.

Macd. What should he be?

Mal. It is myself I mean; in whom I know 50
All the particulars of vice so grafted
That, when they shall be opened, black Macbeth
Will seem as pure as snow, and the poor state
Esteem him as a lamb, being compared
With my confineless harms.

Macd. Not in the legions 55
Of horrid hell can come a devil more damned
In evils to top Macbeth.

Mal. I grant him bloody,
Luxurious, avaricious, false, deceitful,
Sudden, malicious, smacking of every sin
That has a name. But there's no bottom, none, 60
In my voluptuousness. Your wives, your daughters,
Your matrons, and your maids could not fill up
The cistern of my lust; and my desire
All continent impediments would o'erbear
That did oppose my will. Better Macbeth 65
Than such an one to reign.

Macd. Boundless intemperance
In nature is a tyranny. It hath been
The untimely emptying of the happy throne
And fall of many kings. But fear not yet
To take upon you what is yours. You may 70
Convey your pleasures in a spacious plenty,
And yet seem cold—the time you may so hoodwink.
We have willing dames enough. There cannot be
That vulture in you to devour so many
As will to greatness dedicate themselves, 75
Finding it so inclined.

Mal. With this there grows
In my most ill-composed affection such
A stanchless avarice that, were I King,
I should cut off the nobles for their lands,
Desire his jewels, and this other's house, 80
And my more-having would be as a sauce
To make me hunger more, that I should forge
Quarrels unjust against the good and loyal,
Destroying them for wealth.

Macd. This avarice
Sticks deeper, grows with more pernicious root 85
Than summer-seeming lust; and it hath been
The sword of our slain kings. Yet do not fear.
Scotland hath foisons to fill up your will
Of your mere own. All these are portable,
With other graces weighed. 90

Mal. But I have none. The king-becoming graces,
As justice, verity, temp'rance, stableness,
Bounty, perseverance, mercy, lowliness,
Devotion, patience, courage, fortitude,
I have no relish of them, but abound 95
In the division of each several crime,
Acting it many ways. Nay, had I pow'r, I should
Pour the sweet milk of concord into hell,
Uproar the universal peace, confound
All unity on earth.

Macd. O Scotland, Scotland! 100

Mal. If such a one be fit to govern, speak.
I am as I have spoken.

Macd. Fit to govern?
No, not to live. O nation miserable,
With an untitled tyrant bloody-scept'red,
When shalt thou see thy wholesome days again,
Since that the truest issue of thy throne 106
By his own interdiction stands accursed
And does blaspheme his breed? Thy royal father

26. **rawness:** exposed state
27. **motives:** inspirations
29. **Let . . . dishonors:** do not regard my suspicions as reflections on yourself
30. **rightly just:** truly honorable
32. **basis:** foundation
33. **wrongs:** stolen honors
34. **title:** legal right; **affeered:** certified by law
37. **to boot:** in addition
43. **England:** the King of England
52. **opened:** revealed
55. **confineless harms:** unlimited evils
58. **Luxurious:** lustful
59. **Sudden:** violent
64. **continent:** (1) restraining; (2) chaste
71. **Convey:** contrive stealthily
77. **affection:** disposition
86. **summer-seeming:** quick and brief
88. **foisons:** plenty
89. **mere:** very; **portable:** tolerable
90. **With . . . weighed:** balanced against other virtues
95. **relish:** taste; touch
96. **several:** individual
107. **interdiction:** ban
108. **blaspheme:** slander

Was a most sainted king; the queen that bore thee,
Oft'ner upon her knees than on her feet, 110
Died every day she lived. Fare thee well!
These evils thou repeatst upon thyself
Have banished me from Scotland. O my breast,
Thy hope ends here!

Mal. Macduff, this noble passion,
Child of integrity, hath from my soul 115
Wiped the black scruples, reconciled my thoughts
To thy good truth and honor. Devilish Macbeth
By many of these trains hath sought to win me
Into his power; and modest wisdom plucks me
From over-credulous haste; but God above 120
Deal between thee and me! for even now
I put myself to thy direction and
Unspeak mine own detraction, here abjure
The taints and blames I laid upon myself
For strangers to my nature. I am yet 125
Unknown to woman, never was forsworn,
Scarcely have coveted what was mine own,
At no time broke my faith, would not betray
The devil to his fellow, and delight 129
No less in truth than life. My first false speaking
Was this upon myself. What I am truly,
Is thine and my poor country's to command;
Whither indeed, before thy here-approach,
Old Siward with ten thousand warlike men
Already at a point was setting forth. 135
Now we'll together; and the chance of goodness
Be like our warranted quarrel! Why are you silent?

Macd. Such welcome and unwelcome things at once
'Tis hard to reconcile.

Enter a DOCTOR.

Mal. Well, more anon.
Comes the King forth, I pray you? 140

Doct. Ay, sir. There are a crew of wretched souls
That stay his cure. Their malady convinces
The great assay of art; but at his touch,
Such sanctity hath heaven given his hand,
They presently amend.

Mal. I thank you, doctor. 145

Exit [*Doctor*].

Macd. What's the disease he means?

Mal. 'Tis called the evil:
A most miraculous work in this good king,
Which often since my here-remain in England
I have seen him do. How he solicits heaven
Himself best knows; but strangely-visited people,
All swol'n and ulcerous, pitiful to the eye, 151
The mere despair of surgery, he cures,
Hanging a golden stamp about their necks,
Put on with holy prayers; and 'tis spoken,
To the succeeding royalty he leaves 155
The healing benediction. With this strange virtue,
He hath a heavenly gift of prophecy,
And sundry blessings hang about his throne
That speak him full of grace.

Enter ROSS.

Macd. See who comes here.

Mal. My countryman; but yet I know him not.

Macd. My ever gentle cousin, welcome hither.

Mal. I know him now. Good God betimes remove 162
The means that makes us strangers!

Ross. Sir, amen.

Macd. Stands Scotland where it did?

Ross. Alas, poor country,
Almost afraid to know itself! It cannot 165
Be called our mother, but our grave; where nothing,
But who knows nothing, is once seen to smile;
Where sighs and groans, and shrieks that rent the air,
Are made, not marked; where violent sorrow seems
A modern ecstasy. The dead man's knell 170
Is there scarce asked for who; and good men's lives
Expire before the flowers in their caps,
Dying or ere they sicken.

Macd. O, relation 173
Too nice, and yet too true!

Mal. What's the newest grief?

Ross. That of an hour's age doth hiss the speaker:
Each minute teems a new one.

Macd. How does my wife?

Ross. Why, well.

Macd. And all my children?

Ross. Well too.

Macd. The tyrant has not battered at their peace?

Ross. No, they were well at peace when I did leave 'em.

Macd. Be not a niggard of your speech. How goes't? 180

111. Died: denied earthly pleasures
116. scruples: doubts
118. these trains: tricks such as I have suspected you of
119. modest: prudent
135. at . . . point: fully prepared
136–37. the . . . quarrel: may our luck equal the justice of our cause
142. stay: await; **convinces:** defeats
143. great . . . art: medicine's best efforts
146. evil: scrofula. Curing scrofula by the royal touch was begun by Edward the Confessor. James I also performed the ritual, though rarely and reluctantly.
150. strangely-visited: severely afflicted
152. mere: downright
153. stamp: coin. usually the coin known as an "angel"
156. virtue: healing power
163. The . . . strangers: i.e., Macbeth
169. Are . . . marked: go unnoticed
170. modern ecstasy: ordinary emotion
173. or ere: before
175. doth . . . speaker: earns the speaker hisses for telling an old story
176. teems: gives birth to

Ross. When I came hither to transport the tidings
Which I have heavily borne, there ran a rumor
Of many worthy fellows that were out;
Which was to my belief witnessed the rather
For that I saw the tyrant's power afoot. 185
Now is the time of help. Your eye in Scotland
Would create soldiers, make our women fight
To doff their dire distresses.
Mal. Be't their comfort
We are coming thither. Gracious England hath
Lent us good Siward and ten thousand men. 190
An older and a better soldier none
That Christendom gives out.
Ross. Would I could answer
This comfort with the like! But I have words
That would be howled out in the desert air,
Where hearing should not latch them.
Macd. What concern they?
The general cause? or is it a fee-grief 196
Due to some single breast?
Ross. No mind that's honest
But in it shares some woe, though the main part
Pertains to you alone.
Macd. If it be mine,
Keep it not from me, quickly let me have it. 200
Ross. Let not your ears despise my tongue forever,
Which shall possess them with the heaviest sound
That ever yet they heard.
Macd. Humh! I guess at it.
Ross. Your castle is surprised; your wife and babes
Savagely slaughtered. To relate the manner 205
Were, on the quarry of these murdered deer,
To add the death of you.
Mal. Merciful heaven!
What, man! Ne'er pull your hat upon your brows.
Give sorrow words. The grief that does not speak
Whispers the o'erfraught heart and bids it break.
Macd. My children too?
Ross. Wife, children, servants, all
That could be found.
Macd. And I must be from thence?
My wife killed too?
Ross. I have said.
Mal. Be comforted. 213
Let's make us med'cines of our great revenge
To cure this deadly grief. 215
Macd. He has no children. All my pretty ones?
Did you say all? O hell-kite! All?
What, all my pretty chickens and their dam
At one fell swoop?
Mal. Dispute it like a man.
Macd. I shall do so; 220
But I must also feel it as a man.
I cannot but remember such things were
That were most precious to me. Did heaven look on
And would not take their part? Sinful Macduff,
They were all struck for thee! Naught that I am,
Not for their own demerits, but for mine, 226
Fell slaughter on their souls. Heaven rest them now!
Mal. Be this the whetstone of your sword. Let grief
Convert to anger; blunt not the heart, enrage it.
Macd. O, I could play the woman with mine eyes
And braggart with my tongue! But, gentle heavens,
Cut short all intermission. Front to front 232
Bring thou this fiend of Scotland and myself.
Within my sword's length set him. If he scape,
Heaven forgive him too!
Mal. This tune goes manly. 235
Come, go we to the King. Our power is ready;
Our lack is nothing but our leave. Macbeth
Is ripe for shaking, and the pow'rs above
Put on their instruments. Receive what cheer you may.
The night is long that never finds the day. 240
Exeunt.

182. **heavily:** sorrowfully
183. **out:** in rebellion
184. **witnessed:** attested to
185. **power:** army
191–92. **none . . . out:** there is none proclaimed in Christendom
195. **latch:** catch
196. **fee-grief:** private sorrow
197. **Due:** belonging
206. **on:** on top of; **quarry:** heap of dead
210. **o'erfraught:** overburdened
220. **Dispute:** contend with
225. **Naught:** worthless
226. **demerits:** deserts, not faults
232. **Front:** face
237. **leave:** leave-taking of the King
239. **Put . . . instruments:** incite their agents

ACT V

Scene I. [*Dunsinane. Macbeth's Castle.*]

Enter a Doctor of Physic *and a* Waiting Gentlewoman.

Doct. I have two nights watched with you, but can perceive no truth in your report. When was it she last walked?

Gent. Since his Majesty went into the field I have seen her rise from her bed, throw her night- 5 gown upon her, unlock her closet, take forth paper, fold it, write upon't, read it, afterwards seal it, and again return to bed; yet all this while in a most fast sleep.

Doct. A great perturbation in nature, to re- 10 ceive at once the benefit of sleep and do the effects of watching! In this slumb'ry agitation, besides her walking and other actual performances, what (at any time) have you heard her say?

Gent. That, sir, which I will not report after 15 her.

Doct. You may to me, and 'tis most meet you should.

Gent. Neither to you nor any one, having no witness to confirm my speech. 20

Enter Lady [Macbeth], *with a taper.*

Lo you, here she comes! This is her very guise, and, upon my life, fast asleep! Observe her; stand close.

Doct. How came she by that light?

Gent. Why, it stood by her. She has light by her continually. 'Tis her command. 25

Doct. You see her eyes are open.

Gent. Ay, but their sense is shut.

Doct. What is it she does now? Look how she rubs her hands.

Gent. It is an accustomed action with her to 30 seem thus washing her hands. I have known her continue in this a quarter of an hour.

Lady. Yet here's a spot.

Doct. Hark, she speaks! I will set down what comes from her, to satisfy my remembrance 35 the more strongly.

Lady. Out, damned spot! out, I say! One; two. Why then 'tis time to do't. Hell is murky. Fie, my lord, fie! a soldier, and afeard? What need we fear who knows it, when none can call our pow'r to 40 accompt? Yet who would have thought the old man to have had so much blood in him?

Doct. Do you mark that?

Lady. The Thane of Fife had a wife. Where is she now? What, will these hands ne'er be clean? No 45 more o' that, my lord, no more o' that! You mar all with this starting.

Doct. Go to, go to! You have known what you should not.

Gent. She has spoke what she should not, I 50 am sure of that. Heaven knows what she has known.

Lady. Here's the smell of the blood still. All the perfumes of Arabia will not sweeten this little hand. Oh, oh, oh!

Doct. What a sigh is there! The heart is 55 sorely charged.

Gent. I would not have such a heart in my bosom for the dignity of the whole body.

Doct. Well, well, well.

Gent. Pray God it be, sir. 60

Doct. This disease is beyond my practice. Yet I have known those which have walked in their sleep who have died holily in their beds.

Lady. Wash your hands, put on your nightgown, look not so pale! I tell you yet again, Banquo's 65 buried. He cannot come out on's grave.

Doct. Even so?

Lady. To bed, to bed! There's knocking at the gate. Come, come, come, come, give me your hand! What's done cannot be undone. To bed, to bed, 70 to bed! *Exit.*

Doct. Will she go now to bed?

Gent. Directly.

Doct. Foul whisp'rings are abroad. Unnatural deeds
Do breed unnatural troubles. Infected minds 75
To their deaf pillows will discharge their secrets.
More needs she the divine than the physician.
God, God forgive us all! Look after her;
Remove from her the means of all annoyance,
And still keep eyes upon her. So good night. 80

6. closet: chest for personal possessions
11–12. do . . . watching: act as though awake
22. close: hidden
41. accompt: account
48. Go to: for shame
79. annoyance: injury

My mind she has mated, and amazed my sight.
I think, but dare not speak.
Gent. Good night, good doctor.
Exeunt.

Scene II. [*The country near Dunsinane.*]

Drum and Colors. Enter MENTEITH, CAITHNESS, ANGUS, LENNOX, SOLDIERS.

Ment. The English pow'r is near, led on by Malcolm,
His uncle Siward, and the good Macduff.
Revenges burn in them; for their dear causes
Would to the bleeding and the grim alarm
Excite the mortified man.
Ang. Near Birnam Wood 5
Shall we well meet them; that way are they coming.
Caith. Who knows if Donalbain be with his brother?
Len. For certain, sir, he is not. I have a file
Of all the gentry. There is Siward's son
And many unrough youths that even now 10
Protest their first of manhood.
Ment. What does the tyrant?
Caith. Great Dunsinane he strongly fortifies.
Some say he's mad; others, that lesser hate him,
Do call it valiant fury; but for certain
He cannot buckle his distempered cause 15
Within the belt of rule.
Ang. Now does he feel
His secret murders sticking on his hands.
Now minutely revolts upbraid his faith-breach.
Those he commands move only in command,
Nothing in love. Now does he feel his title 20
Hang loose about him, like a giant's robe
Upon a dwarfish thief.
Ment. Who then shall blame
His pestered senses to recoil and start,
When all that is within him does condemn
Itself for being there?
Caith. Well, march we on 25
To give obedience where 'tis truly owed.
Meet we the med'cine of the sickly weal;
And with him pour we in our country's purge
Each drop of us.
Len. Or so much as it needs
To dew the sovereign flower and drown the weeds.
Make we our march towards Birnam. 31
Exeunt, marching.

Scene III. [*Dunsinane. A room in the Castle.*]

Enter MACBETH, DOCTOR, *and* ATTENDANTS.

Macb. Bring me no more reports. Let them fly all!
Till Birnam Wood remove to Dunsinane,
I cannot taint with fear. What's the boy Malcolm?
Was he not born of woman? The spirits that know
All mortal consequences have pronounced me thus:
"Fear not, Macbeth. No man that's born of woman
Shall e'er have power upon thee." Then fly, false thanes, 7
And mingle with the English epicures.
The mind I sway by and the heart I bear
Shall never sag with doubt nor shake with fear. 10

Enter SERVANT.

The devil damn thee black, thou cream-faced loon!
Where gotst thou that goose look?
Serv. There is ten thousand—
Macb. Geese, villain?
Serv. Soldiers, sir.
Macb. Go prick thy face and over-red thy fear,
Thou lily-livered boy. What soldiers, patch? 15
Death of thy soul! Those linen cheeks of thine
Are counselors to fear. What soldiers, whey-face?
Serv. The English force, so please you.
Macb. Take thy face hence. [*Exit Servant.*]
Seyton!—I am sick at heart,
When I behold—Seyton, I say!—This push 20
Will cheer me ever, or disseat me now.
I have lived long enough. My way of life
Is fallen into the sere, the yellow leaf;
And that which should accompany old age,
As honor, love, obedience, troops of friends, 25
I must not look to have; but, in their stead,
Curses not loud but deep, mouth-honor, breath,

81. **mated:** bewildered; **amazed:** dumfounded
3. **dear:** grievous
4. **bleeding . . . alarm:** bloody and desperate attack
5. **mortified:** paralyzed or dead
6. **well:** surely
8. **file:** list
10. **unrough:** beardless
11. **Protest:** affirm
15–16. **buckle . . . rule:** i.e., his cause is so corrupt that he cannot prosecute it temperately.
18. **minutely:** every minute
23. **pestered:** harassed
24. **all . . . him:** i.e., guilty recollections
27. **med'cine:** Malcolm
28. **purge:** curative bloodletting
30. **dew:** moisten; **sovereign flower:** bud of royalty (Malcolm)
3. **taint:** be tainted
5. **mortal consequences:** human events
8. **English epicures:** expressive of the Scots' contempt for what they believed was the English fondness for rich food
9. **sway:** rule
11. **loon:** lout
15. **patch:** clown; fool
27. **breath:** mere words

Which the poor heart would fain deny, and dare not.
Seyton!

Enter SEYTON.

Sey. What's your gracious pleasure?
Macb. What news more? 30
Sey. All is confirmed, my lord, which was reported.
Macb. I'll fight, till from my bones my flesh be hacked.
Give me my armor.
Sey. 'Tis not needed yet.
Macb. I'll put it on.
Send out mo horses, skirr the country round; 35
Hang those that talk of fear. Give me mine armor.
How does your patient, doctor?
Doct. Not so sick, my lord,
As she is troubled with thick-coming fancies
That keep her from her rest.
Macb. Cure her of that!
Canst thou not minister to a mind diseased, 40
Pluck from the memory a rooted sorrow,
Raze out the written troubles of the brain,
And with some sweet oblivious antidote
Cleanse the stuffed bosom of that perilous stuff
Which weighs upon the heart?
Doct. Therein the patient 45
Must minister to himself.
Macb. Throw physic to the dogs, I'll none of it!—
Come, put mine armor on. Give me my staff.
Seyton, send out.—Doctor, the thanes fly from me.—
Come, sir, dispatch.—If thou couldst, doctor, cast
The water of my land, find her disease, 51
And purge it to a sound and pristine health,
I would applaud thee to the very echo,
That should applaud again.—Pull't off, I say.—
What rhubarb, senna, or what purgative drug, 55
Would scour these English hence? Hearest thou of them?
Doct. Ay, my good lord. Your royal preparation
Makes us hear something.
Macb. Bring it after me!
I will not be afraid of death and bane
Till Birnam Forest come to Dunsinane. 60
Doct. [*Aside*] Were I from Dunsinane away and clear,
Profit again should hardly draw me here.
Exeunt.

35. **mo:** more; **skirr:** scour
43. **oblivious:** productive of oblivion
48. **staff:** lance
50. **cast:** analyze
51. **water:** urine
55. **senna:** a cathartic herb. This is the reading of the Second Folio; the First Folio reads "cyme," a name for colewort, another cathartic.
58. **it:** i.e., his armor
59. **bane:** destruction

Scene IV. [*Country near Birnam Wood.*]

Drum and Colors. Enter MALCOLM, SIWARD, MACDUFF, SIWARD'S SON, MENTEITH, CAITHNESS, ANGUS, [LENNOX, ROSS,] *and* SOLDIERS, *marching.*

Mal. Cousins, I hope the days are near at hand
That chambers will be safe.
Ment. We doubt it nothing.
Siw. What wood is this before us?
Ment. The wood of Birnam.
Mal. Let every soldier hew him down a bough
And bear't before him. Thereby shall we shadow 5
The numbers of our host and make discovery
Err in report of us.
Soldiers. It shall be done.
Siw. We learn no other but the confident tyrant
Keeps still in Dunsinane and will endure
Our setting down before't.
Mal. 'Tis his main hope; 10
For where there is advantage to be given,
Both more and less have given him the revolt;
And none serve with him but constrained things,
Whose hearts are absent too.
Macd. Let our just censures
Attend the true event, and put we on 15
Industrious soldiership.
Siw. The time approaches
That will with due decision make us know
What we shall say we have, and what we owe.
Thoughts speculative their unsure hopes relate,
But certain issue strokes must arbitrate; 20
Towards which advance the war.
Exeunt, marching.

Scene V. [*Dunsinane. Within the Castle.*]

Enter MACBETH, SEYTON, *and* SOLDIERS, *with Drum and Colors.*

Macb. Hang out our banners on the outward walls.
The cry is still, "They come!" Our castle's strength
Will laugh a siege to scorn. Here let them lie
Till famine and the ague eat them up.

2. **chambers:** i.e., sleeping chambers, remembering his father's murder
5. **shadow:** camouflage
9. **endure:** withstand
11. **advantage:** opportunity
12. **more . . . less:** greater and lesser; men of all classes
14–15. **our . . . event:** our judgments await the actual outcome
20. **certain . . . arbitrate:** the definite outcome must be decided by blows
21. **which:** the **certain issue**

Were they not forced with those that should be ours,
We might have met them dareful, beard to beard, 6
And beat them backward home.

A cry within of women.

What is that noise?

Sey. It is the cry of women, my good lord. [*Exit.*]

Macb. I have almost forgot the taste of fears.
The time has been, my senses would have cooled 10
To hear a night-shriek, and my fell of hair
Would at a dismal treatise rouse and stir
As life were in't. I have supped full with horrors.
Direness, familiar to my slaughterous thoughts,
Cannot once start me.

[*Enter* SEYTON.]

Wherefore was that cry? 15

Sey. The Queen, my lord, is dead.

Macb. She should have died hereafter;
There would have been a time for such a word.
Tomorrow, and tomorrow, and tomorrow
Creeps in this petty pace from day to day 20
To the last syllable of recorded time;
And all our yesterdays have lighted fools
The way to dusty death. Out, out, brief candle!
Life's but a walking shadow, a poor player,
That struts and frets his hour upon the stage 25
And then is heard no more. It is a tale
Told by an idiot, full of sound and fury,
Signifying nothing.

Enter a MESSENGER.

Thou comest to use thy tongue. Thy story quickly!

Mess. Gracious my lord, 30
I should report that which I say I saw,
But know not how to do't.

Macb. Well, say, sir!

Mess. As I did stand my watch upon the hill,
I looked toward Birnam, and anon methought
The wood began to move.

Macb. Liar and slave! 35

Mess. Let me endure your wrath if't be not so.
Within this three mile may you see it coming;
I say, a moving grove.

Macb. If thou speakst false,
Upon the next tree shalt thou hang alive,
Till famine cling thee. If thy speech be sooth, 40
I care not if thou dost for me as much.
I pull in resolution, and begin
To doubt the equivocation of the fiend,
That lies like truth. "Fear not, till Birnam Wood
Do come to Dunsinane!" and now a wood 45
Comes toward Dunsinane. Arm, arm, and out!
If this which he avouches does appear,
There is nor flying hence nor tarrying here.
I 'gin to be aweary of the sun,
And wish the estate o' the world were now undone.
Ring the alarum bell! Blow wind, come wrack, 51
At least we'll die with harness on our back!

Exeunt.

5. forced: reinforced
6. dareful: defiantly
11. fell: pelt
12. dismal treatise: tale of horror
14. Direness: horror
17. hereafter: i.e., at a more suitable time
40. cling: wither; **sooth:** truth
42. pull: rein
43. doubt: fear
52. harness: armor

Scene VI. [*Dunsinane. Before the Castle.*]

Drum and Colors. Enter MALCOLM, SIWARD, MACDUFF, *and their* ARMY, *with boughs.*

Mal. Now near enough. Your leavy screens throw down
And show like those you are. You, worthy uncle,
Shall with my cousin, your right noble son,
Lead our first battle. Worthy Macduff and we
Shall take upon's what else remains to do, 5
According to our order.

Siw. Fare you well.
Do we but find the tyrant's power tonight,
Let us be beaten if we cannot fight.

Macd. Make all our trumpets speak, give them all breath,
Those clamorous harbingers of blood and death. 10

Exeunt. Alarums continued.

2. show: appear
4. battle: battleline
6. order: plan of battle

Scene VII. [*Another part of the field.*]

Enter MACBETH.

Macb. They have tied me to a stake. I cannot fly,
But bearlike I must fight the course. What's he
That was not born of woman? Such a one
Am I to fear, or none.

Enter YOUNG SIWARD.

Y. Siw. What is thy name?

Macb. Thou'lt be afraid to hear it. 5

Y. Siw. No; though thou callst thyself a hotter name
Than any is in hell.

Macb. My name's Macbeth.

2. bearlike: like a bear about to be baited by dogs in the popular sport of bearbaiting

Y. Siw. The devil himself could not pronounce a title
More hateful to mine ear.
Macb. No, nor more fearful.
Y. Siw. Thou liest, abhorred tyrant! With my sword 10
I'll prove the lie thou speakst.
Fight, and Young Siward slain.
Macb. Thou wast born of woman.
But swords I smile at, weapons laugh to scorn,
Brandished by man that's of a woman born. *Exit.*

Alarums. Enter MACDUFF.

Macd. That way the noise is. Tyrant, show thy face!
If thou beest slain and with no stroke of mine, 15
My wife and children's ghosts will haunt me still.
I cannot strike at wretched kerns, whose arms
Are hired to bear their staves. Either thou, Macbeth,
Or else my sword with an unbattered edge
I sheathe again undeeded. There thou shouldst be.
By this great clatter one of greatest note 21
Seems bruited. Let me find him, Fortune!
And more I beg not. *Exit. Alarums.*

Enter MALCOLM *and* SIWARD.

Siw. This way, my lord. The castle's gently rendered:
The tyrant's people on both sides do fight; 25
The noble thanes do bravely in the war;
The day almost itself professes yours,
And little is to do.
Mal. We have met with foes
That strike beside us.
Siw. Enter, sir, the castle.
Exeunt. Alarum.

Scene VIII. [*Another part of the field.*]

Enter MACBETH.

Macb. Why should I play the Roman fool and die
On mine own sword? Whiles I see lives, the gashes
Do better upon them.

Enter MACDUFF.

Macd. Turn, hellhound, turn!
Macb. Of all men else I have avoided thee.
But get thee back! My soul is too much charged 5
With blood of thine already.
Macd. I have no words;
My voice is in my sword, thou bloodier villain
Than terms can give thee out! *Fight. Alarum.*
Macb. Thou loseth labor.
As easy mayst thou the intrenchant air
With thy keen sword impress as make me bleed. 10
Let fall thy blade on vulnerable crests.
I bear a charmed life, which must not yield
To one of woman born.
Macd. Despair thy charm!
And let the angel whom thou still hast served
Tell thee, Macduff was from his mother's womb 15
Untimely ripped.
Macb. Accursed be that tongue that tells me so,
For it hath cowed my better part of man!
And be these juggling fiends no more believed,
That palter with us in a double sense, 20
That keep the word of promise to our ear
And break it to our hope! I'll not fight with thee!
Macd. Then yield thee, coward,
And live to be the show and gaze o' the time!
We'll have thee, as our rarer monsters are, 25
Painted upon a pole, and underwrit
"Here may you see the tyrant."
Macb. I will not yield,
To kiss the ground before young Malcolm's feet
And to be baited with the rabble's curse.
Though Birnam Wood be come to Dunsinane, 30
And thou opposed, being of no woman born,
Yet I will try the last. Before my body
I throw my warlike shield. Lay on, Macduff,
And damned be him that first cries "Hold, enough!"
Exeunt fighting. Alarums.

Retreat and flourish. Enter, with Drum and Colors, MALCOLM, SIWARD, ROSS, THANES, *and* SOLDIERS.

Mal. I would the friends we miss were safe arrived. 35
Siw. Some must go off; and yet, by these I see,
So great a day as this is cheaply bought.
Mal. Macduff is missing, and your noble son.
Ross. Your son, my lord, has paid a soldier's debt.
He only lived but till he was a man, 40
The which no sooner had his prowess confirmed
In the unshrinking station where he fought
But like a man he died.
Siw. Then he is dead?

18. **staves:** lances
20. **undeeded:** unused
22. **bruited:** proclaimed
24. **gently rendered:** surrendered without resistance
27. **itself professes:** announces itself
29. **strike beside us:** join our side
2. **lives:** living enemies

8. **give . . . out:** report thee
9. **intrenchant:** untrenchable; i.e., invulnerable
20. **palter:** equivocate
25. **monsters:** freaks
36. **go off:** die
37. **cheaply bought:** acquired with little cost
42. **unshrinking station:** spot where he fought without shrinking

Ross. Ay, and brought off the field. Your cause of sorrow
Must not be measured by his worth, for then 45
It hath no end.
Siw. Had he his hurts before?
Ross. Ay, on the front.
Siw. Why, then, God's soldier be he!
Had I as many sons as I have hairs,
I would not wish them to a fairer death.
And so his knell is knolled.
Mal. He's worth more sorrow, 50
And that I'll spend for him.
Siw. He's worth no more.
They say he parted well and paid his score,
And so, God be with him! Here comes newer comfort.

Enter MACDUFF, *with Macbeth's head.*

Macd. Hail, King! for so thou art. Behold where stands
The usurper's cursed head. The time is free. 55
I see thee compassed with thy kingdom's pearl,
That speak my salutation in their minds;
Whose voices I desire aloud with mine—
Hail, King of Scotland!
All. Hail, King of Scotland! *Flourish.*
Mal. We shall not spend a large expense of time
Before we reckon with your several loves 61
And make us even with you. My Thanes and kinsmen,
Henceforth be Earls, the first that ever Scotland
In such an honor named. What's more to do
Which would be planted newly with the time— 65
As calling home our exiled friends abroad
That fled the snares of watchful tyranny,
Producing forth the cruel ministers
Of this dead butcher and his fiendlike queen,
Who (as 'tis thought) by self and violent hands 70
Took off her life—this, and what needful else
That calls upon us, by the grace of Grace
We will perform in measure, time, and place.
So thanks to all at once and to each one,
Whom we invite to see us crowned at Scone. 75
Flourish. Exeunt omnes.

52. **parted:** departed
55. **The time:** our age
56. **compassed:** surrounded; **pearl:** chief ornaments; noblest men
62. **make . . . with:** repay
65. **would . . . time:** should be done immediately
70. **self . . . hands:** her own violent hands

Victors and Vanquished
From John Derricke, *The Image of Ireland*
(1581; 1883 reprint)

Cleopatra Triumphant in Death

Engraved by one of the Brothers Dalziel.

The Tragedy of ANTONY AND CLEOPATRA

INTRODUCTION

A reasonable date for the first performance of *Antony and Cleopatra* is 1607. Three great tragedies, *Othello, King Lear,* and *Macbeth,* had preceded it in the two previous years, and Shakespeare was in the full swing of his tragic vein when he went back to the classical world for a theme. The story of Antony and Cleopatra was already well known. Chaucer had used it in his *Legend of Good Women,* in which he transformed Cleopatra from a calculating enchantress to an example of faithful love. Elizabethan audiences had also seen the famous lovers on the stage. Samuel Daniel in 1594 had written a play entitled *The Tragedy of Cleopatra,* which he revised and published in 1607 with changes suggested by Shakespeare's play. Other dramatists found Cleopatra's love a fitting subject for plays. Samuel Brandon, shifting his emphasis somewhat, wrote *The Virtuous Octavia* (*ca.* 1594). Mary Herbert, the Countess of Pembroke, translated from the French Robert Garnier's *Marc-Antoine,* which she published under the title of *Antony* (1592). Fulke Greville wrote a play, *Antony and Cleopatra,* but he burned the manuscript in 1603. Shakespeare's age, like others before and since, found in the story of Cleopatra a fascination that insured the success of a play by one of the master dramatists of the day.

Antony and Cleopatra is one of the longest of Shakespeare's plays, being exceeded in length only by *Hamlet* and *Richard III*. Even if one makes allowance for the bare Shakespearean stage with its rapid entrances and exits, it is obvious that these plays required drastic cutting. The time covered in *Antony and Cleopatra* extends historically from Fulvia's death in 40 B.C. to Cleopatra's death on August 29, 30 B.C. Shakespeare's play telescopes this decade into twelve days.

Critics have complained about the multiplicity of scenes in this play, which has constant shifts back and forth between Rome and Egypt. The division into acts and scenes is the work of later editors, who, following Nicholas Rowe, gave a fresh scene division to each new episode. Since Elizabethan producers were not concerned with the paraphernalia of realistic stage scenery attempted in the nineteenth-century theatre, the constant changes of scenes bothered neither them nor the audience. The dialogue made clear the whereabouts of the characters involved in any particular scene.

In *Antony and Cleopatra,* Shakespeare put behind him idyllic love, which he had treated earlier in *Romeo and Juliet,* and turned his attention to the consuming passion of two characters who had already run the gamut of human emotions. Six or seven years before, Shakespeare had portrayed Antony as the devoted friend of Julius Cæsar, the orator at his funeral, and the leader of a faction that put to rout his assassins. Now we see Antony, an older if not a wiser man, a leader who could still command the allegiance of half the Roman world, exuberant in all of his emotions, great of soul and equally great in his vices, who matches his wit, his courage, and his passion with the most cunning siren of the East, Cleopatra.

Shakespeare might have employed a morality-play motif as he did in his previous play, *Macbeth,* and made the conflict in *Antony and Cleopatra* a struggle between good and evil for the soul of Antony, or universal man. Instead, he decided upon a treatment more complex and subtle than a morality play. Like a clinical psychologist he studies the impact upon each other of two characters who are themselves complex and subtle. In his hands Antony and Cleopatra become not only prototypes of universal man and woman but symbols of West and East, of Roman and Eastern civilizations. In his person Antony sums up the good and bad of Roman life; Cleopatra is the essence of the mystery of the East. Yet the tragic struggle in the play is not between Antony and Cleopatra, for Antony does not try to resist the serpent of the Nile. The struggle is rather in Antony's own soul as at intervals he remembers his duty as a Roman and a soldier in the face of the enervations of Eastern luxury and lust. In the end, Antony's passion for Cleopatra merely completes his ruin, a ruin to which Shakespeare contrives to give an air of grandeur.

Shakespeare changed the historical concept of Cleopatra as the wily sovereign, intent upon maintaining the power of her dynasty, to make her the epitome of feminine sorcery. The interest of the audience naturally focuses upon Cleopatra, the sum of all passionate women, the object of Antony's own grand passion. She is distinctly not the calculating Egyptian queen of history who could murder a brother to keep him from sharing her throne and employ her talents to outwit the Roman conquerors. Shakespeare makes her first and foremost a woman in love, a realistic woman who recognizes her status as mistress instead of wife and voices her spite at those women who occupy more favored positions. She has a contempt for Octavia and hates the memory of the dead Fulvia.

As in all of his plays, Shakespeare gives to the protagonists and to the lesser characters human qualities such as his audience could comprehend. They do not move in an Olympian world incomprehensible to ordinary mortals; they exemplify the emotions and the qualities understood by us all.

The poetry of *Antony and Cleopatra* has received high praise from critics who admire the compactness of the verse and find much to commend in the language and phrasing of even the most difficult passages. Shakespeare in this play was not writing with the lyrical abandon or the youthful exuberance that he had shown, let us say, in *Romeo and Juliet*. His lines now are not only tense with emotion but packed with meaning. Sometimes this compactness leads to obscurity, and occasionally the verse is too cryptic for clear comprehension and too filled with a diversity of ideas and metaphors to please all tastes.

SOURCE, HISTORY, AND TEXT

Shakespeare's source for *Antony and Cleopatra* was North's translation of Plutarch. He may have picked up ideas from other classical works and from earlier plays on the theme, but there is little evidence of any source other than Plutarch in the words of the play. Shakespeare does not follow Plutarch slavishly but selects his material carefully and reworks it into his own dramatic pattern.

Surviving records of the Jacobean theatre do not mention Shakespeare's *Antony and Cleopatra,* but it is safe to assume that it met with success. So far as we know, Shakespeare's version was not acted during the Restoration period because Sir Charles Sedley with an independent play of *Antony and Cleopatra* (1677) and John Dryden with *All for Love* (1678), written, as the author declared, "in imitation of Shakespeare's style," pre-empted the stage. Indeed, Dryden's *All for Love* long remained popular, and in the eighteenth century even revivals of Shakespeare's play often included bits from Dryden's. David Garrick in 1759 revived Shakespeare's original, but it ran for only six nights. John Philip Kemble in 1813 produced a mixture of Shakespeare, Dryden, and spectacle, including a realistic Battle of Actium and a great deal of extraneous music. Nineteenth- and early-twentieth-century versions of Shakespeare's *Antony and Cleopatra* continued to emphasize scenery and elaborate productions that attempted to give visions of Oriental luxury with a voluptuous siren in the role of Cleopatra.

But on neither side of the Atlantic has this play been consistently successful. After a performance in New York on April 2, 1859, in which a plump actress billed as Madame Ponisi took the part of Cleopatra, the New York *Herald* commented that she was "not quite fascinating enough to make one throw away an empire." Nevertheless, the role of Cleopatra has lured many actresses into attempting it. Tallulah Bankhead tried it in New York in the season of 1937–38, but the play lasted only five performances. Katharine Cornell played the part in 1947–48 with somewhat greater success. Despite the difficulty of staging and the long record of ill success, the play has had frequent revivals.

One fact about its original staging at the Globe should be emphasized. Since female parts in his theatre were played by boys, Shakespeare wrote no scenes requiring physical contact between Antony and Cleopatra. The quality of their love affair is suggested entirely by the magic of words.

Although *Antony and Cleopatra* was entered in the *Stationers' Register* on May 20, 1608, no quarto version of the play is known to exist. The first known printing occurred in the First Folio, and that text is the basis of modern editions.

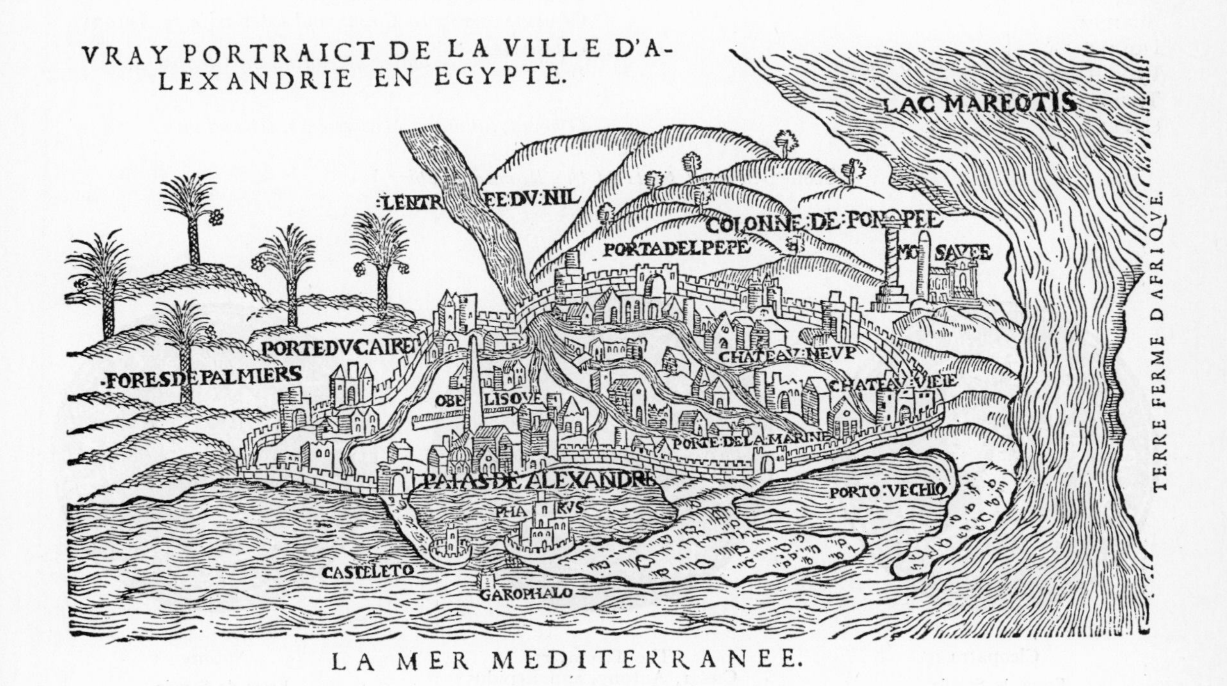

Ancient Alexandria

From Pierre Belon, *Les observations de plusieurs singularités* (1588).

[Dramatis Personæ

MARK ANTONY, OCTAVIUS CÆSAR, M. ÆMILIUS LEPIDUS, — *Triumvirs.*

SEXTUS POMPEIUS.

DOMITIUS ENOBARBUS, VENTIDIUS, EROS, SCARUS, DERCETAS, DEMETRIUS, PHILO, — *friends to Antony.*

CANIDIUS, *Lieutenant General to Antony.*

MÆCENAS, AGRIPPA, DOLABELLA, PROCULEIUS, THIDIAS, GALLUS, — *friends to Cæsar.*

TAURUS, *Lieutenant General to Cæsar.*

MENAS, MENECRATES, VARRIUS, — *friends to Pompey.*

SILIUS, *an Officer in the army of Ventidius.*

EUPHRONIUS, *an Ambassador from Antony to Cæsar.*

ALEXAS, MARDIAN, SELEUCUS, DIOMEDES, — *attendants on Cleopatra.*

A SOOTHSAYER.

A CLOWN.

CLEOPATRA, *Queen of Egypt.*

OCTAVIA, *sister to Cæsar and later wife to Antony.*

CHARMIAN, IRAS, — *ladies attending on Cleopatra.*

Officers, Soldiers, Messengers, Attendants.

Scene: *Several parts of the Roman Empire.*]

Cleopatra
From de Strada.

The Triumvirs,
Cæsar, Antony, and Lepidus
From Jacobus de Strada,
Epitome thesauri antiquitatum (1557).

Antony
From de Strada.

The Tragedy of
ANTONY AND CLEOPATRA

ACT I

Scene I. [*Alexandria. A room in Cleopatra's Palace.*]

Enter DEMETRIUS *and* PHILO.

Philo. Nay, but this dotage of our general's
O'erflows the measure. Those his goodly eyes
That o'er the files and musters of the war
Have glowed like plated Mars, now bend, now turn
The office and devotion of their view 5
Upon a tawny front. His captain's heart,
Which in the scuffles of great fights hath burst
The buckles on his breast, reneges all temper,
And is become the bellows and the fan
To cool a gypsy's lust.

Flourish. Enter ANTONY, CLEOPATRA, *her* LADIES, *the* TRAIN, *with* EUNUCHS *fanning her.*

Look where they come! 10
Take but good note, and you shall see in him
The triple pillar of the world transformed
Into a strumpet's fool. Behold and see.
Cleo. If it be love indeed, tell me how much.
Ant. There's beggary in the love that can be reckoned. 15
Cleo. I'll set a bourn how far to be beloved.
Ant. Then must thou needs find out new heaven, new earth.

Enter a MESSENGER.

Mess. News, my good lord, from Rome.
Ant. Grates me! The sum.
Cleo. Nay, hear them, Antony.
Fulvia perchance is angry; or who knows 20
If the scarce-bearded Cæsar have not sent
His pow'rful mandate to you: Do this, or this;
Take in that kingdom, and enfranchise that;
Perform't, or else we damn thee.
Ant. How, my love?
Cleo. Perchance? Nay, and most like: 25
You must not stay here longer; your dismission
Is come from Cæsar; therefore hear it, Antony.
Where's Fulvia's process? Cæsar's I would say. Both?
Call in the messengers. As I am Egypt's Queen,
Thou blushest, Antony, and that blood of thine 30
Is Cæsar's homager! Else so thy cheek pays shame
When shrill-tongued Fulvia scolds. The messengers!
Ant. Let Rome in Tiber melt and the wide arch
Of the ranged empire fall! Here is my space.
Kingdoms are clay; our dungy earth alike 35

3. files . . . musters: assembled troops
4. plated: armored
5. office . . . devotion: devoted service
6. front: forehead; face
8. reneges: renounces; **temper:** his usual self-control
10. gypsy's: Egyptian's
12. triple: i.e., third; one of the triumvirate composed of Octavius Cæsar, Antony, and Lepidus
16. bourn: limit
21. scarce-bearded: i.e., youthful
24. damn: condemn
28. process: summons
31. homager: slave
33-34. wide . . . empire: keystone of the wide-ranging empire

Feeds beast as man. The nobleness of life
Is to do thus [*Embracing her*] when such a mutual pair
And such a twain can do't, in which I bind,
On pain of punishment, the world to weet
We stand up peerless.

Cleo. Excellent falsehood! 40
Why did he marry Fulvia, and not love her?
I'll seem the fool I am not. Antony
Will be himself.

Ant. But stirred by Cleopatra.
Now for the love of Love and her soft hours, 44
Let's not confound the time with conference harsh.
There's not a minute of our lives should stretch
Without some pleasure now. What sport tonight?

Cleo. Hear the ambassadors.

Ant. Fie, wrangling queen!
Whom every thing becomes—to chide, to laugh,
To weep; whose every passion fully strives 50
To make itself, in thee, fair and admired!
No messenger but thine, and all alone
Tonight we'll wander through the streets and note
The qualities of people. Come, my queen;
Last night you did desire it.—Speak not to us. 55

Exeunt [*Antony and Cleopatra*] *with the Train.*

Dem. Is Cæsar with Antonius prized so slight?

Philo. Sir, sometimes when he is not Antony
He comes too short of that great property
Which still should go with Antony.

Dem. I am full sorry
That he approves the common liar, who 60
Thus speaks of him at Rome; but I will hope
Of better deeds tomorrow. Rest you happy!

Exeunt.

[Scene II. *Alexandria. Another room in Cleopatra's Palace.*]

Enter a SOOTHSAYER, CHARMIAN, IRAS, *and* ALEXAS.

Char. Lord Alexas, sweet Alexas, most anything Alexas, almost most absolute Alexas, where's the soothsayer that you praised so to the Queen? O that I knew this husband which, you say, must charge his horns with garlands! 5

Alex. Soothsayer!

Sooth. Your will?

Char. Is this the man? Is't you, sir, that know things?

Sooth. In nature's infinite book of secrecy
A little I can read.

Alex. Show him your hand. 10

[*Enter* ENOBARBUS.]

Eno. Bring in the banquet quickly; wine enough
Cleopatra's health to drink.

Char. Good sir, give me good fortune.

Sooth. I make not, but foresee.

Char. Pray then, foresee me one. 15

Sooth. You shall be yet far fairer than you are.

Char. He means in flesh.

Iras. No, you shall paint when you are old.

Char. Wrinkles forbid!

Alex. Vex not his prescience; be attentive. 20

Char. Hush!

Sooth. You shall be more beloving than beloved.

Char. I had rather heat my liver with drinking.

Alex. Nay, hear him.

Char. Good now, some excellent fortune! Let 25 me be married to three kings in a forenoon and widow them all. Let me have a child at fifty, to whom Herod of Jewry may do homage. Find me to marry me with Octavius Cæsar, and companion me with my mistress. 30

Sooth. You shall outlive the lady whom you serve.

Char. O excellent! I love long life better than figs.

Sooth. You have seen and proved a fairer former fortune
Than that which is to approach.

Char. Then belike my children shall have no 35 names. Prithee, how many boys and wenches must I have?

Sooth. If every of your wishes had a womb,
And fertile every wish, a million.

Char. Out, fool! I forgive thee for a witch. 40

Alex. You think none but your sheets are privy to your wishes.

Char. Nay, come, tell Iras hers.

Alex. We'll know all our fortunes.

Eno. Mine, and most of our fortunes, to- 45 night, shall be—drunk to bed.

Iras. There's a palm presages chastity, if nothing else.

Char. E'en as the o'erflowing Nilus presageth famine. 50

Iras. Go, you wild bedfellow, you cannot soothsay.

Char. Nay, if an oily palm be not a fruitful prog-

38. bind: challenge
39. weet: acknowledge
45. confound: waste
58. great property: greatness
59. still: always
60. approves: confirms
2. absolute: perfect
4. charge: load; Lewis Theobald's correction of the Folio's "change"
5. horns: i.e., the horns of the cuckold (deceived husband)

23. drinking: that is, instead of by love
25. Good now: if you will be so good, tell me now
33. proved: experienced
40. forgive . . . witch: absolve you of sorcery
52. oily palm: believed to be an indication of a lustful nature

nostication, I cannot scratch mine ear. Prithee tell her but a workyday fortune.

Sooth. Your fortunes are alike. 55

Iras. But how, but how? Give me particulars.

Sooth. I have said.

Iras. Am I not an inch of fortune better than she?

Char. Well, if you were but an inch of fortune better than I, where would you choose it? 60

Iras. Not in my husband's nose.

Char. Our worser thoughts heavens mend! Alexas —come, his fortune, his fortune! O, let him marry a woman that cannot go, sweet Isis, I beseech thee! and let her die too, and give him a worse! and 65 let worse follow worse till the worst of all follow him laughing to his grave, fiftyfold a cuckold! Good Isis, hear me this prayer, though thou deny me a matter of more weight; good Isis, I beseech thee!

Iras. Amen. Dear goddess, hear that prayer 70 of the people! For, as it is a heartbreaking to see a handsome man loose-wived, so it is a deadly sorrow to behold a foul knave uncuckolded. Therefore, dear Isis, keep decorum, and fortune him accordingly!

Char. Amen. 75

Alex. Lo now, if it lay in their hands to make me a cuckold, they would make themselves whores but they'ld do't!

Eno. Hush! Here comes Antony.

Enter CLEOPATRA.

Char. Not he! the Queen.

Cleo. Saw you my lord?

Eno. No, lady.

Cleo. Was he not here?

Char. No, madam. 81

Cleo. He was disposed to mirth; but on the sudden
A Roman thought hath struck him. Enobarbus!

Eno. Madam?

Cleo. Seek him, and bring him hither. Where's Alexas? 85

Alex. Here at your service. My lord approaches.

Enter ANTONY *with a* MESSENGER [*and* ATTENDANTS].

Cleo. We will not look upon him. Go with us.
Exeunt [*Cleopatra, Enobarbus and the rest*].

Mess. Fulvia thy wife first came into the field.

Ant. Against my brother Lucius?

Mess. Ay. 90
But soon that war had end, and the time's state
Made friends of them, jointing their force 'gainst Cæsar,
Whose better issue in the war from Italy
Upon the first encounter drave them.

Ant. Well, what worst?

Mess. The nature of bad news infects the teller.

Ant. When it concerns the fool or coward. On!
Things that are past are done with me. 'Tis thus:
Who tells me true, though in his tale lie death, 98
I hear him as he flattered.

Mess. Labienus—
This is stiff news—hath with his Parthian force
Extended Asia from Euphrates, 101
His conquering banner shook from Syria
To Lydia and to Ionia,
Whilst—

Ant. Antony, thou wouldst say.

Mess. O, my lord!

Ant. Speak to me home. Mince not the general tongue. 105
Name Cleopatra as she is called in Rome.
Rail thou in Fulvia's phrase, and taunt my faults
With such full license as both truth and malice
Have power to utter. O, then we bring forth weeds
When our quick minds lie still, and our ills told us
Is as our earing. Fare thee well awhile. 111

Mess. At your noble pleasure. *Exit.*

Ant. From Sicyon, ho, the news! Speak there!

1. Att. The man from Sicyon—is there such an one?

2. Att. He stays upon your will.

Ant. Let him appear.
These strong Egyptian fetters I must break 116
Or lose myself in dotage.

Enter ANOTHER MESSENGER, *with a letter.*

What are you?

Mess. Fulvia thy wife is dead.

Ant. Where died she?

Mess. In Sicyon.
Her length of sickness, with what else more serious
Importeth thee to know, this bears.
[*Gives the letter.*]

Ant. Forbear me. 121
[*Exit Messenger.*]
There's a great spirit gone! Thus did I desire it.
What our contempts doth often hurl from us,

54. **workyday:** ordinary
64. **go:** (1) walk (?); (2) bear children (?)
70–71. **prayer . . . people:** common prayer
73. **foul:** ugly
74. **keep decorum:** act appropriately
93. **better issue:** greater success
101. **Extended:** seized forcibly; a legal term
105. **home:** frankly; **Mince . . . tongue:** do not gloss over what everyone is saying.
110. **ills:** faults
111. **earing:** plowing. When we neglect to reflect on our behavior we do nothing of value; but when we are forced to think of our faults we can begin to make better use of our abilities.
115. **stays upon:** awaits
121. **Importeth . . . know:** concerns thee; **Forbear:** leave

We wish it ours again. The present pleasure,
By revolution low'ring, does become 125
The opposite of itself. She's good, being gone;
The hand could pluck her back that shoved her on.
I must from this enchanting queen break off.
Ten thousand harms more than the ills I know
My idleness doth hatch. How now, Enobarbus!

[*Re-*]*enter* ENOBARBUS.

Eno. What's your pleasure, sir? 131
Ant. I must with haste from hence.
Eno. Why, then we kill all our women. We see how mortal an unkindness is to them. If they suffer our departure, death's the word. 135
Ant. I must be gone.
Eno. Under a compelling occasion let women die. It were pity to cast them away for nothing, though between them and a great cause they should be esteemed nothing. Cleopatra, catching but the 140 least noise of this, dies instantly. I have seen her die twenty times upon far poorer moment. I do think there is mettle in death, which commits some loving act upon her, she hath such a celerity in dying.
Ant. She is cunning past man's thought. 145
Eno. Alack, sir, no! Her passions are made of nothing but the finest part of pure love. We cannot call her winds and waters sighs and tears. They are greater storms and tempests than almanacs can report. This cannot be cunning in her; if it be, 150 she makes a shower of rain as well as Jove.
Ant. Would I had never seen her!
Eno. O, sir, you had then left unseen a wonderful piece of work, which not to have been blest withal would have discredited your travel. 155
Ant. Fulvia is dead.
Eno. Sir?
Ant. Fulvia is dead.
Eno. Fulvia?
Ant. Dead. 160
Eno. Why, sir, give the gods a thankful sacrifice. When it pleaseth their deities to take the wife of a man from him, it shows to man the tailors of the earth; comforting therein, that when old robes are worn out, there are members to make new. If 165 there were no more women but Fulvia, then had you indeed a cut, and the case to be lamented. This grief is crowned with consolation; your old smock brings forth a new petticoat; and indeed the tears live in an onion that should water this sorrow. 170
Ant. The business she hath broached in the state
Cannot endure my absence.
Eno. And the business you have broached here cannot be without you; especially that of Cleopatra's, which wholly depends on your abode. 175
Ant. No more light answers. Let our officers
Have notice what we purpose. I shall break
The cause of our expedience to the Queen
And get her leave to part. For not alone
The death of Fulvia, with more urgent touches,
Do strongly speak to us, but the letters too 181
Of many our contriving friends in Rome
Petition us at home. Sextus Pompeius
Hath given the dare to Cæsar and commands
The empire of the sea. Our slippery people, 185
Whose love is never linked to the deserver
Till his deserts are past, begin to throw
Pompey the Great and all his dignities
Upon his son; who, high in name and power,
Higher than both in blood and life, stands up 190
For the main soldier; whose quality, going on,
The sides o' the world may danger. Much is breeding
Which, like the courser's hair, hath yet but life
And not a serpent's poison. Say our pleasure
To such whose places under us require, 195
Our quick remove from hence.
Eno. I shall do't.
[*Exeunt.*]

[Scene III. *Alexandria. Another room in Cleopatra's Palace.*]

Enter CLEOPATRA, CHARMIAN, ALEXAS, *and* IRAS.

Cleo. Where is he?
Char. I did not see him since.
Cleo. See where he is, who's with him, what he does.
I did not send you. If you find him sad,
Say I am dancing; if in mirth, report
That I am sudden sick. Quick, and return! 5
[*Exit Alexas.*]
Char. Madam, methinks if you did love him dearly,
You do not hold the method to enforce
The like from him.
Cleo. What should I do, I do not?

125. By . . . low'ring: turning to a lower point on Fortune's wheel
127. could: would willingly
134. mortal: deadly
143. mettle: ardent spirit
171. broached: opened

178. expedience: haste
179. leave: Alexander Pope's reading. The Folio reads "love."
180. touches: concerns
183. at home: to return home
190. blood . . . life: spirit and energy
190–91. stands . . . soldier: takes his place as the model warrior
191. quality: warlike inclination
193. courser's hair: a horse's hair, which in popular belief would turn to a snake if placed in water
3. sad: grave

Char. In each thing give him way, cross him in nothing.
Cleo. Thou teachest like a fool. The way to lose him! 10
Char. Tempt him not so too far; I wish, forbear.
In time we hate that which we often fear.

Enter ANTONY.

But here comes Antony.
Cleo. I am sick and sullen.
Ant. I am sorry to give breathing to my purpose—
Cleo. Help me away, dear Charmian! I shall fall.
It cannot be thus long; the sides of nature 16
Will not sustain it.
Ant. Now, my dearest queen—
Cleo. Pray you stand farther from me.
Ant. What's the matter?
Cleo. I know by that same eye there's some good news.
What says the married woman? You may go. 20
Would she had never given you leave to come!
Let her not say 'tis I that keep you here.
I have no power upon you; hers you are.
Ant. The gods best know—
Cleo. O, never was there queen
So mightily betrayed! Yet at the first 25
I saw the treasons planted.
Ant. Cleopatra—
Cleo. Why should I think you can be mine, and true,
Though you in swearing shake the throned gods,
Who have been false to Fulvia? Riotous madness,
To be entangled with those mouth-made vows 30
Which break themselves in swearing!
Ant. Most sweet queen—
Cleo. Nay, pray you seek no color for your going,
But bid farewell and go. When you sued staying,
Then was the time for words. No going then!
Eternity was in our lips and eyes, 35
Bliss in our brows' bent, none our parts so poor
But was a race of heaven. They are so still,
Or thou, the greatest soldier of the world,
Art turned the greatest liar.
Ant. How now, lady?
Cleo. I would I had thy inches! Thou shouldst know 40
There were a heart in Egypt.
Ant. Hear me, Queen.
The strong necessity of time commands
Our services awhile; but my full heart
Remains in use with you. Our Italy
Shines o'er with civil swords. Sextus Pompeius 45
Makes his approaches to the port of Rome.
Equality of two domestic powers
Breed scrupulous faction. The hated, grown to strength,
Are newly grown to love. The condemned Pompey,
Rich in his father's honor, creeps apace 50
Into the hearts of such as have not thrived
Upon the present state, whose numbers threaten;
And quietness, grown sick of rest, would purge
By any desperate change. My more particular,
And that which most with you should safe my going,
Is Fulvia's death. 56
Cleo. Though age from folly could not give me freedom,
It does from childishness. Can Fulvia die?
Ant. She's dead, my queen.
Look here, and at thy sovereign leisure read 60
The garboils she awaked. At the last, best,
See when and where she died.
Cleo. O most false love!
Where be the sacred vials thou shouldst fill
With sorrowful water? Now I see, I see,
In Fulvia's death, how mine received shall be. 65
Ant. Quarrel no more, but be prepared to know
The purposes I bear; which are, or cease,
As you shall give the advice. By the fire
That quickens Nilus' slime, I go from hence
Thy soldier, servant, making peace or war 70
As thou affects.
Cleo. Cut my lace, Charmian, come!
But let it be. I am quickly ill and well—
So Antony loves.
Ant. My precious queen, forbear,
And give true evidence to his love, which stands
An honorable trial.
Cleo. So Fulvia told me. 75
I prithee turn aside and weep for her;
Then bid adieu to me, and say the tears
Belong to Egypt. Good now, play one scene
Of excellent dissembling, and let it look 79
Like perfect honor.
Ant. You'll heat my blood. No more!
Cleo. You can do better yet; but this is meetly.

13. sullen: melancholy
14. breathing: voice
30. mouth-made: insincere
32. color: excuse
35. our: my
36. brows' bent: eyebrows' arch; **parts:** features; characteristics
37. a . . . heaven: heavenly in origin; divine
44. in . . . you: entrusted to you for your use (legal terminology)
45. civil: domestic
47–48. Equality . . . faction: the two domestic parties are so evenly matched that the uncommitted are cautious about joining either.
54. particular: personal motive
60. at . . . leisure: when you please (complete mistress of yourself as you are)
61. garboils: disorders
71. affects: prefer
74. give . . . to: acknowledge the truth of
81. meetly: suitably acted

Ant. Now by my sword—
Cleo. And target. Still he mends;
But this is not the best. Look, prithee, Charmian,
How this Herculean Roman does become
The carriage of his chafe. 85
Ant. I'll leave you lady.
Cleo. Courteous lord, one word.
Sir, you and I must part—but that's not it.
Sir, you and I have loved—but there's not it.
That you know well. Something it is I would—
O, my oblivion is a very Antony, 90
And I am all forgotten!
Ant. But that your royalty
Holds idleness your subject, I should take you
For idleness itself.
Cleo. 'Tis sweating labor
To bear such idleness so near the heart
As Cleopatra this. But, sir, forgive me; 95
Since my becomings kill me when they do not
Eye well to you. Your honor calls you hence;
Therefore be deaf to my unpitied folly,
And all the gods go with you! Upon your sword
Sit laurel victory, and smooth success 100
Be strewed before your feet!
Ant. Let us go. Come.
Our separation so abides and flies
That thou, residing here, goes yet with me,
And I, hence fleeting, here remain with thee.
Away! 105
Exeunt.

[Scene IV. *Rome. Cæsar's house.*]

Enter OCTAVIUS [CÆSAR], *reading a letter,* LEPIDUS, *and their* TRAIN.

Cæs. You may see, Lepidus, and henceforth know,
It is not Cæsar's natural vice to hate
Our great competitor. From Alexandria
This is the news: he fishes, drinks, and wastes
The lamps of night in revel; is not more manlike 5
Than Cleopatra, nor the queen of Ptolemy
More womanly than he; hardly gave audience, or
Vouchsafed to think he had partners. You shall find
there
A man who is the abstract of all faults
That all men follow.
Lep. I must not think there are 10
Evils enow to darken all his goodness.
His faults, in him, seem as the spots of heaven,
More fiery by night's blackness; hereditary
Rather than purchased; what he cannot change
Than what he chooses. 15
Cæs. You are too indulgent. Let's grant it is not
Amiss to tumble on the bed of Ptolemy,
To give a kingdom for a mirth, to sit
And keep the turn of tippling with a slave,
To reel the streets at noon, and stand the buffet 20
With knaves that smell of sweat. Say this becomes
him
(As his composure must be rare indeed
Whom these things cannot blemish), yet must Antony
No way excuse his foils when we do bear
So great weight in his lightness. If he filled 25
His vacancy with his voluptuousness,
Full surfeits and the dryness of his bones
Call on him for't! But to confound such time
That drums him from his sport and speaks as loud
As his own state and ours—'tis to be chid 30
As we rate boys who, being mature in knowledge,
Pawn their experience to their present pleasure
And so rebel to judgment.

Enter a MESSENGER.

Lep. Here's more news.
Mess. Thy biddings have been done, and every
hour,
Most noble Cæsar, shalt thou have report 35
How 'tis abroad. Pompey is strong at sea,
And it appears he is beloved of those
That only have feared Cæsar. To the ports
The discontents repair, and men's reports
Give him much wronged.
Cæs. I should have known no less.
It hath been taught us from the primal state 41
That he which is was wished until he were;
And the ebbed man, ne'er loved till ne'er worth love,

82. target: shield
84–85. does . . . chafe: pretends suitable anger
90. oblivion: forgetfulness
91–93. But . . . itself: if you were not so well able to command folly to serve you, I should think you the personification of folly.
93–94. 'Tis . . . heart: it's hard work to trifle about a matter so dear to me; a double entendre
96. my becomings: even my most attractive wiles
3. Our: my; the Folio reads "one"; **competitor:** associate; partner
6. the . . . Ptolemy: Cleopatra, her brother Ptolemy's widow
9. abstract: epitome
18. for . . . mirth: in exchange for diversion
19. keep . . . tippling: match drink for drink
20. stand . . . buffet: mingle familiarly
22. As: although
24. foils: disgraces
26. vacancy: leisure
27–28. Full . . . for't: I would be content to let the physical consequences of debauchery be his sole punishment.
28. confound: waste
29. drums . . . from: calls him as urgently as a martial drum
31. rate: scold
32. Pawn . . . to: hazard the benefits of experience in exchange for
41. primal state: first government
42. he . . . is: the man in power
43. the . . . man: the man whose power has waned

Comes deared by being lacked. This common body,
Like to a vagabond flag upon the stream, 45
Goes to and back, lackeying the varying tide,
To rot itself with motion.

Mess. Cæsar, I bring thee word,
Menecrates and Menas, famous pirates,
Makes the sea serve them, which they ear and wound
With keels of every kind. Many hot inroads 50
They make in Italy; the borders maritime
Lack blood to think on't, and flush youth revolt.
No vessel can peep forth but 'tis as soon
Taken as seen; for Pompey's name strikes more
Than could his war resisted.

Cæs. Antony, 55
Leave thy lascivious wassails. When thou once
Wast beaten from Modena, where thou slewst
Hirtius and Pansa, consuls, at thy heel
Did famine follow, whom thou foughtst against
(Though daintily brought up) with patience more
Than savages could suffer. Thou didst drink 61
The stale of horses and the gilded puddle
Which beasts would cough at. Thy palate then did deign
The roughest berry on the rudest hedge. 64
Yea, like the stag when snow the pasture sheets,
The barks of trees thou browsedst. On the Alps
It is reported thou didst eat strange flesh,
Which some did die to look on. And all this
(It wounds thine honor that I speak it now)
Was borne so like a soldier that thy cheek 70
So much as lanked not.

Lep. 'Tis pity of him.

Cæs. Let his shames quickly
Drive him to Rome. 'Tis time we twain
Did show ourselves i' the field, and to that end
Assemble we immediate council. Pompey 75
Thrives in our idleness.

Lep. Tomorrow, Cæsar,
I shall be furnished to inform you rightly
Both what by sea and land I can be able
To front this present time.

Cæs. Till which encounter,
It is my business too. Farewell. 80

Lep. Farewell, my lord. What you shall know meantime
Of stirs abroad, I shall beseech you, sir,
To let me be partaker.

Cæs. Doubt not, sir;
I knew it for my bond.

Exeunt.

[Scene V. *Alexandria. A room in Cleopatra's Palace.*]

Enter Cleopatra, Charmian, Iras, *and* Mardian.

Cleo. Charmian!

Char. Madam?

Cleo. Ha, ha!
Give me to drink mandragora.

Char. Why, madam?

Cleo. That I might sleep out this great gap of time
My Antony is away.

Char. You think of him too much. 6

Cleo. O, 'tis treason!

Char. Madam, I trust not so.

Cleo. Thou, eunuch Mardian!

Mar. What's your Highness' pleasure?

Cleo. Not now to hear thee sing. I take no pleasure
In aught an eunuch has. 'Tis well for thee 10
That, being unseminared, thy freer thoughts
May not fly forth of Egypt. Hast thou affections?

Mar. Yes, gracious madam.

Cleo. Indeed?

Mar. Not in deed, madam; for I can do nothing
But what indeed is honest to be done. 16
Yet have I fierce affections, and think
What Venus did with Mars.

Cleo. O, Charmian!
Where thinkst thou he is now? Stands he, or sits he?
Or does he walk? or is he on his horse? 20
O happy horse, to bear the weight of Antony!
Do bravely, horse! for wotst thou whom thou mov'st?
The demi-Atlas of this earth, the arm
And burgonet of men. He's speaking now,
Or murmuring "Where's my serpent of old Nile?"
For so he calls me. Now I feed myself 26
With most delicious poison. Think on me,
That am with Phœbus' amorous pinches black
And wrinkled deep in time. Broad-fronted Cæsar,
When thou wast here above the ground, I was 30
A morsel for a monarch; and great Pompey
Would stand and make his eyes grow in my brow;

44. Comes . . . lacked: is valued when he is gone
45. flag: iris
46. lackeying: following in servile fashion
49. ear: plow
52. blood: courage; **flush youth:** the high-spirited young
54–55. Pompey's . . . resisted: i.e., Pompey's name alone is so effective that he conquers without attacking.
56. wassails: carouses
62. stale: urine; **gilded:** scum-covered
71. lanked: thinned
79. front: oppose

84. bond: duty
4. mandragora: *Mandragora officinarum,* used for sleeping potions
11. unseminared: castrated; rendered impotent
16. honest: chaste
22. wotst: knowest
23. demi-Atlas: supporter of half the world (Cæsar supporting the other half)
24. burgonet: helmet

There would he anchor his aspect, and die
With looking on his life.

Enter ALEXAS.

Alex. Sovereign of Egypt, hail! 34
Cleo. How much unlike art thou Mark Antony!
Yet, coming from him, that great med'cine hath
With his tinct gilded thee.
How goes it with my brave Mark Antony?
Alex. Last thing he did, dear Queen,
He kissed—the last of many doubled kisses— 40
This orient pearl. His speech sticks in my heart.
Cleo. Mine ear must pluck it thence.
Alex. "Good friend," quoth he,
"Say the firm Roman to great Egypt sends
This treasure of an oyster; at whose foot,
To mend the petty present, I will piece 45
Her opulent throne with kingdoms. All the East,
Say thou, shall call her mistress." So he nodded,
And soberly did mount an arm-gaunt steed,
Who neighed so high that what I would have spoke
Was beastly dumbed by him.
Cleo. What, was he sad or merry?
Alex. Like to the time o' the year between the extremes 51
Of hot and cold. He was nor sad nor merry.

33. aspect: gaze
36–37. that . . . thee: his great power has transmuted you (in the same way as the alchemist's tincture was supposed to change baser metals into gold).
38. brave: splendid; gallant
41. orient: lustrous
43. firm: constant; **Egypt:** queen of Egypt
45. piece: add to (and make opulent)
48. arm-gaunt: precise meaning uncertain; "armored and trained down for battle" (?). M. R. Ridley's edition in the new Arden series (Cambridge, Mass., 1956) contains a two-page appendix discussing the possible meanings of this word.
50. dumbed: silenced
52. nor . . . nor: neither . . . nor

Cleo. O well-divided disposition! Note him,
Note him, good Charmian; 'tis the man; but note him!
He was not sad, for he would shine on those 55
That make their looks by his; he was not merry,
Which seemed to tell them his remembrance lay
In Egypt with his joy; but between both.
O heavenly mingle! Beest thou sad or merry,
The violence of either thee becomes, 60
So does it no man else.—Metst thou my posts?
Alex. Ay, madam, twenty several messengers.
Why do you send so thick?
Cleo. Who's born that day
When I forget to send to Antony
Shall die a beggar. Ink and paper, Charmian. 65
Welcome, my good Alexas. Did I, Charmian,
Ever love Cæsar so?
Char. O that brave Cæsar!
Cleo. Be choked with such another emphasis!
Say "the brave Antony."
Char. The valiant Cæsar!
Cleo. By Isis, I will give thee bloody teeth 70
If thou with Cæsar paragon again
My man of men!
Char. By your most gracious pardon,
I sing but after you.
Cleo. My salad days,
When I was green in judgment, cold in blood,
To say as I said then. But come, away! 75
Get me ink and paper.
He shall have every day a several greeting,
Or I'll unpeople Egypt.
Exeunt.

62. several: separate
65. die . . . beggar: because it will be a very unlucky day
71. paragon: parallel
73. sing . . . you: echo your own words

[ACT II]

[Scene I. *Messina. Pompey's house.*]

Enter POMPEY, MENECRATES, *and* MENAS, *in warlike manner.*

Pom. If the great gods be just, they shall assist
The deeds of justest men.
Menec. Know, worthy Pompey,
That what they do delay, they not deny.
Pom. Whiles we are suitors to their throne, decays
The thing we sue for.
Menec. We, ignorant of ourselves, 5
Beg often our own harms, which the wise pow'rs

4–5. decays . . . for: i.e., the ripe moment for victory is passing.

Deny us for our good: so find we profit
By losing of our prayers.
Pom. I shall do well.
The people love me, and the sea is mine;
My powers are crescent, and my auguring hope 10
Says it will come to the full. Mark Antony
In Egypt sits at dinner, and will make
No wars without doors. Cæsar gets money where
He loses hearts. Lepidus flatters both,
Of both is flattered; but he neither loves, 15
Nor either cares for him.
Menas. Cæsar and Lepidus
Are in the field; a mighty strength they carry.
Pom. Where have you this? 'Tis false.
Menas. From Silvius, sir.
Pom. He dreams. I know they are in Rome together,
Looking for Antony. But all the charms of love,
Salt Cleopatra, soften thy waned lip! 21
Let witchcraft join with beauty, lust with both!
Tie up the libertine in a field of feasts,
Keep his brain fuming. Epicurean cooks
Sharpen with cloyless sauce his appetite, 25
That sleep and feeding may prorogue his honor
Even till a Lethe'd dullness!

Enter VARRIUS.

How now, Varrius?
Var. This is most certain that I shall deliver:
Mark Antony is every hour in Rome
Expected. Since he went from Egypt 'tis 30
A space for farther travel.
Pom. I could have given less matter
A better ear. Menas, I did not think
This amorous surfeiter would have donned his helm
For such a petty war. His soldiership
Is twice the other twain. But let us rear 35
The higher our opinion, that our stirring
Can from the lap of Egypt's widow pluck
The ne'er-lust-wearied Antony.
Menas. I cannot hope
Cæsar and Antony shall well greet together.
His wife that's dead did trespasses to Cæsar; 40
His brother warred upon him; although, I think,
Not moved by Antony.
Pom. I know not, Menas,
How lesser enmities may give way to greater.
Were't not that we stand up against them all,
'Twere pregnant they should square between themselves, 45
For they have entertained cause enough
To draw their swords; but how the fear of us
May cement their divisions and bind up
The petty difference we yet not know.
Be't as our gods will have't! It only stands 50
Our lives upon to use our strongest hands.
Come, Menas.
Exeunt.

[Scene II. *Rome. The house of Lepidus.*]

Enter ENOBARBUS *and* LEPIDUS.

Lep. Good Enobarbus, 'tis a worthy deed,
And shall become you well, to entreat your captain
To soft and gentle speech.
Eno. I shall entreat him
To answer like himself. If Cæsar move him,
Let Antony look over Cæsar's head 5
And speak as loud as Mars. By Jupiter,
Were I the wearer of Antonius' beard,
I would not shave't today!
Lep. 'Tis not a time
For private stomaching.
Eno. Every time
Serves for the matter that is then born in't. 10
Lep. But small to greater matters must give way.
Eno. Not if the small come first.
Lep. Your speech is passion;
But pray you stir no embers up. Here comes
The noble Antony.

Enter ANTONY *and* VENTIDIUS.

Eno. And yonder, Cæsar.

Enter CÆSAR, MÆCENAS, *and* AGRIPPA.

Ant. If we compose well here, to Parthia. 15
Hark, Ventidius.
Cæs. I do not know,
Mæcenas. Ask Agrippa.
Lep. Noble friends,
That which combined us was most great, and let not
A leaner action rend us. What's amiss,
May it be gently heard. When we debate 20
Our trivial difference loud, we do commit

10. crescent: increasing; **auguring hope:** prophesying expectation
21. Salt: lustful
26–27. prorogue . . . dullness: delay remembrance of his honor to the point of complete forgetfulness. Lethe is the river in Hades containing the waters of oblivion.
31. A space: i.e., time enough
36. opinion: self-esteem
38. hope: expect
39. well . . . together: agree among themselves
45. pregnant: extremely probable; **square:** quarrel
50–51. stands . . . upon: vitally concerns us
9. stomaching: resentment
15. compose: agree
19. leaner: slighter

Murder in healing wounds. Then, noble partners,
The rather for I earnestly beseech,
Touch you the sourest points with sweetest terms,
Nor curstness grow to the matter.

Ant. 'Tis spoken well.
Were we before our armies, and to fight, 26
I should do thus. *Flourish.*

Cæs. Welcome to Rome.

Ant. Thank you.

Cæs. Sit.

Ant. Sit, sir.

Cæs. Nay then.

[*They seat themselves.*]

Ant. I learn you take things ill which are not so,
Or being, concern you not.

Cæs. I must be laughed at 30
If, or for nothing or a little, I
Should say myself offended, and with you
Chiefly i' the world; more laughed at that I should
Once name you derogately when to sound your name
It not concerned me.

Ant. My being in Egypt, Cæsar, 35
What was't to you?

Cæs. No more than my residing here at Rome
Might be to you in Egypt. Yet if you there
Did practice on my state, your being in Egypt 39
Might be my question.

Ant. How intend you, practiced?

Cæs. You may be pleased to catch at mine intent
By what did here befall me. Your wife and brother
Made wars upon me, and their contestation
Was theme for you; you were the word of war.

Ant. You do mistake your business. My brother never 45
Did urge me in his act. I did inquire it
And have my learning from some true reports
That drew their swords with you. Did he not rather
Discredit my authority with yours,
And make the wars alike against my stomach, 50
Having alike your cause? Of this my letters
Before did satisfy you. If you'll patch a quarrel,
As matter whole you have to make it with,
It must not be with this.

Cæs. You praise yourself
By laying defects of judgment to me; but 55
You patched up your excuses.

Ant. Not so, not so!
I know you could not lack, I am certain on't,
Very necessity of this thought, that I,
Your partner in the cause 'gainst which he fought,
Could not with graceful eyes attend those wars 60
Which fronted mine own peace. As for my wife,
I would you had her spirit in such another!
The third o' the world is yours, which with a snaffle
You may pace easy, but not such a wife.

Eno. Would we had all such wives, that the 65
men might go to wars with the women!

Ant. So much uncurbable, her garboils, Cæsar,
Made out of her impatience—which not wanted
Shrewdness of policy too—I grieving grant
Did you too much disquiet. For that you must 70
But say I could not help it.

Cæs. I wrote to you
When, rioting in Alexandria, you
Did pocket up my letters, and with taunts
Did gibe my missive out of audience.

Ant. Sir,
He fell upon me ere admitted. Then 75
Three kings I had newly feasted, and did want
Of what I was i' the morning; but next day
I told him of myself, which was as much
As to have asked him pardon. Let this fellow
Be nothing of our strife. If we contend, 80
Out of our question wipe him.

Cæs. You have broken
The article of your oath, which you shall never
Have tongue to charge me with.

Lep. Soft, Cæsar!

Ant. No,
Lepidus; let him speak.
The honor is sacred which he talks on now, 85
Supposing that I lacked it. But on, Cæsar.
The article of my oath—

Cæs. To lend me arms and aid when I required them,
The which you both denied.

Ant. Neglected rather;
And then when poisoned hours had bound me up
From mine own knowledge. As nearly as I may, 91
I'll play the penitent to you; but mine honesty
Shall not make poor my greatness, nor my power
Work without it. Truth is, that Fulvia,
To have me out of Egypt, made wars here, 95
For which myself, the ignorant motive, do
So far ask pardon as befits mine honor
To stoop in such a case.

Lep. 'Tis noble spoken.

25. **Nor . . . matter:** and do not add hostility to the discussion
34. **derogately:** disparagingly
39. **practice on:** plot against
40. **question:** concern
44. **you . . . war:** the war was made in your name
46. **urge:** mention
47. **true reports:** honest informants
50. **stomach:** liking; pleasure
52. **satisfy:** fully inform; **patch:** improvise from bits and pieces
53. **As:** whereas
60. **with . . . attend:** regard favorably
61. **fronted:** opposed
63. **snaffle:** bridle
74. **missive:** messenger
92–94. **mine . . . it:** my honor (which compels me to confess my fault) will not allow me to be abject in my apologies, nor can I retain my power without honor.

Mæc. If it might please you to enforce no further
The griefs between ye—to forget them quite 100
Were to remember that the present need
Speaks to atone you.

Lep. Worthily spoken, Mæcenas.

Eno. Or, if you borrow one another's love for the instant, you may, when you hear no more words of Pompey, return it again. You shall have time 105
to wrangle in when you have nothing else to do.

Ant. Thou art a soldier only. Speak no more.

Eno. That truth should be silent I had almost forgot.

Ant. You wrong this presence; therefore speak no more. 110

Eno. Go to, then! your considerate stone.

Cæs. I do not much dislike the matter, but
The manner of his speech; for 't cannot be
We shall remain in friendship, our conditions
So diff'ring in their acts. Yet if I knew 115
What hoop should hold us staunch, from edge to edge
O' the world I would pursue it.

Agr. Give me leave, Cæsar.

Cæs. Speak, Agrippa.

Agr. Thou hast a sister by the mother's side,
Admired Octavia. Great Mark Antony 120
Is now a widower.

Cæs. Say not so, Agrippa.
If Cleopatra heard you, your reproof
Were well deserved of rashness.

Ant. I am not married, Cæsar. Let me hear
Agrippa further speak. 125

Agr. To hold you in perpetual amity,
To make you brothers, and to knit your hearts
With an unslipping knot, take Antony
Octavia to his wife; whose beauty claims
No worse a husband than the best of men; 130
Whose virtue and whose general graces speak
That which none else can utter. By this marriage
All little jealousies, which now seem great,
And all great fears, which now import their dangers,
Would then be nothing. Truths would be tales, 135
Where now half-tales be truths. Her love to both
Would each to other, and all loves to both,
Draw after her. Pardon what I have spoke;
For 'tis a studied, not a present thought,
By duty ruminated.

Ant. Will Cæsar speak? 140

Cæs. Not till he hears how Antony is touched
With what is spoke already.

Ant. What power is in Agrippa,
If I would say "Agrippa, be it so,"
To make this good?

Cæs. The power of Cæsar, and
His power unto Octavia.

Ant. May I never 145
To this good purpose, that so fairly shows,
Dream of impediment! Let me have thy hand.
Further this act of grace; and from this hour
The heart of brothers govern in our loves
And sway our great designs!

Cæs. There is my hand.
A sister I bequeath you, whom no brother 151
Did ever love so dearly. Let her live
To join our kingdoms and our hearts; and never
Fly off our loves again!

Lep. Happily, amen!

Ant. I did not think to draw my sword 'gainst Pompey; 155
For he hath laid strange courtesies and great
Of late upon me. I must thank him only,
Lest my remembrance suffer ill report;
At heel of that, defy him.

Lep. Time calls upon's.
Of us must Pompey presently be sought, 160
Or else he seeks out us.

Ant. Where lies he?

Cæs. About the Mount Misenum.

Ant. What is his strength by land?

Cæs. Great and increasing; but by sea
He is an absolute master.

Ant. So is the fame. 165
Would we had spoke together! Haste we for it.
Yet, ere we put ourselves in arms, dispatch we
The business we have talked of.

Cæs. With most gladness;
And do invite you to my sister's view,
Whither straight I'll lead you.

Ant. Let us, Lepidus, 170
Not lack your company.

Lep. Noble Antony,
Not sickness should detain me.

Flourish. Exeunt. Manent Enobarbus, Agrippa, Mæcenas.

Mæc. Welcome from Egypt, sir.

Eno. Half the heart of Cæsar, worthy Mæcenas!
My honorable friend, Agrippa! 175

Agr. Good Enobarbus!

99. enforce: emphasize
102. atone: reconcile
111. Go . . . stone: very well, I will be silent (but continue to reflect on what I see). **Considerate** is used in a double sense.
114–15. our . . . acts: since our temperaments are so different
131–32. speak . . . utter: i.e., are in themselves her highest praise
134. import . . . dangers: carry their own dangers with them
146. so . . . shows: appears so fair
153–54. never . . . again: may our friendship never again be interrupted.
156. strange: extraordinary
165. fame: rumor
170. straight: immediately

Mæc. We have cause to be glad that matters are so well disgested. You stayed well by't in Egypt.

Eno. Ay, sir; we did sleep day out of countenance and made the night light with drinking. 180

Mæc. Eight wild boars roasted whole at a breakfast, and but twelve persons there. Is this true?

Eno. This was but as a fly by an eagle. We had much more monstrous matter of feast, which worthily deserved noting. 185

Mæc. She's a most triumphant lady, if report be square to her.

Eno. When she first met Mark Antony, she pursed up his heart, upon the river of Cydnus.

Agr. There she appeared indeed; or my 190
reporter devised well for her.

Eno. I will tell you.
The barge she sat in, like a burnished throne,
Burned on the water. The poop was beaten gold;
Purple the sails, and so perfumed that 195
The winds were lovesick with them; the oars were silver,
Which to the tune of flutes kept stroke, and made
The water which they beat to follow faster,
As amorous of their strokes. For her own person,
It beggared all description. She did lie 200
In her pavilion, cloth-of-gold of tissue,
O'erpicturing that Venus where we see
The fancy outwork Nature. On each side her
Stood pretty dimpled boys, like smiling Cupids,
With divers-colored fans, whose wind did seem 205
To glow the delicate cheeks which they did cool,
And what they undid did.

Agr. O, rare for Antony!

Eno. Her gentlewomen, like the Nereides,
So many mermaids, tended her i' the eyes,
And made their bends adornings. At the helm 210
A seeming mermaid steers. The silken tackle
Swell with the touches of those flower-soft hands
That yarely frame the office. From the barge
A strange invisible perfume hits the sense
Of the adjacent wharfs. The city cast 215
Her people out upon her; and Antony,
Enthroned i' the market place, did sit alone,
Whistling to the air; which, but for vacancy,
Had gone to gaze on Cleopatra too,
And made a gap in nature.

Agr. Rare Egyptian! 220

Eno. Upon her landing, Antony sent to her,
Invited her to supper. She replied,
It should be better he became her guest;
Which she entreated. Our courteous Antony,
Whom ne'er the word of "no" woman heard speak,
Being barbered ten times o'er, goes to the feast,
And for his ordinary pays his heart 227
For what his eyes eat only.

Agr. Royal wench!
She made great Cæsar lay his sword to bed.
He plowed her, and she cropped.

Eno. I saw her once
Hop forty paces through the public street; 231
And having lost her breath, she spoke, and panted,
That she did make defect perfection
And, breathless, pow'r breathe forth.

Mæc. Now Antony must leave her utterly. 235

Eno. Never! He will not.
Age cannot wither her nor custom stale
Her infinite variety. Other women cloy
The appetites they feed, but she makes hungry
Where most she satisfies; for vilest things 240
Become themselves in her, that the holy priests
Bless her when she is riggish.

Mæc. If beauty, wisdom, modesty, can settle
The heart of Antony, Octavia is
A blessed lottery to him.

Agr. Let us go. 245
Good Enobarbus, make yourself my guest
Whilst you abide here.

Eno. Humbly, sir, I thank you.

Exeunt.

[Scene III. *Rome. Cæsar's house.*]

Enter ANTONY, CÆSAR, OCTAVIA *between them.*

Ant. The world, and my great office, will sometimes
Divide me from your bosom.

Octa. All which time
Before the gods my knee shall bow my prayers
To them for you.

Ant. Good night, sir. My Octavia,
Read not my blemishes in the world's report. 5
I have not kept my square; but that to come
Shall all be done by the rule. Good night, dear lady.

178. disgested: settled
186. triumphant: spectacular
201. cloth-of-gold . . . tissue: a fine silk woven with gold threads
202–3. O'erpicturing . . . Nature: surpassing in loveliness the most superlative picture of Venus that ever outdid Nature's handiwork
208. Nereides: sea nymphs, daughters of Nereus
209. eyes: areas in the bows of the ship
210. bends: planks at the ship's sides, which were adorned by Cleopatra's attendants
213. yarely: skillfully; **frame:** perform; **office:** function

227. ordinary: meal; a set meal obtainable at an inn or tavern
237. custom: familiarity
242. riggish: wanton
245. lottery: prize
6. kept . . . square: kept to the straight and narrow path. **Square** equals "foot rule."

Octa. Good night, sir.
Cæs. Good night. *Exit* [*with Octavia*].

Enter SOOTHSAYER.

Ant. Now, sirrah, you do wish yourself in Egypt?
Sooth. Would I had never come from thence, nor you thither! 11
Ant. If you can, your reason!
Sooth. I see it in my motion, have it not in my tongue.
But yet hie you to Egypt again.
Ant. Say to me,
Whose fortunes shall rise higher, Cæsar's or mine?
Sooth. Cæsar's. 16
Therefore, O Antony, stay not by his side!
Thy daemon, that thy spirit which keeps thee, is
Noble, courageous, high, unmatchable,
Where Cæsar's is not; but near him thy angel 20
Becomes afeard, as being o'erpow'red. Therefore
Make space enough between you.
Ant. Speak this no more.
Sooth. To none but thee; no more but when to thee.
If thou dost play with him at any game,
Thou art sure to lose; and of that natural luck 25
He beats thee 'gainst the odds. Thy luster thickens
When he shines by. I say again, thy spirit
Is all afraid to govern thee near him;
But he away, 'tis noble.
Ant. Get thee gone.
Say to Ventidius I would speak with him. 30
Exit [*Soothsayer*].
He shall to Parthia.—Be it art or hap,
He hath spoken true. The very dice obey him,
And in our sports my better cunning faints
Under his chance. If we draw lots, he speeds;
His cocks do win the battle still of mine 35
When it is all to naught, and his quails ever
Beat mine, inhooped, at odds. I will to Egypt;
And though I make this marriage for my peace,
I' the East my pleasure lies.

Enter VENTIDIUS.

O, come, Ventidius,
You must to Parthia. Your commission's ready; 40
Follow me, and receive't.
Exeunt.

13. see . . . motion: perceive it intuitively
18. daemon: guardian spirit
25. of: because of
26. thickens: dims
34. speeds: prospers
35. still: ever
36. it . . . naught: the odds are all in my favor
37. inhooped: i.e., when they fight in a ring

[Scene IV. *Rome. A street.*]

Enter LEPIDUS, MÆCENAS, *and* AGRIPPA.

Lep. Trouble yourselves no further. Pray you, hasten
Your generals after.
Agr. Sir, Mark Antony
Will e'en but kiss Octavia, and we'll follow.
Lep. Till I shall see you in your soldier's dress,
Which will become you both, farewell.
Mæc. We shall, 5
As I conceive the journey, be at the Mount
Before you, Lepidus.
Lep. Your way is shorter;
My purposes do draw me much about.
You'll win two days upon me.
Both. Sir, good success!
Lep. Farewell. 10
Exeunt.

[Scene V. *Alexandria. Cleopatra's Palace.*]

Enter CLEOPATRA, CHARMIAN, IRAS, *and* ALEXAS.

Cleo. Give me some music! music, moody food
Of us that trade in love.
Omnes. The music, ho!

Enter MARDIAN, *the Eunuch*.

Cleo. Let it alone! Let's to billiards. Come, Charmian.
Char. My arm is sore; best play with Mardian.
Cleo. As well a woman with an eunuch played 5
As with a woman. Come, you'll play with me, sir?
Mar. As well as I can, madam.
Cleo. And when good will is showed, though't come too short,
The actor may plead pardon. I'll none now.
Give me mine angle! we'll to the river. There, 10
My music playing far off, I will betray
Tawny-finned fishes. My bended hook shall pierce
Their slimy jaws; and as I draw them up,
I'll think them every one an Antony,
And say, "Ah, ha! y'are caught!"
Char. 'Twas merry when 15
You wagered on your angling, when your diver
Did hang a salt fish on his hook, which he
With fervency drew up.
Cleo. That time? O times!
I laughed him out of patience; and that night
I laughed him into patience; and next morn 20

Ere the ninth hour I drunk him to his bed,
Then put my tires and mantles on him, whilst
I wore his sword Philippan.

Enter a MESSENGER.

O, from Italy!
Ram thou thy fruitful tidings in mine ears,
That long time have been barren.
Mess. Madam, madam—
Cleo. Antony's dead! If thou say so, villain, 26
Thou killst thy mistress; but well and free,
If thou so yield him, there is gold, and here
My bluest veins to kiss—a hand that kings
Have lipped, and trembled kissing. 30
Mess. First, madam, he is well.
Cleo. Why, there's more gold.
But, sirrah, mark, we use
To say the dead are well. Bring it to that,
The gold I give thee will I melt and pour
Down thy ill-uttering throat. 35
Mess. Good madam, hear me.
Cleo. Well, go to, I will.
But there's no goodness in thy face. If Antony
Be free and healthful, why so tart a favor
To trumpet such good tidings? If not well,
Thou shouldst come like a Fury crowned with snakes, 40
Not like a formal man.
Mess. Will't please you hear me?
Cleo. I have a mind to strike thee ere thou speakst.
Yet, if thou say Antony lives, is well,
Or friends with Cæsar or not captive to him,
I'll set thee in a shower of gold and hail 45
Rich pearls upon thee.
Mess. Madam, he's well.
Cleo. Well said.
Mess. And friends with Cæsar.
Cleo. Th'art an honest man.
Mess. Cæsar and he are greater friends than ever.
Cleo. Make thee a fortune from me!
Mess. But yet, madam—
Cleo. I do not like "but yet." It does allay 50
The good precedence. Fie upon "but yet"!
"But yet" is as a jailer to bring forth
Some monstrous malefactor. Prithee, friend,
Pour out the pack of matter to mine ear, 54
The good and bad together. He's friends with Cæsar;
In state of health thou sayst; and thou sayst free.
Mess. Free, madam? No; I made no such report
He's bound unto Octavia.
Cleo. For what good turn?
Mess. For the best turn i' the bed.
Cleo. I am pale, Charmian.
Mess. Madam, he's married to Octavia. 60
Cleo. The most infectious pestilence upon thee!
Strikes him down.
Mess. Good madam, patience.
Cleo. What say you?
Strikes him.
Hence,
Horrible villain! or I'll spurn thine eyes
Like balls before me. I'll unhair thy head!
She hales him up and down.
Thou shalt be whipped with wire and stewed in brine, 65
Smarting in ling'ring pickle.
Mess. Gracious madam,
I that do bring the news made not the match.
Cleo. Say 'tis not so, a province I will give thee
And make thy fortunes proud. The blow thou hadst
Shall make thy peace for moving me to rage; 70
And I will boot thee with what gift beside
Thy modesty can beg.
Mess. He's married, madam.
Cleo. Rogue, thou hast lived too long.
Draw a knife.
Mess. Nay, then I'll run.
What mean you, madam? I have made no fault. *Exit.*
Char. Good madam, keep yourself within yourself.
The man is innocent. 76
Cleo. Some innocents scape not the thunderbolt.
Melt Egypt into Nile! and kindly creatures
Turn all to serpents! Call the slave again.
Though I am mad, I will not bite him. Call! 80
Char. He is afeard to come.
Cleo. I will not hurt him.
These hands do lack nobility, that they strike
A meaner than myself; since I myself
Have given myself the cause.

Enter the MESSENGER *again.*

Come hither, sir.
Though it be honest, it is never good 85
To bring bad news. Give to a gracious message
An host of tongues, but let ill tidings tell
Themselves when they be felt.
Mess. I have done my duty.
Cleo. Is he married?
I cannot hate thee worser than I do 90
If thou again say yes.
Mess. He's married, madam.

22. tires: headdresses
23. sword Philippan: the sword he used at the battle of Philippi (Brutus' defeat)
28. yield: report
38. favor: face
41. formal: normal; in the usual form
50. allay: modify
63. spurn: kick
71. boot: reward
83–84. I . . . cause: i.e., it is my own doting fondness that causes my anger.
86. gracious: pleasing

Cleo. The gods confound thee! Dost thou hold there still?
Mess. Should I lie, madam?
Cleo. O, I would thou didst,
So half my Egypt were submerged and made
A cistern for scaled snakes! Go get thee hence! 95
Hadst thou Narcissus in thy face, to me
Thou wouldst appear most ugly. He is married?
Mess. I crave your Highness' pardon.
Cleo. He is married?
Mess. Take no offense that I would not offend you.
To punish me for what you make me do 100
Seems much unequal. He's married to Octavia.
Cleo. O, that his fault should make a knave of thee,
That art not what th'art sure of! Get thee hence.
The merchandise which thou hast brought from Rome 104
Are all too dear for me. Lie they upon thy hand,
And be undone by 'em! [*Exit Messenger.*]
Char. Good your Highness, patience.
Cleo. In praising Antony I have dispraised Cæsar.
Char. Many times, madam.
Cleo. I am paid for't now.
Lead me from hence,
I faint. O Iras, Charmian! 'Tis no matter. 110
Go to the fellow, good Alexas. Bid him
Report the feature of Octavia, her years,
Her inclination; let him not leave out
The color of her hair. Bring me word quickly.
[*Exit Alexas.*]
Let him forever go!—let him not!—Charmian,
Though he be painted one way like a Gorgon, 116
The other way's a Mars.—[*To Mardian*] Bid you Alexas
Bring me word how tall she is.—Pity me, Charmian,
But do not speak to me. Lead me to my chamber.
Exeunt.

[Scene VI. *Near Misenum.*]

Flourish. Enter POMPEY *at one door, with a Drum and Trumpet: at another* CÆSAR, LEPIDUS, ANTONY, ENOBARBUS, MÆCENAS, AGRIPPA, [*and*] MENAS *with* SOLDIERS *marching.*

Pom. Your hostages I have, so have you mine;
And we shall talk before we fight.
Cæs. Most meet
That first we come to words; and therefore have we
Our written purposes before us sent;
Which if thou hast considered, let us know 5
If 'twill tie up thy discontented sword
And carry back to Sicily much tall youth
That else must perish here.
Pom. To you all three,
The senators alone of this great world,
Chief factors for the gods: I do not know 10
Wherefore my father should revengers want,
Having a son and friends, since Julius Cæsar,
Who at Philippi the good Brutus ghosted,
There saw you laboring for him. What was't
That moved pale Cassius to conspire? and what 15
Made the all-honored honest Roman, Brutus,
With the armed rest, courtiers of beauteous freedom,
To drench the Capitol, but that they would
Have one man but a man? And that is it
Hath made me rig my navy, at whose burden 20
The angered ocean foams; with which I meant
To scourge the ingratitude that despiteful Rome
Cast on my noble father.
Cæs. Take your time.
Ant. Thou canst not fear us, Pompey, with thy sails. 24
We'll speak with thee at sea. At land thou knowst
How much we do o'ercount thee.
Pom. At land indeed
Thou dost o'ercount me of my father's house!
But since the cuckoo builds not for himself,
Remain in't as thou mayst.
Lep. Be pleased to tell us
(For this is from the present) how you take 30
The offers we have sent you.
Cæs. There's the point.
Ant. Which do not be entreated to, but weigh
What it is worth embraced.
Cæs. And what may follow,
To try a larger fortune.
Pom. You have made me offer
Of Sicily, Sardinia; and I must 35
Rid all the sea of pirates; then, to send
Measures of wheat to Rome; this 'greed upon,
To part with unhacked edges and bear back
Our targes undinted.
Omnes. That's our offer.

92. confound: destroy
101. unequal: unfair
103. what . . . of: i.e., his bad news
113. inclination: temperament
116. a Gorgon: a fabulous creature of Greek mythology; a woman with a terrifying face that turned the beholder to stone

7. tall: brave
10. factors: agents
16. honest: honorable
24. fear: frighten
26. o'ercount: outnumber
27. o'ercount . . . house: Antony bought Pompey's house at public auction but refused to pay for it. Pompey uses the word **o'ercount** in the sense "cheat."
28. builds not: the cuckoo lays its eggs in the nests of other birds.
30. from . . . present: irrelevant
33. embraced: accepted
33–34. what . . . fortune: the result of holding out for more
39. targes: targets; **undinted:** undented by use; unscarred

Pom. Know then,
I came before you here a man prepared 40
To take this offer; but Mark Antony
Put me to some impatience. Though I lose
The praise of it by telling, you must know,
When Cæsar and your brother were at blows,
Your mother came to Sicily and did find 45
Her welcome friendly.
Ant. I have heard it, Pompey,
And am well studied for a liberal thanks,
Which I do owe you.
Pom. Let me have your hand.
I did not think, sir, to have met you here.
Ant. The beds i' the East are soft; and thanks to
you, 50
That called me timelier than my purpose hither;
For I have gained by't.
Cæs. Since I saw you last
There is a change upon you.
Pom. Well, I know not
What counts harsh Fortune casts upon my face;
But in my bosom shall she never come 55
To make my heart her vassal.
Lep. Well met here.
Pom. I hope so, Lepidus. Thus we are agreed.
I crave our composition may be written,
And sealed between us.
Cæs. That's the next to do.
Pom. We'll feast each other ere we part, and let's
Draw lots who shall begin.
Ant. That will I, Pompey. 61
Pom. No, Antony, take the lot;
But, first or last, your fine Egyptian cookery
Shall have the fame. I have heard that Julius Cæsar
Grew fat with feasting there.
Ant. You have heard much. 65
Pom. I have fair meanings, sir.
Ant. And fair words to them.
Pom. Then so much have I heard;
And I have heard Apollodorus carried—
Eno. No more of that! He did so.
Pom. What, I pray you?
Eno. A certain queen to Cæsar in a mattress. 70
Pom. I know thee now. How farest thou, soldier?
Eno. Well;
And well am like to do, for I perceive
Four feasts are toward.
Pom. Let me shake thy hand.
I never hated thee. I have seen thee fight
When I have envied thy behavior.
Eno. Sir, 75
I never loved you much; but I ha' praised ye
When you have well deserved ten times as much
As I have said you did.
Pom. Enjoy thy plainness;
It nothing ill becomes thee.
Aboard my galley I invite you all. 80
Will you lead, lords?
All. Show us the way, sir.
Pom. Come.
Exeunt. Manent Enobarbus and Menas.
Menas. [*Aside*] Thy father, Pompey, would ne'er have made this treaty.—You and I have known, sir.
Eno. At sea, I think.
Menas. We have, sir. 85
Eno. You have done well by water.
Menas. And you by land.
Eno. I will praise any man that will praise me; though it cannot be denied what I have done by land.
Menas. Nor what I have done by water. 90
Eno. Yes, something you can deny for your own safety. You have been a great thief by sea.
Menas. And you by land.
Eno. There I deny my land service. But give me your hand, Menas. If our eyes had authority, 95 here they might take two thieves kissing.
Menas. All men's faces are true, whatsome'er their hands are.
Eno. But there is never a fair woman has a true face. 100
Menas. No slander. They steal hearts.
Eno. We came hither to fight with you.
Menas. For my part, I am sorry it is turned to a drinking. Pompey doth this day laugh away his fortune. 105
Eno. If he do, sure he cannot weep't back again.
Menas. Y'have said, sir. We looked not for Mark Antony here. Pray you, is he married to Cleopatra?
Eno. Cæsar's sister is called Octavia.
Menas. True, sir. She was the wife of Caius 110 Marcellus.
Eno. But she is now the wife of Marcus Antonius.
Menas. Pray ye, sir?
Eno. 'Tis true.
Menas. Then is Cæsar and he forever knit 115 together.
Eno. If I were bound to divine of this unity, I would not prophesy so.
Menas. I think the policy of that purpose made more in the marriage than the love of the 120 parties.
Eno. I think so too. But you shall find the band that seems to tie their friendship together will be the

47. studied: prepared
54. counts: marks (used in keeping accounts)
58. composition: compact
68. Appollodorus: the story of how Cleopatra was smuggled into Cæsar's presence wrapped in a mattress is told in Plutarch.
73. toward: impending
95. authority: the authority to make arrests
97. true: honest
107. Y'have said: you speak truly.
122. band: bond

very strangler of their amity. Octavia is of a holy, cold, and still conversation. 125

Menas. Who would not have his wife so?

Eno. Not he that himself is not so; which is Mark Antony. He will to his Egyptian dish again. Then shall the sighs of Octavia blow the fire up in Cæsar, and, as I said before, that which is the 130 strength of their amity shall prove the immediate author of their variance. Antony will use his affection where it is. He married but his occasion here.

Menas. And thus it may be. Come, sir, will you aboard? I have a health for you. 135

Eno. I shall take it, sir. We have used our throats in Egypt.

Menas. Come, let's away.

Exeunt.

[Scene VII. *On board Pompey's galley, off Misenum.*]

Music plays. Enter Two or Three Servants, *with a banquet.*

1. Serv. Here they'll be, man. Some o' their plants are ill-rooted already; the least wind i' the world will blow them down.

2. Serv. Lepidus is high-colored. 4

1. Serv. They have made him drink alms drink.

2. Serv. As they pinch one another by the disposition, he cries out "No more!" reconciles them to his entreaty and himself to the drink.

1. Serv. But it raises the greater war between him and his discretion. 10

2. Serv. Why, this it is to have a name in great men's fellowship. I had as lief have a reed that will do me no service as a partisan I could not heave.

1. Serv. To be called into a huge sphere and not to be seen to move in't, are the holes where eyes 15 should be, which pitifully disaster the cheeks.

A sennet sounded. Enter Cæsar, Antony, Pompey, Lepidus, Agrippa, Mæcenas, Enobarbus, Menas, *with other* Captains.

Ant. [*To Cæsar*] Thus do they, sir: they take the flow o' the Nile
By certain scales i' the pyramid. They know
By the height, the lowness, or the mean, if dearth
Or foison follow. The higher Nilus swells, 20
The more it promises. As it ebbs, the seedsman
Upon the slime and ooze scatters his grain,
And shortly comes to harvest.

Lep. Y'have strange serpents there.

Ant. Ay, Lepidus. 25

Lep. Your serpent of Egypt is bred now of your mud by the operation of your sun; so is your crocodile.

Ant. They are so.

Pom. Sit—and some wine! A health to 30 Lepidus!

Lep. I am not so well as I should be, but I'll ne'er out.

Eno. Not till you have slept. I fear me you'll be in till then. 35

Lep. Nay, certainly, I have heard the Ptolemies' pyramises are very goodly things. Without contradiction I have heard that.

Menas. [*Aside to Pompey*] Pompey, a word.

Pom. [*Aside to Menas*] Say in mine ear. What is't?

Menas. [*Aside to Pompey*] Forsake thy seat, I do beseech thee, Captain, 40
And hear me speak a word.

Pom. [*Aside to Menas*] Forbear me till anon.

Whispers in's ear.

This wine for Lepidus!

Lep. What manner o' thing is your crocodile?

Ant. It is shaped, sir, like itself, and it is as broad as it hath breadth. It is just so high as it is, and 45 moves with it own organs. It lives by that which nourisheth it, and the elements once out of it, it transmigrates.

Lep. What color is it of?

Ant. Of it own color too. 50

Lep. 'Tis a strange serpent.

Ant. 'Tis so. And the tears of it are wet.

Cæs. Will this description satisfy him?

Ant. With the health that Pompey gives him; else he is a very epicure. 55

Pom. [*Aside to Menas*] Go hang, sir, hang! Tell me of that? Away!
Do as I bid you.—Where's this cup I called for?

Menas. [*Aside to Pompey*] If for the sake of merit thou wilt hear me,
Rise from thy stool.

Pom. [*Aside to Menas*] I think th'art mad.

[*Rises and walks aside.*]

The matter? 59

Menas. I have ever held my cap off to thy fortunes.

125. conversation: behavior
133. occasion: advantage
1. plants: i.e., feet
5. alms drink: i.e., even the leavings
13. partisan: a long-handled weapon like a pike
14–15. not . . . in't: play no significant part
16. disaster: ruin
S.D. 16. sennet: trumpet call

20. foison: plenty
33. out: pass out
34. in: in liquor
37. pyramises: pyramids
46. it: its
47. elements: vital elements; the four components of life: earth, air, fire, and water

Pom. Thou hast served me with much faith. What's else to say?—
Be jolly, lords.
Ant. These quicksands, Lepidus,
Keep off them, for you sink.
Menas. Wilt thou be lord of all the world?
Pom. What sayst thou?
Menas. Wilt thou be lord of the whole world? That's twice. 65
Pom. How should that be?
Menas. But entertain it,
And though thou think me poor, I am the man
Will give thee all the world.
Pom. Hast thou drunk well?
Menas. No, Pompey, I have kept me from the cup.
Thou art, if thou darest be, the earthly Jove. 70
Whate'er the ocean pales, or sky inclips,
Is thine, if thou wilt ha't.
Pom. Show me which way.
Menas. These three world-sharers, these competitors,
Are in thy vessel. Let me cut the cable;
And when we are put off, fall to their throats. 75
All there is thine.
Pom. Ah, this thou shouldst have done,
And not have spoke on't! In me 'tis villainy;
In thee't had been good service. Thou must know,
'Tis not my profit that does lead mine honor;
Mine honor it. Repent that e'er thy tongue 80
Hath so betrayed thine act. Being done unknown,
I should have found it afterwards well done,
But must condemn it now. Desist, and drink.
Menas. [*Aside*] For this,
I'll never follow thy palled fortunes more. 85
Who seeks, and will not take when once 'tis offered,
Shall never find it more.
Pom. This health to Lepidus!
Ant. Bear him ashore. I'll pledge it for him, Pompey.
Eno. Here's to thee, Menas!
Menas. Enobarbus, welcome!
Pom. Fill till the cup be hid. 90
Eno. There's a strong fellow, Menas.
[*Points to the Servant who carries off Lepidus.*]
Menas. Why?
Eno. 'A bears the third part of the world, man; seest not?
Menas. The third part, then, is drunk. Would it were all,
That it might go on wheels! 95
Eno. Drink thou. Increase the reels.
Menas. Come.
Pom. This is not yet an Alexandrian feast.
Ant. It ripens towards it. Strike the vessels, ho!
Here's to Cæsar!
Cæs. I could well forbear't. 100
It's monstrous labor when I wash my brain
And it grows fouler.
Ant. Be a child o' the time.
Cæs. Possess it; I'll make answer.
But I had rather fast from all four days 104
Than drink so much in one.
Eno. [*To Antony*] Ha, my brave emperor!
Shall we dance now the Egyptian Bacchanals
And celebrate our drink?
Pom. Let's ha't, good soldier.
Ant. Come, let's all take hands
Till that the conquering wine hath steeped our sense
In soft and delicate Lethe.
Eno. All take hands. 110
Make battery to our ears with the loud music,
The while I'll place you; then the boy shall sing.
The holding every man shall bear as loud
As his strong sides can volley.
Music plays. Enobarbus places them hand in hand.

The Song.

Come, thou monarch of the vine, 115
Plumpy Bacchus with pink eyne!
In thy fats our cares be drowned,
With thy grapes our hairs be crowned.
Cup us till the world go round,
Cup us till the world go round! 120

Cæs. What would you more? Pompey, good night. Good brother,
Let me request you off. Our graver business
Frowns at this levity. Gentle lords, let's part;
You see we have burnt our cheeks. Strong Enobarb
Is weaker than the wine, and mine own tongue 125
Splits what it speaks. The wild disguise hath almost
Anticked us all. What needs more words? Good night.
Good Antony, your hand.
Pom. I'll try you on the shore.
Ant. And shall, sir.—Give's your hand.
Pom. O Antony,

66. entertain: accept
71. pales: encloses; **inclips:** embraces
73. competitors: partners
85. palled: weakened
93. 'A: he
95. on wheels: i.e., quickly and smoothly; cf. the proverbial saying "The world runs on wheels."
96. the reels: the number of those reeling
99. Strike . . . vessels: empty the vessels; "drink up"
101. monstrous: outrageously absurd
103. Possess . . . answer: finish your drink and I'll do likewise.
109. Till that: until
113. holding: burden; refrain
116. pink eyne: blinking eyes
117. fats: vats
126. the . . . disguise: intoxication
127. Anticked: make buffoons of
128. try you: test your capacity for drink
129. And shall: agreed

You have my father's house—but what? We are friends! 130
Come, down into the boat.
Eno. Take heed you fall not.
[*Exeunt all but Enobarbus and Menas.*]
Menas, I'll not on shore.
Menas. No, to my cabin.
These drums! these trumpets, flutes! what!
Let Neptune hear we bid a loud farewell 134
To these great fellows. Sound and be hanged, sound out! *Sound a flourish, with drums.*
Eno. Hoo! says 'a. There's my cap.
Menas. Hoo! Noble Captain, come.
Exeunt.

136. **Hoo:** hurrah! Enobarbus mimics the salute of the trumpets honoring the departing triumvirs.

[ACT III]

[Scene I. *A plain in Syria.*]

Enter VENTIDIUS *as it were in triumph,* [*with* SILIUS *and other* ROMANS, OFFICERS, *and* SOLDIERS;] *the dead body of* PACORUS *borne before him.*

Ven. Now, darting Parthia, art thou stroke, and now
Pleased fortune does of Marcus Crassus' death
Make me revenger. Bear the King's son's body
Before our army. Thy Pacorus, Orodes,
Pays this for Marcus Crassus.
Silius. Noble Ventidius, 5
Whilst yet with Parthian blood thy sword is warm,
The fugitive Parthians follow. Spur through Media,
Mesopotamia, and the shelters whither
The routed fly. So thy grand captain, Antony,
Shall set thee on triumphant chariots and 10
Put garlands on thy head.
Ven. O Silius, Silius,
I have done enough. A lower place, note well,
May make too great an act. For learn this, Silius:
Better to leave undone than by our deed
Acquire too high a fame when him we serve's away.
Cæsar and Antony have ever won 16
More in their officer than person. Sossius,
One of my place in Syria, his lieutenant,
For quick accumulation of renown, 19
Which he achieved by the minute, lost his favor.
Who does i' the wars more than his captain can
Becomes his captain's captain; and ambition,
The soldier's virtue, rather makes choice of loss
Than gain which darkens him.
I could do more to do Antonius good, 25
But 'twould offend him; and in his offense
Should my performance perish.
Silius. Thou hast, Ventidius, that
Without the which a soldier and his sword
Grants scarce distinction. Thou wilt write to Antony?
Ven. I'll humbly signify what in his name, 30
That magical word of war, we have effected;
How with his banners and his well-paid ranks
The ne'er-yet-beaten horse of Parthia
We have jaded out o' the field.
Silius. Where is he now?
Ven. He purposeth to Athens; whither, with what haste 35
The weight we must convey with 's will permit,
We shall appear before him.—On, there! Pass along!
Exeunt.

1. **darting Parthia:** the Parthian horsemen, armed with darts, were famed for their speed and skill.
2. **Marcus Crassus:** a member of the first triumvirate, killed by the Parthians
4. **Pacorus:** son of Orodes, King of Parthia
12. **lower place:** subordinate
18. **his:** i.e., Antony's
24. **darkens him:** overshadows his commander (and thus displeases him)
27–29. **Thou . . . distinction:** i.e., you have wisdom, the lack of which would make you indistinguishable from your sword as a weapon of war.
34. **jaded:** routed like jades (nags)

[Scene II. *Rome. Cæsar's house.*]

Enter AGRIPPA *at one door,* ENOBARBUS *at another.*

Agr. What, are the brothers parted?
Eno. They have dispatched with Pompey; he is gone;

1. **brothers:** brothers-in-law

The other three are sealing. Octavia weeps
To part from Rome; Cæsar is sad; and Lepidus
Since Pompey's feast, as Menas says, is troubled 5
With the greensickness.

Agr. 'Tis a noble Lepidus.

Eno. A very fine one. O, how he loves Cæsar!

Agr. Nay, but how dearly he adores Mark Antony!

Eno. Cæsar? Why, he's the Jupiter of men.

Agr. What's Antony? The god of Jupiter. 10

Eno. Spake you of Cæsar? Hoo! the nonpareil!

Agr. O Antony! O thou Arabian bird!

Eno. Would you praise Cæsar, say "Cæsar"—go no further.

Agr. Indeed he plied them both with excellent praises. 14

Eno. But he loves Cæsar best. Yet he loves Antony!
Hoo! hearts, tongues, figures, scribes, bards, poets, cannot
Think, speak, cast, write, sing, number—hoo!—
His love to Antony. But as for Cæsar,
Kneel down, kneel down, and wonder!

Agr. Both he loves.

Eno. They are his shards, and he their beetle.
[*Trumpet within.*] So: 20
This is to horse. Adieu, noble Agrippa.

Agr. Good fortune, worthy soldier, and farewell!

Enter CÆSAR, ANTONY, LEPIDUS, *and* OCTAVIA.

Ant. No further, sir.

Cæs. You take from me a great part of myself;
Use me well in't. Sister, prove such a wife 25
As my thoughts make thee, and as my farthest band
Shall pass on thy approof. Most noble Antony,
Let not the piece of virtue which is set
Betwixt us as the cement of our love
To keep it builded be the ram to batter 30
The fortress of it; for better might we
Have loved without this mean, if on both parts
This be not cherished.

Ant. Make me not offended
In your distrust.

Cæs. I have said.

Ant. You shall not find,
Though you be therein curious, the least cause 35
For what you seem to fear. So the gods keep you
And make the hearts of Romans serve your ends!
We will here part.

Cæs. Farewell, my dearest sister, fare thee well.
The elements be kind to thee and make 40
Thy spirits all of comfort! Fare thee well.

Octa. My noble brother!

Ant. The April's in her eyes. It is love's spring,
And these the showers to bring it on. Be cheerful.

Octa. Sir, look well to my husband's house; and—

Cæs. What,
Octavia? 46

Octa. I'll tell you in your ear.

Ant. Her tongue will not obey her heart, nor can
Her heart inform her tongue—the swan's-down feather
That stands upon the swell at full of tide, 50
And neither way inclines.

Eno. [*Aside to Agrippa*] Will Cæsar weep?

Agr. [*Aside to Enobarbus*] He has a cloud in's face.

Eno. [*Aside to Agrippa*] He were the worse for that were he a horse;
So is he being a man.

Agr. [*Aside to Enobarbus*] Why, Enobarbus, 55
When Antony found Julius Cæsar dead,
He cried almost to roaring; and he wept
When at Philippi he found Brutus slain.

Eno. [*Aside to Agrippa*] That year indeed he was troubled with a rheum.
What willingly he did confound he wailed, 60
Believe't, till I wept too.

Cæs. No, sweet Octavia,
You shall hear from me still. The time shall not
Outgo my thinking on you.

Ant. Come, sir, come.
I'll wrestle with you in my strength of love.
Look, here I have you; thus I let you go, 65
And give you to the gods.

Cæs. Adieu, be happy!

Lep. Let all the number of the stars give light
To thy fair way!

Cæs. Farewell, farewell! *Kisses Octavia.*

Ant. Farewell!

Trumpets sound. Exeunt.

[Scene III. *Alexandria. Cleopatra's Palace.*]

Enter CLEOPATRA, CHARMIAN, IRAS, *and* ALEXAS.

Cleo. Where is the fellow?

Alex. Half afeard to come.

Cleo. Go to, go to!

3. sealing: signing their agreement
6. greensickness: anemia (associated with lovesick maidens)
12. Arabian bird: i.e., phoenix, a legendary bird which existed in only one exemplar
20. shards: fragments of dung; **beetle:** tumblebug or dung beetle
26–27. as . . . approof: as I would be willing to stake my uttermost that you will prove
28. piece: masterpiece
35. curious: minutely attentive

43. The April's: i.e., tears
59. rheum: head cold
60. confound: destroy
62. still: ever
62–63. The . . . you: you shall be ever in my thoughts.
64. in . . . love: i.e., lovingly, by an embrace

Enter the MESSENGER, *as before.*

Come hither, sir.
Alex. Good Majesty,
Herod of Jewry dare not look upon you
But when you are well pleased.
Cleo. That Herod's head
I'll have! But how, when Antony is gone 5
Through whom I might command it? Come thou near.
Mess. Most gracious Majesty!
Cleo. Didst thou behold Octavia?
Mess. Ay, dread Queen.
Cleo. Where? 10
Mess. Madam, in Rome.
I looked her in the face, and saw her led
Between her brother and Mark Antony.
Cleo. Is she as tall as me?
Mess. She is not, madam.
Cleo. Didst hear her speak? Is she shrill-tongued or low? 15
Mess. Madam, I heard her speak. She is low-voiced.
Cleo. That's not so good! He cannot like her long.
Char. Like her? O Isis! 'tis impossible.
Cleo. I think so, Charmian. Dull of tongue, and dwarfish!
What majesty is in her gait? Remember, 20
If e'er thou lookst on majesty.
Mess. She creeps!
Her motion and her station are as one.
She shows a body rather than a life,
A statue than a breather.
Cleo. Is this certain?
Mess. Or I have no observance.
Char. Three in Egypt 25
Cannot make better note.
Cleo. He's very knowing;
I do perceive't. There's nothing in her yet.
The fellow has good judgment.
Char. Excellent.
Cleo. Guess at her years, I prithee.
Mess. Madam,
She was a widow—
Cleo. Widow? Charmian, hark! 30
Mess. And I do think she's thirty.
Cleo. Bearst thou her face in mind? Is't long or round?
Mess. Round even to faultiness.
Cleo. For the most part, too, they are foolish that are so.
Her hair, what color? 35
Mess. Brown, madam; and her forehead
As low as she would wish it.

22. **station:** standing position
23. **shows:** appears

Cleo. There's gold for thee.
Thou must not take my former sharpness ill.
I will employ thee back again; I find thee
Most fit for business. Go, make thee ready; 40
Our letters are prepared. [*Exit Messenger.*]
Char. A proper man.
Cleo. Indeed he is so. I repent me much
That so I harried him. Why, methinks, by him,
This creature's no such thing.
Char. Nothing, madam.
Cleo. The man hath seen some majesty, and should know. 45
Char. Hath he seen majesty? Isis else defend,
And serving you so long!
Cleo. I have one thing more to ask him yet, good Charmian.
But 'tis no matter. Thou shalt bring him to me
Where I will write. All may be well enough. 50
Char. I warrant you, madam.
Exeunt.

[Scene IV. *Athens. Antony's house.*]

Enter ANTONY *and* OCTAVIA.

Ant. Nay, nay, Octavia; not only that—
That were excusable, that and thousands more
Of semblable import—but he hath waged
New wars 'gainst Pompey; made his will, and read it
To public ear; 5
Spoke scantly of me: when perforce he could not
But pay me terms of honor, cold and sickly
He vented them, most narrow measure lent me;
When the best hint was given him, he not took't,
Or did it from his teeth.
Octa. O, my good lord, 10
Believe not all; or if you must believe,
Stomach not all. A more unhappy lady,
If this division chance, ne'er stood between,
Praying for both parts.
The good gods will mock me presently 15
When I shall pray "O, bless my lord and husband!"
Undo that prayer by crying out as loud
"O, bless my brother!" Husband win, win brother,
Prays, and destroys the prayer; no midway
'Twixt these extremes at all.

41. **proper:** fine; excellent
44. **no . . . thing:** nothing much
46. **defend:** forbid
3. **semblable:** similar
8. **vented:** uttered
9. **hint:** opportunity
9–10. **he . . . teeth:** he neglected it or took it reluctantly.
12. **Stomach:** resent
15. **presently:** at once

Ant. Gentle Octavia, 20
Let your best love draw to that point which seeks
Best to preserve it. If I lose mine honor,
I lose myself. Better I were not yours
Than yours so branchless. But, as you requested,
Yourself shall go between's. The meantime, lady,
I'll raise the preparation of a war 26
Shall stain your brother. Make your soonest haste;
So your desires are yours.
Octa. Thanks to my lord.
The Jove of power make me most weak, most weak,
Your reconciler! Wars 'twixt you twain would be
As if the world should cleave, and that slain men
Should solder up the rift. 32
Ant. When it appears to you where this begins,
Turn your displeasure that way, for our faults
Can never be so equal that your love 35
Can equally move with them. Provide your going;
Choose your own company, and command what cost
Your heart has mind to.
Exeunt.

[Scene V. *Athens. Another room in Antony's house.*]

Enter ENOBARBUS *and* EROS.

Eno. How now, friend Eros?
Eros. There's strange news come, sir.
Eno. What, man?
Eros. Cæsar and Lepidus have made wars upon Pompey. 5
Eno. This is old. What is the success?
Eros. Cæsar, having made use of him in the wars 'gainst Pompey, presently denied him rivality, would not let him partake in the glory of the action; and not resting here, accuses him of letters he had 10 formerly wrote to Pompey; upon his own appeal, seizes him. So the poor third is up till death enlarge his confine.
Eno. Then, world, thou hast a pair of chaps, no more;
And throw between them all the food thou hast, 15
They'll grind the one the other. Where's Antony?
Eros. He's walking in the garden thus, and spurns
The rush that lies before him; cries "Fool Lepidus!"
And threats the throat of that his officer
That murd'red Pompey.
Eno. Our great navy's rigged.
Eros. For Italy and Cæsar. More, Domitius: 21
My lord desires you presently. My news
I might have told hereafter.
Eno. 'Twill be naught;
But let it be. Bring me to Antony.
Eros. Come, sir. 25
Exeunt.

[Scene VI. *Rome. Cæsar's house.*]

Enter AGRIPPA, MÆCENAS, *and* CÆSAR.

Cæs. Contemning Rome, he has done all this and more
In Alexandria. Here's the manner of't:
I' the market place on a tribunal silvered
Cleopatra and himself in chairs of gold
Were publicly enthroned. At the feet sat 5
Cæsarion, whom they call my father's son,
And all the unlawful issue that their lust
Since then hath made between them. Unto her
He gave the stablishment of Egypt; made her
Of lower Syria, Cyprus, Lydia, 10
Absolute queen.
Mæc. This in the public eye?
Cæs. I' the common show place, where they exercise.
His sons he there proclaimed the kings of kings:
Great Media, Parthia, and Armenia
He gave to Alexander; to Ptolemy he assigned 15
Syria, Cilicia, and Phoenicia. She
In the habiliments of the goddess Isis
That day appeared; and oft before gave audience,
As 'tis reported, so.
Mæc. Let Rome be thus informed.
Agr. Who, queasy with his insolence 20
Already, will their good thoughts call from him.
Cæs. The people know it, and have now received
His accusations.
Agr. Who does he accuse?
Cæs. Cæsar; and that, having in Sicily
Sextus Pompeius spoiled, we had not rated him 25
His part o' the isle. Then does he say he lent me
Some shipping unrestored. Lastly, he frets

24. branchless: stripped of branches; unadorned (perhaps referring to "branch embroidery," patterns of foliage and branches used on garments)
28. So: i.e., by thus making haste; otherwise you may be too late.
33. where . . . begins: the origin of this rift
6. success: outcome
8. rivality: partnership
11. appeal: accusation
12. up: in custody
14. chaps: jaws
17. spurns: kicks
19. that . . . officer: that officer of his own
23–24. 'Twill . . . be: the expedition will come to nothing; but never mind.
3. tribunal: platform
6. Cæsarion: son of Cleopatra and Julius Cæsar. Octavius was Cæsar's adopted son.
9. stablishment: government
25. spoiled: looted; **rated:** allotted

That Lepidus of the triumvirate
Should be deposed; and, being, that we detain
All his revenue.

Agr. Sir, this should be answered. 30

Cæs. 'Tis done already, and the messenger gone.
I have told him Lepidus was grown too cruel,
That he his high authority abused
And did deserve his change. For what I have conquered,
I grant him part; but then in his Armenia, 35
And other of his conquered kingdoms, I
Demand the like.

Mæc. He'll never yield to that.

Cæs. Nor must not then be yielded to in this.

Enter OCTAVIA *with her* TRAIN.

Octa. Hail, Cæsar, and my lord! hail, most dear Cæsar!

Cæs. That ever I should call thee castaway! 40

Octa. You have not called me so, nor have you cause.

Cæs. Why have you stol'n upon us thus? You come not
Like Cæsar's sister. The wife of Antony
Should have an army for an usher, and
The neighs of horse to tell of her approach 45
Long ere she did appear. The trees by the way
Should have borne men, and expectation fainted,
Longing for what it had not. Nay, the dust
Should have ascended to the roof of heaven,
Raised by your populous troops. But you are come
A market-maid to Rome, and have prevented 51
The ostentation of our love, which, left unshown,
Is often left unloved. We should have met you
By sea and land, supplying every stage
With an augmented greeting.

Octa. Good my lord, 55
To come thus was I not constrained, but did it
On my free will. My lord, Mark Antony,
Hearing that you prepared for war, acquainted
My grieved ear withal; whereon I begged
His pardon for return.

Cæs. Which soon he granted, 60
Being an abstract 'tween his lust and him.

Octa. Do not say so, my lord.

Cæs. I have eyes upon him,
And his affairs come to me on the wind.
Where is he now?

Octa. My lord, in Athens.

Cæs. No, my most wronged sister. Cleopatra 65
Hath nodded him to her. He hath given his empire
Up to a whore, who now are levying
The kings o' the earth for war. He hath assembled
Bocchus, the king of Libya; Archelaus,
Of Cappadocia; Philadelphos, king 70
Of Paphlagonia; the Thracian king, Adallas;
King Malchus of Arabia; King of Pont;
Herod of Jewry; Mithridates, king
Of Comagene; Polemon and Amyntas,
The kings of Mede and Lycaonia, with a 75
More larger list of scepters.

Octa. Ay me most wretched,
That have my heart parted betwixt two friends
That do afflict each other!

Cæs. Welcome hither.
Your letters did withhold our breaking forth,
Till we perceived both how you were wronged 80
And we in negligent anger. Cheer your heart!
Be you not troubled with the time, which drives
O'er your content these strong necessities;
But let determined things to destiny
Hold unbewailed their way. Welcome to Rome, 85
Nothing more dear to me! You are abused
Beyond the mark of thought; and the high gods,
To do you justice, make them ministers
Of us and those that love you. Best of comfort,
And ever welcome to us!

Agr. Welcome, lady. 90

Mæc. Welcome, dear madam.
Each heart in Rome does love and pity you.
Only the adulterous Antony, most large
In his abominations, turns you off
And gives his potent regiment to a trull 95
That noises it against us.

Octa. Is it so, sir?

Cæs. Most certain. Sister, welcome. Pray you
Be ever known to patience. My dear'st sister!

Exeunt.

[Scene VII. *Near Actium. Antony's camp.*]

Enter CLEOPATRA *and* ENOBARBUS.

Cleo. I will be even with thee, doubt it not.

Eno. But why, why, why?

Cleo. Thou hast forspoke my being in these wars,
And sayst it is not fit.

Eno. Well, is it, is it?

53. unloved: unfelt; **should:** would
61. abstract: separation. Octavia herself is probably the **abstract.**
67. who: Antony and Cleopatra together

81. in . . . danger: endangered by negligence
83. content: happiness
84. determined . . . destiny: predetermined things
87. mark: bound; limit
88. make . . . ministers: create their own agents of punishment
93. large: free and open
96. noises it: causes disturbances
3. forspoke: criticized

Cleo. If not, denounced against us, why should not we 5
Be there in person?

Eno. [*Aside*] Well, I could reply:
If we should serve with horse and mares together,
The horse were merely lost; the mares would bear
A soldier and his horse.

Cleo. What is't you say?

Eno. Your presence needs must puzzle Antony;
Take from his heart, take from his brain, from's time, 11
What should not then be spared. He is already
Traduced for levity, and 'tis said in Rome
That Photinus an eunuch and your maids
Manage this war.

Cleo. Sink Rome, and their tongues rot
That speak against us! A charge we bear i' the war
And, as the president of my kingdom, will 17
Appear there for a man. Speak not against it.
I will not stay behind!

Enter ANTONY *and* CANIDIUS.

Eno. Nay, I have done.
Here comes the Emperor.

Ant. Is it not strange, Canidius, 20
That from Tarentum and Brundusium
He could so quickly cut the Ionian sea
And take in Toryne?—You have heard on't, sweet?

Cleo. Celerity is never more admired
Than by the negligent.

Ant. A good rebuke, 25
Which might have well becomed the best of men
To taunt at slackness. Canidius, we
Will fight with him by sea.

Cleo. By sea? What else?

Can. Why will my lord do so?

Ant. For that he dares us to't.

Eno. So hath my lord dared him to single fight.

Can. Ay, and to wage this battle at Pharsalia, 31
Where Cæsar fought with Pompey. But these offers,
Which serve not for his vantage, he shakes off;
And so should you.

Eno. Your ships are not well manned;
Your mariners are muleteers, reapers, people 35
Engrossed by swift impress. In Cæsar's fleet
Are those that often have 'gainst Pompey fought;
Their ships are yare; yours, heavy. No disgrace
Shall fall you for refusing him at sea,
Being prepared for land.

Ant. By sea, by sea! 40

Eno. Most worthy sir, you therein throw away
The absolute soldiership you have by land;
Distract your army, which doth most consist
Of war-marked footmen; leave unexecuted
Your own renowned knowledge; quite forgo 45
The way which promises assurance, and
Give up yourself merely to chance and hazard
From firm security.

Ant. I'll fight at sea.

Cleo. I have sixty sails, Cæsar none better.

Ant. Our overplus of shipping will we burn, 50
And with the rest full-manned, from the head of Actium
Beat the approaching Cæsar. But if we fail,
We then can do't at land.

Enter a MESSENGER.

Thy business?

Mess. The news is true, my lord. He is descried;
Cæsar has taken Toryne. 55

Ant. Can he be there in person? 'Tis impossible;
Strange that his power should be! Canidius,
Our nineteen legions thou shalt hold by land
And our twelve thousand horse. We'll to our ship.
Away, my Thetis!

Enter a SOLDIER.

How now, worthy soldier? 60

Sold. O noble Emperor, do not fight by sea!
Trust not to rotten planks. Do you misdoubt
This sword and these my wounds? Let the Egyptians
And the Phoenicians go a-ducking. We
Have used to conquer standing on the earth 65
And fighting foot to foot.

Ant. Well, well. Away!

Exeunt Antony, Cleopatra, and Enobarbus.

Sold. By Hercules, I think I am i' the right.

Can. Soldier, thou art; but his whole action grows
Not in the power on't. So our leader's led,
And we are women's men.

Sold. You keep by land 70
The legions and the horse whole, do you not?

Can. Marcus Octavius, Marcus Justeius,
Publicola, and Cælius are for sea;
But we keep whole by land. This speed of Cæsar's
Carries beyond belief.

Sold. While he was yet in Rome, 75

5. denounced . . . us: i.e., since it is declared against myself
8. merely: completely; **lost:** useless
16. charge: responsibility
29. For that: because
36. Engrossed: amassed; **impress:** conscription
38. yare: light and easily maneuvered
42. absolute: perfect
43. Distract: divide
51. head: headland
57. power: army
60. Thetis: a Nereid, whose son was Achilles
68–69. his . . . on't: the planning of his whole campaign disregards the proper use of his strength.
75. Carries: extends

His power went out in such distractions as
Beguiled all spies.
Can. Who's his lieutenant, hear you?
Sold. They say, one Taurus.
Can. Well I know the man.

Enter a MESSENGER.

Mess. The Emperor calls Canidius.
Can. With news the time's with labor and throes forth 80
Each minute some.
Exeunt.

[Scene VIII. *Actium. A plain.*]

Enter CÆSAR, *with his* ARMY, *marching.*

Cæs. Taurus!
Taur. My lord?
Cæs. Strike not by land; keep whole: provoke not battle
Till we have done at sea. Do not exceed
The prescript of this scroll. Our fortune lies 5
Upon this jump.
Exeunt.

[Scene IX. *The same.*]

Enter ANTONY *and* ENOBARBUS.

Ant. Set we our squadrons on yond side o' the hill
In eye of Cæsar's battle; from which place
We may the number of the ships behold,
And so proceed accordingly.
Exeunt.

[Scene X. *The same.*]

CANIDIUS *marcheth with his land army one way over the stage, and* TAURUS, *the Lieutenant of Cæsar, the other way. After their going in is heard the noise of a sea fight.*

Alarum. Enter ENOBARBUS.

Eno. Naught, naught, all naught! I can behold no longer.
The Antoniad, the Egyptian admiral,
With all their sixty, fly and turn the rudder.
To see't mine eyes are blasted.

Enter SCARUS.

Scar. Gods and goddesses,
All the whole synod of them!
Eno. What's thy passion?
Scar. The greater cantle of the world is lost 6
With very ignorance. We have kissed away
Kingdoms and provinces.
Eno. How appears the fight?
Scar. On our side like the tokened pestilence
Where death is sure. Yon ribald-rid nag of Egypt
(Whom leprosy o'ertake!) i' the midst o' the fight,
When vantage like a pair of twins appeared, 12
Both as the same, or rather ours the elder—
The breeze upon her, like a cow in June—
Hoists sails, and flies.
Eno. That I beheld. 15
Mine eyes did sicken at the sight and could not
Endure a further view.
Scar. She once being luffed,
The noble ruin of her magic, Antony,
Claps on his sea-wing, and (like a doting mallard)
Leaving the fight in heighth, flies after her. 20
I never saw an action of such shame.
Experience, manhood, honor, ne'er before
Did violate so itself.
Eno. Alack, alack!

Enter CANIDIUS.

Can. Our fortune on the sea is out of breath
And sinks most lamentably. Had our general 25
Been what he knew himself, it had gone well.
O, he has given example for our flight
Most grossly by his own!
Eno. Ay, are you thereabouts?
Why then, good night indeed.
Can. Toward Peloponnesus are they fled. 30
Scar. 'Tis easy to't; and there I will attend
What further comes.
Can. To Cæsar will I render

76. distractions: scatterings
80. throes forth: painfully produces
5. prescript: direction
6. jump: hazard; dangerous venture
2. battle: forces in battle array

2. admiral: flagship
5. passion: cause of grief
6. cantle: portion
9. tokened: indicated by characteristic "tokens" (spots)
10. ribald-rid: Nicholas Rowe's emendation of the Folio's "ribaudred"; the meaning is probably "lust-driven."
12–13. When . . . elder: when our advantage seemed somewhat better than the enemy's
14. breeze: gadfly
17. luffed: headed into the wind
20. in heighth: at its height
26. Been . . . himself: lived up to his personal standard of courage
28. thereabouts: i.e., thinking of flight
32. render: surrender

My legions and my horse. Six kings already
Show me the way of yielding.
Eno. I'll yet follow
The wounded chance of Antony, though my reason
Sits in the wind against me. 36
[*Exeunt.*]

[Scene XI. *Alexandria. Cleopatra's Palace.*]

Enter ANTONY *with* ATTENDANTS.

Ant. Hark! the land bids me tread no more upon't!
It is ashamed to bear me! Friends, come hither.
I am so lated in the world that I
Have lost my way forever. I have a ship
Laden with gold. Take that; divide it. Fly, 5
And make your peace with Cæsar.
Omnes. Fly? Not we!
Ant. I have fled myself, and have instructed cowards
To run and show their shoulders. Friends, be gone.
I have myself resolved upon a course
Which has no need of you. Be gone. 10
My treasure's in the harbor. Take it! O,
I followed that I blush to look upon.
My very hairs do mutiny; for the white
Reprove the brown for rashness, and they them
For fear and doting. Friends, be gone. You shall 15
Have letters from me to some friends that will
Sweep your way for you. Pray you look not sad
Nor make replies of loathness. Take the hint
Which my despair proclaims. Let that be left
Which leaves itself. To the seaside straightway! 20
I will possess you of that ship and treasure.
Leave me, I pray, a little; pray you now!
Nay, do so; for indeed I have lost command;
Therefore I pray you. I'll see you by-and-by.
Sits down.

Enter CLEOPATRA *led by* CHARMIAN *and* EROS, [IRAS *following*].

Eros. Nay, gentle madam, to him! comfort him!
Iras. Do, most dear Queen. 26
Char. Do! Why, what else?
Cleo. Let me sit down. O Juno!
Ant. No, no, no, no, no!
Eros. See you here, sir? 30
Ant. O fie, fie, fie!
Char. Madam!
Iras. Madam, O good Empress!
Eros. Sir, sir!
Ant. Yes, my lord, yes! He at Philippi kept 35
His sword e'en like a dancer, while I struck
The lean and wrinkled Cassius; and 'twas I
That the mad Brutus ended. He alone
Dealt on lieutenantry and no practice had
In the brave squares of war. Yet now—No matter.
Cleo. Ah, stand by! 41
Eros. The Queen, my lord, the Queen!
Iras. Go to him, madam, speak to him.
He is unqualitied with very shame.
Cleo. Well then, sustain me. O! 45
Eros. Most noble sir, arise. The Queen approaches.
Her head's declined, and death will seize her, but
Your comfort makes the rescue.
Ant. I have offended reputation—
A most unnoble swerving.
Eros. Sir, the Queen. 50
Ant. O, whither hast thou led me, Egypt? See
How I convey my shame out of thine eyes
By looking back what I have left behind
Stroyed in dishonor.
Cleo. O my lord, my lord,
Forgive my fearful sails! I little thought 55
You would have followed.
Ant. Egypt, thou knewst too well
My heart was to thy rudder tied by the strings,
And thou shouldst tow me after. O'er my spirit
Thy full supremacy thou knewst, and that
Thy beck might from the bidding of the gods 60
Command me.
Cleo. O, my pardon!
Ant. Now I must
To the young man send humble treaties, dodge
And palter in the shifts of lowness, who
With half the bulk o' the world played as I pleased,
Making and marring fortunes. You did know 65
How much you were my conqueror, and that
My sword, made weak by my affection, would
Obey it on all cause.
Cleo. Pardon, pardon!
Ant. Fall not a tear, I say. One of them rates
All that is won and lost. Give me a kiss. 70

36. Sits . . . against: strongly opposes
3. lated: belated, like a traveler overtaken by night
13–15. the . . . doting: i.e., mature wisdom criticizes his rashness, while youthful spirit calls him a cowardly dotard.
19. that: i.e., Antony, who has been untrue to his own nature

35–36. kept . . . dancer: i.e., avoided personal action. A sword was an accessory of the Elizabethan gentleman's costume, even at a ball.
38. ended: Antony was not the direct agent of Brutus' death, and it is unlikely that such a meaning is intended; his conduct of the war against Brutus is probably referred to.
39. Dealt . . . lieutenantry: relied on underlings to fight his battles
40. brave: splendid; **squares:** battle formations; squadrons
44. unqualitied: unmanned
54. Stroyed: destroyed
62. treaties: entreaties
63. palter: haggle; **lowness:** base creatures
69. rates: is worth

Even this repays me. We sent our schoolmaster.
Is 'a come back? Love, I am full of lead.
Some wine, within there, and our viands! Fortune knows
We scorn her most when most she offers blows.
Exeunt.

[Scene XII. *Egypt. Cæsar's camp.*]

Enter Cæsar, Agrippa, Dolabella, [Thidias], *with others.*

Cæs. Let him appear that's come from Antony.
Know you him?
Dol. Cæsar, 'tis his schoolmaster.
An argument that he is plucked, when hither
He sends so poor a pinion of his wing,
Which had superfluous kings for messengers 5
Not many moons gone by.

Enter [Euphronius,] Ambassador *from Antony.*

Cæs. Approach and speak.
Amb. Such as I am, I come from Antony.
I was of late as petty to his ends
As is the morn-dew on the myrtle leaf
To his grand sea.
Cæs. Be't so. Declare thine office. 10
Amb. Lord of his fortunes he salutes thee, and
Requires to live in Egypt; which not granted,
He lessens his requests and to thee sues
To let him breathe between the heavens and earth,
A private man in Athens. This for him. 15
Next, Cleopatra does confess thy greatness,
Submits her to thy might, and of thee craves
The circle of the Ptolemies for her heirs,
Now hazarded to thy grace.
Cæs. For Antony,
I have no ears to his request. The Queen 20
Of audience nor desire shall fail, so she
From Egypt drive her all-disgraced friend
Or take his life there. This if she perform,
She shall not sue unheard. So to them both.
Amb. Fortune pursue thee!
Cæs. Bring him through the bands.
[*Exit Ambassador.*]
[*To Thidias*] To try thy eloquence now 'tis time. Dispatch. 26
From Antony win Cleopatra. Promise,
And in our name, what she requires; add more,
From thine invention, offers. Women are not
In their best fortunes strong, but want will perjure
The ne'er-touched Vestal. Try thy cunning, Thidias.
Make thine own edict for thy pains, which we 32
Will answer as a law.
Thid. Cæsar, I go.
Cæs. Observe how Antony becomes his flaw,
And what thou thinkst his very action speaks 35
In every power that moves.
Thid. Cæsar, I shall.
Exeunt.

12. **Requires:** requests
19. **grace:** mercy
25. **Bring:** escort; **bands:** troops
30. **perjure:** make a perjurer of; cause to break the oath
34. **becomes . . . flaw:** endures his disgrace

[Scene XIII. *Alexandria. Cleopatra's Palace.*]

Enter Cleopatra, Enobarbus, Charmian, *and* Iras

Cleo. What shall we do, Enobarbus?
Eno. Think, and die.
Cleo. Is Antony or we in fault for this?
Eno. Antony only, that would make his will
Lord of his reason. What though you fled
From that great face of war whose several ranges
Frighted each other? Why should he follow? 6
The itch of his affection should not then
Have nicked his captainship, at such a point,
When half to half the world opposed, he being
The meered question. 'Twas a shame no less 10
Than was his loss, to course your flying flags
And leave his navy gazing.
Cleo. Prithee peace!

Enter the Ambassador [Euphronius] *with* Antony.

Ant. Is that his answer?
Amb. Ay, my lord.
Ant. The Queen shall then have courtesy, so she
Will yield us up.
Amb. He says so.
Ant. Let her know't. 16
To the boy Cæsar send this grizzled head,
And he will fill thy wishes to the brim
With principalities.
Cleo. That head, my lord?
Ant. To him again! Tell him he wears the rose
Of youth upon him; from which the world should note 21

1. **Think . . . die:** pine away from sheer dejection
3. **will:** lust
8. **nicked:** marred
10. **meered question:** specific subject. The word **meered** has been the source of much speculation; if **meered** is right, the derivation must be from "meer" (boundary). Samuel Johnson suggested "mooted," which could have been misread as "meered."
11. **course:** pursue

Something particular. His coin, ships, legions
May be a coward's, whose ministers would prevail
Under the service of a child as soon
As i' the command of Cæsar. I dare him therefore
To lay his gay comparisons apart 26
And answer me declined, sword against sword,
Ourselves alone. I'll write it. Follow me.
[*Exeunt Antony and Ambassador.*]
Eno. [*Aside*] Yes, like enough high-battled Cæsar will
Unstate his happiness and be staged to the show
Against a sworder! I see men's judgments are 31
A parcel of their fortunes, and things outward
Do draw the inward quality after them
To suffer all alike. That he should dream,
Knowing all measures, the full Cæsar will 35
Answer his emptiness! Cæsar, thou hast subdued
His judgment too.

Enter a SERVANT.

Serv. A messenger from Cæsar.
Cleo. What, no more ceremony? See, my women!
Against the blown rose may they stop their nose
That kneeled unto the buds. Admit him, sir. 40
[*Exit Servant.*]
Eno. [*Aside*] Mine honesty and I begin to square.
The loyalty well held to fools does make
Our faith mere folly. Yet he that can endure
To follow with allegiance a fall'n lord
Does conquer him that did his master conquer 45
And earns a place i' the story.

Enter THIDIAS.

Cleo. Cæsar's will?
Thid. Hear it apart.
Cleo. None but friends. Say boldly.
Thid. So haply are they friends to Antony.
Eno. He needs as many, sir, as Cæsar has,
Or needs not us. If Cæsar please, our master 50
Will leap to be his friend. For us, you know
Whose he is we are, and that is Cæsar's.
Thid. So.
Thus then, thou most renowned: Cæsar entreats
Not to consider in what case thou standst
Further than he is Cæsar.
Cleo. Go on. Right royal! 55
Thid. He knows that you embrace not Antony
As you did love, but as you feared him.
Cleo. O!
Thid. The scars upon your honor, therefore, he
Does pity, as constrained blemishes,
Not as deserved.
Cleo. He is a god, and knows 60
What is most right. Mine honor was not yielded,
But conquered merely.
Eno. [*Aside*] To be sure of that,
I will ask Antony. Sir, sir, thou art so leaky
That we must leave thee to thy sinking, for
Thy dearest quit thee. *Exit.*
Thid. Shall I say to Cæsar 65
What you require of him? For he partly begs
To be desired to give. It much would please him
That of his fortunes you should make a staff
To lean upon. But it would warm his spirits
To hear from me you had left Antony 70
And put yourself under his shroud,
The universal landlord.
Cleo. What's your name?
Thid. My name is Thidias.
Cleo. Most kind messenger,
Say to great Cæsar this: in deputation
I kiss his conqu'ring hand. Tell him I am prompt
To lay my crown at's feet, and there to kneel. 76
Tell him, from his all-obeying breath I hear
The doom of Egypt.
Thid. 'Tis your noblest course.
Wisdom and fortune combating together,
If that the former dare but what it can, 80
No chance may shake it. Give me grace to lay
My duty on your hand.
Cleo. Your Cæsar's father oft,
When he hath mused of taking kingdoms in,
Bestowed his lips on that unworthy place
As it rained kisses.

Enter ANTONY *and* ENOBARBUS.

Ant. Favors, by Jove that thunders!
What art thou, fellow?

22. particular: singular; remarkable
26. gay: splendid; **comparisons:** marks of superiority; i.e., trappings that surpass Antony's own. A combination of the meanings of **comparisons** and "caparisons" may be intended.
29. high-battled: equipped with great armies
30. Unstate . . . happiness: renounce his advantage
31. sworder: professional swordsman. Fencing exhibitions were among the public entertainments of the Elizabethan period.
32. A . . . of: consistent with
35. Knowing . . . measures: knowing the value of things
36. Answer: accept the challenge of
39. blown: decaying
41. honesty: honor; **square:** quarrel
50. Or . . . us: Enobarbus is adept at equivocal speech; without denying allegiance to Antony, he suggests a willingness to desert him for Cæsar.
54-55. Not . . . Cæsar: i.e., have no fear of your fate, since Cæsar will decide it.
59. constrained: involuntary
71. shroud: shelter
72. universal landlord: world's master
77. breath: voice; utterance
79-81. Wisdom . . . it: trust to discretion for your safety; submission to Cæsar is your safest course.
81. grace: favor
82. duty: i.e., a respectful kiss
85. As: as if

Thid. One that but performs 86
The bidding of the fullest man, and worthiest
To have command obeyed.
Eno. [*Aside*] You will be whipped.
Ant. Approach there!—Ah, you kite!—Now, gods and devils!
Authority melts from me. Of late, when I cried "Ho!" 90
Like boys unto a muss, kings would start forth
And cry "Your will?" Have you no ears? I am
Antony yet.

Enter SERVANTS.

Take hence this Jack and whip him.
Eno. [*Aside*] 'Tis better playing with a lion's whelp
Than with an old one dying.
Ant. Moon and stars! 95
Whip him. Were't twenty of the greatest tributaries
That do acknowledge Cæsar, should I find them
So saucy with the hand of she here—what's her name
Since she was Cleopatra? Whip him, fellows,
Till like a boy you see him cringe his face 100
And whine aloud for mercy. Take him hence.
Thid. Mark Antony—
Ant. Tug him away. Being whipped,
Bring him again. This Jack of Cæsar's shall
Bear us an errand to him.
Exeunt [*Servants*] *with Thidias.*
You were half blasted ere I knew you. Ha! 105
Have I my pillow left unpressed in Rome,
Forborne the getting of a lawful race,
And by a gem of women, to be abused
By one that looks on feeders?
Cleo. Good my lord—
Ant. You have been a boggler ever. 110
But when we in our viciousness grow hard
(O misery on't!) the wise gods seel our eyes,
In our own filth drop our clear judgments, make us
Adore our errors, laugh at's while we strut
To our confusion.
Cleo. O, is't come to this? 115
Ant. I found you as a morsel cold upon
Dead Cæsar's trencher. Nay, you were a fragment
Of Gnæus Pompey's, besides what hotter hours,
Unregist'red in vulgar fame, you have
Luxuriously picked out: for I am sure, 120
Though you can guess what temperance should be,
You know not what it is.
Cleo. Wherefore is this?
Ant. To let a fellow that will take rewards,
And say "God quit you!" be familiar with
My playfellow, your hand, this kingly seal 125
And plighter of high hearts! O that I were
Upon the hill of Bashan to outroar
The horned herd! for I have savage cause,
And to proclaim it civilly were like
A haltered neck which does the hangman thank
For being yare about him.

Enter a SERVANT *with* THIDIAS.

Is he whipped? 131
Serv. Soundly, my lord.
Ant. Cried he? and begged 'a pardon?
Serv. He did ask favor.
Ant. If that thy father live, let him repent
Thou wast not made his daughter; and be thou sorry
To follow Cæsar in his triumph, since 136
Thou hast been whipped for following him. Henceforth
The white hand of a lady fever thee!
Shake thou to look on't! Get thee back to Cæsar;
Tell him thy entertainment. Look thou say 140
He makes me angry with him; for he seems
Proud and disdainful, harping on what I am,
Not what he knew I was. He makes me angry;
And at this time most easy 'tis to do't,
When my good stars that were my former guides
Have empty left their orbs and shot their fires 146
Into the abysm of hell. If he mislike
My speech and what is done, tell him he has
Hipparchus, my enfranched bondman, whom
He may at pleasure whip or hang or torture, 150
As he shall like, to quit me. Urge it thou.
Hence with thy stripes, be gone! *Exit Thidias.*
Cleo. Have you done yet?
Ant. Alack, our terrene moon
Is now eclipsed, and it portends alone
The fall of Antony!

89. **kite:** wanton
91. **muss:** a game involving the scattering of objects to be scrambled for
93. **Jack:** impudent fellow; rascal
94. **a . . . whelp:** i.e., Octavius Cæsar
99. **was:** ceased to be
104. **errand:** message
105. **blasted:** blighted
109. **feeders:** menials; hangers-on
110. **boggler:** dissembler
112. **seel:** sew up, from the French *cil* ("eyelash"). The eyelids of hawks were sewed up in order to train them to wear a hood.
115. **confusion:** destruction
119. **Unregist'red . . . fame:** not entered in the common report
120. **Luxuriously:** lustfully
124. **quit:** repay
126. **high:** noble
127. **the . . . Bashan:** cf. Psalms 68:15 and 22:12–13.
128. **horned herd:** i.e., common run of cuckolds
131. **yare:** deft
132. **'a:** he
140. **entertainment:** reception
146. **orbs:** spheres
149. **enfranched:** freed
153. **our . . . moon:** Cleopatra, incarnation of Isis, the moon-goddess

Cleo. I must stay his time. 155
Ant. To flatter Cæsar, would you mingle eyes
With one that ties his points?
Cleo. Not know me yet?
Ant. Cold-hearted toward me?
Cleo. Ah, dear, if I be so,
From my cold heart let heaven engender hail,
And poison it in the source, and the first stone 160
Drop in my neck; as it determines, so
Dissolve my life! The next Cæsarion smite!
Till by degrees the memory of my womb,
Together with my brave Egyptians all,
By the discandying of this pelleted storm, 165
Lie graveless, till the flies and gnats of Nile
Have buried them for prey!
Ant. I am satisfied.
Cæsar sits down in Alexandria, where
I will oppose his fate. Our force by land
Hath nobly held; our severed navy too 170
Have knit again, and fleet, threat'ning most sea-like.
Where hast thou been, my heart? Dost thou hear, lady?
If from the field I shall return once more
To kiss these lips, I will appear in blood.
I and my sword will earn our chronicle. 175
There's hope in't yet.
Cleo. That's my brave lord!
Ant. I will be treble-sinewed, hearted, breathed,
And fight maliciously. For when mine hours
Were nice and lucky, men did ransom lives 180
Of me for jests; but now I'll set my teeth
And send to darkness all that stop me. Come,
Let's have one other gaudy night. Call to me
All my sad captains; fill our bowls once more. 184
Let's mock the midnight bell.
Cleo. It is my birthday.
I had thought t' have held it poor; but since my lord
Is Antony again, I will be Cleopatra.
Ant. We will yet do well.
Cleo. Call all his noble captains to my lord.
Ant. Do so, we'll speak to them; and tonight I'll force 190
The wine peep through their scars. Come on, my queen,
There's sap in't yet! The next time I do fight,
I'll make Death love me; for I will contend
Even with his pestilent scythe.
Exeunt [*all but Enobarbus*].
Eno. Now he'll outstare the lightning. To be furious 195
Is to be frighted out of fear, and in that mood
The dove will peck the estridge. I see still
A diminution in our captain's brain
Restores his heart. When valor preys on reason,
It eats the sword it fights with. I will seek 200
Some way to leave him.
Exit.

155. **stay . . . time:** wait for him to calm down
157. **points:** laces that fastened his clothes together
161. **determines:** terminates
165. **discandying:** melting
169. **fate:** victorious destiny
171. **fleet:** float
179. **maliciously:** violently
179–80. **when . . . lucky:** i.e., when I was master of my fate. Among the many senses in which **nice** was used are "dainty," "fastidious," and "finicky"—all implying freedom to please oneself.
183. **gaudy:** festive
197. **estridge:** this word can mean either "ostrich" or "goshawk"; it is uncertain which meaning Shakespeare intended.

[ACT IV]

[Scene I. *Alexandria. Cæsar's camp.*]

Enter CÆSAR, AGRIPPA, *and* MÆCENAS, *with his* ARMY; CÆSAR *reading a letter.*

Cæs. He calls me boy, and chides as he had power
To beat me out of Egypt. My messenger
He hath whipped with rods; dares me to personal combat,
Cæsar to Antony. Let the old ruffian know
I have many other ways to die, meantime 5
Laugh at his challenge.
Mæc. Cæsar must think,
When one so great begins to rage, he's hunted
Even to falling. Give him no breath, but now
Make boot of his distraction. Never anger
Made good guard for itself.

8. **breath:** breathing space
9. **boot:** profit

Cæs. Let our best heads 10
Know that tomorrow the last of many battles
We mean to fight. Within our files there are,
Of those that served Mark Antony but late,
Enough to fetch him in. See it done;
And feast the army. We have store to do't, 15
And they have earned the waste. Poor Antony!

Exeunt.

[Scene II. *Alexandria. Cleopatra's Palace.*]

Enter ANTONY, CLEOPATRA, ENOBARBUS, CHARMIAN, IRAS, ALEXAS, *with others.*

Ant. He will not fight with me, Domitius?
Eno. No.
Ant. Why should he not?
Eno. He thinks, being twenty times of better fortune,
He is twenty men to one.
Ant. Tomorrow, soldier,
By sea and land I'll fight. Or I will live, 5
Or bathe my dying honor in the blood
Shall make it live again. Woo't thou fight well?
Eno. I'll strike, and cry "Take all!"
Ant. Well said. Come on.
Call forth my household servants. Let's tonight
Be bounteous at our meal.

Enter THREE OR FOUR SERVITORS.

Give me thy hand, 10
Thou hast been rightly honest. So hast thou;
And thou, and thou, and thou. You have served me well,
And kings have been your fellows.
Cleo. [*Aside to Enobarbus*] What means this?
Eno. [*Aside to Cleopatra*] 'Tis one of those odd tricks which sorrow shoots
Out of the mind.
Ant. And thou art honest too. 15
I wish I could be made so many men,
And all of you clapped up together in
An Antony, that I might do you service
So good as you have done.
Omnes. The gods forbid!
Ant. Well, my good fellows, wait on me tonight.
Scant not my cups, and make as much of me 21
As when mine empire was your fellow too
And suffered my command.
Cleo. [*Aside to Enobarbus*] What does he mean?
Eno. [*Aside to Cleopatra*] To make his followers weep.
Ant. Tend me tonight.
Maybe it is the period of your duty. 25
Haply you shall not see me more; or if,
A mangled shadow. Perchance tomorrow
You'll serve another master. I look on you
As one that takes his leave. Mine honest friends,
I turn you not away; but, like a master 30
Married to your good service, stay till death.
Tend me tonight two hours, I ask no more,
And the gods yield you for't!
Eno. What mean you, sir,
To give them this discomfort? Look, they weep,
And I, an ass, am onion-eyed. For shame! 35
Transform us not to women.
Ant. Ho, ho, ho!
Now the witch take me if I meant it thus!
Grace grow where those drops fall! My hearty friends,
You take me in too dolorous a sense;
For I spake to you for your comfort, did desire you
To burn this night with torches. Know, my hearts,
I hope well of tomorrow, and will lead you 42
Where rather I'll expect victorious life
Than death and honor. Let's to supper, come,
And drown consideration.

Exeunt.

[Scene III. *Alexandria. Before Cleopatra's Palace.*]

Enter a COMPANY OF SOLDIERS.

1. Sold. Brother, good night. Tomorrow is the day.
2. Sold. It will determine one way. Fare you well.
Heard you of nothing strange about the streets?
1. Sold. Nothing. What news?
2. Sold. Belike 'tis but a rumor. Good night to you. 5
1. Sold. Well, sir, good night.

They meet other soldiers.

2. Sold. Soldiers, have careful watch.
3. Sold. And you. Good night, good night.

They place themselves in every corner of the stage.

2. Sold. Here we. And if tomorrow
Our navy thrive, I have an absolute hope
Our landmen will stand up.

7. Woo't: wilt
8. Take all: "Winner take all."
11. honest: faithful

25. period: end
33. yield: reward
45. consideration: contemplation
5. Belike: most likely

1. Sold. 'Tis a brave army, 10
And full of purpose.

Music of the hautboys is under the stage.

2. Sold. Peace! What noise?
1. Sold. List, list!
2. Sold. Hark!
1. Sold. Music i' the air.
3. Sold. Under the earth.
4. Sold. It signs well, does it not?
3. Sold. No.
1. Sold. Peace, I say!
What should this mean?
2. Sold. 'Tis the god Hercules, whom Antony loved, 15
Now leaves him.
1. Sold. Walk. Let's see if other watchmen
Do hear what we do.
2. Sold. How now, masters?

Speak together.

Omnes. How now?
How now? Do you hear this?
1. Sold. Ay. Is't not strange?
3. Sold. Do you hear, masters? Do you hear?
1. Sold. Follow the noise so far as we have quarter. 20
Let's see how it will give off.
Omnes. Content. 'Tis strange.

Exeunt.

[Scene IV. *Alexandria. Cleopatra's Palace.*]

Enter ANTONY *and* CLEOPATRA, [CHARMIAN, IRAS,] *with others.*

Ant. Eros! mine armor, Eros!
Cleo. Sleep a little.
Ant. No, my chuck. Eros! Come, mine armor, Eros!

Enter EROS [*with armor*].

Come, good fellow, put mine iron on.
If Fortune be not ours today, it is 5
Because we brave her. Come.
Cleo. Nay, I'll help too.
What's this for?
Ant. Ah, let be, let be! Thou art
The armorer of my heart. False, false! This, this!
Cleo. Sooth, la, I'll help. Thus it must be.

Ant. Well, well,
We shall thrive now. Seest thou, my good fellow?
Go put on thy defenses.
Eros. Briefly, sir. 11
Cleo. Is not this buckled well?
Ant. Rarely, rarely!
He that unbuckles this, till we do please
To daff't for our repose, shall hear a storm.
Thou fumblest, Eros, and my queen's a squire 15
More tight at this than thou. Dispatch. O love,
That thou couldst see my wars today, and knewst
The royal occupation! Thou shouldst see
A workman in't.

Enter an ARMED SOLDIER.

Good morrow to thee! Welcome.
Thou lookst like him that knows a warlike charge.
To business that we love we rise betime 21
And go to't with delight.
Sold. A thousand, sir,
Early though't be, have on their riveted trim
And at the port expect you.

Shout. Trumpets. Flourish. Enter CAPTAINS *and* SOLDIERS.

Capt. The morn is fair. Good morrow, General.
All. Good morrow, General.
Ant. 'Tis well blown, lads.
This morning, like the spirit of a youth 27
That means to be of note, begins betimes.
So, so. Come, give me that! This way. Well said.
Fare thee well, dame, whate'er becomes of me. 30
This is a soldier's kiss. Rebukable
And worthy shameful check it were to stand
On more mechanic compliment. I'll leave thee
Now like a man of steel. You that will fight,
Follow me close; I'll bring you to't. Adieu. 35

Exeunt [Antony, Eros, Captains, and Soldiers].

Char. Please you retire to your chamber?
Cleo. Lead me.
He goes forth gallantly. That he and Cæsar might
Determine this great war in single fight!
Then Antony—but now—Well, on!

Exeunt.

S.D. 11. hautboys: oboes
13. signs: portends
20. noise: music; **so . . . quarter:** to the limits of our appointed station
21. give off: conclude
9. Sooth: truly

11. Briefly: shortly
14. daff't: doff it
16. tight: competent
19. workman: craftsman
20. charge: task
21. betime: early; promptly
23. riveted trim: armor
24. port: gate
29. Well said: well done
32. check: rebuke
32–33. stand . . . compliment: insist upon the sentimental ceremony usual with lovers of lower station

[Scene V. *Alexandria. Antony's camp.*]

Trumpets sound. Enter ANTONY *and* EROS, [*a* SOLDIER *meeting them*].

Sold. The gods make this a happy day to Antony!
Ant. Would thou and those thy scars had once prevailed
To make me fight at land!
Sold. Hadst thou done so,
The kings that have revolted and the soldier
That has this morning left thee would have still 5
Followed thy heels.
Ant. Who's gone this morning?
Sold. Who?
One ever near thee. Call for Enobarbus,
He shall not hear thee, or from Cæsar's camp
Say "I am none of thine."
Ant. What sayest thou?
Sold. Sir,
He is with Cæsar.
Eros. Sir, his chests and treasure 10
He has not with him.
Ant. Is he gone?
Sold. Most certain.
Ant. Go, Eros, send his treasure after. Do it;
Detain no jot, I charge thee. Write to him
(I will subscribe) gentle adieus and greetings.
Say that I wish he never find more cause 15
To change a master. O, my fortunes have
Corrupted honest men! Dispatch. Enobarbus!
Exeunt.

[Scene VI. *Alexandria. Cæsar's camp.*]

Flourish. Enter AGRIPPA, CÆSAR, *with* ENOBARBUS, *and* DOLABELLA.

Cæs. Go forth, Agrippa, and begin the fight.
Our will is Antony be took alive.
Make it so known.
Agr. Cæsar, I shall. [*Exit.*]
Cæs. The time of universal peace is near. 5
Prove this a prosp'rous day, the three-nooked world
Shall bear the olive freely.

Enter a MESSENGER.

Mess. Antony
Is come into the field.

6. **three-nooked:** three-cornered (Europe, Asia, and Africa)

Cæs. Go charge Agrippa
Plant those that have revolted in the van,
That Antony may seem to spend his fury 10
Upon himself. *Exeunt* [*all but Enobarbus*].
Eno. Alexas did revolt and went to Jewry on
Affairs of Antony; there did dissuade
Great Herod to incline himself to Cæsar
And leave his master Antony. For this pains 15
Cæsar hath hanged him. Canidius and the rest
That fell away have entertainment, but
No honorable trust. I have done ill,
Of which I do accuse myself so sorely
That I will joy no more.

Enter a SOLDIER OF CÆSAR'S.

Sold. Enobarbus, Antony 20
Hath after thee sent all thy treasure, with
His bounty overplus. The messenger
Came on my guard and at thy tent is now
Unloading of his mules.
Eno. I give it you!
Sold. Mock not, Enobarbus. 25
I tell you true. Best you safed the bringer
Out of the host. I must attend mine office
Or would have done't myself. Your emperor
Continues still a Jove. *Exit.*
Eno. I am alone the villain of the earth, 30
And feel I am so most. O Antony,
Thou mine of bounty, how wouldst thou have paid
My better service, when my turpitude
Thou dost so crown with gold! This blows my heart.
If swift thought break it not, a swifter mean 35
Shall outstrike thought; but thought will do't, I feel.
I fight against thee? No! I will go seek
Some ditch wherein to die; the foul'st best fits
My latter part of life.
Exit.

[Scene VII. *Field of battle between the camps.*]

Alarum. Drum and Trumpets. Enter AGRIPPA [*and others*].

Agr. Retire. We have engaged ourselves too far.
Cæsar himself has work, and our oppression
Exceeds what we expected. *Exeunt.*

Alarums. Enter ANTONY, *and* SCARUS, *wounded.*

9. **van:** vanguard; front
17. **entertainment:** employment
26. **safed:** provided safe passage for
33. **turpitude:** baseness
34. **blows:** swells
35. **thought:** sorrow
2. **has work:** is hard pressed

Scar. O my brave Emperor, this is fought indeed!
Had we done so at first, we had droven them home
With clouts about their heads.
Ant. Thou bleedst apace.
Scar. I had a wound here that was like a T, 7
But now 'tis made an H. [*Retreat sounded*] *far off.*
Ant. They do retire.
Scar. We'll beat 'em into bench holes. I have yet
Room for six scotches more. 10

Enter EROS.

Eros. They are beaten, sir, and our advantage serves
For a fair victory.
Scar. Let us score their backs
And snatch 'em up, as we take hares, behind!
'Tis sport to maul a runner.
Ant. I will reward thee
Once for thy sprightly comfort, and tenfold 15
For thy good valor. Come thee on!
Scar. I'll halt after.
Exeunt.

[Scene VIII. *Under the walls of Alexandria.*]

Alarum. Enter ANTONY *again in a march;* SCARUS, *with others.*

Ant. We have beat him to his camp. Run one before
And let the Queen know of our gests. Tomorrow,
Before the sun shall see's, we'll spill the blood
That has today escaped. I thank you all;
For doughty-handed are you, and have fought 5
Not as you served the cause, but as't had been
Each man's like mine. You have shown all Hectors.
Enter the city, clip your wives, your friends,
Tell them your feats, whilst they with joyful tears
Wash the congealment from your wounds and kiss
The honored gashes whole.

Enter CLEOPATRA [*attended*].

[*To Scarus*] Give me thy hand.—
To this great fairy I'll commend thy acts, 12
Make her thanks bless thee. [*To Cleopatra*] O thou day o' the world,
Chain mine armed neck! Leap thou, attire and all,
Through proof of harness to my heart, and there
Ride on the pants triumphing!
Cleo. Lord of lords! 16
O infinite virtue, comest thou smiling from
The world's great snare uncaught?
Ant. My nightingale,
We have beat them to their beds. What, girl! though grey
Do something mingle with our younger brown, yet ha' we 20
A brain that nourishes our nerves, and can
Get goal for goal of youth. Behold this man.
Commend unto his lips thy favoring hand.—
Kiss it, my warrior!—He hath fought today
As if a god in hate of mankind had 25
Destroyed in such a shape.
Cleo. I'll give thee, friend,
An armor all of gold. It was a king's.
Ant. He has deserved it, were it carbuncled
Like holy Phœbus' car. Give me thy hand.
Through Alexandria make a jolly march; 30
Bear our hacked targets like the men that owe them.
Had our great palace the capacity
To camp this host, we all would sup together
And drink carouses to the next day's fate,
Which promises royal peril. Trumpeters, 35
With brazen din blast you the city's ear;
Make mingle with our rattling taborins,
That heaven and earth make strike their sounds together,
Applauding our approach.
Exeunt.

[Scene IX. *Cæsar's camp.*]

Enter a SENTRY *and his* COMPANY. ENOBARBUS *follows.*

Sent. If we be not relieved within this hour,
We must return to the court of guard. The night
Is shiny, and they say we shall embattle
By the second hour i' the morn.

6. clouts: bandages
8. H: a pun; "ache" was pronounced like the letter "H."
9. bench holes: privies
10. scotches: slashes
15. sprightly: cheerful
16. halt: limp
2. gests: exploits
7. shown . . . Hectors: appeared as valiant as Hector
8. clip: embrace
12. fairy: enchantress

13. day: i.e., light
15. proof . . . harness: proof (impenetrable) armor
17. virtue: valor
20. something: somewhat
23. Commend: entrust
28. carbuncled: gem-studded
29. Phœbus' car: described as set with gems in Ovid, *Metamorphoses,* bk. ii.
30. jolly: triumphant
31. owe: own
37. taborins: drums
2. court . . . guard: guard room

1. Watch. This last day was
A shrewd one to's.
Eno. O, bear me witness, night— 5
2. Watch. What man is this?
1. Watch. Stand close, and list him.
Eno. Be witness to me, O thou blessed moon,
When men revolted shall upon record
Bear hateful memory, poor Enobarbus did
Before thy face repent!
Sent. Enobarbus?
2. Watch. Peace! 10
Hark further.
Eno. O sovereign mistress of true melancholy,
The poisonous damp of night disponge upon me,
That life, a very rebel to my will,
May hang no longer on me! Throw my heart 15
Against the flint and hardness of my fault,
Which, being dried with grief, will break to powder,
And finish all foul thoughts. O Antony,
Nobler than my revolt is infamous,
Forgive me in thine own particular, 20
But let the world rank me in register
A master-leaver and a fugitive!
O Antony! O Antony! [*Dies.*]
1. Watch. Let's speak
To him.
Sent. Let's hear him, for the things he speaks 25
May concern Cæsar.
2. Watch. Let's do so. But he sleeps.
Sent. Swoons rather; for so bad a prayer as his
Was never yet for sleep.
1. Watch. Go we to him.
2. Watch. Awake, sir, awake! Speak to us!
1. Watch. Hear you, sir?
Sent. The hand of death hath raught him.
Drums afar off.
Hark! The drums
Demurely wake the sleepers. Let us bear him 31
To the court of guard. He is of note. Our hour
Is fully out.
2. Watch. Come on then.
He may recover yet.
Exeunt [*with the body*].

[Scene X. *Between the two camps.*]

Enter ANTONY *and* SCARUS, *with their* ARMY.

Ant. Their preparation is today by sea;
We please them not by land.
Scar. For both, my lord.
Ant. I would they'ld fight i' the fire or i' the air;
We'ld fight there too. But this it is, our foot
Upon the hills adjoining to the city 5
Shall stay with us. Order for sea is given;
They have put forth the haven,
Where their appointment we may best discover
And look on their endeavor.
Exeunt.

[Scene XI. *Between the camps.*]

Enter CÆSAR *and his* ARMY.

Cæs. But being charged, we will be still by land,
Which, as I tak't, we shall; for his best force
Is forth to man his galleys. To the vales,
And hold our best advantage.
Exeunt.

[Scene XII. *Alexandria. A hill overlooking the harbor.*]

Enter ANTONY *and* SCARUS.

Ant. Yet they are not joined. Where yond pine does stand
I shall discover all. I'll bring thee word
Straight how 'tis like to go. *Exit.*
Scar. Swallows have built
In Cleopatra's sails their nests. The augurers
Say they know not, they cannot tell; look grimly 5
And dare not speak their knowledge. Antony
Is valiant, and dejected; and by starts
His fretted fortunes give him hope and fear
Of what he has and has not.
Alarum afar off, as at a sea fight.

Enter ANTONY.

Ant. All is lost!
This foul Egyptian hath betrayed me! 10
My fleet hath yielded to the foe, and yonder
They cast their caps up and carouse together
Like friends long lost. Triple-turned whore! 'tis thou
Hast sold me to this novice, and my heart
Makes only wars on thee. Bid them all fly! 15

5. shrewd: grievous
6. close: concealed
12. melancholy: attributed to the moon's influence
13. disponge: squeeze out
20. in . . . particular: personally
30. raught: grasped (the past participle of "reach")
31. Demurely: gently

4. foot: foot soldiers
1. But . . . charged: unless we are charged
4. hold . . . advantage: take up the best strategic position
1. joined: embattled
3. Straight: directly
8. fretted: checkered

For when I am revenged upon my charm,
I have done all. Bid them all fly; begone!
[*Exit Scarus.*]

O sun, thy uprise shall I see no more.
Fortune and Antony part here; even here
Do we shake hands. All come to this? The hearts
That spanieled me at heels, to whom I gave 21
Their wishes, do discandy, melt their sweets
On blossoming Cæsar; and this pine is barked,
That overtopped them all. Betrayed I am.
O this false soul of Egypt! this grave charm— 25
Whose eye becked forth my wars and called them home,
Whose bosom was my crownet, my chief end—
Like a right gypsy hath at fast and loose
Beguiled me to the very heart of loss!
What, Eros, Eros!

Enter CLEOPATRA.

Ah, thou spell! Avaunt! 30
Cleo. Why is my lord enraged against his love?
Ant. Vanish, or I shall give thee thy deserving
And blemish Cæsar's triumph. Let him take thee
And hoist thee up to the shouting plebeians.
Follow his chariot, like the greatest spot 35
Of all thy sex. Most monsterlike be shown
For poor'st diminutives, for doits, and let
Patient Octavia plough thy visage up
With her prepared nails. *Exit Cleopatra.*
'Tis well th'art gone,
If it be well to live; but better 'twere 40
Thou fellst into my fury, for one death
Might have prevented many. Eros, ho!
The shirt of Nessus is upon me. Teach me,
Alcides, thou mine ancestor, thy rage.
Let me lodge Lichas on the horns o' the moon, 45
And with those hands that grasped the heaviest club
Subdue my worthiest self. The witch shall die.

16. **charm:** charmer
22. **discandy:** dissolve
25. **grave charm:** deadly witch
28. **right:** veritable; **fast . . . loose:** a mountebank's trick with a knot that appeared securely tied but loosened at a touch
29. **Beguiled:** cheated; **very . . . loss:** absolute ruin
33. **blemish . . . triumph:** i.e., by killing Cleopatra, who would otherwise be its finest ornament
35. **spot:** disgrace
36. **monsterlike:** like a freak
37. **diminutives:** pittances; **doits:** copper coins of slight value
41–42. **one . . . many:** her present death would save her from the many deaths of shame and humiliation she might expect as a captive.
43. **Nessus:** a centaur who revenged himself upon Hercules by sending him a shirt impregnated with poison, which consumed Hercules when he donned it. The shirt was delivered by Lichas, whom Hercules in his agony threw into the sea.
44. **Alcides:** a Greek name for Hercules (descendant of Alcæus)

To the young Roman boy she hath sold me, and I fall
Under this plot. She dies for't. Eros, ho!
Exit.

[Scene XIII. *Alexandria. Cleopatra's Palace.*]

Enter CLEOPATRA, CHARMIAN, IRAS, MARDIAN.

Cleo. Help me, my women! O, he is more mad
Than Telamon for his shield. The boar of Thessaly
Was never so embossed.
Char. To the monument!
There lock yourself, and send him word you are dead.
The soul and body rive not more in parting 5
Than greatness going off.
Cleo. To the monument!
Mardian, go tell him I have slain myself.
Say that the last I spoke was "Antony"
And word it, prithee, piteously. Hence, Mardian,
And bring me how he takes my death. To the monument! 10
Exeunt.

[Scene XIV. *Another room in Cleopatra's Palace.*]

Enter ANTONY *and* EROS.

Ant. Eros, thou yet beholdst me?
Eros. Ah, noble lord.
Ant. Sometime we see a cloud that's dragonish;
A vapor sometime like a bear or lion,
A towered citadel, a pendent rock,
A forked mountain, or blue promontory 5
With trees upon't that nod unto the world
And mock our eyes with air. Thou hast seen these signs;
They are black Vesper's pageants.
Eros. Ay, my lord.
Ant. That which is now a horse, even with a thought
The rack dislimns, and makes it indistinct 10
As water is in water.

2. **Telamon:** Ajax, son of Telamon, who coveted the armor of Achilles and went mad when it was awarded to Ulysses; **boar . . . Thessaly:** a ferocious beast loosed on Calydon as Diana's revenge for the neglect of her worship
3. **embossed:** driven to extremity, like a hunted animal; desperately enraged; **monument:** Cleopatra's tomb
5–6. **The . . . off:** the rupture between soul and body at death is less violent than the inner disturbance of a man who sees his greatness departing.
8. **Vesper's:** night's; **pageants:** i.e., spectacles that herald his arrival
10. **rack:** cloud drift; **dislimns:** effaces

Eros. It does, my lord.
Ant. My good knave Eros, now thy captain is
Even such a body. Here I am Antony;
Yet cannot hold this visible shape, my knave.
I made these wars for Egypt; and the Queen— 15
Whose heart I thought I had, for she had mine,
Which, whilst it was mine, had annexed unto't
A million mo, now lost—she, Eros, has
Packed cards with Cæsar and false-played my glory
Unto an enemy's triumph. 20
Nay, weep not, gentle Eros. There is left us
Ourselves to end ourselves.

Enter MARDIAN.

O, thy vile lady!
She has robbed me of my sword.
Mar. No, Antony.
My mistress loved thee and her fortunes mingled
With thine entirely.
Ant. Hence, saucy eunuch! Peace!
She hath betrayed me and shall die the death. 26
Mar. Death of one person can be paid but once,
And that she has discharged. What thou wouldst do
Is done unto thy hand. The last she spake
Was, "Antony! most noble Antony!" 30
Then in the midst a tearing groan did break
The name of Antony; it was divided
Between her heart and lips. She rend'red life,
Thy name so buried in her.
Ant. Dead, then?
Mar. Dead.
Ant. Unarm, Eros. The long day's task is done,
And we must sleep. [*To Mardian*] That thou departst hence safe 36
Does pay thy labor richly. Go. *Exit Mardian.*
Off, pluck off!
The sevenfold shield of Ajax cannot keep
The battery from my heart. O, cleave, my sides!
Heart, once be stronger than thy continent, 40
Crack thy frail case! Apace, Eros, apace.—
No more a soldier. Bruised pieces, go;
You have been nobly borne.—From me awhile.
Exit Eros.
I will o'ertake thee, Cleopatra, and
Weep for my pardon. So it must be, for now 45
All length is torture. Since the torch is out,
Lie down, and stray no farther. Now all labor
Mars what it does; yea, very force entangles
Itself with strength. Seal then, and all is done.
Eros!—I come, my queen.—Eros!—Stay for me.
Where souls do couch on flowers, we'll hand in hand 51
And with our sprightly port make the ghosts gaze.
Dido and her Æneas shall want troops,
And all the haunt be ours.—Come, Eros, Eros!

Enter EROS.

Eros. What would my lord?
Ant. Since Cleopatra died
I have lived in such dishonor that the gods 56
Detest my baseness. I, that with my sword
Quartered the world and o'er green Neptune's back
With ships made cities, condemn myself to lack
The courage of a woman—less noble mind 60
Than she which by her death our Cæsar tells
"I am conqueror of myself." Thou art sworn, Eros,
That, when the exigent should come (which now
Is come indeed) when I should see behind me
The inevitable prosecution of 65
Disgrace and horror, that, on my command,
Thou then wouldst kill me. Do't; the time is come.
Thou strikest not me; 'tis Cæsar thou defeatst.
Put color in thy cheek.
Eros. The gods withhold me!
Shall I do that which all the Parthian darts, 70
Though enemy, lost aim and could not?
Ant. Eros,
Wouldst thou be windowed in great Rome and see
Thy master thus with pleached arms, bending down
His corrigible neck, his face subdued
To penetrative shame, whilst the wheeled seat 75
Of fortunate Cæsar, drawn before him, branded
His baseness that ensued?
Eros. I would not see't.
Ant. Come then; for with a wound I must be cured.
Draw that thy honest sword, which thou hast worn
Most useful for thy country.
Eros. O sir, pardon me! 80
Ant. When I did make thee free, sworest thou not then

18. mo: more
19. Packed cards: joined in stacking the deck
20. triumph: pun on the trump card in the game of "triumph"
23. robbed . . . sword: destroyed my career
33. rend'red: surrendered
38. sevenfold shield: a shield made of seven folds of oxhide
40. continent: container
46. length: lingering; **the torch:** Cleopatra, light of his life
48–49. very . . . strength: sheer violence of effort defeats the effect of strength.
49. Seal: i.e., finish the job. The **seal** is the finishing touch on a document.
51. Where . . . flowers: in the Elysian Fields; **hand . . . hand:** walk hand in hand
52. port: behavior
53. want troops: lack visitors (followers)
54. haunt: resort
63. exigent: exigency; crisis
65. inevitable prosecution: inescapable pursuit
73. pleached: crossed and tied in the attitude of a captive
74. corrigible: submissive to correction
74–75. subdued . . . shame: conquered by acute shame

To do this when I bade thee? Do it at once,
Or thy precedent services are all
But accidents unpurposed. Draw, and come.

Eros. Turn from me then that noble countenance
Wherein the worship of the whole world lies. 86

Ant. Lo thee! [*Turns from him.*]

Eros. My sword is drawn.

Ant. Then let it do at once
The thing why thou hast drawn it.

Eros. My dear master,
My captain, and my emperor, let me say, 90
Before I strike this bloody stroke, farewell.

Ant. 'Tis said, man; and farewell.

Eros. Farewell, great chief. Shall I strike now?

Ant. Now, Eros.

Eros. Why, there then! Thus I do escape the sorrow
Of Antony's death. *Kills himself.*

Ant. Thrice nobler than myself! 95
Thou teachest me, O valiant Eros, what
I should, and thou couldst not. My queen and Eros
Have by their brave instruction got upon me
A nobleness in record. But I will be
A bridegroom in my death and run into't 100
As to a lover's bed. Come then; and, Eros,
Thy master dies thy scholar. To do thus
[*Falls on his sword.*]
I learned of thee. How? not dead? not dead?—
The guard, ho! O, dispatch me!

Enter [DERCETAS *and*] *a* GUARD.

1. Guard. What's the noise?

Ant. I have done my work ill, friends. O, make an end 105
Of what I have begun.

2. Guard. The star is fall'n.

1. Guard. And time is at his period.

All. Alas, and woe!

Ant. Let him that loves me strike me dead.

1. Guard. Not I.

2. Guard. Nor I. 109

3. Guard. Nor anyone. *Exeunt* [*Guard*].

Der. Thy death and fortunes bid thy followers fly.
This sword but shown to Cæsar, with this tidings,
Shall enter me with him.

Enter DIOMEDES.

Dio. Where's Antony?

Der. There, Diomed, there.

Dio. Lives he?
Wilt thou not answer, man? [*Exit Dercetas.*]

Ant. Art thou there, Diomed? Draw thy sword and give me 116
Sufficing strokes for death.

Dio. Most absolute lord,
My mistress Cleopatra sent me to thee.

Ant. When did she send thee?

Dio. Now, my lord.

Ant. Where is she?

Dio. Locked in her monument. She had a prophesying fear 120
Of what hath come to pass; for when she saw
(Which never shall be found) you did suspect
She had disposed with Cæsar, and that your rage
Would not be purged, she sent you word she was dead;
But, fearing since how it might work, hath sent
Me to proclaim the truth; and I am come, 126
I dread, too late.

Ant. Too late, good Diomed. Call my guard, I prithee.

Dio. What ho! the Emperor's guard! the guard, what ho!
Come, your lord calls! 130

Enter FOUR OR FIVE OF THE GUARD OF ANTONY.

Ant. Bear me, good friends, where Cleopatra bides.
'Tis the last service that I shall command you.

1. Guard. Woe, woe are we, sir, you may not live to wear
All your true followers out.

All. Most heavy day!

Ant. Nay, good my fellows, do not please sharp fate 135
To grace it with your sorrows. Bid that welcome
Which comes to punish us, and we punish it,
Seeming to bear it lightly. Take me up.
I have led you oft; carry me now, good friends,
And have my thanks for all. 140
Exeunt, bearing Antony.

[Scene XV. *Alexandria. A monument.*]

Enter CLEOPATRA *and her* MAIDS *aloft, with* CHARMIAN *and* IRAS.

Cleo. O Charmian, I will never go from hence.

Char. Be comforted, dear madam.

Cleo. No, I will not.
All strange and terrible events are welcome,
But comforts we despise. Our size of sorrow,

86. **Wherein . . . lies:** which all the world reverences
98 99. **got . . . record:** outrun me in recording their nobility
S.D. 104. **Guard:** body of guards
107. **his period:** its end
113. **enter . . . with:** gain me favor with
122. **found:** adjudged true on examination of the facts
123. **disposed:** composed; compacted
134. **heavy:** sorrowful
136. **To grace:** by honoring

Proportioned to our cause, must be as great 5
As that which makes it.

Enter DIOMEDES [*below*].

How now? Is he dead?

Dio. His death's upon him, but not dead.
Look out o' the other side your monument.
His guard have brought him thither.

Enter, [*below,*] ANTONY *and the* GUARD [*bearing him*].

Cleo. O sun,
Burn the great sphere thou movest in! Darkling stand 10
The varying shore o' the world! O Antony,
Antony, Antony! Help, Charmian; help, Iras; help!
Help, friends below! Let's draw him hither.

Ant. Peace!
Not Cæsar's valor hath o'erthrown Antony,
But Antony's hath triumphed on itself. 15

Cleo. So it should be, that none but Antony
Should conquer Antony; but woe 'tis so!

Ant. I am dying, Egypt, dying; only
I here importune death awhile, until
Of many thousand kisses the poor last 20
I lay upon thy lips.

Cleo. I dare not, dear.
Dear my lord, pardon! I dare not,
Lest I be taken. Not the imperious show
Of the full-fortuned Cæsar ever shall
Be brooched with me! If knife, drugs, serpents have
Edge, sting, or operation, I am safe. 26
Your wife Octavia, with her modest eyes
And still conclusion, shall acquire no honor
Demuring upon me. But come, come, Antony!
Help me, my women. We must draw thee up. 30
Assist, good friends.

Ant. O, quick, or I am gone.

Cleo. Here's sport indeed! How heavy weighs my lord!
Our strength is all gone into heaviness:
That makes the weight. Had I great Juno's power,
The strong-winged Mercury should fetch thee up
And set thee by Jove's side. Yet come a little! 36
Wishers were ever fools. O, come, come, come!

They heave Antony aloft to Cleopatra.

And welcome, welcome! Die where thou hast lived!
Quicken with kissing. Had my lips that power,
Thus would I wear them out.

All. A heavy sight! 40

Ant. I am dying, Egypt, dying.
Give me some wine, and let me speak a little.

Cleo. No, let me speak; and let me rail so high
That the false huswife Fortune break her wheel,
Provoked by my offense.

Ant. One word, sweet queen.
Of Cæsar seek your honor, with your safety. O! 46

Cleo. They do not go together.

Ant. Gentle, hear me.
None about Cæsar trust but Proculeius.

Cleo. My resolution and my hands I'll trust;
None about Cæsar. 50

Ant. The miserable change now at my end
Lament nor sorrow at; but please your thoughts
In feeding them with those my former fortunes,
Wherein I lived the greatest prince o' the world,
The noblest; and do now not basely die, 55
Not cowardly put off my helmet to
My countryman—a Roman by a Roman
Valiantly vanquished. Now my spirit is going.
I can no more.

Cleo. Noblest of men, woo't die?
Hast thou no care of me? Shall I abide 60
In this dull world, which in thy absence is
No better than a sty? O, see, my women,

[*Antony dies.*]

The crown o' the earth doth melt. My lord!
O, withered is the garland of the war,
The soldier's pole is fall'n! Young boys and girls
Are level now with men. The odds is gone, 66
And there is nothing left remarkable
Beneath the visiting moon. [*Swoons.*]

Char. O quietness; lady!

Iras. She's dead too, our sovereign.

Char. Lady!

Iras. Madam!

Char. O madam, madam, madam!

Iras. Royal Egypt!
Empress! 71

Char. Peace, peace, Iras!

Cleo. No more but e'en a woman, and commanded
By such poor passion as the maid that milks
And does the meanest chares. It were for me 75
To throw my scepter at the injurious gods,
To tell them that this world did equal theirs
Till they had stol'n our jewel. All's but naught.
Patience is sottish, and impatience does
Become a dog that's mad. Then is it sin 80

10. Darkling: in darkness
25. brooched: ornamented
28. still conclusion: quiet condemnation
29. Demuring: looking demurely
33. heaviness: sorrow
39. Quicken: revive

43. rail: scold; **high:** loudly
44. huswife: housewife; hussy; **wheel:** secondary meaning, "spinning wheel"
64–65. withered . . . fall'n: victorious wreaths are meaningless, since Antony, who once wore such wreaths, is dead.
66. odds: standard of comparison
68. visiting: paying regular calls according to its phases
74. passion: grief
75. chares: chores
79. sottish: stupid

To rush into the secret house of death
Ere death dare come to us? How do you, women?
What, what! good cheer! Why, how now, Charmian?
My noble girls! Ah, women, women, look! 84
Our lamp is spent, it's out! Good sirs, take heart.
We'll bury him; and then, what's brave, what's noble,
Let's do it after the high Roman fashion
And make death proud to take us. Come, away!
This case of that huge spirit now is cold.
Ah, women, women! Come; we have no friend 90
But resolution and the briefest end.
Exeunt; [*those above*] *bearing off Antony's body.*

[ACT V]

[Scene I. *Alexandria. Cæsar's camp.*]

Enter Cæsar, Agrippa, Dolabella, Mæcenas, [Gallus, Proculeius, *and others*], *his Council of War.*

Cæs. Go to him, Dolabella; bid him yield.
Being so frustrate, tell him, he mocks
The pause that he makes.
Dol. Cæsar, I shall. [*Exit.*]

Enter Dercetas, *with the sword of Antony.*

Cæs. Wherefore is that? And what art thou that darest
Appear thus to us?
Der. I am called Dercetas. 5
Mark Antony I served, who best was worthy
Best to be served. Whilst he stood up and spoke,
He was my master, and I wore my life
To spend upon his haters. If thou please
To take me to thee, as I was to him 10
I'll be to Cæsar; if thou pleasest not,
I yield thee up my life.
Cæs. What is't thou sayst?
Der. I say, O Cæsar, Antony is dead.
Cæs. The breaking of so great a thing should make
A greater crack. The round world 15
Should have shook lions into civil streets
And citizens to their dens. The death of Antony
Is not a single doom; in the name lay
A moiety of the world.
Der. He is dead, Cæsar,
Not by a public minister of justice 20
Nor by a hired knife; but that self hand
Which writ his honor in the acts it did
Hath, with the courage which the heart did lend it,
Splitted the heart. This is his sword.
I robbed his wound of it. Behold it stained 25
With his most noble blood.
Cæs. Look you sad, friends?
The gods rebuke me but it is tidings
To wash the eyes of kings!
Agr. And strange it is
That nature must compel us to lament
Our most persisted deeds.
Mæc. His taints and honors 30
Waged equal with him.
Agr. A rarer spirit never
Did steer humanity; but you gods will give us
Some faults to make us men. Cæsar is touched.
Mæc. When such a spacious mirror's set before him,
He needs must see himself.
Cæs. O Antony, 35
I have followed thee to this! But we do lanch
Diseases in our bodies. I must perforce
Have shown to thee such a declining day
Or look on thine: we could not stall together
In the whole world. But yet let me lament 40
With tears as sovereign as the blood of hearts
That thou, my brother, my competitor
In top of all design, my mate in empire,
Friend and companion in the front of war,
The arm of mine own body, and the heart 45

2–3. **Being . . . makes:** since he is completely checked, his delay in submitting himself is futile.
16. **civil:** civilized; urban
19. **moiety:** half
21. **self:** same
30. **most . . . deeds:** deeds accomplished with the greatest persistence
31. **Waged . . . with:** contended equally in
32. **humanity:** a human being
36. **lanch:** lance
39. **stall:** dwell
41. **sovereign:** masterful; overwhelming
42. **competitor:** partner
43. **In . . . design:** in the highest enterprises

Where mine his thoughts did kindle—that our stars,
Unreconciliable, should divide
Our equalness to this. Hear me, good friends—

Enter an EGYPTIAN.

But I will tell you at some meeter season.
The business of this man looks out of him; 50
We'll hear him what he says. Whence are you?
Egyp. A poor Egyptian yet. The Queen my mistress,
Confined in all she has, her monument,
Of thy intents desires instruction,
That she preparedly may frame herself 55
To the way she's forced to.
Cæs. Bid her have good heart.
She soon shall know of us, by some of ours,
How honorable and how kindly we
Determine for her; for Cæsar cannot live
To be ungentle.
Egyp. So the gods preserve thee! *Exit.*
Cæs. Come hither, Proculeius. Go and say 61
We purpose her no shame. Give her what comforts
The quality of her passion shall require,
Lest, in her greatness, by some mortal stroke
She do defeat us; for her life in Rome 65
Would be eternal in our triumph. Go,
And with your speediest bring us what she says
And how you find of her.
Pro. Cæsar, I shall. *Exit.*
Cæs. Gallus, go you along. [*Exit Gallus.*] Where's Dolabella,
To second Proculeius?
All. Dolabella! 70
Cæs. Let him alone, for I remember now
How he's employed. He shall in time be ready.
Go with me to my tent; where you shall see
How hardly I was drawn into this war,
How calm and gentle I proceeded still 75
In all my writings. Go with me and see
What I can show in this.
Exeunt.

[Scene II. *Alexandria. The monument.*]

Enter CLEOPATRA, CHARMIAN, IRAS, *and* MARDIAN.

Cleo. My desolation does begin to make
A better life. 'Tis paltry to be Cæsar.
Not being Fortune, he's but Fortune's knave,
A minister of her will. And it is great
To do that thing that ends all other deeds, 5
Which shackles accidents and bolts up change,
Which sleeps, and never palates more the dung,
The beggar's nurse and Cæsar's.

Enter PROCULEIUS.

Pro. Cæsar sends greeting to the Queen of Egypt,
And bids thee study on what fair demands 10
Thou meanst to have him grant thee.
Cleo. What's thy name?
Pro. My name is Proculeius.
Cleo. Antony
Did tell me of you, bade me trust you; but
I do not greatly care to be deceived,
That have no use for trusting. If your master 15
Would have a queen his beggar, you must tell him
That majesty, to keep decorum, must
No less beg than a kingdom. If he please
To give me conquered Egypt for my son,
He gives me so much of mine own as I 20
Will kneel to him with thanks.
Pro. Be of good cheer.
Y'are fall'n into a princely hand; fear nothing.
Make your full reference freely to my lord,
Who is so full of grace that it flows over
On all that need. Let me report to him 25
Your sweet dependency, and you shall find
A conqueror that will pray in aid for kindness,
Where he for grace is kneeled to.
Cleo. Pray you tell him
I am his fortune's vassal and I send him
The greatness he has got. I hourly learn 30
A doctrine of obedience, and would gladly
Look him i' the face.
Pro. This I'll report, dear lady.
Have comfort, for I know your plight is pitied
Of him that caused it. 34

[*Enter* GALLUS *and* SOLDIERS.]

Gal. You see how easily she may be surprised.
Guard her till Cæsar come. [*Exit.*]
Iras. Royal Queen!
Char. O Cleopatra! thou art taken, Queen!

46. **Where . . . kindle:** which inspired the feelings of my own heart
47–48. **divide . . . this:** so divide two equals
49. **meeter:** more suitable
59. **live:** Nicholas Rowe; the Folio reads "leave."
63. **passion:** grief
65–66. **her . . . triumph:** i.e., her living presence in Rome at my triumph would be ever remembered.

3. **knave:** menial
6. **accidents:** happenings
7. **palates:** tastes; **dung:** earth
14–15. **I . . . trusting:** I care not whether I am deceived since I have no hope of escaping.
20. **as:** that
23. **Make . . . freely:** surrender yourself completely
26. **sweet dependency:** gentle submission
27. **pray . . . kindness:** beg your assistance in showing him how to be kind. **Pray in aid** is a legal term.
29–30. **send . . . got:** acknowledge him my conqueror
35. **surprised:** captured

Cleo. Quick, quick, good hands! [*Draws a dagger*.]
Pro. Hold, worthy lady, hold!
[*Disarms her*.]
Do not yourself such wrong, who are in this 40
Relieved, but not betrayed.
Cleo. What, of death too,
That rids our dogs of languish?
Pro. Cleopatra,
Do not abuse my master's bounty by
The undoing of yourself. Let the world see
His nobleness well acted, which your death 45
Will never let come forth.
Cleo. Where art thou, death?
Come hither, come! Come, come, and take a queen
Worth many babes and beggars!
Pro. O, temperance, lady!
Cleo. Sir, I will eat no meat; I'll not drink, sir;
If idle talk will once be necessary, 50
I'll not sleep neither. This mortal house I'll ruin,
Do Cæsar what he can. Know, sir, that I
Will not wait pinioned at your master's court
Nor once be chastised with the sober eye
Of dull Octavia. Shall they hoist me up 55
And show me to the shouting varletry
Of censuring Rome? Rather a ditch in Egypt
Be gentle grave unto me! Rather on Nilus' mud
Lay me stark-naked and let the waterflies
Blow me into abhorring! Rather make 60
My country's high pyramides my gibbet
And hang me up in chains!
Pro. You do extend
These thoughts of horror further than you shall
Find cause in Cæsar.

Enter Dolabella.

Dol. Proculeius,
What thou hast done thy master Cæsar knows, 65
And he hath sent me for thee. For the Queen,
I'll take her to my guard.
Pro. So, Dolabella,
It shall content me best. Be gentle to her.
[*To Cleopatra*] To Cæsar I will speak what you shall please,
If you'll employ me to him.
Cleo. Say, I would die. 70
Exeunt Proculeius [*and Soldiers*].
Dol. Most noble Empress, you have heard of me?
Cleo. I cannot tell.
Dol. Assuredly you know me.

Cleo. No matter, sir, what I have heard or known.
You laugh when boys or women tell their dreams;
Is't not your trick?
Dol. I understand not, madam. 75
Cleo. I dreamt there was an Emperor Antony—
O, such another sleep, that I might see
But such another man!
Dol. If it might please ye—
Cleo. His face was as the heav'ns, and therein stuck 79
A sun and moon, which kept their course and lighted
The little O, the earth.
Dol. Most sovereign creature—
Cleo. His legs bestrid the ocean: his reared arm
Crested the world. His voice was propertied
As all the tuned spheres, and that to friends;
But when he meant to quail and shake the orb, 85
He was as rattling thunder. For his bounty,
There was no winter in't; an autumn 'twas
That grew the more by reaping. His delights
Were dolphin-like: they showed his back above
The element they lived in. In his livery 90
Walked crowns and crownets. Realms and islands were
As plates dropped from his pocket.
Dol. Cleopatra—
Cleo. Think you there was or might be such a man
As this I dreamt of?
Dol. Gentle madam, no.
Cleo. You lie, up to the hearing of the gods! 95
But, if there be or ever were one such,
It's past the size of dreaming. Nature wants stuff
To vie strange forms with fancy; yet, t'imagine
An Antony were nature's piece 'gainst fancy,
Condemning shadows quite.
Dol. Hear me, good madam.
Your loss is as yourself, great; and you bear it 101
As answering to the weight. Would I might never
O'ertake pursued success but I do feel,
By the rebound of yours, a grief that smites
My very heart at root.
Cleo. I thank you, sir. 105
Know you what Cæsar means to do with me?

46. come forth: appear
48. temperance: calm yourself
50. If . . . necessary: needless to say
56. varletry: rabble
60. Blow . . . abhorring: swell my body until it becomes an abhorrent thing
66. For: as for

75. trick: habit
82–83. his . . . world: his might dominated the world. The image was probably suggested by a heraldic crest.
83–84. was . . . spheres: was as harmonious as the music of the spheres
85. quail . . . shake: cause to quail and shake; **orb:** earth
88–90. His . . . in: i.e., Antony's nobility was such that he was never subdued by his pleasures; like a dolphin cresting the water he rose above them.
90–91. In . . . crownets: his followers wore crowns and coronets; he mastered kings and peers.
92. plates: silver coins (Spanish *real de plata*)
97. wants: lacks
98. vie . . . fancy: compete with fancy in creating remarkable forms
98–100. t' imagine . . . quite: when we recreate an Antony in our imagination, we have a masterpiece of nature that quite puts to shame the shadowy creations of fancy.
103. but . . . do: if I do not

Dol. I am loath to tell you what I would you knew.
Cleo. Nay, pray you, sir.
Dol. Though he be honorable—
Cleo. He'll lead me, then, in triumph?
Dol. Madam, he will. I know't. *Flourish.*
[*Shout within.*] "Make way there! Cæsar!" 111

Enter PROCULEIUS; CÆSAR [*with*] GALLUS, MÆCENAS, *and others of his* TRAIN, [SELEUCUS *following*].

Cæs. Which is the Queen of Egypt?
Dol. It is the Emperor, madam. *Cleopatra kneels.*
Cæs. Arise! You shall not kneel.
I pray you rise. Rise, Egypt.
Cleo. Sir, the gods 115
Will have it thus. My master and my lord
I must obey.
Cæs. Take to you no hard thoughts.
The record of what injuries you did us,
Though written in our flesh, we shall remember
As things but done by chance.
Cleo. Sole sir o' the world,
I cannot project mine own cause so well 121
To make it clear, but do confess I have
Been laden with like frailties which before
Have often shamed our sex.
Cæs. Cleopatra, know
We will extenuate rather than enforce. 125
If you apply yourself to our intents,
Which towards you are most gentle, you shall find
A benefit in this change; but if you seek
To lay on me a cruelty by taking
Antony's course, you shall bereave yourself 130
Of my good purposes, and put your children
To that destruction which I'll guard them from
If thereon you rely. I'll take my leave.
Cleo. And may, through all the world! 'Tis yours, and we, 134
Your scutcheons and your signs of conquest, shall
Hang in what place you please. Here, my good lord.
Cæs. You shall advise me in all for Cleopatra.
Cleo. This is the brief of money, plate, and jewels
I am possessed of. 'Tis exactly valued,
Not petty things admitted. Where's Seleucus? 140
Sel. Here, madam.
Cleo. This is my treasurer. Let him speak, my lord,
Upon his peril, that I have reserved
To myself nothing. Speak the truth, Seleucus.
Sel. Madam, 145
I had rather seel my lips than to my peril
Speak that which is not.
Cleo. What have I kept back?
Sel. Enough to purchase what you have made known.
Cæs. Nay, blush not, Cleopatra. I approve 149
Your wisdom in the deed.
Cleo. See, Cæsar! O, behold,
How pomp is followed! Mine will now be yours;
And should we shift estates, yours would be mine.
The ingratitude of this Seleucus does
Even make me wild. O slave, of no more trust
Than love that's hired! What, goest thou back? Thou shalt 155
Go back, I warrant thee; but I'll catch thine eyes,
Though they had wings. Slave, soulless villain, dog!
O rarely base!
Cæs. Good Queen, let us entreat you.
Cleo. O Cæsar, what a wounding shame is this,
That thou vouchsafing here to visit me, 160
Doing the honor of thy lordliness
To one so meek, that mine own servant should
Parcel the sum of my disgraces by
Addition of his envy! Say, good Cæsar,
That I some lady trifles have reserved, 165
Immoment toys, things of such dignity
As we greet modern friends withal; and say
Some nobler token I have kept apart
For Livia and Octavia, to induce
Their mediation—must I be unfolded 170
With one that I have bred? The gods! It smites me
Beneath the fall I have. [*To Seleucus*] Prithee go hence!
Or I shall show the cinders of my spirits
Through the ashes of my chance. Wert thou a man,
Thou wouldst have mercy on me.
Cæs. Forbear, Seleucus.
[*Exit Seleucus.*]
Cleo. Be it known that we, the greatest, are misthought 176
For things that others do; and, when we fall,
We answer others' merits in our name,
Are therefore to be pitied.

122. **clear:** blameless
125. **extenuate:** excuse; **enforce:** emphasize
126. **apply:** submit
135. **scutcheons:** armorial shields; trophies
138. **brief:** list
140. **Not . . . admitted:** excluding petty things
146. **seel:** sew up
151. **How . . . followed:** how faithfully great ones are served
152. **estates:** conditions
163–64. **Parcel . . . envy:** add to my misfortunes with his malice
166. **Immoment toys:** inconsequential trifles; **dignity:** value
167. **modern:** ordinary
169. **Livia:** Octavius' wife
170–71. **unfolded/With:** revealed by
175. **Forbear:** leave us
176. **misthought:** blamed
178. **merits:** deserts

Cæs. Cleopatra,
Not what you have reserved, nor what acknowledged, 180
Put we i' the roll of conquest. Still be't yours,
Bestow it at your pleasure; and believe
Cæsar's no merchant, to make prize with you
Of things that merchants sold. Therefore be cheered;
Make not your thoughts your prisons. No, dear Queen; 185
For we intend so to dispose you as
Yourself shall give us counsel. Feed and sleep.
Our care and pity is so much upon you
That we remain your friend; and so adieu. 189

Cleo. My master and my lord!

Cæs. Not so. Adieu.

Flourish. Exeunt Cæsar and his Train.

Cleo. He words me, girls, he words me, that I should not
Be noble to myself! But hark thee, Charmian.
[*Whispers to Charmian.*]

Iras. Finish, good lady. The bright day is done,
And we are for the dark.

Cleo. Hie thee again.
I have spoke already, and it is provided. 195
Go put it to the haste.

Char. Madam, I will.

[*Re-*]*enter* DOLABELLA.

Dol. Where is the Queen?

Char. Behold, sir. [*Exit.*]

Cleo. Dolabella!

Dol. Madam, as thereto sworn, by your command
(Which my love makes religion to obey)
I tell you this: Cæsar through Syria 200
Intends his journey, and within three days
You with your children will he send before.
Make your best use of this. I have performed
Your pleasure and my promise.

Cleo. Dolabella,
I shall remain your debtor.

Dol. I your servant. 205
Adieu, good Queen; I must attend on Cæsar.

Cleo. Farewell, and thanks. *Exit* [*Dolabella*].
Now, Iras, what thinkst thou?
Thou, an Egyptian puppet, shall be shown
In Rome as well as I. Mechanic slaves,
With greasy aprons, rules, and hammers, shall 210
Uplift us to the view. In their thick breaths,
Rank of gross diet, shall we be enclouded,
And forced to drink their vapor.

Iras. The gods forbid!

Cleo. Nay, 'tis most certain, Iras. Saucy lictors
Will catch at us like strumpets, and scald rhymers
Ballad us out o' tune. The quick comedians 216
Extemporally will stage us and present
Our Alexandrian revels. Antony
Shall be brought drunken forth, and I shall see
Some squeaking Cleopatra boy my greatness 220
I' the posture of a whore.

Iras. O the good gods!

Cleo. Nay, that's certain.

Iras. I'll never see't; for I am sure my nails
Are stronger than mine eyes.

Cleo. Why, that's the way
To fool their preparation and to conquer 225
Their most absurd intents.

[*Re-*]*enter* CHARMIAN.

Now, Charmian!
Show me, my women, like a queen. Go fetch
My best attires. I am again for Cydnus,
To meet Mark Antony. Sirrah Iras, go.
Now, noble Charmian, we'll dispatch indeed; 230
And when thou hast done this chare, I'll give thee leave
To play till doomsday.—Bring our crown and all.
[*Exit Iras.*]
A noise within.

Wherefore's this noise?

Enter a GUARDSMAN.

Guard. Here is a rural fellow
That will not be denied your Highness' presence.
He brings you figs. 235

Cleo. Let him come in. *Exit Guardsman.*
What poor an instrument
May do a noble deed! He brings me liberty.
My resolution's placed, and I have nothing
Of woman in me. Now from head to foot
I am marble-constant. Now the fleeting moon 240
No planet is of mine.

Enter GUARDSMAN *and* CLOWN [*with basket*].

Guard. This is the man.

Cleo. Avoid, and leave him. *Exit Guardsman.*
Hast thou the pretty worm of Nilus there
That kills and pains not?

183. **make prize:** bargain
209. **Mechanic slaves:** base workingmen
212. **Rank:** foul-smelling

214. **lictors:** magistrates' assistants, who apprehended offenders. Shakespeare apparently equates them with the Elizabethan beadles.
215. **scald:** scurvy; contemptible
216. **quick:** inventive; **comedians:** actors
221. **posture:** conduct
229. **Sirrah:** a form of familiar address for both sexes
236. **What:** how
238. **placed:** fixed
240. **fleeting:** inconstant
242. **Avoid:** withdraw

Clown. Truly I have him. But I would not 245
be the party that should desire you to touch him, for his biting is immortal. Those that do die of it do seldom or never recover.

Cleo. Rememberst thou any that have died on't?

Clown. Very many, men and women too. I 250
heard of one of them no longer than yesterday—a very honest woman, but something given to lie, as a woman should not do but in the way of honesty—how she died of the biting of it, what pain she felt. Truly, she makes a very good report o' the 255
worm; but he that will believe all that they say shall never be saved by half that they do. But this is most falliable, the worm's an odd worm.

Cleo. Get thee hence; farewell.

Clown. I wish you all joy of the worm. 260
[*Sets down his basket.*]

Cleo. Farewell.

Clown. You must think this, look you, that the worm will do his kind.

Cleo. Ay, ay; farewell.

Clown. Look you, the worm is not to be 265
trusted but in the keeping of wise people, for indeed there is no goodness in the worm.

Cleo. Take thou no care; it shall be heeded.

Clown. Very good. Give it nothing, I pray you, for it is not worth the feeding. 270

Cleo. Will it eat me?

Clown. You must not think I am so simple but I know the devil himself will not eat a woman. I know that a woman is a dish for the gods, if the devil dress her not. But truly, these same whoreson devils 275
do the gods great harm in their women; for in every ten that they make, the devils mar five.

Cleo. Well, get thee gone; farewell.

Clown. Yes, forsooth. I wish you joy o' the worm.
Exit.

[*Enter* IRAS *with a robe, crown, etc.*]

Cleo. Give me my robe, put on my crown. I have
Immortal longings in me. Now no more 281
The juice of Egypt's grape shall moist this lip.
Yare, yare, good Iras; quick. Methinks I hear
Antony call. I see him rouse himself
To praise my noble act. I hear him mock 285
The luck of Cæsar, which the gods give men
To excuse their after wrath. Husband, I come!
Now to that name my courage prove my title!
I am fire and air; my other elements
I give to baser life. So, have you done? 290
Come then and take the last warmth of my lips.
Farewell, kind Charmian. Iras, long farewell.
[*Kisses them. Iras falls and dies.*]
Have I the aspic in my lips? Dost fall?
If thou and nature can so gently part,
The stroke of death is as a lover's pinch, 295
Which hurts, and is desired. Dost thou lie still?
If thus thou vanishest, thou tellst the world
It is not worth leave-taking.

Char. Dissolve, thick cloud, and rain, that I may
say
The gods themselves do weep!

Cleo. This proves me base.
If she first meet the curled Antony, 301
He'll make demand of her, and spend that kiss
Which is my heaven to have. Come, thou mortal
wretch,
[*To an asp, which she applies to her breast.*]
With thy sharp teeth this knot intrinsicate
Of life at once untie. Poor venomous fool, 305
Be angry, and dispatch. O, couldst thou speak,
That I might hear thee call great Cæsar ass
Unpolicied!

Char. O Eastern star!

Cleo. Peace, peace!
Dost thou not see my baby at my breast, 309
That sucks the nurse asleep?

Char. O, break! O, break!

Cleo. As sweet as balm, as soft as air, as gentle—
O Antony! Nay, I will take thee too:
[*Applies another asp to her arm.*]
What should I stay— *Dies.*

Char. In this vile world? So fare thee well.
Now boast thee, death, in thy possession lies 315
A lass unparalleled. Downy windows, close;
And golden Phœbus never be beheld
Of eyes again so royal! Your crown's awry.
I'll mend it, and then play— 319

Enter the GUARD, *rustling in.*

1. Guard. Where's the Queen?

Char. Speak softly, wake her not.

1. Guard. Cæsar hath sent—

Char. Too slow a messenger.
[*Applies an asp.*]
O, come apace, dispatch. I partly feel thee.

1. Guard. Approach, ho! All's not well. Cæsar's
beguiled.

252. honest: respectable
253. honesty: honor; i.e., to guard her honor
258. falliable: infallible
263. do . . . kind: perform his natural function
274. dress: prepare
275. whoreson: a jocular epithet not meant literally
281. Immortal longings: longings for death
288. title: right
293. aspic: variant of "asp"
303. mortal: fatal
304. intrinsicate: intricate
308. Unpolicied: wanting in cunning
314. vile: Edward Capell's reading. The Folio reads "wilde."

2. Guard. There's Dolabella sent from Cæsar. Call him.
1. Guard. What work is here! Charmian, is this well done? 325
Char. It is well done, and fitting for a princess
Descended of so many royal kings.
Ah, soldier! *Charmian dies.*

Enter DOLABELLA.

Dol. How goes it here?
2. Guard. All dead.
Dol. Cæsar, thy thoughts
Touch their effects in this. Thyself art coming 330
To see performed the dreaded act which thou
So soughtst to hinder.
[*Shout within.*] "A way there, a way for Cæsar!"

Enter CÆSAR *and all his* TRAIN.

Dol. O sir, you are too sure an augurer:
That you did fear is done.
Cæs. Bravest at the last!
She leveled at our purposes, and being royal, 335
Took her own way. The manner of their deaths?
I do not see them bleed.
Dol. Who was last with them?
1. Guard. A simple countryman, that brought her figs.
This was his basket.
Cæs. Poisoned, then.
1. Guard. O Cæsar,
This Charmian lived but now; she stood and spake.
I found her trimming up the diadem 341
On her dead mistress. Tremblingly she stood,
And on the sudden dropped.
Cæs. O noble weakness!
If they had swallowed poison, 'twould appear
By external swelling; but she looks like sleep, 345
As she would catch another Antony
In her strong toil of grace.
Dol. Here on her breast
There is a vent of blood, and something blown;
The like is on her arm.
1. Guard. This is an aspic's trail; and these fig leaves 350
Have slime upon them, such as the aspic leaves
Upon the caves of Nile.
Cæs. Most probable
That so she died; for her physician tells me
She hath pursued conclusions infinite
Of easy ways to die. Take up her bed, 355
And bear her women from the monument.
She shall be buried by her Antony.
No grave upon the earth shall clip in it
A pair so famous. High events as these
Strike those that make them; and their story is
No less in pity than his glory which 361
Brought them to be lamented. Our army shall
In solemn show attend this funeral,
And then to Rome. Come, Dolabella, see
High order in this great solemnity. 365
Exeunt omnes.

330. **Touch . . . effects:** are realized
334. **Bravest:** noblest
335. **leveled:** guessed
341. **trimming up:** putting straight
346. **As:** as if
347. **toil:** snare
348. **something blown:** somewhat swollen
354. **conclusions:** experiments
358. **clip:** enclose
360. **those . . . them:** the agents responsible, i.e., Cæsar and his allies

Octavius Cæsar

From Thomas Treterus, *Romanorum imperatorum effigies* (1590).

Coriolanus with Volumnia and Virgilia

Engraved by J. Bauer after a painting by H. A. Bone.

The Tragedy of CORIOLANUS

INTRODUCTION

Coriolanus, the last of Shakespeare's tragedies, probably dates from 1608, but evidence for a precise date is lacking. It is one of Shakespeare's more puzzling plays, and its interpretations have been varied and sometimes contradictory. Some critics have seen in the play evidence of an antidemocratic spirit on the part of the author; others have seen it as a tract against fascist dictators; a few have traced in the play reflections of political events of Shakespeare's time: the career of Raleigh, for example, or the fall of the Earl of Essex; still others deny any political meaning whatever.

Similarly, critics have had divergent views about the quality of the play. A few have expressed the opinion that the play shows evidence of Shakespeare's exhaustion and a failing of his dramatic art. To others, including Mr. T. S. Eliot, *Coriolanus* is Shakespeare's "most assured artistic success." But Sir Edmund Chambers comments that "For the first time since some of the painful humors and strained wit-combats of his early experiments, Shakespeare has become tedious. Perhaps that is why the schoolmasters are so fond of the play."

The play is puzzling in its meaning and often compact and elliptical in its expression, but to interpret *Coriolanus* as an obscure and mediocre play, turned out as a perfunctory theatrical piece merely because the company needed another classical tragedy, is to do less than justice to the drama and the dramatist.

Coriolanus is the work of Shakespeare's maturity and shows, it is true, none of the ebullience of his earlier drama, but it is nonetheless an effective and thoughtful play with many scenes of dramatic power. Whatever may have been Shakespeare's mood when he wrote it, he was not weary and bored, as some critics have implied. As Shakespeare in *Antony and Cleopatra* studied a great character who allowed pleasure and sensuality to encompass his ruin, so in *Coriolanus* he analyzes a noble character who lets pride and a perverted sense of honor destroy him.

In appraising *Coriolanus* we would do well to remember the enormous emphasis that the Renaissance placed upon honor. The Renaissance man was expected to strive for honor and fame. Despite the Roman atmosphere with which Shakespeare superficially surrounds Coriolanus, he is essentially a Renaissance character, acting as the Italian courtesy books prescribed. Many of these books had been translated into English and were well known to Shakespeare and his contemporaries. Curtis B. Watson in *Shakespeare and the Renaissance Concept of Honor* makes this comment:

> For the Renaissance aristocracy, honor, good name, credit, reputation, and glory come close to the very center of their ethical values and receive expression almost wherever we look in the records of the nobility of that age. For this class, these values are so popular, so widespread, so trite, that they pass into its literature almost without definition, particularly into the drama of the age [pp. 63–64].

Coriolanus' overweening pride in his honor determines his attitude toward every action. Although he displays great bravery, risking his life for Rome, one feels that he is thinking less of Rome than of the glory accruing to himself. Although he goes through the motions of deprecating the praise that his colleagues bestow upon him for his courage in the face of the Volsces, he is so conscious of his own worth that he reveals a resentment that anyone should presume to evaluate his conduct. Coriolanus' pride in his position as the first among the patricians of Rome, his sense of honor that will not permit him to demean himself by seeking the favor of anyone, much less the favor of the sweaty populace, makes abhorrent the thought that he must put on a gown of humility and beg the people for their suffrage. His haughty pride keeps him from compromising with the realities of Roman politics.

Explanations for Coriolanus' actions can be found in aristocratic Italian conduct books which discuss the problem of honor and fame. As always in his great tragedies, Shakespeare is concerned with the effect upon his chief protagonist of some significant motivation. The motivations of Coriolanus are less familiar and less easily understood by a modern audience than are those of most of Shakespeare's tragic heroes. Although we can sympathize with him in his contempt for demagogues, his declamatory outbursts about his honor ring strangely in our ears. Nevertheless, he does provide a subject for the kind of morbid analysis that is popular today. It was the study of Coriolanus as a special type, one who was a prey to egotism and pride, that must have fascinated his creator.

In an informal talk before the Shakespeare Conference at Stratford-upon-Avon on August 28, 1961, J. B. Priestley commented upon Shakespeare's ability to express the views of the average Englishman. One remark has pertinence to *Coriolanus:* "The Englishman is at heart a snob," Mr. Priestley observed. "It is a trait that runs through the English from top to bottom. Shakespeare was a characteristic Englishman in this respect. Shakespeare distrusted the faceless, nameless mass—the mob." In *Coriolanus* Shakespeare is not glorifying a dictator who can control the masses; indeed, if anything, he is emphasizing the folly of Coriolanus' actions. Nor is Shakespeare an opponent of democracy—something neither he nor his contemporaries knew or dreamed of. As Mr. Priestley points out, he merely reflected the Englishman's distrust of mobocracy.

SOURCE, HISTORY, AND TEXT

Coriolanus, a mythical figure from Roman legend, found a place in Plutarch, and it was from North's translation of Plutarch that Shakespeare took his plot and some phraseology. But he deleted incidents not pertinent to the dramatic presentation and altered others to suit his purposes. For example, in Plutarch Menenius is wooden and insignificant; Shakespeare made him a lifelike and important character who gives a touch of comedy to the play. He also develops Volumnia far beyond Plutarch's conception and builds up Aufidius to make him a worthy opponent of Coriolanus. A study of the use that Shakespeare made of his Plutarchan material provides one more insight into the way a playwright of his ability could transmute prose into poetical drama.

Shakespeare could have found the story of Coriolanus in William Painter's *Palace of Pleasure* (1566–67) but there is little to show that he used Painter. The fable of the rebellion of the body's members against the belly is told in William Camden's *Remains* (1605), but it is also in Plutarch and in Livy as well.

Records of the early performances of *Coriolanus* are lacking, and we do not know how it was received on the pre-Restoration stage. In 1681–82 Nahum Tate made an adaptation for performance at Drury Lane under the title *The Ingratitude of a Commonwealth, or, The Fall of Caius Martius Coriolanus.* Tate made his version a tract for the times by identifying the demagogic tribunes with the Whig politicians of his day. Despite this infusion of topical interest, Tate's effort was a failure. In 1719 John Dennis prepared another adaptation with political overtones inspired by the Jacobite rebellion of 1715. His play, called *The Invader of His Country, or, The Fatal Resentment,* also failed. In 1720 Shakespeare's *Coriolanus* unaltered was revived at Lincoln's Inn Fields, and it was again revived by Garrick at Drury Lane in 1754 to forestall a rival version at Covent Garden combining elements from Shakespeare's play and from one written on the same subject by James Thomson and performed in 1749. John Philip Kemble made a new adaptation and produced it in 1789. Edmund Kean revived Shakespeare's version in 1820 and played the title role himself. Since the mid-nineteenth century, *Coriolanus* has been seen on the stage at fairly frequent intervals. Although it is not one of Shakespeare's most popular plays, it has retained an interest for both playgoers and readers through the centuries.

Coriolanus first appeared in print in the Folio of 1623, and the Folio version is therefore the basis of modern texts. Somewhat elaborate stage directions suggest that the copy for the Folio was the author's own manuscript. Because of the mislineations in the Folio text, some scholars have argued that Shakespeare in this period wrote in a freer form and that the mislineations are often deliberate.

A Roman Tribune

From Guillaume Du Choul, *Discours de la religion des anciens Romains* (1556).

[Dramatis Personæ

Caius Marcius, *afterward* Caius Marcius Coriolanus.
Titus Lartius, Cominius, } *generals against the Volscians.*
Menenius Agrippa, *friend to Coriolanus.*
Sicinius Velutus, Junius Brutus, } *tribunes of the people.*
Young Marcius, *son to Coriolanus.*
A Roman Herald.
Tullus Aufidius, *general of the Volscians.*
Lieutenant *to Aufidius.*
Conspirators *with Aufidius.*
Nicanor, *a Roman in the service of the Volscians.*
Adrian, *a Volscian.*
A Citizen of Antium.
Two Volscian Guards.

Volumnia, *mother to Coriolanus.*
Virgilia, *wife to Coriolanus.*
Valeria, *friend to Virgilia.*
Gentlewoman *attending on Virgilia.*

Roman and Volscian Senators, Patricians, Ædiles, Lictors, Soldiers, Citizens, Messengers, Servants to Aufidius, and other Attendants.

Scene: *Rome and the neighborhood; Corioli and the neighborhood; Antium.*]

A Roman Patrician
From Cesare Vecellio,
Degli habiti antichi et moderni (1590).

The Tragedy of CORIOLANUS

ACT I

Scene I. [*Rome. A street.*]

Enter a company of mutinous CITIZENS, *with staves, clubs, and other weapons.*

1. Cit. Before we proceed any further, hear me speak.

All. Speak, speak.

1. Cit. You are all resolved rather to die than to famish? 5

All. Resolved, resolved.

1. Cit. First, you know Caius Marcius is chief enemy to the people.

All. We know't, we know't.

1. Cit. Let us kill him, and we'll have corn 10 at our own price. Is't a verdict?

All. No more talking on't; let it be done. Away, away!

2. Cit. One word, good citizens.

1. Cit. We are accounted poor citizens, the 15 patricians good. What authority surfeits on would relieve us; if they would yield us but the superfluity while it were wholesome, we might guess they relieved us humanely; but they think we are too dear. The leanness that afflicts us, the object of our 20 misery, is as an inventory to particularize their abundance; our sufferance is a gain to them. Let us revenge this with our pikes ere we become rakes; for the gods know I speak this in hunger for bread, not in thirst for revenge. 25

2. Cit. Would you proceed especially against Caius Marcius?

1. Cit. Against him first; he's a very dog to the commonalty.

2. Cit. Consider you what services he has 30 done his country?

1. Cit. Very well, and could be content to give him good report for't but that he pays himself with being proud.

2. Cit. Nay, but speak not maliciously. 35

1. Cit. I say unto you, what he hath done famously he did it to that end; though soft-conscienced men can be content to say it was for his country, he did it to please his mother and to be partly proud, which he is, even to the altitude of his virtue. 40

2. Cit. What he cannot help in his nature you account a vice in him. You must in no way say he is covetous.

1. Cit. If I must not, I need not be barren of accusations; he hath faults, with surplus, to tire in 45 repetition. *Shouts within.* What shouts are these? The other side o' the city is risen. Why stay we prating here? To the Capitol!

All. Come, come.

1. Cit. Soft! Who comes here? 50

Enter MENENIUS AGRIPPA.

10. corn: grain (not Indian corn)
12. on't: of it
18. guess: think
19. dear: expensive
20. object: spectacle
22. sufferance: suffering

23. rakes: cf. the proverbial "As lean as a rake."
28. dog: hound; persecutor

2. Cit. Worthy Menenius Agrippa; one that hath always loved the people.

1. Cit. He's one honest enough; would all the rest were so!

Men. What work's, my countrymen, in hand? Where go you 55
With bats and clubs? The matter? Speak, I pray you.

1. Cit. Our business is not unknown to the Senate; they have had inkling this fortnight what we intend to do, which now we'll show 'em in deeds. They say poor suitors have strong breaths; they shall 60 know we have strong arms too.

Men. Why, masters, my good friends, mine honest neighbors,
Will you undo yourselves?

1. Cit. We cannot, sir; we are undone already.

Men. I tell you, friends, most charitable care 65
Have the patricians of you. For your wants,
Your suffering in this dearth, you may as well
Strike at the heaven with your staves as lift them
Against the Roman state, whose course will on
The way it takes, cracking ten thousand curbs 70
Of more strong link asunder than can ever
Appear in your impediment. For the dearth,
The gods, not the patricians, make it, and
Your knees to them, not arms, must help. Alack,
You are transported by calamity 75
Thither where more attends you; and you slander
The helms o' the state, who care for you like fathers,
When you curse them as enemies.

1. Cit. Care for us! True, indeed! They ne'er cared for us yet. Suffer us to famish, and their store- 80 houses crammed with grain; make edicts for usury, to support usurers; repeal daily any wholesome act established against the rich, and provide more piercing statutes daily to chain up and restrain the poor. If the wars eat us not up, they will; and there's 85 all the love they bear us.

Men. Either you must
Confess yourselves wondrous malicious,
Or be accused of folly. I shall tell you
A pretty tale. It may be you have heard it; 90
But, since it serves my purpose, I will venture
To stale't a little more.

1. Cit. Well, I'll hear it, sir; yet you must not think to fob off our disgrace with a tale. But, an't please you, deliver. 95

Men. There was a time when all the body's members
Rebelled against the belly; thus accused it:
That only like a gulf it did remain
I' the midst o' the body, idle and unactive,
Still cupboarding the viand, never bearing 100
Like labor with the rest; where the other instruments
Did see and hear, devise, instruct, walk, feel,
And, mutually participate, did minister
Unto the appetite and affection common
Of the whole body. The belly answered— 105

1. Cit. Well, sir, what answer made the belly?

Men. Sir, I shall tell you. With a kind of smile,
Which ne'er came from the lungs, but even thus—
For look you, I may make the belly smile
As well as speak—it tauntingly replied 110
To the discontented members, the mutinous parts
That envied his receipt; even so most fitly
As you malign our senators for that
They are not such as you.

1. Cit. Your belly's answer—What?
The kingly crowned head, the vigilant eye, 115
The counselor heart, the arm our soldier,
Our steed the leg, the tongue our trumpeter,
With other muniments and petty helps
In this our fabric, if that they—

Men. What then? 119
Fore me, this fellow speaks. What then? What then?

1. Cit. Should by the cormorant belly be restrained,
Who is the sink o' the body—

Men. Well, what then?

1. Cit. The former agents, if they did complain,
What could the belly answer?

Men. I will tell you; 124
If you'll bestow a small—of what you have little—
Patience awhile, you'st hear the belly's answer.

1. Cit. Y'are long about it.

Men. Note me this, good friend:
Your most grave belly was deliberate,
Not rash like his accusers, and thus answered.
"True is it, my incorporate friends," quoth he, 130
"That I receive the general food at first
Which you do live upon; and fit it is,
Because I am the storehouse and the shop
Of the whole body. But, if you do remember,
I send it through the rivers of your blood, 135
Even to the court, the heart, to the seat o' the brain;
And, through the cranks and offices of man,
The strongest nerves and small inferior veins
From me receive that natural competency 139
Whereby they live. And though that all at once
You, my good friends"—this says the belly; mark me—

77. **helms:** pilots
92. **stale't:** Theobald's emendation of the Folio's "scale't."
94. **fob off:** set aside; gloss over; **disgrace:** misfortune
98. **gulf:** voracious appetite

103. **participate:** participating
104. **affection:** taste
113. **for that:** because
118. **muniments:** defenses
121. **cormorant:** insatiable
126. **you'st:** thou shalt
130. **incorporate:** united in a single body
137. **cranks:** winding passages; **offices:** organs
138. **nerves:** sinews
139. **competency:** sufficiency

1. Cit. Ay, sir; well, well.
Men. "Though all at once cannot
See what I do deliver out to each,
Yet I can make my audit up, that all
From me do back receive the flour of all, 145
And leave me but the bran." What say you to't?
1. Cit. It was an answer. How apply you this?
Men. The senators of Rome are this good belly,
And you the mutinous members; for, examine 149
Their counsels and their cares, digest things rightly
Touching the weal o' the common, you shall find
No public benefit which you receive
But it proceeds or comes from them to you,
And no way from yourselves. What do you think,
You, the great toe of this assembly? 155
1. Cit. I the great toe? Why the great toe?
Men. For that, being one o' the lowest, basest, poorest,
Of this most wise rebellion, thou goest foremost.
Thou rascal, that art worst in blood to run,
Leadst first to win some vantage. 160
But make you ready your stiff bats and clubs.
Rome and her rats are at the point of battle;
The one side must have bale.

Enter CAIUS MARCIUS.

Hail, noble Marcius!
Mar. Thanks. What's the matter, you dissentious rogues
That, rubbing the poor itch of your opinion, 165
Make yourselves scabs?
1. Cit. We have ever your good word.
Mar. He that will give good words to thee will flatter
Beneath abhorring. What would you have, you curs,
That like nor peace nor war? The one affrights you,
The other makes you proud. He that trusts to you,
Where he should find you lions, finds you hares;
Where foxes, geese; you are no surer, no, 172
Than is the coal of fire upon the ice
Or hailstone in the sun. Your virtue is
To make him worthy whose offense subdues him,
And curse that justice did it. Who deserves greatness
Deserves your hate; and your affections are 177
A sick man's appetite, who desires most that
Which would increase his evil. He that depends
Upon your favors swims with fins of lead, 180
And hews down oaks with rushes. Hang ye! Trust ye?
With every minute you do change a mind
And call him noble that was now your hate,
Him vile that was your garland. What's the matter
That in these several places of the city 185
You cry against the noble Senate, who,
Under the gods, keep you in awe, which else
Would feed on one another? What's their seeking?
Men. For corn at their own rates, whereof they say
The city is well stored.
Mar. Hang 'em! They say! 190
They'll sit by the fire and presume to know
What's done i' the Capitol, who's like to rise,
Who thrives and who declines; side factions, and give out
Conjectural marriages, making parties strong,
And feebling such as stand not in their liking 195
Below their cobbled shoes. They say there's grain enough!
Would the nobility lay aside their ruth
And let me use my sword, I'd make a quarry
With thousands of these quartered slaves, as high
As I could pick my lance. 200
Men. Nay, these are almost thoroughly persuaded;
For though abundantly they lack discretion,
Yet are they passing cowardly. But, I beseech you,
What say the other troop?
Mar. They are dissolved. Hang 'em!
They said they were an-hungry; sighed forth proverbs— 205
That hunger broke stone walls, that dogs must eat,
That meat was made for mouths, that the gods sent not
Corn for the rich men only. With these shreds
They vented their complainings; which being answered,
And a petition granted them—a strange one, 210
To break the heart of generosity
And make bold power look pale—they threw their caps
As they would hang them on the horns o' the moon,
Shouting their emulation.
Men. What is granted them?
Mar. Five tribunes, to defend their vulgar wisdoms,
Of their own choice. One's Junius Brutus— 216
Sicinius Velutus, and I know not. 'Sdeath!
The rabble should have first unroofed the city
Ere so prevailed with me; it will in time

151. **weal . . . common:** general welfare
159. **rascal:** an immature or inferior specimen of a deer; **worst . . . blood:** in poorest physical condition
163. **bale:** poison
165. **opinion:** self-love
174. **virtue:** valor
176. **that justice:** the justice that
177. **affections:** inclinations
198. **quarry:** heap of dead
199. **quartered:** cut in quarters (perhaps thinking of the punishment of traitors)
200. **pick:** pitch
203. **passing:** exceedingly
209. **answered:** satisfied
211. **generosity:** i.e., the nobles
214. **Shouting . . . emulation:** expressing triumph at their victory
217. **'Sdeath:** God's death

Win upon power and throw forth greater themes
For insurrection's arguing.

Men. This is strange. 221

Mar. Go get you home, you fragments.

Enter a MESSENGER, *hastily.*

Mess. Where's Caius Marcius?

Mar. Here. What's the matter?

Mess. The news is, sir, the Volsces are in arms.

Mar. I am glad on't; then we shall ha' means to vent 225
Our musty superfluity. See, our best elders.

Enter COMINIUS, TITUS LARTIUS, *with other* SENATORS; JUNIUS BRUTUS *and* SICINIUS VELUTUS.

1. Sen. Marcius, 'tis true that you have lately told us:
The Volsces are in arms.

Mar. They have a leader,
Tullus Aufidius, that will put you to't.
I sin in envying his nobility; 230
And were I anything but what I am,
I would wish me only he.

Com. You have fought together?

Mar. Were half to half the world by the ears, and he
Upon my party, I'd revolt, to make
Only my wars with him. He is a lion 235
That I am proud to hunt.

1. Sen. Then, worthy Marcius,
Attend upon Cominius to these wars.

Com. It is your former promise.

Mar. Sir, it is;
And I am constant. Titus Lartius, thou
Shalt see me once more strike at Tullus' face. 240
What, art thou stiff? Standst out?

Lar. No, Caius Marcius;
I'll lean upon one crutch and fight with t'other
Ere stay behind this business.

Men. O, true bred!

1. Sen. Your company to the Capitol; where, I know,
Our greatest friends attend us.

Lar. [*To Cominius*] Lead you on. 245
[*To Marcius*] Follow Cominius; we must follow you;
Right worthy you priority.

Com. Noble Marcius!

1. Sen. [*To the Citizens*] Hence to your homes; be gone.

Mar. Nay, let them follow.
The Volsces have much corn: take these rats thither
To gnaw their garners. Worshipful mutineers, 251
Your valor puts well forth; pray follow.

Citizens steal away.

Exeunt all but Sicinius and Brutus.

Sic. Was ever man so proud as is this Marcius?

Bru. He has no equal.

Sic. When we were chosen tribunes for the people— 255

Bru. Marked you his lip and eyes?

Sic. Nay, but his taunts!

Bru. Being moved, he will not spare to gird the gods.

Sic. Bemock the modest moon.

Bru. The present wars devour him! He is grown
Too proud to be so valiant.

Sic. Such a nature, 260
Tickled with good success, disdains the shadow
Which he treads on at noon. But I do wonder
His insolence can brook to be commanded
Under Cominius.

Bru. Fame, at the which he aims—
In whom already he is well graced—cannot 265
Better be held nor more attained than by
A place below the first; for what miscarries
Shall be the general's fault, though he perform
To the utmost of a man, and giddy censure
Will then cry out of Marcius, "O, if he 270
Had borne the business!"

Sic. Besides, if things go well,
Opinion, that so sticks on Marcius, shall
Of his demerits rob Cominius.

Bru. Come.
Half all Cominius' honors are to Marcius, 274
Though Marcius earned them not; and all his faults
To Marcius shall be honors, though indeed
In aught he merit not.

Sic. Let's hence and hear
How the dispatch is made, and in what fashion,
More than his singularity, he goes
Upon this present action.

Bru. Let's along. 280

Exeunt.

220. **Win . . . power:** prevail by sheer force of numbers
220–21. **themes . . . arguing:** reasons for rebellion
225. **vent:** get rid of
226. **musty superfluity:** stale (idle) and foul-smelling excess of population
229. **put . . . to't:** tax your utmost effort

252. **puts . . . forth:** is well pretended
257. **gird:** taunt
260. **to be:** of being
263. **brook:** endure
269. **giddy:** unreliable; **censure:** judgment
272. **sticks on:** favors
273. **demerits:** deserts
278. **dispatch . . . made:** business is handled
279. **singularity:** superiority. Sicinius means that they can be sure that Marcius will set out arrogantly, but he is curious about the details of his departure.

[Scene II. *Corioli. The Senate House.*]

Enter TULLUS AUFIDIUS *with* SENATORS *of Corioli.*

1. Sen. So, your opinion is, Aufidius,
That they of Rome are ent'red in our counsels
And know how we proceed.
Auf. Is it not yours?
What ever have been thought on in this state
That could be brought to bodily act ere Rome 5
Had circumvention? 'Tis not four days gone
Since I heard thence; these are the words—I think
I have the letter here; yes, here it is:
[*Reads*] "They have pressed a power, but it is not known
Whether for east or west. The dearth is great, 10
The people mutinous; and it is rumored,
Cominius, Marcius, your old enemy,
Who is of Rome worse hated than of you,
And Titus Lartius, a most valiant Roman,
These three lead on this preparation 15
Whither 'tis bent. Most likely 'tis for you;
Consider of it."
1. Sen. Our army's in the field;
We never yet made doubt but Rome was ready
To answer us.
Auf. Nor did you think it folly
To keep your great pretenses veiled till when 20
They needs must show themselves; which in the hatching,
It seemed, appeared to Rome. By the discovery
We shall be short'ned in our aim, which was
To take in many towns ere almost Rome
Should know we were afoot.
2. Sen. Noble Aufidius, 25
Take your commission; hie you to your bands;
Let us alone to guard Corioli.
If they set down before's, for the remove
Bring up your army; but I think you'll find
Th' have not prepared for us.
Auf. O, doubt not that! 30
I speak from certainties. Nay, more,
Some parcels of their power are forth already,
And only hitherward. I leave your honors.
If we and Caius Marcius chance to meet,
'Tis sworn between us we shall ever strike 35
Till one can do no more.
All. The gods assist you!
Auf. And keep your honors safe!
1. Sen. Farewell.
2. Sen. Farewell.
All. Farewell.
Exeunt.

[Scene III. *Rome. Marcius' house.*]

Enter VOLUMNIA *and* VIRGILIA, *mother and wife to Marcius; they set them down on two low stools and sew.*

Vol. I pray you, daughter, sing, or express yourself in a more comfortable sort. If my son were my husband, I should freelier rejoice in that absence wherein he won honor than in the embracements of his bed where he would show most love. When yet he 5 was but tender-bodied, and the only son of my womb; when youth with comeliness plucked all gaze his way; when, for a day of kings' entreaties, a mother should not sell him an hour from her beholding; I, considering how honor would become 10 such a person—that it was no better than picturelike to hang by the wall, if renown made it not stir—was pleased to let him seek danger where he was to find fame. To a cruel war I sent him, from whence he returned his brows bound with oak. I tell thee, 15 daughter, I sprang not more in joy at first hearing he was a man-child than now in first seeing he had proved himself a man.
Vir. But had he died in the business, madam, how then? 20
Vol. Then his good report should have been my son; I therein would have found issue. Hear me profess sincerely: had I a dozen sons, each in my love alike, and none less dear than thine and my good Marcius, I had rather had eleven die nobly for 25 their country than one voluptuously surfeit out of action.

Enter a GENTLEWOMAN.

Gent. Madam, the Lady Valeria is come to visit you.
Vir. Beseech you give me leave to retire myself.
Vol. Indeed you shall not. 31
Methinks I hear hither your husband's drum;
See him pluck Aufidius down by the hair;
As children from a bear, the Volsces shunning him.
Methinks I see him stamp thus, and call thus: 35
"Come on, you cowards! You were got in fear,

9. pressed: conscripted; **power:** army
13. of: by
28. remove: repulse
32. parcels: portions

11. person: i.e., handsome presence
15. oak: a victorious garland of oak leaves
34. shunning: fleeing
36. got: begot

Though you were born in Rome." His bloody brow
With his mailed hand then wiping, forth he goes,
Like to a harvestman that's tasked to mow
Or all or lose his hire. 40

Vir. His bloody brow? O Jupiter, no blood!

Vol. Away, you fool! It more becomes a man
Than gilt his trophy. The breasts of Hecuba,
When she did suckle Hector, looked not lovelier
Than Hector's forehead when it spit forth blood
At Grecian sword, contemning. Tell Valeria 46
We are fit to bid her welcome. *Exit Gentlewoman.*

Vir. Heavens bless my lord from fell Aufidius!

Vol. He'll beat Aufidius' head below his knee
And tread upon his neck. 50

[*Re-*]*enter* GENTLEWOMAN, *with* VALERIA *and an* USHER.

Val. My ladies both, good day to you.

Vol. Sweet madam!

Vir. I am glad to see your ladyship.

Val. How do you both? You are manifest housekeepers. What are you sewing here? A fine spot, 55
in good faith. How does your little son?

Vir. I thank your ladyship; well, good madam.

Vol. He had rather see the swords and hear a drum than look upon his schoolmaster.

Val. O' my word, the father's son! I'll swear 60
'tis a very pretty boy. O' my troth, I looked upon him a Wednesday half an hour together; has such a confirmed countenance! I saw him run after a gilded butterfly; and when he caught it he let it go again, and after it again, and over and over he comes, 65
and up again, catched it again; or whether his fall enraged him, or how 'twas, he did so set his teeth and tear it. O, I warrant, how he mammocked it!

Vol. One on's father's moods.

Val. Indeed, la, 'tis a noble child. 70

Vir. A crack, madam.

Val. Come, lay aside your stitchery; I must have you play the idle huswife with me this afternoon.

Vir. No, good madam; I will not out of doors.

Val. Not out of doors! 75

Vol. She shall, she shall.

Vir. Indeed, no, by your patience; I'll not over the threshold till my lord return from the wars.

Val. Fie, you confine yourself most unreasonably; come, you must go visit the good lady that lies in. 80

Vir. I will wish her speedy strength, and visit her with my prayers; but I cannot go thither.

Vol. Why, I pray you?

Vir. 'Tis not to save labor, nor that I want love.

Val. You would be another Penelope; yet 85
they say all the yarn she spun in Ulysses' absence did but fill Ithaca full of moths. Come, I would your cambric were sensible as your finger, that you might leave pricking it for pity. Come, you shall go with us.

Vir. No, good madam, pardon me; indeed I 90
will not forth.

Val. In truth, la, go with me; and I'll tell you excellent news of your husband.

Vir. O, good madam, there can be none yet.

Val. Verily, I do not jest with you; there 95
came news from him last night.

Vir. Indeed, madam?

Val. In earnest, it's true; I heard a senator speak it. Thus it is: the Volsces have an army forth; against whom Cominius the general is gone, with one 100
part of our Roman power. Your lord and Titus Lartius are set down before their city Corioli; they nothing doubt prevailing and to make it brief wars. This is true, on mine honor; and so, I pray, go with us. 105

Vir. Give me excuse, good madam; I will obey you in everything hereafter.

Vol. Let her alone, lady; as she is now, she will but disease our better mirth.

Val. In troth, I think she would. Fare you 110
well, then. Come, good sweet lady. Prithee, Virgilia, turn thy solemnness out o' door and go along with us.

Vir. No, at a word, madam; indeed I must not. I wish you much mirth.

Val. Well then, farewell. 115

Exeunt.

[Scene IV. *Before Corioli.*]

Enter MARCIUS, TITUS LARTIUS, *with drum and colors, with* CAPTAINS *and* SOLDIERS. *To them a* MESSENGER.

Mar. Yonder comes news; a wager—they have met.

Lar. My horse to yours, no.

Mar. 'Tis done.

Lar. Agreed.

Mar. Say, has our general met the enemy?

Mess. They lie in view, but have not spoke as yet.

Lar. So, the good horse is mine.

40. Or: either
43. gilt: gilding; **trophy:** monument
46. contemning: expressing disdain
47. fit: ready
48. fell: savage
55. spot: pattern or stitch
63. confirmed: resolute
68. mammocked: tore to pieces
69. on's: of his
71. crack: rogue
73. huswife: housewife
84. want: lack
88. sensible: sensitive
113. at . . . word: in a word
1. met: fought
4. spoke: encountered

Mar. I'll buy him of you.
Lar. No, I'll not sell nor give him; lend you him I will 6
For half a hundred years. Summon the town.
Mar. How far off lie these armies?
Mess. Within this mile and half.
Mar. Then shall we hear their 'larum, and they ours.
Now, Mars, I prithee, make us quick in work, 10
That we with smoking swords may march from hence
To help our fielded friends! Come, blow thy blast.

They sound a parley. Enter TWO SENATORS *with others, on the walls of Corioli.*

Tullus Aufidius, is he within your walls?
1. Sen. No, nor a man that fears you less than he:
That's lesser than a little. (*Drum afar off.*) Hark, our drums 15
Are bringing forth our youth. We'll break our walls
Rather than they shall pound us up; our gates,
Which yet seem shut, we have but pinned with rushes;
They'll open of themselves. (*Alarum far off.*) Hark you far off!
There is Aufidius. List what work he makes 20
Amongst your cloven army.
Mar. O, they are at it!
Lar. Their noise be our instruction. Ladders, ho!

Enter the ARMY OF THE VOLSCES.

Mar. They fear us not, but issue forth their city.
Now put your shields before your hearts, and fight
With hearts more proof than shields. Advance, brave Titus. 25
They do disdain us much beyond our thoughts,
Which makes me sweat with wrath. Come on, my fellows.
He that retires, I'll take him for a Volsce,
And he shall feel mine edge. 29

Alarum. The Romans are beat back to their trenches. [*Re-*]*enter* MARCIUS, *cursing.*

Mar. All the contagion of the south light on you,
You shames of Rome! You herd of—Boils and plagues
Plaster you o'er, that you may be abhorred
Farther than seen, and one infect another
Against the wind a mile! You souls of geese
That bear the shapes of men, how have you run 35
From slaves that apes would beat! Pluto and hell!
All hurt behind! Backs red, and faces pale
With flight and agued fear! Mend and charge home,
Or, by the fires of heaven, I'll leave the foe 39
And make my wars on you. Look to't. Come on;
If you'll stand fast we'll beat them to their wives,
As they us to our trenches followed.

Another alarum. [*The Volsces fly,*] *and Marcius follows them to the gates.*

So, now the gates are ope; now prove good seconds;
'Tis for the followers fortune widens them,
Not for the fliers. Mark me, and do the like. 45
[*Marcius*] *enters the gates.*
1. Sol. Foolhardiness; not I.
2. Sol. Nor I.
[*Marcius is shut in.*]
1. Sol. See, they have shut him in.
All. To the pot, I warrant him. *Alarum continues.*

[*Re-*]*enter* TITUS LARTIUS.

Lar. What is become of Marcius?
All. Slain, sir, doubtless.
1. Sol. Following the fliers at the very heels, 50
With them he enters; who, upon the sudden,
Clapped to their gates. He is himself alone,
To answer all the city.
Lar. O noble fellow!
Who sensibly outdares his senseless sword, 54
And when it bows stands up. Thou art left, Marcius;
A carbuncle entire, as big as thou art,
Were not so rich a jewel. Thou wast a soldier
Even to Cato's wish, not fierce and terrible
Only in strokes, but with thy grim looks and
The thunderlike percussion of thy sounds 60
Thou madest thine enemies shake, as if the world
Were feverous and did tremble.

[*Re-*]*enter* MARCIUS, *bleeding, assaulted by the enemy.*

1. Sol. Look, sir.
Lar. O, 'tis Marcius!
Let's fetch him off, or make remain alike.
They fight, and all enter the city.

9. 'larum: trumpet signal to begin fighting
12. fielded: embattled
17. pound . . . up: impound us
21. cloven: split; scattered
25. proof: invulnerable; cf. "proof armor."
30. contagion . . . south: unwholesome damp borne by the south wind
38. agued: shaking as with ague; **home:** i.e., the heart of the enemy
48. To . . . pot: i.e., to destruction. The metaphor presumably comes from the cutting up of meat and vegetables for the pot.
54. sensibly: possessed of full comprehension; **senseless:** insensitive
55. Thou . . . left: you stand unmatched in courage
58. Cato's: Theobald's correction of the Folio's "Calues"
63. fetch . . . off: rescue him; **make . . . alike:** stay with him

[Scene V. *Corioli. A street.*]

Enter CERTAIN ROMANS, *with spoils.*

1. Rom. This will I carry to Rome.
2. Rom. And I this.
3. Rom. A murrain on't! I took this for silver.
Alarum continues still afar off.

Enter MARCIUS *and* TITUS [LARTIUS] *with a* TRUMPET.

Mar. See here these movers that do prize their hours
At a cracked drachma! Cushions, leaden spoons, 5
Irons of a doit, doublets that hangmen would
Bury with those that wore them, these base slaves,
Ere yet the fight be done, pack up. Down with them!
Exeunt [pillagers].
And hark, what noise the general makes! To him!
There is the man of my soul's hate, Aufidius, 10
Piercing our Romans; then, valiant Titus, take
Convenient numbers to make good the city;
Whilst I, with those that have the spirit, will haste
To help Cominius.
Lar. Worthy sir, thou bleedst;
Thy exercise hath been too violent 15
For a second course of fight.
Mar. Sir, praise me not;
My work hath yet not warmed me. Fare you well;
The blood I drop is rather physical
Than dangerous to me. To Aufidius thus 19
I will appear, and fight.
Lar. Now the fair goddess Fortune
Fall deep in love with thee, and her great charms
Misguide thy opposers' swords! Bold gentleman,
Prosperity be thy page!
Mar. Thy friend no less
Than those she placeth highest! So farewell. 24
Lar. Thou worthiest Marcius! [*Exit Marcius.*]
Go sound thy trumpet in the market place;
Call thither all the officers o' the town,
Where they shall know our mind. Away!
Exeunt.

3. murrain: plague
Ent. 3. Trumpet: i.e., trumpeter
5. drachma: a Greek coin valued at six obols or less than ten cents
6. Irons . . . doit: swords worth a doit (one-fourth of an English farthing in value)
12. Convenient: appropriate
16. praise: appraise
18. physical: beneficial, like medicine
23. be . . . page: i.e., attend thee

[Scene VI. *Near the camp of Cominius.*]

Enter COMINIUS, *as it were in retire, with* SOLDIERS.

Com. Breathe you, my friends. Well fought; we are come off
Like Romans, neither foolish in our stands
Nor cowardly in retire. Believe me, sirs,
We shall be charged again. Whiles we have struck,
By interims and conveying gusts we have heard 5
The charges of our friends. The Roman gods
Lead their successes as we wish our own,
That both our powers, with smiling fronts encoun-t'ring,
May give you thankful sacrifice!

Enter a MESSENGER.

Thy news?
Mess. The citizens of Corioli have issued 10
And given to Lartius and to Marcius battle;
I saw our party to their trenches driven,
And then I came away.
Com. Though thou speakst truth,
Methinks thou speakst not well. How long is't since?
Mess. Above an hour, my lord. 15
Com. 'Tis not a mile; briefly we heard their drums.
How couldst thou in a mile confound an hour,
And bring thy news so late?
Mess. Spies of the Volsces
Held me in chase, that I was forced to wheel
Three or four miles about; else had I, sir, 20
Half an hour since brought my report.

Enter MARCIUS.

Com. Who's yonder
That does appear as he were flayed? O gods!
He has the stamp of Marcius, and I have
Beforetime seen him thus.
Mar. Come I too late?
Com. The shepherd knows not thunder from a tabor 25
More than I know the sound of Marcius' tongue
From every meaner man.
Mar. Come I too late?
Com. Ay, if you come not in the blood of others,
But mantled in your own.
Mar. O! let me clip ye
In arms as sound as when I wooed; in heart 30

5. By . . . gusts: borne by intermittent gusts of wind
8. fronts: foreheads; faces
10. issued: come forth
16. briefly: not long ago
17. confound: expend
25. tabor: small drum
29. clip: embrace

As merry as when our nuptial day was done,
And tapers burned to bedward.

Com. Flower of warriors,
How is't with Titus Lartius?

Mar. As with a man busied about decrees:
Condemning some to death and some to exile; 35
Ransoming him or pitying, threat'ning the other;
Holding Corioli in the name of Rome
Even like a fawning greyhound in the leash,
To let him slip at will.

Com. Where is that slave 39
Which told me they had beat you to your trenches?
Where is he? Call him hither.

Mar. Let him alone;
He did inform the truth. But for our gentlemen,
The common file—a plague! Tribunes for them!
The mouse ne'er shunned the cat as they did budge
From rascals worse than they.

Com. But how prevailed you? 45

Mar. Will the time serve to tell? I do not think.
Where is the enemy? Are you lords o' the field?
If not, why cease you till you are so?

Com. Marcius,
We have at disadvantage fought, and did
Retire to win our purpose. 50

Mar. How lies their battle? Know you on which side
They have placed their men of trust?

Com. As I guess, Marcius,
Their bands i' the vaward are the Antiates,
Of their best trust; o'er them Aufidius,
Their very heart of hope.

Mar. I do beseech you, 55
By all the battles wherein we have fought,
By the blood we have shed together, by the vows
We have made to endure friends, that you directly
Set me against Aufidius and his Antiates;
And that you not delay the present, but, 60
Filling the air with swords advanced and darts,
We prove this very hour.

Com. Though I could wish
You were conducted to a gentle bath
And balms applied to you, yet dare I never
Deny your asking: take your choice of those 65
That best can aid your action.

Mar. Those are they
That most are willing. If any such be here—
As it were sin to doubt—that love this painting
Wherein you see me smeared; if any fear
Lesser his person than an ill report; 70
If any think brave death outweighs bad life
And that his country's dearer than himself;
Let him alone, or so many so minded,
Wave thus to express his disposition,
And follow Marcius. 75

They all shout and wave their swords, take him up in their arms and cast up their caps.

O, me alone! Make you a sword of me?
If these shows be not outward, which of you
But is four Volsces? None of you but is
Able to bear against the great Aufidius
A shield as hard as his. A certain number, 80
Though thanks to all, must I select from all; the rest
Shall bear the business in some other fight,
As cause will be obeyed. Please you to march;
And four shall quickly draw out my command, 84
Which men are best inclined.

Com. March on, my fellows;
Make good this ostentation, and you shall
Divide in all with us.

Exeunt.

[Scene VII. *The gates of Corioli.*]

TITUS LARTIUS, *having set a guard upon Corioli, going with drum and trumpet toward Cominius and Caius Marcius, enters with a* LIEUTENANT, *other* SOLDIERS, *and a* SCOUT.

Lar. So, let the ports be guarded; keep your duties
As I have set them down. If I do send, dispatch
Those centuries to our aid; the rest will serve
For a short holding. If we lose the field
We cannot keep the town.

Lieut. Fear not our care, sir. 5

Lar. Hence, and shut your gates upon's.
Our guider, come; to the Roman camp conduct us.

Exeunt.

[Scene VIII. *A field of battle.*]

Alarum, as in battle. Enter MARCIUS *and* AUFIDIUS *at several doors.*

Mar. I'll fight with none but thee, for I do hate thee
Worse than a promise-breaker.

Auf. We hate alike:
Not Afric owns a serpent I abhor
More than thy fame and envy. Fix thy foot.

51. **How . . . battle:** how are their forces deployed?
53. **vaward:** vanguard; forefront
58. **endure:** remain
61. **advanced:** raised
62. **prove:** make trial
83. **cause . . . obeyed:** occasion requires
86. **Make . . . ostentation:** confirm this display of courage
3. **centuries:** companies of one hundred men
4. **fame . . . envy:** envied fame; **Fix . . . foot:** take your stance for combat.

Mar. Let the first budger die the other's slave, 5
And the gods doom him after!
Auf. If I fly, Marcius,
Halloa me like a hare.
Mar. Within these three hours, Tullus,
Alone I fought in your Corioli walls, 8
And made what work I pleased. 'Tis not my blood
Wherein thou seest me masked. For thy revenge
Wrench up thy power to the highest.
Auf. Wert thou the Hector
That was the whip of your bragged progeny,
Thou shouldst not scape me here.

Here they fight, and certain Volsces come in the aid of Aufidius. Marcius fights till they be driven in breathless.

Officious, and not valiant, you have shamed me
In your condemned seconds. 15

Exeunt.

[Scene IX. *The Roman camp.*]

Flourish. Alarum. A retreat is sounded. Enter, at one door, COMINIUS *with the* ROMANS; *at another door,* MARCIUS, *with his arm in a scarf.*

Com. If I should tell thee o'er this thy day's work,
Thou't not believe thy deeds; but I'll report it
Where senators shall mingle tears with smiles;
Where great patricians shall attend and shrug,
I' the end admire; where ladies shall be frighted
And, gladly quaked, hear more; where the dull tribunes, 6
That with the fusty plebeians hate thine honors,
Shall say against their hearts, "We thank the gods
Our Rome hath such a soldier."
Yet camest thou to a morsel of this feast, 10
Having fully dined before.

Enter TITUS [LARTIUS,] *with his* POWER, *from the pursuit.*

Lar. O General,
Here is the steed, we the caparison.
Hadst thou beheld—

Mar. Pray now, no more; my mother,
Who has a charter to extol her blood, 14
When she does praise me grieves me. I have done
As you have done—that's what I can; induced
As you have been—that's for my country.
He that has but effected his good will
Hath overta'en mine act.
Com. You shall not be
The grave of your deserving; Rome must know 20
The value of her own. 'Twere a concealment
Worse than a theft, no less than a traducement,
To hide your doings and to silence that
Which to the spire and top of praises vouched
Would seem but modest. Therefore, I beseech you,
In sign of what you are, not to reward 26
What you have done, before our army hear me.
Mar. I have some wounds upon me, and they smart
To hear themselves rememb'red.
Com. Should they not,
Well might they fester 'gainst ingratitude 30
And tent themselves with death. Of all the horses—
Whereof we have ta'en good, and good store—of all
The treasure in this field achieved and city,
We render you the tenth; to be ta'en forth
Before the common distribution at 35
Your only choice.
Mar. I thank you, General,
But cannot make my heart consent to take
A bribe to pay my sword. I do refuse it,
And stand upon my common part with those
That have beheld the doing. 40

A long flourish. They all cry "Marcius, Marcius!" cast up their caps and lances. Cominius and Lartius stand bare.

May these same instruments which you profane
Never sound more! When drums and trumpets shall
I' the field prove flatterers, let courts and cities be
Made all of false-faced soothing. When steel grows
Soft as the parasite's silk, let him be made 45
An overture for the wars. No more, I say.
For that I have not washed my nose that bled,
Or foiled some debile wretch, which without note
Here's many else have done, you shout me forth
In acclamations hyperbolical, 50
As if I loved my little should be dieted
In praises sauced with lies.
Com. Too modest are you;
More cruel to your good report than grateful

12. bragged progeny: boasted progenitors. The Trojan Æneas was supposed to have founded Rome. Hector was Troy's mightiest warrior, hence the **whip** with which the Trojans scourged the Greeks.
15. In . . . seconds: by violating the rules of single combat in supporting me
2. Thou't: thou wouldst
7. fusty: stale-smelling
8. against . . . hearts: grudgingly
10–11. camest . . . before: this action was slight in comparison with the deeds you had already performed.
12. steed: referring to Marcius; **caparison:** horse trapping; accessory

14. charter: privilege; **blood:** kin
24. spire . . . top: topmost spire
31. tent: probe (used to cleanse and treat wounds)
35–36. at . . . choice: as you alone choose
44. soothing: flattering
45. him: i.e., the parasite
46. overture: offer. That is, let the parasite be called upon to fight.
48. Or foiled: or because I have defeated; **debile:** weak
50. hyperbolical: extravagant
51. dieted: feasted

To us that give you truly. By your patience, 54
If 'gainst yourself you be incensed, we'll put you—
Like one that means his proper harm—in manacles,
Then reason safely with you. Therefore be it known,
As to us, to all the world, that Caius Marcius
Wears this war's garland; in token of the which,
My noble steed, known to the camp, I give him, 60
With all his trim belonging; and from this time,
For what he did before Corioli, call him
With all the applause and clamor of the host,
Caius Marcius Coriolanus.
Bear the addition nobly ever! 65

Flourish. Trumpets sound, and drums.

All. Caius Marcius Coriolanus!

Cor. I will go wash;
And when my face is fair you shall perceive
Whether I blush or no. Howbeit, I thank you;
I mean to stride your steed, and at all times 70
To undercrest your good addition
To the fairness of my power.

Com. So, to our tent;
Where, ere we do repose us, we will write
To Rome of our success. You, Titus Lartius,
Must to Corioli back. Send us to Rome 75
The best, with whom we may articulate
For their own good and ours.

Lar. I shall, my lord.

Cor. The gods begin to mock me. I, that now
Refused most princely gifts, am bound to beg 79
Of my Lord General.

Com. Take 't; 'tis yours; what is't?

Cor. I sometime lay here in Corioli
At a poor man's house; he used me kindly.
He cried to me; I saw him prisoner;
But then Aufidius was within my view, 84
And wrath o'erwhelmed my pity. I request you
To give my poor host freedom.

Com. O, well begged!
Were he the butcher of my son, he should
Be free as is the wind. Deliver him, Titus.

Lar. Marcius, his name?

Cor. By Jupiter, forgot!
I am weary; yea, my memory is tired. 90
Have we no wine here?

Com. Go we to our tent.
The blood upon your visage dries; 'tis time
It should be looked to. Come.

Exeunt.

[Scene X. *The Camp of the Volsces.*]

A flourish. Cornets. Enter TULLUS AUFIDIUS *bloody, with* TWO OR THREE SOLDIERS.

Auf. The town is ta'en.

1. Sol. 'Twill be delivered back on good condition.

Auf. Condition!
I would I were a Roman; for I cannot,
Being a Volsce, be that I am. Condition? 5
What good condition can a treaty find
I' the part that is at mercy? Five times, Marcius,
I have fought with thee; so often hast thou beat me;
And wouldst do so, I think, should we encounter
As often as we eat. By the elements, 10
If e'er again I meet him beard to beard,
He's mine or I am his. Mine emulation
Hath not that honor in't it had; for where
I thought to crush him in an equal force, 14
True sword to sword, I'll potch at him some way;
Or wrath or craft may get him.

1. Sol. He's the devil.

Auf. Bolder, though not so subtle. My valor's poisoned
With only suff'ring stain by him; for him
Shall fly out of itself. Nor sleep nor sanctuary,
Being naked, sick, nor fane nor Capitol, 20
The prayers of priests nor times of sacrifice,
Embarquements all of fury, shall lift up
Their rotten privilege and custom 'gainst
My hate to Marcius. Where I find him, were it
At home, upon my brother's guard, even there, 25
Against the hospitable canon, would I
Wash my fierce hand in's heart. Go you to the city;
Learn how 'tis held, and what they are that must
Be hostages for Rome.

1. Sol. Will not you go?

Auf. I am attended at the cypress grove; I pray you— 30
'Tis south the city mills—bring me word thither
How the world goes, that to the pace of it
I may spur on my journey.

1. Sol. I shall, sir.

Exeunt.

54. **give:** describe
56. **proper:** personal
59. **garland:** victorious wreath
65. **addition:** title
71–72. **undercrest . . . power:** merit the honored title to the best of my ability
75. **us:** for us
76. **articulate:** discuss terms
81. **sometime:** once
88. **Deliver:** release

4–5. **I . . . am:** being a defeated Volsce, I cannot be a merciless victor.
12. **emulation:** envious rivalry
15. **potch:** thrust
19. **fly . . . itself:** renounce its character
20. **fane:** temple (the restraints of religion); **Capitol:** i.e., governmental control
22. **Embarquements:** embargoes; restraints
25. **upon . . . guard:** in my brother's custody
26. **hospitable canon:** law of hospitality

ACT II

[Scene I. *Rome. A public place.*]

Enter MENENIUS, *with the two Tribunes of the people,* SICINIUS *and* BRUTUS.

Men. The augurer tells me we shall have news to-night.

Bru. Good or bad?

Men. Not according to the prayer of the people, for they love not Marcius. 5

Sic. Nature teaches beasts to know their friends.

Men. Pray you, who does the wolf love?

Sic. The lamb.

Men. Ay, to devour him, as the hungry plebeians would the noble Marcius. 10

Bru. He's a lamb indeed, that baes like a bear.

Men. He's a bear indeed, that lives like a lamb. You two are old men; tell me one thing that I shall ask you.

Both Trib. Well, sir. 15

Men. In what enormity is Marcius poor in that you two have not in abundance?

Bru. He's poor in no one fault, but stored with all.

Sic. Especially in pride.

Bru. And topping all others in boasting. 20

Men. This is strange now. Do you two know how you are censured here in the city—I mean of us o' the right-hand file? Do you?

Both Trib. Why, how are we censured?

Men. Because you talk of pride now—will 25 you not be angry?

Both Trib. Well, well, sir, well.

Men. Why, 'tis no great matter; for a very little thief of occasion will rob you of a great deal of patience. Give your dispositions the reins, and be 30 angry at your pleasures—at the least, if you take it as a pleasure to you in being so. You blame Marcius for being proud?

Bru. We do it not alone, sir.

Men. I know you can do very little alone; 35 for your helps are many, or else your actions would grow wondrous single: your abilities are too infant-like for doing much alone. You talk of pride. O that you could turn your eyes toward the napes of your necks, and make but an interior survey of your 40 good selves! O that you could!

Both Trib. What then, sir?

Men. Why, then you should discover a brace of unmeriting, proud, violent, testy magistrates—alias fools—as any in Rome. 45

Sic. Menenius, you are known well enough too.

Men. I am known to be a humorous patrician, and one that loves a cup of hot wine with not a drop of allaying Tiber in't; said to be something imperfect in favoring the first complaint, hasty and tin- 50 derlike upon too trivial motion; one that converses more with the buttock of the night than with the forehead of the morning. What I think I utter, and spend my malice in my breath. Meeting two such wealsmen as you are—I cannot call you Ly- 55 curguses—if the drink you give me touch my palate adversely, I make a crooked face at it. I cannot say your worships have delivered the matter well when I find the ass in compound with the major part of your syllables; and though I must be content to bear 60 with those that say you are reverend grave men, yet they lie deadly that tell you you have good faces. If you see this in the map of my microcosm, follows it that I am known well enough too? What harm can your bisson conspectuities glean out of this 65 character, if I be known well enough too?

Bru. Come, sir, come; we know you well enough.

Men. You know neither me, yourselves, nor any thing. You are ambitious for poor knaves' caps and legs; you wear out a good wholesome forenoon 70 in hearing a cause between an orangewife and a fosset-seller, and then rejourn the controversy of threepence to a second day of audience. When you

16–17. In . . . abundance: what monstrous fault has Marcius that you have not to a greater degree?
22. censured: judged
23. right-hand file: patricians
29. occasion: opportunity

37. single: puny
47. humorous: whimsical
49. allaying: diluting
51. motion: incitement
55. wealsmen: statesmen
55–56. Lycurguses: lawgivers. Lycurgus devised the Spartan constitution.
63. the . . . microcosm: my face. Man was considered a microcosm, the universe the "macrocosm."
65. bisson conspectuities: blinded visions; faulty perceptions
69–70. caps . . . legs: hat-doffing and bowing
72. fosset-seller: seller of barrel taps; **rejourn:** adjourn

are hearing a matter between party and party, if you chance to be pinched with the colic, you 75 make faces like mummers, set up the bloody flag against all patience, and, in roaring for a chamber pot, dismiss the controversy bleeding, the more entangled by your hearing. All the peace you make in their cause is calling both the parties knaves. 80 You are a pair of strange ones.

Bru. Come, come, you are well understood to be a perfecter giber for the table than a necessary bencher in the Capitol.

Men. Our very priests must become mockers 85 if they shall encounter such ridiculous subjects as you are. When you speak best unto the purpose, it is not worth the wagging of your beards; and your beards deserve not so honorable a grave as to stuff a botcher's cushion or to be entombed in an ass's 90 packsaddle. Yet you must be saying Marcius is proud, who, in a cheap estimation, is worth all your predecessors since Deucalion; though peradventure some of the best of 'em were hereditary hangmen. Godden to your worships. More of your conversation 95 would infect my brain, being the herdsmen of the beastly plebeians. I will be bold to take my leave of you. [*Brutus and Sicinius go aside.*]

Enter VOLUMNIA, VIRGILIA, *and* VALERIA.

How now, my as fair as noble ladies—and the moon, were she earthly, no nobler—whither do you 100 follow your eyes so fast?

Vol. Honorable Menenius, my boy Marcius approaches; for the love of Juno, let's go.

Men. Ha! Marcius coming home?

Vol. Ay, worthy Menenius, and with most 105 prosperous approbation.

Men. Take my cap, Jupiter, and I thank thee. Hoo! Marcius coming home!

Vol., Vir. Nay, 'tis true.

Vol. Look, here's a letter from him; the 110 state hath another, his wife another; and I think there's one at home for you.

Men. I will make my very house reel tonight. A letter for me?

Vir. Yes, certain, there's a letter for you; I 115 saw't.

Men. A letter for me! It gives me an estate of seven years' health; in which time I will make a lip at the physician. The most sovereign prescription in Galen is but empiricutic and, to this preserva- 120 tive, of no better report than a horse drench. Is he not wounded? He was wont to come home wounded.

Vir. O, no, no, no.

Vol. O, he is wounded, I thank the gods for't.

Men. So do I too, if it be not too much. 125 Brings a victory in his pocket? The wounds become him.

Vol. On's brows, Menenius; he comes the third time home with the oaken garland.

Men. Has he disciplined Aufidius soundly? 130

Vol. Titus Lartius writes they fought together, but Aufidius got off.

Men. And 'twas time for him too, I'll warrant him that; an he had stayed by him, I would not have been so fidiused for all the chests in Corioli 135 and the gold that's in them. Is the Senate possessed of this?

Vol. Good ladies, let's go. Yes, yes, yes: the Senate has letters from the general, wherein he gives my son the whole name of the war; he hath in this ac- 140 tion outdone his former deeds doubly.

Val. In troth, there's wondrous things spoke of him.

Men. Wondrous! Ay, I warrant you, and not with out his true purchasing. 145

Vir. The gods grant them true!

Vol. True! Pow, waw.

Men. True! I'll be sworn they are true. Where is he wounded? [*To the Tribunes*] God save your good worships! Marcius is coming home; he has 150 more cause to be proud. Where is he wounded?

Vol. I' the shoulder and i' the left arm; there will be large cicatrices to show the people when he shall stand for his place. He received in the repulse of Tarquin seven hurts i' the body. 155

Men. One i' the neck and two i' the thigh—there's nine that I know.

Vol. He had before this last expedition twenty-five wounds upon him.

Men. Now it's twenty-seven; every gash 160 was an enemy's grave. (*A shout and flourish.*) Hark! The trumpets.

Vol. These are the ushers of Marcius. Before him he carries noise, and behind him he leaves tears;
Death, that dark spirit, in's nervy arm doth lie, 165
Which, being advanced, declines, and then men die.

76. mummers: pantomime actors; **bloody flag:** standard of war
84. bencher: magistrate
90. botcher: clumsy tailor or maker of repairs
94. Godden: God give you good evening
96. being: since you are
105–6. most . . . approbation: great success and applause
108. Hoo: hurrah!
119. sovereign: powerful
120. empiricutic: quackish; **to:** compared to
121. drench: medicinal draught
135. fidiused: i.e., treated as Aufidius could expect to be by Marcius
136. possessed: informed
140. whole . . . of: complete credit for
145. true purchasing: honest acquiring
147. Pow, waw: Volumnia dismisses contemptuously the possibility of their being untrue.
155. Tarquin: the tyrant Tarquinius Superbus
165. nervy: powerful

A sennet. Trumpets sound. Enter COMINIUS *the General, and* TITUS LARTIUS; *between them,* CORIOLANUS, *crowned with an oaken garland; with* CAPTAINS *and* SOLDIERS *and a* HERALD.

Her. Know, Rome, that all alone Marcius did fight
Within Corioli gates, where he hath won,
With fame, a name to Caius Marcius; these
In honor follows Coriolanus. 170
Welcome to Rome, renowned Coriolanus! *Flourish.*
All. Welcome to Rome, renowned Coriolanus!
Cor. No more of this, it does offend my heart.
Pray now, no more.
Com. Look, sir, your mother!
Cor. O,
You have, I know, petitioned all the gods 175
For my prosperity! *Kneels.*
Vol. Nay, my good soldier, up;
My gentle Marcius, worthy Caius, and
By deed-achieving honor newly named—
What is it? Coriolanus must I call thee?
But, O, thy wife!
Cor. My gracious silence, hail! 180
Wouldst thou have laughed had I come coffined home,
That weepst to see me triumph? Ah, my dear,
Such eyes the widows in Corioli wear,
And mothers that lack sons.
Men. Now the gods crown thee!
Cor. And live you yet? [*To Valeria*] O my sweet lady, pardon. 185
Vol. I know not where to turn.
O, welcome home! And welcome, General.
And y'are welcome all.
Men. A hundred thousand welcomes. I could weep
And I could laugh; I am light and heavy. Welcome!
A curse begin at very root on's heart 191
That is not glad to see thee! You are three
That Rome should dote on; yet, by the faith of men,
We have some old crab trees here at home that will not
Be grafted to your relish. Yet welcome, warriors.
We call a nettle but a nettle, and 196
The faults of fools but folly.
Com. Ever right.
Cor. Menenius, ever, ever.
Her. Give way there, and go on.
Cor. [*To his wife and mother*] Your hand, and yours. 200
Ere in our own house I do shade my head,
The good patricians must be visited;
From whom I have received not only greetings,
But with them change of honors.

Vol. I have lived
To see inherited my very wishes, 205
And the buildings of my fancy; only
There's one thing wanting, which I doubt not but
Our Rome will cast upon thee.
Cor. Know, good mother,
I had rather be their servant in my way 209
Then sway with them in theirs.
Com. On, to the Capitol.
Flourish. Cornets. Exeunt in state, as before.

BRUTUS *and* SICINIUS [*come forward*].

Bru. All tongues speak of him and the bleared sights
Are spectacled to see him. Your prattling nurse
Into a rapture lets her baby cry
While she chats him; the kitchen malkin pins
Her richest lockram 'bout her reechy neck, 215
Clamb'ring the walls to eye him; stalls, bulks, windows,
Are smothered up, leads filled and ridges horsed
With variable complexions, all agreeing
In earnestness to see him. Seld-shown flamens
Do press among the popular throngs and puff 220
To win a vulgar station; our veiled dames
Commit the war of white and damask in
Their nicely gauded cheeks to the wanton spoil
Of Phœbus' burning kisses. Such a pother,
As if that whatsoever god who leads him 225
Were slyly crept into his human powers,
And gave him graceful posture.
Sic. On the sudden
I warrant him consul.
Bru. Then our office may
During his power go sleep. 229
Sic. He cannot temp'rately transport his honors
From where he should begin and end but will
Lose those he hath won.
Bru. In that there's comfort.
Sic. Doubt not
The commoners, for whom we stand, but they
Upon their ancient malice will forget 234
With the least cause these his new honors; which

190. **light:** merry; **heavy:** grave
195. **to . . . relish:** to have a taste for you

205. **inherited:** possessed
210. **sway:** rule
213. **rapture:** fit
214. **chats him:** chats about him; **malkin:** wench
215. **lockram:** fabric; **reechy:** greasy
216. **bulks:** shop fronts
217. **leads:** roofs (usually sheeted with lead); **ridges horsed:** roof-ridges straddled
218. **variable complexions:** people of various kinds
219. **Seld-shown:** seldom seen; **flamens:** priests
222–24. **Commit . . . kisses:** offer their cleverly painted red and white complexions to the mercy of the sun's rays
224. **pother:** commotion
227. **graceful:** divine
230–31. **temp'rately . . . end:** carry his burden of honors modestly from first to last
235. **which:** referring to **cause**

That he will give them make I as little question
As he is proud to do't.
Bru. I heard him swear,
Were he to stand for consul, never would he
Appear i' the market place, nor on him put
The napless vesture of humility; 240
Nor, showing, as the manner is, his wounds
To the people, beg their stinking breaths.
Sic. 'Tis right.
Bru. It was his word. O, he would miss it rather
Than carry it but by the suit of the gentry to him
And the desire of the nobles.
Sic. I wish no better 245
Than have him hold that purpose and to put it
In execution.
Bru. 'Tis most like he will.
Sic. It shall be to him then as our good wills:
A sure destruction.
Bru. So it must fall out
To him or our authorities. For an end, 250
We must suggest the people in what hatred
He still hath held them; that to's power he would
Have made them mules, silenced their pleaders, and
Dispropertied their freedoms, holding them
In human action and capacity 255
Of no more soul nor fitness for the world
Than camels in their war, who have their provand
Only for bearing burdens and sore blows
For sinking under them.
Sic. This, as you say, suggested
At some time when his soaring insolence 260
Shall touch the people—which time shall not want,
If he be put upon't, and that's as easy
As to set dogs on sheep—will be his fire
To kindle their dry stubble; and their blaze
Shall darken him forever.

Enter a MESSENGER.

Bru. What's the matter? 265
Mess. You are sent for to the Capitol. 'Tis thought
That Marcius shall be consul.
I have seen the dumb men throng to see him and
The blind to hear him speak; matrons flung gloves,
Ladies and maids their scarfs and handkerchers,
Upon him as he passed; the nobles bended 271
As to Jove's statue, and the commons made
A shower and thunder with their caps and shouts.
I never saw the like.
Bru. Let's to the Capitol,
And carry with us ears and eyes for the time, 275
But hearts for the event.
Sic. Have with you.
Exeunt.

[Scene II. *The same. The Capitol.*]

Enter TWO OFFICERS, *to lay cushions, as it were in the Capitol.*

1. Off. Come, come, they are almost here. How many stand for consulships?
2. Off. Three, they say; but 'tis thought of every one Coriolanus will carry it.
1. Off. That's a brave fellow; but he's vengeance proud and loves not the common people. 5
2. Off. Faith, there have been many great men that have flattered the people who ne'er loved them; and there be many that they have loved they know not wherefore; so that, if they love they know not 10 why, they hate upon no better a ground. Therefore, for Coriolanus neither to care whether they love or hate him manifests the true knowledge he has in their disposition, and out of his noble carelessness lets them plainly see't. 15
1. Off. If he did not care whether he had their love or no, he waved indifferently 'twixt doing them neither good nor harm; but he seeks their hate with greater devotion than they can render it him and leaves nothing undone that may fully discover 20 him their opposite. Now to seem to affect the malice and displeasure of the people is as bad as that which he dislikes, to flatter them for their love.
2. Off. He hath deserved worthily of his country; and his ascent is not by such easy degrees as 25 those who, having been supple and courteous to the people, bonneted, without any further deed to have them at all, into their estimation and report; but he hath so planted his honors in their eyes and his actions in their hearts that for their tongues to be 30 silent and not confess so much were a kind of ingrateful injury; to report otherwise were a malice that, giving itself the lie, would pluck reproof and rebuke from every ear that heard it.

240. **napless vesture:** worn clothing
242. **breaths:** voices of approval
244. **but:** other than
247. **like:** likely
248. **as . . . wills:** as we would wish
250. **For . . . end:** to settle the matter
252. **still:** always
254. **Dispropertied . . . freedoms:** deprived them of their liberties
257. **provand:** provender
261. **want:** be lacking
262. **put upon't:** incited to it
275. **time:** present occasion
276. **event:** ultimate outcome; **Have . . . you:** let's go.
5–6. **vengeance:** excessively; cf. the phrase "with a vengeance"
20. **discover:** reveal
21. **opposite:** enemy; **affect:** desire
26. **supple:** compliant
27. **bonneted:** won favor by deference
28. **estimation . . . report:** popularity

1. Off. No more of him; he's a worthy man. 35
Make way, they are coming.

A sennet. Enter the PATRICIANS *and the* TRIBUNES *of the People,* LICTORS *before them;* CORIOLANUS, MENENIUS, COMINIUS *the Consul.* SICINIUS *and* BRUTUS *take their places by themselves.* CORIOLANUS *stands.*

Men. Having determined of the Volsces, and
To send for Titus Lartius, it remains,
As the main point of this our after-meeting,
To gratify his noble service that 40
Hath thus stood for his country. Therefore, please you,
Most reverend and grave elders, to desire
The present consul and last general
In our well-found successes to report
A little of that worthy work performed 45
By Caius Marcius Coriolanus; whom
We met here both to thank and to remember
With honors like himself. [*Coriolanus sits.*]
1. Sen. Speak, good Cominius.
Leave nothing out for length, and make us think
Rather our state's defective for requital 50
Than we to stretch it out. Masters o' the people,
We do request your kindest ears; and, after,
Your loving motion toward the common body,
To yield what passes here.
Sic. We are convented
Upon a pleasing treaty, and have hearts 55
Inclinable to honor and advance
The theme of our assembly.
Bru. Which the rather
We shall be blessed to do, if he remember
A kinder value of the people than 59
He hath hereto prized them at.
Men. That's off, that's off;
I would you rather had been silent. Please you
To hear Cominius speak?
Bru. Most willingly.
But yet my caution was more pertinent
Than the rebuke you give it.
Men. He loves your people;
But tie him not to be their bedfellow. 65
Worthy Cominius, speak.
Coriolanus rises, and offers to go away.
Nay, keep your place.

1. Sen. Sit, Coriolanus, never shame to hear
What you have nobly done.
Cor. Your Honors' pardon.
I had rather have my wounds to heal again 70
Than hear say how I got them.
Bru. Sir, I hope
My words disbenched you not.
Cor. No, sir; yet oft,
When blows have made me stay, I fled from words.
You soothed not, therefore hurt not. But your people,
I love them as they weigh—
Men. Pray now, sit down.
Cor. I had rather have one scratch my head i' the sun 76
When the alarum were struck than idly sit
To hear my nothings monstered. *Exit.*
Men. Masters of the people,
Your multiplying spawn how can he flatter— 79
That's thousand to one good one—when you now see
He had rather venture all his limbs for honor
Than one on's ears to hear it? Proceed, Cominius.
Com. I shall lack voice; the deeds of Coriolanus
Should not be uttered feebly. It is held
That valor is the chiefest virtue and 85
Most dignifies the haver. If it be,
The man I speak of cannot in the world
Be singly counterpoised. At sixteen years,
When Tarquin made a head for Rome, he fought
Beyond the mark of others; our then dictator, 90
Whom with all praise I point at, saw him fight
When with his Amazonian chin he drove
The bristled lips before him; he bestrid
An o'erpressed Roman and i' the consul's view
Slew three opposers; Tarquin's self he met, 95
And struck him on his knee. In that day's feats,
When he might act the woman in the scene,
He proved best man i' the field, and for his meed
Was brow-bound with the oak. His pupil age
Man-ent'red thus, he waxed like a sea, 100
And in the brunt of seventeen battles since
He lurched all swords of the garland. For this last,
Before and in Corioli, let me say
I cannot speak him home. He stopped the fliers,

40. gratify: reward
44. well-found: notable
48. like himself: worthy of him
50–51. Rather . . . out: we are deficient rather in the means to reward him adequately than in the will to do so.
53–54. Your . . . here: your favorable report to the people concerning this matter
54. convented: convened
55. Upon . . . treaty: for a pleasant purpose
58. blessed: happy
60. off: irrelevant
74. soothed: flattered
75. weigh: merit
78. monstered: displayed as wonders
80. That's . . . one: among whom there is only one good man in a thousand
88. singly counterpoised: equaled by any other
89. made . . . for: raised an army to attack
92. Amazonian: i.e., beardless
93. bestrid: straddled the fallen body of
96. on: onto
98. meed: reward
99–100. His . . . Man-ent'red: his apprenticeship entered in manly fashion
100. waxed: grew
102. lurched . . . garland: cheated all other soldiers of the victor's wreath
104. speak . . . home: describe him thoroughly

And by his rare example made the coward 105
Turn terror into sport; as weeds before
A vessel under sail, so men obeyed
And fell below his stem. His sword, death's stamp,
Where it did mark, it took; from face to foot
He was a thing of blood, whose every motion 110
Was timed with dying cries. Alone he ent'red
The mortal gate of the city, which he painted
With shunless destiny; aidless came off,
And with a sudden reinforcement struck
Corioli like a planet. Now all's his. 115
When by-and-by the din of war 'gan pierce
His ready sense, then straight his doubled spirit
Requick'ned what in flesh was fatigate,
And to the battle came he; where he did
Run reeking o'er the lives of men as if 120
'Twere a perpetual spoil; and till we called
Both field and city ours he never stood
To ease his breast with panting.
Men. Worthy man!
1. Sen. He cannot but with measure fit the honors
Which we devise him.
Com. Our spoils he kicked at, 125
And looked upon things precious as they were
The common muck of the world. He covets less
Than misery itself would give, rewards
His deeds with doing them, and is content
To spend the time to end it.
Men. He's right noble; 130
Let him be called for.
1. Sen. Call Coriolanus.
Off. He doth appear.

[*Re-*]*enter* CORIOLANUS.

Men. The Senate, Coriolanus, are well pleased
To make thee consul.
Cor. I do owe them still
My life and services.
Men. It then remains 135
That you do speak to the people.
Cor. I do beseech you
Let me o'erleap that custom; for I cannot
Put on the gown, stand naked, and entreat them
For my wounds' sake to give their suffrage. Please you
That I may pass this doing.
Sic. Sir, the people 140
Must have their voices; neither will they bate
One jot of ceremony.
Men. Put them not to't.
Pray you go fit you to the custom, and
Take to you, as your predecessors have,
Your honor with your form.
Cor. It is a part 145
That I shall blush in acting, and might well
Be taken from the people.
Bru. Mark you that?
Cor. To brag unto them, "Thus I did, and thus!"
Show them the unaching scars which I should hide,
As if I had received them for the hire 150
Of their breath only!
Men. Do not stand upon't.
We recommend to you, tribunes of the people,
Our purpose to them; and to our noble consul
Wish we all joy and honor.
Sen. To Coriolanus come all joy and honor! 155
Flourish. Cornets. Then exeunt [*all but Sicinius and Brutus.*]
Bru. You see how he intends to use the people.
Sic. May they perceive's intent! He will require them
As if he did contemn what he requested
Should be in them to give.
Bru. Come, we'll inform them
Of our proceedings here. On the market place 160
I know they do attend us.
Exeunt.

[Scene III. *The same. The Forum.*]

Enter SEVEN OR EIGHT CITIZENS.

1. Cit. Once, if he do require our voices, we ought not to deny him.
2. Cit. We may, sir, if we will.
3. Cit. We have power in ourselves to do it, but it is a power that we have no power to do; for if he 5 show us his wounds and tell us his deeds, we are to put our tongues into those wounds and speak for them; so, if he tell us his noble deeds, we must also tell him our noble acceptance of them. Ingratitude is monstrous, and for the multitude to be ingrate- 10 ful were to make a monster of the multitude; of the which we being members should bring ourselves to be monstrous members.
1. Cit. And to make us no better thought of, a little help will serve; for once we stood up about 15

108. stem: prow
112. mortal: fatal
118. fatigate: fatigued
120. reeking: smelling of blood
124. with measure: proportionately; adequately
128. misery: miserliness
141. bate: omit

142. Put . . . to't: don't anger them.
145. with . . . form: with the prescribed formality
151. breath: approval; **stand upon't:** make an issue of it
152–53. recommend . . . them: submit to you the announcement to the people of our purpose
157. require: ask
1. Once: in the first place

the corn, he himself stuck not to call us the many-headed multitude.

3. Cit. We have been called so of many; not that our heads are some brown, some black, some abram, some bald, but that our wits are so diversely 20 colored; and truly I think if all our wits were to issue out of one skull, they would fly east, west, north, south, and their consent of one direct way should be at once to all the points o' the compass.

2. Cit. Think you so? Which way do you 25 judge my wit would fly?

3. Cit. Nay, your wit will not so soon out as another man's will—'tis strongly wedged up in a blockhead; but if it were at liberty 'twould sure southward. 30

2. Cit. Why that way?

3. Cit. To lose itself in a fog; where being three parts melted away with rotten dews, the fourth would return for conscience' sake, to help to get thee a wife.

2. Cit. You are never without your tricks; 35 you may, you may.

3. Cit. Are you all resolved to give your voices? But that's no matter, the greater part carries it. I say, if he would incline to the people, there was never a worthier man. 40

Enter CORIOLANUS, *in a gown of humility, with* MENENIUS.

Here he comes, and in the gown of humility. Mark his behavior. We are not to stay all together, but to come by him where he stands, by ones, by twos, and by threes. He's to make his requests by particulars, wherein every one of us has a single honor, in 45 giving him our own voices with our own tongues; therefore follow me, and I'll direct you how you shall go by him.

All. Content, content. [*Exeunt Citizens.*]

Men. O sir, you are not right; have you not known
The worthiest men have done't?

Cor. What must I say?
"I pray, sir"—Plague upon't! I cannot bring 52
My tongue to such a pace. "Look, sir, my wounds!
I got them in my country's service, when
Some certain of your brethren roared and ran 55
From the noise of our own drums."

Men. O me, the gods!
You must not speak of that. You must desire them
To think upon you.

Cor. Think upon me? Hang 'em!
I would they would forget me, like the virtues
Which our divines lose by 'em.

Men. You'll mar all. 60
I'll leave you. Pray you speak to 'em, I pray you,
In wholesome manner. *Exit.*

[*Re-*]*enter* THREE OF THE CITIZENS.

Cor. Bid them wash their faces
And keep their teeth clean. So, here comes a brace.
You know the cause, sir, of my standing here.

3. Cit. We do, sir; tell us what hath brought 65 you to't.

Cor. Mine own desert.

2. Cit. Your own desert?

Cor. Ay, not mine own desire.

3. Cit. How, not your own desire? 70

Cor. No, sir, 'twas never my desire yet to trouble the poor with begging.

3. Cit. You must think, if we give you anything, we hope to gain by you.

Cor. Well then, I pray, your price o' the con- 75 sulship?

1. Cit. The price is to ask it kindly.

Cor. Kindly, sir, I pray let me ha't. I have wounds to show you, which shall be yours in private. Your good voice, sir; what say you? 80

2. Cit. You shall ha' it, worthy sir.

Cor. A match, sir. There's in all two worthy voices begged. I have your alms. Adieu.

3. Cit. But this is something odd.

2. Cit. An 'twere to give again—but 'tis no 85 matter. *Exeunt* [*the three Citizens*].

[*Re-*]*enter* TWO OTHER CITIZENS.

Cor. Pray you now, if it may stand with the tune of your voices that I may be consul, I have here the customary gown.

4. Cit. You have deserved nobly of your 90 country, and you have not deserved nobly.

Cor. Your enigma?

4. Cit. You have been a scourge to her enemies; you have been a rod to her friends. You have not indeed loved the common people. 95

Cor. You should account me the more virtuous that I have not been common in my love. I will, sir, flatter my sworn brother, the people, to earn a dearer estimation of them; 'tis a condition they account gentle; and since the wisdom of their choice is 100 rather to have my hat than my heart, I will practice the insinuating nod and be off to them most counterfeitly. That is, sir, I will counterfeit the bewitchment

19. abram: auburn
23. consent: agreement
36. you may: you may have your little joke.
44. by particulars: of each individual
59–60. like . . . 'em: as they forget the pious teachings of our clergy
62. wholesome: favorable
82. A match: then it's a bargain.
87–88. stand . . . voices: meet with your approval
99. of: from; **condition:** conduct
100. gentle: gentlemanly
102. insinuating: ingratiating

of some popular man and give it bountiful to the desirers. Therefore, beseech you I may be consul. 105

5. Cit. We hope to find you our friend; and therefore give you our voices heartily.

4. Cit. You have received many wounds for your country.

Cor. I will not seal your knowledge with 110
showing them. I will make much of your voices, and so trouble you no farther.

Both Cit. The gods give you joy, sir, heartily!

[*Exeunt Citizens.*]

Cor. Most sweet voices!
Better it is to die, better to starve, 115
Than crave the hire which first we do deserve.
Why in this wolvish toge should I stand here
To beg of Hob and Dick that do appear
Their needless vouches? Custom calls me to't.
What custom wills, in all things should we do't,
The dust on antique time would lie unswept, 121
And mountainous error be too highly heaped
For truth to o'erpeer. Rather than fool it so,
Let the high office and the honor go
To one that would do thus. I am half through: 125
The one part suffered, the other will I do.

Enter THREE CITIZENS *more.*

Here come mo voices.
Your voices. For your voices I have fought;
Watched for your voices; for your voices bear
Of wounds two dozen odd; battles thrice six 130
I have seen and heard of; for your voices have
Done many things, some less, some more. Your voices?
Indeed, I would be consul.

6. Cit. He has done nobly, and cannot go without any honest man's voice. 135

7. Cit. Therefore let him be consul. The gods give him joy, and make him good friend to the people!

All. Amen, amen. God save thee, noble consul!

[*Exeunt Citizens.*]

Cor. Worthy voices!

[*Re-*]*enter* MENENIUS *with* BRUTUS *and* SICINIUS.

Men. You have stood your limitation, and the tribunes 140
Endue you with the people's voice. Remains
That, in the official marks invested, you
Anon do meet the Senate.

Cor. Is this done?

Sic. The custom of request you have discharged.
The people do admit you, and are summoned 145
To meet anon, upon your approbation.

Cor. Where? At the Senate House?

Sic. There, Coriolanus.

Cor. May I change these garments?

Sic. You may, sir.

Cor. That I'll straight do, and, knowing myself again,
Repair to the Senate House. 150

Men. I'll keep you company. Will you along?

Bru. We stay here for the people.

Sic. Fare you well.

Exeunt Coriolanus and Menenius.

He has it now; and by his looks methinks
'Tis warm at's heart.

Bru. With a proud heart he wore 155
His humble weeds. Will you dismiss the people?

[*Re-enter* CITIZENS.]

Sic. How now, my masters! Have you chose this man?

1. Cit. He has our voices, sir.

Bru. We pray the gods he may deserve your loves.

2. Cit. Amen, sir. To my poor unworthy notice,
He mocked us when he begged our voices.

3. Cit. Certainly;
He flouted us downright. 162

1. Cit. No, 'tis his kind of speech; he did not mock us.

2. Cit. Not one amongst us, save yourself, but says
He used us scornfully. He should have showed us
His marks of merit, wounds received for's country.

Sic. Why, so he did, I am sure. 167

All. No, no; no man saw 'em.

3. Cit. He said he had wounds which he could show in private,
And with his hat, thus waving it in scorn, 170
"I would be consul," says he; "aged custom
But by your voices will not so permit me;
Your voices therefore." When we granted that,
Here was, "I thank you for your voices. Thank you,
Your most sweet voices. Now you have left your voices, 175
I have no further with you." Was not this mockery?

Sic. Why either were you ignorant to see't,
Or, seeing it, of such childish friendliness
To yield your voices?

Bru. Could you not have told him—
As you were lessoned—when he had no power 180
But was a petty servant to the state,

104. popular man: seeker of popularity
110. seal: confirm
116. crave: request
117. wolvish toge: garb of hypocritical humility (like the wolf in sheep's clothing). This is Steevens' emendation of the Folio's "tongue"; later Folios read "gowne."
127. mo: more
129. Watched: kept watch (guard)
141. Endue: endow; **voice:** approval
142. official marks: robes of office
146. upon . . . approbation: for approval of your appointment
156. weeds: garments
180. lessoned: instructed

He was your enemy; ever spake against
Your liberties and the charters that you bear
I' the body of the weal; and now, arriving
A place of potency and sway o' the state, 185
If he should still malignantly remain
Fast foe to the plebeii, your voices might
Be curses to yourselves? You should have said
That as his worthy deeds did claim no less
Than what he stood for, so his gracious nature 190
Would think upon you for your voices, and
Translate his malice towards you into love,
Standing your friendly lord.

Sic. Thus to have said,
As you were foreadvised, had touched his spirit
And tried his inclination; from him plucked 195
Either his gracious promise, which you might,
As cause had called you up, have held him to;
Or else it would have galled his surly nature,
Which easily endures not article
Tying him to aught. So, putting him to rage, 200
You should have ta'en the advantage of his choler
And passed him unelected.

Bru. Did you perceive
He did solicit you in free contempt
When he did need your loves; and do you think
That his contempt shall not be bruising to you 205
When he hath power to crush? Why, had your bodies
No heart among you? Or had you tongues to cry
Against the rectorship of judgment?

Sic. Have you
Ere now denied the asker, and now again,
Of him that did not ask but mock, bestow 210
Your sued-for tongues?

3. Cit. He's not confirmed: we may deny him yet.

2. Cit. And will deny him;
I'll have five hundred voices of that sound.

1. Cit. I twice five hundred, and their friends to
piece 'em. 215

Bru. Get you hence instantly, and tell those friends
They have chose a consul that will from them take
Their liberties, make them of no more voice
Than dogs, that are as often beat for barking
As therefore kept to do so.

Sic. Let them assemble; 220
And, on a safer judgment, all revoke
Your ignorant election. Enforce his pride
And his old hate unto you; besides, forget not
With what contempt he wore the humble weed;
How in his suit he scorned you; but your loves,
Thinking upon his services, took from you 226
The apprehension of his present portance,
Which, most gibingly, ungravely, he did fashion
After the inveterate hate he bears you.

Bru. Lay
A fault on us, your tribunes, that we labored, 230
No impediment between, but that you must
Cast your election on him.

Sic. Say you chose him
More after our commandment than as guided
By your own true affections; and that your minds,
Preoccupied with what you rather must do 235
Than what you should, made you against the grain
To voice him consul. Lay the fault on us.

Bru. Ay, spare us not. Say we read lectures to you,
How youngly he began to serve his country, 239
How long continued; and what stock he springs of—
The noble house o' the Marcians; from whence came
That Ancus Marcius, Numa's daughter's son,
Who, after great Hostilius, here was king;
Of the same house Publius and Quintus were, 244
That our best water brought by conduits hither;
And [Censorinus,] nobly named so,
Twice being [by the people chosen] censor,
Was his great ancestor.

Sic. One thus descended,
That hath beside well in his person wrought
To be set high in place, we did commend 250
To your remembrances; but you have found,
Scaling his present bearing with his past,
That he's your fixed enemy, and revoke
Your sudden approbation.

Bru. Say you ne'er had done't—
Harp on that still—but by our putting on; 255
And presently, when you have drawn your number,
Repair to the Capitol.

Cit. We will so; almost all
Repent in their election. *Exeunt* [*Citizens*].

Bru. Let them go on;
This mutiny were better put in hazard
Than stay, past doubt, for greater. 260
If, as his nature is, he fall in rage
With their refusal, both observe and answer
The vantage of his anger.

Sic. To the Capitol, come.
We will be there before the stream o' the people;
And this shall seem, as partly 'tis, their own, 265
Which we have goaded onward.

Exeunt.

183. charters: privileges
184. weal: commonwealth
194. touched: tested
199. article: condition
203. free: open
207. heart: courage
208. rectorship: rule; **judgment:** wisdom
215. piece: add to
222. Enforce: emphasize
227. apprehension: understanding; **portance:** behavior
230–32. we . . . him: we did all in our power to see that nothing prevented your electing him.
246–47. [Censorinus] . . . censor: the bracketed words, supplied to complete the sense, are not in the Folio.
252. Scaling: weighing in the scales
254. sudden: hasty
256. drawn . . . number: gathered sufficient support
263. vantage . . . anger: opportunity his anger will give us

ACT III

[Scene I. *Rome. A street.*]

Cornets. Enter CORIOLANUS, MENENIUS, ALL THE GENTRY, COMINIUS, TITUS LARTIUS, *and other* SENATORS.

Cor. Tullus Aufidius, then, had made new head?
Lar. He had, my lord; and that it was which caused
Our swifter composition.
Cor. So then the Volsces stand but as at first, 4
Ready, when time shall prompt them, to make road
Upon's again.
Com. They are worn, Lord Consul, so
That we shall hardly in our ages see
Their banners wave again.
Com. Saw you Aufidius?
Lar. On safeguard he came to me, and did curse
Against the Volsces, for they had so vilely 10
Yielded the town. He is retired to Antium.
Cor. Spoke he of me?
Lar. He did, my lord.
Cor. How? What?
Lar. How often he had met you, sword to sword;
That of all things upon the earth he hated 14
Your person most; that he would pawn his fortunes
To hopeless restitution, so he might
Be called your vanquisher.
Cor. At Antium lives he?
Lar. At Antium.
Cor. I wish I had a cause to seek him there, 20
To oppose his hatred fully. Welcome home.

Enter SICINIUS *and* BRUTUS.

Behold, these are the tribunes of the people,
The tongues o' the common mouth. I do despise them,
For they do prank them in authority,
Against all noble sufferance.
Sic. Pass no further. 25
Cor. Ha! What is that?
Bru. It will be dangerous to go on—no further.

1. made . . . head: raised a new force
3. composition: settlement
9. On safeguard: in protective custody
24. prank them: dress themselves
25. noble sufferance: the nobility's tolerance

Cor. What makes this change?
Men. The matter?
Com. Hath he not passed the noble and the common? 30
Bru. Cominius, no.
Cor. Have I had children's voices?
1. Sen. Tribunes, give way: he shall to the market place.
Bru. The people are incensed against him.
Sic. Stop,
Or all will fall in broil.
Cor. Are these your herd? 34
Must these have voices, that can yield them now
And straight disclaim their tongues? What are your offices?
You being their mouths, why rule you not their teeth?
Have you not set them on?
Men. Be calm, be calm.
Cor. It is a purposed thing, and grows by plot,
To curb the will of the nobility; 40
Suffer't, and live with such as cannot rule
Nor ever will be ruled.
Bru. Call't not a plot.
The people cry you mocked them; and of late,
When corn was given them gratis, you repined; 44
Scandaled the suppliants for the people, called them
Time-pleasers, flatterers, foes to nobleness.
Cor. Why, this was known before.
Bru. Not to them all.
Cor. Have you informed them sithence?
Bru. How? I inform them!
Com. You are like to do such business.
Bru. Not unlike
Each way to better yours. 50
Cor. Why then should I be consul? By yond clouds,
Let me deserve so ill as you, and make me
Your fellow tribune.
Sic. You show too much of that
For which the people stir; if you will pass 54
To where you are bound, you must inquire your way,
Which you are out of, with a gentler spirit,

36. offices: functions
41. Suffer't: allow it
45. Scandaled: slandered
48. sithence: since
49. like: likely
49–50. Not . . . yours: likely to perform any business better than you
55. inquire: request; **way:** passage

Or never be so noble as a consul,
Nor yoke with him for tribune.
Men. Let's be calm.
Com. The people are abused; set on. This palt'ring
Becomes not Rome; nor has Coriolanus 60
Deserved this so dishonored rub, laid falsely
I' the plain way of his merit.
Cor. Tell me of corn!
This was my speech, and I will speak't again—
Men. Not now, not now.
1. Sen. Not in this heat, sir, now.
Cor. Now, as I live, I will. 65
My nobler friends, I crave their pardons.
For the mutable, rank-scented meinie, let them
Regard me as I do not flatter, and
Therein behold themselves. I say again,
In soothing them we nourish 'gainst our Senate 70
The cockle of rebellion, insolence, sedition,
Which we ourselves have plowed for, sowed, and scattered,
By mingling them with us, the honored number,
Who lack not virtue, no, nor power, but that 74
Which they have given to beggars.
Men. Well, no more.
1. Sen. No more words, we beseech you.
Cor. How! no more!
As for my country I have shed my blood,
Not fearing outward force, so shall my lungs
Coin words till their decay against those measles
Which we disdain should tetter us, yet sought 80
The very way to catch them.
Bru. You speak o' the people
As if you were a god to punish, not
A man of their infirmity.
Sic. 'Twere well
We let the people know't.
Men. What, what? his choler?
Cor. Choler! 85
Were I as patient as the midnight sleep,
By Jove, 'twould be my mind!
Sic. It is a mind
That shall remain a poison where it is,
Not poison any further.
Cor. Shall remain! 89
Hear you this Triton of the minnows? Mark you
His absolute "shall"?
Com. 'Twas from the canon.
Cor. "Shall"!
O good but most unwise patricians! Why,
You grave but reckless senators, have you thus
Given Hydra here to choose an officer
That with his peremptory "shall," being but 95
The horn and noise o' the monster's, wants not spirit
To say he'll turn your current in a ditch,
And make your channel his? If he have power,
Then vail your ignorance; if none, awake
Your dangerous lenity. If you are learned, 100
Be not as common fools; if you are not,
Let them have cushions by you. You are plebeians
If they be senators; and they are no less,
When, both your voices blended, the great'st taste
Most palates theirs. They choose their magistrate;
And such a one as he, who puts his "shall," 106
His popular "shall," against a graver bench
Than ever frowned in Greece. By Jove himself,
It makes the consuls base; and my soul aches
To know, when two authorities are up, 110
Neither supreme, how soon confusion
May enter 'twixt the gap of both and take
The one by the other.
Com. Well, on to the market place.
Cor. Whoever gave that counsel to give forth
The corn o' the storehouse gratis, as 'twas used 115
Sometime in Greece—
Men. Well, well, no more of that.
Cor. Though there the people had more absolute pow'r—
I say they nourished disobedience, fed
The ruin of the state.
Bru. Why, shall the people give 119
One that speaks thus their voice?
Cor. I'll give my reasons,
More worthier than their voices. They know the corn
Was not our recompense, resting well assured
They ne'er did service for't; being pressed to the war,
Even when the navel of the state was touched, 124
They would not thread the gates. This kind of service
Did not deserve corn gratis. Being i' the war,
Their mutinies and revolts, wherein they showed
Most valor, spoke not for them. The accusation
Which they have often made against the Senate,
All cause unborn, could never be the native 130
Of our so frank donation. Well, what then?
How shall this bosom multiplied digest
The Senate's courtesy? Let deeds express
What's like to be their words: "We did request it;

59. abused: deceived; **palt'ring:** haggling
61. dishonored rub: dishonorable obstacle
64. heat: anger
67. meinie: common herd
71. cockle: weed
80. tetter: afflict with a skin eruption
90. Triton: sea-god
91. from: contrary to
94. Hydra: the many-headed multitude. **Hydra** was a legendary serpent with numerous heads.
96. horn . . . noise: noisy voice; **wants:** lacks
99. vail . . . ignorance: let your ignorance (that gave him power) humble itself to him
99–100. awake . . . lenity: realize the danger created by your lenience.
102. have . . . you: i.e., sit in assembly with you as equals
104–5. the . . . theirs: i.e., their pleasure is decisive.
111. confusion: destruction
125. thread . . . gates: leave the city to fight
130. All . . . unborn: without any cause; **native:** natural result
132. this . . . multiplied: these multiple hearts

We are the greater poll, and in true fear 135
They gave us our demands." Thus we debase
The nature of our seats, and make the rabble
Call our cares fears; which will in time
Break ope the locks o' the Senate and bring in
The crows to peck the eagles.

Men. Come, enough. 140

Bru. Enough, with over measure.

Cor. No, take more.
What may be sworn by, both divine and human,
Seal what I end withal! This double worship,
Where one part does disdain with cause, the other
Insult without all reason; where gentry, title, wisdom, 145
Cannot conclude but by the yea and no
Of general ignorance—it must omit
Real necessities, and give way the while
To unstable slightness. Purpose so barred, it follows
Nothing is done to purpose. Therefore, beseech you—
You that will be less fearful than discreet; 151
That love the fundamental part of state
More than you doubt the change on't; that prefer
A noble life before a long, and wish
To jump a body with a dangerous physic 155
That's sure of death without it—at once pluck out
The multitudinous tongue; let them not lick
The sweet which is their poison. Your dishonor
Mangles true judgment and bereaves the state
Of that integrity which should become't, 160
Not having the power to do the good it would,
For the ill which doth control't.

Bru. Has said enough.

Sic. Has spoken like a traitor and shall answer
As traitors do.

Cor. Thou wretch, despite o'erwhelm thee!
What should the people do with these bald tribunes,
On whom depending, their obedience fails 166
To the greater bench? In a rebellion,
When what's not meet, but what must be, was law,
Then were they chosen; in a better hour
Let what is meet be said it must be meet, 170
And throw their power i' the dust.

Bru. Manifest treason!

Sic. This a consul? No.

Bru. The ædiles, ho!

Enter an ÆDILE.

Let him be apprehended.

Sic. Go call the people, [*Exit Ædile.*] in whose name myself
Attach thee as a traitorous innovator, 175
A foe to the public weal. Obey, I charge thee,
And follow to thine answer.

Cor. Hence, old goat!

Patrician. We'll surety him.

Com. Aged sir, hands off.

Cor. Hence, rotten thing! Or I shall shake thy bones
Out of thy garments.

Sic. Help, ye citizens! 180

Enter a rabble of PLEBEIANS, *with the* ÆDILES.

Men. On both sides more respect.

Sic. Here's he that would take from you all your power.

Bru. Seize him, ædiles.

Pleb. Down with him! Down with him!

2. Sen. Weapons, weapons, weapons! 185

They all bustle about Coriolanus.

All. Tribunes! Patricians! Citizens! What, ho! Sicinius! Brutus! Coriolanus! Citizens!

Patrician. Peace, peace, peace; stay, hold, peace!

Men. What is about to be? I am out of breath;
Confusion's near; I cannot speak. You tribunes
To the people—Coriolanus, patience! 190
Speak, good Sicinius.

Sic. Hear me, people; peace!

Pleb. Let's hear our tribune. Peace! Speak, speak, speak.

Sic. You are at point to lose your liberties.
Marcius would have all from you; Marcius, 194
Whom late you have named for consul.

Men. Fie, fie, fie!
This is the way to kindle, not to quench.

1. Sen. To unbuild the city, and to lay all flat.

Sic. What is the city but the people?

Pleb. True,
The people are the city. 199

Bru. By the consent of all we were established
The people's magistrates.

Pleb. You so remain.

Men. And so are like to do.

Com. That is the way to lay the city flat,
To bring the roof to the foundation,
And bury all which yet distinctly ranges 205
In heaps and piles of ruin.

Sic. This deserves death.

Bru. Or let us stand to our authority
Or let us lose it. We do here pronounce,

138. cares: concern for their welfare
143. Seal: confirm; **double worship:** dual rule
145. gentry: gentlemen; **title:** nobility; **wisdom:** wise men
147. general ignorance: the ignorant commonalty; **omit:** neglect
149. unstable slightness: giddy triviality; **Purpose . . . barred:** purposeful planning thus prevented
153. doubt: fear
155. jump: jolt
160. integrity: singleness (of purpose or action)
167. greater bench: higher officials (the Senate)
170. Let . . . meet: let them be told what is appropriate
175. Attach: arrest; **innovator:** revolutionary
177. to . . . answer: to defend the charge
193. at point: about
205. ranges: stands in proper order

Upon the part o' the people, in whose power
We were elected theirs, Marcius is worthy 210
Of present death.

Sic. Therefore lay hold of him;
Bear him to the rock Tarpeian, and from thence
Into destruction cast him.

Bru. Ædiles, seize him.

Pleb. Yield, Marcius, yield. 214

Men. Hear me one word; beseech you, tribunes,
Hear me but a word.

Æd. Peace, peace!

Men. Be that you seem, truly your country's friend,
And temp'rately proceed to what you would
Thus violently redress.

Bru. Sir, those cold ways, 220
That seem like prudent helps, are very poisonous
Where the disease is violent. Lay hands upon him
And bear him to the rock.

Coriolanus draws his sword.

Cor. No: I'll die here.
There's some among you have beheld me fighting;
Come, try upon yourselves what you have seen me.

Men. Down with that sword! Tribunes, withdraw awhile. 226

Bru. Lay hands upon him.

Men. Help Marcius, help,
You that be noble; help him, young and old.

Pleb. Down with him, down with him! 229

In this mutiny the Tribunes, the Ædiles, and the people are beat in.

Men. Go, get you to your house; be gone, away.
All will be nought else.

2. Sen. Get you gone.

Cor. Stand fast;
We have as many friends as enemies.

Men. Shall it be put to that?

1. Sen. The gods forbid!
I prithee, noble friend, home to thy house; 234
Leave us to cure this cause.

Men. For 'tis a sore upon us
You cannot tent yourself; be gone, beseech you.

Com. Come, sir, along with us.

Cor. I would they were barbarians, as they are,
Though in Rome littered; not Romans, as they are not, 239
Though calved i' the porch o' the Capitol.

Men. Be gone.
Put not your worthy rage into your tongue;
One time will owe another.

Cor. On fair ground
I could beat forty of them.

Men. I could myself
Take up a brace o' the best of them; yea, the two tribunes.

Com. But now 'tis odds beyond arithmetic, 245
And manhood is called foolery when it stands
Against a falling fabric. Will you hence,
Before the tag return? whose rage doth rend
Like interrupted waters, and o'erbear
What they are used to bear.

Men. Pray you be gone. 250
I'll try whether my old wit be in request
With those that have but little; this must be patched
With cloth of any color.

Com. Nay, come away.

Exeunt Coriolanus and Cominius, [*with others*].

Patrician. This man has marred his fortune.

Men. His nature is too noble for the world: 255
He would not flatter Neptune for his trident,
Or Jove for's power to thunder. His heart's his mouth;
What his breast forges, that his tongue must vent;
And, being angry, does forget that ever 259
He heard the name of death. *A noise within.*
Here's goodly work!

Patrician. I would they were a-bed.

Men. I would they were in Tiber.
What the vengeance, could he not speak 'em fair?

Enter BRUTUS *and* SICINIUS, *with the* RABBLE *again.*

Sic. Where is this viper
That would depopulate the city and 265
Be every man himself?

Men. You worthy tribunes—

Sic. He shall be thrown down the Tarpeian rock
With rigorous hands; he hath resisted law,
And therefore law shall scorn him further trial
Than the severity of the public power, 270
Which he so sets at nought.

1. Cit. He shall well know
The noble tribunes are the people's mouths,
And we their hands.

Pleb. He shall, sure on't.

Men. Sir, sir—

Sic. Peace! 274

Men. Do not cry havoc, where you should but hunt
With modest warrant.

Sic. Sir, how comes't that you
Have holp to make this rescue?

212. the . . . Tarpeian: a rock on the Capitoline Hill, from which criminals were hurled to their deaths
231. nought: wrecked
236. tent: treat
242. One . . . another: i.e., a better time will come.
248. tag: rabble
249. interrupted: erupted from their confines
275. cry havoc: order merciless slaughter. In war, the cry of "Havoc!" was the signal to give no quarter.
276. modest warrant: moderate license; temperance
277. holp: helped

Men. Hear me speak.
As I do know the consul's worthiness,
So can I name his faults.
Sic. Consul! What consul?
Men. The consul Coriolanus.
Bru. He consul! 280
Pleb. No, no, no, no, no.
Men. If, by the tribunes' leave, and yours, good people,
I may be heard, I would crave a word or two;
The which shall turn you to no further harm
Than so much loss of time.
Sic. Speak briefly, then, 285
For we are peremptory to dispatch
This viperous traitor; to eject him hence
Were but one danger, and to keep him here
Our certain death; therefore it is decreed
He dies tonight.
Men. Now the good gods forbid 290
That our renowned Rome, whose gratitude
Towards her deserved children is enrolled
In Jove's own book, like an unnatural dam
Should now eat up her own!
Sic. He's a disease that must be cut away. 295
Men. O, he's a limb that has but a disease:
Mortal to cut it off; to cure it easy.
What has he done to Rome that's worthy death?
Killing our enemies, the blood he hath lost—
Which I dare vouch is more than that he hath 300
By many an ounce—he dropped it for his country;
And what is left, to lose it by his country
Were to us all that do't and suffer it
A brand to the end o' the world.
Sic. This is clean kam.
Bru. Merely awry. When he did love his country,
It honored him.
Sic. The service of the foot, 306
Being once gangrened, is not then respected
For what before it was.
Bru. We'll hear no more.
Pursue him to his house and pluck him thence,
Lest his infection, being of catching nature, 310
Spread further.
Men. One word more, one word:
This tiger-footed rage, when it shall find
The harm of unscanned swiftness, will, too late,
Tie leaden pounds to's heels. Proceed by process,
Lest parties—as he is beloved—break out, 315
And sack great Rome with Romans.
Bru. If it were so—
Sic. What do ye talk?
Have we not had a taste of his obedience—
Our ædiles smote, ourselves resisted? Come! 319

Men. Consider this: he has been bred i' the wars
Since 'a could draw a sword, and is ill schooled
In bolted language; meal and bran together
He throws without distinction. Give me leave,
I'll go to him and undertake to bring him
Where he shall answer by a lawful form, 325
In peace, to his utmost peril.
1. Sen. Noble tribunes,
It is the humane way; the other course
Will prove too bloody, and the end of it
Unknown to the beginning.
Sic. Noble Menenius,
Be you then as the people's officer. 330
Masters, lay down your weapons.
Bru. Go not home.
Sic. Meet on the market place. We'll attend you there;
Where, if you bring not Marcius, we'll proceed
In our first way.
Men. I'll bring him to you.
[*To the Senators*] Let me desire your company; he must come, 335
Or what is worst will follow.
1. Sen. Pray you let's to him.
Exeunt.

[Scene II. *The same. A room in Coriolanus' house.*]

Enter CORIOLANUS *with* NOBLES.

Cor. Let them pull all about mine ears, present me
Death on the wheel or at wild horses' heels;
Or pile ten hills on the Tarpeian rock,
That the precipitation might downstretch
Below the beam of sight; yet will I still 5
Be thus to them.
1. Pat. You do the nobler.
Cor. I muse my mother
Does not approve me further, who was wont
To call them woolen vassals, things created
To buy and sell with groats; to show bare heads 10
In congregations, to yawn, be still, and wonder,
When one but of my ordinance stood up
To speak of peace or war.

Enter VOLUMNIA.

I talk of you:
Why did you wish me milder? Would you have me

286. peremptory: resolved
304. clean kam: quite askew
305. Merely: absolutely
314. process: due legal form

322. bolted: refined
7. muse: wonder
9. woolen: woolen-clad
10. groats: coins worth about fourpence each
12. ordinance: rank

False to my nature? Rather say I play 15
The man I am.

Vol. O, sir, sir, sir,
I would have had you put your power well on
Before you had worn it out.

Cor. Let go.

Vol. You might have been enough the man you are
With striving less to be so; lesser had been 20
The thwartings of your dispositions if
You had not showed them how ye were disposed,
Ere they lacked power to cross you.

Cor. Let them hang.

Vol. Ay, and burn too.

Enter MENENIUS *with the* SENATORS.

Men. Come, come, you have been too rough, something too rough; 25
You must return and mend it.

1. Sen. There's no remedy,
Unless, by not so doing, our good city
Cleave in the midst and perish.

Vol. Pray be counseled;
I have a heart as little apt as yours,
But yet a brain that leads my use of anger 30
To better vantage.

Men. Well said, noble woman!
Before he should thus stoop to the herd, but that
The violent fit o' the time craves it as physic
For the whole state, I would put mine armor on,
Which I can scarcely bear.

Cor. What must I do? 35

Men. Return to the tribunes.

Cor. Well, what then, what then?

Men. Repent what you have spoke.

Cor. For them! I cannot do it to the gods;
Must I then do't to them?

Vol. You are too absolute;
Though therein you can never be too noble 40
But when extremities speak. I have heard you say
Honor and policy, like unsevered friends,
I' the war do grow together; grant that, and tell me
In peace what each of them by the other lose
That they combine not there.

Cor. Tush, tush!

Men. A good demand.

Vol. If it be honor in your wars to seem 46
The same you are not, which for your best ends
You adopt your policy, how is it less or worse
That it shall hold companionship in peace
With honor as in war; since that to both 50
It stands in like request?

Cor. Why force you this?

Vol. Because that now it lies you on to speak
To the people, not by your own instruction,
Nor by the matter which your heart prompts you,
But with such words that are but roted in 55
Your tongue, though but bastards and syllables
Of no allowance to your bosom's truth.
Now, this no more dishonors you at all
Than to take in a town with gentle words,
Which else would put you to your fortune and 60
The hazard of much blood.
I would dissemble with my nature where
My fortunes and my friends at stake required
I should do so in honor. I am in this
Your wife, your son, these senators, the nobles; 65
And you will rather show our general louts
How you can frown than spend a fawn upon 'em
For the inheritance of their loves and safeguard
Of what that want might ruin.

Men. Noble lady!
Come, go with us, speak fair; you may salve so, 70
Not what is dangerous present, but the loss
Of what is past.

Vol. I prithee now, my son,
Go to them with this bonnet in thy hand; 73
And thus far having stretched it, here be with them,
Thy knee bussing the stones—for in such business
Action is eloquence, and the eyes of the ignorant
More learned than the ears—waving thy head,
Which often, thus correcting thy stout heart,
Now humble as the ripest mulberry
That will not hold the handling. Or say to them 80
Thou art their soldier and, being bred in broils,
Hast not the soft way which, thou dost confess,
Were fit for thee to use as they to claim,
In asking their good loves; but thou wilt frame
Thyself, forsooth, hereafter theirs, so far 85
As thou hast power and person.

Men. This but done
Even as she speaks, why, their hearts were yours;
For they have pardons, being asked, as free
As words to little purpose.

Vol. Prithee now,
Go, and be ruled; although I know thou hadst rather

21. **thwartings:** Theobald's reading for the Folio's "things"; **dispositions:** wishes
23. **Ere . . . power:** before they lost the power
29. **apt:** flexible
32. **herd:** Warburton's reading. The Folio reads "heart."
39. **absolute:** inflexible
41. **extremities speak:** emergency requires
42. **policy:** discretion
51. **stands . . . request:** is equally required; **force:** emphasize
52. **lies . . . on:** is incumbent upon you
57. **Of . . . to:** not sanctioned by
64. **am:** represent
68. **inheritance:** possession
70. **salve:** cure; mitigate
71–72. **Not . . . past:** not only the present danger but the loss of the consulship
74. **here . . . them:** act thus with them
75. **bussing:** kissing
77. **waving:** bowing
78. **Which often:** which do often
90. **ruled:** ruly; tractable

Follow thine enemy in a fiery gulf 91
Than flatter him in a bower.

Enter COMINIUS.

Here is Cominius.

Com. I have been i' the market place; and, sir, 'tis fit
You make strong party, or defend yourself
By calmness or by absence; all's in anger. 95

Men. Only fair speech.

Com. I think 'twill serve, if he
Can thereto frame his spirit.

Vol. He must and will.
Prithee now, say you will, and go about it.

Cor. Must I go show them my unbarbed sconce? Must I
With my base tongue give to my noble heart 100
A lie that it must bear? Well, I will do't;
Yet, were there but this single plot to lose,
This mold of Marcius, they to dust should grind it,
And throw't against the wind. To the market place!
You have put me now to such a part which never
I shall discharge to the life.

Com. Come, come, we'll prompt you. 106

Vol. I prithee now, sweet son, as thou hast said
My praises made thee first a soldier, so,
To have my praise for this, perform a part
Thou hast not done before.

Cor. Well, I must do't. 110
Away, my disposition, and possess me
Some harlot's spirit! My throat of war be turned,
Which quired with my drum, into a pipe
Small as an eunuch or the virgin voice
That babies lulls asleep! The smiles of knaves 115
Tent in my cheeks, and schoolboys' tears take up
The glasses of my sight! A beggar's tongue
Make motion through my lips, and my armed knees,
Who bowed but in my stirrup, bend like his
That hath received an alms! I will not do't, 120
Lest I surcease to honor mine own truth,
And by my body's action teach my mind
A most inherent baseness.

Vol. At thy choice, then.
To beg of thee, it is my more dishonor
Than thou of them. Come all to ruin. Let 125
Thy mother rather feel thy pride than fear
Thy dangerous stoutness; for I mock at death
With as big heart as thou. Do as thou list.
Thy valiantness was mine, thou suckedst it from me;
But owe thy pride thyself.

Cor. Pray be content. 130
Mother, I am going to the market place;
Chide me no more. I'll mountebank their loves,
Cog their hearts from them, and come home beloved
Of all the trades in Rome. Look, I am going.
Commend me to my wife. I'll return consul, 135
Or never trust to what my tongue can do
I' the way of flattery further.

Vol. Do your will. *Exit.*

Com. Away! The tribunes do attend you. Arm yourself
To answer mildly; for they are prepared
With accusations, as I hear, more strong 140
Than are upon you yet.

Cor. The word is "mildly." Pray you let us go.
Let them accuse me by invention; I
Will answer in mine honor.

Men. Ay, but mildly.

Cor. Well, mildly be it then—mildly. 145
Exeunt.

[Scene III. *The same. The Forum.*]

Enter SICINIUS *and* BRUTUS.

Bru. In this point charge him home, that he affects
Tyrannical power. If he evade us there,
Enforce him with his envy to the people,
And that the spoil got on the Antiates
Was ne'er distributed.

Enter an ÆDILE.

What, will he come? 5

Æd. He's coming.

Bru. How accompanied?

Æd. With old Menenius, and those senators
That always favored him.

Sic. Have you a catalogue
Of all the voices that we have procured,
Set down by the poll?

Æd. I have; 'tis ready. 10

Sic. Have you collected them by tribes?

Æd. I have.

Sic. Assemble presently the people hither;
And when they hear me say, "It shall be so

94. make . . . party: have strong support
99. unbarbed sconce: unhelmeted head
102. plot: piece of earth
112. harlot's spirit: the spirit of one whose vocation is to please
113. quired: sounded in harmony
116. Tent: lodge
121. surcease: cease
130. owe: own
132. mountebank . . . loves: win their love with a mountebank's tricks
133. Cog: swindle
135. Commend: offer my greetings
138. attend: await
12. presently: at once

I' the right and strength o' the commons," be it either
For death, for fine, or banishment, then let them,
If I say fine, cry "Fine!"—if death, cry "Death!"
Insisting on the old prerogative 17
And power i' the truth o' the cause.
Æd. I shall inform them.
Bru. And when such time they have begun to cry,
Let them not cease, but with a din confused 20
Enforce the present execution
Of what we chance to sentence.
Æd. Very well.
Sic. Make them be strong and ready for this hint,
When we shall hap to give't them.
Bru. Go about it.
[*Exit Ædile.*]
Put him to choler straight. He hath been used 25
Ever to conquer, and to have his worth
Of contradiction; being once chafed, he cannot
Be reined again to temperance; then he speaks
What's in his heart, and that is there which looks
With us to break his neck.

Enter CORIOLANUS, MENENIUS, *and* COMINIUS, *with others.*

Sic. Well, here he comes. 30
Men. Calmly, I do beseech you.
Cor. Ay, as an ostler, that for the poorest piece
Will bear the knave by the volume. The honored gods
Keep Rome in safety, and the chairs of justice
Supplied with worthy men! Plant love among's!
Throng our large temples with the shows of peace,
And not our streets with war!
1. Sen. Amen, amen! 37
Men. A noble wish.

[*Re-*]*enter the* ÆDILE, *with the* PLEBEIANS.

Sic. Draw near, ye people.
Æd. List to your tribunes. Audience! Peace, I say! 40
Cor. First, hear me speak.
Both Trib. Well, say. Peace, ho!
Cor. Shall I be charged no further than this present?
Must all determine here?
Sic. I do demand,
If you submit you to the people's voices,
Allow their officers, and are content 45
To suffer lawful censure for such faults
As shall be proved upon you.
Cor. I am content.
Men. Lo, citizens, he says he is content.
The warlike service he has done, consider; think
Upon the wounds his body bears, which show 50
Like graves i' the holy churchyard.
Cor. Scratches with briers,
Scars to move laughter only.
Men. Consider further,
That when he speaks not like a citizen,
You find him like a soldier; do not take
His rougher accents for malicious sounds, 55
But, as I say, such as become a soldier
Rather than envy you.
Com. Well, well! No more.
Cor. What is the matter,
That being passed for consul with full voice,
I am so dishonored that the very hour 60
You take it off again?
Sic. Answer to us.
Cor. Say then; 'tis true, I ought so.
Sic. We charge you that you have contrived to take
From Rome all seasoned office, and to wind
Yourself into a power tyrannical; 65
For which you are a traitor to the people.
Cor. How! Traitor!
Men. Nay, temperately! Your promise.
Cor. The fires i' the lowest hell fold in the people!
Call me their traitor! Thou injurious tribune!
Within thine eyes sat twenty thousand deaths, 70
In thy hands clutched as many millions, in
Thy lying tongue both numbers, I would say
"Thou liest" unto thee with a voice as free
As I do pray the gods.
Sic. Mark you this, people?
Pleb. To the rock, to the rock with him! 75
Sic. Peace!
We need not put new matter to his charge.
What you have seen him do and heard him speak,
Beating your officers, cursing yourselves,
Opposing laws with strokes, and here defying 80
Those whose great power must try him—even this,
So criminal and in such capital kind,
Deserves the extremest death.
Bru. But since he hath
Served well for Rome—
Cor. What do you prate of service?
Bru. I talk of that that know it.
Cor. You! 85
Men. Is this the promise that you made your mother?

23. **hint:** opportunity
25. **Put . . . straight:** anger him at once.
26–27. **have . . . contradiction:** indulge his contrariness to the full
32. **ostler:** groom
33. **bear . . . volume:** endure being called a knave to the limit
36. **shows:** spectacles
43. **determine:** conclude
45. **Allow:** acknowledge
54. **find:** judge
57. **envy you:** dislike of you
64. **seasoned:** either "well-established" or "equitable"; i.e., a government in which the people are represented
69. **injurious:** insulting

Com. Know, I pray you—
Cor. I'll know no further.
Let them pronounce the steep Tarpeian death,
Vagabond exile, flaying, pent to linger
But with a grain a day, I would not buy 90
Their mercy at the price of one fair word,
Nor check my courage for what they can give,
To have't with saying, "Good morrow."
Sic. For that he has,
As much as in him lies, from time to time 95
Envied against the people, seeking means
To pluck away their power; as now at last
Given hostile strokes, and that not in the presence
Of dreaded justice, but on the ministers
That do distribute it—in the name o' the people,
And in the power of us the tribunes, we, 101
Ev'n from this instant, banish him our city,
In peril of precipitation
From off the rock Tarpeian, never more
To enter our Rome gates. I' the people's name, 105
I say it shall be so.
Pleb. It shall be so, it shall be so! Let him away!
He's banished, and it shall be so.
Com. Hear me, my masters and my common friends— 109
Sic. He's sentenced; no more hearing.
Com. Let me speak.
I have been consul, and can show for Rome
Her enemies' marks upon me. I do love
My country's good with a respect more tender,
More holy and profound, than mine own life,
My dear wife's estimate, her womb's increase 115
And treasure of my loins. Then if I would
Speak that—

89. pent: confined
94. For that: because
115. estimate: reputation

Sic. We know your drift. Speak what?
Bru. There's no more to be said, but he is banished,
As enemy to the people and his country.
It shall be so.
Pleb. It shall be so, it shall be so. 120
Cor. You common cry of curs, whose breath I hate
As reek o' the rotten fens, whose loves I prize
As the dead carcasses of unburied men
That do corrupt my air—I banish you.
And here remain with your uncertainty! 125
Let every feeble rumor shake your hearts;
Your enemies, with nodding of their plumes,
Fan you into despair! Have the power still
To banish your defenders, till at length
Your ignorance, which finds not till it feels, 130
Making but reservation of yourselves,
Still your own foes, deliver you
As most abated captives to some nation
That won you without blows! Despising
For you the city, thus I turn my back; 135
There is a world elsewhere. *Exeunt Coriolanus, Cominius, Menenius,* [*with the other Patricians*].
Æd. The people's enemy is gone, is gone!
They all shout and throw up their caps.
Pleb. Our enemy is banished, he is gone! Hoo-oo!
Sic. Go see him out at gates, and follow him,
As he hath followed you, with all despite; 140
Give him deserved vexation. Let a guard
Attend us through the city.
Pleb. Come, come, let's see him out at gates; come!
The gods preserve our noble tribunes! Come.
Exeunt.

121. cry: pack
130. finds . . . feels: is not discovered until its effect is felt
131. Making . . . yourselves: i.e., retaining yourselves only
133. abated: humiliated
140. despite: spite

ACT IV

[Scene I. *Rome. Before a gate of the city.*]

Enter CORIOLANUS, VOLUMNIA, VIRGILIA, MENENIUS, COMINIUS, *with the young* NOBILITY *of Rome.*

Cor. Come, leave your tears; a brief farewell. The beast
With many heads butts me away. Nay, mother,
Where is your ancient courage? You were used
To say extremities was the trier of spirits;
That common chances common men could bear; 5
That when the sea was calm all boats alike
Showed mastership in floating; fortune's blows,
When most struck home, being gentle wounded craves
A noble cunning. You were used to load me

7–9. fortune's . . . cunning: when fortune's blows have hit with their full force, only a noble heart can endure without complaint.

With precepts that would make invincible 10
The heart that conned them.
Vir. O heavens! O heavens!
Cor. Nay, I prithee, woman—
Vol. Now the red pestilence strike all trades in Rome,
And occupations perish!
Cor. What, what, what! 14
I shall be loved when I am lacked. Nay, mother,
Resume that spirit when you were wont to say,
If you had been the wife of Hercules,
Six of his labors you'd have done, and saved
Your husband so much sweat. Cominius, 19
Droop not; adieu. Farewell, my wife, my mother.
I'll do well yet. Thou old and true Menenius,
Thy tears are salter than a younger man's
And venomous to thine eyes. My sometime General,
I have seen thee stern, and thou hast oft beheld
Heart-hard'ning spectacles; tell these sad women
'Tis fond to wail inevitable strokes, 26
As 'tis to laugh at 'em. My mother, you wot well
My hazards still have been your solace; and
Believe't not lightly, though I go alone,
Like to a lonely dragon, that his fen 30
Makes feared and talked of more than seen, your son
Will or exceed the common or be caught
With cautelous baits and practice.
Vol. My first son,
Whither wilt thou go? Take good Cominius
With thee awhile; determine on some course 35
More than a wild exposture to each chance
That starts i' the way before thee.
Vir. O the gods!
Com. I'll follow thee a month, devise with thee
Where thou shalt rest, that thou mayst hear of us,
And we of thee; so, if the time thrust forth 40
A cause for thy repeal, we shall not send
O'er the vast world to seek a single man,
And lose advantage, which doth ever cool
I' the absence of the needer.
Cor. Fare ye well; 44
Thou hast years upon thee, and thou art too full
Of the wars' surfeits to go rove with one
That's yet unbruised; bring me but out at gate.
Come, my sweet wife, my dearest mother, and
My friends of noble touch; when I am forth,
Bid me farewell, and smile. I pray you come. 50
While I remain above the ground you shall
Hear from me still, and never of me aught
But what is like me formerly.
Men. That's worthily
As any ear can hear. Come, let's not weep.
If I could shake off but one seven years 55
From these old arms and legs, by the good gods,
I'd with thee every foot.
Cor. Give me thy hand.
Come.
Exeunt.

11. **conned:** learned
26. **fond:** foolish; **inevitable:** unavoidable
27. **wot:** know
29. **Believe't . . . lightly:** be certain of this
33. **cautelous:** crafty; **practice:** trickery
36. **exposture:** exposure
41. **repeal:** recall
43. **advantage:** opportunity
47. **bring:** escort
49. **noble touch:** tried and true nobility

[Scene II. *The same. A street near the gate.*]

Enter the two Tribunes, SICINIUS *and* BRUTUS, *with the* ÆDILE.

Sic. Bid them all home; he's gone, and we'll no further.
The nobility are vexed, whom we see have sided
In his behalf.
Bru. Now we have shown our power,
Let us seem humbler after it is done
Than when it was a-doing.
Sic. Bid them home. 5
Say their great enemy is gone, and they
Stand in their ancient strength.
Bru. Dismiss them home.
Exit Ædile.
Here comes his mother.

Enter VOLUMNIA, VIRGILIA, *and* MENENIUS.

Sic. Let's not meet her.
Bru. Why?
Sic. They say she's mad. 9
Bru. They have ta'en note of us; keep on your way.
Vol. O, y'are well met; the hoarded plague o' the gods
Requite your love!
Men. Peace, peace, be not so loud.
Vol. If that I could for weeping, you should hear—
Nay, and you shall hear some. [*To Brutus*] Will you be gone?
Vir. [*To Sicinius*] You shall stay too. I would I had the power 15
To say so to my husband.
Sic. Are you mankind?
Vol. Ay, fool; is that a shame? Note but this, fool:

16. **mankind:** masculine (?); mad (?)
17. **is . . . shame:** Volumnia chooses to answer as though he had asked whether she were of the human race.

Was not a man my father? Hadst thou foxship
To banish him that struck more blows for Rome
Than thou hast spoken words?
Sic. O blessed heavens! 20
Vol. Mo noble blows than ever thou wise words;
And for Rome's good. I'll tell thee what—yet go!
Nay, but thou shalt stay too. I would my son
Were in Arabia, and thy tribe before him, 24
His good sword in his hand.
Sic. What then?
Vir. What then!
He'd make an end of thy posterity.
Vol. Bastards and all.
Good man, the wounds that he does bear for Rome!
Men. Come, come, peace.
Sic. I would he had continued to his country 30
As he began, and not unknit himself
The noble knot he made.
Bru. I would he had.
Vol. "I would he had!" 'Twas you incensed the rabble—
Cats that can judge as fitly of his worth
As I can of those mysteries which heaven 35
Will not have earth to know.
Bru. Pray, let's go.
Vol. Now, pray, sir, get you gone;
You have done a brave deed. Ere you go, hear this:
As far as doth the Capitol exceed
The meanest house in Rome, so far my son— 40
This lady's husband here, this, do you see?—
Whom you have banished does exceed you all.
Bru. Well, well, we'll leave you.
Sic. Why stay we to be baited
With one that wants her wits? *Exeunt Tribunes.*
Vol. Take my prayers with you.
I would the gods had nothing else to do 45
But to confirm my curses. Could I meet 'em
But once a day, it would unclog my heart
Of what lies heavy to't.
Men. You have told them home,
And, by my troth, you have cause. You'll sup with me?
Vol. Anger's my meat; I sup upon myself, 50
And so shall starve with feeding. Come, let's go.
Leave this faint puling and lament as I do,
In anger, Juno-like. Come, come, come.
Exeunt [Volumnia and Virgilia].
Men. Fie, fie, fie!
[Exit.]

24. **in Arabia:** i.e., in some wild desert where he would be defenseless; **tribe:** family
32. **The . . . made:** the bonds with Rome created by his noble actions
38. **brave:** noble
47. **unclog:** unburden
52. **faint puling:** weak whimpering

[Scene III. *A highway between Rome and Antium.*]

Enter a Roman *and a* Volsce, [*meeting*].

Rom. I know you well, sir, and you know me; your name, I think, is Adrian.
Vols. It is so, sir. Truly, I have forgot you.
Rom. I am a Roman; and my services are, as you are, against 'em. Know you me yet? 5
Vols. Nicanor? No!
Rom. The same, sir.
Vols. You had more beard when I last saw you, but your favor is well appeared by your tongue. What's the news in Rome? I have a note from the Volscian state to find you out there. You have well saved me a day's journey. 10
Rom. There hath been in Rome strange insurrections: the people against the senators, patricians, and nobles. 15
Vols. Hath been! It is ended, then? Our state thinks not so; they are in a most warlike preparation, and hope to come upon them in the heat of their division.
Rom. The main blaze of it is past, but a small thing would make it flame again; for the nobles receive so to heart the banishment of that worthy Coriolanus that they are in a ripe aptness to take all power from the people and to pluck from them their tribunes forever. This lies glowing, I can tell you, and is almost mature for the violent breaking out. 20 25
Vols. Coriolanus banished!
Rom. Banished, sir.
Vols. You will be welcome with this intelligence, Nicanor.
Rom. The day serves well for them now. I have heard it said the fittest time to corrupt a man's wife is when she's fall'n out with her husband. Your noble Tullus Aufidius will appear well in these wars, his great opposer, Coriolanus, being now in no request of his country. 30 35
Vols. He cannot choose. I am most fortunate thus accidentally to encounter you; you have ended my business, and I will merrily accompany you home.
Rom. I shall between this and supper tell you most strange things from Rome, all tending to the good of their adversaries. Have you an army ready, say you? 40
Vols. A most royal one: the centurions and their charges, distinctly billeted, already in the entertainment, and to be on foot at an hour's warning. 45

9. **your . . . tongue:** your identity is displayed by your speech.
36. **choose:** fail (to appear well)
44. **distinctly billeted:** enrolled by companies
44-45. **in . . . entertainment:** hired

Rom. I am joyful to hear of their readiness, and am the man, I think, that shall set them in present action. So, sir, heartily well met, and most glad of your company.

Vols. You take my part from me, sir. I have 50 the most cause to be glad of yours.

Rom. Well, let us go together.

Exeunt.

[Scene IV. *Antium. Before Aufidius' house.*]

Enter CORIOLANUS, *in mean apparel, disguised and muffled.*

Cor. A good city is this Antium. City,
'Tis I that made thy widows: many an heir
Of these fair edifices fore my wars
Have I heard groan and drop. Then know me not,
Lest that thy wives with spits and boys with stones,
In puny battle slay me.

Enter a CITIZEN.

Save you, sir. 6

Cit. And you.

Cor. Direct me, if it be your will,
Where great Aufidius lies. Is he in Antium?

Cit. He is, and feasts the nobles of the state 10
At his house this night.

Cor. Which is his house, beseech you?

Cit. This here before you.

Cor. Thank you, sir; farewell.

Exit Citizen.

O world, thy slippery turns! Friends now fast sworn,
Whose double bosoms seems to wear one heart, 14
Whose hours, whose bed, whose meal and exercise
Are still together, who twin, as 'twere, in love
Unseparable, shall within this hour,
On a dissension of a doit, break out
To bitterest enmity; so fellest foes, 19
Whose passions and whose plots have broke their sleep
To take the one the other, by some chance,
Some trick not worth an egg, shall grow dear friends
And interjoin their issues. So with me:
My birthplace hate I, and my love's upon
This enemy town. I'll enter. If he slay me, 25
He does fair justice: if he give me way,
I'll do his country service.

Exit.

18. On . . . doit: over a trivial difference
19. fellest: fiercest
22. trick: toy; trifle
23. interjoin . . . issues: make common cause
26. way: admittance

[Scene V. *The same. A hall in Aufidius' house.*]

Music plays. Enter a SERVINGMAN.

1. Ser. Wine, wine, wine! What service is here! I think our fellows are asleep. [*Exit.*]

Enter ANOTHER SERVINGMAN.

2. Ser. Where's Cotus? My master calls for him. Cotus! [*Exit.*]

Enter CORIOLANUS.

Cor. A goodly house. The feast smells well, but I
Appear not like a guest. 6

[*Re-*]*enter the* FIRST SERVINGMAN.

1. Ser. What would you have, friend?
Whence are you? Here's no place for you: pray go to the door. [*Exit.*]

Cor. I have deserved no better entertainment
In being Coriolanus. 10

[*Re-*]*enter* SECOND SERVINGMAN.

2. Ser. Whence are you, sir? Has the porter his eyes in his head that he gives entrance to such companions? Pray get you out.

Cor. Away!

2. Ser. Away? Get you away. 15

Cor. Now th' art troublesome.

2. Ser. Are you so brave? I'll have you talked with anon.

Enter a THIRD SERVINGMAN. *The first meets him.*

3. Ser. What fellow's this?

1. Ser. A strange one as ever I looked on. I 20 cannot get him out o' the house. Prithee call my master to him.

3. Ser. What have you to do here, fellow? Pray you avoid the house. 24

Cor. Let me but stand; I will not hurt your hearth.

3. Ser. What are you?

Cor. A gentleman.

3. Ser. A marv'lous poor one.

Cor. True, so I am.

3. Ser. Pray you, poor gentleman, take up 30 some other station; here's no place for you. Pray you avoid. Come.

9. entertainment: reception
12–13. companions: base fellows
17. brave: defiant
24. avoid: vacate

Cor. Follow your function, go and batten on cold bits. *Pushes him away from him.*

3. Ser. What, you will not? Prithee tell my master what a strange guest he has here. 35

2. Ser. And I shall. *Exit.*

3. Ser. Where dwellst thou?

Cor. Under the canopy.

3. Ser. Under the canopy? 40

Cor. Ay.

3. Ser. Where's that?

Cor. I' the city of kites and crows.

3. Ser. I' the city of kites and crows! 44
What an ass it is! Then thou dwellst with daws too?

Cor. No, I serve not thy master.

3. Ser. How, sir! Do you meddle with my master?

Cor. Ay; 'tis an honester service than to meddle with thy mistress. Thou pratest and pratest; serve with thy trencher; hence! *Beats him away.*

Enter AUFIDIUS *with the* [SECOND] SERVINGMAN.

Auf. Where is this fellow? 51

2. Ser. Here, sir; I'd have beaten him like a dog but for disturbing the lords within.

Auf. Whence comest thou? What wouldst thou? Thy name? 54
Why speakst not? Speak, man. What's thy name?

Cor. [*Unmuffling*] If, Tullus,
Not yet thou knowst me, and, seeing me, dost not
Think me for the man I am, necessity
Commands me name myself.

Auf. What is thy name?

Cor. A name unmusical to the Volscians' ears, 60
And harsh in sound to thine.

Auf. Say, what's thy name?
Thou hast a grim appearance, and thy face
Bears a command in't; though thy tackle's torn,
Thou showst a noble vessel. What's thy name?

Cor. Prepare thy brow to frown—knowst thou me yet? 65

Auf. I know thee not. Thy name?

Cor. My name is Caius Marcius, who hath done
To thee particularly, and to all the Volsces,
Great hurt and mischief; thereto witness may
My surname, Coriolanus. The painful service, 70
The extreme dangers, and the drops of blood
Shed for my thankless country, are requited
But with that surname—a good memory
And witness of the malice and displeasure
Which thou shouldst bear me. Only that name remains; 75
The cruelty and envy of the people,
Permitted by our dastard nobles, who
Have all forsook me, hath devoured the rest,
And suffered me by the voice of slaves to be
Whooped out of Rome. Now this extremity 80
Hath brought me to thy hearth; not out of hope,
Mistake me not, to save my life; for if
I had feared death, of all the men i' the world
I would have 'voided thee; but in mere spite,
To be full quit of those my banishers, 85
Stand I before thee here. Then if thou hast
A heart of wreak in thee, that wilt revenge
Thine own particular wrongs and stop those maims
Of shame seen through thy country, speed thee straight
And make my misery serve thy turn. So use it 90
That my revengeful services may prove
As benefits to thee; for I will fight
Against my cank'red country with the spleen
Of all the under fiends. But if so be 94
Thou darest not this, and that to prove more fortunes
Th'art tired, then, in a word, I also am
Longer to live most weary, and present
My throat to thee and to thy ancient malice;
Which not to cut would show thee but a fool,
Since I have ever followed thee with hate, 100
Drawn tuns of blood out of thy country's breast,
And cannot live but to thy shame, unless
It be to do thee service.

Auf. O Marcius, Marcius!
Each word thou hast spoke hath weeded from my heart
A root of ancient envy. If Jupiter 105
Should from yond cloud speak divine things,
And say, " 'Tis true," I'd not believe them more
Than thee, all noble Marcius. Let me twine
Mine arms about that body, where against
My grained ash an hundred times hath broke 110
And scarred the moon with splinters; here I clip
The anvil of my sword, and do contest
As hotly and as nobly with thy love
As ever in ambitious strength I did
Contend against thy valor. Know thou first, 115
I loved the maid I married; never man
Sighed truer breath; but that I see thee here,
Thou noble thing, more dances my rapt heart
Than when I first my wedded mistress saw 119
Bestride my threshold. Why, thou Mars, I tell thee
We have a power on foot, and I had purpose

33. **batten:** glut yourself
45. **daws:** jackdaws
64. **showst:** appearest

85. **full . . . of:** fully revenged upon
87. **heart . . . wreak:** vengeful heart
88. **particular:** personal
88–89. **maims . . . shame:** shameful injuries
93. **cank'red:** spiteful; **spleen:** rage
95. **prove:** attempt; **fortunes:** martial victories
105. **envy:** hostility
110. **grained ash:** ashen spear
111. **clip:** embrace
112. **The . . . sword:** the object against which I have beat my sword

Once more to hew thy target from thy brawn,
Or lose mine arm for't. Thou hast beat me out
Twelve several times, and I have nightly since
Dreamt of encounters 'twixt thyself and me— 125
We have been down together in my sleep,
Unbuckling helms, fisting each other's throat—
And waked half dead with nothing. Worthy Marcius,
Had we no other quarrel else to Rome but that
Thou art thence banished, we would muster all 130
From twelve to seventy, and, pouring war
Into the bowels of ungrateful Rome,
Like a bold flood o'erbeat. O, come; go in,
And take our friendly senators by the hands,
Who now are here, taking their leaves of me 135
Who am prepared against your territories,
Though not for Rome itself.

Cor. You bless me, gods!

Auf. Therefore, most absolute sir, if thou wilt have
The leading of thine own revenges, take
The one half of my commission, and set down, 140
As best thou art experienced, since thou knowst
Thy country's strength and weakness, thine own ways,
Whether to knock against the gates of Rome,
Or rudely visit them in parts remote
To fright them ere destroy. But come in; 145
Let me commend thee first to those that shall
Say yea to thy desires. A thousand welcomes!
And more a friend than e'er an enemy;
Yet, Marcius, that was much. Your hand; most welcome! *Exeunt* [*Coriolanus and Aufidius*].

[*The* TWO SERVINGMEN *come forward.*]

1. Ser. Here's a strange alteration! 150

2. Ser. By my hand, I had thought to have strucken him with a cudgel; and yet my mind gave me his clothes made a false report of him.

1. Ser. What an arm he has! He turned me about with his finger and his thumb, as one would set 155 up a top.

2. Ser. Nay, I knew by his face that there was something in him; he had, sir, a kind of face, methought—I cannot tell how to term it.

1. Ser. He had so, looking as it were— 160 Would I were hanged, but I thought there was more in him than I could think.

2. Ser. So did I, I'll be sworn. He is simply the rarest man i' the world.

1. Ser. I think he is; but a greater soldier 165 than he you wot on.

2. Ser. Who, my master?

1. Ser. Nay, it's no matter for that.

2. Ser. Worth six on him.

1. Ser. Nay, not so neither; but I take him 170 to be the greater soldier.

2. Ser. Faith, look you, one cannot tell how to say that; for the defense of a town our general is excellent.

1. Ser. Ay, and for an assault too. 175

[*Re-*]*enter the* THIRD SERVINGMAN.

3. Ser. O slaves, I can tell you news—news, you rascals!

Both. What, what, what? Let's partake.

3. Ser. I would not be a Roman, of all nations; I had as lief be a condemned man. 180

Both. Wherefore? wherefore?

3. Ser. Why, here's he that was wont to thwack our general—Caius Marcius.

1. Ser. Why do you say "thwack our general"?

3. Ser. I do not say "thwack our general," 185 but he was always good enough for him.

2. Ser. Come, we are fellows and friends. He was ever too hard for him, I have heard him say so himself.

1. Ser. He was too hard for him directly, to 190 say the troth on't; before Corioli he scotched him and notched him like a carbonado.

2. Ser. An he had been cannibally given, he might have broiled and eaten him too.

1. Ser. But more of thy news! 195

3. Ser. Why, he is so made on here within as if he were son and heir to Mars; set at upper end o' the table; no question asked him by any of the senators but they stand bald before him. Our general himself makes a mistress of him, sanctifies himself 200 with's hand, and turns up the white o' the eye to his discourse. But the bottom of the news is, our general is cut i' the middle and but one half of what he was yesterday, for the other has half by the entreaty and grant of the whole table. He'll go, he says, and 205 sowl the porter of Rome gates by the ears; he will mow all down before him, and leave his passage polled.

2. Ser. And he's as like to do't as any man I can imagine. 210

3. Ser. Do't! He will do't; for look you, sir, he has as many friends as enemies; which friends, sir, as it were, durst not—look you, sir—show themselves, as we term it, his friends, whilst he's in directitude.

122. **target:** shield
127. **helms:** helmets
138. **absolute:** perfect
146. **commend:** present
152. **my . . . me:** I suspected

190. **directly:** completely
191. **scotched:** scored
192. **carbonado:** piece of meat, slashed in preparation for broiling
199. **bald:** bareheaded
200–201. **sanctifies . . . hand:** holds his hand reverently
201. **turns . . . eye:** lends admiring attention
206. **sowl:** pull
208. **polled:** cropped; cleared
214. **directitude:** probably a comic error for "discredit"

1. Ser. Directitude? What's that? 215

3. Ser. But when they shall see, sir, his crest up again and the man in blood, they will out of their burrows, like conies after rain, and revel all with him.

1. Ser. But when goes this forward?

3. Ser. Tomorrow; today; presently. You 220 shall have the drum struck up this afternoon; 'tis as it were a parcel of their feast, and to be executed ere they wipe their lips.

2. Ser. Why, then we shall have a stirring world again. This peace is nothing but to rust iron, 225 increase tailors, and breed ballad-makers.

1. Ser. Let me have war, say I; it exceeds peace as far as day does night; it's spritely, waking, audible, and full of vent. Peace is a very apoplexy, lethargy; mulled, deaf, sleepy, insensible; a getter of 230 more bastard children than war's a destroyer of men.

2. Ser. 'Tis so; and as war in some sort may be said to be a ravisher, so it cannot be denied but peace is a great maker of cuckolds.

1. Ser. Ay, and it makes men hate one 235 another.

3. Ser. Reason: because they then less need one another. The wars for my money. I hope to see Romans as cheap as Volscians. They are rising, they are rising. 240

Both. In, in, in, in!

Exeunt.

[Scene VI. *Rome. A public place.*]

Enter the two Tribunes, SICINIUS *and* BRUTUS.

Sic. We hear not of him, neither need we fear him.
His remedies are tame. The present peace
And quietness of the people, which before
Were in wild hurry, here do make his friends
Blush that the world goes well; who rather had, 5
Though they themselves did suffer by't, behold
Dissentious numbers pest'ring streets than see
Our tradesmen singing in their shops, and going
About their functions friendly.

Enter MENENIUS.

Bru. We stood to't in good time. Is this Menenius?

Sic. 'Tis he, 'tis he. O, he is grown most kind 11
Of late. Hail, sir!

Men. Hail to you both!

Sic. Your Coriolanus is not much missed
But with his friends. The commonwealth doth stand,
And so would do, were he more angry at it. 15

Men. All's well, and might have been much better if
He could have temporized.

Sic. Where is he, hear you?

Men. Nay, I hear nothing; his mother and his wife
Hear nothing from him.

Enter THREE OR FOUR CITIZENS.

Cit. The gods preserve you both! 20

Sic. Godden, our neighbors.

Bru. Godden to you all, godden to you all.

1. Cit. Ourselves, our wives, and children, on our knees
Are bound to pray for you both.

Sic. Live and thrive!

Bru. Farewell, kind neighbors; we wished Coriolanus 25
Had loved you as we did.

Cit. Now the gods keep you!

Both Trib. Farewell, farewell. *Exeunt Citizens.*

Sic. This is a happier and more comely time
Than when these fellows ran about the streets
Crying confusion.

Bru. Caius Marcius was 30
A worthy officer i' the war, but insolent,
O'ercome with pride, ambitious past all thinking,
Self-loving—

Sic. And affecting one sole throne,
Without assistance.

Men. I think not so. 34

Sic. We should by this, to all our lamentation,
If he had gone forth consul, found it so.

Bru. The gods have well prevented it, and Rome
Sits safe and still without him.

Enter an ÆDILE.

Æd. Worthy tribunes,
There is a slave, whom we have put in prison,
Reports the Volsces with two several powers 40
Are ent'red in the Roman territories,
And with the deepest malice of the war
Destroy what lies before 'em.

Men. 'Tis Aufidius,
Who, hearing of our Marcius' banishment,
Thrusts forth his horns again into the world, 45
Which were inshelled when Marcius stood for Rome,
And durst not once peep out.

Sic. Come, what talk you of Marcius?

Bru. Go see this rumorer whipped. It cannot be
The Volsces dare break with us.

217. in blood: primed for bloodshed
222. parcel: portion
229. vent: utterance
230. mulled: deadened
234. cuckolds: betrayed husbands
2. His . . . tame: there is no further harm in him.
7. pest'ring: crowding
10. stood to't: took a stand about Coriolanus

33. affecting: desiring
45. horns: i.e., like a snail

Men. Cannot be! 50
We have record that very well it can;
And three examples of the like hath been
Within my age. But reason with the fellow
Before you punish him, where he heard this,
Lest you shall chance to whip your information 55
And beat the messenger who bids beware
Of what is to be dreaded.
Sic. Tell not me.
I know this cannot be.
Bru. Not possible.

Enter a MESSENGER.

Mess. The nobles in great earnestness are going
All to the Senate House; some news is come 60
That turns their countenances.
Sic. 'Tis this slave—
Go whip him fore the people's eyes—his raising,
Nothing but his report.
Mess. Yes, worthy sir,
The slave's report is seconded, and more,
More fearful, is delivered.
Sic. What more fearful? 65
Mess. It is spoke freely out of many mouths—
How probable I do not know—that Marcius,
Joined with Aufidius, leads a power 'gainst Rome,
And vows revenge as spacious as between 69
The young'st and oldest thing.
Sic. This is most likely!
Bru. Raised only that the weaker sort may wish
Good Marcius home again.
Sic. The very trick on't.
Men. This is unlikely.
He and Aufidius can no more atone
Than violent'st contrariety. 75

Enter [*a* SECOND] MESSENGER.

2. Mess. You are sent for to the Senate.
A fearful army, led by Caius Marcius
Associated with Aufidius, rages
Upon our territories, and have already 79
O'erborne their way, consumed with fire, and took
What lay before them.

Enter COMINIUS.

Com. O, you have made good work!
Men. What news? What news?
Com. You have holp to ravish your own daughters and
To melt the city leads upon your pates,
To see your wives dishonored to your noses— 85
Men. What's the news? What's the news?
Com. Your temples burned in their cement, and
Your franchises, whereon you stood, confined
Into an auger's bore.
Men. Pray now, your news? 89
You have made fair work, I fear me. Pray, your news.
If Marcius should be joined wi' the Volscians—
Com. If!
He is their god; he leads them like a thing
Made by some other deity than Nature,
That shapes man better; and they follow him
Against us brats with no less confidence 95
Than boys pursuing summer butterflies,
Or butchers killing flies.
Men. You have made good work,
You and your apron men; you that stood so much
Upon the voice of occupation and
The breath of garlic-eaters! 100
Com. He'll shake your Rome about your ears.
Men. As Hercules
Did shake down mellow fruit. You have made fair work!
Bru. But is this true, sir?
Com. Ay; and you'll look pale
Before you find it other. All the regions
Do smilingly revolt, and who resists 105
Are mocked for valiant ignorance,
And perish constant fools. Who is't can blame him?
Your enemies and his find something in him.
Men. We are all undone unless
The noble man have mercy.
Com. Who shall ask it? 110
The tribunes cannot do't for shame; the people
Deserve such pity of him as the wolf
Does of the shepherds; for his best friends, if they
Should say, "Be good to Rome," they charged him even
As those should do that had deserved his hate, 115
And therein showed like enemies.
Men. 'Tis true;
If he were putting to my house the brand
That should consume it, I have not the face
To say, "Beseech you, cease." You have made fair hands,
You and your crafts! You have crafted fair!
Com. You have brought
A trembling upon Rome, such as was never 121
So incapable of help.
Both Trib. Say not we brought it.

53. reason: discuss
65. delivered: reported
74. atone: reconcile
88. franchises: privileges; **whereon . . . stood:** on which you insisted
89. bore: hole
98. apron men: artisans
99. voice: say-so; **occupation:** workingmen
107. constant: loyal

Men. How! Was't we? We loved him, but, like beasts
And cowardly nobles, gave way unto your clusters,
Who did hoot him out o' the city.
Com. But I fear 125
They'll roar him in again. Tullus Aufidius,
The second name of men, obeys his points
As if he were his officer. Desperation
Is all the policy, strength, and defense,
That Rome can make against them. 130

Enter a Troop of Citizens.

Men. Here come the clusters.
And is Aufidius with him? You are they
That made the air unwholesome when you cast
Your stinking greasy caps in hooting at
Coriolanus' exile. Now he's coming, 135
And not a hair upon a soldier's head
Which will not prove a whip; as many coxcombs
As you threw caps up will he tumble down,
And pay you for your voices. 'Tis no matter;
If he could burn us all into one coal, 140
We have deserved it.
Pleb. Faith, we hear fearful news.
1. Cit. For mine own part,
When I said banish him, I said 'twas pity.
2. Cit. And so did I.
3. Cit. And so did I; and, to say the truth, 145
so did very many of us. That we did, we did for the best; and though we willingly consented to his banishment, yet it was against our will.
Com. Y'are goodly things, you voices!
Men. You have made
Good work, you and your cry! Shall's to the Capitol?
Com. O, ay, what else? 151
Exeunt [Cominius and Menenius].
Sic. Go, masters, get you home; be not dismayed;
These are a side that would be glad to have
This true which they so seem to fear. Go home,
And show no sign of fear. 155
1. Cit. The gods be good to us! Come, masters, let's home. I ever said we were i' the wrong when we banished him.
2. Cit. So did we all. But come, let's home.
Exeunt Citizens.
Bru. I do not like this news. 160
Sic. Nor I.
Bru. Let's to the Capitol. Would half my wealth
Would buy this for a lie!
Sic. Pray let's go.
Exeunt.

124. clusters: mobs
127. The . . . men: the man whose reputation is second to that of Coriolanus; **points:** trumpeted orders
150. cry: pack of curs

[Scene VII. *A camp at a short distance from Rome.*]

Enter Aufidius *with his* Lieutenant.

Auf. Do they still fly to the Roman?
Lieut. I do not know what witchcraft's in him, but
Your soldiers use him as the grace fore meat,
Their talk at table, and their thanks at end;
And you are dark'ned in this action, sir, 5
Even by your own.
Auf. I cannot help it now,
Unless by using means I lame the foot
Of our design. He bears himself more proudlier,
Even to my person, than I thought he would
When first I did embrace him; yet his nature 10
In that's no changeling, and I must excuse
What cannot be amended.
Lieut. Yet I wish, sir—
I mean, for your particular—you had not
Joined in commission with him, but either
Had borne the action of yourself, or else 15
To him had left it solely.
Auf. I understand thee well; and be thou sure,
When he shall come to his account, he knows not
What I can urge against him. Although it seems,
And so he thinks, and is no less apparent 20
To the vulgar eye, that he bears all things fairly
And shows good husbandry for the Volscian state,
Fights dragonlike, and does achieve as soon
As draw his sword; yet he hath left undone
That which shall break his neck or hazard mine 25
Whene'er we come to our account.
Lieut. Sir, I beseech you, think you he'll carry Rome?
Auf. All places yield to him ere he sits down,
And the nobility of Rome are his; 30
The senators and patricians love him too.
The tribunes are no soldiers, and their people
Will be as rash in the repeal as hasty
To expel him thence. I think he'll be to Rome
As is the osprey to the fish, who takes it 35
By sovereignty of nature. First he was
A noble servant to them, but he could not
Carry his honors even. Whether 'twas pride,
Which out of daily fortune ever taints
The happy man; whether defect of judgment, 40

5. dark'ned: overshadowed
6. your own: your own men
7. I lame: i.e., by which I lame
13. particular: personal sake
22. husbandry: management
23. achieve: conquer
29. sits down: besieges
36. sovereignty . . . nature: natural supremacy
38. even: temperately

To fail in the disposing of those chances
Which he was lord of; or whether nature,
Not to be other than one thing, not moving
From the casque to the cushion, but commanding
peace
Even with the same austerity and garb 45
As he controlled the war; but one of these—
As he hath spices of them all—not all,
For I dare so far free him—made him feared,
So hated, and so banished; but he has a merit
To choke it in the utt'rance. So our virtues 50
Lie in the interpretation of the time;
And power, unto itself most commendable,
Hath not a tomb so evident as a chair
T' extol what it hath done.
One fire drives out one fire; one nail, one nail; 55
Rights by rights falter, strengths by strengths do fail.
Come, let's away. When, Caius, Rome is thine,
Thou art poor'st of all; then shortly art thou mine.
Exeunt.

44. casque: helmet; **cushion:** symbolic of peace
45. austerity . . . garb: stern manner (a hendiadys)
47. spices: tastes; slight traces
48. free: acquit
49–50. he . . . utt'rance: his merit should have spoken louder than the fault with which he was charged.
52–54. power . . . done: praise will be the certain destruction of the superior man. Whether the passage implies self-praise is uncertain. Coriolanus up to this point has shunned praise, but his boastful response to Aufidius' taunts ultimately provokes his murderers to strike.
56. falter: Alexander Dyce's reading. The Folio reads "fouler."

ACT V

[Scene I. *Rome. A public place.*]

Enter MENENIUS, COMINIUS, SICINIUS *and* BRUTUS, *the two Tribunes, with others.*

Men. No, I'll not go. You hear what he hath said
Which was sometime his general, who loved him
In a most dear particular. He called me father;
But what o' that? Go, you that banished him:
A mile before his tent fall down, and knee 5
The way into his mercy. Nay, if he coyed
To hear Cominius speak, I'll keep at home.
Com. He would not seem to know me.
Men. Do you hear?
Com. Yet one time he did call me by my name.
I urged our old acquaintance, and the drops 10
That we have bled together. "Coriolanus"
He would not answer to; forbade all names;
He was a kind of nothing, titleless,
Till he had forged himself a name i' the fire 14
Of burning Rome.
Men. Why, so! You have made good work,
A pair of tribunes that have wracked for Rome
To make coals cheap—a noble memory!
Com. I minded him how royal 'twas to pardon
When it was less expected; he replied,
It was a bare petition of a state 20
To one whom they had punished.
Men. Very well.
Could he say less?
Com. I offered to awaken his regard
For's private friends; his answer to me was,
He could not stay to pick them in a pile 25
Of noisome musty chaff. He said 'twas folly,
For one poor grain or two, to leave unburnt
And still to nose the offense.
Men. For one poor grain or two!
I am one of those. His mother, wife, his child,
And this brave fellow too—we are the grains: 30
You are the musty chaff, and you are smelt
Above the moon. We must be burnt for you.
Sic. Nay, pray be patient; if you refuse your aid
In this so never-needed help, yet do not
Upbraid's with our distress. But sure, if you 35
Would be your country's pleader, your good tongue,
More than the instant army we can make,
Might stop our countryman.
Men. No; I'll not meddle.
Sic. Pray you go to him.

2. Which: who; common Elizabethan usage
6. coyed: disdained
16. wracked: striven
17. noble memory: fine memorial
20. bare: empty
23. offered: attempted
28. nose: smell
30. brave: noble
37. instant: quickly assembled

Men. What should I do?
Bru. Only make trial what your love can do 40
For Rome, towards Marcius.
Men. Well, and say that Marcius
Return me, as Cominius is returned,
Unheard—what then?
But as a discontented friend, grief-shot
With his unkindness? Say't be so? 45
Sic. Yet your good will
Must have that thanks from Rome after the measure
As you intended well.
Men. I'll undertake 't;
I think he'll hear me. Yet to bite his lip
And hum at good Cominius much unhearts me. 50
He was not taken well: he had not dined;
The veins unfilled, our blood is cold, and then
We pout upon the morning, are unapt
To give or to forgive; but when we have stuffed
These pipes and these conveyances of our blood 55
With wine and feeding we have suppler souls
Than in our priestlike fasts. Therefore I'll watch him
Till he be dieted to my request,
And then I'll set upon him. 59
Bru. You know the very road into his kindness
And cannot lose your way.
Men. Good faith, I'll prove him,
Speed how it will. I shall ere long have knowledge
Of my success. *Exit.*
Com. He'll never hear him.
Sic. Not?
Com. I tell you he does sit in gold, his eye
Red as 'twould burn Rome, and his injury 65
The jailer to his pity. I kneeled before him;
'Twas very faintly he said, "Rise"; dismissed me
Thus with his speechless hand. What he would do
He sent in writing after me; what he would not,
Bound with an oath to yield to his conditions; 70
So that all hope is vain,
Unless his noble mother and his wife,
Who, as I hear, mean to solicit him
For mercy to his country. Therefore let's hence,
And with our fair entreaties haste them on. 75
Exeunt.

[Scene II. *The Volscian camp before Rome.*]

Enter MENENIUS *to the* WATCH *on guard.*

1. Watch. Stay. Whence are you?
2. Watch. Stand, and go back.
Men. You guard like men, 'tis well; but, by your leave,
I am an officer of state and come
To speak with Coriolanus.
1. Watch. From whence?
Men. From Rome.
1. Watch. You may not pass; you must return. Our general 5
Will no more hear from thence.
2. Watch. You'll see your Rome embraced with fire before
You'll speak with Coriolanus.
Men. Good my friends,
If you have heard your general talk of Rome
And of his friends there, it is lots to blanks 10
My name hath touched your ears: it is Menenius.
1. Watch. Be it so; go back. The virtue of your name
Is not here passable.
Men. I tell thee, fellow,
Thy general is my lover. I have been
The book of his good acts whence men have read
His fame unparalleled haply amplified; 16
For I have ever verified my friends,
Of whom he's chief, with all the size that verity
Would without lapsing suffer. Nay, sometimes,
Like to a bowl upon a subtle ground, 20
I have tumbled past the throw, and in his praise
Have almost stamped the leasing; therefore, fellow,
I must have leave to pass.
1. Watch. Faith, sir, if you had told as many lies in his behalf as you have uttered words in your 25 own, you should not pass here; no, though it were as virtuous to lie as to live chastely. Therefore go back.
Men. Prithee, fellow, remember my name is Menenius, always factionary on the party of your general.
2. Watch. Howsoever you have been his liar, 30 as you say you have, I am one that, telling true under him, must say you cannot pass. Therefore go back.
Men. Has he dined, canst thou tell? For I would not speak with him till after dinner.
1. Watch. You are a Roman, are you? 35
Men. I am as thy general is.
1. Watch. Then you should hate Rome, as he does. Can you, when you have pushed out your gates the very defender of them, and in a violent popular ignorance given your enemy your shield, think to 40 front his revenges with the easy groans of old

61. prove: try
62. Speed . . . will: however it may succeed
70. Bound . . . conditions: i.e., in setting terms, Coriolanus was limited by his oath to the Volsces.
72. Unless: except by means of

10. lots . . . blanks: more than likely
12. virtue: power
14. lover: friend
15. book: recorder
17. verified: supported by testimony
18–19. with . . . suffer: as largely as possible without lapsing into falsehood
20. a bowl: the cast of a bowling ball; **subtle:** tricky; irregular
22. stamped . . . leasing: circulated a lie as true
29. factionary on: partial to
41. front: confront

women, the virginal palms of your daughters, or with the palsied intercession of such a decayed dotant as you seem to be? Can you think to blow out the intended fire your city is ready to flame in with 45 such weak breath as this? No, you are deceived; therefore back to Rome and prepare for your execution. You are condemned; our general has sworn you out of reprieve and pardon.

Men. Sirrah, if thy captain knew I were here, 50 he would use me with estimation.

1. Watch. Come, my captain knows you not.

Men. I mean thy general.

1. Watch. My general cares not for you. Back, I say; go, lest I let forth your half pint of blood. 55 Back—that's the utmost of your having. Back.

Men. Nay, but fellow, fellow—

Enter CORIOLANUS *with* AUFIDIUS.

Cor. What's the matter?

Men. Now, you companion, I'll say an errand for you; you shall know now that I am in estima- 60 tion; you shall perceive that a Jack guardant cannot office me from my son Coriolanus. Guess but by my entertainment with him if you standst not i' the state of hanging, or of some death more long in spectatorship and crueler in suffering; behold now pres- 65 ently, and swoon for what's to come upon thee. [*To Coriolanus*] The glorious gods sit in hourly synod about thy particular prosperity, and love thee no worse than thy old father Menenius does! O my son! my son! Thou art preparing fire for us; look 70 thee, here's water to quench it. I was hardly moved to come to thee; but, being assured none but myself could move thee, I have been blown out of your gates with sighs, and conjure thee to pardon Rome and thy petitionary countrymen. The good gods as- 75 suage thy wrath, and turn the dregs of it upon this varlet here; this, who, like a block, hath denied my access to thee.

Cor. Away!

Men. How! Away! 80

Cor. Wife, mother, child, I know not. My affairs
Are servanted to others. Though I owe
My revenge properly, my remission lies
In Volscian breasts. That we have been familiar,
Ingrate forgetfulness shall poison rather 85
Than pity note how much. Therefore be gone.
Mine ears against your suits are stronger than
Your gates against my force. Yet, for I loved thee,
Take this along; I writ it for thy sake 89
[*Gives a letter.*]
And would have sent it. Another word, Menenius,
I will not hear thee speak. This man, Aufidius,
Was my beloved in Rome; yet thou beholdst.

Auf. You keep a constant temper.

Exeunt [*Coriolanus and Aufidius*].

1. Watch. Now, sir, is your name Menenius?

2. Watch. 'Tis a spell, you see, of much 95 power! You know the way home again.

1. Watch. Do you hear how we are shent for keeping your greatness back?

2. Watch. What cause, do you think, I have to swoon? 100

Men. I neither care for the world nor your general; for such things as you, I can scarce think there's any, y'are so slight. He that hath a will to die by himself fears it not from another. Let your general do his worst. For you, be that you are, long; 105 and your misery increase with your age! I say to you, as I was said to: Away! *Exit.*

1. Watch. A noble fellow, I warrant him.

2. Watch. The worthy fellow is our general; he's the rock, the oak not to be wind-shaken. 110

Exeunt.

[Scene III. *The tent of Coriolanus.*]

Enter CORIOLANUS, AUFIDIUS, [*and others*].

Cor. We will before the walls of Rome tomorrow
Set down our host. My partner in this action,
You must report to the Volscian lords how plainly
I have borne this business.

Auf. Only their ends
You have respected; stopped your ears against 5
The general suit of Rome; never admitted
A private whisper—no, not with such friends
That thought them sure of you.

Cor. This last old man,
Whom with cracked heart I have sent to Rome,
Loved me above the measure of a father; 10
Nay, godded me indeed. Their latest refuge
Was to send him; for whose old love I have,
Though I showed sourly to him, once more offered
The first conditions, which they did refuse
And cannot now accept. To grace him only, 15
That thought he could do more, a very little

43. dotant: dotard; old fool
51. estimation: esteem
59. companion: base fellow; **say . . . errand:** deliver a message
61. Jack: knave; **guardant:** on guard
67. synod: assembly
82. servanted: subordinate, or hired
83. properly: personally; **remission:** power to forgo (revenge)

88. for: because
93. constant: resolute
97. shent: scolded
2. host: army
3. plainly: honestly
11. godded: idolized
15. grace: honor

I have yielded to; fresh embassies and suits,
Nor from the state nor private friends, hereafter
Will I lend ear to. (*Shout within.*) Ha! What shout is this?
Shall I be tempted to infringe my vow 20
In the same time 'tis made? I will not.

Enter, [*in mourning habits,*] VIRGILIA, VOLUMNIA, VALERIA, YOUNG MARCIUS, *with* ATTENDANTS.

My wife comes foremost, then the honored mold
Wherein this trunk was framed, and in her hand
The grandchild to her blood. But out, affection!
All bond and privilege of nature, break! 25
Let it be virtuous to be obstinate.
What is that curtsy worth? or those doves' eyes,
Which can make gods forsworn? I melt, and am not
Of stronger earth than others. My mother bows,
As if Olympus to a molehill should 30
In supplication nod; and my young boy
Hath an aspect of intercession which
Great nature cries, "Deny not." Let the Volsces
Plow Rome and harrow Italy; I'll never
Be such a gosling to obey instinct, but stand 35
As if a man were author of himself
And knew no other kin.
Vir. My lord and husband!
Cor. These eyes are not the same I wore in Rome.
Vir. The sorrow that delivers us thus changed
Makes you think so.
Cor. Like a dull actor now 40
I have forgot my part and I am out,
Even to a full disgrace. Best of my flesh,
Forgive my tyranny; but do not say,
For that, "Forgive our Romans." O, a kiss
Long as my exile, sweet as my revenge! 45
Now, by the jealous queen of heaven, that kiss
I carried from thee, dear, and my true lip
Hath virgined it e'er since. You gods! I prate,
And the most noble mother of the world 49
Leave unsaluted. Sink, my knee, i' the earth; *Kneels.*
Of thy deep duty more impression show
Than that of common sons.
Vol. O, stand up blest!
Whilst with no softer cushion than the flint
I kneel before thee, and unproperly
Show duty, as mistaken all this while 55
Between the child and parent. [*Kneels.*]
Cor. What's this?
Your knees to me, to your corrected son?
Then let the pebbles on the hungry beach
Fillip the stars; then let the mutinous winds
Strike the proud cedars 'gainst the fiery sun, 60
Murd'ring impossibility, to make
What cannot be slight work.
Vol. Thou art my warrior;
I holp to frame thee. Do you know this lady?
Cor. The noble sister of Publicola,
The moon of Rome, chaste as the icicle 65
That's curdied by the frost from purest snow,
And hangs on Dian's temple—dear Valeria!
Vol. This is a poor epitome of yours,
Which by the interpretation of full time
May show like all yourself.
Cor. The god of soldiers, 70
With the consent of supreme Jove, inform
Thy thoughts with nobleness, that thou mayst prove
To shame unvulnerable, and stick i' the wars
Like a great seamark, standing every flaw,
And saving those that eye thee!
Vol. Your knee, sirrah.
Cor. That's my brave boy. 76
Vol. Even he, your wife, this lady, and myself,
Are suitors to you.
Cor. I beseech you, peace!
Or, if you'd ask, remember this before:
The thing I have forsworn to grant may never 80
Be held by you denials. Do not bid me
Dismiss my soldiers, or capitulate
Again with Rome's mechanics. Tell me not
Wherein I seem unnatural; desire not
T'allay my rages and revenges with 85
Your colder reasons.
Vol. O, no more, no more!
You have said you will not grant us anything—
For we have nothing else to ask but that
Which you deny already; yet we will ask,
That, if you fail in our request, the blame 90
May hang upon your hardness; therefore hear us.
Cor. Aufidius, and you Volsces, mark; for we'll
Hear nought from Rome in private. Your request?
Vol. Should we be silent and not speak, our raiment
And state of bodies would bewray what life 95
We have led since thy exile. Think with thyself
How more unfortunate than all living women
Are we come hither; since that thy sight, which should
Make our eyes flow with joy, hearts dance with comforts,
Constrains them weep and shake with fear and sorrow, 100
Making the mother, wife, and child, to see
The son, the husband, and the father, tearing
His country's bowels out. And to poor we

23. **trunk:** body
41. **out:** at a loss for words
46. **the . . . heaven:** Juno
59. **Fillip:** beat
66. **curdied:** congealed
68. **epitome:** abstract (his son)
74. **flaw:** tempest
95. **bewray:** betray
100. **Constrains them:** forces them to

Thine enmity's most capital: thou barrest us
Our prayers to the gods, which is a comfort 105
That all but we enjoy. For how can we,
Alas, how can we for our country pray,
Whereto we are bound, together with thy victory,
Whereto we are bound? Alack, or we must lose
The country, our dear nurse, or else thy person,
Our comfort in the country. We must find 111
An evident calamity, though we had
Our wish which side should win; for either thou
Must as a foreign recreant be led
With manacles through our streets, or else 115
Triumphantly tread on thy country's ruin,
And bear the palm for having bravely shed
Thy wife and children's blood. For myself, son,
I purpose not to wait on fortune till
These wars determine; if I cannot persuade thee
Rather to show a noble grace to both parts 121
Than seek the end of one, thou shalt no sooner
March to assault thy country than to tread—
Trust to't, thou shalt not—on thy mother's womb
That brought thee to this world.

Vir. Ay, and mine, 125
That brought you forth this boy to keep your name
Living to time.

Boy. 'A shall not tread on me!
I'll run away till I am bigger, but then I'll fight.

Cor. Not of a woman's tenderness to be
Requires nor child nor woman's face to see. 130
I have sat too long. [*Rising.*]

Vol. Nay, go not from us thus.
If it were so that our request did tend
To save the Romans, thereby to destroy
The Volsces whom you serve, you might condemn us
As poisonous of your honor. No, our suit 135
Is that you reconcile them: while the Volsces
May say, "This mercy we have showed," the Romans,
"This we received," and each in either side
Give the all-hail to thee, and cry "Be blest 139
For making up this peace!" Thou knowst, great son,
The end of war's uncertain; but this certain,
That if thou conquer Rome the benefit
Which thou shalt thereby reap is such a name
Whose repetitition will be dogged with curses; 144
Whose chronicle thus writ: "The man was noble,
But with his last attempt he wiped it out,
Destroyed his country, and his name remains
To the ensuing age abhorred." Speak to me, son.
Thou hast affected the fine strains of honor,
To imitate the graces of the gods, 150
To tear with thunder the wide cheeks o' the air,
And yet to charge thy sulphur with a bolt
That should but rive an oak. Why dost not speak?
Thinkst thou it honorable for a noble man 154
Still to remember wrongs? Daughter, speak you:
He cares not for your weeping. Speak thou, boy;
Perhaps thy childishness will move him more
Than can our reasons. There's no man in the world
More bound to's mother, yet here he lets me prate
Like one i' the stocks. Thou hast never in thy life
Showed thy dear mother any courtesy, 161
When she, poor hen, fond of no second brood,
Has clucked thee to the wars, and safely home
Loaden with honor. Say my request's unjust,
And spurn me back; but if it be not so 165
Thou art not honest, and the gods will plague thee,
That thou restrainst from me the duty which
To a mother's part belongs. He turns away.
Down, ladies; let us shame him with our knees.
To his surname Coriolanus 'longs more pride 170
Than pity to our prayers. Down. An end;
This is the last. So we will home to Rome,
And die among our neighbors. Nay, behold's!
This boy, that cannot tell what he would have
But kneels and holds up hands for fellowship, 175
Does reason our petition with more strength
Than thou hast to deny't. Come, let us go.
This fellow had a Volscian to his mother;
His wife is in Corioli, and his child
Like him by chance. Yet give us our dispatch. 180
I am hushed until our city be afire,
And then I'll speak a little.

Holds her by the hand, silent.

Cor. O mother, mother!
What have you done? Behold, the heavens do ope,
The gods look down, and this unnatural scene
They laugh at. O my mother, mother! O! 185
You have won a happy victory to Rome;
But for your son—believe it, O, believe it!—
Most dangerously you have with him prevailed,
If not most mortal to him. But let it come.
Aufidius, though I cannot make true wars, 190
I'll frame convenient peace. Now, good Aufidius,
Were you in my stead, would you have heard
A mother less, or granted less, Aufidius?

Auf. I was moved withal.

Cor. I dare be sworn you were!
And, sir, it is no little thing to make 195
Mine eyes to sweat compassion. But, good sir,
What peace you'll make, advise me. For my part,
I'll not to Rome, I'll back with you; and pray you
Stand to me in this cause. O mother! Wife!

Auf. [*Aside*] I am glad thou hast set thy mercy and thy honor 200
At difference in thee. Out of that I'll work
Myself a former fortune.

Cor. [*To the ladies*] Ay, by-and-by;
But we will drink together; and you shall bear

104. capital: deadly
114. recreant: traitor
117. palm: victorious symbol
191. convenient: appropriate

A better witness back than words, which we,
On like conditions, will have countersealed. 205
Come, enter with us. Ladies, you deserve
To have a temple built you. All the swords
In Italy, and her confederate arms,
Could not have made this peace.
Exeunt.

[Scene IV. *Rome. A public place.*]

Enter MENENIUS *and* SICINIUS.

Men. See you yond coign o' the Capitol, yond cornerstone?

Sic. Why, what of that?

Men. If it be possible for you to displace it with your little finger, there is some hope the ladies of 5 Rome, especially his mother, may prevail with him. But I say there is no hope in't; our throats are sentenced, and stay upon execution.

Sic. Is't possible that so short a time can alter the condition of a man? 10

Men. There is differency between a grub and a butterfly; yet your butterfly was a grub. This Marcius is grown from a man to dragon; he has wings, he's more than a creeping thing.

Sic. He loved his mother dearly. 15

Men. So did he me; and he no more remembers his mother now than an eight-year-old horse. The tartness of his face sours ripe grapes; when he walks, he moves like an engine and the ground shrinks before his treading. He is able to pierce a corselet with 20 his eye, talks like a knell, and his hum is a battery. He sits in his state as a thing made for Alexander. What he bids be done is finished with his bidding. He wants nothing of a god but eternity, and a heaven to throne in. 25

Sic. Yes—mercy, if you report him truly.

Men. I paint him in the character. Mark what mercy his mother shall bring from him. There is no more mercy in him than there is milk in a male tiger; that shall our poor city find. And all this is 'long 30 of you.

Sic. The gods be good unto us!

Men. No, in such a case the gods will not be good unto us. When we banished him we respected not them; and, he returning to break our necks, 35 they respect not us.

Enter a MESSENGER.

Mess. Sir, if you'd save your life, fly to your house.
The plebeians have got your fellow tribune
And hale him up and down; all swearing if
The Roman ladies bring not comfort home 40
They'll give him death by inches.

Enter ANOTHER MESSENGER.

Sic. What's the news?

2. Mess. Good news, good news! The ladies have prevailed,
The Volscians are dislodged, and Marcius gone.
A merrier day did never yet greet Rome,
No, not the expulsion of the Tarquins.

Sic. Friend, 45
Art thou certain this is true? Is't most certain?

2. Mess. As certain as I know the sun is fire.
Where have you lurked, that you make doubt of it?
Ne'er through an arch so hurried the blown tide
As the recomforted through the gates. Why, hark you! 50
Trumpets, hautboys, drums beat, all together.
The trumpets, sackbuts, psalteries, and fifes,
Tabors and cymbals, and the shouting Romans,
Make the sun dance. Hark you! *A shout within.*

Men. This is good news.
I will go meet the ladies. This Volumnia
Is worth of consuls, senators, patricians, 55
A city full; of tribunes such as you,
A sea and land full. You have prayed well today:
This morning for ten thousand of your throats
I'd not have given a doit. Hark, how they joy!
Sound still with the shouts.

Sic. First, the gods bless you for your tidings; next,
Accept my thankfulness.

2. Mess. Sir, we have all 61
Great cause to give thanks.

Sic. They are near the city?

Mess. Almost at point to enter.

Sic. We'll meet them,
And help the joy.
Exeunt.

[Scene V. *Rome. A street near the gate.*]

Enter TWO SENATORS *with* LADIES, [VOLUMNIA, VIRGILIA, VALERIA,] *passing over the stage, with other* LORDS.

1. Sen. Behold our patroness, the life of Rome!
Call all your tribes together, praise the gods,

8. stay upon: await
10. condition: character
17. than . . . horse: than a horse remembers its dam
19. engine: war machine
20. corselet: body armor
22. state: chair of state; **as . . . Alexander:** like an image of Alexander the Great

51. sackbuts: instruments like trombones; **psalteries:** stringed instruments

And make triumphant fires; strew flowers before them.
Unshout the noise that banished Marcius,
Repeal him with the welcome of his mother; 5
Cry "Welcome, ladies, welcome!"
All. Welcome, ladies, welcome!
A flourish with drums and trumpets. [*Exeunt.*]

[Scene VI. *Antium. A public place.*]

Enter TULLUS AUFIDIUS, *with* ATTENDANTS.

Auf. Go tell the lords o' the city I am here;
Deliver them this paper; having read it,
Bid them repair to the market place, where I,
Even in theirs and in the commons' ears,
Will vouch the truth of it. Him I accuse 5
The city ports by this hath entered and
Intends t' appear before the people, hoping
To purge himself with words. Dispatch.
[*Exeunt attendants.*]

Enter THREE OR FOUR CONSPIRATORS *of Aufidius' faction.*

Most welcome!
1. Con. How is it with our general?
Auf. Even so
As with a man by his own alms empoisoned, 10
And with his charity slain.
2. Con. Most noble sir,
If you do hold the same intent wherein
You wished us parties, we'll deliver you
Of your great danger.
Auf. Sir, I cannot tell;
We must proceed as we do find the people. 15
3. Con. The people will remain uncertain whilst
'Twixt you there's difference; but the fall of either
Makes the survivor heir of all.
Auf. I know it;
And my pretext to strike at him admits 19
A good construction. I raised him, and I pawned
Mine honor for his truth; who being so heightened,
He watered his new plants with dews of flattery,
Seducing so my friends; and to this end
He bowed his nature, never known before
But to be rough, unswayable, and free. 25
3. Con. Sir, his stoutness
When he did stand for consul, which he lost
By lack of stooping—
Auf. That I would have spoke of.
Being banished for't, he came unto my hearth, 30
Presented to my knife his throat. I took him;
Made him joint servant with me; gave him way
In all his own desires; nay, let him choose
Out of my files, his projects to accomplish, 34
My best and freshest men; served his designments
In mine own person; holp to reap the fame
Which he did end all his, and took some pride
To do myself this wrong. Till, at the last,
I seemed his follower, not partner; and
He waged me with his countenance as if 40
I had been mercenary.
1. Con. So he did, my lord.
The army marveled at it; and, in the last,
When he had carried Rome, and that we looked
For no less spoil than glory—
Auf. There was it; 44
For which my sinews shall be stretched upon him.
At a few drops of women's rheum, which are
As cheap as lies, he sold the blood and labor
Of our great action; therefore shall he die,
And I'll renew me in his fall. But, hark! 49
Drums and trumpets sound, with great shouts of the people.
1. Con. Your native town you entered like a post,
And had no welcomes home; but he returns
Splitting the air with noise.
2. Con. And patient fools,
Whose children he hath slain, their base throats tear
With giving him glory.
3. Con. Therefore, at your vantage,
Ere he express himself or move the people 55
With what he would say, let him feel your sword,
Which we will second. When he lies along,
After your way his tale pronounced shall bury
His reasons with his body.
Auf. Say no more:
Here come the lords. 60

Enter the LORDS *of the city.*

Lords. You are most welcome home.
Auf. I have not deserved it.
But, worthy lords, have you with heed perused
What I have written to you?
Lords. We have.

8. purge: clear
12. wherein: to which
19–20. admits . . . construction: can be favorably interpreted

34. files: ranks of soldiers
37. Which . . . his: which was all his in the end
40–41. waged . . . mercenary: patronized me as though I were only a hired soldier
45. my . . . him: I shall exert myself to destroy him.
46. rheum: moisture; tears
50. post: messenger
54. vantage: opportunity
57. along: prone
58–59. After . . . body: when you have told his story in your fashion, any justification he could have made will be buried with him.

1. Lord. And grieve to hear't.
What faults he made before the last, I think 65
Might have found easy fines; but there to end
Where he was to begin, and give away
The benefit of our levies, answering us
With our own charge, making a treaty where
There was a yielding—this admits no excuse. 70
Auf. He approaches; you shall hear him.

Enter CORIOLANUS, *marching with drum and colors; the* COMMONERS *being with him.*

Cor. Hail, lords! I am returned your soldier;
No more infected with my country's love
Than when I parted hence, but still subsisting
Under your great command. You are to know 75
That prosperously I have attempted, and
With bloody passage led your wars even to
The gates of Rome. Our spoils we have brought home
Doth more than counterpoise a full third part
The charges of the action. We have made peace 80
With no less honor to the Antiates
Than shame to the Romans; and we here deliver,
Subscribed by the consuls and patricians,
Together with the seal o' the Senate, what 84
We have compounded on.
Auf. Read it not, noble lords;
But tell the traitor in the highest degree
He hath abused your powers.
Cor. Traitor! How now?
Auf. Ay, traitor, Marcius.
Cor. Marcius!
Auf. Ay, Marcius, Caius Marcius! Dost thou think
I'll grace thee with that robbery, thy stol'n name
Coriolanus, in Corioli? 91
You lords and heads o' the state, perfidiously
He has betrayed your business and given up,
For certain drops of salt, your city Rome—
I say your city—to his wife and mother; 95
Breaking his oath and resolution like
A twist of rotten silk; never admitting
Counsel o' the war; but at his nurse's tears
He whined and roared away your victory,
That pages blushed at him, and men of heart 100
Looked wond'ring each at others.
Cor. Hearst thou, Mars?
Auf. Name not the god, thou boy of tears—
Cor. Ha!
Auf. —no more.
Cor. Measureless liar, thou hast made my heart
Too great for what contains it. "Boy"! O slave!
Pardon me, lords, 'tis the first time that ever 105
I was forced to scold. Your judgments, my grave lords,
Must give this cur the lie; and his own notion—
Who wears my stripes impressed upon him, that
Must bear my beating to his grave—shall join
To thrust the lie unto him. 110
1. Lord. Peace, both, and hear me speak.
Cor. Cut me to pieces, Volsces; men and lads,
Stain all your edges on me. "Boy"! False hound!
If you have writ your annals true, 'tis there
That, like an eagle in a dovecote, I 115
Fluttered your Volscians in Corioli.
Alone I did it. "Boy"!
Auf. Why, noble lords,
Will you be put in mind of his blind fortune,
Which was your shame, by this unholy braggart,
Fore your own eyes and ears?
Conspirators. Let him die for't. 120
All People. Tear him to pieces.—Do it presently.—He killed my son.—My daughter.—He killed my cousin Marcus.—He killed my father.
2. Lord. Peace, ho! No outrage! Peace!
The man is noble, and his fame folds in 125
This orb o' the earth. His last offenses to us
Shall have judicious hearing. Stand, Aufidius,
And trouble not the peace.
Cor. O that I had him,
With six Aufidiuses, or more—his tribe,
To use my lawful sword!
Auf. Insolent villain! 130
Conspirators. Kill, kill, kill, kill, kill him!
The Conspirators draw and kill Coriolanus, who falls. Aufidius stands on him.
Lords. Hold, hold, hold, hold!
Auf. My noble masters, hear me speak.
1. Lord. O Tullus!
2. Lord. Thou hast done a deed whereat valor will weep.
3. Lord. Tread not upon him. Masters all, be quiet;
Put up your swords. 135
Auf. My lords, when you shall know—as in this rage,
Provoked by him, you cannot—the great danger
Which this man's life did owe you, you'll rejoice
That he is thus cut off. Please it your honors
To call me to your Senate, I'll deliver 140
Myself your loyal servant, or endure
Your heaviest censure.
1. Lord. Bear from hence his body,
And mourn you for him. Let him be regarded
As the most noble corse that ever herald
Did follow to his urn.

66. fines: punishment
68–69. answering . . . charge: returning us no profit for our outlay
83. Subscribed: signed
85. compounded: agreed
107. notion: understanding
118. blind fortune: sheer luck
125–26. folds . . . earth: encompasses the universe
138. owe you: cause you to have

2. Lord. His own impatience 145
Takes from Aufidius a great part of blame.
Let's make the best of it.
Auf. My rage is gone,
And I am struck with sorrow. Take him up.
Help, three o' the chiefest soldiers; I'll be one.
Beat thou the drum, that it speak mournfully; 150
Trail your steel pikes. Though in this city he
Hath widowed and unchilded many a one,
Which to this hour bewail the injury,
Yet he shall have a noble memory.
Assist. 155

Exeunt, bearing the body of Coriolanus. A dead march sounded.

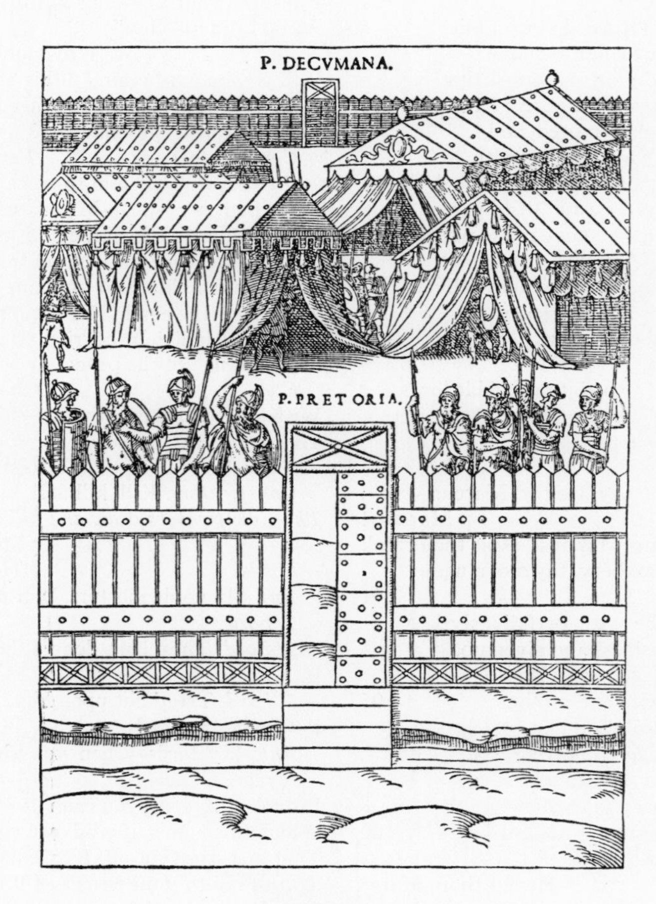

A Roman Camp

From Guillaume Du Choul, *Discours de la religion des anciens Romains* (1556).

A Ship in a Storm

From Guillaume de la Perrière, *La morosophie* (1553). [Although published long before *The Tempest* was written, this picture uncannily suggests Prospero, with Ariel hovering over the laboring ship.]

THE TEMPEST

INTRODUCTION

In *The Tempest,* dating from 1611, the last entire play that Shakespeare wrote, was the great dramatist's farewell to the stage. Many critics, including Sir Edmund Chambers, have seen in the episode of Prospero's breaking of his staff and burying his book Shakespeare's renunciation of his active life in London and his return to his "dukedom of Milan" at Stratford. The life of an actor and dramatist in Jacobean England was not one to be envied. Actors still occupied no position of respectability, and theatrical writing was still, in 1611, hardly considered literature. For a man who could afford to say good-by to the strenuous life of the theatre, there was little temptation to remain, even though Shakespeare himself must have been conscious that his plays possessed a charm that made him a magician among writers. It is not hard to believe that Shakespeare gladly gave up that magic for a better life in the pleasant town of Stratford. Although the staff-breaking episode occurs elsewhere in the literature of the day, Shakespeare could easily have seen in the incident a symbolism parallel to his own plans.

The Tempest apparently was originally written for presentation at court on November 1, 1611. It was again performed at court in the winter of 1612–13, probably as part of the wedding festivities of King James's daughter Elizabeth to Frederick, the Elector of the Palatinate and briefly King of Bohemia. The play has some of the qualities characteristic of the courtly entertainments and masques that Ben Jonson and Inigo Jones were making popular. The masque was a pageant-like production of dance, music, dialogue, and spectacle, frequently with scenes taken from mythology. The typical masque has dainty and graceful music and dance numbers followed by an antimasque of grotesque characters who serve as foils and as contrast. In *The Tempest* Shakespeare presents Ariel and the courtly figures in contrast with Caliban and the drunken sailors, who provide comic effects. In Act IV, Prospero by his magic calls up a formal mythological pageant characteristic of the court masque. Indeed, some critics have argued that Act IV was a later insertion by another hand, perhaps written in for Princess Elizabeth's wedding. But since Act IV supplies precisely the kind of spectacle that was fashionable, there is no reason to believe that it is not Shakespeare's. In other court plays, for example in *A Midsummer Night's Dream* and *As You Like It,* he had employed with dramatic effectiveness similar techniques.

Scholars and critics have long debated the possible allegorical interpretations of *The Tempest.* Whether Shakespeare intended to endow his play with deep allegorical significance may be doubted. With the common sense that always characterizes his observations, Sir Edmund Chambers has written:

> I have rejected the temptation to suggest that just as Ariel symbolizes the spirit of poetry brought by Shakespeare into the service of the creative imagination, so Caliban signifies the spirit of prose, born of Sycorax who is controversial theology, and imperfectly subdued by Shakespeare to the same purpose. There are some who follow Renan in taking Caliban for a type of Demos, and regard his desire to "nor scrape trenchering nor wash dish" as eminently characteristic of political ideals which aim at nothing higher than the escape from reasonable labor. Of any political intention on Shakespeare's part in *The Tempest* I am profoundly skeptical.

Others have not been so chary of allegorical interpretation. Someone has even seen Caliban as Shakespeare's prophetic anticipation of Darwin's missing link, and others have found sundry meanings in the dramatist's contrast between this earthy, half-human creature and the ethereal Ariel. Whatever allegorical interpretation later critics may find for Caliban, Shakespeare's audiences probably saw him as a stage representation of the type of monstrous creature described by travelers from Mandeville to Raleigh. Shakespeare's age had heard many strange tales of the world beyond the seas and could accept as veritable any monster or marvel, however fantastic.

SOURCES, HISTORY, AND TEXT

The Tempest has a peculiar interest for Americans because it is the only play of Shakespeare's that reflects the impact of the New World on the dramatist. Shakespeare's imagination, we know, was stimulated by stories of the wreck on Bermuda in 1609 of part of the expedition to Virginia led by Sir Thomas Gates. Accounts of the wreck of Gates's ship, the "Sea Adventure," were soon available in London, and Shakespeare shows evidence of having read Silvester Jourdain's *A Discovery of the Barmudas* (1610), which gave an eyewitness report and attracted much attention. The Virginia Company of London brought out an official statement as *A True Declaration of the Estate of the Colony in Virginia* (1610), and Richard Rich wrote a ballad on the subject, *News from Virginia* (1610). But the account that seems to have colored Shakespeare's thinking more than any other was William Strachey's *A True Reportory of the Wrack and Redemption of Sir Thomas Gates, Knight,* which first appeared in print in 1625 in Samuel Purchas' *Hakluytus Posthumus, or Purchas His Pilgrims.* Strachey, however, was a friend of members of Shakespeare's theatrical group, and his *True Reportory,* sent back to England soon after the wreck, was doubtless read by Shakespeare in manuscript. The colonization of Virginia had stirred the imagination of many writers and had excited the interest of men in all walks of life. The Earl of Southampton, Shakespeare's patron, was an investor in the Virginia Company and was deeply concerned with the ventures overseas. With all the talk and writing about the New World, it is strange that Shakespeare did not reflect this interest in other plays, but by 1610, when he was gathering material for a new play to appeal to the court, he could hardly have overlooked the excitement over the adventures of Sir Thomas Gates and Sir George Somers on the devil-infested island of Bermuda.

The Tempest shows evidence of other reading in the travel literature of the day. From Richard Eden's *History of Travel* (1577) Shakespeare may have taken the name of a Patagonian god, Setebos. From John Florio's translation of Montaigne, in the essay "Of Cannibals," he borrowed material for Gonzalo's description (II.i) of an idealized Golden Age. Although *The Tempest* shows that at last the New World had stirred Shakespeare's imagination, patriotic Americans have perhaps read more into the play than the words warrant. Actually, the travel literature merely suggested a shipwreck, a magic isle, and the strangely assorted inhabitants of the island.

Perhaps we can credit most of *The Tempest* to Shakespeare's own fecund imagination. Plot elements in the play are common to fiction and folklore. It is possible that some forgotten story or play suggested the main outlines to Shakespeare. A German play, *Die schöne Sidea,* by Jacob Ayrer of Nuremberg, dating from sometime before 1605, has a magician whose daughter falls in love with his enemy's son; some of the situations are similar to those in *The Tempest,* but there is no evidence that Shakespeare ever saw the German play. Perhaps Ayrer and Shakespeare drew their inspiration from some common source. In 1913 Ferdinando Neri published from a Renaissance manuscript four Italian *scenari* for *commedia dell' arte* performances. These contain scenes that resemble comic situations in *The Tempest.* Since *commedia dell' arte* performances were known in Shakespeare's London, some scholars have argued that these *scenari* may have suggested material for his play. But the parallels are not close enough to be convincing. Like any creative artist, Shakespeare was capable of drawing upon his memory and his imagination without depending upon an exact source for every idea and scene.

The Tempest has enjoyed a long and deserved popularity, but producers have found it hard to resist adapting the play into a spectacle. In 1667 Sir William Davenant and John Dryden prepared an adaptation for presentation at Lincoln's Inn Fields. Among their "improvements" was the addition of a man who had never seen a woman, a sister for Miranda, a sister for Caliban, a sprite in love with Ariel, and comic additions to the sailor scenes. Grotesque as was this hodgepodge, it was so popular that Thomas Shadwell in 1674 further "improved" it into an opera, with music by Henry Purcell. This version, dependent upon scenery and music rather than upon Shakespeare's original poetry, was long popular and was seen in the theatre until late in the eighteenth century. David Garrick wrote a libretto for a new operatic version for Drury Lane, and this was performed in 1756 with music by John Christopher Smith.

Frederick Reynolds was responsible for a third operatic version, performed in London in 1821. The two older operatic versions, which had continued to flourish, were finally eliminated by Reynolds' musical play and by a revival of Shakespeare's original work by Charles William Macready in 1838.

During the nineteenth and early twentieth centuries *The Tempest* appeared with a fair degree of regularity on both sides of the Atlantic, but producers usually depended upon spectacular staging for their effects. Before condemning the adapters out of hand, one should remember that Shakespeare himself had designed the play for a certain amount of spectacle. Inigo Jones had already shown writers of masques that elaborate "spectaculars" were possible. A television production of *The Tempest* in 1960 introduced many tricks of illusion, with a miniscule Ariel flitting through the air and a very fishy Caliban creeping about in the slime, but the effect was less than satisfactory. Although *The Tempest* is a difficult play to stage and to interpret, it has remained popular with both spectators and readers.

The Tempest was first printed in the Folio of 1623, where it was given the place of honor at the beginning of the volume. The Folio text appears to have been set from a manuscript more carefully edited than most. Stage directions are more elaborate than is customary in most of the plays. The present edition is based on the Folio text with a minimum of emendations and corrections.

Names of the Actors

ALONSO, *King of Naples.*
SEBASTIAN, *his brother.*
PROSPERO, *the right Duke of Milan.*
ANTONIO, *his brother, the usurping Duke of Milan.*
FERDINAND, *son to the King of Naples.*
GONZALO, *an honest old counselor.*
ADRIAN *and* FRANCISCO, *lords.*
CALIBAN, *a savage and deformed slave.*
TRINCULO, *a jester.*
STEPHANO, *a drunken butler.*
MASTER *of a ship.*
BOATSWAIN.
MARINERS.

MIRANDA, *daughter to Prospero.*
ARIEL, *an airy spirit.*
IRIS,
CERES,
JUNO, } [*spirits*].
NYMPHS,
REAPERS,

[*Other Spirits serving Prospero.*]

The Scene: [*A ship at sea; afterwards*] *an uninhabited island.*

Iris
From Vincenzo Cartari,
Imagini de gli dei delli antichi (1615).

THE TEMPEST

ACT I

Scene I. [*A ship at sea.*]

A tempestuous noise of thunder and lightning heard. Enter a SHIPMASTER *and a* BOATSWAIN.

Mast. Boatswain!

Boats. Here, master. What cheer?

Mast. Good, speak to the mariners; fall to't yarely, or we run ourselves aground! Bestir, bestir! *Exit.*

Enter MARINERS.

Boats. Heigh, my hearts! Cheerly, cheerly, 5 my hearts! Yare, yare! Take in the topsail! Tend to the master's whistle! Blow till thou burst thy wind, if room enough!

Enter ALONSO, SEBASTIAN, ANTONIO, FERDINAND, GONZALO, *and others.*

Alon. Good boatswain, have care. Where's the master? Play the men. 10

Boats. I pray now, keep below.

Ant. Where is the master, bos'n?

Boats. Do you not hear him? You mar our labor. Keep your cabins: you do assist the storm!

Gon. Nay, good, be patient. 15

Boats. When the sea is. Hence! What cares these roarers for the name of king? To cabin! Silence! Trouble us not!

Gon. Good, yet remember whom thou hast aboard.

Boats. None that I more love than myself. 20 You are a counselor: if you can command these elements to silence and work the peace of the present, we will not hand a rope more; use your authority. If you cannot, give thanks you have lived so long, and make yourself ready in your cabin for the mis- 25 chance of the hour, if it so hap.—Cheerly, good hearts!—Out of our way, I say. *Exit.*

Gon. I have great comfort from this fellow. Methinks he hath no drowning mark upon him; his complexion is perfect gallows. Stand fast, good 30 Fate, to his hanging! Make the rope of his destiny our cable, for our own doth little advantage. If he be not born to be hanged, our case is miserable. *Exeunt.*

[*Re-*]*enter* BOATSWAIN.

Boats. Down with the topmast! Yare! Lower, lower! Bring her to try with main course! 35 (*A cry within.*) A plague upon this howling! They are louder than the weather or our office.

Enter SEBASTIAN, ANTONIO, *and* GONZALO.

3. Good: my good fellow; **yarely:** speedily
6. Tend: hearken
7. Blow: addressing the storm
7–8. if . . . enough: if the sea room is sufficient to prevent running aground

16. cares: disagreement in number of verb and subject was common usage.
28–30. Methinks . . . gallows: proverbial: "He that is born to be hanged shall never be drowned."
29–30. complexion: temperament; nature
35. Bring . . . course: heave her to with only the mainsail set.
37. our office: our duty of shouting orders to the seamen

Yet again? What do you here? Shall we give o'er and drown? Have you a mind to sink?

Seb. A pox o' your throat, you bawling, blasphemous, incharitable dog! 40

Boats. Work you then.

Ant. Hang, cur, hang, you whoreson, insolent noisemaker! We are less afraid to be drowned than thou art. 45

Gon. I'll warrant him for drowning, though the ship were no stronger than a nutshell and as leaky as an unstanched wench.

Boats. Lay her ahold, ahold! Set her two courses! Off to sea again! Lay her off! 50

Enter MARINERS, *wet.*

Mariners. All lost! To prayers, to prayers! All lost! [*Exeunt.*]

Boats. What, must our mouths be cold?

Gon. The King and Prince at prayers! Let's assist them,
For our case is as theirs.

Seb. I am out of patience.

Ant. We are merely cheated of our lives by drunkards. 55
This wide-chopped rascal—would thou mightst lie drowning
The washing of ten tides!

Gon. He'll be hanged yet,
Though every drop of water swear against it
And gape at wid'st to glut him.

A confused noise within: "Mercy on us— 60
We split, we split!—Farewell, my wife and children!—
Farewell, brother!—We split, we split, we split!"
[*Exit Boatswain.*]

Ant. Let's all sink with the King.

Seb. Let's take leave of him.
Exeunt [*Antonio and Sebastian*].

Gon. Now would I give a thousand furlongs of sea for an acre of barren ground—long heath, 65 brown furze, anything. The wills above be done, but I would fain die a dry death.
Exit.

46. **warrant . . . drowning:** guarantee him against drowning
48. **unstanched:** loose
49. **ahold:** close to the wind; **two courses:** foresail and mainsail
50. **off:** away from shore
55. **merely:** completely
56. **wide-chopped:** big-mouthed
57. **ten tides:** pirates were hanged at the low-tide line and left to drown through the washing of three tides.

Scene II. [*The island. Before Prospero's cell.*]

Enter PROSPERO *and* MIRANDA.

Mir. If by your art, my dearest father, you have
Put the wild waters in this roar, allay them.
The sky, it seems, would pour down stinking pitch
But that the sea, mounting to the welkin's cheek,
Dashes the fire out. O, I have suffered 5
With those that I saw suffer! a brave vessel
(Who had no doubt some noble creature in her)
Dashed all to pieces! O, the cry did knock
Against my very heart! Poor souls, they perished!
Had I been any god of power, I would 10
Have sunk the sea within the earth or ere
It should the good ship so have swallowed and
The fraughting souls within her.

Pros. Be collected.
No more amazement. Tell your piteous heart
There's no harm done.

Mir. O, woe the day!

Pros. No harm. 15
I have done nothing but in care of thee,
Of thee my dear one, thee my daughter, who
Art ignorant of what thou art, naught knowing
Of whence I am; nor that I am more better
Than Prospero, master of a full poor cell, 20
And thy no greater father.

Mir. More to know
Did never meddle with my thoughts.

Pros. 'Tis time
I should inform thee farther. Lend thy hand
And pluck my magic garment from me. So,
[*Takes off his magic robe.*]
Lie there, my art. Wipe thou thine eyes; have comfort. 25
The direful spectacle of the wrack, which touched
The very virtue of compassion in thee,
I have with such provision in mine art
So safely ordered that there is no soul—
No, not so much perdition as an hair 30
Betid to any creature in the vessel
Which thou heardst cry, which thou sawst sink. Sit down;
For thou must now know farther.

Mir. You have often
Begun to tell me what I am, but stopped

4. **welkin's:** heaven's
6. **brave:** splendid
13. **fraughting souls:** human freight
14. **amazement:** dismay
22. **meddle:** mix
27. **virtue:** essence
30. **perdition:** loss
31. **Betid:** befallen

And left me to a bootless inquisition, 35
Concluding, "Stay! Not yet."
Pros. The hour's now come;
The very minute bids thee ope thine ear.
Obey, and be attentive. Canst thou remember
A time before we came unto this cell?
I do not think thou canst, for then thou wast not 40
Out three years old.
Mir. Certainly, sir, I can.
Pros. By what? By any other house or person?
Of anything the image tell me that
Hath kept with thy remembrance.
Mir. 'Tis far off,
And rather like a dream than an assurance 45
That my remembrance warrants. Had I not
Four or five women once that tended me?
Pros. Thou hadst, and more, Miranda. But how is it
That this lives in thy mind? What seest thou else
In the dark backward and abysm of time? 50
If thou remember'st aught ere thou camest here,
How thou camest here thou mayst.
Mir. But that I do not.
Pros. Twelve year since, Miranda, twelve year since,
Thy father was the Duke of Milan and
A prince of power.
Mir. Sir, are not you my father? 55
Pros. Thy mother was a piece of virtue, and
She said thou wast my daughter; and thy father
Was Duke of Milan; and his only heir
A princess—no worse issued.
Mir. O the heavens! 59
What foul play had we that we came from thence?
Or blessed was't we did?
Pros. Both, both, my girl!
By foul play, as thou sayst, were we heaved thence,
But blessedly holp hither.
Mir. O, my heart bleeds
To think o' the teen that I have turned you to, 64
Which is from my remembrance! Please you, farther.
Pros. My brother, and thy uncle, called Antonio—
I pray thee mark me—that a brother should
Be so perfidious!—he whom next thyself
Of all the world I loved, and to him put
The manage of my state, as at that time 70
Through all the seigniories it was the first,
And Prospero the prime duke, being so reputed
In dignity, and for the liberal arts
Without a parallel; those being all my study,
The government I cast upon my brother 75
And to my state grew stranger, being transported
And rapt in secret studies—thy false uncle—
Dost thou attend me?
Mir. Sir, most heedfully.
Pros. Being once perfected how to grant suits,
How to deny them, who t' advance, and who 80
To trash for overtopping, new-created
The creatures that were mine, I say, or changed 'em,
Or else new-formed 'em; having both the key
Of officer and office, set all hearts i' the state
To what tune pleased his ear, that now he was 85
The ivy which had hid my princely trunk
And sucked my verdure out on't. Thou attendst not!
Mir. O, good sir, I do.
Pros. I pray thee mark me.
I thus neglecting worldly ends, all dedicated
To closeness, and the bettering of my mind 90
With that which, but by being so retired,
O'erprized all popular rate, in my false brother
Awaked an evil nature, and my trust,
Like a good parent, did beget of him
A falsehood in its contrary as great 95
As my trust was, which had indeed no limit,
A confidence sans bound. He being thus lorded,
Not only with what my revenue yielded
But what my power might else exact, like one
Who having unto truth, by telling of it, 100
Made such a sinner of his memory
To credit his own lie, he did believe
He was indeed the Duke, out o' the substitution
And executing the outward face of royalty 104
With all prerogative. Hence his ambition growing—
Dost thou hear?
Mir. Your tale, sir, would cure deafness.
Pros. To have no screen between this part he played
And him he played it for, he needs will be
Absolute Milan. Me (poor man) my library 109
Was dukedom large enough! Of temporal royalties
He thinks me now incapable; confederates

35. bootless: unavailing
41. Out: quite
46. remembrance warrants: memory certifies
50. backward: past
56. piece: masterpiece
59. issued: descended; born
63. holp: obsolete past tense of "help"
64. teen: trouble; **turned . . . to:** reminded you of
65. from: out of
71. seigniories: dominions
74. study: employment
79. perfected: skilled
81. trash . . . overtopping: check for advancing presumptuously. The metaphor was applied to overeager hounds.
85. that: so that
85–87. now . . . on't: he obscured my royal self and stole my power.
90. closeness: seclusion
91–92. but . . . rate: had it not been so foreign to common understanding, would have been prized beyond anything
93–94. trust . . . parent: proverbial: "Trust is the mother of deceit."
97. lorded: given lordly power
103. out . . . substitution: because of being made the deputy
107. screen: barrier
109. Absolute Milan: the actual Duke of Milan
110. temporal: worldly

(So dry he was for sway) with the King of Naples
To give him annual tribute, do him homage,
Subject his coronet to his crown, and bend
The dukedom yet unbowed (alas, poor Milan!) 115
To most ignoble stooping.

Mir. O the heavens!

Pros. Mark his condition, and the event; then tell me
If this might be a brother.

Mir. I should sin
To think but nobly of my grandmother.
Good wombs have borne bad sons.

Pros. Now the condition.
This King of Naples, being an enemy 121
To me inveterate, hearkens my brother's suit;
Which was, that he, in lieu o' the premises,
Of homage and I know not how much tribute,
Should presently extirpate me and mine 125
Out of the dukedom and confer fair Milan,
With all the honors, on my brother. Whereon,
A treacherous army levied, one midnight
Fated to the purpose, did Antonio open
The gates of Milan; and, i' the dead of darkness,
The ministers for the purpose hurried thence 131
Me and thy crying self.

Mir. Alack, for pity!
I, not rememb'ring how I cried out then,
Will cry it o'er again. It is a hint 134
That wrings mine eyes to't.

Pros. Hear a little further,
And then I'll bring thee to the present business
Which now's upon's; without the which this story
Were most impertinent.

Mir. Wherefore did they not
That hour destroy us?

Pros. Well demanded, wench.
My tale provokes that question. Dear, they durst not, 140
So dear the love my people bore me; nor set
A mark so bloody on the business; but
With colors fairer painted their foul ends.
In few, they hurried us aboard a bark,
Bore us some leagues to sea; where they prepared
A rotten carcass of a butt, not rigged, 146
Nor tackle, sail, nor mast; the very rats
Instinctively have quit it. There they hoist us,
To cry to the sea, that roared to us; to sigh
To the winds, whose pity, sighing back again, 150
Did us but loving wrong.

Mir. Alack, what trouble
Was I then to you!

Pros. O, a cherubin
Thou wast that did preserve me! Thou didst smile,
Infused with a fortitude from heaven,
When I have decked the sea with drops full salt, 155
Under my burden groaned; which raised in me
An undergoing stomach, to bear up
Against what should ensue.

Mir. How came we ashore?

Pros. By providence divine.
Some food we had, and some fresh water, that 160
A noble Neapolitan, Gonzalo,
Out of his charity, who being then appointed
Master of this design, did give us, with
Rich garments, linens, stuffs, and necessaries 164
Which since have steaded much. So, of his gentleness,
Knowing I loved my books, he furnished me
From mine own library with volumes that
I prize above my dukedom.

Mir. Would I might
But ever see that man!

Pros. Now I arise.
Sit still, and hear the last of our sea-sorrow. 170
Here in this island we arrived; and here
Have I, thy schoolmaster, made thee more profit
Than other princess can, that have more time
For vainer hours, and tutors not so careful.

Mir. Heavens thank you for't! And now I pray you, sir,— 175
For still 'tis beating in my mind,—your reason
For raising this sea-storm?

Pros. Know thus far forth.
By accident most strange, bountiful Fortune
(Now my dear lady) hath mine enemies
Brought to this shore; and by my prescience 180
I find my zenith doth depend upon
A most auspicious star, whose influence
If now I court not, but omit, my fortunes
Will ever after droop. Here cease more questions.
Thou art inclined to sleep. 'Tis a good dullness, 185
And give it way. I know thou canst not choose.
[*Miranda sleeps.*]
Come away, servant, come! I am ready now.
Approach, my Ariel. Come!

Enter ARIEL.

Ariel. All hail, great master! Grave sir, hail! I come

112. **dry:** avid; **sway:** rule
117. **condition:** character; **event:** outcome
118. **might:** could
123. **in . . . premises:** in return for fulfilling premised terms
125. **presently:** at once; **extirpate:** root out
134. **hint:** suitable occasion
138. **impertinent:** irrelevant
146. **butt:** old tub
148. **hoist:** hoisted
157. **undergoing stomach:** courage to endure
165. **steaded:** assisted; **gentleness:** nobility
173. **princess:** princesses
174. **vainer:** more uselessly spent
178. **accident:** happening
181. **zenith:** height of fortune
183. **omit:** neglect
186. **give . . . way:** yield to it
189. **Grave:** reverend

To answer thy best pleasure; be't to fly, 190
To swim, to dive into the fire, to ride
On the curled clouds. To thy strong bidding task
Ariel and all his quality.

Pros. Hast thou, spirit,
Performed to point the tempest that I bade thee?

Ariel. To every article. 195
I boarded the King's ship. Now on the beak,
Now in the waist, the deck, in every cabin,
I flamed amazement. Sometime I'ld divide
And burn in many places; on the topmast, 199
The yards, and bowsprit would I flame distinctly,
Then meet and join. Jove's lightnings, the precursors
O' the dreadful thunderclaps, more momentary
And sight-outrunning were not. The fire and cracks
Of sulphurous roaring the most mighty Neptune
Seem to besiege and make his bold waves tremble;
Yea, his dread trident shake.

Pros. My brave spirit! 206
Who was so firm, so constant, that this coil
Would not infect his reason?

Ariel. Not a soul
But felt a fever of the mad and played
Some tricks of desperation. All but mariners 210
Plunged in the foaming brine and quit the vessel,
Then all afire with me. The King's son Ferdinand,
With hair up-staring (then like reeds, not hair),
Was the first man that leapt; cried "Hell is empty,
And all the devils are here!"

Pros. Why, that's my spirit!
But was not this nigh shore?

Ariel. Close by, my master. 216

Pros. But are they, Ariel, safe?

Ariel. Not a hair perished.
On their sustaining garments not a blemish,
But fresher than before; and as thou badest me,
In troops I have dispersed them 'bout the isle. 220
The King's son have I landed by himself,
Whom I left cooling of the air with sighs
In an odd angle of the isle, and sitting,
His arms in this sad knot.

Pros. Of the King's ship
The mariners say how thou hast disposed, 225
And all the rest o' the fleet.

Ariel. Safely in harbor
Is the King's ship; in the deep nook where once
Thou calledst me up at midnight to fetch dew
From the still-vexed Bermoothes, there she's hid;
The mariners all under hatches stowed, 230
Who, with a charm joined to their suff'red labor,
I have left asleep; and for the rest o' the fleet,
Which I dispersed, they all have met again,
And are upon the Mediterranean float
Bound sadly home for Naples, 235
Supposing that they saw the King's ship wracked
And his great person perish.

Pros. Ariel, thy charge
Exactly is performed; but there's more work.
What is the time o' the day?

Ariel. Past the mid season.

Pros. At least two glasses. The time 'twixt six and now 240
Must by us both be spent most preciously.

Ariel. Is there more toil? Since thou dost give me pains,
Let me remember thee what thou hast promised,
Which is not yet performed me.

Pros. How now? moody?
What is't thou canst demand?

Ariel. My liberty. 245

Pros. Before the time be out? No more!

Ariel. I prithee,
Remember I have done thee worthy service,
Told thee no lies, made no mistakings, served
Without or grudge or grumblings. Thou didst promise
To bate me a full year.

Pros. Dost thou forget 250
From what a torment I did free thee?

Ariel. No.

Pros. Thou dost; and thinkst it much to tread the ooze
Of the salt deep,
To run upon the sharp wind of the North,
To do me business in the veins o' the earth 255
When it is baked with frost.

Ariel. I do not, sir.

Pros. Thou liest, malignant thing! Hast thou forgot
The foul witch Sycorax, who with age and envy
Was grown into a hoop? Hast thou forgot her?

Ariel. No, sir.

Pros. Thou hast. Where was she born? Speak! Tell me! 260

Ariel. Sir, in Argier.

Pros. O, was she so? I must
Once in a month recount what thou hast been,
Which thou forgetst. This damned witch Sycorax,

192. task: tax
193. quality: kind; i.e., his associate spirits
194. to point: exactly
196. beak: prow
197. waist: middle
198. flamed amazement: burned to the consternation of the beholders
200. distinctly: severally; at one and the same time
207. constant: self-controlled; **coil:** uproar
209. fever . . . mad: fit of madness
218. sustaining: buoying
224. in . . . knot: crossed, an attitude of melancholy to the Elizabethans
229. still-vexed: perpetually storm-ridden; **Bermoothes:** Bermudas
234. float: sea
241. preciously: i.e., as one would spend something precious
242. pains: painful tasks
250. bate: abate; shorten
258. envy: malice
261. Argier: Algiers

For mischiefs manifold, and sorceries terrible
To enter human hearing, from Argier 265
Thou knowst was banished. For one thing she did
They would not take her life. Is not this true?
Ariel. Ay, sir.
Pros. This blue-eyed hag was hither brought with child 269
And here was left by the sailors. Thou, my slave,
As thou reportst thyself, wast then her servant;
And, for thou wast a spirit too delicate
To act her earthy and abhorred commands,
Refusing her grand hests, she did confine thee,
By help of her more potent ministers, 275
And in her most unmitigable rage,
Into a cloven pine; within which rift
Imprisoned thou didst painfully remain
A dozen years; within which space she died
And left thee there; where thou didst vent thy groans 280
As fast as mill wheels strike. Then was this island
(Save for the son that she did litter here,
A freckled whelp, hag-born) not honored with
A human shape.
Ariel. Yes, Caliban, her son.
Pros. Dull thing, I say so! he, that Caliban 285
Whom now I keep in service. Thou best knowst
What torment I did find thee in. Thy groans
Did make wolves howl and penetrate the breasts
Of ever-angry bears. It was a torment
To lay upon the damned, which Sycorax 290
Could not again undo. It was mine art,
When I arrived and heard thee, that made gape
The pine, and let thee out.
Ariel. I thank thee, master.
Pros. If thou more murmurst, I will rend an oak
And peg thee in his knotty entrails till 295
Thou hast howled away twelve winters.
Ariel. Pardon, master.
I will be correspondent to command
And do my spriting gently.
Pros. Do so; and after two days
I will discharge thee.
Ariel. That's my noble master!
What shall I do? Say what! What shall I do? 300
Pros. Go make thyself like a nymph o' the sea. Be subject
To no sight but thine and mine; invisible
To every eyeball else. Go take this shape
And hither come in't. Go! Hence with diligence! 304
Exit [*Ariel*].
Awake, dear heart, awake! Thou hast slept well.
Awake!
Mir. The strangeness of your story put
Heaviness in me.
Pros. Shake it off. Come on.
We'll visit Caliban, my slave, who never
Yields us kind answer.
Mir. 'Tis a villain, sir, 310
I do not love to look on.
Pros. But as 'tis,
We cannot miss him. He does make our fire,
Fetch in our wood, and serves in offices
That profit us. What, ho! slave! Caliban! 314
Thou earth, thou! Speak!
Cal. (*Within*) There's wood enough within.
Pros. Come forth, I say! There's other business for thee.
Come, thou tortoise! When?

Enter ARIEL *like a water nymph.*

Fine apparition! My quaint Ariel,
Hark in thine ear.
Ariel. My lord, it shall be done. *Exit.*
Pros. Thou poisonous slave, got by the devil himself 320
Upon thy wicked dam, come forth!

Enter CALIBAN.

Cal. As wicked dew as e'er my mother brushed
With raven's feather from unwholesome fen
Drop on you both! A southwest blow on ye
And blister you all o'er! 325
Pros. For this, be sure, tonight thou shalt have cramps,
Side-stitches that shall pen thy breath up; urchins
Shall, for that vast of night that they may work,
All exercise on thee; thou shalt be pinched 329
As thick as honeycomb, each pinch more stinging
Than bees that made 'em.
Cal. I must eat my dinner.
This island's mine by Sycorax my mother,
Which thou takest from me. When thou camest first,
Thou strokedst me and made much of me; wouldst give me
Water with berries in't; and teach me how 335

269. blue-eyed: i.e., having blue-shadowed eyes
274. grand hests: important tasks
275. ministers: agents
281. strike: i.e., against the grain hopper to shake the grain to the grinding surfaces
295. his: its; the common neuter genitive
297. correspondent: responsive
298. do . . . gently: perform the duties of a spirit graciously
312. miss: lack
317. When: an exclamation of impatience
318. quaint: clever; ingenious
322. wicked: baneful; poisonous
324. southwest: southwest wind, traditionally believed **to** carry infection with it
327. urchins: goblins. Such evil imps sometimes took the form of hedgehogs, also called **urchins.**

To name the bigger light, and how the less,
That burn by day, and night; and then I loved thee
And showed thee all the qualities o' the isle,
The fresh springs, brine-pits, barren place and fertile.
Cursed be I that did so! All the charms 340
Of Sycorax—toads, beetles, bats light on you!
For I am all the subjects that you have,
Which first was mine own king; and here you sty me
In this hard rock, whiles you do keep from me
The rest o' the island.

Pros. Thou most lying slave, 345
Whom stripes may move, not kindness! I have used thee
(Filth as thou art) with humane care, and lodged thee
In mine own cell till thou didst seek to violate
The honor of my child.

Cal. O ho, O ho! Would't had been done! 350
Thou didst prevent me; I had peopled else
This isle with Calibans.

Mir. Abhorred slave,
Which any print of goodness wilt not take,
Being capable of all ill! I pitied thee,
Took pains to make thee speak, taught thee each hour 355
One thing or other. When thou didst not, savage,
Know thine own meaning, but wouldst gabble like
A thing most brutish, I endowed thy purposes
With words that made them known. But thy vile race,
Though thou didst learn, had that in't which good natures 360
Could not abide to be with. Therefore wast thou
Deservedly confined into this rock, who hadst
Deserved more than a prison.

Cal. You taught me language, and my profit on't
Is, I know how to curse. The red plague rid you 365
For learning me your language!

Pros. Hag-seed, hence!
Fetch us in fuel; and be quick, thou'rt best,
To answer other business. Shrugst thou, malice?
If thou neglectst or dost unwillingly 369
What I command, I'll rack thee with old cramps,
Fill all thy bones with aches, make thee roar
That beasts shall tremble at thy din.

Cal. No, pray thee.
[*Aside*] I must obey. His art is of such pow'r
It would control my dam's god, Setebos,
And make a vassal of him.

Pros. So, slave; hence! 375
Exit Caliban.

Enter FERDINAND; *and* ARIEL, *invisible, playing and singing.*

365. red: bubonic; **rid:** kill

Ariel's song.

Come unto these yellow sands,
And then take hands.
Curtsied when you have and kissed,
The wild waves whist,
Foot it featly here and there; 380
And, sweet sprites, the burden bear.
Hark, hark!

Burden dispersedly. Bow, wow!
The watchdogs bark.

Burden dispersedly. Bow, wow! 385

Ariel. Hark, hark! I hear
The strain of strutting chanticleer
Cry, cock-a-diddle-dowe.

Fer. Where should this music be? I' the air, or the earth?
It sounds no more; and sure it waits upon 390
Some god o' the island. Sitting on a bank,
Weeping again the King my father's wrack,
This music crept by me upon the waters,
Allaying both their fury and my passion
With its sweet air. Thence I have followed it, 395
Or it hath drawn me rather; but 'tis gone.
No, it begins again.

Ariel's song.

Full fathom five thy father lies;
Of his bones are coral made;
Those are pearls that were his eyes; 400
Nothing of him that doth fade
But doth suffer a sea-change
Into something rich and strange.
Sea nymphs hourly ring his knell:

Burden. Ding-dong. 405

Hark! now I hear them—Ding-dong bell.

Fer. The ditty does remember my drowned father.
This is no mortal business, nor no sound
That the earth owes. I hear it now above me. 409

Pros. The fringed curtains of thine eye advance
And say what thou seest yond.

Mir. What is't? a spirit?
Lord, how it looks about! Believe me, sir,
It carries a brave form. But 'tis a spirit.

379. whist: hushed
380. featly: nimbly
381. burden: refrain
S.D. 383. dispersedly: from several directions
394. passion: grief
409. owes: owns
410. advance: raise
413. brave: handsome

Pros. No, wench. It eats, and sleeps, and hath such senses 414
As we have, such. This gallant which thou seest
Was in the wrack; and, but he's something stained
With grief (that's beauty's canker), thou mightst call him
A goodly person. He hath lost his fellows
And strays about to find 'em.

Mir. I might call him
A thing divine, for nothing natural 420
I ever saw so noble.

Pros. [*Aside*] It goes on, I see,
As my soul prompts it. Spirit, fine spirit! I'll free thee
Within two days for this.

Fer. Most sure, the goddess
On whom these airs attend! Vouchsafe my pray'r
May know if you remain upon this island, 425
And that you will some good instruction give
How I may bear me here. My prime request,
Which I do last pronounce, is (O you wonder!)
If you be maid or no?

Mir. No wonder, sir,
But certainly a maid.

Fer. My language? Heavens! 430
I am the best of them that speak this speech,
Were I but where 'tis spoken.

Pros. How? the best?
What wert thou if the King of Naples heard thee?

Fer. A single thing, as I am now, that wonders
To hear thee speak of Naples. He does hear me; 435
And that he does I weep. Myself am Naples,
Who with mine eyes, never since at ebb, beheld
The King, my father, wracked.

Mir. Alack, for mercy!

Fer. Yes, faith, and all his lords, the Duke of Milan 439
And his brave son being twain.

Pros. [*Aside*] The Duke of Milan
And his more braver daughter could control thee,
If now 'twere fit to do't. At the first sight
They have changed eyes. Delicate Ariel,
I'll set thee free for this!—A word, good sir. 444
I fear you have done yourself some wrong. A word!

Mir. Why speaks my father so ungently? This
Is the third man that e'er I saw; the first
That e'er I sighed for. Pity move my father
To be inclined my way!

Fer. O, if a virgin, 449
And your affection not gone forth, I'll make you
The Queen of Naples.

Pros. Soft, sir! one word more.
[*Aside*] They are both in either's pow'rs. But this swift business
I must uneasy make, lest too light winning
Make the prize light.—One word more! I charge thee
That thou attend me. Thou dost here usurp 455
The name thou owest not, and hast put thyself
Upon this island as a spy, to win it
From me, the lord on't.

Fer. No, as I am a man!

Mir. There's nothing ill can dwell in such a temple.
If the ill spirit have so fair a house, 460
Good things will strive to dwell with't.

Pros. Follow me.—
Speak not you for him; he's a traitor.—Come!
I'll manacle thy neck and feet together;
Sea water shalt thou drink; thy food shall be 464
The fresh brook mussels, withered roots, and husks
Wherein the acorn cradled. Follow.

Fer. No.
I will resist such entertainment till
Mine enemy has more power.

He draws, and is charmed from moving.

Mir. O dear father,
Make not too rash a trial of him, for
He's gentle, and not fearful.

Pros. What, I say, 470
My foot my tutor?—Put thy sword up, traitor!
Who makest a show but darest not strike, thy conscience
Is so possessed with guilt. Come, from thy ward!
For I can here disarm thee with this stick 474
And make thy weapon drop.

Mir. Beseech you, father!

Pros. Hence! Hang not on my garments.

Mir. Sir, have pity.
I'll be his surety.

Pros. Silence! One word more
Shall make me chide thee, if not hate thee. What,
An advocate for an impostor? Hush! 479
Thou thinkst there is no more such shapes as he,
Having seen but him and Caliban. Foolish wench!
To the most of men this is a Caliban,
And they to him are angels.

Mir. My affections
Are then most humble. I have no ambition
To see a goodlier man.

Pros. Come on, obey! 485

416. something: somewhat; **stained:** marred
425. remain: reside
427. bear me: conduct myself
429. maid: a mortal (rather than a divine creature)
434. single: solitary
436. Naples: King of Naples
441. control thee: correct your mistake
443. changed: exchanged
445. done . . . wrong: told an untruth
467. entertainment: treatment
470. gentle . . . fearful: a gentleman, not a coward
471. My . . . tutor: my inferior instructing me
473. from . . . ward: abandon your fighting stance
483. affections: tastes

Thy nerves are in their infancy again
And have no vigor in them.
Fer. So they are.
My spirits, as in a dream, are all bound up.
My father's loss, the weakness which I feel, 489
The wrack of all my friends, nor this man's threats
To whom I am subdued, are but light to me,
Might I but through my prison once a day
Behold this maid. All corners else o' the earth
Let liberty make use of; space enough
Have I in such a prison.

486. nerves: strength; sinews
488. spirits: energies

Pros. [*Aside*] It works. [*To Ferdinand*]
Come on.— 495
Thou hast done well, fine Ariel! [*To Ferdinand*]
Follow me.—
[*To Ariel*] Hark what thou else shalt do me.
Mir. Be of comfort.
My father's of a better nature, sir,
Than he appears by speech. This is unwonted 499
Which now came from him.
Pros. Thou shalt be as free
As mountain winds; but then exactly do
All points of my command.
Ariel. To the syllable.
Pros. Come, follow.—Speak not for him.
Exeunt.

ACT II

Scene I. [*Another part of the island.*]

Enter Alonso, Sebastian, Antonio, Gonzalo, Adrian, Francisco, *and others.*

Gon. Beseech you, sir, be merry. You have cause
(So have we all) of joy; for our escape
Is much beyond our loss. Our hint of woe
Is common. Every day some sailor's wife,
The master of some merchant, and the merchant, 5
Have just our theme of woe; but for the miracle,
I mean our preservation, few in millions
Can speak like us. Then wisely, good sir, weigh
Our sorrow with our comfort.
Alon. Prithee peace.
Seb. He receives comfort like cold porridge. 10
Ant. The visitor will not give him o'er so.
Seb. Look, he's winding up the watch of his wit; by-and-by it will strike.
Gon. Sir—
Seb. One. Tell. 15
Gon. When every grief is entertained that's offered,
Comes to the entertainer—

1. merry: cheerful
3. hint: cause
5. some merchant: some merchant ship
11. visitor: comforter
15. Tell: keep count
16. entertained: accepted

Seb. A dollar.
Gon. Dolor comes to him, indeed. You have spoken truer than you proposed. 20
Seb. You have taken it wiselier than I meant you should.
Gon. Therefore, my lord—
Ant. Fie, what a spendthrift is he of his tongue!
Alon. I prithee spare. 25
Gon. Well, I have done. But yet—
Seb. He will be talking.
Ant. Which, of he or Adrian, for a good wager, first begins to crow?
Seb. The old cock. 30
Ant. The cock'rel.
Seb. Done! The wager?
Ant. A laughter.
Seb. A match!
Adr. Though this island seem to be desert— 35
Ant. Ha, ha, ha!
Seb. So, you're paid.
Adr. Uninhabitable and almost inaccessible—
Seb. Yet—
Adr. Yet— 40
Ant. He could not miss't.
Adr. It must needs be of subtle, tender, and delicate temperance.
Ant. Temperance was a delicate wench.

33. laughter: good laugh
42–43. subtle . . . temperance: temperate climate
44. Temperance: a contemporary feminine name; also the virtue personified as a woman

Seb. Ay, and a subtle, as he most learnedly 45
delivered.

Adr. The air breathes upon us here most sweetly.

Seb. As if it had lungs, and rotten ones.

Ant. Or as 'twere perfumed by a fen.

Gon. Here is everything advantageous to life. 50

Ant. True; save means to live.

Seb. Of that there's none, or little.

Gon. How lush and lusty the grass looks! how green!

Ant. The ground indeed is tawny. 55

Seb. With an eye of green in't.

Ant. He misses not much.

Seb. No; he doth but mistake the truth totally.

Gon. But the rarity of it is—which is indeed almost beyond credit— 60

Seb. As many vouched rarities are.

Gon. That our garments, being, as they were, drenched in the sea, hold, notwithstanding, their freshness and gloss, being rather new-dyed than stained with salt water. 65

Ant. If but one of his pockets could speak, would it not say he lies?

Seb. Ay, or very falsely pocket up his report.

Gon. Methinks our garments are now as fresh as when we put them on first in Afric, at the mar- 70
riage of the King's fair daughter Claribel to the King of Tunis.

Seb. 'Twas a sweet marriage, and we prosper well in our return.

Adr. Tunis was never graced before with 75
such a paragon to their queen.

Gon. Not since widow Dido's time.

Ant. Widow? A pox o' that! How came that "widow" in? Widow Dido!

Seb. What if he had said "widower Æneas" 80
too? Good Lord, how you take it!

Adr. "Widow Dido," said you? You make me study of that. She was of Carthage, not of Tunis.

Gon. This Tunis, sir, was Carthage.

Adr. Carthage? 85

Gon. I assure you, Carthage.

Ant. His word is more than the miraculous harp.

Seb. He hath raised the wall, and houses too.

Ant. What impossible matter will he make easy next? 90

Seb. I think he will carry this island home in his pocket and give it his son for an apple.

Ant. And, sowing the kernels of it in the sea, bring forth more islands.

Gon. Ay! 95

Ant. Why, in good time!

Gon. Sir, we were talking that our garments seem now as fresh as when we were at Tunis at the marriage of your daughter, who is now Queen.

Ant. And the rarest that e'er came there. 100

Seb. Bate, I beseech you, widow Dido.

Ant. O, widow Dido? Ay, widow Dido.

Gon. Is not, sir, my doublet as fresh as the first day I wore it? I mean, in a sort.

Ant. That "sort" was well fished for. 105

Gon. When I wore it at your daughter's marriage.

Alon. You cram these words into mine ears against
The stomach of my sense. Would I had never
Married my daughter there! for, coming thence,
My son is lost; and, in my rate, she too, 110
Who is so far from Italy removed
I ne'er again shall see her. O thou mine heir
Of Naples and of Milan, what strange fish
Hath made his meal on thee?

Fran. Sir, he may live.
I saw him beat the surges under him 115
And ride upon their backs. He trod the water,
Whose enmity he flung aside, and breasted
The surge most swol'n that met him. His bold head
'Bove the contentious waves he kept, and oared
Himself with his good arms in lusty stroke 120
To the shore, that o'er his wave-worn basis bowed,
As stooping to relieve him. I not doubt
He came alive to land.

Alon. No, no, he's gone.

Seb. Sir, you may thank yourself for this great loss,
That would not bless our Europe with your daughter,
But rather lose her to an African, 126
Where she, at least, is banished from your eye
Who hath cause to wet the grief on't.

Alon. Prithee peace.

Seb. You were kneeled to and importuned otherwise
By all of us; and the fair soul herself 130
Weighed, between loathness and obedience, at
Which end o' the beam should bow. We have lost your son,
I fear, forever. Milan and Naples have
Mo widows in them of this business' making
Than we bring men to comfort them. 135
The fault's your own.

Alon. So is the dear'st o' the loss.

46. delivered: reported
53. lusty: plentiful
56. eye: touch
61. vouched rarities: i.e., the curiosities vouched for by travelers
68. pocket up: accept without protest
77. widow Dido: the widowed Queen of Carthage
87. the . . . harp: the legendary poet Amphion was reported to have raised the walls of Thebes by playing his harp.

101. Bate: except
104. in . . . sort: more or less
107–8. against . . . sense: i.e., the subject matter is distasteful.
110. in . . . rate: as I see it
121. basis: base; ground
131. Weighed: balanced; **loathness:** reluctance
134. Mo: more, from Old English *mā*

Gon. My Lord Sebastian,
The truth you speak doth lack some gentleness,
And time to speak it in. You rub the sore
When you should bring the plaster.

Seb. Very well. 140

Ant. And most chirurgeonly.

Gon. It is foul weather in us all, good sir,
When you are cloudy.

Seb. Foul weather?

Ant. Very foul.

Gon. Had I plantation of this isle, my lord—

Ant. He'd sow't with nettle seed.

Seb. Or docks, or mallows. 145

Gon. And were the king on't, what would I do?

Seb. 'Scape being drunk, for want of wine.

Gon. I' the commonwealth I would by contraries
Execute all things; for no kind of traffic
Would I admit; no name of magistrate; 150
Letters should not be known; riches, poverty,
And use of service, none; contract, succession,
Bourn, bound of land, tilth, vineyard, none;
No use of metal, corn, or wine, or oil;
No occupation; all men idle, all; 155
And women too, but innocent and pure;
No sovereignty.

Seb. Yet he would be king on't.

Ant. The latter end of his commonwealth forgets the beginning.

Gon. All things in common nature should produce
Without sweat or endeavor. Treason, felony, 161
Sword, pike, knife, gun, or need of any engine
Would I not have; but nature should bring forth,
Of it own kind, all foison, all abundance,
To feed my innocent people. 165

Seb. No marrying 'mong his subjects?

Ant. None, man! All idle—whores and knaves.

Gon. I would with such perfection govern, sir,
T'excel the golden age.

Seb. Save his Majesty!

Ant. Long live Gonzalo!

Gon. And—do you mark me, sir? 170

Alon. Prithee no more. Thou dost talk nothing to me.

Gon. I do well believe your Highness; and did it to minister occasion to these gentlemen, who are of such sensible and nimble lungs that they always use to laugh at nothing. 175

Ant. 'Twas you we laughed at.

Gon. Who in this kind of merry fooling am nothing to you. So you may continue, and laugh at nothing still. 180

Ant. What a blow was there given!

Seb. An it had not fall'n flatlong.

Gon. You are gentlemen of brave metal. You would lift the moon out of her sphere if she would continue in it five weeks without changing. 185

Enter ARIEL, [*invisible*], *playing solemn music.*

Seb. We would so, and then go a-batfowling.

Ant. Nay, good my lord, be not angry.

Gon. No, I warrant you. I will not adventure my discretion so weakly. Will you laugh me asleep, for I am very heavy? 190

Ant. Go sleep, and hear us.

[*All sleep except Alonso, Sebastian, and Antonio.*]

Alon. What, all so soon asleep? I wish mine eyes
Would, with themselves, shut up my thoughts. I find
They are inclined to do so.

Seb. Please you, sir,
Do not omit the heavy offer of it. 195
It seldom visits sorrow; when it doth,
It is a comforter.

Ant. We two, my lord,
Will guard your person while you take your rest,
And watch your safety.

Alon. Thank you. Wondrous heavy.
[*Alonso sleeps. Exit Ariel.*]

Seb. What a strange drowsiness possesses them!

Ant. It is the quality o' the climate.

Seb. Why 201
Doth it not then our eyelids sink? I find not
Myself disposed to sleep.

Ant. Nor I. My spirits are nimble.
They fell together all, as by consent. 204
They dropped as by a thunderstroke. What might,
Worthy Sebastian—O, what might?—No more!
And yet methinks I see it in thy face,
What thou shouldst be. The occasion speaks thee, and
My strong imagination sees a crown
Dropping upon thy head.

Seb. What? Art thou waking? 210

Ant. Do you not hear me speak?

Seb. I do; and surely
It is a sleepy language, and thou speakst
Out of thy sleep. What is it thou didst say?
This is a strange repose, to be asleep 214

139. time: suitable time
141. most chirurgeonly: spoken like a proper surgeon
145. docks, mallows: two common weeds
151. Letters: literary interests
153. Bourn: boundary; **tilth:** tillage
162. engine: military machine
164. it: its; **foison:** plenty
174. minister occasion: give opportunity
175. sensible: responsive
183. brave: fine
186. a-batfowling: a night sport in which the roosting birds were confused by lights and struck down with bats. Sebastian would use the moon for his light.
188. adventure: risk
189. discretion: reputation for discretion
195. omit: neglect
208. occasion . . . thee: opportunity calls thy name

With eyes wide open; standing, speaking, moving—
And yet so fast asleep.

Ant. Noble Sebastian,
Thou letst thy fortune sleep—die, rather; winkst
Whiles thou art waking.

Seb. Thou dost snore distinctly;
There's meaning in thy snores.

Ant. I am more serious than my custom. You 220
Must be so too, if heed me; which to do
Trebles thee o'er.

Seb. Well, I am standing water.

Ant. I'll teach you how to flow.

Seb. Do so. To ebb
Hereditary sloth instructs me.

Ant. O,
If you but knew how you the purpose cherish 225
Whiles thus you mock it! how, in stripping it,
You more invest it! Ebbing men indeed
(Most often) do so near the bottom run
By their own fear or sloth.

Seb. Prithee say on.
The setting of thine eye and cheek proclaim 230
A matter from thee; and a birth, indeed,
Which throes thee much to yield.

Ant. Thus, sir:
Although this lord of weak remembrance, this
Who shall be of as little memory
When he is earthed, hath here almost persuaded 235
(For he's a spirit of persuasion, only
Professes to persuade) the King his son's alive,
'Tis as impossible that he's undrowned
As he that sleeps here swims.

Seb. I have no hope
That he's undrowned.

Ant. O, out of that no hope 240
What great hope have you! No hope that way is
Another way so high a hope that even
Ambition cannot pierce a wink beyond,
But doubts discovery there. Will you grant with me
That Ferdinand is drowned?

Seb. He's gone.

Ant. Then tell me,
Who's the next heir of Naples?

Seb. Claribel. 246

Ant. She that is Queen of Tunis; she that dwells
Ten leagues beyond man's life; she that from Naples
Can have no note, unless the sun were post—
The man i' the moon's too slow—till newborn chins
Be rough and razorable; she that from whom 251
We all were sea-swallowed, though some cast again,
And, by that destiny, to perform an act
Whereof what's past is prologue, what to come,
In yours and my discharge.

Seb. What stuff is this? How say you? 255
'Tis true my brother's daughter's Queen of Tunis;
So is she heir of Naples; 'twixt which regions
There is some space.

Ant. A space whose ev'ry cubit
Seems to cry out "How shall that Claribel
Measure us back to Naples? Keep in Tunis, 260
And let Sebastian wake!" Say this were death
That now hath seized them, why, they were no worse
Than now they are. There be that can rule Naples
As well as he that sleeps; lords that can prate
As amply and unnecessarily 265
As this Gonzalo. I myself could make
A chough of as deep chat. O, that you bore
The mind that I do! What a sleep were this
For your advancement! Do you understand me?

Seb. Methinks I do.

Ant. And how does your content
Tender your own good fortune?

Seb. I remember 271
You did supplant your brother Prospero.

Ant. True.
And look how well my garments sit upon me,
Much feater than before! My brother's servants
Were then my fellows; now they are my men. 275

Seb. But, for your conscience—

Ant. Ay, sir! Where lies that? If 'twere a kibe,
'Twould put me to my slipper; but I feel not
This deity in my bosom. Twenty consciences 279
That stand 'twixt me and Milan, candied be they
And melt, ere they molest! Here lies your brother,
No better than the earth he lies upon
If he were that which now he's like—that's dead;
Whom I with this obedient steel (three inches of it)
Can lay to bed forever; whiles you, doing thus, 285
To the perpetual wink for aye might put
This ancient morsel, this Sir Prudence, who
Should not upbraid our course. For all the rest,
They'll take suggestion as a cat laps milk;
They'll tell the clock to any business that 290
We say befits the hour.

217. **winkst:** close your eyes
222. **Trebles . . . o'er:** increases you threefold; **standing water:** i.e., receptive
232. **throes:** pains
234. **of . . . memory:** as little remembered
237. **Professes . . . persuade:** makes persuasion his business
243. **wink:** the least bit
244. **doubts . . . there:** doubts that revelation; disbelieves what he sees
248. **man's life:** i.e., the distance it is possible to travel in a man's lifetime
249. **note:** information; **post:** messenger
251. **from whom:** traveling from whom
252. **cast:** cast up
260. **us:** i.e., the cubits
267. **chough:** jackdaw
270–71. **how . . . fortune:** how does your good fortune please you?
274. **feater:** more aptly
277. **kibe:** chilblain
280. **candied:** frozen
287–88. **who . . . not:** lest he should
289. **suggestion:** evil prompting
290. **tell . . . clock:** keep time with; fall in with

Seb. Thy case, dear friend,
Shall be my precedent. As thou gotst Milan,
I'll come by Naples. Draw thy sword. One stroke
Shall free thee from the tribute which thou payest,
And I the King shall love thee.
Ant. Draw together; 295
And when I rear my hand, do you the like,
To fall it on Gonzalo. [*They draw.*]
Seb. O, but one word!
[*They converse apart.*]

Enter ARIEL, [*invisible*], *with music and song.*

Ariel. My master through his art foresees the danger
That you, his friend, are in, and sends me forth
(For else his project dies) to keep them living. 300
Sings in Gonzalo's ear.
While you here do snoring lie,
Open-eyed conspiracy
His time doth take.
If of life you keep a care,
Shake off slumber and beware. 305
Awake, awake!
Ant. Then let us both be sudden.
Gon. [*Wakes*] Now good angels preserve the King!
Alon. [*Wakes*] Why, how now? Ho, awake! Why are you drawn? 309
Wherefore this ghastly looking?
Gon. What's the matter?
Seb. Whiles we stood here securing your repose,
Even now, we heard a hollow burst of bellowing
Like bulls, or rather lions. Did't not wake you?
It struck mine ear most terribly.
Alon. I heard nothing.
Ant. O, 'twas a din to fright a monster's ear, 315
To make an earthquake! Sure it was the roar
Of a whole herd of lions.
Alon. Heard you this, Gonzalo?
Gon. Upon mine honor, sir, I heard a humming,
And that a strange one too, which did awake me.
I saw their weapons drawn. There was a noise; 320
That's verily. 'Tis best we stand upon our guard,
Or that we quit this place. Let's draw our weapons.
Alon. Lead off this ground, and let's make further search
For my poor son.
Gon. Heavens keep him from these beasts!
For he is sure i' the island.
Alon. Lead away. 325
Ariel. Prospero my lord shall know what I have done.
So, King, go safely on to seek thy son.
Exeunt.

311. **securing:** guarding
312. **Even:** just
321. **verily:** truth

Scene II. [*Another part of the island.*]

Enter CALIBAN *with a burden of wood. A noise of thunder heard.*

Cal. All the infections that the sun sucks up
From bogs, fens, flats, on Prosper fall and make him
By inchmeal a disease! His spirits hear me,
And yet I needs must curse. But they'll not pinch,
Fright me with urchin-shows, pitch me i' the mire,
Nor lead me, like a firebrand, in the dark 6
Out of my way, unless he bid 'em; but
For every trifle are they set upon me;
Sometime like apes that mow and chatter at me,
And after bite me; then like hedgehogs which 10
Lie tumbling in my barefoot way and mount
Their pricks at my footfall; sometime am I
All wound with adders, who with cloven tongues
Do hiss me into madness.

Enter TRINCULO.

Lo, now, lo!
Here comes a spirit of his, and to torment me 15
For bringing wood in slowly. I'll fall flat;
Perchance he will not mind me. [*Lies down.*].
Trin. Here's neither bush nor shrub to bear off any weather at all, and another storm brewing. I hear it sing i' the wind. Yond same black cloud, yond 20 huge one, looks like a foul bombard that would shed his liquor. If it should thunder as it did before, I know not where to hide my head. Yond same cloud cannot choose but fall by pailfuls. What have we here? a man or a fish? dead or alive? A fish: he 25 smells like a fish; a very ancient and fishlike smell; a kind of, not of the newest, Poor John. A strange fish! Were I in England now, as once I was, and had but this fish painted, not a holiday fool there but would give a piece of silver. There would this monster 30 make a man. Any strange beast there makes a man. When they will not give a doit to relieve a lame beggar, they will lay out ten to see a dead Indian. Legged like a man! and his fins like arms! Warm, o' my troth! I do now let loose my opinion, hold it 35 no longer: this is no fish, but an islander, that hath lately suffered by a thunderbolt. [*Thunder.*] Alas, the storm is come again! My best way is to creep

3. **By inchmeal:** inch by inch
5. **urchin-shows:** visitations by imps
6. **firebrand:** will-o'-the-wisp
9. **mow:** grimace
17. **mind:** notice
21. **bombard:** leather drinking-vessel
27. **Poor John:** dried salt fish
29. **painted:** advertised on a sign to attract the curious
31. **make . . . man:** make a man's fortune
32. **doit:** coin of little value

under his gaberdine. There is no other shelter hereabout. Misery acquaints a man with strange 40
bedfellows. I will here shroud till the dregs of the storm be past. [*Creeps under Caliban's garment.*]

Enter STEPHANO, *singing;* [*a bottle in his hand*].

Ste. I shall no more to sea, to sea;
Here shall I die ashore.

This is a very scurvy tune to sing at a man's 45
funeral. Well, here's my comfort. *Drinks.*

The master, the swabber, the boatswain, and I,
The gunner, and his mate,
Loved Mall, Meg, and Marian, and Margery,
But none of us cared for Kate. 50
For she had a tongue with a tang,
Would cry to a sailor "Go hang!"
She loved not the savor of tar nor of pitch;
Yet a tailor might scratch her where'er she did itch.
Then to sea, boys, and let her go hang! 55

This is a scurvy tune too; but here's my comfort. *Drinks.*

Cal. Do not torment me! O!

Ste. What's the matter? Have we devils here? Do you put tricks upon's with savages and men of Inde, ha? I have not 'scaped drowning to be afeard 60
now of your four legs; for it hath been said, "As proper a man as ever went on four legs cannot make him give ground"; and it shall be said so again, while Stephano breathes at nostrils.

Cal. The spirit torments me. O! 65

Ste. This is some monster of the isle, with four legs, who hath got, as I take it, an ague. Where the devil should he learn our language? I will give him some relief, if it be but for that. If I can recover him, and keep him tame, and get to Naples with 70
him, he's a present for any emperor that ever trod on neat's leather.

Cal. Do not torment me prithee! I'll bring my wood home faster.

Ste. He's in his fit now and does not talk 75
after the wisest. He shall taste of my bottle. If he have never drunk wine afore, it will go near to remove his fit. If I can recover him and keep him tame, I will not take too much for him; he shall pay for him that hath him, and that soundly. 80

Cal. Thou dost me yet but little hurt. Thou wilt anon; I know it by thy trembling. Now Prosper works upon thee.

Ste. Come on your ways. Open your mouth. Here is that which will give language to you, cat. 85
Open your mouth. This will shake your shaking, I can tell you, and that soundly. [*Gives Caliban drink.*] You cannot tell who's your friend. Open your chaps again.

Trin. I should know that voice. It should be 90
—but he is drowned; and these are devils. O, defend me!

Ste. Four legs and two voices—a most delicate monster! His forward voice now is to speak well of his friend; his backward voice is to utter foul 95
speeches and to detract. If all the wine in my bottle will recover him, I will help his ague. Come! [*Gives drink.*] Amen! I will pour some in thy other mouth.

Trin. Stephano! 100

Ste. Doth thy other mouth call me? Mercy, mercy! This is a devil, and no monster. I will leave him; I have no long spoon.

Trin. Stephano! If thou beest Stephano, touch me and speak to me; for I am Trinculo—be not 105
afeard—thy good friend Trinculo.

Ste. If thou beest Trinculo, come forth. I'll pull thee by the lesser legs. If any be Trinculo's legs, these are they. [*Pulls him out.*] Thou art very Trinculo indeed! How camest thou to be the 110
siege of this mooncalf? Can he vent Trinculos?

Trin. I took him to be killed with a thunderstroke. But art thou not drowned, Stephano? I hope now thou art not drowned. Is the storm overblown? I hid me under the dead mooncalf's gaberdine for 115
fear of the storm. And art thou living, Stephano? O Stephano, two Neapolitans 'scaped?

Ste. Prithee do not turn me about. My stomach is not constant.

Cal. [*Aside*] These be fine things, and if 120
they be not sprites. That's a brave god and bears celestial liquor. I will kneel to him.

Ste. How didst thou 'scape? How camest thou hither? Swear by this bottle how thou camest hither. I escaped upon a butt of sack which the sail- 125
ors heaved o'erboard, by this bottle, which I made of the bark of a tree with mine own hands since I was cast ashore.

Cal. I'll swear upon that bottle to be thy true subject, for the liquor is not earthly. 130

Ste. Here! Swear then how thou escapedst.

Trin. Swum ashore, man, like a duck. I can swim like a duck, I'll be sworn.

Ste. Here, kiss the book. [*Gives him drink.*]

39. gaberdine: cloak
45. scurvy: contemptible
61. your . . . legs: four-legged creatures
72. neat's: cow's
79. I . . . him: no price will be too high to ask for him
80. hath: i.e., buys

84–85. Here . . . cat: proverbial: "Good ale will make a cat speak."
89. chaps: jaws
102–3. devil . . . spoon: cf. the proverb, "He should have a long spoon that sups with the devil."
111. siege: excrement; **mooncalf:** freak
125. butt: barrel; **sack:** sherry

Though thou canst swim like a duck, thou art 135
made like a goose.

Trin. O Stephano, hast any more of this?

Ste. The whole butt, man. My cellar is in a rock by the seaside, where my wine is hid. How now, mooncalf? How does thine ague? 140

Cal. Hast thou not dropped from heaven?

Ste. Out o' the moon, I do assure thee. I was the Man i' the Moon when time was.

Cal. I have seen thee in her, and I do adore thee.
My mistress showed me thee, and thy dog, and thy bush. 145

Ste. Come, swear to that; kiss the book. I will furnish it anon with new contents. Swear.

[*Caliban drinks.*]

Trin. By this good light, this is a very shallow monster! I afeard of him? A very weak monster! The Man i' the Moon? A most poor credulous 150
monster! Well drawn, monster, in good sooth.

Cal. I'll show thee every fertile inch o' the island; and I will kiss thy foot. I prithee be my god.

Trin. By this light, a most perfidious and drunken monster! When's god's asleep he'll rob his bot- 155
tle.

Cal. I'll kiss thy foot. I'll swear myself thy subject.

Ste. Come on then. Down, and swear!

Trin. I shall laugh myself to death at this 160
puppy-headed monster. A most scurvy monster! I could find in my heart to beat him—

Ste. Come, kiss.

Trin. But that the poor monster's in drink. An abominable monster! 165

Cal. I'll show thee the best springs; I'll pluck thee berries;
I'll fish for thee, and get thee wood enough.
A plague upon the tyrant that I serve!
I'll bear him no more sticks, but follow thee,
Thou wondrous man. 170

Trin. A most ridiculous monster, to make a wonder of a poor drunkard!

Cal. I prithee let me bring thee where crabs grow;
And I with my long nails will dig thee pignuts,
Show thee a jay's nest, and instruct thee how 175
To snare the nimble marmoset; I'll bring thee
To clust'ring filberts, and sometimes I'll get thee
Young scamels from the rock. Wilt thou go with me?

Ste. I prithee now lead the way without any more talking. Trinculo, the King and all our com- 180
pany else being drowned, we will inherit here. Here, bear my bottle. Fellow Trinculo, we'll fill him by-and-by again. *Caliban sings drunkenly.*

Cal. Farewell, master; farewell, farewell!

Trin. A howling monster! a drunken monster! 185

Cal. No more dams I'll make for fish,
Nor fetch in firing
At requiring,
Nor scrape trenchering, nor wash dish.
'Ban, 'Ban, Ca—Caliban 190
Has a new master. Get a new man.

Freedom, highday! highday, freedom! freedom, highday, freedom!

Ste. O brave monster! lead the way.

Exeunt.

143. when . . . was: at one time
145. thy . . . bush: the Man in the Moon, according to an old story, was a human punished for gathering wood on Sunday by transportation to the moon. He took with him his bundle of faggots and dog.
148. shallow: stupid
151. Well drawn: a fine draught
173. crabs: crab apples
174. pignuts: edible tubers
178. scamels: not definitely identified; possibly a misprint for "seamels" (seamews)
189. scrape trenchering: trencher-scraping
192. highday: heyday

ACT III

Scene I. [*Before Prospero's cell.*]

Enter FERDINAND, *bearing a log.*

Fer. There be some sports are painful, and their labor
Delight in them sets off; some kinds of baseness
Are nobly undergone, and most poor matters
Point to rich ends. This my mean task
Would be as heavy to me as odious, but 5
The mistress which I serve quickens what's dead
And makes my labors pleasures. O, she is
Ten times more gentle than her father's crabbed;

And he's composed of harshness! I must remove
Some thousands of these logs and pile them up, 10
Upon a sore injunction. My sweet mistress
Weeps when she sees me work, and says such baseness
Had never like executor. I forget;
But these sweet thoughts do even refresh my labors.
Most busy least when I do it.

Enter MIRANDA; *and* PROSPERO [*behind, unseen*].

Mir. Alas, now pray you 15
Work not so hard! I would the lightning had
Burnt up those logs that you are enjoined to pile!
Pray set it down and rest you. When this burns,
'Twill weep for having wearied you. My father
Is hard at study; pray now rest yourself; 20
He's safe for these three hours.

Fer. O most dear mistress,
The sun will set before I shall discharge
What I must strive to do.

Mir. If you'll sit down,
I'll bear your logs the while. Pray give me that.
I'll carry it to the pile.

Fer. No, precious creature. 25
I had rather crack my sinews, break my back,
Than you should such dishonor undergo
While I sit lazy by.

Mir. It would become me
As well as it does you; and I should do it
With much more ease; for my good will is to it, 30
And yours it is against.

Pros. [*Aside*] Poor worm, thou art infected!
This visitation shows it.

Mir. You look wearily.

Fer. No, noble mistress. 'Tis fresh morning with me
When you are by at night. I do beseech you,
Chiefly that I might set it in my prayers, 35
What is your name?

Mir. Miranda. O my father,
I have broke your hest to say so!

Fer. Admired Miranda!
Indeed the top of admiration, worth
What's dearest to the world! Full many a lady
I have eyed with best regard, and many a time 40
The harmony of their tongues hath into bondage
Brought my too diligent ear; for several virtues
Have I liked several women; never any
With so full soul but some defect in her
Did quarrel with the noblest grace she owed, 45
And put it to the foil; but you, O you,
So perfect and so peerless, are created
Of every creature's best!

Mir. I do not know
One of my sex; no woman's face remember,
Save, from my glass, mine own; nor have I seen 50
More that I may call men than you, good friend,
And my dear father. How features are abroad
I am skill-less of; but, by my modesty
(The jewel in my dower), I would not wish
Any companion in the world but you; 55
Nor can imagination form a shape,
Besides yourself, to like of. But I prattle
Something too wildly, and my father's precepts
I therein do forget.

Fer. I am, in my condition,
A prince, Miranda; I do think, a king 60
(I would not so!), and would no more endure
This wooden slavery than to suffer
The flesh fly blow my mouth. Hear my soul speak!
The very instant that I saw you, did
My heart fly to your service, there resides, 65
To make me slave to it; and for your sake
Am I this patient log-man.

Mir. Do you love me?

Fer. O heaven, O earth, bear witness to this sound,
And crown what I profess with kind event
If I speak true! if hollowly, invert 70
What best is boded me to mischief! I,
Beyond all limit of what else i' the world,
Do love, prize, honor you.

Mir. I am a fool
To weep at what I am glad of.

Pros. [*Aside*] Fair encounter
Of two most rare affections! Heavens rain grace 75
On that which breeds between 'em!

Fer. Wherefore weep you?

Mir. At mine unworthiness, that dare not offer
What I desire to give, and much less take
What I shall die to want. But this is trifling;
And all the more it seeks to hide itself, 80
The bigger bulk it shows. Hence, bashful cunning!
And prompt me plain and holy innocence!
I am your wife, if you will marry me;
If not, I'll die your maid. To be your fellow
You may deny me; but I'll be your servant, 85
Whether you will or no.

Fer. My mistress, dearest!
And I thus humble ever.

Mir. My husband then?

11. Upon . . . injunction: for fear of grievous punishment
15. Most . . . it: i.e., when I think such sweet thoughts, I am unaware how hard I am working.
21. safe: not to be feared
37. Admired: admirable
40. best regard: closest attention
45. owed: owned
46. put . . . foil: foiled it; offset it
52. abroad: in the world at large
69. event: outcome
74. Fair encounter: even match
79. want: lack
81. cunning: cleverness
84. fellow: mate

Fer. Ay, with a heart as willing
As bondage e'er of freedom. Here's my hand.
Mir. And mine, with my heart in't; and now farewell 90
Till half an hour hence.
Fer. A thousand thousand!
Exeunt [Ferdinand and Miranda severally].
Pros. So glad of this as they I cannot be,
Who are surprised withal; but my rejoicing
At nothing can be more. I'll to my book;
For yet ere suppertime must I perform 95
Much business appertaining.
Exit.

Scene II. [*Another part of the island.*]

Enter CALIBAN, STEPHANO, *and* TRINCULO.

Ste. Tell not me! When the butt is out, we will drink water; not a drop before. Therefore bear up and board 'em! Servant monster, drink to me.
Trin. Servant monster? The folly of this island! They say there's but five upon this isle. We are 5 three of them. If the other two be brained like us, the state totters.
Ste. Drink, servant monster, when I bid thee. Thy eyes are almost set in thy head.
Trin. Where should they be set else? He 10 were a brave monster indeed if they were set in his tail.
Ste. My man-monster hath drowned his tongue in sack. For my part, the sea cannot drown me. I swam, ere I could recover the shore, five-and-thirty 15 leagues off and on, by this light. Thou shalt be my lieutenant, monster, or my standard.
Trin. Your lieutenant, if you list; he's no standard.
Ste. We'll not run, Monsieur Monster.
Trin. Nor go neither; but you'll lie like dogs, 20 and yet say nothing neither.
Ste. Mooncalf, speak once in thy life, if thou beest a good mooncalf.
Cal. How does thy honor? Let me lick thy shoe.
I'll not serve him; he is not valiant. 25
Trin. Thou liest, most ignorant monster! I am in case to justle a constable. Why, thou deboshed fish thou, was there ever man a coward that hath drunk so much sack as I today? Wilt thou tell a monstrous lie, being but half a fish and half a monster? 30

Cal. Lo, how he mocks me! Wilt thou let him, my lord?
Trin. "Lord" quoth he? That a monster should be such a natural!
Cal. Lo, lo, again! Bite him to death I prithee.
Ste. Trinculo, keep a good tongue in your 35 head. If you prove a mutineer—the next tree! The poor monster's my subject, and he shall not suffer indignity.
Cal. I thank my noble lord. Wilt thou be pleased
To hearken once again to the suit I made to thee? 40
Ste. Marry, will I. Kneel and repeat it; I will stand, and so shall Trinculo.

Enter ARIEL, *invisible.*

Cal. As I told thee before, I am subject to a tyrant,
A sorcerer, that by his cunning hath
Cheated me of the island. 45
Ariel. Thou liest.
Cal. Thou liest, thou jesting monkey thou!
I would my valiant master would destroy thee.
I do not lie.
Ste. Trinculo, if you trouble him any more in's tale, by this hand, I will supplant some of your 50 teeth.
Trin. Why, I said nothing.
Ste. Mum then, and no more.—Proceed.
Cal. I say by sorcery he got this isle;
From me he got it. If thy greatness will 55
Revenge it on him—for I know thou darest,
But this thing dare not—
Ste. That's most certain.
Cal. Thou shalt be lord of it, and I'll serve thee.
Ste. How now shall this be compassed? 60
Canst thou bring me to the party?
Cal. Yea, yea, my lord! I'll yield him thee asleep,
Where thou mayst knock a nail into his head.
Ariel. Thou liest; thou canst not.
Cal. What a pied ninny's this! Thou scurvy patch!
I do beseech thy greatness give him blows 66
And take his bottle from him. When that's gone,
He shall drink naught but brine, for I'll not show him
Where the quick freshes are.
Ste. Trinculo, run into no further danger. 70
Interrupt the monster one word further and, by this hand, I'll turn my mercy out o' doors and make a stockfish of thee.

2–3. bear . . . 'em: act like a man; drink up
9. set: closed
11. brave: fine
17. standard: standard-bearer
18. list: please; **no standard:** (1) unable to stand upright; (2) abnormal
26–27. in . . . constable: i.e., pot-valiant
27. deboshed: debauched

33. natural: idiot, with a pun on the usual meaning
41. Marry: indeed ("by the Virgin Mary")
60. compassed: achieved
65. pied ninny: parti-colored fool; **patch:** another name for a jester
69. quick freshes: fresh-water springs
73. stockfish: dried salt fish, usually beaten to soften it for cooking

Trin. Why, what did I? I did nothing. I'll go farther off. 75

Ste. Didst thou not say he lied?

Ariel. Thou liest.

Ste. Do I so? Take thou that! [*Strikes Trinculo.*]
As you like this, give me the lie another time.

Trin. I did not give thee the lie. Out o' your 80
wits, and hearing too? A pox o' your bottle! This can sack and drinking do. A murrain on your monster, and the devil take your fingers!

Cal. Ha, ha, ha!

Ste. Now forward with your tale.—Prithee 85
stand further off.

Cal. Beat him enough. After a little time
I'll beat him too.

Ste. Stand farther.—Come, proceed.

Cal. Why, as I told thee, 'tis a custom with him
I' the afternoon to sleep. There thou mayst brain
him, 90
Having first seized his books, or with a log
Batter his skull, or paunch him with a stake,
Or cut his weasand with thy knife. Remember
First to possess his books; for without them
He's but a sot, as I am, nor hath not 95
One spirit to command. They all do hate him
As rootedly as I. Burn but his books.
He has brave utensils (for so he calls them)
Which, when he has a house, he'll deck withal.
And that most deeply to consider is 100
The beauty of his daughter. He himself
Calls her a nonpareil. I never saw a woman
But only Sycorax my dam and she;
But she as far surpasseth Sycorax
As great'st does least.

Ste. Is it so brave a lass? 105

Cal. Ay, lord. She will become thy bed, I warrant,
And bring thee forth brave brood.

Ste. Monster, I will kill this man. His daughter and I will be king and queen, save our Graces! and Trinculo and thyself shall be viceroys. Dost 110
thou like the plot, Trinculo?

Trin. Excellent.

Ste. Give me thy hand. I am sorry I beat thee; but while thou livest, keep a good tongue in thy head.

Cal. Within this half hour will he be asleep. 115
Wilt thou destroy him then?

Ste. Ay, on mine honor.

Ariel. This will I tell my master.

Cal. Thou makest me merry; I am full of pleasure.
Let us be jocund. Will you troll the catch
You taught me but whilere? 120

Ste. At thy request, monster, I will do reason, any reason. Come on, Trinculo, let us sing. *Sings.*

Flout 'em and scout 'em
And scout 'em and flout 'em!
Thought is free. 125

Cal. That's not the tune.

Ariel plays the tune on a tabor and pipe.

Ste. What is this same?

Trin. This is the tune of our catch, played by the picture of Nobody.

Ste. If thou beest a man, show thyself in 130
thy likeness. If thou beest a devil, take 't as thou list.

Trin. O, forgive me my sins!

Ste. He that dies pays all debts. I defy thee.
Mercy upon us!

Cal. Art thou afeard? 135

Ste. No, monster, not I.

Cal. Be not afeard. The isle is full of noises,
Sounds, and sweet airs that give delight and hurt not.
Sometimes a thousand twangling instruments 139
Will hum about mine ears; and sometime voices
That, if I then had waked after long sleep,
Will make me sleep again; and then, in dreaming,
The clouds methought would open and show riches
Ready to drop upon me, that, when I waked,
I cried to dream again. 145

Ste. This will prove a brave kingdom to me, where I shall have my music for nothing.

Cal. When Prospero is destroyed.

Ste. That shall be by-and-by. I remember the story.

Trin. The sound is going away. Let's follow 150
it, and after do our work.

Ste. Lead, monster; we'll follow. I would I could see this taborer! He lays it on.

Trin. Wilt come? I'll follow Stephano.

Exeunt.

Scene III. [*Another part of the island.*]

Enter Alonso, Sebastian, Antonio, Gonzalo, Adrian, Francisco, *etc.*

Gon. By'r Lakin, I can go no further, sir!
My old bones ache. Here's a maze trod indeed
Through forthrights and meanders. By your patience,
I needs must rest me.

82. murrain: plague
92. paunch: stab
93. weasand: windpipe
95. sot: blockhead
98. brave utensils: splendid furnishings
119. troll . . . catch: sing the round
120. whilere: a while ago

121. reason: anything reasonable
123. Flout: mock; **scout:** deride
125. Thought . . . free: proverbial
S.D. 126. tabor: small drum; **pipe:** fife
129. Nobody: a man with only head and limbs, depicted on the title page of a play *Nobody and Somebody* (1606), probably originally an inn sign
1. By'r Lakin: by our little lady (the Virgin)
3. forthrights: straight ways

Alon. Old lord, I cannot blame thee,
Who am myself attached with weariness 5
To the dulling of my spirits. Sit down and rest.
Even here I will put off my hope, and keep it
No longer for my flatterer. He is drowned
Whom thus we stray to find; and the sea mocks
Our frustrate search on land. Well, let him go. 10

Ant. [*Aside to Sebastian*] I am right glad that he's so out of hope.
Do not for one repulse forego the purpose
That you resolved t' effect.

Seb. [*Aside to Antonio*] The next advantage
Will we take throughly. 15

Ant. [*Aside to Sebastian*] Let it be tonight;
For, now they are oppressed with travel, they
Will not nor cannot use such vigilance
As when they are fresh.

Seb. [*Aside to Antonio*] I say tonight. No more.

Solemn and strange music; and PROSPERO *on the top (invisible).*

Alon. What harmony is this? My good friends, hark! 21

Gon. Marvelous sweet music!

Enter several strange SHAPES, *bringing in a banquet; and dance about it with gentle actions of salutations; and, inviting the King, etc., to eat, they depart.*

Alon. Give us kind keepers, heavens! What were these?

Seb. A living drollery. Now I will believe
That there are unicorns; that in Arabia 25
There is one tree, the phoenix' throne, one phoenix
At this hour reigning there.

Ant. I'll believe both;
And what does else want credit, come to me,
And I'll be sworn 'tis true. Travelers ne'er did lie,
Though fools at home condemn 'em.

Gon. If in Naples 30
I should report this now, would they believe me?
If I should say, I saw such islanders
(For certes these are people of the island),
Who, though they are of monstrous shape, yet, note,
Their manners are more gentle, kind, than of 35
Our human generation you shall find
Many—nay, almost any.

Pros. [*Aside*] Honest lord,
Thou hast said well; for some of you there present
Are worse than devils.

Alon. I cannot too much muse
Such shapes, such gesture, and such sound, expressing 40
(Although they want the use of tongue) a kind
Of excellent dumb discourse.

Pros. [*Aside*] Praise in departing.

Fran. They vanished strangely.

Seb. No matter, since
They have left their viands behind; for we have stomachs.
Will't please you taste of what is here?

Alon. Not I. 45

Gon. Faith, sir, you need not fear. When we were boys,
Who would believe that there were mountaineers
Dewlapped like bulls, whose throats had hanging at 'em
Wallets of flesh? or that there were such men
Whose heads stood in their breasts? which now we find 50
Each putter-out of five for one will bring us
Good warrant of.

Alon. I will stand to, and feed;
Although my last, no matter, since I feel
The best is past. Brother, my lord the Duke,
Stand to, and do as we. 55

Thunder and lightning. Enter ARIEL, *like a harpy; claps his wings upon the table; and with a quaint device the banquet vanishes.*

Ariel. You are three men of sin, whom destiny—
That hath to instrument this lower world
And what is in't—the never-surfeited sea
Hath caused to belch up you, and on this island,
Where man doth not inhabit—you 'mongst men 60
Being most unfit to live. I have made you mad;
And even with suchlike valor men hang and drown
Their proper selves.

[*Alonso, Sebastian, etc., draw their swords.*]

5. attached: seized
10. frustrate: frustrated
15. throughly: thoroughly
17. oppressed: overpowered
S.D. 20. invisible: wearing a cloak to represent invisibility
23. Give . . . heavens: heaven protect us
24. drollery: puppet show
26. one phoenix: the legendary phoenix inhabited Arabia. One specimen existed at a time; when it grew old, it burned itself, and a new specimen rose from the ashes.
28. what . . . else: whatever else; **want credit:** lack belief
39. muse: wonder at
40. gesture: behavior
42. Praise . . . departing: proverbial, a caution against premature praise
47–49. mountaineers . . . flesh: probably men of Switzerland, where goiter is common; monkey-men with **wallets of flesh** at the neck were also described by travelers
49–50. men . . . breasts: also referred to by Othello; see that play I.iii.145–46
51. putter-out . . . one: insurance underwriter who undertook to pay travelers five to one if they proved they had completed stipulated journeys. Such a man would have heard many tales of wonder.
52. stand to: fall to
S.D. 55. quaint: clever
57. hath . . . instrument: manipulates
63. proper: emphatic: own

You fools! I and my fellows
Are ministers of Fate. The elements, 64
Of whom your swords are tempered, may as well
Wound the loud winds, or with bemocked-at stabs
Kill the still-closing waters, as diminish
One dowle that's in my plume. My fellow ministers
Are like invulnerable. If you could hurt, 69
Your swords are now too massy for your strengths
And will not be uplifted. But remember
(For that's my business to you) that you three
From Milan did supplant good Prospero;
Exposed unto the sea, which hath requit it, 74
Him and his innocent child; for which foul deed
The powers, delaying (not forgetting), have
Incensed the seas and shores, yea, all the creatures,
Against your peace. Thee of thy son, Alonso,
They have bereft; and do pronounce by me
Ling'ring perdition (worse than any death 80
Can be at once) shall step by step attend
You and your ways; whose wraths to guard you from,
Which here, in this most desolate isle, else falls
Upon your heads, is nothing but heart's sorrow
And a clear life ensuing. 85

He vanishes in thunder; then, to soft music, enter the SHAPES *again, and dance, with mocks and mows, and carrying out the table.*

Pros. [*Aside*] Bravely the figure of this harpy hast thou
Performed, my Ariel; a grace it had, devouring.
Of my instruction hast thou nothing bated
In what thou hadst to say. So, with good life
And observation strange, my meaner ministers 90
Their several kinds have done. My high charms work,
And these, mine enemies, are all knit up
In their distractions. They now are in my pow'r;
And in these fits I leave them, while I visit 94
Young Ferdinand, whom they suppose is drowned,
And his and mine loved darling. [*Exit above.*]

Gon. I' the name of something holy, sir, why stand you
In this strange stare?

Alon. O, it is monstrous, monstrous!
Methought the billows spoke and told me of it;
The winds did sing it to me; and the thunder, 100
That deep and dreadful organ pipe, pronounced
The name of Prosper. It did bass my trespass.
Therefore my son i' the ooze is bedded; and
I'll seek him deeper than e'er plummet sounded
And with him there lie mudded. *Exit.*

Seb. But one fiend at a time,
I'll fight their legions o'er!

Ant. I'll be thy second. 106
Exeunt [*Sebastian and Antonio*].

Gon. All three of them are desperate. Their great guilt,
Like poison given to work a great time after,
Now 'gins to bite the spirits. I do beseech you,
That are of suppler joints, follow them swiftly 110
And hinder them from what this ecstasy
May now provoke them to.

Adr. Follow, I pray you.
Exeunt omnes.

66. **bemocked-at:** ineffectual
67. **still-closing:** ever-closing
68. **dowle:** small feather
70. **massy:** heavy
74. **requit it:** repaid it (your deed)
80. **perdition:** destruction
85. **clear:** pure; blameless
86. **Bravely:** excellently
88. **bated:** omitted
89. **good life:** lifelike realism
90. **observation strange:** extraordinary care; **meaner ministers:** lesser spirits
91. **kinds:** offices
98. **monstrous:** extremely unnatural
102. **bass . . . trespass:** voice my sin in deep tones
106. **their . . . o'er:** all their legions. See Mark 5:9.
111. **ecstasy:** madness

ACT IV

Scene I. [*Before Prospero's cell.*]

Enter PROSPERO, FERDINAND, *and* MIRANDA.

Pros. If I have too austerely punished you,
Your compensation makes amends; for I
Have given you here a third of mine own life,
Or that for which I live; who once again
I tender to thy hand. All thy vexations 5
Were but my trials of thy love, and thou
Hast strangely stood the test. Here, afore heaven,

5. **tender:** offer
7. **strangely:** remarkably

I ratify this my rich gift. O Ferdinand,
Do not smile at me that I boast her off,
For thou shalt find she will outstrip all praise 10
And make it halt behind her.
Fer. I do believe it
Against an oracle.
Pros. Then, as my gift, and thine own acquisition
Worthily purchased, take my daughter. But
If thou dost break her virgin-knot before 15
All sanctimonious ceremonies may
With full and holy rite be minist'red,
No sweet aspersion shall the heavens let fall
To make this contract grow; but barren hate,
Sour-eyed disdain, and discord shall bestrew 20
The union of your bed with weeds so loathly
That you shall hate it both. Therefore take heed,
As Hymen's lamp shall light you!
Fer. As I hope
For quiet days, fair issue, and long life,
With such love as 'tis now, the murkiest den, 25
The most opportune place, the strong'st suggestion
Our worser genius can, shall never melt
Mine honor into lust, to take away
The edge of that day's celebration
When I shall think or Phœbus' steeds are foundered
Or Night kept chained below.
Pros. Fairly spoke. 31
Sit then and talk with her; she is thine own.
What, Ariel! my industrious servant, Ariel!

Enter ARIEL.

Ariel. What would my potent master? Here I am.
Pros. Thou and thy meaner fellows your last service 35
Did worthily perform; and I must use you
In such another trick. Go bring the rabble,
O'er whom I give thee pow'r, here to this place.
Incite them to quick motion; for I must
Bestow upon the eyes of this young couple 40
Some vanity of mine art. It is my promise,
And they expect it from me.
Ariel. Presently?
Pros. Ay, with a twink.
Ariel. Before you can say "Come" and "go,"
And breathe twice and cry, "So, so," 45
Each one, tripping on his toe,
Will be here with mop and mow.
Do you love me master? No?
Pros. Dearly, my delicate Ariel. Do not approach
Till thou dost hear me call.
Ariel. Well! I conceive. 50
Exit.
Pros. Look thou be true. Do not give dalliance
Too much the rein. The strongest oaths are straw
To the fire i' the blood. Be more abstemious,
Or else good night your vow!
Fer. I warrant you, sir.
The white cold virgin snow upon my heart 55
Abates the ardor of my liver.
Pros. Well.
Now come, my Ariel! Bring a corollary
Rather than want a spirit. Appear, and pertly!
No tongue! All eyes! Be silent. *Soft music.*

Enter IRIS.

Iris. Ceres, most bounteous lady, thy rich leas 60
Of wheat, rye, barley, fetches, oats, and pease;
Thy turfy mountains, where live nibbling sheep,
And flat meads thatched with stover, them to keep;
Thy banks with pioned and twilled brims,
Which spongy April at thy hest betrims 65
To make cold nymphs chaste crowns; and thy broom groves,
Whose shadow the dismissed bachelor loves,
Being lasslorn; thy pole-clipt vineyard;
And thy sea-marge, sterile and rocky-hard,
Where thou thyself dost air—the queen o' the sky,
Whose wat'ry arch and messenger am I, 71
Bids thee leave these, and with her sovereign Grace,
Juno descends.
Here on this grass-plot, in this very place,
To come and sport. Her peacocks fly amain;
Approach, rich Ceres, her to entertain. 75

Enter CERES.

Ceres. Hail, many-colored messenger, that ne'er
Dost disobey the wife of Jupiter,

9. **boast . . . off:** boast of her
12. **Against . . . oracle:** though an oracle should deny it
14. **purchased:** acquired
16. **sanctimonious:** holy
18. **aspersion:** besprinkling (holy water/rain)
23. **Hymen's lamp:** Hymen, god of marriage, conferred happy married life with his bright torches.
26. **suggestion:** temptation
27. **worser . . . can:** worser nature is capable of
30. **or:** either; **foundered:** lamed
41. **vanity:** trifling show; **art:** magic
42. **Presently:** at once
43. **with . . . twink:** in a twinkling
47. **mop . . . mow:** grimaces
50. **conceive:** understand
51. **true:** faithful
56. **liver:** the organ believed to be the seat of passion
57. **corollary:** surplus
58. **pertly:** quickly
S.D. 59. **Iris:** personification of the rainbow and messenger of the gods
61. **fetches:** vetches; hay
63. **thatched:** covered; **stover:** crops for cattle feed
64. **pioned . . . twilled:** perhaps, "furrowed"
65. **betrims:** i.e., with flowers
66–67. **broom . . . loves:** cf. the "Willow Song" from *Othello:* "The poor soul sat sighing by a sycamore tree."
68. **pole-clipt:** i.e., in which the vines twine on poles
70. **queen . . . sky:** Juno
74. **peacocks:** fowl sacred to Juno; **amain:** apace
75. **entertain:** welcome

Who, with thy saffron wings, upon my flow'rs
Diffusest honey drops, refreshing show'rs,
And with each end of thy blue bow dost crown 80
My bosky acres and my unshrubbed down,
Rich scarf to my proud earth—why hath thy queen
Summoned me hither to this short-grassed green?

Iris. A contract of true love to celebrate
And some donation freely to estate 85
On the blest lovers.

Ceres. Tell me, heavenly bow,
If Venus or her son, as thou dost know,
Do now attend the queen. Since they did plot
The means that dusky Dis my daughter got,
Her and her blind boy's scandaled company 90
I have forsworn.

Iris. Of her society
Be not afraid. I met her Deity
Cutting the clouds towards Paphos, and her son
Dove-drawn with her. Here thought they to have done
Some wanton charm upon this man and maid, 95
Whose vows are, that no bed-right shall be paid
Till Hymen's torch be lighted; but in vain.
Mars's hot minion is returned again;
Her waspish-headed son has broke his arrows, 99
Swears he will shoot no more, but play with sparrows
And be a boy right out.

[*Enter* JUNO.]

Ceres. Highest queen of state,
Great Juno, comes; I know her by her gait.

Juno. How does my bounteous sister? Go with me
To bless this twain, that they may prosperous be
And honored in their issue. 105

They sing.

Juno. Honor, riches, marriage blessing,
Long continuance, and increasing,
Hourly joys be still upon you!
Juno sings her blessings on you.

Ceres. Earth's increase, foison plenty, 110
Barns and garners never empty,
Vines with clust'ring bunches growing,
Plants with goodly burden bowing;
Spring come to you at the farthest
In the very end of harvest! 115
Scarcity and want shall shun you,
Ceres' blessing so is on you.

Fer. This is a most majestic vision, and
Harmonious charmingly. May I be bold
To think these spirits?

Pros. Spirits, which by mine art
I have from their confines called to enact 121
My present fancies.

Fer. Let me live here ever!
So rare a wond'red father and a wise
Makes this place Paradise.

Juno and Ceres whisper, and send Iris on employment.

Pros. Sweet now, silence!
Juno and Ceres whisper seriously. 125
There's something else to do. Hush and be mute,
Or else our spell is marred.

Iris. You nymphs, called Naiads, of the wind'ring brooks,
With your sedged crowns and ever-harmless looks,
Leave your crisp channels, and on this green land
Answer your summons. Juno does command. 131
Come, temperate nymphs, and help to celebrate
A contract of true love. Be not too late.

Enter certain NYMPHS.

You sunburned sicklemen, of August weary,
Come hither from the furrow and be merry. 135
Make holiday. Your rye-straw hats put on,
And these fresh nymphs encounter every one
In country footing.

Enter certain REAPERS, *properly habited. They join with the* NYMPHS *in a graceful dance; towards the end whereof Prospero starts suddenly and speaks; after which, to a strange, hollow, and confused noise, they heavily vanish.*

Pros. [*Aside*] I had forgot that foul conspiracy
Of the beast Caliban and his confederates 140
Against my life. The minute of their plot
Is almost come.—[*To the Spirits*] Well done! Avoid! No more!

Fer. This is strange. Your father's in some passion
That works him strongly.

Mir. Never till this day
Saw I him touched with anger so distempered. 145

81. bosky: wooded
85. estate: bestow
89. Dis: Pluto, king of the underworld, who abducted Ceres' daughter, Proserpine
90. scandaled: scandalous
92. Deity: Divine Majesty
93. Paphos: a town in Cyprus where Venus landed after her birth from the foam of the sea, thereafter a center of her worship
94. Dove-drawn: doves drew Venus' chariot
98. minion: mistress, referring to Venus, who once had a love affair with Mars
99. waspish-headed: ill-tempered
101. right out: completely; renounce his godhead
114–15. Spring . . . harvest: i.e., with no barren winter intervening
123. So . . . father: a father so rarely wonderful
128. wind'ring: meandering
130. crisp: curly; rippling
S.D. 138. heavily: slowly and sadly
142. Avoid: avaunt; be off!

Pros. You do look, my son, in a moved sort,
As if you were dismayed. Be cheerful, sir.
Our revels now are ended. These our actors,
As I foretold you, were all spirits and
Are melted into air, into thin air; 150
And, like the baseless fabric of this vision,
The cloud-capped towers, the gorgeous palaces,
The solemn temples, the great globe itself,
Yea, all which it inherit, shall dissolve,
And, like this insubstantial pageant faded, 155
Leave not a rack behind. We are such stuff
As dreams are made on, and our little life
Is rounded with a sleep. Sir, I am vexed.
Bear with my weakness. My old brain is troubled.
Be not disturbed with my infirmity. 160
If you be pleased, retire into my cell
And there repose. A turn or two I'll walk
To still my beating mind.

Fer., *Mir.* We wish your peace. *Exeunt.*

Enter Ariel.

Pros. Come with a thought! I thank thee, Ariel. Come. 165

Ariel. Thy thoughts I cleave to. What's thy pleasure?

Pros. Spirit, we must prepare to meet with Caliban.

Ariel. Ay, my commander. When I presented Ceres,
I thought to have told thee of it, but I feared
Lest I might anger thee. 170

Pros. Say again, where didst thou leave these varlets?

Ariel. I told you, sir, they were redhot with drinking;
So full of valor that they smote the air
For breathing in their faces, beat the ground
For kissing of their feet; yet always bending 175
Towards their project. Then I beat my tabor;
At which like unbacked colts they pricked their ears,
Advanced their eyelids, lifted up their noses
As they smelt music. So I charmed their ears 179
That calf-like they my lowing followed through
Toothed briers, sharp furzes, pricking goss, and thorns,
Which ent'red their frail shins. At last I left them
I' the filthy mantled pool beyond your cell,
There dancing up to the chins, that the foul lake
O'erstunk their feet.

Pros. This was well done, my bird.
Thy shape invisible retain thou still. 186
The trumpery in my house, go bring it hither
For stale to catch these thieves.

Ariel. I go, I go. *Exit.*

Pros. A devil, a born devil, on whose nature
Nurture can never stick! on whom my pains, 190
Humanely taken, all, all lost, quite lost!
And as with age his body uglier grows,
So his mind cankers. I will plague them all,
Even to roaring.

Enter Ariel, *loaden with glistening apparel, etc.*

Come, hang them on this line.
[*Prospero and Ariel remain, invisible.*]

Enter Caliban, Stephano, *and* Trinculo, *all wet.*

Cal. Pray you tread softly, that the blind mole may not 195
Hear a foot fall. We now are near his cell.

Ste. Monster, your fairy, which you say is a harmless fairy, has done little better than played the Jack with us.

Trin. Monster, I do smell all horse-piss, at 200
which my nose is in great indignation.

Ste. So is mine. Do you hear, monster? If I should take a displeasure against you, look you—

Trin. Thou wert but a lost monster.

Cal. Good my lord, give me thy favor still. 205
Be patient, for the prize I'll bring thee to
Shall hoodwink this mischance. Therefore speak softly.
All's hushed as midnight yet.

Trin. Ay, but to lose our bottles in the pool—

Ste. There is not only disgrace and dis- 210
honor in that, monster, but an infinite loss.

Trin. That's more to me than my wetting. Yet this is your harmless fairy, monster.

Ste. I will fetch off my bottle, though I be o'er ears for my labor. 215

Cal. Prithee, my king, be quiet. Seest thou here?
This is the mouth o' the cell. No noise, and enter.
Do that good mischief which may make this island
Thine own forever, and I, thy Caliban,
For aye thy foot-licker. 220

151. **baseless:** insubstantial
154. **all . . . inherit:** all that possess it; all earthly creatures
155. **pageant:** spectacle
156. **rack:** wisp of cloud
157. **on:** of
171. **varlets:** rogues
175. **bending:** aiming themselves
178. **Advanced:** raised
181. **furzes:** spiny plants similar to **goss** (gorse)
183. **mantled:** covered with scum
187. **trumpery:** trash
188. **stale:** bait
190. **Nurture:** moral training or discipline
193. **cankers:** festers with malice
194. **line:** linden tree
198. **Jack:** knave
207. **hoodwink:** cover from sight; blot out
214. **fetch off:** rescue
218. **good:** beneficial

Ste. Give me thy hand. I do begin to have bloody thoughts.

Trin. O King Stephano! O peer! O worthy Stephano, look what a wardrobe here is for thee!

Cal. Let it alone, thou fool! It is but trash.

Trin. O ho, monster! we know what belongs 225
to a frippery. O King Stephano!

Ste. Put off that gown, Trinculo. By this hand, I'll have that gown!

Trin. Thy Grace shall have it.

Cal. The dropsy drown this fool! What do you mean 230
To dote thus on such luggage? Let't alone,
And do the murder first. If he awake,
From toe to crown he'll fill our skins with pinches,
Make us strange stuff.

Ste. Be you quiet, monster. Mistress line, is 235
not this my jerkin? [*Takes it down.*] Now is the jerkin under the line. Now, jerkin, you are like to lose your hair and prove a bald jerkin.

Trin. Do, do! We steal by line and level, an't like your Grace. 240

Ste. I thank thee for that jest. Here's a garment for't. Wit shall not go unrewarded while I am king of this country. "Steal by line and level" is an excellent pass of pate. There's another garment for't.

Trin. Monster, come put some lime upon 245
your fingers, and away with the rest!

Cal. I will have none on't. We shall lose our time
And all be turned to barnacles, or to apes
With foreheads villainous low.

Ste. Monster, lay-to your fingers. Help to 250
bear this away where my hogshead of wine is, or I'll turn you out of my kingdom. Go to, carry this.

Trin. And this.

Ste. Ay, and this.

A noise of hunters heard. Enter divers SPIRITS *in shape of dogs and hounds, hunting them about,* PROSPERO *and* ARIEL *setting them on.*

Pros. Hey, Mountain, hey! 255

Ariel. Silver! there it goes, Silver!

Pros. Fury, Fury! There, Tyrant, there! Hark, hark!

[*Caliban, Stephano, and Trinculo are driven out.*]

Go, charge my goblins that they grind their joints
With dry convulsions, shorten up their sinews
With aged cramps, and more pinch-spotted make them 260
Than pard or cat o' mountain.

Ariel. Hark, they roar.

Pros. Let them be hunted soundly. At this hour
Lie at my mercy all mine enemies.
Shortly shall all my labors end, and thou
Shalt have the air at freedom. For a little 265
Follow, and do me service.

Exeunt.

222. King Stephano: a reference to the song "King Stephen was and a worthy peer"; the last line reads "Then take thy old cloak about thee." Cf. *Othello* II.iii.90–97.
226. frippery: old-clothes shop
231. luggage: rubbish
236. jerkin: jacket
237. line: equator; possibly a reference to the loss of hair from fever, which afflicted many sailors who made the long voyage across the equator
239. by . . . level: methodically
244. pass . . . pate: thrust of wit
245. lime: birdlime, a gluey substance used to catch birds
248. barnacles: barnacle geese, supposed to have been hatched from barnacles
249. villainous: wretchedly
261. pard: leopard

ACT V

Scene I. [*Before the cell of Prospero.*]

Enter PROSPERO *in his magic robes, and* ARIEL.

Pros. Now does my project gather to a head.
My charms crack not, my spirits obey, and Time
Goes upright with his carriage. How's the day?

Ariel. On the sixth hour, at which time, my lord,
You said our work should cease.

Pros. I did say so 5
When first I raised the tempest. Say, my spirit,
How fares the King and 's followers?

Ariel. Confined together

2–3. Time . . . carriage: Time does not bend under his burden; all is going on schedule.

In the same fashion as you gave in charge,
Just as you left them—all prisoners, sir,
In the line grove which weather-fends your cell. 10
They cannot budge till your release. The King,
His brother, and yours abide all three distracted,
And the remainder mourning over them,
Brimful of sorrow and dismay; but chiefly 14
Him that you termed, sir, the good old Lord Gonzalo.
His tears run down his beard like winter's drops
From eaves of reeds. Your charm so strongly works 'em,
That if you now beheld them, your affections
Would become tender.

Pros. Dost thou think so, spirit?

Ariel. Mine would, sir, were I human.

Pros. And mine shall. 20
Hast thou, which art but air, a touch, a feeling
Of their afflictions, and shall not myself,
One of their kind, that relish all as sharply
Passion as they, be kindlier moved than thou art?
Though with their high wrongs I am struck to the quick, 25
Yet with my nobler reason 'gainst my fury
Do I take part. The rarer action is
In virtue than in vengeance. They being penitent,
The sole drift of my purpose doth extend
Not a frown further. Go, release them, Ariel. 30
My charms I'll break, their senses I'll restore,
And they shall be themselves.

Ariel. I'll fetch them, sir. *Exit.*

Pros. [*Makes a magic circle with his staff*] Ye elves of hills, brooks, standing lakes, and groves,
And ye that on the sands with printless foot
Do chase the ebbing Neptune, and do fly him 35
When he comes back; you demipuppets that
By moonshine do the green sour ringlets make,
Whereof the ewe not bites; and you, whose pastime
Is to make midnight mushrumps, that rejoice
To hear the solemn curfew; by whose aid 40
(Weak masters though ye be) I have bedimmed
The noontide sun, called forth the mutinous winds,
And 'twixt the green sea and the azured vault
Set roaring war; to the dread rattling thunder
Have I given fire and rifted Jove's stout oak 45
With his own bolt; the strong-based promontory
Have I made shake and by the spurs plucked up
The pine and cedar; graves at my command
Have waked their sleepers, oped, and let 'em forth
By my so potent art. But this rough magic 50
I here abjure; and when I have required
Some heavenly music (which even now I do)
To work mine end upon their senses that
This airy charm is for, I'll break my staff,
Bury it certain fathoms in the earth, 55
And deeper than did ever plummet sound
I'll drown my book. *Solemn music.*

Here enters Ariel *before; then* Alonso, *with a frantic gesture, attended by* Gonzalo; Sebastian *and* Antonio *in like manner, attended by* Adrian *and* Francisco. *They all enter the circle which Prospero had made, and there stand charmed; which Prospero observing, speaks.*

A solemn air, and the best comforter
To an unsettled fancy, cure thy brains,
Now useless, boiled within thy skull! There stand,
For you are spell-stopped. 61
Holy Gonzalo, honorable man,
Mine eyes, ev'n sociable to the show of thine,
Fall fellowly drops. The charm dissolves apace;
And as the morning steals upon the night, 65
Melting the darkness, so their rising senses
Begin to chase the ignorant fumes that mantle
Their clearer reason. O good Gonzalo,
My true preserver, and a loyal sir
To him thou followst! I will pay thy graces 70
Home both in word and deed. Most cruelly
Didst thou, Alonso, use me and my daughter.
Thy brother was a furtherer in the act.
Thou art pinched for't now, Sebastian. Flesh and blood,
You, brother mine, that entertained ambition, 75
Expelled remorse and nature; who, with Sebastian
(Whose inward pinches therefore are most strong),
Would here have killed your king, I do forgive thee,
Unnatural though thou art. Their understanding
Begins to swell, and the approaching tide 80
Will shortly fill the reasonable shore,
That now lies foul and muddy. Not one of them
That yet looks on me or would know me. Ariel,
Fetch me the hat and rapier in my cell.
I will discase me, and myself present 85
As I was sometime Milan. Quickly, spirit!
Thou shalt ere long be free.

[*Exit* Ariel *and returns immediately.*]

10. weather-fends: protects from the weather
12. abide: remain
18. affections: feelings
23. relish: feel
24. Passion: strong emotion; grief
36. demipuppets: fairies
37. ringlets: fairy rings
39. mushrumps: mushrooms
47. spurs: roots
S.D. 57. gesture: manner
63. ev'n sociable: exactly sympathetic
64. fellowly: companionable
67. ignorant fumes: fumes of ignorance
69. sir: gentleman
70. graces: favors
71. Home: thoroughly
76. remorse: pity
85. discase me: discard my magician's robe
86. sometime Milan: the former Duke of Milan

Ariel sings and helps to attire him.

Where the bee sucks, there suck I;
In a cowslip's bell I lie;
There I couch when owls do cry. 90
On the bat's back I do fly
After summer merrily.
Merrily, merrily shall I live now
Under the blossom that hangs on the bough.

Pros. Why, that's my dainty Ariel! I shall miss thee, 95
But yet thou shalt have freedom. So, so, so.
To the King's ship, invisible as thou art!
There shalt thou find the mariners asleep
Under the hatches. The master and the boatswain
Being awake, enforce them to this place, 100
And presently, I prithee.
Ariel. I drink the air before me, and return
Or ere your pulse twice beat. *Exit.*
Gon. All torment, trouble, wonder, and amazement
Inhabits here. Some heavenly power guide us 105
Out of this fearful country!
Pros. Behold, sir King,
The wronged Duke of Milan, Prospero.
For more assurance that a living prince
Does now speak to thee, I embrace thy body,
And to thee and thy company I bid 110
A hearty welcome.
Alon. Whe'r thou beest he or no,
Or some enchanted trifle to abuse me,
As late I have been, I not know. Thy pulse
Beats, as of flesh and blood; and, since I saw thee,
The affliction of my mind amends, with which, 115
I fear, a madness held me. This must crave
(An if this be at all) a most strange story.
Thy dukedom I resign and do entreat
Thou pardon me my wrongs. But how should Prospero
Be living and be here?
Pros. First, noble friend, 120
Let me embrace thine age, whose honor cannot
Be measured or confined.
Gon. Whether this be
Or be not, I'll not swear.
Pros. You do yet taste
Some subtleties o' the isle, that will not let you
Believe things certain. Welcome, my friends all.
[*Aside to Sebastian and Antonio*] But you, my brace of lords, were I so minded, 126
I here could pluck his Highness' frown upon you,
And justify you traitors. At this time
I will tell no tales.
Seb. [*Aside*] The devil speaks in him.
Pros. No.
For you, most wicked sir, whom to call brother 130
Would even infect my mouth, I do forgive
Thy rankest fault—all of them; and require
My dukedom of thee, which perforce I know
Thou must restore.
Alon. If thou beest Prospero,
Give us particulars of thy preservation; 135
How thou hast met us here, who three hours since
Were wracked upon this shore; where I have lost
(How sharp the point of this remembrance is!)
My dear son Ferdinand.
Pros. I am woe for't, sir.
Alon. Irreparable is the loss, and patience 140
Says it is past her cure.
Pros. I rather think
You have not sought her help, of whose soft grace
For the like loss I have her sovereign aid
And rest myself content.
Alon. You the like loss?
Pros. As great to me as late; and, supportable 145
To make the dear loss, have I means much weaker
Than you may call to comfort you; for I
Have lost my daughter.
Alon. A daughter?
O heavens, that they were living both in Naples,
The King and Queen there! That they were, I wish
Myself were mudded in that oozy bed 151
Where my son lies. When did you lose your daughter?
Pros. In this last tempest. I perceive these lords
At this encounter do so much admire
That they devour their reason, and scarce think 155
Their eyes do offices of truth, their words
Are natural breath. But, howsoev'r you have
Been justled from your senses, know for certain
That I am Prospero, and that very duke 159
Which was thrust forth of Milan, who most strangely
Upon this shore, where you were wracked, was landed
To be the lord on't. No more yet of this;
For 'tis a chronicle of day by day,
Not a relation for a breakfast, nor
Befitting this first meeting. Welcome, sir. 165
This cell's my court. Here have I few attendants,
And subjects none abroad. Pray you look in.

103. Or ere: before
111. Whe'r: whether
112. enchanted trifle: trick of magic; **abuse:** deceive
116. crave: require
121. thine age: your aged self
124. subtleties: a pun on a special meaning: pastries in fancy shapes created for festive occasions
128. justify: prove
139. woe: woeful
144. rest . . . content: remain happy
146. dear: bitter
154. admire: wonder
156. do . . . truth: serve truthfully
156–57. their . . . breath: their efforts at speech result only in gasps.

My dukedom since you have given me again,
I will requite you with as good a thing,
At least bring forth a wonder to content ye 170
As much as me my dukedom.

Here PROSPERO *discovers* FERDINAND *and* MIRANDA *playing at chess.*

Mir. Sweet lord, you play me false.
Fer. No, my dearest love,
I would not for the world.
Mir. Yes, for a score of kingdoms you should wrangle,
And I would call it fair play.
Alon. If this prove 175
A vision of the island, one dear son
Shall I twice lose.
Seb. A most high miracle!
Fer. Though the seas threaten, they are merciful.
I have cursed them without cause. [*Kneels.*]
Alon. Now all the blessings
Of a glad father compass thee about! 180
Arise, and say how thou camest here.
Mir. O, wonder!
How many goodly creatures are there here!
How beauteous mankind is! O brave new world
That has such people in't!
Pros. 'Tis new to thee.
Alon. What is this maid with whom thou wast at play? 185
Your eld'st acquaintance cannot be three hours.
Is she the goddess that hath severed us
And brought us thus together?
Fer. Sir, she is mortal;
But by immortal providence she's mine.
I chose her when I could not ask my father 190
For his advice, nor thought I had one. She
Is daughter to this famous Duke of Milan,
Of whom so often I have heard renown
But never saw before; of whom I have
Received a second life; and second father 195
This lady makes him to me.
Alon. I am hers.
But, O, how oddly will it sound that I
Must ask my child forgiveness!
Pros. There, sir, stop.
Let us not burden our remembrance with
A heaviness that's gone.
Gon. I have inly wept, 200
Or should have spoke ere this. Look down, you gods,
And on this couple drop a blessed crown!
For it is you that have chalked forth the way
Which brought us hither.
Alon. I say amen, Gonzalo. 204
Gon. Was Milan thrust from Milan that his issue
Should become kings of Naples? O, rejoice
Beyond a common joy, and set it down
With gold on lasting pillars: In one voyage
Did Claribel her husband find at Tunis,
And Ferdinand her brother found a wife 210
Where he himself was lost; Prospero his dukedom
In a poor isle; and all of us ourselves
When no man was his own.
Alon. [*To Ferdinand and Miranda*] Give me your hands.
Let grief and sorrow still embrace his heart 215
That doth not wish you joy.
Gon. Be it so! Amen!

Enter ARIEL, *with the* MASTER *and* BOATSWAIN *amazedly following.*

O, look, sir; look, sir! Here is more of us!
I prophesied, if a gallows were on land, 218
This fellow could not drown. Now, blasphemy,
That swearest grace o'erboard, not an oath on shore?
Hast thou no mouth by land? What is the news?
Boats. The best news is that we have safely found
Our king and company; the next, our ship,
Which, but three glasses since, we gave out split,
Is tight and yare and bravely rigged as when 225
We first put out to sea.
Ariel. [*Aside to Prospero*] Sir, all this service
Have I done since I went.
Pros. [*Aside to Ariel*] My tricksy spirit!
Alon. These are not natural events; they strengthen 230
From strange to stranger. Say, how came you hither?
Boats. If I did think, sir, I were well awake,
I'ld strive to tell you. We were dead of sleep
And (how we know not) all clapped under hatches,
Where, but even now, with strange and several noises 235
Of roaring, shrieking, howling, jingling chains,
And mo diversity of sounds, all horrible,
We were awaked; straightway at liberty;
Where we, in all her trim, freshly beheld
Our royal, good and gallant ship, our master 240
Cap'ring to eye her. On a trice, so please you,
Even in a dream, were we divided from them
And were brought moping hither.
Ariel. [*Aside to Prospero*] Was't well done?

170. content: please
S.D. 171. discovers: reveals (by drawing a curtain or the like)
196. hers: i.e., her second father
200. heaviness: sorrow
219. blasphemy: blasphemous one
224. glasses: hours; **since:** ago
225. yare: seaworthy
229. tricksy: clever
241. On . . . trice: in a moment
243. moping: in a semiconscious state

Pros. [*Aside to Ariel*] Bravely, my diligence.
Thou shalt be free. 245
Alon. This is as strange a maze as e'er men trod,
And there is in this business more than nature
Was ever conduct of. Some oracle
Must rectify our knowledge.
Pros. Sir, my liege,
Do not infest your mind with beating on 250
The strangeness of this business. At picked leisure,
Which shall be shortly, single I'll resolve you
(Which to you shall seem probable) of every
These happened accidents; till when, be cheerful
And think of each thing well. [*Aside to Ariel*]
Come hither, spirit. 255
Set Caliban and his companions free.
Untie the spell. [*Exit Ariel.*] How fares my gracious sir?
There are yet missing of your company
Some few odd lads that you remember not.

Enter ARIEL, *driving in* CALIBAN, STEPHANO, *and* TRINCULO, *in their stol'n apparel.*

Ste. Every man shift for all the rest, and let 260
no man take care for himself; for all is but fortune.
Coragio, bully-monster, coragio!
Trin. If these be true spies which I wear in my
head, here's a goodly sight.
Cal. O Setebos, these be brave spirits indeed!
How fine my master is! I am afraid 266
He will chastise me.
Seb. Ha, ha!
What things are these, my Lord Antonio?
Will money buy 'em?
Ant. Very like. One of them
Is a plain fish and no doubt marketable. 270
Pros. Mark but the badges of these men, my lords,
Then say if they be true. This misshapen knave,
His mother was a witch, and one so strong
That could control the moon, make flows and ebbs,
And deal in her command without her power. 275
These three have robbed me, and this demidevil
(For he's a bastard one) had plotted with them
To take my life. Two of these fellows you
Must know and own; this thing of darkness I
Acknowledge mine.
Cal. I shall be pinched to death. 280
Alon. Is not this Stephano, my drunken butler?
Seb. He is drunk now. Where had he wine?
Alon. And Trinculo is reeling ripe. Where should they
Find this grand liquor that hath gilded 'em?
How camest thou in this pickle? 285
Trin. I have been in such a pickle, since I saw you
last, that I fear me will never out of my bones. I
shall not fear fly-blowing.
Seb. Why, how now, Stephano?
Ste. O, touch me not! I am not Stephano, but a
cramp. 290
Pros. You'ld be king o' the isle, sirrah?
Ste. I should have been a sore one then.
Alon. This is as strange a thing as e'er I looked on.
Pros. He is as disproportioned in his manners
As in his shape. Go, sirrah, to my cell; 295
Take with you your companions. As you look
To have my pardon, trim it handsomely.
Cal. Ay, that I will! and I'll be wise hereafter,
And seek for grace. What a thrice-doubled ass
Was I to take this drunkard for a god 300
And worship this dull fool!
Pros. Go to! Away!
Alon. Hence, and bestow your luggage where you
found it.
Seb. Or stole it rather.
[*Exeunt Caliban, Stephano, and Trinculo.*]
Pros. Sir, I invite your Highness and your train
To my poor cell, where you shall take your rest
For this one night; which, part of it, I'll waste 306
With such discourse as, I not doubt, shall make it
Go quick away—the story of my life,
And the particular accidents gone by
Since I came to this isle; and in the morn 310
I'll bring you to your ship, and so to Naples,
Where I have hope to see the nuptial
Of these our dear-beloved solemnized;
And thence retire me to my Milan, where
Every third thought shall be my grave.
Alon. I long 315
To hear the story of your life, which must
Take the ear strangely.
Pros. I'll deliver all;
And promise you calm seas, auspicious gales,
And sail so expeditious that shall catch
Your royal fleet far off.—My Ariel, chick, 320
That is thy charge. Then to the elements
Be free, and fare thou well.—Please you draw near.
Exeunt omnes.

244. diligence: diligent one
247–48. there . . . of: this business is beyond the natural.
250. infest: disturb: **beating:** harping
252. single: alone (without an oracle)
254. accidents: occurrences
266. fine: finely dressed
271. Mark: note; **badges:** signs that associate them with particular masters
272. true: honest; loyal
283. reeling ripe: ripe for reeling
284. gilded: flushed (the effect of liquor)
317. Take: charm

EPILOGUE

Spoken by PROSPERO.

Now my charms are all o'erthrown,
And what strength I have's mine own,
Which is most faint. Now 'tis true
I must be here confined by you,
Or sent to Naples. Let me not, 5
Since I have my dukedom got
And pardoned the deceiver, dwell
In this bare island by your spell;
But release me from my bands
With the help of your good hands. 10
Gentle breath of yours my sails
Must fill, or else my project fails,
Which was to please. Now I want
Spirits to enforce, art to enchant;
And my ending is despair 15
Unless I be relieved by prayer,
Which pierces so that it assaults
Mercy itself and frees all faults.
As you from crimes would pardoned be,
Let your indulgence set me free. 20
Exit.

The Immortal Phoenix
Rising from Its Own Ashes
(*Tempest,* III.iii.25–27)
From Claude Paradin, *Devises héroïques* (1557).

WILLIAM SHAKESPEARE:

SUMMARY OF BIOGRAPHICAL FACTS

In the parish records of Trinity Church, Stratford-upon-Avon, in the county of Warwickshire, one may still see the entry for the baptism on Wednesday, April 26, 1564, of William Shakespeare, son of John and Mary Arden Shakespeare. Since it was the normal custom to baptize a child within two or three days after birth, April 23 has been conventionally accepted as the date of Shakespeare's birth.

John Shakespeare, the future poet's father, was a fairly prosperous tradesman of Stratford. By trade a glover and a dealer in wool, grains, and timber, he was a member of the Guild of Glovers, Whittawers, and Collar Makers, one of Stratford's most important trade guilds. At various times he served as a burgess, constable, chamberlain, high bailiff, alderman, and chief alderman of the town. John Shakespeare had married Mary Arden, daughter of Robert Arden of Wilmcote, a village near Stratford. The Ardens were an old and substantial family, who owned farm lands and occupied an important place in the community. John Shakespeare bought property in Stratford and in 1590 is recorded as the owner of two adjoining houses in Henley Street, one of which is now called the "Birthplace" and the other the "Woolshop." Although there is some doubt as to which house John Shakespeare was occupying when William was born, evidence points to the one now designated as the birthplace.

The fact that on April 29, 1552, John Shakespeare was fined a shilling for maintaining an unauthorized dunghill in Henley Street has been cited by uninformed commentators as evidence of John's shiftlessness and Stratford's backwardness. The possession of a compost pile merely indicates that he was a provident gardener; and Stratford was not less backward in this respect than London or Paris in the sixteenth century.

Stratford, indeed, was a bustling little town, the market center for Warwickshire, a rich agricultural county on the edge of the Cotswolds, which were noted for sheep-raising. It was a pleasant town on the north bank of the Avon, then as now a beautiful willow-lined river. A native of Stratford, Sir Hugh Clopton, a wealthy merchant and Lord Mayor of London in the year of America's discovery, built a stone bridge across the river and made other benefactions to his home town. A religious and fraternal organization known as the Guild of the Holy Cross had long maintained a grammar school and almshouse. After the religious foundations were dissolved by Henry VIII, the grammar school was refounded under Edward VI and had a good reputation; it paid its schoolmaster a higher salary than was customary in most Elizabethan grammar schools. Good roads connected Stratford and Oxford, and regular carriers plied between Stratford and London. The town had two annual fairs and a weekly market. Its industries included weaving, glove-making, tanning of hides, leather-working, shoemaking, cloth-dyeing, brewing, and woodworking of timber from nearby woodlands. In short, Stratford was a thriving town in contact with London and the larger world that it represented. Shakespeare was not brought up in a backwater of provincial barbarism, as some unhistorical writers would have us believe.

Since his father was a burgess of the town, young William undoubtedly attended the local grammar school, where he learned Latin and read such Latin classics as Ovid, Plautus, and Terence. He probably began studying Greek in the fifth form. It may be significant that one of his earliest plays, *The Comedy of Errors,* is based on a play by Plautus, which he may have read first in school. The grammar school was the place where an Englishman received his basic education in classical literature. If he later went on to the university, he received little instruction there that would be beneficial to a writer for the public stage. The university curriculum in the sixteenth century was better adapted to provide instruction for future parsons and lawyers than to stimulate the imaginations of poets and dramatists. There is no record of Shakespeare's matriculation at either university, and his plays do not show any evidence of university training, for they are not burdened with the particular kind of pedantic learning characteristic of university teaching in this period. It was fortunate that Shakespeare escaped the university curriculum and acquired instead the deep perception and understanding of human nature that illuminate his plays.

According to Nicholas Rowe, Shakespeare's first biographer, he left school prematurely to assist his father in his business. Certainly John Shakespeare had run into difficulties. In 1587 he was replaced as alderman for failure to attend meetings in the town hall, and in 1592 he was listed in a group of nine persons charged with not attending church for fear of being arrested for debt. Precisely when William left grammar school to help his father in his business, no one knows. Gossipy John Aubrey reported more than a century after Shakespeare's birth that young Shakespeare followed his father's trade of butcher and when he killed a calf "would do it in a high style and make a speech." It would be pleasant to believe that the lad was already thinking of the stage and acting out a part, but Aubrey is not a reliable witness and there is no evidence that John Shakespeare combined the trade of butcher with his other activities, even though the anti-Shakespeareans like to refer to William Shakespeare as the "ignorant butcher's boy of Stratford."

No records are left to document Shakespeare's boyhood. There is no reason why any should exist. No one knew that centuries later the world would treasure his works; and like most citizens of the sixteenth century, even those of more prominence than he, he went his way without leaving many written records. He was doubtless an active and vigorous youth, working in his father's shop and enjoying the pleasures that came to most healthy country boys.

In 1582 he married Anne Hathaway, which event is a matter of record. On November 27, the Bishop of Worcester, who had jurisdiction over Stratford, issued a license for the marriage of William Shakespeare and Anne Whateley of Temple Grafton after reading the banns once instead of the usual three times. The clerk who wrote out the license had got the name of the bride wrong. The next day a bond was given by two friends of Shakespeare to insure the Bishop against suits that might arise because of the omission of the banns. This time the bride's name was spelled "Anne Hathwey of Stratford." Anne's father, the evidence indicates, was Richard Hathaway of Shottery. His house is now called "Anne Hathaway's Cottage." At the time of their marriage, William had not yet reached his nineteenth birthday; Anne was already twenty-six.

The need for haste in performing the marriage ceremony was explained on May 26, 1583, when the christening of Susanna, daughter of William and Anne Shakespeare, was recorded in Trinity Church, Stratford. Two years later, on February 2, 1585, the parish records show the christening of twins, a son and daughter, Hamnet and Judith.

We have no precise information concerning Shakespeare's occupation and activities in Stratford after his marriage or the date when he left Stratford for London. It has been conjectured that he tried his hand at schoolteaching, but that is a mere guess. There is a legend that he left Stratford to escape a charge of poaching deer from Sir Thomas Lucy of Charlecote, but that too is based on local gossip that first appears about 1695 in some notes left by Richard Davies, rector of Saperton in Gloucestershire. One difficulty with this story is that Sir Thomas Lucy had no proper deer park.

Sometime in the late 1580's Shakespeare went up to London and managed to get his foot on the theatrical ladder, where and how we do not know. One legend says he made his living at first by holding horses outside a playhouse and presently was given employment inside, but there is nothing but eighteenth-century hearsay for this. But lack of information is not surprising. We have little or no information of this kind about most of Shakespeare's contemporaries. Elizabethans did not write their autobiographies, and no Boswells were standing around to take down their words and report their deeds. We know even less about many of the important writers of the day and some of the men of affairs than we know about Shakespeare. By 1592 he was sufficiently popular to incur the envy of the dramatist and pamphleteer Robert Greene, who referred to him as an "upstart crow . . . in his own conceit the only Shake-scene in a country." After this date contemporary allusions and references in legal documents provide more accurate information about Shakespeare's career than we have for most other dramatists of the period.

By 1594 Shakespeare had joined the company of actors known as the Lord Chamberlain's Men, which became the King's Men after the accession of James I in 1603. During his years of connection with the London theatre, Shakespeare not only was a playwright, an actor, and a member of the dramatic company, but he was also one of the shareholders or "householders" who leased the Globe and the Blackfriars playhouses, a group to whom the acting company had to pay a proportion of the receipts. Thus Shakespeare had an income from various sources in the theatrical world. As an actor he apparently was not a star, possibly because he was busy with other duties in the playhouse. Tradition has assigned to him the roles of Adam in *As You Like It* and the Ghost in *Hamlet*.

Shakespeare began his career as a playwright in

1590–91 with *Henry VI, Part 2,* which was quickly followed by *Henry VI, Part 3,* and a little later, 1591–92, with *Henry VI, Part 1.* The precise order in which he wrote his plays has been the subject of much detailed investigation, and not all scholars are in agreement. The latest research indicates that the plays after *Henry VI* were probably performed in the following chronological sequence, though not all scholars are in agreement on the dates of first performance:

1592–93	*Richard III*
1592–93	*Comedy of Errors*
1593–94	*Titus Andronicus*
1593–94	*Taming of the Shrew*
1594–95	*Two Gentlemen of Verona*
1594–95	*Love's Labor's Lost*
1594–95	*Romeo and Juliet*
1595–96	*Richard II*
1595–96	*A Midsummer Night's Dream*
1596–97	*King John*
1596–97	*The Merchant of Venice*
1596–97	*Henry IV, Part 1*
1597–98	*Henry IV, Part 2*
1598–99	*Much Ado about Nothing*
1599	*Henry V*
1599–1600	*Julius Cæsar*
1599–1600	*As You Like It*
1600	*Hamlet*
1600–1601	*Twelfth Night*
1600–1601	*The Merry Wives of Windsor*
1601–2	*Troilus and Cressida*
1602–3	*All's Well That Ends Well*
1604–5	*Measure for Measure*
1604	*Othello*
1605	*King Lear*
1606	*Macbeth*
1607	*Antony and Cleopatra*
1608	*Coriolanus*
1608	*Timon of Athens*
1608–9	*Pericles*
1609–10	*Cymbeline*
1610–11	*The Winter's Tale*
1611	*The Tempest*
1612–13	*Henry VIII*

Shakespeare's career as a playwright and as a member of London's leading dramatic company brought him wealth as well as fame. On May 4, 1597, he bought New Place, the second-largest house in Stratford, with a handsome garden. In 1602 he purchased 107 acres of farm land near Stratford and a few months later a cottage and gardens across the alley from New Place. In 1612 a legal document describes him as "William Shakespeare of Stratford-upon-Avon . . . gentleman," which suggests that by this time he had retired to Stratford. During his years of activity in London his wife and children apparently had remained in Stratford. His only son, Hamnet, died in 1612.

Shakespeare's designation as "gentleman" results from the College of Heralds' grant of a coat-of-arms to his father in 1596. Although actors in the sixteenth and seventeenth centuries occupied a low social status, Shakespeare could claim to be a second-generation gentleman.

Sketch of Shakespeare's Coat of Arms
From a sixteenth-century manuscript (Folger V.a.156).

In 1607 Susanna Shakespeare married a prosperous Stratford physician, Dr. John Hall. Judith remained unwed until she was thirty-two years old, when she married Thomas Quiney, a Stratford vintner. The couple were excommunicated by the Bishop of Worcester for marrying in Trinity Church during Lent and without a license. There is reason to believe that Shakespeare had little liking for his younger daughter's match.

On March 25, 1616, Shakespeare made his will, leaving his landed property to Susanna, £300 to Judith, certain sums to other relatives, and his second-best bed with its furnishings to his wife. The latter bequest probably indicates that Anne had expressed a desire for the bed; common law insured her a dower right of one-third for life in the real estate left by her husband. On April 23, 1616, William

Shakespeare died and was buried on April 25 within the chancel of Trinity Church, as befitted an honored citizen of Stratford. Anne Shakespeare survived until August 6, 1623, a few months before the publication of the First Folio of her husband's works.

Shakespeare has no direct descendants. His daughter Susanna and Dr. John Hall had one daughter, who became Lady Bernard of Abingdon, but she died childless in 1670. His younger daughter, Judith, had three children, but they all died young without issue.

There is no evidence that Shakespeare made any effort to publish his plays during his lifetime. Since plays were not considered "literature" any more than modern radio and television scripts are considered literature, and since playwrights sold their scripts outright to acting companies, it is not surprising that the author had no hand in their publication. His ambition to be considered a man of letters as well as a popular playwright is indicated by the publication of his narrative poems *Venus and Adonis* (1593) and *The Rape of Lucrece* (1594), which he probably saw through the press himself. The *Sonnets* (printed in 1609) probably circulated in manuscript and were apparently published without his permission.

We owe the publication of the First Folio to the industry of two of Shakespeare's colleagues in the King's Men, John Heminges and Henry Condell. In their preface, "To the great variety of readers," Heminges and Condell promise that "whereas you were abused with divers stolen and surreptitious copies, maimed and deformed by the frauds and stealths of injurious impostors that exposed them, even those are now offered to your view cured and perfect of their limbs; and all the rest, absolute in their numbers, as he conceived them." It was true that some of the previously printed quarto texts had been pirated or printed from memorial reconstructions, but whether the editors of the Folio used playhouse scripts or whether they corrected quartos by comparing the texts with copies used in the playhouse we cannot now tell with certainty. Their promise of providing accurate texts was unfortunately not carried out, since Heminges and Condell were not editors by profession and the proofreading of the Folio was careless. *Mr. William Shakespeare's Comedies, Histories, and Tragedies. Published according to the True Original Copies* (1623) contained eighteen plays not previously printed and eighteen plays that existed in previous quarto versions. The only play usually attributed to Shakespeare omitted from the Folio was *Pericles*.

It is believed that the First Folio was printed in an edition of 1,000–1,250 copies and sold for about £1 (the equivalent of $40–$50 in modern purchasing power). The fact that it was a large and expensive book may account for the fact that it is not rare as seventeenth-century books go. Something like 238 copies are known to exist, and the Folger Shakespeare Library in Washington, D.C., possesses seventy-nine copies, which the founder, Henry Clay Folger, collected because he believed that a collation of as many copies as possible would bring to light significant information about Shakespeare's text. Dr. Charlton Hinman has collated all the copies of the Folio owned by the Folger Library, using a machine he invented for mechanical comparison of texts, and has made interesting discoveries about printing practices of Shakespeare's period.

The popularity of Shakespeare's works is indicated by the publication of a Second Folio in 1632, followed by a Third in 1663–64 and a Fourth in 1685. The Third and Fourth Folios contained *Pericles* and six additional plays not included in the First Folio, which are considered apocryphal.

Notes on the Authorship Controversy

Shakespeare has been the focus for one of the most curious and, in many respects, one of the most unenlightened controversies in the history of literature. No contemporary of Shakespeare's thought of questioning the authenticity of his works. But a little over a century ago several writers began to speculate that Shakespeare's plays were written by somebody else, and since that time a vast literature on this theme has developed. It is true that a few scattered comments after the middle of the eighteenth century question the authorship of plays attributed to Shakespeare, but by and large the controversy is a phenomenon of the nineteenth and twentieth centuries.

Let it suffice to say that there is contemporary evidence that Shakespeare of Stratford is the author of Shakespeare's plays and that actor and playwright are the same person. Shakespeare's own age believed this, and there is no valid reason to question it. Perhaps no one would have questioned it if Shakespeare idolaters had not endowed the dramatist with such superhuman qualities of learning and godlike omniscience that their extravagance produced a natural reaction. Skeptics set out to prove that a youth from a country town like Stratford could not have written the plays; instead they must have been written by some noble lord, or at least a learned lawyer like Francis Bacon. During the past century an incredible list of candidates has been proposed, regardless of the logic of chronology. These include Cardinal Wolsey, a nun named Anne Whateley, a parcel of Jesuits, Mary Queen of Scots, Francis Bacon, Queen Elizabeth I, the Earl of Oxford, the Earl of Derby, the Earl of Rutland, Christopher Marlowe, Sir Edward Dyer, and a score of others. An Arab student at the University of London in 1962 set forth the thesis that Shakespeare was not an Englishman at all but one Sheik Zubair from Basra, in southern Iraq, who came to London in the late sixteenth century. In recent years the most strident and verbose advocates have been those who have tried to establish the claims of the Earl of Oxford. The candidate with the longest roster of distinguished names among his advocates, however, is Francis Bacon. Distinguished lawyers on both sides of the Atlantic have argued that Bacon must be the author.

In spite of the energy expended by these amateurs in the fields of Elizabethan literature and history, no one has produced a single new fact to disprove Shakespeare's authorship or a single authenticated fact that proves anyone else to have been the author. All of the theories rest on mere hypothesis and speculation.

The anti-Shakespeareans base their arguments upon a few simple premises, all of which are false. These false premises are that Shakespeare was an unlettered yokel without any schooling, that nothing is known about him, and that only a noble lord or an equivalent in background could have written the plays. The facts are that more is known about Shakespeare than about many other writers of even greater prominence at the time, that he had a very good education (better than that possessed by some members of the nobility), which he probably received at the Stratford Grammar School, that the plays show no evidence of profound book learning, that the knowledge of kings and courts evident in the plays is no greater than that which any intelligent young playwright could have picked up at second hand. Indeed, some of the "intimate acquaintance of kings and noble persons" that the anti-Shakespeareans talk about is taken almost word for word from Holinshed's *Chronicles*. But perhaps Holinshed also was written by Bacon or the Earl of Oxford!

Some of the anti-Shakespeareans write plausibly if one grants their false premises and can believe statements quoted out of context or distorted to prove what they want to believe. They betray such ignorance of the ordinary facts of sixteenth- and seventeenth-century history, literary conventions of the day, and the ordinary practices of actors, printers, and publishers that no professional historian can take them seriously. The refusal of professional historians to waste time in arguing with the anti-Shakespeareans may account in part for the surly truculence and abuse that characterize much of their writing.

A considerable literature has been written to show the folly of their contentions. One of the best books in refutation is R. C. Churchill, *Shakespeare and His Betters* (Bloomington, Ind., 1959). Mr. Churchill with excessive politeness analyzes each of the major theories and concludes that not one has any genuine evidence to substantiate it. He provides a useful bibliography of works pro and con. Gerald E. Bentley, *Shakespeare: A Biographical Handbook* (New Haven, 1961), pp. 16–21, gives a succinct statement of some of the chief theories. A highly useful brief analysis of the facts is James G. McManaway, *The Authorship of Shakespeare* ("Folger Booklets on Tudor and Stuart Civilization"; Washington and Ithaca, N.Y.: Cornell University Press, 1962). See also Louis B. Wright, "The Anti-Shakespeare Industry," *Virginia Quarterly Review,* XXXV (1959), 289–303. The most recent work on the subject is H. N. Gibson, *The Shakespeare Claimants: A Critical Study of the Four Principal Theories concerning the Authorship of the Shakespearian Plays* (London, 1962).

London Bridge

From Visscher's "View of London" (1616).

SHAKESPEARE'S THEATRE AND THE DRAMATIC TRADITION *

For many years the characteristics of Shakespeare's stage have excited the interest of scholars. In thousands of pages of learned commentary they have discussed the history of Elizabethan theatres, the physical conditions of the stage, the composition of the companies of actors, the influence of the physical nature of the stage upon the quality of the drama, and scores of related topics. In an area where precise documentary evidence is scanty, many topics have aroused controversies that cannot be resolved dogmatically. For example, blueprints for the original construction of the Globe playhouse do not exist, and our knowledge of it is based on a variety of evidence, much of which is inconclusive.

Though scholars may not agree on every detail of stage construction, they have accumulated enough evidence to permit the reconstruction of a characteristic theatre in its essential outlines. The public theatres were not exact replicas of each other, of course, and the so-called "private" theatres showed many differences. We would do well to remember that, then as now, individual theatres varied considerably in their appointments and equipment, and a generalization about the staging of a play in one theatre may not precisely fit conditions in another. Nevertheless, the conditions of staging in all of the public playhouses had a general similarity, and certain theatrical practices were common to them all.

Traditionally the English had found pleasure and delight in dramatic entertainment. For centuries before the development of Elizabethan drama, folk games, pageantry, and processions had been a part of English life. Wandering entertainers had been a familiar sight in both manor houses and town halls. Jugglers, sleight-of-hand artists, acrobats, rope dancers, bear-leaders, and fortunetellers, who belong to an ancient profession antedating recorded history, roamed the English countryside and regularly turned up at fairs and festivals. When performers of rude dramatic skits first appeared in England, no man can say. Mimes and clowns performing impromptu roles probably date from the Roman occupation. Certainly the clown has an ancient if not an honorable lineage. In the country, the mummers' play and other types of folk drama go back to an early date.

The theatre proper, however, traces its origins back to the Church, even to the most solemn part of the liturgy, the Easter Mass. Between the ninth and the eleventh centuries throughout Europe the Easter Mass acquired richness and variety. In some churches, a brief text, or "trope," attached itself to the beginning portion of the Mass called the *Introit* and served as a kind of dramatic introduction to the service. In the Easter Mass this trope began, *Quem quaeritis in sepulchro, O Christicolae?* ["Whom seek ye in the sepulcher, O followers of Christ?"]; and when the three Marys replied that they sought Jesus of Nazareth who had been crucified, the angel responded that he was not there, that they should go forth and say that he had risen as it had been prophesied. This bit of liturgical decoration gave rise to other dramatic episodes, notably to a similar playlet attached to the Christmas Mass. Liturgical drama of this type was acted throughout the European Church until the middle of the fifteenth century, by which time religious plays had already become secularized and had passed from the church into the streets and market place.

Precisely when or how this secularization came about, no one knows. A summer feast day, that of Corpus Christi, first established by the Church in 1264 and revived in 1311, provided an ideal time for an outdoor celebration and was soon the occasion for the performances of secularized Biblical plays. Since Corpus Christi Day falls on the Thursday after Trinity Sunday (the eighth Sunday after Easter), the performers could count on a long summer's day with a chance for good weather. In many towns throughout England on Corpus Christi Day associa-

* Material in this section is adapted by permission from a booklet by Louis B. Wright with the same title, published by the Folger Library.

tions of tradesmen known as guilds made themselves responsible for the presentation of cycles of plays based on the Bible, beginning with the Creation and ending with the Last Judgment. When possible, particular guilds chose plays that suited their callings. At Newcastle, York, and elsewhere, for example, the Shipwrights were responsible for the play concerned with building Noah's Ark. Corpus Christi Day was not the only occasion for the performance of guild plays. At Chester, for example, the plays were given during the week following Whitsunday. Although in some places the plays might be performed on stationary platforms, the general practice was to use "pageant wagons"—which in America would be called "floats"—platforms or structures on wheels which could go from place to place about the town until the whole cycle had been seen in sequence at several stations. When an entire cycle was given in one day, the performances had to start early and end late. The York cycle numbered at one time at least fifty plays, forty-eight of which have survived. If the audience tired of them, the records do not show it, and the cyclic plays, given in the language of the people, continued in popular esteem in some places until Shakespeare's time. Plays were acted at Chester in the 1570's, and at Coventry, only a few miles from Stratford, until 1580.

These cyclic plays performed by the trade guilds are usually called miracle or mystery plays (the latter probably from an old French word for "trade"). Literary historians have sometimes tried to make a distinction between mystery and miracle plays. They would restrict mystery plays to those based on episodes in the lives of the saints, but the distinction has not gained currency, and both terms are used to describe the guild plays. Saints plays were never so popular in England as in France and elsewhere on the Continent.

The significant fact about the guild plays in the growth of the dramatic tradition in England is their popularity over a great span of years and their dissemination throughout the country. As late as the mid-sixteenth century, even many small towns had a summer festival of drama in which large numbers of citizens participated. Gradually non-Biblical material crept into the stories, particularly in certain roles that offered possibilities for comedy. Noah had trouble getting his wife into the Ark, for instance, and had to beat her "black and blue," to the jollification of the spectators. The raging of King Herod became a comic scene, and the devils in the Last Judgment made much comic by-play as they snatched urchins from the street and carried them off to Hell Mouth. Finally, in a sheepstealing episode in the Second Shepherd's Play in the Towneley (or Wakefield) Cycle, we have a fully developed comedy taken from the folklore of the countryside.

Still another type of drama, also religious in its beginnings, flourished in the fifteenth century. This was the morality play, an allegorical drama in which the characters are personified abstractions such as Envy, Pride, Mercy, Repentance, and the like. The conflict in this type of drama is between Good and Evil for the Soul of Man, with a variety of situations precipitated by such characters as the Seven Deadly Sins, who are opposed by the Seven Virtues.

The longest morality play (more than 3,600 lines) and one of the most comprehensive in theme is *The Castle of Perseverance,* extant in a manuscript now in the Folger Library. Dating from about 1425, it exemplifies most of the situations found in this type of play. Human Kind, the hero, tempted by the World, the Flesh, and the Devil, takes refuge in the Castle of Perseverance, where he is besieged by the Seven Deadly Sins and defended by the Seven Virtues. Having grown old during a long war of words, Human Kind is tempted to leave the Castle of Covetousness, the sin peculiar to old age, but he soon repents, and after Mercy, Truth, Justice, and Peace have delivered sermons, God the Father pardons Human Kind, and the play closes with advice to the audience to "think on your last ending."

The manuscript contains an interesting diagram showing the method of staging. A rough drawing of the Castle occupies the center of the arena with fixed scaffolds at intervals around the circumference for other scenes as they would be required. This multiple-set type of staging was common in the medieval drama and persisted to the Elizabethan period, particularly in plays at court. The audience conveniently forgot the other sets while action was taking place on the one required at the moment.

Despite the unpromising subject matter of the morality plays, they were popular in the second half of the fifteenth century, and they continued in favor down to the accession of Queen Elizabeth. Indeed, some belated moralities were acted during her reign, and morality-play elements occasionally appear in the fully matured Elizabethan drama.

One reason for the popularity of the moralities was the amount of comedy that the actors managed to introduce. Even in so early a play as *The Castle of Perseverance* the personified abstractions were qualified slightly by the comic appearance of Belial, a devil equipped with bizarre fireworks. In the somewhat later play of *Mankind* (*ca.* 1475), the chief interest is in the clownery of Titivillus, the great devil, and his cohorts. At one point the comic characters Nought, New Guise, and Now-A-Days sing a travesty of a Christmas carol that must have delighted unsqueamish audiences, though a modern editor simply prints a series of dots and says, "The song is unprintable."

Mankind also illustrates the development of a professional class of actors. No longer is drama left to the auspices of clerks attached to religious establishments, to trade guilds, or to any other amateurs. As early as the last quarter of the fifteenth century, town records in many parts of England show that professional actors were strolling from town to town with amusing plays in their repertories. In *Mankind* even the collection of money is made a scene of comedy as Titivillus passes his hat and solicits the audience to pay. The most popular characters in the morality plays were the devils and their assistants. From an early date these comedians were responsible for the enduring popularity of theatrical performances throughout the country. During the half-century after *Mankind,* professional troupes of actors multiplied, and during the reign of Henry VIII the country swarmed with players who acted out of doors or in manor houses, castles, and town halls to the increasing delight of the spectators.

A new type of play, generally called an "interlude," developed in this period and gained popularity. The term is not precise and scholars debate about its meaning. Interludes were usually short dramatic pieces, frequently corresponding in length to a one-act play, and were often performed in the halls of great houses, sometimes as part of the entertainment offered at a dinner for some visiting dignitary. They were secular in tone, though some interludes continued to use personified abstractions of a sort. In one of the most curious of the type, *A New Interlude and a Merry of the Nature of the Four Elements,* attributed to John Rastell and written soon after the accession of Henry VIII, we are treated to a long dramatized lesson in science.

The more popular interludes, however, abandoned teaching in favor of sheer entertainment; the best of the writers in this kind was John Heywood, who provided short comic plays and farces for Henry VIII and his noblemen. Although Heywood was not an innovator and was content to borrow from Chaucer and to adapt French farcical stories to dramatic form, his interludes have a freshness and a vitality not found in morality plays, with which they competed for favor. Among the better known of Heywood's interludes is the *Play of the Weather,* in which Jupiter decides to let people choose their own weather but has to return to arbitrary methods when no two can agree on what they want. Another of his interludes, the *Four P's,* exemplifies an ancient but still popular comic device, the contest to see who can tell the biggest lie.

Many interludes and belated morality plays on a wide variety of themes survive from the first half of the sixteenth century. They include political satires, like John Skelton's *Magnificence* and Sir David Lindsay's *Satire of the Three Estates;* dramatized tracts concerned with religious controversy, like John Bale's *God's Promises* and other works from his vitriolic pen; and plays entirely for entertainment, like those of Heywood and such embryonic comedies as *Tom Tyler and His Wife.* The secular interludes made a significant contribution to the comic tradition, and the satiric moralities gave a new dramatic purpose to the stage. The somewhat amorphous drama of the early sixteenth century stimulated the continued development of a popular taste for plays.

The players of interludes did not confine their performances to the great halls of the nobility but often took to the road. Entries in the town records of the visits of players increased markedly in the 1530's and continued through the rest of the century. Scarcely a town was too small to have a visit from a group of strolling players, who frequently described themselves as the servants of some noble lord. This designation merely meant that the nobleman had consented to become the patron of the company of players and thus to lend them his name as a measure of protection against harassment from local authorities, for players occupied a low position in the social scale and were frequently classified in civic regulations with vagabonds and sturdy beggars, a situation that prevailed until Shakespeare's lifetime.

Although relics of the old types of drama cropped up now and then throughout the sixteenth century, by the early years of Elizabeth's reign mature secular drama had come into being. The earliest type to develop was comedy, partly because of a strong native tradition of comic stage situations and partly because the new learning of the Renaissance had familiarized academic audiences with Roman comedy. It was not mere chance that one of Shakespeare's earliest plays, *The Comedy of Errors,* was an adaptation from the *Menaechmi* of Plautus, for he may have remembered the Roman dramatist from his grammar-school studies. As early as 1553 Nicholas Udall, a former headmaster at Eton, composed a play on a Roman model and gave it the title of *Ralph Roister Doister.* Though it owes much to Plautine comedy, it is recognizably English in spirit. Sometime about 1553–54 the students of Christ's College, Cambridge, saw performed in their college hall another English comedy, *Gammer Gurton's Needle,* by an unidentified "Mr. S., Master of Arts." This play is still amusing enough to gain an audience.

On January 18, 1562, two years before Shakespeare was born, the young gentlemen of the Inner Temple, one of the Inns of Court where law students received their training, presented before Queen Elizabeth the first fully developed English tragedy of which we have record, *The Tragedy of Gorboduc.* The authors, Thomas Sackville, later Earl of Dorset, and Thomas Norton, modeled their play after the style of the Roman writer Seneca, but they also showed a familiarity with Italian dramatists. Though

Elizabethan drama had not yet reached full maturity, the forms of both tragedy and comedy were now established, and the development of both types shows rapid progress during the next three decades to culminate in the work of Shakespeare and his contemporaries.

The growing demand for plays and the development of full-length drama had created such a need for professional playhouses by the late 1570's that in 1576 a cabinetmaker-turned-actor named James Burbage erected the first building in London designed exclusively for the use of players. To it he gave the descriptive name The Theatre. Its site was east of Finsbury Fields, a park area to the northward of the city proper, on land leased from one Giles Alleyn. Burbage had been careful to choose a site just outside the jurisdiction of the city authorities yet close enough to be accessible to playgoers. Within a year another playhouse called the Curtain (from the name of the estate on which it was located) opened nearby. London now had two professional public playhouses, both outside the city's jurisdiction. It was important to be beyond the reach of the aldermen of London, for they maintained an inveterate hostility to the players on the grounds that they caused disturbances, brought together crowds that spread the plague, lured apprentices from their work, and were generally ungodly.

An early attempt to open a playhouse within the city was made by Richard Farrant, Master of the Children of Windsor Chapel. For a long time the choirboys of Windsor Chapel, like the choirboys of the Chapel Royal and St. Paul's Cathedral, had been accustomed to performing plays and to taking part in other entertainments at Court. Farrant conceived the notion of renting a hall in part of the old Blackfriars Monastery and of fitting it up for a playhouse on the pretext of rehearsing plays to be performed before the Queen. Although the Blackfriars property was within the walls of the city of London, not far from St. Paul's Cathedral, it retained its ancient exemption from the jurisdicton of the city's aldermen. Even so, Farrant did not dare try to open a public theatre but announced that it would be a "private" house though open to paying customers. This distinction between "public" and "private" theatres would persist throughout the Elizabethan period. Farrant's subterfuge worked, and he opened his playhouse late in 1576 or early in 1577. Despite trouble with his landlord, his theatre was a modest success until his death in 1580. The Blackfriars Theatre operated for another four years under the direction of William Hunnis, Master of the Children of the Chapel Royal, with the help for a time of John Lyly, a young novelist and dramatist. There Lyly's own plays were performed by the boy actors.

From the time of the opening of the earliest formal theatres, the public and the private houses differed widely in physical characteristics and methods of staging. The public theatres, for all we know, may have been influenced in their shape and construction by the circular arenas, like those on the Bankside across the Thames, which were used for bull- and bearbaiting. A more significant influence on their architecture, however, came from the inns. Long before the erection of regular theatres, players had used the yards of inns, and in London certain inns like the Cross Keys, the Bell, and the Bull were noted as playing places for professional actors. At the inns, the players had been accustomed to set up a stage at one end of the open courtyard and to accommodate spectators in the courtyard, which was open to the weather, and in the surrounding galleries.

The public theatres for many years retained this open courtyard feature. There the "groundlings" for the price of a penny could stand, while more opulent spectators could pay a higher fee for the privilege of sitting in the galleries. Plays were performed in the daytime, beginning in the early afternoon, for the stage had no means of artificial lighting. The public theatres could not be used in the worst weather or in the dead of winter. The private houses were enclosed halls in which plays could be given at night. They could be used in winter and in all weathers. The stage was lighted by candles, lamps, or torches. The private houses were not private in the sense of restricting audiences to any special groups, but prices were higher than in the public playhouses, a fact that may have given the private houses a somewhat more select audience.

A place of recreation long popular with the citizens of London was the Bankside, an extensive area on the Southwark side of the Thames and west of what is now Southwark Cathedral. Much of this territory consisted of land that had formerly belonged to the Church or the Crown, and the aldermen of London had no authority over certain areas, like the Manor of Paris Garden and the Liberty of the Clink. These and other localities beyond the jurisdiction of the city became the sites for a variety of amusements.

To the Bankside, Londoners went to witness bear- and bullbaitings at arenas erected for the purpose. After one of the old arenas collapsed in 1583 with some loss of life, a polygonal amphitheatre, called the New Bear Garden, was erected. Other even less savory enticements brought Londoners to the Bankside. This area by the 1580's was attracting the interest of theatrical entrepreneurs. One of these was Philip Henslowe, a semiliterate but shrewd businessman, who in 1587 was instrumental in building the Rose playhouse, not far from the Bear Garden. Henslowe has earned the gratitude of literary historians because he kept an account book, usually described as his "Diary," which preserves much the-

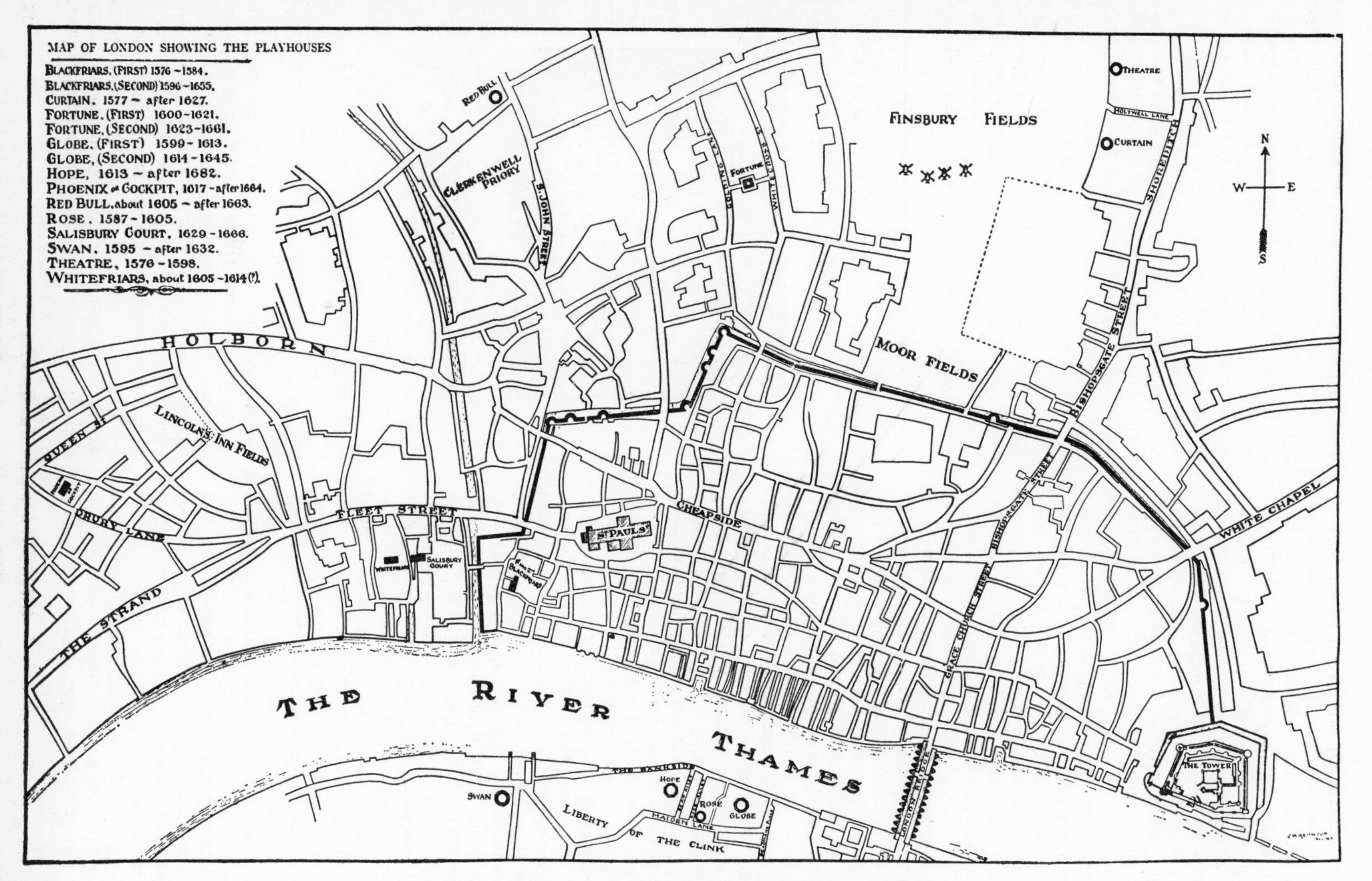

Map of London, Showing the Playhouses of Shakespeare's Time

From J. Q. Adams, *Shakespearean Playhouses* (1917).

atrical and dramatic history. His son-in-law, Edward Alleyn, was one of the most famous actors and stage managers of the day.

The popularity of Henslowe's Rose stimulated another businessman, Francis Langley, goldsmith, to purchase the Manor of Paris Garden, west of the site of the Rose and the Bear Garden. There he erected in 1595 a new theatre which he called the Swan. This playhouse is of interest to historians because in 1596 a Dutch priest, Johannes de Witt, saw a performance at the Swan and described the stage to a friend, Arend van Buchell, who made a drawing that is the earliest visual representation of an Elizabethan stage in use.

The Globe Playhouse

From Visscher's "View of London" (1616).

Because of its association with Shakespeare, the best known of the Bankside theatres is the Globe. The Globe was erected in 1599, in part from timbers of The Theatre, which the lessees, Cuthbert and Richard Burbage, moved across the Thames on December 28, 1598, to a site in Maiden Lane which they had chosen when their landlord made trouble over the lease of The Theatre. To be owners of the new playhouse, the Burbages organized a stock company consisting of themselves and four actors, including Shakespeare and John Heminges, who was later to be one of the editors of the 1623 collection of Shakespeare's plays. The theatre-owners, or "housekeepers" as they were then called, received half the receipts from the galleries. The acting company received the other half and all the receipts taken at the door. Thus Shakespeare, who was a housekeeper, a member of the acting company, and a dramatist, received income from all three sources. The Globe was completed in 1599 and lasted until 1613, when it burned down after a piece of wadding from a cannon fired during a performance of *Henry VIII* ignited its thatched roof. A second Globe was soon erected to take its place. The first Globe is usually pictured as octagonal on the outside, but despite the octagonal pictures in seventeenth-century views of London, some evidence points to a circular shape. The interior may have been circular. The Globe was the model for the Fortune Theatre, which Henslowe and Alleyn erected in 1600 north of the city on the opposite side of Finsbury Fields from the site of The Theatre and the Curtain. In only one essential did they change the design. The Fortune was square. The builder's specifications for the Fortune, which have survived, provide the best existing information about Elizabethan theatrical construction.

A playhouse that combined the functions of a theatre with those of an arena for bear- and bullbaiting was the Hope, erected in 1613 on the site of the Bear Garden, which had fallen into decay and was torn down to make way for the new building. The owners of the Hope were Philip Henslowe and a partner, Jacob Meade. The contract which the partners signed with the carpenter-contractor exists and throws some light on its construction. The Hope had a portable stage which could be removed when the building was required for other purposes. Over the stage area was a permanent canopy. But details of the construction of the stage and the entry doors that we would like to have are omitted. The contract specifies that the contractor is to build the Hope "of such large compass, form, wideness, and height as the playhouse called the Swan."

One other public theatre needs to be mentioned. This was the Red Bull, built about 1605 in the upper end of St. John's Street, Clerkenwell, about a mile from the old Curtain. This theatre was a favorite with London apprentices and was the place where some of the more boisterous of Elizabethan plays were performed.

Almost as important as the Globe in the history of Shakespeare's company was the second Blackfriars Theatre. In 1596 James Burbage purchased a portion of the Frater building in the rambling old Blackfriars Monastery and remodeled it for a theatre. Like the earlier Blackfriars, it was a covered hall, but it was more elaborately designed, with galleries for spectators and a better-equipped stage at one end. The precise construction of the stage we do not know. Burbage leased the theatre for several years to the managers of the boy actors of the Chapel Royal, but in 1608, when the lease expired, a syndicate of seven actors, including Shakespeare, took it over. Henceforth Shakespeare's company operated the Blackfriars as a "private" theatre, but in actuality it was the playhouse regularly used by the company in winter.

Both the Blackfriars and the Globe stages, like other Elizabethan stages, were platform stages without the familiar proscenium arch of the modern theatre and of course without a curtain to come down between the acts and at the end of the play. These stages lacked painted and movable scenery, though Elizabethan theatres made considerably more use of stage properties than we have been led to believe. The question that has aroused the greatest controversy concerns the use of an inner stage and the location of entry doors and balconies in the back of the stage. The Swan drawing shows a projecting platform stage with two doors flat against the rear wall. People, presumably spectators, are shown in the balcony over the rear stage doors. The Swan drawing also shows a canopy supported by columns over a portion of the stage and a room above that. The canopy and room above were characteristics of the public theatres. The upper room, called the "tiring house," was used for dressing and storage. From a trap door in the canopy, called the "heavens," gods and angels might descend when the action required it.

Most modern reconstructions of the stage of the Globe provide an inner stage, useful for bedroom or "study" scenes, with an upper stage above it. Both of these are closed with curtains. Stage doors open obliquely on each side, with boxes or balconies above. This type of construction would best suit a scene like the balcony scene in *Romeo and Juliet*. Some scholars insist that the inner stage was too deeply recessed to permit many in the audience to see properly and that bedroom scenes must have been staged farther forward on the platform, with properties brought into use as they were required. There is no convincing evidence that the regular Elizabethan theatres were designed for performances in the round. There is much evidence for the use of an inner and upper stage with entry doors set either flat against the back or diagonally on the sides. It should be pointed out, however, that the text and directions of many plays seem to indicate the use of the main stage for scenes that editors like to relegate to an inner stage. Such use of the main stage suggests that necessary properties and equipment could be set up in advance and ignored by the audience until time for their use, as in the simultaneous stage settings in medieval drama.

Where there are so many suggestions of both types of staging, one cannot escape the conclusion that usage varied and that stage construction in the theatres may have differed in some important details. Actors have always been skilled in improvising, and Elizabethan players had to be unusually adroit in this respect in order to adapt their plays to a wide variety of conditions: performances in the great hall at Court, in a public theatre in the daytime, in a private theatre at night, or on some makeshift stage in a country town when the plague closed the London theatres and sent the players strolling through the provinces.

During Shakespeare's lifetime the principal theatres were occupied by companies of actors organized under the patronage of various titled personages. The company with which Shakespeare was associated for most of his active career had for its earliest patron Henry Carey, Lord Hunsdon, the Lord Chamberlain. Hence they were known as the Lord Chamberlain's Men. After the accession of James I, the King became their patron and they were known as the King's Men. They were the great rivals of the Lord Admiral's Men, managed by Henslowe and Alleyn. Competitors of all the adult companies were the child actors drawn from the choirboys of the Chapel Royal, Windsor, and St. Paul's. These actors are referred to in *Hamlet* as "an aery of children, little eyases, that cry out on the top of question, and are most tyrannically clapped for't." The adult companies recruited some of their best impersonators of fe-

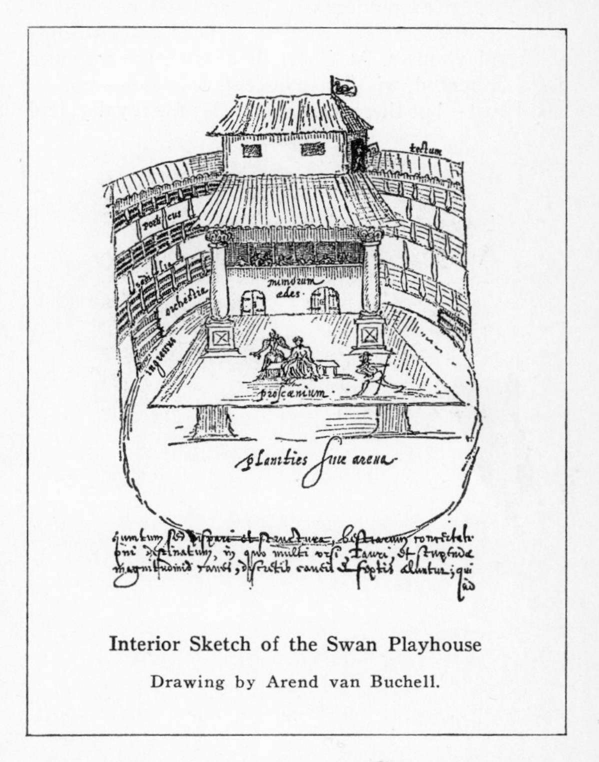

Interior Sketch of the Swan Playhouse

Drawing by Arend van Buchell.

male roles from the children's companies, for the Elizabethan stage never employed women as players. That innovation had to wait until the Restoration.

Elizabethan acting must have been skillful and effective. To hold the attention of a restless and unruly audience in close proximity, the actors had to speak their lines well and simulate their parts to perfection. The impersonation of women's roles by boys seems to us the least satisfactory element in Elizabethan acting, but there is ample evidence that youths succeeded in these parts. No Elizabethan complained that a boy spoiled the role of Juliet.

Elizabethan audiences were not accustomed to the conventions of modern staging and did not expect realistic stage sets and colorful scenery in the professional playhouses. At Court, it is true, the masques were mounted with magnificent splendor—and at great cost—but these were spectacles for royalty, and few who witnessed plays in the theatres ever saw a masque. We have perhaps overemphasized the bareness of the Elizabethan stage, and we may forget that Elizabethan producers made adequate use of stage properties. Nevertheless we are correct in insisting that Elizabethan plays were written primarily for the ear rather than the eye. It was not always necessary to stick up a board reading "The Forest of Arden" or other locale. The poetry frequently conveyed the description adequately for the audience to comprehend both the place and the atmosphere that the dramatist wanted to suggest. In the age of Shakespeare poetic drama reached its greatest height, and one can speculate as to whether Shakespeare would have written so vividly if he could have left to the carpenter and the scene-painter the effects that he achieved in words.

EARLY COMMENT ON SHAKESPEARE

Shakespeare in his own time was a popular and respected playwright, but, as Professor Gerald E. Bentley points out in his excellent little volume, *Shakespeare: A Biographical Handbook,* his reputation was not so great as Ben Jonson's, and after his death it was eclipsed by the fame of Beaumont and Fletcher. By the time of the publication of the First Folio in 1623, however, one can discern evidence of his increasing reputation.

Significantly, it was Ben Jonson, the most learned of the dramatists, who wrote the finest tribute to Shakespeare in the prefatory matter in the First Folio. Other discriminating writers, including Milton, recognized Shakespeare's greatness, but it was not until the time of David Garrick, after the middle of the eighteenth century, that Shakespeare became the subject of idolatrous commentary. John Dryden, the great poet of the Restoration period, recognized Shakespeare's stature, but Dryden was far from an idolater. In general, the neoclassic poets and critics regarded Shakespeare as a genius in spite of his barbaric disregard of the classic unities and the rules of decorum in writing.

The most intelligent observations on Shakespeare in the Garrick period came from the pen of Dr. Samuel Johnson. Johnson's criticism is opinionated and in a few instances eccentric, but for the most part he writes with common sense and penetration. The great age of Shakespearean criticism came in the nineteenth century, but the early comments are significant as foreshadowing the growth of the poet's reputation.

The Droeshout Engraving of William Shakespeare

From the title page of the First Folio.

Comments in the Prefatory Material Printed in the First Folio of 1623

TO THE READER

This figure that thou here seest put,
It was for gentle Shakespeare cut;
Wherein the graver had a strife
With nature to outdo the life.
O, could he but have drawn his wit
As well in brass as he hath hit
His face, the print would then surpass
All that was ever writ in brass!
But since he cannot, reader, look
Not on his picture but his book.

B. I.
[Ben Jonson]

TO THE GREAT VARIETY OF READERS

From the most able to him that can but spell: there you are numbered. We had rather you were weighed. Especially when the fate of all books depends upon your capacities, and not of your heads alone but of your purses. Well! it is now public and you will stand for your privileges, we know, to read and censure. Do so, but buy it first. That doth best commend a book, the stationer says. Then, how odd soever your brains be or your wisdoms, make your license the same and spare not. Judge your six-penny'orth, your shilling's worth, your five shillings' worth at a time, or higher, so you rise to the just rates, and welcome; but whatever you do, buy. Censure will not drive a trade or make the jack go. And though you be a magistrate of wit and sit on the stage at Blackfriars or the Cockpit to arraign plays daily, know, these plays have had their trial already and stood out all appeals, and do now come forth quitted rather by a decree of court than any purchased letters of commendation.

It had been a thing, we confess, worthy to have been wished that the author himself had lived to have set forth and overseen his own writings; but since it hath been ordained otherwise, and he by death departed from that right, we pray you, do not envy his friends the office of their care and pain to have collected and published them; and so to have published them as where before you were abused with divers stolen and surreptitious copies, maimed and deformed by the frauds and stealths of injurious impostors that exposed them; even those are now offered to your view cured and perfect of their limbs, and all the rest, absolute in their numbers, as he conceived them. Who, as he was a happy imitator of nature, was a most gentle expresser of it. His mind and hand went together, and what he thought he uttered with that easiness that we have scarce received from him a blot in his papers. But it is not our province, who only gather his works and give them you, to praise him. It is yours that read him. And there we hope, to your divers capacities, you will find enough both to draw and hold you, for his wit can no more lie hid than it could be lost. Read him, therefore, and again and again; and if then you do not like him, surely you are in some manifest danger not to understand him. And so we leave you to other of his friends who, if you need, can be your guides; if you need them not, you can lead yourselves and others. And such readers we wish him.

JOHN HEMINGES
HENRY CONDELL

TO THE MOST NOBLE AND INCOMPARABLE PAIR OF BRETHREN, WILLIAM, EARL OF PEMBROKE, ETC., LORD CHAMBERLAIN TO THE KING'S MOST EXCELLENT MAJESTY, AND PHILIP, EARL OF MONTGOMERY, ETC., GENTLEMAN OF HIS MAJESTY'S BEDCHAMBER, BOTH KNIGHTS OF THE MOST NOBLE ORDER OF THE GARTER AND OUR SINGULAR GOOD LORDS.

Right Honorable:

Whilst we study to be thankful in our particular for the many favors we have received from your Lordships, we are fallen upon the ill fortune to mingle two the most diverse things that can be, fear and rashness—rashness in the enterprise and fear of the success. For when we value the places your Honors sustain, we cannot but know their dignity greater than to descend to the reading of these trifles; and, while we name them trifles, we have deprived ourselves of the defense of our dedication. But since your Lordships have been pleased to think these trifles something heretofore, and have prosecuted both them and their author living with so much favor, we hope that (they outliving him, and he not having the fate, common with some, to be executor to his own writings) you will use the like indulgence toward them you have done unto their parent. There is a great difference whether any book choose his patrons or find them: this hath done both. For, so much were your Lordships' likings of the several parts when they were acted, as before they were published the volume asked to be yours. We have but collected them and done an office to the dead to procure his orphans guardians, without ambition either of self-profit or fame, only to keep the memory of so worthy a friend and fellow alive as was our Shakespeare by humble offer of his plays to your most noble patronage. Wherein, as we have justly observed no man to come near your Lordships but with a kind of religious address, it hath been the height of our care who are the presenters to make the present worthy of your Honors by the perfection. But there we must also crave our abilities to be considered, my Lords. We cannot go beyond our own powers. Country hands reach forth milk, cream, fruits, or what they have; and many nations, we have heard, that had not gums and incense, obtained their requests with a leavened cake. It was no fault to approach their gods by what means they could. And the most, though meanest, of things are made more precious when they are dedicated to temples. In that name, therefore, we most humbly consecrate to your Honors these remains of your servant Shakespeare; that what delight is in them may be ever your Lordships', the reputation his, and the faults ours, if any be committed by a pair so careful to show their gratitude both to the living and the dead, as is

Your Lordships' most bounden

JOHN HEMINGES
HENRY CONDELL

TO THE MEMORY OF MY BELOVED, THE AUTHOR, MR. WILLIAM SHAKESPEARE, AND WHAT HE HATH LEFT US

To draw no envy, Shakespeare, on thy name,
Am I thus ample to thy book and fame;
While I confess thy writings to be such
As neither man nor Muse can praise too much;
'Tis true, and all men's suffrage. But these ways
Were not the paths I meant unto thy praise,
For seeliest ignorance on these may light,
Which when it sounds at best but echoes right;
Or blind affection, which doth ne'er advance
The truth, but gropes and urgeth all by chance;
Or crafty malice might pretend this praise,
And think to ruin where it seemed to raise.
These are as some infamous bawd or whore
Should praise a matron; what could hurt her more?
But thou art proof against them, and indeed
Above th' ill fortune of them, or the need.
I therefore will begin. Soul of the age!
The applause, delight, the wonder of our stage!
My Shakespeare, rise; I will not lodge thee by
Chaucer, or Spenser, or bid Beaumont lie
A little further to make thee a room;
Thou art a monument without a tomb,
And art alive still while thy book doth live,
And we have wits to read and praise to give.
That I not mix thee so, my brain excuses—
I mean with great but disproportioned Muses—
For if I thought my judgment were of years
I should commit thee surely with thy peers,
And tell how far thou didst our Lyly outshine,
Or sporting Kyd, or Marlowe's mighty line.
And though thou hadst small Latin and less Greek,
From thence to honor thee I would not seek
For names but call forth thund'ring Æschylus,
Euripides, and Sophocles to us,
Pacuvius, Accius, him of Cordova dead,
To life again, to hear thy buskin tread
And shake a stage; or, when thy socks were on,
Leave thee alone for the comparison
Of all that insolent Greece or haughty Rome
Sent forth, or since did from their ashes come.
Triumph, my Britain, thou hast one to show
To whom all scenes of Europe homage owe.
He was not of an age but for all time!
And all the Muses still were in their prime,
When like Apollo he came forth to warm
Our ears, or like a Mercury to charm!
Nature herself was proud of his designs
And joyed to wear the dressing of his lines,
Which were so richly spun, and woven so fit,
As, since, she will vouchsafe no other wit;
The merry Greek, tart Aristophanes,
Neat Terence, witty Plautus, now not please,
But antiquated and deserted lie
As they were not of Nature's family.
Yet must I not give Nature all; thy art,
My gentle Shakespeare, must enjoy a part;
For though the poet's matter nature be,
His art doth give the fashion; and that he
Who casts to write a living line must sweat—
Such as thine are—and strike the second heat
Upon the Muses' anvil, turn the same,
And himself with it, that he thinks to frame;
Or for the laurel he may gain a scorn,
For a good poet's made as well as born;
And such wert thou. Look how the father's face
Lives in his issue; even so the race
Of Shakespeare's mind and manners brightly shines
In his well-turned and true-filed lines,
In each of which he seems to shake a lance,
As brandished at the eyes of ignorance.
Sweet swan of Avon! what a sight it were
To see thee in our waters yet appear
And make those flights upon the banks of Thames
That so did take Eliza and our James!
But stay, I see thee in the hemisphere
Advanced and made a constellation there!
Shine forth, thou star of poets, and with rage
Or influence chide or cheer the drooping stage,
Which since thy flight from hence hath mourned like night,
And despairs day but for thy volume's light.

BEN JONSON

TO THE MEMORY OF THE DECEASED AUTHOR, MASTER W. SHAKESPEARE

Shakespeare, at length thy pious fellows give
The world thy works: thy works, by which outlive
Thy tomb thy name must. When that stone is rent,
And time dissolves thy Stratford monument,
Here we alive shall view thee still. This book,
When brass and marble fade, shall make thee look
Fresh to all ages; when posterity
Shall loathe what's new, think all is prodigy
That is not Shakespeare's, every line, each verse,
Here shall revive, redeem thee from thy hearse.
Nor fire nor cankering age, as Naso said
Of his, thy wit-fraught book shall once invade.
Nor shall I e'er believe, or think, thee dead,
Though missed, until our bankrout stage be sped
(Impossible) with some new strain t' outdo
Passions of Juliet and her Romeo;
Or till I hear a scene more nobly take,
Than when thy half-sword parleying Romans spake.
Till these, till any of thy volume's rest
Shall with more fire, more feeling, be expressed,
Be sure, our Shakespeare, thou canst never die,
But, crown'd with laurel, live eternally.

LEONARD DIGGES

Post-1623 Commentary

AN EPITAPH ON THE ADMIRABLE DRAMATIC POET, W. SHAKESPEARE

What needs my Shakespeare for his honored bones
The labor of an age in piled stones?
Or that his hallowed relics should be hid
Under a star-ypointing pyramid?
Dear son of Memory, great heir of Fame,
What needst thou such dull witness of thy name?
Thou in our wonder and astonishment
Hast built thyself a lasting monument.
For whilst, to the shame of slow-endeavoring art,
Thy easy numbers flow, and that each part
Hath from the leaves of thy unvalued book
Those Delphic lines with deep impression took,
Then thou, our fancy of herself bereaving,
Dost make us marble with too much conceiving,
And, so sepulchered, in such pomp dost lie
That kings for such a tomb would wish to die.

[JOHN MILTON, a prefatory poem in the Second Folio of Shakespeare's *Works,* 1632. The poem was written in 1630.]

DE SHAKESPEARE NOSTRATI

I remember the players have often mentioned it as an honor to Shakespeare that in his writing, whatsoever he penned, he never blotted out line. My answer hath been, "Would he had blotted a thousand," which they thought a malevolent speech. I had not told posterity this but for their ignorance who choose that circumstance to commend their friend by wherein he most faulted, and to justify mine own candor, for I loved the man and do honor his memory, on this side idolatry, as much as any. He was, indeed, honest and of an open and free nature; had an excellent fancy, brave notions, and gentle expressions, wherein he flowed with that facility that sometimes it was necessary he should be stopped. *Sufflaminandus erat,* as Augustus said of Haterius. His wit was in his own power; would the rule of it had been so too. Many times he fell into those things could not escape laughter, as when he said in the person of Cæsar, one speaking to him: "Cæsar, thou dost me wrong," he replied, "Cæsar did never wrong but with just cause"; and suchlike, which were ridiculous. But he redeemed his vices with his virtues. There was ever more in him to be praised than to be pardoned.

[BEN JONSON, *Timber: or, Discoveries; Made upon Men and Matter,* 1641.]

AUBREY ON SHAKESPEARE

Master William Shakespeare was born at Stratford-upon-Avon, in the county of Warwick. His father was a butcher, and I have been told heretofore by some of the neighbors that when he was a boy he exercised his father's trade, but when he killed a calf he would do it in a high style and make a speech. There was at that time another butcher's son in this town that was held not at all inferior to him for a natural wit, his acquaintance and coetanean, but died young. This William, being inclined naturally to poetry and acting, came to London, I guess, about 18, and was an actor at one of the playhouses and did act exceedingly well. (Now Ben Jonson was never a good actor but an excellent instructor.) He began early to make essays at dramatic poetry, which at that time was very low; and his plays took well. He was a handsome, well-shaped man, very good company, and of a very ready and pleasant smooth wit. The humor of ——— the constable in *Midsummer Night's Dream* he happened to take at Grendon in Bucks (I think it was Midsummer Night that he happened to lie there), which is the road from London to Stratford, and there was living that constable about 1642 when I first came to Oxford. Master Josias Howe is of that parish and knew him. Ben Jonson and he did gather humors of men daily wherever they came. One time, as he was at the tavern at Stratford-super-Avon, one Combes, an old rich usurer, was to be buried. He makes there this extemporary epitaph:

Ten in the hundred the devil allows,
But Combes will have twelve, he swears and vows:
If anyone asks who lies in this tomb:
"Ho!" quoth the devil, "'tis my John o' Combe."

He was wont to go to his native country once a year. I think I have been told that he left two or three hundred pounds per annum there and thereabout to a sister. (Vide his epitaph in Dugdale's Warwickshire.) I have heard Sir William Davenant and Master Thomas Shadwell (who is counted the best comedian we have now) say that he had a most prodigious wit, and did admire his natural parts beyond all other dramatical writers. He was wont to say that he never blotted out a line in his life. . . . Said Ben Jonson, "I wish he had blotted out a thousand." His comedies will remain wit as long as the English tongue is understood, for that he handles *mores hominum.* Now our present writers reflect so much upon particular persons and coxcombities that twenty years hence they will not be understood. Though, as Ben Jonson says of him, that he had but little Latin and less Greek, he understood Latin pretty well, for he had been in his younger years a schoolmaster in the country.

[JOHN AUBREY, *Brief Lives,* written *ca.* 1681.]

THE REVEREND JOHN WARD COMMENTS ON SHAKESPEARE

Shakespeare had but two daughters, one whereof Master Hall, the physician, married, and by her had one daughter, to wit, the Lady Bernard of Abingdon. . . .

I have heard that Master Shakespeare was a natural wit, without any art at all. He frequented the plays all his younger time, but in his elder days lived at Stratford and supplied the stage with two plays every year, and for that had an allowance so large that he spent at the rate of a thousand pounds a year, as I have heard. . . .

Shakespeare, Drayton, and Ben Jonson had a merry meeting, and it seems drank too hard, for Shakespeare died of a fever there contracted.

[From JOHN WARD'S "Notebooks," now preserved in the Folger Shakespeare Library. The excerpts date from sometime between 1661 and 1663.]

WILLIAM SHAKESPEARE OF STRATFORD

William Shakespeare was born at Stratford-on-Avon in this county, in whom three eminent poets may seem in some sort to be compounded:

1. Martial, in the warlike sound of his surname (whence some may conjecture him of a military extraction) *Hasti-vibrans,* or Shakespeare;

2. Ovid, the most natural and witty of all poets; and hence it was that Queen Elizabeth, coming into a grammar school, made this extemporary verse:

"Persius a crab-staff, bawdy Martial,
Ovid a fine wag."

3. Plautus, who was an exact comedian yet never any scholar, as our Shakespeare (if alive) would confess himself. Add to all these that though his genius generally was jocular and inclining him to festivity, yet he could (when so disposed) be solemn and serious, as appears by his tragedies; so that Heraclitus himself (I mean if secret and unseen) might afford to smile at his comedies, they were so merry; and Democritus scarce forbear to sigh at his tragedies, they were so mournful.

He was an eminent instance of the truth of that rule, *Poeta non fit, sed nascitur* (one is not made but born a poet). Indeed his learning was very little; so that, as Cornish diamonds are not polished by any lapidary but are pointed and smoothed even as they are taken out of the earth, so nature itself was all the art which was used upon him.

Many were the wit-combats betwixt him and Ben Jonson; which two I behold like a Spanish great galleon and an English man-of-war; Master Jonson (like the former) was built far higher in learning; solid, but slow in his performances. Shakespeare, with the English man-of-war, lesser in bulk, but lighter in sailing, could turn with all tides, tack about, and take advantage of all winds by the quickness of his wit and invention. He died *anno Domini* 16——, and was buried at Stratford-upon-Avon, the town of his nativity.

[THOMAS FULLER, *The History of the Worthies of England,* 1662.]

DRYDEN'S PRAISE

To begin then with Shakespeare: he was the man who of all modern and, perhaps, ancient poets had the largest and most comprehensive soul. All the images of nature were still present to him and he drew them not laboriously but luckily. When he describes anything you more than see it—you feel it too. Those who accuse him to have wanted learning give him the greater commendation. He was naturally learned; he needed not the spectacles of books to read Nature; he looked inwards and found her there. I cannot say he is everywhere alike; were he so, I should do him injury to compare him with the greatest of mankind. He is many times flat, insipid; his comic wit degenerating into clenches, his serious swelling into bombast. But he is always great when some great occasion is presented to him. No man can say he ever had a fit subject for his wit and did not then raise himself as high above the rest of poets, *Quantum lenta solent inter viburna cupressi.*

The consideration of this made Mr. Hales of Eton say that there was no subject of which any poet ever writ but he would produce it much better treated of in Shakespeare; and however others are now generally preferred before him, yet the age wherein he lived, which had contemporaries with him Fletcher and Jonson, never equaled them to him in their esteem. And in the last king's court when Ben's reputation was at highest, Sir John Suckling, and with him the greater part of the courtiers, set our Shakespeare far above him.

. . . .

Shakespeare was the Homer or father of our dramatic poets; Jonson was the Vergil—the pattern of elaborate writing; I admire him, but I love Shakespeare.

[JOHN DRYDEN, *Of Dramatic Poesy, An Essay,* 1668.]

THE DUCHESS OF NEWCASTLE'S OPINION OF SHAKESPEARE

Madam:

I wonder how that person you mention in your letter could either have the conscience or confidence to dispraise Shakespeare's plays as to say they were made up only with clowns, fools, watchmen, and the like. But to answer that person—though Shakespeare's wit will answer for himself—I say that it seems by his judging or censuring he understands not plays or wit, for to express properly, rightly, usually, and naturally a clown's or fool's humor, expressions, phrases, garbs, manners, actions, words, and course of life is as witty, wise, judicious, ingenious, and observing as to write and express the expressions, phrases, garbs, manners, actions, words, and course of life of kings and princes, and to express naturally to the life a mean country wench as a great lady, a courtesan as a chaste woman, a madman as a man in his right reason and senses, a drunkard as a sober man, a knave as an honest man, and so a clown as a well-bred man, and a fool as a wise man. Nay, it expresses and declares a greater wit to express and deliver to posterity the extravagancies of madness, the subtlety of knaves, the ignorance of clowns, and the simplicity of naturals, or the craft of feigned fools, than to express regularities, plain honesty, courtly garbs, or sensible discourses, for 'tis harder to express nonsense than sense and ordinary conversations than that which is unusual, and 'tis harder and requires more wit to express a jester than a grave statesman. Yet Shakespeare did not want wit to express to the life all sorts of persons of what quality, profession, degree, breeding, or birth soever, nor did he want wit to express the diverse and different humors or natures or several passions in mankind; and so well he hath expressed in his plays all sorts of persons as one would think he had been transformed into every one of those persons he hath described, and as sometimes one would think he was really himself the clown or jester he feigns, so one would think he was also the king and privy councilor; also as one would think he were really the coward he feigns, so one would think he were the most valiant and experienced soldier. Who would not think he had been such a man as his Sir John Falstaff? and who would not think he had been Harry the Fifth? And certainly Julius Cæsar, Augustus Cæsar, and Antonius did never really act their parts better—if so well—as he hath described them, and I believe that Antonius and Brutus did not speak better to the people than he hath feigned them. Nay, one would think that he had been metamorphosed from a man to a woman, for who could describe Cleopatra better than he hath done and many other females of his own creating, as Nan Page, Mrs. Page, Mrs. Ford, the Doctor's maid, Beatrice, Mrs. Quickly, Doll Tearsheet, and others too many to relate? And in his tragic vein he presents passions so naturally and misfortunes so probably as he pierces the souls of his readers with such a true sense and feeling thereof that it forces tears through their eyes and almost persuades them they are really actors, or at least present at those tragedies. Who would not swear he had been a noble lover that could woo so well? And there is not any person he hath described in his book but his readers might think they were well acquainted with them.

Indeed, Shakespeare had a clear judgment, a quick wit, a spreading fancy, a subtle observation, a deep apprehension, and a most eloquent elocution. Truly, he was a natural orator as well as a natural poet, and he was not an orator to speak well only on some subjects, as lawyers who can make eloquent orations at the bar and plead subtly and wittily in law cases, or divines that can preach eloquent sermons or dispute subtly and wittily in theology, but take them from that and put them to other subjects and they will be to seek. But Shakespeare's wit and eloquence was general for and upon all subjects. He rather wanted subjects for his wit and eloquence to work on, for which he was forced to take some of his plots out of history—where he only took the bare designs, the wit and language being all his own—and so much he had above others that those who writ after him were forced to borrow of him, or rather to steal from him. I could mention divers places that others of our famous poets have borrowed or stolen, but lest I should discover the persons I will not mention the places or parts but leave it to those that read his plays and others to find them out. I should not have needed to write this to you, for his works would have declared the same truth. But I believe those that dispraised his plays dispraised them more out of envy than simplicity or ignorance. . . . But leaving Shakespeare's works to their own defense and his detractors to their envy, and you to your better employments than reading my letter, I rest

Madam, your faithful friend and humble servant.

[*CCXI Sociable Letters,* by MARGARET CAVENDISH, Marchioness, later Duchess of Newcastle, 1664.]

COMMENTS BY SHAKESPEARE'S FIRST EDITOR, NICHOLAS ROWE

He was the son of Mr. John Shakespeare, and was born at Stratford-upon-Avon, in Warwickshire, in April, 1564. His family, as appears by the Register and public writings relating to that town, were of good figure and fashion there, and are mentioned as gentlemen. His father, who was a considerable dealer in wool, had so large a family, ten children in all, that though he was his eldest son he could give him no better education than his own employment. He had bred him, 'tis true, for some time at a free school, where 'tis probable he acquired that little Latin he was master of. But the narrowness of his circumstances, and the want of his assistance at home, forced his father to withdraw him from thence, and unhappily prevented his further proficiency in that language. . . .

Upon his leaving school, he seems to have given entirely into that way of living which his father proposed to him; and in order to settle in the world after a family manner he thought fit to marry while he was yet very young. His wife was the daughter of one Hathaway, said to have been a substantial yeoman in the neighborhood of Stratford. In this kind of settlement he continued for some time, till an extravagance that he was guilty of forced him both out of his country and that way of living which he had taken up; and though it seemed at first to be a blemish upon his good manners, and a misfortune to him, yet it afterwards happily proved the occasion of exerting one of the greatest geniuses that ever was known in dramatic poetry. He had, by a misfortune common enough to young fellows, fallen into ill company; and amongst them some that made a frequent practice of deer-stealing engaged him with them more than once in robbing a park that belonged to Sir Thomas Lucy of Charlecote, near Stratford. For this he was prosecuted by that gentleman, as he thought, somewhat too severely; and in order to revenge that ill usage he made a ballad upon him. And though this, probably the first essay of his poetry, be lost, yet it is said to have been so very bitter that it redoubled the prosecution against him to that degree that he was obliged to leave his business and family in Warwickshire for some time and shelter himself in London.

It is at this time, and upon this accident, that he is said to have made his first acquaintance in the playhouse. He was received into the company then in being at first in a very mean rank; but his admirable wit and the natural turn of it to the stage soon distinguished him, if not as an extraordinary actor, yet as an excellent writer. His name is printed, as the custom was in those times, amongst those of the other players before some old plays, but without any particular account of what sort of parts he used to play; and though I have inquired, I could never meet with any further account of him this way than that the top of his performance was the Ghost in his own *Hamlet*. . . .

Besides the advantages of his wit, he was in himself a good-natured man, of great sweetness in his manners, and a most agreeable companion; so that it is no wonder if with so many good qualities he made himself acquainted with the best conversations of those times. Queen Elizabeth had several of his plays acted before her and without doubt gave him many gracious marks of her favor. It is that maiden Princess, plainly, whom he intends by

> A fair Vestal, throned by the West.
>
> *Midsummer Night's Dream.*

And that whole passage is a compliment very properly brought in, and very handsomely applied to her. She was so well pleased with that admirable character of Falstaff in the two parts of *Henry the Fourth* that she commanded him to continue it for one play more, and to show him in love. This is said to be the occasion of his writing *The Merry Wives of Windsor*. How well she was obeyed, the play itself is an admirable proof. . . .

He had the honor to meet with many great and uncommon marks of favor and friendship from the Earl of Southampton, famous in the histories of that time for his friendship to the unfortunate Earl of Essex. It was to that noble Lord that he dedicated *Venus and Adonis,* the only piece of his poetry which he ever published himself, though many of his plays were surreptitiously and lamely printed in his lifetime. There is one instance so singular in the magnificence of this patron of Shakespeare's that if I had not been assured that the story was handed down by Sir William Davenant, who was probably very well acquainted with his affairs, I should not have ventured to have inserted—that my Lord Southampton at one time gave him a thousand pounds to enable him to go through with a purchase which he heard he had a mind to. . . .

His acquaintance with Ben Jonson began with a remarkable piece of humanity and good nature: Mr. Jonson, who was at that time altogether unknown to the world, had offered one of his plays to the players in order to have it acted; and the persons into whose hands it was put, after having turned it carelessly and superciliously over, were just upon returning it to him with an ill-natured answer that it would be of no service to their company, when Shakespeare luckily cast his eye upon it and found something so well in it as to engage him first to read it through and afterwards to recommend Mr. Jonson and his writings to the public. After this they were professed friends. . . .

Jonson was certainly a very good scholar, and in that had the advantage of Shakespeare; though at the same time I believe it must be allowed that what Nature gave the latter was more than a balance for what books had given the former. . . .

I cannot leave *Hamlet* without taking notice of the advantage with which we have seen this masterpiece of Shakespeare distinguish itself upon the stage by Mr. Betterton's fine performance of that part—a man who, though he had no other good qualities, as he has a great many, must have made his way into the esteem of all men of letters by this only excellency. . . .

I must own a particular obligation to him for the most considerable part of the passages relating to his life which I have here transmitted to the public; his veneration for the memory of Shakespeare having engaged him to make a journey into Warwickshire on purpose to gather up what remains he could of a name for which he had so great a value. . . .

The latter part of his life was spent, as all men of

good sense will wish theirs may be, in ease, retirement, and the conversation of his friends. He had the good fortune to gather an estate equal to his occasion, and, in that, to his wish; and is said to have spent some years before his death at his native Stratford. His pleasurable wit and good nature engaged him in the acquaintance, and entitled him to the friendship, of the gentlemen of the neighborhood. . . .

He died in the fifty-third year of his age and was buried on the north side of the chancel in the great church at Stratford, where a monument, as engraved in the plate, is placed in the wall. . . .

He had three daughters [*sic!*], of which two lived to be married: Judith, the elder, to one Mr. Thomas Quiney, by whom she had three sons who all died without children; and Susanna, who was his favorite, to Dr. John Hall, a physician of good reputation in that country. She left one child only, a daughter, who was married first to Thomas Nash, Esq., and afterwards to Sir John Bernard of Abingdon, but died likewise without issue.

This is what I could learn of any note, either relating to himself or family. The character of the man is best seen in his writings. . . .

[From introductory material in Volume 1 of NICHOLAS ROWE's edition of Shakespeare's *Works,* 1709.]

ALEXANDER POPE'S VIEWS ON SHAKESPEARE

It is not my design to enter into a criticism upon this author, though to do it effectually and not superficially would be the best occasion that any just writer could take to form the judgment and taste of our nation. For of all English poets Shakespeare must be confessed to be the fairest and fullest subject for criticism, and to afford the most numerous as well as most conspicuous instances both of beauties and faults of all sorts. But this far exceeds the bounds of a preface, the business of which is only to give an account of the fate of his works and the disadvantages under which they have been transmitted to us. We shall hereby extenuate many faults which are his and clear him from the imputation of many which are not—a design which, though it can be no guide to future critics to do him justice in one way, will at least be sufficient to prevent their doing him an injustice in the other.

I cannot, however, but mention some of his principal and characteristic excellencies for which (notwithstanding his defects) he is justly and universally elevated above all other dramatic writers. Not that this is the proper place of praising him, but because I would not omit any occasion of doing it.

If ever any author deserved the name of an original, it was Shakespeare. Homer himself drew not his art so immediately from the fountains of Nature; it proceeded through Egyptian strainers and channels and came to him not without some tincture of the learning or some cast of the models of those before him. The poetry of Shakespeare was inspiration indeed. He is not so much an imitator as an instrument of Nature, and 'tis not so just to say that he speaks from her as that she speaks through him.

His characters are so much Nature herself that 'tis a sort of injury to call them by so distant a name as copies of her. Those of other poets have a constant resemblance, which shows that they received them from one another and were but multipliers of the same image; each picture, like a mock rainbow, is but the reflection of a reflection. But every single character in Shakespeare is as much an individual as those in life itself; it is as impossible to find any two alike, and such as from their relation or affinity in any respect appear most to be twins will upon comparison be found remarkably distinct. To this life and variety of character we must add the wonderful preservation of it, which is such throughout his plays that had all the speeches been printed without the very names of the persons, I believe one might have applied them with certainty to every speaker.

The power over our passions was never possessed in a more eminent degree or displayed in so different instances. Yet all along there is seen no labor, no pains to raise them, no preparation to guide our guess to the effect or be perceived to lead toward it. But the heart swells and the tears burst out just at the proper places. We are surprised the moment we weep, and yet upon reflection find the passion so just that we should be surprised if we had not wept, and wept at that very moment.

How astonishing is it, again, that the passions directly opposite to these, laughter and spleen, are no less at his command! that he is not more a master of the great than of the ridiculous in human nature, of our noblest tendernesses than of our vainest foibles, of our strongest emotions than of our idlest sensations!

Nor does he only excel in the passions: in the coolness of reflection and reasoning he is full as admirable. His sentiments are not only in general the most pertinent and judicious upon every subject, but by a talent very peculiar—something between penetration and felicity—he hits upon that particular point on which the bent of each argument turns or the force of each motive depends. This is perfectly amazing from a man of no education or experience in those great and public scenes of life which are usually the subject of his thoughts. So that he seems to have known the world by intuition, to have looked through human nature at one glance, and to be the only author that gives ground for a very new opinion, that the philosopher and even the man of the world may be born as well as the poet.

It must be owned that with all these great excellencies, he has almost as great defects; and that as he has certainly written better, so he has perhaps written worse than any other. But I think I can in some measure account for these defects from several causes and accidents, without which it is hard to imagine that so large and so enlightened a mind could ever have been susceptible of them. That all these contingencies should unite to his disadvantage seems to me almost as singularly unlucky as that so many various—nay, contrary—talents should meet in one man was happy and extraordinary.

It must be allowed that stage poetry of all other is more particularly leveled to please the populace and its success more immediately depending upon the common suffrage. One cannot therefore wonder if Shakespeare, having at his first appearance no other aim in his writings than to procure a subsistence, directed his endeavors solely to hit the taste and humor that then prevailed. The audience was generally composed of the meaner sort of people, and therefore the images of life were to be drawn from those of their own rank. Accordingly we find that not our author's only but almost all the old comedies have their scene among tradesmen and mechanics, and even their historical plays strictly follow the common old stories or vulgar traditions of that kind of people. In tragedy nothing was so sure to surprise and cause admiration as the most strange, unexpected, and, consequently, most unnatural events and incidents; the most exaggerated thoughts; the most verbose and bombast expression; the most pompous rhymes and thundering versification. In comedy nothing was so sure to please as mean buffoonery, vile ribaldry, and unmannerly jests of fools and clowns. Yet even in these our author's wit buoys up and is borne above his subject. His genius in those low parts is like some prince of a romance in the disguise of a shepherd or peasant: a certain greatness and spirit now and then break out which manifest his higher extraction and qualities.

It may be added that not only the common audience had no notion of the rules of writing, but few even of the better sort piqued themselves upon any great degree of knowledge or nicety that way, till Ben Jonson, getting possession of the stage, brought critical learning into vogue. And that this was not done without difficulty may appear from those frequent lessons—and, indeed, almost declamations—which he was forced to prefix to his first plays and put into the mouth of his actors, the *grex,* chorus, etc., to remove the prejudices and inform the judgment of his hearers. Till then our authors had no thoughts of writing on the model of the ancients; their tragedies were only histories in dialogue, and their comedies followed the thread of any novel as they found it no less implicitly than if it had been true history.

To judge, therefore, of Shakespeare by Aristotle's rules is like trying a man by the laws of one country who acted under those of another. He writ to the people, and writ at first without patronage from the better sort and therefore without aims of pleasing them; without assistance or advice from the learned, as without the advantage of education or acquaintance among them; without that knowledge of the best models, the ancients, to inspire him with an emulation of them; in a word, without any views of reputation and of what poets are pleased to call immortality: some or all of which have encouraged the vanity or animated the ambition of other writers.

Yet it must be observed that when his performances had merited the protection of his prince, and when the encouragement of the court had succeeded to that of the town, the works of his riper years are manifestly raised above those of his former. The dates of his plays sufficiently evidence that his productions improved in proportion to the respect he had for his auditors. And I make no doubt this observation would be found true in every instance were but editions extant from which we might learn the exact time when every piece was composed and whether writ for the town or the court.

Another cause—and no less strong than the former—may be deduced from our author's being a player and forming himself first upon the judgments of that body of men whereof he was a member. They have ever had a standard to themselves upon other principles than those of Aristotle. As they live by the majority, they know no rule but that of pleasing the present humor and complying with the wit in fashion, a consideration which brings all their judgment to a short point. Players are just such judges of what is right as tailors are of what is graceful. And in this view it will be but fair to allow that most of our author's faults are less to be ascribed to his wrong judgment as a poet than to his right judgment as a player. . . .

But as to his want of learning it may be necessary to say something more. There is certainly a vast difference between learning and languages. How far he was ignorant of the latter, I cannot determine, but 'tis plain he had much reading at least, if they will not call it learning. Nor is it any great matter, if a man has knowledge, whether he has it from one language or from another. Nothing is more evident than that he had a taste of natural philosophy, mechanics, ancient and modern history, poetical learning, and mythology. We find him very knowing in the customs, rites, and manners of antiquity. . . .

I will conclude by saying of Shakespeare that with all his faults, and with all the irregularity of his drama, one may look upon his works in comparison of those that are more finished and regular as upon an ancient majestic piece of Gothic architecture compared with a neat modern building: the latter is more elegant and glaring, but the former is more strong and more solemn. It must be allowed that in one of these there are materials enough to make many of the other. It has much the greater variety and much the nobler apartments, though we are often conducted to them by dark, odd, and uncouth passages. Nor does the whole fail to strike us with greater reverence, though many of the parts are childish, ill placed, and unequal to its grandeur.

[Preface to ALEXANDER POPE, *The Works of Shakespeare,* 1725.]

DR. SAMUEL JOHNSON ON SHAKESPEARE

. . . The poet of whose works I have undertaken the revision may now begin to assume the dignity of an ancient and claim the privilege of established fame and prescriptive veneration. He has long outlived his century, the term commonly fixed as the test of literary merit. Whatever advantages he might once derive from personal allusions, local customs, or temporary opinions have for many years been lost; and every topic of merriment or motive of sorrow which the modes of artificial life afforded him now only obscure the scenes which they once illuminated. The effects of favor and competition are at an end; the tradition of his friendships and his enmities has perished; his works support no opinion with arguments nor supply any faction with invectives; they can neither indulge vanity nor gratify malignity, but are read without any other reason than the desire of pleasure, and are therefore praised only as pleasure is obtained; yet, thus unassisted by interest or passion, they have passed through variations of taste and changes of manners, and as they devolved from one generation to another have received new honors at every transmission.

But because human judgment, though it be gradually gaining upon certainty, never becomes infallible, and approbation, though long continued, may yet be only the approbation of prejudice or fashion, it is proper to inquire by what peculiarities of excellence Shakespeare has gained and kept the favor of his countrymen.

Nothing can please many and please long but just representations of general nature. Particular manners can be known to few, and therefore few only can judge how nearly they are copied. The irregular combinations of fanciful invention may delight awhile, by that novelty of which the common satiety of life sends us all in quest, but the pleasures of sudden wonder are soon exhausted and the mind can only repose on the stability of truth.

Shakespeare is above all writers—at least above all modern writers—the poet of nature; the poet that holds up to his readers a faithful mirror of manners and of life. His characters are not modified by the customs of particular places unpracticed by the rest of the world, by the peculiarities of studies or professions which can operate but upon small numbers, or by the accidents of transient fashions or temporary opinions; they are the genuine progeny of common humanity such as the world will always supply and observation will always find. His persons act and speak by the influence of those general passions and principles by which all minds are agitated and the whole system of life is continued in motion. In the writings of other poets a character is too often an individual; in those of Shakespeare it is commonly a species.

It is from this wide extension of design that so much instruction is derived. It is this which fills the plays of Shakespeare with practical axioms and domestic wisdom. It was said of Euripides that every verse was a precept, and it may be said of Shakespeare that from his works may be collected a system of civil and economical prudence. Yet his real power is not shown in the splendor of particular passages but by the progress of his fable and the tenor of his dialogue, and he that tries to recommend him by select quotations will succeed like the pedant in Hierocles who, when he offered his house to sale, carried a brick in his pocket as a specimen.

It will not easily be imagined how much Shakespeare excels in accommodating his sentiments to real life but by comparing him with other authors. It was observed of the ancient schools of declamation that the more diligently they were frequented the more was the student disqualified for the world, because he found nothing there which he should ever meet in any other place. The same remark may be applied to every stage but that of Shakespeare. The theatre, when it is under any other direction, is peopled by such characters as were never seen, conversing in a language which was never heard, upon topics which will never arise in the commerce of mankind. But the dialogue of this author is often so evidently determined by the incident which produces it, and is pursued with so much ease and simplicity, that it seems scarcely to claim the merit of fiction but to have been gleaned by diligent selection out of common conversation and common occurrences. . . .

Other dramatists can only gain attention by hyperbolical or aggravated characters, by fabulous and unexampled excellence or depravity, as the writers of barbarous romances invigorated the reader by a giant and a dwarf; and he that should form his expectations of human affairs from the play or from the tale would be equally deceived. Shakespeare has no heroes; his scenes are occupied only by men who act and speak as the reader thinks that he should himself have spoken or acted on the same occasion; even where the agency is supernatural the dialogue is level with life. Other writers disguise the most natural passions and most frequent incidents so that he who contemplates them in the book will not know them in the world. Shakespeare approximates the remote and familiarizes the wonderful. The event which he represents will not happen, but, if it were possible, its effects would probably be such as he has assigned; and it may be said that he has not only shown human nature as it acts in real exigencies but as it would be found in trials to which it cannot be exposed.

This, therefore, is the praise of Shakespeare: that his drama is the mirror of life; that he who has mazed his imagination in following the phantoms which other writers raise up before him may here be cured of his delirious ecstasies by reading human sentiments in human language, by scenes from which a hermit may estimate the transactions of the world and a confessor predict the progress of the passions.

His adherence to general nature has exposed him to the censure of critics who form their judgments upon narrower principles. Dennis and Rhymer think his Romans not sufficiently Roman, and Voltaire censures his kings as not completely royal. Dennis is offended that Menenius, a senator of Rome, should play the buffoon, and Voltaire perhaps thinks decency violated when the Danish usurper is represented as a drunkard. But Shakespeare always makes nature predominate over accident; and if he preserves the essential character is not very careful of distinctions superinduced and adventitious. His story requires Romans or kings, but he thinks only on men. He knew that Rome like every other city had men of all dispositions, and, wanting a buffoon, he went into the senate house for that which the senate house would certainly have afforded him. He was inclined to show an usurper and a murderer not only odious but despicable; he therefore added drunkenness to his other qualities, knowing that kings love wine like other men and that wine exerts its natural power upon kings. These are the petty cavils of petty minds; a poet overlooks the casual distinction of country and condition as a painter satisfied with the figure neglects the drapery.

The censure which he has incurred by mixing comic and tragic scenes, as it extends to all his works, deserves more consideration. Let the fact be first stated and then examined.

Shakespeare's plays are not in the rigorous and critical sense either tragedies or comedies but compositions of a distinct kind; exhibiting the real state of sublunary nature which partakes of good and evil, joy and sorrow, mingled with endless variety of proportion and innumerable modes of combination, and expressing the course of the world in which the loss of one is the gain of another; in which at the same time the reveler is hasting to his wine and the mourner burying his friend; in which the malignity of one is sometimes defeated by the frolic of another; and many mischiefs and many benefits are done and hindered without design.

Out of this chaos of mingled purposes and casualties the ancient poets, according to the laws which custom had prescribed, selected some the crimes of men and some their absurdities, some the momentous vicissitudes of life and some the lighter occurrences, some the terrors of distress and some the gaieties of prosperity. Thus arose the two modes of imitation known by the names of tragedy and comedy—compositions intended to promote different ends by contrary means and considered as so little allied that I do not recollect among the Greeks or Romans a single writer who attemped both.

Shakespeare has united the powers of exciting laughter and sorrow not only in one mind but in one composition. Almost all his plays are divided between serious and ludicrous characters, and in the successive evolutions of the design sometimes produce seriousness and sorrow and sometimes levity and laughter.

That this is a practice contrary to the rules of criticism will be readily allowed, but there is always an appeal open from criticism to nature. The end of writing is to instruct; the end of poetry is to instruct by pleasing. That the mingled drama may convey all the instruction of tragedy or comedy cannot be denied, because it includes both in its alterations of exhibition and approaches nearer than either to the appearance of life by showing how great machinations and slender designs may promote or obviate one another and the high and the low co-operate in the general system by unavoidable concatenation.

It is objected that by this change of scenes the passions are interrupted in their progression, and that the principal event, being not advanced by a due gradation of preparatory incidents, wants at last the power to move which constitutes the perfection of dramatic poetry. This reasoning is so specious that it is received as true even by those who in daily experience feel it to be false. The interchanges of mingled scenes seldom fail to produce the intended vicissitudes of passion. Fiction cannot move so much but that the attention may be easily transferred; and though it must be allowed that pleasing melancholy be sometimes interrupted by unwelcome levity, yet let it be considered likewise that melancholy is often not pleasing and that the disturbance of one man may be the relief of another, that different auditors have different habitudes, and that, upon the whole, all pleasure consists in variety.

The players, who in their edition divided our author's works into comedies, histories, and tragedies, seem not to have distinguished the three kinds by any very exact or definite ideas. . . .

Through all these denominations of the drama Shakespeare's mode of composition is the same: an interchange of seriousness and merriment by which the mind is softened at one time and exhilarated at another. But whatever be his purpose, whether to gladden or depress, or to conduct the story without vehemence or emotion through tracts of easy and familiar dialogue, he never fails to attain his purpose; as he commands us, we laugh or mourn or sit silent with quiet expectation in tranquillity without indifference.

When Shakespeare's plan is understood, most of the criticisms of Rhymer and Voltaire vanish away. The play of *Hamlet* is opened without impropriety by two sentinels; Iago bellows at Brabantio's window without injury to the scheme of the play, though in terms which a modern audience would not easily endure; the character of Polonius is seasonable and useful; and the Gravediggers themselves may be heard with applause.

Shakespeare engaged in dramatic poetry with the world open before him; the rules of the ancients were yet known to few; the public judgment was unformed; he had no example of such fame as might force him upon imitation nor critics of such authority as might restrain his extravagance. He therefore indulged his natural disposition, and his disposition, as Rhymer has remarked, led him to comedy. In tragedy he often writes with great appearance of toil and study what is written at last with little felicity; but in his comic scenes he seems to produce without labor what no labor can improve. In tragedy he is always struggling after some occasion to be comic, but in comedy he seems to repose or to luxuriate, as in a mode of thinking congenial to his nature. In his tragic scenes there is always something wanting, but his comedy often surpasses expectation or desire. His comedy pleases by the thoughts and the language, and his tragedy for the greater part by incident and action. His tragedy seems to be skill, his comedy to be instinct.

The force of his comic scenes has suffered little diminution from the changes made by a century and a half in manners or in words. As his personages act upon principles arising from genuine passion very little modified by particular forms, their pleasures and vexations are communicable to all times and to all places; they are natural and therefore durable; the adventitious peculiarities of personal habits are only superficial dyes, bright and pleasing for a little while, yet soon fading to a dim tinct without any remains of former luster; but the discriminations of true passion are the colors of nature; they pervade the whole mass and can only perish with the body that exhibits them. . . .

Shakespeare with his excellencies has likewise faults, and faults sufficient to obscure and overwhelm any other merit. I shall show them in the proportion in which they appear to me without envious malignity or superstitious veneration. No question can be more innocently discussed than a dead poet's pretensions to renown, and little regard is due to that bigotry which sets candor higher than truth.

His first defect is that to which may be imputed most of the evil in books or in men. He sacrifices virtue to convenience, and is so much more careful to please than to instruct that he seems to write without any moral purpose. From his writings, indeed, a system of social duty may be selected, for he that thinks reasonably must think morally; but his precepts and axioms drop casually from him; he makes no just distribution of good or evil, nor is always careful to show in the virtuous a disapprobation of the wicked; he carries his persons indifferently through right and wrong, and at the close dismisses them without further care and leaves their examples to operate by chance. This fault the barbarity of his age cannot extenuate, for it is always a writer's duty to make the world better, and justice is a virtue independent on time or place.

The plots are often so loosely formed that a very slight consideration may improve them, and so carelessly pursued that he seems not always fully to comprehend his own design. He omits opportunities of instructing or delighting which the train of his story seems to force upon him, and apparently rejects those exhibitions which would be more affecting for the sake of those which are more easy.

It may be observed that in many of his plays the latter part is evidently neglected. When he found himself near the end of his work and in view of his reward, he shortened the labor to snatch the profit. He therefore remits his efforts where he should most vigorously exert them, and his catastrophe is improbably produced or imperfectly represented.

He had no regard to distinction of time or place, but gives to one age or nation, without scruple, the customs, institutions, and opinions of another at the expense not only of likelihood but of possibility. These faults Pope has endeavored with more zeal than judgment to transfer to his imagined interpolaters. We need not wonder to find Hector quoting Aristotle when we see the loves of Theseus and Hippolyta combined with the Gothic mythology of fairies. Shakespeare, indeed, was not the only violator of chronology, for in the same age Sidney, who wanted not the advantages of learning, has in his *Arcadia* confounded the pastoral with the feudal times, the days of innocence, quiet, and security with those of turbulence, violence, and adventure.

In his comic scenes he is seldom very successful when he engages his characters in reciprocations of smartness and contests of sarcasm; their jests are commonly gross and their pleasantry licentious; neither his gentlemen nor his ladies have much delicacy nor are sufficiently distinguished from his clowns by any appearance of refined manners. Whether he represented the real conversation of his time is not easy to determine; the reign of Elizabeth is commonly supposed to have been a time of stateliness, formality, and reserve, yet perhaps the relaxations of that severity were not very elegant. There must, however, have been always some modes of gaiety preferable to others, and a writer ought to choose the best.

In tragedy his performance seems constantly to be worse as his labor is more. The effusions of passion which exigence forces out are for the most part striking and energetic, but whenever he solicits his invention or strains his faculties, the offspring of his throes is tumor, meanness, tediousness, and obscurity.

In narration he affects a disproportionate pomp of diction and a wearisome train of circumlocution, and tells the incident imperfectly in many words which might have been more plainly delivered in few. Narration in dramatic poetry is naturally tedious, as it is unanimated and inactive and obstructs the progress of the action; it should therefore always be rapid and enlivened by frequent interruption. Shakespeare found it an encumbrance, and instead of lightening it by brevity endeavored to recommend it by dignity and splendor.

His declamations or set speeches are commonly cold and weak, for his power was the power of nature; when he endeavored like other tragic writers to catch opportunities of amplification, and instead of inquiring what the occasion demanded to show how much his stores of knowledge could supply, he seldom escapes without the pity or resentment of his reader.

It is incident to him to be now and then entangled with an unwieldy sentiment which he cannot well express and will not reject; he struggles with it awhile, and if it continues stubborn, comprises it in words such as occur, and leaves it to be disentangled and evolved by those who have more leisure to bestow upon it.

Not that always where the language is intricate the thought is subtle, or the image always great where the line is bulky; the equality of words to things is very often neglected, and trivial sentiments and vulgar ideas disappoint the attention to which they are recommended by sonorous epithets and swelling figures.

But the admirers of this great poet have never less reason to indulge their hopes of supreme excellence than when he seems fully resolved to sink them in dejection and mollify them with tender emotions by the fall of greatness, the danger of innocence, or the crosses of love. He is not long soft and pathetic without some idle conceit or contemptible equivocation. He no sooner begins to move than he counteracts himself, and terror and pity, as they are rising in the mind, are checked and blasted by sudden frigidity.

A quibble is to Shakespeare what luminous vapors are to the traveler; he follows it at all adventures; it is sure to lead him out of his way and sure to engulf him in the mire. It has some malignant power over his mind and its fascinations are irresistible. Whatever be the dignity or profundity of his disquisition —whether he be enlarging knowledge or exalting affection, whether he be amusing attention with incidents or enchaining it in suspense, let but a quibble spring up before him and he leaves his work unfinished. A quibble is the golden apple for which he will always turn aside from his career or stoop from his elevation. A quibble, poor and barren as it is, gave him such delight that he was content to purchase it by the sacrifice of reason, propriety, and truth. A quibble was to him the fatal Cleopatra for which he lost the world, and was content to lose it.

It will be thought strange that in enumerating the defects of this writer I have not yet mentioned his neglect of the unities, his violation of those laws which have been instituted and established by the joint authority of poets and of critics.

For his other deviations from the art of writing I resign him to critical justice, without making any other demand in his favor than that which must be indulged to all human excellence: that his virtues be rated with his failings. But, from the censure which this irregularity may bring upon him, I shall, with due reverence to that learning which I must oppose, adventure to try how I can defend him. . . . [A long passage follows in which Johnson defends Shakespeare by showing that though he violates the unities of time, place, and action, his plays are of such imaginative quality that they transcend the classical rules.]

The English nation in the time of Shakespeare was yet struggling to emerge from barbarity. . . . Nations, like individuals, have their infancy. A people newly awakened to literary curiosity, being yet unacquainted with the true state of things, knows not how to judge of that which is proposed as its resemblance. Whatever is remote from common appearances is always welcome to vulgar as to childish credulity, and of a country unenlightened by learning the whole people is the vulgar. The study of those who then aspired to plebeian learning was laid out upon adventures, giants, dragons, and enchantments. *The Death of Arthur* was the favorite volume. . . .

His plots, whether historical or fabulous, are always crowded with incidents by which the attention of a rude people was more easily caught than by sentiment or argumentation, and such is the power of the marvelous even over those who despise it that every man finds his mind more strongly seized by the tragedies of Shakespeare than of any other writer. Others please us by particular speeches, but he always makes us anxious for the event, and has perhaps excelled all but Homer in securing the first purpose of a writer: by exciting restless and unquenchable curiosity and compelling him that reads his work to read it through.

The shows and bustle with which his plays abound have the same original. As knowledge advances, pleasure passes from the eye to the ear, but returns, as it declines, from the ear to the eye. Those to whom our author's labors were exhibited had more skill in pomps or processions than in poetical language, and perhaps wanted some visible and discriminated events as comments on the dialogue. He knew how he should most please; and whether his practice is more agreeable to nature or whether his example has prejudiced the nation we still find that on our stage something must be done as well as said, and inactive declamation is very coldly heard, however musical or elegant, passionate or sublime.

Voltaire expresses his wonder that our author's extravagances are endured by a nation which has seen the tragedy of *Cato*. Let him be answered that Addison speaks the language of poets and Shakespeare of men. . . .

There has always prevailed a tradition that Shakespeare wanted learning, that he had no regular education nor much skill in the dead languages. Jonson, his friend, affirms that "he had small Latin and no Greek"; who, besides that he had no imaginable temptation to falsehood, wrote at a time when the character and acquisitions of Shakespeare were known to multitudes. His evidence ought therefore to decide the controversy, unless some testimony of equal force could be opposed.

Some have imagined that they have discovered deep learning in many imitations of old writers; but the examples which I have known urged were drawn from books translated in his time, or were such easy coincidences of thought as will happen to all who consider the same subjects, or such remarks on life or axioms of morality as float in conversation and are transmitted through the world in proverbial sentences. . . .

There is, however, proof enough that he was a very diligent reader, nor was our language then so indigent of books but that he might very liberally indulge his curiosity without excursion into foreign literature. Many of the Roman authors were translated, and some of the Greek; the Reformation had filled the kingdom with theological learning; most of the topics of human disquisition had found English writers; and poetry had been cultivated not only with diligence but success. This was a stock of knowledge sufficient for a mind so capable of appropriating and improving it.

But the greater part of his excellence was the product of his own genius. He found the English stage in a state of the utmost rudeness; no essays either in tragedy or comedy had appeared from which it could be discovered to what degree of delight either one or other might be carried. Neither character nor dialogue were yet understood. Shakespeare may be truly said to have introduced them both amongst us and in some of his happier scenes to have carried them both to the utmost height. . . .

It does not appear that Shakespeare thought his works worthy of posterity, that he levied any ideal tribute upon future times, or had any further prospect than of present popularity and present profit. When his plays had been acted, his hope was at an end; he solicited no addition of honor from the reader. He therefore made no scruple to repeat the same jests in many dialogues or to entangle different plots by the same knot of perplexity, which may be at least forgiven him by those who recollect that of Congreve's four comedies two are concluded by a marriage in a mask, by a deception which perhaps never happened and which, whether likely or not, he did not invent.

So careless was this great poet of future fame that, though he retired to ease and plenty while he was yet little declined into the vale of years, before he could be disgusted with fatigue or disabled by infirmity, he made no collection of his works, nor desired to rescue those that had been already published from the depravations that obscured them, or secure to the rest a better destiny by giving them to the world in their genuine state. . . .

It is to be lamented that such a writer should want a commentary; that his language should become obsolete or his sentiments obscure. But it is vain to carry wishes beyond the condition of human things; that which must happen to all has happened to Shakespeare by accident and time; and more than has been suffered by any other writer since the use of types has been suffered by him through his own negligence of fame, or perhaps by that superiority of mind which despised its own performances when it compared them with its powers, and judged those works unworthy to be preserved which the critics of following ages were to contend for the fame of restoring and explaining.

Among these candidates of inferior fame I am now to stand the judgment of the public and wish that I could confidently produce my commentary as equal to the encouragement which I have had the honor of receiving. Every work of this kind is by its nature deficient, and I should feel little solicitude about the sentence were it to be pronounced only by the skillful and the learned.

[Preface to SAMUEL JOHNSON, *The Plays of William Shakespeare,* 1765. A convenient collection of Johnson's commentary on Shakespeare is that edited by Sir Walter Raleigh, *Johnson on Shakespeare* (Oxford, 1946).]

SELECTED BIBLIOGRAPHY

Since the eighteenth century scholars, critics, and amateurs have turned out a vast literature concerned with Shakespeare. These writers have produced books and articles on almost every topic that can be imagined. The sheer quantity of publication about Shakespeare is overwhelming. Fortunately a few guides through the morass of writing will help the student of Shakespeare to pick out significant works that he may need. One of the most useful introductions is Gerald E. Bentley, *Shakespeare: A Biographical Handbook* (New Haven, 1961). This succinct volume gives essential information in the light of the most recent scholarship and provides a brief but well-chosen list of books for further consultation. Another brief handbook is Gerald Sanders, *A Shakespeare Primer* (New York, 1950). Somewhat longer but useful, especially for facts about the history of play performances, is Hazelton Spencer, *The Art and Life of William Shakespeare* (New York, 1940). Valuable for the variety of its information is *A Companion to Shakespeare Studies,* edited by Harley Granville-Barker and G. B. Harrison (Cambridge, 1934). Convenient and useful is F. E. Halliday, *A Shakespeare Companion, 1550–1950* (London, 1952). The most complete factual treatment of Shakespeare's biography and the writing and production of his plays remains Sir Edmund Chambers, *William Shakespeare: A Study of Facts and Problems* (2 vols., Oxford, 1930). Although much has been written since the first publication of Chambers' two volumes more than thirty years ago, most of his observations remain valid today.

Bibliographical Guides

Since no single volume can list all of the works about Shakespeare, the student in search of specialized information will have to consult Shakespeare bibliographies. The most elaborate and detailed of modern guides is Walther Ebisch and Levin L. Schücking, *A Shakespeare Bibliography* (Oxford, 1931) and a *Supplement for the Years 1930–1935* (Oxford, 1937). William Jaggard, *Shakespeare Bibliography* (Stratford-upon-Avon, 1911) is long out of date, but it contains a vast and indiscriminate listing of editions of Shakespeare and works about him. *The Cambridge Bibliography of English Literature* (Cambridge, 1941), I, 539–608, has a well-selected list of Shakespearean items. Various annual bibliographies in literature contain sections on current Shakespeare scholarship. See especially *The Annual Bibliography of English Language and Literature,* published by the Modern Humanities Research Association (1920——); *The Bulletin of the Shakespeare Association of America* (1926–1949); *Shakespeare Quarterly* (1950——); *Studies in Philology,* published by the University of North Carolina (1922——); *The Year's Work in English Studies* (1921——); and *Shakespeare Survey: An Annual Survey of Shakespearian Study and Production,* ed. Allardyce Nicoll (Cambridge and New York, 1948——).

Biography

The essential facts about Shakespeare are set down carefully in Chambers, *William Shakespeare,* previously cited. This is the standard reference work and is not likely to be superseded. The most readable and accurate of the recent biographies is Marchette Chute, *Shakespeare of London* (New York, 1949; paperback reprint, Dutton Everyman, 1957). The most readable of the older biographies is Joseph Q. Adams, *A Life of William Shakespeare* (Boston, 1923). Sidney Lee, *A Life of William Shakespeare* (London, 1898; 14th ed., London and New York, 1931), long regarded as the standard biography but now out of date, has useful information. J. O. Halliwell-Phillipps, *Outlines of the Life of Shakespeare* (7th rev. ed., 1887) contains valuable documentary material. Mark Eccles, *Shakespeare in Warwickshire* (Madison, Wis., 1961) supplies information about contemporaries of Shakespeare in his native county. Shakespeare's learning is treated in great detail by T. W. Baldwin, *William Shakspere's Small Latine and Lesse Greeke* (2 vols., Urbana, Ill., 1944). The question of alleged ciphers in Shakespeare's works indicating other authorship is disposed of with finality in William and Elizebeth Friedman, *The Shakespeare Ciphers Examined* (Cambridge, 1957).

Modern Editions

Editions of Shakespeare are numbered by the thousands. One of the best modern editions is John Munro (ed.), *The London Shakespeare* (6 vols., London and New York, 1957). The new English Arden series now in progress in single-play volumes is one of the most scholarly of the recent editions. Many single-play versions are appearing in paperbacks. The Washington Square Press is publishing individual plays in paper covers, edited by Louis B. Wright and Virginia A. LaMar. The best modern edition of all of Shakespeare in one volume is George Lyman Kittredge (ed.), *The Complete Works of Shakespeare* (Boston, 1936). A summary of modern scholarship will be found in the New Variorum Shakespeare editions begun by H. H. Furness and continued under the auspices of the Modern Language Association of America.

Textual Problems and Printing

The textual problems posed by Shakespeare's plays are intricate and have occupied the attention of many able scholars since the time of Edmond Malone in the eighteenth century. The undergraduate student of Shakespeare may want to gain some knowledge of bibliographical and textual problems in Shakespeare's age. The most concise and sensible treatment for the beginning student—or for anyone else—is R. B. McKerrow, *An Introduction to Bibliography for Literary Students* (London, 1927). Various aspects of the textual problems are treated in the following books:

Evelyn M. Albright, *Dramatic Publication in England, 1580–1640: A Study of Conditions Affecting Content and Form of Drama* (New York and London, 1927).

Edward Arber, ed., *A Transcript of the Registers of the Company of Stationers of London, 1554–1640 A.D.* (5 vols., London, 1875–94).

Henrietta C. Bartlett, *Mr. William Shakespeare: Original and Early Editions of His Quartos and Folios, His Source Books, and Those Containing Contemporary Notices* (New Haven, 1922).

Henrietta C. Bartlett and A. W. Pollard, *A Census of Shakespeare's Plays in Quarto, 1594–1709* (New Haven, 1916; rev. ed., 1939).

M. W. Black and M. A. Shaaber, *Shakespeare's Seventeenth-Century Editors, 1632–1685* (New York and London, 1937).

Fredson T. Bowers, *On Editing Shakespeare and the Elizabethan Dramatists* (Philadelphia, 1955).

C. F. Tucker Brooke, *The Shakespeare Apocrypha: Being a Collection of Fourteen Plays Which Have Been Ascribed to Shakespeare* (Oxford, 1908).

Sir Walter Greg, *Dramatic Documents from the Elizabethan Playhouses* (Oxford, 1931).

———, *A Bibliography of the English Printed Drama to the Restoration* (4 vols., London, 1939–59).

———, *The Editorial Problem in Shakespeare: A Survey of the Foundations of the Text* (London, 1942).

———, *The Shakespeare First Folio: Its Bibliographical and Textual History* (Oxford, 1955).

C. J. K. Hinman, *The Printing and Proof-Reading of the First Folio of Shakespeare* (Oxford, 1962).

Leo Kirschbaum, *Shakespeare and the Stationers* (Columbus, Ohio, 1955).

Baldwin Maxwell, *Studies in the Shakespeare Apocrypha* (New York, 1956).

A. W. Pollard, *The Foundations of Shakespeare's Text*. British Academy Annual Shakespeare Lecture (London, 1923).

———, *Shakespeare Folios and Quartos: A Study in the Bibliography of Shakespeare's Plays, 1594–1685* (London, 1909).

———, *Shakespeare's Fight with the Pirates and the Problem of the Transmission of His Text* (Cambridge, 1920).

Alice Walker, *Textual Problems of the First Folio* (Cambridge, 1953).

Growth of Shakespeare's Reputation

Most of the books dealing with the history of Shakespearean criticism treat the growth of Shakespeare's reputation. A recent brief account is F. E. Halliday, *The Cult of Shakespeare* (London, 1957). Older and more detailed is Robert W. Babcock, *The Genesis of Shakespeare Idolatry* (Chapel Hill, N.C., 1931), which contains a long bibliography of the subject. See also Ivor Brown and George Fearon, *Amazing Monument: A Short History of the Shakespeare Industry* (London, 1939). The growth of Shakespearean citation may be traced in John Munro (ed.), *The Shakspere Allusion-Book: A Collection of Allusions to Shakspere from 1591 to 1700* (2 vols., Oxford, 1932). See also Gerald E. Bentley, *Shakespeare and Jonson: Their Reputations in the Seventeenth Century Compared* (2 vols., Chicago, 1945).

Shakespeare Criticism

The mass of critical material on Shakespeare published during the past twenty years alone would fill a sizable library. A recent critic has observed that *Hamlet* alone has accounted for a publication every twelve days since 1877. Obviously only a few works of general utility to the student can be cited here. For the development of criticism see Augustus Ralli, *A History of Shakespearian Criticism* (2 vols., Oxford, 1932; New York, 1958). More recent and more succinct is F. E. Halliday, *Shakespeare and His Critics* (London, 1949; rev. ed., 1958).

The following titles treat various aspects of Shakespeare:

C. L. Barber, *Shakespeare's Festive Comedy: A Study of Dramatic Form and Its Relation to Social Custom* (Princeton, 1959).

Muriel C. Bradbrook, *Shakespeare and Elizabethan Poetry* (Oxford, 1951).

A. C. Bradley, *Shakespearean Tragedy: Lectures on Hamlet, Othello, King Lear, Macbeth* (London, 1904; many later editions including paperback reprint, Noonday Press, 1955).

C. F. Tucker Brooke, *Essays on Shakespeare and Other Elizabethans* (New Haven, 1948).

———, *Shakespeare's Sonnets* (London, 1936).

John Russell Brown, *Shakespeare and His Comedies* (London, 1957).

Lily Bess Campbell, *Shakespeare's "Histories": Mirrors of Elizabethan Policy* (Cambridge, 1947).

———, *Shakespeare's Tragic Heroes: Slaves of Passion* (Cambridge, 1940; paperback reprint, Barnes and Noble, 1959).

Oscar J. Campbell, *Shakespeare's Satire* (London and New York, 1943).

Sir Edmund Chambers, *Shakespeare: A Survey* (London, 1935; paperback reprint, Hill and Wang, 1958).

W. H. Clemen, *The Development of Shakespeare's Imagery* (Cambridge, Mass., 1951).

H. B. Charlton, *Shakespearian Comedy* (London, 1938; 4th ed., 1949).

———, *Shakespearian Tragedy* (Cambridge, 1948).

Coleridge's Shakespearian Criticism, ed. T. M. Raysor (2 vols., London, 1930).

Coleridge's Writings on Shakespeare, ed. Terence Hawkes (paperback, Capricorn, 1959).

Milton Crane, *Shakespeare's Prose* (Chicago, 1951).

B. Ifor Evans, *The Language of Shakespeare's Plays* (London, 1952; 2d ed., 1959).

Willard Farnham, *The Medieval Heritage of Elizabethan Tragedy* (Berkeley, 1936).

———, *Shakespeare's Tragic Frontier: The World of His Final Tragedies* (Berkeley, 1950).

Helen Gardner, *The Business of Criticism* (Oxford, 1959).

Harley Granville-Barker, *Prefaces to Shakespeare* (5 vols., London, 1927–48; 2 vols., London, 1958).

Alfred Harbage, *As They Liked It: An Essay on Shakespeare and Morality* (New York, 1947).

———, *Shakespeare and the Rival Traditions* (New York, 1952).

William Hazlitt, *Characters of Shakespeare's Plays.* World Classics (Oxford, 1917, and later eds.).

Edward Hubler, *The Sense of Shakespeare's Sonnets* (Princeton, 1952).

Samuel Johnson, *Johnson on Shakespeare: Essays and Notes Selected,* ed. Walter Raleigh (London, 1908, and later eds.).

———, *Preface to Shakespeare With Proposals for Printing the Dramatic Works of William Shakespeare* (Oxford, 1957).

———, *Samuel Johnson on Shakespeare,* ed. W. K. Wimsatt, Jr. (paperback, Hill and Wang, 1960).

W. W. Lawrence, *Shakespeare's Problem Comedies* (New York, 1931).

M. W. MacCallum, *Shakespeare's Roman Plays and Their Background* (London, 1910).

John Palmer, *The Comic Characters of Shakespeare* (London, 1946).

———, *Political Characters of Shakespeare* (London, 1945; 1961).

Thomas M. Parrott, *Shakespearean Comedy* (New York, 1949).

Levin L. Schücking, *Character Problems in Shakespeare's Plays* (London, 1922).

George Bernard Shaw, *Dramatic Opinions and Essays* (2 vols., New York, 1907).

———, *Shaw on Shakespeare: An Anthology of Bernard Shaw's Writings on the Plays and Production of Shakespeare* (New York, 1961; paperback, Dutton Everyman, 1961).

David Nichol Smith, ed., *Eighteenth Century Essays on Shakespeare* (Glasgow, 1903).

Hallett Smith, *Elizabethan Poetry* (Cambridge, Mass., 1952).

Logan Pearsall Smith, *On Reading Shakespeare* (New York, 1933).

Theodore Spencer, *Shakespeare and the Nature of Man* (New York, 1942; 2d ed., 1960).

Caroline F. E. Spurgeon, *Shakespeare's Imagery and What It Tells Us* (New York and Cambridge, 1936; paperback reprint, Beacon, 1958).

Elmer E. Stoll, *Art and Artifice in Shakespeare* (Cambridge, 1933).

———, *Shakespeare Studies* (New York, 1927; corr. ed., 1960).

J. A. K. Thomson, *Shakespeare and the Classics* (London, 1952).

E. M. W. Tillyard, *Shakespeare's Problem Plays* (London, 1950).

F. P. Wilson, *Marlowe and the Early Shakespeare* (Oxford, 1953).

Harold S. Wilson, *On the Design of Shakespearian Tragedy* (Toronto, 1957).

Structure and History of the Theatre

The physical characteristics of the Elizabethan playhouse have been the subject of infinite controversy. Scholars do not agree about such matters as the placement of the doors, the use of an inner stage, and other problems of the physical arrangement. One of the most sensible books is C. Walter Hodges, *The Globe Restored* (London, 1953). Although not all scholars agree with his reconstruction, John C. Adams provides plausible explanations in *The Globe Playhouse: Its Design and Equipment* (Cambridge, Mass., 1942; 2d ed., 1962). A description with excellent drawings, based on the Adams model, is Irwin Smith, *Shakespeare's Globe Playhouse: A Modern Reconstruction* (New York, 1956). A lucid synthesis of available information is provided by A. M. Nagler, *Shakespeare's Stage* (New Haven, 1958). Bernard Beckerman, *Shakespeare at the Globe, 1599–1609* (New York, 1962) is written from the point of view of a teacher of practical play production.

Encyclopedic detail about all aspects of Shakespeare's theatre will be found in Sir Edmund Chambers, *The Elizabethan Stage* (4 vols., Oxford, 1923) and Gerald E. Bentley, *The Jacobean and Caroline Stage* (5 vols., Oxford, 1941–56). For detailed information on players and performances from the Restoration to 1800 see *The London Stage, 1660–1800: A Calendar of Plays, Entertainments & Afterpieces,* four volumes of which have been published to date: Part 2, *1700–1729,* ed. Emmett L. Avery, and Part 3, *1729–1747,* ed. Arthur H. Scouten (Carbondale, Ill., 1960).

Further material on the history of the theatre and related topics will be found in the following titles:

Joseph Q. Adams, *Shakespearean Playhouses: A History of English Theatres from the Beginnings to the Restoration* (Boston, 1917).

T. W. Baldwin, *The Organization and Personnel of the Shakespearean Company* (Princeton, 1927).

George C. Branam, *Eighteenth-Century Adaptations of Shakespeare's Tragedies* (Berkeley, 1956).

Lily Bess Campbell, *Scenes and Machines on the English Stage during the Renaissance* (Cambridge, 1923).

Sir Edmund Chambers, *The Medieval Stage* (2 vols., Oxford, 1903).

Esther C. Dunn, *Shakespeare in America* (New York, 1939).

Alfred Harbage, *Shakespeare's Audience* (New York, 1941).

Henslowe's Diary, ed. R. A. Foakes and R. T. Rickert (Cambridge, 1961).

C. Walter Hodges, *Shakespeare and the Players* (London, 1948).

C. Beecher Hogan, *Shakespeare in the Theatre, 1701–1800* (Oxford, 1957).

Martin R. Holmes, *Shakespeare's Public: The Touchstone of His Genius* (London, 1960).

J. L. Hotson, *The Commonwealth and Restoration Stage* (Cambridge, Mass., 1928).

B. L. Joseph, *Elizabethan Acting* (Oxford, 1951).

W. J. Lawrence, *The Physical Conditions of the Elizabethan Playhouse* (Cambridge, Mass., 1927).

George C. D. Odell, *Shakespeare from Betterton to Irving* (2 vols., London, 1921).

Richard Southern, *The Medieval Theatre in the Round* (London, 1947).

Robert Speaight, *William Poel and the Elizabethan Revival* (London, 1954).

Hazelton Spencer, *Shakespeare Improved: The Restoration Versions in Quarto and on the Stage* (Cambridge and London, 1927).

Arthur C. Sprague, *Shakespeare and the Actors: The Stage Business in His Plays, 1660–1905* (Cambridge, Mass., 1944).

———, *Shakespearian Players and Performances* (Cambridge, Mass., 1953).

Alwin Thaler, *Shakspere to Sheridan: A Book about the Theatre of Yesterday and To-day* (Cambridge, Mass., 1922).

Ashley H. Thorndike, *Shakespeare's Theater* (New York, 1916; paperback reprint, Macmillan, 1960).

Sources

The following titles provide material for a study of Shakespeare's use of some of his sources:

H. R. D. Anders, *Shakespeare's Books: A Dissertation on Shakespeare's Reading and the Immediate Sources of His Works* (Berlin, 1904).

W. G. Boswell-Stone, ed., *Shakespeare's Holinshed* (London, 1907).

C. F. Tucker Brooke, ed., *Shakespeare's Plutarch* (2 vols., London, 1909).

Geoffrey Bullough, ed., *Narrative and Dramatic Sources of Shakespeare.* I. *Early Comedies, Poems, and Romeo and Juliet* (London and New York, 1957); II. *Comedies, 1597–1603* (London and New York, 1957); III. *Earlier English History Plays: Henry VI, Richard III, Richard II* (London and New York, 1960); IV. *Later English History Plays: King John, Henry IV, Henry V, Henry VIII* (London and New York, 1962).

Douglas Bush, *Mythology and the Renaissance Tradition in English Poetry* (Minneapolis, 1932).

John P. Collier, ed., *Shakespeare's Library* (2 vols., London, 1850).

Israel C. Gollancz, ed., *The Shakespeare Classics* (12 vols., London, 1907–26).

W. C. Hazlitt, ed., *Shakespeare's Library* (6 vols., London, 1875).

Kenneth Muir, *Shakespeare's Sources: Comedies and Tragedies* (London, 1957).

Allardyce and Josephine Nicoll, eds., *Holinshed's Chronicle as Used in Shakespeare's Plays* (London, 1955).

R. K. Root, *Classical Mythology in Shakespeare* (New York, 1903).

Language

The language used by Shakespeare and his contemporaries has undergone many changes since Shakespeare's times. *The New English Dictionary on Historical Principles,* edited by James A. H. Murray (Oxford, 1888–1928) is the most convenient source for Elizabethan usage of words. Other works that will be helpful are:

E. A. Abbot, *A Shakespearian Grammar* (London, 1872).

Albert C. Baugh, *A History of the English Language* (New York and London, 1935).

Helge Kökeritz, *Shakespeare's Pronunciation* (New Haven, 1953).

Robert Nares, *A Glossary; or, Collection of Words, Phrases, Names, and Allusions to Customs, Proverbs, etc.,* ed. J. O. Halliwell-Phillipps and T. Wright (2 vols., London, 1872).

C. T. Onions, *A Shakespeare Glossary* (2d ed. rev., Oxford, 1925).

Eric Partridge, *Shakespeare's Bawdy* (New York, 1948; paperback reprint, Dutton Everyman, 1960).

Sister Miriam Joseph, *Shakespeare's Use of the Arts of Language* (New York, 1947).

M. P. Tilley, *A Dictionary of the Proverbs in England in the Sixteenth and Seventeenth Centuries* (Ann Arbor, Mich., 1950).

———, *Elizabethan Proverb Lore in Lyly's Euphues and Pettie's Petite Pallace, with Parallels from Shakespeare* (New York and London, 1926).

General Background

A knowledge of Shakespeare's age helps to increase one's appreciation and enjoyment of the plays. Interesting essays on a variety of subjects pertaining to the intellectual and social history of the period will be found in *Shakespeare's England,* edited by C. T. Onions (2 vols., Oxford, 1916) and in *Life and Letters in Tudor and Stuart England,* edited by Louis B. Wright and Virginia A. LaMar (published for the Folger Shakespeare Library by Cornell University Press, 1962 and subsequently). Each essay is fully illustrated with contemporary pictures. The following individual essays in the series, "Folger Booklets on Tudor and Stuart Civilization," are available from the Cornell University Press:

Giles E. Dawson, *The Life of William Shakespeare* (1958).

John R. Hale, *The Art of War and Renaissance England* (1961).

Virginia A. LaMar, *English Dress in the Age of Shakespeare* (1958).

———, *Travel and Roads in England* (1960).

James G. McManaway, *The Authorship of Shakespeare* (1962).

Dorothy E. Mason, *Music in Elizabethan England* (1958).

Boies Penrose, *Tudor and Early Stuart Voyaging* (1962).

Conyers Read, *The Government of England under Elizabeth* (1960).

Albert J. Schmidt, *The Yeoman in Tudor and Stuart England* (1961).

Lilly C. Stone, *English Sports and Recreations* (1960).

Craig R. Thompson, *The Bible in English, 1525–1611* (1958).

———, *The English Church in the Sixteenth Century* (1958).

———, *Schools in Tudor England* (1958).

———, *Universities in Tudor England* (1958).

Louis B. Wright, *Shakespeare's Theatre and the Dramatic Tradition* (1958).

The Shakespeare Institute of Stratford-upon-Avon is issuing a series of collected essays under the general editorship of John Russell Brown and Bernard Harris, three volumes of which have been published to date:

Jacobean Theatre (London, 1960).

Elizabethan Poetry (London, 1960).

Early Shakespeare (London, 1961).

Other useful titles are:

J. W. Allen, *A History of Political Thought in the Sixteenth Century* (New York, 1928).

Lawrence Babb, *The Elizabethan Malady: A Study of Melancholia in English Literature* (East Lansing, Mich., 1951).

S. T. Bindoff, *The Tudors* (Penguin paperback, 1950).

J. B. Black, *The Reign of Elizabeth, 1558–1603* (Oxford, 1936; 2d ed., 1959).

Muriel St. C. Byrne, *Elizabethan Life in Town and Country* (London, 1925; rev. ed., 1954; paperback reprint, University, 1961).

Edward P. Cheyney, *A History of England from the Defeat of the Armada to the Death of Elizabeth* (2 vols., New York, 1914–26).

S. K. Heninger, Jr., *A Handbook of Renaissance Meteorology* (Durham, N.C., 1960).

Paul A. Jorgensen, *Shakespeare's Military World* (Berkeley and Los Angeles, 1956).

A. V. Judges, *The Elizabethan Underworld* (London, 1930).

C. S. Lewis, *English Literature in the Sixteenth Century Excluding Drama.* Oxford Hist. of Eng. Lit. (Oxford, 1954).

Norman E. McClure, ed., *The Letters of John Chamberlain* (2 vols., Philadelphia, 1939).

D. H. Madden, *The Diary of Master William Silence: A Study of Shakespeare and of Elizabethan Sport* (London, 1897).

Sir John Neale, *Queen Elizabeth* (London and New York, 1934; paperback reprint, Anchor, 1957).

Sir Charles Oman, *The Sixteenth Century* (New York, 1937).

A. L. Rowse, *The England of Elizabeth* (London, 1950; paperback reprint, Macmillan, 1961).

Felix E. Schelling, *Elizabethan Drama, 1558–1642* (2 vols., Boston, 1908).

De Witt T. Starnes and Ernest W. Talbert, *Classical Myth and Legend in Renaissance Dictionaries* (Chapel Hill, N.C., 1956).

John Stow, *A Survey of London,* ed. C. L. Kingsford (2 vols., Oxford, 1908).

Henry O. Taylor, *Thought and Expression in the Sixteenth Century* (2 vols., New York, 1920).

E. M. W. Tillyard, *The Elizabethan World Picture* (London, 1943).

G. M. Trevelyan, *The History of England* (London, 1926; many eds. including paperbacks since).

———, *English Social History* (London, 1942; many later editions).

F. P. Wilson, *The Plague in Shakespeare's London* (Oxford, 1927).

Louis B. Wright, *Middle-Class Culture in Elizabethan England* (Chapel Hill, N.C., 1935; Ithaca, 1958).

———, ed., *Advice to a Son: Precepts of Lord Burghley, Sir Walter Raleigh, and Francis Osborne* (Ithaca, 1962).

Individual Plays

Titles already listed in the preceding bibliography are cited in abbreviated form under individual plays. Titles not previously cited are given with full bibliographical details when first mentioned; thereafter they appear in a short form.

RICHARD III

Peter Alexander, *Shakespeare's Henry VI and Richard III* (Cambridge, 1929).

Robert W. Babcock, "An Introduction to the Study of the Text of *Richard III,*" *Studies in Philology,* XXIV (1927), 243–60.

Geoffrey Bullough, *Narrative and Dramatic Sources . . . ,* Vol. I.

James Gairdner, *History of the Life and Reign of Richard III* (rev. ed., Cambridge, 1898).

H. C. Hart, *Stolne and Surreptitious Copies, a Comparative Study of Shakespeare's Bad Quartos* (Melbourne, Aus., 1942).

William Hutton, *The Battle of Bosworth Field* (Birmingham, 1788; rev. ed., ed. J. G. Nichols, London, 1813).

Paul Murray Kendall, *Richard the Third* (New York, 1956).

———, *Warwick the Kingmaker* (New York, 1957).

Sir Thomas More, *The History of King Richard III,* ed. J. R. Lumby (Cambridge, 1833).

David L. Patrick, *The Textual History of Richard III* (Stanford, 1936).

Horace Walpole, *Historic Doubts on the Life and Reign of King Richard the Third* (London, 1768).

Alice I. P. Wood, *The Stage History of Shakespeare's King Richard the Third* (New York, 1909).

LOVE'S LABOR'S LOST

C. L. Barber, *Shakespeare's Festive Comedy.*

Oscar J. Campbell, "*Love's Labor's Lost* Re-studied," in *Studies in Shakespeare, Milton, and Donne* (New York, 1925).

H. B. Charlton, "The Date of *Love's Labor's Lost,*" *Modern Language Review,* XIII (1918), 257–66, 387–400.

W. Schrickx, *Shakespeare's Early Contemporaries: The Background of the Harvey-Nashe Polemic and Love's Labor's Lost* (Antwerp, 1956).

Ernest A. Strathmann, *Sir Walter Ralegh: A Study in Elizabethan Skepticism* (New York, 1951).

See also works on Shakespeare's comedies under "Shakespeare Criticism."

ROMEO AND JULIET

Brooke's "Romeus and Juliet," Being the Original of Shakespeare's "Romeo and Juliet," ed. J. J. Munro. The Shakespeare Classics (London, 1908).

Geoffrey Bullough, *Narrative and Dramatic Sources . . . ,* Vol. I.

Harry R. Hoppe, *The Bad Quarto of Romeo and Juliet* (Ithaca, 1948).

Olin H. Moore, *The Legend of Romeo and Juliet* (Columbus, Ohio, 1950).

Kenneth Muir, *Shakespeare's Sources.*

MIDSUMMER NIGHT'S DREAM

C. L. Barber, *Shakespeare's Festive Comedy.*

William Bell, *Shakespeare's Puck and His Folks-lore, Illustrated from the Superstitions of All Nations* (3 vols., London, 1852).

K. M. Briggs, *The Anatomy of Puck* (London, 1959).

Geoffrey Bullough, *Narrative and Dramatic Sources . . .*, Vol. II.

James O. Halliwell-Phillipps, *Illustrations of the Fairy Mythology of A Midsummer Night's Dream* (London, 1845).

Kenneth Muir, *Shakespeare's Sources.*

George C. D. Odell, "'A Midsummer Night's Dream' on the New York Stage," in *Shakesperian Studies,* ed. Brander Matthews and Ashley H. Thorndike (New York, 1916), pp. 119–62.

Frank Sidgwick, ed., *The Sources and Analogues of "A Midsummer Night's Dream."* The Shakespeare Library (London, 1908).

THE MERCHANT OF VENICE

The Merchant of Venice, ed. John Russell Brown. Arden Shakespeare (London, 1955).

C. L. Barber, *Shakespeare's Festive Comedy.*

Geoffrey Bullough, *Narrative and Dramatic Sources . . .*, Vol. II.

J. L. Cardozo, "The Background of Shakespeare's *Merchant of Venice,*" *English Studies,* XIV (1932), 177–86.

———, *The Contemporary Jew in the Elizabethan Drama* (Amsterdam, 1925).

Bernard Grebanier, *The Truth about Shylock* (New York, 1962).

M. J. Landa, *The Shylock Myth* (London, 1942).

Sidney Lee, "Elizabethan England and the Jew," *Transactions of the New Shakespeare Society* (London, 1888).

Lucien Wolff, "Jews in Elizabethan England," The Jewish Historical Society of England, *Transactions, Sessions 1924–1927* (London, 1928), pp. 1–91.

HENRY IV, PART 1

The First Part of the History of King Henry IV, ed. Arthur R. Humphreys. Arden Shakespeare (London, 1960).

C. L. Barber, *Shakespeare's Festive Comedy.*

W. G. Bowling, "The Wild Prince Hal in Legend and Literature," *Washington University Studies,* XIII, Hum. ser., No. 2 (1925–26), 305–34.

W. G. Boswell-Stone, *Shakespeare's Holinshed.*

Geoffrey Bullough, *Narrative and Dramatic Sources . . .*, Vol. IV.

H. Edward Cain, "Further Light on the Relation of *1* and *2 Henry IV,*" *Shakespeare Quarterly,* III (1952), 21–38.

Samuel Daniel, *The Civil Wars,* ed. Laurence Michel (New Haven, 1958).

The Famous Victories of Henry the Fifth: The Earliest Known Quarto, 1598, a Facsimile, ed. P. A. Daniel (London, 1887).

Holinshed's Chronicle, ed. Nicoll.

Robert A. Law, "Structural Unity in the Two Parts of *Henry the Fourth,*" *Studies in Philology,* XXIV (1927), 223–42.

Maurice Morgann, *An Essay on the Dramatic Character of Sir John Falstaff* (London, 1777; reprinted, ed. W. A. Gill, London, 1912).

M. A. Shaaber, "The Unity of *Henry IV,*" *Joseph Quincy Adams: Memorial Studies* (Washington, 1948).

J. Dover Wilson, *The Fortunes of Falstaff* (Cambridge and New York, 1944).

J. H. Wylie, *The History of England under Henry the Fourth* (4 vols., London, 1884–98).

HENRY V

W. G. Boswell-Stone, *Shakespeare's Holinshed.*

Geoffrey Bullough, *Narrative and Dramatic Sources . . .*, Vol. IV.

The Famous Victories . . ., ed. P. A. Daniel.

Holinshed's Chronicle, ed. Nicoll.

E. F. Jacob, *Henry V and the Invasion of France* (New York, 1950).

Hereward T. Price, *The Text of Henry V* (Newcastle-under-Lyme, 1921).

J. H. Wylie, *Reign of Henry the Fifth* (3 vols., Cambridge, 1914–29).

JULIUS CÆSAR

Julius Cæsar, ed. T. S. Dorsch. Arden Shakespeare (London, 1955).

H. M. Ayres, "Shakespeare's *Julius Cæsar* in the Light of Some Other Versions," *Publications of the Modern Language Association of America,* XXV (1910), 183–227.

C. F. Tucker Brooke, ed., *Shakespeare's Plutarch.*

M. W. MacCallum, *Shakespeare's Roman Plays.*

George Bernard Shaw, "Better than Shakespear," in *Three Plays for Puritans* (London, 1900 and later eds.; reprinted in *Shaw on Shakespeare,* ed. Edwin Wilson).

Neil S. Snodgrass, *Plutarch and Shakespeare* (New York, n.d.).

T. J. B. Spencer, "Shakespeare and the Elizabethan Romans," *Shakespeare Survey X* (Cambridge, 1957), 27–38.

AS YOU LIKE IT

C. L. Barber, *Shakespeare's Festive Comedy.*

Geoffrey Bullough, *Narrative and Dramatic Sources . . .*, Vol. II.

Oscar J. Campbell, "Jaques," *Huntington Library Bulletin,* No. 8 (Cambridge, Mass., 1935), 71–102.

Cumberland Clark, *A Study of "As You Like It"* (London, 1932).

Lodge's Rosalynde, Being the Original of Shakespeare's As You Like It, ed. Sir Walter Greg. Shakespeare Classics (London, 1907).

Kenneth Muir, *Shakespeare's Sources.*

Elmer E. Stoll, "Jaques, and the Antiquaries," *Modern Language Notes,* LIV (1939), 79–85.

Ashley H. Thorndike, "The Relation of 'As You Like It' to Robin Hood Plays," *Journal of English and Germanic Philology,* IV, (1902), 59–69.

HAMLET

Peter Alexander, *Hamlet; Father and Son* (Oxford, 1955).

A. C. Bradley, *Shakespearean Tragedy.*

Lily Bess Campbell, "Polonius: The Tyrant's Ears," *Adams Memorial Studies,* pp. 295–313.

———, *Shakespeare's Tragic Heroes.*

J. Corbin, *The Elizabethan Hamlet: A Study . . . to Show That the Mad Scenes Had a Comic Aspect Now Ignored* (London, 1895).

John W. Draper, *The Hamlet of Shakespeare's Audience* (Durham, N.C., 1938).

G. I. Duthie, *The "Bad" Quarto of Hamlet: A Critical Study* (Cambridge, 1941).

Israel Gollancz, ed., *The Sources of Hamlet.* The Shakespeare Classics (London, 1926).

Harley Granville-Barker, *Preface to Hamlet* (paperback reprint, Hill and Wang, 1957).

Ernest Jones, *Hamlet and Oedipus* (London, 1949).

Bertram Joseph, *Conscience and the King: A Study of Hamlet* (Oxford, 1953).

Robert A. Law, "Belleforest, Shakespeare, and Kyd," *Adams Memorial Studies,* pp. 279–94.

Kenneth Muir, *Shakespeare's Sources.*

Ludwig Lavater, *Of Ghostes and Spirites Walking by Nyght, 1572,* ed. J. Dover Wilson and May Yardley (Oxford, 1929).

Gilbert Murray, *Hamlet and Orestes* (London, 1914).

Levin L. Schücking, *The Meaning of Hamlet* (Oxford, 1937).

Hazelton Spencer, "Seventeenth-Century Cuts in Hamlet's Soliloquies," *Review of English Studies,* IX (1933), 257–65.

Elmer E. Stoll, *Hamlet: An Historical and Comparative Study* (Minneapolis, 1919).

A. J. A. Waldock, *Hamlet, a Study in Critical Method* (Cambridge, 1931).

J. Dover Wilson, *The Manuscript of Shakespeare's Hamlet and the Problem of Its Transmission* (2 vols., Cambridge and New York, 1934).

———, *What Happens in Hamlet* (Cambridge and New York, 1935; paperback reprint, Cambridge, 1959).

SPECIAL BIBLIOGRAPHICAL AIDS

Paul S. Conklin, *A History of Hamlet Criticism, 1601–1821* (New York, 1947).

Russell E. Leavenworth, *Interpreting Hamlet: Materials for Analysis* (paperback, Howard Chandler, 1960. Contains excerpts from classic comment on *Hamlet* by Goethe, Coleridge, Bradley, Eliot, etc.).

A. A. Raven, *Hamlet Bibliography and Reference Guide, 1877–1935* (Chicago, 1936).

Claude C. H. Williamson, *Readings on the Character of Hamlet, 1661–1947* (London, 1950).

TWELFTH NIGHT

C. L. Barber, *Shakespeare's Festive Comedy.*

Geoffrey Bullough, *Narrative and Dramatic Sources . . .*, Vol. II.

John W. Draper, *The Twelfth Night of Shakespeare's Audience* (Stanford, 1950).

J. L. Hotson, *The First Night of Twelfth Night* (London, 1954).

Kenneth Muir, *Shakespeare's Sources.*

Rich's Farewell to Military Profession, ed. T. M. Cranfill (Austin, Tex., 1959). (Contains "Of Apolonius and Silla.")

OTHELLO

Othello, ed. M. R. Ridley. Arden Shakespeare (London, 1958).

A. C. Bradley, *Shakespearean Tragedy.*

John W. Draper, *The "Othello" of Shakespeare's Audience* (Paris, 1952).

G. R. Elliott, *Flaming Minister: A Study of Othello* (Durham, N.C., 1953).

G. B. Giraldi (Cinthio), *Hecatommithi* (Venice, 1566; reprinted with translation in New Variorum *Othello,* ed. H. H. Furness, Philadelphia, 1886).

Robert B. Heilman, *Magic in the Web: Action and Language in Othello* (Lexington, Ky., 1956).

C. J. K. Hinman, "The 'Copy' for the Second Quarto of *Othello,*" *Adams Memorial Studies,* pp. 373–89.

Kenneth Muir, *Shakespeare's Sources.*

Elmer E. Stoll, "Another *Othello* Too Modern," *Adams Memorial Studies,* pp. 351–71.

———, *Art and Artifice in Shakespeare.*

———, *Othello: An Historical and Comparative Study* (Minneapolis, 1915).

KING LEAR

King Lear, ed. Kenneth Muir. Arden Shakespeare (London, 1952).

John C. Adams, "The Original Staging of *King Lear,*" *Adams Memorial Studies,* pp. 315–35.

A. C. Bradley, *Shakespearean Tragedy.*

C. F. Tucker Brooke, "*King Lear* on the Stage," in *Essays on Shakespeare and Other Elizabethans,* pp. 57–70.

Lily Bess Campbell, *Shakespeare's Tragic Heroes.*

B. A. P. van Dam, *The Text of Shakespeare's Lear* (Louvain, 1935).

Madeleine Doran, "The Quarto of *King Lear* and Bright's Shorthand," *Modern Philology,* XXXIII (1935), 139–57.

———, *The Text of King Lear* (Stanford Univ., 1931).

G. I. Duthie, *Elizabethan Shorthand and the First Quarto of King Lear* (Oxford, 1949).

———, *Shakespeare's King Lear, a Critical Study* (Cambridge, 1941).

Sir Walter Greg, "The Function of Bibliography in Literary Criticism Illustrated in a Study of the Text of King Lear," *Neophilologus,* XVIII (1933), 241–62.

———, *The Variants in the First Quarto of "King Lear"* (London, 1940).

Robert B. Heilman, *This Great Stage: Image and Structure in King Lear* (Baton Rouge, La., 1948).

Sidney Lee, ed., *The Chronicle History of King Leir: The Original of Shakespeare's King Lear.* The Shakespeare Classics (London, 1909).

Kenneth Muir, *Shakespeare's Sources.*

W. Perrett, *The Story of King Lear from Geoffrey of Monmouth to Shakespeare* (Weimar, 1903).

R. W. Zandvoort, *King Lear: The Scholars and the Critics* (Amsterdam, 1956).

MACBETH

Macbeth, ed. Kenneth Muir. Arden Shakespeare (London, 1953).

W. G. Boswell-Stone, *Shakespeare's Holinshed.*

A. C. Bradley, *Shakespearean Tragedy.*

Lily Bess Campbell, *Shakespeare's Tragic Heroes.*

Holinshed's Chronicle, ed. Nicoll.

G. L. Kittredge, *Witchcraft in Old and New England* (Cambridge, Mass., 1929; New York, 1956).

Kenneth Muir, *Shakespeare's Sources.*

Henry N. Paul, *The Royal Play of Macbeth* (New York, 1950).

Elmer E. Stoll, *Art and Artifice in Shakespeare.*

ANTONY AND CLEOPATRA

Antony and Cleopatra, ed. M. R. Ridley. Arden Shakespeare (London, 1954).

C. F. Tucker Brooke, *Shakespeare's Plutarch.*

Harley Granville-Barker, *Prefaces to Shakespeare.*

M. W. MacCallum, *Shakespeare's Roman Plays.*

J. C. Maxwell, "Shakespeare's Roman Plays, 1900–1956," *Shakespeare Survey X.*

George Bernard Shaw, "Better than Shakespear."

Neil S. Snodgrass, *Plutarch and Shakespeare.*

CORIOLANUS

See general titles under *Antony and Cleopatra* and following:

A. C. Bradley, "Coriolanus," *Proceedings of the British Academy, 1911–1912* (London, 1912), pp. 457–73. (Reprinted in Bradley's *A Miscellany* [London, 1929], pp. 73–104.)

Hermann Heuer, "From Plutarch to Shakespeare: A Study of Coriolanus," *Shakespeare Survey X,* pp. 50–59.

THE TEMPEST

The Tempest, ed. Frank Kermode. Arden Shakespeare (London, 1954).

R. R. Cawley, "Shakspere's Use of the Voyagers in *The Tempest,*" *Publications of the Modern Language Association of America,* XLI (1926), 688–726.

———, *The Voyagers and Elizabethan Drama* (Boston and London, 1938).

Sir Edmund Chambers, "The Integrity of *The Tempest,*" *Review of English Studies,* I (1925), 129–50.

H. D. Gray, "Some Indications That *The Tempest* Was Revised," *Studies in Philology,* XVIII (1921), 129–40.

Rudyard Kipling, *How Shakspere Came to Write "The Tempest"* (New York, 1916).

Kathleen M. Lea, *Italian Popular Comedy* (2 vols., Oxford, 1935). (See Vol. II, pp. 443–53 for possible relation between *Tempest* and *commedia dell' arte.*)

Elmer E. Stoll, "*The Tempest,*" *Publications of the Modern Language Association of America,* XLVII (1932), 699–726.